The World Almanac of Islamism
Volume I

2019 Edition

Table of Contents

3 Preface

Welcome to the 2019 edition of the American Foreign Policy Council's World Almanac of Islamism. The Almanac is a unique compilation designed to examine the current status of the political phenomenon of Islamism worldwide. It is intended to provide a snapshot of contemporary Islamism, as well as of the movements it motivates and the governments it impacts.

For the purposes of this collection, the term Islamist is used to describe movements, groups, and individuals which harness religious values and ideals in the service of a political agenda aimed at spreading or imposing Islamic law locally, regionally, or internationally. While it showcases a broad spectrum of Islamist thought and ideology, and touches more briefly upon more moderate Muslim movements, the Almanac does not—and is not meant to—provide a comprehensive chronicle of the full range of Islamic political thought.

The past year has brought with it considerable changes to the Islamist milieu, as well as in the international responses to Islamic radicalism being marshalled by foreign governments. Arguably of most note has been the advent of the Trump administration in the United States, which has brought with it a reinvigoration of U.S. counterterrorism efforts against the Islamic State (ISIS) and other radical groupings, as well as an abandonment of the 2015 nuclear agreement with Iran known as the Joint Comprehensive Plan of Action and its replacement with a new strategy aimed at curtailing Iran's malign international behavior. That strategy, now unfolding, will have significant implications for the behavior and capabilities of the Islamic Republic of Iran, which continues to rank as the world's leading state sponsor of terrorism.

In the Middle East, the strategic fortunes of the Islamic State have suffered a catastrophic decline. The terrorist group's once-robust "caliphate" in Iraq and Syria has been almost completely degraded territorially, thanks to the concerted military campaign that has been waged by the United States and its international partners in the Global Coalition. So, too, have ISIS resources, which have been progressively degraded as a result of the group's loss of territorial control. As it has, the group has demonstrated a notable shift in tactics, refocusing its attention on disseminating its message via social media platforms and by spurring its adherents to migrate foreign theaters (such as Libya) as well as to carry out "jihad in place" against soft targets in the West.

ISIS' deteriorating fortunes have closely mirrored the course of the Syrian civil war. Once in danger of losing his grip on the country, Syrian dictator Bashar al-Assad now appears to be firmly ensconced in Damascus as a result of military assistance provided to his regime by both Russia and Iran. That support has proven decisive in tilting the strategic balance of power in the nearly eight-year-old conflict firmly back toward the Syrian regime. It has also had the corollary effect of ensconcing Iran firmly in the Syrian theater, where it now boasts an extensive military footprint as a result of the materiel and fighters that it has mobilized to date in support of the Syrian regime.

At the same time, Africa – and particularly sub-Saharan Africa – remains fertile soil for a range of Islamist movements, most notably Nigeria's Boko Haram and Somalia's al-Shabaab. The ongoing threat to regional stability posed by these groups has created significant population displacement, as civilians have fled local unrest and broader political instability. As they have, they have contributed to ongoing refugee flows from the African continent into Europe.

In Europe, in turn, the migrant question remains a topic of considerable controversy. The rise of far-right parties throughout the Continent (in places such as Austria, Germany and Italy) has led to an expansion of protectionist, anti-immigration policies and attitudes in those places. At the same time, sporadic terrorist attacks in a number of European locales have further hardened attitudes toward Middle Eastern refugees among local populations, while demonstrating the continued ability of Islamist groups to carry out attacks against "soft targets" throughout the Eurozone.

The countries of Eurasia cumulatively continue to serve as a major source of Islamist mobilization, with the five nations of Central Asia and the Russian Federation estimated to have supplied a quarter of all foreign fighters that have joined the Islamic State's ranks to date. These conditions, however, may be changing. In Russia, the unrepresentative, ultra-nationalist rule of President Vladimir Putin, as well as his government's continued involvement in the Syrian civil war, continues to spur disaffection and mobilization among the country's growing Muslim minority. However, in Uzbekistan, new reforms now being implemented by the government of President Shavkat Mirziyoyev include a significant focus on promoting and popularizing a tolerant interpretation of the Muslim faith. This stands in contrast with Afghanistan, where the fragile central government in Kabul still struggles to contain the Taliban movement, as well as to counter a growing presence by ISIS on its soil.

Islamism continues to impact Asia as well. In Indonesia, the world's largest majority-Muslim nation, tolerant interpretations of the Muslim faith continue to predominate, spearheaded and buttressed by the country's largest mass Muslim movements, the Nahdlatul Ulama (NU) and Muhammadiyah. However, alarming signs of growing religious intolerance and rising Islamist activity have appeared there, placing strain on the traditionally inclusive, inter-confessional nature of Indonesia's politics. The Communist Party of China, meanwhile, has stepped up its pressure on – and repression of – that country's Uighur Muslim minority as part of a stepped-up effort to contain manifestations of Islam viewed as nonconformist or threatening. This policy, as yet poorly defined by Beijing, has created growing alarm in Washington and foreign capitals, and has the potential to serve as a significant political flashpoint in the future.

Islamist tactics and behavior continue to evolve. As the world becomes increasingly globalized, Islamist movements are in increasing competition with one another for both resources and recruits. But that are also in greater communication than ever before, a dynamic evident in the growing sophistication of extremist media and messaging. Islamist thought, as well as the operations and objectives of Islamist groups themselves, continues to evolve as well, as groups such as the Islamic State and al-Qaeda adapt militarily, politically and ideologically to preserve and expand their appeal.

The Almanac represents our attempt to track and codify those changes as a way of assisting policymakers in the United States and elsewhere to develop more comprehensive approaches to that ever-evolving challenge. In this undertaking, a number of people deserve special thanks, including AFPC's Vice President of Operations, Richard Harrison, AFPC Research Fellow Amanda Azinheira, and a talented crop of interns and rising researchers, including Diana Biya, Diane Cardon, and Cannon Counselor. And, as always, we are also deeply indebted to AFPC President Herman Pirchner, Jr. for providing the original vision for this project, as well as for supplying the ongoing guidance and support necessary for its success.

Ilan Berman, Executive Editor
Chloe Thompson, Managing Editor

Washington, DC
October 2018

North America

5 Canada

Quick Facts

Population: 35,623,680 (July 2017 est.)
Area: 9,984,670 sq km
Ethnic Groups: Canadian 32.2%, English 19.8%, French 15.5%, Scottish 14.4%, Irish 13.8%, German 9.8%, Italian 4.5%, Chinese 4.5%, North American Indian 4.2%, other 50.9%
GDP (official exchange rate):$1.652 trillion (2017 est.)

Source: CIA World FactBook (Last Updated August 2018)

Introduction

Canada is a free and peaceful society, with a large and generally successful immigration program. Newcomers to Canada tend to learn the local language (English or French), integrate into the economy, adopt Canadian values, and develop a positive Canadian identity. Muslims are no exception, and most Muslim communities in Canada are better integrated than their European counterparts. That said, Canada has also earned the unsavory reputation of being a terrorist haven, thanks to decades of political inaction and a weak legal framework to stop terrorist activities. A succession of terrorist groups flocked to Canada in the decades prior to 9/11. Following the September 2001 attacks on Washington and New York, Canada finally enacted stricter anti-terrorism laws. In the years since, however, Islamist, jihadist and other terrorist groups have been able to hide amid Canada's immigrant communities – including its Muslim population of just over 1 million.[1] Stubborn and subversive Islamist groups have penetrated the community and established terrorist cells, fundraising operations, communal organizations, mosques, and schools.

Following two attacks against members of the Canadian Forces in 2014, the Canadian government once again strengthened its response to these developments through legislation (including the 2015 Anti-Terrorism Act, known as Bill C51) which created new tools for the Canadian government to fight terrorism and the ideology responsible for it. Canada's approach to combatting Islamism has shifted under current Prime Minister Justin Trudeau, who has been accused of building alliances with Islamist organizations and turning a blind eye to extremism in Canada in an attempt to court Muslim and Arab voters.[2] *Trudeau has also pledged to welcome returned Islamic State fighters in the hopes of "de-radicalizing" and "re-integrating" them into Canadian society.*[3]

ISLAMIST ACTIVITY OVERVIEW

Exploiting the lack of anti-terrorism legislation that existed until 2001, terrorist groups traditionally used Canada's immigrant communities as safe havens and, occasionally, as bases of operations. These groups included, among others, the Armenian Secret Army for the Liberation of Armenia (ASALA),[4] Sri Lanka's Liberation Tigers of Tamil Eelam (LTTE),[5] and Sikh extremists.[6] More recently, these organizations and groups have been joined and outpaced by Islamist cells of various political and ideological stripes.

Canada's Islamist terrorists fall into three broad camps: (1) Salafist, including the new and enthusiastic supporters of the Islamic State, (2) Shiite, and (3) Palestinian. Salafists belong primarily to the Islamic State, al-Qaeda, and Armed Islamic Group (GIA), an Algerian group striving to turn Algeria into a theocratic Islamic state.

Al-Qaeda

Al-Qaeda has a persistent presence in Canada, and terrorism from al-Qaeda extremists remains a serious threat. According to the Canadian Security Intelligence Service (CSIS)[7], there are three primary ways in which terrorism threatens Canadian safety and security: 1) terrorists continue to plot direct attacks against Canada and its allies, at home and abroad, with the intent of causing death, disruption and fear; 2) terrorists conduct activities in Canada to support terrorist activity globally, namely fundraising to support attacks and military groups; and 3) terrorists use social media to reach and radicalize individual Canadians, who are then convinced to travel abroad to join a terrorist army and commit attacks, or to receive training on terrorist methods.

One of the most prominent examples of al-Qaeda in Canada is the Khadr family. Ahmed Said Khadr, the patriarch of the family, raised extensive funding for al-Qaeda and was the highest-ranking member of the group in Canada at one point. He died in a 2003 confrontation with the Pakistani military,[8] but his Islamist legacy lives on through his children. Two sons, Omar and Abdul Rahman, attended al-Qaeda training camps, fought for the Taliban and spent time in Guantanamo for terrorism. Omar killed an American medic, Spt. 1st Class Christopher J. Speer, during a gun battle in Afghanistan in July 2002. He was arrested and sent to Guantanamo Bay. In 2003, the U.S. released Abdul Rahman and he returned to Canada.[9]

In October 2010, Omar Khadr pleaded guilty to murder in violation of the laws of war, attempted murder in violation of the laws of war, conspiracy, two counts of providing material support for terrorism, and spying in the United States.[10] In exchange for his guilty plea, the military tribunal sentenced him to eight years in prison and promised to repatriate him to Canada after he had served the first year of his sentence at Guantanamo. The U.S. finally repatriated Omar Khadr to Canada on September 29, 2012,[11] and he was released on bail from an Edmonton prison and put on "house arrest" in May 2015. He has since had his bail conditions relaxed to include visiting his still-radicalized family members in Toronto, become engaged to a Palestinian activist, graced the front cover of Canada's cultural magazine, Maclean's, and filed a $20 million lawsuit against the Canadian government.[12]

In July 2017, Canadian media reported that the Trudeau government had secretly settled this lawsuit, awarded Khadr $10.5 million (CAD) and issued an official apology on behalf of the Government of Canada.[13] Trudeau confirmed this payout, stating that the decision came as a result of a court decision that sided with Khadr. The court ruling, however, only stated that Khadr's rights had been violated in 2003 when he was sent to Guantanamo and did not order the government to pay him or apologize. Public opinion in Canada has been critical of the Trudeau government and its decision to pay an admitted al-Qaeda terrorist.[14]

Two Canadian men participated in the In Amenas hostage crisis in January 2013, when an al-Qaeda-linked terrorist group took over

800 hostages at a gas facility in In Amenas, Algeria. Ultimately, at least 38 civilians and 29 terrorists died during the siege.[15] Two of the terrorists, Ali Medlej and Xristos Katsiroubas, were Canadian men and high school classmates from London South Collegiate Institute in London, Ontario. Both men were killed in the attack.[16] Mauritanian authorities had previously arrested a third classmate, Aaron Yoon, who was convicted in July 2012 of having ties to al-Qaeda and of posing a danger to national security and sentenced to two years in prison.[17] Yoon was transferred back to London, Canada in July 2013. [18]

Increasingly, al-Qaeda cells in Canada have graduated from planning attacks abroad to planning attacks against Canada itself. In 2006, the Royal Canadian Mounted Police (RCMP) arrested eighteen men plotting to bomb the Toronto Stock Exchange, a military base located off Highway 401 between Toronto and Ottawa, and Front Street offices of CSIS, Canada's security and intelligence agency.[19] They also intended to storm the Canadian Broadcasting Corporation (CBC) and Canadian Parliament, take hostages, and decapitate the leaders of each party, including the Prime Minister. They planned to demand that Canada withdraw her troops from Afghanistan.[20]

Of the 18 men arrested, eleven have been convicted of terrorism offences and two have been sentenced to life in prison.[21] The ring-leader, Zakaria Amara, pled guilty, received a life sentence and was stripped of his Canadian citizenship under a new law passed by the Harper government. Harper's successor, Justin Trudeau, has reversed this law and overhauled the government's ability to strip citizenship from foreign-born dual citizens convicted on terrorism charges.

Another al-Qaeda connected plot was thwarted on April 22, 2013, after an eight-month investigation. The RCMP arrested Tunisian-born Chiheb Esseghaier and Raed Jaser, a Palestinian from the United Arab Emirates, for plotting to derail a VIA Rail passenger train near Toronto. Police claim that the pair received guidance from members of al-Qaeda living in Iran.[22]

A final example of an al-Qaeda connected terrorist cell was that headed up by Hiva Mohammad Alizadeh in Ottawa. The Iranian-born Kurdish refugee to Canada is considered the ringleader of an

Ottawa al-Qaeda cell. He pled guilty to a terror plot in 2014 and was sentenced to 24 years in a federal prison.[23] Alizadeh admitted that he spent two months in an al-Qaeda terrorist training camp in Afghanistan in 2009, where he received training on using firearms and assembling improvised explosive devices, and smuggled 56 circuit boards, capable of triggering remote bombs, back to Canada.[24]

The Islamic State

The Islamic State has garnered interest in Canada since its emergence in 2014. Recent estimates suggested that over 180 Canadians have left their homes to fight overseas, particularly in the Islamic State's jihad. Several were arrested before they could leave, and there have been at least four attacks in Canada, using lone wolf tactics, carried out by men who had sworn allegiance to the Islamic State.

The first attack was carried out by Canadian-born Martin Couture-Rouleau, who, on October 20, 2014, intentionally rammed his car into a pair of Canadian Forces soldiers in a shopping mall parking lot in Saint-Jean-sur-Richelieu, Quebec, killing one of them. Couture-Rouleau converted from Christianity to Islam in 2013, and began regularly posting pro-Islamic State and anti-Semitic messages on his Facebook page.[25]

Just two days later, a second Islamist attack took place on Parliament Hill in Ottawa. Islamist terrorist Michael Zehaf-Bibeau shot and killed Corporal Nathan Cirillo, who was standing ceremonially on guard at the Canadian War Memorial. After the shooting, Zehaf-Bibeau reportedly raises his gun in the air and shouted, "For Iraq." He then stormed the Centre Block building of the Canadian Parliament, shot a security guard and made his way towards the Library of Parliament before being fatally shot by parliamentary security guards. Prime Minister Stephen Harper and Leader of Her Majesty's Royal Opposition Thomas Mulcair were in adjacent rooms when the terrorist was killed.[26]

On August 10, 2016, another would-be ISIS jihadist was shot and killed by Canadian police while in a taxi near his home in small-town Ontario. Twenty-five-year-old Aaron Driver, a Muslim-convert who was known to authorities, had recorded a homemade video and strapped on a home-made bomb. He was headed to busy

Union Station in downtown Toronto,[27] but thankfully, the Canadian police were tipped off by their counterparts in the FBI and his attack was thwarted. In Driver's video, he didn't mince words: "I give my pledge of allegiance to (ISIS leader) Abu Bakr al-Baghdadi, who's called for jihad in the lands of crusaders, and I respond to this call," said a masked river.[28] The driver was a known Islamist radical, and had been issued a Peace Bond by police to limit his communication with the outside world. And yet, he was able to build a bomb and record a video despite this order.

Finally, on October 1, 2017, Somali national Abdulahi Hasan Sharif engaged in an ISIS terrorist attack in Edmonton, Alberta. He drove a truck through a crowd, rammed a police officer and then stabbed him repeatedly, all while hanging an ISIS flag from his car window. Sharif illegally entered the U.S. from Mexico and was issued a deportation order before showing up in Canada and asking for asylum.[29] Oddly, the Canadian government did not stop Sharif from entering Canada, despite not having a passport and using different spelling for his name, and later awarded him with refugee status.[30]

On top of these attacks at home, a sizeable number of young Canadians have taken up arms to fight alongside Islamic State militants in Iraq, Syria and beyond. According to the Minister of Public Safety, at least 180 individuals with a connection to Canada are currently overseas fighting alongside Islamist terrorist organizations, primarily the Islamic State.[31] There are also at least 60 known returned foreign fighters in Canada, most of them living freely.[32] The reason is that, according to Larry Brooks, a former Center for Strategic and International Studies (CSIS) counter-terrorism official, it's nearly impossible to prove to a Canadian judge, in a Canadian court, that an individual has participated in terrorist activities overseas. "It's tremendously difficult to collect credible evidence that could satisfy a Canadian court for prosecution," Brooks has said.[33]

In 2017, Public Safety Minister Ralph Goodale stated that the number of returned jihadists remained at 60. Against the backdrop of the collapse of the ISIS "caliphate" in Iraq and Syria, many observers were skeptical and believe the number is higher. Prime Minister Trudeau's administration appears to be taking a more conciliatory approach to dealing with returning Islamic State fighters. In a 2017 year-end interview, Trudeau stated "We know that actually someone who has engaged and turned away from that hateful ideology can be an extraordinarily powerful voice for preventing radicalization."[34] He also pledged millions to a "de-radicalization" program for returned ISIS terrorists.

Hezbollah

Canada was an important source of financing and operational organizing for Hezbollah, prior to it being banned as a terrorist entity in 2002.[35] Before being outlawed, the Lebanese Shiite militia raised funds, bought equipment, and hid wanted terrorists in Canada.

In 1998, the RCMP uncovered a car theft ring run by members of the Iranian-backed terrorist organization to raise money for its global operations. Mohamed Dbouk managed one of the most lucrative Hezbollah cells. After seeking refugee status in Canada, he raised cash through credit card and banking scams, as well as cigarette smuggling, and used the proceeds to purchase high-tech military supplies and ship them to Lebanon. After Dbouk was indicted in Canada, he returned to Lebanon.

Although officially banned, Hezbollah continues its subversive reach into Canada. In 2011, the U.S. Treasury Department identified the Lebanese Canadian Bank SAL, along with its subsidiaries, as a "financial institution of primary money laundering concern under Section 311 of the USA PATRIOT Act for the bank's role in facilitating the money laundering activities of an international narcotics trafficking and money laundering network.[36] Its network traffics illegal narcotics from South America to Europe and the Middle East and laundered hundreds of millions monthly through bank accounts and other assets including U.S. used car dealerships, according the U.S. Treasury.[37] The U.S. government found that Hezbollah derived direct "financial support from the criminal activities of [this] network.[38]

Hezbollah has also been known to hide terrorists wanted by other countries in Canada. Hani Abd al-Rahim al-Sayegh, a leader of Saudi Hezbollah involved in the 1996 Khobar Towers bombing that killed nineteen American Air Force personnel, made a refugee claim in Canada using a false name and settled in Ottawa, where he was arrested a year later.[39]

The Iranian embassy in Ottawa had a history of funding and aiding a controversial cultural center with ties to Hezbollah, and was increasingly considered an outpost for espionage and subversion by the Iranian regime. The Iran embassy regularly hosted and funded conferences for Iranian Canadians and invited guests only. These events sought to reach sympathetic members of the Muslim community—to recruit, persuade, and intimidate them to join the Islamic Republic's network.[40] In 2012, the Canadian government posted a notice on the Iranian embassy door ordering all Iranian officials to leave the country within five days. The government also closed Canada's embassy in Tehran, recalling all Canadian diplomats, cutting diplomatic ties with Iran, and officially listing Iran as a state sponsor of terrorism. The Trudeau government has somewhat softened Canada's hardline stance against Iran, for instance by lifting some sanctions in February 2016.[41] Trudeau has pledged rapprochement with Iran, however, has yet to follow through with re-opening official diplomatic ties.[42]

Canada went further by amending the *State Immunity Act* and adopting the *Justice for the Victims of Terrorism Act*, both of which allowed the families and victims of terrorism to take legal action and seek damages from the perpetrators of terrorism and those who support them, including the government of Iran. This effectively eliminated the legal distinction between terrorist groups and the states that bankroll them, extinguishing the sovereign immunity protection typically granted to governments. To assist victims in identifying and locating Iran's state assets, the government released a list of known Iranian state-owned property in Canada. In 2014, an Ontario judge ordered the seizure of more than $7 million in bank accounts and property belonging to Iran. The historic ruling validated the Harper government's legal changes. Currently over 90 Canadian victims of terrorism have launched claims in Ontario's Superior Court seeking compensation from Iran for its role in training, arming, and financing Islamic terror networks.[43]

Palestinian Islamists

Hamas, the most influential Palestinian Islamist group, has a history of using Canada as a fundraising base, even after the government designated it a terrorist organization in November 2002.[44] A May 2000 Privy Council Office memo to Prime Minister Jean Chrétien identified the Jerusalem Fund for Human Services (Jerusalem Fund) as a fundraising entity for Hamas.[45]

The Canadian Coalition for Democracies alleges that the Jerusalem Fund responded to the flagging by merely changing its name to the International Relief Fund for the Afflicted and Needy (IRFAN) in 2001-2002. The Canadian Jewish News discovered that the Jerusalem Fund and IRFAN shared a mailing address in Mississauga, as well as a fax number.[46]

In 2004, IFRAN came under scrutiny from the Canada Revenue Agency and its auditors over fundraising links to Hamas, but was able to keep its charitable status by signing an agreement stating it would not fund any organization linked to Hamas.[47] A later audit found that, between 2004 and 2009, IFRAN had "openly supported and provided funding to Hamas" while also engaging in "deceptive and misleading fundraising."[48] A Charities Branch document highlight how IFRAN sent almost $15 million to Hamas and related agencies during this period, leading to the government's decision to strip IFRAN of its charity status in 2011, and, in 2014, to add IFRAN to Canada's official list of terrorist groups. [49]

Hamas also has raised hundreds of thousands of dollars in Canada through the Texas-headquartered Holy Land Foundation (HLF).[50] The U.S., which designated Hamas a terrorist organization in 1995, shut down HLF in 2008 and, in 2009, sentenced five of its leaders to prison terms ranging from 15 to 65 years.[51]

Additionally, Hamas is known to have recruited Canadians to commit attacks within Canada. In 2003, for instance, Israel arrested a Canadian man in Gaza who pled guilty to conspiracy and illegal military training for planning attacks against Jews in Canada and the U.S.[52] Hamas denied recruiting him, claiming that they limit their attacks to Middle Eastern targets.[53]

The smaller Palestinian Islamic Jihad (PIJ) has also tried to penetrate Canada—albeit on a much more modest scale. The group is known to have long collected and laundered money in Canada, and even attempted to acquire a fraudulent visa so that its treasurer, Muhammed Tasir Hassan Al-Khatib, could visit Canada.[54]

Additional details of PIJ activity inside Canada remain spotty, but the country's intelligence service has warned that the group could expand its current, minimal activity in the years ahead; a confidential 2003 CSIS report notes that the discovery of a PIJ fundraising network in Florida "raises the possibility of PIJ elements crossing the border to develop a similar infrastructure in Canada."[55] To date, however, here is no evidence that the PIJ has done so. Like Hamas, PIJ was designated a foreign terrorist organization by the Canadian government in November 2002, and its activities have waned in Canada since this designation.[56]

Islamist community organizations

Though it is not the norm for the Canadian Muslim community, a number of Islamic community organizations that have been infiltrated with radical extremists. The most prominent example was the Canadian Islamic Congress (CIC), which called itself "Canada's largest national non-profit and wholly independent Islamic organization."[57] After a number of controversies, the CIC finally closed its doors in 2014, and is now defunct. The CIC had a history of demonizing Israel, fabricating lies about opponents, and apologizing for hardline Islamist groups.[58] This incitement foments anti-Semitism and justifies the violence committed by Islamist groups against Israel. The CIC's leadership has further validated terrorism by denouncing the Canadian government's decision to designate Hamas and Hezbollah as terrorist groups, calling it an "unconscionable act of hypocrisy and a mockery of justice."[59]

The Islamist Muslim Students' Association (MSA) has chapters at many Canadian universities. Muslim Brotherhood activists founded the MSA in 1963 at the University of Illinois Urbana-Champaign[60] to help Muslims "practice Islam as a complete way of life."[61] Chapters of the MSA have raised funds for the Hamas-linked Holy Land Foundation,[62] as well as the Benevolence International Foundation and the Global Relief Foundation (both of which were later outlawed by the U.S. government for their links to al-Qaeda).[63]

In September 2017, the Islamic Society of British Columbia was penalized by the Canadian Revenue Agency (CRA) and alleged to have a relationship with a Qatari organization that supports jihadist terrorism. CRA audit documents obtained by Global News[64] found that the Eid Foundation of Qatar "maintained some level of control or influence over the affairs" of the Islamic Society, while also having alleged ties to terrorist organization.

Radicalism can be found in Canadian places of worship as well, with certain mosques and Islamic schools indoctrinating their parishioners and students. The Salaheddin Islamic Center and Al-Rahman Islamic Centre, both in Toronto, are examples of this trend. The Khadr family frequented the former, and six of the terrorists in the cell that planned to storm parliament and decapitate the Prime Minister prayed at the latter.[65]

Islamism and Society

Canada's 2011 National Household Survey, the most recent data available from the Government of Canada, recorded 1.05 million Muslims in the country, equaling 3.2 percent of the total population.[66] Sixty-eight percent of Canada's Muslims are immigrants, and more than 387,000 Muslims have entered Canada since 2001. A majority of Muslim-Canadians live in the province of Ontario (581,950) and most of those are located in the city of Toronto (424,930). The province of Quebec hosts the second largest Muslim community (243,430), 221,040 of whom live in Montreal, and it is home to many immigrants from the former French colonies of Algeria and Lebanon. Sizeable Muslim populations also reside in the provinces of Alberta (113,445) and British Columbia (79,310).

According to a 2007 Environics poll, 81 percent of Canadian Muslims "felt satisfied with the way things were going in their country."[67] Unfortunately, the same Environics poll highlighted a troubling propensity for radicalism among respondents, with about 12 percent of Canadian Muslims polled saying that the terrorist plot to storm Parliament and behead the Prime Minister was justified.[68]

Perhaps that often-vocal minority explains why a 2010 Leger Marketing poll found that 55 percent of Canadians disagreed when asked whether "Muslims share our values."[69] A subsequent 2009 Angus Reid Strategies poll uncovered similar opinions, with only 28 percent of Canadians polled viewing Islam favorably, compared with 72 percent approval for Christianity and 53 percent approval for Judaism.[70]

The updated 2016 Environics report on Muslims in Canada found similarly mixed results. On the one hand, it found that 83 percent of Muslims polled were "very proud to be Canadian," compared to 73 percent of non-Muslims in Canada. However, when it comes to social views, on issues such as acceptance of homosexuals in society, and the dominance of men in the household, for instance, Muslims and non-Muslims have very diverging opinions. While 80 percent of Canadians believe that homosexuality should be accepted by society, only 36 percent of Muslims agree with that statement. [71]

In March 2017, the House of Commons passed Motion 103, a non-binding resolution to condemn Islamophobia and religious discrimination in general. Critics have argued that the law could potentially limit free speech and grant Muslim citizens special privileges. Furthermore, the motion did not define Islamophobia in a concrete way, which could lead to confusion in the future.[72] Some analysis indicates that hate crimes against Muslims have declined in Canada. [73]

Islamism and the State

Canada passed its first anti-terrorism legislation, the *Canadian Anti-Terrorism Act* (Bill C-36), in the wake of the September 11th terrorist attacks on the United States. Before the *Anti-Terrorism Act* received the Royal Assent on December 18, 2001, the Canadian criminal code did not even formally define "terrorist activity." The *Anti-Terrorism Act* rectified this deficiency, providing a definition of both "terrorist activity" and "terrorist group,"[74] and authorizing the Governor in Council, on the recommendation of the Solicitor General, to designate an entity as a terrorist group.[75]

The *Anti-Terrorism Act*'s prohibition of providing financial services to terrorist groups represented Canada's first measure aimed at curbing terrorist financing. Before the *Act*, people could legally raise money for terrorist groups in Canada and the Crown could only prosecute people for directly funding a terrorist attack. However, as a practical matter, because of the opaque manner in which terrorist groups use banks and financial markets, it had proven to be almost impossible to connect donors to attacks.[76]

The *Anti-Terrorism Act* equipped authorities with several new tools to fight terrorism, including investigative hearings, preventive arrests, and new rules concerning information disclosure and rescinding a group's charity status. The *Act* amended the *Proceeds of Crime (Money Laundering) Act* to provide authorities with a scheme for monitoring suspicious financial transactions that could be tied to terrorism. The *Act* also established a mechanism for rescinding organizations' charitable status if there are reasonable grounds to believe that it has or will fund a terrorist group.[77]

However, in the wake of the 2013 Boston Marathon Bombing, Liberals and Conservatives united to pass, by a vote of 183 to 93, the *Combating Terrorism Act*. The bill revives the investigative hearing and preventive detention practices discontinued in 2007. Authorities may compel someone to submit to interrogation if he is suspected of having knowledge of a terrorist act and may imprison any who refuse to cooperate for up to twelve months. Authorities may also detain someone for up to three days and impose probationary conditions for up to a year on anyone suspected of engaging in terrorist activity.[78]

In the wake of the two Islamist terrorist attacks that resulted in the death of two members of the Canadian Forces in October 2014, the Harper government introduced updates to the *Anti-Terrorism Act* in January 2015, through Bill C-51. The bill sought to broaden the mandate of CSIS and to allow various Canadian government agencies to share information more easily, with the goal of proactively thwarting attacks before they happen.[79] While Bill C-51 sparked some controversy, it was passed and received royal assent in June 2015. During the 2015 Canadian election campaign, current Prime Minister Justin Trudeau pledged to amend the bill in order to strike a greater balance between promoting security and respecting civil liberties. Despite this pledge, the Trudeau government has not taken steps to amend the *Act* since forming government in late 2015.[80]

Prime Minister Trudeau, much like former U.S. President Barack Obama, is reluctant to discuss the threat posed by Islamists in Canada, and avoids using the term Islamist terrorism. In September 2016, Trudeau visited a gender-segregated mosque, the Ottawa Muslim Association, whose imam is a member of a group considered by some to be a terrorist organization. Trudeau met with Samy Metwally, who is a member of the International Union for Muslim Scholars (IUMS), which was founded by Yusuf al-Qaradawi, the Muslim Brotherhood's leading ideological figure. In 2014, the United Arab Emirates listed IUMS on its list of designated terrorist organizations.[81]

Trudeau's candidate selection and subsequent members of the Liberal caucus have also raised some concerns. Two members of his Liberal caucus, MPs Ali Ehassi and Majid Jowhari, have been lobbying to re-open diplomatic ties with Iran. The two men hosted an invitation-only roundtable event in Toronto in November 2016 to discuss Canadian-Iranian relations. The event was criticized for being stacked with pro-regime voices and not discussing Iran's human rights violations.[82] When anti-regime protests broke out in early 2018, Jowhari stated on Twitter that the Islamic Republic's dictatorship was an "elected government." [83] Another example is Mississauga Liberal MP Omar Alghabra, who Trudeau appointed as the Parliamentary Secretary to the Minister of Foreign Affairs. The Saudi-born Syrian Alghabra is the former president of the Canadian Arab Federation (CAF), an organization that was defunded by the Canadian government in 2009 over its participation in a conference with Hamas and Hezbollah delegates and for comparing Israelis to Nazis. In 2014, a Federal Court ruling upheld the decision, citing evidence that included a sign threatening to murder a Jewish child and a CAF-sponsored essay contest on the topic of "ethnic cleansing" in Israel. Alghabra once wrote an open letter calling Israel "a country that is conducting a brutal and the longest contemporary occupation in the world."[84]

ENDNOTES

1. Statistics Canada, "2011 National Household Survey: Data tables," https://www12.statcan.gc.ca/nhs-enm/2011/dp-pd/dt-td/Rp-eng.cfm?LANG=E&APATH=3&DETAIL=0&DIM=0&FL=A&FREE=0&GC=0&GID=0&GK=0&GRP=0&PID=105399&PRID=0&PTYPE=105277&S=0&SHOWALL=0&SUB=0&Temporal=2013&THEME=95&VID=0&VNAMEE=&VNAMEF=.
2. Gatestone Institute, "Canada: Trudeau's Support for Is-

lamists a Warning to America," January 2018, www.gatestoneinstitute.org/11679/trudeau-support-islamists. Tarek Fatah, "Islamist groups eligible for share of $23M in federal funding?," *Toronto Sun*, July 3, 2018, torontosun.com/opinion/columnists/fatah-islamic-relief-and-other-islamist-groups-to-receive-23m.

3. Alison Crawford, "Deradicalization must be tailored to Canadian cities, says expert," CBC News, October 7, 2017, https://www.cbc.ca/news/politics/deradicalization-terrorism-extremism-1.4343689. Amanda Connolly, "Conservatives accuse Trudeau of smug approach to returning foreign fighters," Global News, December 4, 2017, https://globalnews.ca/news/3895418/conservatives-accuse-trudeau-of-smug-approach-to-returning-foreign-fighters/.
4. Andrew Millie and Dilip K. Das, Contemporary Issues in Law Enforcement and Policing (Boca Raton: CRC Press, 2008), 88.
5. Stewart Bell, Cold Terror: How Canada Nurtures and Exports Terrorism Around the World (Ontario: Wiley, 2005), 42.
6. "In Depth: Air India, The Victims," CBC News, March 16, 2005, http://www.cbc.ca/news/background/airindia/victims.html.
7. Canadian Security Intelligence Service, Public Report, 2013-2014, February 2015. https://www.csis.gc.ca/pblctns/nnlrprt/2013-2014/2013-2014_Public_Report_Inside_ENG.pdf.
8. "Khadr Family," Global Jihad, September 15, 2010, http://www.globaljihad.net/view_page.asp?id=902.
9. Anti-Defamation League, "Canada And Terrorism," January 2004, http://www.adl.org/terror/tu/tu_0401_canada.asp.
10. "Youngest Guantanamo Detainee Pleads Guilty," CNN, October 25, 2010, http://www.cnn.com/2010/US/10/25/khadr.plea/.
11. Michelle Shephard, "Omar Khadr Repatriated to Canada," *Toronto Star*, September 29, 2012. http://www.thestar.com/news/2012/09/29/omar_khadr_repatriated_to_canada.html
12. Colin Perkel, "Omar Khadr wins right to expand $20M

suit vs. Canadian government," The Canadian Press, October 23, 2014, http://www.cbc.ca/news/politics/omar-khadr-wins-right-to-to-expand-20m-suit-vs-canadian-government-1.2811226.

13. Paul Waldie. "Trudeau defends apology and $10.5-million payment to Omar Khadr," *The Globe and Mail*, July 8, 2017, www.theglobeandmail.com/news/national/trudeau-defends-apology-and-105-million-payment-to-omar-khadr/article35623594/.
14. Éric Grenier, "Majority of Canadians oppose Omar Khadr settlement, poll suggests," CBC News, July 10, 2017, https://www.cbc.ca/news/politics/grenier-khadr-poll-1.4198306.
15. Angelique Chrisafis, Julian Borger, Justin McCurry, and Terry Macalister, "In Amenas: Timeline of Four-Day Siege in Algeria," *Guardian* (London), January 25, 2013, https://www.theguardian.com/world/2013/jan/25/in-amenas-timeline-siege-algeria.
16. Tonda MacCharles, "'Clear leader of raid on Algerian plant was Ali Medlej, Canadian officials believe," *Toronto Star*, September 19, 2013, https://www.thestar.com/news/canada/2013/09/19/clear_leader_of_raid_on_algerian_plant_was_ali_medlej_canadian_officials_believe.html.
17. Tonda MacCharles, "Mauritania Jailed Canadian Aaron Yoon for Al Qaeda Ties, Says Amnesty," *Toronto Star*, April 5, 2013, http://www.thestar.com/news/canada/2013/04/05/aaron_yoon_serving_twoyear_sentence_in_mauritania_for_al_qaeda_ties_amnesty_international.html.
18. "Aaron Yoon trying to readjust to life in London after time in Mauritanian prison," *CTV London*, September 18, 2013, http://london.ctvnews.ca/aaron-yoon-trying-to-readjust-to-life-in-london-after-time-in-mauritanian-prison-1.1460730.
19. "Toronto 18 Bomb Plot Chief' Jailed," *Al-Jazeera* (Doha), September 28, 2010, http://english.aljazeera.net/news/americas/2010/01/201011935438946391.html
20. "Another 'Toronto 18' Member Pleads Guilty," *CBC News*, September 28, 2010, http://www.cbc.ca/canada/

toronto/story/2010/01/20/toronto-18-plea941.html.

21. Christie Blatchford, "'Toronto 18' Case Our First Sign that 'Good Canadian Boys' are being Radicalized Too," *National Post*, April 2, 2013, http://fullcomment.nationalpost.com/2013/04/02/christie-blatchford-toronto-18-case-our-first-sign-that-good-canadian-boys-are-being-radicalized-too/.
22. Megan O'Toole, Stewart Bell and Adrian Humphreys, "I Don't Want a Book Written By Humans: VIA Terror Plot Accused again Rejects Criminal Code," *National Post*, May 23, 2013, http://news.nationalpost.com/2013/05/23/i-dont-want-a-book-written-by-humans-via-terror-plot-accused-again-rejects-criminal-code/.
23. Robert Bostelaar, "Hiva Alizadeh pleads guilty to terror plot," *Ottawa Citizen*, September 18, 2014, http://ottawacitizen.com/news/local-news/hiva-alizadeh-pleads-guilty-to-terror-plot.
24. "Hiva Alizadeh pleads guilty in Ottawa terrorism trial" *CBC News*, September 17, 2014, http://www.cbc.ca/beta/news/canada/ottawa/hiva-alizadeh-pleads-guilty-in-ottawa-terrorism-trial-1.2768944.
25. Erika Tucker, "Who is Quebec terror-linked suspect Martin Rouleau?" *Global News*, November 30, 2014, http://globalnews.ca/news/1626457/who-is-quebec-terror-linked-suspect-martin-rouleau/.
26. Evan Solomon, "Ottawa shooting: The face-to-face encounter that ended the attack on Parliament," *CBC News*, October 24, 2014, http://www.cbc.ca/news/politics/ottawa-shooting-the-face-to-face-encounter-that-ended-the-attack-on-parliament-1.2812802.
27. The Canadian Press, "Toronto's Union Station was target in foiled terror plot in 2016, Goodale confirms," *Toronto Star*, March 9, 2018, http://www.cbc.ca/news/politics/ottawa-shooting-the-face-to-face-encounter-that-ended-the-attack-on-parliament-1.2812802.
28. Candice Malcolm, "Bill C-51 played a part in thwarting Driver's attack," *Toronto Sun*, August 12, 2016, http://torontosun.com/2016/08/12/bill-c-51-played-a-part-in-thwarting-drivers-attack/wcm/9cd11f57-7882-4941-ad93-f2fd61b1caf5.

29. Candice Malcolm, "Refugee system even worse than I thought," *Toronto Sun*, October 25, 2017, http://torontosun.com/opinion/columnists/columnist-refugee-system-even-worse-than-i-thought.
30. Malcolm, "Refugee system even worse than I thought."
31. Rachel Aiello, "Chance of reintegrating Canadian ISIS fighters 'pretty remote': Goodale," CTV News, November 26, 2017, https://www.ctvnews.ca/politics/chance-of-reintegrating-canadian-isis-fighters-pretty-remote-goodale-1.3693559.
32. Department of Public Safety, "2016 Public Report on the Terrorist Threat to Canada."
33. Stewart Bell, "About 180 'individuals with a nexus to Canada' suspected of participating in terrorist activities oversea," *National Post*, August 25, 2016, http://news.nationalpost.com/news/canada/canada-a-target-of-direct-threats-from-isil-and-other-extremists-government-says-in-overdue-report
34. "Trudeau talks Trump, Khadr, ISIS and pot in exclusive interview with CTV News," *CTV News*. December 15, 2017, https://www.ctvnews.ca/canada/trudeau-talks-trump-khadr-isis-and-pot-in-exclusive-interview-with-ctv-news-1.3723920.
35. Stewart Bell, "Canada pushed EU to add Hezbollah to list of banned terrorist organizations, officials says," July 24, 2013, http://news.nationalpost.com/news/canada-pushed-eu-to-add-hezbollah-to-list-of-banned-terrorist-organizations-official-says
36. U.S. Department of the Treasury, "Treasury Identifies Lebanese Canadian Bank Sal as a 'Primary Money Laundering Concern,'" February 10, 2011, https://www.treasury.gov/press-center/press-releases/Pages/tg1057.aspx.
37. "Treasury Identifies Lebanese Canadian Bank Sal as a 'Primary Money Laundering Concern.'"
38. "Treasury Identifies Lebanese Canadian Bank Sal as a 'Primary Money Laundering Concern.'"
39. Bell, *Cold Terror*, 107.
40. Michael Petrou, "Iran's long reach into Canada," *Macleans*, June 20, 2012, http://www.macleans.ca/authors/michael-petrou/irans-long-reach-into-canada/.

41. John Paul Tasker, "Iran sanctions lifted by Canada, but Justin Trudeau still faces 'delicate dance'," CBC News, February 13, 2016, https://www.cbc.ca/news/politics/trudeau-iran-sanctions-1.3442614.
42. Sohrab Ahmari, "Canada comes to its sense," Commentary Magazine, June 13, 2018, https://www.commentarymagazine.com/foreign-policy/middle-east/iran/canada-comes-senses-iran/
43. Candice Malcolm, "A hawk among doves," *C2C Journal*, March 1, 2016, http://www.c2cjournal.ca/2016/03/a-hawk-among-doves/.
44. Department of Public Safety, Government of Canada, "Currently Listed Entities," October 20, 2010 http://www.publicsafety.gc.ca/prg/ns/le/cle-eng.aspx - Hamas.
45. Paul Lungen, "Group Claims Hamas Raising Funds in Canada," *Canadian Jewish News*, November 22, 2004, http://www.cjnews.com/index.php?option=com_content&task=view&id=5971&Itemid=86.
46. Bell, *Cold Terror*, 107.
47. Stewart Bell, "Muslim group appealing Ottawa's 'unreasonable' and 'unconstitutional' decision to list it as a terrorist entity," *National Post*, May 4, 2014, http://news.nationalpost.com/news/canada/muslim-non-profit-appealing-ottawas-unreasonable-and-unconstitutional-decision-to-list-it-as-a-terrorist-group.
48. Bell, "Muslim group appealing Ottawa's 'unreasonable' and 'unconstitutional' decision to list it as a terrorist entity."
49. Bell, "Muslim group appealing Ottawa's 'unreasonable' and 'unconstitutional' decision to list it as a terrorist entity."
50. Anti-Defamation League, "Canada And Terrorism."
51. Anti-Defamation League, "Backgrounder: The Holy Land Foundation for Relief And Development," May 28, 2009, http://www.adl.org/main_Terrorism/backgrounder_holyland.htm.
52. "Canadian Pleads Guilty In Plot To Kill Jews," *CBC News*, November 24, 2004, http://www.cbc.ca/world/story/2004/11/24/akkal-israel041124.html.
53. Rami Amichai, "Israel Remands Canadian In Al-

leged Attack Plot," *The Age* (Melbourne), December 16, 2003, http://www.theage.com.au/articles/2003/12/15/1071336890251.html.

54. Stewart Bell, "The Holy War Comes To Canada," *National Post*, October 23, 2003, http://archive.frontpagemag.com/readArticle.aspx?ARTID=15775.
55. Bell, "The Holy War Comes To Canada."
56. Department of Public Safety, Government of Canada, "Listed Terrorist Entities," https://www.publicsafety.gc.ca/cnt/ntnl-scrt/cntr-trrrsm/lstd-ntts/index-en.aspx.
57. Canadian Islamic Congress, "Facts About the CIC," September 10, 2010, http://www.canadianislamiccongress.com/cicfacts.php.
58. Wahida Valiante, "The New Syndrome - F.e.a.r. -- Fear Everything Anxiety Reaction," *Friday Magazine* 9, iss. 60 (2006), http://www.canadianislamiccongress.com/opeds/article.php?id=2840; Canadian Islamic Congress, "Islamic Congress And Arab Federation Call On All Canadians To Condemn Continuing Israeli War Crimes In Gaza," January 21, 2008, http://www.canadianislamiccongress.com/mc/media_communique.php?id=985.
59. Canadian Islamic Congress, "Islamic Congress Urges Government to Take Hezbollah And Hamas Off Terrorist' List," August 22, 2006, http://www.canadianislamiccongress.com/mc/media_communique.php?id=814.
60. The Investigative Project on Terrorism, "Muslim Student's Association," January 1, 2008, http://www.investigativeproject.org/profile/166.
61. Muslim Student's Association, "Constitution/Bylaws," October 25, 2010, http://www.msanational.org/about/constitution.
62. Jonathan Dowd-Gailey, "Islamism's Campus Club: The Muslim Students' Association," *Middle East Quarterly* 11, no. 1 (2004), 63-72.
63. Dowd-Gailey, "Islamism's Campus Club: The Muslim Students' Association."
64. Stewart Bell and Rumina Day, "Audit of B.C. Mosque charity alleges personal spending, 'relationship' with Qatar group accused of supporting terror." *Global News,* September 27, 2017. https://globalnews.ca/

news/3762864/bc-mosque-qatar-terror-relationship/

65. Anthony DePalma, "Six of 17 Arrested In Canada's Antiterror Sweep Have Ties To Mosque Near Toronto," *New York Times*, June 5, 2006.
66. Statistics Canada, "2011 National Household Survey: Data tables," http://www12.statcan.gc.ca/nhs-enm/2011/dp-pd/dt-td/Rp-eng.cfm?LANG=E&APATH=3&DETAIL=0&DIM=0&FL=A&FREE=0&GC=0&GID=0&GK=0&GRP=0&PID=105399&PRID=0&PTYPE=105277&S=0&SHOWALL=0&SUB=0&Temporal=2013&THEME=95&VID=0&VNAMEE=&VNAMEF=..
67. "Canada's Muslims: An International Comparison," *CBC News*, February 13, 2007, http://www.cbc.ca/news/background/islam/muslim-survey.html.
68. David B. Harris, "Is Canada Losing The Balance Between Liberty And Security?" in Alexander Moens and Martin Collacott, eds., *Immigration Policy and the Terrorist Threat in Canada and the United States* (Vancouver: Fraser Institute, 2008), 137.
69. Elizabeth Thompson, "Canadians Don't Believe That Muslims Share Their Values," National Post, September 10, 2010, http://www.nationalpost.com/Canadians+believe+Muslims+share+their+values+poll/3508281/story.html.
70. John Geddes, "What Canadians Think Of Sikhs, Jews, Christians, Muslims," *Maclean's*, April 28, 2009, http://www2.macleans.ca/2009/04/28/what-canadians-think-of-sikhs-jews-christians-muslims/.
71. Environics, "Survey of Muslims in Canada, 2016," http://www.environicsinstitute.org/uploads/institute-projects/survey%20of%20muslims%20in%20canada%202016%20-%20final%20report.pdf.
72. "House of Commons passes anti-Islamophobia motion," Canadian Broadcasting Corporation, March 23, 2017, http://www.cbc.ca/news/politics/m-103-islamophobia-motion-vote-1.4038016.
73. Candice Malcolm "What hate crime statistics really say," *Toronto Sun,* December 13, 2017, http://torontosun.com/opinion/columnists/malcolm-what-hate-crime-statistics-really-say.

74. Department of Justice, "About the *Anti-terrorism Act,*" http://www.justice.gc.ca/eng/cj-jp/ns-sn/act-loi.html.
75. "About the *Anti-terrorism Act.*"
76. Bell, *Cold Terror*, 97.
77. Department of Justice, Government of Canada, "About the *Anti-terrorism Act,*" http://www.justice.gc.ca/eng/cj-jp/ns-sn/act-loi.html.
78. "Controversial Anti-terrorism Tools Revived as Bill Passes," *CBC News*, April 24, 2013, http://www.cbc.ca/news/politics/controversial-anti-terrorism-tools-revived-as-bill-passes-1.1414767.
79. Parliament of Canada, *Statutes of Canada 2015*, Chapter 20, Second Session, Forty-first Parliament, http://www.parl.gc.ca/HousePublications/Publication.aspx-?Language=E&Mode=1&DocId=8056977&File=4.
80. Chris Hall, "Trudeau tracker: Promised changes to anti-terrorism law C-51 still months away," *CBC News*, May 17, 2016, http://www.cbc.ca/news/politics/trudeau-tracker-anti-terrorism-bill-1.3586337.
81. Anthony Furey, "Trudeau visits mosque with terror connections," *Toronto Sun*, September 12, 2016, http://www.torontosun.com/2016/09/12/trudeau-visits-mosque-with-terror-connections.
82. Michael Petrou, "Liberal MPs defend invitation list for Stephane Dion roundtable on Iran," *CBC News*, November 4, 2016, http://www.cbc.ca/news/politics/iran-canada-dion-engagement-1.3834592.
83. Evan Dyer, "Liberal MP Majid Jowhari's Iran tweets roil his heavily Iranian riding," *CBC News*, January 4, 2018, http://www.cbc.ca/news/politics/majid-jowhari-iran-tweet-1.4473817.
84. Ari Yashar, "Is Trudeau's new Foreign Minister Secretary a Hamas backer?" *Israel National News*, April 12, 2016, http://www.israelnationalnews.com/News/News.aspx/204406.

6 United States

Quick Facts

Population: 326,625,791 (July 2017 est.)
Area: 9,833,517 sq km
Ethnic Groups: white 72.4%, black 12.6%, Asian 4.8%, Amerindian and Alaska native 0.9%, native Hawaiian and other Pacific islander 0.2%, other 6.2%, two or more races 2.9% (2010 est.)
GDP (official exchange rate): $19.36 trillion (2017 est.)

Source: CIA World FactBook (Last Updated June 2018)

Introduction

Despite significant advances in the U.S.-led fight against the Islamic State terrorist group in Iraq and Syria throughout 2017, the broader threat posed by militant Islamists and terrorist networks remains a challenge to U.S. national security. In November 2017, National Counterterrorism Center (NCTC) Director Nicholas Rasmussen told the House Committee on Homeland Security that "ISIS and al-Qa'ida have proven to be extremely resilient organizations" and terrorist groups "continue to exploit safe havens created by ungoverned spaces and threaten the United States and our allies."[1] *The threat from the Islamic State's "virtual caliphate" likewise continues to grow and expand, as the terrorist group makes savvy use of social media to continue to recruit terrorists and motivate individuals to perpetrate attacks in the United States and other Western nations.*[2] *Although the Trump administration has yet to release a comprehensive counterterrorism strategy, it has taken significant steps to bolster counterterrorism operations in conflict zones. These have included easing the rules of engagement for U.S. troops battling enemy forces in Afghanistan, Iraq, and Syria*[3] *and loosening restrictions on drone strikes and commando raids.*[4] *The United States has also deployed combat-equipped forces to conduct counterterrorism operations and assist counterterrorism capabilities of partner countries in Afghanistan, Iraq, Syria, Yemen, Somalia, Libya, and elsewhere.*[5]

Islamist Activity

Contemporary Islamist activity in the United States can be understood in the context of five loose conceptual groupings:

The Ikhwan-Jama'at duopoly[6]

The Ikhwan-Jama'at duopoly is the largest and most influential grouping of organized Islamist activism in the United States. In the 1950s and 1960s, Muslim Brotherhood activists fled repression in Egypt and sought refuge in Gulf countries, including Saudi Arabia. Wahhabi authorities took advantage of their organizational experience, placing them in key positions at major Islamic NGOs. With Saudi backing, these Brotherhood activists, joined by Jama'at-e-Islami[7] cadres, propagated Islamist thought and institutions all over the world, including the United States and the wider Western world.[8]

The structure of the U.S.-based Ikhwan-Jama'at duopoly can be understood on three levels: 1) a covert vanguard, 2) professional activist organizations with formalized membership schemes, and 3) the related grassroots they seek to mobilize. The vanguard consists of Brotherhood and Jama'at leaders in North America who hold key leadership positions in a network of overlapping activist organizations. These activist organizations are the most prominent Islamic groups in American civil society. They are influential in local, state, and national politics and have established relationships with editorial boards and news producers at media outlets throughout the country.

Internal U.S. Brotherhood records released as evidence in the terrorism financing trial of the Holy Land Foundation for Relief and Development (HLF) reveal that a covert vanguard of Muslim Brotherhood activists founded and directed the most influential Muslim-American civil society groups in the United States, including the Muslim Students' Association (MSA) the Islamic Society of North America (ISNA), the North American Islamic Trust (NAIT), the International Institute of Islamic Thought (IIIT), the Council on American-Islamic Relations (CAIR) and the Muslim American Society (MAS).[9] The Islamic Circle of North America (ICNA) similarly has been identified as a "front" for Jama'at-e-Islami.[10]

The public faces of these groups are professionally-led activist organizations that are purportedly concerned with civil rights, religious education, political awareness, grass-roots organization, and other seemingly benign activities.[11] However, internal Brotherhood documents reveal another use for these organizations: promoting "the main goal of Islamic activism," which is "establishing the nation of Islam, the rule of God in the lives of humans, making people worship their Creator and cleansing the earth from the tyrants who assault God's sovereignty, the abominators in His earth and the suppressors of His creation."[12] Brotherhood officials have done so by promoting the creation of civic organizations with a covert—and occasionally an overt—political agenda, an activity described by one Brotherhood official in the 1980s as "energizing political work fronts."[13] Such groups include:

The Muslim Student Association ("MSA")

Founded in 1963 by Brotherhood activists at the University of Illinois Urbana-Champaign, the MSA, or MSA National, served as a coordinating committee for Brotherhood activities during the organization's formative years in the United States. During this early era, all Brotherhood activists in the U.S. had to be active in the MSA.[14] Now a national organization, the MSA has about 98 affiliated university chapters in the United States and Canada.[15]

Like all member organizations of the Ikhwan-Jama'at duopoly, the MSA proclaims "moderation," but public statements by MSA activists reveal an Islamist agenda and ideology. For instance, MSA officials have espoused the desire "to restore Islam to the leadership of society" and to be working toward "the reestablishment of the Islamic form of government."[16] They have likewise emphasized the importance of dawah (propagation of faith) as a vehicle for the spread of Islam in the United States, with the ultimate goal of making America "a Muslim country."[17]

The North American Islamic Trust ("NAIT")

NAIT was founded in 1973 as a "national waqf (trust) organization" by the Muslim Students Association of the United States and Canada ("MSA") to ensure continuity of Islamic centers in North America. NAIT's website states: "Even though Muslims have been immigrating to the United States since the founding of the nation, many people and communities ultimately lost or abandoned their Islamic heritage due to social, and political reasons. Indeed, many indigenous masajid [mosque] and [Islamic] centers were lost or forgotten. To prevent this in the future, the organizers believed that creating a waqf or general trust to safeguard the properties if masajid and Islamic centers would be vital for the growth and maintenance of the American Muslim community."[18] NAIT continues to retain its "foundational supporting relationship with MSA and the Islamic Society of North America (ISNA)."[19]

NAIT is a non-profit 501(c) (3) organization and "holds titles to the real estate assets of Islamic centers and schools in more than forty states,"[20] making it, according to some analysts, a holding company and financial hub for various Muslim Brotherhood-tied groups in North America.[21] It also manages the Iman Fund, a no-load mutual fund, and runs American Trust Publications (which publishes Islamic literature, including the works of Brotherhood luminary Yusuf al Qaradawi[22]) and the Islamic Book Service.[23] A 1987 FBI investigation of NAIT concluded that the organization supported the "Islamic Revolution." "Their support of JIHAD (a holy war) in the U.S. has been evidenced by the financial and organizational support provided through NAIT from Middle East countries to Muslims residing in the U.S. and Canada," the FBI report continued. The countries named as providing this support were Iran, Libya, Kuwait, and Saudi Arabia. "The organizational support provided by NAIT includes planning, organizing, and funding anti-U.S. and anti-Israel demonstrations, pro-PLO [Palestine Liberation Organization] demonstrations and the distribution of political propaganda against U.S. policies in the Middle East and in support of the Islamic Revolution as advocated by the [Government of Iran]. NAIT also supports the recruitment, training and funding of black Muslims in the U.S. who support the Islamic Revolution."[24]

The Islamic Society of North America (ISNA)

ISNA, which emerged out of the MSA in 1981, was named as an unindicted co-conspirator in the Hamas financing trial against the Holy Land Foundation.[25] Like NAIT, ISNA is included among the "individuals/entities who are and/or were members of the US

Muslim Brotherhood."[26] There is no evidence that ISNA currently provides material support to terrorist organizations. However, as recently as November 2016, key U.S. Brotherhood activists held leadership positions in ISNA. ISNA's board of directors (Majlis Ash-Shura) included the chairman of NAIT, the president of the MSA, and the heads of ISNA's other "constituent organizations": the Association of Muslim Scientists, Engineers and Technology Professionals, the Islamic Medical Association of North America, the Canadian Islamic Trust, Muslim Youth of North America, and the Council of Islamic Schools of North America—some of which are explicitly named as Brotherhood-allied groups in internal Brotherhood documents.[27]

The Islamic Circle of North America (ICNA)

ICNA is the successor to the Pakistani-American organization Halaqa Ahbabe Islami, which sought to recruit "Islamic movement oriented Urdu speaking Muslims and to strengthen the Jama'at-e-Islami Pakistan."[28] In 1977, Halaqa Ahbabe Islami formally changed its name to ICNA.[29] ICNA's charter calls for the "establishment of the Islamic system of life" in the world, "whether it pertains to beliefs, rituals and morals or to economic, social or political spheres."[30] The organization's curriculum promotes[31] the teachings of Islamist scholar and Jama'at-e-Islami founder Maulana Sayyid Abdul Ala Maududi[32] who wrote that "the objective of the Islamic 'Jihad' is to eliminate the rule of an un-Islamic system and establish in its stead [sic] an Islamic system of state rule."[33]The organization's 2010 *Member's Hand Book* lists five stages that involve going through the individual, family, societal, state, and global levels "to establish [a] true Islamic society" that "will lead to the unity of the Ummah [global Muslim community] and towards the establishment of the Khilafah [Caliphate]."[34] ICNA has also been closely affiliated with Islamist radicals and extremists. A former president of ICNA's New York chapter, Ashrafuz Zaman Khan, was convicted for committing war crimes in the name of Maududi's pan-Islamist ideology during Bangladesh's 1971 war of independence.[35] ICNA is a strong advocate of the separatist movement in Kashmir.[36] A 1997 article in its magazine, *The Message*, featured an exclusive interview with U.S.-designated Kashmiri terrorist Syed Salahuddin, praised him as the "undisputed leader of the mujahideen struggling to liberate the territory of Kashmir from brutal Indian occupation."[37] Its overseas charitable arm, Helping Hands for Relief and Development, works closely with the Pakistani Jamaat charity, Al Khidmat Foundation, that has close ties to Kashmiri jihadists.[38]

The Council on American-Islamic Relations (CAIR)

CAIR's mission statement is "to enhance understanding of Islam, encourage dialogue, protect civil liberties, empower American Muslims, and build coalitions that promote justice and mutual understanding."[39] This statement is misleading and a closer look at the organization raises troubling questions about its stated purpose and origins in a Hamas-support network in the United States. CAIR was founded in 1994 by three leaders of the Islamic Association for Palestine (IAP)—Nihad Awad, Omar Ahmad, and Rafeeq Jaber.[40] IAP, which is now defunct, was a central player in the Muslim Brotherhood's "Palestine Committee" created to advance Hamas' political and financial agenda in the United States.[41] It is worth noting that soon after its founding, CAIR was added to a Palestine Committee meeting agenda.[42]

IAP served as the Committee's propaganda arm and its primary role involved organizing rallies and publishing magazines supporting Hamas. Other members of the Committee included its fundraising branch, the Holy Land for Relief and Development (HLF),[43] which was convicted in 2008 along with five senior officials of illegally routing more than $12 million to Hamas.[44] A Northern Virginia think tank called the United Association for Studies and Research (UASR) was "involved in passing Hamas communiques to the United States-based Muslim Brotherhood community and relaying messages from the community back to Hamas"[45] and was headed by Hamas leader Mousa Abu Marzook.[46]

CAIR has defended convicted terrorists and other radicals and opposed U.S. government prosecution of alleged terrorist financiers and supporters.[47] CAIR also claims that the "war on terrorism" is a "war on Islam" and has made repeated statements that reflect the group's extremist and anti-Semitic positions.[48] CAIR was named an unindicted co-conspirator in the HLF trial[49] and during testimony FBI agent Lara Burns described CAIR as a front organization for

Hamas.[50] In 2009, the Federal Bureau of Investigation (FBI) cut off contacts with CAIR over concerns the group had roots in a Hamas-support network.[51]

The Muslim American Society (MAS)

The Northern Virginia-based MAS was founded in 1993 as the Muslim Brotherhood's arm in the U.S.[52] Among its founding members was Ahmed Elkadi, who supposedly led the Brotherhood in the U.S. from 1984 to 1994.[53] Mohammad Mehdi Akef, the Supreme Guide of the global Muslim Brotherhood in Egypt from 2004 to 2010, claims to have played a role in founding MAS in a push for more "openness" in the Brotherhood's activities in the U.S.[54]

MAS is reported to have instructed its leaders to distance themselves publicly from the Brotherhood. If a leader was asked about MAS' ties to the Muslim Brotherhood, he was to say that MAS was an independent organization.[55] Former MAS Secretary General Shaker El Sayed once said that: "MAS, like the Brotherhood, believes in the teachings of Brotherhood founder Hassan al-Banna, which are 'the closest reflection of how Islam should be in this life.'"[56]

MAS' ties to the Muslim Brotherhood were reaffirmed by convicted terrorist financier Abdurrahman Alamoudi, who told federal investigators in a 2012 interview that "[e]veryone knows that MAS is the Muslim Brotherhood."[57] Alamoudi, the former head of the American Muslim Council, was sentenced to 23 years in prison for illegal financial dealings with Libya. Alamoudi also confessed to taking part in a Libyan plot to assassinate the then crown Prince of Saudi Arabia.[58] MAS annually partners with ICNA to host its national conventions,[59] which feature extremist speakers who support jihad[60] and advocate for Israel's destruction.[61]

The International Institute of Islamic Thought (IIIT)

Conceived at a 1977 Islamic conference in Lugano, Switzerland, IIIT was founded four years later in Pennsylvania as "a private, non-profit, academic, cultural and educational institution, concerned with general issues of Islamic thought and education."[62] It is now based in Herndon, Virginia. IIIT ostensibly "promotes academic research on the methodology and philosophy of various disciplines, and gives special emphasis to the development of Islamic scholarship in contemporary social sciences."[63] However, IIIT has been accused by the U.S. government of contributing funds to the World and Islam Studies Enterprise (WISE), which was founded to support the Palestinian Islamic Jihad terrorist organization.[64] IIIT is a part of a network of companies and not-for-profit organizations based in Northern Virginia known as the SAAR Network or the Safa Group, which was under investigation by the U.S. Department of Justice since at least 2003, although no charges have been filed.[65] In May 2009, Ishaq Farhan, a trustee of IIIT, was chosen to head the Islamic Action Front (IAF)—the political party of the Jordanian Muslim Brotherhood—a post he had held before.[66] Farhan had long been associated with the IAF and is said to be one of the key figures behind its formation.[67] (Since then, Farhan has been replaced as head of the IAF by Hamza Mansour.[68] Ostensibly, however, Farhan still retains an affiliation—and a position of prominence—with the organization.)

American Muslims for Palestine (AMP)

AMP is a virulently anti-Israeli group that actively seeks to delegitimize the Jewish state,[69] and has defended Hamas[70] as well as advocated in support of convicted terrorists.[71] In 2015, the Investigative Project on Terrorism first identified connections between AMP and a now-defunct network called the Palestine Committee.[72] Foundation for the Defense of Democracies Vice President Jonathan Schanzer expanded on those connections in congressional testimony a year later.[73] The Palestine Committee was created by the Muslim Brotherhood to advance Hamas' agenda politically and financially in the United States.[74] A lawsuit filed in Chicago federal court in May 2017 alleges that AMP and several of its activists are "alter egos and/or successors" of a Hamas-support network that was found liable for an American teen's death in a 1996 terrorist attack in Israel.[75] AMP hosts conferences[76] that feature anti-Israel speakers and supports "resistance" against the "Zionist state."[77] The organization is also one of the main supporters of the Boycott, Divestment, and Sanctions (BDS) Movement against the Jewish state.

Jamaat al Fuqra

Jama'at al Fuqra (JF, Arabic for "Community of the Impoverished") was founded in New York in 1980 by Pakistani religious leader Sheikh Mubarak Ali Gilani.[78] JF has been described as a splinter group of Jaish-e-Mohammad (JeM).[79] Daniel Pearl, the late *Wall Street Journal* reporter, was on his way to interview Gilani in 2002 when he was kidnapped in Pakistan and subsequently beheaded.

In the U.S., JF is a loosely structured movement primarily composed of African-American converts to Islam. JF functions officially through Muslims of the Americas, a non-profit organization, and the International Quranic Open University.[80] JF also operates a news publication called *The Islamic Post*.[81] JF runs a network of rural compounds in New York, Maryland, Pennsylvania, Arizona, Oregon, South Carolina, California and Colorado. Members of the group were involved in a wave of violent crime and fraud—including murder and arson—in the 1980s and 1990s.[82] Some members have also been known to attack Hindu places of worship.[83] Over the past decade, the group has been fairly quiet in the U.S. It received some attention in 2008 and 2009 as a result of a documentary on the group produced by the Christian Action Network entitled "Homegrown Jihad."[84]

Hizb ut-Tahrir

Hizb ut-Tahrir in America (HTA) has been led by Middle Eastern activists who moved to the U.S. in the 1980s. For most of its history, it has met with little success in expanding its native activist base. This has been attributed to competition from other Islamist groups (mainly the Brotherhood); the limited ability of an older leadership to connect with the younger generation; and a level of paranoia and secrecy among the leadership that have limited outreach efforts, hindered online interaction, and may have turned off potential recruits.[85]

The HTA website states that the organization's aim is "to resume the Islamic way of life and to convey the Islamic da'wah to the world."[86] HTA is currently well-networked and connected with the larger global presence of HuT. Their three-stage methodology for taking power is the same as that promoted by the global movement:

> The First Stage: The stage of culturing to produce people who believe in the idea and the method of the Party, so that they form the Party group.
>
> The Second Stage: The stage of interaction with the Ummah (global Muslim community), to let the Ummah embrace and carry Islam, so that the Ummah takes it up as its issue, and thus works to establish it in the affairs of life.
>
> The Third Stage: The stage of establishing government, implementing Islam generally and comprehensively, and carrying it as a message to the world.[87]

In the West, HuT seeks to foster a mass movement toward revolution, while in Muslim-majority countries it attempts to recruit members of the military for the purpose of carrying out a military coup.[88] According to one specialist, HTA "counts well-educated professionals who are influential in their communities among their members" and in recent years the group has expanded beyond their main hubs of activity in New York, Orange County (California), Chicago, and Milwaukee.[89]

The jihadist-activist milieu

There are a number of small U.S.-based formal and informal groups and networks that support violent jihad in America and elsewhere, but do not necessarily engage in it themselves. Most of their activities are political and social in nature, consisting of provocative public statements and demonstrations. Two particularly prominent groups deserve mention in this regard.

Revolution Muslim [RM] was a New York-based jihadist-activist group. Founded in 2007 "to invite people to proper Islam... and command the good... while forbidding the falsehood," RM's mission "is to one day see the Muslims united under one Khalifah and under the commands of Allah."[90] RM maintained an active blog and website, which serves as a forum for a dissemination of its views, proselytization, condemnation of U.S. policies, and even support for violence. In April 2014, Revolution Muslim co-founder Yousef al-Khattab was sentenced to two-and-a-half years in prison for advocating violence against the Chabad Jewish organization's headquarters in Brooklyn.[91] Khattab posted a photograph of the building, along with a map, to Revolution Muslim's website, and pointed out that "the man temple was always full at prayer times." In the past, he had told his readers to "deal with" prominent Jewish leaders "directly at their homes."[92]

One of Revolution Muslim's other co-founders was Jesse Morton. Morton was arrested in 2011 after one of his associates published the home addresses of the writers of *South Park,* after an episode of the cartoon show mocked the Prophet Muhammad. Before that time, Morton was one of the most prolific recruiters for al-Qaeda in the United States.[93] After his arrest, Morton worked as an informant for the Federal Bureau of Investigation (FBI) and made contact with several of his former recruits.[94] In September 2016, Morton began a job as a researcher at George Washington University's Program on Extremism.[95] This affiliation, however, proved to be short-lived; Morton's affiliation with the University was severed after he was arrested in late 2016 on drug possession and solicitation of prostitution charges.[96]

Homegrown jihadist cells and networks

Jihadi plots inspired by terrorist groups such as al Qaeda and the Islamic State continue to pose a threat to the United States. In a 2017 report, George Washington University's Program on Extremism identified 51 "successful" attacks in North America and Europe from the time of declaration of the Islamic Caliphate in June 2014 until June 2017. The highest number of attacks were in France (17) followed by the United States (16).[97]

In December 2017, Bangladeshi immigrant Akayed Ullah set off a homemade pipe bomb at the Port Authority Bus Terminal in New York City. Five people were injured in the attack and Ullah sustained minor injuries. Ullah who had pled allegiance to ISIS, said the suicide bombing was in retaliation to U.S. bombing of ISIS-controlled territory in Syria and Iraq.[98] Earlier, in October 2017,

Uzbek national Sayfullo Habibullaevich Saipov drove a rented pickup truck into cyclists and runners on a bike lane and pedestrian walkway in New York City. The attack killed eight people and injured 12 others. A flag and document indicating allegiance to the Islamic State were found in the truck.[99] In October 2017, Talha Haroon, along with Abdurahman El Bahnasawy and Russell Salic, were arrested for plotting to carry out terror attacks in New York City for the Islamic State. Haroon was a U.S. citizen residing in Pakistan and El Bahnasawy and Salic were from Canada and the Philippines, respectively. The three men plotted through Internet messaging applications to target concerts, subways and other landmarks in the name of ISIS in NYC during the Islamic holy month of Ramadan.[100]

A large number of Islamist terrorist plots in the U.S. have been thwarted or uncovered over the past decade. Many of these were planned by cells of Muslims who were either born in the U.S. or lived there for many years. There were also episodes of Americans planning attacks against U.S. interests abroad and/or going to fight with foreign Islamist movements. These included:

- Daniel P. Boyd, an American convert to Islam, was accused in 2009 of heading a seven-man North Carolina-based cell that allegedly planned to provide material support to al-Qaeda, murder, kidnap, maim and injure persons in Israel and elsewhere, and kill U.S. military personnel stationed at Quantico, Virginia.[101] Boyd pleaded guilty to conspiracy to commit murder and conspiracy to provide material support to terrorists in U.S. District Court in February 2011, and subsequently cooperated with the government, providing testimony at trial against several of his co-conspirators, who were convicted that October.[102]
- Hosam Maher Husein Smadi, a Jordanian national, was found guilty of planning to blow up the Fountain Place office complex in downtown Dallas with a vehicle bomb in 2009, and in 2010 was sentenced to twenty-four years in prison.[103] He also reportedly considered attacking a National Guard Armory and the Dallas Airport.[104]
- In August 2013, a U.S. citizen and a foreign national were

charged in a Miami federal court with providing financing and recruits to al-Qaeda and two other designated other foreign terrorist organizations. Gufran Ahmed Kauser Mohammed, a naturalized U.S. citizen born in India, and Mohamed Hussein Said, a Kenyan, were charged on a fifteen-count indictment after being arrested in Saudi Arabia and transferred to the U.S. The two men allegedly wired a total of $96,000 to an al-Qaeda affiliate in Syria, the al Nusra Front, and to the militant group al Shabaab in Somalia.[105]

- There was also a "lone wolf" Islamist terrorist attack launched at Fort Hood, Texas on November 5, 2011 by Major Nidal Malik Hasan, a U.S. Army psychiatrist, who had been in regular contact with Anwar al-Awlaki, an American-born imam of Yemeni descent who served as one of al-Qaeda's main ideologues before his death in September 2011 in an American drone strike. Hasan opened fire on the base, killing thirteen people and wounding 31 others. Hasan was shot multiple times, but survived.[106] In August 2013, Hasan was unanimously convicted by a jury of army officers.[107] Hasan's defense lawyer asked the judge to spare Hasan's life, but the request was denied and Hasan is scheduled to die by lethal injection (although a date for his execution has not been set).[108] The Department of Defense and White House declined to classify Hasan as a terrorist, however, instead labeled the Fort Hood incident as a case of workplace violence.[109] Numerous members of Congress have objected to this description, asserting that the attack was clearly one of "homegrown terror[ism]" and have urged the U.S. government to recognize this fact.[110]
- In April 2013, brothers Dzhokar Tsarnaev and Tamerlane Tsarnaev planted bombs at the annual Boston Marathon race. The resulting explosion killed three and injured more than 170.[111] Dzhorkar was captured by police, and Tamerlane died after being shot several times and being run over by Dzhorkar in his attempt to escape.[112] After his capture, the surviving Tsarnaev claimed that he and his brother were motivated by extremist Islamic beliefs, but that they were

not connected to any militant group in particular. He also claimed they learned to build bombs through the website of the al-Qaeda affiliate in Yemen.[113] In May 2015, a federal jury sentenced Tsarnaev to death.[114]

- In December 2015, married couple Syed Rizwan Farook and Tashfeen Malik killed 14 people and injured 22 at a Christmas office party at Farook's employment in San Bernardino, California. The couple was killed in a shootout with police that afternoon.[115] The Islamic State later released a statement claiming responsibility for the attack, referring to Farook and Malik as "'soldiers of the caliphate,'" a term used to describe its soldiers.[116]
- In June 2016, Omar Mateen shot and killed 49 people in a gay nightclub in Orlando, Florida. Mateen himself was shot and killed by Orlando police.[117] During the massacre, Mateen called 911. In the recording, he identified himself, claimed responsibility for the shootings, and pledged allegiance to "Abu Bakr al-Baghdadi of the Islamic State."[118] Mateen also called Orlando news station News 13 and claimed his actions had been motivated by loyalty to the Islamic State.[119]
- In November 2016, Abdul Razak Ali Artan injured 11 people at Ohio State University before being shot by a police officer. Artan rammed a car into a crowd on campus and then stabbed several people with a butcher knife. Shortly before the attack, Artan posted angrily on Facebook about American interference in Muslim countries, referencing radical cleric Anwar al-Awlaki and lone wolf attacks.[120]

Islamism and Society

The U.S. has the most diverse Muslim population in the Western world. In 2016, the Pew Research Center estimated that 3.3 million Muslims live in the United States, equaling about 1 percent of the U.S. population.[121] Sixty-five percent of U.S. Muslims identify themselves as Sunnis, 11 percent as Shia, and 24 percent as having no specific affiliation (describing themselves as "just a Muslim").[122] A large proportion of Muslims in the U.S. are first generation immigrants (63 percent), and 37 percent are native-born, with 15 percent being second generation.[123] Foreign-born Muslim Americans have come from at least 77 different countries. Twenty-six percent of Muslim immigrants to the United States come from the Arab world (Middle East and North Africa), nine percent from Pakistan, seven percent from other South Asian countries (including Pakistan, India, Bangladesh and Afghanistan), three percent come from Iran, five percent come from Europe, and seven percent come from Sub-Saharan Africa. One-third of all Muslim immigrants came to the U.S. during the 1990s and 40 percent have come after 2000. Over three-quarters (81 percent) of all Muslim-Americans are U.S. citizens.[124] At 30 percent, whites make up the largest proportion of Muslims in America.[125] Muslims in America, as a group, are younger than other major religious groups in the U.S.[126]

Seventy percent of Muslim Americans hold very unfavorable views of al-Qaeda, and 81 percent of Muslims in the United States say that violence against civilians and suicide bombings are never justified. Furthermore, 21 percent of American Muslims believe there is either a great deal or a fair amount of support for extremism within their community. Forty-eight percent say that Muslim leaders are not doing enough to challenge extremists.[127]

The fact that the most influential and well-resourced Muslim-American civil society groups are, in a very concrete sense, affiliated with the Muslim Brotherhood and Jama'at-e-Islami is not widely held knowledge. This is partially because Islamist organizations have successfully framed themselves as "moderate," "mainstream," and representative American Muslim religious and civil rights organizations. This has allowed them to avoid widespread public distrust and frame criticism of them as Islamophobia targeting the Muslim-American community rather than criticism of the organizations themselves.

Islamism and the State

Defeating jihadist terrorists is a top priority for President Donald Trump's administration, as ISIS and al-Qaeda continue to ideologically inspire Americans and others to perpetrate terror attacks. The National Security Strategy released by the White House in December 2017 describes the threat from Islamist terrorism and its ideology as follows: "America, alongside our allies and partners, is fighting a long war against these fanatics who advance a totalitarian vision for a global Islamist caliphate that justifies murder and slavery, promotes repression, and seeks to undermine the American way of life. Jihadist terrorists use virtual and physical networks around the world to radicalize isolated individuals, exploit vulnerable populations, and inspire and direct plots."[128] The strategy details the administration's "priority actions" to defeat the threat, including efforts to disrupt terror plots, eliminate terrorist safe havens, and combat radicalization and recruitment in communities.[129]

The Department of Homeland Security (DHS) has set up the Terrorism Prevention Partnerships (TPP) "to address the root causes of violent extremism by providing resources to communities to build and sustain local prevention efforts and promote the use of counter-narratives to confront violent extremist messaging online."[130] In July 2016, DHS announced the Countering Violent Extremism ("CVE") Grant Program that seeks to provide grants to "state, local and tribal partners and community groups—religious groups, mental health and social service providers, educators and other NGOs—with the ability to build prevention programs that address the root causes of violent extremism and deter individuals who may already be radicalizing to violence."[131]

The U.S. government has moved aggressively to disrupt homegrown terror plots and since March 2014, a total of 153 individuals have been charged in the United States on terrorism offenses related to the Islamic State.[132] 32% of the individuals charged were alleged to have been involved in plots targeting the U.S. homeland and 58% were arrested in government sting operations.[133]

Soon after assuming office in January 2017, President Trump signed an executive order which immediately barred entry of individuals into the U.S. from seven Muslim-majority nations—Iran, Iraq, Libya, Somalia, Sudan, Syria, and Yemen. The order dubbed "Protecting the Nation from Foreign Terrorist Entry into the United States" also put a hold on the U.S. refugee program for 120 days and indefinitely barred Syrian refugees from entering the country.[134]

The travel ban generated widespread controversy among the American public resulting in President Trump issuing Executive

Order 13780 on March 6, 2017 that took into consideration certain legal objections and removed Iraq from the list of affected countries.[135] On September 24, 2017, Presidential Proclamation 9645 superseded Executive Order 13780 and North Korea and Venezuela were added to the list of countries impacted by the travel ban.[136] The Supreme Court upheld President Trump's controversial travel ban in a landmark decision on June 26, 2018.[137]

A report released in January 2018 by the Departments of Justice and Homeland Security found that a majority of terrorists convicted of "international terrorism-related charges" in the U.S. since 2001 were foreign-born. Out of 549 convictions for international terrorism-related charges in U.S. federal courts between September 11, 2001 and December 31, 2016, approximately 73 percent (402 of the 549 individuals) were foreign-born.[138]

Designation of the Muslim Brotherhood as an international terrorist organization has been the topic of considerable debate[139] in Washington since Sen. Ted Cruz (R-TX) and Rep. Mario Diaz-Balart (R-FL) introduced a bill called the "Muslim Brotherhood Terrorist Designation Act" in January 2017.[140] The debate lost steam after an internal State Department report "advised against it because of the movement's loose-knit structure and far-flung political ties across the Middle East."[141] However, such a designation, or lesser related actions that might be undertaken by the Administration, remain actively discussed within the Administration and the Washington policy community.[142]

Endnotes

1. Nicholas J. Rasmussen, "World Wide Threats: Keeping America Secure in the New Age of Terror," Hearing before the House Committee on Homeland Security, November 30, 2017, http://docs.house.gov/meetings/HM/HM00/20171130/106651/HHRG-115-HM00-Wstate-RasmussenN-20171130.pdf.
2. Mina Hamblet, "The Islamic State's Virtual Caliphate: Jihad in the West," *Middle East Quarterly* (Fall 2017), http://www.meforum.org/6894/the-islamic-state-virtu-

al-caliphate#_ftnref6.

3. Aaron Mehta, "Mattis reveals new rules of engagement," *Military Times*, Oct. 3, 2017, https://www.militarytimes.com/flashpoints/2017/10/03/mattis-reveals-new-rules-of-engagement/
4. Charlie Savage and Eric Schmitt, "Trump Poised to Drop Some Limits on Drone Strikes and Commando Raids," *Nee York Times*, Sept. 17, 2017, https://www.nytimes.com/2017/09/21/us/politics/trump-drone-strikes-commando-raids-rules.html
5. "Text of Letter from the President to the Speaker of the House of Representatives and the President Pro Tempore of the Senate," Dec. 11, 2017, https://www.whitehouse.gov/briefings-statements/text-letter-president-speaker-house-representatives-president-pro-tempore-senate-2/.
6. This term was coined in Kalim Siddiqui, *Stages of Islamic Revolution* (London: The Open Press, 1996). It refers to groups tied to the Muslim Brotherhood (*Al-Ikhwan al-Muslimeen*) and the Pakistani Islamist party, *Jama'at al-Islami.*
7. *Jama'at-e Islami* is a South Asian Islamist movement founded in 1941 by Syed Abul A'ala Maududi, who was perhaps the most influential Islamist thinker of the 20th Century.
8. Giles Kepel, *The War for Muslim Minds: Islam and the West* (Cambridge, MA: Belknap Press, 2006); Lorenzo Vidino, *The New Western Brothers* (New York: Columbia University Press, forthcoming 2010); Lorenzo Vidino, "Aims and Methods of Europe's Muslim Brotherhood," *Current Trends in Islamist Ideology* 4 (2006); Allison Pargeter, *The New Frontiers of Jihad: Radical Islam in Europe* (Philadelphia: University of Pennsylvania Press, 2008), 20.
9. "Elbarasse Search 1," *U.S. v. Holy Land Foundation et al.*, 3:04-CR-240-G (N.D. Tex. 2008), http://www.txnd.uscourts.gov/judges/hlf2/09-25-08/Elbarasse Search 1.pdf; "Elbarasse Search 3," *U.S. v. Holy Land Foundation et al.*, http://www.txnd.uscourts.gov/judges/hlf2/09-25-08/Elbarasse Search 3.pdf; "Elbarasse Search 19," *U.S. v. Holy Land Foundation et al.*,

http://www.txnd.uscourts.gov/judges/hlf2/09-29-08/Elbarasse Search 19.pdf; "Elbarasse Search 2," *U.S. v. Holy Land Foundation et al.*, http://www.txnd.uscourts.gov/judges/hlf2/09-25-08/Elbarasse Search 2.pdf; Esam Omeish, Letter to the *Washington Post*, September 16, 2004, http://www.unitedstatesaction.com/documents/omeish/www-masnet-org_pressroom_release-asp_nycmexs4.pdf; Noreen S. Ahmed-Ullah et al., "A Rare Look at the Secretive Brotherhood in America," *Chicago Tribune*, September 19, 2004, http://www.chicagotribune.com/news/watchdog/chi-0409190261sep19,0,3008717.story.

10. Stephen P. Cohen, *The Idea of Pakistan* (Washington, DC: Brookings Institution, 2004), 348, n. 7; Vali Reza Nasr, *The Vanguard of the Islamic Revolution: The Jama'at-I Islami of Pakistan* (Berkeley: University of California Press, 1994).
11. See, for example: Esam Omeish, "MAS President Letter to the Washington Post," Muslim American Society Website, September 16, 2004, http://www.unitedstatesaction.com/documents/omeish/www-masnet-org_pressroom_release-asp_nycmexs4.pdf
12. "Exhibit 0003918-0003919," (Letter from "The Political Office" re: the founding of the Islamic Association for Palestine by "the Group"), *U.S. v. Holy Land Foundation et al.*, 5.
13. Zeid al-Noman, as quoted in "Elbarasse Search 2," *U.S. v. Holy Land Foundation et al.*
14. "Elbarasse Search 2," *U.S. v. Holy Land Foundation et al.*
15. "MSA MAP," MSA National, accessed January 22, 2018, http://msanational.org/msa-map/
16. Ahmed Shama, Speech before the 7th Annual MSA West Conference, University of Southern California, January 2005.
17. Shah Imam, Speech before the MSA 2006 East Zone Conference, University of Maryland, March 2006
18. "About NAIT," accessed January 22, 2018, http://islamicbookservice.org/index.php/about-nait/about
19. "The North American Islamic Trust-NAIT," accessed January 22, 2018, http://islamicbookservice.org/

20. "The North American Islamic Trust-NAIT," accessed January 22, 2018, http://islamicbookservice.org/
21. "The North American Islamic Trust – NAIT," North American Islamic Trust Website, n.d., http://www.nait.net/NAIT_about_ us.htm; See also John Mintz and Douglas Farah, "In Search of Friends Among the Foes," *Washington Post*, September 11, 2004, http://www.washingtonpost.com/wp-dyn/articles/A12823-2004Sep10.html; Zeyno Baran, "The Muslim Brotherhood's U.S. Network," *Current Trends in Islamist Ideology* 6 (2008); Steven Merley, "The Muslim Brotherhood in the United States," Hudson Institute *Research Monographs on the Muslim World Series* no. 2, paper no. 3, April 2009.
22. Yusuf Al-Qaradawi, *The Lawful and the Prohibited in Islam (Al-Halal Wal Haram Fil Islam)*(American Trust Publications, 1999), https://books.google.com/books/about/The_Lawful_and_the_Prohibited_in_Islam_A.html?id=v21NCwAAQBAJ.
23. NAIT Website, http://islamicbookservice.org/.
24. Federal Bureau of Investigation, Indianapolis, Indiana, "North American Islamic Trust (NAIT)," December 15, 1987, http://www.investigativeproject.org/documents/misc/148.pdf
25. "List of Unindicted Co-Conspirators and Joint Venturers," *U.S. v. Holy Land Foundation et al.*, http://www.investigativeproject.org/documents/case_docs/423.pdf.
26. "List of Unindicted Co-Conspirators and Joint Venturers," *U.S. v. Holy Land Foundation et al.*
27. "ISNA Board of Directors (Majlis Ash-Shura)," ISNA Website, ,November 14, 2016, accessed January 22, 2018, https://web.archive.org/web/20161114145902/http://www.isna.net/board-of-directors.html; "Elbarasse Search 3," *U.S. v. Holy Land Foundation et al.*
28. Zaheer Uddin, "ICNA: A Successful Journey and a Promising Road Ahead." *The Message International* 23, no. 8 (1999), 24.
29. "The Charter And By-Laws," Islamic Circle of North America, accessed January 22, 2018, https://web.archive.org/web/20101227052638/http:/www.icnasisterswing.com/charterbylawfiles/ICNA_CBL.pdf.

30. "The Charter And By-Laws," Islamic Circle of North America, accessed January 22, 2018, https://web.archive.org/web/20101227052638/http:/www.icnasisterswing.com/charterbylawfiles/ICNA_CBL.pdf.
31. "Promoting Radical Ideas—What ICNA Demands of its Members," *IPT News*, August 10, 2010, https://www.investigativeproject.org/2098/promoting-radical-ideas-what-icna-demands-of-its; "ICNA Still Promotes Radical Texts," *IPT News*, September 9, 2011, https://www.investigativeproject.org/3155/icna-still-promotes-radical-texts; "ICNA's Radical Reading List," *IPT News*, April 27, 2010, https://www.investigativeproject.org/1919/icnas-radical-reading-list.
32. Nadeem F. Paracha, "Abdul Ala Maududi: An existentialist history," *Dawn*, January 1, 2015, https://www.dawn.com/news/1154419.
33. Paulo Casaca, "Maududi: The founder of modern Jihadism," *New Delhi Times*, March 3, 2017, http://www.newdelhitimes.com/maududi-the-founder-of-modern-jihadism123/,
34. "Member's Hand Book," *Islamic Circle of North America*, pp. 9-10, https://www.investigativeproject.org/documents/misc/475.pdf.
35. "ICNA Leader Convicted in 1971 Bangladesh Massacres," *IPT News*, November 3, 2013, https://www.investigativeproject.org/4204/icna-leader-convicted-in-1971-bangladesh-massacres.
36. Naeem Baig, "Kashmir needs immediate attention of Pres. Obama," *Islamic Circle of North America*, July 12, 2016, http://www.icna.org/kashmir-needs-immediate-attention-of-obama-administration/.
37. "Kashmir Commander Speaks," Interview with Syed Salahuddin Ahmed, Supreme Commander, Hizbul Mujahideen, *The Message*, October 1997, https://www.investigativeproject.org/documents/misc/963.pdf.
38. Abha Shankar, "IPT Investigation Reveals ICNA Partner's Close Ties to Kashmiri Jihadists," *IPT News*, December 5, 2017, https://www.investigativeproject.org/7011/ipt-investigation-reveals-icna-partner-close-ties.
39. "Vision, Mission, Core Principles," Council on Amer-

ican-Islamic Relations (CAIR) Website, accessed January 22, 2018, https://www.cair.com/about-us/vision-mission-core-principles.html.

40. "Articles of Incorporation, Council of American-Islamic Relations," September 15, 1994.
41. "Elbarasse Search 13," *U.S. v. Holy Land Foundation et al.*, https://www.investigativeproject.org/documents/case_docs/1536.pdf.
42. Government Exhibit 003-0078, *U.S. v. Holy Land Foundation et al.*, https://www.investigativeproject.org/documents/case_docs/717.pdf.
43. "Federal Judge Hands Down Sentences in Holy Land Foundation Case," *Department of Justice Press Release*, May 27, 2009, https://www.justice.gov/opa/pr/federal-judge-hands-downs-sentences-holy-land-foundation-case.
44. "Jury Verdict," *U.S. v. Holy Land Foundation et al.*, https://www.investigativeproject.org/documents/case_docs/741.pdf.
45. "Government's Second Supplemental Trial Brief," *U.S. v. Holy Land Foundation et al.*, pp. 7-8, https://www.investigativeproject.org/documents/case_docs/658.pdf.
46. "Government's Second Supplemental Trial Brief," *U.S. v. Holy Land Foundation et al.*, pp. 7-8, https://www.investigativeproject.org/documents/case_docs/658.pdf.
47. "CAIR and Terrorism: Blanket Opposition to U.S. Investigations, Equivocal Condemnations for Plots Against America," Investigative Project on Terrorism, n.d., https://www.investigativeproject.org/documents/misc/116.pdf.
48. "CAIR's Extremism and anti-Semitism," Investigative Project on Terrorism, n.d., https://www.investigativeproject.org/documents/misc/120.pdf.
49. "List of Unindicted Co-Conspirators and Joint Venturers," *U.S. v. Holy Land Foundation et al.*, http://www.investigativeproject.org/documents/case_docs/423.pdf.
50. "FBI: CAIR is a front group, and Holy Land Foundation tapped Hamas clerics for fundraisers," *Dallas Morning News*, October 7, 2008, https://www.dallasnews.com/news/crime/2008/10/07/fbi-cair-is-a-front-group-and.

51. Mary Jacoby, "FBI Cuts Off CAIR Over Hamas Questions," *IPT News*, January 29, 2009, https://www.investigativeproject.org/985/fbi-cuts-off-cair-over-hamas-questions.
52. Noreen S. Ahmed-Ullah, Roe and Cohen, "A rare look at secretive Brotherhood in America."
53. Noreen S. Ahmed-Ullah, Roe and Cohen, "A rare look at secretive Brotherhood in America."
54. Noreen S. Ahmed-Ullah, Roe and Cohen, "A rare look at secretive Brotherhood in America."
55. Noreen S. Ahmed-Ullah, Roe and Cohen, "A rare look at secretive Brotherhood in America."
56. Noreen S. Ahmed-Ullah, Roe and Cohen, "A rare look at secretive Brotherhood in America."
57. "IPT Exclusive: Under Oath, Alamoudi Ties MAS to Brotherhood," *IPT News*, March 14, 2012, https://www.investigativeproject.org/3486/under-oath-alamoudi-ties-mas-to-brotherhood.
58. "Abdurahman Alamoudi Sentenced to Jail in Terrorism Financing Case," *Department of Justice Press Release*, October 15, 2004, https://www.justice.gov/archive/opa/pr/2004/October/04_crm_698.htm.
59. "American Muslims: Shaping the Future Through Faith Vision," 16th Annual MAS-ICNA Convention, Chicago, December 28-30, 2017, http://www.masicna.com/.
60. "CAIR Protests Saudi Radical's Exclusion from U.S.," *IPT News*, December 27, 2012, https://www.investigativeproject.org/3864/cair-protests-saudi-radical-exclusion-from-us.
61. "Conference Make AMP's Destructive Ambition Clear," *IPT News*, December 30, 2010, https://www.investigativeproject.org/2462/conferences-make-amp-destructive-ambition-clear.
62. "About IIIT," IIIT Website, n.d., http://www.iiit.org/AboutUs/AboutIIIT/tabid/66/Default.aspx
63. "About IIIT," IIIT Website, n.d.
64. "Affidavit of SA David Kane," In the Matter Involving 555 Grove Street, Herndon, Virginia, and Related Locations, 02-MG-114 (E.D.V.A. March 2002), 49–50. (Hereinafter "Kane Affidavit").
65. Kane Affidavit.

66. Mintz and Farah, "In Search Of Friends Among The Foes"; "Jordan's Islamic Action Front picks up New Leadership," Deutsche Presse-Agentur, May 31, 2009.
67. Syed Saleem Shahzad, "Jordan's Islamic Front rallies Muslims," *Asia Times Online*, March 7, 2003, http://www.atimes.com/atimes/Middle_East/EC07Ak01.html.
68. See, for example, Jamal Halaby, "Jordan Islamists to Step up Anti-Election Campaign," Associated Press, January 15, 2013, http://news.yahoo.com/jordan-islamists-step-anti-election-campaign-114524529.html.
69. "Conferences Make AMP's Destructive Ambition Clear," *IPT News*, December 30, 2010, https://www.investigativeproject.org/2462/conferences-make-amp-destructive-ambition-clear.
70. "AMP Official Defends Hamas, Praises Israeli Casualties," *IPT News*, July 21, 2014, https://www.investigativeproject.org/4470/amp-official-defends-hamas-praises-israeli.
71. "IPT Exclusive: AMP's Telling Choice of Heroes," *IPT News*, April 8, 2014, https://www.investigativeproject.org/4346/ipt-exclusive-amp-telling-choice-of-heroes.
72. "Investigation Exposes AMP Leaders' Ties to Former US-Based Hamas-Support Network," *IPT News*, June 24, 2015, https://www.investigativeproject.org/4891/investigation-exposes-amp-leaders-ties-to-former.
73. Jonathan Schanzer, "Israel Imperiled: Threats to the Jewish State," Joint Hearing before House Foreign Affairs Committee, Subcommittee on Terrorism, Nonproliferation, and Trade and the Subcommittee on the Middle East and North Africa, Washington, DC, April 19, 2016, http://docs.house.gov/meetings/FA/FA18/20160419/104817/HHRG-114-FA18-Wstate-SchanzerJ-20160419.pdf.
74. "Islamic Action for Palestine—An Internal Memo (Government Exhibit 003-0015," *U.S. v. Holy Land Foundation, et al.*, https://www.investigativeproject.org/documents/misc/23.pdf#page=11.
75. Abha Shankar, "Judge Reinstates Hamas/AMP Lawsuit," *IPT News*, January 8, 2018, https://www.investigativeproject.org/7204/judge-reinstates-hamas-amp-

lawsuit.

76. "Conferences Make AMP's Destructive Ambition Clear," *IPT News*, December 30, 2010, https://www.investigativeproject.org/2462/conferences-make-amp-destructive-ambition-clear.
77. "AMP Official Defends Hamas, Praises Israeli Casualties," *IPT News*, July 21, 2014, https://www.investigativeproject.org/4470/amp-official-defends-hamas-praises-israeli.
78. "Jamaat ul-Fuqra," South Asia Terrorism Portal (SATP), n.d., http://www.satp.org/satporgtp/countries/pakistan/terroristoutfits/jamaat-ul-fuqra.htm
79. Richard Sale, "Pakistan ISI link to Pearl kidnap probed," United Press International, January 29, 2002, http://www.upi.com/Business_News/Security-Industry/2002/01/29/Pakistan-ISI-link-to-Pearl-kidnap-probed/UPI-22581012351784/. JeM is designated as a Foreign Terrorist Organization by the U.S. government. JeM seeks to liberate Kashmir and reunite it with Pakistan.
80. "Welcome to the International Quranic Open University," International Quranic Open University Website, n.d., http://www.iqou-moa.org/.
81. The online edition of *The Islamic Post* can be accessed at http://islamicpostonline.com/.
82. Colorado Attorney General Press Release, "Attorney General Salazar announces 69 Year Sentence for 'Fuqra' defendant convicted of racketeering and conspiracy to commit murder," March 16, 2001.
83. "United States: The Jamaat al-Fuqra Threat," *Stratfor*, June 2, 2005, http://www.stratfor.com/memberships/61912/united_states_jamaat_al_fuqra_threat.
84. "'Homegrown Jihad: The Terrorist Camps Around U.S.' Hits Cable TV," Christian Action Network Website, n.d., http://www.christianaction.org/homegrown-jihad/.
85. Madeleine Gruen, "Hizb ut Tahrir's Activities in the United States," Jamestown Foundation *Terrorism Monitor* 5, no. 16, August 22, 2007, http://www.jamestown.org/single/?no_cache=1&tx_ttnews%5Btt_news%5D=4377

86. "Hizb ut Tahrir," Hizb ut Tahrir America Website, n.d., http://www.hizb-america.org/index.php/aboutus/hizbuttahrir.
87. "Hizb ut Tahrir," Hizb ut Tahrir America Website, n.d.
88. Houriya Ahmed and Hannah Stuart, *Hizb ut Tahrir: Ideology and Strategy* (London: Centre for Social Cohesion, 2009).
89. Gruen, "Hizb ut Tahrir's Activities in the United States"
90. "Mission Statement," Revolution Muslim Website, n.d., http://www.revolutionmuslim.com/index.php?option=com_content&view=article&id=3&Itemid=17
91. Matt Zapotosky, "New Jersey man sentenced to prison for extremist Islamic Web posts," *Washington Post,* April 25, 2014, https://www.washingtonpost.com/local/crime/new-jersey-man-to-be-sentenced-for-extremist-islamic-web-posts/2014/04/24/406e65a8-cbc4-11e3-93eb-6c0037dde2ad_story.html?utm_term=.95898084ffe5.
92. Matt Zapotosky, "New Jersey man sentenced to prison for extremist Islamic Web posts"
93. Rukmini Callimachi, "Once a Qaeda Recruiter, Now a Voice Against Jihad," *New York Times,* August 29, 2016, https://www.nytimes.com/2016/08/30/us/al-qaeda-islamic-state-jihad-fbi.html?_r=0.
94. Matt Zapotosky, "The feds billed him as a threat to American freedom. Now they're paying him for help," *Washington Post,* February 5, 2016, https://www.washingtonpost.com/local/public-safety/the-feds-billed-him-as-a-threat-to-american-freedom-now-theyre-paying-him-for-help/2016/02/04/32be460a-c6c5-11e5-a4aa-f25866ba0dc6_story.html?utm_term=.f1f753576d06.
95. Callimachi, "Once a Qaeda Recruiter, Now a Voice Against Jihad."
96. Rachel Weiner, "Man Who Turned Away from Radical Islam Arrested on Drug, Prostitution Charges," *Washington Post*, January 25, 2017, https://www.washingtonpost.com/local/public-safety/man-who-turned-away-from-radical-islam-arrested-on-drug-prostitution-charges/2017/01/25/70a9627e-de7a-11e6-ad42-f3375f271c9c_story.html .

97. Lorenzo Vidino, Francesco Marone and Eva Entenmann, "Fear Thy Neighbor: Radicalization and Jihadist Attacks in the West," Program of Extremism, The George Washington University & The International Centre for Counter-Terrorism—The Hague (ICCT), 2017, pp. 15-16, https://extremism.gwu.edu/sites/extremism.gwu.edu/files/FearThyNeighbor%20RadicalizationandJihadistAttacksintheWest.pdf.
98. Tom Winter, Jonathan Dienst and Tracy Connor, "NYC blast suspect Akayed Ullah aimed to avenge Muslim deaths, sources say," *NBC News*, December 12, 2017, https://www.nbcnews.com/news/us-news/akayed-ullah-nyc-explosion-suspect-identified-27-year-old-brooklyn-n828361.
99. Peter Martinez, "New York attack suspect: Who is Sayfullo Habibullaevic Saaipov?," *CBS News*, November 1, 2017, https://www.cbsnews.com/news/new-york-terror-attack-suspect-who-is-sayfullo-habibullaevic-saipov/.
100. Denis Slattery, et al., "Terrorist plot targeting NYC concerts, subways and landmarks foiled by investigators," *New York Daily News*, Oct. 6, 2017, http://www.nydailynews.com/new-york/terror-plot-targeting-concerts-subways-nyc-foiled-article-1.3546153.
101. U.S. Department of Justice Press Release, "Seven Charged with Terrorism Violations in North Carolina," July 27, 2009; U.S. Department of Justice Press Release, "Superseding Indictment in Boyd Matter Charges Defendants with Conspiring to Murder U.S. Military Personnel, Weapons Violations," September 24, 2009.
102. U.S. Attorney's Office, Eastern District of North Carolina, "North Carolina Resident Daniel Patrick Boyd Sentenced for Terrorism Violations," August 24, 2012, http://www.fbi.gov/charlotte/press-releases/2012/north-carolina-resident-daniel-patrick-boyd-sentenced-for-terrorism-violations
103. United States Department of Justice, "Man Sentenced to 24 Years in Prison for Attempting to Use a Weapon of Mass Destruction to Bomb Skyscraper in Downtown Dallas," October 19, 2010, http://www.justice.gov/opa/pr/2010/October/10-nsd-1170.html.

104. "Criminal Complaint," *U.S. v. Smadi*, 3:09-MT-286 (N.D. Tex. September 24, 2009).
105. Zachary Fagenson, "Two men charged in Miami with financing foreign terrorist groups," Reuters, August 13, 2013, http://www.reuters.com/article/2013/08/13/us-usa-florida-suspects-idUSBRE97C0ZL20130813.
106. Philip Sherwell and Alex Spillius, "Fort Hood Shooting: Texas Army Killer Linked to September 11 Terrorists," *Telegraph* (London), November 7, 2009.
107. "Judge Denies Defense Lawyers' Request in Fort Hood Case," *New York Times*, August 27, 2013, http://www.nytimes.com/2013/08/28/us/judge-denies-defense-lawyers-request-in-fort-hood-case.html.
108. "Death Penalty for Rampage at Fort Hood," *New York Times*, August 28, 2013, http://www.nytimes.com/2013/08/29/us/jury-weighs-sentence-for-fort-hood-shooting.html?pagewanted=all
109. See, for example, "Pentagon Will Not Classify Fort Hood Shootings as Terrorism -- or Anything Else," *CNS News*, October 22, 2012, http://cnsnews.com/news/article/pentagon-will-not-classify-fort-hood-shootings-terrorism-or-anything-else - sthash.YWjerBq9.dpuf.
110. "Lawmakers Call Ft. Hood Shootings 'Terrorism,'" *New York Times*, November 19, 2009, http://www.nytimes.com/2009/11/20/us/politics/20hood.html.
111. Katherine Q. Seelye, William K. Rashbaum, and Michael Cooper, "2nd Bombing Suspect Caught After Frenzied Hunt Paralyzes Boston," *New York Times,* April 19, 2013, http://www.nytimes.com/2013/04/20/us/boston-marathon-bombings.html?hp.
112. Katherine Q. Seelye, et al., "2nd Bombing Suspect Caught After Frenzied Hunt Paralyzes Boston."
113. Michael Cooper, Michael S. Schmidt, and Eric Schmidt, "Boston Suspects Are Seen as Self-Taught and Fueled by Web," *New York Times,* April 23, 2013, http://www.nytimes.com/2013/04/24/us/boston-marathon-bombing-developments.html?hp&pagewanted=all.
114. Ann O'Neill, Aaron Cooper and Ray Sanchez, "Boston Marathon bombing Dzhokar Tsarnaev sentenced to death," *CNN,* May 17, 2015, http://www.cnn.

com/2015/05/15/us/boston-bombing-tsarnaev-sentence/.

115. Joe Mozingo, "'The worst thing imaginable:' Bodies and blood everywhere after San Bernardino terrorist attack, DOJ report shows," *Los Angeles Times,* September 9, 2016, http://www.latimes.com/local/lanow/la-me-san-bernardino-terror--20160909-snap-story.html.
116. Rukmini Callimachi, "Islamic State Says 'Soldiers of Caliphate' Attacked in San Bernardino," *New York Times,* December 5, 2015, https://www.nytimes.com/2015/12/06/world/middleeast/islamic-state-san-bernardino-massacre.html.
117. AnneClaire Stapleton and Ralph Ellis, "Timeline of Orlando nightclub shooting," *CNN,* June 17, 2016, http://www.cnn.com/2016/06/12/us/orlando-shooting-timeline/.
118. United States Department of Justice, Office of Public Affairs, "Joint Statement From the Justice Department and FBI Regarding Transcript Related to Orlando Terror Attack," June 20, 2016, https://www.justice.gov/opa/pr/joint-statement-justice-department-and-fbi-regarding-transcript-related-orlando-terror-attack.
119. Scott Fais, "Mateen to News 13 producer: 'I'm the shooter. It's me,'" *News 13,* June 15, 2016, http://www.mynews13.com/content/news/cfnews13/news/article.html/content/news/articles/cfn/2016/6/14/orlando_shooting_oma.html.
120. Pete Williams, Tom Winter, Andrew Blankstein and Tracy Connor, "Suspect Identified in Ohio State Attack as Abdul Razak Ali Artan," *NBC News,* November 28, 2016, http://www.nbcnews.com/news/us-news/suspect-dead-after-ohio-state-university-car-knife-attack-n689076.
121. Besheer Mohamed, "A new estimate of the U.S. Muslim population," Pew Research Center, January 6, 2016, http://www.pewresearch.org/fact-tank/2016/01/06/a-new-estimate-of-the-u-s-muslim-population/.
122. Michael Lipka, "Muslims and Islam: Key findings in the U.S. and around the world," Pew Research Center, February 27, 2017, http://www.pewresearch.org/fact-tank/2017/02/27/muslims-and-islam-key-findings-in-

the-u-s-and-around-the-world/.
123. Pew Research Center, "Muslim Americans: No Signs of Growth in Alienation or Support for Extremism," August 30, 2011, http://people-press.org/files/2011/08/muslim-american-report.pdf.
124. Pew Research Center, "Muslim Americans: No Signs of Growth in Alienation or Support for Extremism".
125. Pew Research Center, "Muslim Americans: No Signs of Growth in Alienation or Support for Extremism".
126. Pew Research Center, "Muslim Americans: No Signs of Growth in Alienation or Support for Extremism".
127. Pew Research Center, "Muslim Americans: No Signs of Growth in Alienation or Support for Extremism".
128. "National Security Strategy of the United States of America," December 2017, p. 10, https://www.whitehouse.gov/wp-content/uploads/2017/12/NSS-Final-12-18-2017-0905.pdf.
129. "National Security Strategy of the United States of America," December 2017, p. 11, https://www.whitehouse.gov/wp-content/uploads/2017/12/NSS-Final-12-18-2017-0905.pdf.
130. "Terrorism Prevention Partnerhips," Department of Homeland Security, https://www.dhs.gov/terrorism-prevention-partnerships.
131. "Terrorism Prevention Partnerhips," Department of Homeland Security, https://www.dhs.gov/terrorism-prevention-partnerships.
132. "GW Extremism Tracker: The Islamic State in America," Program on Extremism, The George Washington University, https://extremism.gwu.edu/sites/extremism.gwu.edu/files/Dec%202017%20Update.pdf.
133. "GW Extremism Tracker: The Islamic State in America," Program on Extremism, The George Washington University, https://extremism.gwu.edu/sites/extremism.gwu.edu/files/Dec%202017%20Update.pdf.
134. "Executive Order Protecting the Nation from Foreign Terrorist Entry into the United States," *The White House*, January 27, 2017, https://www.whitehouse.gov/presidential-actions/executive-order-protecting-nation-foreign-terrorist-entry-united-states/.
135. "Executive Order Protecting The Nation From For-

eign Terrorist Entry Into The United States," *The White House*, March 6, 2017, https://www.whitehouse.gov/presidential-actions/executive-order-protecting-nation-foreign-terrorist-entry-united-states-2/

136. "Presidential Proclamation Enhancing Vetting Capabilities and Processes for Detecting Attempted Entry Into the United States by Terrorists or Other Public-Safety Threats," *The White House*, September 24, 2017, https://www.whitehouse.gov/presidential-actions/presidential-proclamation-enhancing-vetting-capabilities-processes-detecting-attempted-entry-united-states-terrorists-public-safety-threats/
137. Brent Kendall and Jess Bravin, "Supreme Court Upholds Trump Travel Ban," *Wall Street Journal*, June 26, 2018, https://www.wsj.com/articles/supreme-court-upholds-trump-travel-ban-1530022794
138. "Executive Order 13780: *Protecting the Nation from Foreign Terrorist Entry Into the United States*," Department of Homeland Security and Department of Justice, January 2018, p. 2, https://www.dhs.gov/sites/default/files/publications/Executive%20Order%2013780%20Section%2011%20Report%20-%20Final.pdf.
139. Mark Hosenball, "Trump administration debates designating Muslim Brotherhood as terrorist group," *Reuters*, January 29, 2017, https://www.reuters.com/article/us-usa-trump-muslimbrotherhood/trump-administration-debates-designating-muslim-brotherhood-as-terrorist-group-idUSKBN15D0VV.
140. Christine Rousselle, "Ted Cruz Introduces Bill to Designate Muslim Brotherhood As Terrorist Organization," *Townhall*, January 11, 2017, https://townhall.com/tipsheet/christinerousselle/2017/01/11/ted-cruz-introduces-bill-to-designate-muslim-brotherhood-as-terrorist-organization-n2269714.
141. Guy Taylor, "How to deal with Muslim Brotherhood triggers Trump White House infighting," *Washington Times*, March 27, 2017, https://www.washingtontimes.com/news/2017/mar/27/muslim-brotherhood-listing-as-terror-group-delayed/.
142. Jonathan Schanzer, "The careful way to go after Muslim Brotherhood radicals," *New York Post*, February 12,

2017, https://nypost.com/2017/02/12/the-careful-way-to-go-after-muslim-brotherhood-radicals/

Latin America

8 Argentina

Quick Facts

Population: 44,293,293 (July 2017 est.)
Area: 2,780,400 sq km
Ethnic Groups: European (mostly Spanish and Italian descent) and mestizo (mixed European and Amerindian ancestry) 97.2%, Amerindian 2.4%, African 0.4% (2010 est.)
Religions: Nominally Roman Catholic 92% (less than 20% practicing), Protestant 2%, Jewish 2%, other 4%
Government Type: Presidential republic
GDP (official exchange rate): $619.9 billion (2017 est.)

Source: CIA World FactBook (Last Updated March 2018)

Introduction

Argentina is home to one of the largest Muslim populations in Latin America. A growing percentage of this community is made up of Argentine converts to Islam, a significant number of whom have been recruited and radicalized by Islamist operatives working throughout the country.

The Argentine Muslim community has gone largely unnoticed since its establishment in the 19th century, but questionable financial investments, such as those from Libya and Saudi Arabia tied to Carlos Menem's administration and bombings in Buenos Aires in the early 1990s—the largest terror attacks in the region at the time—brought it into the national spotlight. Since then, the community has been stigmatized for its connection to radical Islamist networks tied to Iran and its proxy, Hezbollah. Through these networks, Iran has used intelligence operatives to infiltrate Muslim society and recruit members from a community that shows signs of increasing radicalization.

These networks pose a significant danger to Argentina, whose policy toward Iran and other Arab states has often been ambivalent and inconsistent. Moreover, Argentina's failing economy and its strained relationships with Western allies during the presidency of Cristina Fernández de Kirchner made it even more vulnerable to Iranian advances and activities in the region.

Islamist Activity

Radical Islamist activity has been growing throughout Argentina since at least the early 1980s, when the Iranian Revolution was "exported" to the Americas. Iranian interest in the American continent at large dates to the 1850s. Then known as Persia and controlled by the Qajar Dynasty, the nation sought U.S. help in constraining European powers. In later years, Persia fostered diplomatic relationships with a variety of other nations such as Argentina, Brazil, and Mexico. However, Iran's political objectives changed with the 1979 Revolution, resulting in a break in ties with the United States and an eventual shift toward Latin America, particularly toward countries antagonistic to "American imperialism." According to Alberto Nisman, the special prosecutor for the AMIA attack, Iran and Hezbollah saw Argentina as a land of opportunity for spreading radical Islam due to the large number of Muslim communities in the region, particularly the Tri-Border Area at the crossroads of Argentina, Brazil, and Paraguay. Nisman cited documents seized from Iranian operatives identifying high-density areas of Muslim population to be used "as centers of penetration of Islam" throughout South America. Since then, Argentina in particular has served as one of the main hubs through which Shi'a radicals have developed an extensive network of terrorists, clergymen and recruiters, money launderers, and other operatives all dedicated to "exporting the revolution" throughout the region.

The result of this growing network was the execution of Latin America's most notorious Islamist terrorist attack—the July 18, 1994 bombing in Buenos Aires, Argentina of the Asociación Mutual Israelita Argentina (AMIA), which killed 85 civilians and injured hundreds more. Two years earlier, on March 17, 1992, a similar attack had been carried out against Israel's embassy in Buenos Aires, murdering 29 people and injuring over two hundred. These twin attacks awoke Argentina to the real threat of Islamist activity within and around its borders.

According to Nisman, Iran's Islamist terrorist network in Argentina was first established in 1983 with the arrival of Iranian operative Mohsen Rabbani. Originally sent to Argentina under the guise of a commercial representative of the Iranian meat industry, Rabbani quickly established himself as a leader within the country's Shi'ite Muslim community and began leading prayers at the At-Tauhid mosque in the Floresta neighborhood of Buenos Aires. In his role as a prayer leader, Rabbani was able to address believers at will, inserting radical political rhetoric into his sermons and developing relationships with young "disciples" who would later become operatives within his evolving terror network.

The network Rabbani established throughout the Shi'ite Muslim community in Buenos Aires grew to include more than 40 Islamic associations, including schools, media outlets, and charity organizations that are used today as backdoor channels through which the Islamic Republic and Hezbollah perform intelligence and covert operations. It spans across state borders, allowing Iran and its proxies to pursue various terror operations in the region as a part of their political expansion. The most well-known of these operations is the 1994 AMIA attack in Buenos Aires, of which Nisman identified Rabbani as "the mastermind." Though Rabbani escaped justice in Argentina by leaving the country in 1997, Interpol has since placed him on a "red alert" list, barring his travel to the region. However, the Islamist terror network he established continues to grow under the supervision of his numerous disciples.

According to a recent report by the Center for a Secure Free Society (SFS), Rabbani's Argentine connections can be broken down into three different types of actors: shadow facilitators, "super fixers," and "fixers." While prohibited from entering Argentina, Rabbani still acts as a shadow facilitator from Iran, providing guidance and funding to various Islamist activities in Argentina. His disciples act as "super fixers," moving across countries throughout Latin America and acting as point persons for the "fixers," or local Argentine agents who have access to or knowledge of targeted communities in the country. Perhaps the two most infamous Rabbani disciples and "super fixers" are Abdul Karim Paz and Edgardo Ruben "Suhail" Assad. According to Nisman, Karim Paz is Rabbani's first convert and has been described as his "right-hand man" and immediate successor as the Imam of the At-Tauhid mosque. Similarly, Suhail Assad is known as a prominent leader in the local Shi'a community, with strong connections to the government of former Argentine president Cristina Fernández de Kirchner. Some of these connections come from Suhail Assad's cousin, Jorge Alejandro "Yussuf" Khalil, who was accused by Nisman of conspiring with the Fernández de Kirchner regime to cover up Iran's involvement in the AMIA attack through a controversial agreement signed between both countries in 2013. Yussuf Khalil is currently the General Secretary of the At-Tauhid Mosque.

Together, Yussuf Khalil, Abdul Karim Paz and Suhail Assad serve as Iran's "informal ambassadors" in Argentina, continuing to recruit and radicalize Islamic communities to join the revolution. Under their supervision, the radical Islamist network in Argentina grows stronger and more expansive behind its façade of Muslim community and religious centers, cultural associations, and seemingly innocuous development of diplomatic and trade relations with Argentine leaders. So does its influence on the local Muslim population, susceptible to radicalization and recruitment to Islamic extremism through proselytizing in mosques, schools, and cultural events in Argentine society.

Rabbani and his disciples have paved the way for other extremist groups to target Argentina, most notably the Islamic State. In September of 2016, Secretary of National Security Eugenio Burzaco mentioned the possibility of ISIS operatives in Corrientes. While he later announced that national security forces had investigated and found no evidence of an ISIS cell in the region, he nevertheless maintained that the Argentine government remained worried that Argentines who travelled to Syria and Iraq to join ISIS might return to form terrorist cells within Argentina. President Mauricio Macri has also received threats from individuals possibly linked to ISIS, implying that Argentina is under threat of imminent attack. In 2017, the Argentine Army's website was briefly hacked by unknown individuals who displayed a pro-ISIS message that claimed the organization was in the country. Argentine World Cup matches and high-profile players have also been the targets of ISIS propaganda.

While these individuals may be acting independently and an organized threat has so far not materialized, they nonetheless reflect an alarming degree of infiltration and activism by Islamist elements—a level of activity influenced and encouraged by the inroads created by Mohsen Rabbani and his network.

Islamism and Society

The date of Islam's first appearance in Argentina is unknown. Early records remain unreliable since Muslims were listed as "other," along with Jews and Catholics, and did not receive a special category. Some believe the first Muslims to arrive in Argentina were descendants from the Moors who came to the Americas with the Spanish conquistadors, though this theory has not been verified. The first official data possibility mentioning Arabs in Argentina comes from 1887 when 17 "Ottomans" were listed as arrivals at the port of Buenos Aires. Later records indicate a wave of Arab/Islamic migration to Argentina, comprised primarily of Syrian and Lebanese immigrants, during the mid- to late-19th century. This population continued to grow through the 20th century to an estimated 700,000 Muslims, mainly of Arab descent. In 2010, the Pew Forum estimated Argentina's Muslim community to have grown to almost 1 million people, or 2.5 percent of the country's population of approximately 41 million. Approximately 70% of this population is Sunni, with the Shi'ite community making up the remaining 30%. However, within the Muslim community itself, the Arab population is starting to shrink as immigration from Arab countries like Syria and Lebanon is replaced by increasing immigration from West Africa. Furthermore, the current growth of Islam in Argentina owes less to immigration from Arab states than to converts from within Argentina itself, thus changing the cultural demographic of the country's Muslim community from primarily Arab to a more diverse group.

Islam's spread to populations beyond the Arab community can be credited to the proliferation of Islamic centers and schools that have been established since the late 20th century. Though the Arab immigrant community originally established organizations and centers focused on preserving cultural rather than religious identity (Jews and Christians of Arab origin also participated in these groups), certain centers devoted to religious instruction. The foundation of the Centro de Estudios Islámicos (Center of Islamic Studies), headed by Imam Mahmoud Hussein, initiated the process of "diffusion of Islam" in 1973 and began to attract converts of non-Arab origin. Since then, several mosques and Islamic centers have emerged throughout Argentina, though the Islamic community remains overwhelmingly concentrated in Buenos Aires.

One such mosque is the King Fahd mosque in Palermo, the largest mosque and Muslim cultural center in Latin America. Inaugurated in 2000, the mosque is notable for the fact that the approximately $15 million in building costs were paid for by King Fahd himself, and the land, formerly property of the Argentine state, was donated to King Fahd in the mid-1990s by ex-President Carlos Menem.Despite the presence of multiple mosques and Muslim cultural centers in Buenos Aires, the Argentine Congress passed a bill approving the construction of the mosque, which drew criticism from members of the community who cited it as an example of Menem's tendency to favor pro-Arab or pro-Muslim ventures in Argentina, while failing to support other faiths with donations in cash or land.

Despite its size and international connections, until Menem's election as president in 1989, the Muslim population went largely unnoticed by the rest of Argentine society. Though Menem maintained his identity as a Catholic convert, his Arab background and family's continued ties to Islam brought the Muslim community into the public eye. As Menem raised the Muslim community to political prominence by adding members of the community, including his own family, to high-ranking positions within his cabinet, scandal and controversy also dominated his administration, resulting in a rejection of the Muslim community by certain sectors of Argentine society.

After the bombings in Buenos Aires in the early 1990s, anti-Arab and anti-Muslim sentiment within Argentine society intensified. Argentina, which had until then considered itself safe from international terrorism, turned against its Muslim population. Muslims and Arabs were stigmatized for their community's ties to the perpetrators of the AMIA attack, most notably the leader of the Shi'ite Muslim community in Argentina, Mohsen Rabbani. Muslims in Argentina also faced considerable public discrimination following the September 11, 2001 attacks, according to Alexis El-Sayer of the Centro Islámico de la República Argentina (CIRA). At that time, Muslims often hesitated to identify themselves publicly, though by 2012 the community had largely overcome this challenge and continued to practice Islam in peace, despite widespread ignorance about the Islamic faith and community in Argentina.

Though the Islamic community remains a small minority within larger Argentine society, the Arab community continues to grow and is now the third largest community in Argentina, after Italians and Spaniards. Islamic leaders hope that the proliferation of Islamic/ Arab cultural centers and increased Islamic influence on society, particularly in Buenos Aires, will help "create a new bond between Islam and Latin America" and help spread a positive, unbiased image of Islam.

The Argentine government also makes an effort to help the Muslim community feel like a part of Argentine society. The Argentine Secretariat of Worship under the Office of Foreign Affairs maintains a close relationship with leaders of the Islamic community and seeks to promote religious harmony by sending government officials to religious celebrations of all faiths. The Islamic community has seen the attendance of government officials, including ex-President Cristina Fernández de Kirchner, at Muslim celebrations and events as "recognition… of our existence within Argentine society."

The familiarity with which the Fernández de Kirchner administration treated the Muslim community can be attributed to the influence of a major cultural organization known as the Federación de Entidades Arabes, or FEARAB. Originally founded in 1972 to represent Muslim immigrant communities in Latin America, the organization has offices throughout the region and its leaders maintain strong relationships with local governments. In Argentina especially, FEARAB leadership was successful in developing relationships with the federal government during the Fernández de Kirchner era. This access to high-ranking Argentine officials allowed FEARAB to supersede its original social and cultural spheres and become a political entity. This ascent is cause for concern, because at least some of the leaders of FEARAB, the ranks of which include Abdul Karim Paz and Yussuf Khalil, maintain connections with Mohsen Rabbani's Islamist network. A series of Argentine government wiretaps reveal that these individuals took advantage of the organization's access to top Argentine officials to implement Iran's political agenda and further extend Iranian influence in Argentine politics—resulting in the Kirchner government's introduction of a controversial Memorandum of Understanding in 2013, under which the two countries agreed to work together to investigate the perpetrators of the 1994 AMIA attack.

ISLAMISM AND THE STATE

Argentina's policy towards Arab or Middle East states has historically been seen as rather ambivalent, particularly on controversial issues such as the Israeli-Palestinian conflict. Yet, tacit support for the Arab World among Peronistas can be traced back decades.

Many scholars continue to interpret Argentina's decision to abstain from voting on the UN resolution to partition Palestine in 1947 as an unwillingness to pick a side in the conflict. But the vote actually helped the Palestinian cause, and the Arab World recognized the benefit of the vote. The Syrian-Lebanese Society of Santiago de Estero, the Syrian-Lebanese Club of San Juan, and the Arab-Muslim society in the Cordoba province, among other notable Arab civic organizations, forwarded notes of gratitude to government leaders and the Central Arab Committee for Aid to Palestine expressed their gratitude for a position "before the assembly of the U.N., in defense of the Palestine sovereignty."

Syrian leadership awarded Perón the Grand Order of the Umayyads during an Argentine delegation visit to Syria in 1950 and renamed a main street in Damascus after Argentina, explaining that "when Arabs lost friends in the east and the west, Argentina was the first state to answer the call of duty… by sticking to the Arab side in the United Nations."

Yet neutrality in Middle East issues remained a fairly consistent position after the 1950s, with only intermittent support for Palestinian issues. Argentina enacted policies in favor of the Palestinians in order to avoid oil embargos from OPEC nations, but subsequently adopted a more moderate stance toward Israel after public outcry from the Argentine Jewish community. Since then, Argentina has typically sought to balance support for the Palestinians with its backing of Israel.

This duality of Argentina's stance toward Arab/Muslim and Jewish/Western issues became even more pronounced during the presidency of Carlos Menem, who offered to mediate the Arab-Israeli conflict and extended links to Israel by becoming the first Argentine president to visit the country, despite his ties to the Arab/Muslim community both in Argentina and abroad. Official attitudes toward Arab and Islamic elements were further confused by the revelation that Libyan leader Muammar Ghadafi had contributed $4 million to Menem's electoral campaign and of the president's "donation" of state property, valued at $10 million, to the Saudi Arabian Islamic Affairs Department for the construction of what is today the Fahd center in Buenos Aires. Meanwhile, Menem had terminated Argentina's cooperation with Iran's nuclear program in 1992, the same year that the Israeli embassy in Buenos Aires was bombed by a group linked to Iran and Hezbollah and two years before the 1994 AMIA attack that led to a break in diplomatic ties between Argentina and Iran.

Argentina's relationship with Iran is one of the longest-standing in the region, beginning in 1902, but the 1992 and 1994 terror attacks in Buenos Aires resulted in a cooling of diplomatic relations between the two countries as Argentina sought the extradition of the high-ranking Iranian officials linked to the attacks. With the advent of the Kirchner government (2007-2015), however, Argentine policy shifted dramatically, abandoning its traditional pro-Western, pro-United States orientation in favor of warmer ties with anti-U.S. regional governments such as Cuba, Venezuela and other "Bolivarian" states, as well as with Iran.

Energy deficits and mounting debt alienated Argentina from its former Western allies, nudging the Kirchner administration toward "friendlier" governments in Venezuela and Cuba. The Chávez administration in particular served as a new political ally and source of economic support to Argentina and provided further incentive for Fernández de Kirchner to distance herself from the U.S.

Iran took this shift as an opportunity to re-open relations with Argentina. In 2007, then-Iranian President Mahmoud Ahmedinejad allegedly asked Venezuela's Hugo Chávez to reach out to Kirchner with the aim of "changing Argentine policy and allowing Iran access to Argentine nuclear technology." The result was a gradual re-establishment of diplomatic ties between Argentina and Iran, a development that allowed Iran to increase its trade opportunities in the region and further strengthen its proxy terrorist network in the country.

As part of this process, then-Foreign Minister Héctor Timerman broke with the Argentine Jewish community in 2012 in order to pursue ties with Iran, and Fernández de Kirchner offered to freeze the longstanding federal investigation into the AMIA bombing in exchange for expanded bilateral trade with the Islamic Republic. This move was partly motivated by Argentina's increasing political and economic desperation, and its growing dependence on alternative sources of trade. It had the effect of making Argentina one of Iran's largest trade partners in the hemisphere, providing the Islamic Republic with long sought-after agricultural commodities. Meanwhile, Argentina's dependence on oil and gas, which make up 90 percent of the country's primary energy sources, intensified its dependence on imports from Iran. This warming of ties culminated with the announcement of the 2013 Memorandum of Understanding between Argentina and Iran, which further normalized relations between the two countries.

This normalization proved to be short lived, however. Just half a year later, Argentina voted against Iran at the UN Human Rights Council, and in 2014 Fernández de Kirchner announced the abrogation of the Memorandum due to lack of progress and internal opposition. A series of back and forth maneuvers followed, with Kirchner alternately courting the country's Jewish community and contesting a decision by the country's Federal Criminal Appeals Court that declared the MOU unconstitutional. This inconsistent attitude toward Iran remained in place until the end of her tenure in 2015.

Meanwhile, under Kirchner's leadership, Argentina continued to develop relationships with other anti-Western Arab nations. In

2010, Syrian President Bashar Al-Assad visited Buenos Aires and was warmly received by the President, who never acknowledged him as a dictator. In the years following, Foreign Minister Timerman would make various trips to Aleppo to meet with Syrian officials, arranged by pro-Iran Ambassador to Syria Roberto Ahuad. This rapprochement and Argentina's reluctance to denounce the Syrian civil war in late 2012 demonstrated an effort to maintain a positive relationship with a Syrian government closely allied to Iran.

The election of Mauricio Macri to the Argentine presidency in late 2015 signaled yet another change in Argentina's rather disjointed policy toward Iran. Macri expressed disgust at Iran's involvement in the AMIA case and the relationship that Fernández de Kirchner's administration had developed with the Islamic Republic. In the first weeks of his presidency, he ordered the withdrawal of the appeal filed by his predecessor's government regarding the federal ruling of the MOU's unconstitutionality. Additionally, Macri called for the use of Mercosur's Democracy Clause to expel Venezuela from the economic bloc for its human rights abuses, thus striking another blow to Iranian influence in the region. This signified a clear break from the previous administration's policies towards Iran and its anti-Western allies and set a precedent for Argentina's realignment with the United States, Europe, and Israel.

However, Macri's attitude toward other Middle Eastern and Arab states, particularly the Gulf States, has not been as clear. Since Macri took office in late 2015, his most notable actions toward the Middle East have included the signing of a controversial commercial treaty with Qatar, aimed at encouraging and protecting bilateral investment, and the announcement that Argentina would accept at least 3,000 Syrian refugees in cooperation with the European Union.

This announcement reflected a continuation of the previous administration's policy toward the Syrian conflict, which had entailed the creation of Program Siria (Syria Program) by the previous administration, in which Syrians affected or displaced by the country's civil war were granted residency in Argentina for up to two years. Palestinian nationals that had been residing in Syria were also eligible to participate in this program. Under Macri's administration, the refugee acceptance program has been augmented by the creation of the Gabinete Nacional del Programa Siria (National Cabinet for the Syria Program), an inter-departmental entity whose main goal is establishing guidelines for the country's reception of refugees and facilitating their social integration.

Like his predecessors, Macri has demonstrated a certain level of ambivalence in his policies toward Arab and Muslim nations, attempting to balance criticism of one with support for another The knowledge that Iranian terror agents have been operating within these communities and have used them to gain access to government officials, radicalize and recruit members, and raise funds has made this decision a potential security risk.

Kirchner's questionable dealings while in office followed by the still–unsolved murder of Nisman culminated in December 2017 when an Argentine judge issued an arrest warrant for the former President, who had recently won a seat in the Senate. Back in January 2015, authorities had discovered Nisman dead in his apartment from apparent gunshot wound to the head a mere hours before his scheduled testimony to Argentine parliament regarding an alleged conspiracy by government officials to cover-up Iran's participation in AMIA bombing. Nisman's 300-page dossier contained years of damning wiretap transcripts that revealed "Kirchner and several of her governmental colleagues [had] whitewash[ed] Iranian involvement, in order to secure much-needed oil deliveries."

The judge who issued the arrest warrant cited treason, calling the AMIA attack an "act of war" by Iran and accused now-Senator Kirchner of covering up the role of Iranian leaders and their Hezbollah proxies in favor of a lucrative trade deal. The judge requested Congress vote to remove her immunity as an elected official. Macri's emphasis also resulted in new investigations by the Argentine national police into the death of Nisman, leading to the finding that the prosecutor had been drugged with ketamine before being brutally assaulted and shot.

Argentina is not yet free from the threat of radical Islamist terrorism, nor are its Arab and Muslim communities rid of the terror network still operating in their midst today. But Macri's reversal of a previously pro-Iran agenda and his rapprochement with Israel and Western allies represents a concrete step in this direction.

ENDNOTES

1. The Argentine national census does not record religious data, so statistics vary by source, with some reports citing Argentina as home to the largest Muslim population in Latin America (1,000,000 members) and others citing Brazil (35,000 to 1.5 million members). For more information, see the US Department of State International Religious Freedom Report for 2015, accessed October 27, 2016, http://www.state.gov/j/drl/rls/irf/religiousfreedom/index.htm#wrapper.
2. As described in the 2013 Nisman Dictum, the "export of the revolution" is Iran's official policy of extending its political-religious view beyond its borders. Alberto Nisman, *Report on Terrorist Networks in Latin America*, pg. 10, May 2013, accessed October 12, 2016, http://albertonisman.org/nisman-report-dictamina-on-sleeper-cells-full-text/.
3. Stephen Johnson, *Iran's Influence in the Americas* Center for Strategic and International Studies, February 2012, http://csis.org/files/publication/120223_Johnson_IranInfluence_ExecSumm_Web.pdf.
4. Johnson, *Iran's Influence in the Americas*.
5. Nisman, 2013 Dictum, op cit., p. 59, 72, 180-181.
6. Marcelo Martinez Burgos and Alberto Nisman, Office of Criminal Investigations: AMIA CASE; Investigations Unit of the Office of the Attorney General (Argentina), October 25, 2006, accessed October 27, 2016, http://www.peaceandtolerance.org/docs/nismanindict.pdf.
7. Matthew Levitt, "Exporting Terror in America's Backyard," *Foreign Policy*, June 14, 2013, http://foreignpolicy.com/2013/06/14/exporting-terror-in-americas-backyard/.
8. Levitt, "Exporting Terror in America's Backyard."
9. US Department of State. "Patterns of Global Terrorism: 1992," accessed October 27, 2016, http://fas.org/irp/threat/terror_92/chron.html.
10. Nisman's report indicates that this role was merely a front; Rabbani was already a member of Iran's intelligence bureau upon his arrival in Argentina.
11. Alberto Nisman, 2013 Dictum, op cit., p. 56, 58-59.

12. Douglas Farah, *Back to the Future: Argentina Unravels* (Inter-American Institute for Democracy, 2013), 75.
13. Alberto Nisman, 2013 Dictum, op. cit.
14. Douglas Farah, *Fixers, Super Fixers and Shadow Facilitators: How Networks Connect*, International Assessment and Strategy Center, April 23, 2012, http://www.strategycenter.net/docLib/20120423_Farah_FixersSuperFixersShadow.pdf.
15. Joseph Humire, *After Nisman: How the death of a prosecutor revealed Iran's growing influence in the Americas*, Center for a Secure Free Society, 2016, 17.
16. Alberto Nisman, *Complaint of Criminal Plot*, p. 96, 2015, accessed October 27, 2016, http://albertonisman.org/nisman-complaint-denuncia/.
17. Humire, *After Nisman*, p. 19-20.
18. Humire, *After Nisman*, 17.
19. Humire, *After Nisman*, 17.
20. "Eugenio Burzaco descartó presencia demiembros de Isis en Argentina," *El Día*, September 11, 2016, accessed October 27, 2016, http://www.eldia.com/el-pais/el-gobierno-detecto-argentinos-formados-por-el-estado-islamico-164431.
21. Jerry Nelson, "ISIS to Argentina: We're Coming to See You," *Huffington Post*, October 27, 2016, http://www.huffingtonpost.com/entry/isis-to-argentina-were-coming-to-see-you_us_57dfb7d0e4b0d5920b5b3054.
22. Demian Bio, "Argentine Army Website Hacked With Alleged Threat From ISIS," *Bubble*, June 19, 2017, http://www.thebubble.com/argentine-army-website-hacked-with-alleged-threat-from-isis/
23. Marissa Payne, "Pro-ISIS poster threatening World Cup terrorist attack depicts Lionel Messi crying blood," *Washington Post*, October 24, 2017, https://www.washingtonpost.com/news/early-lead/wp/2017/10/24/pro-isis-poster-threatening-world-cup-terrorist-attack-depicts-lionel-messi-crying-blood/?utm_term=.26c5f5426bff.
24. Pedro Brieger, "Muslims in Argentina," ISIM Newsletter, June 2000, 33, https://openaccess.leidenuniv.nl/bitstream/handle/1887/17433/ISIM_6_Muslims_in_Argentina.pdf?sequence=1.

25. Chris Moss, "Latin America's First Mega-Mosque," *Hispanic Muslims*, May 16, 2016, http://hispanicmuslims.com/articles/other/openseyes.html.
26. "Table: Muslim Population by Country," The Pew Center, January 27, 2011, http://www.pewforum.org/2011/01/27/table-muslim-population-by-country/?utm_expid=53098246-2.Lly4CFSVQG2lphsg-KopIg.0.
27. The World Bank cites Argentina's population at 41,222,875 people in 2010. For more information, please see World Bank population data, accessed December 9, 2016, http://data.worldbank.org/indicator/SP.POP.TOTL?end=2010&locations=AR&start=2010&view=bar.
28. "International Religious Freedom Report—Argentina," The United States Department of State, November 17, 2010, http://www.state.gov/j/drl/rls/irf/2010/148731.htm.
29. *The Argentina Independent*, "Ramadan Mubarak: Observing the Month-Long Fast in Buenos Aires," July 20, 2012, http://www.argentinaindependent.com/life-style/ramadan-mubarak-observing-the-month-long-fast-in-buenos-aires/.
30. Rosemary Pennington, "Is there Islam in Latin America?," *Muslim Voices*, n.d., http://muslimvoices.org/islam-latin-america/.
31. Brieger, "Muslims in Argentina," 33.
32. Moss, "Latin America's First Mega-Mosque;" Clarín, "Se inaugura la mezquita más grande de Sudamérica," September 9, 2000, http://edant.clarin.com/diario/2000/09/25/s-03801.htm.
33. Brieger, "Muslims in Argentina," 33.
34. Moss, "Latin America's First Mega-Mosque."
35. Brieger, "Muslims in Argentina," 33.
36. *The Argentina Independent*, "Ramadan Mubarak."
37. *The Argentina Independent*, "Ramadan Mubarak."
38. Moss, "Latin America's First Mega-Mosque."
39. "Argentina," *International Religious Freedom Report 2010*, U.S. Department of State Bureau of Democracy, Human Rights, and Labor, November 27, 2010, http://www.state.gov/j/drl/rls/irf/2010/148731.htm.
40. *The Argentina Independent*, op.cit.

41. Jose R. Cardenas and Roger Noriega, *The Mounting Hezbollah Threat in Latin America*, American Enterprise Institute, October 6, 2011, http://www.aei.org/publication/the-mounting-hezbollah-threat-in-latin-america/.
42. For more information on the FEARAB relationship with the Argentine government, see Humire's special report After Nisman.
43. Humire, *After Nisman*.
44. Humire, *After Nisman*.
45. Delegacion de Asociaciones Israelitas Argentinas, "Anti-Jewish Activities of the Arabs in Argentine" (Buenos Aires: DAIA, 1958), 9.
46. Abdel Latif Yunes quoted in Campodónico to Paz, July 4, 1950, *División de Política*, Syria, 1950, Box 7, Folder "Politíca Interna," AMREC.
47. Cecilia Baeza, "América Latina y la cuestión palestina (1947-2012)," Araucaria Revista Iberoamericana de Filosofia, Política y Humanidades 14/28 (2012): 111-131.
48. Baeza, "América Latina y la cuestión palestina (1947-2012)."
49. Brieger, "Muslims in America," 33.
50. Moss, "Latin America's First Mega-Mosque."
51. Cardenas and Roger Noriega, *The Mounting Hezbollah Threat in Latin America*.
52. The United States Department of State, "The Year in Review," *Patterns of Global Terrorism: 1992*, April 30, 1993, https://fas.org/irp/threat/terror_92/review.html.
53. Ilan Berman and Joseph M. Humire, *Iran's Strategic Penetration of Latin America* (London: Lexington Books, 2014), 35, 81.
54. Berman and Humire, 82.
55. Roger F. Noriega, *Argentina's Secret Deal with Iran?*, (American Enterprise Institute), n.d., https://www.aei.org/publication/argentinas-secret-deal-with-iran/.
56. Berman and Humire, 86.
57. Ilan Berman, "The Dangerous Iran Flirtation," *The Washington Times*, September 27, 2012, http://www.washingtontimes.com/news/2012/sep/27/at-first-blush-argentina-seems-like-an-odd-choice-/.
58. Jaime Darenblum, "How Argentina and Brazil Help

Iran," *The Weekly Standard*, accessed May 16, 2016, http://www.weeklystandard.com/article/how-argentina-and-brazil-help-iran/659920.
59. Berman and Humire, 82.
60. Johnson, *Iran's Influence in the Americas*.
61. Berman and Humire, 82.
62. Berman and Humire, 82.
63. *Buenos Aires Herald*, "Argentina votes against Irán at UN Human Rights Council," n.d., http://www.buenosairesherald.com/article/127012/argentina-votes-against-irán-at-un-human-rights-council.
64. *Buenos Aires Herald*, "Appeals Court declares unconstitutional deal with Iran on AMIA attack probe," n.d., http://www.buenosairesherald.com/article/159604/appeals-court-declares-unconstitutional-deal-with-iran-on-amia-attack-probe-.
65. Pepe Eliaschev, "El Gobierno negocia un pacto secreto con Irán para 'olvidar' los atentados," *Perfil*, n.d. http://www.perfil.com/politica/El-Gobierno-negocia-un-pacto-secreto-con-Iran-para-olvidar-los-atentados-20110326-0004.html.
66. Eliaschev, "El Gobierno negocia un pacto secreto con Irán."
67. Dana Chocron, "Argentina: A New Foreign Policy?," *Young Diplomats*, accessed October 10, 2016, http://www.young-diplomats.com/argentinas-promised-foreign-policy/.
68. Uki Goñi and Jonathan Watts, "Argentina president-elect pledges radical policy changes in shift to right," *The Guardian*, November 23, 2015, https://www.theguardian.com/world/2015/nov/23/argentina-president-elect-mauricio-macri-iran-venezuela.
69. Eamonn MacDonagh, "Analysis: Macri Victory in Argentina Marks Setback for Iranian Ambitions in Latin America," *The Tower*, n.d., http://www.thetower.org/2600-macri-victory-in-argentina-election-marks-setback-for-iranian-ambitions-in-latin-america/.
70. Ramón Indart, "Qué dice el polémico memorándum que firmó el gobierno de Macri con Qatar," *Perfil*, November 17, 2016, accessed January 16, 2017, http://www.

perfil.com/politica/que-dice-el-polemico-memorandum-que-firmo-el-gobierno-de-macri-con-qatar.phtml.

71. Amanda Blohm, “Argentina will accept 3,000 Syrian refugees,” *PanAm Post*, July 7, 2016, accessed January 5, 2017, https://panampost.com/amanda-blohm/2016/07/07/argentina-will-receive-3000-syrian-refugees/.
72. *La Nación*, "La Argentina también recibirá refugiados sirios,” October 22, 2014, http://www.lanacion.com.ar/1737801-la-argentina-tambien-recibira-refugiados-sirios.
73. *La Nación*, "La Argentina también recibirá refugiados sirios.”
74. *Telam*, “El gobierno creará un gabinete para atender a las necesidades de los refugiados sirios,” September 22, 2016, http://www.telam.com.ar/notas/201609/164023-gabinete-nacional-programa-siria-refugiados.html.
75. Jonathan Gilbert and Simon Romero, “Argentine Phone Calls Details Efforts to Shield Iran,” *New York Times*, January 21, 2015.
76. Harriet Alexander, “Argentine prosecutor who accused Cristina Kirchner over 1994 bombing found dead,” *Telegraph*, January 19, 2015.
77. Harriet Alexander, “Argentine judge issues arrest warrant for Cristina Kirchner over terror attack cover-up,” *Telegraph*, December 7, 2017, http://www.telegraph.co.uk/news/2017/12/07/argentine-judge-issues-arrest-warrant-cristina-kirchner-terror/.
78. Mark Dubowitz and Toby Dershowitz, “Iranian Terror. Argentinian Cover Up. Justice at Last?” *New York Times*, December 11, 2017, https://www.nytimes.com/2017/12/11/opinion/argentina-kirchner-iran-nisman.html.

9 Bolivia

Quick Facts

Population: 11,138,234 (July 2017 est.)
Area: 1,098,581 sq km
Ethnic Groups: Mestizo (mixed white and Amerindian ancestry) 68%, indigenous 20%, white 5%, cholo/chola 2%, black 1%, other 1%, unspecified 3% ; 44% of respondents indicated feeling part of some indigenous group, predominantly Quechua or Aymara
GDP (official exchange rate): $37.78 billion (2017 est.)

Source: CIA World FactBook (Last Updated June 2018)

Introduction

Bolivia, a country of over 10.8 million people, has a Muslim population of approximately 2,000. But while the practice of the religion in Bolivia remains small and dispersed, the election of President Evo Morales in 2005 brought about a more amiable relationship with Islamic countries in the Middle East, and significantly opened Bolivia's official policy towards Islam in the years since.[1]

Bolivia's Muslim population counts among its members' descendants from Bangladesh, Pakistan, Egypt, the Palestinian territories, Iran, Syria, and Lebanon. These communities are generally spread out between the major cities of La Paz and Santa Cruz, with a smaller presence in Sucre, Cochabamba, and Oruro and other remote cities throughout the country. There are at least fifteen different Islamic organizations, both Shia and Sunni, operating within Bolivia, funded primarily by either Saudi Arabia or the Islamic Republic of Iran.

Since opening an embassy in La Paz in 2008, Iran has been a driving force in increasing the Islamic presence in Bolivia, within both society and the state. Iran has proposed several bilateral agreements with Bolivia, ranging from economic development projects to military-to-military exchanges. Iran has also reportedly funded state-owned media networks in the country. In return, Bolivia has lifted visa restrictions for Iranian citizens, supported its efforts in the UN, and facilitated the increased presence of Iranian officials in this Andean nation.

ISLAMIST ACTIVITY

Given that Bolivia has a small Islamic population its community is susceptible to influence from Islamist elements from abroad, notably sponsored by Iran and Hezbollah. In recent years, the number of mosques and Islamic cultural centers has increased drastically in this small Andean nation. Iran's presence and activities has grown at a commensurate rate. As in the rest of Latin America, Iran's modus operandi in Bolivia is to establish Islamist networks through mosques and cultural centers run by Bolivian converts to Shia Islam, while Hezbollah gets involved in the illicit narcotics and arms trade in Bolivia.

In La Paz, the capital of Bolivia, a prominent local Islamist is known to boast ties to the Islamic Republic of Iran and its proxies. The leader of the Association of the Islamic Community of Bolivia (ACIB) Ahlul Bait, and of the Bolivian Shia community writ large, is Roberto Chambi Calle, a Bolivian lawyer who converted to Islam in 1996. Chambi also goes by the name of Yousef, and simultaneously runs another Shia organization—the Bolivia Islamic Cultural Foundation (FCIB in its Spanish acronym). Also based in La Paz, the FCIB was founded in August 2007 with the support of the Iranian government.

Chambi and his wife, Sdenka Saavedra Alfaro, a journalist and author, actively promote an Islamist message through seminars and small meetings that they organize in Bolivia. They have invited imams from neighboring Latin American countries, such as Argentina, Peru, Chile, and Brazil, to these gatherings, and have a longstanding relationship with Shia spiritual leader Sheikh Abdul Karim Paz from Buenos Aires, Argentina. Karim Paz is a direct disciple of Iranian intelligence operative Mohsen Rabbani, and was his successor at the At Tawhid mosque in Buenos Aires after Rabbani left Argentina following his involvement in the 1994 bombing of the Argentine-Jewish Mutual Association (AMIA) building.[2]

The Bolivian couple currently resides in Iran, studying under Karim Paz and Rabbani at the Al Mustafa University in Qom, Iran, but continues to actively help in the spread of an Islamist message to the indigenous peoples of Bolivia. The Iranian government, meanwhile, has further enhanced these efforts via its work with state-owned media. In 2008, for instance, the Iranian government attempted to build a television station in Bolivia's coca-growing region of Chapare.[3] Although that project did not materialize, Iran did succeed in launching a broader, Spanish language television network in 2011. Known as HispanTV, it is owned and operated by the Islamic Republic of Iran Broadcasting (IRIB) conglomerate and is based out of Tehran.[4] HispanTV currently broadcasts Islamist-leaning programming 24 hours a day in several countries throughout Latin America and the Caribbean. The channel's local Bolivian correspondent was an Argentine journalist, Andrés Sal-lari, who used to work for Bolivia's state-owned Canal 7.[5] The current Bolivian correspondent for Iran's HispanTV is Mariano Vázquez, another Argentine journalist who also works for state-owned BoliviaTV.[6]

Andrés Sal-lari and Mariano Vazquez also worked for another state-controlled media outlet believed to be financed by the Iranian government to the tune of approximately $3 million.[7] In 2012, President Evo Morales reportedly received a monetary gift from his then-Iranian counterpart, Mahmud Ahmadinejad, to launch Abya Yala, a new multimedia television network. Initially financed through one of Morales' foundations, the Abya Yala TV network has benefited from large amounts of government advertising and preferential contracts with various government agencies, notably the hydrocarbons agency, among other public entities. As of 2015, Abya Yala had 135 hours of national programming a week through a major telecommunications firm, and in the western cities of La Paz and El Alto broadcast 24-hour coverage through an open signal on channel 41 and on Bolivian cable on channel 91.

According to Bolivian journalist Amalia Pando, the Abya Yala TV network's rapid expansion raises at least some suspicion: "here are two immoralities, first that the president receives three million dollars from a foreign power to launch a TV channel, then that the channel, which does not have a significant audience, receives such large amounts of public contracts and advertising."[8] Abya Yala's meteoric rise in Bolivia is due, in part, to its integrated programming with Venezuela's state-owned Telesur network, AnnurTV in Argentina, Russia Today, and the Iranian-owned HispanTV. In the case of Iran, Abya Yala provides an authentic way to reach Bolivia's largely indigenous population to propagate an Islamist message.

For instance, in July 2015, the Abya Yala TV network broadcast the opening of a new Iranian-funded hemodialysis center, The Red Crescent Society, in the city of Cochabamba. Nevertheless, the broadcast omitted the fact that the women working at The Red Crescent Society were forced to wear hijabs, to the displeasure of many Bolivians. Lourdes Millares, the deputy for an opposition party in Bolivia, subsequently called this Iranian demand an "assault on the dignity of women…" and excoriated President Morales for, "…submission to the rules of another government."[9]

Further criticism arose in 2016, when opposition Senator Arturo Murillo issued a complaint to the Bolivian Attorney General against then Minister of the Presidency and Evo Morales strongman, Juan Ramon Quintana, for "donating" three vehicles to the Abya Yala TV network. Senator Murillo claimed this was "influence peddling" on behalf of the Bolivian government and suggested that Abya Yala TV is simply used to spread Iranian propaganda in Bolivia.[10]

The opposition Senator hit the headlines once again in 2017, when he denounced the presence of Canadian-Venezuelan-Lebanese businessman Khaled Khalil Majzoub. Senator Murillo suggested that Majzoub is under investigation in Bolivia for alleged involvement in drug trafficking. [11] The Bolivian government denied any investigation against Majzoub or his involvement in illicit activity and stated that he is in Bolivia under legal pretenses.[12] Majzoub became well known to U.S. counter-narcotics authorities after the narco-sobrinos case involving the arrest of the nephews of Venezuelan President Nicolás Maduro and first lady Cilia Flores in 2015. The plane used by the nephews to traffic drugs in Haiti was registered to one of Majzoub's companies in Venezuela.[13]

These accusations against Majzoub elevated a concern in Bolivia about Hezbollah's' involvement in the country. In March 2017, Bolivian security forces raided a warehouse in the suburbs of La Paz, seizing bomb-making materials and a four-wheel drive vehicle suspected to be used in a terrorist attack. According to several press reports, regional intelligence agencies believe the raid in La Paz thwarted potential terrorist plots by Hezbollah in Bolivia, Chile, and Peru.[14]

Islamism and Society

Bolivia has a small Islamic community, numbering approximately two thousand, most of whose members are Sunni, with a smaller number of Shia followers. Altogether, Muslims in Bolivia account for less than 0.1% of the total population. However, they are increasingly active.

Most of the established members of the Islamic community in Bolivia were born in the country and converted, or are the descendants of Palestinian or Lebanese immigrants who have lived in Bolivia for decades. The traditional Islamic community in Bolivia is primarily Sunni, and typically adheres to the local Bolivian style of dress and culture. They do not practice fundamentalist Islamic traditions, nor do they actively proselytize. Nevertheless, there has been a recent influx of Pakistanis and Iranians that follow a more fundamentalist line, and are actively recruiting and proselytizing among Bolivian youth and women, causing some friction with the established Muslim community in Bolivia.[15]

Islamic proselytization (da'wah) began in Bolivia in the early 1970s, during the economic boom that integrated Santa Cruz into national and international markets. Over the ensuing years, Santa Cruz became the financial hub of Bolivia and in the 1990s the department's local economy was greatly bolstered by the capitalization of the country's petroleum and gas industry. This spurred a mass wave of immigration that flooded Santa Cruz, of which an initial influx of Islamic immigrants was also a part.

In 1974, Bolivia's Islamic community began its Islamic proselytization (da'wah) after Mahmud Amer Abusharar arrived from the Palestinian territories. Almost immediately after arriving, Amer started gathering Muslims from around Bolivia and inviting them to his home for prayer. He quickly became the leader of the small but emerging Islamic community in Bolivia, particularly in Santa Cruz, and in 1986 registered the first Bolivian Islamic organization—which was officially recognized by Bolivia's Ministry of Foreign Affairs Office of Religion three years later, in 1989.[16]

This organization, the Bolivian Islamic Center (CIB is its Spanish acronym), based in the country's commercial capital, Santa Cruz, claims to have founded Bolivia's first fully operational mosque in 1994, serving some 300 congregants. The CIB claims to support "open-mindedness and peace," but does appear to espouse an anti-U.S. political position closely aligned with that of the Bolivian government.[17]

On May 14, 2011, Mahmud Amer Abusharar died of natural causes. One of his disciples, Isa Amer Quevedo, stepped in to serve as Director of the CIB. Quevedo has a degree in Islamic jurisprudence from the University of Medina in Saudi Arabia, and used to be the CIB's administrative director and translator. Anecdotal evidence suggests that Quevedo supports his predecessor's anti-U.S. stance, as he offered criticism of the United States on the CIB website immediately after the September 11th attacks.[18]

The CIB has grown over the years to become Bolivia's largest Islamic organization, and is known to receive support from the Saudi-based Islamic Organization for Latin America and the Muslim World League. The Egyptian Embassy in Bolivia and the Gulf Cooperation Council both also have helped to fund the CIB's first mosque. Moreover, the CIB has an affiliation with the World Assembly of Muslim Youth, acting as this organization's headquarters in Bolivia.

Also, connected with the Muslim World League is the Bolivian Muslim Cultural Association (ACBM is its Spanish acronym), located in Sucre, the constitutional capital of Bolivia. A Palestinian doctor and lawyer, Fayez Rajab Khedeer Kannan, runs this organization. Kannan espouses an extreme worldview, and has, among other things, openly praised the late Libyan leader Muammar al-Qadhafi.[19] In 1998, he received a 30-year grant from the Sucre city council to use five acres of land in the Los Libertadores neighborhood to construct an educational center and clinic, with additional funding for the effort coming from the Muslim World League and the Islamic Development Bank. By 2003, ACBM had built a private Islamic school, which led to some legal disputes over a revoked title transfer (disputes which were finally resolved in 2006, in favor of ACBM).

It is not clear whether this school is still active.

More recently, in 2016, an Indian couple, Ghalib Ataul and Nayara Zafar, built a new mosque in the Paititi district of Warnes, a small town outside the city of Santa Cruz de la Sierra. The mosque adheres to the creed of the Ahmadiyya, a small sect of Islam from the late 19th century in northern India, and, according to Ghalib Ataul, will serve all faiths, both Muslim and non-Muslim. The mosque, however, has generated some negative reaction, as noted by Bolivian journalist Magali Sánchez: "As long as they respect our customs and our creed, no problem. But do not try to change us. They should not think that the women of Warnes want to wear hijabs and burkas."[20] The new mosque in Warnes is emblematic of the small but notable growth of Islamic communities within remote eastern regions of Bolivia, including in San Borja and Riberalta, Beni, where there are practicing Muslims.

Moving north along the Andean ridge, in La Paz, is the Association of the Islamic Community of Bolivia (ACIB is its Spanish acronym). It is believed that the origin of Islam in La Paz dates to 1995, when Moumin Candia, a Bolivian trained in an Argentine mosque, brought Islam to the city. A Bolivian convert and the former president of ACIB, Gerardo Cutipa Trigo is educated as an engineer, and was an atheist through most of his college years in Bolivia, assuming leadership roles in leftist student unions. It wasn't until the late 1990s that Cutipa converted to Islam while working in Spain, where he first was exposed to the religion. The ACIB is now led by Ahmad Ali, who claims to informally represent a community of approximately 300 Muslims, of which around 70 regularly attend service at the ACIB's mosque, called Masjidum Jbelannur.[21]

In 2006, a more fundamentalist mosque was opened in La Paz by a group of Pakistanis that had arrived in Bolivia three years earlier. This small Pakistani community, known as the Islamic Association of Bolivia, operates the Masjid As-Salam mosque, and has offered prayer services to other Muslims, including many Bolivian-born Muslim converts in La Paz. The imam of the Masjid As-Salam mosque was Mahmud Ali Teheran, a Peruvian-born son of Iranian immigrants who converted to Sunni Islam. Prior to this, Ali Teheran lead the Babu Ul-Islam mosque in Tacna, Peru and as of 2008 has left Bolivia to lead the Islamic community in Uruguay.[22]

La Paz is also a hub for a small but growing Shia community, which is much smaller than its Sunni counterparts. This small influx of Shia Muslims is primarily due to the newfound Iranian presence in Bolivia, as the more visible Shia organizations have ties to the Iranian Embassy in La Paz.

The oldest Shia organization has a name like the Sunni ACIB; however, it adds the suffix "Ahlul Bait" which literally means "family of the House." This has an important distinction for Shia Muslims because the term refers to the family of the Islamic prophet Muhammad, and is generally where Shia Muslims derive their hadiths. It is unclear how this organization was founded, but it appears to have been operational since 2000. For at least some time, however, it seems to have operated under a different name (Shia Islamic Community of Bolivia), until resurfacing with its original name in 2006.

During the brief time that the ACIB Ahlul Bait was organized under a different name, it was run by a licensed psychologist named Tommy Nelson Salgueiro Criales, a former Jesuit who converted to Islam in the mid-1990s while living in Australia. ACIB Ahlul Bait is known for its publications and translations of Islamic text into Spanish, and was the first to introduce Islamic literature to the 15th annual international book fair in 2010, where they presented Bolivian Vice President Alvaro Garcia Linera with their own in-house publication, "La Revolución de la Mano de Dios," written by resident Islamic scholar Sergio Grover Dueñas Calle.

ACIB Ahlul Bait has an associated mosque purchased with the help of the Iranian government. The first Shia mosque in Bolivia, As-Salam, is a three-story building in the heart of La Paz with a large prayer hall that was inaugurated in 2006. The mosque is meant to serve a growing Shia community in La Paz, and other smaller Islamic communities nearby.

The Iranian-supported Abya Yala TV channel dedicates programming targeted towards the diverse indigenous peoples of the Americas. The term Abya Yala means "land in its full maturity" or "land of vital blood" in its indigenous Kuna language. The Kuna are indigenous people that used to inhabit the Darién Gap, which is today in northwest Colombia and southeast Panama. Abya Yala TV consistently propagates the message that consumerism and the exploitation of natural resources leads to the erosion of biodiversity and the loss of indigenous culture.

Many of the organizations mentioned above have created their own websites, radio broadcasts, and/or social media outlets. Social media plays a significant part in spreading the Islamic message throughout Bolivia, as many communities have a virtual presence on Facebook, Twitter and YouTube. Roberto Chambi and his colleagues at ACIB Ahlul Bait are arguably the most active in both mainstream and social media, establishing a local radio program, "Al-Islam," that broadcasts every weekday morning on 107.3 FM. Chambi is also a regular on HispanTV's local broadcasts and is featured in ACIB's web portal Islam en Bolivia (www.islam.org.bo). This portal is frequently updated, largely with articles claiming Israeli atrocities against Palestinians, and recently launched an effort to proselytize in Aymara, one of Bolivia's mayor indigenous languages and culture. It currently offers a translation of the tract "What is Islam?" in the Aymara language.[23]

In 2014, according to an interview with Ahmad Ali, an American student researching Islam in Bolivia discovered that Aymara and Quechua Indians had begun converting to Islam.[24] This represents an important advance for the Islamic community, because Aymara indigenous groups hold important political currency with the current government and society. Establishing a footprint with this group would help advance Islam (and, potentially, Islamism) to a significant degree within Bolivian society.

Islamism and the State

The growing political and strategic ties between La Paz and Tehran dominate Bolivia's contemporary relationship with Islam. Bolivian President Evo Morales first met former Iranian President Mahmoud Ahmadinejad at the inauguration of Ecuadorian President Rafael Correa in mid-January 2007. At the time, the two leaders showed unprecedented interest in bringing their respective countries closer together politically, culturally, and economically. Ahmadinejad focused on agriculture, gas, and oil, referring to "academic potentials" in Iran for "improving the technical knowledge of Bolivia experts... in accordance with our Islamic teachings and duties."[25]

Months later, in September 2007, Bolivia's then-Foreign Minister, David Choquehuanca, visited Tehran to meet with his then-counterpart, Manuchehr Mottaki, to build upon the January meeting with firm commitments outlined in a strategic agreement to broaden political and economic relations. Later in the month, the first bilateral agreement was drafted. It provided a strategic framework for future collaborative ventures in the hydrocarbons, extractive, agriculture, oil and gas industries, as well as science, culture and technology. There were also several side agreements made to implement the importation and installation of six Iranian milk-processing plants in Bolivia. But the larger strategic agreement was the focus of the effort, and was announced on September 27, 2007 during Ahmadinejad's first official visit to Bolivia. At the time, Morales noted: "we are interested in broadening relations with Iran, starting in the trade area with a view to continuing and consolidating relations of friendship, understanding and diplomacy."[26]

The agreement, however, was not ratified by the Bolivian Congress until three years later, in 2010. Nevertheless, this did not stop the two countries from continuing to foster their diplomatic relationship, and the first Embassy of the Islamic Republic of Iran was inaugurated in La Paz in February 2008. Evo Morales announced later that year that Bolivia would move its only embassy in the Middle East from Cairo to Tehran (such a move, however, never happened, likely due to a lack of resources on Bolivia's part).

By March 2008, Iran's relationship with Bolivia had developed an economic facet as well. News sources out of Tehran reported that Iran had signed several joint projects with Bolivia worth some $1 billion in total.[27]

Morales finally reciprocated Ahmadinejad's Bolivian visit when he arrived in Tehran on September 1, 2008. Brief meetings with the Iranian president and the country's Minister of Mining and Industry punctuated his short stay in the Islamic Republic, where he focused on persuading Ahmadinejad to accelerate payments under Iran's promise to invest $1 billion in Bolivia.

By the end of September 2008, Bolivia and Iran had exchanged technical delegations, with one Hojatollah Soltani emerging as Iran's business attaché to Bolivia. Soltani pledged that, apart from the promised investment of $1 billion, Iran would also invest some $230 million in a cement factory and another $3 million to build dairy farms.[28] A month later, Soltani announced that Iran would use Bolivia as the base for a planned Red Crescent health clinic expansion across Latin America.[29] The announcement coincided with Bolivia signing a credit agreement with Venezuela and Iran for $115 million, reportedly to cooperate in mineral exploration in Coroma, a mineral rich region in southern Bolivia. This cooperation created suspicion of a dual-use effort, because—according to a retired Bolivian mining engineer—Coroma covers more than 100,000 hectares where there are uranium and other dispersed minerals.[30]

By February 2009, pledges from Iran to invest in economic development projects had yet to materialize, but the milk processing plants were already under construction. Some Iranian funding had found its way to Bolivia, but much of what was promised had not yet been delivered. This gap between rhetoric and action, however, did not appear to dampen relations between the two countries. In July 2009, Bolivia announced that it would receive a $280 million loan from the Islamic Republic. Iran's top diplomat in Bolivia, Masoud Edrisi, stated at the time that the money was to be used as President Morales saw fit.[31] The loan was part of the $1 billion originally promised when Ahmadinejad first met Morales in 2007. Later in 2009, a new Iranian-funded maternal care health clinic was opened in the poor municipality of El Alto, on the outskirts of La Paz. The health clinic reportedly cost $2.5 million and filled a gap in community healthcare despite some controversy over a requirement that female nurses wear hijabs, or head covering.[32]

In 2010, some of the original financial promises made by Iran began to materialize, albeit quite slowly and extremely inconsistently. By the middle of that year, more agreements were signed, particularly in the extractive industry, as Iran began to look at Bolivia's strategic resource wealth. Bolivia is one of Latin America's most resource-rich countries, and possesses some of the world's largest reserves of lithium chloride. Knowing this, Iran made a move to become Bolivia's co-developer of this resource, to include the production of lithium batteries. This resource exploitation project, in turn, has prompted speculation that other strategic minerals, namely uranium, would be exploited. To date, however, it has been difficult to prove that Iran has effectively received any uranium ore from Bolivia.[33]

This is not to say, however, that Iran is not exploring or exploiting other strategic resources from Bolivia. In 2010, the Bolivian government awarded six new oil and gas exploration blocks to Iran and later signed an agreement to train Bolivian technicians in petroleum drilling and petrochemical operations. By July 2011, 26 Bolivian technicians had completed their first petrochemical training in Iran.[34] While the Islamic Republic was training Bolivian engineers, and exploring the country's strategic mineral deposits, a more nefarious relationship began to form through military-to-military exchanges between both countries. This bilateral military relationship was highlighted when Bolivia's Defense Ministry invited then-Iranian Minister of Defense, Ahmad Vahidi, one of the accused masterminds of the bombings of the AMIA community center in Buenos Aires in 1994, to attend the inauguration of a new regional defense school for the Bolivarian Alliance of the Americas (ALBA in its Spanish acronym). Iran reportedly helped finance this regional defense school to the tune of approximately $1.8 million. Argentine foreign minister Hector Timmerman immediately sent a complaint to his Bolivian counterpart, and Vahidi had to make a hasty exit from the country, leaving President Morales to do damage control by apologizing to Argentina for the fiasco.[35]

Vahidi's trip sparked many questions as to what type of military relationship exists between the two countries, and it was subsequently discovered that Bolivia had bought a package of military equipment from Iran just a year earlier, in October 2010. The items procured included a FAJR-3 piston trainer, an S-68 turboprop trainer, and the Iran-140 light transport (a licensed version of the Russia Antonov An-140 light transport).[36]

Once the aftermath and embarrassment of Vahidi's trip to Bolivia had subsided, the Bolivian government re-established military ties with Iran. On June 20, 2012, during Ahmadinejad's third official visit to Bolivia, an anti-narco trafficking accord was signed to help Bolivia in its "fight" against drug trafficking. This accord created the political and legal groundwork for Iran to have a military footprint in Bolivia, and the Islamic Republic is currently rumored to be helping Bolivia set up a new unit within one of their military special operations wing.[37]

A few months prior to Ahaminejad's visit, on April 2, 2012, news surfaced that a Bolivian-flagged vessel had been seized by Somali pirates off the coast of Maldives. After learning that the vessel, the MV Eglantine, belonged to Iran, it was freed by the pirates and continued its route to deliver sugar to Brazil. The incident sparked speculation that the Bolivian government maybe violating international sanctions then in effect against Iran by helping its sanctioned ships sail through strategic ports using a Bolivian flag. Later that month, Reuters reported that 15 vessels linked to IRISL, the UN-sanctioned Iranian shipping conglomerate, carried the Bolivian flag.[38] The Bolivian government responded by saying that it would revoke the Bolivian flag license and remove these Iranian vessels from its shipping register, but it was never confirmed that this took place.

Bolivia has become one of Iran's most important strategic partners in Latin America. This relationship has fostered and enhanced a greater Islamic presence in this plurinational state—one that is unprecedented in size and scope. Growing alongside this presence is the size of Iran's official mission in the country—which has been linked to the propagation of an increasingly active Islamist element there. The Spanish daily El Pais reported in 2012 that Bolivia has at least 145 registered Iranian diplomats in country.[39] By comparison, Spain has only ten. On the surface, Bolivia appears to be the beneficiary of this relationship, but upon closer examination one can determine that for every Iranian investment or action into this Andean nation, there is a reciprocal action by Bolivia.

Some analysts speculated that this strategic relationship had been prompted by aggressive outreach of the Ahmadinejad regime, and would dissipate with Ahmadinejad's departure from power in 2013. However, more recent Iranian activity suggests otherwise. For example, on August 25, 2016, Iranian Foreign Minister Mohammed Javad Zarif arrived in Santa Cruz, Bolivia along with a delegation of at least 70 executives of Iranian state-owned firms for a series of events with prominent Bolivian businessman. Against the backdrop of Iran's 2015 nuclear deal with the West, known as the Joint Comprehensive Plan of Action (JCPOA), Zarif's visit was a clear signal that Iran is back in business in Bolivia. In a concrete demonstration of his government's commitment to Iran, Bolivian President Evo Morales flew from La Paz to Santa Cruz to meet with Zarif and decorated him with the Order of the Condor of the Andes, a state medal awarded for exceptional merit to Bolivians or foreign nationals.[40]

The current Iranian ambassador to Bolivia, Reza Tabatabayee Shafiyee, has been even more active at enhancing cultural, commercial, diplomatic, technological and military ties with the Andean nation. The results have yielded a series of additional agreements, including in non-traditional areas such as space and nano-technology, and has also produced at least two high-level visits to Bolivia by Iranian Foreign Minister Mohammad Javad Zarif and the third head-of-state bilateral visit to Tehran by President Evo Morales. Bolivia also sent its Minister of Justice, Hector Arce, to Iran for the inauguration ceremony of Rouhani's 2017 re-election as president.

More notably, however, has been the increased military-to-military cooperation between the two nations. This cooperation culminated in a recent visit by the Bolivian Armed Forces Joint Chief Admiral Yamil Borda Sosa to Tehran for a series of meetings with his Iranian counterparts, including Iran's Defense Minister Brigadier General Amir Hatami in May 2018. The Bolivian army has reportedly expressed an interest to Iran in providing housing projects for its armed forces and increased training for its anti-narcotic and special operations units.[41] If this cooperation materializes it would mean a greater presence of Iranian (likely IRGC) military trainers in Bolivia, dispelling any suggestion that Iran's interests in Latin America, and Bolivia are tied to previous governments.

Endnotes

1. Pew Research Center, "Global Muslim Population: A Report on the Size and Distribution of the World's Muslim Population," October 2009.
2. "Bolivia – Key Muslim Converts Assert Local Peril, Ally with Zealots Abroad," Open Source Center Report, May 12, 2009, https://fas.org/irp/dni/osc/bolivia.pdf.
3. "Iran's Bolivian TV venture to 'interface' with Venezuela's Telesur," *Fars* (Tehran), March 19, 2008.
4. Adam Housley, "Iran moving in on Latin American television market," *Fox News Latino*, March 20, 2012,http://latino.foxnews.com/latino/news/2012/03/20/iran-moving-in-on-latin-american-television-market/.
5. Andrés Sal-lari has his own blog (http://andressallari.blogspot.com/) where he posts interviews and media appearances for both the Iranian-owned HispanTV and the Bolivian-controlled National Corporation for Bolivian Television (ENTVB), which operates the Canal 7 television station.
6. See this abbreviated bio of Mariano Vázquez here: http://www.agenciacta.org/spip.php?auteur428
7. Bolivian journalist Raúl Peñaranda made the initial claim that Iran provided $3 million to the Juan Evo Morales Ayma (JEMA) Foundation in his book, *Remote Control*, published in May 2014.
8. Amalia Pando, "El Canal de TV de Evo Morales ganó más de Bs 2,1 milliones con la propaganda del Estado," *Cabildeo* (La Paz, Bolivia), March 17, 2016, http://www.amaliapandocabildeo.com/2016/03/el-canal-de-tv-de-evo-morales-gano-mas.html
9. Ann "Babe" Huggett, "Iran Demands Nurses in Bolivia Wear Hijabs," *Red State*, Dec. 3, 2009, http://www.redstate.com/diary/annbabehuggett/2009/12/03/iran-demands-nurses-in-bolivia-wear-hijabs/
10. Wendy Pinto, "Murillo denuncia que Gobierno donó tres vehículos a Abya Yala," *Pagina Siete* (La Paz, Bolivia), August 25, 2016. Accessed: http://www.paginasiete.bo/nacional/2016/8/25/murillo-denuncia-gobierno-dono-tres-vehiculos-abya-yala-107494.html
11. Beatriz Layme, "UD liga a empresario con drogas y

dice que trabaja con el Estado," *Pagina Siete* La Paz, Bolivia, September 27, 2017, http://www.paginasiete.bo/nacional/2017/9/27/liga-empresario-drogas-dice-trabaja-estado-153641.html

12. ANF, "Gobierno a Murillo: Majzoub no tiene orden de arraigo y su situación en Bolivia es legal," *Los Tiempos* (Santa Cruz, Bolivia), September 27, 2017, http://www.lostiempos.com/actualidad/nacional/20170927/gobierno-murillo-majzoub-no-tiene-orden-arraigo-su-situacion-bolivia-es
13. Reporting of the arrest of Efrain Antonio Campo Flores and Franqui Francisco Flores de Freitas (nephews of First Lady Cilia Flores, wife of President Nicolas Maduro) cited an airplane Citation 500 with tail number YV2030 that was seized by the DEA. This plane is registered to Inversiones Sabenpe C.A. a Venezuelan company created in 1980 under the leadership of Khaled Khalil Majzoub.
14. The Saudi Arabian daily newspaper Okaz first reported on this potential terrorist plot by Hezbollah in their March 16, 2017 edition. Subsequent media outlets, such as Aurora (in Israel) picked up on this reporting: http://aurora-israel.co.il/hezbollah-en-bolivia-desbaratan-atentados-masivos-en-sudamerica/
15. U.S. Ambassador Phillip Goldberg, "Bolivia's Tiny Muslim Community," WikiLeaks cable 08LAPAZ872 dated April 16, 2008, http://wikileaks.org/cable/2008/04/08LAPAZ872.html.
16. Rinat Sueiro-Phillips, "El Centro Islámico Boliviano busca promover la realidad del Islam," *El Mundo* (Santa Cruz), July 10, 2011, http://www.elmundo.com.bo/Secundaria.asp?edicion=10/07/2011&Tipo=Comunidad&Cod=15149.
17. The CIB was reported on by the Open Source Center (OSC) of the Office of the Directorate of National Intelligence (ODNI) in the U.S., and the Federation of American Scientists released the official report in 2009. "Bolivia – Key Muslim Converts Assert Local Peril, Ally with Zealots Abroad."
18. Ally with Zealots Abroad, 3.
19. Ally with Zealots Abroad, 4.

20. Quote taken from an interview with El Deber newspaper in Santa Cruz, Bolivia published on Aug. 9, 2015. Online link is no longer active, however, the article has been reposted on Eju.tv: http://eju.tv/2015/08/ahmadies-quieren-aportar-en-la-construccion-de-una-bolivia-mas-multicultural/
21. Goldberg, WikiLeaks cable 08LAPAZ872.
22. Victor Rodriguez, "La voz de Islam' llego a Durazno," *El Pais* (Uruguay), October 24, 2008, http://historico.elpais.com.uy/08/10/24/pciuda_377459.asp.
23. Diana Rojas, "El Islam de los Aymaras en Bolivia," Islamico.org, April 12, 2012.
24. This statement is from Ahmad Ali, when giving an interview on April 20, 2014, to Andrea Estéfany Caballero for Erbol, a digital platform in Bolivia. Ahmad Ali is the president of the Asociación de la Comunidad Islámica de Bolivia. See here: http://www.erbol.com.bo/noticia/indigenas/20042014/hay_aymaras_y_quechuas_que_se_convierten_al_islam
25. "President of Iran, Bolivia ask for Higher Level Ties," IRNA (Tehran), January 16, 2007.
26. "President Makes Agreement with Iran Official," *La Razón* (La Paz), September 9, 2007.
27. At the time, Morales announced that Bolivia would remove visa restrictions for Iranian nationals traveling to Bolivia. See John Kiriakou, "Iran's Latin America Push: As the U.S. ignores its neighbors to the south, Tehran has been making friends and influencing nations," *Los Angeles Times*, November 18, 2008.
28. Faramarz Asghari, "Iran-Bolivia Strategic Interaction," *Siyasat-e Ruz* (Tehran), September 1, 2008.
29. "Iran to open two clinics in Bolivia," *Moj News Agency* (Tehran), October 11, 2008, http://www.presstv.com/Detail.aspx?id=71865§ionid=351020706.
30. "Detectaron uranio en la zona que controlan Irán y Venezuela en Bolivia," *Infobae*, Aug. 30, 2010, http://www.infobae.com/2010/08/30/534064-detectaron-uranio-la-zona-que-controlan-iran-y-venezuela-bolivia/
31. "Iran Approves US$280 Million Loan for Bolivia," Associated Press, July 29, 2009.
32. "Iran to open two clinics in Bolivia."

33. Stephen Johnson, *Iran's Influence in the Americas* (Washington, DC: Center for Strategic & International Studies, March 2012).
34. *Iran's Influence in the Americas*, 67.
35. Ilan Berman, "Iran Woos Bolivia for Influence in Latin America," *Newsweek/Daily Beast*, May 20, 2012, http://www.thedailybeast.com/articles/2012/05/20/iran-woos-bolivia-for-influence-in-latin-america.html.
36. Johnson, *Iran's Influence in the Americas*.
37. Author's interviews with retired military officials in Bolivia, October 2012.
38. Daniel Fineren, "Exclusive: Bolivia says may de-flag Iranian ships," *Reuters*, Apr. 18, 2012, http://www.reuters.com/article/us-iran-ships-bolivia-idUSBRE83H10H20120418
39. Jorge Marirrodriga, "Irán se lanza a la conquista de Latinoamérica" *El Pais* (Spain), June 23, 2012, http://internacional.elpais.com/internacional/2012/06/23/actualidad/1340465739_921466.html.
40. "Zarif recibe la medulla más prestigiosa del Gobierno de Bolivia," *HispanTV*, Aug. 26, 2016, http://www.hispantv.com/noticias/diplomacia/286074/iran-zarif-bolivia-medalla-prestigiosa-morales
41. Tehran Times, "Iran says welcomes co-op with Bolivian army," *Tehran Times* (Iran), May 12, 2018. Accessed: http://www.tehrantimes.com/news/423489/Iran-says-welcomes-co-op-with-Bolivian-army

10 Brazil

Quick Facts

Population: 207,353,391 (July 2017 est.)
Area: 8,515,770 sq km
Ethnic Groups: White 47.7%, mulatto (mixed white and black) 43.1%, black 7.6%, Asian 1.1%, indigenous 0.4% (2010 est.)
Religions: Roman Catholic 64.6%, other Catholic 0.4%, Protestant 22.2%, other Christian 0.7%, Spiritist 2.2%, other 1.4%, none 8%, unspecified 0.4% (2010 est.).
Government Type: Federal presidential republic
GDP (official exchange rate): $2.081 trillion (2017 est.)

Source: CIA World FactBook (Last Updated March 2018)

Introduction

The Federative Republic of Brazil is Latin America's largest country, both in geographical size and in terms of population, and subsequently has the largest Islamic population in the region, hovering at around one million. A growing portion of this population is made up of converts to Islam, as da'wah (Islamic proselytization activities) is in full effect in most major cities within Brazil.

With antecedents going back 500 years to the founding of the state of Brazil, Islam is generally accepted within society, and there are many successful Muslim entrepreneurs who have assimilated into Brazilian culture. Unfortunately, however, a radical element is forming within the larger Muslim population, fueled by ties to Islamist terrorist networks from the Middle East. Iran and Hezbollah have historically been major propagators of these networks in Brazil. However, recent years have seen a rise in followers and sympathizers of the Islamic State terrorist group within the country.

Considered an important logistical center and recognized "safe haven" by extremist groups, Brazil enacted its first piece of national antiterrorism legislation in March 2016, providing the government with legal authority to surveil, apprehend, and arrest members of

Islamist terrorist organizations. Just four months after the creation of the anti-terror law, the Brazilian Federal Police foiled a major terrorist plot by ISIS affiliate Ansar al-Khilafah targeting the 2016 Summer Olympic Games in Rio de Janeiro. These arrests stopped what would have been the worst Islamic terrorist attack in Latin America in the last twenty years. In May of 2017, the Brazilian Federal Court convicted eight Brazilians of terrorist activity, constituting that country's first sentence of its kind.

Islamist Activity

Since the mid-1980s, an Islamist movement has been steadily growing within Brazil. This movement consists of radical clergymen, terrorists, influence peddlers and money laundering "fixers" who use the country as a logistics hub for many of their regional operations, which stretch from the Southern Cone to the Andes. The most prominent of these operations was the 1994 bombing of the Asociación Mutual Israelita Argentina (AMIA) Jewish community center in Buenos Aires, Argentina, which in part was supported by radical Islamist elements in Brazil and the Triple Frontier, or Tri-Border Area (TBA) where Argentina, Paraguay and Brazil meet.

According to the late Argentine prosecutor of the AMIA case, Alberto Nisman, Iran's intelligence apparatus first engaged Brazil in 1984 by sending operative Mohammad Tabataei Einaki to its capital, Brasilia. Some years later, Einaki was expelled for his involvement in political activities incompatible with the role he had declared upon entering the country. Nevertheless, Iranian intelligence continued to operate through the early 1990s from the Embassy of the Islamic Republic in Brasilia via a Civil Attaché, Jaffar Saadat Ahmad-Nia. To local authorities, Jaffar Saadat was known as a "fixer" for regional logistical problems. This would come to light when Ahmad-Nia was implicated in the 1992 bombing of the Israeli Embassy in Argentina, which preceded the larger attack on AMIA a couple of years later.

Part of the reason Iranian intelligence targeted Brazil as an area of support for regional operations is because of the heavy Islamic presence in the southern city of Foz do Iguaçu (state of Paraná). Historically, Foz do Iguaçu, which is within the TBA, has one of the largest Lebanese enclaves in Latin America, and is in close proximity, across the Parana River, to the largest free trade zone in South America—Ciudad del Este, Paraguay. Combined, these conditions provide a permissive environment for recruitment, proselytizing, fundraising and other terrorist operations by a variety of Islamist terrorist groups.

Most notable is Iranian terror proxy Hezbollah, which has had a presence in the TBA since the mid-1980s, at the height of the Lebanese civil war. Hezbollah's decision to establish its presence in the TBA, and in Foz do Iquaço in particular, turned out to be a lucrative one, allowing the group to reportedly funnel between $15 million and $150 million annually to Lebanon through a variety of illicit activities, including drugs and arms trafficking as well as counterfeit and contraband operations. Hezbollah, however, is not the only Islamist terrorist group operating in Foz do Iquaço; Egypt's al-Gama'a al-Islamiyya (Islamic Group) and al-Jihad (Islamic Jihad), as well as the Palestinian Hamas movement, have all established themselves to some degree in the area.

Al-Qaeda likewise has an interest and presence in the TBA. Both Osama bin Laden and 9/11 mastermind Khaled Sheikh Mohammed (KSM) reportedly visited Foz do Iguaço in 1995 to attend meetings at the local mosque there. KSM returned to this mosque three years later in 1998 to connect with other radical elements throughout Brazil. The Islamist presence in Brazil originated in the TBA but began to spread north into major cities, such as Sao Paulo, in the 21st century. In 2011, reports re-surfaced of al-Qaeda cells on the move in western Brazil, when a Lebanese man, Khaled Hussein Ali, was discovered to be running an Internet café in Sao Paulo, Brazil's largest city. According to *Veja*, the prominent newsweekly that ran the story, the Internet café controlled an online communications arm of al-Qaeda called the Jihad Media Battalion.

These terrorist groups have planned several operations over the years, most of which have been foiled by authorities. Yet some have succeeded, such as the infamous AMIA attack, in which one of the mobile phones used by the suspects was purchased in Foz do Iguaço. Coincidentally, a Colombian citizen of Lebanese descent, Samuel Salman El Reda, had residence in Foz do Iguaço, and was accused of coordinating the logistics of the attacks from Brazil. He later fled to Lebanon to escape detention for his role in the AMIA attack.

A more recent terrorist plot was foiled in the summer of 2016, when 12 Brazilian Islamists were arrested on suspicion of being linked to ISIS and planning terrorist attacks during the 2016 Summer Olympic Games in Rio de Janeiro. These arrests were the first high-profile use of Brazil's new anti-terrorism law, passed earlier in 2016. Former Brazilian Justice Minister Alexandre de Moraes hailed the new law as an important tool that empowered Brazilian authorities to coordinate effectively across nine Brazilian states to neutralize the terrorist plot against the Olympic games.

However, the true test of the new law came fourteen months after its ratification, when the Brazilian judiciary began carrying out trials against the 12 arrested Brazilians. According to the indictment presented by the Federal Public Prosecutor's Office, the defendants had demonstrated an explicit intention to commit terrorist attacks at the Rio Summer Olympics. On May 4, 2017, Federal Judge Marcos Josegrei da Silva sentenced eight of them for promoting an Islamist terrorist organization. Leonid El Kadre de Melo was the leader of the ISIS affiliate in Brazil, earning him the longest sentence: 15 years, ten months, and five days in prison. The other members of the ISIS cell received sentences ranging between five years and six months and 6 years, 11 months. In June 2017, Josegrei da Silva upheld charges of terrorism against five more operatives that formed the ISIS cell.

Appropriate anti-terrorism laws are a strong step in addressing the counterterrorism challenge in Brazil. The country's porous borders, weak institutions, and recent influx of Syrian refugees, however, present additional challenges. Due to these conditions, over the years Brazil has become a hub for Islamism in South America. High levels of public and private corruption and organized crime compound this challenge. These factors have catalyzed a growing crime-terror nexus that facilitates increased arms, drugs, and human trafficking, along with new avenues for terror finance and immigration fraud.

The most notable example of the criminal-terrorist convergence in Brazil is the infamous Barakat brothers, who lead a Lebanese clan prevalent in the Tri-Border Area (TBA) and prominent within

Hezbollah. Assad Ahmad Barakat has been identified by the U.S. Treasury Department as one of Hezbollah's most prominent members, raising some $50 million for the terrorist organization from the TBA. In 2004, he was arrested and extradited to Paraguay for tax evasion. A decade later, in 2014, Brazilian police arrested Assad's brother, Hamze Ahmad Barakat, and convicted him of embezzling money from fellow Lebanese immigrants, and creating false documents to create companies to cover for trafficking in arms and drugs. Reportedly, the proceeds from these illicit activities went to Hezbollah, which contacted a well-known Brazilian criminal gang known as the "First Capital Command" to establish an arms-for-drugs pipeline in Brazil. Today, the Barakat brothers have been released from prison and are back on the streets of Brazil.

Hezbollah remains the most active foreign terrorist organization in South America. However, recent years have seen an uptick in Islamic State followers and sympathizers within Brazil's borders. The use of social media and modern pop culture provides increased avenues for Islamists to attract Brazilian youth. For instance, the following of Saudi extremist Muhammad Al Arifi, who is banned from 30 countries in Europe, has grown exponentially over the years to include some young Brazilians appearing in ISIS propaganda videos. According to Brazilian intelligence, the most active Brazilian Islamist propagandist on the web is Ismail Abdul-Jabbar al-Brazili, aka "the Brazilian." Intelligence officials believe Abu-Khalid Al-Amriki, an American ISIS fighter who died in Syria, recruited al-Brazili. Al-Brazili's virtual profile provides Portuguese content on social media in support of ISIS. The account uses the hashtags: #EstadoIslâmico (Islamic State) and #CalifadoPT (Caliphate PT—in this case, PT refers to the Portuguese language, not to Partido dos Trabalhadores (Workers Party)).

The increase in Islamist social media in Brazil led to the creation of an encrypted channel on the messaging app Telegram called Ansar al-Khilafah, which officially pledged allegiance to ISIS in 2016. One message on this channel read: "If the French police cannot stop attacks on its territory, training given to the Brazilian police will not do anything." Ansar al-Khilafah was created in response to a call from an ISIS-linked Telegram account named Online Dawah Operations, which requested its supporters with Spanish or Portuguese skills to contact a local Brazilian militant and join its ranks. This call to action sparked an internal discussion within Brazilian intelligence on handling ISIS recruitment in Brazil, resulting in a report on the phenomenon entitled *Islamic State: Reflections for Brazil.* The findings of the report led to more aggressive surveillance by Brazilian authorities and subsequently more arrests of Islamists in Brazil prior to the Rio 2016 Olympic Games.

In July 2016, authorities uncovered a terrorist plot targeting the Olympic Games through potential small arms attacks at various locations, emulating the 2015 Paris attacks carried out by ISIS. For the period that the Olympics took place, more than 110 intelligence agencies from around the world were installed in Rio de Janeiro. They augmented the 85,000 security personnel employed by the Brazilian government as force protection for the Games. Empowered by recently enacted antiterrorism legislation, Brazilian authorities thwarted what could have been the worst Islamist terrorist attack in its history.

Argentine intelligence has been monitoring Brazil since the Buenos Aires bombings in the 1990s. Intelligence analysts have determined that pro-Iranian Shiite groups, such as the Islamic Jihad and Lebanese Hezbollah, which normally work separately from orthodox Sunni groups, have been collaborating and cooperating with their Sunni rivals within Brazil. This Sunni-Shiite collaboration is embodied in the work of Khaled Taki el-Dyn, formerly from the Al Murabitun Mosque in Guarulhos, Sao Paulo. Taki el-Dyn is a Sunni of Egyptian origin who was the Director of Islamic Affairs of the Brazilian Muslim Associations Federation. He is believed to be a member of the Egyptian Islamic Jihad, and to have coordinated the visit of Bin Laden and KSM to Foz do Iquaço in the mid-1990s. Although Taki el-Dyn is believed to be an al-Qaeda sympathizer, he has maintained a long-standing relationship with, and even received support from, Mohsen Rabbani, the Iranian Shiite cleric labeled the mastermind of the AMIA attack.

This Sunni-Shi'ite nexus is even more pronounced when dissecting the money-laundering network of the Barakat brothers, who laundered millions of dollars for both Osama bin Laden of al-

Qaeda and Imad Mughniyah of Hezbollah through a construction company with offices in Ciudad del Este and Beirut. There are unconfirmed reports that Barakat organized a "terrorist summit" in 2002 in the TBA, with high-level officials from al-Qaeda and Hezbollah in attendance to discuss cooperation in casing U.S. and Israeli targets throughout the Western Hemisphere.

Two key events in 2016 and 2017 highlighted growing acceptance of Islamist radicalism in Brazilian Muslim communities. In January 2016, Saudi Sheikh Muhammad al-Arifi visited Brazil for ten days, during which he met behind closed doors with local leaders and Brazilian converts. Al-Arifi is known for his inflammatory speeches, which contain jihadist propaganda in favor of Sunni (ISIS) combatants against the regime of Syrian President Bashar al-Assad, and which are often cited by other radical groups. In July 2017, the Shiite community in Brazil also received a visit from another spokesman of extremism. Ayatollah Mohsen Araki participated in a summit in São Paulo attended by several high-profile members of Mohsen Rabbani's Iran-backed network in Latin America.

The tacit acceptance of these radical leaders by Muslim communities could be due in part to the influence that local leaders and organizers have over vulnerable populations, such as refugees. According to Brazilian authorities, between 2010 and 2017 over four thousand Syrian citizens applied for refugee status in Brazil. The latest migratory wave has attracted growing numbers of Muslim refugees to local mosques in search of support. The mosques receiving the largest numbers of refugees are located primarily in the São Paulo area, where el-Dyn (mentioned above to have connections to Mohsen Rabbani and the Egyptian Islamic Jihad) serves as one of the main organizers of refugee reception. As local mosques continue to operate under leaders with ties to radical elements, vulnerable populations such as refugees and other disenfranchised groups face increased risk of radicalization, presenting extremist groups with the opportunity to expand their reach across Brazil.

Since the mid-1980s, this Islamist mobilization has intruded into Brazilian society through an array of mosques, Islamic cultural centers and commercial endeavors. Its stealthy presence provides its members with the ability to move freely within Brazil, and to continue their attempts to unify and radicalize other Muslim populations throughout the country. As one prominent former Brazilian official has described it: "Without anyone noticing, a generation of Islamic extremists is emerging in Brazil."

Islamism and Society

Islam in Brazil has been present since the founding of the country over 500 years ago, and was first practiced by African slaves who led the largest urban slave revolt in Latin America. This uprising in Bahia, known as the Malé Revolt of 1835, involved 300 African slaves who stormed the streets of Salvador, Bahia and confronted soldiers and Brazilian authorities. Although the revolt was short-lived (spanning just a few hours), its implications would impact Islamic propagation in Brazil in future years, when authorities began to monitor the Malé people and made efforts to force them to convert to Catholicism.

The Islamic community, however, was not erased and dawah in Brazil continued into the late 19th century, when an imam, born in Baghdad and educated in Damascus, arrived in Rio de Janeiro. This imam, Al-Baghdadi al-Dimachqi, would connect with small Islamic communities in Salvador, Bahia and later was invited to Recife to continue his proselytization work. There are conflicting reports as to when the first mosque in Brazil was built, but around the same time Al-Baghdadi al-Dimachqi moved to Recife, the Brazilian government passed a resolution to allow for temples other than Catholic churches to be built. More than a century later, Brazil's first contemporary mosque, the so-called Mesquita Brasil (Brazil Mosque) was built on Avenida do Estado in Sao Paulo. It remains one of Brazil's largest mosques, but as Sao Paulo continued to grow, it became more difficult for congregants to attend. Thus, smaller mosques were built in surrounding neighborhoods.

Today, there are over 115 active mosques and 94 cultural centers and Islamic associations in the country, and it is estimated that there are over 100,000 Muslim converts living in Brazil. Moreover, Islam is increasingly noticeable in Brazilian society, not only through the presence of mosques, but also Islamic libraries, newspapers, and schools. But it wasn't until a telenovela (soap opera) called "The

Clone" was launched in 2001 that Islam hit the Brazilian mainstream. This soap opera centered around showing the difference between Islam and the Western world and was such a success that *Globo*, the most prominent TV channel in Brazil, dedicated a half-hour weekly show to talk about a variety of Muslim issues.

Islam has experienced comparatively rapid growth in recent years in Brazil relative to other countries in Latin America, even though Muslims still make up a small percentage of the overall population.

The majority of the Muslim community in Brazil is Sunni, and most have assimilated into Brazilian society. There are smaller and more reclusive Shiite communities, which remain somewhat insular, located in Sao Paulo, Curitiba and Foz do Iguaçu. The Sunnis, however, have been able to accumulate wealth, which has allowed them to organize and represent their political interests in Brasilia. For instance, in the first half of 2013, legislation was proposed in the Brazilian parliament to create a "national day of Islam" as a federal holiday in Brazil. Although the legislative proposal failed, it highlights that an Islamic lobby of sorts is active in Brasilia.

Brazil already has a major problem with drug trafficking/consumption and organized crime, and the addition of Islamist terror networks to this mix would dramatically complicate the country's security environment. Unfortunately, the radical Islamist actors described in the previous section are all too aware of these conditions, and have begun outreach to disenfranchised communities within Brazil in order to proselytize and radicalize them. The goal is not to assimilate into Brazilian society and culture, but rather to assimilate Brazil into the global jihadist movement.

Islamism and the State

Under President Luiz Inácio Lula da Silva of the Workers' Party (Partido dos Trabalhadores, PT), Brazil engaged in a new foreign policy paradigm known as the "South-South Strategy." This paradigm was part of Lula's vision to align African and Middle Eastern nations to Brazil, and his successor, Dilma Rousseff, largely continued his pursuit of a multi-polar world.

Emblematic of Brazil's growing support for Islamic nations in the Middle East and North Africa (MENA) was Lula's controversial intervention in the Iranian nuclear dispute in May 2010. To help Iran avoid further UN Security Council sanctions, in April 2010 Lula attempted to negotiate an agreement between Iran and the P5+1 countries (the U.S., UK, France, China, Russia and Germany) to swap low-enriched uranium for higher-enriched uranium. The deal, however, eventually broke down, and the UN Security Council adopted another resolution calling on Iran to suspend all enrichment activity that could be used to support their nuclear program. While this activism shocked some in the U.S. foreign policy community, Brazil's political ties to the Middle East and North Africa had grown stronger under Lula's tenure.

Dilma Rousseff built on Lula's foreign policy paradigm while prioritizing social spending during her term as president (January 2011 – August 2016). Under the control of the PT for over a decade, the state expanded massive welfare programs and crowded out private enterprise. The result was Brazil's private sector struggled, while the state rewarded crooked businessmen and created a culture of corruption within the government.

This reached a boiling point in 2014, when the largest corruption scandal in Brazil's history erupted after known money launderer Alberto Youssef implicated the state-run energy giant Petrobras in a massive public corruption scheme. Upwards of $5 billion was believed to have changed hands between corrupt public and private actors as kickbacks and bribes. In 2015, this scandal implicated top politicians in Brazil, including the former president Lula da Silva. Throughout the year, massive public protests spread throughout Brazil calling for Rousseff's impeachment or resignation. By December, the Brazilian Parliament answered the protestors' call to action by filing for the impeachment of President Rousseff. On August 31, 2016, the Brazilian Senate voted by a 61-20 margin to remove Rousseff from office, finding her guilty of breaking budgetary laws. Acting President Michel Temer, who took office after Rousseff's impeachment, appears committed to establishing fiscal discipline but is also realigning Brazil's foreign policy priorities.

One of the last governmental initiatives of the Rousseff administration was to begin talks with Germany, the European

Union, and the United Nations to consider accepting Syrian refugees. As of November 2017, Brazil had agreed to accept 9,151 Syrian refugees with humanitarian visas, and had already granted 2,696 Syrians full asylum. Following calls from various sectors of society for the Brazilian government to welcome additional Syrian refugees, Rousseff responded. Eugenio Aragao, the former justice minister, said the country could welcome "up to 100,000 Syrians, in groups of 20,000 per year," before leaving his post in May. Following the suspension—and later impeachment—of Rousseff as Brazil's president, the new Temer government has decided to abandon discussions of taking in more Syrian refugees, citing security concerns.

Suspending the Syrian refugee issue symbolizes a wider pivot in foreign policy being taken by the interim President Temer and his foreign minister, Jose Serra. In his first act as minister, Serra revamped Brazil's foreign policy priorities. His new strategy aimed to strengthen Brazil's relationships with traditional economic and trade partners: Europe, the U.S., and Japan. This was a significant shift from the previous governments' engagement with Middle Eastern and developing nations. This shift resulted in Brazil withdrawing its vote in support of a UNESCO resolution that described Israel as an "occupying power." While marginal in its effect, the decision to realign foreign relations closer to Israel broke Brazil's longstanding supportive attitude toward the Palestinian Authority. Under Rousseff, Brazil had become home to the first Palestinian Authority embassy in the Western Hemisphere, which opened in early 2016 in Brasilia.

Brazil's future is uncertain, as acting President Michel Temer is also facing potential corruption charges. The Attorney General has twice attempted to obtain authorization from the National Congress to prosecute him. Both requests have been denied. Elections in 2018 will define the leadership of the country and renew Brazil's foreign policy priorities. The critical issue of Syrian refugees and large public corruption scandals have highlighted the importance of paying attention to the rise of Islamism in Brazil, a phenomenon still largely misunderstood in Brazil, Latin America, and the world writ large.

Endnotes

1. The Brazilian Census of 2010 puts the number of Muslims in Brazil at 35,207, while religious authorities speak of far higher numbers: between one and two million. Based on the scope of Islamic activities in Brazil, the number of one million seems a more plausible estimate.
2. Julia Corthian, "Brazilian Police Arrest 10 Suspected of Plotting Olympics Terror Attack" TIME magazine, July 21, 2016, http://time.com/4417762/rio-olympics-brazil-terror-plot/
3. Ricardo Brandt, Luiz Vassallo, Julia Affonso and Fausto Macedo, "Juiz usa Lei Antiterror pela 1ª vez para condenar réus da Hashtag" O Estado de S. Paulo, May 7, 2017, http://politica.estadao.com.br/blogs/fausto-macedo/juiz-usa-lei-antiterror-pela-1a-vez-para-condenar-reus-da-hashtag/
4. Marcelo Martinez Burgos and Alberto Nisman, Office of Criminal Investigations: AMIA CASE; Investigations Unit of the Office of the Attorney General (Argentina), October 25, 2006, http://www.peaceandtolerance.org/docs/nismanindict.pdf.
5. Alberto Nisman released a special follow-on 502-page report on May 29, 2013 that discussed Iran's clandestine intelligence structure in Latin America. An English translation of this report can be found at www.albertonisman.org (http://albertonisman.org/nisman-report-dictamina-on-sleeper-cells-full-text/)
6. Rex Hudson, *Terrorist and Organized Crime Groups in the Tri-Border Area (TBA) of South America*, (Congressional Research Service, July 2003 (revised December 2010)), http://www.loc.gov/rr/frd/pdf-files/TerrOrg-Crime_TBA.pdf.
7. *Terrorist and Organized Crime Groups in the Tri-Border Area*, 5.
8. *Terrorist and Organized Crime Groups in the Tri-Border Area* , 20.
9. *Terrorist and Organized Crime Groups in the Tri-Border Area*, 25.
10. Leonardo Coutinho, "A Rede do Terror Finca Bases no Brasil," VEJA (Brazil), April 6, 2011.

11. Burgos & Nisman, Office of Criminal Investigations: AMIA CASE, 64 .
12. Holly Yan, Julia Jones, and Shasta Darlington, "Brazilian police arrest 12 suspected of planning terrorist acts during Olympics," *CNN World*, July 25, 2016, http://www.cnn.com/2016/07/21/americas/brazil-olympics-terror-arrests/index.html
13. "Brazil: New Anti-Terrorism Law Enacted," Global Legal Monitor, Library of Congress, Apr. 15, 2016; http://www.loc.gov/law/foreign-news/article/brazil-new-anti-terrorism-law-enacted/; On Terrorism and Rio 2016 Olympic Games, Center for a Secure Free Society, August 2016, http://www.securefreesociety.org/wp-content/uploads/2016/08/SITREP-AUG-2016-Rio-Olympics.pdf.
14. For more information on the ISIS terrorist plot in Brazil, please see the Situation Report (SITREP) from the Center for a Secure Free Society (SFS) published on August 2016.
15. Marcelo Toledo, "Courts Sentence Eight Men for Planning Terrorist Attack in Brazil," *Folha de S. Paulo*, May 05, 2017, http://www1.folha.uol.com.br/internacional/en/brazil/2017/05/1881372-courts-sentence-eight-men-for-planning-terrorist-attack-in-brazil.shtml
16. Leonardo Coutinho, *Turning the Tables: How Brazil Defeated an ISIS Threat,* Secure Free Society, September 2017, Issue 5, http://www.securefreesociety.org/wp-content/uploads/2017/09/SFS-Global-Dispatch-Issue-5-1.pdf.
17. Leonardo Coutinho, "Justiça aceita denúncia contra mais 5 investigados de terrorismo," VEJA, São Paulo, June 20, 2017, https://veja.abril.com.br/blog/radar/justica-aceita-denuncia-contra-mais-5-investigados-de-terrorismo/.
18. Press Release, "Treasury Targets Hizballah Fundraising Network in the Triple Frontier of Argentina, Brazil, and Paraguay," Dec. 6, 2006, https://www.treasury.gov/press-center/press-releases/Pages/hp190.aspx
19. Simon Romero, "Businessman Linked by U.S. to Hezbollah Is Arrested in Brazil in a Fraud Scheme," *The New York Times*, May 20, 2013, http://www.nytimes.

com/2013/05/21/world/americas/man-linked-by-us-to-hezbollah-is-arrested-in-brazil.html

20. "Hezbollah has ties to Brazil's largest criminal gang; group also found active in Peru," *Fox News World*, November 11, 2014, http://www.foxnews.com/world/2014/11/11/hezbollah-has-ties-to-brazil-largest-criminal-gang-group-also-found-active-in.html.
21. Jack Moore, "ISIS Calls for Recruitment of Portuguese 'Brothers' Ahead of Rio Olympics," *Newsweek*, June 21, 2016, http://www.newsweek.com/isis-calls-recruitment-portuguese-brothers-ahead-rio-olympics-472649
22. Christine Williams, "Jihadists pledge loyalty to Islamic State in first public declaration in South America," *Jihad Watch*, July 19, 2016, https://www.jihadwatch.org/2016/07/jihadists-pledge-loyalty-to-islamic-state-in-first-public-declaration-in-south-america-weeks-before-olympics.
23. This report is in the author's possession. For more information please see the SFS SITREP from August 2016.
24. "Ten People Arrested on Suspicion of Terrorism," *Global Legal Monitor*, Library of Congress, July 26, 2016, http://www.loc.gov/law/foreign-news/article/brazil-ten-people-arrested-on-suspicion-of-terrorism/.
25. Robert Windrem and William Arkin, "More than 1,000 U.S. Spies Protecting Rio Olympics," *NBC News*, Aug. 5, 2016, http://www.nbcnews.com/storyline/2016-rio-summer-olympics/more-1-000-u-s-spies-brazil-protecting-rio-olympics-n623186
26. Jose R. Cardenas, Roger F. Noriega, "The mounting Hezbollah threat in Latin America," American Enterprise Institute, October 6, 2011, https://www.aei.org/publication/the-mounting-hezbollah-threat-in-latin-america/.
27. Cyrus Miryekta, "Hezbollah in the Tri-Border Area of South America," *Small Wars Journal*, September 10, 2010, http://usacac.army.mil/cac2/call/docs/11-15/ch_11.asp.
28. Allegretti and Coutinho (2016).
29. Leonardo Coutinho, "Aiatolá que prega a destruição de Israel já está no Brasil," VEJA, São Paulo, July 27,

2017, https://veja.abril.com.br/mundo/aiatola-que-prega-a-destruicao-de-israel-ja-esta-no-brasil/

30. Ministério da Justiça. Brasília. December (2017)
31. Diego Zerbato, "Refugiados sírios encontram abrigo em mesquitas de SP," *Folha de S. Paulo*, São Paulo, March 24, 2014, http://www1.folha.uol.com.br/mundo/2014/03/1429884-refugiados-sirios-encontram-abrigo-em-mesquitas-de-sp.shtml.
32. Leonardo Coutinho, "Bem-vindos ao Brasil. E virem-se," VEJA, São Paulo, June 4, 2015, https://veja.abril.com.br/brasil/bem-vindos-ao-brasil-e-virem-se/.
33. Robin Yapp, "Brazil Latest Base for Islamic Extremists," *Telegraph* (London), April 3, 2011, http://www.telegraph.co.uk/news/worldnews/southamerica/brazil/8424929/Brazil-latest-base-for-Islamic-extremists.html.
34. Cristina Maria de Castro, *The Construction of Muslim Identities in Contemporary Brazil* (Lanham, MD: Lexington Books, 2013).
35. De Castro, *The Construction of Muslim Identities*, 17.
36. Rodrigo Cardoso, "Os caminhos do Islã no Brasil," Istoé, São Paulo, February 21, 2017, http://istoe.com.br/349181_OS+CAMINHOS+DO+ISLA+NO+BRASIL/.
37. Paulo G. Pinto, *Muslim Identities in Brazil: Shared Traditions and Cultural Creativity in the Making of Islamic Communities* (Florida International University Applied Research Center, April 2010), http://strategicculture.fiu.edu/LinkClick.aspx?fileticket=jDk1ZPpNivg%3D&tabid=89.
38. Robert Plummer, "Giving Brazil a taste of Arabia," *BBC*, December 11, 2005, http://news.bbc.co.uk/2/hi/business/4468070.stm.
39. Pinto, *Muslim Identities in Brazil*, 46.
40. Jaime Darenblum, "How Argentina and Brazil help Iran," *Weekly Standard*, November 1, 2012, http://www.weeklystandard.com/blogs/how-argentina-and-brazil-help-iran_659920.html.
41. Jackson Diehl, "Has Brazil's Lula Become Iran's Useful Idiot?" *Washington Post*, May 6, 2010, http://voices.washingtonpost.com/postpartisan/2010/05/has_bra-

zils_lula_become_irans.html.

42. Helio Bicudo, Miguel Reale Jr, Janaína Paschoal, "Pedido de impeachment da presidente Dilma Rousseff" [Impeachment request of President Dilma Rousseff] (PDF) (in Portuguese)., 11, December 3, 2015, http://ep00.epimg.net/descargables/2015/12/03/753f58eed8d66adf4ad11129cb833401.pdf.
43. CNN, Catherine E. Shoichet and Euan McKirdy, "Brazil's Senate ousts Rousseff in impeachment vote," *CNN*, September 1, 2016, http://www.cnn.com/2016/08/31/americas/brazil-rousseff-impeachment-vote/index.html.
44. "New Brazilian government suspends plans to welcome Syrian refugees," *Deutsche Welle*, June 26, 2016, http://www.dw.com/en/new-brazilian-government-suspends-plans-to-welcome-syrian-refugees/a-19353345.
45. "New Brazilian government suspends plans," *Deutsche Welle*.
46. "New Brazilian government suspends plans," *Deutsche Welle*.
47. Raphael Ahren, "Support for UNESCO Temple Mount resolution was 'error,' Brazil says," *The Times of Israel*, June 13, 2016, http://www.timesofisrael.com/support-for-unesco-temple-mount-resolution-was-error-brazil-says/
48. JTA, "Palestinians Open Embassy in Brazil, First in Western Hemisphere," *Forward*, Feb. 4, 2016; http://forward.com/news/world/332909/palestinians-open-embassy-in-brazil-first-in-western-hemisphere/.

11 Nicaragua

Quick Facts

Population: 6,025,951 (July 2017 est.)
Area:130,370 sq km
Ethnic Groups: Mestizo (mixed Amerindian and white) 69%, white 17%, black 9%, Amerindian 5%
Government Type: Presidential republic
GDP (official exchange rate): $13.69 billion (2017 est.)

Source: CIA World FactBook (Last Updated April 2018)

Introduction

Islam has had a presence in Nicaragua since the late 19th century, when Muslims from the territories of what was then known as Palestine placed a particular focus on Central America as an immigration destination. According to one estimate, as many as 40 families from Palestine settled in Nicaragua during this period.[1] *However, this first wave of immigration, and a subsequent second wave that took place in the 1960s, did little to establish Islam in Nicaragua. The most recent group of Middle Eastern immigrants arrived in the early 1990s, however, and this group helped establish what is today a small but thriving Islamic community.*

Nicaragua's Islamic community consists of Muslim descendants of Arab emigrants from the territory of Palestine and Lebanon. There are likewise a relatively small number of Nicaraguan nationals who have converted to the Muslim faith. According to 2011 statistics released by the U.S. State Department, there were approximately 300 Muslims, mostly Sunnis, who were either resident aliens or naturalized citizens in Nicaragua. Most Nicaraguan Muslims originated from Palestine, Libya, and Iran, or are natural-born Nicaraguan citizens born into one or more of those groups. [2] *There are also Shia Muslims in Nicaragua, mainly of Iranian origin.*[3] *While the Muslim population remains relatively small, it nonetheless has demonstrated notable religious activity, with prayer centers established in private residences around the country, including in Masaya, Leon and Granada.*[4]

The first mosque that was built in Nicaragua was constructed in 1999 with local funding, as well as the assistance of Panamanian Muslims. Construction on a second mosque was completed in 2009. The resumption of power by President Daniel Ortega in 2006 brought with it a positive change in the relationship between Nicaragua's Muslim community and the government, including considerably better treatment than under past regimes, when Muslims were forced into hiding or made to convert to Christianity. In January 2007, then-Iranian President Mahmoud Ahmadinejad visited the country's first mosque, signaling a growing international recognition of Nicaragua's Islamic community.

ISLAMIST ACTIVITY

Native Islamist activity in Nicaragua has been limited. The Muslim community in Nicaragua is small and generally moderate. Nicaragua's Islamic Cultural Association in Managua serves as the focal point of the country's Muslim population. The U.S. Department of State reported that the Sunni leader of the prayer center was dismissed in May of 2007 due to increasing Iranian and Shia influence in the Muslim community, but no Shia leader was identified.[5] The following year, the State Department's International Religious Freedom report stated that a new Sunni leader from Egypt had been appointed.[6] Run by Fahmi Hassan and his staff, the center also operates the country's first mosque. Apart from traditional prayer activities, the center maintains an office, a library, a children's area, and a school, and offers the use of its basketball court and soccer field to local residents. Religious seminars are available for men and women and Spanish-language literature is made available for the community and visitors.

Hassan arrived in Nicaragua in 1960 and has remained in the country since, with one exception. During the Sandinista Revolution, he lived in Saudi Arabia and Jordan, but as he explains in an interview, he left for business reasons.[7]

In 2007, the Nicaraguan Islamic Cultural Center opened in Managua with the purpose of spreading Islamic teachings. Founded by Carlos Arana, a Palestinian descendant,[8] the center was set up to organize seminars and to maintain a library and website. While the establishment of the new Center was said to be backed by the Iranian embassy in Managua, there is no indication at this point that the Cultural Center was used for anything other than non-radical Islamic teaching and, according to Hassan, it closed months later, with both the Sunni majority and Shia minority choosing the already-existing Islamic Cultural Association.[9]

In 2014, Nicaragua was visited by Sheikh Suhail Assad, a member of Iranian cleric Mohsen Rabbani's Islamist operative network in Latin America. Based out of the Center for Iranian-Latin American Cultural Exchange in Caracas, Venezuela, Assad serves as one of Iran's "informal ambassadors" for Islamism in Latin America.[10] His appearance at a conference at the Universidad Politécnica de Nicaragua in May 2014[11] denotes an increased openness on the part of Nicaraguan society to accept Islamist discourse. In more recent years, an Afghan man with terrorist ties was caught in 2016 after passing through Nicaragua en route to the U.S.,[12] but no significant presence of ISIS or other radical cells are reported to be operating in Nicaragua in the past year.

Islamism and Society

Throughout much of Nicaragua's history, Muslim citizens have been victims, off-and-on, of government repression, largely due to rejection by the country's dominant Catholic society. Muslim immigration to Nicaragua occurred largely in the late 19th century, when Palestinian Arab Muslims emigrated during the final decline of the Ottoman Empire.[13] This first wave quickly assimilated into the local culture, some of them adopting Christianity via intermarriage or due to government pressure. During this time, Nicaragua joined several Latin American countries in establishing laws that restricted the entry of Arabs, forbade the stay of Arabs already arrived in the country, or restricted their commercial activities.[14]

The peak of this repression occurred just before the beginning of the Sandinista Revolution in the late 1970s. During the Revolution, however, Nicaragua's government treated the Muslim community, especially Palestinian Arabs, exceptionally well. It was during this time that Nicaragua welcomed a wave of Iranian immigrants escaping the Iranian Revolution of 1979 and the Iran-Iraq War of

1980, establishing a Shia minority within the Muslim community as Nicaragua-Iran ties strengthened under President Daniel Ortega.

Most men and women who immigrate to Nicaragua from the Middle East choose to settle in the country, and leave only when they are old because they would prefer to die in their homeland.[15] This trend suggests a high level of acceptance of Islam within Nicaraguan society. Another indication of Islamic acceptance is Managua's Arabic business district. All along a road known as Casa de los Encajes, in the Ciudad Jardin section of the capital, there is a concentration of Arab stores, most of them owned by Palestinians who sell Arab rugs, home decoration, clothing, and fabrics. Hassan owns a rug store located in this small district, which by 2003 had been in place for "many years."[16] Hassan was also quoted in 2003 as saying that Muslims "have lived here for a long time we don't get involved in politics and at no time have we felt threatened or afraid" in response to media reports of tension between the Muslim community and the Bolaños government.[17]

More recently, historical pressures have all but disappeared as President Ortega has focused on bringing the Central American country closer to Middle Eastern states, especially Iran.

Islamism and the State

The Islamist activity that does occur in Nicaragua tends to occur in political spheres, rather than in grassroots organizations or local communities. The two main instances of Islamism in Nicaragua are the connection between the revolutionary Sandinista party and the Palestine Liberation Organization (PLO), and Iran's growing interest and interference in Nicaraguan affairs.

Current President Daniel Ortega led the Sandinistas to power in 1979. The relationship between the Sandinistas and the PLO was already well established at that point, as PLO fighters had trained Sandinista guerrillas before the Sandinista Revolution. Once the Sandinistas seized power, the PLO sent a 25-man team to train Sandinista soldiers in the use of Eastern-bloc weapons, and provided a loan of $12 million.[18] Yasser Arafat, then head of the PLO, visited Managua in 1980. By 1982, some 70 high-ranking PLO officers were assisting with special infantry training for the

Nicaraguan army.[19] In return, Ortega and the Sandinistas granted the PLO full diplomatic status. The Sandinista regime, from the time it came into power, has considered Israel an enemy. For its part, the Israeli government shipped weapons to the Contras in 1983, to aid the U.S.-backed resistance fighters in their fight against the Soviet-backed Sandinistas.[20]

In 1989, Ortega visited Europe and the Middle East in search of support, with stops in Qatar, Kuwait, and Bahrain. During a layover in Newfoundland, he announced that he had secured significant financing and aid for his country, presumably from patrons in the Middle East.[21] When Ortega unexpectedly lost the historic elections of 1990 to Violeta Chamorro, the Nicaraguan attitude toward the Islamic world changed dramatically. One of the first things Chamorro's administration did was close the Iranian embassy in Managua as well as the Nicaraguan embassy in Tehran. In addition, Chamorro renewed relations with Israel and significantly reduced the presence of the PLO and Libya in Nicaragua.

However, Chamorro's acquiescence to entreaties from the international community for reconciliation resulted in a number of Sandinista holdovers serving in her government. *The Economist* magazine noted the result of this decision in June 1998:

> ...One relic of Nicaragua's 11 years under far-left government remains—more exactly, at least 1,000 relics: sympathisers, militants, actual terrorists of half-a-dozen extremist movements who found a welcome and have extended it, despite the election of right-wing governments in 1990 and later. Beside sundry Latin Americans, they include left-overs of Germany's Baader-Meinhof gang, Italy's Red Brigades, Basque separatists, Islamic fundamentalists, Palestinian extremists and others. They have been able to stay because the Sandinistas, in their last weeks of power, gave them Nicaraguan passports.[22]

Support in the form of providing government documents and identification to enable unfettered travel to radical Islamists continued throughout the 1990s. When Saddam Hussein's troops retreated from Kuwait in 1991, they also left a cache of Nicaraguan passports behind, and the terrorists who set off a bomb under the World Trade Center in 1993 were found to have five Nicaraguan passports in their possession.[23]

Chamorro's policy of refocusing Nicaraguan attention on Latin America and the United States continued until Ortega's reelection in November 2006. During his second tenure as president, Daniel Ortega redirected Nicaragua's attention back on the Middle East. One of Ortega's first official acts was to reestablish diplomatic ties with Iran, waiving visa requirements for Iranian travelers and authorizing Iran to reopen its embassy in Managua. In a sign of this growing warmth, then-Iranian President Mahmoud Ahmadinejad attended Ortega's inauguration ceremony in January 2007 before visiting the country's mosque. President Ortega has also visited Iran, where on June 10, 2007 he met with Supreme Leader Ali Khamenei to mutually criticize "American imperialism" and secure Iranian support for a raft of foreign direct investment projects. While in Tehran, Ortega declared that the Iranian revolution and Nicaragua's Sandinista revolution were "practically twins" because they shared not only the same birth year (1979) but the same goals of "justice, self-determination and the struggle against imperialism."[24]

The meeting yielded concrete dividends. In August of that year, Iran's Deputy Minister of Energy, Hamid Chitchian, visited Nicaragua with a delegation of 21 businessmen. Ortega presented the delegation with a long list of discussed projects: a deep-water port, a wharf at Port Corinto and Monkey Point, a 70-kilometer highway on the Caribbean coast, improvements to Managua's drinking water system, six hydraulic plants, a plan for the mechanization of the country's agricultural sector, assembly plants for tractors and other agricultural machinery, five milk processing plants, ten milk storage centers, and a health clinic in Managua. In exchange, Ortega offered meat, plantains, and coffee exports to Iran.[25]

Since then, Iran has moved forward on studies for a $350 million deep-water port in Nicaragua, [26] but as of this writing construction on the project has yet to begin. And of the six hydroelectric plants, Iran has agreed to assist with four, but had the funding to invest only in one. Construction on the $120 million hydroelectric plant remains delayed.[27]

In the wake of the April 2013 death of Venezuelan strongman Hugo Chavez, many speculated that Ortega would attempt to fill the resulting regional leadership void, possibly through closer ties to the Iranian regime. Contacts between Managua and Tehran, however, remain largely unchanged, with hardly a mention of unfulfilled agreements between the two nations during subsequent diplomatic visits.

In a December 2014 meeting, the Nicaraguan Foreign Minister and Iranian Energy Minister discussed issues of mutual interest, including the expansion of bilateral industrial and commercial ties. In the years that followed, Nicaragua has reiterated its support for Iran's right to use nuclear energy and supported the Islamic Republic in other public fora such at the United Nations.[28] While Iran will not pardon Nicaragua's $160 million dollar debt, the country has indeed followed through with some initial investments.[29] 1,000 of the 10,000 promised "social housing" units have been slated for construction, according to an agreement signed between President Ortega and Iranian Deputy Energy Minister Hamid Chitchian.[30]

In August 2016, Iranian Foreign Minister Mohammad Javad Zarif made a trip to Nicaragua with a high-ranking "politico-economic delegation" that consisted of 120 businessmen and financial executives from the Iranian government and private sectors. Zarif indicated that Iran "greatly values its relationship with Latin American nations, including Nicaragua."[31]

Although there was no reported discussion of unfulfilled previous commitments, Zarif stated that: "Cooperation between Iran and Nicaragua can include collaboration in the construction of the [Grand] Interoceanic Canal to the areas of agriculture, energy production, petrochemistry, banking, credit, transportation, food and pharmaceutical industries, and science and technology."[32] The Interoceanic Canal has long been touted by the Nicaraguan government to compete with the Panama Canal, but it has mostly been promoted in fits and starts. As of December 2014, the government had broken ground on the project, but has since claimed to be awaiting environmental impact studies in order to continue construction. It has issued some ancillary concessions based on where the proposed canal would be placed, though even these have caused controversy, creating growing doubt about the country's ability to see the project through to completion.[33]

The Joint Comprehensive Plan of Action (JCPOA, or the Iran nuclear deal), signed between the five permanent members of the United Nations Security Council—China, France, Russia, United Kingdom, United States—plus Germany) and the European Union in July 2015, has received plaudits from Nicaraguan officials. Edwin Castro, head of the Sandinista bloc and co-chair of the Iran-Nicaragua Friendship group in the Nicaraguan parliament, said that the Nicaraguan government welcomed lifting the "unfair" sanctions imposed on Iran "in contravention of international law."[34] However, though Iran has seen an infusion of cash since the JCPOA was signed, it has not significantly increased its economic investment with Nicaragua nor made overtures toward completing earlier trade and construction commitments.

Earlier rumors of Iran operating the largest embassy in Central America in Managua have proven untrue,[35] and a 2012 revelation by Israeli media that Iran had established a Hezbollah training base close to the Nicaragua-Honduras border[36] has likewise been shown to be unfounded.[37] Nicaragua, however, opened an embassy office in Tehran, and sent Mario Antonio Barquero Baltadano to serve as ambassador in 2015. Through President Ortega's efforts, the Central American country continues to be an international partner for the Iranian regime, and has joined the other ALBA nations in supporting Iran's allies in the Middle East, particularly Syria.[38] While Saudi Arabia originally ideologically opposed the Sandinista regime, President Ortega's second administration has expressed interest in strengthening bilateral relations with the Middle Eastern country, echoing this sentiment with Kuwait.[39] By contrast, Nicaragua's contacts with Lebanon, Libya, and the Palestinian Territories—where most of the country's Muslim population retains some connection—are limited. Ortega's administration has maintained vociferous support for Palestinian causes,[40] even holding an international conference in support of the Palestinian Authority and the Palestinian diaspora in Managua in early 2017.[41] A month later, however, the administration announced the reestablishment of diplomatic relations with Israel, signifying a change in Nicaragua's stance toward Israel since the two countries broke diplomatic ties in 2010.[42]

Endnotes

1. Roberto Marín Guzmán, *A Century of Palestinian Immigration into Central America: A Study of Their Economic and Cultural Contributions* (Editorial Universidad de C.R., 2000), 49–59.
2. "International Religious Freedom Report," *U.S. Department of* State, September 13, 2011, https://www.state.gov/j/drl/rls/irf/2010_5/168223.htm
3. Roberto Tottoli (editor), *Routledge Handbook of Islam in the West*, (Routledge, 2015), p. 166.
4. "International Religious Freedom Report," *U.S. Department of* State, October 26, 2009, https://www.state.gov/j/drl/rls/irf/2009/127398.htm
5. "International Religious Freedom Report," *U.S. Department of* State, 2007, https://www.state.gov/j/drl/rls/irf/2007/90261.htm
6. "International Religious Freedom Report," *U.S. Department of* State, 2008, https://www.state.gov/j/drl/rls/irf/2008/108533.htm
7. Edwin Sanchez, "El Ramadan de un musulman en El Oriental," *El Nuevo Diario*, October 9, 2005, http://impreso.elnuevodiario.com.ni/2005/10/09/nacionales/2967
8. Doren Roa, "Inauguran Centro Cultural Islámico," *El Nuevo Diario*, September 15, 2007, http://tinyurl.com/yeqmsnu
9. Steve Stecklow, "A New Mosque in Nicaragua Fires Up the Rumor Mill," *The Wall Street Journal*, November 10, 2009, https://www.wsj.com/articles/SB125772737927737439
10. Joseph Humire testimony at joint hearing of the House of Representatives Committee on Foreign Affairs Subcommittee on the Western Hemisphere and

Subcommittee on the Middle East and North Africa and Subcommittee entitled "Iran and Hezbollah in the Western Hemisphere," March 18, 2015, http://albertonisman.org/wp-content/uploads/2015/03/March-18-2015-Testimony-of-J.-Humire-Hearing-on-Iran-and-Hezbollah-in-the-Western-Hemisphere.pdf

11. "Teólogo Sheij Suhail Assad analiza el islam en la UPOLI," *Universidad Politécnica de Nicaragua*, May 15, 2014, https://www.upoli.edu.ni/noticias/verNoticia/articulo:158-teologo-sheij-suhail-assad-analiza-el-islam-en-la-upoli-
12. "Smuggling network guided illegals from Middle East terror hotbeds to U.S. border," *The Washington Times*, June 2, 2016, http://www.washingtontimes.com/news/2016/jun/2/smuggling-network-guided-illegal-immigrants-from-m/
13. Guzmán, *A Century of Palestinian Immigration,* 49–59.
14. Christina Civantos, *Between Argentines and Arabs: Argentine orientalism, Arab immigrants, and the writing of identity*, (SUNY Press 2005), 224.
15. Sanchez, "El Ramadan de un musulman en El Oriental."
16. Eduardo Tercero Marenco, "La defensa de Irak es obligatoria y necesaria," *La Prensa*, April 6, 2003, http://tinyurl.com/yzjhlp3
17. Valeria Imhof, "Urcuyo calam a los árabes," *El Nuevo Diario*, April 2, 2003, https://web.archive.org/web/20070310212305/http://archivo.elnuevodiario.com.ni/2003/abril/02-abril-2003/nacional/nacional17.html
18. Robert Fisk, "Long link with Middle East / Nicaraguan involvement in US-Iran arms deal," *Times of London*, November 28, 1986.
19. George Gedda, "Administration Worried About Sandinista Ties to Middle East 'Radicals,'" Associated Press, July 10, 1985.
20. Robert Fisk, "Long link with Middle East / Nicaraguan involvement in US-Iran arms deal," *Times of London*, November 28, 1986.
21. "Nicaragua Ortega on results of Middle East tour," *Voz de Nicaragua*, October 20, 1989.

22. "Nicaragua: Rest Home for Revolutionaries," *The Economist*, June 18, 1998, http://www.economist.com/node/136402
23. Larry Rohter, "New Passports Being Issued By Nicaragua to Curb Fraud," *New York Times*, January 28, 1996.
24. "Nicaragua e Iran: 'Union Invencible,'" BBC Mundo.com, June 11, 2007, http://news.bbc.co.uk/hi/spanish/latin_america/newsid_6741000/6741829.stm
25. Revista Envio, *Nicaragua Briefs* 313, August 2007, http://www.envio.org.ni/articulo/3628
26. "Latin America warms to Iran amid anti-U.S. sentiment," Reuters, August 29, 2007, https://www.reuters.com/article/us-latinamerica-iran/latin-america-warms-to-iran-amid-anti-u-s-sentiment-idUSN2929293420070829
27. JoAnn Fagot Aviel, "Nicaraguan Foreign Policy Toward the Middle East," *Latin American Foreign Policies towards the Middle East: Actors, Contexts, and Trends* (Palgrave Macmillian US, 2016) Edited, Marta Tawil Kuri.
28. Fagot Aviel, "Nicaraguan Foreign Policy Toward the Middle East."
29. Ludwin Lopez Loaisiga, "Iran sin perdonar US$160 millones," *La Prensa*, February 7, 2009, http://tinyurl.com/yj79tcr.
30. Ludwin Loaisiga Lopez, "Iran hace promesas de ayudas millonarias," *La Prensa*, August 2007, http://eldiarioexterior.com/iran-hace-promesas-de-ayudas-15621.htm
31. "Iran Greatly Values Latin America Ties: Zarif In Nicaragua," *Press TV*, August 24, 2016, http://www.caribflame.com/2016/08/iran-greatly-values-latin-america-ties-zarif-in-nicaragua/.
32. "Iran Greatly Values Latin America Ties: Zarif In Nicaragua," *Press TV*.
33. Edwin Nieves, "The Canal Stuck in a Quagmire," Council On Hemispheric Affairs, April 25, 2016, http://www.coha.org/the-canal-stuck-in-a-quagmire/

34. "Nicaraguan MP: Latin American states welcome JCPOA," IRNA, August 24, 2016, https://www3.irna.ir/en/News/82201646/
35. Anne-Marie O'Connor and Mary Beth Sheridan, "Iran's Invisible Nicaraguan Embassy," *Washington Post*, July 13, 2009, http://tinyurl.com/knfpyt
36. Philip Podolsky, "Iran, Hezbollah establish training base in Nicaragua," *The Times of Israel*, September 6, 2012, https://www.timesofisrael.com/iran-hezbollah-establish-training-base-in-nicaragua/
37. Tim Rogers, "Hezbollah rumors continue to hound Nicaragua," *The Tico Times*, September 28, 2012, http://www.ticotimes.net/2012/09/28/hezbollah-rumors-continue-to-hound-nicaragua
38. Fagot Aviel, "Nicaraguan Foreign Policy Toward the Middle East."
39. Fagot Aviel, "Nicaraguan Foreign Policy Toward the Middle East."
40. "Nicaragua expresses solidarity with Palestinians," *The Jerusalem Post,* February 5, 2017, http://www.jpost.com/Arab-Israeli-Conflict/Nicaragua-expresses-solidarity-with-Palestinians-480596
41. "Nicaragua Supports Palestine Resistance Amid Israel Colonization," *TeleSUR*, February 2, 2017, https://www.telesurtv.net/english/news/Nicaragua-Supports-Palestine-Resistance-Amid-Israel-Colonization-20170202-0039.html
42. Raphael Ahren, "Israel set to renew diplomatic ties with Nicaragua," *The Times of Israel,* March 28, 2017, https://www.timesofisrael.com/israel-said-to-renew-diplomatic-ties-with-nicaragua/

12 Venezuela

Quick Facts

Population: 31,304,016 (July 2017 est.)
Area: 912,050 sq km
Ethnic Groups: Spanish, Italian, Portuguese, Arab, German, African, indigenous people
GDP (official exchange rate): $210.1 billion (2017 est.)

Source: CIA World FactBook (Last Updated August 2018)

Introduction

President Nicolas Maduro has continued his predecessor Hugo Chavez's welcoming stance toward the propaganda, recruitment, and fundraising of Islamist groups that fit into the anti-U.S. and anti-Semitic worldview inherent in the anti-imperialist "Bolivarian" ideology of the Venezuelan government. Maduro continues to provide various Islamist elements with assistance and safe havens for a range of financial and extra-territorial activities in Latin America and beyond.

The roots of this Islamist affinity stretch back to Chavez's years as a revolutionary in the 4-F movement, during which time the future Venezuelan president fell under the sway of individuals with a sympathetic view of a variety of "non-aligned" Middle Eastern rogues. Members of that group included now-embattled Syrian despot Bashar al-Assad, the late Libyan dictator Muammar Qadhafi, former Iraqi strongman Saddam Hussein, and the leaders of the Iranian Revolution.[1] These early lessons provided the basis for the foreign policy that Chavez pursued from the start of his presidency in 1999—a foreign policy that has been perpetuated by Maduro, and which made Venezuela a close ally of the Islamic Republic of Iran and an array of radical Islamist groups, chief among them Hezbollah.

Islamist Activity

Venezuela is an attractive way station for Islamist groups, which have a quiet but longstanding and profitable presence there that includes fundraising, smuggling, money laundering, and training. The U.S. Southern Command (SOUTHCOM) estimates that "Islamist terrorist groups raise between three hundred million and five hundred million dollars per year in the Triple Frontier and the duty-free zones of Iquique, Colon, Maicao, and Margarita Island, Venezuela."[2]

There is a special relationship between the Venezuelan government and Iran's chief terrorist proxy, Hezbollah. Venezuela provides political, diplomatic, material and logistical support to Hezbollah. As it is in most of Latin America, Hezbollah is the primary Islamist force in Venezuela. Capitalizing on the network of enterprising Lebanese Shiamerchants throughout the country's larger cities, the group uses the South American country for fundraising and various forms of money-laundering, smuggling, and fraud. The basic model is a simple "pay to play" system, in which local Lebanese Shiamerchants are persuaded by Hezbollah agents and financiers, through varying degrees of coercion, to "tithe" to Hezbollah.[3] Most worrisome, however, is the network of underworld connections that Hezbollah is building throughout the hemisphere from its base in Venezuela.

There have been several reports of the Venezuelan government providing identification documents to suspected members of Hezbollah, and other Islamist terrorist organizations from the Middle East. One former director of Venezuela's immigration agency has suggested that the number of documents provided to Islamist militants number in the tens of thousands.[4] Another official, a former legal attaché to the Bolivarian Republic's embassy in Iraq named Misael Lopez-Soto, provided even more damning evidence. In a special CNN documentary, Lopez-Soto provided an eyewitness account and documentary evidence that the Venezuelan embassy in Baghdad was selling passports to suspected members of Hezbollah.[5] In one case, Lopez-Soto identified an acquaintance of one of the 9/11 hijackers who fled to Venezuela after the attack on the World Trade Center and Pentagon.

The CNN documentary pointed to the country's former Vice President (and current Minister of Industry and Production), Tareck El-Aissami, as the most prominent government official involved in this alleged passports-for-terrorists scheme. The son of Syrian-Lebanese parents, El Aissami was groomed as an ardent supporter of Islamists and has used his political prominence to establish conduits to several Islamic governments. He has helped create a criminal-terrorist pipeline funneling illicit funds and drugs to the Middle East and facilitating the movement of Islamists into the Western Hemisphere.[6] One intelligence report cited by the CNN documentary estimates that at least 173 Islamist militants from the Middle East received identification documents from the government of Venezuela. These militants capitalized on a sophisticated, multi-layered money-laundering network established by El Aissami and his family while he was the Interior Minister from 2008-2012.[7]

One of the individuals benefitting from El Aissami's financial network is the former Venezuelan diplomat, Ghazi Nassereddine, who is sanctioned as a "Specially Designated Global Terrorist" by the U.S. Treasury Department's Office of Financial Assets and Control (OFAC).[8] The Nassereddine's are a prominent Lebanese family in Venezuela with close ties to Hezbollah. They are believed to have facilitated travel to, and logistical support in, Venezuela for Hezbollah operatives for several decades, establishing a real estate footprint on Margarista Island, off the Caribbean coast.[9] Ghazi Nasserredine, who is also wanted by the FBI, and Tareck El Aissami are both sanctioned by OFAC. Ghazi in 2008 and Tareck in February 2017 as a "Specially Designated Narcotics Trafficker."[10]

Walid Makled Garcia, a noted Syrian-Venezuelan drug kingpin incarcerated in 2011, identified Tareck El Aissami and his brother Feras as former clients.[11] Makled claimed that the El Aissami brothers would pay him to create spaces for the Venezuelan armed forces to move illicit products from Venezuela to the Middle East and West Africa. With more than 40 Venezuelan generals on his payroll, Makled had strategic access to ports, airports, national airlines, and fertilizer plants, to cover and conceal the movement of illicit narcotics and launder the funds for several Drug Trafficking Organizations, including Hezbollah.[12]

Islamism and Society

Venezuela's Muslim population is small but influential. According to the conservative estimate of the U.S. State Department in its 2017 *International Religious Freedom Report*, there are more than 100,000 Muslims in Venezuela, primarily of Lebanese and Syrian descent, and concentrated in Nueva Esparta and Caracas.[13] While Margarita Island's Muslim population is almost entirely Lebanese Shi'a, there are Sunni Muslims elsewhere in the country, and Caracas has a largely Sunni population of 15,000 that is served by one of the largest mosque in Latin America, built by the Saudis as a sister mosque to the Sheikh Ibrahim Al-Ibrahim mosque in Gibraltar.[14] There are other mosques in the major cities of Maracaibo, Valencia, Vargas, Punto Fijo, and Bolivar. Local cable television outlets in Margarita carry *Al-Jazeera* and the Lebanese Hezbollah outlet LBC, while on the mainland the Saudi Channel is available via satellite as well.[15]

The picture of Islamism and society in Venezuela resembles that of much of Latin America. While there is a vague anti-globalist sense that pervades society, actual friendship with Islamist aims is at the political, rather than the religious, level.[16] While the Latin American left at times can sound Islamist in its politics and its understanding of who the "enemy" is, apart from one-off episodes, there is no mass conversion to Islam taking place in Venezuela—or, indeed, in the region. This is not to say that efforts have not been made, especially among indigenous and Creole groups whose Christianity has never been especially solid. To the contrary, in the past 150 years of immigration from the Middle East to the New World, the opposite trend has held sway. Many prominent turcos (immigrants and their descendants from the Middle East) originally were Muslim, but have been genuine conversos (converts to Christianity) for generations.

Thus, the presence in Caracas of the largest mosque in Latin America may give Muslim proselytizers the right to say they have penetrated the region, but it reflects Venezuela's cosmopolitan self-image more than it serves as evidence of an Islamic trajectory. Nonetheless, one should not dismiss the larger fact that Islam does play a significant—if not central—role in Venezuela's anti-globalist and anti-hegemonic culture, which post-colonial critic Robert Young notes incarnates a "tricontinental counter-modernity" that combines diaspora and local cultural elements, and blends Arab, Islamic, black and Hispanic factors to generate "a revolutionary black, Asian and Hispanic globalization, with its own dynamic counter-modernity... constructed in order to fight global imperialism."[17]

However, there has been at least one instance of a radical Islamist group that was based in Venezuela and seemingly concerned with Venezuelan social issues. The group advertised itself as Hezbollah en América Latina ("Hezbollah in Latin America.") Though it was largely eclipsed in the news media by the U.S. 2006 mid-term elections, Hezbollah en América Latina's failed attempt in October 2006 to bomb the U.S. (and perhaps the Israeli) embassy in Caracas was a significant event. The group, based within the country's Wayuu Indian population, boasts of activity in Argentina, Chile, Colombia, El Salvador and Mexico on their website,[18] which is written in Spanish and Chapateka (a combination of the Wayuu language and Spanish). However, the backbone of the organization is in Venezuela on the country's western border with Colombia. The group's members are local Venezuelans without Muslim heritage, and claim to be Shiite supporters of Hezbollah and Iran.[19]

In its manifesto, the organization asserted that Venezuelan society, with its interest in sex, money, industry and commerce, has become a "swamp of immorality and corruption."[20] It claimed that political movements and parties could not provide an answer to these challenges because they were also part of the problem. Thus, only "a theocratic, Political-Islamic force can liberate society from this situation."[21] By contrast, Hezbollah en América Latina "respect[ed] the Venezuelan revolutionary process, and support[ed] its social policies as well as its anti-Zionism and anti-Americanism," even as it rejected socialism in favor of an Islamic order. Tellingly, the group urged everyone to vote for and support Chavez.[22]

Islamism and the State

Ever since Hugo Chavez took his first trip to Iran in 2001, close relations with the Islamic Republic have been a cardinal tenet of Venezuela's foreign policy. During Iran's 2009 elections, Chavez offered "total solidarity" to Iranian president Mahmoud Ahmadinejad, equating attacks on him as an assault by "global capitalism,"[23] and condoned the brutal tactics of Iran's domestic militia, the *Basij*, in their crackdown on opposition protesters.[24] Iran reciprocated these friendly feelings when Hugo Chávez was decorated with the Higher Medal of the Islamic Republic of Iran in 2008, Mahmoud Ahmadinejad called Chávez "my brother… a friend of the Iranian nation and the people seeking freedom around the world. He works perpetually against the dominant system. He is a worker of God and servant of the people."[25] Ahmadinejad even risked a public embrace of Chavez's grieving mother at the caudillo's funeral, a move which scandalized the mullahs back home.

This relationship manifested itself in a series of agreements over the years. Venezuela announced the agreement to purchase Unmanned Aerial Vehicles (UAVs) from Iran in 2007. But this drone cooperation, troubling enough in and of itself, may mask still more sinister cooperation. There has been speculation, albeit never corroborated, that Venezuela and Iran signed an agreement to construct a joint missile base in Venezuela and co-develop ballistic missiles.[26] Notably, however, the State Department claimed that it had "no evidence to support this claim and therefore no reason to believe the assertions made in the article are credible."[27]

In November 2008, Iranian and Venezuelan officials signed a secret "science and technology" agreement formalizing cooperation "in the field of nuclear technology."[28] As part of that outreach, then-Iranian Minister of Science, Research and Technology Mohammad-Mehdi Zahedi led a delegation to Caracas and held talks with high-ranking Venezuelan officials. The delegation visited the Venezuelan Foundation for Seismological Research, Caracas Central University, the Simon Bolivar University, and the Venezuelan Institute for Scientific Research.[29] During the visit, Chavez promised to provide the Islamic Republic with 20,000 barrels of petrol a day, despite the sanctions on Iran's economy being contemplated by much of the world and despite Venezuela's own problems in supplying its domestic markets with fuel.[30]

In January 2010, the two countries launched a bi-national bank with $200 million of initial capital—with each country contributing half—and a final goal of $1.2 billion.[31] The Iran Venezuela Bi-

National Bank (IVBB) is the first non-governmental bi-national bank in Iran supposedly financing projects of mutual benefit to the two countries. Based in Tehran, it offers a convenient channel for Iran and Venezuela to sidestep U.S. sanctions along with the several branches of Iran's Saderat Bank already open in Venezuela.[32] Furthermore, U.S. State Department cables, published by Wikileaks, reveal an Iranian shipment of *Mohajer*-2 unmanned aerial vehicles in violation of UNSCR 1747 bound for Venezuela sometime before May 2009.[33] Subsequently, a visit to Iran by Chavez in September 2009 yielded a new deal on nuclear cooperation.[34] The agreement was an addition to a rapidly growing list of bilateral pacts between Caracas and Tehran. Despite U.S. sanctions, in November 2011, the first *Mohajer* was spotted at El Libertador airbase in Ochoa. In the summer of 2012, a Spanish news source, ABC.es, broke a story about U.S. investigations into the program and Chavez admitted and shared pictures of the UAVs, according to a Reuters report.[35]

Other violations of UNSCR 1747 included a more alarming Iranian enterprise in Venezuela. Parchin Chemical Industries (PCI) is part of Iran's Defense Industries Organization's Chemical Industries Group, and specializes in the production of ammunition, explosives, as well as the solid propellants for rockets and missiles. It is prominently listed in the annex to United Nations Security Council Resolution 1747, as an entity that is involved in Iran's missile and WMD programs.[36] In April 2007, U.S. officials identified PCI "as the final recipient of sodium perchlorate monohydrate, a chemical precursor for solid propellant oxidizer, possibly to be used for ballistic missiles,"[37] and subsequently added them to the specially designated national and blocked persons list of the Department of Treasury's Office of Foreign Asset Control.[38] In addition, the Parchin military complex approximately 20 kilometers southeast of Tehran (where PCI is believed to be located) is suspected to be a testing site for explosives used in the detonation of nuclear weapons. PCI and CAVIM, Venezuela's state-owned weapons manufacturer, were constructing plants to produce nitroglycerine and nitrocellulose (both active ingredients for manufacturing explosives and propellants), as well as a gunpowder factory in the state of Falcón.[39] These joint military projects led the U.S. State Department to sanction CAVIM in 2011 – penalties which it renewed in 2013 that are still active today.[40]

The relationship between Iran and Venezuela has now persisted for four years beyond the personal bond between late president Chavez and former president Ahmadinejad. The joint ventures erected between Caracas and Tehran, and the purchase of Venezuelan enterprises, allow Iran to do business with U.S. companies and even within the United States itself. Because of the direct connection between Caracas and Tehran, efforts to contain trade with Iran are futile without cutting off the billions of dollars of legitimate U.S. trade with Venezuela, according to Manhattan District Attorney Robert Morganthau.[41] In June of 2015, Iran and Venezuela signed a series of agreements, complete with a $500 million line of credit. The scope of the agreement included drugs and surgical equipment, along with joint nanotechnology research.[42]

Iran and Venezuela have continued to strengthen ties under the leadership of Hassan Rouhani and Nicolás Maduro. In August 2016, Iranian Foreign Minister Mohamad Javad Zarif took a six-country tour of Latin America, culminating in a visit to Venezuela to meet with President Maduro.[43] The Foreign Minister's trip was to prepare for Iran's President Hassan Rouhani's first and only official visit to the region. Rouhani attended the 17th summit of the Non-Aligned Movement (NAM) in September 2016, before traveling New York for the UN General Assembly.[44]

2017 began with a period of instability for Venezuela as street protests and social uprisings spread throughout the country. Amid the political and economic crisis in Venezuela, the spokesperson for Iran's Foreign Ministry stated "the continuation of instability in Venezuela does not benefit anyone, but could only serve to heighten the pressure felt by citizens. The stability and security of Latin America, especially that of our friend Venezuela, is of great importance to Iran."[45] This show of solidarity was followed by pledge of military support from Iran's Defense Minister Brigadier General Hossein Dehqan, who met with Venezuela's Defense Minister Vladimir Padrino López at the Moscow International Security Conference.[46]

Venezuela and Iran are experiencing similar political and

economic crises, fueled by hyperinflation, high levels of corruption, and plunging oil prices. Iran and Venezuela, both OPEC members, remain key suppliers to world oil markets and have been cooperating to drive oil prices up. Venezuela's crisis, however, has reached historic proportions rivaling Syria's humanitarian situation, with refugee outflows upwards of 1.5 million leaving since 2014.[47] The Trump administration has sanctioned some 70 regime officials in Venezuela to date for corruption, drug trafficking, and human rights abuses.[48] It has also begun to re-impose sanctions on Iran after the May 2018 U.S. withdrawal from the nuclear deal known as the JCPOA.

After years of investments in Venezuela, the Iranian regime will not let its stake in the country go to waste. To this end, Iran's Vice Minister of Foreign Affairs Morteza Sarmadi recently called for "closer cooperation" with Venezuela in standing against the Trump administration.[49] For his part, President Maduro reassured his Iranian allies that Venezuela will remain steadfast in partnership with the Islamic Republic against "U.S. aggression," stating that "[Iran and Venezuela] must firmly stand against U.S. patronizing policies in OPEC and coordinate the policies of OPEC and non-OPEC members against Washington."[50] Indeed, as of July 2018, the Iranian government had already dispatched top diplomats to Venezuela to rekindle the relationship, indicating that strategic ties between Tehran and Caracas are hardly a thing of the past.

Endnotes

1. Alberto Garrido, *Las Guerras de Chavez* (Rayuela: Taller de Ediciones, 2006), 17.
2. Paul D. Taylor, ed., "Latin American Security Challenges: A Collaborative Inquiry from North and South," Naval War College *Newport Paper* no. 21, 2004.
3. U.S. Department of the Treasury, Office of Public Affairs, "Treasury Designates Islamic Extremist, Two Companies Supporting Hezbollah in Tri-border Area," June 10, 2004, http://www.treas.gov/press/releases/js1720.htm.

4. Antonio María Delgado, "Régimen chavista otorgó ilegalmente 10,000 pasaportes venezolanos a sirios, iraníes," *El Nuevo Herald*, April 16, 2017, https://www.elnuevoherald.com/noticias/mundo/america-latina/venezuela-es/article144934809.html.
5. The documentary, titled "Passports in the Shadows" aired simultaneously on AC360° and Conclusiones of CNN en Español on Feb. 14, 2017, https://www.cnn.com/videos/world/2017/02/14/fraudulent-venezuelan-passports-griffin-dnt-ac.cnn.
6. "Passports in the Shadows," AC360.
7. "Passports in the Shadows," AC360.
8. US Department of Treasury Press Center: "Treasury Targets Hizballah in Venezuela," June 18, 2008, https://www.treasury.gov/press-center/press-releases/Pages/hp1036.aspx.
9. Emili J. Blasco, *Boomerang Chavez: The Fraud that Led to Venezuela's Collapse*, June 15, 2016 (CreateSpace Independent Publishing Platform).
10. US Department of Treasury Press Center, "Treasury Sanctions Prominent Venezuelan Drug Trafficker Tareck El Aissami and his Primary Frontman Samark Lopez Bello," February 13, 2017, https://www.treasury.gov/press-center/press-releases/Pages/as0005.aspx.
11. Joseph Humire, "Chapter 8, Venezuela: Trends in Organized Crime," *Re-conceptualizing Security in the Americas in the 21st Century*, Published in August 2016 by Lexington Books.
12. See Interview with Walid Makled on "Aqui y Ahora" news program on Spanish-language network *Univision*, March 31, 2011, Accessed: https://www.univision.com/shows/aqui-y-ahora/exclusiva-con-walid-makled-el-narcotraficante-que-quieren-extraditar-eu-y-venezuela
13. U.S. Department of State, Bureau of Democracy, Human Rights and Labor, *Venezuela*: *2011 Report on International Religious Freedom*, September 2011, https://www.state.gov/j/drl/rls/irf/2011/wha/193009.htm.
14. *Venezuela: 2011.*
15. *Venezuela: 2011.*
16. Hezbollah Venezuela's website: http://

hezboallahpartidoislamico.blogspot.es/1149260280/hezboallah-grupo-islamico-venezolano/ (in Spanish).

17. Robert Young, *Postcolonialism: An Historical Introduction* (London: Blackwell Publishers, 2001), 2.
18. The organization's website was previously located at http://groups.msn.com/AutonomiaIslamicaWayuu. It currently appears to be housed at http://autonomiaislamicawayuu.blogspot.com/.
19. Manuel Torres Soriano, "La Fascinación por el éxito: Hezbollah en América Latina," *Jihad Monitor*, October 17, 2006.
20. Soriano, 2.
21. Gustavo Coronel, "Chávez Joins the Terrorists: His Path to Martyrdom," *Venezuela Today*, September 2, 2006.
22. Gustavo Coronel, "The Hezbollah Venezuelan Metastasis," *Venezuela Today*, September 4, 2006, 3.
23. "Iran-Venezuela Ties Serve Strategic Aims," United Press International, August 14, 2009, http://www.upi.com/Top_News/Special/2009/08/14/Iran-Venezuela-ties-serve-strategic-aims/UPI-91201250266165.
24. "Iran-Venezuela Ties Serve Strategic Aims," United Press International.
25. "Chávez decorated in Iran; initials cooperation pacts," *El Universal* (Caracas), July 31, 2006, http://english.eluniversal.com/2006/07/31/en_pol_art_31A756133.shtml.
26. Von C. Wergin and H. Stausberg, "Iran plant Bau einer Raketenstellung in Venezuela," *Die Welt* (Hamburg), November25,2010,http://www.welt.de/politik/ausland/article11219574/Iran-plant-Bau-einer-Raketenstellung-in-Venezuela.html; Von Clemens Wergin, "Iranische Raketenbasis in Venezuela in Planungsphase" *Die Welt* (Hamburg), May 15, 2011, http://www.welt.de/politik/ausland/article13366204/Iranische-Raketenbasis-in-Venezuela-in-Planungsphase.html.
27. CNN Wire Staff, "U.S. knocks down report of Iran, Venezuela missile base," *CNN*, March 21, 2011, http://www.cnn.com/2011/WORLD/americas/05/21/venezuela.iran.missiles/.
28. Roger F. Noriega, "Chávez's Secret Nuclear

Program" *Foreign Policy*, October 5, 2010, http://www.foreignpolicy.com/files/fp_uploaded_documents/101004_0_Acuerdos_Ciencia_y_Tecnologia.pdf.

29. "Iranian Delegation In Venezuela," *Mathaba* (London), November 17, 2008, http://mathaba.net/news/?x=611701.
30. Robert M. Morgenthau, "The Emerging Axis Of Iran And Venezuela," *Wall Street Journal*, September 8, 2009, http://online.wsj.com/article/SB10001424052970203440104574400792835972018.html.
31. Morgenthau, "The Emerging Axis Of Iran And Venezuela."
32. "Iran Raises Profile In Latin America," *Washington Post*, November 22, 2008.
33. "Shipment of UAVs from Iran to Venezuela," State Department cable dated March 24, 2009, http://www.wikileaks.ch/cable/2009/03/09STATE28302.html; "Additional information on Shipment of UAVs from Iran to Venezuela," State Department cable dated April 14, 2009, http://wikileaks.org/cable/2009/04/09STATE36825.html.
34. "Venezuela's President Wants to Marshal the Forces of Anti-Imperialism," *The Economist*, September 15, 2009, http://www.economist.com/displayStory.cfm?story_id=14444403.
35. Brian Ellsworth, "Venezuela says Building Drones with Iran's Help", Reuters, June 14, 2012, http://www.reuters.com/article/2012/06/14/us-venezuela-iran-drone-idUSBRE85D14N20120614.
36. United Nations, "Security Council Toughens Sanctions Against Iran, Adds Arms Embargo, With Unanimous Adoption of Resolution 1747," 24 March, 2007, https://www.un.org/press/en/2007/sc8980.doc.htm.
37. U.S. Department of Treasury, "Treasury designates Iranian proliferation Individuals, Entities," July 8, 2008, http://www.treasury.gov/press-center/press-releases/Pages/hp1071.aspx.
38. "Treasury designates Iranian proliferation Individuals, Entities," July 8, 2008.
39. "The mysterious Venezuelan-Iranian gunpowder

plant," *Univision News*, January 13, 2012, http://news.univision.com/article/2012-01-13/the-mysterious-venezuelan-iranian-gunpowder-plant-casto-ocando.
40. U.S. Department of State, "U.S. Relations With Venezuela," August 31, 2016, https://2009-2017.state.gov/r/pa/ei/bgn/35766.htm.
41. Robert M. Morgenthau, "The Link between Iran and Venezuela: A Crisis in the Making?" Briefing before the Brookings Institution, Washington, DC, September 8, 2009.
42. Aditya Tejas, "Venezuela, Iran Sign Economic Cooperation Deals; Venezuela Signs $500M Credit Line With Iran," *International Business Times,* June 2015, http://www.ibtimes.com/venezuela-iran-sign-economic-cooperation-deals-venezuela-signs-500m-credit-line-iran-1986665.
43. "Zarif, Rodriguez stress expansion of Iran-Venezuela ties," MEHR News Agency (Iran), August 16, 2016, https://en.mehrnews.com/news/118959/Zarif-Rodr%C3%ADguez-stress-expansion-of-Iran-Venezuela-ties.
44. "Iran's Rouhani arrives in Venezuela for NAM summit," Press TV (Iran), September 16, 2016, https://www.presstv.com/Detail/2016/09/16/485036/Iran-Venezuela-Rouhani-Nicols-Maduro-NAM.
45. Correo del Orinoco, "Irán rechaza cualquier intervención extranjera en los asuntos internos de Venezuela," Apporea (Venezuela), April 14, 2017, https://www.aporrea.org/internacionales/n307038.html.
46. "Iran discusses Defense Ties with Serbia, Venezuela," Tasnim News Agency (Iran), April 26, 2017, https://www.tasnimnews.com/en/news/2017/04/26/1390155/iran-discusses-defense-ties-with-serbia-venezuela.
47. USAID Venezuela Regional Crisis Fact Sheet #1, April 18, 2018
48. José Cardenas, "It's Time for a Coup in Venezuela," June 5, 2018, Foreign Policy, Accessed: https://foreignpolicy.com/2018/06/05/its-time-for-a-coup-in-venezuela-trump/
49. "Iran, Venezuela need closer joint cooperation against

Trump's policies," MEHR News Agency (Iran), July 1, 2018, https://en.mehrnews.com/news/135272/Iran-Venezuela-need-closer-joint-coop-against-Trump-s-policies.

50. "Iran, Venezuela need closer joint cooperation against Trump's policies," MEHR News Agency (Iran), July 1, 2018, https://en.mehrnews.com/news/135272/Iran-Venezuela-need-closer-joint-coop-against-Trump-s-policies.

Middle East and North Africa

14 Algeria

Quick Facts

Population: 40,969,443 (July 2017 est.)
Area: 2,381,741 sq km
Ethnic Groups: Arab-Berber 99%, European less than 1%
Government Type: Presidential republic
GDP (official exchange rate): $175.5 billion (2017 est.)

Source: CIA World FactBook (Last Updated April 2018)

Introduction

Algeria declared its independence from France in 1962. Since then, Islamist parties and armed groups have made up the major opposition to successive Algerian governments. Between 1991 and 1999, civil strife between violent Islamist extremists and security forces plagued Algeria and claimed over 150,000 lives. The majority of those killed were civilians. Despite the brutality of that conflict, conservative Islamism still holds appeal for many in Algeria. The Algerian government's attempts at reconciliation in 1999 and again in 2005 have aided the decline of violent extremist groups but have unwittingly legitimated and empowered political Islamism. Both Islamism and Salafist Islam rose in the Algerian political sphere, with Islamist parties multiplying and gaining parliamentary seats in national elections. While these parties have of late declined in stature and appeal, as evidenced by their dwindling power and dismal electoral results, Islamist ideas and underlying social conservatism nonetheless remain widespread throughout the country.

Islamist Activity

The exact numbers of armed Islamist militants operating in any country are difficult to discern. Algeria is no different, and estimates vary from around 300 and 1,000.[1] Many of these militants shift their affiliation between more established groups and splinter groups in the region—of which al-Qaeda in the Islamic Maghreb (AQIM) is one of the most significant.

GSPC/AQIM

The Salafist Group for Preaching and Combat (GSPC) in Algeria was a militant organization that focused on waging jihad against the Algerian government and trying to implement sharia there.[2] In 2006, the GSPC merged with al-Qaeda and in 2007, it renamed itself al-Qaeda in the Islamic Maghreb (AQIM). AQIM follows GSPC's basic tenet of resisting the Algerian government, but now as a part of al-Qaeda's global network rather than a solely domestic organization.[3] Since the rise of the so-called Islamic State in 2013, AQIM has competed with it for influence in the Maghreb-Sahel region. However, AQIM has retained its hegemony in the area.

AQIM is primarily concentrated in the ethnically Kabylie region in northeastern Algeria (where the GSPC originally established its headquarters), and in the Algerian desert along the Sahara-Sahel in northern Mali. However, the Algerian government's successful attacks there have compelled AQIM to move into Algeria's southern territory, before eventually settling in northern Mali. The operations of Algerian security forces have greatly reduced the number of fighters in the north of the country. However, AQIM's sporadic attacks continued despite this pressure.[4] The most important such attack occurred in January 2013, when AQIM militants attacked the In Amenas gas plant in southern Algeria. The group had entered the country through Libya, which has faced civil war since 2014. The attack resulted in the death of 40 staff members (mostly foreigners) of the gas plant and at least 29 militants.[5] AQIM assassinations of police and military officers likewise have been ongoing.[6]

By 2013, the number of victims of terrorism from disparate armed groups had decreased substantially, with 30 to 40 a month–a considerable drop from the 1990s, when the number had reached 1,000 per month.[7] In 2015, 62 terrorist attacks took place, resulting in several dozen victims.[8] Security forces were quite successful in 2016 as they neutralized 350 terrorists, of whom 125 killed and 225 arrested.[9] Generally, Algerian security forces do not reveal the names of the groups that carry out these terrorists attacks; both AQIM and the so-called Islamic State have claimed responsibility for some of their operations. Other, smaller armed groups also claim responsibility for the sporadic attacks, but it is not clear how realistic the existence of these groups is. With the exception of AQIM, the current extremist groups operating in Algeria have limited means, no popular support, and little impact.

In 2017, dozens of Algerian militants surrendered in the south and southeast of Algeria after fleeing northern Mali, Niger, and Libya. The military neutralized 161- armed insurgents, of whom 91 killed, 40 arrested, while 30 surrendered. The authorities arrested 214 individuals for supporting terrorist groups, as well as 19 arms smugglers. They also arrested 549 narco-traffickers.[10] A high-level security source in Algeria revealed to the newspaper *Elkhabar* that the militants belonged to a variety of groups, not solely AQIM. Some of those whom Algerian criminal courts or courts in Mali and Niger had sentenced to death in abstensia on charges of arms smuggling or of belonging to armed criminal groups.[11]

AQIM receives considerable amounts of money from drug trafficking.[12] Thus, although AQIM does not traffic drugs directly, it provides safe passage for smugglers through the desert. It also provides protection to the drug traffickers in exchange for large sums of money. AQIM has also provided storage facilities for drugs in exchange for payment.[13] However, AQIM also has connections with weapons trafficking, and in the past, some instances of kidnapping for ransom. It is common for terrorist groups to pursue multiple forms of illicit income: "Activities of terrorists and organized criminals frequently reinforce each other, where terrorists engage either directly or indirectly in organized crime activities such as trafficking, smuggling, extortion, kidnapping for ransom and the illicit trade of natural resources, for financial and/or material benefits."[14]

An analysis of the security situation in Algeria indicates that the threat of AQIM has diminished inside Algeria, in large part due to the security forces' efforts. However, the threat of AQIM and other jihadist groups operating at Algeria's southern borders remains as potent as ever and represents great concern for various countries in and outside the Sahel region. The communiqués of the Ministry of Defense are primary indicators of the considerable decline of terrorism in the country. The head of AQIM, Abdel-Malek Droukdel, who operated out of the mountains of Kabylia for more than 15 years, has allegedly fled to neighboring Tunisia[15] to avoid death or capture in Algeria. Furthermore, most of the militants arrested in recent years are well over thirty-years old, indicating that many groups are struggling with recruitment. (Though AQIM leaders hope that the defeat of the Islamic State, despite its rivalry with AQIM, may provide some new recruits).[16] Most militants no longer carry the heavy weapons that were available following the collapse of the Qaddafi regime; many only have access to shotguns and a few AK-47s.[17] The Algerian military has cut off the supply networks that terrorist groups had used to equip their troops. Algerian security forces are today not only adequately equipped in counterterrorism operations, but they have reconciled with the population, which has become averse to terrorism, having suffered from a decade of bloodshed.

ISIS

ISIS militants have made many attempts to infiltrate Algeria through the Tunisian western border, but there too the Algerian army has repeatedly repelled or killed those militants. IS has repeatedly sought to establish a presence in Algeria; however, the military has successfully countered emerging IS cells.[18] Jihadism in Algeria is no longer what it was in the 1990s, when its thousands of troops were supported by the population and when there existed a huge pool of young people to join the multitude of groups, such as the GIAs, the AIS, and the GSPC (now AQIM). These groups or IS do not have any support among the population anymore. Today, it is difficult to imagine IS, an alien organization, coming to Algeria to recruit young people to join jihad. True, the civil war in Libya has worried Algerian officials, which explains their mediation efforts to bring about a political solution, which would in turn help in eliminating the terrorist threat. Algerians have feared a spillover effect; thus, they have secured their border with Libya and assisted Tunisia in doing the same. In Libya, ISIS no longer represents the threat it once did (2016-2017), although the return of ISIS troops from Iraq and Syria, where they have suffered defeat, has caused understandable concern.

Political Parties: FIS, MSP, Nahda, MRN, and the Small Islamist Formations

The emergence of Islamist political parties in Algeria is a comparatively recent phenomenon.[19] Religious political parties only became legal after the regime consented to political liberalization, prompted by bloody riots in October 1988. Most of the Islamist parties born in the period between 1989 and 1991 emerged out of a heterogeneous Islamist movement that took root in the 1960s. The most powerful and radical of them was the Islamic Salvation Front (FIS), banned in March 1992 following its overwhelming victory in the first round of the legislative elections the previous December. Notwithstanding FIS' popularity (it won overwhelming victories in the 1990 municipal elections and in the 1991 legislative elections), its impressive organization, and its capacity to mobilize large segments of society, authorities banned the group because of its radical ideology and the threat it purportedly posed to the state and society. Although the FIS is defunct today, its influence has not completely vanished. Some of its members joined the still-legal Islamist parties and/or voted for them during elections, while others joined the multitude of armed groups that have fought the state since the 1990s.

Today, numerous legal Islamist parties remain active on the national political scene, including the Movement for Society and Peace (MSP), the Movement for Islamic Renaissance (*Nahda*), and its offshoot, the Movement for National Reform (MRN), and the recent ones legalized on the eve of the May 2012 legislative elections, namely, the Party for Liberty and Justice (PLJ), the Front for Justice and Development (FJD—El Adala), the Front for New Algeria (FAN), and the Front for Change (FC).[20] All endorse the eventual application of sharia law. However, unlike the FIS, which wished to implement it immediately, these parties (the MSP in particular) seek a gradual implementation of Islamic principles.

The MSP, the largest legal Islamist party in Algeria, was created in 1990 as the Movement for Islamic Society/HAMAS, but changed its name to conform to the 1996 constitution, which forbade religious political expression. The group belonged to the "presidential alliance," a conservative mixture of nationalist, Islamist, and technocratic parties. In early January 2012, the MSP withdrew from the presidential alliance, and pulling its four ministers out of the government. In March 2012, the MSP, with El Islah and Ennahda, formed the Green Alliance. The three parties ran on the same ticket in the country's subsequent legislative election. However, the Green Alliance did quite poorly in the 2012 legislature, garnering only 48 seats out of an expanded field of 462.

Nahda split in 1999 when its charismatic founding leader, Abdallah Djaballah, created yet another party, the Movement for National Reform (MRN or Islah). The MRN did very well in the 2002 local elections, coming in ahead of both the MSP and Nahda, after which it demanded a ban on the import of alcoholic beverages in 2004. However, Djaballah did quite poorly in the 2004 presidential election, receiving only 5 percent of the votes.[21] The party has undergone further crises, and it is not clear what influence either Nahda or MSN now have—for, like most Algerian political parties, the fate of the parties is often tied to the individual that founded them. In the 2007 legislative election, the two parties garnered only five and three parliamentary seats, respectively. These parties did not gain many votes in the legislative election in May 2017. Indeed, in the legislative elections of May 2017, the Islamic Movement coalition ranked third with 33 out of 462 seats, a score that indicates some stagnation when compared to the results they obtained in 2012.

The three older parties had worked with the Algerian government, and abided by its constraints on political participation. In 2009, all three had endorsed the candidacy of sitting President Abdelaziz Bouteflika for a third term in office.[22] That cooperation was a product of the comparative decline in popularity experienced by Islamist political parties in recent years, as well as their internal turmoil. For example, the MSP split into two factions in 2009 due to the loss of popularity of its president, Aboudjera Soltani, who served as a minister under various governments. Many members of the party did not agree with Soltani's unconditional support for President Abdelaziz Bouteflika, and in June 2009 orchestrated a revolt inside the MSP. Following the dissensions and eventual split of the party, the MSP is no longer the force it once represented.

Algerian Islamist parties have lost their appeal.[23]

Before the May 2017 elections, the Islamist parties, such as the MSP and the FC, among others, sought to unify their forces with the hope of garnering more votes. However, despite these efforts, the Islamist political parties did poorly at the polls. The legislative elections in May 2017 signaled that the domesticated Islamists parties had weakened considerably. Local elections in November 2017 continued that trend. The regime has succeeded in not only taming the political Islamist parties, but also in fragmenting them, as was the case on the eve of the 2012 legislative election.[24] Indeed, many of these parties experienced internal ruptures,[25] which however does not necessarily mean that Islamist socio-political dynamics have broken down.[26]

In addition to these party splits, there has been an unmistakable rise of quietist Salafists who refuse to partake in political life, considering it anathema, a 'bid'a (heretical innovation). Although they do not represent a threat to the incumbent regime, they have nevertheless ascertained their presence in many mosques throughout the country. They do represent a challenge to the MSP because of the uncompromising nature of their discourse. While this state of affairs is favorable to the regime, as it plays Islamists against one another, large segments of society resent the growth of quietist Salafism; they see the conservative ideas of quietist Islamists as a potential danger.

Islamism and Society

Islam in Algeria is not simply the main religion of the population; it constitutes the primary foundation of identity and culture. Islamic beliefs and practices regulate social behavior and, largely, govern social relations. While the socioeconomic failure of the 1980s provided a trigger for the emergence of Islamism in Algerian society, its doctrinal aspects derive at least in part from the crisis of identity generated by 132 years of colonial rule. France's brutal colonialism served to undermine the principal local religious institutions: mosques and religious schools were turned into churches or even bars, religious lands were expropriated, and Islamic culture was openly held up to be inferior to Christian/Western civilization. Because French colonialists treated the native population and values with contempt, the overwhelming majority of Algerians turned to Islam to establish their cultural identity. The country's nationalist movement itself, though secular, used Arab-Islamic values as symbols for popular mobilization against colonialism. Contemporary Islamists often claim that they are the legitimate offspring of that effort.

Islamism is still prevalent in Algeria. However, with few exceptions, Algerians do not support armed groups, as many did in the early and mid-1990s. The brutal massacres that armed groups committed in 1996-1999 alienated large segments of the population, and authorities continue to dismantle progressively the small number of die-hard support groups. Rather, Islamism today has turned to social conservativism with no institutional or partisan attachment.[27]

Nevertheless, Islamist parties continue to do poorly in local and legislative elections. The local elections held in November 2017 confirmed the regression of Islamist parties in Algeria.[28] This decline was already perceptible in the April 2009 presidential election, during which the Islamist candidates were marginalized, with the Nahda candidate Djahid Younsi garnering a mere 1.3 percent of the votes and others even less.[29]

Therefore, while it is hard to gauge the present popularity of Islamism as a social and political movement, what is certain is that the institutional parties as well as the armed groups have lost the appeal that they had had throughout the 1990s and even in the early 2000s. One can advance four reasons for such decline: 1) the legacy of the civil strife which left more than 150,000 dead, mostly innocent civilians, 2) the relative loss of legitimacy on the part of armed groups like the GIAs and AQIM, which resorted to barbaric methods to impose their will upon the population; the methods were criticized by the leadership of Al-Qaida central itself because those methods could alienate the population and lose its support 3) the relative success of the 2005 National Reconciliation, which led to the surrender of thousands of armed militants and the extension of amnesty to numerous Islamists, and, 4) general disappointment with Islamist political parties, which are perceived as opportunistic and self-serving.

Islamism and the State

In 1989, Algerian authorities, in violation of a constitution that forbade the existence of parties based on religion, legalized the Islamic Salvation Front (FIS), a radical Islamist party. A front made up of a variety of forces, including alumni of the Afghan jihad, the FIS eventually became one of the most potent force against the state. In June 1990, the government organized nationwide municipal elections, the first pluralist elections in the country, and then cancelled the second round 1991 elections when it appeared that the FIS would win overwhelmingly. It cancelled the election, claiming that the victory of the FIS would have ended the democratic process altogether. The government banned the FIS shortly thereafter—and imprisoned its leaders—, which resulted in a crisis of the state. The civil strife that ensued not only pitted the security forces against armed groups but also spilled over to ravage the civilian population, notably in the horrible collective massacres of 1997 and 1998.

The intensity of the armed Islamist insurrection of the 1990s took Algeria's security forces by surprise. Authorities never envisioned the remarkable degree of organization prevalent among jihadist groups, or the significant resources available to them. The level of unrestrained destruction that these armed groups inflicted upon the state structures, personnel, intellectuals, journalists, moderate Islamists, and the various strata of society was intense, such that some spoke of the demise of the Algerian state.[30]

Aware of the near-collapse of the state and its institutions, civilian and military authorities took measures to safeguard the state. The first action was to remove elected Islamist officials from the municipalities and replace them with state-appointed officials. Armed Islamists eventually assassinated many of those replacements. The state also decided to arm thousands of people, many of them unemployed youths, throughout the country to serve as auxiliary forces for regular troops. These security agents, known as *gardes communaux* [municipal sentries], played a critical role in fighting Islamist insurgents, especially in the suburbs.

Moreover, the government increased the size of the police force and provided new recruits with more competent antiterrorist training, both in Algeria and abroad.[31] The police force acquired some adapted equipment imported from the former Soviet bloc, South Africa, and elsewhere. The state also took measures to thwart the financing of the insurgency. It incorporated a series of decisions, notably "La lutte contre le blanchiment (LAB) et contre le financement du terrorisme (CFT)," into the 2003 Finance Act (*Loi de Finance*)[32] to combat the funding of terrorist groups and money laundering. These laws allow authorities to trace the financial sources of the terrorist networks through numerous methods, from the freezing of suspicious assets and to the use of intelligence procedures to prevent suspicious financial operations.[33] Algeria is a member of the Middle East and North Africa Financial Action Task Force (MENA-FATF), a Financial Action Task Force-style regional body.[34]

The 2005 Law on National Reconciliation offered clemency measures and/or pardon for those Islamist fighters who surrendered to the state. In October 2010, authorities declared that 7,500-armed insurgents had surrendered.[35] The law was relatively successful. However, it did not contain provisions through which it was possible to seek justice against Islamists or members of security forces who committed crimes during the bloody decade of the 1990s. As the fates of thousands of people who were disappeared during the conflict are still unknown, this lack of closure continues to rankle many in the population. In 2016, the government added new articles to the penal code to strengthen measures against foreign terrorists, individuals who support or finance foreign violent extremists, and the usage of information technology in violent extremist recruiting and support. The law also targets internet service providers who do not abide by legal duties to store information or to hinder access to criminal material. The expansion of the legal measures aims at executing UN Security Council resolutions (UNSCR) 2178 (2014) and 2199 (2015), and the UN Security Council (UNSC) ISIL (ISIS) and al-Qaeda sanctions regime.[36]

The Algerian government cooperates closely with the governments of countries in the Sahel, such as Mali and Niger, in its counterterrorism efforts. The most noteworthy pursuit is its participation in the U.S.-led Trans-Saharan Counter-Terrorism Partnership to fight terrorism in the Maghreb-Sahel region.[37] Algeria has also sought to create a quasi-collective security community with the Sahel states, namely, Mali, Mauritania, and Niger to counter the terrorist threat in the region. Unfortunately, the fragility of those states undermined the potential capabilities of the General Staff Joint-Operations Committee (CEMOC) and the Algiers-based Joint-Intelligence Centre (CRC).[38] However, like other initiatives in the region, CEMOC is a rather ineffective alliance due to the lack of trust among the members, as well as foreign interference. In December 2017, French president Emmanuel Macron added a military component to the G5, which regroups Burkina Faso, Chad, Mali, Mauritania and Niger. Algeria has refused to join because it sees it as foreign interference in the region. Most analysts agree that the G5 might fail not only because it needs substantial funding (it is not United Nations-supported grouping) but also because Algeria, a key player in the Sahel, is absent from it.

A war has been ongoing in northern Mali since January 2013, and Algeria has played a small but significant role. It has allowed French warplanes to overfly its territory to dislodge AQIM and other groups from the cities they had occupied hitherto. It likewise has closed its long border with Mali, to prevent jihadists from fleeing the conflict and seeking refuge on Algerian territory. Algeria has also helped broker a deal between the various Tuareg factions and between those factions and the central government in Bamako.[39] In July 2015, the Tuareg factions and Bamako signed a peace deal; the deal so far has been unsuccessful. Peace has not been restored and the groups continue their activities because of the persistent absence of the state in the north of the country,[40] and despite France's presence. Furthermore, Algeria is helping Tunisia protect its borders against assaults from ISIS and has deployed thousands of troops along both its Tunisian and Libya borders.

Indeed, Algeria has sealed military border areas (Libya, Niger, and Mali), adding more observer stations along the Tunisian and Libyan borders.[41] After the attack against the gas plant in 2013, the authorities have since fortified the oil and gas installations, imported sophisticated aerial-based surveillance technologies and greatly improved the country's communication systems.[42] Overall, Algerian authorities have taken serious measures to counter terrorism, enacting a multitude of laws and erecting safeguards to thwart the reemergence of jihadism inside Algeria's borders.

Morocco has continuously accused Algeria of not cooperating on counterterrorism initiatives in the Sahel. Moroccan Foreign Minister Nasser Bourita stated during a meeting of the G5 that the "Sahel is not the preserve of anyone,"[43] suggesting that Algeria cannot exclude Morocco from being a player in the Sahel. Algerians, for their part, argue that events in the Sahel should be the responsibility of the Sahelian states, and that Moroccan is not a Sahelian state.[44] This reflects the enduring rivalry between Algeria and Morocco since their independence from colonial France.[45] However, there is some cooperation between the two countries against terrorism. For instance, as mentioned above, both participate in the US-led Trans-Saharan Counterterrorism Partnership as well as in the Global Forum on International Terrorism. Furthermore, Algerian authorities have informed their counterparts about Moroccans seeking to join ISIS in Syria. Algerian security forces repatriated these would-be jihadists to Morocco. One argument Algerian officials make in private is that Algeria guarantees Morocco's security at no cost to Morocco and at a great expense to Algeria, which has deployed thousands of troops to thwart the threats coming from the Sahel.[46] No matter the public mutual recriminations, both cooperate, albeit at a minimum, when it comes to their common security.

Algeria watchers wonder what the succession to the ailing Bouteflika would mean for Islamism and counterterrorism in the country. In view of the tragedy that Algeria underwent in the 1990s, it is certain that there will be little or no change to the current security policy, which consists of an implacable war on the jihadists while focusing on development and programs of deradicalization to prevent the youth from succumbing to the influence of jihadi ideology. Counterterrorism has in fact become one of the components of Algeria's foreign policy. Non-violent, domesticated Islamism will remain part of the societal evolution that Algeria has witnessed in recent decades. Short of a cataclysmic ideological break—similar to what might be happening in Saudi Arabia—Algerians will continue to view social conservatism, rightly or wrongly, as part of their identity. However, the reminiscences of the 1990s will likely prevent the conversion of this social conservatism into jihadism.

Endnotes

1. Author's interview with Algerian senior military officers, Algiers, January and September 2016. See also, Hebba Selim, "Des chiffres très précis sur le nombre de terroristes en Algérie: 304 dont 73 à Jund Al-Khilafa (Journal)," *HuffPost Algérie*, May 3, 2016, http://www.huffpostmaghreb.com/2016/05/03/terrorisme-effectifs-aqmi-jound-al-khilafa_n_9826062.html.
2. Zachary Laub and Jonathan Masters, "Al-Qaeda in the Islamic Maghreb (AQIM)," *Council on Foreign Relations*, March 27, 2015, http://www.cfr.org/terrorist-organizations-and-networks/al-qaeda-islamic-maghreb-aqim/p12717.
3. Zachary Laub and Jonathan Masters, "Al-Qaeda in the Islamic Maghreb (AQIM)," *Council on Foreign Relations*, March 27, 2015, http://www.cfr.org/terrorist-organizations-and-networks/al-qaeda-islamic-maghreb-aqim/p12717.
4. Djallil Lounnas and Yahia H. Zoubir, "L'Algérie face à l'arc des menaces: Quelle stratégie?" *Stratégie et Sécurité* (forthcoming16); Stefano Maria Torelli, "Jihadism and Counterterrorism Policy in Algeria: New Responses to New Challenges," *Terrorism Monitor*, Volume 11, Issue 19, October 7, 2013, https://jamestown.org/program/jihadism-and-counterterrorism-policy-in-algeria-new-responses-to-new-challenges/.
5. "In Amenas inquest: British victims of Algeria attack," *BBC News,* November 28, 2014, http://www.bbc.com/news/uk-29127935.
6. R.P., "Deux militaires et un civil tués--L'inquiétant faux barrage de Aïn Defla," *El-Wa*tan, November 16, 2016, http://www.elwatan.com/actualite/l-inquietant-faux-barrage-de-ain-defla-16-11-2016-332966_109.php.
7. A.F., "Me Merouane Azzi à propos du dossier Réconciliation Nationale: 'Le nombre de victimes du terrorisme décroît,'" *Liberté* (Algiers), March 4, 2013, http://www.liberte-algerie.com/actualite/le-nombre-de-victimes-du-terrorisme-decroit-120259 .
8. "Country Reports on Terrorism 2015," United States Department of State, June 2016, http://www.state.gov/documents/organization/258249.pdf.

9. *El-Djeich*, No. 641, December 2016, p. 20, available at: http://www.mdn.dz/site_principal/sommaire/revue/images/EldjeichDec2016Fr.pdf.
10. "Bilan opérationnel 2017-Résultats probants dans le combat antiterroriste," *El-Djeich* N° 654 (Janvier 2018), p. 22.
11. Mohamed Ben-Ahmed, "Details of the surrender of terrorists in northern Mali and Libya," *Elkhabar* (Algiers), 20 January 2018, http://www.elkhabar.com/press/article/132201/تفاصيل-استسلام-إرهابيين-في-شمال-مالي-وليبيا/.
12. Mohamed Mokeddem. *Al-Qaïda au Maghreb islamique-Contrebande au nom de l'islam* (Algiers: Casbah Editions, 2010), esp. 37-68.
13. Brisard, "Terrorism Financing in North Africa"; "Al-Qaeda in the Islamic Maghreb and the Africa-to-Europe Narco-Trafficking Connection," Jamestown Foundation *Terrorism Monitor* 8, iss. 43, November 24, 2010, http://www.jamestown.org/single/?no_cache=1&tx_ttnews[tt_news]=37207.
14. "Examining the Nexus between Organised Crime and Terrorism
and its implications for EU Programming," *CT Morse Counterterrorism Monitorism, Reporting and Support Mechanism*, 2 April 2017, https://icct.nl/publication/examining-the-nexus-between-organised-crime-and-terrorism-and-its-implications-for-eu-programming/.
15. Ikram Ghioua, "Les dessous d'un regain terroriste aux frontières et les alertes de L'Algérie--Et l'on reparle de Droukdel," *L'Expression* (Algiers), 18 October 2016,
http://www.lexpressiondz.com/actualite/252251-et-l-on-reparle-de-droukdel.html?print.
16. "Al-Qaida Is Trying to Recruit Algerians to Strengthen Its Strongholds After ISIS Collapse," *Echoroukonline*, 19 January 2018, https://www.echoroukonline.com/ara/articles/546432.html.
17. Author interviews with Algerian officials. Furthermore, the communiqués of the Algerian Ministry of Defense reveal that the type of weapons the security forces have seized do not include heavy weaponry. Algerian TV and the Military magazine, *Eldjeich*, frequently publish

pictures of the weapons the security forces uncover or capture during their unrelenting operations.

18. Dalia Ghanem-Yazbeck, "Obstacles to ISIS Expansion," *Cipher Brief*, 1 September 2016, https://www.thecipherbrief.com/obstacles-to-isis-expansion
19. Yahia H. Zoubir, "Islamist Political Parties in Contemporary Algeria," in Ibrahim M. Abu-Rabi', ed., *The Contemporary Arab Reader on Political Islam* (London: Pluto Press/University of Alberta Press, 2010).
20. Ahmed Aghrout and Yahia H. Zoubir, "Algeria: Reforms without change?" In, Yahia H. Zoubir and Gregory White, *North African Politics: Change and Continuity* (London & New York: Routledge, 2016), pp. 145-155.
21. For a detailed analysis, see Yahia H. Zoubir and Louisa Dris-Aït-Hamadouche, "L'islamisme en Algérie: institutionnalisation du politique et déclin du militaire," *Maghreb-Machrek* no. 188 (Summer 2006), 63-86.
22. Louisa Aït-Hamadouche and Yahia H. Zoubir, "The Fate of Political Islam in Algeria," in Bruce Maddy-Weitzman and Daniel Zisenwine, eds., *The Maghrib in the New Century-Identity, Religion, and Politics* (Gainesville: University of Florida Press, 2007), 103-131.
23. Saïd Boucetta, "Après L'abdication des Tunisiens, l'effacement des Marocains et la dérive des Turcsles islamistes algériens dans la galère," *L'Expression* (Algiers), November 5, 2016, http://www.lexpressiondz.com/actualite/253382-les-islamistes-algeriens-dans-la-galere.html.
24. The results of the 2012 local elections are available in "Elections locales : le ministère algérien de l'Intérieur rend public les résultats de chaque parti," SIWEL, December 1, 2012, http://www.siwel.info/Elections-locales-le-ministere-algerien-de-l-Interieur-rend-public-les-resultats-de-chaque-parti_a4325.html.
25. Yahia H. Zoubir and Ahmed Aghrout, "Algeria's Path to Political Reforms: Authentic Change?" *Middle East Policy*, 19, No. 2, (2012): 66-83.
26. Ahmed Aghrout and Yahia H. Zoubir, "Algeria: Reforms without change?" *North African Politics: Change*

and Continuity, New York, 2016, 145-155.

27. Rachid Tlemçani, "Les islamistes échappent aujourd'hui à tout contrôle institutionnel ou partisan," *El Watan* (Algiers), April, 23, 2009 , http://www.elwatan.com/Les-islamistes-echappent-aujourd.
28. For an analysis of the decline of the Islamists in elections, see, M. Kebci, "Ils ne cessent de perdre du terrain : L'irrésistible déclin des islamistes," *Le Soir d'Algérie*, 8 January 2018. http://lesoirdalgerie.com/articles/2018/01/08/article.php?sid=240&cid=2.
29. See, Louisa Dris-Aït-Hamadouche, "Régime et islamistes en Algérie: un échange politique asymétrique?" *Maghreb-Machrek* (Paris) no. 200 (Summer 2009), 43.
30. Graham Fuller, *Algeria: The Next Fundamentalist State?* (Santa Barbara: RAND, 1996).
31. Yahia H. Zoubir and Louisa Aït-Hamadouche, "Penal Reform in Algeria," in Chris Ferguson and Jeffrey O. Isima, eds., *Providing Security for People: Enhancing Security through Police, Justice and Intelligence Reform in Africa* (London: Global Facilitation Network for Security Sector Reform, 2004), 75-84.
32. Abbas Aït-Hamlat, "Terrorisme au Maghreb-Al-Qaîda menace et l'UE resserre l'étau, " *L'Expression* (Algiers), September 24, 2008, http://www.lexpressiondz.com/article/2/2008-09-24/56544.html.
33. See "Lutte contre le financement du terrorisme et le blanchiment d'argent. La fin du secret bancaire pour l'argent suspect," *Le Quotidien d'Oran*, January 8, 2003; See also Algeria's National Report, "Mise en œuvre de la Résolution 1373 (2001) Adoptée par le Conseil de Sécurité des Nations-Unies le 28 septembre 2001," which describes at length the actions taken by the Algerian government to implement UN Resolution 1373 on terrorism. See also Yazid F. "Algérie: Le Gouvernement durcit la législation sur les changes, " Ministère de l'Economie et des Finances, *Cellule nationale du traitement des informations financières*, September 13, 2010, http://www.centif.ci/news.php?id_news=67.
34. "Country Reports on Terrorism 2015," United States Department of State, June 2016, http://www.state.gov/documents/organization/258249.pdf.

35. Souhil B. "Bilan de la réconciliation nationale-7500 terroristes ont bénéficié des dispositions de la charte, " *El Watan* (Algiers), October 4, 2010, http://www.elwatan.com/actualite/7500-terroristes-ont-beneficie-des-dispositions-de-la-charte-04-10-2010-93047_109.php.
36. United States Department of State, *Country Reports on Terrorism*, 2016, https://www.state.gov/j/ct/rls/crt/2016/272232.htm#ALGERIA.
37. Yahia H. Zoubir, "The United States and Maghreb-Sahel Security," *International Affairs* 85, no. 5 (Fall 2009), 977-995.
38. Yahia H. Zoubir, "The Sahara-Sahel Quagmire: Regional and International Ramifications," *Mediterranean Politics*, 17:3 (November 2012), 452-458.
39. See, "Accord pour la paix et la réconciliation au Mali issu du processus d'Alger," http://photos.state.gov/libraries/mali/328671/peace-accord-translations/1-accord-paix-et-reconciliation-francais.pdf. See also, Benjamin Roger, "Accord d'Alger pour la paix au Mali : le plus dur reste à faire,"*Jeune Afrique*, 1 July 2015, http://www.jeuneafrique.com/mag/241413/politique/accord-dalger-pour-la-paix-mali-le-plus-dur-reste-a-faire/.
40. Selma Mihoubi, "Mali: un an après la signature de l'Accord d'Alger, quel avenir pour le Nord?" *Jeune Afrique*, 20 juin 2016, http://www.jeuneafrique.com/334516/politique/mali-paix-ans-apres-signature-de-laccord-dalger/
41. Abdennour Benantar, "Sécurité aux frontières : Portée et limites de la stratégie algérienne" *L'Année du Maghreb*, 14, 2016, p. 147-163; Lyes Khaldoun, "L'Algérie élève d'un cran le niveau de sécurité à ses frontières avec la Tunisie, la Libye et le Mali, *L'Authentique* (Algiers), 8 September 2017. https://www.algeriepatriotique.com/2017/09/08/algerie-eleve-securite-frontieres/
42. "Country Reports on Terrorism 2015," United States Department of State, June 2016, http://www.state.gov/documents/organization/258249.pdf
43. Mohammed Jaabouk, "En l'absence d'Alger, Bourita affirme que le 'Sahel n'est le champ exclusif de personne'," *Yabiladi* (Morocco), 23 February 2018, https://www.yabiladi.com/articles/details/62141/l-absence-d-

alger-bourita-affirme-sahel.html

44. Interviews with Algerian security and diplomatic officials.
45. See, Yahia H. Zoubir, "The Algerian-Moroccan Rivalry: Constructing the Imaginary Enemy," in William Thompson and Imad Mansour, Eds. Shocks and Rivalry in the Middle East and North Africa. Washington, DC. Georgetown University Press, forthcoming. See also, Yahia H. Zoubir, Yahia H. Zoubir, "Algerian-Moroccan Relations and Their Impact on Maghrebi Integration," *Journal of North African Studies*, Vol. 5, No. 3, Fall 2000 (2001), pp. 43-74. Although this latter article is old, the core arguments have remained virtually intact.
46. Author's interview with high-level officials in Algeria and abroad in 2016 and 2017.

15 Bahrain

Quick Facts

Population: 1,410,942 (July 2017 est.)
Area: 760 sq km
Ethnic Groups: Bahraini 46%, Asian 45.5%, other Arab 4.7%, African 1.6%, European 1%, other 1.2% (includes Gulf Co-operative country nationals, North and South Americans, and Oceanians) (2010 est.)
Government Type: Constitutional monarchy
GDP (official exchange rate): $33.87 billion (2017 est.)

Source: CIA World FactBook (Last Updated April 2018)

Introduction

Bahrain has traditionally been something of an anomaly among the Arab states of the Persian Gulf. While its ruling al-Khalifa family and as much as 30 percent of its population are Sunni Muslims, a substantial majority of its citizens are Shiites. One of the first major oil exporters in the region, it was also the first of the Gulf "oil sheikhdoms" to face significant depletion of its petroleum reserves and the need to develop a non-resource-based economy. Further, although it has never been close to qualifying as a truly free country, Bahrain traditionally stood apart from other Gulf states in its relatively high degree of social and cultural openness. Unfortunately, freedom of the press, latitude for NGOs to operate, and what elements of democracy existed in the past have been degraded in recent years, to the point where Bahrain is now considered one of the region's most repressive states.[1]

Islamism in Bahrain has traditionally maintained an almost exclusively domestic focus, largely directed at confronting economic and morality issues through political action rather than violence. There are indications, however, that this relatively peaceful type of Islamism may be giving way, at least in part, to more violent forms: while in the past only a few Bahrainis traveled overseas to join in jihad, and some others were involved in providing financial or logistical support for al-Qaeda, there are now accusations that

Bahrainis have joined ISIS, received combat training, and attempted to form local terrorist cells.[2] Shiite attacks on Bahraini security forces also show signs of increasing sophistication.[3] While the presence of the U.S. Fifth Fleet in Bahrain would appear to make the country an attractive target for anti-American terrorism, neither Bahrain's government nor its traditional Islamists appear ready to condone or facilitate such attacks.

The Bahraini government's response to the Arab Spring protests often consisted of brutal repression, coupled with occasional promises of a reconciliation dialogue that became less and less convincing over the succeeding years.[4] As of late 2017, Bahrain remains locked in an uneasy stasis, with attitudes among both Sunni and Shiite residents hardened to such an extent that it is difficult to imagine how the country can resume even the semblance of a functioning democracy.[5] Bahrain's domestic impasse, along with the intensifying regional conflict between the Iran-led Shiite bloc and the Saudi-led Sunni bloc, will strengthen the appeal and extremism of both Sunni and Shia Islamist forces. And despite the country's tiny size, the failure of major powers and international organizations to exert effective pressure on the Bahraini government to reform has had significant regional implications.

Islamist Activity

Bahrain's majority Shiite population is significantly poorer than its Sunni minority counterpart, and complains of discrimination in employment (particularly with regard to senior-level government and security-service jobs—a significant issue given the government's dominant status as an employer, not to mention the importance such jobs have in influencing the nature of life in Bahrain), housing, immigration policy, and government services. Accordingly, the Shiite opposition—which is almost entirely Islamist in character—has an agenda largely based around the attempt to redress these inequalities, in addition to more traditional Islamist goals, such as the imposition of sharia law. The political and economic goals of the Shiite opposition include:

- Genuine democracy, in which the Shiite community, as

the majority population, would have a much greater say in legislating and setting policy. This would necessitate the rewriting of Bahrain's constitution, as well as revising an electoral-district system that favors Sunni candidates.[6]

- The dismantling, or at least a substantial weakening, of Bahrain's internal-security apparatus, and the release of political prisoners.
- Economic justice, including equality of opportunity in employment and equal provision of government services.
- Equal access to positions of authority in the government bureaucracy and the military/security services.
- An end to Bahrain's policy of facilitating Sunni immigration, which is perceived as a governmental effort to reduce or eliminate the Shiite demographic advantage. (Participants in the country's February 2011 demonstrations noted that many of the security personnel confronting them were immigrants from other Arab countries, and even Urdu-speaking Pakistanis, who had been granted Bahraini citizenship as an inducement to serve in the Bahraini security services.)[7]
- Traditional Islamist moral and social issues, such as the elimination of alcohol, prostitution, and other evils from the kingdom, the application of sharia law, etc

It is worth noting that most Bahraini Shiites are adherents of the Akhbari school of Twelver Shi'ism, as opposed to Iranian Shiites (and most Iraqi Shiites), who are members of the more common Usuli Twelver faction. Among other differences, Akhbaris believe that while clerics can and should advise political leaders, they should not seek or be given direct political power. As Akhbaris, Bahraini Shiites traditionally claimed that they were loyal to the state and to its ruling family, seeking change within the system rather than wanting to overthrow it.[8] The Bahraini Shiite community does not have its own marja ("source of emulation") or any other religious figure of sufficient stature to constitute a Khomeini-style threat to the Bahraini establishment. However, the Bahraini government's heavy-handed response to Shiite protests and political activism has significantly radicalized Shiite political discourse, to the extent that overt calls for the overthrow of the monarchy are now common.[9]

Despite the Shiite community's past assertions of loyalty to Bahrain and its governing family (if not to its Constitution, which provides some semblance of democracy but effectively leaves the monarchy and the Sunni minority in firm control of the country), many Bahraini Sunnis have long accused the Shiites of being suspiciously close, culturally and politically, to Iran; the fact that Bahraini Shiite clerics are often trained in Iran adds some credibility to this accusation. Shiites have often responded by pointing out that many Bahraini Sunnis have just as much cultural connection to Iran, and that quite a few of these Sunnis in fact speak Farsi, rather than Arabic, at home. The ongoing government repression of Bahraini Shiites, as well as Bahrain's participation in the Saudi-led campaign against the Shiite Houthi in Yemen, have increased the community's identification with Iran, as well as Iranians' feelings of solidarity with Bahraini Shiites.[10]

The Bahraini government and others in the Sunni elite, as well as outside commentators concerned about Iranian influence in the region, have repeatedly claimed that Shiite unrest in Bahrain is the product of Iranian scheming, aided by allies and proxies such as Syria and Hezbollah. At first glance, such accusations are plausible: Iran is certainly not averse to meddling in other countries' affairs, and Iranian officials occasionally reassert their country's historical claim on Bahrain as Iranian territory.[11] However, little to no concrete, convincing evidence has ever been produced to back these claims of Iranian interference; and neutral observers have pointed out that Shiite unrest can be quite adequately explained by the genuine grievances of Bahraini Shiites.[12] The protests that began in February 2011 did not strengthen the case for an Iranian conspiracy to destabilize Bahrain; nothing in the protestors' goals, capabilities, or tactics at that time was inconsistent with what would be expected from an entirely domestic movement.[13] The use of more sophisticated explosives in recent Shiite attacks does, however, strengthen the case for Iranian involvement, if not instigation.[14]

Ultimately, as long as Bahrain's Shiites are kept relatively powerless, there is no way to validate their claims of loyalty to the country and its al-Khalifa rulers; and no matter how enthusiastically Shiite demonstrators wave Bahraini flags, many Bahraini Sunnis will continue to believe that the country's Shiites are, at best, a potential pro-Iranian fifth column. Even if Bahrain's Shiites are sincere in their expressions of patriotism, there is no question that, should they achieve significant political power, Iran will view Bahrain as "low-hanging fruit" and likely attempt to gain their allegiance;[15] In any case, the Bahraini government seems intent on doing everything in its power to destroy whatever loyalty the country's Shiites still have to the ruling regime.

Shiite Organizations

The most prominent Bahraini Shiite political "society" is the al-Wefaq National Islamic Society (Jam'īyat al-Wifāq al-Watanī al-Islāmīyah, also known as the Islamic National Accord Association), led by Qom-educated cleric Sheikh Ali Salman, with at least 1,500 active members.[16] (Salman himself is considered a "mid-level" cleric. Bahrain's most prominent Shia cleric, Ayatollah Isa Qassim, a disciple of Iraqi Grand Ayatollah Ali al-Sistani, is generally considered al-Wefaq's spiritual leader, although this is not an official position; in 2005 he publicly endorsed the group's decision to register as a "political society" and enter the Council of Representatives.)[17] After boycotting the 2002 elections to protest the new constitution's failure to provide a fully democratic constitutional monarchy, al-Wefaq decided to compete in the 2006 elections, and scored a resounding success: out of 17 candidates fielded by the group, 16 won their districts outright in the first round of voting (and the 17th candidate won his seat in a second-round run-off), making al-Wefaq by far the largest bloc in the Council of Representatives.[18] The group repeated this success in the 2010 elections, winning all 18 seats it contested; and were the Bahraini electoral system not gerrymandered to favor Sunni candidates, there is little question that, given the country's demographics, al-Wefaq would have easily won a commanding majority of the Council's 40 seats.[19]

Until the 2011 Arab Spring protests and the government's violent response to them, al-Wefaq had consistently positioned itself as a loyal opposition, working to achieve equality for Bahraini Shiites while maintaining allegiance to Bahrain and its monarchy, if not to the current Constitution and Cabinet. This stance has since largely evaporated. All 18 al-Wefaq members of the Council of Representatives resigned in protest in early 2011, and the group's leaders initially refused to enter a dialogue with the government until Prime Minister Khalifa al-Khalifa, perceived to be the primary driving force behind the marginalization of Bahraini Shiites, was replaced.[20] Al-Wefaq, partly in response to American and British persuasion, did agree to participate in a government-organized "national consensus dialogue" that began in July 2011; but the group's representatives walked out about a week later, frustrated at the allocation of only 25 out of 300 seats to the opposition, and the failure of the "dialogue" effectively to address Shiite grievances.[21]

Al-Wefaq, along with the rest of the opposition, boycotted the September-October 2011 by-election called to fill the seats it had vacated.[22] Protests were violently suppressed,[23] and, despite government claims backed by some rather odd mathematics,[24] the vast majority of Shiite voters obeyed calls to boycott the vote.[25] With no opposition representation, the Council of Representatives could no longer claim to provide even a skewed representation of the citizens of Bahrain. Matters did not improve with the next elections in 2014, when Al-Wefaq, along with other opposition groups, boycotted the vote.[26]

In 2016, the government significantly escalated its conflict with al-Wefaq, first suspending its activities and freezing its funds, and then in July ordering the organization dissolved and its assets turned over to the national treasury.[27] Ayatollah Isa Qassim was accused of financial misdeeds[28] and stripped of his citizenship,[29] and Sheikh Ali Salman and other leaders of the group were imprisoned.[30] Al-Wefaq appealed this decision, but in February 2017 its appeal was rejected.[31] Ali Salman, already serving a nine-year prison sentence for "inciting hatred, promoting disobedience and insulting public institutions"[32] (apparently later changed to "inciting hatred and calling for forceful regime change,"[33]) was further accused in November 2017 of spying and colluding with Qatar to carry out "hostile acts" and "damage Bahrain's prestige."[34] The U.S. and other Western powers have condemned the suppression of al-Wefaq, but Bahraini authorities remain unmoved.[35] In May 2017, Ayatollah

Qassim and two aides were convicted, fined, and given one-year suspended sentences;[36] two days later, a raid on his home town of Diraz to "maintain security and public order" resulted in the killing of at least five protestors and the arrest of several hundred.[37] The government promised an investigation of these killings;[38] but given the government's recent track record, it is unlikely that security forces will be held accountable, and "security and public order" in the town do not appear to have improved.[39]

Haq Movement for Liberty and Democracy

Al-Wefaq's main competition for the loyalty of Bahraini Shiites is the Haq Movement for Liberty and Democracy, founded in 2005 by a group consisting mostly of al-Wefaq's more radical leaders, who objected to al-Wefaq's decision to participate in the 2006 elections and thus grant an appearance of legitimacy to Bahrain's quasi-democratic constitution. Haq's agenda is more specifically targeted at achieving full democracy, and the group is less identified with morality issues and Shiite sectarianism than its parent movement; in fact, one of Haq's leaders, Sheikh Isa Abdullah al-Jowder (who died in September 2011), was a Sunni cleric, and another founder (who eventually left the movement)[40], Ali Qasim Rabea, is a secular leftist nationalist.[41] Nonetheless, Haq is generally thought of as both Shia and Islamist, even though its leader, Hasan Mushaima, is a layman and the group is not endorsed by any senior Bahraini Shiite cleric.[42]

Haq has unquestionably benefited from the breakdown in the relationship between the Bahraini government and Bahraini Shiites, since—unlike al-Wefaq—Haq never invested its credibility in a political process that it perceived (and loudly denounced) as inherently unfair and dishonest. (In fact, Haq has consistently refused even to register as an official "political society,"[43] even though its rejectionist record is not absolute: Mushaima met with King Hamad in London in March, 2008).[44] While al-Wefaq spent four years in the Council of Representatives ineffectually working for the Shiite community's interests, Haq (or, at least, groups of young Shiites apparently inspired by low-level Haq activists) was out on the streets throwing rocks at the police,[45] and Haq itself was submitting petitions to the United Nations and the United States calling for condemnation of the Bahraini government.[46] While the rocks and petitions accomplished no more at the time than did al-Wefaq's political maneuvering, they established Haq as a genuine "fighting opposition"—one respected by Shiites and feared (and persecuted) by the Bahraini government. The fact that Haq leaders Hasan Mushaima and Abdeljalil al-Singace were among the opposition leaders imprisoned by the government in the aftermath of the 2011 protests only reinforced the movement's credibility.[47]

As part of the Bahraini government's efforts to confront Haq, officials have accused the organization's leaders of being in the pay of Iran, either directly or through Hezbollah intermediaries. While it is very difficult to prove that such a relationship does not exist, and many in the Sunni community take it as an article of faith that Bahraini Shiites are more loyal to Iran than to Bahrain, disinterested observers, including the U.S. Embassy in Bahrain, have pointed out that no convincing evidence has ever been produced to back these accusations.[48]

Haq Secretary General Hasan Mushaima (one of the founders of al-Wefaq, who left that group to co-found Haq) returned to Bahrain from Great Britain in late February 2011 to a "rapturous" welcome; he had previously been charged and tried in absentia for conspiring against the government, but the charges against him were dropped as part of a package of government concessions aimed at establishing a dialogue with the Bahraini opposition.[49] Upon his return, Mushaima attempted, together with other opposition leaders, to formulate a unified platform of demands and expectations.[50] As the government crackdown continued, Mushaima was again brought to trial and imprisoned, along with many other protest leaders.[51]

Wafa'

A third Shiite opposition movement, Wafa' ("Loyalty"), was founded in early 2009 by Abdulwahab Hussain, a cleric who had been a leading Shia activist in the 1990s and a co-founder of al-Wefaq. Unlike Haq, Wafa' enjoys the open backing of senior cleric (and rival of Ayatollah Isa Qassim) Sheikh Abduljalil al-Maqdad. And unlike al-Wefaq, Wafa' has consistently and firmly opposed participation in Bahrain's quasi-democratic constitutional government.

The period when Haq leader Hasan Mushaima was in a brief self-imposed exile should have presented something of an opportunity for Wafa' to attract support from Shia rejectionists. However, despite the fact that Wafa' has the clerical backing Haq lacks and has credible, experienced leadership, it does not appear so far to have gained much traction among Bahraini Shiites. Now that Hasan Mushaima has returned to Bahrain (and is unlikely to be able to leave any time soon) and al-Wefaq has quit the Council of Representatives, Wafa' is likely to have a great deal of difficulty finding a meaningful niche for itself in Bahraini Shiite politics.[52]

Amal

Yet another rejectionist Shiite Islamist "political society" is Amal (the "Islamic Action Society," Jam'iyyat al-Amal al-Islami, also referred to by Bahrainis as "the Shirazi faction"). This group is "the non-violent heir to the defunct Islamic Front for the Liberation of Bahrain, which launched a failed uprising in 1981 inspired by Iran's Islamic revolution."[53] Amal refused to register as a "legal" faction before the 2002 election, did not win any seats in the 2006 election,[54] and decided not to participate in the 2010 election. The society's Secretary General, Sheikh Mohammed al-Mahfoodh, justified this decision by citing the usual objections to Bahrain's political system, claiming that: "We don't want to just be employees... the members of parliament are just employees who get a big salary."[55] (It is not entirely clear, however, if Sheikh al-Mahfoodh's feelings would have been the same had there been a significant likelihood of his actually becoming one of these "employees.") Amal was apparently considered enough of a threat to the Bahraini government that the movement was effectively shut down in July 2012.[56]

The challenge for the official organized Shiite opposition (both legal and illegal), as well as for leaders of the young, self-organizing protestors (known for using Twitter and social media) and the leftist secular organizations that have joined the anti-government protests, was to agree on a set of demands that were ambitious enough to maintain the enthusiasm of the protestors (and, of course, to offer a realistic hope of solving the genuine problems facing Bahraini Shiites) but could also be palatable to Bahrain's ruling family and its Sunni allies.[57] This challenge has only become more intractable as the conflict has drawn on.

Sunni Organizations

Unlike the country's Shiite majority, Bahrain's Sunni community is not overwhelmingly Islamist in its beliefs. This means that Sunni Islamist "political societies" must compete with secular groups and independent candidates for voter support. Further, Sunni Islamist groups are constrained in their ambitions by Bahrain's demographic and economic situation: because Sunnis are a relatively wealthy, privileged minority, Sunni Islamists do not join their Shiite colleagues in calling for genuine democratic reform (which would effectively disempower Sunni politicians and their supporters). While they may aspire to "increase the standard of living for Bahrainis; strengthen political, social and economic stability; and enhance financial and administrative oversight of the government and industry"[58], they do not agitate for fully equal opportunity for Bahrain's Shiites. Because the American military presence contributes to Bahrain's economy and provides a bulwark against supposed Iranian designs on their country, the mainstream Sunni Islamist groups do not oppose the presence of the infidels on Bahrain's territory.

In short, Bahrain's organized Sunni Islamist "societies" have traditionally been seen as basically pro-government parties, working at times for incremental modifications to the status quo but not advocating full democracy or other large-scale, disruptive changes. Further, as the ongoing protests assumed an increasingly sectarian character, what goodwill and cooperation there was between Sunni and Shiite Islamists largely disappeared,[59] and the government used Sunni Islamists as a counter to Shiite agitation.

More recently, however, it appears that the relationship between local Sunni Islamists and Bahrain's government may be becoming slightly less cozy, largely as a result of outside pressure. The Muslim Brotherhood, which has a branch in Bahrain, is increasingly seen by status quo Sunni-dominated states as an antagonist; and given its substantial dependency on Saudi and Emirati support, official Bahrain policy has little to no choice but to toe the line, or at least create some anti-Brotherhood atmospherics.[60], This dilemma (for both the Bahraini government and Bahraini Sunni Islamists) became even more extreme in 2017, with Bahrain joining Saudi Arabia, the United Arab Emirates, and other Sunni countries in an outright diplomatic break with Qatar—precipitated mostly by the latter's support for the Muslim Brotherhood.[61] The most viable outcome for both the local Sunni Islamists and the government is for both to continue to assert that while the local organizations may share the Brotherhood's foundational ideas and ideology, they are not in fact part of the international Brotherhood. This allows the two sides to support each other[62] even as the government loudly condemns the external Muslim Brotherhood.[63]

There are two principal Sunni-Islamist "political societies" in Bahrain. The first is the al-Menbar National Islamic Society (al-Minbar al-Islami), the political wing of the al-Eslah Society, which is generally seen as Bahrain's branch of the Muslim Brotherhood. The second is the al-Asala Political Society, which in turn is the political wing of the Islamic Education Society (al-Tarbiya al-Islamiya), a conservative Salafist organization. Al-Menbar is the more liberal of the two Sunni Islamist parties, and has, for example, taken positions in favor of women's rights.[64] However, this liberalism has its limits: in 2006 the group's Council of Representatives members formed part of a bloc that prevented Bahrain from ratifying the government's signature on the International Covenant on Civil and Political Rights, on the basis that the Covenant would mean "that Muslims could convert to another religion, something against the Islamic law, since those who do so should be beheaded."[65] Al-Menbar had promised to field several female candidates for the 2006 election, but as part of an electoral pact with al-Asala, which does not approve of women's standing for political office, this pledge was dropped. Further, al-Menbar's parent organization (with "support" from the Islamic Education Society) held a 2008 workshop opposing government efforts to promote gender equality.[66]

Its association with al-Eslah, which runs a network of mosques, gives al-Menbar a solid social support base among Bahraini Sunnis. Furthermore, al-Eslah (and, by extension, al-Menbar) benefits from the official patronage of the Bahraini royal family (its President is Sheikh Isa bin Mohammed al-Khalifa), as well as from some of Bahrain's largest businesses.[67] While charitable contributions to al-Eslah do not necessarily provide direct support for al-Menbar's political activity, they unquestionably contribute to al-Eslah's standing in society, and thus to al-Menbar's credibility.

Al-Asala takes a harder line than al-Menbar on various issues. As noted above, al-Asala does not approve of fielding female candidates, and the group is, in general, opposed to Bahrain's comparatively modern, freewheeling character. It has also taken positions opposed to U.S. military action in Iraq. Despite their differences, however, al-Menbar and al-Asala have often cooperated; and, like al-Menbar, al-Asala cannot be accurately described as an opposition "society" even though it dissents from some Bahraini government policies.

In the 2006 elections, al-Menbar and al-Asala agreed to divide the Sunni electoral districts between them in order not to compete with each other and split the Sunni Islamist vote.[68] This strategy worked well, with the two groups winning seven seats each.[69] In 2010, however, they failed to organize a similar arrangement. As a result, the two "societies" ran against each other in many districts, and the consequence was the loss of most of their seats. Al-Menbar won only two seats in the Council of Representatives, and al-Asala received just three.[70] Furthermore, the Sunni Islamist "societies" lost two seats in the 2014 election, perhaps in part as a result of government redistricting.[71]

Unsurprisingly, Sunni Islamist organizations have not participated in the anti-government demonstrations in Bahrain; if anything, they may have been one of the forces behind several pro-government rallies that took place while Bahrain's Shiites were protesting against government policies.[72] While these pro-government rallies were not openly acknowledged as al-Menbar or al-Asala events, there is no question that Bahrain's Sunnis consider Shiite protests to be a threat to their privileged situation, and Sunni "societies," like all political parties, need to be seen as promoting the interests of their constituents. Beyond any such cynical calculations, Sunni Islamists would be justifiably concerned that a Shiite-Islamist-governed Bahrain would be much less hospitable to Sunni practices and beliefs than a relatively liberal Sunni-dominated Bahrain—despite the latter's tolerance of various social vices. (It is also worth noting that these pro-government rallies may not have been quite the "spontaneous outpouring of affection" that they appeared to be; Bangladeshi expatriate workers claimed that they had been forced to participate.[73])

Traditionally, then, Sunni Islamists were seen as a "loyal opposition" to the al-Khalifa rulers of Bahrain, if they were properly considered an opposition at all; any more militant expressions of Sunni extremism were directed outward. There is now concern that Bahrainis drawn to fight for ISIS and other Sunni extremist groups in Syria may return to their country radicalized not only against Shiites, but also against the status quo in Bahrain.[74] The al-Khalifa regime is far enough from sharia compliance that it is easily classified as kafir (infidel) and thus in need of overthrow. It has been further pointed out that the government's policy of recruiting foreign Sunnis to join the security forces and receive Bahraini citizenship could ultimately backfire, as some of these recruits may be easily (or already) radicalized, and are likely to lack any personal feelings of loyalty to the al-Khalifa family.[75] One irony in this situation is that while Bahrain is officially part of the international coalition fighting ISIS, those native-born Bahrainis joining the organization are typically from social strata close to the al-Khalifa monarchy.[76] To date, at least 24 Bahrainis have been accused of joining ISIS, and have been sentenced to prison and, in many cases, to loss of Bahraini citizenship.[77] (As of 2017, there have also been at least some cases of foreign workers becoming radicalized in Bahrain and joining ISIS.[78]) But at the same time, the Bahraini government has failed to demonstrate consistent attitudes and policies to counter Sunni radicalization, apparently preferring to attempt to use it against Shiites while preventing it from becoming too much of a threat to the monarchy.[79]

Islamism and Society

In addition to political activities, many of the established Islamist groups in Bahrain engage in conventional charitable and outreach work: supporting widows, orphans, and other poor people, operating mosques and providing religious education, and proselytizing for their particular brand of Islam. Al-Eslah, in particular, runs a large charitable enterprise, supported by corporate zakat as well as private contributions. Notably, al-Eslah has also made a number of prominent humanitarian contributions to the Gaza Strip, including funding construction of a building at the Islamic University there in 2005 and sending five ambulances to Gaza in 2009.[80] The particular affinity of al-Eslah for aid to Gaza is explained by the fact that both al-Eslah and Hamas are offshoots of the Muslim Brotherhood, that Hamas has ruled the Gaza Strip since 2007, and that the Islamic University there has been associated with Hamas since its founding. (In fact, Sheikh Ahmed Yassin founded the university, ten years before he founded Hamas.)

As bitter rivals for political and economic power, Shiite and Sunni Islamists in Bahrain are not particularly comfortable cooperating, even when they agree. However, some issues are uncontroversial enough (at least within Islamist circles) that Shiite and Sunni leaders have joined forces to fight for their shared ideals, or at least have managed not to interfere with each others' efforts:

- While they have not been successful in completely banning the sale and consumption of alcohol in Bahrain, Islamists have done what they can to impose limits on drinking in the kingdom. Islamist organizations supported a government move to close bars in cheap (two-star) hotels in 2009;[81] this partial ban was extended to three-star hotels in mid-2014, but "viral" social-media rumors in late 2017 that the ban was to be imposed on all hotels, along with a ban on hotel discos and night clubs, appear—at least as of early 2018—to be false.[82]
- Horrified by reports that Manama had been ranked as one of the top ten "vice cities" in the world, Islamists have attempted to eliminate prostitution—either by banning female entertainers in cheap hotels or by attempting to prevent the issuance of visas to women from Russia, Thailand, Ethiopia, and China. (The latter measure, proposed by the Salafist al-Asala "society," fell flat; even other Islamists in the Council of Representatives pointed out that it would cause diplomatic damage if passed, and probably not be very effective in any case.)[83]
- In 2007, Islamist parliamentarians condemned a performance by Lebanese composer/oudist Marcel Khalife and Bahraini

poet Qassim Haddad that was presented as part of a government-sponsored culture festival, complaining that it included "sleazy dance moves" that would "encourage debauchery." It appears the show went ahead as planned.[84] A year later, the same Council members united again to attempt to ban a show by provocative Lebanese singer Haifa Wehbe; this show also went ahead, although Wehbe did tone down her act a bit in response.[85]

- In late 2012, between 50 and 100 "hardline" Islamists protested U.S. celebrity Kim Kardashian's visit to Bahrain to open a milkshake shop. Among the signs at the protest was one asserting that: "[n]one of our customs and traditions allow us to receive stars of porn movies." The government responded with tear gas.[86] (In fact, it is unclear whether the protesters in this case were Sunni or Shiite, or both. At the very least, one can say that there were no reports of Islamist pro-Kardashian demonstrations.)

Traditionally, Bahraini Sunnis and Shiites lived and worked together with minimal friction. However, the recent Shia protests and the Sunni government's response to them (including, in at least some cases, Sunni vigilante participation)[87] have done a great deal to damage the relationship between the two communities. Within a week of the February 14, 2011 onset of Shiite protests, Sunnis had begun to mount counter demonstrations,[88] and as the crisis continued, confrontations between Sunni and Shiite groups became more frequent and more violent. Some Sunni groups explicitly came out against government-Shiite dialogue; apparently preferring the status quo to a resolution they felt would favor Shiites over their own community.[89] Even assuming that a political settlement is someday reached between Bahrain's government and the organizations representing the Shiite majority, it is difficult to imagine that Bahrain's social atmosphere will quickly return to the comfortable status quo ante.[90]

Islamism and the State

After a turbulent period during the 1990s, the country's new king,

Hamad bin Isa al-Khalifa, restored constitutional government in 2002. From then until January 2011, Bahrain's government was largely successful in channeling the energies of the country's Islamists into non-violent political activity rather than terrorism or major civil unrest. In accordance with the 2002 constitution, elections with universal suffrage are held every four years (most recently in November 2014) for the lower chamber of the National Assembly, the Council of Representatives (Majlis an-Nuwab); all members of the upper chamber, the Consultative Council (Majlis al-Shura), are appointed by the King. Both chambers must approve any legislation, giving each one effective veto power over proposed laws. As a result, since the one national body that is democratically elected has such limited ability to accomplish anything against the wishes of the ruling establishment, Bahrain's version of democracy has never been entirely satisfactory to the majority of the country's citizens. Still, for a few years, even this limited form of democracy provided the people of Bahrain with a voice and hope for future improvement.

Nevertheless, Bahrain has retained most of the essential characteristics of traditional Gulf emirate governance. Real power is concentrated in the ruling al-Khalifa family, members of which occupy the most important governmental positions, including 20 of the country's 25 Cabinet seats.[91] The Prime Minister, Prince Khalifa ibn Sulman al-Khalifa, has held office since the country was granted independence in 1971, and is currently the world's longest-serving Prime Minister. He is the uncle of King Hamad, and is also thought to be one of the wealthiest people in Bahrain.[92] Even the Council of Representatives' ability to block legislation is not really much of a constraint on royal power; under the Constitution, the King retains the right to rule by royal decree, bypassing the legislature entirely.[93]

While the ongoing Shiite unrest in Bahrain has eclipsed most other news about Bahraini Islamism, earlier news stories paint a more complex picture of a government quite willing to work with Islamists to achieve its goals, but equally willing to take strong measures to limit the actions and influence of Islamist forces. The Bahraini government is generally perceived as working against Islamism (or at least working to limit Islamists to minor victories while preserving Bahrain's modern, relatively open character). However, it is not above using Sunni Islamists as weapons against the Shiite community. In a 2006 report, the Gulf Centre for Democratic Development detailed a government effort led by Sheikh Ahmed bin Ateyatalla al-Khalifa to "manipulate the results of… elections, maintain sectarian distrust and division, and to ensure that Bahrain's Shias remain oppressed and disenfranchised." The initiative reportedly involved government payments to a number of individuals and NGOs, including both al-Eslah/al-Menbar and the Islamic Education Society/al-Asala. Among the tasks to be achieved by the various participants in this scheme were "running websites and Internet forums which foment sectarian hatred," and running "Sunni Conversion" and "Sectarian Switch" projects.[94]

The foreign-policy implications of Islamism can sometimes create problems for the Bahraini government. Al-Eslah's affinity for the Gaza Strip has already been mentioned, and is harmless enough when it involves sending ambulances and other forms of aid there. But when, in late 2009, al-Eslah leader Sheikh Fareed Hadi gave a sermon condemning the Egyptian government for building a steel barricade across the Egypt-Gaza Strip border, Bahrain's government, not wishing to ruffle feathers, stepped in and suspended him from delivering further sermons. The eloquently named "Bahraini Society to Resist Normalization with the Zionist Enemy" promptly objected, reminding Bahrain's government and citizens of "the dangers of Zionism and its drive to infiltrate Arab and Islamic societies and influence them."[95] Anti-Zionism continues to serve as one of the few factors uniting Bahraini Sunnis and Shiites: in the midst of the government's dissolution of al-Wefaq, the Shiite organization's Deputy Secretary General, Sheikh Hussein al-Daihi, found time to condemn the government's permission for an Israeli delegation to attend an international conference of the world soccer association FIFA to be held in Manama in May 2017.[96]

Nevertheless, Bahrain is not usually considered a major source of mujahideen, terrorists, or financial/logistical support for overseas jihad in its various forms. Much of this is probably due to the fact that Sunni Bahrainis are neither especially impoverished nor exposed to the more radical forms of Wahhabi Islamic fundamentalism—and, of course, they are also not very numerous. Still, a number of Bahrainis have traveled abroad to participate in jihad. One, Khalil Janahi, was arrested by Saudi authorities in the course of his religious studies in Riyadh, and was accused of being one of a group of 172 al-Qaeda militants planning "to storm Saudi prisons to free militants and attack oil refineries and public figures."[97] Another was royal family member Sheikh Salman Ebrahim Mohamed Ali al-Khalifa, who was captured near the Pakistan-Afghanistan border and held by the United States in Guantanamo Bay, Cuba as a Taliban/al-Qaeda supporter before eventually being released to return to Bahrain.[98] The Bahraini government is actively concerned about the trend toward increasing Sunni radicalization through participation in fighting abroad, as well as radicalization through the internet.

Inside Bahrain itself, the government has acted against individuals providing funding or other support to al-Qaeda, ISIS, and other radical Sunni organizations. For example, two men associated with a small Salafist movement known as "National Justice" were arrested in June 2008 for sending money to al-Qaeda; one was released shortly afterwards for lack of evidence,[99] and the other was among a group of prisoners officially pardoned in mid-2009.[100] Some other Bahrainis have been implicated in plots to support or engage in terrorism,[101] but until recently, the Bahraini government had far more serious problems dealing with domestic Shiite popular unrest than it does with the global jihad.

In the months leading up to the country's 2010 elections, Bahrain's government instituted a crackdown on many political organizations and news outlets, and vigorously suppressed demonstrations and civil unrest.[102] The ostensible justification was that Shiite opposition leaders were planning to lead a revolt against the government. In February 2011, Bahrain experienced a new and significant round of demonstrations and rioting by Shiite citizens, triggered by this apparent rollback of democratic reforms, and by the revolutions in Tunisia and Egypt. The beginning of the mass demonstrations also coincided with the February 14th anniversary of the restoration of constitutional government in 2002 and the referendum in 2001 that approved the new constitution.[103]

The government's initial reaction to these demonstrations was an indecisive and unproductive vacillation between brutal suppression and attempts at conciliation. But after seven demonstrators had been killed and many more injured, Bahrain's rulers decided to back down from lethal confrontation, and on February 19th began a concerted effort, led by Crown Prince Salman bin Hamad al-Khalifa, to de-escalate the crisis and promote a "national dialogue" to iron out a solution.[104] At first, it appeared likely that such a dialogue would soon take place.[105] But Shiite leaders demanded substantial concessions before talks could begin, and when a dialogue was eventually begun in July 2011, its mechanism—apparently dictated by the hardline faction of the royal family—was clearly not intended to facilitate a genuine airing and resolution of Bahrain's problems, and ended with no accomplishments.[106] Calls for dialogue continued to be made on occasion, but some seven years after the beginning of the "Arab Spring," it still seems impossible for the faction-ridden royal family, the disparate opposition, and loyalist groups to agree on conditions that would enable a meaningful and productive dialogue to take place.[107]

Clearly, even once negotiations begin, they will be difficult; after years of protests, repression, killings, torture,[108] mass dismissal of Shiites from their jobs,[109] revocation of citizenship,[110] and demolition of Shiite mosques,[111] there is very little good will or mutual trust between Bahrain's Shiites and their government.[112]

The Bahraini government has a number of factors in its favor as it attempts to maintain the status quo:

- It appears to have solid support from almost all members of the country's Sunni minority, which holds most economic power and controls all of Bahrain's security forces.
- It enjoys substantial outside support from neighboring Sunni states—particularly Saudi Arabia, which is concerned about the possibility of unrest or even rebellion by its own large Shiite minority and has a history of intervention to preserve Bahrain's Sunni regime. In March of 2012, a 1,500-strong force of Gulf Cooperation Council troops and policemen (which may in fact have been as large as 5000 or more men),[113] headed by Saudi Arabia, entered Bahrain to assist

government forces in restoring order. In all likelihood, the Saudis will quickly return at any time they (or the al-Khalifas) feel that the existing order is threatened.

- It is backed by the United States. Although the U.S. has in the past been critical of the Bahraini government's more extreme measures to confront unrest, and has called for more democratic rule and better protection of human rights, Bahrain's importance as a naval base and the dangers a regime collapse would pose to other Persian Gulf governments give Washington little real maneuvering room.[114] In the words of one anonymous U.S. official, Bahrain is "just too important to fail;"[115] and the current U.S. administration does not appear to be strongly motivated to pressure Bahrain's government about human-rights abuses in any case.

Nonetheless, it is clear that the Bahraini government has done tremendous damage to its own perceived legitimacy, both at home and abroad. While it would appear unlikely that the regime faces any real danger of being overthrown in the near future, it is equally true that unless it can find some way to regain the trust of the country's Shiite community, Bahrain's ruling class will have a difficult time maintaining long-term stability when and if the conditions promoting outside support for the *status quo* change. Lastly, as the regional Sunni-Shia conflict has intensified, Bahrain's rulers may face challenges even assuring the loyalty of their Sunni subjects.

ENDNOTES

1. "Bahrain", Freedom House, 2017, https://freedomhouse.org/report/freedom-world/2017/bahrain; "Bahrain 2016/2017", Amnesty International, https://www.amnesty.org/en/countries/middle-east-and-north-africa/bahrain/report-bahrain/.
2. "Bahrain jails 24 for forming ISIS cell," *The Daily* Star (Lebanon), June 23, 2016, http://www.dailystar.com.lb/News/Middle-East/2016/Jun-23/358553-bahrain-jails-24-for-forming-isis-cell.ashx.
3. *Bahrain 2016 Crime & Safety Report*, U.S.

Department of State, n.d., https://www.osac.gov/pages/ContentReportDetails.aspx?cid=19255.

4. Andrew Hammond, "Bahrain Says Will Hold Dialogue to End Crisis Soon," *Reuters*, March 10, 2012, http://www.reuters.com/article/2012/03/10/us-bahrain-protest-talks-idUSBRE8290A420120310; Bill Law, "Time running out as Bahrain tries to revive national dialogue", *BBC*, January 30, 2014, http://www.bbc.com/news/world-middle-east-25918628.
5. "Bahrain is still hounding its Shia," *The Economist,* January 19, 2017, https://www.economist.com/news/middle-east-and-africa/21715023-protesters-are-cowed-repression-carries-bahrain-still-hounding-its.
6. Mahjoob Zweiri and Mohammed Zahid, *The victory of Al Wefaq: The rise of Shiite politics in Bahrain*, Research Institute for European and American Studies (RIEAS) *Research Paper* no. 108, April 2007, http://rieas.gr/images/rieas108.pdf; "Bahrain Split by Electoral Boundaries," Al Wefaq National Islamic Society, June 9, 2010, http://alwefaq.net/~alwefaq/index.php?show=news&action=article&id=4723; "Bahrain Opposition Representation: Was it a Silent Majority or is it now a Loud Minority?" n.p., n.d., http://www.scribd.com/doc/49888133/Bahrain-Opposition-Representation.
7. Robert Fisk, "Abolish Bahrain's Monarchy, Chant Shia Muslims," *New Zealand Herald*, February 21, 2011, http://www.nzherald.co.nz/democracy/news/article.cfm?c_id=171&objectid=10707688; "Several Hurt as Sunnis. Shiites Clash in Bahrain," *Reuters*, March 4, 2011, http://tribune.com.pk/story/127573/several-hurt-as-sunnis-shiites-clash-in-bahrain/.
8. "Bahrain Shiites Eye Easing of Sunni Grip," *Agence France Presse*, October 23, 2010, http://www.arabtimesonline.com/NewsDetails/tabid/96/smid/414/ArticleID/161106/reftab/73/t/Bahrain-Shiites-eye-easing-of-Sunni-grip/Default.aspx.
9. Joost Hiltermann and Toby Matthiesen,"Bahrain Burning," *New York Review of Books*, August 18, 2011, http://www.tobymatthiesen.com/wp/newspaper_articles/bahrain-burning/.

10. Imran Khan, "Inside Friday prayer in Tehran," *Al Jazeera* (Doha), May 18, 2012, http://blogs.aljazeera.com/blog/middle-east/inside-friday-prayer-tehran.
11. "Bahrain WikiLeaks Cables: Bahrain as 'Iran's Fourteenth Province,'" *Telegraph* (London), February 18, 2011, http://www.telegraph.co.uk/news/wikileaks-files/bahrain-wikileaks-cables/8334785/GENERAL-PETRAEUS-VISIT-TO-BAHRAIN.html.
12. Christopher Hope, "WikiLeaks: Bahrain Opposition 'Received Training from Hezbollah,'" *Telegraph* (London), February 18, 2011, http://www.telegraph.co.uk/news/worldnews/wikileaks/8333686/WikiLeaks-Bahrain-opposition-received-training-from-Hizbollah.html; "US Embassy Cables: Bahrainis Trained by Hezbollah, Claims King Hamad," *Guardian* (London), February 15, 2011, http://www.guardian.co.uk/world/us-embassy-cables-documents/165861.
13. *Report of the Bahrain Independent Commission of Inquiry*, paragraphs 1584 and 1585, p. 387, http://www.bici.org.bh/BICIreportEN.pdf.
14. *Bahrain 2016 Crime & Safety Report*, U.S. Department of State.
15. Jonathan Spyer, "Gulf Regimes: The Real Game – Saudi Arabia," *Jerusalem Post*, March 11, 2011, http://www.jpost.com/Features/FrontLines/Article.aspx?id=211679. According to Spyer, "Iran… is adept, however, at turning political chaos into gain… If the Gulf regimes fail to effectively navigate the current unrest, Iran is fair set to begin to apply these practices in this area."
16. Zweiri and Zahid, "The Victory of Al Wefaq," p. 9.
17. "US Embassy Cables: Guide to Bahrain's Politics," *Guardian* (London), February 15, 2011, http://www.guardian.co.uk/world/us-embassy-cables-documents/168471; "Bahrain WikiLeaks Cables: Wafa': A New Shia Rejectionist Movement," *Telegraph* (London), February 18, 2011, http://www.telegraph.co.uk/news/wikileaks-files/bahrain-wikileaks-cables/8334607/WAFA-A-NEW-SHIA-REJECTIONIST-MOVEMENT.html.
18. Zweiri and Zahid, "The Victory of Al Wefaq," p. 11.

19. Al Wefaq National Islamic Society, "Bahrain Split by Electoral Boundaries." Note that in addition to having district lines that separate Sunni and Shia populations in order to create Sunni-majority districts, the population size of the districts drawn varies widely: some Sunni-majority districts have as few as 1,000 voters, while some Shiite-majority districts have as many as 15,000 voters.
20. "MPs Urge Al Wefaq to Rethink Resignation," *Gulf Daily News*, March 9, 2011, http://www.gulf-daily-news.com/NewsDetails.aspx?storyid=301425; Adrian Bloomfield, "Bahrain King under Pressure to Sack Prime Minister Uncle," *Telegraph* (London), February 20, 2011, http://www.telegraph.co.uk/news/worldnews/middleeast/bahrain/8336934/Bahrain-king-under-pressure-to-sack-prime-minister-uncle.html.
21. Sara Sorcher,"What's The State of Play In Bahrain's Protests?" *National Journal*, July 18, 2011, http://www.nationaljournal.com/nationalsecurity/what-s-the-state-of-play-in-bahrain-s-protests--20110718; Hiltermann and Matthiesen, "Bahrain Burning."
22. Reuters, "Bahrain holds vote to fill seats vacated during unrest," *AhramOnline*, September 24, 2011, http://english.ahram.org.eg/~/NewsContent/2/8/22324/World/Region/Bahrain-holds-vote-to-fill-seats-vacated-during-un.aspx.
23. Ethan Bronner, "Bahrain Vote Erupts in Violence," *New York Times*, September 24, 2011, http://www.nytimes.com/2011/09/25/world/middleeast/bahrain-protesters-and-police-clash-during-election.html.
24. Mohammed A'Ali,"Thousands defy threats and flock to the polls," *Gulf Daily News*, September 25, 2011,http://www.gulf-daily-news.com/NewsDetails.aspx?storyid=314082.
25. Andrew Hammond,"UPDATE 1-Fewer than 1 in 5 vote in Bahrain by-elections," *Reuters*, September 25, 2011,http://www.reuters.com/article/2011/09/25/bahrain-vote-results-idUSL5E7KP13G20110925.
26. "Bahrain opposition groups announce elections boycott", *BBC*, October 11, 2014, http://www.bbc.com/news/world-middle-east-29583378.

27. Associated Press, "Bahrain court orders Shia opposition group to be dissolved", *The Guardian,* July 17, 2016, https://www.theguardian.com/world/2016/jul/17/bahrain-al-wefaq-shia-opposition-group-sunni; "Bahrain regime to auction Al-Wefaq's seized assets", *Al Masdar News,* October 22, 2016, https://www.almasdarnews.com/article/bahrain-regime-auction-al-wefaqs-seized-assets/.
28. "Bahrain's leading Shia cleric charged with corruption", *Middle East Eye*, July 18, 2016, http://www.middleeasteye.net/news/bahrain-s-leading-shias-religious-leader-charged-corruption-1212082735.
29. "Bahrain strips Sheikh Isa Qassim of nationality," *Al Jazeera,* June 21, 2016, http://www.aljazeera.com/news/2016/06/bahrain-strips-religious-leader-nationality-160620122338238.html.
30. Associated Press, "Bahrain court orders Shia opposition group to be dissolved."
31. "Bahrain opposition loses appeal against dissolution," *Al Araby*, February 6, 2017, https://www.alaraby.co.uk/english/news/2017/2/6/bahrain-opposition-loses-appeal-against-dissolution
32. Kate Kizer & Michael Payne, "Bahrain's five-year plan of repression", *Middle East Eye,* February 14, 2016, http://www.middleeasteye.net/columns/bahrain-s-five-year-plan-repression-1903103504.
33. "Bahrain court overturns jail term of opposition chief," *Middle East Eye,* October 17, 2016, http://www.middleeasteye.net/news/bahrain-court-overturns-jail-term-opposition-chief-215996772.
34. "Bahrain charges opposition leader with 'spying,'" *Al Jazeera,* November 1, 2017, http://www.aljazeera.com/news/2017/11/bahrain-charges-opposition-leader-spying-171101182543073.html
35. "Closure of Opposition Political Society Al-Wefaq in Bahrain," U.S. Department of State, June 14, 2016, http://www.state.gov/r/pa/prs/ps/2016/06/258464.htm; "Bahrain snubs Western allies' condemnation of opposition ban", *Middle East Eye,* July 19, 2016, http://www.middleeasteye.net/news/bahrain-rejects-us-and-uk-condemnation-opposition-ban-517968328.

36. "Bahrain's top Shi'ite cleric gets one year suspended jail sentence", *Reuters*, May 21, 2017, https://www.reuters.com/article/us-bahrain-security-trial/bahrains-top-shiite-cleric-gets-one-year-suspended-jail-sentence-idUSKBN18H07C.
37. Jon Gambrell, "Bahrain Raid on Shiite Cleric's Town: 5 Killed, 286 Arrested", *Associated Press*, May 23, 2017, https://www.bloomberg.com/news/articles/2017-05-24/bahrain-raid-on-shiite-cleric-s-town-5-killed-286-arrested; Kareem Fahim, "After assurances by Trump, Bahrain mounts deadliest raid in years on opposition", *The Washington Post*, May 24, 2017, https://www.washingtonpost.com/world/after-assurances-by-trump-bahrain-mounts-deadliest-raid-in-years-on-pro-opposition-shiite-neighborhood/2017/05/24/6995e954-4067-11e7-9851-b95c40075207_story.html.
38. Sami Aboudi, "Bahrain says five died during raid on Shi'ite Muslim leader's hometown", *Reuters*, May 25, 2017, http://www.reuters.com/article/us-bahrain-security/bahrain-says-five-died-during-raid-on-shiite-muslim-leaders-hometown-idUSKBN18L0T2.
39. Celine Aswad, "Suspects arrested over Bahrain blast in village of Shi'ite cleric: ministry", *Reuters*, June 20, 2017, http://www.reuters.com/article/us-bahrain-security/suspects-arrested-over-bahrain-blast-in-village-of-shiite-cleric-ministry-idUSKBN19B0ED.
40. "Bahrain WikiLeaks Cables: Wafa': A New Shia Rejectionist Movement," *Telegraph* (London).
41. "Shaikh Isa Al Jowder and the Haq Movement," *Chan'ad* Bahraini blog, May 31, 2006, http://chanad.weblogs.us/?p=487.
42. "Bahrain WikiLeaks Cables: Wafa': A New Shia Rejectionist Movement," *Telegraph* (London).
43. "US Embassy Cables: Guide to Bahrain's Politics," *Guardian* (London).
44. "Bahrain WikiLeaks Cables: Wafa': A New Shia Rejectionist Movement," *Telegraph* (London).
45. "Bahrain – Political Parties," globalsecurity.org, n.d., http://www.globalsecurity.org/military/world/gulf/bahrain-politics-parties.htm.

46. "US Embassy Cables: Guide to Bahrain's Politics," *Guardian* (London).
47. "Bahrain Appeal Court Upholds Activists' Convictions," *BBC*, September 4, 2012, http://www.bbc.co.uk/news/world-middle-east-19474026.
48. "US Embassy Cables: Guide to Bahrain's Politics," *Guardian* (London).
49. "Bahrain Unrest: Shia Dissident Hassan Mushaima Returns," *BBC*, February 26, 2011, http://www.bbc.co.uk/news/world-middle-east-12587902.
50. "Bahraini Shia Groups Seek to Unify Demands," *Financial Times*, February 27, 2011, http://www.ft.com/cms/s/0/a5766674-429e-11e0-8b34-00144feabdc0.html.
51. "Bahrain Appeal Court Upholds Activists' Convictions," *BBC*.
52. "Bahrain WikiLeaks Cables: Wafa," *Telegraph* (London): A New Shia Rejectionist Movement"; "Wafa' ('loyalty')," globalsecurity.org, n.d., http://www.globalsecurity.org/military/world/gulf/bahrain-politics-parties-wafa.htm.
53. "US Embassy Cables: Guide to Bahrain's Politics," *Guardian* (London).
54. "US Embassy Cables: Guide to Bahrain's Politics," *Guardian* (London).
55. Zoi Constantine, "Opposition Party Votes against Bahrain Election," *The National* (UAE), August 26, 2010, https://www.thenational.ae/world/mena/opposition-party-votes-against-bahrain-election-1.537990.
56. "The Opposition Parties: The Decision to Dissolve Amal Society is a Deliberate Attack on Political Activity in Bahrain," *Al Wefaq*, July 12, 2012, http://alwefaq.net/index.php?show=news&action=article&id=6664.
57. Joe Parkinson, "Bahrain is Roiled by Return of Shiite," *Wall Street Journal*, February 28, 2011, http://online.wsj.com/article/SB10001424052748704430304576170661773277324.html; Joe Parkinson and Nour Malas, "Bahrain Opposition Steps Up Pressure," *Wall Street Journal*, March 7, 2011, http://online.wsj.com/article/SB10001424052748704504404576183972416733938.html?mod=WSJEurope_hpp_LEFTTopStories.

58. "US Embassy Cables: Guide to Bahrain's Politics," *Guardian* (London).
59. Hussein Ibish, "The Bahrain Stalemate," *The Atlantic*, July 18, 2011, http://www.theatlantic.com/international/archive/2011/07/the-bahrain-stalemate/242086/.
60. Alex MacDonald, "Sunni Islamists could face uphill struggle in Bahrain elections," *Middle East Eye*, February 13, 2015, http://www.middleeasteye.net/in-depth/features/sunni-islamists-could-face-uphill-struggle-bahrain-elections-1404489268; "Bahrain FM: Muslim Brotherhood is a terrorist group", *Al Jazeera*, July 6, 2017, http://www.aljazeera.com/news/2017/07/bahrain-fm-muslim-brotherhood-terrorist-group-170706140931861.html.
61. Eric Trager, "The Muslim Brotherhood Is the Root of the Qatar Crisis", *The Atlantic*, July 2, 2017, https://www.theatlantic.com/international/archive/2017/07/muslim-brotherhood-qatar/532380/.
62. "Muslim Brotherhood in Bahrain Urges Gulf Leaders to Reunite their Countries," *Bahrain Mirror*, July 12, 2017, http://bhmirror.myftp.biz/en/news/40410.html.
63. Courtney Freer and Giorgio Cafiero, "Is the Bahraini Muslim Brotherhood's 'special status' over?" *The New Arab*, August 7, 2017, https://www.alaraby.co.uk/english/Comment/2017/8/7/Is-the-Bahraini-Muslim-Brotherhoods-special-status-over; Kylie Moore-Gilbert, "A Band of (Muslim) Brothers? Exploring Bahrain's Role in the Qatar Crisis," Middle East Institute, August 3, 2017, http://www.mei.edu/content/map/band-muslim-brothers-exploring-bahrain-s-role-qatar-crisis.
64. Zweiri and Zahid, "The Victory of Al Wefaq," p. 7.
65. Zweiri and Zahid, "The Victory of Al Wefaq," p. 7.
66. Suad Hamada, "Anti-Gender Equality Campaign Starts," womangateway.com, August 4, 2008, http://www.womengateway.com/NR/exeres/7A81C4CA-5539-4C3D-9F97-38EB79F2A735.htm.
67. National Bank of Bahrain, "Social Responsibility," n.d., http://www.nbbonline.com/default.asp?action=category&id=6; "Sakana Contributes Zakat to Al Eslah Society," sakanaonline.com, October 7,

2010, http://www.sakanaonline.com/en/press-releases/sakana-zakat-al-eslah-society.html.

68. Kenneth Katzman "Bahrain: The Political Structure, Reform and Human Rights," *Eurasia Review*, February 28, 2011, http://www.eurasiareview.com/28022011-bahrain-the-political-structure-reform-and-human-rights/.
69. Kenneth Katzman, "Bahrain: The Political Structure, Reform and Human Rights."
70. Kenneth Katzman, "Bahrain: The Political Structure, Reform and Human Rights."; Habib Toumi, "Al Asala, Islamic Menbar Join Forces in Bahrain," *Gulf News*, October 29, 2010, http://gulfnews.com/news/gulf/bahrain/al-asala-islamic-menbar-join-forces-in-bahrain-1.703600.
71. Habib Toumi, "Bahrain's political societies lose big in polls", *Gulf News,* November 30, 2014, http://gulfnews.com/news/gulf/bahrain/bahrain-s-political-societies-lose-big-in-polls-1.1420042.
72. Michael Slackman and Nadim Audi, "Protests in Bahrain Become Test of Wills," *New York Times*, February 22, 2011, http://www.nytimes.com/2011/02/23/world/middleeast/23bahrain.html; Nancy Youssef, "Huge Bahraini Counter-Protest Reflects Rising Sectarian Strife," McClatchy, February 21, 2011, http://www.mcclatchydc.com/2011/02/21/109155/huge-bahraini-counter-protest.html.
73. "Bangladeshis Say Being Forced to take Part in Bahrain Pro Government Rally," ANI, March 18, 2011, http://www.sify.com/news/bangladeshis-say-being-forced-to-take-part-in-bahrain-pro-government-rally-news-international-ldsrkjcfgba.html.
74. Husain Marhoon, "Bahraini Salafists in Spotlight," *Al-Monitor,* June 18, 2013, http://www.al-monitor.com/pulse/originals/2013/06/bahrain-jihadists-syria-salafism.html.
75. Bill Law, "Bahrain: The Islamic State threat within," *Middle East Eye,* October 14, 2014, http://www.middleeasteye.net/columns/bahrain-islamic-state-threat-within-884335108.
76. Sayed Ahmed Alwadaei, "The Islamic State's Bahraini

Backers," *New York Times,* November 25, 2015, http://www.nytimes.com/2015/11/26/opinion/the-islamic-states-bahraini-backers.html.

77. Obaid al-Suhaymi, "Bahrain Revokes Nationality of 13 ISIS Members, Postpones Session to Dissolve Wefaq Islamic Society", Asharq al-Awsat, June 24, 2016, http://english.aawsat.com/2016/06/article55353290/bahrain-revokes-nationality-13-isis-members-postpones-session-dissolve-wefaq-islamic-society; Bahrain Mirror, "Appeals Court Adjourns Case of Bahrain ISIS cell until Jan. 12," January 3, 2017, http://mirror.no-ip.org/en/news/35796.html.
78. Prashanth MP, "Keralites killed in Syria had joined Bahrain Salafi group,", *The Times of India* (Kochi), July 6, 2017, http://epaperbeta.timesofindia.com/Article.aspx?eid=31811&articlexml=Keralites-killed-in-Syria-had-joined-Bahrain-Salafi-06072017004043
79. Giorgio Cafiero and Daniel Wagner, "Bahrain's Daesh Dilemma," The World Post, January 15 / March 17 2015, http://www.huffingtonpost.com/giorgio-cafiero/bahrains-daesh-dilemma_b_6462998.html.
80. Aniqa Haider, "Society Sends Five Ambulances," *Gulf Daily News*, January 15, 2009, http://www.gulf-daily-news.com/NewsDetails.aspx?storyid=240214.
81. Habib Toumi, "Bahraini Islamist Societies Press for Closure of Bars, Discos," *Gulf News*, April 22, 2009, http://gulfnews.com/news/gulf/bahrain/bahrain-islamist-societies-press-for-closure-of-bars-discos-1.1880.
82. "Liquor ban in Bahrain rumours go viral", DT News / News of Bahrain, November 14, 2017, http://www.newsofbahrain.com/viewNews.php?ppId=39521&TYPE=Posts&pid=21&MNU=2&-SUB=2
83. Habib Toumi, "Bahraini Islamist Societies Press for Closure of Bars, Discos."; Alexandra Sandels, "BAHRAIN: Islamists Seeking to Curb Prostitution Fail in Bid to Ban Women From 4 Countries," *Los Angeles Times Babylon & Beyond* blog, December 15, 2009, http://latimesblogs.latimes.com/babylonbeyond/2009/12/bahrain-conservatives-

seeking-to-curb-prostitution-fail-in-bid-to-ban-visas-for-women-from-russia-thailand-ethiopia-and-china.html.

84. "Marcel Khalife and Qassim Haddad Cause Fury in Bahrain's Parliament," FREEMUSE, March 27, 2007, http://www.freemuse.org/sw18500.asp.
85. "Haifa Wehbe Sings in Bahrain," *Middle East Online*, May 2, 2008, http://www.middle-east-online.com/english/?id=25672.
86. "Bahrain Police Deploy Teargas at anti-Kim Kardashian Protest," *USA Today*, December 1, 2012, http://www.usatoday.com/story/life/people/2012/12/01/bahrain-kardashian-protest/1739609/; Robert Mackey, "Bahrain's Embrace of Kim Kardashian," *New York Times*, December 3, 2012, http://thelede.blogs.nytimes.com/2012/12/03/bahrains-embrace-of-kim-kardashian/.
87. "Bahrain Protesters March on Palace as Gates Visits," Associated Press, March 12, 2011, http://www.washingtonpost.com/wp-dyn/content/article/2011/03/12/AR2011031201563.html.
88. Youssef, "Huge Bahraini Counter-Protest Reflects Rising Sectarian Strife."
89. "Bahrain's Sunni party rejects dialogue, calls for end to street violence," *Global Times* (China), December 27, 2012, http://www.globaltimes.cn/content/752643.shtml; Justin Gengler, "Look Who's Boycotting Dialogue Now," *Religion and Politics in Bahr*ain, March 25, 2012, http://bahrainipolitics.blogspot.co.il/2012/03/look-whos-boycotting-dialogue-now.html.
90. "Bahrain is still hounding its Shia", *The Economist,* January 19, 2017, https://www.economist.com/news/middle-east-and-africa/21715023-protesters-are-cowed-repression-carries-bahrain-still-hounding-its
91. "Factsheet: Bahrain Protests Feb. 2011," Canadians for Justice and Peace in the Middle East *CJPME Factsheet Series* no. 114, February 22, 2011, http://www.cjpme.org/fs_114.
92. Bloomfield, "Bahrain King under Pressure to Sack Prime Minister Uncle."
93. "Bahrain Opposition Representation."

94. *'Al Bander Report': Demographic Engineering in Bahrain and Mechanisms of Exclusion,* Bahrain Center for Human Rights, September 30, 2006, http://www.bahrainrights.org/node/528.
95. Habib Toumi, "Call to Reinstate Imam Who Criticised Egypt's Steel Fence," *Gulf News*, December 25, 2009, http://gulfnews.com/news/gulf/bahrain/call-to-reinstate-imam-who-criticised-egypt-s-steel-fence-1.557927.
96. "Al-Wefaq: Bahrain will always support Palestine", *Press TV,* October 19, 2016, http://presstv.ir/Detail/2016/10/19/489831/wefaq-bahrain-fifa-israeli.
97. Sandeep Singh Grewal, "UAE Releases Suspected Al Qaeda Militant of Bahraini Origin," NewsBlaze, June 12, 2009, http://newsblaze.com/story/20090612184137sand.nb/topstory.html.
98. "The Guantanamo Docket: Sheikh Salman Ebrahim Mohamed Ali al Khalifa," *New York Times*, n.d., http://projects.nytimes.com/guantanamo/detainees/246-sheikh-salman-ebrahim-mohamed-ali-al-khalifa/documents/2/pages/1781.
99. Bahrain Freedom Movement, "Two Men Accused of Funding al-Qaeda Groups," June 25, 2008, http://www.vob.org/en/index.php?show=news&action=article&id=324.
100. Grewal, "UAE Releases Suspected Al Qaeda Militant of Bahraini Origin."
101. Grewal, "UAE Releases Suspected Al Qaeda Militant of Bahraini Origin."
102. See, for example, Jon Marks, "Bahrain returns to the bad old days," *Guardian* (London), September 13, 2010, http://www.guardian.co.uk/commentisfree/2010/sep/13/bahrain-opposition-protests.
103. Canadians for Justice and Peace in the Middle East, "Factsheet: Bahrain Protests Feb. 2011"; Simeon Kerr, Robin Wigglesworth and Abigail Fielding-Smith, "Arab Regimes Brace for 'Days of Rage,'" *Financial Times*, February 3, 2011, http://www.ft.com/cms/s/0/63ce290c-2ef1-11e0-88ec-00144feabdc0.html#axzz1G7GakJjJ.
104. "Bahrain King Orders Release of Political Prisoners," *Associated Press*, February 22, 2011, http://www.

independent.co.uk/news/world/middle-east/bahrain-king-orders-release-of-political-prisoners-2222371.html.

105. "Bahrain's Shiite Opposition Set to Talk to Rulers," *Associated Press*, March 3, 2011, http://www.cbsnews.com/stories/2011/03/03/ap/world/main20038661.shtml.
106. See Note 22.
107. Shahira Salloum,"Bahrain: A Return to Dialogue?" *Al-Akhbar*, December 14, 2012, http://english.al-akhbar.com/node/14375; Bill Law, "Bahrain Minister Plays Down Dialogue Calls," *BBC*, December 17, 2012, http://www.bbc.co.uk/news/world-middle-east-20757862.
108. Kristen Chick, "Bahrain Rights Activist's Wife Details Torture, Unfair Trial," *Christian Science Monitor*, May 16, 2011, http://www.csmonitor.com/World/Middle-East/2011/0516/Bahrain-rights-activist-s-wife-details-torture-unfair-trial.
109. Kristen Chick, "Amid Unrest, Bahrain Companies Fire Hundreds of Shiites," *Christian Science Monitor*, April 7, 2011, http://www.csmonitor.com/World/Middle-East/2011/0407/Amid-unrest-Bahrain-companies-fire-hundreds-of-Shiites.
110. Human Rights Watch, "Bahrain – Events of 2015", n.d., https://www.hrw.org/world-report/2016/country-chapters/bahrain. See also Amnesty International, "Bahrain 2015/2016," n.d., https://www.amnesty.org/en/countries/middle-east-and-north-africa/bahrain/report-bahrain/.
111. "Mosques Under Construction Re-Demolished by Authorities in Bahrain," Bahrain Center for Human Rights, December 9, 2012, http://www.bahrainrights.org/en/node/5550.
112. Roy Gutman,"U.S. Warns Bahrain's Society 'Could Break Apart,'" McClatchy, November 20, 2012, http://www.mcclatchydc.com/2012/11/20/175207/us-warns-bahrains-society-could.html.
113. "Gulf State Troops to Remain in Bahrain in 2011," *World Tribune*, May 13, 2011, http://www.worldtribune.com/worldtribune/WTARC/2011/me_gulf0577_05_13.

asp.

114. Thomas Fuller, "Bahrainis Fear the U.S. Isn't Behind Their Fight for Democracy," *New York Times*, March 5, 2011, http://www.nytimes.com/2011/03/05/world/middleeast/05bahrain.html.
115. Adam Entous and Julian E. Barnes, "U.S. Wavers on 'Regime Change,'" *Wall Street Journal*, March 5, 2011, http://online.wsj.com/article/SB10001424052748703580004576180522653787198.html?mod=WSJEUROPE_hpp_MIDDLETopNews.

16 Egypt

Quick Facts

Population: 97,041,072 (July 2017 est.)
Area: 1,001,450 sq km
Ethnic Groups: Egyptian 99.6%, other 0.4% (2006 census)
GDP (official exchange rate): $237.1 billion (2017 est.)

Source: CIA World FactBook (Last Updated September 2018)

Introduction

Egypt has played a central role in the history and the development of Islamism. In 1928, an Egyptian teacher named Hassan al-Banna founded the Muslim Brotherhood, the world's first modern Islamist movement, and the most prominent Islamist force in Egypt. The Brotherhood soon conceived an ideological framework that would go on to inspire most contemporary Islamists, and eventually became the main political opposition force against successive governments in Egypt. From the time of President Gamal Abdel Nasser through the era of President Hosni Mubarak, the Muslim Brotherhood was outlawed but tolerated to varying extents.

Following the 1952 Free Officers Revolution in Egypt, during which a small group of military officers ousted King Farouk, the Brotherhood and the military-led government enjoyed a short period of cooperation. This ended with an attempt on Nasser's life in 1954, whereupon the organization was outlawed and a number of prominent Brotherhood members were imprisoned, including al-Banna's ideological descendant, Sayyid Qutb. In the late 1970s, the Muslim Brothers officially renounced violence at the insistence of President Anwar Sadat, temporarily easing their relationship with Egyptian authorities. The movement was granted enough space to expand its influence on civil society through social services and other outreach activities. This distinguished the Brotherhood at the time from jihadist groups, such Islamic Jihad (Al-Jihad), whose members assassinated President Sadat in 1981, bringing Hosni Mubarak to power. Mubarak cracked down on more radical Islamist currents such as the Islamic Jihad, and rhetorically justified the slow pace of democratic reforms by pointing to the security threat posed by extremists. The Muslim Brotherhood remained tolerated by the Mubarak regime (though still illegal), as Mubarak viewed the organization as a useful counter to the spread of those more radical ideologies.

Mubarak's ouster in 2011 marked a turning point for Islamists, with many Islamist groups establishing legal political parties to participate in post-uprising politics. In the parliamentary elections held between November 2011 and January 2012, Islamists won nearly three-quarters of all seats in the new Egyptian parliament. A Muslim Brotherhood leader, Mohammed Morsi, was elected Egypt's president on June 30, 2012, in the country's first democratic presidential election. However, in the wake of mass protests against Morsi's increasingly authoritarian and incompetent government in late June and early July of 2013, the Egyptian military ousted the new president and replaced him with an interim government tasked with drafting a new constitution, which was approved in a popular referendum in January 2014. Meanwhile, the government severely repressed the Muslim Brotherhood, imprisoning tens of thousands of its leaders and members. Since Morsi's overthrow, Egypt has contended with an upsurge in jihadist violence in the Sinai Peninsula, where the main militant group has been a formal affiliate of the Islamic State terrorist group since November 2014.[1].

Islamist Activity

Egyptian Islamism has always spanned a diverse ideological and operational spectrum, the entirety of which is reflected in the post-Mubarak era.

The most prominent Egyptian Islamist movement is the Muslim Brotherhood (Al-Ikhwan al-Muslimun), founded in 1928 by Hassan al-Banna. Its ideology states that a true "Islamic society" is one in which state institutions and the government follow the principles of the Qur'an, and in which laws follow sharia, or "Islamic law."[2] Al-Banna, a teacher from a modest background, was heavily influenced by Syrian-Egyptian thinker Mohammed Rashid Rida, who believed that a return to the Islam of the 7th and 8th century was the only way for Muslim societies to regain strength and to escape Western colonialism and cultural hegemony.[3] Al-Banna viewed Islam as an "all-embracing concept," meant to govern every aspect of life, and he constructed the Muslim Brotherhood to advance this totalitarian interpretation within Egypt from the grassroots up. Specifically, he sought to "reform" the individual through the Brotherhood's multi-year indoctrination process, those individuals would then form families, and the families would then spread the message within Egyptian society. Once Egyptian society was "Islamized," an Islamic state would emerge, and once this happened throughout the Muslim world, the states would unify under a new caliphate.

Muslim Brotherhood cells spread rapidly throughout Egypt in the 1920s and 1930s. Amid episodic government crackdowns, the Brotherhood formed a violent "secret apparatus," which was implicated in multiple assassinations and terrorist attacks. Al-Banna was assassinated in February 1949, and while the Brotherhood initially cooperated with Egypt's military following the July 1952 Free Officers' revolution, the new regime cracked down on it severely following an attempt on President Gamal Abdel Nasser's life. During this period, the Brotherhood's chief ideologue, Sayyid Qutb, authored the famous Islamist manifesto *Milestones Along The Way* (Ma'alim fi-l-Tariq) while in prison in 1964. In *Milestones*, Qutb claims that all non-Muslim societies, and indeed those societies that are only Muslim in name but not in practice, are in a state of "ignorance" (jahiliyya). Jahili societies are those that do not strictly follow revelation, and Qutb called on Muslims to wage offensive jihad against jahiliyya until they established a united Islamic community worldwide. This was interpreted as a call to arms against the Egyptian state, and Qutb was executed in 1966.[4]

Following Nasser's death in 1970, his successor, Anwar al-Sadat, lifted restrictions on Islamist activism, viewing Islamists as useful counters to the leftists who challenged his authority. During this period, a wide variety of Islamist groups emerged on Egyptian campuses, and as the Egyptian government liberated Brotherhood leaders during the 1970s, the Brotherhood integrated many of these young Islamists as the organization rebuilt itself. The Brotherhood ultimately renounced violence, thereby distinguishing itself from other Islamist movements, such as the Islamic Group (Al-Gama'a al-Islamiyya), which recruited on university campuses, in Egyptian prisons, and in the country's poor urban and rural areas.

The Islamic Group was involved in a series of attacks during the 1980s and 1990s aimed at deposing Egypt's secular, autocratic government and replacing it with an Islamic theocracy. These attacks included the 1997 killing of Western tourists in Luxor, the attempted assassination of President Hosni Mubarak in Ethiopia in 1995, the Cairo bombings of 1993, and several other armed operations against Egyptian intellectuals and Coptic Christians. The movement's spiritual leader, Umar Abd al-Rahman, was connected to Ramzi Yusuf, the perpetrator of the first World Trade Center bombing in 1993.[5] Rahman and nine followers were subsequently arrested and convicted of plotting to blow up the United Nations headquarters in New York, the New York Federal Reserve Building, the George Washington Bridge, and the Holland and Lincoln Tunnels. In 1999, the Islamic Group declared a unilateral ceasefire in its longstanding struggle against Cairo. This declaration marked a major ideological shift and was accompanied by a steady drift away from the use of violence, which was completed in 2002. The Islamic Group's members have not claimed responsibility for any armed attack since.[6] Subsequent moves to diminish radicalism within the party drove a faction of the Islamic Group's more violent adherents to join al-Qaeda in 2006.[7] In the 2011-2012 parliamentary elections, the Islamic Group ran under the Building and Development Party and won thirteen seats in the lower house.[8] Members of the Islamic group have protested the Egyptian military's deposing of Morsi and the dissolution of his government, but in February 2014 the organization announced it was ready to engage with the interim government to end Egypt's political impasse.[9]

The third Islamist group that has played a major role in recent Egyptian history is the Islamic Jihad (Al-Jihad). Active since the 1970s, it was officially formed in 1980 as a result of the merger of two Islamist cells led by Karam Zuhdi and Muhammad Abd al-Salam Faraj. Faraj's famous manifesto, *The Absent Duty* (Al-Farida al-Ghaiba), outlined the new movement's ideology.[10] Like those affiliated with the Islamic Group, members of the Islamic Jihad represent a relative minority within Egypt's Islamist spectrum and are mostly former members of the Brotherhood. Some are believed to have fought alongside the Afghan mujahideen in the 1980s against the Soviet Union. The organization's stated objective was to overthrow the Egyptian "infidel" regime and establish an Islamic government in its place. The Islamic Jihad also sought to attack U.S. and Israeli interests in Egypt and abroad. The group is infamous for assassinating President Anwar Sadat in 1981 and for additional attacks on Egyptian government officials in the early 1990s. It is also believed to have attacked Egypt›s embassy in Pakistan in 1995 and to have been involved in planning bombings against U.S. embassies in Kenya and Tanzania in 1998. In June 2001, the group merged with al-Qaeda to form a new entity, called Gama'a Qa'idat al-Jihad, headed by Osama bin Laden's second-in-command, Ayman al-Zawahiri.

Over time, Egypt's Islamist landscape has evolved considerably. While the ideology of Egyptian Islamist groups remains radical and anti-democratic in nature, many of them have changed their tactics, favoring elections rather than revolution and/or violence as a means for achieving power.

In this vein, during the late 1970s and early 1980s, the Muslim Brotherhood increasingly disavowed jihad in favor of political participation. The process began with the release of a text entitled *Preachers, Not Judges* in 1969, which was likely written by multiple individuals but has been attributed to supreme guide Hassan al-Hudaybi. In this tract, al-Hudaybi developed a series of theological counterarguments to Qutb's radical views.[11] Under the influence of al-Hudaybi and his successor, Umar al-Tilmisani, the Brotherhood gradually distanced itself from armed action, gave an oath to Sadat not to use violence against his regime, and even named him a "martyr" after he was killed in 1981. Under Mubarak, the Brotherhood participated in most parliamentary elections, sometimes in partnership with legal parties, including non-Islamist ones. However, it remained an illegal organization, and the government used its illegality as a pretext for cracking down on it whenever it appeared to be gaining strength, such as during the run-up to the 1995 elections and following the Brotherhood's success in the 2005 elections, when it won 88 of 444 contested seats.

The Brotherhood's ideological shift drew condemnation from other Islamist groups, most notably the Islamic Jihad and its commander Ayman al-Zawahiri, who severely criticized the Brotherhood's reorientation in a book entitled *The Bitter Harvest: The Muslim Brotherhood in Sixty Years* (Al-Hasad al-Murr: Al-Ikhwan al-Muslimun fi Sittin 'Aman).[12] In it, al-Zawahiri condemned the Brotherhood's good relations with King Farouk and Presidents Nasser, Sadat, and Mubarak:

> The Muslim Brotherhood, by recognizing the tyrants' legitimacy and sharing constitutional legitimacy with them, has become a tool in the tyrants' hands to strike jihadist groups in the name of [fighting] extremism and disobeying sharia *[Islamic law].* There should be no doubt that we are proud to be outside of this "legitimacy of disbelief," which the Muslim Brotherhood has accepted and approved.[13]

The Egyptian government's success in combating jihadist trends during the 1990s compelled some of these groups to offer theological arguments against political violence. One of the most prominent instances of this trend occurred within the Islamic Group. In July 1997, during a military tribunal, one of the group's activists, Muhammad al-Amin Abd al-Alim, read a statement signed by six other Islamist leaders that called on their affiliates to cease all armed operations in Egypt and abroad.[14] While it elicited considerable controversy within the movement, the statement heralded the beginning of the group's renunciation of violence. In March 1999, the group's leadership launched an "Initiative for Ceasing Violence" and declared a unilateral ceasefire. Ideologues and leaders were mostly successful in convincing their base to renounce armed struggle and support a non-violent approach by authoring a series of texts to provide the ideological justification for their rejection of violence. Leaders published four books in January 2002 under the title of *Correcting Conceptions* (Silsilat Tashih al-Mafahim), addressing the reasons behind the Islamic Group's ideological reorientation and explaining why jihad in Egypt had failed. Twelve other books followed, developing a critique of al-Qaeda's extreme ideology.[15]

In addition to ideological revisionism within these groups, the increasing interactions of radical Islamists with non-violent ones, as well as with non-Islamists, helped the process of embracing politics over violence to take root. This, surprisingly, occurred within Egypt's prison facilities, where inmates discussed their beliefs and tactics. The Muslim Brothers were the first to undergo such a process following the execution of Sayyid Qutb in 1966. Members of the movement began questioning the relevance of jihad as a way to combat the government, and many chose to reject violence. Another notable example of this dynamic was the interaction between the Islamic Group and the smaller, more radical Islamic Jihad that began in the 1990s and culminated in 2007, when the latter embraced non-violence to some degree. These efforts were led by the movement's former leader Sayyid Imam al-Sharif—also known as Abd al-Qadir Ibn Abd al-Aziz, or "Dr. Fadl." His *Document for the Right Guidance of Jihad in Egypt and the World* (Tarshid al-'Amal al-Jihadi fi Misr wa-l-'Alam) had an enormous impact within prisons and led numerous inmates to reject violent jihad.[16]

The state's use of repression and positive incentives vis-à-vis jihadist groups escalated following the September 11, 2001 terrorist attacks. In the case of the Islamic Group, the regime provided fighters with pensions, and the Interior Ministry offered other incentives such as business grants to reformed jihadists.[17] In addition, the heavy-handed approach of Egyptian security forces to radical movements encouraged the view that armed resistance was no longer a promising method for these elements to achieve their goals.

To be sure, these efforts to dissuade violence did not always resonate with group members. The case of Islamic Jihad, for which deradicalization has only been partially successful, illustrates this point. While the group's leaders have publicly abandoned violence, some affiliated factions continue to advocate jihad, sometimes even leaving the movement to join other groups more closely aligned with their beliefs. One cell of Islamic Jihad, for example, joined al-Qaeda in the early 2000s and was likely involved in the wave of attacks that hit Egypt after 2003. The Islamic Group faced similar difficulties. In a 2010 interview, Nagih Ibrahim, one of its former ideologues, emphasized that although the group's formal rejection of violence had obviously helped limit the spread of violent Islamism in Egypt, such ideological revisions had had less impact on the younger generations, especially those sympathetic toward or active within hardline jihadist groups such as al-Qaeda.[18]

By the same token, the Brotherhood's renunciation of violence was limited to the domestic sphere. The organization otherwise continued to praise terrorist acts conducted by its Palestinian off-shoot Hamas, as well as by the Iranian-backed Shi'ite militia Hezbollah. Several little-known violent groups, like the jihadist "Abdallah Azzam Brigades in Egypt" or the "Holy Warriors of Egypt,"[19] also emerged in the 2000s, spreading radical and extremist ideologies, conducting anti-regime activity, and accusing society and state institutions of "apostasy."[20] Another group calling itself "Monotheism and Holy War" (Tawhid wa-l-Jihad), which was connected to al-Qaeda, emerged during that period in the Sinai. It targeted the country's tourism sector in a wave of bombings that first hit the town of Taba in 2004 and then the resort towns of Sharm al-Sheikh and Dahab in 2005 and 2006.

The Sinai Peninsula, in particular, has been a hotbed for Islamic extremism for years. The Peninsula has been largely neglected by the state for decades, and clauses in the 1979 Egypt-Israel peace treaty restrict Egyptian security operations in the Sinai, though the two sides negotiated massive Egyptian deployments to combat jihadists in recent years under one of the treaty's annexes. During the 2000s, however, the mix of state neglect and insufficient security control enabled groups to develop smuggling networks, plan attacks, and develop local support, and a number of militant groups have expressed the goal of creating an independent Islamic Emirate in the Peninsula.

When Mubarak was ousted following Egypt's 2011 "Arab Spring" uprising, Islamic extremist activities there took on a new intensity. On multiple occasions, armed fighters attacked Egyptian security forces, police stations, and the al Arish-Ashkelon pipeline exporting natural gas to Israel and Jordan. Other operations targeted Israeli patrols and soldiers.[21] New jihadist groups emerged, such as the "Supporters of Holy War" (Ansar al-Jihad), while other existing groups like "Excommunication and Exodus" (Takfir wa-l-Hijra),[22] established in 1965 by Muslim Brother Shukri Mustafa, were reconstituted.[23] After the military ousted President Mohammed Morsi on July 3, 2013, violence surged, mostly propelled by relatively small insurgent groups, the most prominent of which was Ansar Beit al-Maqdis, which swore allegiance to the Islamic State in November 2014 and renamed itself Wilayat Sinai (Sinai Province).[24] On August 7, 2013, the army launched an operation into the Sinai and killed sixty suspected terrorists, losing thirty from its own ranks.[25] The Egyptian military remains engaged in an offensive counterterrorism campaign against these groups as of this writing.[26] Overall, the Sinai region with its mountainous terrain, particularly in the areas of Rafah and Sheikh Zuwaid, provides vast hideouts for jihadist networks and has become increasingly unstable since the July 3, 2013 coup. Egyptian authorities have since declared victory in their Sinai campaign,[27] but the Egyptian government's tight control over news regarding its operations in the Sinai make it difficult to assess the military's performance – or how lasting any order that the Egyptian government has managed to reestablish is liable to be.

Islamism and Society

Since the 1950s, failures in governance, economic stagnation, and political exclusion have provided opportunities for reactionary Islamists to expand their influence in Egyptian society. Islamists have used their politicized interpretation of Islam as a source of legitimacy, and they have set up a number of informal institutions (charities, educational organizations, health services) to advance their ideology within various sectors.[28] While some extremist groups started to renounce violence in the 1970s, this rejection almost always catalyzed the emergence of violent groups that rejected the renunciations. As a result, radical discourse perpetuated within Islamist circles even when groups were technically non-violent. For example, the Brotherhood continued to read and teach Sayyid Qutb's works even while claiming to have disavowed them.

Meanwhile, political stagnation and poor economic conditions under Mubarak generated sympathy for the Muslim Brotherhood and Salafist groups, which offered social services, religious education, and preaching.[29] Salafists inherit their name from the Arabic term "al-salaf al-salih," meaning the "righteous ancestors," a phrase referring to the first generations of Muslims after the Prophet Mohammed's death who sought to emulate his practices and maintained a literalist reading of the Qur'an and the hadith (the sayings of the Prophet). Salafists regard deviations from this literalist approach as bida'a (innovation), and therefore tantamount to kufr (apostasy). Under Mubarak, Salafists were strictly prohibited from political activities – in stark contrast to the Brotherhood, which was at times tolerated within formal politics and at other times repressed. Salafists therefore focused almost exclusively on social work and spiritual development, and were permitted to launch television networks dedicated to preaching. At the same time, the most prominent Salafist groups such as Salafist Call (al-Dawa al-Salfiyya) encouraged allegiance to the state, including at the height of the 2011 uprising, though some (typically younger) Salafists rejected this and joined the protests.

The presence of Salafists in Egypt began in the early 20th century. The first Salafist association, the "Sharia Assembly," was created in 1912, even before the formation of the Muslim Brotherhood. Another group, named the "Supporters of the Sunna" (Ansar Al-Sunna), was founded by Sheikh Mohammed Hamid al-Fiqi in 1926. Its members were focused on protecting monotheism and fighting un-Islamic practices and beliefs.

Salafism became more visible in Egypt during the 1970s and 1980s, for two reasons. First, as previously mentioned, President Sadat permitted Islamists greater freedom during this period to counter the leftists domestically. Second, Egyptians working abroad in Saudi Arabia and other Persian Gulf states returned home to Egypt. It was during this period that the organization "Salafist Call" was established. The Salafist Call is the preeminent Salafist organization in Egypt, and in the past has focused primarily on preaching and social service, but recently has shifted to focus on politics. In 1980, the Salafists institutionalized their activities, and the Salafist Call became active in education and charity. Yet the Egyptian state soon outlawed the movement, and regularly arrested its members.

Although few Egyptians openly identified as Salafists under the Mubarak regime, there were signs that their puritanical interpretation of Islam was gaining ground among the general public. This was, for instance, evidenced by the growing number of women wearing the niqab (full veil) and men growing their beards. Beyond the traditional role of radical imams in mosques, satellite television channels also started to adopt explicitly Salafist rhetoric, and widened their audience in the process.[30] The phenomenon was worrisome to a number of secular Egyptians, especially as it related to the protection of women's and minority rights, which most Salafists reject.

Radical Islamists have openly targeted religious minorities for years in an attempt to provoke sectarian warfare in Egypt. Coptic Christians, a community that represents 10 percent of the population, has been a special target of Salafist bigotry, though anti-Christian (and anti-Semitic) ideas also pervade Brotherhood teachings. Militant Salafists commonly portray Christians as "infidels" who conspire against Islam, and have regularly called for violent attacks on them.[31] The rise of Islamists following Mubarak's ouster brought these attitudes to the fore, as radical preachers called minorities "heretics" and threatened to expel them if they did not pay the jizya, a tax levied on non-Muslims, in certain instances.[32]

Since the 2011 uprising, Salafists have engaged in a massive anti-Coptic hate campaign. As a result, many Egyptian Christians left the country during this period, fearing for their future under Islamist rule.[33] In 2012, several Salafists accused Copts of being "traitors" for voting against Islamists in the presidential polls.[34] Then following Morsi's ouster in July 2013, dozens of churches were torched nationwide. Unfortunately, these types of attacks have continued under the rule of President Abdel Fattah al-Sisi, despite the fact that he is not an Islamist and the Coptic Orthodox Church's close official relations with him.

Salafists have also targeted other sects of Islam, such as the

Shi'a, Baha'i and Sufis, viewing them as un-Islamic because of their beliefs.[35] Before 2011, Salafists managed to ban the dhikr (a devotional act of Sufi orders) and continued to call for the prohibition of all Sufi ceremonies. In addition to labeling Sufis as "infidels," Salafists accuse them of encouraging sin and debauchery by mixing the sexes at shrines and during their rituals—a practice that Salafists consider improper. They have, for example, regularly pointed to the mosque of Ahmad al-Badawi in Tanta—where the founder of the Sufi Ahmadiyya order is buried—which does not enforce segregation between men and women, except during prayers, as one instance of un-Islamic behavior. Salafists also view ancient Egyptian monuments as idolatrous, and various Salafist groups threatened to cover the pyramids in wax following Mubarak's overthrow, when these groups appeared to be on the threshold of power.[36]

Finally, Salafists have increasingly targeted Egyptian women. Egyptian law requires that at least one candidate from each party be a woman. The Salafist Al-Nour party responded by running female candidates, but replacing their pictures with either a rose or a logo. On multiple occasions, Salafist leaders who have appeared on political talk shows insist either that they be separated from female hosts by a screen, or that the female hosts wear the veil. In 2011, the spokesman of the Salafist Daawa party, Abdel Moneim Alshahat, requested that host Iman al-Israf wear a headscarf during their interview. Al-Ishraf consented. After the interview, he told her that she should: "wear the veil now voluntarily before you have to wear it by force."[37]

Islamism and the State

From the 1970s until the overthrow of Mubarak, the Egyptian state actively fought violent Islamists who acted locally, but tolerated other Islamist groups at certain points while repressing them at others. The Muslim Brotherhood in particular used moments of tolerance to build its nationwide organization and win parliamentary seats, and it frequently generated public sympathy when the regime then cracked down on it.

The Brotherhood's greatest political success during these years came in 2005, when it fielded approximately 150 candidates in the parliamentary elections and won 88 of 444 contested seats, making it the largest opposition bloc. The regime viewed these gains as threatening, and it responded with a series of constitutional amendments in 2007 that limited the political participation of religious groups. The following year, these restrictions resulted in the rejection of more than 800 Muslim Brothers as candidates for local council elections. Additional constitutional changes further extended the "temporary" emergency law enforced after the assassination of President Anwar Sadat in 1981. And the adoption of a new anti-terrorism law (Article 179) gave security forces extensive powers to crack down on Islamists. During the November 2010 parliamentary elections, the repression worsened: hundreds of Muslim Brothers were arrested, and the organization's parliamentary candidates lost the most forged elections in Egypt's contemporary history.[38]

While the fraudulence of the late 2010 parliamentary elections contributed to the January 2011 uprising, the Brotherhood and Salafist groups largely stayed on the sidelines during its earliest days. Salafist groups largely preached fealty to the state, while the Brotherhood feared that its participation in the protests would catalyze an even more severe crackdown. (Indeed, the Mubarak regime warned the Brotherhood prior to the protests that it would decapitate the organization if it got involved.) Moreover, the Brotherhood's leaders were skeptical of the mostly non-Islamist youth activists who called for the protests.[39] After massive protests on January 25, 2011, however, the Brotherhood endorsed the pivotal January 28th "Friday of Rage" protests, during which protesters overwhelmed the police and forced the military to take control of the streets. The Brotherhood attempted to negotiate with the regime on at least two occasions during the uprising, but faced criticism from its youth members and revolutionary groups for doing so, and ultimately called for Mubarak's overthrow on February 7, 2011, four days before the Egyptian president was forced from power.[40]

Following Mubarak's overthrow and the collapse of his ruling National Democratic Party, Egypt's Islamist groups were the only political forces capable of mobilizing their members nationwide. Non-Islamist groups, by contrast, had been weakened after decades of mostly working within the regime's legal constraints. So when the

Supreme Council of the Armed Forces (SCAF) took control of the country on February 11, 2011 and opened Egypt's political arena, many of these Islamist groups quickly established legal political parties. In this vein, the Brotherhood announced in late April 2011 the creation of its "Freedom and Justice Party" (FJP), stating that its policies would be grounded in Islamic principles, but that the party would be non-confessional and tolerant, including both women and Christians in its ranks. In June 2011, the FJP received official recognition as a political party, enabling it to run candidates in the 2011-2012 parliamentary elections.

In a surprising and unexpected move,[41] the Salafist Call also entered party politics, establishing the "Light Party" (Hizb al-Nour), led by Imad Abd al-Ghaffour, as did the Islamic Group with its "Building and Development Party" (Hizb al-Bina' wa-l-Tanmia). The new Salafist end of the political spectrum also included smaller movements such as the ultraconservative "Al-Asala Party" in Cairo, founded by Adil Abd al-Maqsoud Afifi. This marked a considerable historical departure for Salafist groups, which had always been apolitical. Members of the groups generally refused to work with un-Islamic state institutions, dismissing the concept of democracy as "alien."[42] But under the guidance of charismatic preachers, Salafist movements opted for participation because they saw it as an opportunity to implement sharia and feared that their failure to participate would lead to Egypt's secularization.[43] Salafists also sought to provide ideological justification for their entry into politics. One important concern for leaders was to make sure that its members did not view the decision to enter the political arena as an abandonment of religious principles. Their arguments hinged on pointing to the duty incumbent on Muslims to try and implement sharia law wherever possible. Given the contested political environment of post-Mubarak Egypt, this duty was now achievable, and the alternative (namely, a secular regime) would constitute negligence of that duty.

Non-Islamist political parties, some of which had only recently been established and others whose growth was stunted during Mubarak's rule, fared poorly in the parliamentary elections of late 2011 and early 2012. By contrast, Islamists did extremely well: the

FJP-led Democratic Alliance for Egypt won 47 percent of the seats, while the Light Part-dominated Islamic Bloc, which included the Islamic Group's Building and Development Party, won 24 percent. The Wasat Party, an offshoot of the Brotherhood, won another two percent of the parliament.[44] The Salafists' electoral gains were by far the most unanticipated development of the election.[45]

The most critical issue before the resulting parliament was selecting the members of the Constituent Assembly, as that body would draft Egypt's new constitution. Muslim Brotherhood leader Saad al-Katatny was appointed parliamentary speaker, and Muslim Brothers became either the chairman or deputy chairman of 18 out of 19 total committees, and Salafist Ministers of Parliament had the chairmanships of three committees.[46] Though the Brotherhood and the Salafists certainly had their differences, both factions wanted a Constituent Assembly that was as Islamist as possible. The two groups collaborated to produce an Assembly that was roughly 65 percent Islamist. Non-Islamist Assembly members were alarmed by this turn of events, and responded by boycotting the Assembly. A court disbanded the Assembly just two weeks after it had been formed.

However, the Assembly was not the Brotherhood's last attempt to use its dominance in parliament to its advantage. The group did its best to undermine the SCAF's political legitimacy, including trying to use the parliament to declare no confidence in the SCAF-backed government. In response, the SCAF issued a statement that tacitly threatened with a major crackdown.[47]

In 2011, just before the collapse of Mubarak's regime, the Muslim Brotherhood had promised not to run a presidential candidate. The simmering tensions between the military and the Brotherhood, combined with the threat of a new crackdown, propelled the group into breaking that promise. Furthermore, former Muslim Brotherhood leader Abdel Moneim Abouel Fotouh had emerged as a dominant candidate in the presidential elections of May/June 2012. The Brotherhood had banished Abouel Fotouh from its ranks for declaring his intention to run for president, despite the group's orders not to do so. The Brotherhood was concerned that if it did not run its own approved candidate, its members would vote for a disgraced former member and cause chaos in the ranks.[48]

The Brotherhood's initial candidate was disqualified due to his incarceration during the Mubarak regime, as were several other leading candidates, for a variety of reasons. The Brotherhood nominated FJP chairman Mohammed Morsi.[49] The final list of candidates included thirteen people, including members of former governments. Hamdeen Sabbahi was a member of parliament during Nasser's time, Ahmed Shafiq was Mubarak's Prime Minister, and Amr Moussa was a former Foreign Minister. Morsi won with 24 percent of the vote,[50] and then won the run-off election against Shafik with 51.7 percent of the vote.

In June of 2012, a court disbanded the FJP-controlled parliament on the grounds that its election was unconstitutional, because the electoral format did not give political independents an equal opportunity to win. Also in June, the SCAF issued a constitutional declaration that protected the military from the president's oversight and granted itself legislative authority, to prevent Morsi from gaining power. In response, the Brotherhood and its allies occupied Cairo's Tahrir Square and threatened mass protests if Morsi did not become Egypt's president.

The constitutional declaration had significant impact. When Morsi was sworn in on June 30th, 2012, there was no parliament and no new constitution, and his exact powers were poorly defined.[51] On August 12, however, Morsi used a major attack in the Sinai that had taken place the previous week as a pretext for firing the SCAF's leaders, promoting director of military intelligence Abdel Fatah al-Sisi to defense minister, and issuing a new constitutional declaration granting himself legislative power until a new parliament was sworn in.[52]

This made Morsi Egypt's undisputed power holder, at least legally. But in November 2012, it appeared as though a second Constituent Assembly, which parliament had appointed before it was disbanded in June, was going to be nullified by the courts much as the first one had been. Morsi responded by issuing another constitutional declaration that protected the Constituent Assembly from the courts, but also placed his own edicts above any judicial oversight. It was effectively a total power grab, and when mass protests broke out, Morsi used the ensuing political crisis to ram through the ratification of a theocratic constitution.[53]

While the new constitution passed by 64 percent via referendum,[54] the political crisis persisted for months, with increasingly violent protests against Morsi erupting with greater regularity. Meanwhile, the economy plummeted, lines for gas extended around city blocks, and power shortages created outages lasting many hours on end.[55] As a result, on June 30, 2013, millions of Egyptians took to the streets to demand Morsi's ouster. When Morsi refused to compromise, the military responded by ousting Morsi on July 3, 2013.

In the wake of the coup, the Brotherhood gathered is members and allies in northern Cairo's Rabaa al-Adawiya Square and Giza's al-Nahda Square. Protesters denounced the interim government installed to replace Morsi as illegitimate. After negotiations between the new government and the Brotherhood broke down, security forces violently cleared these protests on August 14, 2013, killing at least 800 civilians, according to Human Rights Watch.[56]

After the clearing of Rabaa, the government arrested tens of thousands of Brotherhood leaders and supporters. Then, following a massive terrorist incident in al-Mansoura in December 2013, the government labeled the Muslim Brotherhood as a terrorist group.[5754] Ultimately, the government's crackdown on the Brotherhood appears to have been successful: with its leaders in prison, exile, or hiding, the organization has been decapitated, rendering it incapable of executing a nationwide strategy within Egypt.[58]

Meanwhile, the Brotherhood faces a significant internal crisis pitting younger members, who want to fight the current government with violence, against older leaders, who fear that Brotherhood violence will legitimate the regime's crackdown. The Brotherhood youth's wing appears to have won internal elections that were held in 2014, which explains the Brotherhood's January 2015 statement calling for jihad and martyrdom in fighting the regime. For a time, the "revolutionary" wing was backed by senior Brotherhood leader Mohamed Kamal, who endorsed and encouraged the use of violence against Egyptian security forces and state infrastructure, and commissioned a Brotherhood sharia body to draft an Islamic legal defense of his faction's violence, which was titled *The Jurisprudence of Popular Resistance to the Coup*.[59] This pitted him and his faction against the Brotherhood's "old guard," nominally headed by deputy supreme guide Mahmoud Ezzat, which has argued that the "revolutionary" wing's violence would legitimate the state's violence and accused Kamal's wing of defying the Brotherhood's internal hierarchy.[60]

The rift deepened following the arrest of several "old guard" leaders who had remained in hiding within Egypt in mid-2015, as the "old guard" blamed the "revolutionary" wing's violence for endangering senior leaders. For a brief period, however, the "revolutionary" wing appeared to have the upper hand, and took control of the organization's main web portal, ikhwanonline.com. But following Kamal's killing during an October 2016 raid, the "old guard" retook control of ikhwanonline.com. This did little to dampen the rift, however, and in early 2017, the Brotherhood's "revolutionary" wing launched a series of online pamphlets harshly criticizing the "old guard" leaders' conduct since the 2011 uprising, and called for establishing new structures for confronting the Egyptian regime.[61]

Due to these internal disagreements as well as the Egyptian government's repression, the Brotherhood no longer represents a significant threat to the current regime. The regime has sought to prevent the Brotherhood's possible reemergence by shutting down its social services and implementing strict restrictions on mosque preaching. In this vein, in mid-2016, the Egyptian government mandated that imams read government-approved sermons in Friday prayers. This edict was also intended to constrain Salafist preachers, despite the fact that the leading Salafist party—the Light Party—supported Morsi's overthrow and is the only Islamist group still participating in Egyptian politics.

In the Brotherhood's absence, however, other Islamist groups have emerged. Islamist youths who appear to have been affiliated with the Brotherhood have formed a variety of low-level insurgency groups, such as the Molotov Movement, Revolutionary Punishment, Liwaa al-Thawra, and Hassm, which focus their attacks on state infrastructure and security forces. At the same time, Sinai-based jihadists used the coup as a pretext for escalating their attacks on security forces. These groups also benefitted from the regional environment: state breakdown in Libya made weapons more available and therefore cheaper to acquire. These groups also aligned to varying extents with groups in Gaza, such as Hamas, in trying to destabilize the Egyptian government.

The most significant jihadist group is Ansar Bayt al-Maqdis (Supporters of Jerusalem). Ansar Bayt al-Maqdis started its violent operations immediately following Mubarak's ouster in 2011, targeting Israel and Israeli interests in Egypt, such as the al Arish-Ashkelon natural gas pipeline, which has been bombed repeatedly since 2011. Since the 2013 coup, however, the Egyptian military has been the organization's primary target and, as previously mentioned, the Egyptian military has been actively fighting ABM since September 2013.[62] Another jihadist group is Ajnad Misr ("Soldiers of Egypt"), which emerged in late January 2014, saying that it was targeting "criminal" elements of the regime. As of early February 2014, the group has claimed responsibility for seven attacks in Cairo.[63] Ansar Bayt al-Maqdis has referred to Ajnad Misr as "brothers" and suggested[64] that the two organizations have cooperated on attacks in the past, but neither the extent nor the nature of the collaboration is currently known.

While the rise of jihadist groups within Egypt since Morsi's ouster bodes ill for the country's long-term stability, Islamists overall exert less influence in Egypt today than they have in nearly five decades. The Brotherhood's rapid failure in power, combined with a broad anti-Brotherhood media campaign within Egypt, badly damaged the organization's image. And despite the attempts of some Brotherhood leaders to exert influence from exile in Istanbul, London, and elsewhere, they are increasingly detached from events on the ground. Moreover, the government's severe repression of the organization has deterred other Islamist organizations from escalating their activities, and many of the Brotherhood's initial allies in the "Coalition for Legitimacy" have either been imprisoned or resigned from the coalition. For this reason, those Islamists who have not joined jihadist movements have deferred their political ambitions until the current regime falls. They seek power in the long run, but for the time being are prioritizing their personal survival. Meanwhile, in November 2017, the Islamic State launched an attack on a mosque in Ismailia. Over 300 people were killed in what was called "the worst bloodshed of its kind in Egypt's modern history."[65] The attack was a stark reminder of the limits of the regime's ability to contain all Islamist groups operating in and around its borders.

In March 2018, President Al Sisi won reelection with a reported 97% of the vote.[66] Following his second term, Sisi has continued the crackdown of the Muslim Brotherhood, as well as other dissidents. Continued state repression of Islamists has also extended into the legal system. On July 5, 2018, 14 alleged members of the Muslim Brotherhood were sentenced to life in prison for their association with the now-outlawed organization.[67] Three weeks later, on July 28, 2018, an Egyptian court sentenced 75 people to death for their role in the 2013 protests. Despite the continued crackdown, however, reports have begun to circulate speculating a potential reconciliation between the Muslim Brotherhood and Sisi's regime. In July 2018, spokesman of the FJP, Dr. Hamza Zawba, confirmed that talks between the Brotherhood and Sisi regime had occurred in private.[68] Amid July 2018 court sentencings of Brotherhood members and demonstrators, an Egyptian appeals court overturned the verdict that placed 1,500 Brotherhood members on the national terror list.[69] The verdict was seen as a potential shift in attitudes regarding the Brotherhood, although its impact still remains unclear. As of August 2018, no official talks of reconciliation between the Muslim Brotherhood and Sisi's government have occurred.

Sisi's strategy in the Sinai has also undergone changes in recent months. Prior to his reelection, Sisi repeatedly spoke of the challenge posed by militants in the Sinai Peninsula. In February 2018, the Egyptian government launched Operation Sinai 2018 intended to eradicate Islamic State fighters and reinforce the army units already there.[70] Following mild success in suppressing terrorist activity in the Sinai, Sisi's government appears to be formulating a new strategy for counterterrorism in the region. Development projects, supported by a LE175 ($10 million) allocation for 2018 were announced in March. Projects are set to include "the electricity sector, roads, improving the environment, strengthening local units, and strengthening security, traffic, and fire departments' services."[71] Such regional buildup of infrastructure and local rule of law, it is hoped, will strengthen the regime's grip on the notoriously challenging region and further consolidate Sisi's power.

Endnotes

1. "Who are Egypt's militant groups?" BBC News, November 24, 2017, https://www.bbc.com/news/world-middle-east-34751349.
2. For an overview of the Muslim Brotherhood's formative ideology, see Hassan al-Banna's writings and memoirs, among which the *Letter To A Muslim Student* posits the core principles of the movement. For the English translation, see http://www.jannah.org/articles/letter.html.
3. For a detailed biography, see "Muhammad Rashid Rida," Encyclopedia Britannica online, n.d., http://www.britannica.com/EBchecked/topic/491703/Rashid-Rida.
4. Sayyid Qutb, *Milestones* (Kazi Publications, 2007).
5. "The Trial Of Omar Abdel Rahman," *New York Times*, October 3, 1995, http://www.nytimes.com/1995/10/03/opinion/the-trial-of-omar-abdel-rahman.html.
6. Holly Fletcher, "Jamaat al-Islamiyya," Council on Foreign Relations (CFR) *Backgrounder*, May 30, 2008, http://www.cfr.org/publication/9156/jamaat_alislamiyya.html.
7. Dana J Suster, "Egyptian political party wants off U.S. terrorist list," *Foreign Policy*, May 14, 2013, http://blog.foreignpolicy.com/posts/2013/05/14/egyptian_political_party_wants_off_us_terrorist_list.
8. "Egypt: 2011/2012 People's Assembly elections results," *Electoral Institute for Sustainable Democracy in Africa*, January 2013, http://www.eisa.org.za/WEP/egy2012results1.htm.
9. Kamel Kamel and Ramy Nawar, "Gamaa Islamiyya seeking political solution to current crisis," *The Cairo Post*, February 20, 2014, http://thecairopost.com/news/92346/news/gamaa-islamiyya-seeking-politi-

cal-solution-to-current-crisis.

10. Youssef H. Aboul-Enein, “Al-Ikhwan Al-Muslimeen: the Muslim Brotherhood,” *Military Review*, July-August 2003, 26-31, http://www.ikhwanweb.com/print.php?id=5617.
11. Barbara Zollner, *The Muslim Brotherhood: Hasan al-Hudaybi and Ideology* (London: Routledge, 2008).
12. This book was first published in 1991 and attacked the Brotherhood for its “betrayal” after “recognizing the legitimacy of secular institutions” in Egypt and “helping the Tyrants [the government]” repress *jihadists*. Ayman al-Zawahiri, *The Bitter Harvest: The Muslim Brotherhood in Sixty Years*, trans. Nadia Masid, (Egypt: n.p., 1991).
13. Ayman al-Zawahiri, *The Bitter Harvest: The Muslim Brotherhood in Sixty Years*, trans. Nadia Masid, (Egypt: n.p., 1991).
14. Omar Ashour, “Lions tamed? An inquiry into the causes of de-radicalization of armed Islamist movements: the case of the Egyptian Islamic Group,” *Middle East Journal* 61, no. 4, 2007, 596-597; Rohan Gunaratna and Mohamed Bin Ali, “De-Radicalization Initiatives in Egypt: A Preliminary Insight,” *Studies in Conflict & Terrorism* 32, no. 4, 2009, 277-291.
15. Among these are Karam Zuhdi, *The Strategy and the Bombings of Al-Qaeda: Mistakes and Dangers* (*Istratijiyyat wa Tajjirat al-Qa‘ida: Al-Akhta’ wa-l-Akhtar*) (Cairo: Al-Turath al-Islami, 2002); Nagih Ibrahim and Ali al-Sharif, *Banning Extremism in Religion and the Excommunication of Muslims* (*Hurmat al-Ghuluw fi-l-Din wa Takfir al-Muslimin*) (Cairo: Al-Turath al-Islami, 2002).
16. On this interactional process, see Omar Ashour, “De-Radicalization of Jihad? The Impact of Egyptian Islamist Revisionists on Al-Qaeda,” *Perspectives on Terrorism* II, no. 5, 2008, http://www.terrorismanalysts.com/pt/index.php?option=com_rokzine&view=article&id=39&Itemid=54. See also Lawrence Wright, “The Rebellion Within: An Al Qaeda mastermind questions terrorism,” *The New Yorker*, June 2, 2008, http://www.newyorker.com/reporting/2008/06/02/080602fa_

fact_wright?currentPage=all.

17. Ashour, "Lions tamed?"
18. See "Another Salafi-Jihadi Cell Arrested In Egypt," Middle East Media Research Institute *MEMRI TV* no. 5017, January 4, 2010, http://www.memritv.org/report/en/4193.htm.
19. Mohammad Mahmoud, "Islamic Group theorist: al-Qaeda's ideology in a state of decline," *Al-Shorfa.com*, August 2, 2010, http://www.al-shorfa.com/cocoon/meii/xhtml/en_GB/features/meii/features/main/2010/08/02/feature-01.
20. "Who are the Abdullah Azzam Brigades?" Reuters, August 4, 2010, http://uk.reuters.com/article/idUKTRE6733QJ20100804; Hugh Roberts, "Egypt's Sinai Problem," *The Independent*(London), April 26, 2006, http://www.crisisgroup.org/en/regions/middle-east-north-africa/egypt-syria-lebanon/egypt/egypts-sinai-problem.aspx.
21. "Egypt army dispatches team to Sinai following Eilat attack," *Ahram Online* (Cairo), April 17, 2013, http://english.ahram.org.eg/News/69484.aspx; Jodi Rudoren, "Sinai Attack Tests New Egyptian President's Relationship With Israel," *New York Times*, August 6, 2012, http://www.nytimes.com/2012/08/07/world/middleeast/sinai-attack-a-test-for-israel-egypt-and-gaza.html; "Pipeline Supplying Israel Is Attacked," Agence France Presse, February 4, 2012, http://www.nytimes.com/2012/02/05/world/middleeast/egyptian-pipeline-supplying-israel-is-attacked.html?_r=0.
22. See Bill Roggio, "Ansar al Jihad swears allegiance to al Qaeda's emir," *Long War Journal*, January 24, 2012, http://www.longwarjournal.org/archives/2012/01/ansar_al_jihad_swear.php.
23. See Abigail Hauslohner, "What Scares the Sinai Bedouin: the Rise of the Radical Islamists," *Time*, August 10, 2011, http://www.time.com/time/world/article/0,8599,2087797,00.html.
24. Abigail Hauslohner, "In Egypt's Sinai, insurgency taking root," *Washington Post*, July 28, 2013, http://www.washingtonpost.com/world/insurgency-takes-root-in-egypts-sinai/2013/07/28/2e3e01da-f7a4-11e2-

a954-358d90d5d72d_story.html; Stephanie McCrummen, "Car bombs hit military site in Egypt's Volatile Sinai Peninsula," *Washington Post*, September 11, 2013, http://www.washingtonpost.com/world/middle_east/car-bombs-hit-military-sites-in-egypts-volatile-sinai-peninsula/2013/09/11/53f6d30e-1ae3-11e3-80ac-96205cacb45a_story.html.

25. "Egypt since Mohammed Morsi was ousted: timeline" *ABC News*, August 15, 2013, http://www.abc.net.au/news/2013-08-15/egypt-since-mohammed-morsi-was-ousted3a-timeline/4887986.
26. Jacob Wirtschafter, "Egypt's Operation Sinai 2018 is an all-out war on militants," *The National*, February 10, 2018, https://www.thenational.ae/world/mena/egypt-s-operation-sinai-2018-is-all-out-war-on-militants-1.703394.
27. Jack Clause, "IS-Sinai Peninsula Hit by Egyptian Raids," *Center for Security Policy*, August 6, 2018, https://www.centerforsecuritypolicy.org/2018/08/06/is-sinai-peninsula-hit-by-egyptian-raids/.
28. See Samir Amin, "Egypt: Muslim Brotherhood - Revolutionary or Anti-Revolutionary?" *Pambazuka News*, July 4, 2012, http://www.pambazuka.org/en/category/features/83202.
29. On the rise and spread of Salafism in Egyptian society, see Nathan Field and Ahmed Hamem, "Egypt: Salafism Making Inroads," Carnegie Endowment for International Peace *Arab Reform Bulletin*, March 9, 2009, http://www.carnegieendowment.org/arb/?fa=-show&article=22823; Saif Nasrawi, "Egypt's Salafis: When My Enemy's Foe Isn't My Friend," *Al-Masry al-Youm* (Cairo), April 27, 2010, http://www.egyptindependent.com/news/egypt%E2%80%99s-salafis-when-my-enemy%E2%80%99s-foe-isn%E2%80%99t-my-friend.
30. On the media dimension, see Nathan Field and Ahmed Hamam, "Salafi Satellite TV In Egypt," *Arab Media & Society* no. 8, Spring 2009, http://www.arabmediasociety.com/?article=712.
31. See "Salafi Violence against Copts," *Islamopedia online*, n.d., http://www.islamopediaonline.org/country-profile/egypt/salafists/salafi-violence-against-copts.

32. See "Coptic (Catholic) priest: We will resist reimposition of jizya to the point of martyrdom," *Jihad Watch*, January 2, 2012, http://www.jihadwatch.org/2012/01/coptic-priest-we-will-resist-reimposition-of-jizya-to-the-point-of-martyrdom.html.
33. André Aciman, "After Egypt's Revolution, Christians Are Living in Fear," *New York Times*, November 19, 2011, http://www.nytimes.com/2011/11/20/opinion/sunday/after-egypts-revolution-christians-are-living-in-fear.html?pagewanted=all.
34. "Islamists in Egypt Blame Christians for Voting," *Assyrian International News Agency (AINA)*, May 29, 2012, http://www.aina.org/news/20120528191505.htm.
35. See Baher Ibrahim, "Salafi Intolerance Threatens Sufis," *The Guardian* (London), May 10, 2010, http://www.guardian.co.uk/commentisfree/belief/2010/may/10/islam-sufi-salafi-egypt-religion.
36. See Sarah Sheffer, "Salafi group reaffirms call to set Egypt's Pharaonic relics in wax," *bikyarmasr.com*, December 6, 2011, http://www.masress.com/en/bikyamasr/50394.
37. Raymond Ibrahim, "Calls to Destroy Egypt's Great Pyramids Begin," *Counter Jihad Report*, July 10, 2012, http://counterjihadreport.com/2012/07/10/calls-to-destroy-egypts-great-pyramids-begin/.
38. Mohammad Abdel Rahman, "Effacing Women in Salafi Campaign Bid," *Al-Akhbar*, November 15, 2011, http://english.al-akhbar.com/node/1505.
39. Yasmine Fathi, "Another Round of MB Arrests," Ahram Online (27 Nov. 2010): <http://english.ahram.org.eg/NewsContent/1/5/677/Egypt/Egypt-Elections-/Another-round-of-MB-arrests.aspx>.
40. "Egyptian Elections Watch: Al-Nour Party,", *Ahram Online* (Cairo), December 4, 2011, http://english.ahram.org.eg/NewsContentPrint/33/0/26693/Elections-/0/Al-Nour-Party.aspx.
41. Eric Trager, *Arab Fall: How the Muslim Brotherhood Won and Lost Egypt in 891 Days* (Washington: Georgetown University Press, 2016) 32-25.
42. See Omar Ashour, "The unexpected rise of Salafists has complicated Egyptian politics," *Daily Star*, January

6, 2012, http://www.dailystar.com.lb/Opinion/Commentary/2012/Jan-06/159027-the-unexpected-rise-of-salafists-has-complicated-egyptian-politics.ashx#ixzz1iz2mHPKa.

43. The Islamic Group declared: "We believe that the suffering we endured during the past years was due to neglecting religion and putting those who don't fear [God] in power (…) Islam can contain everyone and respects the freedom of followers of other religions to refer to their own Sharia in private affairs." See "Al-Gamaa Al-Islamiya calls for unity, says minority rights guaranteed," *Daily News Egypt*, September 1, 2011, http://www.dailynewsegypt.com/2011/09/01/al-gamaa-al-islamiya-calls-for-unity-says-minority-rights-guaranteed/.
44. Salafist cleric Yasser Burhami, who was instrumental in the establishment of the al-Nour party, declared that, "Islam must become involved of all aspects of life, even the political, and the Islamic movement must unite." See Hani Nasira, "The Salafist movement in Egypt" (*Al-Salafiyya fi Misr*), Al-Ahram Center for Political and Strategic Studies *Strategic Note* no. 46, 2011.
45. Jasmine Coleman, "Egypt election results show firm win for Islamists," *The Guardian* (London), January 21, 2012, http://www.theguardian.com/world/2012/jan/21/egypt-election-clear-islamist-victory.
46. Yolande Knell, "What will Salafists' election success mean for Egypt?" *BBC News*, December 12, 2011, http://www.bbc.co.uk/news/world-middle-east-16112833.
47. Sherif Tarek, "El-Katatni: From prisoner to speaker of parliament," *Ahram Online* (Cairo), January 24, 2012, http://english.ahram.org.eg/NewsContent/1/0/32600/Egypt//ElKatatni-from-prisoner-to-speaker-of-parliament.aspx.
48. Trager (2016) 122-124.
49. Trager (2016) 129-130.
50. Muslim Brotherhood and Salafists excluded from presidential poll," *Asia News*, April 16, 2012, http://www.asianews.it/news-en/Muslim-Brotherhood-and-Salafists-excluded-from-presidential-poll-24512.html.
51. Although some contest the electoral results. See Borzou

Daragahi, "Egypt nervously awaits election results," *Financial Times*, June 22, 2012, http://www.ft.com/cms/s/0/a17de564-bc5b-11e1-a470-00144feabdc0.html#axzz21WobfdCf.

52. Trager (2016) 145; Eric Trager, "Egypt," *World Almanac of Islamism,* March 2017.
53. Trager (2016) 157-160; Trager, *World Almanac of Islamism*
54. Trager (2016) 175-177; Trager, *World Almanac of Islamism.*
55. Trager (2016) 186-187; Trager, *World Almanac of Islamism.*
56. Trager (2016) 209; Trager, *World Almanac of Islamism.*
57. Ali Omar, "Muslim Brotherhood responds to NCHR Rabaa report," *Daily News Egypt*, March 8, 2014, http://www.dailynewsegypt.com/2014/03/08/muslim-brotherhood-responds-nchr-rabaa-report/.
58. Salma Abdelaziz and Steve Almasy, "Egypt's interim Cabinet officially labels Muslim Brotherhood a terrorist group," *CNN,* December 25, 2013, http://www.cnn.com/2013/12/25/world/africa/egypt-muslim-brotherhood-terrorism/.
59. Trager, *World Almanac of Islamism.*
60. Mohktar Awad, "The Rise of the Violent Muslim Brotherhood," Current Trends (27 Jul. 2017): <https://www.hudson.org/research/13787-the-rise-of-the-violent-muslim-brotherhood>.
61. Trager, *World Almanac of Islamism.*
62. These pamphlets are accessible at https://vision-28.com; Trager, *World Almanac of Islamism.*
"Profile: Egypt's militant Ansar Beit al-Maqdis group," *BBC News*, January 24, 2014, http://www.bbc.com/news/world-middle-east-25882504.
63. David Barnett, "Ajnad Misr claims 7th Cairo area attack, 6 wounded," *The Long War Journal*, February 7, 2014, http://www.longwarjournal.org/threat-matrix/archives/2014/02/ajnad_misr_claims_7th_cairo_ar.php.
64. Hamdi Alkhshali and Nadeem Muaddi, "Egyptian court sentences 75 people to death over 2013 demonstration," *CNN*, July 29, 2018, https://www.cnn.com/2018/07/28/middleeast/egypt-muslim-brotherhood-death-sentences/

index.html.

65. Yursi Mohamed and Mahmoud Mourad, "Islamic State raises stakes with Egypt mosque attack," *Reuters*, November 26, 2017, https://www.reuters.com/article/us-egypt-security-mosque/islamic-state-raises-stakes-with-egypt-mosque-attack-idUSKBN1DQ0K0.
66. John Davison and Ahmed Tolba, "Egypt's Sisi wins 97 percent in election with no real opposition," *Reuters*, April 2, 2018, https://www.reuters.com/article/us-egypt-election-result/egypts-sisi-wins-97-percent-in-election-with-no-real-opposition-idUSKCN1H916A.
67. "Egypt sentences 14 to life for belonging to banned Islamists," *The Associated Press*, July 5, 2018, https://wtop.com/middle-east/2018/07/egypt-sentences-14-to-life-for-belonging-to-banned-islamists/.
68. Murat Sofuoglu, "Will Egypt's Sisi ever reconcile with the Muslim Brotherhood?" *TRT World*, July 12, 2018, https://www.trtworld.com/magazine/will-egypt-s-sisi-ever-reconcile-with-the-muslim-brotherhood--18865.
69. "Egypt's top appeals court overturns 'terror list' ruling on Morsi," *Al Jazeera*, July 4, 2018, https://www.aljazeera.com/news/2018/07/egypt-top-appeals-court-overturns-terror-list-ruling-morsi-180704171711654.html.
70. Zvi Mazel, "Five years after the revolution: Is Egyptian President El-Sisi winning the battle?" *Jewish News Syndicate*, July 15, 2018, https://www.jns.org/opinion/five-years-after-the-revolution-is-egyptian-president-al-sisi-winning-the-battle/.
71. Al-Masry Al-Youm, "Govt allocates LE174.5 mn for this year's North Sinai development projects," *Egypt Independent*, March 22, 2018, https://www.egyptindependent.com/govt-allocates-le174-5-mn-years-north-sinai-development-projects/.

Quick Facts

Population: 54,841,552
Area: 1,219,090 sq km
Ethnic Groups: Black African 80.2%, white 8.4%, colored 8.8%, Indian/Asian 2.5%
Government Type: Parliamentary republic
GDP (official exchange rate): $344.1 billion (2017 est.)

Source: CIA World FactBook (Last Updated April 2018)

Introduction

Although there was a strong Islamist current in the Palestinian national movement of the British Mandate Period, the Israeli War of Independence (1947–49) and subsequent policies adopted by the Israeli government kept Islamism largely at bay until the 1970s. Islamism regained popularity in the wake of Iran's 1979 Islamic Revolution, spreading to the Palestinian Territories and even into Israel itself as Israeli Arabs have shown increasing identification with their Palestinian cousins in the West Bank and Gaza Strip. Israeli preoccupation with secular Arab nationalist groups in the 1970s and 80s enabled Islamism to metastasize unfettered. In recent years, the phenomenon is manifested most concretely in the Islamic Movement of Israel. Today, the lack of strong governmental oversight in the Sinai Province has led to militant Islamist infiltration of the area, and poses significant threats to Israeli national security.

Islamist Activity

Hamas

The Islamist group known by the acronym HAMAS ("the Islamic resistance movement" in Arabic) is the premier Islamist faction in the Palestinian Territories, and the principal extremist threat to the state of Israel. Its precursor was an Islamist group known as

Mujama al-Islamiya. In the 1970s, over the objections of moderate Palestinians,[1] the Israeli government permitted Sheikh Ahmed Yassin, the leader of the Muslim Brotherhood in the Gaza Strip, to register Mujama al-Islamiya, first as a charity and then, in 1979, as an association.[2] At first, the group devoted itself primarily to building schools, clinics, and libraries. Mujama al-Islamiya refrained from anti-Israel violence in its early years, but when the First Intifada erupted in December 1987, Yassin and some of his Mujama al-Islamiya colleagues founded Hamas. Hamas promotes fundamentalist Islamic norms, such as requiring women to wear the hijab and allowing polygamous unions. Furthermore, Hamas has committed itself to waging an armed struggle to obliterate Israel and to establish an Islamic state governed by sharia law "from the Jordan River to the Mediterranean Sea."[3] To that end, Hamas engineered dozens of suicide bombings that killed hundreds of Israelis. Hamas carried out almost 40 percent of suicide attacks during the Second Intifada (2000-2005), far more than any other group.[4]

Hamas, despite being a Sunni movement, benefits significantly from Iranian support. Iran has provided military assistance to Hamas since the early 1990s. It has also provided both rhetorical and logistical support to the group in its operations. In 2002, Israel captured the *Karine A,* a ship destined for the Gaza Strip and carrying 50 tons of advanced weaponry on board. The ship had been stocked in Iranian waters.[5] Iran has also provided substantial financial aid to Hamas. In December 2006, Hamas reported on its website that Iran had provided the organization with $250 million.[6] After Operation Cast Lead in 2008–2009, Iran provided Hamas with a variety of weapons, including Grad rockets with range of 20–40 km, anti-tank missiles and others. Along with the military aid, Iran has provided advanced training for Hamas operatives with instructors from the Iranian Revolutionary Guards, as well as propaganda support.[7]

The Syrian civil war initially proved detrimental to the relationship between Hamas and Iran. Hamas refused to support Syrian dictator Bashar al-Assad, one of Iran's key allies.[8] In response to this refusal, Tehran cut off Hamas's funding, which amounted to about $23 million per month.[9] This move forced Hamas to seek out alternative sources of funding, including from wealthy Sunni states such as Qatar[10] and Saudi Arabia. However, Hamas and Iran eventually reconciled, and in 2015 Iran began supplying Hamas with military technology, helping it repair tunnels destroyed in the 2014 conflict with Israel, and hosting Hamas delegations in Iran.[11]

Like many militant groups, Hamas has secured popular support among Palestinians and pursued recruitment through community service and engagement. Hamas provides schools, hospitals, and other necessary social services. Hamas guarantees to the family of its suicide bombers economic assistance, including education, healthcare, and funeral expenses. This financial support—especially in impoverished communities—serves as a continuing recruitment driver.[12]

Though Hamas is more active and powerful in Palestinian communities, Israeli Arabs have also been involved with the organization. In May 2011, the Haifa District Court sentenced an Israeli Arab to five years in prison for conspiring with his brother-in-law to gather an arms cache in Israel for Hamas.[13] The same year, Israeli authorities arrested two Arab residents of East Jerusalem holding Israeli citizenship who were planning to attack Jerusalem's Teddy Stadium during a Premier League soccer match. Authorities divulged that the two men had longstanding ties with Hamas.[14]

In the face of international pressure, Hamas cosmetically modified its charter to make it appear more moderate. The amended charter still refuses to relinquish the claim to every part of British Mandate Palestine. However, it acknowledges "the establishment of a fully sovereign and independent Palestinian state, with Jerusalem as its capital along the lines of the 4th of June 1967, with the return of the refugees and the displaced to their homes from which they were expelled, to be a formula of national consensus."[15]

Islamic Movement in Israel

The Islamic Movement in Israel is a Sunni group, founded by Abdullah Darwish, that advocates for the vital role of Islam in public life in Israel. Much like Hamas, the Islamic Movement courts favor from local populations through providing social services. During the First Intifada, the Islamic Movement established the Islamic Relief Committee, the stated purpose of which was to provide assistance to injured Palestinians. In 1993, the Islamic Movement split in response to internal discord over the Oslo Accords. Darwish supported accepting the accords, while more hardline members, such as Sheikh Ra'ed Salah and Sheikh Kemal Khatib, did not support the agreement. The hardline faction became known as the Northern Branch (as the majority of its leaders came from northern Israel).[16] Darwish led the more moderate Southern Branch. The Northern Branch played a part in inciting the Second Intifada in 2000. Specifically, incitement by the group helped instigate clashes between Israeli Arabs and police in the Wadi Ara region in October 2000—clashes that left 13 protesters dead.[17]

Most of the Islamic Movement's support within Israel comes from the Bedouin community (discussed further below). In November 2015, the Israeli government designated the Northern Branch of the Islamic Movement and its 17 affiliated charities illegal, and jailed its leader, Ra'ed Salah. To circumvent the ban, members of the Northern Branch of the Islamic Movement founded a new group, the Trust and Reform Party, in 2016. The head of the party, Husam Abu Leil, was the second deputy head of the Islamic Movement's Northern Branch.[18] In November 2016, the Shin Bet arrested two Israeli Arabs who were planning an attack on Israeli Defense Forces (IDF) troops in retaliation for the Northern Branch's proscription.[19]

Palestinian Islamic Jihad (PIJ)

Palestinian Islamic Jihad emerged in Gaza in 1981 as a fusion of the Islamism advocated by Omar Abdel-Rahman, the spiritual leader of Egyptian Islamic Jihad, with Palestinian nationalism. Its founders included Fathi Shaqaqi and Abd al-Aziz al-Awda, who were affiliated with Egyptian Islamic Jihad until their expulsion from Egypt after Sadat's assassination,[20] as well as several members of the secular Popular Liberation Forces. PIJ quickly became one of the most violent Palestinian factions, assassinating the commander of the Israeli military police in the Gaza Strip in August 1987 and launching a wave of suicide bombings.[21]

Israel deported Shaqaqi and al-Awda to southern Lebanon in 1988, and in 1989 Shaqaqi decided to relocate the official command to Damascus.[22] According to the U.S. State Department, PIJ's high-ranking leadership is located in Syria while some leaders live in Lebanon, though most of its affiliates live in Gaza.[23] After the Mossad killed Shaqaqi in 1995, Ramadan Shallah, previously a professor at the University of South Florida, became head of the organization.[24] PIJ is much smaller than Hamas and consists of around 1,000 members[25] (although in 2011, the organization was reported to have at least 8,000 fighters in Gaza).[26] The PIJ, like Hamas, is ardently committed to the violent destruction of Israel,[27] but unlike Hamas spends little time on social services for Palestinians in Gaza and the West Bank, where it is active today. The organization's armed wing is called the al-Quds Brigades and, despite its small size, was responsible for more than a quarter of the suicide bombings during the Second Intifada.[28] In recent years, the organization has intensified its firing of rockets from Gaza into Israel.[29]

PIJ maintains a degree of support from Israeli Arabs. In August 2008, Israeli authorities arrested a five-man PIJ cell, which included two Israeli Arabs accused of planning an attack on an army checkpoint near Ramallah and of planning to assassinate Israeli pilots, scientists, and university professors.[30] Then, in January 2013, Israeli police detained three members of a PIJ cell at the Eyal Junction in the Sharon region. The men, including two Palestinians from Jenin and an Israeli Arab from Tira, planned to kidnap an Israeli soldier and trade him for the release of incarcerated Palestinian terrorists.[31]

Though the group is Sunni, PIJ is nonetheless strongly influenced by the model of Islamic political activism embodied by Iran's 1979 Revolution.[32] As a result, Iran has historically provided extensive support to the group via funding, as well as military equipment and training. In 1998 it was revealed that Iran had allocated $2 million to PIJ's annual budget. Since then, the Iranian support to PIJ has been much higher. In 2013 PIJ sources stated that they received from Iran around $3 million per month.[33] According to Ali Nourizadeh, director of the Center for Iranian Studies in London, Iran at the time transferred to the organization $100–150 million every year.[34]

However, in 2015, tensions between the group and Iran began to appear, due to PIJ's refusal to condemn the Sunni Gulf state attacks, led by Saudi Arabia, against the Houthi rebels in Yemen.[35] In 2015, a senior leader at PIJ acknowledged that the organization was suffering from the worst financial catastrophe since its foundation due to Iran curtailing its financial support.[36] According to various reports in 2016, Iran cut its support for the organization by 90 percent.[37] However, Iran resumed funding PIJ in 2016 to the tune of $70 million a year, compared with $50 million for Hamas.[38]

Hezbollah

Hezbollah is a Shia Muslim militia that engages in terrorist activity while maintaining a robust political/social-welfare wing.[39] The organization was founded in 1982 during the Lebanese Civil War with significant support from the Iranian Revolutionary Guard Corps (IRGC).[40] In its founding statement,[41] Hezbollah professes its loyalty to Iran's supreme leader, Ayatollah Ruhollah Khomeini; calls for the establishment of an Islamic regime; and demands the removal of the United States, France, and Israel from Lebanon, in addition to the annihilation of Israel.[42] Iran regards Hezbollah as a proxy and vehicle for spreading its influence through the region. The Islamic Republic provides financial support, training, and advanced weaponry to Hezbollah.[43] In total, Iran's support is estimated at $100–200 million per year, including weaponry, training, and logistical support. In addition, Iran funds Hezbollah's television channel *Al-Manar*, providing approximately $15 million annually.[44]

Hezbollah coalesced following the 1982 Israeli invasion of Lebanon to oust the Palestinian Liberation Organization (PLO). Soon after the PLO evacuated Beirut for Tunis, Shia militias began attacking the IDF. Hezbollah was formed through the amalgamation of some of the aforementioned Shia militias and launched a guerilla war to expel the IDF from Lebanon. In 1985, the IDF withdrew to the "security belt" in southern Lebanon, where it proceeded to fight a 15-year war against Hezbollah. Then-Israeli Prime Minister Ehud Barak attempted to alter this equation in 2000 by removing Israel's remaining forces from Lebanon. Following Israel's withdrawal, however, Hezbollah quickly became the dominant political force in the country.[45] Hezbollah officially entered politics in the 1992 parliamentary elections, and has continued to grow in influence and power since, to the point that it is now represented in the Lebanese cabinet.

According to Israeli Security Agency (ISA) assessments, following Israel's withdrawal from Lebanon in 2000, Hezbollah began to focus on penetrating the Israeli Arab population. Hezbollah sees Israeli Arabs as valuable operatives because they have the advantage of being Israeli citizens who enjoy freedom of movement and accessibility to targets.[46] While the majority of its activities are affiliated with Fatah's al-Aqsa Martyrs Brigades, Hezbollah also cooperates with Hamas, PIJ, and the Popular Front for the Liberation of Palestine (PFLP).[47] Hezbollah uses its international presence to recruit Israeli Arabs when they travel outside of Israel.[48]

Hezbollah is known for its cross-border operations in addition to extensive terrorist activities abroad, such as attacks in Argentina targeting the Israeli embassy in Buenos Aires and the Jewish community center there, in 1992 and 1994, respectively,[49] as well as an attack against a bus carrying Israeli tourists in Burgas, Bulgaria, in 2012. Hezbollah maintains a large presence of supporters and operatives all around the world, including North and South America, Africa, Asia, and Europe.[50] Some of the attacks carried out by the organization were initiated and directed by Iran, such as the Khobar Towers bombing in Saudi Arabia in 1996 and the attacks in Argentina.[51]

After Hezbollah operatives killed eight Israeli soldiers and captured two more in 2006, Israel and Hezbollah descended into a 33-day war.[52] During the conflict, Hezbollah launched thousands of rockets into Israel.[53] Although the war ended in a stalemate,[54] given Israel's overwhelming military advantage, Hezbollah could portray the outcome as a victory. Since 2006, the northern border has seen relatively little terrorist activity.[55] In February 2017, Hezbollah leader Hassan Nasrallah threatened to attack Israel's nuclear reactor in Dimona, and has previously threatened to attack ammonia supplies in Haifa.[56]

Along with Iran, Syria has historically been a key supporter of Hezbollah. When the Arab Spring threatened the stability of the Assad dictatorship, both Iran and Hezbollah intervened to support the regime. Hezbollah has lost approximately 1,800 fighters in the Syrian Civil War[57] and has squandered most of the popularity among Sunnis won during the 2006 war with Israel.[58] As the Syrian regime and Hezbollah wrest control of more of the Syrian-Israeli border from the rebels, Jerusalem fears that Israel will become more vulnerable to Hezbollah terrorism.[59]

Al-Qaeda and the Islamic State

Israel has more often been a rhetorical target of al-Qaeda than an actual one.[60] In almost every one of his public statements between 1990 and 2011, Osama bin Laden referenced the Palestinian issue. A 2001 Treasury Department report reveals that the group's Iraqi emir, Abu Musab al-Zarqawi, had received more than $35,000 for training Jordanian and Palestinian operatives in Afghanistan and enabling their travel to the Levant with assurances that he would receive more funding for attacks against Israel.[61] However, nothing came of these attacks and "al Qaeda's plotting against Israel has never matched its anti-Israel propaganda."[62]

However, there have been some exceptions. In 2010, four Israeli Arabs were among those charged by Israeli authorities with establishing a terror cell and killing a taxi driver.[63] Two of the plaintiffs had trained at an al-Qaeda camp in Somalia.[64] In January 2014, Israeli officials revealed an al-Qaeda plot in Israel with a direct involvement of senior leaders of the organization. According to the reports, an al-Qaeda operative in Gaza run by Zawahiri recruited three men (two from East Jerusalem and one from the West Bank) through Skype and Facebook. All four operators were arrested. [65]

More recently, the Islamic State (ISIS) has likewise emerged as a threat to Israeli security. An offshoot of al-Qaeda,[66] in 2014 ISIS managed to occupy vast areas in the region of Iraq and Syria and to take control over the population in its territory. However, American and European airstrikes completely cleared ISIS from Iraq while reducing its domain in Syria to less than 5% of the nation's territory,[67] forcing the organization to expand into secondary territories, such as in Libya and the Sinai.[68]

The affiliate that proves most dangerous for Israel is the Sinai Province of the Islamic State, formerly known as Ansar Bayt al-Maqdis. The organization is located in the Sheikh Zweid area in the northern Sinai Peninsula, near the border with Israel,[69] and commands approximately 1,500 members.[70] The group pledged allegiance to ISIS on November 2014 with an emphasis on the importance of fighting the Jews:

> After decades . . . Allah ordered the flag of jihad to be raised in our land and gave us the honor of being

> the soldiers [Allah] chose to fight the nation's most bitter enemies . . . the Jews. . . . Our swords will be extended against them until Allah is victorious.[71]

The Sinai Province affiliate has launched several attacks against Israel over the past few years, including a combined attack that was carried out against a bus in Eilat in August 2011, several rocket attacks on Eilat, and attacks against the gas pipeline between Egypt and Israel in north Sinai.[72]

Israeli Arabs have not proven immune to ISIS's appeal. At least 60 Israelis, including two Jewish converts to Islam, have traveled to Syria or Iraq to fight with jihadist groups, leading Israel to revoke the citizenship of 19 known to be fighting with ISIS.[73] And, in October 2017, Israel sentenced a resident of Sakhnin, Wissam Zbedat, to nearly six years in prison for fighting with ISIS. His wife, who accompanied him to the Islamic State, was sentenced to four years.[74] Also, since the beginning of 2015, a number of Israeli citizens were arrested for supporting ISIS. In June 2015, the Israeli Security Agency uncovered six Hura residents, including several teachers, spreading ISIS's ideology in the Israeli school system and planning to join ISIS in Syria.[75] Even as ISIS territory shrank in Syria and Iraq, support for the group grew in some Arab Israeli quarters. In 2017, the Shin Bet arrested two 17-year-old boys from Barta'a and another minor from East Barta'a in the West Bank, who swore allegiance to ISIS and manufactured an improvised explosive device.[76] Then, the Shin Bet arrested two 19-year-old Bedouin women, Rahma and Tasnin al-Assad, from the village of Lakia in January 2018 for providing intelligence to a foreign ISIS handler and planning attacks in Israel, including one on a New Year's celebration.[77]

Uncoordinated Terrorism

Greater security cooperation between Israel and the Palestinian Authority since the end of the Second Intifada has greatly diminished the number of bombings and other coordinated attacks. Today, lone wolf attacks predominate. In recent years, there have been several spikes in lone wolf attacks, mostly committed by Palestinian residents of East Jerusalem. One spike was in the summer of 2014 after the murder and immolation of a Muslim teenager, Mohammad

Abu Khdeir, by Jewish terrorists in retaliation for the kidnapping and murder of three Jewish teenage hitchhikers at Alon Shvut.[78] The violence took the form of vehicular assault, stabbings, stone throwing, and arson. The use of firecrackers was particularly prominent.[79] Rioters also targeted East Jerusalem infrastructure, destroying three light rail stations.[80] Some of the attacks were more deadly, such as the November 18, 2014, Jerusalem synagogue attack in which two cousins from East Jerusalem massacred five civilians and a police officer with a gun, knives, and axes.[81] In the previous weeks a member of Hamas killed a three-month-old girl in a vehicular assault at a Jerusalem train station while others committed fatal stabbing attacks in Alon Shvut and Tel Aviv.[82]

Another spike in terrorism occurred during the 2017 Temple Mount Crisis. Accusations that Israel will annul the Supreme Muslim Council's control of the Temple Mount often provoke violence. On July 14, 2017, three Israeli Muslims from Umm al-Fahm who were affiliated with the Northern Branch of the Islamic Movement murdered two policemen at the Temple Mount. The Israeli government responded by placing metal detectors at the entrances to the site. The security measure elicited a furious reaction, expressed through terrorism. One particularly gruesome attack involved the fatal stabbing of three people during a Shabbat dinner in Halamish. After the attack, police found the perpetrator's suicide note, which explicitly cited the Temple Mount controversy as justification for the murders.[83] Ultimately, the Israeli Cabinet voted to remove all security measures introduced at the Temple Mount after the 14 July attack.

The Palestinian Authority exacerbated the violence by calling for a "day of rage" in East Jerusalem and the West Bank in response to the metal detectors,[84] approving demonstrations organized by the Fatah affiliated Tanzim militia against the Israeli security measures,[85] and offering free university tuition to students participating in the subsequent rioting.[86] PA incitement against Israel stretches back to its establishment, when it assumed responsibility for the Palestine Mujahidin and Martyrs Fund, renamed the Palestinian Authority Martyrs Fund, which pays stipends to families of Palestinians imprisoned, injured, or killed for terrorism against Israelis. In

2017, the fund paid terrorists and their families over $347 million according to PA records.[87]

Islamism and Society

Israel's population numbers nearly 8.6 million people, 74.6 percent of which is Jewish,[88] and 17.7 percent is Muslim.[89] Within this body politic, however, deep divisions exist over the future of the state. According to a study conducted by Pew Research Center in 2015, 76 percent of Israeli Jews believe that Israel can simultaneously be a Jewish state and a democracy, whereas only 27 percent of Israeli Arabs agree with this sentiment. However, 60 percent of Israeli Arabs have a positive view of the state and 49 percent of Israeli Muslims do.[90]

The tension between Israel and its Arab citizens is also evident in the traditionally nomadic Bedouin community. Official Israeli neglect of the Bedouin communities in the Negev and difficulty transitioning from a nomadic to a sedentary lifestyle has spawned increasing alienation from the state among that community—an alienation that the Northern Branch of the Islamic Movement is exploiting. Thus, when the military planned a parade through Rahat, Israel's largest Bedouin town, to celebrate Israel's 63rd independence day in 2011, the town's mayor, Faiz Abu Sahiban, who belongs to the Islamic Movement, objected, preferring to commemorate the 1948 exodus of the Palestinian refugees instead.[91] This came in the wake of violent resistance to the Israeli government demolishing a mosque built illegally on public land in 2010 by the Northern Branch of the Islamic Movement.[92]

Concerns that Bedouin alienation might breed violence increased when two Bedouin from the Negev, Mahmoud Abu Quider, aged 24, and his 21-year-old brother Samah, confessed in January 2013 to planning to fire rockets, mount a suicide bombing at the Beer Sheba Central Bus Station, and launch other attacks. Before their arrest, the brothers built several explosive devices and traded drugs for an IDF soldier's rifle.[93] In another incident in 2015, Bedouin teachers from the South were suspected of promoting the ideology of the Islamic State in a local school.[94] The perpetrator of a deadly terrorist attack in Beer Sheba in October 2015 attended the same school.[95]

Then, in December 2017, two Bedouin stabbed to death an Israeli soldier at an Arad bus stop.[96]

The Northern Branch is increasingly penetrating the Negev and successfully discouraging Bedouin from joining the IDF, where a high percentage of Bedouin have historically served, mainly in scouting or tracking capacities. Furthermore, as the Islamic Movement has gained control of more town councils in Bedouin areas, they have been able to use their authority to obstruct the hiring of Bedouin who serve in the military.[97] There has been a public debate over whether young Arab Israelis should be perform mandatory military or national service. In this case, opinions are significantly divided between Jewish and Arab respondents; the majority of the Jews polled support this requirement (74.1 percent) while the majority of Arabs oppose it (71.8 percent).[98]

Despite the growth of the Islamic Movement, the Israeli Muslim community remains less religious than the Palestinians of the West Bank and Gaza. According to a 2016 Pew survey, 68 percent of Israeli Muslims say religion is very important in their lives, while the corresponding number among Palestinians is 85 percent.[99] Likewise, support for terrorism is much lower among Israeli Muslims. A 2014 Pew Research Center poll found that while 46 percent of Palestinians in the West Bank and Gaza believe suicide bombings can be justified to defend Islam "often" or "sometimes," only 16 percent of Israeli Muslims feel that way.[100]

Islamism and the State

Israel has struggled with Islamism and Islamist sentiment both internally and externally. Officially, Israel sees the political-legal status of Israeli Arabs as a purely domestic matter without strategic implications. At the same time, however, it has traditionally refused to recognize Israeli Arabs as a national minority possessing collective rights apart from specific cases (such as in the education system and family law, each religious community being subject to its own clerics). This opening in the education system has enabled Israeli Arabs to cultivate a separate national identity—and created an ideological space in which Islamism can increasingly take root.

The country's Education Ministry has attempted to counter

Islamism by banning the teaching of the Nakba ("catastrophe," the common Arabic reference for the establishment of Israel in 1948) in schools, by forcing students to sing Hatikva (the Israeli national anthem) and by rewarding schools that encourage military and national service. Many Israeli Arab leaders have voiced opposition to the campaign to promote Israeli Arab participation in national service, terming it a veiled attempt by the government to erode the community's sense of unity.[101]

Externally, Israel's national security was deeply and negatively impacted by the Arab Spring in 2011. First and foremost, the overthrow of the Mubarak regime in Egypt in February 2011 undermined law and order in the Sinai Peninsula, enabling al-Qaeda to develop a base there. As of May 2011, senior Egyptian security officials estimated that over 400 al-Qaeda militants were then operating in the Sinai Peninsula.[102] The growing Islamist presence in the Sinai resulted in increasing terrorism originating from the territory. In August 2011, eight Israelis were killed in a cross border attack by militants belonging to the Mujahideen Shura Council from the Environs of Jerusalem, an al-Qaeda affiliate founded in 2011 and operational in Gaza and Sinai. The Mujahideen Shura Council launched rocket attacks on Sderot in August 2012[103] and March 2013, during President Obama's visit to Israel,[104] as well as to Eilat in April 2013.[105] However, today, the main threat to Israel from its southern border is Sinai Province.

Islamist militants have also attacked key infrastructure that lies outside Israel's borders. As of April 2012, Islamic militants have carried out at least fourteen attacks on the Egyptian pipeline passing through the Sinai that previously provided Israel with 40 percent of its natural gas.[106] From the end of the Mubarak regime until June 2012, there was a significant increase in the number of attacks against the gas pipelines in the region and terrorist infiltration to Israel.[107] Salafi-jihadists see the pipelines as an instance of an Islamic resource sold to the Zionist enemy.[108]

Smuggling is another issue of concern to the Israeli security forces. Israel's withdrawal from the Gaza Strip significantly increased the smuggling of weapons, food and fuel to Gaza.[109] This was much intensified after Hamas takeover of Gaza in 2007.[110]

Alongside the smuggling, the organization created an extensive network of tunnels contributing to the Gazan economy $230 million per month.[111] During Operation Protective Edge in 2014, one of Israel's goals was to terminate cross border tunnels, which were widely used for smuggling arms and people. The IDF destroyed of 32 tunnels. Unfortunately, Israel has not yet fully succeeded in developing technology to deal with the tunnels.[112] IDF officials and residents living near the Gazan border have expressed worry that Hamas is reconstructing its tunnels demolished in 2014.[113] The Israeli-Egyptian border (around 230 kilometers in length) is also characterized by extensive smuggling of people, drugs, weapons, and goods. After the Israeli disengagement, the Israeli-Egyptian border has also become a transit point of two types of terrorists: specialists in the manufacture of weapons and terrorists on their way to attack Israel.[114]

There are several looming threats to Israel's security. First is a more powerful Hezbollah, which gained valuable battlefield experience in Syria and may entrench itself on the Syrian-Israeli border after the Assad regime regains control of the area. Second, the deteriorating economic situation in Gaza, where more than 60% of the population is dependent on humanitarian aid,[115] increases the likelihood of another war between Israel and Hamas, which desperately wants to break the naval blockade of the Strip. The current Hamas-orchestrated demonstrations along the Gaza-Israel border wall, which have already resulted in 25 Palestinian fatalities, also risk igniting another war.[116] Lastly, Israel must confront greater radicalization of its Arab citizens, particularly the Bedouin, long the country's poorest group by several orders of magnitude.[117]

Endnotes

1. Anat Kurz and Nahman Tal, “Hamas: Radical Islam in a National Struggle,” Tel Aviv University Jaffee Center for Strategic Studies Memorandum no. 48, July 1997.
2. Andrew Higgins, “How Israel Helped to Spawn Hamas,” *Wall Street Journal*, January 24, 2009, http://online.wsj.com/article/SB123275572295011847.html.
3. Khaled Mash’al, “We Will Not Relinquish an Inch of Palestine, from the River to the Sea,” speech, Al-Aqsa TV, December 7, 2012, Middle East Media Research Institute, https://www.memri.org/tv/hamas-leader-khaled-mashal-we-will-not-relinquish-inch-palestine-river-sea/transcript.
4. Efraim Benmelech and Claude Berrebi, “Human Capital and the Productivity of Suicide Bombers,” p. 227, *Journal of Economic Perspectives* 21, no. 3, Summer 2007.
5. Rachel Brandenburg, “Iran and the Palestinians,” *The Iran Primer*, United States Institute of Peace, 2010, updated by Cameron Glenn and Garrett Nada in January 2016, http://iranprimer.usip.org/resource/iran-and-palestinians.
6. *Iranian Support of Hamas*, Intelligence and Terrorism Information Center at the Israel Intelligence Heritage & Commemoration Center (IICC), January 12, 2008, http://www.terrorism-info.org.il/data/pdf/PDF_09_019_2.pdf.
7. *Iranian Support of Hamas*.
8. Matthew Levitt, “Iran’s Support for Terrorism Under the JCPOA,” The Washington Institute, July 8, 2016, http://www.washingtoninstitute.org/policy-analysis/view/irans-support-for-terrorism-under-the-jcpoa.
9. Harriet Sherwood, “Hamas and Iran Rebuild Ties Three Years After Falling out over Syria,” *The Guardian*, January 9, 2014, https://www.theguardian.com/world/2014/jan/09/hamas-iran-rebuild-ties-falling-out-syria.
10. Rachel Brandenburg, “Iran and the Palestinians.”
11. Matthew Levitt, “Iran’s Support for Terrorism Under the JCPOA.”
12. *“Dawa” – Hamas’ Civilian Infrastructure and its Role in Terror Financing*, Israeli Security Agency, https://www.shabak.gov.il/SiteCollectionImages/english/Ter-

rorInfo/dawa-en.pdf.

13. "Israeli Arab Gets 5 Years for Hamas Plot," *UPI*, May 11, 2011, http://www.upi.com/Top_News/World-News/2011/05/11/Israeli-Arab-gets-5-years-for-Hamas-plot/UPI-54921305125753/.
14. "Israeli Arab Gets 5 Years for Hamas Plot."
15. "Hamas in 2017: The Document in Full," *Middle East Eye*, May 1, 2017, http://www.middleeasteye.net/news/hamas-charter-1637794876.
16. Hillel Frisch, "Israel and Its Arab Citizens," in *Israeli Democracy at the Crossroads*, p. 216, Routledge, 2005.
17. Jonathan Lis, "Salah Calls for 'Intifada' against Temple Mount Excavation," *Haaretz*, February 16, 2007, https://www.haaretz.com/news/salah-calls-for-intifada-against-temple-mount-excavation-1.213221.
18. Ariel Ben Solomon, "Israel's Islamic Movement: Overcoming Obstacles," *The Jerusalem Post,* May 15, 2016. http://www.jpost.com/Arab-Israeli-Conflict/Israels-Islamic-Movement-Overcoming-obstacles-453861.
19. Gili Cohen and Almog Ben Zikri, "Shin Bet: Two Israelis Plotted Attack Against Soldiers," *Haaretz*, Dec. 27, 2016. https://www.haaretz.com/israel-news/.premium-1.761709.
20. Monte Palmer and Princess Palmer, *Islamic Extremism: Causes, Diversity, and Challenges*, p. 142, Rowman and Littlefield, 2008.
21. Holly Fletcher, *Palestinian Islamic Jihad*, Council on Foreign Relations, April 10, 2008, http://www.cfr.org/israel/palestinian-islamic-jihad/p15984.
22. Holly Fletcher, *Palestinian Islamic Jihad.*
23. "Country Reports on Terrorism 2013: Chapter 6. Foreign Terrorist Organizations," U.S. Department of State, April 30, 2014, http://www.state.gov/j/ct/rls/crt/2013/224829.htm.
24. Susan Aschoff, "Jihad Leader Emerged from Shadows of USF," *St. Petersburg Times*, February 21, 2003, http://www.sptimes.com/2003/02/21/TampaBay/Jihad_leader_emerged_.shtml.
25. Holly Fletcher, *Palestinian Islamic Jihad.*
26. *Palestinian Islamic Jihad*, The Counter Extremism Project, 2017, https://www.counterextremism.com/

threat/palestinian-islamic-jihad#overview.

27. The Meir Amit Intelligence and Terrorism Information Center, "The Palestinian Islamic Jihad", http://www.terrorism-info.org.il/he/%D7%94%D7%92%60%D7%94%D7%90%D7%93_%D7%94%D7%90%D7%A1%D7%9C%D7%90%D7%9E%D7%99_%D7%91%D7%A4%D7%9C%D7%A1%D7%98%D7%99%D7%9F?page=8
28. Efraim Benmelech and Claude Berrebi, "Human Capital and the Productivity of Suicide Bombers," p. 227.
29. Raymond Ibrahim, Jonathan Schanzer, David Barnett, and Grant Rumley, "Palestinian Territories," *The World Almanac of Islamism*, 2017, http://almanac.afpc.org/palestinian-territories.
30. Jack Khoury and Yuval Azoulay, "2 Israeli Arabs Arrested over Suspected Jihad Plot to Kill Pilots, Scientists," *Haaretz*, August 28, 2008, http://www.haaretz.com/news/2-israeli-arabs-arrested-over-suspected-jihad-plot-to-kill-pilots-scientists-1.252814.
31. Yaniv Kubovich and Gili Cohen, "Shin Bet Nabs Islamic Jihad Cell Plotting to Kidnap Israelis," *Haaretz*, February 3, 2013, http://www.haaretz.com/news/diplomacy-defense/shin-bet-nabs-islamic-jihad-cell-plotting-to-kidnap-israelis-1.501107.
32. Holly Fletcher, *Palestinian Islamic Jihad.*
33. Hazem Balousha, "Islamic Jihad May Respond If Israel Enters Syria War," *Al-Monitor*, September 2, 2013, http://www.al-monitor.com/pulse/originals/2013/09/islamic-jihad-syria-us-strike.html.
34. Joshua Levitt, "Expert: Hamas Received $2 Billion from Iran; Islamic Jihad Gets $150 Million Annually," *The Algemeiner*, February 11, 2014, http://www.algemeiner.com/2014/02/11/expert-hamas-received-2-billion-from-iran-islamic-jihad-gets-150-million-annually/.
35. Rachel Brandenburg, "Iran and the Palestinians."
36. Hazem Balousha, "Islamic Jihad's Coffers Run Dry," *Al-Monitor*, June 2, 2015, http://www.al-monitor.com/pulse/originals/2015/06/palestine-islamic-jihad-financial-crisis-money-iran-hezbolla.html.
37. "Iran cuts 90% of support for Palestinian Islamic Ji-

had," *Middle East Monitor*, January 11, 2016, https://www.middleeastmonitor.com/20160111-iran-cuts-90-of-support-for-palestinian-islamic-jihad/.

38. Yonah Jeremy Bob, "Massive Iranian Funding for Anti-Israel Groups Revealed," *The Jerusalem Post*, June 23, 2017, http://www.jpost.com/Middle-East/Iran-News/Massive-Iranian-funding-for-anti-Israel-terror-groups-revealed-497703?utm_source=dlvr.it&utm_medium=twitter.
39. Matthew Levitt, "Hezbollah Finances: Funding the Party of God," the Washington Institute, February 2005, http://www.washingtoninstitute.org/policy-analysis/view/hezbollah-finances-funding-the-party-of-god
40. Matthew Levitt, "Hezbollah Finances: Funding the Party of God."
41. http://www.cfr.org/terrorist-organizations-and-networks/open-letter-hizballah-program/p30967
42. Jonathan Masters and Zachary Laub, *Hezbollah*, Council on Foreign Relations, January 3, 2014, https://www.cfr.org/backgrounder/hezbollah.
43. *Hezbollah*, The Counter Extremism Project, 2017, https://www.counterextremism.com/threat/hezbollah#overview.
44. Matthew Levitt, "Hezbollah Finances: Funding the Party of God."
45. http://www.terrorism-info.org.il/en/Hezbollah
46. Israel Security Agency, "Terror Data and Trends: Hizballa Activity involving Israeli Arabs," http://www.shabak.gov.il/ENGLISH/ENTERRORDATA/REVIEWS/Pages/HizballaActivity.aspx
47. The Knesset Research and Information Center, "Terrorist Organizations fighting Israel," July 2004, https://www.knesset.gov.il/mmm/data/pdf/m01057.pdf (in Hebrew)
48. Shabak website, Hizballah Recruiting Activity of Israeli-Arabs, https://www.shabak.gov.il/English/EnTerrorData/Reviews/Pages/HizballahRecruitingActivityofIsraeli-Arabs.aspx.
49. http://www.terrorism-info.org.il/en/Hezbollah
50. Matthew Levitt, "Hezbollah," *The World Almanac of Islamism*, 2017, http://almanac.afpc.org/Hezbollah.

51. Matthew Levitt, "Hezbollah Finances: Funding the Party of God."
52. "2006: Lebanon war," *BBC News,* May 6, 2008, http://news.bbc.co.uk/2/hi/middle_east/7381389.stm.
53. Dov Leiber and Alexander Fulbright, "Hezbollah Chief Threatens Israel's Dimona Nuclear Reactor," *The Times of Israel*, February 16, 2017, http://www.timesofisrael.com/hezbollah-chief-threatens-israels-dimona-nuclear-reactor/.
54. "2006: Lebanon war," *BBC News*.
55. http://www.terrorism-info.org.il/en/Hezbollah
56. Dov Leiber and Alexander Fulbright, "Hezbollah Chief Threatens Israel's Dimona Nuclear Reactor."
57. "Report: Hezbollah to leave Syria to prepare for conflict with Israel,'" *Israel HaYom*, October 25, 2017, http://www.israelhayom.com/2017/10/25/report-hezbollah-to-leave-syria-to-prepare-for-conflict-with-israel/.
58. Rola el-Husseini, "The Muslim World is Turning on Hezbollah," *The National Interest*, April 13, 2015, http://nationalinterest.org/feature/the-muslim-world-turning-hezbollah-12608.
59. "Netanyahu Warns Iran Filling the Void Left by IS on Golan," *Times of Israel*, July 25, 2017, https://www.timesofisrael.com/netanyahu-says-iran-filling-the-void-left-by-is-in-golan/.
60. Matthew Levitt, "Zawahiri Aims at Israel," *Foreign Affairs*, February 3, 2014, https://www.foreignaffairs.com/articles/israel/2014-02-03/zawahiri-aims-israel.
61. Matthew Levitt, "Zawahiri Aims at Israel."
62. Matthew Levitt, "Zawahiri Aims at Israel."
63. Eli Ashkenazi, "Israeli Arabs 'Inspired by Global Jihad' Charged with Taxi Driver Murder," *Haaretz*, June 28, 2010, https://www.haaretz.com/israel-news/israeli-arabs-inspired-by-global-jihad-charged-with-taxi-driver-murder-1.298736.
64. "Shin Bet Arrests Eight Israeli Arabs for Illicit Arms Trading," *Haaretz*, July 15, 2010, https://www.haaretz.com/israel-news/shin-bet-arrests-eight-israeli-arabs-for-illicit-arms-trading-1.302156.
65. Matthew Levitt, "Zawahiri Aims at Israel."
66. Alberto Fernandez, "Islamic State," *The World Alma-*

nac of Islamism, 2017, http://almanac.afpc.org/islamic-state.

67. "Less Than 5 Percent of Syria Under ISIS Control, Russia Says," *Haaretz*, October 24, 2017, https://www.haaretz.com/middle-east-news/syria/less-than-5-percent-of-syria-under-isis-control-russia-says-1.5459980.
68. Eitan Azani, Jonathan Fighel, and Lorena Atiyas Lvovsky, "The Islamic State's Threat to Israel: Challenges and Coping Mechanisms," The International Institute for Counter-Terrorism (ICT), February 17, 2016, https://www.ict.org.il/Article/1612/The-Islamic-States-Threat-to-Israel
69. Borzou Daragahi, "Sinai Jihadi Group Emerges at Forefront of Egypt Violence," *Financial Times*, January 31, 2014. http://www.ft.com/cms/s/0/b5ad40d0-8a7b-11e3-9c29-00144feab7de.html#axzz3RfJCfft2
70. Taylor Luck, "Why Sinai mosque attack is seen as a major ISIS miscalculation," *The Christian Science Monitor*, November 27, 2017, https://www.csmonitor.com/World/Middle-East/2017/1127/Why-Sinai-mosque-attack-is-seen-as-a-major-ISIS-miscalculation.
71. *ISIS: Portrait of a Jihadi Terrorist Organization*, The Meir Amit Intelligence and Terrorism Information Center (ITIC), November 2014, http://www.terrorism-info.org.il/Data/articles/Art_20733/101_14_Ef_1329270214.pdf
72. *A History of Terrorism in Egypt's Sinai*, Middle East Institute, http://www.mei.edu/sinai-terrorism.
73. Anna Ahronheim, "19 Israelis to have citizenship revoked for fighting with ISIS," *The Jerusalem Post*, August 22, 2017, http://www.jpost.com/Arab-Israeli-Conflict/19-Israelis-to-have-citizenship-revoked-for-fighting-with-ISIS-503145.
74. "Israeli Arabs Sentenced to Prison Time for Joining ISIS," *Israel Today*, October 20, 2017, http://www.israeltoday.co.il/NewsItem/tabid/178/nid/32587/Default.aspx.
75. Israeli Security Agency, "2015 Annual Summary Terrorism and CT Activity Data and Trends," March 2016, http://www.shabak.gov.il/English/EnTerrorData/Archive/Annual/Pages/2015AnnualSummary.aspx

76. Anna Ahronheim, "Shin Bet arrests three Arab-Israelis suspected of supporting ISIS," *The Jerusalem Post*, June 12, 2017, http://www.jpost.com/Arab-Israeli-Conflict/Shin-Bet-arrests-three-Arab-Israelis-suspected-of-supporting-ISIS-496673.
77. Anna Ahronheim, "Israel's Shin Bet arrests 2 Beduin women on suspicion of planning ISIS attacks," The *Jerusalem Post*, January 8, 2018, http://www.jpost.com/Arab-Israeli-Conflict/Israeli-Beduin-women-arrested-on-suspicion-of-planning-attacks-for-ISIS-533118.
78. Ruth Eglash and Griff Witte, "Clashes in East Jerusalem After Teen's Burial Revive Intifada Fears for Middle East," *The Washington Post*, July 5, 2014, https://www.washingtonpost.com/world/2014/07/05/a9f5c538-d2a8-463d-b5cb-ec5f4fa0ab37_story.html?utm_term=.ed34ce5d8249.
79. Nir Hasson, ""Firecrackers: The Newest Popular Weapon, and the Newest Threat, in Jerusalem," *Haaretz*. November 4, 2014, https://www.haaretz.com/israel-news/.premium-1.624446.
80. Daniel K. Eisenbud and Lahav Harkov, "Minister of Public Security Blasts Barkat for Blaming Ministry for 'Silent Intifada,'" *The Jerusalem Post*, October 5, 2014, http://www.jpost.com/Israel-News/Minister-of-Public-Security-blasts-Barkat-for-blaming-ministry-for-silent-intifada-378102.
81. Jodi Rudoren and Isabel Kershner, "Israel Shaken by Five Deaths in Synagogue Assault," *New York Times*, November 14, 2014, https://www.nytimes.com/2014/11/19/world/middleeast/killings-in-jerusalem-synagogue-complex.html.
82. Itay Blumental and Omri Efraim, "Dalia Lemkus Survived 2006 Attack, but Was Murdered in Another Stabbing," *Ynet News*, October 11, 2014, https://www.ynetnews.com/articles/0,7340,L-4590480,00.html; Yonah Jeremy Bob, "Palestinian Sentenced to Life for Murder of Soldier Almog Shiloni," *The Jerusalem Post*, September 14, 2016, http://www.jpost.com/Arab-Israeli-Conflict/Palestinian-sentenced-to-life-for-murder-of-soldier-Almog-Shiloni-467753.
83. Rotem Elizera, Yoav Zitun, Shahar Hay, and Elior Levy,

"Deadly Halamish Attack Hits Family Celebrating Grandson's Birth," *YNet News*, July 22, 2017, https://www.ynetnews.com/articles/0,7340,L-4992716,00.html.

84. "Abbas' Fatah party calls for 'day of rage' following Temple Mount clashes," *Jewish Telegraph Agency*, July 18, 2017, https://www.jta.org/2017/07/18/news-opinion/israel-middle-east/abbas-fatah-party-calls-for-day-of-rage-following-temple-mount-clashes.
85. Avi Issacharoff, "Mobilizing militia, Abbas approves mass protests Friday over Temple Mount," *Times of Israel*, July 26, 2017, http://www.timesofisrael.com/mobilizing-militia-abbas-orders-mass-protests-friday-over-temple-mount/.
86. David Rosenberg, "Report: Mahmoud Abbas funding Jerusalem riots," *Israel National News,* July 30, 2017, http://www.israelnationalnews.com/News/News.aspx/233175.
87. Lahav Harkov, "Palestinian Authority paid terrorists nearly $350 million in 2017," *The Jerusalem Post*, January 9, 2018, http://www.jpost.com/Arab-Israeli-Conflict/Palestinian-Authority-paid-terrorists-nearly-350-million-in-2017-533227.
88. Lidar Gravé-Lazi, "Ahead of Jewish New Year, Israel's Population Stands at 8.585 Million," *The Jerusalem Post*, September 27, 2016, http://www.jpost.com/Israel-News/Ahead-of-Jewish-New-Year-Israels-population-stands-at-8585-million-468809.
89. Ahiya Raved, "Central Bureau of Statistics Reports Muslim Growth Rate Still Highest in Israel," *Ynet News*, August 30, 2017, https://www.ynetnews.com/articles/0,7340,L-5009798,00.html.
90. Ben Lynfield, "Survey: 60% of Arab Israelis Have Positive View of State," *The Jerusalem Post*, September 27, 2017, http://www.jpost.com/Israel-News/Survey-60-percent-of-Arab-Israelis-have-positive-view-of-state-506150
91. Ilana Curiel, "Rahat objects to IDF Independence Day exhibit," *Ynet News*, May 9, 2011, http://www.ynetnews.com/articles/0,7340,L-4066563,00.html.
92. Yaakov Lappin, "Israel Lands Authority Demolishes

Illegal Rahat Mosque," *The Jerusalem Post*, November 7, 2010, http://www.jpost.com/Israel/Article.aspx?id=194375.

93. Yoav Zitun, "2 Bedouins Confess to Plotting Terror Attacks," *Ynet News*, January 20, 2013, http://www.ynetnews.com/articles/0,7340,L-4334793,00.html.
94. "Promoting the 'Islamic State' ideology in the educational system," The Knesset Committee on Education, Culture and Sport, November 10, 2015, http://main.knesset.gov.il/Activity/committees/Education/Conclusion/161115.pdf#search=%D7%91%D7%93%D7%95%D7%90%D7%99%D7%9D
95. "Promoting the 'Islamic State' ideology in the educational system," The Knesset Committee on Education, Culture and Sport.
96. Judah Ari Gross, "2 Bedouin Israelis suspected of killing soldier in terror attack," *Times of Israel*, December, 4, 2017, https://www.timesofisrael.com/2-bedouin-israelis-suspected-of-killing-soldier-in-terror-attack/.
97. Donna Rosenthal, *The Israelis: Ordinary People in an Extraordinary Land*, 2nd ed., p. 300, Free Press, 2008.
98. Tamar Hermann, Chanan Cohen, Ella Heller, and Dana Bublil, *The Israeli Democracy Index 2015*, The Israel Democracy Institute, http://en.idi.org.il/analysis/idi-press/publications/english-books/the-israeli-democracy-index-2015/.
99. *Israel's Religiously Divided Society*, p. 40, Pew Research Center, March 8, 2016, http://www.pewforum.org/2016/03/08/israels-religiously-divided-society/.
100. Frida Ghitis, "A Spark of Good News from the Middle East," *CNN*, July 10 2014, http://www.cnn.com/2014/07/10/opinion/ghitis-mideast-polls/index.html.
101. Gil Shefler, "Israeli Arab Volunteers Rising," *JTA*, August 27, 2009, http://www.jta.org/news/article/2009/08/27/1007492/israeli-arab-volunteers-rising.
102. Ilan Berman, "Al-Qaeda's Newest Outpost," *Forbes*, December 29, 2011, http://www.forbes.com/sites/ilanberman/2011/12/29/al-qaedas-newest-outpost/.
103. Elad Benari, "Salafi Terrorists: Jihad Against Criminal Jews is a Duty," *Israel National News*, August 27,

2012, http://www.israelnationalnews.com/News/News.aspx/159309#.UXOET4VHqkB.

104. Yaakov Lappin, "IDF Decreases Gazan Fishing Zone after Rockets," *The Jerusalem Post*, March 21, 2013, http://www.jpost.com/National-News/Two-rockets-slam-into-Sderot-during-Obama-visit-307212.
105. Aaron Kalman, "Gazan Salafist Vows to Keep Attacking Israel," *Times of Israel*, April 18, 2013, http://www.timesofisrael.com/gazan-salafist-vows-to-keep-attacking-israel/.
106. "Egypt Scraps Israel Gas Supply Deal," *BBC*, April 23, 2012, http://www.bbc.co.uk/news/world-middle-east-17808954.
107. Holly Cramer, Tim Harper, Samantha Moog, and Eric Spioch, *A History of Terrorism in Egypt's Sinai*, Middle East Institute, n.d., http://www.mei.edu/sinai-terrorism.
108. Zach Gold, *Security in the Sinai: Present and Future*, International Center for Counter-Terrorism, March 2014, http://www.icct.nl/download/file/ICCT-Gold-Security-In-The-Sinai-March-2014.pdf.
109. Zack Gold, *Sinai Security: Opportunities for Unlikely Cooperation Among Egypt, Israel, and Hamas*, The Saban Center for Middle East Policy at Brookings, Analysis Paper Number 30, October 2013, https://www.brookings.edu/wp-content/uploads/2016/06/22-sinai-hamas-egypt-israel-gold.pdf.
110. Holly Cramer, Tim Harper, Samantha Moog, and Eric Spioch, *A History of Terrorism in Egypt's Sinai.*
111. Zachary Laub, *Security in Egypt's Sinai Peninsula*, Council of Foreign Relations, December 11, 2013, http://www.cfr.org/egypt/egypts-sinai-peninsula-security/p32055.
112. Efraim Inbar, "The Gaza Tunnels Get Too Much Attention," BESA Center Perspectives Paper No. 369, October 6, 2016, https://besacenter.org/wp-content/uploads/2016/10/Inbar-Efraim-Gaza-Tunnels-Get-Too-Much-Attention-PP-369-6-Oct-2016a.pdf.
113. "Netanyahu Threatens to Eclipse 2014 War to Destroy Gaza Tunnels," *The Times of Israel*, January 31, 2016, http://www.timesofisrael.com/netanyahu-threatens-to-eclipse-2014-war-to-destroy-gaza-tunnels/.

114. "Smuggling through Israel-Egypt border," The Knesset Research and Information Center, 2006, https://www.knesset.gov.il/mmm/data/pdf/m01667.pdf (in Hebrew).
115. Beverly Milton-Edwards, "Gaza protests highlight humanitarian crisis and lack of political progress to peace," *Brookings Institution*, April 5, 2018, https://www.brookings.edu/opinions/gaza-protests-highlight-humanitarian-crisis-and-lack-of-political-progress-to-peace/.
116. Hazem Balousha and Peter Beaumont, "Palestinian death toll mounts as thousands protest on Gaza border," *The Guardian*, April 6, 2018, https://www.theguardian.com/world/2018/apr/06/israel-warned-un-protesters-head-for-gaza-demonstrations.
117. Meirav Arlosoroff, "Settling the Bedouin Question," *Haaretz*, December 27, 2012, https://www.haaretz.com/.premium-meirav-arlosoroff-bitter-lives-of-the-bedouin-1.5282742.

18 Iran

Quick Facts

Population: 82,021,564 (2017 est)
Area: 1,648,195 sq km
Ethnic Groups: Persian, Azeri, Kurd, Lur, Baloch, Arab, Turkmen and Turkic tribes
Religions: Muslim (official) 99.4% (Shia 90-95%, Sunni 5-10%), other (includes Zoroastrian, Jewish, and Christian) 0.3%, unspecified 0.4%
Government Type: Theocratic Republic
GDP (official exchange rate): $431.9 billion (2017 est)

Map and Quick Facts Courtesy of the CIA World Factbook (Last Updated September 2018)

Introduction

Since its founding in February of 1979, the Islamic Republic of Iran has consistently ranked as the world's most active state sponsor of terrorism, according to the estimates of the United States government. Iran's support for terrorism is both pervasive and ideological, encompassing a vast array of official and quasi-official institutions, individuals and policies. It finds its roots in the ideas of the Ayatollah Ruhollah Khomeini, the founder of the Islamic Revolution, who espoused the need to "export" Iran's successful religious model the world over. Nearly three decades after Khomeini's death, that priority continues to animate Iran's leaders and guide their sponsorship of instability, both in Iran's immediate geographic neighborhood and far beyond.

Today, Iran's capabilities to do so have expanded significantly. In the decade between 2003 and 2013, the Iranian regime's persistent pursuit of a nuclear capability engendered escalating pressure from the United States and international community in the form of economic sanctions and diplomatic isolation. Over time, these measures took their toll, progressively isolating the Islamic Republic and severely impacting its economic fortunes. However, the successful conclusion of a nuclear deal between Iran and the P5+1 powers in July of 2015 fundamentally altered this dynamic, *providing the Islamic Republic with massive direct economic relief, totaling upwards of $100 billion[1], and a surge in post-sanctions trade with a range of international partners. This served to greatly expand the resources available to the Islamic Republic to support terror proxies in the region and beyond, and breathed new life into Tehran's longstanding efforts to reshape the global order in its own image.*

The advent of the Trump administration has been followed by a new, more robust U.S. approach toward Iran. The centerpiece of this new strategy has been a U.S. withdrawal from the 2015 Iran nuclear deal, and the reimposition of a range of sanctions on the Iranian regime. That process – underway as of this writing – has significantly impacted Iran's economic fortunes, precipitating an exodus of international commerce from the Islamic Republic and causing a massive devaluation of Iran's national currency, the rial. As of yet, however, it has not caused a material change in Iran's regional behavior, or its persistent sponsorship of terrorism, both in its immediate neighborhood and more globally.

Islamist Activity

The Iranian regime's support for international terrorism predates the establishment of the Islamic Republic itself. In the 1960s and 1970s, while in exile in Iraq and in France, the Ayatollah Ruhollah Khomeini formulated his ideas about the need for a radical Islamic transformation in his home country, Iran, and of subsequently "exporting" this system of government throughout the Middle East and beyond.[2] In keeping with this thinking, Khomeini's political manifesto, *Islamic Government*, extolled the virtues of "a victorious and triumphant Islamic political revolution" that would go on "to unite the Moslem nation, [and] to liberate [all] its lands."[3]

When the Ayatollah and his followers subsequently swept to power in Tehran in the spring of 1979, this principle became a cardinal regime priority. The preamble of the country's formative constitution, adopted in October 1979, outlines that the country's military would henceforth "be responsible not only for guarding and preserving the frontiers of the country, but also for fulfilling the ideological mission of jihad in God's way; that is, extending the sovereignty of God's law throughout the world."[4] These words were backed by concrete regime action, with Khomeini consolidating the country's various radical religious militias into an ideological army known as the Islamic Revolutionary Guard Corps (IRGC, or Pasdaran), tasked with promoting his revolutionary message abroad, with violence if necessary.

The nearly-four decades since have seen a consistent regime commitment to international terrorism. In the early years of the Islamic Republic, Iran is known to have ordered, orchestrated or facilitated a series of terrorist attacks in the Middle East, among them the 1983 U.S. Embassy and Marine Barracks bombings in Beirut, Lebanon, as well as abortive coup attempts and bombings in Bahrain, the United Arab Emirates and Kuwait.[5] These activities, and the rationale behind them, were reinforced by the outcome of the country's bloody eight-year war with Iraq, which strengthened the Iranian government's belief that radical proxies could serve as an attractive, low-cost substitute for direct military action. As a result, the principle of "exporting the revolution" remained a vibrant element of regime policy after the death of Khomeini in 1989. In the decade that followed, the Islamic Republic continued to bankroll assassinations and terrorist acts on foreign soil, aided the infiltration of countries in Europe, Africa and Latin America by radical Islamic groups, and assisted irregulars in various international conflict zones.[6]

In the aftermath of the September 11, 2001 terrorist attacks, the Islamic Republic chose to dramatically strengthen its links to international terrorism, redoubling its support for Lebanon's Hezbollah militia and Palestinian rejectionist groups, expanding its footprint in the Palestinian territories, maintaining at least low-level links to the al-Qaeda network, and becoming heavily involved in the bankrolling of radical Shi'ite militias and activities aimed at hindering the U.S.-led Coalition in post-Saddam Iraq. This support for terrorism, while ideologically driven, was and remains rooted in pragmatism. While Khomeini's Islamic Revolution was a distinctly Shi'a one, in the nearly four decades since its establishment, the Islamic Republic has embraced a more universalist conception of its international role, aspiring to serve as the vanguard of Islamic revolution worldwide.[7] The Iranian regime today funds a broad range of both Sunni and Shi'a groups throughout the greater Middle East and beyond. The critical determinant appears to be the degree to which these movements and organizations can reinforce Iran's leading role in the "Shi'a revival" taking place in the Muslim world, and their shared animosity toward the West, most directly Israel and the United States.

The scope of Iran's support of violent Islamism is global in nature, and so is its reach. In the decade that followed the 9/11 attacks, it encompassed: ongoing support for Hezbollah in Lebanon and a reconstitution of the Shi'ite militia's strategic capabilities;[8] extensive involvement in post-Saddam Iraq, first through the provision of arms and materiel to the country's various Shi'a militias and later through political and strategic support of various forces both inside and outside of the government of Iraqi Prime Minister Nouri al-Maliki;[9] the provision of significant military and operational assistance to the insurgency in Afghanistan, increasing the lethality of forces arrayed against the government of President Hamid Karzai and Coalition authorities there;[10] exerting influence in the Palestinian arena through financial aid and support to Palestinian rejectionist groups, chief among them Hamas and the Palestinian Islamic Jihad[11] and; bankrolling terrorist and subversive activities in various countries, including Egypt.[12]

The onset of the Arab Spring in early 2011 marked a turning point for Iranian activities—and for its regional standing. In the early stages of the "Spring," Iranian officials sought to take credit for the anti-regime sentiment sweeping the region, depicting it as the belated product of the Ayatollah Khomeini's successful Islamic revolution in 1979 and heralding an "Islamic awakening" in which Iran would inevitably play a leading role.[13] Iran's stance was not simply rhetorical; the Islamic Republic became a political supporter of various regional insurgent causes, from protests by Bahrain's majority-Shi'ite population against the country's ruling al-Khalifa family[14] to the successful struggle by Yemen's al-Houthi rebellion against the central government in Sana'a.[15]

Iran's most conspicuous initiative, however, was to assume the role of a lifeline for the regime of Syrian dictator Bashar al-Assad.

Shortly after the eruption of anti-regime unrest in Syria in March 2011, Iran took on a major role in bolstering and strengthening Assad's hold on power. It did so through extensive financial assistance, as well as the provision of forces to augment Syria's military in its fight against the country's disparate opposition elements. This has included the deployment of a large IRGC contingent to the Syrian battlefield, including hundreds of trained snipers who have helped to reinforce Syrian forces and increase their lethality against Syria's opposition. [16] Together with its Lebanese proxy Hezbollah, it has also played a key role in organizing pro-Assad militias among the country's Alawite and Shi'a communities, as well as coordinating pro-regime foreign fighters from Iraq, Yemen, Lebanon and Afghanistan.[17] Over time, this migration of Shi'ite militants eclipsed the broad-based mobilization of Sunni jihadists in the Muslim World in both size and scope. As of April 2018, the size of this jihadi legion was estimated at around 80,000[18], or twice the size of the foreign fighter contingent believed to have been mobilized up to that point by the Islamic State terrorist group.[19]

Iran's objectives in this effort are two-fold. Most immediately, Iran's aid is intended to shore up the stability of the Assad regime, its most important regional partner. More broadly, however, Iran sees its involvement in Syria as a direct blow against the "Great Satan," the United States. "Since Syria was and continues to be part of the Islamic resistance front and the Islamic Revolution, it provokes the anger of the Americans," IRGC commander Mohammad Ali Jafari explained on Iranian television in April of 2014.[20] Additionally, Iranian leaders view the Islamic State and its exclusionary, aggressive Sunni interpretation of the Islamic faith, as something approaching an existential threat to the Islamic Republic, and accordingly have marshalled massive resources against the group, both within their national territory and beyond it.[21]

Broadly construed, Iran's regional efforts have been singularly successful. The Iranian regime can now be said to control four regional capitals in the Middle East. The first is Damascus, where Iranian (as well as Russian) support has been instrumental to keeping the Assad regime in power to date. The second is Baghdad, where Iran simultaneously wields extensive influence among the country's political elites and supports an extensive network of powerful Shi'a militias, collectively known as the hashd al-shaabi. The third is Lebanon, where the group's principal terrorist proxy, Hezbollah, maintains a powerful grip on national politics. The fourth is Sana'a, Yemen, where since the spring of 2015, Iranian-supported rebels have effectively taken over the national government, precipitating a pitched civil war that – some three years on – has created the world's worst humanitarian catastrophe.

The financial scope of these activities is enormous. In the past, U.S. officials have estimated that the Islamic Republic boasts "a nine-digit line item in its budget for support to terrorist organizations."[22] More recently, in the summer of 2015, in the aftermath of the conclusion of the JCPOA, the Congressional Research Service estimated that the Islamic Republic was spending between $3.5 billion and $16 billion annually on support for terrorism and insurgency worldwide.[23]

This funding remains pervasive—at least for the moment. In August 2018, Brian Hook, the Trump administration's Special Representative for Iran, estimated that "Iran provides Lebanese Hezbollah about $700 million per year," and that the Iranian regime had spent "at least $16 billion on supporting its proxies in Syria, Iraq and Yemen" to that point.[24] Additionally, Hook stressed, "Iran has historically provided over $100 million per year to Palestinian groups, including Hamas and Palestinian Islamic Jihad."[25] Accordingly, Trump administration efforts are focused in large part on curtailing the funds available to the Iranian regime to engage in terror sponsorship, albeit without measurable results so far.

Islamism and Society

While "exporting the revolution" was and remains a persistent regime objective, involvement and investment on the part of the Iranian population in this pursuit is far from universal. There is little empirical data to suggest that ordinary Iranians share the depth of their regime's commitment to the exportation of radical Islam. To the contrary, terrorism funding in Iran remains an elite—rather than popular—undertaking, directed through state institutions rather than non-governmental organizations, and overseen at an official, not a grassroots, level.

At times, Iran's involvement in the support of radical groups abroad has served as a significant bone of contention between the Iranian regime and its population. In the wake of Hezbollah's summer 2006 war with Israel, for example, Iran's extensive financial support for Lebanon's Shi'ites became a domestic flashpoint, with ordinary Iranians publicly questioning—and condemning—their government's skewed strategic priorities.[26] More recently, the Iranian regime's foreign adventurism – and its support for radical proxies – has emerged as prominent anti-regime narrative in the persistent protests that have taken place throughout the Islamic Republic since late 2017.

Support for radical Islamic causes is eroded by Iran's complex ethno/religious composition. Although the country is overwhelmingly (98 percent) Muslim and predominantly (89 percent) Shi'a, as of 2013 ethnic Persians were estimated to hold only a modest majority (61 percent) in Iran's population of almost 80 million. The remainder is Azeri (16 percent), Kurdish (10 percent), Baloch (2 percent), Arab (2 percent), and a range of other minorities,[27] many of which are systematically discriminated against by the Islamic Republic and feel little or limited allegiance to it. The base of support for Islamic radicalism—and other governmental priorities—in Iranian society is further weakened by the regime's persecution of religious minorities, which, according to the U.S. State Department, has created "a threatening atmosphere for nearly all non-Shi'a religious groups" in the Islamic Republic.[28]

Social and economic malaise has historically served to dilute identification with regime ideals and principles, something that was encapsulated in the mass uprising (colloquially known as the "Green Movement") that emerged in Iran in mid-2009. Back then, the protests were successfully quashed by the Iranian regime, but these underlying factors – including unemployment, poverty and widespread regime corruption – remain potent drivers of domestic politics. This has been evident since late 2017, which has seen Iran convulsed by persistent protests that have presented its leaders with the greatest challenge to their legitimacy since the 1979 Islamic Revolution. The initial period that followed the passage of the JCPOA in 2015 was greeted with considerable euphoria by ordinary Iranians, who were hopeful that the agreement would be accompanied by an economic "peace dividend" of sorts.[29] This, however, did not materialize, notwithstanding a surge in trade and investment into the Islamic Republic. The Iranian regime chose not to parlay the economic benefits of JCPOA-enabled trade into meaningful, sustained investments in infrastructure and prosperity within the Islamic Republic—with pronounced results.

Officially, unemployment in Iran now stands at some 12.5 percent, but unofficially is gauged to be significantly higher.[30] It is also endemic, reaching as high as 60 percent in some cities within the Islamic Republic.[31] Youth unemployment is particularly widespread, and in 2017 measured nearly 29 percent.[32] Poverty within the Islamic Republic remains pervasive as well, with some 33 percent of the country's population (26 million Iranians) suffering from "absolute poverty" and six percent facing starvation.[33] Meanwhile, commodity prices have risen significantly (with staple goods such as eggs and chicken increasing in cost by 40 percent or more), while purchasing power has declined as Iran's national currency, the *rial*, has plummeted in value in recent months. Yet, rather than focus on the country's deleterious domestic conditions, Iran's leaders systematically prioritized guns over butter. Between 2016 and 2017, Iran's national defense budget increased by some 20 percent, while its defense budget for 2018-2019 further hikes spending by nearly 90 percent.[34] Iran also significantly expanded its foreign activism in places like Bahrain, Yemen and (most conspicuously) Syria, at considerable cost to the regime. The Islamic Republic's ongoing campaign in Syria alone is estimated to cost the country between $15-$20 billion annually – roughly equivalent to Iran's total national healthcare budget of $16.3 billion.[35]

This combination of domestic neglect and foreign adventurism has generated a massive domestic backlash within Iran. Prominent among the slogans in the current cycle of protests within the Islamic Republic have been calls of "Leave Syria, think about us!" and "Death to Hezbollah!"[36] – chants that reflect a fundamental dissatisfaction with, and rejection of, the prevailing priorities of the Iranian regime.

ISLAMISM AND THE STATE

Iran's support for Islamism is channeled through an elaborate infrastructure of institutions and governmental bodies tasked with the promotion of radical Islamic thought and action. These include:

The Islamic Revolutionary Guard Corps (IRGC, or Pasdaran)

At home, the IRGC, in addition to its professional military duties, has become the guardian of the regime's ballistic missile and weapons of mass destruction programs.[37] The agenda of Iran's ideological army, however, is global in scope, and so is its reach. Over the past three-and-a-half decades, the IRGC has emerged as the shock troops of Iran's Islamic Revolution, training terrorist organizations both within Iran and in specialized training camps in places like Lebanon and Sudan, as well as providing assistance to radical movements and terrorist proxies throughout the Middle East, Africa, Europe and Asia via specialized paramilitary units.[38] The most notorious of these is the Quds Force, a crack military battalion formed in 1990 and dedicated to carrying out "extra-regional operations of the Islamic Revolutionary Guard Corps"—namely, terrorism and insurgency in the name of the Islamic Republic.[39] Since the 2003 ouster of Saddam Hussein, this unit has played a leading role in Iraq as part of what analysts have characterized as an "open-ended, resilient, and well-funded" covert effort on the part of the Iranian regime to extend its influence into the former Ba'athist state.[40] More recently, the IRGC has become a principal player in the Iranian government's ongoing assistance to Syrian dictator Bashar al-Assad.[41]

The IRGC also boasts a dedicated intelligence service, the Protection and Intelligence Department, or Hefazat va Ettelaat-e Sepah-e Pasdaran. Founded in 1980, it encompasses three main functions: intelligence in support of IRGC military operations; political operations at home and abroad; and support to the foreign terrorist operations of the Quds Force.[42]

Ministry of Intelligence and Security (MOIS)

Controlled directly by Supreme Leader Ali Khamenei, the MOIS is used by Iran's ruling clergy to quash domestic opposition and carry out espionage against suspect members of the Iranian government.[43] Abroad, the MOIS plays a key role in planning and carrying out terrorist operations on foreign soil, using Iranian embassies and diplomatic missions as cover.[44] MOIS operatives are also known to operate abroad under unofficial identities—for example, as employees of Iran Air, Iran's official airline.[45] The MOIS conducts a variety of activities in support of the operations of Tehran's terrorist surrogates, ranging from financing actual operations to intelligence collection on potential targets. The Ministry also carries out independent operations, primarily against dissidents of the current regime in Tehran living in foreign countries, at the direction of senior Iranian officials.[46]

Ministry of Foreign Affairs

Iran's Foreign Ministry serves as an important enabler of the Iranian regime's international terrorist presence. Agents of the IRGC and MOIS often operate out of Iranian missions abroad, where they are stationed under diplomatic cover, complete with blanket diplomatic immunity. These agents—and through them Iranian foreign proxies—use the Ministry's auspices to untraceably obtain financing, weapons and intelligence from Tehran (for example, via diplomatic pouch).[47]

Cultural Affairs Ministry

Supplementing the role of the Foreign Affairs Ministry in exporting terrorism is Iran's Ministry of Culture and Guidance. Tasked with overseeing the cultural sections of Iranian foreign missions, as well as free-standing Iranian cultural centers, it facilitates IRGC infiltration of—and terrorist recruitment within—local Muslim populations in foreign nations.[48] The Ministry is particularly influential among majority Muslim countries like the former Soviet Republics, many of which share substantial cultural, religious and ideological bonds with Tehran. Between 1982 and 1992, the official in charge of the Ministry—and of its role in support of Iranian terror abroad—was Mohammed Khatami, Iran's subsequent "reformist" president.

Basij

Formed during the early days of the Islamic Republic and trained by the Pasdaran, this militia represents the Iranian regime's premier tool of domestic terror. During the eight years of the Iran-Iraq war, the organization's cadres were the Islamic Republic's cannon fodder, selected to clear minefields and launch "human wave" attacks against Iraqi forces.[49] With the end of the conflict with Iraq, the role of the Basij was reoriented, and the organization became the watchdog of Iranian society. Today, it is used by the ayatollahs to quell domestic anti-regime protests and eradicate "un-Islamic" behavior. Their role ranges from enforcing modest dress to gathering intelligence on university students, which is handed over to the regime's undercover police.[50] The Basij played a significant role in suppressing domestic dissent through violence and intimidation in the aftermath of the fraudulent reelection of Mahmoud Ahmadinejad to the Iranian presidency in June of 2009.[51] More recently, amid growing protests in and around Tehran and other urban centers beginning in December 2017, the Basij has played an instrumental role in regime repression, including by carrying out mass arrests of demonstrators.[52]

There are reported to be as many as 10 million registered Basij members, though not all are on active service.[53] The Basij also plays an important supporting role in Iran's state sponsorship of terror. It is known to be active in training anti-Israeli forces, including carrying out maneuvers designed to ready Hezbollah and assorted Palestinian militants for guerrilla warfare.

Domestic paramilitaries (guruh-I fishar)

Supplementing the role of the Basij are the numerous vigilante or "pressure" groups that are harnessed by the Iranian government. Though officially independent, these gangs actually operate under the patronage of government officials, the IRGC or the MOIS, and target internal opposition to the clerical regime.[54] The most famous is the Ansar-i Hezbollah, which was responsible for fomenting the July 1999 crisis at Tehran University that led to the bloody governmental crackdown on student opposition forces.

Bonyads

These sprawling socio-religious foundations, which are overseen only by Iran's Supreme Leader, serve as conduits for the Islamic Republic's cause of choice. Arguably the most important is the Bonyad-e Mostazafan (Foundation of the Oppressed), a sprawling network of an estimated 1,200 firms created in 1979 with seed money from the Shah's coffers.[55] Another is the Bonyad-e Shahid (Martyrs' Foundation), an enormous conglomerate of industrial, agricultural, construction and commercial companies with some 350 offices and tens of thousands of employees.[56] The sums controlled by these organs are enormous: more than 30 percent of Iran's national GDP, and as much as two-thirds of the country's non-oil GDP.[57] And while many of their functions are legitimate, they are also used by Iran's religious leaders to funnel money to their pet causes, from financing domestic repression to arming radical groups abroad.

Notably, even as Iran remains complicit in the pervasive sponsorship of international terrorism, it is itself the target of violent activity from a number of quarters.

One is the Free Life Party of Kurdistan, or PJAK. Led by Iranian-born German national Abdul Rahman Haji Ahmadi, PJAK is a violent Kurdish nationalist group that has carried out attacks on Iran from strongholds in neighboring Iraq since its formation in 2004. PJAK, which maintains an affiliation with Turkey's larger Kurdistan Workers Party (PKK), claims to seek "democratic change" and characterizes its actions as a "defense" against Iranian state repression of its Kurdish minority.[58] Iranian regime forces clashed repeatedly with members of PJAK between 2008 and 2011, successfully arresting and killing numerous group members as part of ongoing counterterrorism operations.[59] A major counterterrorism campaign against the group by Iranian security forces followed in the fall of 2011, culminating in a ceasefire between the two parties.[60] This ceasefire held until 2013, when clashes between the group and Tehran began anew,[61] and have continued sporadically until the present day.

More pronounced, however, has been the threat to Iran posed by the Islamic State. Since its ascent to regional prominence in mid-2014, ISIS has targeted Shi'a Muslim communities throughout the Middle East, and has made Iran a key target of its animus. The organization has repeatedly attempted to breach Iran's common border with Iraq, and has identified the Iranian regime as a principal adversary in its communiques and writings. ISIS has likewise proven adept at exploiting Iran's latent ethnic cleavages, and in the past found fertile soil for recruitment among disenfranchised communities, such as Iran's Kurds, who are repressed and/or marginalized by the state.[62]

In response, Iran has mobilized extensive resources to fight the Islamic State, both at home and abroad. Thus, Iran deepened its already extensive involvement in Iraq "in the effort to pre-empt a potential spillover across its borders."[63] It also justified its intervention in Syria as part of a broad counterterrorism offensive against the group.[64] These and other paramilitary activities have been spearheaded by Gen. Qassem Suleimani, the head of the IRGC's Quds Force paramilitary unit, who has emerged as a truly national figure over the past half-decade as a result.

Despite these steps, and notwithstanding the Islamic State's larger path of decline in the Middle East, the organization still poses a threat to Iranian security. This was demonstrated dramatically in the summer of 2017, when gunmen attacked the national parliament and Mausoleum of Ayatollah Khomeini in Tehran in a coordinated attack that left at least 13 dead.[65] More recently, ISIS has claimed credit for a September 23rd attack on an Iranian military parade which resulted in 29 casualties.[66]

Endnotes

1. See, for example, Guy Taylor, "Iran is Banking Billions More Than Expected Thanks to Obama's Deal," *Washington Times*, February 3, 2016, http://www.washingtontimes.com/news/2016/feb/3/iran-claims-100-billion-windfall-from-sanctions-re/.
2. Emmanuel Sivan, *Radical Islam: Medieval Theology and Modern Politics* (New Haven: Yale University Press, 1985), 188–207.
3. Ruhollah Khomeini, *Islamic Government* (New York: Manor Books, 1979).
4. Preamble of the Constitution of the Islamic Republic of Iran, http://www.oefre.unibe.ch/law/icl/ir00000_.html.
5. Robin Wright, *Sacred Rage: The Wrath of Militant Islam* (New York: Simon & Schuster, 1986), 111–21.
6. "Iranian Terrorism in Bosnia and Croatia," *Iran Brief*, March 3, 1997, http://www.lexis-nexis.com; Mike O'Connor, "Spies for Iranians Are Said to Gain a Hold in Bosnia," *New York Times*, November 28, 1997, 1.
7. Vali Nasr, *The Shi'a Revival: How Conflicts within Islam will Shape the Future* (New York: W.W. Norton & Com-

pany, 2006), 137.

8. "Hezbollah has 50,000 Rockets: Report," Agence France Presse, December 7, 2010, http://www.spacewar.com/reports/Hezbollah_has_50000_rockets_report_999.html.
9. Joseph Felter and Brian Fishman, "Iranian Strategy in Iraq: Politics and 'Other Means,'" Combating Terrorism Center at West Point *Occasional Paper*, October 13, 2008, http://ctc.usma.edu/Iran_Iraq/CTC_Iran_Iraq_Final.pdf; Ned Parker, "Ten Years After Iraq War Began, Iran Reaps the Gains," *Los Angeles Times*, March 28, 2013, http://articles.latimes.com/2013/mar/28/world/la-fg-iraq-iran-influence-20130329.
10. "Chapter 3. State Sponsors of Terrorism," in *Country Reports on Terrorism 2012* (Washington, DC: U.S. Department of State, May 2013), http://www.state.gov/j/ct/rls/crt/2012/209985.htm.
11. Ibid.
12. The historically tense relations between Iran and Egypt deteriorated precipitously during 2008-2010, spurred in large part by Egyptian fears of Iranian internal meddling. These worries were showcased in spring of 2009, when Egyptian authorities arrested a total of twenty-six individuals suspected of carrying out espionage for Hezbollah, and of plotting to carry out terrorist attacks within Egypt. The suspects were subsequently formally charged with plotting subversion against the Egyptian state. "Egypt Charges 26 'Hizbullah Spies,'" *Jerusalem Post*, July 26, 2009, http://www.jpost.com/servlet/Satellitecid=1248277893866&pagename=JPost%2FJPArticle%2FShowFull.
13. See, for example, "Lawmaker: Uprisings in Region Promising Birth of Islamic Middle-East," Fars News Agency (Tehran), February 5, 2011, http://english.farsnews.com/newstext.php?nn=8911161168.
14. "Iran's Support for Bahrain Protesters Fuels Regional Tensions," *Deutsche Welle*, April 15, 2011, http://www.dw.de/irans-support-for-bahrain-protesters-fuels-regional-tensions/a-6504403-1.
15. See, for example, Eric Schmitt, and Robert F. Worth, "With Arms for Yemen Rebels, Iran Seeks Wider Mideast Role," *New York Times*, March 15, 2012, http://www.ny-

times.com/2012/03/15/world/middleeast/aiding-yemen-rebels-iran-seeks-wider-mideast-role.html.

16. Luke McKenna, "Syria is Importing Iranian Snipers to Murder Anti-Government Protesters," *Business Insider*, January 27, 2012, http://www.businessinsider.com/syria-is-importing-iranian-snipers-to-murder-anti-government-protesters-2012-1.
17. See, for example, Farnaz Fassihi, "Iran Recruiting Afghan Refugees to Fight for Regime in Syria," *Wall Street Journal*, May 15, 2014.
18. Seth J. Franzman, "Who Are Iran's 80,000 Shi'ite Fighters in Syria?" *Jerusalem Post*, April 28, 2018, https://www.jpost.com/Middle-East/Who-are-Irans-80000-Shiite-fighters-in-Syria-552940
19. Richard Barrett, *Beyond The Caliphate: Foreign Fighters and the Threat of Returnees* (The Soufan Center, October 2017), 5, http://thesoufancenter.org/wp-content/uploads/2017/10/Beyond-the-Caliphate-Foreign-Fighters-and-the-Threat-of-Returnees-TSC-Report-October-2017-v2.pdf.
20. "Iranian Revolutionary Guard Corps Commander Jafari: We Support Resistance to U.S. and Israel in Syria and Elsewhere in the Region," Middle East Media Research Institute *Clip* no. 4272, April 21, 2014, http://www.memritv.org/clip/en/4272.htm.
21. See, for example, Dina Esfandiary and Ariane Tabatabai, "Iran's ISIS Policy," *International Affairs* 91, iss. 1 (2015), https://www.chathamhouse.org/sites/default/files/field/field_publication_docs/INTA91_1_01_Esfandiary_Tabatabai.pdf.
22. Under Secretary of the Treasury for Terrorism and Financial Intelligence Stuart Levey, Remarks before the 5th Annual Conference on Trade, Treasury, and Cash Management in the Middle East, Abu Dhabi, United Arab Emirates, March 7, 2007, http://uae.usembassy.gov/remarks_of_stuart_levey_.html.
23. Carla Humud, Christopher Blanchard, Jeremy Sharp and Jim Zanotti, "Iranian Assistance to Groups in Yemen, Iraq, Syria, and the Palestinian Territories," Congressional Research Service *Memorandum*, July 31, 2015, http://www.kirk.senate.gov/images/PDF/Iran%20

Financial%20Support%20to%20Terrorists%20and%20Militants.pdf.

24. Brian Hook, Remarks at the Foundation for Defense of Democracies, Washington, DC, August 28, 2018, http://www.defenddemocracy.org/content/uploads/documents/FDD-Summit-Brian-Hook.pdf.
25. Ibid.
26. See, for example, Azadeh Moaveni, "The Backlash against Iran's Role in Lebanon," *Time*, August 31, 2006, http://www.time.com/time/world/article/0,8599,1515755,00.html.
27. U.S. Central Intelligence Agency, "Iran," *World Factbook*, August 13, 2013, https://www.cia.gov/library/publications/resources/the-world-factbook/geos/ir.html.
28. U.S. Department of State, Bureau of Democracy, Human Rights and Labor, *International Religious Freedom Report 2008*, n.d., http://www.state.gov/g/drl/rls/irf/2008/108482.htm.
29. See, for example, Ebrahim Mohseni, Nancy Gallagher and Clay Ramsey, *Iranian Public Opinion on the Nuclear Agreement*, Center for International & Security Studies at Maryland, September 2015, http://www.cissm.umd.edu/sites/default/files/CISSM-PA%20Iranian%20Public%20Opinion%20on%20the%20Nuclear%20Agreement%20090915%20FINAL-LR.pdf.
30. Andrew Torchia, "Crisis of Expectations: Iran Protests Mean Economic Dilemma for Government," Reuters, January 1, 2018, https://www.reuters.com/article/us-iran-rallies-economy/crisis-of-expectations-iran-protests-mean-economic-dilemma-for-government-idUSKBN1EQ15S.
31. "Iran Worried as Unemployment Reaches 60% in Some Cities," *Radio Farda*, October 2, 2017, https://en.radiofarda.com/a/iran-unemployment-60-percent/28768226.html.
32. Patrick Cockburn, "Corruption and Inequality Fueling Protests in Iran as Rouhani Faces Pressure to Crack Down," *Independent* (London), January 1, 2018, https://www.independent.co.uk/news/world/middle-east/why-iran-protests-demonstrations-violence-corruption-inequality-hassan-rouhani-donald-trump-a8137051.

html.

33. "26 Million Iranians Suffer Absolute Poverty, Says Prominent Economist," *Radio Farda*, April 10, 2018, https://en.radiofarda.com/a/iran-million-suffer-from-poverty/29156808.html.
34. Chirine Mouchantaf, "Iranian Protest: 'Military Adventurism' at the Core of Citizens Outcry," *Defense News*, January 5, 2018, https://www.defensenews.com/global/mideast-africa/2018/01/05/iranian-protest-military-adventurism-at-the-core-of-citizens-outcry/.
35. Amir Basiri, "Iran Increases its Military Budget in Response to Nationwide Protests," January 30, 2018, https://www.washingtonexaminer.com/iran-increases-its-military-budget-in-response-to-nationwide-protests.
36. Philip Issa, "Iran Protests put Spotlight on Military's Vast and Shadowy War in Syria," Associated Press, January 5, 2018, https://www.thestar.com/news/world/2018/01/05/iran-protests-put-spotlight-on-militarys-vast-and-shadowy-war-in-syria.html.
37. Mohammad Mohaddessin, *Islamic Fundamentalism: The New Global Threat* (Washington: Seven Locks Press, 1993), 132-136.
38. See, for example, Michael Eisenstadt, *Iranian Military Power: Capabilities and Intentions* (Washington: Washington Institute for Near East Policy, 1996), 70-72.
39. Mohaddessin, *Islamic Fundamentalism*, 102.
40. Michael Knights, "Iran's Ongoing Proxy War in Iraq," Washington Institute for Near East Policy *Policywatch* 1492, March 16, 2009, http://www.washingtoninstitute.org/templateC05.php?CID=3029.
41. See, for example, Amir Toumaj, "IRGC Special Officer's Death Highlights Involvement in Syria," *Long War Journal*, October 1, 2016, http://www.longwarjournal.org/archives/2016/10/irgc-special-forces-officers-death-highlights-involvement-in-syria.php.
42. "Rev. Guards Intelligence," *Iran Brief*, January 6, 1997, http://www.lexis-nexis.com.
43. "Ministry of Intelligence and Security [MOIS]: Vezarat-e Ettela'at va Amniat-e Keshvar VEVAK," globalsecurity.org, February 19, 2006, http://www.globalsecurity.org/intell/world/iran/vevak.htm.

44. [Eisenstadt, *Iranian Military Power*, 70.
45. Federation of American Scientists, "Ministry of Intelligence and Security [MOIS]: Organization," n.d., http://www.fas.org/irp/world/iran/vevak/org.htm.
46. See, for example, "Khamene'i Ordered Khobar Towers Bombing, Defector Says," *Iran Brief*, August 3, 1998, http://www.lexis-nexis.com; American intelligence officials have long maintained that Iranian terrorism is authorized at the highest official levels. See, for example, CIA Director R. James Woolsey, "Challenges to Peace in the Middle East," remarks before the Washington Institute for Near East Policy's Wye Plantation Conference, Queenstown, Maryland, September 23, 1994, http://www.washingtoninstitute.org/templateC07.php?CID=66.
47. Eisenstadt, *Iranian Military Power*, 71.
48. Ibid.; Mohaddessin, *Islamic Fundamentalism*, 101-102.
49. Drew Middleton, "5 Years of Iran-Iraq War: Toll May Be Near a Million," *New York Times*, September 23, 1985, 4.
50. Geneive Abdo, "Islam's Warriors Scent Blood," *Observer* (London), July 18, 1999, 26.
51. "Basij Commander Admits Forces Shot at 2009 Protesters," International Campaign for Human Rights in Iran, January 6, 2014, https://www.iranhumanrights.org/2014/01/basij-shot/.
52. See, for example, "Six People Said Killed, 300 Arrests at Sufi Protest in Iran," *Radio Farda*, February 20, 2018, https://www.rferl.org/a/iran-sufi-gonabadi-protests-tehran-deaths/29050268.html
53. Angus McDowall, "Tehran Deploys Islamic Vigilantes to Attack Protesters," *Independent* (London), July 11, 2003, 12.
54. For more on the *guruh-i fishar*, see Michael Rubin, *Into the Shadows: Radical Vigilantes in Khatami's Iran* (Washington: Washington Institute for Near East Policy, 2001).
55. Robert D. Kaplan, "A Bazaari's World," *Atlantic Monthly 277*, iss. 3 (1996), 28.
56. Wilfried Buchta, *Who Rules Iran? The Structure of Power in the Islamic Republic* (Washington: Washington Institute for Near East Policy – Konrad Adenauer Stiftung,

2000), 75.

57. Ibid.; See also Kenneth Katzman, Statement before the Joint Economic Committee of the United States Congress, July 25, 2006.
58. "Tehran Faces Growing Kurdish Opposition," *Washington Times*, April 3, 2006, http://www.washingtontimes.com/news/2006/apr/3/20060403-125601-8453r/.
59. See, for example, "4 Members of PJAK Terrorist Group Arrested in Iran," Fars News Agency (Tehran), November 30, 2010, http://english.farsnews.com/newstext.php?nn=8909091200; See also "Iranian Troops Attack Kurdish PJAK Rebel Bases in Iraq," BBC (London), July 18, 2011, http://www.bbc.co.uk/news/world-middle-east-14189313.
60. "Iran Deploying Troops, Tanks to Kurdistan Border," *World Tribune*, July 19, 2013, http://www.worldtribune.com/2013/07/19/iran-deploying-troops-tanks-to-kurdistan-border/.
61. "Five IRGC Soldiers Killed in Clash with 'Terrorists' in Western Iran," Xinhua, October 11, 2013, http://news.xinhuanet.com/english/world/2013-10/11/c_125510936.htm.
62. See, for example, Fuad Haqaqi, "ISIS Boasts Rising Number of Recruits Among Iranian Kurds," *Rudaw*, November 12, 2014, http://www.rudaw.net/english/middleeast/iran/101220141.
63. Esfandiary and Tabatabai, "Iran's ISIS Policy."
64. Mohamad Bazzi, "Iran Will Do What it Takes to Fight ISIS," *CNN*, April 2015, https://edition.cnn.com/2015/01/03/opinion/bazzi-iran-iraq/.
65. "Gunmen Attack Iran's Parliament, Khomeini Shrine," *Al-Jazeera* (Doha), June 7, 2017, https://www.aljazeera.com/news/2017/06/attacks-reported-iran-parliament-mausoleum-170607063232218.html.
66. "ISIS Releases Video Purporting to Show Iran Military Parade Attackers," Reuters, September 24, 2018, https://www.haaretz.com/middle-east-news/isis-releases-video-purporting-to-show-iran-military-parade-attackers-1.6494383.

19 Iraq

Quick Facts

Population: 39,192,111 (July 2017 est.)
Area: 438,317 sq km
Ethnic Groups: Arab 75-80%, Kurdish 15-20%, other 5% (includes Turkmen, Yezidi, Shabak, Kaka'i, bedouin, Romani, Assyrian, Circassian, Sabaean-Mandaean, Persian)
Religions: Muslim (official) 95-98% (Shia 64-69%, Sunni 29-34%), Christian 1% (includes Catholic, Orthodox, Protestant, Assyrian Church of the East), other 1-4%
Government Type: federal parliamentary republic
GDP (official exchange rate): $197.7 billion (2017 est.)

Map and Quick Facts courtesy of the CIA World Factbook (Last Updated September 2018)

Introduction

Iraq's contemporary history is replete with both secular and Islamist political currents. Shia and Sunni Islamist movements formed in Iraq in response to Saddam Hussein's secular nationalist Ba'athist regime, and as part of the political Islam movement sweeping the larger region. Most of these Islamist parties existed in exile or in hiding for much of 1980s and 1990s, and emerged in Iraq only after the fall of Saddam in 2003. Since that time, both Sunni and Shia Islamist parties have played an important role in Iraq's political system. Although the 2010 parliamentary election saw the rise of secular political coalitions, rising sectarianism gave new life to Islamist currents. An extreme example was the Islamic State, which took Iraqi towns and cities in early 2014; another is the presence of certain Shia paramilitary groups within the Popular Mobilization Units (PMU), an umbrella armed organization formed as a response to the Islamic State.

Sunni and Shia Islamist militant groups active in Iraq continue to fuel sectariaaan violence. In 2015, the Iraqi Security Forces, supported by the PMUs, began re-taking territory from the Islamic State, which at its peak occupied one-third of the country. By the end of 2017, Iraqi forces had retaken most of its lost territory, including Mosul, the country's second largest city. The question of

Shia militant groups, however, remains; some have sought a more prominent political role in Iraqi society, yet remain unwilling to integrate into the state apparatus. As Iraq's nascent democratic system evolves, secular and Islamist forces will continue to vie for influence and power.

Islamist Activity

Islamist activity in Iraq today takes three distinct forms based on ethno-sectarian lines. Given that the Shia population of Iraq is significantly larger than that of Iraq's Sunnis, there exists a wider array of Shia militant groups, ranging from sectarian to nationalist orientations. However, Salafi-jihadi Sunni groups, such as the Islamic State, pose a significant threat to the Iraq state. Additionally, among the country's Kurdish population, Islamic activity exists but is relatively minimal.

Shia Groups

The main Shia political factions in Iraq since 2003 have been the Islamic Dawa Party (Ḥizb al-Daʿwa al-Islamiyya), the Sadrist Trend (al-Tayyar al-Sadri), and the Islamic Supreme Council of Iraq, or ISCI (al-Majlis al-A'ala al-Islami al-Iraqi). Both Dawa and ISCI have recently suffered ruptures. Ammar al-Hakim, who previously led ISCI, split from the group in the summer of 2017 to form the National Wisdom Trend (tayar al-hikmat al-watani). Ahead of the 2018 elections, Abadi decided to form a new electoral list, the Victory Alliance (Tahaluf al-Nasr) to compete against his Dawa compatriot Nouri al-Maliki, who headed the State of Law Coalition (Itilaf Dawlat al-Qanun). The main Shia military factions fall under the Popular Mobilization Units, or PMUs (al-hashd al-shaabi), including the Badr Organization, Asaib ahl al-Haq, Kataib Hezbollah, and others. Many of these paramilitaries have their own political identities. In early 2018, the PMU leadership formed an electoral list named the Conquest Alliance (Tahaluf al-Fatah), which spanned beyond the PMU and includes non-armed Shia Islamists groups such as ISCI. Smaller Islamist groups include the National Reform Trend (led by former Prime Minister Ibrahim al-Jaafari) and the Fadhila (Islamic Virtue) Party.

The Islamic Dawa Party

The Dawa Party is the oldest Shia Islamist party in Iraq. It emerged in the late 1950s in response to the spread of socialist and communist movements in Iraq.[1] Grand Ayatollah Mohammed Baqir al-Sadr, a distinguished Shia scholar, is widely credited as Dawa's founder.[2] Dawa emphasized the promotion of Islamic values and ethics and believed the right to govern was distinct from the juridical function of religious authorities. It believed that both should be subsumed under constitutional mechanisms.[3]

In the 1980s, Sadr split from Dawa due to tensions with the Shia seminary (hawza) in Najaf. Dawa remained the leading Shia Islamist opposition party of the 1970s and 1980s, and therefore suffered fierce persecution from Saddam Hussein's Ba'athist regime. During this time, its members remained active and hid in either Iraq or exile. The main exiled Dawa branches existed in Iran, Syria, and the United Kingdom.

Following the 2003 Iraq war and the establishment of the Coalition Provisional Authority (CPA), Dawa emerged as one of the main Shia political groups in Iraq. The CPA was a transitional government for Iraq that lasted from March 2003 to April 2004. Since the handover of power, all of Iraq's Prime Ministers have been members of Dawa, including Prime Minister Nouri al-Maliki (2006-2014).

Initially, Maliki was selected in 2006 as a compromise candidate because of his reputation for weakness. Until 2008, he relied heavily on other Shia factions, such as ISCI and the Sadrists, for political support. However, with U.S. support in the form of a surge of military personnel, he was able to launch a political and military campaign against both Sunni (AQI) and Shia (the Sadrist Trend's Jaysh al-Mahdi, or JAM) militant groups, thus solidifying his leadership and the political supremacy of Dawa. Maliki then formed the State of Law Coalition (Dawlat al-Qanoon), which has remained the umbrella organization for Dawa. Maliki became the single most powerful political actor in Iraq during his second term as premier (2010-2014), when he centralized power and weakened Sunni and Shia political opponents.[4]

The emergence of the Islamic State, however, caused Maliki

to step down and allow another compromise candidate, Haider al-Abadi, to emerge and assume the premiership. Although they come from the same party, Abadi and Maliki are political rivals. As a result of this schism, and despite continuing to be the strongest party, Dawa has split into two factions. In the 2018 elections, these two groups ran in two separate lists, costing them the victory. Abadi's Nasr won 42 seats (out of 329) and Maliki's State of Law won 25 seats.[5]

The Sadrist Trend

The Sadrist Trend is a nationalist religious movement founded by Shia cleric Mohammed Sadeq al-Sadr (the son of Mohammad Baqir al-Sadr) in the 1990s. Across southern Iraq and in Baghdad, the movement gained widespread support from poor Shia communities that were drawn to its emphasis on economic and social relief, along with its focus on traditional Islamic law and customs.[6] The Sadrists believe that religious leaders should take an active role in political and social affairs. This position aligns the group with the current Iranian regime to a certain extent, but the Sadrists are distinguished by their desire for technocratic ministers.[7] Sadrists oppose the interference of any external actor (including both the United States and Iran) in Iraqi domestic affairs.

In 1999, Saddam Hussein ordered the assassination of Sadeq al-Sadr and his two oldest sons, causing much of the movement's leadership to go into hiding. After the 2003 invasion of Iraq, the Sadrist Trend re-emerged under the leadership of his youngest son, Muqtada al-Sadr. The Sadrists vehemently opposed the presence of U.S. forces in Iraq. They also opposed Baghdad's new elite of exiled returnees who had spent decades away from the country – referring to these leaders as "foreigner Iraqis."[8] Muqtada al-Sadr was able to derive considerable legitimacy on the street by making the claim that he was the only leader who had lived in Iraq under the dictatorship of Saddam Hussein. The Sadrist Trend and its Jaysh al-Mahdi (JAM) militia were a powerful force during the height of sectarian violence in Iraq from 2004 to 2007.

The movement lost significant influence as U.S. and Iraqi forces degraded the JAM during security offensives in 2007 and 2008. Nouri al-Maliki's Saulat al-Fursan (Operation Knights Charge) effectively drove out Sadr, who disbanded the JAM and went into exile in Iran.

In 2011, Sadr returned from exile. His time in Iran had turned his sympathies back toward Iraq, and his public discourse reflected this change in sentiment. He restructured the movement to emphasize political and social programs and a need to combat ineffective governance.[9] Sadr has also presented himself as cross-sectarian – he worked with Kurdistan Regional Government (KRG) President Massoud Barzani and secular leader Ayad Allawi (who represented Iraq's Sunnis) in an effort to depose Maliki in 2012. His emphasis on combatting corruption and calling for a change to the political system of muhasasa, which grants power based on identity, has won Sadr significant support with the population.

Moreover, in 2016, Sadr inspired a protest movement that saw millions take to the street of Baghdad's Tahrir Square.[10] In March 2016, Sadr trespassed into Baghdad's Green Zone, which houses most of the international embassies in the city. Rather than reprimanding or arresting Sadr for trespassing, the Iraqi general in command greeted him respectfully.[11]

Despite opposing the existence of the PMU, the Sadrists continue to maintain a militant wing, called Sarayat al-Salam (the Peace Brigades), which has less sectarian connotations than the previous JAM. The Peace Brigades have fought alongside Sunni tribes in Anbar, and remain skeptical of the better-funded, Iranian-backed Shia paramilitaries – particularly Asaib ahl al-Haq and Kataib Hezbollah. Like Dawa, the Sadrist Trend supports a strong central Iraqi government, but opposes an American or Iranian presence in Iraq. It also opposes the current elite, which it believe is corrupt and unrepresentative of the people.

Sadr has also continued to be against Iranian influence in Iraq, and in the summer of 2017 made visits to Saudi Arabia and the UAE to improve relations with regional Sunni powers. Inside Iraq, Sadr enjoy support from Sunni populations.

In 2018, the Sadrists formed the Revolutionaries for Reform Alliance (Tahaluf al-Sairoon), which included Islamists and secularists linked to the Iraqi Communist Party. The list was based on a renewed conception of political Islam, which according to Iraqi sociologist Faleh Abdul Jabar could bridge together the Islamists and the secularists – who were united against the common enemy, i.e. the post-2003 Iraqi elite.[12] The list won the most seats (54 seats) in the May 2018 elections, giving Sadr the chance to play kingmaker in the future.

The Islamic Supreme Council of Iraq

The third significant Islamist political actor in post-2003 Iraq is the Islamic Supreme Council of Iraq (ISCI), previously known as the Supreme Council for the Islamic Revolution in Iraq (SCIRI). SCIRI was originally founded in Iran in 1982, following Saddam Hussein's crackdown on *Dawa*, and worked closely with the Iranian government during the Iran-Iraq War to support Shia activism against the Saddam regime. It had a militia called the Badr Corps.

Following the 2003 U.S.-led invasion, SCIRI became a dominant political force in the post-CPA government, while maintaining its close relationship with Iran. In the mid 2000s, many Badr members were incorporated into the Iraqi Security Forces, where they retained their fighting status.[13]

As time went on, Iran increased its interference in Iraq. In an effort to distance itself from Iran, SCIRI changed its name to ISCI in 2007.[14] In addition, the group began to focus more heavily on Iraqi nationalism. It also shifted its primary religious allegiance away from Iran's Supreme Leader, the Ayatollah Khamenei, to Grand Ayatollah Ali Sistani, who believes religious leaders should not be involved in the administration of the state. Sistani is the head of the Najaf Shia seminar (hawza) and as such is the head of the Shia religious establishment (marjai'ya).

After the death of ISCI leader Abd al-Aziz al-Hakim in August 2009, his son, Ammar al-Hakim, assumed control of the movement. ISCI has suffered from two key defections. In March 2012, ISCI split from the Badr Organization. The split was partly due to leadership squabbles in the wake of poor performance in the 2010 parliamentary elections.[15] More importantly, the two organizations disagreed over whether to support the incumbent prime minister, Maliki. The Badr organization, under the leadership of Hadi al-Ameri, split off from Hakim's ISCI. Then, in 2017, Hakim left ISCI to form the National Wisdom Trend (tayar al-hikmat al-watani), leaving Humam Hamoudi to take over as leader of ISCI. In his departure, Hakim cited internal power struggles within ISCI's senior leadership, who made running the party difficult.[16]

Eventually, ISCI, now led by Humam al-Hamoudi, would rejoin Ameri's Fateh electoral alliance. Moreover, under the auspices of the PMU, ISCI maintains a military wing, which is active in the fight against the Islamic State. Its militias include the Supporters of the Faith brigades. These groups receive funding and weapons from the prime minister's office, and abide by the central government's policy decisions. They often fight alongside the Iraqi Security Forces.

The ideological concept of leadership by clerics (wilayat al-faqih) divides ISCI from Dawa and the Sadrists. ISCI maintains its belief that clergy should lead society. By contrast, Dawa and the Sadrists, stemming from the influence of Mohammad Baqir al-Sadr, believe that the community should be dominant in society (wilayat al-umma).

The Popular Mobilization Units (PMU)

Following the emergence of the Islamic State, which began taking over Iraqi towns and cities in early 2014, Maliki established the PMU, which was later further legitimized by Sistani's fatwa, which called on Iraqis to volunteer to fight against the group.

The PMU is not a single organization; rather, it consists of some 50 militias, some of which are loyal to Sistani. But the most powerful and formidable PMUs are loyal to and backed by Iran. Those groups tend to be better-funded and better-equipped than their wholly Iraqi counterparts. Hadi al-Ameri's Badr Organization, Abu Muhandis' Kataib Hezbollah (KH), and Qais Khazali's Asaib ahl al-Haq (AAH) are all groups that are fighting in direct coordination with Iran. They are known to receive extensive support from the Qods Force paramilitary unit of Iran's Revolutionary Guard Corps (IRGC-QF), including training, funding, and supplies. They share strong relations with the IRGC-QF's leader, Qassem Solaimani.[17] KH emerged in 2007, and since that time has conducted numerous attacks on U.S. and Iraqi forces.[18] KH has used advanced tactics and systems, including Improvised Rocket-Assisted Mortars (IRAMs).[19] The group has remained active following the withdrawal of U.S. forces from Iraq in 2011.[20] It has reportedly conducted attacks against the camps of the Mujahedeen-e-Khalq, an Iranian dissident group with elements based in Iraq. KH fighters are also fighting in Syria at the behest of the Iranian and Assad regimes.[21]

AAH is an offshoot of JAM and was formed following the split between Muqtada al-Sadr and Qais Khazali.[22] Khazali, who was captured by Coalition forces in March 2007 but subsequently released as part of a prisoner exchange in January 2010, is the leader of AAH.[19] Since the departure of U.S. forces in December 2011, AAH has expressed its desire to participate in Iraqi politics and rebranded itself as a nationalist organization also dedicated to Islamic resistance. It has established political offices throughout the country and has instituted religious and social outreach programs.[23] AAH's turn toward politics has heightened its competition with the Sadrist Trend. Sadr and Khazali have publicly traded accusations and the tensions have even resulted in violent clashes.[24] Maliki cultivated strong ties with AAH as a counterbalance to the Sadrists and other opponents. The second group includes paramilitaries closer to Sistani. The Ali al-Akbar Brigades and the Abbadiyah Brigades are part of this group.

The third group is made up of militias that represent wings of political parties. For instance, the above-mentioned ISCI militias, or Sadr's Sarayat al-Salam, fall into this category.[25]

In November 2016, the Iraqi parliament passed a law that will transform the PMUs into a legal and separate military corps alongside the state's forces.[26] The PMUs also showcase splits within the Shia movement in Iraq.[27] For instance, both Sadr and Sistani remain opposed to the politicization of the PMUs, and both call for the provision of greater power to the state. Sadr, despite being the leader of a militia, has claimed he is willing to disband it if all other paramilitaries are also disbanded and monopoly over the use of legitimate violence is restored to the central government.

Hikmah

As discussed above, in 2017 Ammar al-Hakim broke away from

ISCI to form the National Wisdom Movement (Tayar al-Hikmah al-Watani). In the 2018 election, Hikmeh placed seventh with 19 seats. The group is based on Hakim's ideas for a new form of Islamism that moves past the post-2003 ethno-sectarian based political system. He argues for a bottom-up Islamism that is in tune with wider Iraqi society and is not solely based on Shiism. He also argues in favor of greater independence from Iran.

Sunni Groups

The Sunni political landscape has shifted dramatically in Iraq in recent years. The major ideological debate among the Sunni Islamist community, however, remains the question of cooperating with Baghdad.[28] During the civil war (2006-2007) and then again following the emergence of the Islamic State in Mosul and elsewhere (2014-present), many Sunni Islamists have chosen to reject the central government, which they perceive to be a Shia-Iranian dictatorship. However, during the Anwar Awakening and subsequent period of comparatively good governance in Iraq (2008-2010), Sunni Islamists participated in the political process.

The Iraqi Islamic Party

The only Sunni Islamist political party in Iraq has been the Iraqi Islamic Party (IIP) – although it is not a unified organization and lacks the institutional capacities of most political parties. It is currently led by Ayad al-Samarraie.

The IIP has its roots in the mid-1940s or early 1950s, when Mohammed al-Sawwaf, an Iraqi studying in Egypt, met Muslim Brotherhood founder Hassan al-Banna.[29] Upon his return to Iraq, al-Sawwaf and another activist, Amjad al-Zahawi Mahmood, founded an Iraqi organization modeled on the Muslim Brotherhood, known as the Islamic Brotherhood Society.[30] Later, in 1960, the Iraqi Islamic Party was formally established after Abdul-Karim Qassem's government allowed political parties to form in Iraq.[31] Following the overthrow of Qassem's government by the Ba'ath Party in 1963, the IIP was violently suppressed but continued its operations clandestinely and in exile.[32] Ayad al-Samarraie, who had been the Secretary General of the IIP since 1970, fled Iraq in 1980.[33]

Following the fall of Saddam Hussein's Ba'athist regime in

2003, many IIP leaders, including al-Samarraie, returned to Iraq and the party re-emerged. In the December 2005 parliamentary election, the IIP ran as a party of a Sunni coalition known as Tawafuq (Iraqi Accord Front), which won 44 seats in the 275-member parliament. From 2005 to early 2009, Tawafuq was the dominant Sunni political presence in the parliament, though it was seen by many Sunni Iraqis as an exile party that did not represent their interests. By early 2009, Tawafuq began to disintegrate as its constituent parties left the coalition during the debate over the selection of the parliamentary speaker.[34]

In 2009 and 2010, the IIP lost a considerable portion of its electorate to the secular nationalist coalition of former Prime Minister Allawi's al-Iraqiyya, also called the Iraqiyah list. By the 2010 parliamentary election, the vast number of Sunni political entities joined the Iraqiyah List. Even IIP leader Tariq al-Hashimi left the group to join al-Iraqiyya. IPP was the only party to run under the Tawafuq banner in 2010, and consequently, the total number of seats held by Tawafuq shrank from 44 to just 6.

The Association of Muslim Scholars

The Association of Muslim Scholars (Hay'at al-'Ulama' al-Muslimeen*)* formed immediately after the U.S.-led invasion in April of 2003. The group is not a political party, but rather a group of influential Sunni clerics and scholars seeking to represent the Sunni voice in a Shia-dominated Baghdad. It was initially led by Harith al-Dhari, a cleric who called on Iraqis to boycott the U.S.-led attempts to rebuild the Iraqi government in a fatwa that also called for a "national insurgency."[35] Such sentiments, along with the Iraqi people's fear of retaliation if they participated in the political process, combined to significantly depress voter turnout. For example, Anbar Province, which is 90% Sunni[36] and has often suffered from violence and high levels of insurgency, had a voter turnout of just 1% in the January parliamentary interim elections of 2005.[37] However, by the December 2005 elections, national voter turnout rose to 77%.[38] The group was an important driving force of Sunni insurgency in 2006. However, it came into conflict with AQI and its leader, Abu Musab al-Zarqawi, particularly on the question as to the type and scope of acceptable violence. Following Harith's death, his son, Muthanna, has taken over the organization, which continues to claim to speak on behalf of disenfranchised Sunnis. It also relies on rousing a sense of Iraqi nationalism.

Other groups seek to represent Sunni interests as well. The Sunni Endowment (Waqf al-Sunni) is a government-recognized body tasked with managing holy sites (include thousands of mosques) and distributing resources to the population. It is led by Abdul Latif al-Humayim, who was appointed by Prime Minister Haider al-Abadi. The Fiqih Council of Iraq (Majma al-Faqih al-Iraqi) is another group seeking to represent Sunnis. Its goal is to spread the Islamic call of faith, order, and ethics. The Dar al-Iftah al-Iraqi, which is based in Erbil, is another religious organization seeking to represent Sunnis. Finally, Hayat al-Iftah al-Salafi is a small Salafi organization led by Mahdi al-Subaie, who is opposed to the government in Baghdad.

The Islamic State (formerly al-Qaeda in Iraq - AQI)

The Islamic State initially grew out of an al-Qaeda offshoot, al-Qaeda in Iraq (AQI). AQI members included native Sunni Iraqis, members of the Kurdish Islamist group Ansar Al-Islam, and some foreigners, including its Jordanian-born leader, Abu Musab al-Zarqawi.[39] AQI was responsible for some of the deadliest car bombs and suicide bomb attacks in Iraq, as well as a surge in sectarian violence. AQI became the Islamic State of Iraq (ISI) in 2006. The organization had lost many of its strongholds in northern and western Iraq following the security offensives that began in 2007; however, it continued to operate in areas of northern Iraq, especially the city of Mosul, and in areas of Diyala, Salah ad-Din, Anbar, Baghdad, and its surrounding areas. Though AQI leaders pledged their allegiance to al-Qaeda in 2004, the group lost its affiliation and was no longer able to retain operational links with al-Qaeda leaders based in the tribal areas of Pakistan.[40]

ISI's subsequently transformed into the Islamic State in Iraq and the Levant (ISIL) in 2014. Back in Iraq, the group maintained a largely passive presence, but as Maliki began suppressing and attacking Iraqi Sunnis, the Islamic State grew in numbers. Finally, in early 2014, it began taking over Iraqi territory, beginning in Fallujah and leading to Mosul, Iraq's second largest city, which was taken in June 2014. Following this, ISIL formally declared a Caliphate and changed its name to the Islamic State. The group's leader is currently Abu Bakr al-Baghdadi. By 2017, the group suffered defeats at the hands of the Iraqi security forces, the PMU, and the Kurdish peshmerga, reversing a trend of steady territorial gains and political growth. As of this writing, it has lost control over several major cities, including Mosul (which it claimed as its capital), Ramadi, Fallujah, and Tikrit.

To maintain legitimacy, the group has altered its tactics, reverting to AQI-style guerilla warfare and attacks on civilians in the provinces of Kirkuk, Diyala, Salahadeen, and Anbar. Most of its attacks are against security forces, including checkpoints manned by police or PMU groups. While it remains a threat to Baghdad and other major cities, ISIS has begun to show signs of transitioning back into the role of an underground organization.

Kurdish Groups

Political Islam has also developed extensively in Iraqi Kurdistan, also called the Kurdistan Region, an autonomous region in northern Iraq run by the Kurdistan Regional Government (KRG). It is particularly strong in the city of Halabja, but occurs in other major areas as well. The largest Kurdish Islamist political groups are the Kurdistan Islamic Union (KIU) and the Kurdistan Islamic Group (KIG).[41]

The Kurdistan Islamic Union

The KIU, also known as Yekgirtu, was established in 1994. Principally an adherent to Sunni Islam, the group was closely aligned with the Muslim Brotherhood. The group describes itself as "an Islamic reformative political party that strives to solve all political, social, economic and cultural matters of the people in Kurdistan from an Islamic perspective which can achieve the rights, general freedom, and social justice."[42] It is currently led by Secretary General Sheikh Salah ad-Din Muhammad Baha-al-Din. The KIU has no armed forces of its own, and is most active in charity work.

The Kurdistan Islamic Group

The KIG was established in 2001 as a splinter faction of the KIU. It is led by Mala Ali Bapir. The KIG is believed to have close ties with extremist Islamist armed groups, such as Ansar al-Islam, which has been involved in attacks against leaders of the predominant political parties in Kurdistan, the Kurdistan Democratic Party (KDP) and the Patriotic Union of Kurdistan (PUK).[43] Bapir, however, claims his group has abandoned violence.

Nevertheless, the political influence of the KIU and KIG cannot compete with that of the KDP, PUK, and Change List (Gorran*)*, which dominate Kurdish political and social life. Of the 111 seats in the Kurdish parliament, the KIU and KIG have only four.[44] At the national level, the influence of Kurdish Islamist parties is even further diminished. The KIU has 4 seats in the 325-seat Iraqi parliament, while the KIG has only 2 seats. The emergence of Gorran shifted the balance of power and gave the KIU and KIG another ally in the Kurdish Regional Government parliament with which to challenge the dominant Kurdish parties. However, Kurdish Islamist parties remain only marginal actors in Iraqi political life.

Islamism and Society

97 percent of the Iraqi population is Muslim, and of that group, 60-65 percent are Shia Muslims. [45] Iraqi Shia primarily live in central and southern Iraq, though there are Shia communities in the north. 32-37 percent of Iraqi Muslims are Sunnis, and they are concentrated mainly in central and northern Iraq.[46] Of Iraq's more-than-30 million citizens, 75-80 percent are Arabs; 15-20 percent are Kurds; and Turkmen, Chaldean, Assyrian, Armenians, and other minority groups comprise the remaining 5 percent.[47] Religious minorities, such as Christians, Mandeans, and Yazidis comprise the remaining three percent of Iraq's population; however, these non-dominant ethnic and religious populations have declined significantly since 2003.[48]

According to the U.S. military, more than 77,000 Iraqis were killed during the height of sectarian violence between 2004 and 2008; Iraqi government statistics put that number at over 85,000.[49] According to the UN, the emergence of the Islamic State in Iraq led to "staggering violence," with some 18,800 killed between January

1, 2014 and October 31, 2015.[50] Fortunately, the death toll has since abated. The United Nations Assistance Mission to Iraq estimated that approximately 6,878 Iraqi civilians were killed in 2016 in total, primarily by the Islamic State.[51]

Following the fall of Saddam Hussein's secular regime in 2003, both Sunni and Shia Iraqis were able to openly express their Islamic faith in ways that they had not in decades. This was especially true for Shia Iraqis, who for the first time in decades could take part in the religious pilgrimages to the holy cities of Najaf and Karbala in southern Iraq. Exiled Sunni and Shia Islamist parties and movements returned to Iraq, where they played key roles in shaping Iraq's emerging political system. Iraqi politics, after 2003, became defined by identities – making political Islam an important tool for legitimacy.

Parts in the north of Iraq have, during various periods, fallen under strict Salafi-Jihadi rule. From 2004 to 2007 and from 2014 to 2017, as the security situation has deteriorated and the Iraqi state proved itself unable to capably govern, Sunni Islamist militant groups (namely, AQI then the Islamic State) have grown in strength and violently imposed their strict interpretations of Islamic law. They established strongholds in the predominantly Sunni areas of northern and western Iraq, such as the Anbar or Ninewah province. There, they brutally enforced harsh societal rules, including banning smoking and singing, prohibiting men from shaving their beards, forcing marriages and raping local women, such as Yazidi women, forcing minorities to flee their homes, requiring the wearing of strict Islamic dress by women, and maiming or killing anyone caught violating their radical laws.[52]

In the south, Shia militia groups have also at times enforced strict rules in the areas of Baghdad and southern Iraq that were under their control. During the 2005-2007 civil war, sectarian violence soared, as Shia militia groups violently attacked mixed areas of Baghdad.

At other times, however, sectarianism has been rejected. In 2008, Iraqis of all sects and ethnicities grew frustrated with the years of strife, under which Islamist parties and militias dominated. Sunni tribal leaders in Anbar province rejected AQI rule and took up arms against Sunni extremists, in a movement that became known as the Anbar Awakening. Awakening movements spread across Sunni areas from 2007 to 2008.[53] This, coupled with the U.S.-led security offensive that cleared first Baghdad and later the provinces surrounding the capital, significantly degraded AQI's capabilities and networks. During the Surge, Iraqi forces supported by the U.S. also targeted Shia militia groups in Baghdad and throughout central and southern Iraq. This culminated in the Iraqi-led operations in Basra and Baghdad, which dealt a significant blow to JAM and culminated in Sadr's announcement to disband his once-fearsome militia.[54] By mid-2008, when the last of the Surge forces left Iraq, violence had plummeted by more than 60 percent.[55]

The 2009 and 2010 elections saw the reorientation of Iraqi politics away from Islamism in a manner that reflected changes in society. As discussed above, Islamist exile parties like ISCI and the IIP lost considerable influence.[56] New political realities emerged in Iraq, and there was widespread anti-incumbent sentiment and a growing demand for secular, nationalist, and technocratic government that could preserve security, provide essential services, and reduce corruption.[57] These themes played an important role in the provincial and parliamentary elections.

By 2017, however, the shift from identity to issue-based politics had reappeared, as internal Shia, Kurdish, and Sunni struggles outweighed the sectarian narrative. An NDI poll that year found that most Iraqis blamed corruption and their own leaders, rather than sectarianism, for the rise of groups like ISIS.[58] Moreover, the poll also revealed that Shia leaders such as Abadi or Sadr enjoy considerable popularity in Sunni areas.

Nonetheless, Iraqi society remains heavily fragmented and sectarian divisions still exist, providing an opening for the re-emergence of the Islamic State.[59] Iraq's leading Shia parties, *Dawa* and the Sadrist Trend, retain their Islamist character and have emphasized this identity to shore up support.

Islamism and the State

Iraq is a parliamentary democracy and not a theocratic republic like its neighbor, Iran. The Iraqi Constitution guarantees the democratic rights of all Iraqi citizens as well as "full religious rights to freedom of religious belief and practice of all individuals."[60] Yet the Iraqi Constitution stipulates Islam as the official religion of the state and makes clear that no law may be enacted that contradicts the establish provisions of Islam. The ambiguities inherent in these provisions have led to challenges in interpretation and meaning. In some areas of Iraq, local governments have adopted stricter interpretations of Islamic law. The provincial councils in Basra and Najaf, for instance, have banned the consumption, sales, or transit of alcohol.[61] In November 2010, the Baghdad provincial council used a resolution from 1996 to similarly ban the sale of alcohol. [62] There have been occasional violent raids or attacks on venues believed to be selling alcohol.[63]

The Iraqi government's response to Islamist militant groups has varied. Islamist parties dominated provincial and national governments from 2004 to 2008. During that time, the state was both unwilling and unable to challenge the Islamist militant groups that threatened the state's legitimacy. Shia militia groups penetrated elements of the Iraqi Security Forces, and certain paramilitary and police units were accused of perpetrating brutal sectarian violence.[64] The threat from extremist groups ultimately jeopardized the functioning of the Iraqi state by late 2006. Several months later, in early 2007, U.S. forces announced a change of strategy in Iraq and the deployment of 20,000 additional troops, in what became known as the Surge. As the counterinsurgency offensives of the Surge unfolded, the Iraqi state also became more willing and able to challenge Sunni and Shia extremist groups as their influence and capability waned.[65] U.S. support during this time was critical in giving the Iraqi Security Forces, and even Iraq's political leadership, the confidence to move against extremist groups as well as in preventing the manipulation of the security forces for political ends. U.S. and Iraqi leaders also worked to professionalize the Iraqi Security Forces, expand their capabilities, and root out corrupt or sectarian elements.[66] U.S. and Iraqi operations from 2007 to the present significantly degraded both Sunni and Shia extremist groups and reduced violence, doing so by over 90 percent.[67]

Today, Iraqi forces continue to robustly target the Islamic State in Iraq. Despite the growing influence of the PMU, which Amnesty

International and Human Rights Watch have both criticized for committing war crimes,[68] the government has decided not to act against Shia militant groups. Given the weakness of the central government, it is unclear whether the Iraqi state can maintain the will or muster the ability to sufficiently check Shia militant groups (some of which continue to receive Iranian assistance), or whether political interests will enable such groups to expand.

Endnotes

1. Vali Nasr, *The Shia Revival: How Conflicts within Islam will Shape the Future* (New York: Norton, 2006), 117.
2. Patrick Cockburn, *Muqtada* (New York: Scribner, 2008), 31; Faleh Jabar, *The Shi'ite Movement in*
3. Jabar, *The Shi'ite Movement in Iraq,* 78-80; Islamic Dawa Party, "Party History," n.d.,http://www.islamicdawaparty.com/?module=home&fname=history.php&active=7&show=1.
4. Jabar, Malik, "Maliki and the Rest: A Crisis within a Crisis", *IIST Iraq Crisis Report – 2012,* June 2012, http://iraqstudies.com/books/featured3.pdf
5. Michael Knights, "Iraqi Elections and U.S. Interests: Taking the Long View," *Policy Analysis*, The Washington Institute, May 17, 2018, https://www.washingtoninstitute.org/policy-analysis/view/iraqi-elections-and-u.s.-interests-taking-the-long-view.
6. Jabar, *The Shi'ite Movement in Iraq*, 272-273.
7. Marisa Cochrane Sullivan, "The Fragmentation of the Sadrist Movement," Institute for the Study of War *Iraq Report* 12, January 2009, http://www.understandingwar.org/files/Iraq%20Report%2012.pdf.
8. Makiya, Kanan. *The Rope* (New York : Pantheon Books, 2016).
9. Makiya, Kanan. *The Rope*.
10. Mansour, Renad and Clark, Michael, "Is Muqtada Al-Sadr Good For Iraq?", *War on the Rocks,* May 2016, http://warontherocks.com/2016/05/is-muqtada-al-sadr-good-for-iraq/
11. "Iraqi cleric Muqtada al-Sadr starts Green Zone sit-

in," *Al Jazeera* March 28, 2016, http://www.aljazeera.com/news/2016/03/iraqi-cleric-muqtada-al-sadr-starts-green-zone-sit-160328040820897.html.

12. Jabar A. Faleh, *The Iraqi Protest Movement,* London School of Economics Middle East Centre Paper Series, June 2018, https://eprints.lse.ac.uk/88294/1/Faleh_Iraqi%20Protest%20Movement_Published_English.pdf.
13. "Iraqi cleric Muqtada al-Sadr starts Green Zone sit-in," *Al Jazeera.*
14. "Shiite Politics in Iraq: The Role of the Supreme Council," International Crisis Group *Middle East Report* Number 70, November 15, 2007.
15. "URGENT...SIIC, Badr Organization announce their official split," *All Iraq News*, March 11, 2012,http://www.alliraqnews.com/en/index.php?option=com_content&view=article&id=5847:urgentsiic-badr-organization-announce-their-official-split&catid=35:political&Itemid=2.
16. "الحكيم يعلن تأسيس تيار الحكمة الوطني," السومرية نيوز/, 24 تموز 2017," http://www.alsumaria.tv/news/210878/%D8%A7%D9%84%D8%AD%D9%83%D9%8A%D9%85-%D9%8A%D8%B9%D9%84%D9%86-%D8%AA%D8%A3%D8%B3%D9%8A%D8%B3-%D8%AA%D9%8A%D8%A7%D8%B1-%D8%A7%D9%84%D8-%AD%D9%83%D9%85%D8%A9-%D8%A7%D9%84%D9%88%D8%B7%D9%86%D9%8A/ar.
17. Sullivan, "The Fragmentation of the Sadrist Movement."
18. Yusif Salman: "Leading Figure in the Al-Sadr Trend to Al-Mashriq: Al-Sadr Met Asa'ib Ahl al-Haq Leader in Qom," Al-Mashriq (Iraq), January 18 , 2010; Martin Chulov, "Qais al-Khazali: from Kidnapper and Prisoner to Potential Leader,"*Guardian* (London), December 31, 2009, http://www.guardian.co.uk/world/2009/dec/31/iran-hostages-qais-al-khazali.
19. U.S. Department of the Treasury, "Treasury Designates Individual, Entity Posing Threat to Stability in Iraq."
20. Ashish Kumar Sen, "Dissidents Blame Camp Attack on Iraq," *Washington Times*, February 18, 2013,http://

www.washingtontimes.com/news/2013/feb/18/dissidents-blame-camp-attack-on-iraq/?page=all.

21. Michael Gordon and Steven Lee Myers, "Iran and Hezbollah Support for Syria Complicates Peace-Talk Strategy,"*New York Times*, May 21, 2013, http://www.nytimes.com/2013/05/22/world/middleeast/iran-and-hezbollahs-support-for-syria-complicates-us-strategy-on-peace-talks.html?pagewanted=all; Will Fulton, Joseph Holliday, and Sam Wyer, "Iranian Strategy in Syria," A Joint Report by AEI's Critical Threats Project and the Institute for the Study of War, May 2013, 23-25, http://www.understandingwar.org/sites/default/files/IranianStrategyinSyria-1MAY.pdf.
22. Karin Bruilliard, "Ex-Sadr Aide Held in American Deaths," *Washington Post*, March 23, 2007,http://www.washingtonpost.com/wp-dyn/content/article/2007/03/22/AR2007032200261.html; Felter and Fishman, "Iranian Strategy in Iraq: Politics and 'Other Means,'" 35; Sullivan, "The Fragmentation of the Sadrist Movement."
23. For a detailed analysis of AAH's political activities, see Sam Wyer, "The Resurgence of Asa'ib Ahl al-Haq," Institute for the Study of War *Middle East Security Report* 7, December 2012,http://www.understandingwar.org/sites/default/files/ResurgenceofAAH.pdf.
24. Wyer. 22-25.
25. Habib, Mustafa, "Taming The Beast: Can Iraq Ever Control Its Controversial Volunteer Militias?", *Niqash*, http://www.niqash.org/en/articles/security/5323/
26. "Iraqi parliament passes contested law on Shi'ite paramilitaries," *Reuters,* November 26, 2016, http://www.reuters.com/article/us-mideast-crisis-iraq-military-idUSKBN13L0IE.
27. Renad Mansour, *Iraq After the Fall of ISIS: The Struggle for the State,* July 4, 2017, https://www.chathamhouse.org/publication/iraq-after-fall-isis-struggle-state.
28. Mansour, Renad, "The Sunni Predicament in Iraq", *Carnegie Endowment for International Peace,* March 2016, http://carnegieendowment.org/2016/03/03/sunni-predicament-in-iraq-pub-62924
29. Basim Al-Azami, "The Muslim Brotherhood: Genesis

and Development," in Faleh A. Jabar, ed., *Ayatollahs, Sufis and Ideologues: State, Religion and Social Movements in Iraq* (London: Saqi, 2002), 164.

30. Al-Azami, "The Muslim Brotherhood: Genesis and Development;" Graham Fuller and Rend Rahim Francke, *The Arab Shi'a : The Forgotten Muslims* (Basingstoke, UK: Palgrave Macmillan, 2000); "Iraqi Islamic Party," globalsecurity.org, n.d., http://www.globalsecurity.org/military/world/iraq/iip.htm; Iraqi Islamist Party, "History," n.d., http://www.iraqiparty.com/page/who-are-we/.
31. Thabit Abdullah, *A Short History of Iraq: From 636 to the Present* (London: Longman, 2003).
32. "Iraqi Islamic Party"; Iraqi Islamic Party, "History."
33. "Iraqi Islamic Party"; Iraqi Islamic Party, "History."
34. Domergue and Sullivan, "Balancing Maliki."
35. Meijer, Roel, "The Association of Muslim Scholars in Iraq", *Middle East Research and Information,* http://www.merip.org/mer/mer237/association-muslim-scholars-iraq
36. "Irakische Streitkräfte starten Rückeroberung Ramadis". *Deutsche Welle*, May 26, 2015, http://www.dw.com/de/irakische-streitkr%C3%A4fte-starten-r%C3%BCckeroberung-ramadis/a-18477575.
37. Wong, Edward, "Turnout in the Iraqi Election is Reported at 70 Percent", *The New York Times,* December 2005, http://www.nytimes.com/2005/12/22/world/middleeast/turnout-in-the-iraqi-election-is-reported-at-70-percent.html
38. Anthony H. Cordesman, *Iraq's Evolving Insurgency and the Risk of Civil War*, Center for Strategic and International Studies, 2006, pg, 8, http://reliefweb.int/sites/reliefweb.int/files/resources/1B26E4C64879415AC125715D002C49E3-csis-irq-26apr.pdf.
39. United States Forces-Iraq, "The Insurgency," July 31, 2009, http://www.usf-iraq.com/?option=com_content&task=view&id=729&Itemid=45.
40. Kenneth Katzman, "Al Qaeda in Iraq: Assessment and Outside Links," Congressional Research Service Report for Congress, August 15, 2008, http://www.fas.org/sgp/crs/terror/RL32217.pdf; DoD News Briefing with

Commander, U.S. Forces-Iraq Gen. Raymond Odierno from the Pentagon, June 4, 2010.

41. Rafid Fadhil Ali, "Kurdish Islamist Groups in Northern Iraq," Jamestown Foundation *Terrorism Monitor* 6, iss. 22, November 25. 2008, http://www.jamestown.org/single/?no_cache=1&tx_ttnews[tt_news]=34176.
42. Qassim Khidhir Hamad, "Kurdish Election Lists," *Niqash* (Baghdad), June 30, 2009.
43. Kathleen Ridolfo, "A Survey of Armed Groups in Iraq," Radio Free Europe/Radio Liberty *Iraq Report* 7, no. 20, June 4, 2004.
44. "The Kurdistan Parliament," Kurdistan Regional Government website, accessible athttp://www.krg.org/articles/detail.asp?rnr=160&lngnr=12&smap=04070000&anr=15057; "The Members of the Parliament for Third Term 2009," Kurdistan Parliament website, accessible at http://www.perleman.org/Default.aspx?page=Parliamentmembers&c=Presidency-Member2009&group=40.
45. "The Kurdistan Parliament," Kurdistan Regional Government website.
46. "The Kurdistan Parliament," Kurdistan Regional Government website.
47. "Iraq," CIA World Factbook, updated April 6, 2011, https://www.cia.gov/library/publications/the-world-factbook/geos/iz.html; "Background Note: Iraq," U.S. Department of State, September 17, 2010,http://www.state.gov/r/pa/ei/bgn/6804.htm.
48. "Iraq," CIA World Factbook, updated April 6, 2011.
49. "US military says 77,000 Iraqis killed over 5 years," *Associated Press*, October 15, 2010, http://www.post-journal.com/page/content.detail/id/120540/US-military-says-77-000-Iraqis-killed-over-5-years-.html?isap=1&nav=5030.
50. BBC Middle East, "Iraq Conflict: Civilians suffering 'staggering' violence – UN", *BBC News*, January 2015, http://www.bbc.com/news/world-middle-east-35349861
51. Bethan McKernan, "Scale of Iraqi civilian casualties inflicted by Isis revealed by UN," *The Independent,* January 3, 2017, http://www.independent.co.uk/news/

world/middle-east/iraq-isis-casualties-civilian-islamic-state-un-figures-united-nations-middle-east-mosul-a7507526.html.

52. Rod Nordland, "Despite Gains, Petraeus Cautious About Iraq," *Newsweek,* August 21, 2008,http://www.newsweek.com/2008/08/20/avoiding-the-v-word.html; "Marriages split al Qaeda alliance," *Washington Times*, August 31, 2007, http://www.washingtontimes.com/news/2007/aug/31/marriages-split-al-qaeda-alliance/?page=all#pagebreak; "Severe Islamic law which banned 'suggestive' cucumbers cost Al Qaeda public support in Iraq,"*Daily Mail* (UK), August 10, 2008, http://www.dailymail.co.uk/news/worldnews/article-1043409/Severe-Islamic-law-banned-suggestive-cucumbers-cost-Al-Qaeda-public-support-Iraq.html.
53. John A. McCary, "The Anbar Awakening: An Alliance of Incentives," *The Washington Quarterly*, January 2009,http://www.twq.com/09winter/docs/09jan_mccary.pdf.
54. Marisa Cochrane Sullivan, "The Fragmentation of the Sadrist Movement," Institute for the Study of War *Iraq Report*12, January 2009, 37-38, http://www.understandingwar.org/files/Iraq%20Report%2012.pdf.
55. Viola Gienger, "Iraq Civilian Deaths Drop for Third Year as Toll Eases After U.S. Drawdown," *Bloomberg*, December 29, 2010, http://www.bloomberg.com/news/2010-12-30/iraq-civilian-deaths-drop-for-third-year-as-toll-eases-after-u-s-drawdown.html.
56. Iraqi High Electoral Commission, "Iraqi CoR Election Results," n.d., http://ihec-iq.com/en/results.html.
57. Sullivan, "Iraq's Parliamentary Election."
58. *Improved Security Provides Opening for Cooperation in Iraq: March to April 2017 Survey Findings*, National Democratic Institute, June 7, 2017.
59. Marisa Cochrane Sullivan and James Danly, "Iraq on the Eve of Elections," Institute for the Study of War *Backgrounder*, March 3, 2010, http://www.understandingwar.org/files/IraqEveofElections.pdf.
60. Iraqi Constitution, Section One, Article Two.
61. "Alcohol Banned in Iraq holy Shiite City of Najaf," *Middle East Online*, October 11, 2009, http://

www.middle-east-online.com/english/?id=34869.

62. John Leland, "Baghdad Raids on Alcohol Sellers Stir Fears," *New York Times*, January 15, 2011,http://www.nytimes.com/2011/01/16/world/middleeast/16iraq.html.
63. Leland, "Baghdad Raids on Alcohol Sellers Stir Fears," *New*.; "Kurdish Club Scene Booming as Baghdad Bans Alcohol," *Associated Press*, January 11, 2011.
64. Lionel Beehner, "Shiite Militias and Iraq's Security Forces," Council on Foreign
Relations *Backgrounder*, November 30, 2005, http://www.cfr.org/iraq/shiite-militias-iraqs-security-forces/p9316; "Iraq 'death squad caught in act,'" *BBC*, February 16, 2006, http://news.bbc.co.uk/2/hi/middle_east/4719252.stm; Steve Inskeep, "Riding Herd on the Iraqi Police's Dirty 'Wolf Brigade,'" *National Public Radio*, March 28, 2007, http://www.npr.org/templates/story/story.php?storyId=9170738.
65. Marisa Cochrane Sullivan, "The Fragmentation of the Sadrist Movement," Institute for the Study of War *Iraq Report*12, January 2009, 22, http://www.understandingwar.org/files/Iraq%20Report%2012.pdf.
66. For more information on the growth and professionalization of the Iraqi Security Forces during the Surge, see LTG James Dubik, "Building Security Forces and Ministerial Capacity: Iraq as a Primer," Institute for the Study of War *Best Practices in Counterinsurgency Report* 1, August 2009, http://www.csmonitor.com/World/Middle-East/2011/0208/US-reports-20-percent-drop-in-Iraq-violence.
67. Scott Peterson, "US reports 20 percent drop in Iraq violence," *Christian Science Monitor*, February 8, 2011,http://www.csmonitor.com/World/Middle-East/2011/0208/US-reports-20-percent-drop-in-Iraq-violence.
68. "Iraq: End irresponsible arms transfers fuelling militia war crimes," Amnesty International, January 5, 2017, https://www.amnesty.org/en/latest/news/2017/01/iraq-end-irresponsible-arms-transfers-fuelling-militia-war-crimes/; "Iraq: Possible War Crimes by Shia Militia," Human Rights Watch, January 31, 2016,,

https://www.hrw.org/news/2016/01/31/iraq-possible-war-crimes-shia-militia.

20 Jordan

Quick Facts

Population: 10,248,069
Area: 89,342 sq km
Ethnic Groups: Arab 98%, Circassian 1%, Armenian 1%
Government Type: Parliamentary constitutional monarchy
GDP (official exchange rate): $40.49 billion (2017 est.)

Source: CIA World FactBook (Last Updated April 2018)

Introduction

Seven years into the Arab Spring, the threats facing the Hashemite Kingdom, both from within the country and from outside it, continue to mount. Jordan is the most vulnerable of the monarchies affected by the currents of the Arab Spring, and in recent years has faced a growing challenge to its stability from violent Islamist groups. On the other hand, Jordan has weathered the collapse of both Syria and Iraq, and the takeover by jihadist groups of parts of their territory. These developments have been accompanied by large-scale refugee flows which have upset the Kingdom's demographic balance, and which could in the future destabilize its social structure and invite external interference.

For its part, the Jordanian regime has long waged a wide-ranging and determined ideological struggle against radical Islamic organizations on its soil. In this contest, the Kingdom has sought to de-legitimize Salafi jihadi ideology while disseminating a brand of moderate traditional Islam as a religious "vaccine" against it. The large and easily radicalized Palestinian component of the country's population, the combined influence of the Muslim Brotherhood offshoot in Jordan, and Salafi jihadi trends from Iraq and Syria, all pose real and imminent threat to the stability of the Kingdom.

Islamist Activity

Islam has been a part of the political life of Jordan for its entire history. In 1921, the British crafted the Emirate of Transjordan, with King Abdallah I becoming the new nation's king. Abdallah's Islamic identity, as well as the Hashemite family's connections to the Prophet Muhammad's tribe, was and continues to be a central source of legitimacy for the monarchy. Abdallah and his grandson Hussein presented themselves as deeply religious Muslims, publicly praying and taking part in rituals, as well as preforming the Hajj. In 1952, the Jordanian constitution made Islam the kingdom's official religion and stipulated that the king could only be a Muslim, born of Muslim parents. The constitution also establishes sharia as a key legal framework of the kingdom. However, unlike other Muslim countries, sharia was never considered the sole source of legal legitimacy.[1]

The radical Islamic camp in Jordan is composed of two separate—though frequently overlapping—wings. The first is the main body of Jordanian Islamists, which has been affiliated with the Muslim Brotherhood (MB). The second is the radical jihadi-Salafi movement, which has been traditionally embodied by al-Qaeda and its ideological fellow travelers within Jordan, and more recently also by supporters of ISIS who were either Jordanian or arrived as refugees from Syria.

The radical Islamic camp in Jordan largely draws its strength from a diverse array of sources and circumstances within Jordanian society. Foremost among them are: its own significant organizational infrastructure inside the country; the indirect influence and public sympathy from the wider activities of the MB, which the Jordanian public (both Trans-Jordanian and Palestinian) regards in a positive light; the inflammatory influence of the wars in Iraq and Syria; the ongoing Arab conflict with Israel; and the rise of Islamism across the region following the Arab Spring. Confronting all of these factors is a weak official religious establishment that lacks popular support and is unable to mobilize religious figures of authority to defend the regime's views.

The Muslim Brotherhood

The Muslim Brotherhood is deeply rooted in Jordan and boasts a presence in the country's political arena through the Islamic Action Front (IAF) party and parliamentary faction, as well as in civil society (via mosques, schools, labor and trade unions and universities). Since the birth of the Jordanian MB in the 1940s, internal struggles within the movement have taken place between a "dovish," "moderate" faction that aims to co-exist and maintain good relations with the regime, and a "hawkish," "extremist" wing that draws its ideology from the takfiri doctrine of Egyptian MB leader Sayyid Qutb, and as a result attempts to confront the regime both politically and ideologically.

The Palestinian issue ranks high on the agenda of Jordan's Islamist groups, in particular the MB and its political arm, the IAF; this is so for a number of reasons, including the fact that a sizable portion of the Jordanian MB's leaders are themselves Palestinian. Furthermore, the MB views Jordan's Palestinian population, which traditionally has been estimated to constitute about half of the country's entire population, as its primary constituency. The Jordanian MB also has traditional organizational ties with its counterpart in the Palestinian Territories, Hamas.[2]

Throughout most of the MB's history in Jordan, it was led by the Trans-Jordanian faction and tended to work in cooperation with the regime. This cooperation made the MB the only organized extra-governmental political force in the country and allowed it to establish a broad dawah network of civil society organizations and charities.[3] The extremist wing of the group has usually been affiliated with leaders from Palestinian backgrounds, whose identification with the Hashemite regime was often weaker than that of their Trans-Jordanian compatriots.[4]

In the past, this latter, extremist wing was comparably insignificant in the overall operations of the MB in Jordan. In the 1980s and 1990s, it devoted most of its energies to the jihad in Afghanistan, and subsequently the ones in Chechnya, Bosnia, and other places. Since the early 2000s, however, this more extreme faction has gained in strength and daring, as reflected by the results of the internal leadership elections carried out by the MB in early 2006, and manifested particularly in the composition of the IAF. The MB's religious rulings, or fatwas, express its identification with the Salafi worldview, identifying with the jihadi struggles in Iraq and Syria, and in the Israeli-Palestinian conflict. The top figures of this faction have also been founding members of the Global

Anti-Aggression Campaign (GAAC), an international Salafi-led international umbrella organization that brings under its wings Salafi, Salafi-Jihadi, Muslim Brotherhood and Hamas leaders, aiming to coordinate anti-Western strategies under the premise that the West is at war with Islam. At least seven leading GAAC figures and/or their organizations have been designated as terrorists by the United States, the EU, and/or the United Nations for their support of Al-Qaeda and related groups.[5]

Serious disputes between the two factions continue to this day, and are expected to do so as long as in the post Arab Spring period Islamism advances in the Middle East—and as Hamas continues to gain power in the Palestinian arena.

The rapid political rise and fall of the MB in the Middle East, especially the original Egyptian branch, has had a great effect on the Jordanian MB as well. Internally, the Jordanian Brotherhood now seems more divided than ever. In October 2012, members of the "dovish" faction came up with the Zam Zam Initiative, an "Islamist nationalist framework" of national reconstruction that aspired to return to working more closely with the national establishment. Zam Zam aimed for methodical and systematic change through five phases, which included the recruitment of new cadres and membership, including youth, male and female; launching a manifesto and laying down internal laws; the launch of a new political project and the seeking of participation in national institutions and partnership with the government.[6] In April 2014, three leading members who led the Initiative were expelled from the ranks of the movement, accused of aspiring to establish a new party to compete with the MB,[7] and subsequently took part in the 2016 elections, winning three seats in the parliament.[8]

Another split occurred after Abdul Majid Thneibat, another "hawkish" leader, re-registered the Muslim Brotherhood Society in 2015 as a Jordanian entity with no affiliation to the original Egyptian movement. Altogether, more than 400 members left the Brotherhood during 2015 to join these and other splinter groups.[9] The most recent split took place in October 2016, when a group of elder leaders of the "dovish" trend, headed by former Inspector General Salem Falahat and followed by 400 members, left the IAF to form the Partnership and Rescue Party (Hizb al-Shiraka w'al-Inqadh). Falahat maintained that dawa (proselytizing) should be separated from politics, adding that he aimed to open up the ranks of the new party to everyone, regardless of ideology.[10]

In February 2016, the Jordanian MB formally cut its ties with its parent movement in Egypt.[11] This tactic of separation is not uncommon among Middle Eastern offshoots of the Muslim Brotherhood, and represents an attempt to regain credibility and avoid the ire of their respective governments. However, in all likelihood the split was merely a cosmetic move, and the links between Muslim Brotherhood offshoots and affiliates remain intact.

Salafi jihadism

The Muslim Brotherhood in general, and its "hawkish" faction in particular, have played a pivotal role in the dissemination and acceptance of the Salafi-jihadi message in Jordanian society, especially among the younger generation of citizens. Outbreaks of violence between Israel and the Palestinians, particularly in the Gaza Strip, and the wars in Iraq, Syria and Afghanistan, likewise have served to strengthen Salafi sentiment in Jordan.

The ebb and flow of jihadist activity in Iraq profoundly affected Islamist organizations in Jordan. The 2006 killing of Abu Musab al-Zarqawi, the leader of al-Qaeda in Iraq (which subsequently became the Islamic State in Iraq, which turned into ISIS), and coalition successes against the group thereafter (as a result of the "surge" strategy adopted by the Bush administration), along with local Jordanian pressure, all served to create fissures in the Jordanian jihadist movement. The result was the emergence and rise of a more "pragmatic" wing of the movement, led by the prominent Salafi cleric Abu Muhammad al-Maqdisi. Since his release from Jordanian prison in 2008, and again in 2014, al-Maqdisi has consistently criticized the school of thought epitomized by al-Zarqawi and more recently by Abu Bakr Al-Baghdadi's ISIS, which sanctions intra-Muslim conflict due to ideological and political differences. Al-Maqdisi did not change the principles of takfir, the declaration of Muslims as heretics or apostates. However, he made a case against jihadist attacks inside Jordan, thus revising his own views about the permissibility of collateral casualties among

Muslims (or even their direct targeting) if necessary in order to kill "infidels".[12]

Another prominent figure in the Jordanian scene is Abu Qatada, many years considered a spiritual leader of a European Salafi-Jihadi group. In August 2017, Abu Qatada said on a TV program:

> Our rivals accept only extermination – it's either us or them. If we raise and adopt the true banner of Islam – rather than the forged version of Islam in which the Muslims surrender to non-Muslims – we will be upholding Islam of glory and of an Islamic state, an Islam that implements the noble prophecies about the dominance of the banner of the Muslims in the world, about Islam raiding each and every home, about Islam invading Rome... This would be the glorious Islam. If we accept and believe in that [true] version of Islam, there can only be one outcome: confrontation.[13]

In the past few years, many Salafi-Jihadi Jordanians joined the ranks of jihadi groups in Iraq and Syria, such as al-Qaeda and its affiliate Jabhat Fath Al-Sham (formerly known as Jabhat Al-Nusra), or the Islamic State (ISIS). In early 2015, it was even claimed that Jordanians "have enjoyed the lion's share of power" in Jabhat Al-Nusra's chain of command.[14] At the end of 2015, Jordan came in fourth in the list of countries of origin of ISIS fighters in Iraq and Syria, with an official number of more than 2,000.[15] Towards the end of 2017, some estimated this number in 3,000, at least 200 of whom returned home as bombing campaigns intensified in Syria and Iraq.[16]

IS also gradually gained more popularity within Salafi-Jihadi ranks within Jordan.[17] In addition some feared that among the many Syrian refugees who entered the country, there were also IS sleeper cells. Four areas in Jordan have been identified by experts as hotbeds of radicalization: Rusaifa (in Zarqa district); the northern city of Irbid; Ma'an; and Salt.[18] In March 2016, Jordan's General Intelligence Department (GID) acted for the first time against a suspected ISIS-linked cell in Irbid.[19]

Jordan has been a member in the U.S.-led Coalition to battle the Islamic State, and fierce criticism of the group has proliferated, particularly after the capture and burning alive of Jordanian pilot Mu'ath Safi Yousef al-Kaseasbeh, whose plane went down over the city of Raqqa in Syria in December 2014. In the Spring of 2015, it was found in a poll that 94 percent of the wider Jordanian population viewed IS negatively.[20] In another survey, conducted three times between 2015 and 2017, 89-86% answered they considered IS a terrorist organization, and many viewed IS as a threat to the security of Jordan.[21]

Islamism and Society

The Jordanian population is 98 percent Arab, with Circassians and Armenians each accounting for 1 percent of the population.[22] 97.2 percent of the population is Muslim, and the majority of that population is Sunni, and 2.2 percent of the population is Christian.[23] Strict Islamic codes enjoy a broad popular base among both the country's Trans-Jordanian and Palestinian populace. In recent years, Islamic dress—particularly for women—has become more and more ubiquitous. Islamic bookstores selling radical tracts can now be found near almost any mosque in Amman. Pew polls found that support in Jordan for the enactment of sharia law was widespread. 58 percent of those polled even said sharia law should be extended to apply to all citizens, including non-Muslim, while 67 percent of respondents favored stoning for the crime of adultery and 82 percent approved capital punishment for apostates.[24]

In recent years, support for Salafi-jihadi groups among the wider population appears to be declining. This is true both in the case of IS as already demonstrated, as well as in the case of Al-Qaeda, which in 2014 was found to only be supported by 13 percent of the population.[25] Nevertheless, Salafi-jihadi attitudes have multiple outlets in Jordanian society. Those outlets include popular mosques not under the regime's supervision, and bookstands that propagate a radical, exclusionary religious worldview. The many websites of global jihadist groups provide a method for widespread dissemination of this ideology. Jihadist activists arrested by authorities have been found to be indoctrinated via these outlets. A prominent example is Abed Shahadeh, nicknamed Abu Muhammad al-Tahawi, who was imprisoned for three years in 2005 and has been arrested several times since.

The Palestinian issue is a topic of perennial interest in Jordan's politics, and one of major concern to the public. The MB, as discussed previously, shares and capitalizes upon this focus. As one official with the group has explained, the MB "has a religious and national obligation to support the Palestinians and their problem."[26] Hamam Sa'id has gone further, stating that the MB's involvement in the Palestinian arena serves to provide "the Palestinians [with] *jihadist* assistance and support."[27] Like the Palestinian issue generally, the MB's relationship with Hamas remains an important element of Islamist expression in Jordan, even though Hamas is now considered an independent organization, no longer subordinated to any MB group.

In spite of the decline in the MB's popularity, which also affected its political power in the syndicates, demonstrations were held during October 2016, led by the Teachers' Union against reforms and changes in school textbooks in the Kingdom, which toned down their Islamic content and started showing women without headscarves. This act had been perceived as a threat to the long-term Islamist dominance of the education system.[28]

Islamism and the State

Salafi jihadi organizations in Jordan remain under intense pressure from the Jordanian government, which has succeeded in disrupting numerous attempted terrorist attacks inside the Kingdom in recent years. It has done so through the imprisonment of large numbers of jihadist activists and sympathizers, in the process wreaking havoc on their respective organizations and restricting their activities. A high point was the January 2009 trial of twelve members of a Salafi-jihadi group charged with attacks on a Christian church and cemetery, and with involvement in the shooting of a group of Lebanese musicians performing in downtown Amman.[29]

The real challenge facing the MB, "hawks" and "doves" alike, appears to be the far-reaching reforms of the internal political system announced by King Abdullah II in late November 2009. The MB in particular has had doubts about the regime's intention to implement the genuine political reform it promised the public. From the MB's point of view, the implementation of a thorough political reform that would introduce the principle of "one person, one vote" and pledge to hold "honest and fair elections" is a basic condition for translating their potential electoral power into a significant quota of parliamentary seats, and subsequently making political and public gains. The Brotherhood has accused the regime of not holding fair and transparent elections. Leading figures also referred to the political triumph and rise in power of Islamist movements across the region following the Arab Spring as an issue which could be translated into political leverage at home: "We use the results in the other Arab countries to say to our government: look, when the elections are fair, the Islamists win."[30]

The Arab Spring deeply impacted the debate surrounding governance within Jordan. Initially, the revolutionary currents did not seriously undermine the Jordanian regime. The vanguard of protests in Jordan appeared to be more the *Salafi jihadi* movement than the MB itself. The violence also exposed divisions between this faction and the larger *Salafi* movement. However, the fall of the Egyptian and Tunisian regimes and the continued, unsettled situation in other countries (such as Iraq and Syria) encouraged the Jordanian MB to increase its pressure on the regime. The regime, for its part, accused the protestors of receiving orders from the mother movement in Egypt and elsewhere. It has also animated the normally quiescent East-Jordanian political leadership; according to various reports, tribal leaders have warned the King that they would not tolerate a light hand in dealing with the threat, which they perceived as a Palestinian attempt to topple the Hashemite government.[31] This was expressed in demonstrations under increasingly radicalized slogans, along with the classic demands for an end to corruption and the abrogation of the peace treaty with Israel. These demonstrations escalated in March 2011, resulting in a number of casualties (though far less than in other Arab countries).

The MB boycotted the January 2013 elections, and continued to demand the implementations of "reforms" and the limiting of the King's power. In April 2013, the MB issued a warning letter to the King and the national intelligence services, accusing the regime of corruption and calling on him to change his current policies.[32]

King Abdullah II, like his counterparts in the Gulf States, has expressed concern over the emerging Egypt-Turkey-Qatar "axis" that has materialized from the Arab Spring, and which has promoted Muslim Brotherhood influence throughout the region.[33] The MB, for its part, has pushed back against these concerns, claiming new discrimination. The Kingdom began with a crackdown on the MB which included taking over various social charities, the removal of MB sheikhs from the traditional roles they hold in mosques and more.[34] Irsheid, the MB's Deputy Head, was even imprisoned for several months in 2014-2015 for insulting the UAE.

In a June 2016 interview with the Islamist portal *Middle East Eye*, IAF Spokesman Murad Adaileh maintained that the levels of democracy have receded in the country while critiquing the lack of adequate political reform. Adaileh added that the new constitutional amendments granted King Abdullah II dramatically more power over the security forces. He also noted that the government has continued arresting activists, most notably for criticizing Jordan's war against the Islamic State, which has intensified the Brotherhood's distrust of the government.[35]

The Brotherhood's deteriorating situation in Jordan—both internally and with the government—as well as across the Middle East gradually brought it to take a series of steps to try to amend the situation. The IAF ended its elections boycott in 2016, a decision that was welcomed by Queen Rania[36] and the Brotherhood replied that this was a "positive" step.[37] The IAF joined a wider alliance, the National Coalition for Reform (NCR), which included candidates from various backgrounds, in the September 2016 elections. This coalition gained 16 seats in parliament, 10 of which were won by members of the group and the remaining were won by their allies.[38]

In January 2017, both the MB and the IAF declared that they ended their boycott of the U.S., including its embassy in Amman, 14 years after it commenced following the start of the Second Iraq War.[39] Earlier that month, the IAF announced that it will form coalitions for the upcoming municipal elections, which took place in August 2017 under new law to decentralize power.[40] The IAF-led National Alliance for Reform coalition was successful in winning 76 seats in that election—25 out of 48 in provincial councils and 41 out of 88 in local councils.[41] However, the turnout for the elections was very low (37%),[42] and it is therefore hard to draw any conclusions regarding the MB's popularity. In any case, the MB, which also congratulated "Jordan – the people, Government, political forces and civil society institutions, on the launching of the democratic experience,"[43] appears willing to expand its efforts to gain back popularity and mitigate tensions with the government. In October 2017, the MB held internal discussions, which included the possibility of accepting the model of a "civil state."[44]

Endnotes

1. See Shmuel Bar, "The Muslim Brotherhood in Jordan," *Moshe Dayan Center for Middle Eastern and African Studies Data and Analysis*, June 1998, http://www.dayan.tau.ac.il/d&a-jordan-bar.pdf.
2. According to a senior source in the Muslim Brotherhood, the Brotherhood's Inspector General, Hamam Sa'id, and two members of the Brotherhood's Executive Bureau are also members of the Hamas *Shura* Council and participate in its debates.
3. These were widely referred to and named in Ibrahim Gharaybah, *Jamaat Al-Ikhwan Al-Muslimin fi-l-Urdun 1946-1996* (Amman: Markaz al-Urdun al-Jadid lil-Dirasat: Dar Sindibad lil-Nashr, 1997), 169-185; Quintan Wiktorowicz, *The Management of Islamic Activism* (State University of New York Press, 2001), 83-92
4. Bar, "The Muslim Brotherhood in Jordan, 50-52.
5. Steven Merley, "The Global Anti-Aggression Campaign 2003-2016 A Global Muslim Brotherhood, Salafi and Jihadi Alliance Against The West", 2017. https://www.globalmbresearch.com/wp-content/uploads/2017/02/Global_Anti-Aggression_Campaign_2003-2016.pdf
6. Larbi Sadiki, "Jordan: Arab Spring Washout?" *Al-Jazeera*, January 12, 2013. http://www.aljazeera.com/indepth/opinion/2013/01/201319134753750165.html

7. Tamer Al-Samadi, 'Zamzam' Reveals Divisions in Jordan's Muslim Brotherhood, Al-Monitor, December 5, 2012. http://www.al-monitor.com/pulse/politics/2012/12/divisions-hit-jordanian-muslim-brotherhood.html
8. Taylor Luck, "Muslim Brotherhood expels three over the 'Zamzam' incident," *Jordan Times*, April 21, 2014. http://www.jordantimes.com/news/local/muslim-brotherhood-expels-three-over-zamzam%E2%80%99-initiative
9. Khetum Malkawi, "Muslim Brotherhood ends link with Egyptian mother group," *Jordan Times*, February 14, 2016. http://www.jordantimes.com/news/local/muslim-brotherhood-ends-link-egyptian-mother-group
10. "New party emerges from the splits in the Jordanian MB", *AlJazeera*, October 26, 2016, http://www.aljazeera.net/news/reportsandinterviews/2016/10/26/%D8%AD%D8%B2%D8%A8-%D8%AC%D8%AF%D9%8A%D8%AF-%D9%8A%D8%AE%D8%B1%D8%AC-%D9%85%D9%86-%D8%A7%D9%86%D8%B4%D9%82%D8%A7%-D9%82%D8%A7%D8%AA-%D8%A5%D8%AE%D9%88%D8%A7%D9%86-%D8%A7%D9%84%D8%A3%D8%B1%D8%AF%D9%86.
11. "Jordanian Muslim Brotherhood split from Egyptian parent group," *The New Arab,* February 16, 2016, https://www.alaraby.co.uk/english/news/2016/2/16/jordanian-muslim-brotherhood-split-from-egyptian-parent-group.
12. See al-Maqdisi's website, http://www.tawhed.ws/, and the subsequent debate with other jihadi authorities such as Ma'asari. For a summary of these debates, see Joas Wagemakers, "Reflections on Maqdisi's Arrest," *Jihadica,* October 2, 2010, http://www.jihadica.com/reflections-on-al-maqdisis-arrest/.
13. "Salafi Jordanian Cleric Abu Qatada Al-Filastini: True Islam Leads to Raiding Rome and Confrontation," Middle East Media Research Institute, August 12, 2017, https://www.memri.org/tv/salafi-jordanian-cleric-abu-qatada-true-islam-means-confrontation/transcript.
14. Suhaib Anjarini, How Jordanians Came to Dominate al-Nusra Front, January 16, 2015. http://english.al-akhbar.

com/node/23238

15. *Foreign Fighters; An Updated Assessment of the Flow of Foreign Fighters into Syria and Iraq*, The Soufan Group, December 2015, http://soufangroup.com/wp-content/uploads/2015/12/TSG_ForeignFightersUpdate3.pdf.
16. Russia has the Most Foreign Fighters Joining ISIS in Syria, Report Claims, October 24, 2017. https://www.albawaba.com/news/russia-isis-fighters-1038608
17. See for example a demonstration in support of ISIS, June 2014. http://www.jordanews.com/jordan/27280.html
18. Anne Speckhard, The Jihad in Jordan: Drivers of Radicalization into Violent Extremism in Jordan, The International Center for the Study of Violent Extremism (ICSVE), March 25, 2017, http://www.icsve.org/research-reports/the-jihad-in-jordan-drivers-of-radicalization-into-violent-extremism-in-jordan/
19. Osama Al Sharif, Jordan and the Challenge of Salafi Jihadists, *Middle East Institute*, March 21, 2016. http://www.mei.edu/content/article/jordan-and-challenge-salafi-jihadists
20. Jacob Foushter, In nations with significant Muslim populations, much disdain for ISIS, December 17, 2015. http://www.pewresearch.org/fact-tank/2015/11/17/in-nations-with-significant-muslim-populations-much-disdain-for-isis/
21. Survey of Jordanian Public Opinion, National Poll #15, May 22-25, 2017., Center for Insights in Survey Research (CISR), http://www.iri.org/sites/default/files/2017-7-12_jordan_poll_slides.pdf
22. "Jordan," *The CIA World Factbook,* November, 2016, https://www.cia.gov/library/publications/the-world-factbook/geos/jo.html.
23. "Jordan," *The CIA World Factbook.*
24. The World's Muslims: Religion, Politics and Society, April 30, 2013. http://www.pewforum.org/2013/04/30/the-worlds-muslims-religion-politics-society-beliefs-about-sharia/
25. Jacob Poushter, Support for al Qaeda was low before (and after) Osama bin Laden's death, May 12 2014. http://www.pewresearch.org/fact-tank/2014/05/02/support-for-al-qaeda-was-low-before-and-after-osama-

bin-ladens-death/

26. "Two Dozen Islamists Go on Trial on Corruption Charges," Deutsche Press-Agentur, December 24, 2009. http://monstersandcritics.com/news/middleeast/news/article_1521391.php/Two-dozen-Islamists-go-on-trial-on-corruption-charages.
27. *Al-Kifah al-Arabi* (Beirut), December 21, 2009.
28. Dia Hadid, "Jordan Tones Down Tetbooks' Islamic Content, and Tempers Rise," *The New York Times*, October 14, 2016, http://www.nytimes.com/2016/10/15/world/middleeast/jordan-tones-down-textbooks-islamic-content-and-tempers-rise.html?_r=0.
29. "Two Dozen Islamists Go on Trial on Corruption Charges," Deutsche Press-Agentur, December 24, 2009. http://monstersandcritics.com/news/middleeast/news/article_1521391.php/Two-dozen-Islamists-go-on-trial-on-corruption-charages.
30. Amis, "The Jordanian Brotherhood in the Arab Spring," 42.
31. "Thousands of protesters demanding the 'downfall of the regime' in Jordan," *BBC*, http://www.bbc.co.uk/arabic/middleeast/2012/11/121116_jordan_protest_king.shtml.
32. See, for example, Tim Lister, "Jordanian Tribal Figures Criticize Queen, Demand Reform," CNN, February 6, 2011, http://articles.cnn.com/2011-02-06/world/jordan.monarchy_1_jordanians-king-abdullah-ii-tribal-leaders?_s=PM:WORLD.
33. "Qatari political money in Jordan starts with the support of Islamic Associations and ends with the production of the drama," *Al-Sharq* (Saudi Arabia), December 15, 2012,

http://www.alsharq.net.sa/2012/12/15/626813.

34. Tareq Al Naimat, "The Jordanian regime and the Muslim Brotherhood: a tug of war," *Woodrow Wilson Center* Viewpoints no. 58 (July 2014). https://www.wilsoncenter.org/sites/default/files/jordanian_regime_muslim_brotherhood_tug_of_war.pdf
35. Aaron Magid, "Analysis: Jordan's Muslim Brotherhood comes in from the cold," *Middle East Eye* (London), June 21, 2016. http://www.middleeasteye.net/news/

analysis-jordan-s-muslim-brotherhood-ends-election-boycott-1119065410

36. "'Jordan's Islamists': What are the expectations after their return to Parliament?" *BBC Arabic*, September 22, 2016. http://www.bbc.com/arabic/interactivity/2016/09/160922_comments_jordan_elections
37. "'Spinning political' between brothers Jordan and Queen Rania," *RT Arabic*, September 22, 2016./
38. Hassan Abu Haniya, "Has the Muslim Brotherhood in Jordan overcome the danger of fragmentation and danger?" *Middle East Monitor* (London), October 4, 2016.
https://www.middleeastmonitor.com/20161004-has-the-muslim-brotherhood-in-jordan-overcome-the-danger-of-fragmentation-and-danger/
39. "The Jordanian Brotherhood officially decides to end its boycott on the US", *Quds Press*, January 22, 2017, http://www.qudspress.com/index.php?page=show&id=27780
40. Sawsan Tabazah, Islamic Action Front mulls coalitions as it prepares for local elections, January 17, 2014. http://jordantimes.com/news/local/islamic-action-front-mulls-coalitions-it-prepares-local-elections
41. "Muslim Brotherhood-led coalition wins big in Jordan local polls", *Middle East Monitor*, August 16, 2017, https://www.middleeastmonitor.com/20170816-muslim-brotherhood-led-coalition-wins-big-in-jordan-local-polls/
42. Osama Al Sharif, Jordan's Islamists win big in local polls amid voter apathy, *Al-Monitor*, August 22, 2017, http://www.al-monitor.com/pulse/originals/2017/08/jordan-local-elections-low-turnout-islamists-win.html#ixzz4yPvZweOl
43. "Muslim Brotherhood Congratulates Jordan's Islamic Action Front Party on Elections Win", August 16, 2017, http://www.ikhwanweb.com/article.php?id=32771
44. Fathi Khattab, "Restructuring the Jordanian MB to accompany the concept of 'civil state' ", October 30, 2017.

21 Kuwait

Quick Facts

Population: 2,875,422 (July 2017 est.)
Area: 17,818 sq km
Ethnic Groups: Kuwaiti 31.3%, other Arab 27.9%, Asian 37.8%, African 1.9%, other 1.1% (includes European, North American, South American, and Australian) (2013 est.)
GDP (official exchange rate): $118.3 billion (2017 est.)

Source: CIA World FactBook (Last Updated July 2018)

Introduction

Kuwaiti soldiers, civilians, and U.S. forces have all been the targets of sporadic attacks by radical religious elements in recent years. However, the phenomenon of global jihad is less prevalent in Kuwait than in many of its Gulf neighbors, despite the June 2015 suicide bombing that killed 27 people in a Shia mosque in Kuwait City.[1] *Najd Province, an Islamic State affiliate, claimed responsibility for that attack.*[2] *Nevertheless, ISIS and other terrorist groups more commonly use Kuwaiti soil for logistical activities, such as the recruitment of fighters for arenas of jihad (Iraq, Afghanistan, Syria and so on), and as a hub through which funds, operatives and equipment are transferred to other countries. While counterterrorism measures have been successful in preventing fatal attacks in Kuwait itself, efforts against facilitation networks serving the global jihad have so far been lacking.*

In the political arena, Kuwait preserves a delicate balance: permitting Islamists a presence in the nation's parliament but vesting power in the nation's Emir to dissolve parliament, a power that he exercises whenever Islamist ideas and criticism cross political red lines. Kuwait's Islamists, for their part, have exhibited a subtle approach, working to gradually expand the role of sharia law within the day-to-day life of Kuwaitis while remaining loyal to the country's constitution.

ISLAMIST ACTIVITY

While not a primary target for al-Qaeda, ISIS, and other terror groups, Kuwait does have a place on the global jihadi agenda, for two main reasons. First, its long-standing relationship with the United States, especially since the first Gulf War, symbolizes to a great extent the imperialist presence that Washington allegedly represents on the Arabian Peninsula. Even with cutbacks following the 2011 withdrawal of troops from Iraq, Kuwait currently hosts an extensive American military presence (encompassing some 16 active and 6 inactive bases, and tens of thousands of soldiers) on its soil,[3] which serves as a natural target for organized terror groups and individual extremists driven by Salafi jihadist ideology. Islamists also consider the Kuwaiti regime a target as well, as they perceive it to be pro-U.S. and to an extent apostate (not adhering completely to the Islamic, or sharia, law). Second, and perhaps more important, Kuwait serves as a transit country for money, equipment and operatives into countries in which a war by the West is being waged—mainly Iraq, Pakistan and Afghanistan, but also Syria since 2012.

There is little known about the organized Islamist presence in Kuwait.[4] However, Kuwaiti security forces occasionally respond to terror attacks and expose plots inside the small Gulf country. Notably, however, they failed to predict or prevent the June 2015 ISIS attack perpetrated by a Saudi citizen working with a local support network in Kuwait. In September 2015, a criminal court in Kuwait convicted 15 out of 29 suspects in the bombing, acquitting the other fourteen. The 15 convictions included seven death sentences, of which five were handed down in absentia, as two of the suspects were believed to be fighting for ISIS in Iraq and two others were Saudi citizens arrested in Saudi Arabia.[5]

Al-Qaeda is believed to operate in Kuwait in a clandestine manner. Geographically, al-Qaeda's activity in Kuwait is supposedly subordinate to al-Qaeda in the Arabian Peninsula (AQAP), the official al-Qaeda franchise in the region. AQAP is mainly based in Saudi Arabia and Yemen, and there is little known regarding its actual operational control over jihadist activity in Kuwait. Nonetheless, AQAP's agenda strongly suggests that the organization's reach includes the entire Gulf region. Given the rise in attention garnered by AQAP since 2009, especially in Yemen, it is likely that the organization will be slower to expand its reach to the smaller countries under its supposed authority, including Kuwait.

AQAP's focus on Saudi Arabia and Yemen has opened the door for other actors to take part in planning attacks against Western targets in Kuwait. Such players are often elements with historical ties to core al-Qaeda leaders in Afghanistan and Pakistan, who for years have been operating independently and carrying out sporadic attacks in the country. In this regard, one should remember that the most senior operational figures of al-Qaeda have Kuwaiti connections. The conspirators behind the infamous Bojinka plot, Abd al Karim Murad, Ramzi Yousef, and above all Khalid Sheikh Mohamed (who would later mastermind the September 11 attacks), were all Kuwaiti residents, and their large families still live in the country. Abu Ahmed al-Kuwaiti, a Kuwait-born Pakistani national, was Osama bin Laden's courier and confidante and was killed with him in the Navy SEAL raid on the Abbottabad compound in May 2011.[6] In the years since September 11th, although there have been few and relatively infrequent terror incidents in Kuwait, most of those that have occurred are generally attributed to al-Qaeda (though not always proven to be so).

First and foremost, Kuwait is an important transit point for the transfer of funds, equipment and operatives from the Gulf countries to Pakistan and Afghanistan.[7] This route, only sparsely monitored by Kuwaiti authorities, is a significant pipeline that feeds insurgent and terror groups in the Afghan-Pakistan. Through a network of smugglers and document forgers, Kuwait is used to support these organizations financially and militarily. Operatives of Kuwaiti origin consequently have grown into significant actors within the core al-Qaeda organization in Pakistan, playing both logistical and operational roles.[8]

Similarly, Kuwait served as a source of fighters and suicide bombers for the al-Qaeda franchise in Iraq (al-Qaeda in Iraq or AQI), the precursor to today's Islamic State terrorist group.[9] Kuwaiti youth were recruited and sent to Iraq, usually through Syria, to perform their jihadi duty by fighting Coalition forces. According to one local AQI commander in Iraq, dozens of Kuwaiti nationals were operating in his area of command as of 2008.[10] Although the participation of Kuwaiti nationals in the Iraqi insurgency declined in tandem with the winding down and 2011 withdrawal of U.S. forces from Iraq, the escalation of the civil war in Syria in 2012-13 offered Kuwaitis (along with other foreign nationals) a new platform to engage in jihadist activity, incidentally also boosting the Sunni-led opposition in Iraq to Prime Minister Maliki.[11]

One of the greatest threats to Kuwait's national security stems from veteran jihadists of Kuwaiti nationality who have completed their duty in Afghanistan, Iraq, or Syria, and wish to put to use the lessons they learned against targets in their homeland. These experienced fighters, who have widespread contacts with other militants and the necessary know-how in guerilla fighting and the construction of bombs, can significantly increase the threat to Western and Kuwait government targets in the country. According to some reports, there have been past attempts to use Kuwaiti veterans in attacks, and senior al-Qaeda officials in Pakistan are known to have entrusted Kuwaiti recruits with secret missions to be conducted in Kuwait.[12] However, so long as more attractive jihad arenas exist (such as Iraq, Afghanistan, Somalia, Syria etc.), the phenomenon of experienced Kuwaiti jihadists launching attacks on Kuwaiti soil will remain limited.

Terrorism finance is another critical issue in Kuwait. While the source of the problem mainly lies in neighboring Saudi Arabia, there are also several terror supporters known to be operating in Kuwait, providing global jihadists in the Middle East and Asia with the funds necessary to carry out their terror activities. As official awareness of this phenomenon has grown, more effort has been put into interdicting and stopping illegal financial transfers. Similar initiatives have also been implemented by the UN Security Council's Sanctions Committee that are designed to freeze financial assets and restrict the travel and arms trade of such operatives. The committee's effectiveness, however, is questionable.[13] Moreover, the efficiency and comprehensiveness of Kuwait's own counterterror efforts are hampered by the fact that it has no specific legal framework criminalizing terrorist financing and other terrorist-related activities.[14] Thus the prosecution of any such crimes must take place through alternative statutes.

Since 2012, credible reports have suggested that Kuwait-based actors play a pivotal role in the channeling of funds to rebel groups fighting the Assad regime in Syria. An in-depth investigation by *The National* newspaper in Abu Dhabi found that Kuwait "has emerged as a central fund-raising hub for direct financial support to insurgents" fighting in Syria, compounding the tens of millions of dollars in humanitarian aid raised by private or individual means.[15] Kuwait also hosted the first in what became a series of annual UN donor conferences on Syria that took place in Kuwait City on January 30, 2013. This resulted in pledges totaling more than $1.5 billion, of which $300 million was promised by the Kuwaiti government.[16] Kuwait hosted additional donors' pledging conference on Syria in Kuwait City on January 15, 2014 and March 31, 2015, and co-organized, with the UN, the United Kingdom, Germany, and Norway, further humanitarian support meetings that took place in London on February 4, 2016 and in Brussels (with Qatar an additional co-organizer) on April 5, 2017.[17] In addition to these official and unofficial funding channels, prominent Sunni Islamist politicians and clerics have openly campaigned to arm rebel fighters in Syria. A conservative Islamist former MP, Waleed al-Tabtabie, posted photographs of himself on Twitter wearing combat gear in Syria.[18]

The rapid growth of ISIS and its capture of a swathe of territory linking eastern Syria and western Iraq in 2014 heightened concerns among U.S. policymakers about the extent of illicit funding flowing from Kuwait to the organization. Former U.S. Treasury Undersecretary David Cohen stated bluntly in March 2014 that Kuwait had become "the epicenter of fundraising for terror groups in Syria" and noted more generally that a new financial tracking unit set up by the Kuwaiti government to investigate suspicious financial transactions and money laundering was still not operational. The Treasury Department expressed particular concern over the dual nature of alleged funding flows, in which organizations "to some extent channel money to blankets and bread and schools, and then money also to supporting terrorist activities."[19] Moreover, Kuwait's Justice and Endowments Minister, Nayef al-Ajmi, resigned in May

2014 after being named by Cohen as having a history of promoting terrorism, and with his ministry coming under suspicion for allowing non-profit organizations and charities to collect donations for the Syrian people at Kuwaiti mosques, which Cohen argued was "a measure we believe can be easily exploited by Kuwait-based terrorist fundraisers."[20]

A suicide bombing at a Shia mosque in Kuwait City on June 26, 2015 that left 27 dead and 227 wounded highlighted Kuwait's vulnerability both to the general surge in sectarian tension across the region and to the particular threat posed by the Islamic State. The attack was the worst act of terrorism in Kuwait in more than thirty years, since the coordinated December 12, 1983 bombings that targeted the United States and French Embassies in Kuwait and the headquarters of the Kuwait Petroleum Corporation.[21] The bombing of the Imam al-Sadiq mosque was designed to cause maximum damage to intercommunal relations in Kuwait. The blast, carried out by Fahad Suleiman al-Gabbaa, a Saudi citizen, targeted the center of the Hasawi community of Kuwaiti Shia. Also known as Sheikhis, the Hasawi originally emigrated from the al-Hasa region of Saudi Arabia's Eastern Province in the late-nineteenth and early-twentieth centuries, in part to escape endemic marginalization and discrimination.[22]

The final element of Islamist activity in Kuwait lies in the role of fundamentalist religious scholars. Such figures play a critical role in the education and indoctrination of Kuwaiti Salafis—especially those that join the armed jihadist struggle.[23] The most famous among them is Hamid al-Ali, a Salafi cleric known for his considerable following. Al-Ali, previously a professor of Islamic studies at Kuwait University, has been officially designated by the U.S. government as a global terrorism financier and supporter. His views—at times radical and supportive of al-Qaeda (for instance, issuing fatwas approving of crashing planes into buildings as a form of attack) and at others more aligned with the moderate approach imposed upon him by the regime—reach many young Muslims through the sermons and articles he publishes online.[24] Al-Ali also approves of ISIS, commending the group's success in "the great cleansing of Iraq."[25] Another important radical religious figure is Suleiman Abu Gheith, a former high school religion teacher in Kuwait City who became a leading figure within al-Qaeda. After joining the group in 2000, Abu Gheith was a member of the al-Qaeda quasi-legislative and consultative committee (Majles al Shura). He headed the organization's media committee responsible for propaganda and was one of Osama bin Laden's top aides as well as his son-in-law. Abu Gheith departed for Iran as part of a group of al-Qaeda senior leaders in 2003.[26] Ten years later, in March 2013, he was seized by U.S. Special Forces in Jordan and extradited to the U.S., where he appeared in a federal court in New York and pleaded not guilty to charges of conspiracy to kill Americans ahead of his trial in 2014, which sentenced him to life imprisonment.[27]

Since 2015, Kuwaiti forces have implemented a series of arrests targeting suspected ISIS members.[28] In August 2016, Kuwaiti authorities apprehended a Filipina woman believed to have ties to ISIS. She was later sentenced to ten years in a Kuwaiti prison.[29] Less than a year later in March 2017, a Kuwaiti couple believed to be plotting an attack was arrested in the Philippines.[30]

In its fight against radicalization and as a part of the global effort against al-Qaeda and ISIS, the Kuwaiti regime is implementing policies to control and prevent radical Islamists from engaging in terrorism—although, as previously discussed, not always doing so sufficiently. In addition to outright arrests and the targeting of Islamist financial flows, the Kuwaiti government has also initiated a number of other counterterrorism measures, including a wide-scale educational program aimed at countering the influence of unchecked radicalism. In addition, Kuwaiti imams are sporadically taken to court by the government, which accuses them of "activities contrary to the function of the Ministry of Islamic Affairs and the mosque."[31]

Islamism and Society

Approximately 85 percent of Kuwait's total population of 3.4 million is Muslim, but Kuwaiti citizens (which comprise only 1 million of that total) are nearly all Muslims. While the national census does not distinguish between Sunnis and Shiites, approximately 70-75 percent of citizens, including the ruling family, belong to the Sunni branch of Islam. The remainder, with the exception of about 100-

200 Christians and a few Baha'is, are Shiites.[32]

Despite the sectarian violence in neighboring Iraq, Kuwait manages to maintain a relatively stable sectarian environment, although tensions have risen sharply since 2012 as hardline Sunni and Shiite politicians have publicly favored differing sides in the Syrian civil war. Generally speaking, Shiites in Kuwait are less organized politically than the Sunnis. Their most notable point of contention is their desire to redress longstanding inequalities and obtain an apology for accusations that they constitute a fifth column for Iran (an allegation that surfaced during the 1980-1988 Iran-Iraq War, but which abated as Shiites demonstrated their loyalty during the Iraqi invasion of Kuwait in August 1990).

The general level of public support in Kuwait for Islamist activity and radicalism is hard to determine. Electoral preferences provide only limited insight, as over two-thirds of Kuwait's population consists of non-citizens who lack the right to vote, and organized political parties are banned. As in many other Arab countries, September 11th and the subsequent U.S. invasions of Afghanistan and Iraq ignited and exposed latent feelings of suspicion and hatred in certain quarters towards the West and the U.S. in particular, irrespective of relatively fruitful cooperation at the governmental level. Nevertheless, the U.S.-led invasion of Iraq in 2003 was less controversial in Kuwait than elsewhere in the Arab world, due to the legacy of Kuwaitis suffering at the hands of Saddam Hussein's dictatorship.

Kuwait manages a delicate balance with regard to Islamic devotion. The society remains traditionally Muslim in many ways, although there are no mutawwa (religious police) as in Saudi Arabia, nor are the five daily prayer times strictly observed. The Kuwaiti public, however, generally supports Islamic traditions; alcohol, gambling, mixed dancing, and other such Western symbols are relatively rare. More extreme anti-Western voices are largely censored out of the country's otherwise fairly free press. However, they are still easily available to the public on the Internet or in pan-Arabian media.

A 2007 Pew poll suggested that there is a significant fringe element inside Kuwait that actively supports or sympathizes with more extremist views and activities. According to the survey, 20 percent of Kuwaitis believed that suicide bombings "in defense of Islam" were sometimes justified, and 13 percent expressed "some confidence" in Osama bin Laden, al-Qaeda's founder and general chief.[33] Since 2011, despite comparative polling evidence, the conflict in Syria has brought extremist voices closer to the surface in support of jihadist groups. Even though these views are a minority in Kuwait, they persist under the protective umbrella of some Islamist spokesmen, among them the aforementioned Sheikh Hamid al-Ali. A recent Pew study in 2015 suggests that widespread support for jihadist activity in a variety of Arab countries, including Kuwait, is low.[34] Only two to five percent of those polled expressed support for "IS and its affiliates, al-Qaeda, and other jihadist activity."[35]

Islamism and the State

Kuwait is a constitutional hereditary emirate.[36] The Emir Sabah al-Ahmad al-Jaber Al-Sabah is the head of state, and has the power to appoint the prime minister, dissolve the parliament and even suspend certain parts of the constitution, as occurred between 1976 and 1981 and between 1986 and 1992. Kuwait's constitution, which was approved in 1962, states that "the religion of the state is Islam and the Sharia shall be a main source of legislation." Thus, though driven by Islamic belief, the government is less strict in the enforcement of Islamic law. Sharia, according to the constitution, is a guideline rather than the formal state law. Notably, the first action of the Islamist-dominated parliament elected in February 2012 was to call for an amendment to the constitution to make sharia "the" rather than "a" source of legislation.[37]

The ruling elite has put considerable effort into maintaining order, and is committed to achieving the right balance between emphasizing the importance of Islam to its citizens and ensuring stability by blunting the rise of extremism. The Kuwaiti government exercises direct control over Sunni religious institutions and appoints Sunni imams, monitors their Friday sermons, and pays the salaries of mosque staff. It also finances the building of new Sunni mosques.[38]

The overall number of mosques in Kuwait exceeds 1,100. Only

six of them are Shiite, while the rest are Sunni.[39] There are no official reports delineating the number of mosques open to a radical interpretation of Islam, but several hints can be found on Kuwaiti Internet websites, which suggest the number is derived from the external involvement and financial support of radical elements (mainly from Saudi Arabia).[40]

As no formal political parties are permitted in Kuwait, the 50 seats in the Kuwaiti parliament are occupied by quasi-political societies of Bedouins, merchants, moderate Sunni and Shiite activists, secular liberals, and nationalists. Parliament members either conform to these unofficial national and religiously affiliated blocs or sit as independents.

The Islamist bloc, which functions as a de facto political party, is the most influential group in the Kuwaiti Parliament. It consists mainly of Sunni Salafis and members of Hadas (the Kuwaiti Islamic Constitutional Movement). Its principal long-term goal is to impose sharia law in Kuwait. However, the Islamist bloc operates conservatively in the short-term, attempting to wield influence within parliament in order to pass legislation that conforms to Islamic law. The bloc is composed of devoted Islamists, but not necessarily extremists.

The most prominent Islamic movement in Kuwait remains Al-Haraka al-Dostooriya al-Islamiya, or Hadas, also known as the Islamic Constitutional Movement (ICM).[41] The ICM was established in 1991, following the liberation of Kuwait from Iraqi control in the first Gulf War. The ICM serves as the political front of the Muslim Brotherhood in Kuwait, though in recent years the ICM has grown away from its parent organization. The ICM broke ties with the international Muslim Brotherhood after the latter backed the Iraqi invasion in 1990 and failed to provide sufficient support for the liberation of Kuwait.[42] Neither the ICM nor the Muslim Brotherhood retains any legal status within the country. Instead, the movement's main legally recognized manifestation is the Social Reform Society, a charitable nongovernmental organization.

Salafis are another important Islamist factor in the Kuwaiti political system. Since its founding in the early 1960s, the Salafi movement in Kuwait has focused on dawa ("religious call," or proselytization) and has been active in charities, heritage, relief work, and building schools, universities, mosques, orphanages, and hospitals. In parliament, the movement is represented by two main groups: the Islamic Salafi Grouping (al-Tajamu al-Islami al-Salafi) and the Salafi Movement (al-Haraka al-Salafiyya), an offshoot of the former. Both signify a more extreme—yet far less organized—opposition to the regime. Many other Salafi MPs are independent Islamists. A growth in their numbers, and especially the establishment of a wide and organized political movement for the Salafis to work from, might serve as a prelude for the country's movement down a more fundamentalist path in the future.

Any initiative pursued by Islamists in parliament can be easily blocked, as the Emir's approval is required for all constitutional amendments. For instance, Islamists have long called for an amendment to Article 2 of the constitution, which states that sharia is "a main source of legislation," and to have the article rephrased to read that sharia is "the source of legislation." The amendment passed in parliament, only to be vetoed by the Emir in 2006. It was attempted anew, again without success, in 2012.[43] A similar change requested by the Islamist bloc relates to Article 79, which states that: "No law may be promulgated unless it has been passed by the National Assembly and sanctioned by the Emir." To this the Islamists sought to add "and according to the *Sharia* [sic]."[44] This measure was also rejected by the Emir in May 2012.[45]

The number of parliamentary seats in the Islamist bloc typically fluctuates between 15 and 24 members. Elections have become a common occurrence in recent years, as the parliament was dissolved by the Kuwaiti Emir four times in seven years between 2006 and 2013, most recently due to protests over election laws and allegations of fraud. In addition to repeated dissolution by the Emir, the Constitutional Court also stepped in to annul the two parliaments elected in February and December 2012, owing to technical irregularities in the conduct of the two elections.[46] In the May 2009 elections, Sunni Islamists won only 13 seats (a sharp decrease compared to their rise in power over the previous decade), while Shiite Islamists won six seats and independents, mostly associated with the government, won 21—a significant portion of the total 50 seats of the parliament.[47]

The 2009 elections were likewise significant because they saw the election of four women MPs for the first time in the country's history.[48] Prior to that year, men had filled the seats of Kuwait's parliament exclusively for nearly five decades, and it was only in 2005 that the country granted women the right to vote and run for office.[49] This phenomenon, along with the loss of seats by Islamists, was taken in 2009 to signify a more moderate and liberal approach emerging in already relatively modernized Kuwait, and although no women were elected in the February 2012 election, three subsequently won seats in the December 2012 parliament and two in the July 2013 vote. To further exemplify the trend, Kuwait's highest court judged in 2009 that female MPs are not obliged to wear headscarves, striking yet another blow to Muslim fundamentalists.[50] Though the majority of Kuwaiti women do wear the hijab, it is not compulsory according to the country's law, as it is in the ultra-conservative neighboring Saudi Arabia.

However, relations between the government and the parliament elected in 2009 deteriorated sharply after the start of the Arab Spring in early 2011. Youth movements associated with the Kuwaiti branch of the Muslim Brotherhood as well as with liberal blocs called for the resignation of the unpopular Prime Minister, Sheikh Nasser al-Mohammed Al-Sabah, a nephew of the Emir. In autumn 2011, popular mobilization intersected with the disclosure of a large political corruption scandal, which implicated 16 of the 50 MPs in having allegedly received government payments in return for votes. The resulting anger culminated in the November 2011 storming of the National Assembly building by demonstrators and the subsequent resignation of the Prime Minister a fortnight later.[51]

During 2012, Kuwait witnessed two controversial elections that left the country—and its society—deeply polarized. Elections in February 2012 resulted in an opposition landslide as conservative tribal and Islamist MPs won 35 out of the 50 seats. At least 21 MPs were Sunni Islamists, including four MPs each from the Islamic Salafi Alliance and the ICM. A further five pro-government Sunni politicians and seven Shiites were elected, reinforcing the strongly Islamist character of the parliament. During a turbulent four-month tenure before its annulment by the Constitutional Court in June 2012, Islamist MPs called for the introduction of the death penalty for blasphemy, a move that was particularly significant in the context of the attempt earlier that year to make sharia the sole basis of the constitution.[52]

Sunni Islamists then joined with tribal groups to boycott the December 2012 election. This occurred in protest of a decree issued by the Emir that October amending the electoral law to reduce the number of votes each Kuwaiti could cast from four to one. A series of mass public demonstrations—the largest in Kuwait's history—were organized by the opposition, which argued that only elected parliamentarians and not the Emir could change the electoral law, while the boycott movement was joined by liberal societies in an unlikely alignment of interests. An informal Opposition Coalition formed, consisting of the ICM, the Popular Action Bloc, trade unions, and student groups, which then proceeded to demand an elected government and an end to Al-Sabah control of the executive. Musallim al-Barrak emerged as the charismatic figurehead of the opposition; of Sunni tribal origin, his views are populist rather than ideological or Islamist in nature.[53]

With the opposition boycotting, the December vote resulted in the emergence of a new political class. An unprecedented seventeen Shiites MPs—more than double their usual number—were elected, spread across four ideological groupings. In response, the Islamist and tribal opposition migrated away from the parliamentary chamber toward street politics. This constituted a destabilizing development that signaled a worrying loss of faith in Kuwait's existing political system. Most of the Islamist groups, including the ICM, also boycotted the subsequent election in July 2013, although the Islamic Salafi Alliance broke ranks and gained two parliamentary seats.

When the Emir dissolved the parliament elected in July 2013 and called early elections in November 2016, the ICM and most other groups that had stood aside from the 2013 vote announced their decision to abandon their boycott and return to the political scene. The decision to return to electoral participation reflects the weakening of the oppositional coalition and a judgment that there is more to gain by taking part in the political process than by standing aside. An amendment to the electoral law that prohibited people from standing for election if they have been convicted of slandering the Emir ruled out many potential candidates from ICM and other groups from the opposition, including al-Barrak, who remained in prison until April 2017 serving his two-year sentence for criticizing the Emir.[54] However, opposition politicians still managed to win nearly half—24—of the 50 seats in parliament, taking advantage of the strong anti-austerity mood in Kuwait. Sunni Islamists from the ICM and Salafi groups won twelve seats while Kuwaiti Shia representation fell from nine to six members of parliament.[55]

The ICM traditionally holds only between two and six seats, yet their influence within the Islamist bloc is significant. It is the most popular and powerful—and also by far the best funded and most highly organized—entity of the Islamist movements. The ICM, through the clandestine activity of the Kuwaiti Muslim Brotherhood and through the Social Reform Society, is involved in various social, charitable, educational and economic activities. It recruits its members from mosques and university campuses, adding many doctors and other highly educated academics to its ranks.[56]

The ICM formally seeks the implementation of sharia law and the protection of a fairly conservative vision of Kuwaiti traditions and values. In addition to leading and supporting the amendments mentioned above, the movement has occasionally introduced legislation that aims to implement various sharia provisions, such as a law mandating payment of zakat, a religious tax. It is, however, interested in operating within the Kuwaiti constitutional order rather than overturning it.[57] Relative to other national and trans-national affiliates of the Muslim Brotherhood, the ICM maintains a mild position toward the United States (though not toward Israel) and it has not criticized the security relationship between Kuwait and Washington, DC.[58]

If able to unite with other Islamists, the ICM's electoral power could help the movement achieve its goal of expanding the role of Islamic law in the day-to-day life of Kuwaitis. Kuwaiti political history, however, is reason enough for skepticism on that score, as the opposition has never been able to maintain a united front for long, and the Kuwaiti government has tools at its disposal to easily disperse and even exclude dissenters, evident in 2013 when members of the ruling family reached out to, and detached, selected groups within the broad opposition coalition.[59]

The ICM's gradual success is attributed largely to its discretion in picking its battles with the government and the ruling family. The ICM has strived to position itself simultaneously as an opposition movement and as a party accepting gradualism and the limitations of the Kuwaiti political system. [60] However, many of the occasions on which the Emir dissolved the parliament were precipitated by political disputes with the ICM. Moreover, ties between the ICM and the Kuwaiti government soured after Kuwait extended financial and political support to the military-led interim regime in Egypt that overthrew the democratically elected Muslim Brotherhood-led government of Mohammed Morsi in July 2013.[61]

It is also worth mentioning that, regardless of its relative success, the ICM suffers criticism on multiple fronts. Some critique it for being insufficiently dedicated to the cause of political opposition. A different line of criticism claims the ICM is masking its true, radical sentiments.[62]

In June 2017, Saudi Arabia led a blockade against Qatar, citing the country's continued support of terrorist organizations.[63] Soon after, Saudi Arabia, the United Arab Emirates (UAE), Bahrain, and Egypt formally ended diplomatic relations with Qatar.[64] In the dispute that ensued, Kuwait has attempted to repair relations between the Gulf states.[65] Kuwaiti Emir Jaber Al-Ahmad Al-Sabah has repeatedly stated his country's desire to resolve the crisis, which he claims has severely damaged the region.[66]

Endnotes

1. "Kuwait Shia mosque blast death toll 'rises to 27'" *BBC,* June 25, 2015, http://www.bbc.com/news/world-middle-east-33287136.
2. Scott Neuman, "ISIS Claims Responsibility For Suicide Attack At Kuwait Mosque," *National Public Radio,* June 26, 2015, http://www.npr.org/sections/thetwo-way/2015/06/26/417708840/isis-claims-responsibility-

for-suicide-attack-at-kuwait-mosque.

3. See, for example, "Kuwait Facilities," globalsecurity.org, n.d., http://www.globalsecurity.org/military/facility/kuwait.htm.
4. No comprehensive and reliable database for jihadists in Kuwait exists. The figures provided represent best assessments by the author, based on material relating to arrests and plots that has appeared in the open source.
5. "Seven Sentenced to Death over Kuwait Mosque Bombing." *Al Jazeera* (Doha), September 15, 2015, http://www.aljazeera.com/news/2015/09/sentenced-death-kuwait-mosque-bombing-150915064024530.html.
6. Mark Memmott, "Bin Laden's Courier, Abu Ahmed al-Kuwaiti, Had Several Responsibilities," *National Public Radio*, May 4, 2011, http://www.npr.org/sections/thetwo-way/2011/05/06/135994650/bin-ladens-courier-abu-ahmed-al-kuwaiti-had-several-responsibilities
7. "Walking the Talk: Forum Members Travel to Afghanistan and Iraq (Part 1)," Jihadica.org, June 30, 2008, http://www.jihadica.com/walking-the-talk-forum-members-travel-to-afghanistan-and-iraq-part-1/; "Walking the Talk: Forum Members Travel to Afghanistan and Iraq (Part 2)," Jihadica.org, July 2, 2008, http://www.jihadica.com/walking-the-talk-forum-members-travel-to-afghanistan-and-iraq-pt-2/
8. For example, Abu Obeida Tawari al-Obeidi and Abu Adel al-Kuwaiti, who were killed in Waziristan in early 2009. "Terrorism: Three Al-Qaeda Leaders Killed in US Attack," AKI (Rome), February 5, 2009, http://www.adnkronos.com/AKI/English/Security/?id=1.0.1845929971.
9. "Video Of Former Gitmo Detainee-Turned-Al-Qaida Suicide Bomber In Iraq," NEFA Foundation, January 2009, http://www.nefafoundation.org/multimedia-prop.html
10. "Abu Islam the Iraqi: Kuwaiti Young Men Are Being Manipulated, 25 Of Them Fought With Al-Qaeda in Diyala," *Al-Watan* (Kuwait), July 16, 2008, http://www.elaph.com/ElaphWeb/NewsPapers/2008/7/348810.

htm.

11. Daniel DePetris, "Kuwait's Hidden Hand in Syria," *The National Interest*, July 16, 2013, http://nationalinterest.org/commentary/kuwaits-hidden-hand-syria-8729
12. Walking the Talk: Forum Members Travel to Afghanistan and Iraq."
13. David Pollock and Michael Jacobson, "Blacklisting Terrorism Supporters in Kuwait," Washington Institute for Near East Policy *Policywatch* 1333, January 25, 2008, http://www.washingtoninstitute.org/templateC05.php?CID=2709.
14. U.S. Department of State, "Kuwait," *Country Reports on Terrorism 2012*, May 30, 2013, http://www.refworld.org/docid/51a86e8216.html
15. Elizabeth Dickinson, "Kuwait, 'the back office of logistical support' for Syria's Rebels," *The National*, February 5, 2013, http://www.thenational.ae/news/world/middle-east/kuwait-the-back-office-of-logistical-support-for-syrias-rebels
16. Kristian Coates Ulrichsen, "The Gulf States and Syria," *Open Democracy*, February 11, 2013, https://www.opendemocracy.net/opensecurity/kristian-coates-ulrichsen/gulf-states-and-syria
17. 'Donors Pledge Billions at Syria Aid Conference,' *Kuwait Times*, April 5, 2017. http://news.kuwaittimes.net/website/donors-pledge-billions-syria-aid-conference/.
18. Sylvia Westall and Mahmoud Harby, "Insight: Kuwaitis Campaign Privately to Arm Syrian Rebels," Reuters, June 27, 2013, http://www.reuters.com/article/us-syria-kuwait-insight-idUSBRE95P0TG20130627
19. Kuwait, a U.S. Ally on Syria, Is Also the Leading Funder of Extremist Rebels,' *Washington Post*, April 25, 2014, https://www.washingtonpost.com/world/national-security/kuwait-top-ally-on-syria-is-also-the-leading-funder-of-extremist-rebels/2014/04/25/10142b9a-ca48-11e3-a75e-463587891b57_story.html?utm_term=.92c750d6cf28
20. Habib Toumi, "Kuwait Justice Minister's Resignation Accepted," *Gulf News*, May 12, 2014. http://gulfnews.com/news/gulf/kuwait/kuwaiti-justice-minister-s-

resignation-accepted-1.1331524

21. "Kuwait Attack: Islamic State Suicide Bombing at Shia Mosque Kills 27," Daily Telegraph, June 26, 2015, http://www.telegraph.co.uk/news/worldnews/middleeast/kuwait/11701322/Kuwait-attack-Islamic-State-suicide-bombing-at-Shia-mosque-kills-13-live.html
22. '27 Killed in ISIS Attack on Kuwait Mosque,' *Al Arabiya* (Riyadh), June 26, 2015, http://english.alarabiya.net/en/News/middle-east/2015/06/26/Explosion-hits-mosque-in-Kuwait-during-Friday-prayers-.html
23. Chris Heffelfinger, "Kuwaiti Cleric Hamid al-Ali: The Bridge between Ideology and Action," Jamestown Foundation *Terrorism Monitor* 5, iss. 8, April 26, 2007, http://www.jamestown.org/single/?no_cache=1&tx_ttnews%5Btt_news%5D=4112.
24. "Treasury Designations Target Terrorist Facilitators," U.S. Department of the Treasury, December 7, 2006, https://www.treasury.gov/press-center/press-releases/Pages/hp191.aspx
25. Andrew Gilligan, "How our allies in Kuwait and Qatar funded Islamic State," *The Telegraph,* September 6, 2014, https://www.telegraph.co.uk/news/worldnews/middleeast/kuwait/11077537/How-our-allies-in-Kuwait-and-Qatar-funded-Islamic-State.html.
26. Al-Qaeda Spokesman 'In Iran,'" *BBC*, July 17, 2003, http://news.bbc.co.uk/2/hi/middle_east/3074785.stm.
27. "Abu Ghaith Trial is Proof For Some that Federal Courts Can Better Handle Terror Cases," Washington Post, April 1, 2014, https://www.washingtonpost.com/world/national-security/abu-ghaith-trial-is-proof-for-some-that-federal-courts-can-better-handle-terror-cases/2014/04/01/d15ee8f6-b906-11e3-96ae-f2c36d2b1245_story.html?utm_term=.0f07627cbf8c
28. "Kuwait: Extremism and Counter-Extremism," The Counter Extremism Project, n.d., https://www.counterextremism.com/countries/kuwait.
29. "Kuwait: Extremism and Counter-Extremism," The Counter Extremism Project.
30. "Kuwait: Extremism and Counter-Extremism," The Counter Extremism Project.

31. Ulph, "Terrorism Accelerates in Kuwait."
32. U.S. Department of State, Bureau of Public Affairs, "Background Notes: Kuwait," February 2009, http://www.state.gov/r/pa/ei/bgn/35876.htm.
33. Pollock and Jacobson, "Blacklisting Terrorism Supporters in Kuwait."
34. David Pollock, "Polls Show Most Muslims Reject Both Extremism and Islamic Reform," *Policywatch 2572,* February 25, 2016, https://www.washingtoninstitute.org/policy-analysis/view/polls-show-most-muslims-reject-both-extremism-and-islamic-reform.
35. Pollock, "Polls Show Most Muslims Reject Both Extremism and Islamic Reform."
36. U.S. Department of State, "Background Notes: Kuwait."
37. Sylvia Westall, "Kuwait's Ruler Blocks Parliament's Proposal to Make All Laws Comply with Sharia," *Al Arabiya* (Riyadh), May 17, 2012. http://english.alarabiya.net/articles/2012/05/17/214673.html
38. "Kuwait," in U.S. Department of State, Bureau of Democracy, Human Rights and Labor, *International Religious Freedom Report 2009*, October 26, 2009, http://www.state.gov/g/drl/rls/irf/2009/127351.htm.
39. "Kuwait," in U.S. Department of State, Bureau of Democracy, Human Rights and Labor, *International Religious Freedom Report 2009.*
40. See, for example, "Limadha al-Masajed? [Why The Multiplicity Of Mosques?]" *Al-Jarida* (Kuwait), March 15, 2009, http://www.aljarida.com/aljarida/Article.aspx?id=101363.
41. See ICM's website at http://www.icmkw.org/.
42. Scheherezade Faramarzi, "Kuwait's Muslim Brotherhood," *Jadaliyya*, April 18, 2012, http://www.jadaliyya.com/pages/index/5116/kuwaits-muslim-brotherhood
43. Nathan J. Brown, "Pushing Toward Party Politics? Kuwait's Islamic Constitutional Movement," Carnegie Endowment *Carnegie Papers* no. 79, January 2007, 10.
44. Wendy Kristianasen, "Kuwait's Islamists, Officially Unofficial," *Le Monde Diplomatique* (Paris), June 2002, http://mondediplo.com/2002/06/04kuwait.

45. Sylvia Westall, "Kuwait's Ruler Blocks MP's Islamic law proposal," Reuters, May 17, 2012, http://uk.reuters.com/article/2012/05/17/uk-kuwait-sharia-idUKBRE84G0G42...
46. Kristian Coates Ulrichsen, "Kuwait Votes, Again," *Foreign Pol*icy, July 25, 2013, http://foreignpolicy.com/2013/07/25/kuwait-votes-again/
47. Michael Herb, "Kuwait Politics Database (in Arabic)," n.d., http://www2.gsu.edu/~polmfh/database/database.htm; "Kuwait Parliamentary Election, 2009,"
48. Robert F. Worth, "First Women Win Seats In Kuwait Parliament," *New York Times*, May 17, 2009, http://www.nytimes.com/2009/05/18/world/middleeast/18kuwait.html
49. "Woman Elected In Kuwait Says Gender In Politics Is 'History,'" *CNN*, May 17, 2009, http://edition.cnn.com/2009/WORLD/meast/05/17/kuwait.women.elections/.
50. "Kuwait: Headscarf Not A Must For Female Lawmakers," Associated Press, October 28, 2009, http://gulfnews.com/news/gulf/kuwait/headscarf-not-a-must-for-female-lawmakers-in-kuwait-1.520316
51. Kristin Smith Diwan, "Kuwait's Constitutional Showdown," *Foreign Policy*, November 17, 2011, http://foreignpolicy.com/2011/11/17/kuwaits-constitutional-showdown/
52. Kristian Coates Ulrichsen, "Political Showdown in Kuwait," *Foreign Policy*, June 20, 2012, http://foreignpolicy.com/2012/06/20/political-showdown-in-kuwait/
53. Kristin Smith Diwan, "The Politics of Transgression in Kuwait," *Foreign Pol*icy, April 19, 2013, http://foreignpolicy.com/2013/04/19/the-politics-of-transgression-in-kuwait/
54. Kristin Smith Diwan, 'Parliamentary Boycotts in Kuwait and Bahrain Cost Opposition,' Arab Gulf States Institute in Washington, July 16, 2016, http://www.agsiw.org/parliamentary-boycotts-in-kuwait-and-bahrain-cost-opposition/
55. 'Kuwait Poll: Opposition Wins Nearly Half of Parliament,' *Al Jazeera Online*, November 27, 2016.

http://www.aljazeera.com/news/2016/11/kuwait-poll-opposition-wins-parliament-161127060822207.html.

56. Brown, "Pushing toward Party Politics? Kuwait's Islamic Constitutional Movement," 7.
57. Brown, "Pushing toward Party Politics? Kuwait's Islamic Constitutional Movement,", 11.
58. Scheherezade Faramarzi, "Kuwait's Muslim Brotherhood," *Jadaliyya*, April 18, 2012, http://www.jadaliyya.com/pages/index/5116/kuwaits-muslim-brotherhood.
59. Brown, "Pushing toward Party Politics? Kuwait's Islamic Constitutional Movement," 4.
60. Brown, "Pushing toward Party Politics? Kuwait's Islamic Constitutional Movement," 5.
61. Lori Plotkin Boghardt, "Kuwait's Elections: It's Not What Happens Now, but What Happens Next," Washington Institute for Near East Policy *Policy Watch* 2109, July 26, 2013, http://www.washingtoninstitute.org/policy-analysis/view/kuwaits-elections-its-not-what-happens-now-but-what-happens-next; Faramarzi, "Kuwait's Muslim Brotherhood."
62. Brown, "Pushing toward Party Politics? Kuwait's Islamic Constitutional Movement," 16.
63. Giorgio Cafiero, "ASEAN and the Qatar Crisis," *New Atlanticist,* November 3, 2017, http://www.atlanticcouncil.org/blogs/new-atlanticist/asean-and-the-qatar-crisis.
64. Cafiero, "ASEAN and the Qatar Crisis."
65. Cafiero, "ASEAN and the Qatar Crisis."
66. "GCC News Roundup: Trump meets with Emir of Qatar, Kuwait says Gulf crisis must end, Houthi political chief killed, (April 1-30)," *Up Front,* May 1, 2018, https://www.brookings.edu/blog/up-front/2018/05/01/gcc-news-roundup-trump-meets-with-emir-of-qatar-kuwait-says-gulf-crisis-must-end-houthi-political-chief-killed-april-1-30/.

22 Lebanon

Quick Facts

Population: 6,229,794 (July 2017 est.)
Area: 10,400 sq km
Ethnic Groups: Arab 95%, Armenian 4%, other 1%
Religions: Muslim 54% (27% Sunni, 27% Shia), Christian 40.5% (includes 21%
Maronite Catholic, 8% Greek Orthodox, 5% Greek Catholic, 6.5% other Christian),
Druze 5.6%, very small numbers of Jews, Baha'is, Buddhists, Hindus, and Mormons
Government Type: parliamentary republic
GDP (official exchange rate): $52.7 billion (2017 est.)

Map and Quick Facts courtesy of the CIA World Factbook (June 2018)

Introduction

Islamism in Lebanon is sui generis in a multitude of important respects. The cohabitation of large Sunni Muslim and Shia Muslim populations in relatively close proximity, with neither constituting a national majority (and alongside a comparably sized multidenominational Christian community and smaller minority groups) has meant that few Islamists of either sectarian persuasion have aggressively pursued the establishment of a theocratic state in Lebanon, or even sought the wholesale downfall of the existing political order. Rather, Islamists have typically sought to advance transnational aims of, and secure patronage from, powerful co-religionists abroad, often at the expense of Lebanese stability.

Hezbollah, the dominant Shia Islamist group in Lebanon, has carved out a heavily armed state-within-a-state in Shia-inhabited areas of southern Lebanon, the eastern Beqaa Valley, and suburban Beirut, while commanding sufficient electoral strength to block encroachment by the central government. Though once revered across the predominantly Sunni Arab world for its armed "resistance" to Israel, its blind obedience to Iran and willingness to turn its guns on other Muslims in recent years have increasingly made it a pariah outside of its own constituency.

Sunni Islamist groups are more numerous and ideologically varied, far more politically marginalized, and surprisingly unwilling to work with one another in pursuit of common objectives. Radicalization in impoverished Sunni areas of northern Lebanon has been growing steadily for years, but has not been effectively channeled by Islamist leaders.

The start of the civil war in neighboring Syria in 2011 has progressively drawn both Shia and Sunni Lebanese Islamists into direct combat with each other across the border, and increasingly at home, while instigating an influx of 1.2 million mostly Sunni Syrian refugees into Lebanon.

Notwithstanding the troubling proliferation of terror attacks in Lebanon by local branches of the Nusra Front and the Islamic State group—and the first ever Lebanese-on-Lebanese suicide bombing of civilian targets—a renewed regional and international commitment to support the Lebanese Army appears likely to prevent the country from collapsing further into civil war.

ISLAMIST ACTIVITY

Established in 1920 by the French mandatory authorities after the collapse of the Ottoman Empire, Lebanon gained full independence in 1943. The new state combined the predominantly Maronite Christian and Druze Mount Lebanon region with the largely Sunni coastal cities of Beirut, Sidon, and Tripoli, as well as the predominantly Shia hinterland to the south and east. Under the terms of the 1943 National Pact between Muslim and Christian leaders and subsequent formal and informal adjustments, fixed shares of political power are distributed by sect, with a Maronite Christian as president, a Sunni as prime minister, a Shia as speaker of the National Assembly, and other specific offices falling to various smaller sects. Fixed shares of legislative power are divided among the various groups. While Lebanon's sectarian system (*al-nizam al-ta'ifiyya*) provided for a modicum of democracy and political stability in the decades following independence, it also impeded the development of a shared national identity, limited the power of the state, and facilitated intervention by outside parties sharing ethnic, religious, and cultural ties to particular sectarian groups.

The growth of Islamism in Lebanon is partly rooted in the same regional crisis conditions that fueled its growth throughout the Middle East—the humiliating Arab defeat in the 1967 war with Israel, severe political oppression by autocratic governments, poor economic growth, and gross wealth disparities. Shia Islamism and Sunni Islamism both emerged as a challenge to the existing political order and to secular leftist and nationalist ideologies then prevalent in opposition circles. However, they have followed very different trajectories.

Shia Islamism

Shia Islamism began emerging as a strong socio-political force in Lebanon during the 1970s, under the influence of Lebanese clerics who were radicalized studying in the religious seminaries of Najaf, Iraq (alongside many Iranian students who would play leading roles in their country's 1979 revolution). The most prominent Shia leader at the time was Sayyid Musa al-Sadr, the Iranian-born child of a prominent Lebanese family that had produced many religious scholars over the years. Upon settling in Lebanon during the 1960s, Sadr assumed leadership of the state-sanctioned Supreme Islamic Shiite Council and created a political movement called the Movement of the Dispossessed, which preached a form of moderate Islamism focused mainly on the pursuit of Shiite socio-economic advancement and modest reform of Lebanon's constitution.

With the onset of civil war in 1975 and Sadr's disappearance (and presumed murder) three years later while on a trip to Muammar Qadhafi's Libya, the Sadrist movement was corrupted (and noticeably secularized) by the need to arm itself and accept Syrian patronage, so much so that it has since been popularly known as Amal, the Arabic acronym for the name of its wartime militia.

A more revolutionary wave of Islamism centered around Muhammad Hussein Fadlallah, a distinguished Najaf-trained cleric who called on Shia to fight not for their own communal advancement but on behalf of all Muslims against Israel. Though Fadlallah himself did not embrace Iranian Ayatollah Ruhollah Khomeini's revolutionary doctrine of velayat-e faqih (Guardianship of the Jurisconsult), which forms the basis for Iran's post-1979 Islamic Republic, many younger clerics who followed his guidance did, whether out of genuine conviction or in pursuit of Iranian patronage.

In the early 1980s, Iran saw Lebanon as a vehicle through which to increase its regional influence. Tehran consequently deployed its Iranian Revolutionary Guard Corps (IRGC, or Pasdaran) to train and indoctrinate local Shia. Syrian President Hafez al-Assad, whose army maintained a considerable troop presence in eastern Lebanon, facilitated the infiltration, as he was eager to prevent Lebanon from falling under the orbit of Israel (which had invaded Lebanon in 1982 to eliminate the threat from Palestinian terrorists dominating southern Lebanon) and the West.

Radical Shia fundamentalists from the Beqaa Valley, the south of Lebanon and the Beirut suburb of Dahiyeh flocked to the emerging network, among them a breakaway faction of *Amal* led by Hussein Mussawi. Using aliases such as the Islamic Jihad Organization and the Organization of the Oppressed on Earth, from 1983 to 1985 they carried out a series of deadly suicide bomb attacks against Israeli forces and the Western Multinational Force in Lebanon (MFL) later deployed to assist President Amine Gemayel in restoring government authority in Beirut. Both had incurred the animosity of most Shia and both subsequently withdrew from the capital under the weight of the assault.

In 1985, these disparate underground groups united and issued a manifesto, calling itself Hezbollah (Party of God) and calling for the establishment of an Islamic state in Lebanon.[1] In practice, however, they were concerned first and foremost with advancing more immediate Iranian interests. During the mid-1980s, militants affiliated with Hezbollah kidnapped dozens of Americans and Europeans, allowing Tehran to extract concessions from Western government bargaining for their release. In 1985, they hijacked TWA flight 847. Though the Iranian government denied responsibility, considerable circumstantial evidence pointed to involvement by high-ranking members of the regime in Tehran.[2] Lavish Iranian financing also enabled Hezbollah to build an extensive social welfare network to provide for civilians living in towns and urban neighborhoods under its control.

Under the 1989 Taif Accord that brought most of the Civil War fighting to an end, the Lebanese constitution was amended to equalize Muslim and Christian representation in parliament and transfer most executive authority to the Sunni prime minister. In return for accepting the Taif Accord, Hezbollah was allowed by Damascus to remain armed, unlike other wartime militias, ostensibly for the purpose of "liberating" the border strip in south Lebanon occupied by Israeli forces. Hezbollah also acted as a conduit for Iranian supplies, finance, and training to Palestinian Sunni Islamist groups fighting Israel, notably Hamas and Islamic Jihad.[3]

Hezbollah participated in the electoral process and sent representatives to parliament. In sharp contrast to Sunni Islamists, however, it made only modest efforts to push Islamist socio-political causes in Lebanon and dismissed the viability of an Islamic state,[4] preferring instead a secular appeal for national unity and resistance to oppression that appealed to non-Shia. The withdrawal of Israeli troops from Lebanon in 2000 left Hezbollah enormously popular in Lebanon and the broader Arab world. Although Arab leaders bemoaned what Jordan's King Abdullah famously called a "Shia crescent" extending from Iran through Iraq and Syria to Lebanon,[5] this kind of sect baiting failed to strike a chord with most Sunnis.

Hezbollah's involvement in the February 2005 car bombing that killed former Lebanese Prime Minister Rafiq Hariri, a Saudi-backed Sunni billionaire widely expected to challenge allies of Syrian-backed President Emile Lahoud in that year's parliamentary elections, marked a major watershed for the group. So pristine was Hezbollah's reputation as a selfless "resistance" movement that even its fiercest critics had not imagined that four of its operatives helped carry out the killing, as alleged (convincingly) in the 2011 indictments released by the Special Tribunal for Lebanon (STL), a special court tasked by the Security Council with prosecuting those responsible for the bombing.[6]

Thereafter, Syria's 2005 withdrawal from Lebanon touched off a struggle for control of the state, with the March 14 coalition of Saad Hariri attempting to leverage strong Western support in effecting Hezbollah's disarmament (see below). Hezbollah's self-proclaimed "divine victory" in the 2006 Israel-Lebanon war appealed broadly to Sunnis in Lebanon and across the Arab world. As recently as March 2008, polling showed Nasrallah to be overwhelmingly the most popular public figure throughout the Arab world.[7] This changed in May 2008, when Hezbollah responded to an attempt by Prime Minister Siniora to close its private telecommunications network by briefly seizing control of predominantly Sunni West Beirut.

Though initially reluctant to get involved in Syria's ongoing civil war, strategic necessity forced Nasrallah's hand. A rebel victory in Syria would cut off Iran's ability to resupply the group with weapons (which are flown to Damascus and driven overland across the Syrian-Lebanese border), leaving it vulnerable to Israeli attack and eventually crippling its capacity to resist the Lebanese Army. When the fortunes of war began turning against the Assad regime in 2012, Hezbollah deployed its forces to help retake territory captured by the rebels and to man defenses in important sites such as the Sayyida Zeinab shrine near Damascus or Shia villages east of the Beqaa valley. Importantly, Hezbollah proved vital in the retaking of Qusair, a major point of entry for supplies heading to Syrian rebels.

Hezbollah's engagement is Syria has only deepened since. The group has sent thousands of fighters, who have frequently played a key role on the battlefield, often leading military operations. Hezbollah saw the need to support Syria both to ensure its logistical base, but also out of a recognition that the Islamist violence against the Assad regime would almost certainly strike the Lebanese Shia as well. Current deployments are estimated to be 7,000 at any time. Hezbollah's total forces are believed to be 30,000 to 50,000, with about of them half full-time fighters. The other half are believed to be new recruits, reservists and village guard members.[8]

During the conflict in Syria, Hezbollah's conflict with Israel has, on the whole, been dormant. In January 2015, Israel killed a group of Hezbollah leaders on the Golan Heights. Later that month, Hezbollah fired on IDF troops near the Israeli-Lebanese border, killing two soldiers. But, preoccupied in Syria, Hezbollah has had little energy to confront its primary adversaries. Nonetheless, Israeli strategists are concerned of the potential future effects of Hezbollah's involvement in Syria, since the group has obtained enormous battlefield experience in Syria, more advanced weapons, and has become a mentor to a panoply of Shia militias throughout the greater Middle East.[9]

Sunni Islamism

Broadly speaking, Sunni Islamists in Lebanon fall into two categories. The first consists of various offshoots of the Muslim Brotherhood. The second consists of Salafis.

Political Islamists

Although Sunni Islamic revivalist movements in Lebanon date back to the 1920s, they were largely focused on renewing religious faith through educational, cultural, and social activities, while operating squarely within the existing political system.

The first Islamic group to directly challenge the country's political order was al-Jama'a al-Islamiyah (Islamic Association), the Lebanese chapter of the Muslim Brotherhood. Established in Tripoli in 1964 by Fathi Yakan and Faysal Mawlawi, al-Jama'a called for the establishment of an Islamic state through peaceful means.

After the outbreak of the Lebanese Civil War, al-Jama'a took up arms alongside the leftist National Movement against the Maronite Christians. Following the entry of Syrian troops into Lebanon in the summer of 1976, Yakan and most other al-Jama'a leaders reached an accommodation with the Assad regime, and later with the Iranians. In the early 1980s, al-Jama'a founded a new armed force in Sidon, known as Quwat Fajr (the Fajr Brigades), to fight against Israeli forces in Lebanon. Yakan's pro-Syrian sympathies went so far that he recommended Lebanon merge with Syria as a solution to its confessional problems.[10]

In contrast, breakaway factions of al-Jama'a in the predominantly Sunni northern port of Tripoli, a deeply conservative city home to numerous exiled Syrian Muslim Brotherhood fighters, defied the Syrian occupiers. Most of these merged in 1982 to form Harakat al-Tawhid al-Islami (the Islamic Unification Movement). Led by the popular preacher Said Sha'ban, Tawhid imposed sharia law there and enforced strict Islamic behavior in the city, regardless of sect. Christian women were forced to wear the veil, while liquor stores, clubs, and churches were vandalized or bombed. In the fall of 1985, the Syrian army entered Tripoli and crushed Tawhid. Sha'ban and most Tawhid commanders reached an accommodation the Syrians; those who didn't were hunted down and killed or imprisoned in Damascus.

Thereafter, al-Jama'a and Tawhid both operated squarely within the Iranian-Syrian orbit. Though barred from directly fighting the Israelis after the war ended, they embraced Hezbollah's vision of a society of resistance.[11] Al-Jama'a supported Lebanon's post-Taif political system and participated in municipal and parliamentary elections, with modest success.

After the withdrawal of Syria forces in 2005, al-Jama'a split over political loyalties. Mawlawi and most of its leaders favored the March 14 coalition, while Yakan remained loyal to Syria. After the 2006 war, Yakan resigned and, together with Tawhid leaders Hashem Minqara and Bilal Sha'ban (the son of its late founder) and other pro-Syrian Sunni Islamists, formed Jabhat al-Amal al-Islami (the Islamic Action Front, IAF). In its founding statement, the IAF described its mission as "an affirmation of Islamic and national unity, protecting the Resistance and defending the unity of Lebanon... confronting sectarian and ethnic strife... and rejecting Western and American threats to Arab and Muslim countries."[12] In contrast, Al-Jama'a was rewarded for its allegiance by inclusion in the March 14 electoral coalition for the 2009 elections, which netted the group one seat in parliament. Now led by Ibrahim Masri, it has avoided entanglement in the Syrian Civil War and maintains only a limited armed presence in Lebanon.

IAF factions, on the other hand, have established a significant armed presence in Tripoli, with money and arms provided by Hezbollah. They are closely aligned with the militias of pro-Syrian Sunni clans in Tripoli (especially the Mouri family)[13] and of the small Alawite community in the Jabal Mohsen neighborhood,[14] altogether about 1,500-strong. The Sha'ban wing of Tawhid is said to be financed by Iran, while the Minqara wing is closer to Syria.[15]

During the Syrian civil war, the Assad regime's Islamist allies have been linked to a number of attacks against its enemies in north Lebanon. In August 2013, two major Salafi mosques in Tripoli that supported Syrian rebels were bombed, killing 48 worshippers. Lebanese investigators linked the bombings to Ahmad Gharib, a key Minqara aide close to Syrian intelligence.[16] At least two IAF-affiliated clerics have been assassinated to date: Tawhid preacher Abdul-Razzaq al-Asmar in October 2012, and Saadedine Ghiyyeh, a leading cleric in the IAF, in November 2013.[17]

Al-Ahbash

The Association of Islamic Philanthropic Projects (Jam'iyyat al-Mashari' al-Khairiyya al-Islamiyya) is a comparatively moderate Sufi movement long supported by Syria as a counterweight to radical Islamist forces in Lebanon, and very much corrupted in the process. The movement devoutly follows the teachings of its founder Abdallah al-Harari, popularly known as Abdallah al-Habashi.[18] His school of thought emphasizes Islam's pluralistic nature and mixes elements of Sunni and Shia theological doctrines with Sufi spiritualism. It opposes the use of violence against the ruling authorities and accepts the legitimacy of many Shia and Sufi beliefs typically condemned by Islamists as heresies.[19] During the Syrian occupation, however, the movement adopted thuggish tactics to intimidate opponents.[20] Its influence has sharply diminished since the withdrawal of Syrian forces.

Hizb ut-Tahrir (Party of Liberation)

Hizb ut-Tahrir, a non-denominational Islamist movement founded in Jordan in the early 1950s, has had an active branch in Lebanon since 1959. Although sharing with hardline Salafis (see below) the goal of restoring an Islamic caliphate across the Muslim world, it believes this can be achieved through non-violent persuasion, and its activities in Lebanon (and elsewhere in the Arab world) have been largely peaceful and apolitical. Nevertheless, the group's rhetoric is deeply unsettling to many non-Sunni Lebanese and Westerners alike,[21] and members of the group have gone on to become involved in al-Qaeda-linked jihadist organizations.[22] Judging from the number of attendees at the party's annual conferences and public demonstrations, Hizb ut-Tahrir in Lebanon appears to have several hundred active members.

Traditional Salafis

Salafism is an ultra-orthodox Sunni Islamist current that preaches literal interpretation of the Koran, a return to early Islamic traditions, and the rejection of "innovations" (bidaa) that have taken root in the centuries since—particularly those practiced by non-Sunni Muslims and Sufis, who are viewed as heretics. In sharp contrast to the Muslim Brotherhood and its offshoots, Salafis have traditionally avoided involvement in politics, focusing instead on missionary work (da'wa) to convert Muslim societies to their way of thinking.

Salafism spread rapidly among poor Sunni communities during the 1990s, due in part to the influx of funding from Islamic charities in the Arab Gulf. One of Salem al-Shahal's sons, Dai al-Islam, was the primary recipient of this largesse, notably from the Al-Haramain Islamic Foundation,[23] a Saudi charity later linked to al-Qaeda[24] and closed under American pressure, and Kuwait's Jama'iyat Ihya' Al-Turath Al-Islami (Revival of Islamic Heritage Society, RIHS). Dai al-Islam al-Shahal's charity, Jama'iyat al-Hidaya wa al-Ihsan al-Islami (Islamic Guidance and Charity Association), funded Salafi mosques, schools, and social welfare institutions throughout the country.

Although Shahal does not appear to have explicitly advocated violence during this period, many of the jihadists who ran afoul of authorities during the Syrian occupation (see below) were educated and indoctrinated within his circle. These links led RIHS to cut off most funding to Shahal. In 2000, Lebanese authorities closed his charity and arrested many of his followers, forcing Shahal to flee the country for Saudi Arabia. After this, RIHS directed funding to more quietist Lebanese Salafis, notably Safwan al-Zu'bi, Hassan al-Shahal (a cousin of Dai al-Islam), and Saad al-Din al-Kibbi.

Following the withdrawal of Syrian forces from Lebanon in 2005, Dai-Islam al-Shahal returned to Lebanon, as did other notable Islamists. Selim al-Rafei, a Salafi preacher who has eclipsed Shahal in influence, returned to Lebanon for the first time since the fall of Tripoli to Syrian forces in 1985.

The Salafi movement became involved in politics following the 2005 Hariri assassination and the subsequent withdrawal of Syrian forces. While al-Jama'a boycotted the May/June 2005 parliamentary elections, Salafi preachers in Tripoli roundly endorsed Saad Hariri's Future Movement and its allies, which proved critical to their defeat of Michel Aoun's Free Patriotic Movement (FPM) in mixed Sunni-Christian districts of north Lebanon. Now controlling a parliamentary majority, Hariri designated his father's former finance minister, Fouad Siniora, to head the new government.

In the wake of Hezbollah's May 2008 seizure of West Beirut and widespread disillusionment with Saad Hariri,[25] the Salafi movement has grown more radical. Abu Bakr al-Shahal (another son of Salem al-Shahal) said that jihad is permissible "under the banner of legitimate defense" and that "a reenactment of the May 7 events could certainly prompt a new jihad."[26]

By 2013, a number of Salafi preachers were calling for Lebanese citizens to go fight in Syria. Echoing the views of his peers, Dai al-Islam al-Shahhal told the BBC that people must "sacrifice money and life" to confront what he described as a Shia plan to take over the Middle East. "They will move on to besiege Saudi Arabia and other countries in the Gulf, to control the sacred places and the riches of that region, to rule the Islamic world, if they can, and become a world superpower."[27] The most notable exception to this trend is Imama, who has urged his followers to support the rebels by donating money and sheltering their families, but not by going to fight there.[28] A number of Salafi figures have gone further, however, and sent their sons to fight in Syria. Shahhal's son Zayed fought with the rebels, later bragging to the BBC about killing captured Hezbollah fighters.[29]

Salafi-jihadis

While traditional Salafis have eschewed violence (with the exception of that aimed at Syria), a more radical Salafi current identifying with al-Qaeda's global jihad has operated in under-developed and poor Sunni areas there,[30] drawing members from among Lebanese Sunnis, Palestinian refugees, and various Arab expatriates resident in the country. The return home of Arab mujahideen who fought the Soviet occupation of Afghanistan (1979-1989) was the critical catalyst for the development of this trend.

The first of these groups, Isbat al-Ansar (Band of Partisans), emerged in the Palestinian refugee camp of Ain al-Hilweh near the southern city of Sidon. Led by Muhammad Abd al-Karim al-Saadi (aka Abu Muhjin), Isbat al-Ansar initially gained notoriety for carrying out a number of attacks on Christian religious targets and liquor stores. In 1995, members of the group assassinated Al-Ahbash leader Nizar al-Halabi. Lebanese authorities publicly executed three members of the group for their participation in the plot. In June 1999, the group took revenge by assassinating three Lebanese judges and the chief prosecutor for southern Lebanon at the Justice Palace in Sidon. Following the 2003 U.S.-led occupation of Iraq, several members of the group took part in the jihad against coalition forces there.[31] The group is estimated to command the loyalty of between 100 and 300 fighters.[32] An offshoot of Isbat al-Ansar known as Jund al-Sham also operates in the camp. The Palestinian groups in Ain al-Hilweh have continued to clash both within the camps and without. In May 2015, a Hezbollah member was killed in the refugee camp.[33] In the end of 2016 there were clashes between Isbat al-Ansar and other Palestinian factions that left several dead. Hamas brokered a ceasefire.[34]

In 2006, Shaker al-Absi, a Jordanian-Palestinian best known for organizing the 2002 assassination of U.S. diplomat Lawrence Foley in Amman, infiltrated Lebanon and raised a force of Lebanese, Palestinian, and other Arab fighters who had returned from jihad in Iraq. In November of that year, they seized control of the Palestinian Nahr al-Bared refugee camp near Tripoli and declared the establishment of Fatah al-Islam (Conquest of Islam). The Lebanese government subsequently linked the group to deadly bus bombings in Ain Alaq that killed three people in February 2007. In May 2007, Lebanese troops stationed outside of Nahr al-Bared were ambushed in retaliation for a police raid against suspects in a bank robbery. The Army laid siege to the camp. The fighting lasted until September and claimed the lives of over 160 Lebanese soldiers.

The Abdullah Azzam Brigades, a jihadist terrorist group with branches in Lebanon, Saudi Arabia and Pakistan, has been active since 2009-2010, initially claiming responsibility for sporadic acts of violence against the United Nations Interim Force in Lebanon (UNIFIL) and firing Katyusha rocket attacks into Israel.[35] Since the outbreak of the Syrian Civil War, its operations in Lebanon have focused on Hezbollah and Iranian targets. The group claimed responsibility for the November 2013 double suicide bombing outside the Iranian embassy that left 22 dead and a February 2014 attack on the Iranian Cultural Center in suburban Beirut that killed

11, both ostensibly in retaliation for Iran's support for the Assad regime. Its emir, Sirajeddine Zureiqat, has called for open war against Hezbollah inside Lebanon and urged Sunni soldiers to desert the military.[36]

Syria's two leading Salafi-jihadist groups, Abu Bakr al-Baghdadi's Islamic State (formerly known as the Islamic State in Iraq and Syria, ISIS) and Jabhat al-Nusra, have both built networks of operatives in Lebanon to ferry supplies and men across the border. Two young militia leaders in Tripoli, Shadi al-Mawlawi and Osama Abu Mansour (the nephew and son, respectively, of local Salafi preachers) have pledged loyalty to ISIS. Both were indicted by a military judge for their involvement in an August 2014 bombing that wounded 11 people.[37] ISIS also claimed responsibility for an earlier January 2014 bombing that killed four people outside a Hezbollah office in Beirut. The bomber was believed to be the first Lebanese Sunni to carry out a suicide bombing against fellow Lebanese civilians.[38] That same month, Al-Nusra claimed responsibility for two suicide bombings in the predominantly Shiite border town of Hermel that left eight people dead.[39] In addition, ISIS and al-Nusra have been recruiting in Lebanon, particularly in the Palestinian and Syrian refugee camps.[40]

As the Syrian Civil War has continued and Hezbollah's involvement has deepened, Syrian Salafists have continued to target Hezbollah in its home territory. On September 20, 2014, an al-Nusra suicide bomber struck a Hezbollah checkpoint in the Beqaa, killing three along with the bomber. In Tripoli, in Lebanon's Sunni heartland, a pair of suicide bombers struck a café in the predominantly Alawite neighborhood of Jabal Mohsen, killing nine (including the two bombers) and wounding 36, on January 10, 2015. Al-Nusra claimed responsibility, calling it retaliation for the August 2013 bombings against Sunni mosques in Tripoli (see above) that were attributed to the Syrian regime, which is predominantly Alawite. Later that month, full-blown fighting broke out between the Lebanese Army and the Islamic State on the Syrian-Lebanese border in the Beqaa Valley.

Lebanon was relatively quiet for the rest of 2015, until November 12, when a pair of suicide bombers struck the predominantly Shia neighborhood (and Hezbollah stronghold) of Burj al-Barahneh in Beirut. Over 200 were wounded and forty were killed in the attack. The Islamic State claimed credit, stating that it was undertaken in revenge for Hezbollah's actions in Syria. Although there have been several smaller scale attacks, including a series of suicide bombings in June 2016 targeting a Christian village near the Syrian border that killed five, Lebanon was spared continuing spillover violence from the Syrian Civil War.[41]

Islamism and Society

Shia and Sunni Islamist movements in Lebanon, as elsewhere, have been fueled by acute socio-economic, political, and sectarian grievances. But the success or failure of Islamist movements in channeling grievances into action in the Lebanese arena has depended on a range of factors, including availability of outside financing, the strength of secular rivals, and doctrinal flexibility.

The Shia

Though Lebanon's Shia community had grown to become the country's largest sect by the early 1970s, it was by far the most impoverished and the most politically disenfranchised when the country descended into civil war in 1976. Barred from the nation's two highest political offices and apportioned less than a fifth of parliamentary seats, most Shia came to view the confessional system as fundamentally unfair to Muslims in general, and Shia in particular.

The 1989 Taif Accord slightly amended this imbalance by modestly expanding the speaker's powers and increasing Shia parliamentary representation to 21 percent of the seats. But Sunnis gained the most from the Saudi-brokered accord through a strengthened premiership, and Shia arguably gained the least from the Beirut-centered laissez-faire post-war economic order, which neglected the agricultural sector in which most Shia still worked,[42] invited an influx of unregulated Syrian labor, and spawned systemic corruption. So brazen was the state's failure that former Hezbollah Secretary-General Subhi Toufaili broke with his compatriots and launched an ill-fated "revolution of the hungry" in the late 1990s.

State failure made Hezbollah's Shia constituency easier to co-opt. With Iran providing around $200 million to the group annually,[43] Hezbollah built an expansive social welfare network to provide the country's Shia with education, healthcare, low-interest loans, and myriad other benefits. In a country where it is often impossible to secure government services without paying a bribe, Hezbollah came to be seen by most Shia (and many non-Shia) as having "clean hands." The fact that most Shia continued to support Hezbollah's "resistance" to Israel even after the latter withdrew from Lebanon, and despite having no major territorial disputes with the Jewish state, is a measure of how secure Hezbollah's stature as communal guardian had become.

Hezbollah's political hegemony within the Shia community was at its peak when Syrian troops departed Lebanon in 2005, and it remained unshaken throughout the bruising battle with the March 14 forces for control of government. With the dramatic upsurge in Sunni Islamist violence against Shia in Iraq, Pakistan and Afghanistan during the mid-2000s, even many secular Shia came to think it unwise to surrender their community's one point of leverage when the future was so uncertain. The Hezbollah's involvement in the sectarian violence in Syria and Iraq started to influence the dynamics between the Lebanese Shia community and Hezbollah. Today, the Shia feel more isolated from Sunni Arab states, but more importantly, Hezbollah was forced to sacrifice the social services that had formerly benefited the Shia community for increased military operations in the region, due to budgetary restraints.[44] Hezbollah and Amal won Lebanon's parliamentary elections in May 2019, in part for want of a significant alternative.[45]

The Sunnis

Tragically, Hezbollah's path to Shia empowerment was part and parcel of Syria's brutal subjugation of Lebanon, which in many respects was felt most acutely by Sunnis.

The pre-war years were not a time of prosperity for all Sunnis, the vast majority of whom inhabited one of the country's three largest cities: Beirut, Tripoli, and Sidon. The latter two declined in prosperity relative to Beirut after the establishment of an independent Lebanon severed their trade routes to the Syrian interior.

Moreover, the Sunni community was dominated politically and economically by a handful of powerful families.[46] The latter also unduly influenced the Sunni religious establishment, known as Dar al-Fatwa, and its vast network of mosques, schools, and other institutions by manipulating its internal elections.

Efforts by Al-Jama'a and various secular Sunni opposition groups to channel growing public resentment of the above into effective political mobilization during the 1960s and 1970s were greatly impeded by demography. Though comprising 25-30 percent of the population, Sunnis are concentrated in three noncontiguous urban centers, with substantial cultural and socio-economic differences among them.[47]

No Sunni political party has ever developed strong public support in all three of these areas. Even when the power of traditional elites was broken during the 1976-1990 civil war, each city fell under the sway of Sunni militias with little or no national reach (e.g. the Murabitoun in Beirut, the Popular Nasserite Organization in Sidon).[48] The Syrian occupation created a new sectarian underclass in Lebanon, this time among Sunni Palestinian and Lebanese constituencies.

Most impoverished are the 350-400,000 Palestinian refugees in Lebanon, primarily Sunnis, who live in squalid, overcrowded camps and are barred by law from owning property and working in many professions.[49] For decades, Lebanese authorities have, with few exceptions, declined to enter the camps, for fear of enflaming sectarian tensions. It is no surprise that the Salafi-jihadist current took root there first.

Outside of the camps, the most underprivileged areas are Tripoli and the nearby Akkar region. According to one widely cited study, about 36 percent of the population in the North was living below the poverty line in 2012, more than double the poverty rate in Beirut; more than 20 percent in Mount Lebanon and Nabatieh; about 38 percent in the Beqaa; and 31 percent in the South.[50] Those Sunnis who have risked life and limb fighting the Assad regime in Syria or punishing its supporters in Lebanon come disproportionately from such poor urban neighborhoods and underdeveloped rural areas.

But the proliferation of Salafi networks in recent years masks extraordinary divisions. Sunni Islam lacks the rigid hierarchies linking followers to the clerical establishment that are prevalent in Shi'ism, a major factor accounting for Hezbollah's internal cohesion and public legitimation. In fact, Salafis loathe organizational hierarchies, viewing them as "innovations" (bidaa) that encourage loyalty to the group, rather than to God. "Almost without exception, Salafi groups lack sophisticated organizational strategies," notes scholar Zoltan Pall. "Members are connected to each other through informal networks, and there is no clear, formal hierarchy between them."[51]

The result is that Salafi organizations tend to work at cross-purposes. Some want to convert other Sunnis to their austere doctrines, while others focus their attention on discrediting Shi'ism and other heterodox beliefs. Among the activist (haraki) wing of the jihadists, some think that focusing on the conflict in Syria is the right path, while others want to shake up the system in Lebanon. The former are themselves divided over how to help the rebels (e.g. whether to actively recruit Lebanese volunteers), the latter over whether the Army or just Hezbollah is the enemy.

This same phenomenon was often evident among Salafi-jihadist groups sharing similar aspirations during the 2000s. Isbat al-Ansar, for example, handed over to the Army a Dinniyeh Group fugitive who fled into Ain al-Hilweh in July 2002 and openly disavowed the 2007 Fatah al-Islam uprising (Jund al-Sham expressed support for the latter, but did not join in). Tawhid, though not properly Salafi, succumbed in Tripoli during the mid-1980s in part due to the failure of local "emirs" to consolidate their forces.

Even if Islamist groups in Tripoli were to unite under one banner, it's unlikely that they could build a substantial base of popular support in north Lebanon, let alone in Beirut and the south. "Few Sunnis of any other class or region would join their ranks or accept their leadership," notes scholar Yezid Sayigh.[52]

Islamism and the State

Although nearly all Islamist movements in Lebanon advocate the abolition of the state's confessional system in principle, in practice they have all accommodated it in one way or another. However, Shia and Sunni Islamist movements have had very different experiences interacting with the Lebanese state.

Hezbollah's fortuitous choice of patrons during the 1975-1990 Civil War translated into effective immunity from government interference for the next fifteen years. Year after year of continuous hostilities against Israeli forces in south Lebanon transformed its wartime militia units into an elite fighting force stronger in nearly every respect than the national army. Syrian vetting of appointments to the military-security apparatus ensured that it enjoyed cooperative relations with Hezbollah.

Hezbollah was obliged by the Syrians to maintain rough parity with *Amal* in parliamentary representation, civil service appointments, and other political spoils and pointedly did not join any of the coalition governments that ruled from 1990 to 2005. However, this bolstered Hezbollah's image as rising above partisanship for the good of the nation.

Hezbollah has not found it difficult to preserve these prerogatives since the withdrawal of Syrian forces in 2005. Its electoral clout alone was sufficient to fend off most challenges to its sprawling paramilitary apparatus. Recognizing that Shia votes would likely decide the outcome of the 2005 legislative elections in several important mixed districts, both the Aounists and Saad Hariri's Future Movement gave Nasrallah assurances that they would not seek Hezbollah's disarmament.

Under the Lebanese constitution, a "one-third-plus-one" or "blocking" minority of seats in the cabinet and parliament is sufficient to veto decisions by the majority (either by not showing up to vote or resigning, preventing the necessary two-thirds quorum). Hezbollah's effective monopolization of Shia representation in parliament (since the Syrian withdrawal, *Amal* deputies are squarely subordinate to Nasrallah) and its durable alliance with the FPM and assorted pro-Syrian groups is more than sufficient to veto the formation of any government. This leverage which enables it to demand a blocking cabinet minority up front.

Moreover, the parliamentary and cabinet representation of Hezbollah and its allies enabled them to prevent the Siniora administration from reforming the security apparatus; the Army and military intelligence are still dominated by personnel who rose through their ranks during the Syrian occupation. Hariri and his allies took over (and still hold) key posts in the Internal Security Force (ISF), especially its intelligence branch.[53] Reclaiming these assets is a high priority for Hezbollah leaders.

Hezbollah's May 2008 seizure of West Beirut was necessary only because shifting alliances had left it without a blocking minority in the cabinet—an unusual circumstance that is unlikely to repeat itself now that post-occupation alignments have solidified. Druze leader Walid Jumblatt and his parliamentary bloc gravitated away from March 14 after this, leaving neither Hezbollah nor Nasrallah with reliable majority support in parliament.

In sharp contrast to Hezbollah, Sunni Islamist groups have not come anywhere near exerting decisive influence over the state. Distrusted by both the Syrians and Sunni political elites, and lacking a state sponsor committed to their empowerment, they had little opportunity during the Syrian occupation to gain representation in government or substantially influence its policies.

Since the outbreak of the Syrian civil war, Lebanon's chronic political deadlock has gotten steadily worse. In January 2011, the Hezbollah-led March 8 coalition pulled its ministers out of government when Prime Minister Hariri refused to disavow the "special tribunal" ahead of its expected indictment of Hezbollah operatives. Hariri was replaced by Najib Miqati, a wealthy Sunni businessman friendly to Hezbollah. In March 2013, Hezbollah forced Miqati's resignation to prevent the extension of the term of Major General Ashra Rifi, a close Hariri ally, as head of the ISF.[54]

Lebanon was without a functioning government from March 2013 to February 2014 because the opposing sides could not agree on the composition of Prime Minister-designate Tammam Salam's cabinet. Unable to agree on an electoral law, lawmakers postponed the 2013 legislative elections until 2014 and then postponed them again, until they finally took place in May 2018. Although President Michel Suleiman's term in office came to an end in May 2014, because the Lebanese factions could not agree on his successor, Michel Aoun was only chosen as president in late 2016.[55]

The shocking regional advances of ISIS in 2013 and 2014 led to a strong regional and international consensus in favor of bolstering the Lebanese security forces. American and European states have increased aid and provided unprecedented intelligence cooperation with Lebanese security agencies.[56] In December 2013, Saudi Arabia pledged to give the Lebanese Army $3 billion over five years.[57] But Saudi Arabia has become concerned about increasingly close relations between the Lebanese government and Hezbollah (and its Iranian masters). When Lebanon did not condemn an Iranian mob sacking the Saudi Embassy in Tehran in January 2016, the Saudis froze payments. [58]

In May 2018, Hezbollah and its allies secured a majority of 70 seats out of 128.[59] The group has also managed to entice a significant number of Sunnis to its parliamentarian blocs. Hariri, the current Prime Minister, lost a third of his bloc. Though he retained his position as Prime Minister, he will be more inclined to compromise with Hezbollah, given his smaller bloc and the loss of the March 14 alliance.[60]

In July 2017, Hezbollah launched an offensive along the Lebanese-Syrian border against militants in the Arsal and Qalamoun mountains. The group coordinated its attack with the Lebanese Armed Forces (LAF), which used artillery to target militants during the assault. The coordination between the LAF and Hezbollah caused significant concerns in Washington, especially given that U.S. assistance to the LAF in 2016 topped $150 million.[61]

In April 2018, Lebanon received aid pledges of over $11 billion at a Paris conference. The pledges included $10.2 billion in loans and $860 million in grants, plus $4 billion in loans from the World Bank, and a $1 billion line of credit from Saudi Arabia.[62] Donors indicated that they wished for Lebanon to recommit to its long-postponed reform efforts, and Hariri promised to reduce the budget deficit as a percentage of GDP by 5 percent in the next 5 years. However, given the significant political deadlock and persistent corruption Lebanon faces, such reforms may be difficult to implement.

Endnotes

1 See the text of the open letter by Hezbollah to the oppressed in Lebanon and the world of February 16, 1985,

as reprinted in Joseph Alagha, *The Shifts in Hizbullah's Ideology: Religious Ideology, Political Ideology, and Political Program* (Amsterdam: Amsterdam University Press, 2006), 223-238.

2 For more on this episode, see Augustus Richard Norton, "Walking between Raindrops: Hizballah in Lebanon," *Mediterranean Politics* 3, no. 1 (Summer 1998), and Magnus Ranstorp, *Hizb'allah in Lebanon: The Politics of the Western Hostage Crisis* (New York: St. Martin's Press, 1997).

3 Gary C. Gambill, "Islamist Groups in Lebanon," *Middle East Review of International Affairs* 11, no. 4, December 2007.

4 "We believe the requirement for an Islamic state is to have an overwhelming popular desire, and we're not talking about fifty percent plus one, but a large majority. And this is not available in Lebanon and probably never will be," said Nasrallah in 2004. As cited in Adam Shatz, "In Search of Hezbollah," *New York Review of Books*, April 29, 2004.

5 See Ian Black, "Fear of a Shia full moon," *Guardian* (London), January 26, 2007.

6 "U.N. court indicts Hezbollah members in 2005 assassination in Lebanon," *Washington Post*, August 17, 2011.

7 University of Maryland, "2008 Annual Arab Public Opinion Poll," April 2008, https://www.brookings.edu/wp-content/uploads/2012/04/0414_middle_east_telhami.pdf

8 Nadav Pollack, "The Transformation of Hezbollah by Its Involvement in Syria," Washington Institute for Near East Policy *Research Notes* no. 35, August 2016, http://www.washingtoninstitute.org/uploads/Documents/pubs/ResearchNote35-Pollak-2.pdf

9 Ibid.

10 Fathi Yakan, *al-Masa'la al-Lubnaniyah min Manthur Islami* [The Lebanese Question from an Islamic Perspective] (Beirut: Mu'assassat al-Risalah, 1979), 126-128.

11 For ideological and political details on Fathi Yakan, see Robert G. Rabil, *Religion, National Identity, and Confessional Politics in Lebanon: The Challenge of Islamism* (New York: Palgrave Macmillan, 2011).

12 For details on the founding of the Islamic Action Front, including a list of its members, see "Tashkil Jabhat al-Amal al-Islami" (Forming of the Islamic Action Front), *al-Mustaqbal* (Beirut), August 3, 2006.

13 "The curious case of the Mouri family," Nowlebanon (Beirut), March 8, 2012. https://now.mmedia.me/lb/en/reportsfeatures/the_curious_case_of_the_mouri_family

14 Raphaël Lefèvre, "Tripoli's Fragmented Sunni Islamists," Carnegie Endowment for International Peace, March 13, 2014, http://carnegieendowment.org/syriaincrisis/?fa=54920.

15 "Behind the scenes in Tripoli," Nowlebanon, September 10, 2008, https://now.mmedia.me/lb/en/commentary-analysis/behind_the_scenes_in_tripoli

16 "Pro-Assad sheikh detained over Tripoli blasts," *Daily Star* (Beirut), August 30, 2013.

17 "Tripoli Sheikh Shot Down Inciting Peace," *Al-Akhbar*, October 23, 2012. http://english.al-akhbar.com/node/13080; "Lebanon: Assassination of pro-Hezbollah sheikh pushes Tripoli to the brink," *Asharq al-Awsat* (London), November 13, 2013, http://www.aawsat.net/2013/11/article55322284.

18 Habashi literally means "the Abyssinian." Harari migrated to Beirut from Ethiopia in the 1950s and became a lecturer at al-Azhar University's Lebanese campus.

19 A. Nizar Hamzeh and R. Hrair Dekmejian, "A Sufi Response to Political Islamism," *International Journal of Middle East Studies* 28 (1996), 217-229.

20 See Daniel Nassif, "Al-Ahbash," *Middle East Intelligence Bulletin* 3, no. 4, April 2001, http://www.meforum.org/meib/articles/0104_ld1.htm.

21 At the party's annual conference in 2009, its leader, Sheikh Adnan Mizyan, proclaimed that, "In light of the fact that many countries of Muslims are today under occupation, including Palestine, Iraq, Cyprus, the Balkans, the Caucasus, Afghanistan, and Kashmir, the Islamic Ummah must take Jihad measures in order to free them." As quoted in "Speaker at Hizb al-Tahrir Conference in Lebanon Calls for Jihad in Cyprus, Balkans, Caucasus," *as-Safir* (Beirut), July 20, 2009, http://

www.thememriblog.org/blog_personal/en/18360.htm.

22 In 2005, Lebanese authorities indicted members of the group *in absentia* for their role in planning terror attacks in Iraq. See "Khamsat Kawader fi Hizb al-Tahrir al-Islami Yuhadirun li-Hajamat fi al-Iraq bil-Tansiq Ma'a Isbat al-Ansar" [Five Cadres from Hizb al-Tahrir Plan in Coordination with Isbat al-Ansar Attacks in Iraq], *al-Mustaqbal* (Beirut), August 27, 2005.

23 Zoltan Pall, *Salafism in Lebanon: Local and Transnational Resources*, Ph.D dissertation, Utrecht University, January 14, 2014, 117, http://dspace.library.uu.nl/handle/1874/289260.

24 U.S. Department of the Treasury, "U.S.-Based Branch of Al Haramain Foundation Linked to Terror: Treasury Designates U.S. Branch, Director," September 9, 2004, http://www.treasury.gov/press-center/press-releases/Pages/js1895.aspx.

25 "We have been insulted by what Hizbullah did in Beirut, but much more by what Al-Hariri did not do," said Hassan al-Shahal. "He has done nothing to defend ahl al-Sunna [the Sunnis]." As cited in Omayma Abdel-Latif, "Alliance in question," *Al-Ahram Weekly* (Cairo), June 12-18, 2008, http://weekly.ahram.org.eg/2008/901/re1.htm.

26 Mona Alami, "Radical Islam Comes to Town" Inter Press Service, July 14, 2008, http://www.ipsnews.net/2008/07/lebanon-radical-islam-comes-to-town/

27 "Lebanese families drawn into Syrian conflict," BBC, June 18, 2013, http://www.bbc.com/news/world-middle-east-22938132.

28 Nada, "Lebanon's Sheikhs Take on Assad and Hezbollah."

29 "Lebanese families," *BBC*.

30 Fida' 'Itani, *Al-Jihadiyun fi Lubnan: Min Quwat Fajr ila Fath al-Islam* [The Jihadists in Lebanon: From Fajr Brigades to Fath al-Islam] (Beirut: Dar al-Saqi, 2008); See also Bilal Y. Saab and Magnus Ranstorp, "Securing Lebanon from the Threat of Salafist Jihadism," *Studies in Conflict and Terrorism* 30 (2007).

31 See Thair Abbas, "Al-Qaeda in Lebanon," *Asharq al-Awsat* (London), March 19, 2006.

32 U.S. Department of State, Office of the Coordinator for Counterterrorism, *Country Reports on Terrorism 2009* (Washington, DC: U.S. Department of State, August 2010), 244.

33 Adnan Abu Amer, "Hamas working to lower tensions in Lebanese camps," *Al-Monitor*, June 15, 2015, http://www.al-monitor.com/pulse/originals/2015/06/palestinian-refugee-camps-lebanon-hamas-tension.html

34 Mohammad Zaatar, "Palestinian factions announce cease-fire in south Lebanon camp," *The Daily Star*, December 22, 2016, http://www.dailystar.com.lb/News/Lebanon-News/2016/Dec-22/386357-tensions-mar-south-lebanon-camp.ashx

35 Ali Hashem, "Al Qaeda-affiliated emir arrested in Lebanon," *Al-Monitor*, January 1, 2014, http://www.al-monitor.com/pulse/originals/2013/12/abdullah-azzam-emir-custody-hashem.html

36 "Abdullah Azzam Brigades urges attacks against Hezbollah, not the Army," *Daily Star* (Beirut), October 13, 2014. https://www.dailystar.com.lb/News/Lebanon-News/2014/Oct-13/273917-abdullah-azzam-brigades-urges-attacks-against-hezbollah-not-the-army.ashx

37 "Tripoli's terror duo: Mawlawi and Mansour," *Daily Star* (Beirut), October 3, 2014, http://www.dailystar.com.lb/News/Lebanon-News/2014/Oct-03/272834-tripolis-terror-duo-mawlawi-and-mansour.ashx

38 "The Syria effect: Lebanese Sunnis begin to strap on bombs," *Christian Science Monitor*, January 7, 2014.

39 Bill Roggio, "Al Nusrah Front launches another suicide attack in Lebanon," *Long War Journal*, February 2, 2014, http://www.longwarjournal.org/archives/2014/02/al_nusrah_front_laun_2.php

40 Mark Townsend, "Isis paying smugglers' fees in recruitment drive among child refugees," *The Guardian*, February 4, 2017, https://www.theguardian.com/world/2017/feb/05/isis-recruitment-drive-child-refugees

41 National Consortium for the Study of Terrorism and Responses to Terrorism (START). (2016). Global Terrorism Database [Data file]. Retrieved from https://www.

start.umd.edu/gtd.

42 Gary C. Gambill, "Lebanese Farmers and the Syrian Occupation," *Middle East Intelligence Bulletin*, October 2003, http://www.meforum.org/meib/articles/0310_11.htm.

43 See Matthew Levitt, *Hezbollah: The Global Footprint of Lebanon's Party of God* (Washington, DC: Georgetown University Press, 2013).

44 Hanin Ghaddar, "Shia Unrest in Hezbollah's Beirut Stronghold," *PolicyWatch 2880,* October 30, 2017, http://www.washingtoninstitute.org/policy-analysis/view/shia-unrest-in-hezbollahs-beirut-stronghold.

45 Hanin Ghaddar, "What Does Hezbollah's Election Victory Mean for Lebanon?" *Policywatch 2966,* May 8, 2018, http://www.washingtoninstitute.org/policy-analysis/view/what-does-hezbollahs-election-victory-mean-for-lebanon.

46 Four prominent Sunni families (Solh, Karameh, Yafi, and Salam) held the post of prime minister in forty of the fifty-three cabinets that served from 1943 to 1982. Samir Khalaf, *Lebanon's Predicament* (New York: Columbia University Press, 1987), 106.

47 *The World Factbook* 2013-14. (Washington, DC: Central Intelligence Agency, 2013), https://www.cia.gov/library/publications/the-world-factbook/index.html

48 Yezid Sayigh, "Shadow War, Not Civil War, in Lebanon," *Al-Hayat*, December 12, 2013, http://carnegie-mec.org/2013/12/12/shadow-war-not-civil-war-in-lebanon/gw09.

49 See Are Knudsen, "The Law, the Loss and the Lives of Palestinian Refugees in Lebanon," Chr. Michelson Institute, Bergen, Norway (2007), https://www.cmi.no/publications/2607-the-law-the-loss-and-the-lives-of-palestinian

50 "Snapshot of Poverty and Labor Market Outcomes in Lebanon based on Household Budget Survey 2011/2012," *Central Administration for Statistics and World Bank*, May 25, 2016, http://documents.worldbank.org/curated/en/279901468191356701/pdf/102819-REVISED-PUBLIC-Snapshot-of-Poverty-and-Labor-Market-in-

Lebanon-10.pdf.

51 Pall, *Salafism in Lebanon: Local and Transnational Resources*, 39.

52 Sayigh, "Shadow War, Not Civil War, in Lebanon."

53 Bilal Y. Saab, "Why Lebanon's Najib Mikati Resigned," *Foreign Affairs*, March 25, 2013, https://www.foreignaffairs.com/articles/lebanon/2013-03-25/why-lebanons-najib-mikati-resigned

54 Ahmad K. Majidyar, "Is Deepening Shi'ite-Sunni Tension Plunging Lebanon into a New Civil War?" American Enterprise Institute, March 6, 2014, https://www.aei.org/publication/is-deepening-shiite-sunni-tension-plunging-lebanon-into-a-new-civil-war/

55 Thanassis Cambanis, "Michel Aoun Rises to Lebanese Presidency, Ending Power Vacuum," *The New York Times*, October 31, 2016, https://www.nytimes.com/2016/11/01/world/middleeast/michel-aoun-lebanon-president.html?rref=collection%2Ftimestopic%2FLebanon&action=click&contentCollection=world®ion=stream&module=stream_unit&version=latest&contentPlacement=8&pgtype=collection

56 Nicholas Noe, "The Islamic State effect: Lebanon's new security symbiosis," European Council on Foreign Relations (ECFR), August 28, 2014, http://www.ecfr.eu/article/commentary_the_islamic_state_effect_lebanons_new_security_symbiosis302

57 "Saudis Pledge $3 Billion to Support Lebanon's Army," *Wall Street Journal*, December 28, 2013.

58 Ben Hubbard, "Saudis Cut Off Funding for Military Aid to Lebanon," *The New York Times*, February 19, 2016, https://www.nytimes.com/2016/02/20/world/middleeast/saudis-cut-off-funding-for-military-aid-to-lebanon.html?_r=1

59 "Lebanese parliament re-elects Shi'ite Berri as speaker," Reuters, May 23, 2018, https://af.reuters.com/article/worldNews/
idAFKCN1IO1CK?feedType=RSS&feedName=worldNews.

60 Hanin Ghaddar, "What Does Hezbollah's Election Victory Mean for Lebanon?" The Washington Institute for Near East Policy, *Policywatch 2966,* May 8, 2018, http://www.washingtoninstitute.org/policy-analysis/view/

what-does-hezbollahs-election-victory-mean-for-lebanon.

61 David Schenker, "U.S. Security Assistance to Lebanon at Risk," The Washington Institute for Near East Policy, *PolicyWatch 2840,* http://www.washingtoninstitute.org/policy-analysis/view/u.s.-security-assistance-to-lebanon-at-risk.

62 John Irish and Marine Pennetier, "Lebanon wins pledges exceeding $11 billion in Paris," Reuters, April 6, 2018, https://www.reuters.com/article/us-lebanon-economy-france/lebanon-wins-pledges-exceeding-11-billion-in-paris-idUSKCN1HD0UU.

23 Libya

Quick Facts

Population: 6,653,210 (July 2017 est.)
Area: 1,759,540 sq km
Ethnic Groups: Berber and Arab 97%, other 3% (includes Greeks, Maltese, Italians, Egyptians, Pakistanis, Turks, Indians, and Tunisians)
GDP (official exchange rate): $33.31 billion (2017 est.)

Source: CIA World FactBook (Last Updated May 2018)

Introduction

Libya is a failed North African state home to a wide array of Islamist and Salafi-jihadi groups. Longtime dictator Muammar Qaddafi ruled the oil-rich country for four decades, gaining international notoriety as an eccentric and brutal authoritarian responsible for a number of high-profile international terror attacks. The Arab Spring revolution that toppled Qaddafi in 2011 turned the country into a battleground for small contingents of ideologically diverse militias, military units, tribal forces, and jihadists. The fall of the Qaddafi regime also created the opportunity for Libya's long-suppressed Islamists to wield political power. Libyan Islamists failed to achieve even the temporary political gains of their counterparts in Egypt and Tunisia, however. Successive transitional governments failed, sending the country spiraling into a complex civil war shaped by local grievances, regional power struggles, and ideological divides.

Several Salafi-jihadi groups have taken advantage of the revolution and subsequent civil war to establish and expand safe havens in Libya. These groups include the al-Qaeda-linked Ansar al-Sharia Libya and the Islamic State of Iraq and al-Sham (ISIS). Salafi-jihadi groups in Libya recruit and train militants, govern populations, and prepare attacks on other Maghreb states and Europe. Islamist militants in Libya, including jihadists, suffered major military losses in recent years but remain a formidable destabilizing force in the country. Regional states pursuing their own visions for the future of Islamism through Libyan proxies are also worsening the conflict. The ongoing crisis has destabilized Libya's neighbors, strengthened transnational smuggling networks, and exacerbated massive migrant flows to Europe.

Islamist Activity

Political Islam entered Libya in the mid-20th century, when King Idris I welcomed asylum-seekers from the Egyptian Muslim Brotherhood. This sanctuary period ended in 1969, when Colonel Muammar Qaddafi overthrew the monarchy. Qaddafi violently suppressed all political opposition during his forty-year rule, including Islamist forces. Islamist organizations, nevertheless, challenged the regime through both peaceful and violent means from the 1970s to the 1990s. State oppression fostered the development of Libyan Islamist networks in the country's prisons and beyond its borders—in Afghanistan and London. Qaddafi later sought to co-opt Islamist organizations through a policy of negotiation and de-radicalization spearheaded by his son, Sayf al-Islam, in the early 2000s.

The 2011 Arab Spring protests rallied Islamists and secularists alike against the regime. Qaddafi responded to unrest with a brutal crackdown leading to a civil war and a subsequent NATO intervention that tore apart the state and led to the dictator's death. The resulting power vacuum yielded chronic instability as various groups vied for influence and failed to exert full control. Libya's transitional government struggled to establish order and rebuild state institutions. Militias and other non-state actors proliferated and strengthened during this period.

Rivalries developed into a full-scale civil war by 2014 when Commander Khalifa Haftar, a former regime officer, launched Operation Dignity with the goal of defeating Islamist groups in Libya.[1] An alliance of mainly Islamist militias launched Operation Dawn to counter Haftar's offensive in August 2014, seizing Tripoli's airport and other parts of the capital.[2] Outside actors, such as the United Arab Emirates (UAE), Egypt, Qatar, and Turkey, have since backed various proxies. Ongoing factional conflict has even mobilized formerly nonviolent quietist Islamists to join the fray in defense of their interests.[3]

Post-revolution Libya gained international notoriety as a hotbed for transnational Salafi jihadi organizations like ISIS and al-Qaeda. Ansar al-Sharia, a Salafi-jihadi group formed by members of al-Qaeda and the Libyan Islamic Fighting Group, is likely responsible for the September 2012 attack on U.S. government facilities in Benghazi that killed four Americans, including Ambassador to Libya J. Christopher Stevens.[4] ISIS took root and grew rapidly in Libya in 2014, establishing the first branch of its caliphate outside of Iraq and Syria. ISIS's Libyan branch has also supported terrorist attacks in Europe, especially the May 2017 Manchester bombing.[5]

Islamist militants are currently losing ground in Libya, but remain a threat to the country's stability. The establishment of the UN-backed Government of National Accord in late 2015 widened a split between hardline and moderate Islamists in the Operation Dawn coalition, and ultimately marginalizing hardline forces aligned with a now-defunct pro-Islamist parliament. In December 2016, GNA-allied forces, with U.S. support, ousted ISIS from its stronghold in Sirte.[6] Subsequent U.S. airstrikes hindered ISIS's efforts to reconstitute. Haftar's forces made significant gains against Islamists and jihadists in eastern and central Libya from 2016 to 2017, including retaking Benghazi. Egyptian and Emirati support for Haftar, paired with a downturn in Qatar's regional influence, has further weakened Libya's Islamists. Libya's diverse array of Islamist and jihadist actors continue to be key players in the conflict, however. They will regain and likely retain power as long as Libya lacks effective governance and security structures.

The Muslim Brotherhood

The Muslim Brotherhood is a transnational organization that seeks to establish sharia as the base for the state and society through nonviolent means. The Brotherhood originated in Egypt in the 1920s. It came to Libya in 1949, when King Idris I allowed Egyptian Brotherhood members fleeing political persecution in their country to settle in Benghazi.[7] Several of these asylum-seekers, along with Egyptian cleric Ezadine Ibrahim Mustafa, founded the Libyan Muslim Brotherhood as a branch of the original Egyptian organization. King Idris I allowed the group relative freedom to spread its ideology, and it in turn began to attract local adherents.

Colonel Muammar Qaddafi overthrew the Libyan monarchy in 1969 and promptly cracked down on the Brotherhood as a potential source of opposition, arresting a number of members and returning others to Egypt.[8] The crackdown continued until 1973, when detained and tortured Brotherhood members agreed to dissolve the organization, effectively silencing themselves for the remainder of the 1970s.

The Brotherhood reorganized in the early 1980s and revived its aspirations to replace the Qaddafi regime with sharia law. It renamed itself the Libyan Islamic Group or al-Jama'a al-Islamiyya al-Libiyya. It began to acquire popular support among Libyan students who met exiled members in the U.S. and UK. These students spread the Brotherhood's ideology and joined its covert cells inside of Libya.[9]

The Brotherhood generated much of its popular appeal through charitable and welfare work, despite the state's repression. Its programs drew members of the Libyan middle class in particular. The Brotherhood was strongest in eastern Benghazi, where major tribes historically opposed Qaddafi's rule.[10] The regime either imprisoned or executed most Brotherhood members remaining in Libya by the mid-1980s.[11]

The Brotherhood began to regenerate in 1999 through dialogue with the Qaddafi regime. The talks gained momentum in 2005-2006, when Muammar Qaddafi's son, Sayf al-Islam, assumed an active role in the talks in an effort to co-opt and neutralize opposition groups, especially Islamists. The Brotherhood had roughly 1,000 members within Libya, and 200 more in exile, on the eve of the Libyan uprising in early 2011.[12]

The Libyan Muslim Brotherhood has lost popularity in recent years, however. This decline first manifested in a poor showing in the 2012 parliamentary elections that followed Qaddafi's ouster. This defeat is noteworthy when compared to the success of the Brotherhood's counterparts in Egypt and Tunisia during the same period.[13] The setbacks suffered by the Egyptian Muslim Brotherhood after its electoral victory, most notably the ouster of the Brotherhood-backed president Mohammed Morsi in 2013, emboldened anti-Brotherhood activists in Libya. Support for the Libyan Brotherhood remained limited in 2014, when affiliated candidates and parties secured only 25 of 200 available seats.[14] The public's rejection of the movement reflects the legacy of Qaddafi's demonization of the organization. Resentment toward the Brotherhood also stems from perceptions that it is anti-democratic as well as associations between the Brotherhood and more radical groups like al-Qaeda and Ansar al-Sharia.[15]

The Brotherhood remains a player on the Libyan political scene. It announced its support for the UN-backed Government of National Accord in March 2016.[16] However, the Brotherhood's influence is limited by the fragmentation of the Libyan Islamist movement and the rise of anti-Islamist militia Commander Khalifa Haftar.[17]

Tablighi Jama'at

Tablighi Jama'at (Islamic Transmission Group) is a revivalist and largely apolitical pan-Islamic organization founded in India in the late 19th century.[18] The number of Tablighi supporters in Libya today is relatively small, and there is only one known Tablighi center in the country.[19] The Qaddafi regime arrested and subsequently co-opted many Tablighi members in the 1980s, which led the group to distance itself from politics.[20] Tablighi Jama'at is pursuing active dawa (preaching) campaigns in Libya. Muhammed Jihani, a Libyan Tablighi cleric based in the UK, claimed to have received support from the Libyan minister of religion in June 2016.[21]

The Libyan Islamic Fighting Group (LIFG)

The origins of the Libyan Islamic Fighting Group (LIFG) or al-Jama'a al-Islamiyya al-Muqatila bil-Libiyya, are rooted in an underground jihadi movement formed in 1982 by Iwad al-Zawawi.[22] The LIFG sought to overthrow the Qaddafi regime militarily by plotting attacks against the dictator and other senior regime figures. Authorities captured many LIFG members, including al-Zawawi, after a series of failed attempts to overthrow the regime in 1986, 1987, and 1989.[23] Many escapees fled to Afghanistan and Pakistan.

The Afghan jihad against the Soviets in the 1980s allowed the LIFG to consolidate and train. LIFG members established their own military training camps in the Afghanistan and al-Qaeda provided military training to them.[24] Influential Salafi jihadi clerics, such as Abdullah Azzam, also indoctrinated Libyan recruits.[25]

The LIFG reinvigorated its efforts to overthrow the Qaddafi regime following the Afghan jihad. LIFG members established cells or traveled to London to obtain logistical and financial support. The LIFG also established a base of operations in Sudan in 1993.[26] The group then sent delegations from Sudan to Algeria to continue training. However, the LIFG's interlude in Sudan was independent of the plans of al-Qaeda and Osama bin Laden, who spent five years there in the 1990s.[27]

The LIFG worked to establish its structure and develop leadership capabilities in preparation for a campaign to overthrow the regime.[28] The group accelerated its plans in 1995 due to poor operational security. LIFG members extracted one of their comrades from a hospital in Benghazi, sparking a crackdown by security forces that compelled the group to officially announce itself in October 1995.[29] The Libyan regime pressured the Sudanese regime to eject the LIFG at this time. Many LIFG members returned to Libya, while others escaped to London. Exposure forced the LIFG to intensify its operations. It conducted a series of attacks on the Libyan regime throughout the 1990s, including several failed attempts to assassinate Qaddafi. The Libyan regime fought relentlessly against the LIFG into the late 1990s and killed several of its leaders including one of the group's founding fathers, Salah Fathi bin Sulayman (aka Abu 'Abd al-Rahman al-Khattab).[30]

The LIFG's insurgency and terrorist campaign inside Libya effectively ended by 1998, though the group did not declare an official ceasefire until 2000.[31] Many of the members who escaped death or imprisonment returned to Afghanistan. Those who fled included the LIFG's emir Abdelhakim Belhaj (aka Abu 'Abd Allah al-Sadiq), chief religious official Abu al-Mundhir al-Sa'idi, and Abu Anas al-Libi, an al-Qaeda operative involved in the 1998 bombing of two U.S. embassies in East Africa.[32]

The LIFG has a complex relationship with al-Qaeda and its ideology. The U.S. Treasury Department designated the LIFG as a foreign terrorist organization in 2001for its ties to al-Qaeda.[33] Senior al-Qaeda leaders Ayman al-Zawahiri and Abu Yahya al-Libi announced a merger between the LIFG and al-Qaeda in 2007, but some LIFG senior leaders refused to swear allegiance to al-Qaeda.[34]

The LIFG did not demonstrate significant support for al-Qaeda's attacks on the West.[35] Nonetheless, the group did not contain its activities to Libya. The U.S. State Department listed the LIFG as a foreign terrorist organization for its ties to the 2003 bombings in Casablanca, Morocco.[36] The State Department later delisted the LIFG in 2015.[37]

The Libyan regime began a reconciliation and de-radicalization process at the prompting of Qaddafi's son, Sayf al-Islam, in 2005.[38] This process led the LIFG to revise its definition of jihad to exclude violence against the state. LIFG leaders in Libya released a new code for jihad in the form of a 417-page religious document titled "Corrective Studies" in September 2009.[39] The new code permitted jihad only in the case of the invasion of Muslim lands citing Afghanistan, Iraq, and the Palestinian Territories, as examples.[40] The regime subsequently released many LIFG members in March 2010.[41] Others, such as former LIFG member turned parliamentarian Abd al-Wahab Qa'id, were not released until after the uprising against the Qaddafi regime began in March 2011.[42]

The LIFG network played a prominent role in the swell of Islamist activity that accompanied the Arab Spring and the overthrow of the Qaddafi regime. Elements of the LIFG human network established branches of the al-Qaeda associate Ansar al-Sharia.[43] Other former LIFG members formed political parties. Islamist militias led by former LIFG members also wield significant influence. The presence of the LIFG itself has decreased and the group has shifted its efforts toward providing social services and youth activities. It changed its name to the Libyan Islamic Movement for Change in an effort to further rehabilitate its image as a peaceful organization.

Ansar al-Sharia in Libya (ASL)

During the revolution, new Salafi-jihadi groups seized the opportunity to fill the vacuum created by the LIFG's renunciation of military operations. Al-Qaeda emir Ayman al-Zawahiri charged senior operatives, including Abu Anas al-Libi, with forming a Libyan affiliate in 2011.[44] Former LIFG operatives formed branches of Ansar al-Sharia in the eastern Libyan cities of Benghazi and Derna.[45] Muhammed al-Zahawi, a former LIFG member and prisoner of the regime, led Ansar al-Sharia Benghazi until his death in late 2014 or early 2015.[46] This group remains the primary suspect in the 2012 attack on the U.S. consulate in Benghazi.[47] Ansar al-Sharia Benghazi later changed its name to Ansar al-Sharia in Libya (ASL)—a move that signified its desire to be perceived as a national movement rather than a local rebel force.[48] Ansar al-Sharia developed affiliates and established training camps throughout Libya, Sirte, and Ajdabiya.

The Benghazi-based Ansar al-Sharia is a separate organization from Ansar al-Sharia Derna, despite some crossover in membership and political goals. Former Guantanamo Bay inmate Abu Sufyan bin Qumu led the group in Derna.[49] Bin Qumu's status is unknown following rumors that he defected to ISIS.[50] Both Ansar al-Sharia branches seek to establish sharia law in Libya.[51]

ASL seeks to build popular support through dawa and charity campaigns. The group's dawa campaign increased its size and popularity at home and abroad.[52] Its most effective method to advance its agenda has been the provision of social services.[53] These services include infrastructure repair and development projects, the provision of security, and general aid.[54] One of the group's most successful projects was its anti-drug campaign, orchestrated in cooperation with a local hospital, a soccer club, and telecom and technologies companies in Benghazi.[55]

The ASL branches use local support bases to advance a global violent jihad. They form an important cog in the facilitation and logistics network within the global Salafi jihadi movement and have trained militants to fight in Syria, Mali, and North Africa.[56] The UN listed both Ansar al-Sharia Benghazi and Ansar al-Sharia Derna as terror organizations associated with al-Qaeda in November 2014.[57]

ASL develops battlefield relationships with other Libyan fighting forces to enhance its legitimacy, spread its ideology, and mask its affiliation to al-Qaeda. ASL has known ties to several smaller Salafi jihadi katibas (battalions) in Libya, including Katibat Abu 'Ubaydah al-Jarah and Saraya Raf Allah al-Sahati.[58] These alliances are a force multiplier for ASL, which had a few hundred members in 2012.[59] ASL exploited the chaos and instability in Libya in order to strengthen its presence in Libyan communities and spread its ideology alongside social programs.[60]

In 2014, ASL transitioned to almost exclusively military

operations to defend its position in Benghazi. Also in 2014, former Libyan Army Commander Khalifa Haftar began his self-declared Operation Dignity campaign to defeat terrorists—defined as all Islamists—in eastern Libya, with ASL among his priority targets.[61] ASL launched a violent counteroffensive that caused high civilian and military casualties.[62] It joined with other Islamist militias fighting Haftar to form the Benghazi Revolutionaries Shura Council (BRSC) in June 2014.[63] Shortly thereafter, the new umbrella organization overran several bases in Benghazi, seized a large cache of weapons, and declared the city an Islamic emirate.[64]

General Haftar's foreign-backed campaign gradually wore down the BRSC, which has since lost most of its military strength. The BRSC cooperated with ISIS militants in a last-ditch effort to preserve its strongholds.[65] Ansar al-Sharia officially announced its dissolution in May 2017 citing heavy casualties and leadership attrition.[66] Haftar declared victory in Benghazi in July 2017.[67] ASL and other al-Qaeda-linked militants fled the city to safe havens elsewhere in Libya.[68] Intermittent militant activity continues in Benghazi as of August 2017.[69]

Ansar al-Sharia Derna controls Derna city as part of the Mujahideen Shura Council of Derna (MSCD), which formed in December 2014.[70] The MSCD drove ISIS fighters out of Derna in June 2015.[71] General Haftar's forces tightened a blockade on Derna following the culmination of major operations in Benghazi in July 2017.[72] The MSCD is fighting to hold the city as of August 2017.

Islamic State (ISIS/ISIL)

Persistent chaos in the wake of the 2011 revolution made Libya an ideal place for ISIS to establish its first wilayat (state) in North Africa. The group's aspirations for a Libyan franchise began in 2013, when ISIS leader Abu Bakr al-Baghdadi deployed an emissary to the eastern city of Derna to examine the possibility of expansion.[73] Derna has been hospitable to Islamist militants for several decades. ISIS leadership understood that establishing a presence in the city could provide a necessary fallback option if the group were to lose its base in the Levant.[74] Libyan militants and ideologues with ties to Iraq and Syria began pledging their allegiance to ISIS by late 2014, seeking legitimacy through the group's infamous brutality and claim to have re-established an Islamic caliphate.[75] The establishment of three ISIS wilayat in Libya provided the group with a largely uncontested space in which to gain strategic proximity to Europe and operate a recruitment and training hub for Africa.

ISIS first took root in Derna through an affiliate called the Shura Council of Islamic Youth, later known as ISIS Wilayat Barqah (Cyrenaica). ISIS simultaneously developed outposts elsewhere in Libya such as Sirte, Sabratha, and various Benghazi neighborhoods. ISIS would not succeed in maintaining its first stronghold, however. The Mujahideen Shura Council of Derna (MSCD), which includes Ansar al-Sharia and other LIFG-linked militias, fought back against ISIS in response to its extreme ideology, brutal methods, and the assassination of a MSCD leader.[76] The MSCD ousted ISIS from Derna in June 2015.[77]

ISIS tempered its loss in Derna with its takeover of Sirte on the central Libyan coast in spring 2015.[78] The group conducted a dawa and intimidation campaign in the city, where it also co-opted pre-existing Ansar al-Sharia networks.[79] It gained international notoriety in April 2015 for a video portraying the mass execution of Egyptian Coptic Christians and African migrants.[80] ISIS's propaganda soon featured the Libyan city alongside Raqqa, Syria, and Mosul, Iraq, as a demonstration of the expanding caliphate.[81] ISIS Wilayat Tarablus governed Sirte with the same harshness as its Levantine counterparts, enforcing corporal punishments and violently quashing dissent. ISIS gradually expanded to the east and west of Sirte, controlling a 150-mile stretch of coastline at its peak. It also conducted a campaign of attacks on oil infrastructure in eastern Libya in an effort to deprive the weak Libyan state of revenue.[82]

Experts estimate that ISIS had 3,000 fighters in Sirte, although other reports estimated as many as 6,000 drawn from Libya, the broader Maghreb, and sub-Saharan Africa.[83] ISIS did not gain significant support from Libyan communities, which view it as foreign. Claims of strong ties between pro-Qaddafi groups and ISIS in Libya, akin to those between former Baathists and ISIS in Iraq, are overstated.[84]

ISIS in Libya seeks to attack neighboring states and Europe. Katibat al-Battar, a seasoned ISIS unit compromised mainly of

Libyan and European fighters, deployed from Iraq and Syria to Libya to coordinate attacks on Europe and Tunisia.[85] Libya-based militants conducted the 2015 Bardo and Sousse attacks that devastated Tunisia's tourism economy. ISIS also attempted to use Libya as a launch pad for an ambitious attempt to expand the caliphate to the Tunisian city of Ben Guerdane in March 2016.[86] Members of Katibat al-Battar met in Tripoli with Salman al-Abedi, the British suicide bomber who killed 22 people at a concert in Manchester, England in May 2017.[87]

ISIS suffered a series of defeats that significantly reduced its strength in Libya from 2016 to 2017. Khalifa Haftar's Operation Dignity forces, at times assisted by French Special Operations Forces, drove ISIS from its posts in Benghazi. American airstrikes supported an offensive that ousted ISIS from its base in Sabratha, near the Tunisian border. Sirte and surrounding small towns remained the group's primary stronghold until mid-2016, when ISIS overreached into terrain controlled by forces from the western Libyan city-state of Misrata. Misratan militias, aligned with the UN-backed government and backed by American air power, launched a grueling campaign to recapture Sirte that culminated in December 2016. Many ISIS fighters left the city, but the group still suffered significant casualties.[88]

ISIS in Libya remains a potent threat despite its territorial losses. Former CIA Director John Brennan warned in June 2016 that the branch was ISIS's most developed and dangerous, citing its influence in Africa and ability to stage attacks in Europe.[89] ISIS is reconstituting in central and southwestern Libya, where it has access to lucrative smuggling routes.[90] Intermittent U.S. airstrikes have interrupted the group's resurgence, but it is not defeated.[91] Hundreds of ISIS militants—if not more—remain active as a network of cells and small units throughout the country.[92]

Islamism and Society

Libya has over six and a half million citizens, roughly ninety-seven percent of whom are Sunni Muslim. The dominant school of Sunni thought in Libya is the Maliki School, often considered the most moderate of the four traditional schools of Islamic jurisprudence.[93]

Non-Sunni Muslims in Libya are primarily Ibadi Muslims in the native Amazigh community or foreigners, including Christians, Buddhists, Hindus, and Jews.[94]

Islam permeates everyday life for most Libyans. Religious instruction in Islam is compulsory in all public schools. Sharia governs family matters such as inheritance, divorce, and the right to own property.[95] Libya's draft constitution designates Islam as the official state religion and sharia as the principal source of legislation.[96] The constitution also bars non-Muslims from Libya's parliament and presidency, per a July 2017 draft, though the country's interim laws protect the rights of non-Muslims to practice their beliefs.[97] A protracted and fierce debate over the legal status of sharia reveals persistent cleavages over the role of Islam in Libyan society.[98]

Islamism in Libya has surged since the 2011 revolution. The ideology has traditionally found few followers in the country and the Qaddafi regime staunchly opposed it. Libyans responded enthusiastically to Islamist political parties following Qaddafi's ouster because they promoted a sense of identity and pledged to maintain order.[99] Many Libyans remain skeptical of Islamism but years of failed political transition have emboldened various Islamist factions and militias.[100] Islamist organizations have filled the void left by the collapse of the Libyan state by providing valuable social and governmental services, including health care, youth activity planning, and religious organization. The ability to provide governance has allowed groups like Ansar al-Sharia and the LIFG to gradually move away from their image as global jihadi organizations and gain some domestic support.

Islamism and the State

Libya won its independence from Italy in the aftermath of World War II. It became a constitutional monarchy in 1951 under King Idris I, the head of eastern Libya's Sufi Senussi order. Colonel Muammar Qaddafi overthrew the monarchy in a military coup d'état in September 1969. He established a new political system—the Jamahiriyah or "state of the masses"—an Arab nationalist regime based on an ideology of Islamic socialism. Qaddafi outlawed all political parties and organized political dissent, including Islamist groups.[101]

The Muslim Brotherhood organized in the 1980s with the intent of peacefully replacing the existing regime, despite intense pressure from Qaddafi's security forces. The Brotherhood's failure to achieve peaceful change set conditions for the emergence of the Libyan Islamic Fighting Group (LIFG). The LIFG launched several failed efforts to topple the regime and assassinate Qaddafi in the 1980s and 1990s. The regime decimated the Islamist opposition by 1998. Only small pockets of jihadist resistance remained by the early 2000s.[102]

Qaddafi's son and advisor, Sayf al-Islam, began negotiations with Islamists in the mid-2000s. He brokered a deal to free imprisoned Islamists on the condition that they recognize the legitimacy of Qaddafi's government, renounce violence, and formally revise their doctrines. These negotiations led to the release of more than one hundred Brotherhood members in 2006 and hundreds of LIFG members by 2008.[103] The LIFG also renounced violence against the state. The regime brought quietest Salafi clerics from Saudi Arabia to Libya during this period in order to foster religious discourse that condemned rebellion against the state.[104]

The Arab Spring protests upended Libya in February 2011. The regime cracked down violently on protesters, plunging the country into civil war. The conflict provided an opportunity for Islamist networks to reconstitute in the country bolstered by additional prisoner releases. Qaddafi's fall sent Libya into a turbulent democratic transition and set the stage for a plethora of groups, both Islamist and secular, to vie for power in the resulting vacuum.

Political Islamists participated in parliamentary elections in 2012. The Muslim Brotherhood-affiliated Justice and Construction Party (JCP) faced off against the liberal National Forces Alliance (NFA).[105] The JCP, led by former political prisoner Mohammed Sawan, won 17 of 80 available seats to the NFA's 39.[106] The JCP failed to achieve post-Arab Spring electoral success like that of its model and inspiration, Egypt's Brotherhood-backed Freedom and Justice Party.

Two political factions of the LIFG—the Hizb al-Watan (HW) and Hizb al-Umma al-Wasat (HUW)—also participated in the 2012 legislative elections. Former LIFG emir and Tripoli militia leader Abdelhakim Belhaj led the HW, which ran as a broad-based moderate party. Former LIFG religious official Sami al-Sa'adi led the HUW, which included most former LIFG figures and ran as a more conservative Islamic party.[107] The HW failed to win any seats in the election, while the HUW won a single seat, allocated to Abdul Wahhab al-Qa'id, brother of the late senior al-Qaeda official Abu Yahya al-Libi. Other small Islamist parties also failed to garner significant support. These parties include the Salafi party al-Asala, which won no seats, and the Hizb al-Islah wa-l-Tanmiyya, led by former member of the Muslim Brotherhood Khaled al-Werchefani.

Popular support for Islamist parties increased during June 2014 legislative elections, when Islamist groups or candidates won 30 of the 80 available seats. Low voter turnout and political violence between secular and Islamist forces marred the elections, however, setting the stage for Libya's shaky democratic transition to devolve into open war.[108] Former Libyan Army General Khalifa Haftar began Operation Dignity, a campaign to drive Islamist militias out of Benghazi and eastern Libya in May 2014.[109] The controversial operation preceded a political crisis between two transitional parliaments: the General National Congress (GNC, elected 2012) and the House of Representatives (HoR, elected 2014). Islamist militias affiliated with the GNC ousted the HoR from Tripoli further hardening the divisions between Islamists and their opponents.

Libya has three primary political blocs as of August 2017: two in the west and one in the east. The United Nations-backed Government of National Accord (GNA), established in December 2015, controls Tripoli through a loose coalition of allied militias.[110] The GNA was meant to bring together the warring GNC and HoR into a unity government. In practice, it divided and weakened the GNC's support base, though GNC leadership and armed allies remain spoilers in the peace process. The GNA and HoR have become the two main poles of the Libyan conflict. The HoR, whose leadership is aligned with Haftar, has refused to endorse the GNA.[111] Efforts by GNA Prime Minister-designate Fayez al-Serraj to strike a ceasefire deal with the increasingly powerful Haftar in mid-2017 have legitimized Haftar internationally and furthered his ascendance as a prospective strongman.[112]

Haftar's rise sets the stage for continued Islamist resistance in Libya. Haftar and his external backers, especially Egypt and the UAE, seek to eradicate political Islam and crush Islamist armed groups in Libya. He has simultaneously courted religious conservatives by empowering followers of Madkhalism, a form of quietist Islamism that enshrines loyalty to a political leader.[113] Haftar's campaign mirrors that of Egyptian President Abdel Fatah el-Sisi. Sisi's crackdown on political Islam benefited Salafi jihadi groups that argue for violence as the only meaningful force for change.[114] For the foreseeable future, Islamism will remain a powerful current in Libya, which has become a key front in a broader regional struggle to determine the future of political Islam in the Muslim world.[115]

As of April 2018, Islamists remain key political and security actors in Libya. Tripoli's High Council of State elected a member of the Muslim Brotherhood-affiliated Justice and Construction Party as its head in April 2018, signaling a potential opening for détente between Islamist and anti-Islamist political factions.[116] The reported illness and subsequent return of LNA commander Khalifa Haftar in April 2018 introduces new instability into Libya's political dynamics. The future role of Islamist parties in Libya remains uncertain as the country prepares for elections in 2018 or 2019.[117] At the local level, Salafi militias are taking on increasingly important security and governance roles in Libyan cities. The Salafi Rada Special Deterrence Force in Tripoli, for example, controls the city's one functioning airport and provides security in the name of the UN-backed GNA.[118] Salafi militias in Benghazi are also a powerful bloc within the LNA coalition.[119] Salafi violence targeting Libyan Sufi communities and their heritage is rising.[120]

Libya remains a haven for Salafi-jihadi groups due to ongoing instability in the country. ISIS militants based in central Libya are conducting a campaign of intermittent attacks intended to undermine security and potentially disrupt oil production.[121] A series of bombings and assassination attempts in January 2018 in Benghazi may signal the return of an Islamist insurgency to the city, though they may also reflect broader political unrest.[122] Salafi-jihadi militants continue to operate in Libya's interior, where the U.S. conducted an airstrike targeting al-Qaeda leaders in March 2018.[123]

Endnotes

1. Camille Tawil, "Operation Dignity: General Haftar's Latest Battle May Decide Libya's Future," Terrorism Monitor 12 iss. 11, May 30, 2014, https://jamestown.org/program/operation-dignity-general-haftars-latest-battle-may-decide-libyas-future/.
2. Chris Stephen and Anne Penketh, "Libyan capital under Islamist control after Tripoli airport seized," The Guardian, August 24, 2014, https://www.theguardian.com/world/2014/aug/24/libya-capital-under-islamist-control-tripoli-airport-seized-operation-dawn.
3. Frederic Wehrey, "Quiet No More?" Diwan, Carnegie Middle East Center, October 13, 2016, http://carnegie-mec.org/diwan/64846.
4. Estelle and Zimmerman, "Backgrounder: Fighting Forces in Libya," AEI's Critical Threats Project, March 3, 2016, https://www.criticalthreats.org/analysis/backgrounder-fighting-forces-in-libya.
5. Rukmini Callimachi and Eric Schmitt, "Manchester Bomber Met With ISIS Unit in Libya, Officials Say," New York Times, June 3, 2017, https://www.nytimes.com/2017/06/03/world/middleeast/manchester-bombing-salman-abedi-islamic-state-libya.html.
6. Hani Amara, "Libyan forces clear last Islamic State holdout in Sirte," Reuters, December 6, 2016, http://www.reuters.com/article/us-libya-security-sirte/libyan-forces-clear-last-islamic-state-holdout-in-sirte-idUSKBN13V15R.
7. Omar Ashour, "Libyan Islamists Unpacked: Rise, Transformation, and Future," Brookings Institution Policy Briefing, May 2012, http://www.brookings.edu/~/media/research/files/papers/2012/5/02%20libya%20ashour/omar%20ashour%20policy%20briefing%20english.pdf.
8. Allison Pargeter, "Political Islam in Libya," Jamestown Foundation Terrorism Monitor 3, iss. 6, May 5, 2005, http://www.jamestown.org/single/?no_cache=1&tx_ttnews[tt_news]=306.
9. Pargeter, "Political Islam in Libya."
10. Pargeter, "Political Islam in Libya."
11. Omar Ashour, "Libya's Muslim Brotherhood faces the

future," Foreign Policy, March 9, 2012, http://mideast.foreignpolicy.com/posts/2012/03/09/libya_s_muslim_brotherhood_faces_the_future.

12. Ashour, "Libya's Muslim Brotherhood faces the future."
13. Aaron Y. Zelin, "Jihadism's Foothold in Libya," Washington Institute for Near East Policy PolicyWatch no. 1980, September 12, 2012, http://www.washingtoninstitute.org/policy-analysis/view/jihadisms-foothold-in-libya.
14. Cameron Glenn, "Libya's Islamists: Who They Are - And What They Want," Wilson Center, August 27, 2015, https://www.wilsoncenter.org/libyas-islamists-who-they-are-and-what-they-want.
15. Mary Fitzgerald, "Libya's Muslim Brotherhood Struggles to Grow," Foreign Policy, May 1, 2014, http://www.foreignpolicy.com/articles/2014/05/01/the_rise_of_libyas_muslim_brotherhood_justice_and_construction_party.
16. "Libya's Justice and Construction Party Announces Support for National Unity Government," Ikhwan Web, March 30, 2016, http://www.ikhwanweb.com/article.php?id=32490.
17. Emily Estelle, "The General's Trap in Libya," AEI's Critical Threats Project, August 1, 2017, https://www.criticalthreats.org/analysis/the-generals-trap-in-libya.
18. "Tablighi Jama'at," World Almanac of Islamism, March 22, 2017, http://almanac.afpc.org/tablighi-jamaat.
19. The facility is part of a comprehensive list of Tablighi facilities worldwide that is available at http://adressmarkazjemaahtabligh.blogspot.com.
20. Pargeter, "Political Islam in Libya."
21. Sheikh Jihani, "Dawah—The Life Blood," The Hanafi Fiqh Channel, September 16, 2016, http://www.tablighijamaat.org/dawah-the-life-blood-sheikh-jihani-libya/.
22. Camille Tawil, Brothers in Arms: The Story of al-Qa'ida and the Arab Jihadists (London: Saqi Books, 2010), 33.
23. Tawil, Brothers in Arms, 93-94.

24. Evan F. Kohlmann, "Dossier: Libyan Islamic Fighting Group," NEFA Foundation, October 2007, 3, http://www.nefafoundation.org/miscellaneous/nefalifg1007.pdf.
25. Kohlmann, "Dossier: Libyan Islamic Fighting Group," 4.
26. Tawil, Brothers in Arms, 93-94.
27. James Astill, "Osama: The Sudan Years," The Guardian, October 16, 2001, https://www.theguardian.com/world/2001/oct/17/afghanistan.terrorism3.
28. Kohlmann, "Dossier: Libyan Islamic Fighting Group," 8.
29. Tawil, Brothers in Arms, 65.
30. Kohlmann, "Dossier: Libyan Islamic Fighting Group," 8-11.
31. Tawil, Brothers in Arms, 140.
32. Tawil, Brothers in Arms, 179.
33. "Three LIFG Members Designation for Terrorism," U.S. Department of the Treasury, November 30, 2008, https://www.treasury.gov/press-center/press-releases/Pages/hp1244.aspx.
34. "Libyan Islamic Fighting Group," Mapping Militant Organizations, Stanford University, May 4, 2017, http://web.stanford.edu/group/mappingmilitants/cgi-bin/groups/view/675.
35. "Libyan Islamic Fighting Group," Stanford.
36. "Libyan Islamic Fighting Group," Stanford.
37. "Foreign Terrorist Organizations," U.S. Department of State, accessed August 21, 2017, https://www.state.gov-/j/ct/rls/other/des/123085.htm.
38. Omar Ashour, "Post-Jihadism: Libya and the Global Transformations of Armed Islamist Movements," Studies in Conflict and Terrorism 23, iss. 3, 2011, 384.
39. Ashour, "Post-Jihadism: Libya and the Global Transformations of Armed Islamist Movements," 385. According to Ashour, there were a few bumps in the road: "the six leaders in Abu Selim Prison wanted the decision to be unanimous so as to maximize the impact on the middle-ranks, the grassroots, and the sympathizers, and thus guarantee successful organizational de-radicalization. They thus demanded the involvement of the

LIFG leaders abroad in the dialogue with the regime. Those leaders included two Shura Council members (Abu Layth al-Libi and 'Urwa al-Libi) and two influential members of the LIFG's legitimate (theological) committee: Abu Yahya al-Libi, currently believed to be the third person in al-Qaida, and Abdullah Sa'id, who was killed in December 2009 by a U.S. drone strike in Pakistan. All four rejected the offer."

40. Ashour, "Post-Jihadism: Libya and the Global Transformations of Armed Islamist Movements," 388.
41. Ashour, "Post-Jihadism: Libya and the Global Transformations of Armed Islamist Movements," 384.
42. David D. Kirkpatrick, "Political Islam and the Fate of Two Libyan Brothers," New York Times, October 6, 2012, http://www.nytimes.com/2012/10/07/world/africa/political-islam-and-the-fate-of-two-libyan-brothers.html?pagewanted=all.
43. Estelle and Zimmerman, "Backgrounder: Fighting Forces in Libya."
44. Estelle and Zimmerman, "Backgrounder: Fighting Forces in Libya."
45. Aaron Y. Zelin, "Know Your Ansar al-Sharia," Foreign Policy, September 21, 2012, http://www.washingtoninstitute.org/policy-analysis/view/know-your-ansar-al-sharia.
46. "Libyan militant group says its leader, Mohamed al-Zahawi, was killed," Associated Press, January 24, 2015, https://www.nytimes.com/2015/01/25/world/africa/libyan-militant-group-says-its-leader-mohammed-al-zahawi-was-killed.html.
47. Mary Fitzgerald, "It Wasn't Us," Foreign Policy, September 18, 2012, http://www.foreignpolicy.com/articles/2012/09/18/it_wasn_t_us.
48. Aaron Y. Zelin, "Libya Beyond Benghazi," Journal of International Security Affairs no. 25, Fall/Winter 2013, http://www.securityaffairs.org/sites/default/files/issues/archives/fw2013covertocover_small.pdf.
49. Zelin, "Know Your Ansar al-Sharia."
50. "Abu Sufyan Bin Qumu," Counter Extremism Project, n.d., https://www.counterextremism.com/extremists/abu-sufyan-bin-qumu.

51. Zelin, "Libya Beyond Benghazi."
52. Zelin, "Libya Beyond Benghazi."
53. Zelin, "Libya Beyond Benghazi."
54. Zelin, "Know Your Ansar al-Sharia."
55. Zelin, "Libya Beyond Benghazi."
56. Aaron Y. Zelin, Testimony before the House of Representatives Committee on Foreign Affairs, Subcommittee on Terrorism, Nonproliferation, and Trade and Subcommittee the Middle East and North Africa, July 10, 2013, https://www.washingtoninstitute.org/uploads/Documents/testimony/ZelinTestimony20130710-v2.pdf
57. "U.N. Blacklists Libya's Ansar al-Sharia, Involved in Benghazi Attack," Reuters, November 19, 2014, http://www.reuters.com/article/2014/11/19/us-libya-security-un-idUSKCN0J32KX20141119
58. These battalions participated in ASL's first "annual conference" on June 6, 2012. Other participants included, the Islamic Foundation for Da'wa and Islah, The Supreme Commission for the Protection of Revolution of February 17, Liwa Dara' Libya, Katibat Shuhada Libya al-Hurrah, Katibat Faruq (Misrata), Katibat Thuwar Sirte, Katibat Shuhada al-Khalij al-Nawfaliya, Katibat Ansar al-Huriyya, Katibat Shuhada al-Qawarsha, Katibat al-Shahid Muhammad al-Hami, Katibat al-Jabal, Katibat al-Nur, Katibat Shuhada Abu Salim, Katibat Shuhada Benghazi, the Preventative Security Apparatus, Katibat al-Shahid Salih al-Nas, and other brigades from Darnah, Sabratha, Janzur, and Ajdabiya. Pictures of the conference can be accessed at https://www.facebook.com/media/set/?set=a.373188266078865.86838.156312127766481&type=1.
59. Zelin, "Know Your Ansar al-Sharia."
60. Aaron Zelin, "Libya's jihadists beyond Benghazi," Foreign Policy, August 12, 2013, http://foreignpolicy.com/2013/08/12/libyas-jihadists-beyond-benghazi/.
61. "Profile: Libya's military strongman Khalifa Haftar." BBC, September 15, 2016, http://www.bbc.com/news/world-africa-27492354.
62. "Ansar al-Sharia in Libya (ASL)," Counter Extrem-

ism Project, n.d., https://www.counterextremism.com/threat/ansar-al-sharia-libya-asl.

63. Glenn, "Libya's Islamists: Who They Are - And What They Want."
64. Ansar al-Sharia in Libya (ASL)," Counter Extremism Project.
65. "ISIS in Action," Eyes on ISIS in Libya, June 6, 2017, http://eyeonisisinlibya.com/isis-in-action/31-may-6-june-misratas-security-forces-release-isis-confession-video/.
66. "Libyan Islamist group Ansar al-Sharia says it is dissolving," Reuters, May 27, 2017, http://www.reuters.com/article/us-libya-security-idUSKBN18N0YR.
67. "Libya eastern commander Haftar declares Benghazi 'liberated'," BBC, July 6, 2017, http://www.bbc.com/news/world-africa-40515325.
68. "Militants Find Sanctuary in Libya's Wild South," Associated Press, July 13, 2017, https://www.voanews.com/a/militants-find-sanctuary-in-libya-wild-south/3942381.html.
69. "Blast hits key tribal leader's mosque in Benghazi," Reuters, August 4, 2017, http://www.reuters.com/article/us-libya-security-idUSKBN1AK1Y3.
70. Glenn, "Libya's Islamists: Who They Are - And What They Want."
71. Estelle and Zimmerman, "Backgrounder: Fighting Forces in Libya."
72. Ayman al-Warfalli and Aidan Lewis, "East Libyan city suffers as military forces tighten siege," Reuters, August 7, 2017, http://www.reuters.com/article/us-libya-security-derna-idUSKBN1AN1UR.
73. Geoff D. Porter, "How Realistic Is Libya as an Islamic State "Fallback"?" Combating Terrorism Center at West Point, March 16, 2016, https://www.ctc.usma.edu/posts/how-realistic-is-libya-as-an-islamic-state-fallback.
74. Porter, "How Realistic Is Libya as an Islamic State "Fallback"?"
75. Tarek Kahlaoui, "The rise of ISIS in Libya, explained," Newsweek, May 29, 2016, http://www.newsweek.com/understanding-rise-islamic-state-isis-libya-437931.

76. "ISIS Loses Libyan Stronghold," Institute for the Study of War, June 24, 2015, http://www.understandingwar.org/backgrounder/isis-loses-libyan-stronghold.
77. Porter, "How Realistic Is Libya as an Islamic State "Fallback"?"
78. Aaron Y. Zelin, "The Islamic State's Burgeoning Capital in Sirte, Libya," The Washington Institute for Near East Policy, August 6, 2015, https://news.siteintelgroup.com/Jihadist-News/is-spokesman-rallies-fighters-blasts-u-s-led-campaign-against-is.html.
79. Estelle and Zimmerman, "Backgrounder: Fighting Forces in Libya."
80. David D. Kirkpatrick and Rukhmini Callimachi. "Islamic State Video Shows Beheadings of Egyptian Christians in Libya," New York Times, February 15, 2015, https://www.nytimes.com/2015/02/16/world/middleeast/islamic-state-video-beheadings-of-21-egyptian-christians.html?_r=0.
81. "IS Spokesman Rallies Fighters, Blasts U.S.-Led Campaign Against IS," SITE Intelligence Group, May 21, 2016, https://news.siteintelgroup.com/Jihadist-News/is-spokesman-rallies-fighters-blasts-u-s-led-campaign-against-is.html.
82. "How the Islamic State Rose, Fell, and Could Rise Again in the Maghreb," International Crisis Group, July 24, 2017, https://www.crisisgroup.org/middle-east-north-africa/north-africa/178-how-islamic-state-rose-fell-and-could-rise-again-maghreb.
83. Patrick Wintour, "Isis loses control of Libyan city of Sirte." Guardian (London). December 5, 2016, https://www.theguardian.com/world/2016/dec/05/isis-loses-control-of-libyan-city-of-sirte.
84. "How the Islamic State Rose, Fell, and Could Rise Again in the Maghreb," International Crisis Group.
85. Callimachi and Schmitt, "Manchester Bomber Met With ISIS Unit in Libya, Officials Say."
86. Emily Estelle, "Desknote: ISIS's Tunisian attack cell in Libya," AEI's Critical Threats Project, March 8, 2016, https://www.criticalthreats.org/analysis/desknote-isiss-tunisian-attack-cell-in-libya.
87. Callimachi and Schmitt, "Manchester Bomber Met

With ISIS Unit in Libya, Officials Say."

88. Patrick Wintour, "Isis loses control of Libyan city of Sirte." Guardian (London). December 5, 2016, https://www.theguardian.com/world/2016/dec/05/isis-loses-control-of-libyan-city-of-sirte.
89. John Brennan, Statement before the Senate Select Committee on Intelligence, June 16, 2016, https://www.cia.gov/news-information/speeches-testimony/2016-speeches-testimony/statement-by-director-brennan-as-prepared-for-delivery-before-ssci.html.
90. Jason Pack, Rhiannon Smith, and Karim Mezran, "The Origins and Evolution of ISIS in Libya," Atlantic Council, June 20, 2017, http://www.atlanticcouncil.org/publications/reports/the-origins-and-evolution-of-isis-in-libya.
91. Estelle, "The General's Trap in Libya."
92. Thomas Joscelyn, "How Many Fighters Does the Islamic State Still Have in Libya?" FDD's Long War Journal, July 20, 2017, http://www.longwarjournal.org/archives/2017/07/how-many-fighters-does-the-islamic-state-still-have-in-libya.php.
93. Manal Omar, "The Islamists are Coming," Woodrow Wilson International Center for Scholars, n.d., http://www.wilsoncenter.org/islamists/libya-rebuilding-scratch.
94. U.S. Department of State, Bureau of Democracy, Human Rights and Labor, International Religious Freedom Report for 2013, n.d., http://www.state.gov/j/drl/rls/irf/religiousfreedom/index.htm?year=2013&dlid=222303#sthash.IH9pgQVJ.dpuf; "Libya," Central Intelligence Agency World Factbook, January 12, 2017, https://www.cia.gov/library/publications/the-world-factbook/geos/ly.html
95. U.S. Department of State, International Religious Freedom Report for 2013.
96. Ragab Saad, "A Constitution That Doesn't Protect Rights and Freedoms: Libya Writes Its Constitution," Atlantic Council, Atlantic Council, August 3, 2017, http://www.atlanticcouncil.org/blogs/menasource/a-constitution-that-doesn-t-protect-rights-and-freedoms-libya-writes-its-constitution.

97. U.S. Department of State, International Religious Freedom Report for 2013.
98. Ragab Saad, "A Constitution That Doesn't Protect Rights and Freedoms: Libya Writes Its Constitution."
99. Omar, "The Islamists are Coming."
100. Mohamed Eljarh, "In Post-Qaddafi Libya, It's Stay Silent or Die," Foreign Policy, September 24, 2014, http://transitions.foreignpolicy.com/posts/2014/09/24/in_post_qaddafi_libya_its_stay_silent_or_die.
101. Pargeter, "Political Islam in Libya."
102. Pargeter, "Political Islam in Libya."
103. Manal Omar, "Libya: Rebuilding From Scratch," Woodrow Wilson International Center for Scholars, n.d., https://www.wilsoncenter.org/libya-rebuilding-scratch.
104. Frederic Wehrey, "Quiet No More?"
105. Ashour, "Libya's Muslim Brotherhood faces the future."
106. Mary Fitzgerald, "A Current of Faith," Foreign Policy, July 6, 2012, http://www.foreignpolicy.com/articles/2012/07/06/a_current_of_faith.
107. Camille Tawil, "Tripoli's Islamist Militia Leader Turns to Politics in the New Libya," Jamestown Foundation Terrorism Monitor 10, iss. 11, June 1, 2012, http://www.jamestown.org/single/?no_cache=1&tx_ttnews%5Btt_news%5D=39450.
108. "Libya Publishes Parliamentary Election Results," The Journal of Turkish Weekly, July 22, 2014, http://www.turkishweekly.net/news/169449/-libya-publishes-parliamentary-election-results.html.
109. "Profile: Libya's military strongman Khalifa Haftar," BBC, September 15, 2016, http://www.bbc.com/news/world-africa-27492354.
110. "Profile: Libya's military strongman Khalifa Haftar," BBC.
111. Wolfgang Pusztai, "The Failed Serraj Experiment of Libya," Atlantic Council, March 31, 2017, http://www.atlanticcouncil.org/blogs/menasource/the-serraj-experiment-of-libya.
112. Estelle, "The General's Trap in Libya."
113. Frederic Wehrey, "Whoever Controls Benghazi Controls Libya," The Atlantic, July 1, 2017, https://www.

theatlantic.com/international/archive/2017/07/benghazi-libya/532056/.

114. Emily Estelle, "The General's Trap in Libya."
115. Karim Mezran and Elissa Miller, "Libya: From Intervention to Proxy War," Atlantic Council, July 2017, http://www.atlanticcouncil.org/publications/issue-briefs/libya-from-intervention-to-proxy-war.
116. Karim Mezran and Erin Neale, "Libya: Permanent Limbo or Refreshed Hope?," Atlantic Council, April 11, 2018, http://www.atlanticcouncil.org/blogs/menasource/libya-permanent-limbo-or-refreshed-hope.
117. Emily Estelle, "Libya Update: Exit the General?," AEI's Critical Threats Project, April 11, 2018, https://www.criticalthreats.org/analysis/libya-update-exit-the-general; and Ayman al-Warfalli, "Libyan commander Haftar back in Benghazi after medical treatment," Reuters, April 26, 2018, https://www.reuters.com/article/us-libya-security-haftar/key-libyan-commander-back-in-benghazi-after-medical-treatment-statement-idUSKBN1HX334?il=0.
118. Mary Fitzgerald and Mattia Toaldo, "A quick guide to Libya's main players," European Council on Foreign Relations, 2017, http://www.ecfr.eu/mena/mapping_libya_conflict#.
119. Wehrey, "Whoever Controls Benghazi Controls Libya."
120. Katherine Pollock and Frederic Wehrey, "The Sufi-Salafi Rift," Carnegie Endowment for International Peace, January 23, 2018, https://carnegie-mec.org/diwan/75310.
121. AEI's Critical Threats Project, "Threat Update Situation Report," April 4, 2018, https://www.criticalthreats.org/briefs/threat-update/continuing-iranian-protests-may-pose-an-internal-security-threat-to-regime.
122. Ayman al-Warfalli, "Twin car bombs kill more than 30 in Libya's Benghazi: officials," Reuters, January 23, 2018, https://www.reuters.com/article/us-libya-security/twin-car-bombs-kill-more-than-30-in-libyas-benghazi-officials-idUSKBN1FC2TC.
123. Declan Walsh and Eric Schmitt, "U.S. Strikes Qaeda Target in Southern Libya, Expanding Shadow War

There," New York Times, March 25, 2018, https://www.nytimes.com/2018/03/25/world/middleeast/us-bombs-qaeda-libya.html.

24 Morocco

Quick Facts

Population: 33,986,655 (July 2017 est.)
Area: 446,550 sq km
Ethnic Groups:Arab-Berber 99%, other 1%
GDP (official exchange rate): $110.7 billion (2017 est.)

Source: CIA World FactBook (Last Updated May 2018)

Introduction

Unlike many other Arab and majority-Muslim states, Morocco has integrated Islamist political movements that oppose violence and support the constitutional order into its political process, while relentlessly prosecuting adherents to Salafist and other extremist ideologies. Not surprisingly, the U.S. State Department's 2016 report on global terrorism trends went out of its way to laud the country's "comprehensive counterterrorism strategy that includes vigilant security measures, regional and international cooperation, and counter-radicalization policies."[1] While the reformist course charted by King Mohammed VI has enabled Moroccans to avoid both the revolutionary tumult and violent repression which have characterized their neighbors' attempts to come to terms with the so-called Arab Spring, the North African kingdom nevertheless has been subjected to jihadist attacks and still confronts an Islamist movement that openly calls for the overthrow of the monarchy and creation of an Islamic state, as well as an Algerian-backed separatist group that, while previously secular, has increasingly been linked to al-Qaeda's regional affiliate. Thus, it remains to be seen whether the "Moroccan exception" is ultimately sustainable and, if so, what implications this might have for the region and the wider Arab and Muslim world.

Islamist Activity

A number of Islamist groups and movements, either indigenous or foreign, are currently active in Morocco. Unlike in many other Arab or majority-Muslim nations, however, Islamism in Morocco is quite fragmented. It is also historic in nature, insofar as today's Islamists active in the Kingdom have roots in previous iterations of Islamist activism that has been endemic to the country for decades.

Ash-Shabiba al-Islamiyya ("Islamic Youth")

Founded in 1969, the Association of Islamic Youth (Shabiba, sometimes known by the French acronym AJI) was the first organization in the Maghreb region established with the explicit objective of advancing Islamist politics.[2] The group also opposed the political leftism then in vogue in many Arab countries. Led by Abdelkarim Mouti, a former education ministry inspector, the group attracted support among university and high school students for whom it ran vacation camps where they received training in propaganda and protest techniques. Shabiba also cultivated ties with clandestine Algerian organizations in the early 1970s.

Mouti fled into exile in 1975 following the murder of two prominent leftist political figures, journalist and Socialist Union of the Forces of Progress (USFP) party official Omar Benjelloun and Party for Progress and Socialism (PPS) secretariat member Abderrahim Meniaoui, for which he was blamed by authorities. The investigation of the assassinations revealed that Shabiba had built up a secretive military arm, the al-Mujahidun al-Maghariba ("Moroccan Holy Warriors"), which was headed by a onetime law student named Abdelaziz Naamani. Sentenced to death in abstentia, Mouti spent time in both Saudi Arabia and Libya, but settled in Belgium where he continued to agitate against the Moroccan government, for a while publishing a small magazine, Al-Mujahid ("The Holy Warrior") and garnering a few followers among the immigrant communities in Europe.

Meanwhile, back in Morocco, following the discovery in 1985 of arms caches near the Algerian border and the subsequent arrest, trial, and conviction of more than two dozen militants, including a number who admitted to *Shabiba* membership, authorities set in motion a crackdown that, for all intents and purposes, shut down the group.

Al-Islah wa't-Tajdid ("Reform and Renewal") / At-Tawhid wa'l-Islah ("Unity and Reform")

The Movement for Reform and Renewal was created in 1992 by former Shabiba members who came to reject the group's embrace of violence and sought instead for a way to advance their objectives within Morocco's existing political system; in 1996, they changed the organization's name to the Association for Unity and Reform (at-Tawhid).[3] While King Hassan II tolerated at-Tawhid, he did not accord it legal recognition. Consequently, Abdelilah Benkirane and other at-Tawhid leaders negotiated an arrangement with a longstanding, but minor, political party, the Democratic Constitutional Movement, that enabled them to participate in elections under the aegis of the latter. The merger took place in 1997, and the new political party changed its name the following year to the Justice and Development Party (generally known by its French acronym, PJD).[4] (A full description of the PJD follows below)

Al-Adl Wal-Ihsan ("Justice and Charity")

The Justice and Charity Organization (al-Adl, or JCO), formed in 1988, has been the most virulent Islamist political and religious movement in Morocco. Considered illegitimate and barely tolerated by the Moroccan government, JCO has gained adherents through its role as the sole indigenous Islamist movement challenging the king's political and religious roles and through its extensive social and charitable organizational network. The Moroccan government refuses to recognize JCO as a political party.[5]

JCO advocates a restoration of Islamic law (sharia), but asserts allegiance to democratic principles in order to differentiate itself as a political movement that opposes what it considers to be Morocco's authoritarian political system. Since the 1970s, its leader and founder, Sheikh Abdessalam Yassine, has openly challenged the legitimacy of the Moroccan monarchy. For that stance, he was tried in 1984 and sentenced to house arrest—a sentence that remained in force until 1989.[6] The following year, JCO was officially outlawed pursuant to a ban that would endure until modified by the current king, Mohammed VI, in 2004. Sheikh Yassine's daughter, Nadia Yassine, increasingly emerged as movement's chief political organizational leader as her father slipped into his dotage (he died in 2012).

Openly critical of the monarchy and in almost constant conflict with the Moroccan government, JCO is committed to the dissolution of the country's current constitutional system and its replacement by an Islamic republic. Nevertheless, at least publicly JCO has renounced the use of violence and armed struggle, relying instead on protests and occasional civil disobedience to advance its goals. The scope of support for JCO is a closely guarded secret, both by the organization itself and by the Moroccan government, although some observers consider it to be substantial given the organization's extensive charitable and social network.[7] Unrest in June 2017 allowed the JCO to demonstrate some of this capability, organizing an estimated 10,000 protestors for a march in Rabat, ostensibly in solidarity with poor living conditions in the country's northern Rif region.[8]

Given the Moroccan government's intense opposition to JCO within the country, the group's leadership decided – beginning roughly in 1996 – to export their movement to Europe through the creation of the Muslim Participation and Spirituality (MPS) Association.[9] MPS has established chapters in various European cities, headed by JCO Islamist activists who have fled Morocco. The goal of MPS is to generate opposition to Morocco's king and government through political activities with the goal of winning legal status for the JCO inside Morocco.[10] The French and Belgian MPS branches often organize demonstrations against Morocco. Nadia Yassine also visits Europe regularly to denounce the repression of JCO, and, in 2006 she created the "New Europe-Morocco Friendship"—an association based in Belgium which convened a conference on the theme "Human Rights Flouted in Morocco."[11]

The Party of Justice and Development (PJD)

In order to co-opt Islamist sentiment in Morocco, King Hassan II permitted the emergence of new political movements that incorporated Islamist orientations—the most significant being the Justice and Development Party (PJD), which draws on Islamic values and inspiration from Turkey's Justice and Development Party (AKP), although there is no official connection between the two.

As previously discussed, the Islamist-inspired at-Tawhid entered a decline and fused with the Constitutional Democratic Popular

Movement, emerging as the PJD. The merged group brought together a coalition of small, moderate Islamist organizations, including conservative Islamist, pro-monarchial political figures. In contrast to JCO, the PJD is a political party that has competed in Morocco's parliamentary elections since 1997. In the subsequent 2002 elections, the PJD emerged as the country's leading opposition party, winning 42 of the 325 seats in Morocco's parliament, making it the third-largest group in the national legislature. In the subsequent poll, in 2007, the PJD won the largest percentage of popular vote (10.9 percent on the local and 13.4 percent on the national lists) garnered by any single party.[12]

Unlike JCO, the PJD is non-revolutionary and does not call for the overthrow of the monarchy, and, consequently, does not directly challenge Morocco's constitutional system. Nor does it advocate the creation of an Islamist state, or caliphate, in Morocco. Indeed, PJD intentionally downplays any religious agenda. Nevertheless, it views itself as the guardian of Morocco's Muslim identity and conservative religious traditions, and opposes any effort that would compromise Morocco's Islamic character. Thus, it opposes further westernization of Moroccan society, but it pragmatically recognizes the importance of Morocco's ties to the West. The PJD also regards itself as a bulwark against radical Islamic groups such as JCO.

Since 1997, the PJD has gradually gained popular support throughout Morocco, and has become quite entrenched in Morocco's political process—balancing its participation in legislative affairs with its adherence to an Islamic political agenda. PJD legislators have won plaudits for focusing their attention on ameliorating Morocco's significant social and economic challenges—of course, once they became the governing party (see below), their failure to deliver on those promises also led to a resurgence of other parties to whom dissatisfied voters turned. Nevertheless, during its period in opposition, the party's ability to influence actual policy is limited, with only marginal ability to translate its agenda into meaningful programs that would obtain greater popular support.

The PJD's agenda in parliament has occasionally taken it into pure sharia territory—calling for prohibition against alcohol distribution and consumption, and challenging media that it views as defacing Islamic principles. On other occasions, however, the PJD has trended in the opposite direction. In 2004 for example, the party actively participated in the adoption of a new, more liberal version of the country's code regulating marriage and family life, known as the Moudawana.[13] The revision of the Moudawana greatly improved the social status of women in Morocco, and was ridiculed by more conservative Islamists. However, the PJD's leader at the time, Saad Eddine el-Othmani, defended his party's approval of the code's revision, asserting in 2006 that it had been approved by religious leaders, aided families, and was consistent with Islamic traditions.[14]

In the November 25, 2011 elections—the first held under the new constitution proposed by King Mohammed VI and approved by plebiscite earlier that year—the PJD won 27.1 percent of the vote and came away with 107 seats, making it by far the single largest party in the new legislature. Since the new charter stipulates that the monarch should appoint the prime minister from the largest party in parliament, the mandate to form a government was given to the PJD's Benkirane, who formed a coalition government with support from the venerable conservative nationalist Independence Party (Istiqlal) and two left-leaning parties. The new government was sworn in on January 3, 2012, with the PJD holding eleven of thirty ministerial portfolios.[15]

Five years later, in the October 7, 2016 parliamentary elections, the PJD again emerged as the largest single party in parliament, with 125 seats, after winning a slightly higher proportion of the overall vote at 27.88 percent. However, widespread dissatisfaction with the PJD's management of the government also manifested itself in an even stronger rally behind the Party of Authenticity and Modernity (PAM) which surged from a fourth-place finish in the previous election to second place with 20.95 percent of the vote and thus winning 102 seats in the legislature (up from the 47 it had).

The election results led to five months of parliamentary deadlock, which ended when Benkirane, unable to reconcile with the USFP, failed to form a coalition government and was subsequently dismissed by the King. Saad Eddine el-Othmani, who was most recently serving as the PJD's secretary-general, was appointed Prime Minister on March 17, 2017, and quickly conceded seventeen ministries to the bloc of parties led by conservative National Rally of Independents leader Aziz Akhannouch, including the powerful economy, finance, commerce, and agricultural portfolios. The PJD was left with eleven of thirty-nine ministerial positions, a result that has stirred ire within the party and caused criticism within its ranks of Othmani's leadership, weakening the PJD and calling into question its future.[16]

Salafist Jihadism

Morocco has "numerous small 'grassroots' extremist groups"[17] that collectively adhere to Salafi-jihadi ideology. Indeed, Spanish anti-terror judge Baltazar Garzon has stated that "Morocco is the worst terrorist threat to Europe."[18] He estimated that al-Qaeda-linked cells in Morocco number more than 100 and that at least 1,000 terrorists are now being actively sought by Moroccan authorities.[19] Al-Qaeda's regional offshoot, al-Qaeda in the Islamic Maghreb (AQIM), has had success in recent efforts to bring these disparate groups (which number less than 50 members per grouping, on average) under its umbrella, announcing the merger of four regional militant groups, including Ansar Dine and other elements of AQIM, to form the Group for the Support of Islam and Muslims (GSIM) in March 2017.[20]

AQIM, like its counterpart al-Qaeda in the Arabian Peninsula (AQAP), constitutes a potent regional terrorist threat not only to Morocco but to Algeria, Burkina Faso, Mauritania, Mali, Niger, and Tunisia. Formed when the Salafist Group for Preaching and Combat (GSPC) reconstituted itself into AQIM in early 2007, its goal has been to integrate all of the North African radical movements, including the small Moroccan Islamic Combatant Group (GICM). On September 11, 2013, AQIM released an unprecedented 41-minute video "documentary" attacking Moroccan domestic and foreign policy, especially its counterterrorism efforts. Analysts believe that the production was the result of the terrorist organization's frustration that, while it had recruited some Moroccans, it had largely failed to target the country successfully, much less compromise its institutions.[21]

Salafist jihadis as a whole remain a significant threat to Morocco and the West. Scores of young Moroccans have traveled to Iraq and

Afghanistan to fight Americans, and there are continuing arrests of extremists by authorities.[22] Salafis also represent a challenge to the Moroccan state, as a number of incidents have underscored. On May 16, 2003, terrorists claiming to be members of the GICM launched a series of five coordinated suicide attacks in Casablanca, killing more than 40 people and wounding more than 100. In April 2007, a series of suicide bomb attacks occurred in central Casablanca, one taking place near the U.S. Consulate and one near the American Language Center. In February 2008, Moroccan authorities arrested nearly 40 members of an alleged terrorist network, led by Abdelkader Belliraj, a Belgian-Moroccan suspected of committing multiple assassinations in addition to arms smuggling and money laundering for al-Qaeda.[23] Belliraj was subsequently convicted and sentenced to life in prison. Press reports have at times asserted that more than 100 al-Qaeda-linked cells exist in Morocco, and that Moroccan police have either imprisoned or placed under house arrest/police surveillance over 1,000 Salafist jihadists either openly sympathetic to AQIM or part of other hard-core underground Islamist movements.[24]

On April 28, 2011, the bombing of a popular tourist café in Marrakech left seventeen people dead and at least twenty wounded. Among those killed were eight French nationals, a Briton, an Israeli-Canadian, a Swiss, and a Portuguese. The government accused AQIM of the attack.

In recent years, Islamist activity has generated scores of arrests. In July 2008, Moroccan security services arrested 35 members of an alleged terrorist network specializing in the recruitment of volunteers for Iraq.[25] In August of the same year, another 15-person network calling itself "Fath al-Andalus" was reportedly disbanded in Layoune, the capital of the Western Sahara, for planning attacks on the UN peacekeeping force there.[26] There also have been reports of considerable numbers of Moroccans traveling to Mali and Algeria to receive training from AQIM elements.[27] In more recent years, Moroccans have also traveled to Syria and Iraq—and, more recently, Libya—to join the Islamic State (ISIS). It is estimated by the Moroccan Central Bureau for Judicial Investigations that by July 2017, over 1,600 Moroccans had joined ISIS.[28] If European citizens of Moroccan descent are included, the number rises to between

2,000 and 2,500.[29]

Although Morocco has so far fortunately not seen a successful assault on its soil by ISIS, since 2013, authorities have dismantled more than three dozen cells plotting attacks both within the kingdom and abroad. In July 2016, fifty-two people were arrested and various armaments seized. According to authorities, the militants were planning a string of attacks to inaugurate a "province" (wilayat) of the Islamic State in the country.[30] With the defeat of ISIS in Iraq and Syria in 2017, the group's ideological cachet will be reduced. However, with an estimated 6,000 African militants expected to return from the Middle East, ISIS' Greater Sahara franchise and other existing groups will receive an influx of experienced fighters, raising security threats in North Africa, the Sahel, and Europe.[31]

The impoverished slums in Morocco's inner cities and northern regions have produced many of these extremists, and many of the Moroccan extremist groupings are composed of family members and friends from the same towns and villages. Indeed, the north of Morocco has become an especially fertile ground for Salafists who favored Wahhabism and other extremist creeds over Morocco's more tolerant version of Islam.

Islamism and Society

Under Moroccan law, the monarch is revered as the "Commander of the Faithful" and traces his lineage back to the Prophet Mohammad. Consequently, the majority of Moroccans take great pride in their nation's embrace of moderate, tolerant Islam. It is worth noting that the reformed Moroccan constitution of 2011, unique in the Arab world, explicitly acknowledges that the country's national culture is "enriched and nourished by African, Andalusian, Hebrew, and Mediterranean influences."[32]

Social and economic conditions, however, play a role in Islamist sentiment. Given Morocco's high unemployment rate, year after year thousands of Moroccans risk their lives attempting to illegally immigrate to Europe across the Straits of Gibraltar.[33] Many, however, are left behind, transforming cities like Tangier, Tetouan, or Al Houcema into smuggling centers feeding criminal elements and opponents of the regime. Despite the current king's efforts to promote a legislative agenda to modernize Islamic laws governing civil society in Morocco (detailed below), the continued growth of political parties such as the PJD and continued political activities by JCO, both inside Morocco and in Europe, point to the fractures in Morocco's society between those who favor a more moderate, tolerant Islam and significant elements of Morocco's populace which prefer stronger Islamic control over the nation's society and its political system.

Morocco's urban slums and rural north continue to be fertile ground for extremism and its recruiters to AQIM. Indeed, hundreds of Moroccans have volunteered to fight in Iraq and Afghanistan against the United States.[34] Morocco's north, especially cities such as Tetouan and the surrounding Rif Mountain villages have at times been centers of jihadist agitation. It is in Morocco's north that such sentiment has most successfully taken root, as a result of institutional neglect. Following a Berber rebellion against his rule in the early 1980s, King Hassan II largely abandoned the northern tier of Morocco to its own devices. The King rarely visited the north during his reign. Consequently, government services were severely cut, and Islamists filled the void with a social and charitable network offering food and medical treatment to the population. While King Mohammed has reversed his father's policy of abandonment of the north (and even conducted an ancient traditional ceremony of mutual allegiance there),[35] the region is still relatively underdeveloped and deeply dependent on charitable networks, some with extremist links, for services not provided by the government.

Islamism and the State

Following the 2003 Casablanca bombings, the Moroccan government focused increasing attention on modernizing Islamic teaching and Islamic infrastructure and adopted laws liberalizing civil marriage and the role of women in Morocco's society. The Ministry of Endowments and Islamic Affairs was provided with new funding and authority to train more moderate Islamic clerics and to expand its programs in Morocco's educational system.

In 2004, King Mohammed VI pushed through a reform of the family code (Moudawana), overcoming conservative opposition and mass demonstrations in part by invoking his religious authority as Commander of the Faithful. Among other provisions, the legislation significantly advanced women's rights by elevating the minimum age of marriage to 18, limiting polygamy, granting couples joint rights over their children, and permitting women to initiate divorce proceedings.[36]

One incident in particular points to Morocco's more aggressive stance against ultra-conservative Muslim clerics who oppose the government's efforts to modernize Morocco's Islamic infrastructure and its religious teachings. In September 2008, Sheikh Mohamed Ben Abderrahman Al Maghraoui issued a highly provocative fatwa legitimizing the marriage of underage women as young as nine years old.[37] The Moroccan government sought to discredit the fatwa and ordered the immediate closure of 60 Quranic schools under his control. The government also launched an inquiry into Sheikh Al Maghraoui's competence as an Islamic scholar, and the public prosecutor's office initiated a criminal case against him for encouraging pedophilia.[38]

Following the incident, King Mohammed unveiled his "proximity strategy," which represented a modernization program for Islamic institutions in Morocco. Under the program, 3,180 mosques were designated to be "modernized," (essentially a wholesale replacement of imams deemed by the regime to be opponents of moderate Islamic principles). Thirty-three thousand new imams were to be trained and the number of regional ulama councils (charged with overseeing Islamic teaching and the competency of imams) was increased from 30 to 70. Exceptionally for the Arab world, women also have a place in Morocco's official religious establishment with mourchidates, or female religious guides, trained alongside more traditional male imams.[39]

To counter violent Islamist extremist ideologies, Morocco has developed a national strategy to reaffirm and further institutionalize Moroccans' historically widespread adherence to Sunni Islam's Maliki school of jurisprudence and its Ashari theology, as well as to the mystical spirituality of Sufism.

The aborted terrorist plot in 2007 and the continuing threat of jihadi sentiment in the country's north only briefly arrested the pace of King Mohammed's reform agenda with respect to rights of women and the judiciary, including enacting legislation in 2014 to end the use of military tribunals to try civilians.

Unlike his father, the King has largely refrained from playing an activist role in Middle East diplomacy, focusing his diplomatic efforts closer to home in Africa, which the monarch has repeatedly characterized as the "top priority" of his country's foreign policy, emphasizing that "this multi-dimensional relationship puts Morocco in the center of Africa" and "Africa holds a special place in the heart of Moroccans."[40] On January 30, 2017, Morocco joined the African Union, more than three decades after leaving its predecessor organization, uniting the African continent from the shores of the Mediterranean Sea to its southernmost tip at Cape Agulhas. In addition to extensive partnerships with African countries on a variety of political and economic issues, Morocco's influence is increasingly seen in its efforts to train religious leaders and preachers from across the continent—and, indeed, even some from Europe and beyond—in the kingdom's moderate form of Islam. The Mohammed VI Institute for the Training of Imams, Morchidines, and Morchidates, established in 2015, has enrolled hundreds of students from Mali, Tunisia, Guinea, Côte d'Ivoire, and France.[41]

For many years, Morocco has permitted mainstream Islamic political parties that do not condone extremism and violence to exist and indeed, to participate in elections, although it continues to deny legal status to the JCO. Since the Casablanca bombings in 2003, Moroccan authorities have maintained a vigilant and aggressive stance against any jihadist movement. Moroccan authorities currently have almost 1,000 prisoners considered to be Islamic radicals in jail.[42] And in July 2007, Moroccan authorities jailed six Islamist politicians who were accused of complicity in a major terrorist plot.[43] On the other hand, the Moroccan government has rewarded Islamist parties that have embraced more moderate Islamic principles, such as the PJD. Notwithstanding the ever-present scourge of jihadi operatives in Morocco, the Moroccan government has demonstrated ingenuity in its "divide and conquer" strategy against Islamists who challenge the state. In addition to adopting the above-referenced "proximity strategy" to replace recalcitrant imams, authorities have established a grassroots police operation to report on any suspicious activities by Islamists.[44]

The Moroccan government has also implemented a concerted social development program, the National Initiative for Human Development (INDH), a multibillion-dollar undertaking aimed at generating employment, fighting poverty, and improving infrastructure in both rural areas as well as the sprawling slums on the outskirts of urban centers that have been susceptible to Islamist-oriented charities nurturing radicalism. In the largest "bidonvilles" (shantytowns) in Morocco's cities, significant social welfare, health and education programs have been instituted and many families have been relocated to new affordable housing units.[45] Overall, the U.S. State Department has applauded Morocco for having "a comprehensive strategy for countering violent extremism that prioritizes economic and human development goals in addition to tight control of the religious sphere and messaging."[46]

Amid the reforms that have been adopted in recent years,[47] even the historically delicate issue of Moroccan sovereignty over the former Spanish Sahara has seen progress.[48] In 2007, the government advanced a proposal to break the longstanding impasse over the issue by offering generous autonomy to the area (including not only an elected local administration but also ideas about education and justice and the promise of financial support). Under the plan, the only matters that would remain in Rabat's control would be defense and foreign affairs, as well as the currency. The regional authority, meanwhile, would have broad powers over local administration, the economy, infrastructure, social and cultural affairs, and the environment. Then-Secretary of State Hillary Rodham Clinton described the autonomy proposal as "serious, credible, and realistic."[49]

Nevertheless, now well into its fourth decade, the "question of Western Sahara," as it is termed in the nomenclature of the United Nations, is one of those challenges which, defying multiple efforts by the international community to facilitate its "solution," despite increasingly dire warnings, recently reiterated by former UN Secretary-General Ban Ki-moon and others, that "the rise of instability and insecurity in and around the Sahel" and the risk of "spillover" from the fighting in Mali requires "an urgent settlement" of this "ticking time bomb."[50] Secretary-General António Guterres reiterated these concerns in January 2018, after tensions escalated near Guerguerat.[51]

Supported by Algeria, the Frente Popular de Liberación de Saguía el Hamra y Río de Oro ("Popular Front for the Liberation of Saqiet al-Hamra and Río del Oro," commonly known as the Polisario Front) continues to demand the complete independence of the territory, even though the armed conflict of the late 1970s and early 1980s left Morocco in control of more than 85 percent of it. The construction by the Moroccan government of a "sand berm," (a defensive shield consisting of a series of barriers of sand and stone completed in 1987) and subsequent deployment of a UN monitoring force has largely confined the Polisario Front to a small zone around Tindouf in southwestern Algeria where it has sequestered tens of thousands of Sahrawi refugees in the squalid camps which have recently been the object of former UN Secretary-General Ban Ki-Moon's concerns about conflict spillover.[52]

While for most of its history the Polisario Front has been avowedly secular and, indeed, leftist in its political orientations—many of its leaders studied in the Soviet bloc and fighters received training in Cuba well into the 1990s—there are worrisome indications of growing linkages with AQIM[53] and other Islamist groups in the Maghreb and the Sahel, including providing AQIM's allies in northern Mali with both fighters and, in one notorious case, Western hostages to trade for ransom.[54] Nor are Sunni jihadists the only extremists with whom the Polisario have lately consorted: in May 2018, Morocco broke diplomatic relations with Iran, closing down its embassy in Tehran and ordering the closure of the Iranian mission in Rabat, amid Iran and its Lebanese Shi'ite ally, Hezbollah, were supporting the Polisario by training and arming its fighters via the Iranian embassy in Algeria. According to Moroccan Foreign Minister Nasser Bourita, "Hezbollah sent military officials to Polisario and provided the front with... weapons and trained them on urban warfare."[55] Should this trend continue, it would not only heighten the challenge of Islamist violence for Morocco, but also exacerbate an already volatile security situation for the entire region.

Endnotes

1. U.S. Department of State, Office of the Coordinator for Counterterrorism, "Country Reports: Middle East and North Africa Overview," in *Country Reports on Terrorism 2015*, June 2, 2016, https://www.state.gov/j/ct/rls/crt/2015/257517.htm.
2. John P. Entelis, "Political Islam in the Maghreb," in John P. Entelis, ed., *Islam, Democracy, and the State in North Africa* (Bloomington: Indiana University Press, 1997), 52-53.
3. Amr Hamzawy, "Party for Justice and Development in Morocco: Participation and Its Discontents," Carnegie Endowment for International Peace *Carnegie Paper* no. 93, July 2008, 7-8, http://www.carnegieendowment.org/publications/index.cfm?fa=view&id=20314.
4. Hamzawy, "Party for Justice and Development in Morocco: Participation and Its Discontents," 8.
5. Samir Amghar, "Political Islam in Morocco," Center for European Policy Studies *CEPS Working Document* No. 269, June 2007.
6. Amghar, "Political Islam in Morocco."
7. National Democratic Institute, *Final Report on the Moroccan Legislative Elections*, September 7, 2007.
8. Samia Errazzouki, "Led by Islamists, Thousands of Moroccans Rally in Support of Northern Protests," Reuters, June 11, 2017, https://www.reuters.com/article/us-morocco-protests/led-by-islamists-thousands-of-moroccans-rally-in-support-of-northern-protests-idUSKBN1920X8.
9. Amghar, "Political Islam in Morocco."
10. Amghar, "Political Islam in Morocco."
11. Amghar, "Political Islam in Morocco."
12. Daniel Williams, "Morocco Parliament May be Controlled by Islamic Party," Bloomberg, December 30, 2009, http://www.bloomberg.com/apps/news?pid=newsarchive&sid=aLXRR7EuJeEo.
13. Hamzawy, "Party for Justice and Development in Morocco: Participation and Its Discontents."
14. See Mona Yacoubian, "Engaging Islamists and Promoting Democracy: A Preliminary Assessment," in Daniel Brumberg and Dina Shehata (eds.), *Conflict,*

Identity and Reform in the Muslim World: Challenges for U.S. Engagement (Washington: U.S. Institute of Peace Press, 2009), 420.

15. "Morocco: Islamist Party Takes over New Government," *Al Bawaba*, January 3, 2012, http://www.albawaba.com/news/morocco-islamist-party-takes-over-new-government-407621.
16. Imad Stitou, "Morocco Finally Gets New Government, but at What Cost?" Al-Monitor, April 12, 2017, https://www.al-monitor.com/pulse/originals/2017/04/morocco-government-islamist-party-majority.html.
17. U.S. Department of State, Office of the Coordinator for Counterterrorism, *Country Reports on Terrorism 2008* (Washington, DC: U.S. Department of State, April 2009), 130, http://www.state.gov/documents/organization/122599.pdf.
18. Olivier Guitta, "Morocco Under Fire," *Weekly Standard*, March 29, 2007, http://www.weeklystandard.com/Content/Public/Articles/000/000/013/470ucfqo.asp.
19. Guitta, "Morocco Under Fire."
20. Caleb Weiss, "Analysis: Merger of al-Qaeda Groups Threatens Security in West Africa," *Long War Journal*, March 18, 2017, https://www.longwarjournal.org/archives/2017/03/analysis-merger-of-al-qaeda-groups-threatens-security-in-west-africa.php.
21. Mawassi Lahcen, "AQIM Lashes Out at Morocco," Magharebia, September 16, 2013, http://magharebia.com/en_GB/articles/awi/features/2013/09/16/feature-01.
22. Mustapha Tossa, "Morocco's Fight Against Terrorism," Common Ground News Service, September 2, 2008, http://commongroundnews.org/article.php?id=23883&lan=en&sid=1&sp=0.
23. U.S. Department of State, *Country Reports on Terrorism 2008*.
24. Stephen Erlanger and Souad Mekhennet, "Islamic Radicalism Slows Moroccan Reforms," *New York Times*, August 26, 2009, http://www.nytimes.com/2009/08/27/world/africa/27morocco.html.
25. U.S. Department of State, *Country Reports on*

Terrorism 2008.

26. U.S. Department of State, *Country Reports on Terrorism 2008*.
27. U.S. Department of State, *Country Reports on Terrorism 2008*.
28. Saad Eddine Lamzouwaq, "As ISIS Weakens, Morocco Faces Threat of Returning Fighters," *Morocco World News*, July 12, 2017, https://www.moroccoworldnews.com/2017/07/222883/as-isis-weakens-morocco-faces-threat-of-returning-fighters/.
29. Mohammed Masbah, *Moroccan Foreign Fighters*, German Institute for International and Security Affairs (SWP) Comments, no. 46 (October 2016), https://www.swp-berlin.org/fileadmin/contents/products/comments/2015C46_msb.pdf.
30. "Morocco Foils Terrorist Attacks, Arrests 52 Militants," *Asharq al-Awsat English*, July 27, 2016, http://english.aawsat.com/2016/07/article55355229/morocco-foils-terrorist-attacks-arrests-52-militants.
31. Amira El Masaiti, "ISIS 'Defeated' in Iraq, 6,000 African Fighters to Return to Africa," *Morocco World News*, December 11, 2017, https://www.moroccoworldnews.com/2017/12/236037/isis-defeated-iraq-6000-african-fighters-return-africa/.
32. Moroccan Constitution of 2011, Preamble, http://www.al-bab.com/arab/docs/morocco/constitution_2011.htm.
33. See, for example, Moha Ennaji, "Illegal Migration From Morocco To Europe," Paper presented before the 7th international Metropolis conference, Oslo, Norway, September 10, 2002, http://international.metropolis.net/events/Metromed/Ennaji_e.pdf.
34. Andrea Elliott, "Where Boys Grow Up To Be Jihadis," *New York Times Magazine*, November 25, 2007, 16.
35. Erlanger and Mekhennet, "Islamic Radicalism Slows Moroccan Reforms."
36. Francesco Cavatorta and Emanuela Dalmasso, "Liberal Outcomes through Undemocratic Means: The Reform of the *Code du statut personnel* in Morocco," *Journal of Modern African Studies* 47, no. 4 (2009), 487-506.
37. U.S. Department of State, *Country Reports on Terrorism 2008*.

38. U.S. Department of State, *Country Reports on Terrorism 2008*..
39. Fatima Zahra Salhi, Ilham Chafik, and Nezha Nassi, "The Mourchidates of Morocco," in Maureen E. Fiedler, ed., *Breaking through the Stained Glass Ceiling: Women Religious Leaders in Their Own Words* (New York: Seabury Press, 2010), 28-30.
40. "S.M. le Roi adresse un discours à la Nation à l'occasion du 63ème anniversaire de la Révolution du Roi et du Peuple, " Maghreb Arabe Presse, August 2016, http://www.mapnews.ma/fr/activites-royales/sm-le-roi-adresse-un-discours-la-nation-loccasion-du-63-eme-anniversaire-de-la-rev.
41. Kamailoudini Tagba, "Morocco Sets Up New Foundation for African Ulemas," *North Africa Post*, June 8, 2016, http://northafricapost.com/12452-morocco-sets-new-foundation-african-ulemas.html.
42. Erlanger and Mekhennet, "Islamic Radicalism Slows Moroccan Reforms."
43. Erlanger and Mekhennet, "Islamic Radicalism Slows Moroccan Reforms."
44. Tossa, "Morocco's Fight Against Terrorism."
45. Tossa, "Morocco's Fight Against Terrorism."
46. U.S. Department of State, *Country Reports on Terrorism 2015*.
47. See J. Peter Pham, "Morocco's Momentum," *The Journal of International Security Affairs* 22 (Spring 2012), 13-20.
48. See J. Peter Pham, "Not Another Failed State: Towards a Realistic Solution of the Western Sahara," *Journal of the Middle East and Africa* 1, no. 1 (Spring 2010), 1-24.
49. Secretary of State Hillary Rodham Clinton, Remarks with Moroccan Foreign Minister Taieb Fassi Fihri, March 23, 2011, archived at http://www.state.gov/secretary/rm/2011/03/158895.htm.
50. United Nations Secretary-General Ban Ki-moon, quoted in Tim Witcher, "Ban says Western Sahara Risks being Drawn into Mali War," Agence France-Presse, April 9, 2013, http://www.google.com/hostednews/afp/article/ALeqM5iOnupKvBuc8I_
51. "Western Sahara: UN Chief Urges Morocco and

Polisario Front to De-escalate Tensions in Buffer Strip," UN News Center, Febraury 25, 2017, http://www.firstpost.com/world/un-secretary-general-antonio-guterres-expresses-concerns-over-spike-in-tensions-in-disputed-western-sahara-4291023.html.

52. Tim Witcher, "Ban says Western Sahara Risks being Drawn into Mali War."
53. See J. Peter Pham, "The Dangerous 'Pragmatism' of Al-Qaeda in the Islamic Maghreb," J*ournal of the Middle East and Africa* 2, no. 1 (January-June 2011), 15-29.
54. Three aid workers, one Italian and two Spaniards, were kidnapped from a Polisario-controlled camp in southern Algeria in October 2011 and eventually transferred to the control of the Movement for Unity and Jihad in West Africa (MUJAO), which extorted a ransom of €15 million for their release in July 2012. See "Rebels: $18.4 Million Paid for Hostage Release," Associated Press, July 20, 2012, http://bigstory.ap.org/article/rebels-184-million-paid-hostage-release.
55. Quoted in "Morocco severs ties with Iran, accusing it of backing Polisario Front," Reuters, May 1, 2018, https://www.reuters.com/article/us-morocco-iran/morocco-severs-ties-with-iran-over-support-for-west-sahara-polisario-front-official-idUSKBN1I23VF .

25 The Palestinian Territories

Quick Facts

Population: *West Bank*: 2,747,943, *Gaza Strip*: 1,795,183
Area: *West Bank*: 5,860 sq km *Gaza Strip*: 360 sq km
Ethnic Groups: *West Bank*: Palestinian Arab and others 83%, Jewish 17% *Gaza Strip*: Palestinian Arab
Religions: *West Bank*: Muslim 80-85% (predominately Sunni), Jewish 12-14%, Christian 1-2.5% (mainly Greek Orthodox), other, unaffiliated, unspecified <1% *Gaza Strip*: Muslim (predominately Sunni) 98-99%, Christian<1%, other, unaffiliated, unspecified <1%
Government Type: PLO/Fatah (contested)
GDP (official exchange rate): *West Bank*: $9.828 billion, *Gaza Strip*: $2.938 billion

Map and Quick Facts derived in part from the CIA World Factbook (Last Updated September 2018)

Introduction

The Palestinian National Authority (PA or PNA) was created in accordance with the 1993 Oslo Accords. Under the subsequent "Oslo Process," the PA assumed the responsibilities of Israeli military administration in parts of the West Bank and Gaza Strip ("Area A"), and was expected to expand that territory through final status negotiations. The PA includes a Palestinian Legislative Council (PLC), a legislative body with 132 seats elected from Gaza and the West Bank. As a result of the last Palestinian legislative elections, held in 2006, Hamas became the largest faction in the PLC, with 72 seats. However, the rival Fatah faction, backed by Western governments concerned about Hamas' continued militancy, undermined the rule of subsequent Hamas-dominated governments. After more than a year of tension, Hamas forcibly seized control of Gaza in 2007. The two territories remained under separate rule for seven years. In June 2014, Hamas and Fatah forged an interim unity government, with the aim of holding elections to formally re-unify. But soon thereafter, conflict between Gaza and Israel erupted. It became clear that Hamas remained in full control of the territory, and commanded a formidable rocket arsenal that had the capacity to reach deep into Israeli territory. A follow-up reconciliation agreement in October 2017 also failed to end the division, with Hamas unwilling to relinquish its weapons and the PA/Fatah unwilling to reassume civil control over Gaza. Hamas remains the true power broker in Gaza, while Fatah maintains an iron grip on the West Bank. Moreover, Hamas remains the most influential Islamist movement in the Gaza Strip, but other Islamist groups have also gained support from the Palestinian public.

Islamist Activity

Hamas

"Hamas" means "zeal" in Arabic, and is an Arabic acronym for Ḥarakat al-Muqāwamah al-ʾIslāmiyyah (the Islamic Resistance Movement). The group is primarily concentrated in the Gaza Strip, but does have support in pockets of the West Bank. The group was founded as a splinter group of the Muslim Brotherhood in December 1987, during the early days of the intifada (uprising) against Israel. The Brotherhood refused to engage in violence against Israel, but Hamas' founders believed that it was a duty to engage in "resistance." According to one insider's account, the secretive organization's founders included Sheikh Ahmad Yassin, Hassan Yousef, Ayman Abu Taha, Jamil Hamami, Mahmud Muslih, Muhammed Jamal al-Natsah, and Jamal Mansour.[1]

In addition to its immediate goal of destroying the State of Israel, Hamas' 1988 mithaq (founding charter) illustrates the organization's commitment to universal Islamist principles. This is demonstrated by its slogan: "Allah is its goal [theocratic rule], the Prophet is its model [importance of the Sunna], the Qur'an its Constitution [sharia], Jihad [violence] is its path and death for the sake of Allah is the loftiest of its wishes."[2] While most Hamas members are Palestinian Sunni Arabs, the charter welcomes all Muslims who: "embraces its faith, ideology, follows its program, keeps its secrets, and wants to belong to its ranks and carry out the duty."[3]

The Hamas charter also conveys the conviction that Palestine is waqf, or land endowed to Muslims by Allah because it was "conquered by the companions of the Prophet."[4] Hamas also clearly defines nationalism as "part of the religious creed,"[5] thereby universalizing the notion of "nationalism" to include the entire

Muslim umma (community).[6]

To achieve its immediate goal of an Islamic Palestinian state, Hamas has steadfastly denounced the 1993 Oslo Accords, the 2007 Annapolis conference, and all other diplomatic efforts to establish a lasting peace in the region as a "contradiction to the principles of the Islamic Resistance Movement."[7] However, when addressing Western audiences, Hamas leaders such as Gaza-based Ismail Haniyeh and politburo chief Khaled Meshal have stated that they are willing to recognize Israel along pre-1967 borders.[8] Yet, other senior Hamas officials, such as Mahmoud al Zahar, bluntly state that there are no leaders within Hamas willing to acknowledge the pre-1967 borders or live at peace with Israel.[9]

Hamas gained the support of a significant portion of the Palestinian people by providing social and welfare services and by presenting itself as Israel's implacable foe, as well as a pious opponent of the more corrupt and ossified Fatah faction, whose officials also comprise most of the leadership of the Palestine Liberation Organization (PLO) and the PA. Indeed, Hamas candidates ran under the name "Change and Reform List" in the 2006 legislative elections.[10] Since its violent takeover of Gaza in 2007, Hamas has taken steps to Islamize the society. However, there are indications that this may have only served to undermine the movement's authority.[11] Additionally, press reports indicate that Hamas has been losing popularity as a result of its inability to deal with Gaza's festering economic and social problems, among other issues.[12]

Following the attacks of September 11, 2001, the United States made efforts to cut the flow of cash to countless terror groups, including Hamas. Funds from Saudi Arabia, long identified as a top sponsor of Hamas, slowed following the Kingdom's decision to cut back on funding *jihadi* groups in 2004, after suffering attacks by a local al-Qaeda affiliate.[13] However, Iran, the world's leading state sponsor of terrorism, filled the void.

Iran soon became Hamas' primary state sponsor, with hundreds of millions of dollars pledged and delivered.[14] Iranian largesse was an important source of income for Hamas, and that revenue stream was significantly and adversely impacted over time as U.S.-led sanctions sapped the Islamic Republic's cash reserves. Thereafter, Tehran cut most, if not all, financial assistance when tension arose between it and Hamas over attitudes toward the Assad regime in Syria. The Iranians strongly supported the embattled Syrian leader, even as he slaughtered Sunnis and Palestinians in the country's ongoing civil war. Hamas, however, did not. As a result, it vacated its headquarters in Damascus, where it had been based, and reportedly turned to new patrons, including Qatar and Turkey.[15] Recent press reports indicate that, following the decline of the Muslim Brotherhood regionally in 2013, Hamas and Iran may now be seeking to restore their ties.[16]

Hamas augments its funds from state sponsors with donations from private charities (the most notorious being the Texas-based Holy Land Foundation, now defunct, which channeled $12 million to the organization before it was proscribed[17]), as well as deep-pocketed donors around the world. For more than a decade Hamas also extracted significant tax revenues from the subterranean tunnels connecting the Gaza Strip to the Sinai Peninsula, through which a great many products, including weapons, flowed. However, since the overthrow of the Muslim Brotherhood-affiliated government of Mohammed Morsi in July 2013, Egyptian authorities have shut down hundreds of smuggling tunnels along the Egypt-Gaza border. According to officials in Gaza, the closure of these tunnels is currently causing the Gaza economy to suffer monthly losses of approximately $230 million.[18] More recently, further taxation on wider swathes of Gazan economic life was instituted in order to address the shortfall in funding.[19]

Hamas, along with other like-minded violent factions, has fired more than 15,000 rockets and mortars into Israel since 2001.[20] The group draws a distinction between its political activities and its paramilitary attacks. However, this is a false distinction, as all of the movement's component parts contribute to "resistance" activities.[21] According to Hamas founder Sheikh Ahmad Yassin, "We cannot separate the wing from the body. If we do so, the body will not be able to fly."[22] Since 1993, the military wing of Hamas, the Izz ad-Din al-Qassam Brigades, is believed to have killed over five hundred people in more than 350 separate terrorist attacks, many of them suicide bombings.[23]

Although attacks against Israel from Gaza slowed in 2013, Israeli authorities foiled numerous Hamas terror plots in the West Bank.[24] Israeli officials identified Gaza-based Hamas official Fathi Hamad[25] as well as Turkey-based Hamas leader Saleh al-Aruri[26] as key catalysts for many of these plots.[27] Meanwhile, the rocket war of July-August 2014 revealed that Hamas maintains a significant arsenal, primarily via Iran, which gives the faction the ability to fire deep into Israeli territory.

After the 2014 war, Hamas continued to build tunnels into Israel and attempt to replenish its rocket supply.[28] Hamas regularly uses items meant for humanitarian aid to construct rockets.[29] The group has also carried out attacks across the West Bank, such as the fatal shooting of an Israeli couple in October of 2015.[30] The group has also planned attacks against Palestinian Authority leader Mahmoud Abbas, one of which was foiled by Shin Bet, the Israeli domestic intelligence service.[31] Meanwhile, Hamas' cooperation with the ISIS affiliate group in Sinai, originally known as Ansar Beit al-Maqdis, escalated tensions with the Egyptian government.[32] Hamas had regularly trained and treated Islamic State fighters before sending them back into the Sinai Peninsula.[33] Since 2017, however, these Hamas-ISIS ties have reportedly been eroded at the request of the Egyptian government, amid Hamas efforts to repair relations with Cairo.[34]

Hamas has also tried to rally public support for a third intifada, or uprising, in the West Bank. Since the start of the wave of terror that hit Israel from late-2015 into mid-2016, Hamas has either celebrated terrorists killed in attacks against Israelis or claimed attackers as members of the group. After three Israeli soldiers were wounded in an attack in February 2016, Hamas held a rally in Gaza.[35] A similar rally was held in April 2016 after a member of Hamas blew up a bus in Jerusalem. That attack wounded 21 Israelis.[36] In September 2016, the international NGO World Vision halted funding to Gaza projects after Israel alleged one of its employees, Mohammad el-Halabi, was funneling the foreign funds to Hamas.[37] In December 2016, the Israeli Shin Bet uncovered a 20-member Hamas cell in the West Bank that was plotting suicide bombings in major Israeli cities.[38]

With economic, humanitarian, and social conditions continuing to deteriorate in Gaza, Hamas began supporting protest marches on the border with Israel in March 2018.[39] The goal of the marches was nominally the "right of return" for Palestinians who had been evicted or fled from their lands in 1948, although Hamas' real goal was to increase international attention on Gaza's plight in order to end the Israeli and Egyptian blockade.[40] As of July 2018, after months of weekly demonstrations and over 100 dead due to Israeli fire (including many reported militants), Hamas has still not met this objective. Reports indicate that a long-term truce with Israel may be a possibility, as is another round of direct conflict if conditions in the territory do not improve.[41]

Palestinian Islamic Jihad (PIJ)

Harakat al-Jihād al-Islāmi fi Filastīn (Palestinian Islamic Jihad, or PIJ) was founded sometime between 1979 and 1981 by several Muslim Brotherhood members who, like Hamas, felt that the Brotherhood was too moderate and not fully committed to the principle of jihad and the establishment of a Palestinian state governed according to sharia. In addition, the founding members were also inspired by the 1979 Iranian Revolution.[42] Founders Fathi Shikaki and Abd al-Aziz Awda forged an organization whose ultimate aim was to destroy Israel through jihad. Unlike Hamas, which is amenable to a hudna (tactical truce) with Israel, PIJ explicitly rejects any and all forms of recognition of the Jewish State.[43]

The exact size of PIJ, a highly secretive organization, is unknown. Most estimates suggest that membership ranges from a few hundred to a few thousand.[44] The ethnic make-up of the group is overwhelmingly Palestinian Sunni, though there have been reports of increasing Shi'ite presence, a direct result of Iranian support.[45]

While PIJ was known for its suicide bombing attacks during the Second Intifada (2000-2005), in recent years the group has primarily focused on rocket and sniper attacks, as well as the construction of cross-border attack tunnels, from the Gaza Strip. The IDF has tried to thin PIJ's ranks through targeted killings and arrests in recent years. The effectiveness of these actions is as yet unclear.

In January 2014, the U.S. State Department designated Ziyad al Nakhalah, the Deputy Secretary General of Palestinian Islamic Jihad (PIJ), as a Specially Designated Global Terrorist (SDGT).[46] Other leaders of the group have yet to be designated. Like Hamas, PIJ's activity against Israel from Gaza declined in 2013. However, it continued to plot and carry out attacks from the West Bank.[47] It subsequently played a significant role in the rocket war of July 2014, firing Iranian-made or Iranian-furnished rockets deep into Israeli territory.

PIJ has also been a strong supporter of the wave of violence (known as the "knife intifada" by some) which swept across Israel in late-2015 and into mid-2016. In November 2015, PIJ and Hamas announced "new methods of resistance" against Israel.[48] In May of 2016 it was revealed that Iran would renew its financial support to PIJ after nearly two years.[49] In Tehran, PIJ leader Ramadan Shallah praised Iran for its support of the "Palestinian intifada."[50] When municipal elections were initially announced in the West Bank and Gaza in August 2016, PIJ boycotted the elections and instead urged Palestinians to escalate the violence, to minimal effect.[51]

PIJ has played an integral role in the Gaza marches on the Israel border, begun in March 2018, with several of its members reported killed by Israeli fire during the two months of unrest.[52] More recently, in late May 2018, PIJ was held responsible for starting a major escalation in rocket and mortar fire from Gaza into southern Israel—a sign, according to some, of a renewed Iranian influence on Palestinian politics.[53]

Popular Resistance Committees

The Popular Resistance Committees (PRC) is made up of "former armed activists of different factions,"[54] and is likely the third largest violent group in the Palestinian territories, after Hamas and PIJ. According to the IDF, the PRC often "acts as a sub-contractor" for Iran, and is heavily influenced by Hezbollah.[55]

Since its founding in 2000, through its military wing known as the Al-Nasser Salah al-Din Brigades, the PRC has taken responsibility for a number of terror attacks against Israel,[56] and an attack on U.S. personnel in Gaza in 2003.[57] Some of the group's operations have been conducted jointly with Hamas.[58] It has also reportedly worked with Salafi jihadist groups operating in the Sinai Peninsula abutting Gaza.[59]

In February 2014, the Israeli Air Force targeted a PRC operative who was known to work with the Sinai-based jihadist group Ansar Bayt al Maqdis.[60] In recent years, the group has become increasingly Salafi in outlook, as conveyed through Sunni *jihadist* forums online.[61] In 2006, Israeli officials warned that the PRC's leadership was in contact with "Global Jihad sources in North Africa and the Sinai."[62]

In light of Hamas' attempts to prevent unauthorized rocket attacks against Israel, the group has at times found itself at odds with Hamas. In July 2013, for example, the PRC issued a communiqué that demanded that Hamas stop its arrest of the mujahideen in the Gaza Strip.[63] The PRC maintained a low profile during the 2014 rocket war, although its personnel are still active when trying to provoke Israeli retribution against Hamas. Israel holds Hamas responsible for militant activity emanating from Gaza. An improvised explosive device (IED) detonated on the Israel-Gaza border in February 2018 against Israel Defense Forces (IDF) personnel was deemed to be a PRC operation.[64]

Al Aqsa Martyrs Brigades

The Al Aqsa Martyrs Brigades is the military wing of the secular Fatah faction,[65] which has adopted Islamist symbols and slogans that stand in stark contrast to those of the secular Fatah faction. The group was formally designated as a Foreign Terrorist Organization by the United States in March 2002, largely for its actions inside Israel and the West Bank, where it carried out suicide bombings and small arms attacks against Israel during the second Intifada.[66]

Over the past few years, however, the group has largely remained dormant. The group has primarily operated out of the Gaza Strip, with a handful of operations in the West Bank.[67] According to the U.S. Department of State, "Iran has exploited al-Aqsa's lack of resources and formal leadership by providing funds and guidance, mostly through Hezbollah facilitators."[68]

The primary acts of violence carried out by the group in recent years have been rocket attacks from Gaza into southern Israel.[69] Press reports, however, have suggested that the group may seek a comeback in the West Bank.[70]

Indeed, in March 2016, thirteen Palestinians were injured in firefights between the Palestinian Authority and members of the

Aqsa Martyrs in Nablus.[71] As clashes heated up again in Nablus in August 2016, the PA arrested a local leader of the Brigades, Ahmed Izz Halawa, and beat him to death.[72] Halawa's death sparked mass protests in the West Bank.[73] Concern on the part of the PA was that the group's members, still heavily armed and now operating more as criminal enterprises, were being coopted by exiled Fatah leader Mohammed Dahlan.[74] Gunfights between PA security forces and local gangs erupt sporadically in the wake of PA arrest operations into Nablus' Balata refugee camp, as was the case in February 2018.[75]

Jaysh al-Islam (JI)

Jaysh al-Islam (JI), or "Army of Islam," is closely linked to the Dughmush clan of Gaza, and is believed to have several hundred members.[76] The Salafi group was founded in 2005, and similar to other Palestinian Islamist splinter groups, it has global jihadist objectives and is believed to have ties to al-Qaeda.[77]

The group's most notable action was the March 2007 kidnapping of BBC journalist Alan Johnston in order to negotiate the release of al-Qaeda-affiliated Islamist militant Abu Qatada, who was then jailed in the United Kingdom.[78] The Johnston kidnapping, as well as an attack that killed five senior Hamas officials, led to a clash with Hamas in August 2008 that is said to have weakened the group significantly.[79]

The group's affinity for al-Qaeda has been widely documented. Days after the death of Osama bin Laden in May 2011, the group released a eulogy for the fallen al-Qaeda leader.[80] In May 2011, the group was designated as a terrorist group by the U.S. Department of State. The accompanying press release noted that the group "worked with Hamas and is attempting to develop closer al Qaeda contacts."[81] In 2006, the group sent a letter to senior al-Qaeda leaders, asking whether it was permissible to accept money from other groups in Gaza that did not share their ideology, specifically nationalists or Iranian-backed factions.[82] Israeli officials also noted in 2006, "alleged efforts by Mumtaz Dughmush to make contact with Global Jihad sources, possibly to include those responsible for the bombing of the USS Cole."[83]

During Israel's Operation Pillar of Defense in November 2012, the Mujahideen Shura Council in the Environs of Jerusalem, a consolidation of Salafi jihadist groups in Gaza, and JI conducted joint rocket attacks against Israel.[84] According to Israeli officials, JI operated training camps in Gaza for jihadists who subsequently went to fight in Yemen, Syria, and Egypt's Sinai Peninsula, among other locations.[85] Hamas allowed these camps to operate in Gaza.[86] In more recent years, Hamas has launched a crackdown on Salafist groups operating from Gaza, including most likely JI, in a bid to rehabilitate its relationship with the Egyptian government and curb rocket fire against Israel.[87]

Jaysh al-Ummah (JU)

Ideologically affiliated with al-Qaeda, Jaysh al-Ummah (JU), or the "Army of the Nation," believes that "the sons of Zion are occupiers and they must be uprooted completely… We will fight them as we are ordered by God and the Prophet Mohammad."[88] The Salafi jihadist group was formed in either 2006[89] or 2007,[90] and is led by Abu Hafs al-Maqdisi. While the group's membership number is kept secret, it lacks the capability to strike targets outside of Gaza, suggesting it is small in size.[91]

JU has been very critical of Hamas since its inception. Most notably, it has criticized Hamas for arresting its members as they were attempting to carry out terrorist operations.[92] Hamas does appear to allow the group to conduct *dawa*-related activity in the Gaza Strip, however.[93]

JU has warned against the increasing influence of Iran and its proxy Palestinian Islamic Jihad in the Gaza Strip. While the group has denied an operational connection to al-Qaeda, it has a similar ideological outlook.[94] We are "connected to our brothers in Al Qaeda by our beliefs, we and they are following the great Prophet. Osama bin Laden is our brother and we appreciate him very much," a JU official stated.[95]

Since 2013, the group has issued a number of statements and videos that belie its Salafi beliefs. In January 2013, the jihadist group issued a video urging "all the mujahideen all over Earth to target Iranian interests everywhere."[96] In a separate message released in January 2013, JU called for greater support for jihadists in Mali: "[W]e will support and be loyal and aid our mujahideen monotheist brothers in

Mali without limits."[97] In August 2013, Abu Hafs al Maqdisi, JU's leader, called on Egyptians to wage jihad against Egyptian army chief General Abdel Fattah el-Sisi.[98] And, in November 2013, the group issued a eulogy for Hakeemullah Mehsud, the former emir of the Movement of the Taliban in Pakistan.[99] JU is believed to have fought alongside other militant factions against Israel during the 2014 Gaza War.[100] As of June 2018, JU was still launching fundraising appeals to supporters on various social media platforms.[101]

Hizb-ut-Tahrir (HuT)

The Palestinian "Party of Liberation" is a local affiliate of the larger HuT movement, which has a presence in some 45 countries. The group's immediate aim is to establish a caliphate and implement sharia throughout the Muslim world.[102]

Despite HuT's well-documented enmity toward Israel, the group does not directly engage in terrorism, nor do its branches maintain an armed wing. Rather, HuT seeks to "agitate and educate."[103] While no reliable figures can be found regarding HuT's membership in the Palestinian Territories, it is widely considered to be small, despite its organic base of support.

To voice opposition to the PLO's participation in the 2007 Annapolis peace summit, HuT organized a demonstration with over 2,500 attendees in Hebron, culminating in the killing of one protestor by PA police.[104] Soon after, over 10,000 HuT supporters gathered in Al-Bireh under the slogan: "the caliphate is the rising force."[105] In July 2010, PA security forces arrested thousands of HuT supporters at a rally in Ramallah, which was banned by the PA.[106]

In 2011, PA forces disrupted one of the group's rallies in the West Bank.[107] This was followed by reports of a campaign of arrests of HuT members by the Palestinian Authority.[108] In August 2011, the group slammed Palestinian Authority President Mahmoud Abbas, when he suggested that NATO may have a presence in a future Palestinian state.[109]

Despite intermittent crackdowns by Palestinian security forces in the West Bank, the Islamist movement has continued to hold events there.[110] Most recently, in February 2014, HuT accused Palestinian Authority security forces in the West Bank of arresting its members for criticizing President Abbas.[111] The group had a significant presence (flags, mainly) during the unrest in the Jerusalem neighborhood of Shuafat, following the murder of a Palestinian teenager by Israeli extremists.

Mujahideen Shura Council in the Environs of Jerusalem (MSC)

The MSC, a Salafi *jihadist* group, was formed in the Gaza Strip in 2012. The group is a consolidation of Ansar al Sunnah and the Tawhid and Jihad Group in Jerusalem.[112] In November 2012, one of the group's leaders stated that the MSC aims to "fight the Jews for the return of Islam's rule, not only in Palestine, but throughout the world."[113]

While the exact size of the group is unknown, it has taken responsibility for a number of rocket attacks against Israel,[114] some of which have been carried out with Jaysh al Islam.[115] In addition, MSC took responsibility for a June 2012 bombing and shooting attack that killed one Israeli civilian.[116] According to a video released by the MSC, the June attack was "a gift to our brothers in Qaedat al Jihad [al-Qaeda] and Sheikh [Ayman al-] Zawahiri" and a retaliation for the killing of former al-Qaeda emir Osama bin Laden.[117]

Several Israeli air strikes targeted MSC operatives in 2012. After those attacks, jihadi groups such as al-Qaeda in the Arabian Peninsula (AQAP) and leaders like al-Qaeda head Ayman al-Zawahiri posted eulogies online.

The MSC was one of several Salafi jihadi groups that took part in the November 2012 conflict with Israel. Following the ceasefire, the group said that "[W]e truly are not a party to the signing of this truce between the Palestinian factions and the Jews."[118] Throughout 2013, the MSC, through the Ibn Taymiyyah Media Center, its media wing, promoted the jihad in Syria as well as the efforts of the Sinai-based jihadist group Ansar Bayt al Maqdis.[119] In November 2013, three MSC operatives were reported killed by Israeli security forces in Yatta, near Hebron in the southern West Bank, ahead of planned terrorist attacks by the cell.[120]

Harakat as-Sabirin Nasran li-Filastin

Harakat as-Sabirin Nasran li-Filastin (as-Sabirin), or "The Movement of the Patient Ones for the Liberation of Palestine" is a new, Iran-sponsored terror group in Gaza.[121] Founded in early

2014, the group burst onto the scene when one of its fighters, Nizar Saeed Issa, died in a mysterious explosion in the Gaza refugee camp of Jabalya.[122] Since then, As-Sabirin has lost two fighters, Ahmad Sharif as-Sarhi and Mus'ab al-Khayr al-Sakafi, in apparent clashes with Israel.

As-Sabirin is Shia group in a predominantly Sunni territory. Its flag and logo are derived from those of Hezbollah, and its fighters are pulled from another Iranian proxy: Palestinian Islamic Jihad. Its charter states that "jihad is the way of Allah to open doors to paradise… and in particular our journey faces the might enemies of the racist Zionist body and on its head America the great Satan."[123]

As-Sabirin is headed by Hisham Salem. Formerly a commander in PIJ, Salem hails from a prominent family in the Beit Lahia neighborhood in Gaza.[124] Salem was jailed in 1996 by the Palestinian Authority for organizing suicide attacks in Israel and during the second intifada was placed on Israel's most wanted terrorist list.[125] He has run several charities in the Gaza Strip, one of which, al-Baqiyat al-Salihat, was shut down by Hamas for spreading Shi'ism.[126]

The Iranian proxy group receives approximately $10 million per year from Tehran, which is typically smuggled through tunnels into Gaza.[127] Local reports suggest fighters in the group receive a salary of 250 to 300 U.S. dollars per month, while senior officials make up to 700 dollars a month.[128]

In February 2016, the Palestinian Authority broke up an as-Sabirin cell in Bethlehem.[129] According to PA security officials, the group was attempting to convert families in the West Bank to Shiism.[130] That same month, Salem's home in Gaza was targeted in a bombing attack; no injuries were reported. In January 2018, the U.S. State Department announced that as-Sabirin was now a "Specially-Designated Global Terrorist Group."[131]

Islamism and Society

Evidence suggests that Hamas was, in the past, more popular among Palestinians than its secular rival, Fatah. This was true even before Hamas' unexpected victory in the PA's 2006 legislative election, and this trend continued after the organization's abrupt seizure of power in Gaza in June 2007.

Some analysts contend that such support is attributable more to a rejection of Fatah's alleged corruption than sincere support for Hamas' Islamism and militancy.[132] However, it may also be tied to the lack of popular support for the PLO's peace negotiations with Israel. A 2013 poll from the Palestinian Center for Policy and Survey Research found that more than 54 percent of Palestinians in Gaza oppose the idea of a two-state-solution.[133] Furthermore, data collected the same year by the Pew Research Center found that 62 percent of Muslims in the Palestinian Territories believe suicide bombings can be often or sometimes justified.[134] However, since Hamas' takeover of Gaza in 2007, anecdotal evidence suggests that the daily challenges of governance have eroded some of the popular support Hamas garnered through its resistance of Israel.[135] In other words, it is hard to maintain popular support as a revolutionary movement when saddled with mundane problems. As one senior Hamas leader in the West Bank acknowledged in 2014, "the sovereign loses."[136],

Under both Hamas rule in Gaza and PLO rule in the West Bank, evidence suggests that Christian minorities in both territories suffer discrimination and persecution, including religiously-motivated attacks on churches, destruction of crosses and altars, and the kidnapping and forced conversion of Christian girls.[137] Admittedly, Christians live with significantly more freedom in the West Bank—and are publicly acknowledged by the PA government—especially relative to Gaza since Hamas took control, where Christians reportedly "feel increasingly unwelcome."[138]

Islamism and the State

The active role of violent Islamist groups in the West Bank has dropped precipitously since the 2007 Palestinian civil war. Fearing a Hamas takeover in the West Bank, the United States and other Western states have been furnishing the Palestinian Authority government in the West Bank with military training, weaponry, financing, and intelligence in order to more efficiently battle Hamas and other factions. Moreover, close security coordination between the PA and Israel has remained intact in the battle against what they perceive to be their common Islamist enemies. This approach has undoubtedly been a success, with the West Bank over the past decade relatively stable compared to preceding years.[139]

With Hamas entrenched in Gaza, it appears unlikely that Israel will be able to neutralize the group with stand-off military power alone. This was made clear again during the 2014 conflict; even as Israel pounded hundreds of Hamas targets, long-range rockets continued to strike deep into Israeli territory. This has prompted some to propose that Israel should enter into negotiations with its long-time foe. Others contend that since Hamas is at one of its weakest points, both economically and politically, since its founding, now may be the time to cripple the group. Yet, the question of who would control Gaza after Hamas has prompted the Israelis to tread carefully. The threat of a bloody ground campaign to reoccupy the territory, in addition to potential anarchy afterwards, has counseled for a policy of restraint, at least so far.[140]

Endnotes

1. Mosab Hassan Yousef and Ron Brackin, *Son of Hamas: A Gripping Account of Terror, Betrayal, Political Intrigue, and Unthinkable Choices* (Carol Stream: Tyndale House, 2010), 253-255.
2. "Hamas Covenant 1988," *The Avalon Project*, n.d., http://avalon.law.yale.edu/20th_century/hamas.asp.
3. "Hamas Covenant 1988," *The Avalon Project*, n.d.
4. "Hamas Covenant 1988," *The Avalon Project*, n.d.
5. "Hamas Covenant 1988," *The Avalon Project*, n.d.
6. See, for example, "Hamas MP and Cleric Yunis Al-Astal: The Jews Were Brought to Palestine for the "Great Massacre" Through Which Allah Will "Relieve Humanity of Their Evil"," *Middle East Media Research Institute*, May 11, 2011, http://www.memri.org/clip/en/0/0/0/0/0/0/2934.htm.
7. "Hamas Covenant 1988."
8. Amira Hass, "Haniyeh: Hamas Willing To Accept Palestinian State With 1967 Borders," *Ha'aretz*, September 11, 2008, http://www.haaretz.com/news/haniyeh-hamas-willing-to-accept-palestinian-state-with-1967-borders-1.256915; "Meshal: Hamas Seeks Palestinian State Based on 1967 Borders," *Ha'aretz*,

May 5, 2009, http://www.haaretz.com/news/meshal-hamas-seeks-palestinian-state-based-on-1967-borders-1.275412.

9. Shlomi Eldar, "Hamas Official Says 'Abbas Doesn't Represent Anyone'," *Al Monitor*, February 20, 2014, http://www.al-monitor.com/pulse/originals/2014/02/mahmoud-al-zahar-hamas-recognizing-israel-mahmoud-abbas.html.
10. "Who's Who in the Palestinian Elections," BBC News, January 16, 2006. http://news.bbc.co.uk/2/hi/middle_east/4601420.stm
11. Jonathan Schanzer, "The Talibanization of Gaza: A Liability for the Muslim Brotherhood," Hudson Institute *Current Trends in Islamist Ideology* 9, August 19, 2009, http://www.currenttrends.org/research/detail/the-talibanization-of-gaza-a-liability-for-the-muslim-brotherhood; Abeer Ayyoub, "Hamas Pushes Islamization of Gaza," *Al Monitor*, February 4, 2013, http://www.al-monitor.com/pulse/originals/2013/02/hamas-islamization-gaza.html.
12. Rasha Abou Jalal, "Hamas Sinks in Polls After Cutting Salaries to Public Servants," *Al Monitor*, February 20, 2014, http://www.al-monitor.com/pulse/originals/2014/02/hamas-gaza-salaries-payments-siege.html.
13. Matthew Levitt, "A Hamas Headquarters in Saudi Arabia," Washington Institute for Near East Policy *Policy Watch* 521, September 28, 2005, http://www.washingtoninstitute.org/policy-analysis/view/a-hamas-headquarters-in-saudi-arabia.
14. Nidal al-Mughrabi, "Hamas Gaza Leader Heads for Iran," Reuters, January 30, 2012, http://uk.reuters.com/article/2012/01/30/uk-palestinians-hamas-iran-idUKTRE80T14P20120130.
15. Jonathan Schanzer, "Hamas Rising," *Foreign Policy*, July 25, 2012, http://www.foreignpolicy.com/articles/2012/07/25/hamas_rising.
16. Harriet Sherwood, "Hamas and Iran Rebuild Ties Three Years After Falling Out Over Syria," *Guardian* (London), January 9, 2014, http://www.theguardian.com/world/2014/jan/09/hamas-iran-rebuild-ties-fall-

ing-out-syria.

17. "Five US Men Jailed for Allegedly Funding Hamas," Ma'an News Agency (Ramallah), May 28, 2009, http://maannews.net/eng/ViewDetails.aspx?ID=210849.
18. "Tunnel Closure 'Costs Gaza $230 Million Monthly,'" Agence France Presse, October 27, 2013, http://www.google.com/hostednews/afp/article/ALeqM5gj2-72tPr4jJFBW_e52ASHwGfy8g?docId=aa97be5f-8a83-45b7-9fdd-cf4bc0ec6d74.
19. Rushdi Abu Alouf, "Gazans Squeezed By Triple Taxes As Hamas Replaces Lost Income," *BBC News*, June 20, 2016. https://www.bbc.com/news/world-middle-east-36274631.
20. "Rocket Attacks on Israel From Gaza," *IDF Blog*, n.d, http://www.idfblog.com/facts-figures/rocket-attacks-toward-israel/; "2010 Annual Summary," Israel Security Agency, n.d., http://www.shabak.gov.il/SiteCollectionImages/english/TerrorInfo/reports/2010summary2-en.pdf.
21. Matthew Levitt, *Hamas: Politics, Charity and Terrorism in the Service of Jihad* (New Haven: Yale University Press, 2006).
22. U.S. Department of the Treasury, "U.S. Designates Five Charities Funding Hamas and Six Senior Hamas Leaders as Terrorist Entities," August 22, 2003, http://www.treasury.gov/press-center/press-releases/Pages/js672.aspx.
23. Bryony Jones, "Q&A: What is Hamas?" CNN, November 24, 2012, http://www.cnn.com/2012/11/16/world/meast/hamas-explainer/.
24. See, for example: David Barnett, "Hamas Terror Plot Targeting Jerusalem Mall Foiled," *Long War Journal – Threat Matrix*, September 1, 2013, http://www.longwarjournal.org/threat-matrix/archives/2013/09/hamas_terror_plot_targeting_je.php.
25. David Barnett, "Hamas Interior Minister Behind Terror Group's Activities in West Bank," *Long War Journal – Threat Matrix*, March 13, 2013, http://www.longwarjournal.org/threat-matrix/archives/2013/03/hamas_interior_minister_behind.php.
26. Amos Harel, "Hamas is Alive and Kicking in the West

Bank – But in Remote Control," *Ha'aretz* (Tel Aviv), December 21, 2013, http://www.haaretz.com/weekend/week-s-end/.premium-1.564568.

27. Israel Security Agency, "2013 Annual Summary," n.d., http://www.shabak.gov.il/English/EnTerrorData/Reports/Pages/2013AnnualSummary.aspx.
28. "Hamas Says it Continues to Build Tunnels to Attack Israel," *Huffington Post,* January 29, 2016. (http://www.huffingtonpost.com/huff-wires/20160129/ml-gaza-tunnels/?utm_hp_ref=world&ir=world)
29. "Israel Intercepts Materials for Building Tunnels, Rockets on their Way to Hamas," *The Tower,* May 27, 2016, http://www.thetower.org/3430oc-israel-intercepts-materials-for-building-tunnels-rockets-on-their-way-to-hamas/.
30. "5-Man Hamas Cell that Killed Naama and Eitam Henkin Arrested," *Times of Israel,* October 5, 2015, http://www.timesofisrael.com/shin-bet-terror-cell-behind-henkin-murders-arrested/.
31. Mitch Ginsburg, "Abbas Orders Probe into Hamas Coup Plot Revealed by Israel," *Times of Israel,* August 19, 2014, http://www.timesofisrael.com/abbas-orders-investigation-into-hamas-coup-plot-revealed-by-israel/.
32. Ehud Yaari, "Hamas and the Islamic State: Growing Cooperation in the Sinai," Washington Institute for Near East Policy *Policywatch* 2533, December 15, 2015, http://www.washingtoninstitute.org/policy-analysis/view/hamas-and-the-islamic-state-growing-cooperation-in-the-sinai.
33. "IDF General: IS Fighters Training with Hamas in Gaza," *Times of Israel,* May 13, 2016, http://www.timesofisrael.com/idf-general-is-fighters-entered-gaza-to-train-with-hamas/.
34. Iyad Abuheweila and Isabel Kershner, "ISIS Declares War on Hamas, and Gaza Families Disown Sons in Sinai," *New York Times*, January 10, 2018. https://www.nytimes.com/2018/01/10/world/middleeast/isis-hamas-sinai.html.
35. "Islamic Jihad, Hamas Officials Rally in Gaza to Support West Bank Shooting," Ma'an News Agency (Ramallah), February 1, 2016, http://www.maannews.com/

Content.aspx?id=770075.
36. Jack Moore, "Hamas Says Jerusalem Bus Bomb Shows Commitment to Third Intifada," *Newsweek,* April 29, 2016, http://www.newsweek.com/hamas-says-jerusalem-bus-bomb-shows-commitment-third-intifada-453845.
37. "World Vision Halts Gaza Projects and Cuts Jobs Amid Claims Funds Sent to Hamas," *The Guardian,* September 9, 2016, https://www.theguardian.com/world/2016/sep/10/world-vision-halts-gaza-projects-and-cuts-jobs-amid-claims-funds-sent-to-hamas.
38. Ilan Ben Zion, "Israel Busts Hamas Cell Planning Suicide Bombings in Jerusalem, Haifa," *The Times of Israel,* December 22, 2016, http://www.timesofisrael.com/israel-busts-hamas-cell-planning-suicide-bombings-in-jerusalem-haifa/.
39. Elior Levy and Yoav Zitun, "Situation in Gaza Approaches Critical Point," *Ynet News*, February 5, 2018. https://www.ynetnews.com/articles/0,7340,L-5090907,00.html.
40. Shlomi Eldar, "Hamas Focused on Ending the Blockade," Al Monitor, May 18, 2018. https://www.al-monitor.com/pulse/originals/2018/05/israel-palestinians-hamas-fatah-mahmoud-abbas-idf-border.html
41. Neri Zilber, "Israel and Hamas: Negotiating with Rockets and Bombs, " *The Daily Beast*, May 31, 2018.
42. Asmaa al-Ghoul, "Palestinian Islamic Jihad: Iran Supplies All Weapons in Gaza," *Al Monitor*, May 14, 2013, http://www.al-monitor.com/pulse/originals/2013/05/gaza-islamic-jihad-and-iranian-arms.html.
43. Holly Fletcher, "Palestinian Islamic Jihad," Council on Foreign Relations, April 10, 2008, http://www.cfr.org/israel/palestinian-islamic-jihad/p15984.
44. "Chapter 6. Foreign Terrorist Organizations," in U.S. Department of State, *Country Reports on Terrorism* 2011, July 31, 2012, http://www.state.gov/j/ct/rls/crt/2011/195553.htm; Abeer Ayyoub, "Iran Top Backer of Palestinian Islamic Jihad," *Al Monitor*, January 9, 2013, http://www.al-monitor.com/pulse/originals/2013/01/palestinian-islamic-jihad.html; Crispian Balmer and Nidal al-Mughrabi, "Single-Minded

Islamic Jihad Grows in Gaza's Shadows," Reuters, November 12, 2013, http://www.reuters.com/article/2013/11/12/us-palestinians-islamicjihad-idUSBRE9AB08720131112.

45. Avi Issacharoff, "Hamas Brutally Assaults Shi'ite Worshippers in Gaza." *Ha'aretz* (Tel Aviv), January 17, 2012, http://www.haaretz.com/news/middle-east/hamas-brutally-assaults-shi-ite-worshippers-in-gaza-1.407688.
46. David Barnett, "US Designates Deputy Secretary-General of Palestinian Islamic Jihad," *Long War Journal*, January 23, 2014, http://www.longwarjournal.org/archives/2014/01/us_designates_deputy.php.
47. See, for example, David Barnett, "Palestinian Islamic Jihad Operatives Behind Recent Bus Bombing Near Tel Aviv," *Long War Journal – Threat Matrix*, January 3, 2014, http://www.longwarjournal.org/threat-matrix/archives/2014/01/palestinian_islamic_jihad_oper.php.
48. "Hamas, Islamic Jihad Warn of 'New Methods of Resistance'," *Ma'an News Agency,* November 4, 2015. (http://www.maannews.com/Content.aspx?id=768645)
49. Maayan Groisman, "Iran to Renew Financial Support for Islamic Jihad After Two-Year Hiatus," *Jerusalem Post,* May 25, 2016, http://www.jpost.com/Middle-East/Reembracing-Islamic-Jihad-Iran-to-renew-financial-aid-for-Palestinian-terror-group-454968.
50. Groisman, "Iran to Renew Financial Support for Islamic Jihad After Two-Year Hiatus."
51. Adam Rasgon, "Islamic Jihad Calls to Escalate Intifada and Boycott Palestinian Elections," *The Jerusalem Post,* August 9, 2016, http://www.jpost.com/Arab-Israeli-Conflict/Islamic-Jihad-calls-to-escalate-intifada-as-it-boycotts-Palestinian-elections-463651.
52. Judah Ari Gross, "Hamas Official: 50 of the 62 Gazans Killed in Border Violence Were Our Members," Times of Israel, May 16, 2018. https://www.timesofisrael.com/hamas-official-50-of-the-people-killed-in-gaza-riots-were-members/.
53. Yaniv Kubovich, "Iran's Fighting Force in Gaza, Calling and Firing the Shots: This Is Islamic Jihad in Palestine," Haaretz, June 17, 2018. https://www.haaretz.

com/middle-east-news/iran/.premium-what-is-islamic-jihad-in-palestine-iran-s-fighting-force-in-gaza-calling-and-firing-the-shots-1.6158730.

54. "Who is the Palestinian Group Blamed for the Attacks?" Reuters, August 19, 2011, http://www.haaretz.com/news/diplomacy-defense/who-is-the-palestinian-group-blamed-for-the-attacks-1.379509.
55. "What Is The Popular Resistance Committee?" *IDF Blog*, March 10, 2012, http://www.idfblog.com/2012/03/10/popular-resistance-committee/; "Who is Organizing the PRC," Walla, June 28, 2006, http://news.walla.co.il/?w=//931483.
56. See, for example, Jack Khoury, "Palestinians Release Video Showing Gaza Anti-Tank Missile Hitting IDF Jeep," *Ha'aretz* (Tel Aviv), November 13, 2012, http://www.haaretz.com/news/diplomacy-defense/palestinians-release-video-showing-gaza-anti-tank-missile-hitting-idf-jeep.premium-1.477488.
57. "Palestinians Bomb US Convoy," *Guardian* (London), October 16, 2003, http://www.guardian.co.uk/world/2003/oct/16/israel.
58. "Who is the Palestinian Group Blamed for the Attacks?"
59. David Barnett, "Israeli Intelligence: Sinai is The 'Home of An Independent Jihadist Network,'" *Long War Journal*, October 3, 2012, http://www.longwarjournal.org/archives/2012/10/israeli_intelligence.php; Eli Lake, "Al Qaeda Linked to Israeli Bus Ambush," *Washington Times*, August 22, 2011, http://www.washingtontimes.com/news/2011/aug/22/al-qaeda-linked-to-israeli-bus-ambush/.
60. David Barnett, "Israel Targets Gaza Terror Operative Linked to Sinai-Based Ansar Jerusalem," *Long War Journal – Threat Matrix*, February 9, 2014, http://www.longwarjournal.org/threat-matrix/archives/2014/02/israel_targets_gaza_terror_ope.php.
61. "Category Archives: Nāṣir Ṣalāḥ ad-Dīn Brigades (PRC)," Jihadology, n.d., http://jihadology.net/category/na%E1%B9%A3ir-%E1%B9%A3ala%E1%B8%A5-ad-din-brigades-prc/.
62. Wikileaks, "Frances Townsend's November 12 Meet-

ing With ISA," November 24, 2006, http://wikileaks.org/cable/2006/11/06TELAVIV4603.html.

63. David Barnett, "Popular Resistance Committees Calls on Hamas to Stop Arrests of 'Mujahideen,'" *Long War Journal – Threat Matrix*, July 22, 2013, http://www.longwarjournal.org/threat-matrix/archives/2013/07/popular_resistance_committees.php.
64. Shlomi Eldar, "Hamas' Grip on Gaza Weakens," *Al Monitor*, February 20, 2018. https://www.al-monitor.com/pulse/originals/2018/02/israel-idf-gaza-hamas-popular-resistance-committees-war.html
65. Israel Ministry of Foreign Affairs, "The Involvement of Arafat, PA Senior Officials and Apparatuses in Terrorism against Israel: Corruption and Crime," May 6, 2002, http://www.mfa.gov.il/MFA/MFAArchive/2000_2009/2002/5/The+Involvement+of+Arafat-+PA+Senior+Officials+and.htm.
66. Holly Fletcher, "Al-Aqsa Martyrs Brigade," Council on Foreign Relations, April 2, 2008, http://www.cfr.org/israel/al-aqsa-martyrs-brigade/p9127.
67. See, for example, Ethan Bronner, "Israeli Military Kills 6 Palestinians," *New York Times*, December 26, 2009, http://www.nytimes.com/2009/12/27/world/middleeast/27mideast.html.
68. "Chapter 6. Foreign Terrorist Organizations."
69. See, for example: "Militant Group Claims Responsibility for Projectile," Ma'an News Agency (Ramallah), December 28, 2011, http://www.maannews.net/eng/ViewDetails.aspx?ID=448358.
70. "In Photos: Al-Aqsa Brigades Hold Military Parade in Qalandiam," Ma'an News Agency (Ramallah), November 17, 2013, http://www.maannews.net/eng/ViewDetails.aspx?ID=648178; Naela Khalil, "Is Fatah's Armed Wing Making Comeback?," *Al Monitor*, September 25, 2013, http://www.al-monitor.com/pulse/originals/2013/09/hebron-israeli-soldiers-killed-fatah-intifada.html.
71. Daniel Douek, "13 Injured as Palestinian Police Clash with Gunmen in Nablus," *Times of Israel*, March 29, 2016, http://www.timesofisrael.com/13-injured-as-palestinian-police-clash-with-gunmen-in-nablus/.

72. Adam Rasgon, "PA Official: Top Suspect in Killing of Two PA Officers Arrested and Beaten to Death," *Jerusalem Post,* August 23, 2016, http://www.jpost.com/Arab-Israeli-Conflict/Top-suspect-in-killing-of-two-PA-officers-arrested-and-beaten-to-death-464841.
73. "Mass Protests in West Bank City After Palestinian Detainee Dies," Reuters, August 23, 2016, http://uk.reuters.com/article/uk-palestinians-nablus-death-idUKKCN10Y1FM.
74. Neri Zilber, "Fatah's Civil War," Foreign Affairs, September 29, 2016. https://www.foreignaffairs.com/articles/palestinian-authority/2016-09-29/fatahs-civil-war
75. Adam Rasgon, "Suspected Palestinian Drug Trafficker Killed in Gunfight with PA Forces," Jerusalem Post, February 1, 2018, https://www.jpost.com/Middle-East/Suspected-Palestinian-drug-trafficker-killed-in-gunfight-with-PA-forces-540449
76. "Chapter 6. Foreign Terrorist Organizations."
77. Jonathan Dahoah Halevi, "Al Qaeda Affiliate Jaish al-Islam Receives Formal Sanctuary In Hamas-Ruled Gaza," Jerusalem Center for Public Affairs *Jerusalem Issue Briefs* 8, no. 7, August 20, 2008, http://jcpa.org/article/al-qaeda-affiliate-jaish-al-islam-receives-formal-sanctuary-in-hamas-ruled-gaz/.
78. Halevi, "Al Qaeda Affiliate Jaish al-Islam Receives Formal Sanctuary In Hamas-Ruled Gaza."
79. Halevi, "Al Qaeda Affiliate Jaish al-Islam Receives Formal Sanctuary In Hamas-Ruled Gaza."
80. Bill Roggio, "US Designates Palestinian Salafist Group as a Foreign Terrorist Organization," *Long War Journal*, May 19, 2011, http://www.longwarjournal.org/archives/2011/05/us_designates_palest.php.
81. Roggio, "US Designates Palestinian Salafist Group as a Foreign Terrorist Organization."
82. "SOCOM-2012-0000008," Combating Terrorism Center, n.d., http://www.ctc.usma.edu/posts/socom-2012-0000008-english.
83. Wikileaks, "Frances Townsend's November 12 Meeting With Isa Chief Diskin Focuses On The Palestinians," November 24, 2006, http://wikileaks.org/cable/2006/11/06TELAVIV4603.html.

84. David Barnett, "Gaza-Based Salafi Jihadists Conduct Joint Rocket Attacks, Sinai Jihadists Suppressed," *Long War Journal – Threat Matrix*, November 22, 2012, http://www.longwarjournal.org/threat-matrix/archives/2012/11/salafi-jihadist_groups_in_gaza.php.
85. David Barnett, "Report Provides Insight on Israeli View of Salafi Jihadists in Sinai," *Long War Journal*, August 20, 2013, http://www.longwarjournal.org/archives/2013/08/report_provides_insi.php.
86. Barak Ravid, "Shin Bet Forms New Unit to Thwart Attacks on Israel by Sinai Jihadists," *Ha'aretz* (Tel Aviv), August 20, 2013, http://www.haaretz.com/news/diplomacy-defense/.premium-1.542417.
87. Amos Harel, "Hamas Arrests and Tortures Salafi Militants to Curb Gaza Rocket Fire Into Israel," *Haaretz*, December 19, 2017. https://www.haaretz.com/israel-news/.premium-hamas-tortures-salafis-militants-to-curb-rocket-fire-into-israel-1.5629017.
88. "Pro Al-Qaeda Fighters Train in Gaza Strip," Reuters, September 1, 2008, http://www.alarabiya.net/articles/2008/09/01/55828.html.
89. Yoram Cohen, Matthew Levitt, and Becca Wasser, *Deterred but Determined: Salafi-Jihadi Groups in the Palestinian Arena* (Washington, DC: Washington Institute for Near East Policy, January 2010), http://www.washingtoninstitute.org/uploads/Documents/pubs/PolicyFocus%2099.pdf.
90. "Radical Islam in Gaza," International Crisis Group, March 29, 2011, http://www.crisisgroup.org/~/media/Files/Middle%20East%20North%20Africa/Israel%20Palestine/104%20Radical%20Islam%20in%20Gaza.ashx.
91. Jaysh Al-Ummah Official: Expect Military Operation In South Lebanon Directed At Israel," *NOW Lebanon*, April 11, 2010, https://now.mmedia.me/lb/en/nownews/jaysh_al-ummah_official_expect_military_operation_in_south_lebanon_directed_at_israel.
92. "Jaish Al Ummah To Hamas: 'Whose Side Are You On?'" *CBS News*, May 27, 2009, http://www.cbsnews.com/news/jaish-al-ummah-to-hamas-whose-side-are-you-on/.

93. "Al-Rāyyah Foundation for Media Presents New Pictures From Jaysh al-Ummah: 'The Arrival of Goodness #3'," *Jihadology*, October 13, 2013, http://jihadology.net/2013/10/13/al-rayyah-foundation-for-media-presents-new-pictures-from-jaysh-al-ummah-the-arrival-of-goodness-3/.
94. "Jaysh Al-Ummah Official: Expect Military Operation In South Lebanon Directed At Israel."
95. "Al Qaeda Conducted Attack Against Israel from Gaza," *Ma'ariv* (Tel Aviv), September 2, 2008, http://www.nrg.co.il/online/1/ART1/781/681.html.
96. "Palestinian Faction Urges Help to Sunnis in Ahvaz, Iran, in Audio," SITE Intelligence Group, January 17, 2013, https://news.siteintelgroup.com/index.php/19-jihadist-news/2658-palestinian-faction-urges-help-to-sunnis-in-ahvaz-iran-in-audio.
97. "Palestinian Faction Supports Malian Jihadists, Calls for Attacks on West," SITE Intelligence Group, January 22, 2013, http://news.siteintelgroup.com/index.php/19-jihadist-news/2678-palestinian-faction-supports-malian-jihadists-calls-for-attacks-on-west.
98. David Barnett, "Gaza Jihadists Call for 'Jihad' Against Egypt's El Sisi," *Long War Journal*, August 15, 2013, http://www.longwarjournal.org/archives/2013/08/gaza_jihadists_call.php.
99. David Barnett, "Gaza-Based Jaish al Ummah Praises Hakeemullah Mehsud," *Long War Journal – Threat Matrix*, November 13, 2013, http://www.longwarjournal.org/threat-matrix/archives/2013/11/gaza-based_jaish_al_ummah_prai.php.
100. "Mapping Palestinian Politics: Jaysh al-Umma (Gaza)," European Council on Foreign Relations, https://www.ecfr.eu/mapping_palestinian_politics/detail/jaysh_al_umma_gaza
101. "Jihad and Terrorism Threat Monitor (JTTM) Weekend Summary," The Middle East Media Research Institute, June 9, 2018, https://www.memri.org/reports/jihad-and-terrorism-threat-monitor-jttm-weekend-summary-305
102. "About Us," Hizb Ut Tahrir, n.d., http://english.hizbuttahrir.org/index.php/about-us.

103. Jonathan Spyer, "Hizb ut-Tahrir: A Rising Force In Palestinian Territories," *Global Politician*, December 14, 2007, https://web.archive.org/web/20120202204241/http://globalpolitician.com/23871-palestine.
104. Isabel Kershner, "Palestinian Is Killed in Hebron as Police Disperse Protest Over Mideast Peace Talks," *New York Times*, November 27, 2007, http://www.nytimes.com/2007/11/28/world/middleeast/28palestinians.html.
105. Jonathan Spyer, "A 'Rising Force,'" *Ha'aretz* (Tel Aviv), June 12, 2007, http://www.haaretz.com/hasen/spages/932087.html.
106. "Hizb Ut-Tahrir: PA Attempts Arrest Of Member," Ma'an News Agency (Ramallah), December 17, 2009, http://www.maannews.net/eng/ViewDetails.aspx?ID=247723; "Hizb Ut-Tahrir: PA Arrests Thousands," Ma'an News Agency (Ramallah), July 17, 2010, http://www.maannews.net/eng/ViewDetails.aspx?ID=300222.
107. "PA Forces Disperse Hizb ut-Tahrir Rally in Ramallah," Ma'an News Agency (Ramallah), July 2, 2011, http://www.maannews.net/eng/ViewDetails.aspx?ID=401698.
108. "PA Arrests 13 Islamists in Crackdown," Ma'an News Agency (Ramallah), July 15, 2011, http://www.maannews.net/eng/ViewDetails.aspx?ID=405427.
109. "Hizb ut-Tahrir Accuses PLO of Betrayal," Ma'an News Agency (Ramallah), August 13, 2011, http://www.maannews.net/eng/ViewDetails.aspx?ID=412772.
110. Khaled Abu Toameh, "Radical Islam Arrives in Ramallah," Gatestone Institute, June 5, 2013, http://www.gatestoneinstitute.org/3751/radical-islam-ramallah; "Hizb al-Tahrir Holds West Bank Festival," Ma'an News Agency (Ramallah), June 17, 2012, http://www.maannews.net/eng/ViewDetails.aspx?ID=496157.
111. "Group Says PA Arrested Dozens of Its Members Over Abbas Criticism," Ma'an News Agency (Ramallah), February 9, 2014, http://www.maannews.net/eng/ViewDetails.aspx?ID=672063.
112. David Barnett, "Mujahideen Shura Council is Consolidation of Salafi-Jihadist Groups in Gaza: Sources," *Long War Journal*, October 14, 2012, http://www.

longwarjournal.org/archives/2012/10/mujahideen_shura_cou.php.

113. David Barnett, "Mujahideen Shura Council Leader Slams Hamas, Calls for Public Dialogue," *Long War Journal – Threat Matrix*, November 9, 2012, http://www.longwarjournal.org/threat-matrix/archives/2012/11/mujahideen_shura_council_leade.php.
114. Barnett, "Mujahideen Shura Council Leader Slams Hamas," *Long War Journal.*
115. David Barnett, "Gaza-Based Salafi Jihadists Conduct Joint Rocket Attacks, Sinai Jihadists Suppressed," *Long War Journal – Threat Matrix*, November 22, 2012, http://www.longwarjournal.org/threat-matrix/archives/2012/11/salafi-jihadist_groups_in_gaza.php.
116. Thomas Joscelyn, "Al Qaeda-Linked Group Claims Responsibility for Attack in Israel," *Long War Journal*, June 19, 2012, http://www.longwarjournal.org/archives/2012/06/al_qaeda-linked_grou.php.
117. Bill Roggio, "Mujahideen Shura Council Calls Attack in Israel a 'Gift' to Zawahiri and Al Qaeda 'Brothers,'" *Long War Journal*, July 30, 2012, http://www.longwarjournal.org/archives/2012/07/egyptian_jihadist_gr.php.
118. David Barnett, "Mujahideen Shura Council: We Are Not Truly a Party to the Ceasefire with Israel," *Long War Journal*, November 27, 2012, http://www.longwarjournal.org/archives/2012/11/mujahideen_shura_cou_2.php.
119. David Barnett, "Jihadist Media Unit Urges Fighters to Strike Egyptian Army," *Long War Journal – Threat Matrix*, September 23, 2013, http://www.longwarjournal.org/archives/2013/09/jihadist_media_unit.php; David Barnett, "Jihadist Media Unit Releases Posters for Palestinian Fighters Killed in Syria," *Long War Journal – Threat Matrix*, October 1, 2013, http://www.longwarjournal.org/threat-matrix/archives/2013/10/jihadist_media_unit_releases_p.php.
120. Lihi Ben Shitrit & Mahmoud Jaraba, "The Threat of Jihadism in the West Bank," Sada: Carnegie Endowment for International Peace, February 6, 2014. http://carnegieendowment.org/sada/54455.

121. Jonathan Schanzer & Grant Rumley, "Iran Spawns New Jihadist Group in Gaza," *Long War Journal,* June 18, 2014, http://www.longwarjournal.org/archives/2014/06/by_jonathan_schanzer.php.
122. "Gaza Militant Dies in Apparent Explosives Accident," *Times of Israel,* May 26, 2014, http://www.timesofisrael.com/gaza-militant-dies-in-apparent-explosives-accident/.
123. Al-Sabireen, "Our Charter," n.d., http://alsabireen.ps/ar/page/4/%D9%87%D9%88%D9%8A%D8%AA%D9%86%D8%A7
124. Ehud Yaari, "Replacing Hamas," *Foreign Affairs,* September 28, 2015, https://www.foreignaffairs.com/articles/palestinian-authority/2015-09-28/replacing-hamas.
125. Ehud Yaari, "Replacing Hamas," *Foreign Affairs,* September 28, 2015, https://www.foreignaffairs.com/articles/palestinian-authority/2015-09-28/replacing-hamas.
126. Adnan Abu Amer, "Why Hamas Closed Down Iranian Charity in Gaza," *Al Monitor,* March 22, 2016, http://www.al-monitor.com/pulse/originals/2016/03/gaza-hamas-shut-down-iran-affiliated-charity.html.
127. Yaari, "Replacing Hamas."
128. "Middle East: Iran Back Into Gaza," *Amad*, October 25, 2015, http://www.amad.ps/ar/?Action=Details&ID=95441
129. Khaled Abu Toameh, "Analysis: Iran Infiltrates the West Bank," *Jerusalem Post,* February 9, 2016, http://www.jpost.com/Arab-Israeli-Conflict/Analysis-Iran-Infiltrates-the-West-Bank-444352.
130. "Palestinian Security Sources: The "Patient" Movement Seeks to Stretch from Gaza to the West," *Amad,* May 2, 2016, http://www.amad.ps/ar/?Action=Details&ID=109775
131. Grant Rumley, "Trump Administration Designates Iranian-Spawned Jihadist Faction in Gaza," *Long War Journal*, January 31, 2018, https://www.longwarjournal.org/archives/2018/01/trump-administration-designates-iranian-spawned-jihadist-faction-in-gaza.php
132. Khaled Abu Toameh, "'Corruption Will Let Hamas

Take W. Bank,'" *Jerusalem Post*, January 29, 2010, http://www.jpost.com/Middle-East/Corruption-will-let-Hamas-take-W-Bank.

133. Palestinian Center for Policy and Survey Research, "Palestinian Public Opinion Poll No (48)," June 2013, http://www.pcpsr.org/survey/polls/2013/p48e.html.
134. "Muslim Publics Share Concerns about Extremist Groups," Pew Research Center, September 10, 2013, http://www.pewglobal.org/2013/09/10/muslim-publics-share-concerns-about-extremist-groups/.
135. Hazem Balousha, "Gazans Unimpressed By Hamas Military Parades," *Al Monitor*, November 20, 2013, http://www.al-monitor.com/pulse/originals/2013/11/hamas-islamic-jihad-military-parade-gaza-crisis.html.
136. Neri Zilber, "Hamas on the Ropes," F*oreign Policy*, June 26, 2016. http://foreignpolicy.com/2014/06/26/hamas-on-the-ropes/.
137. Jonathan Schanzer, *Hamas vs. Fatah: The Struggle for Palestine* (New York: Palgrave Macmillan, 2008), 110-111.
138. Ibrahim Barzak and Diaa Hadid, "Gaza Christians Fear for Future of Tiny Community," *Associated Press*, July 25, 2012, http://bigstory.ap.org/article/gaza-christians-fear-future-tiny-community.
139. Neri Zilber and Ghaith al-Omari, *State with No Army, Army with No State: The Evolution of the Palestinian Authority Security Forces 1994-2018* (Washington Institute for Near East Policy, March 2018), pp. 57-59, http://www.washingtoninstitute.org/uploads/Documents/pubs/PolicyFocus154-ZilberOmari.pdf.
140. Peter Beaumont, "No Obvious Alternative to Hamas in Gaza, Says Top Israeli General," *The Guardian*, May 12, 2015. https://www.theguardian.com/world/2015/may/12/idf-no-alternative-to-hamas-in-gaza-top-israeli-general-turgeman-war.

26 Qatar

Quick Facts

Population: 2,314,307
Area: 11,586 sq km
Ethnic Groups: Arab 40%, Indian 18%, Pakistani 18%, Iranian 10%, other 14%
Religions: Muslim 77.5%, Christian 8.5%, other 14%
Government Type: Emirate
GDP (official exchange rate): $166.3 billion (2017 est.)

Map and Quick Facts derived in part from the CIA World Factbook (Last Updated September 2018)

Introduction

The tiny Gulf state of Qatar is a study in contradictions. Considerably more liberal than many of its neighbors, Qatar nevertheless is the only country other than Saudi Arabia to espouse Wahhabism as its official state religion. A traditionally conservative country whose authoritarian tribal rulers brook no opposition, Qatar is nevertheless host to the Al-Jazeera satellite television network, whose independent reporting has occasionally led to diplomatic crises with neighboring countries. Moreover, Qatar plays host to Al Udeid air base, the regional home of U.S. Central Command, yet the Qatari government has also provided money and diplomatic support to Islamists in Syria, Libya, and the Sahel, as well as the Muslim Brotherhood in Egypt.

Domestically, Qatar has no active Islamist opposition, for the simple reason that the state has co-opted and involved Islamism in its governance ever since its establishment. Wahhabi thought is especially influential among the Al Thani clan, which has ruled Qatar since the beginning of the nineteenth century. Its embrace of Wahhabism distinguishes Qatar religiously from its other neighbors, which has traditionally led to an uneasy alliance with Saudi Arabia. However, the June 2017 diplomatic crisis with Saudi Arabia and a dozen other states has led to a growing alliance between Qatar and Iran.

ISLAMIST ACTIVITY

Islamism is very much an in-house phenomenon in Qatar. It has been pointed out that a necessary precondition for the rise of an Islamist opposition is a decline in government legitimacy and efficacy.[1] This, in a nutshell, explains the general lack of robust Islamic opposition to the governments of the Gulf States, and Qatar is no exception. A small, exceptionally wealthy country where the government subsidizes everything from petrol to education, Qatar so far has lacked serious challenges to the Islamic legitimacy of its government.

Likewise, there have been very few reported incidents of anti-Western terrorism in Qatar in recent years. In November 2001, two U.S. contractors were shot at Al Udeid air base, and attackers attempted to ram the base's gate in 2002.[2] These incidents, however, are believed to have been the work of lone attackers.

In March 2005, Omar Ahmed Abdallah Ali, an expatriate Egyptian, blew himself up outside a theater in Doha. The attack, which killed a British school teacher, was the first suicide bombing in Qatar. Ali was believed to have had ties to al-Qaeda in the Arabian Peninsula, whose leader issued a communiqué two days before the attack calling on local citizens of a number of Gulf states, of which Qatar was at the top of his list,[3] to act against Western interests. In the aftermath of this attack, allegations were made that Qatar's rulers had been paying protection money to al-Qaeda. A report in London's *Sunday Times* described an agreement between the government of Qatar and al-Qaeda prior to the 2003 Iraq War, under which millions of dollars were paid annually to the terror network to keep Qatar off of its target list, despite the country's role as a U.S. ally.[4] This money was believed to be channeled via religious leaders sympathetic to al-Qaeda, and used to support the organization's activities in Iraq. After the attack in Doha, the agreement was renewed, according to the *Times*' source, "just to be on the safe side."[5]

The *Times* report highlights the fine line that Qatar treads in its relations with the U.S. and its powerful neighbors. Because it hosts the Al Udeid air base and Camp As Sayliyah, a pre-positioning facility for U.S. military equipment, Qatar is a more attractive target for terrorists than most neighboring countries, whose ties to the U.S.

are less tangible. Qatar pays for the upkeep of the bases used by American military forces on its soil; the U.S. pays neither rent nor utilities on them.[6] While officially these are Qatari bases, there are reportedly some 10,000 U.S and coalition personal stationed at Al Ubeid.[7] The Qatari government has reported that the U.S. is aiming to expand the base, and host a permanent presence in Qatar—reports that have been downplayed by the Pentagon.[8]. As neither Qatar nor the U.S. makes any secret of these ties, it is surprising that Qatar has not been a more frequent target of Islamists. The purported payment of protection money to al-Qaeda is one explanation for Qatar's relative safety; another may be that the absence of social and political discontent within the country's borders deprives al-Qaeda of willing local recruits. Homegrown jihadis are not as common in Qatar as they are in many neighboring countries.

Moreover, politics in the region are often played out in a very subtle way. While Qatar ostensibly enjoys a close relationship with Washington, these ties are balanced by ties with Islamist groups throughout the region. According to a State Department cable released by Wikileaks, Qatar was deemed "the worst in the region" in its counterterrorism efforts.[9] Qatar's security service was described as "hesitant to act against known terrorists out of concern for appearing to be aligned with the U.S. and provoking reprisals."[10]

Nor is this merely a tactic to defuse Islamist hostility; rather it is consistent with Qatar's long-term strategy. The Qatari government has acquired a reputation as a financial backer of Islamist causes abroad, including funding terrorist organizations. Several charities based in Qatar have been accused of actively financing al-Qaeda and other terrorist organizations. One of these, the Qatar Charitable Society (QCS), was set up and operated by an employee of the Qatari government.[11]

At the start of the Arab Spring, Qatar threw its weight behind the protest movements in North Africa and the Middle East, playing a major role in almost all the conflicts in the Arab world. Qatar became the first Arab country to grant official recognition to the Libyan rebels, and contributed six Mirage fighter jets to the Western military campaign to depose Muamar Qadhafi. Its financial support of the revolution in Libya may have reached $2 billion, channelled through various opposition figures.[12]

Doha also provided financial aid to Islamist militants fighting in the Sahel region, including al-Qaeda forces that managed to carve out a state in Mali. In 2015, Qatar deployed troops and materiel to Yemen, as part of the Arab coalition's fight against Houthi rebels.[13]

In the Palestinian arena, Qatar has long been the primary financial and ideological sponsor of Hamas, and has hosted senior Hamas officials on its soil. In October 2012, the emir became the first head of state to visit the Gaza Strip since Hamas took full control of the territory in 2007. At that time, the emir pledged $400 million for infrastructure projects. The timing of the visit, coming just after the upgrade of the Palestinian Authority's status at the United Nations, appears to have been aimed at boosting Hamas's standing against its Fatah rivals.[14] More recently, Doha has coordinated with Israel and the Palestinian Authority to pay Hamas' employees' salaries, and to import construction materials into the Gaza Strip.[15] In July of 2017, Qatari envoy Mohammed El-Amadi reaffirmed support for development projects in the Hamas-ruled Gaza Strip.[16] More recently, in October 2017, Qatar announced that it would fund a new headquarters for the Palestinian Authority in Gaza in support of reconciliation deal between Hamas and Fatah.[17] Furthermore, in 2013, the Taliban opened an official office in Qatar.[18] The office was briefly closed under pressure from the U.S. and the current Afghan government, but has since reopened to serve as a base for negotiations.[19]

But it is in Syria that Qatar's support for Islamists is most controversial. While Qatari jets have provided symbolic participation in the airpower mission against the Islamic State, Qatar has become a significant financial sponsor of the Islamist elements arrayed against President Bashar al-Assad. In particular, Qatar has provided funding and weapons to Ahrar al-Sham—or "Free Men of Syria." Khalid al-Attiyah, then Qatari foreign minister, praised this movement as "purely" Syrian.[20]

Qatar has been openly funding Jabhat al-Nusra since 2013. Much of this funding is provided in the form of "ransom" for Western hostages, kidnapped by the group for exactly this purpose.[21] This is in addition to large sums of money channeled to the group via Qatari charity organizations and individuals, who are allowed to operate freely in the country.[22]

In addition to material support, Doha has provided considerable propaganda support for the Syrian jihadis via *Al Jazeera*. Qatari officials have touted their support of "moderate" jihadi groups as an effective means of fighting the Islamic State. [23] In fact, this support was portrayed in a positive light by the U.S. State Department in its 2014 Country Reports on Terrorism, which cited Qatar's offer "to host a train-and-equip program for moderate Syrian opposition forces."[24]

In fact, with Qatar's help, Jabhat al-Nusra became powerful enough that that U.S. General Petraeus suggested that the U.S. also support the group as the only plausible threat to ISIS in Syria.[25] However, such suggestions ignore the fact that there is no real hierarchy of jihadi groups. Alliances and rivalries between the different "camps" are continually shifting, so that support for one group can reach rival groups via mergers and temporary alliances.

In addition, membership in the different jihadi groups is fluid; senior leaders of Al Nusra were once members of the Islamic State in Iraq.[26] Hundreds of fighters have left al-Nusra to join the Islamic State over the past few years.[27] These defections lead to the transfer of Qatari-supplied weapons and funds to ISIS, a fact that even Qatar's allies have had to acknowledge. A leaked email published by Wikileaks in October 2016 singled out Qatar and Saudi Arabia as "providing clandestine financial and logistic support to ISIL [ISIS] and other radical Sunni groups in the region."[28]

None of the groups fighting in Syria can be seen as "moderate" in any meaningful sense. Ahrar al-Sham fought alongside Jabhat al-Nusra during the battle for Aleppo and has been accused of at least one sectarian massacre.[29] At the time the organization was being openly supported by Qatar, it was also sharing local authority with the ISIS in Raqqa. [30] Meanwhile Jabhat al-Nusra ostensibly split from al-Qaida in mid 2016, rebranding itself as Jabhat Fateh al-Sham. However, the "split" was in name only; the organization's leader did not in fact renounce ties to its parent group.[31]

Qatar's strategy of simultaneously remaining on good terms with Islamists and with the West has facilitated its role as a mediator in the region, including negotiating for the release of captive U.S. servicemen in Afghanistan in exchange for prisoners held by the U.S. This role, as seen in connection with the al-Nusra hostages, has allowed Qatar to openly bankroll jihadi groups through the payment of ransoms for Western hostages.[32] Qatar's role in playing off regional actors against one another, as well as its support of radical groups, has brought it into conflict with its neighbors. The major bone of contention is Qatar's long-standing support of the Muslim Brotherhood, an organization seen by other Sunni states as a danger to their own regimes.

In March 2014, Saudi Arabia, the United Arab Emirates, and Bahrain withdrew their ambassadors due to the Qatar's sponsorship of the Muslim Brotherhood and other Islamist groups.[33] After Egyptian president Mohamed Morsi was overthrown in 2013, several members of the Muslim Brotherhood were asked to leave Qatar, as part of a rapprochement agreement signed between Gulf countries.[34] It is not known whether those expelled eventually reentered the country. In December 2016, Egypt accused Qatar of being indirectly responsible for the bombing of a Coptic church which killed 24 people. A statement by the Egyptian government said that the attacker had been instructed by the Muslim Brotherhood in Qatar to plan and carry out the attack in order to promote sectarian strife.[35]

These tensions have been exacerbated by what the Gulf countries see as Qatar's breach of the Sunni alliance against Iran. Qatar's relationship with Iran is complicated by the fact that the two states share the largest gas field in the world. Qatar has also cooperated with Iran on infrastructure projects.[36] The tensions with the Gulf countries broke out into an open feud at the end of May 2017, when Emir Sheikh Tamim bin Hamad al-Thani was quoted by Qatari state media as claiming "there is no wisdom in harboring hostility towards Iran." Qatar later denied the emir had made the statements, claiming the state media website and Twitter accounts had been hacked, but the damage was done. The statements—whether real or fabricated—provided Qatar's neighbors the excuse they needed to openly strike out against Qatari policies. Saudi Arabia and the United Arab Emirates quickly blocked access to Al Jazeera's website.[37]

On June 5, 2017, Saudi Arabia, Bahrain, Egypt and the United

Arab Emirates (UAE) broke off relations with Qatar and cut off all air, sea, and land routes. Yemen, Mauritania, and the Maldives followed. Qatari citizens were given 14 days to leave Saudi Arabia, Bahrain and the UAE, and those countries also banned their own citizens from entering Qatar. Saudi Arabia, which leads the coalition fighting Iran-backed Houthi rebels in Yemen, expelled Qatar from the coalition. [38]

On June 22, Saudi Arabia, the UAE, and Egypt issued a 13-point list of demands to restore relations and gave Doha 10 days to comply.[39] The demands include Qatar severing ties with jihadist groups, shutting down news outlets (including Al Jazeera), limiting ties with Iran, and expelling Turkish troops stationed in the country. Among the Islamist groups mentioned in the list were the Muslim Brotherhood, Hezbollah, al-Qaeda, and ISIS. As of late 2017, no obvious progress has been made at resolving the dispute.[40]

Qatar's continued support of Islamist elements, despite its negative diplomatic impact, reflects the fact that this support goes beyond mere pragmatism, and has a clear ideological basis.[41] At times, this support has been a matter of personal honor. Qatar's ties to the Libyan rebels, for instance, were reportedly mostly on the level of personal connections.[42] Such ties are nothing new; according to American intelligence officials, Abdallah bin Khalid al-Thani, a member of the Qatari royal family, helped wanted al-Qaeda chief Khaled Sheikh Mohammed elude capture in 1996. Abdallah bin Khalid, who was Qatar's Minister of Religious Affairs at the time, reportedly sheltered the wanted man on one of his own farms.[43] Mohammed is believed to have been employed for some years in Qatar's Department of Public Water Works, before slipping out of the country on a Qatari passport just ahead of an American attempt to capture him.[44]

Abdallah bin Khalid was not alone in his sympathies to al-Qaeda. News reports have cited U.S. officials as saying there were others in the Qatari royal family who provided safe haven for al-Qaeda leaders.[45] In late 2013, the U.S. Treasury Department imposed sanctions on several prominent Qataris for providing funds to al-Qaeda and to jihadis in Syria.[46] One year later, one of those designated was found to be still employed by the Qatari Interior

Ministry, while others were still living at large in the emirate.[47] A U.S.-based think tank has identified over twenty individuals under U.S. or UN sanctions who have benefitted from some form of Qatari negligence or support. [48]

Islamism and Society

Wahhabism—the very strict interpretation of Islam espoused by 18th century preacher Muhammad ibn Abd al Wahhab—has shaped Qatar's history for more than a century. Among the tribes that adopted the Wahhabi interpretation in the late 19th century was the Al Thani— in contrast to the ruling Al Khalifas of Bahrain, who rejected Wahhabism. When the Al Khalifas attempted to invade the peninsula of Qatar in 1867, the Al Thani and their followers, with the help of the British, repelled the invasion. This victory established the Al Thani family as Qatar's ruling clan. Thereafter, Qatar became the only country other than Saudi Arabia to espouse Hanbali Wahhabism as the official state religion.[49] This set the stage for tensions between Qatar and its other neighbors.

Qatar's population is conservative, but overt religious discrimination has been rare. Non-citizens constitute a majority of Qatar's residents, as most are from Southeast Asia or from other Muslim countries, which has minimized the influence of Western culture.[50] Inter-Muslim friction is also minimized by the homogeneity of Qatar's citizenry. Sunni Muslims constitute the overwhelming majority of the population, while Shi'a Muslims account for less than five percent.[51] As a result, the main drivers for Islamist opposition are lacking in Qatar; the government espouses a distinctly Islamist ideology, while social inequities and cultural frictions have been kept to a minimum. While many Qatari citizens express support for jihadists fighting in Syria and Iraq, relatively few have actually joined the fighting. A 2014 study of social media found that of all social media posts originating in Qatar, 47% were supportive of ISIS, a higher percentage than any other Arab state.[52]

However, in contrast to Saudi Arabia, Wahhabi tenets are not officially enforced or strictly adhered to in most public settings in Qatar. Qatari society is generally moderate, and, among Arab countries, its civil liberties are ranked second only to Lebanon.[53]

While instances of overt religious discrimination have been rare, anti-Semitic motifs are common in the mainstream media: Israel and world Jewry are frequently demonized in editorials and cartoons.[54]

The need to keep pace with global social and economic development has pushed Qatar to gradually shift its political structure from a traditional society based on consent and consensus to one based on more formal, though not necessarily democratic, institutions. Qatar's constitution institutionalized the hereditary rule of the Al Thani family, but it also established an elected legislative body and made government ministers accountable to the legislature.[55] While formally accountable to no one, the emir is still bound by the checks and balances of traditional Muslim Arab societies; all decisions must be in accordance with sharia and must not arouse the opposition of the country's leading families.[56]

In June 2013, Hamad bin Khalifa al-Thani abdicated in favor of his son, British-educated Tamim bin Hamad al-Thani. At 36 years old, Emir Tamim is the youngest head of state in the region and has promised to modernize the country's governmental system and reduce his family's presence in the government. Faced with falling oil prices, the new emir reduced the number of government ministries, slashed state institutions' budgets and put various social welfare schemes on hold. This was accompanied by hikes in utility rates, gas prices, government fines and service costs.[57] While these reforms are aimed to provide a smooth transition into a post-oil economy, they could negatively impact the popularity of the regime among its citizens. In addition to economic reforms, Emir al-Thani has loosened strictures on expressions of foreign culture, including allowing state-owned sales of alcohol and pork to the country's foreign residents, and supported religious freedom for non-Muslims, albeit within strictly proscribed limits.

These measures have not been universally popular among citizens. Some have accused the emir of forsaking his own citizens in favor of the migrant workers who make up some 90% of the population. After conservatives threatened a boycott, a plan to offer co-ed lectures at Qatar's public university were cancelled.[58]

Islamism and the State

Qatar's government and ruling family have traditionally been strongly linked to Wahhabi Hanbali Islam. Not only is Wahhabi Islam the official state religion, but Islamic jurisprudence is the basis of Qatar's legal system. Civil courts have jurisdiction only over commercial law.[59] Qatar's governmental structure, despite a written constitution, conforms closely to traditional Islamic constraints, with tribal and family allegiance remaining an influential factor in the country's politics. There is no provision in Qatar's constitution for political parties, and hence there is no official political opposition.[60] Professional associations and societies, which in other Muslim countries play the role of unofficial political parties, are under severe constraints in Qatar, and are forbidden to engage in political activities.[61] While the official policy has been to support the movements behind the Arab Spring abroad, any such aspirations within the state are dealt with harshly, as in the case of poet Mohammed al-Ajami, who was handed a 15-year prison sentence for a poetry reading in which he called all Arab governments "indiscriminate thieves."[62]

This firm hand when it comes to internal dissent should be contrasted with the considerable leniency shown by authorities toward Qataris accused of funding Islamist activities abroad. What the U.S. government has described as a "permissive" environment for terror finance[63] should be seen as part of a deliberate policy: simply put, the Qatari government has preferred to co-opt rather than oppose Islamism.[64] Religious institutions are carefully monitored by the Ministry of Islamic affairs, which oversees mosque construction and Islamic education. The Ministry appoints religious leaders and previews mosque sermons for inflammatory language that might incite listeners to violence.[65]

Qatar has a longstanding tradition of granting asylum to exiled Islamists and radical preachers from other Muslim countries.[66] Following the 1979 attack on the Grand Mosque in Mecca by an extremist group, Qatar took in a number of radical exiles from Saudi Arabia, including Wahhabi scholar Sheikh Abdallah bin Zayd al-Mahmud, who subsequently was appointed Qatar's most senior cleric.[67]

Sympathy for Islamist causes has traditionally been high in Qatari society and among many members of the ruling clan. Sheikh Fahd bin Hamad al-Thani, the second-oldest son of the emir, established a reputation for surrounding himself with jihadist veterans of the Afghan War.[68] A number of al-Qaeda leaders are believed to have travelled through Qatar during the 1990s under the protection of members of the ruling clan, including Abu Mus'ab al-Zarqawi and Osama bin Laden.[69] The Chechen leader Zelimkhan Yandarbiyev, who was killed in Doha in 2004, also found refuge for several years in Qatar.

During the 1980s, many Wahhabi exiles were appointed to senior and mid-level positions in Qatar's Interior Ministry, which controls both the civilian security force and the Mubahathat (secret police office). After 2003, Emir Hamad bin Khalifa began gradually weeding out the more extreme Islamist elements from government ministries, including the Interior Ministry; the Minister of the Interior, Sheikh Abdallah, a member of the Wahhabi clique, was removed from office in 2004. The Interior Ministry was then put under the de facto control of Sheikh Abdallah bin Nasser bin-Khalifa al-Thani, an emir loyalist. However, a large number of Islamist appointees are believed to remain among mid-level Qatari security officials.[70]

In June 2003, the emir created an independent State Security Agency, answerable directly to him. Additionally, all the most important police, military, and internal security services are headed by powerful members of the ruling family, who in turn answer to the emir.[71] The creation of these parallel security agencies effectively bypassed the Interior Ministry's control of police and public security. These shakeups, however, have had more to do with political alliances than with government opposition to Islamists. Most Islamists, both domestic and immigrant, have become well integrated into the top echelons of Qatari society.[72]

Among the political exiles who have sought refuge in Qatar are prominent figures of the Muslim Brotherhood, many of whom fled persecution at the hands of Gamal Abdel Nasser's government in Egypt during the 1950s. Some of these exiles reportedly laid the foundations for the Qatari Education Ministry, and taught at various levels there until the early 1980s.[73] More recently, Hamas political head Khaled Mishaal quit his former headquarters under the wing of Syria's Al Assad regime and relocated to Doha.[74]

Given the great success of these elements, the country has no obvious need for an Islamist opposition. In 2007, Kuwaiti Islamist writer Abd Allah al-Nafisi called for the Egyptian Muslim Brotherhood to follow the lead of the Qatari branch and disband altogether. Al-Nafisi noted that from 1960 to 1980, Qatar went through a period of great Islamist intellectual activity and organization. In contrast to the experience of the Muslim Brotherhood in Egypt, the Qatari Muslim Brothers had no real conflict with the state.[75]

One of the most influential—not to mention controversial—voices in Islamist circles today is Egyptian Sheikh Yusuf al-Qaradawi, who has lived in Qatar since 1961. Qaradawi enjoys worldwide exposure via *Al Jazeera* television, through his weekly program "Sharia and Life" (al-Shari'a wa-al-Hayat). Until recently, he also oversaw the Islamist Web portal IslamOnline, established in 1997.[76] Many consider Sheikh al-Qaradawi to be the most influential Islamic scholar alive today; he is viewed as the spiritual leader of the Muslim Brotherhood, and "sets the tone for Arabic language Sunni sermons across the world."[77] Qaradawi has sparked considerable controversy in the West by his support for suicide bombings in Israel and the killing of American citizens in Iraq. Among Muslim audiences, however, his comparatively moderate views on the acceptability of Muslim participation in Western democracies have brought him both praise and condemnation.[78] This mixture of conservatism and reform informs Qaradawi's politics. He is one of the founders of the wasatiyya ("Middle Way") movement, which attempts to bridge the gap between the various interpretations of Islam.[79] Yet Qaradawi's political proclivities and involvement have led to some questionable connections: Qaradawi is listed as a founder of the Union of Good (Itilaf al-Khayr), a coalition of European Islamic charities now designated by the United States Treasury as a channel for transferring funds to Hamas.[80]

Qaradawi's influence also played a role in the events of the Arab Spring, as his protégés emerged as new leaders, financial backers, religious authorities and politicians.[81] In May 2013, he urged Sunni Muslims to join the jihad in Syria against the Assad regime and against Hezbollah.[82] In a region where educational and media influence can determine the lives of dictators, Sheikh Qaradawi is a significant foreign policy asset.

Qatar's policies, though seemingly contradictory, are consistent with two strategic objectives: to buy influence with a number of different forces, while playing off its stronger neighbours, particularly Saudi Arabia and Iran. Uppermost on Qatar's agenda is the need to protect its sovereignty and natural gas wealth, by means of which the country has emerged as a regional player. This strategy may be one of the motivations for Qatar's recent spending spree in Europe. Qatar invests billions of dollars a year in Europe, in real estate, tourist venues, sports and media sectors.[83] These investments are a tool of foreign policy, but also serve an important function in domestic policy. The greater the stake foreign countries have in the stability of the Al Thani government, the better. By investing heavily abroad, the Al Thanis are buying insurance against an Arab Spring of their own.

This strategy caused a stir when it emerged in 2012 that Qatar had pledged 150 million Euro [$199 million] to investments in French suburbs inhabited by a Muslim majority. While Qatari officials insisted that the move was "just business," critics claimed that the Qataris were using their economic clout to push an Islamist agenda.[84] The issue highlighted the fact that Qatar has become an international superpower when it comes to soft power. The Al Thani regime has established itself as second to none in wielding influence through non-military means. Perhaps the greatest weapon in its arsenal is the *Al Jazeera* satellite television station.

Although the Qatari press is free from official censorship, self-censorship is the norm. Defense and national security matters, as well as stories related to the royal family, are considered strictly out of bounds. The country's major radio and television stations, Qatar Radio and Qatar Television, are both state-owned.[85] Although newspapers in Qatar are all privately owned in principle, many board members and owners are either government officials or have close ties to the government. For example, the chairman of the influential daily *Al-Watan*, Hamad bin Sahim al Thani, is a member of the royal family.[86] Meanwhile, Qatar's Foreign Minister, Hamed bin Jasem bin Jaber al Thani, owns half of the newspaper.

Compared to the traditionally conservative and highly censored Arab press, Qatar's *Al Jazeera* satellite network would appear to be a breath of fresh air. Formed in 1996 from the remnants of BBC Arabic TV, which had just been closed down, the station initially offered the kind of free and unfettered discussion of issues not usually broadcast in the Muslim world. *Al Jazeera* quickly established itself as a major international media player, and is increasingly being viewed as a political actor in its own right. *Al Jazeera* is in fact funded by the Qatari government, with its expenses reimbursed by the Ministry of Finance, and Sheikh Hamid bin Thamer, a member of the royal family, heads the station's board of directors.[87]

In recent years, *Al Jazeera* has undergone a process of increasing "Islamization," with many of its more secular staff replaced by Islamists.[88] This process has been accompanied by subtle—and not-so-subtle—changes in the station's reportage of happenings in the field. *Al Jazeera* is alleged to have moved away from its rather ideologically diverse origins to a more populist—and more Islamist—approach.[89] In addition, *Al Jazeera* is increasingly becoming a participant in the sectarian feud between Shi'as and Sunnis. Qatar itself is right in the middle of this battle; on the one hand, it hosts an American military base on its soil, where tanks and vehicles damaged in the fighting are serviced and sent back into battle to protect the Shiite-led government of Iraq. On the other, Qatar's Sunni majority sees Shiite Iran as the main threat in the region. Qatar supported Saudi Arabia's intervention in neighboring Bahrain to help quell Shiite protests, and sent a small contingent of security personnel to protect government sites.[90]

Al Jazeera's Arabic channel has also been heavily involved in promoting the Muslim Brotherhood as a viable player in Egypt, and may well have been the determining factor in the election of Muhammed Morsi to the Egyptian presidency.[91] Many leading figures at *Al Jazeera* news are Egyptians affiliated with the Brotherhood, and Brotherhood guests and loyalists dominate most of the channel's programs on Egyptian political affairs.[92]

Al Jazeera rarely criticizes Qatar's ruling Al Thani family, although other Arab governments come in for severe censure.[93] This has not only infuriated those Arab governments on the receiving end of the station's critical coverage, but also raised the question of Qatari complicity in the destabilization of its neighbors. Libya, for instance, withdrew its ambassador from Qatar between 2000 and 2002 to protest *Al Jazeera's* less-than-complimentary coverage of the Qadhafi regime.[94] In 2002, Saudi Arabia likewise withdrew its ambassador to Doha, partly in response to *Al Jazeera* reportage. (Relations were restored six years later, and *Al Jazeera* has since toned down its Saudi coverage.) Jordan and Lebanon have accused *Al Jazeera* of actively working to undermine their governments, while uncritically supporting their opposition Islamist movements.[95]

Prior to the fall of the Mubarak regime, the Egyptian government repeatedly complained about the open forum given by *Al Jazeera* to representatives of the Egyptian Muslim Brotherhood.[96] It would appear that *Al Jazeera* was in fact a key player in the events that led to the eventual ouster of Mubarak and his replacement by an Islamist regime. In the aftermath of Morsi's ouster, *Al Jazeera* reportedly experienced a wave of desertions by veteran reporters over "biased coverage" and the station's blatant support of the Brotherhood.[97] In their 13-point ultimatum to Qatar, Saudi Arabia, Bahrain, Egypt and the UAE mentioned shutting down Al Jazeera as one of the key demands for resolving the current boycott of Qatar.[98] Al-Jazeera, meanwhile, mustered a bevy of protest against the demand as an attack on freedom of the press.[99]

It has become increasingly clear that *Al Jazeera's* Islamist shift was a matter of design as much as evolution, reflecting the interests of the Qatari ruling family, as well as the growing popularity of Islamist causes in Arab society. *Al Jazeera* is more than a mirror of public opinion; it is increasingly taking the initiative in influencing events rather than just reporting on them.[100]

For some, there is no doubt that the network is subject to the political dictates of the Qatari government, which has become a significant player in many of the Middle East's disputes despite the country's small size. Al Jazeera, or at least, it's Arabic channels have come to reflect Doha's official policies.[101] Government control over the channel's reporting appeared to U.S. diplomats to be so direct that the channel's output is said to have become a subject of bilateral discussions between Washington and Doha. An American diplomatic dispatch from July 2009 noted that *Al Jazeera* could be used as a bargaining tool to repair Qatar's relationships with other countries, and called the station "one of Qatar's most valuable political and diplomatic tools."[102]

Al Jazeera's influence reflects the reality of an increasingly media-driven Middle East. The station's rivalry with the newer Saudi *Al Arabiya* satellite channel is indicative of a deeper competition for regional influence. *Al Jazeera* may be seen as an arm of Qatari foreign policy, a sort of electronic da'wah (missionary activity). In effect, these governments use their control of the media to create a monopoly on reporting, making the reportage itself a tool in regional rivalries.

Although *Al-Jazeera* wielded tremendous influence during the events of the "Arab Spring," the fall of the Morsi government in 2013 showed the risks of Qatar's over-reaching itself in "making the news" rather than just reporting it. Al Jazeera's reputation in the Arab world suffered from its blatant support of the Brotherhood-affiliated regime. The station's English language staff members in Egypt were arrested and charged with disseminating "false news." Qatar was eventually forced to close its pro-Brotherhood Arabic service to repair relations with Egypt.[103]

However, *Al-Jazeera* is only one of the means by which Qatar achieves influence. Qatari soft power has increasingly been augmented by investments in arms for Islamist militants in Arab conflicts. Libya was a case in point; by channeling weapons and money to Islamist rebels through personal channels, and largely bypassing the National Transitional Council, Qatar effectively limited the governing body's monopoly on the use of force. This has given Qatar a veto on violence in the country, allowing Qatar to back up its soft power with hard power. In Syria too, Qatar's backing of the insurgency against Assad has gained the country a key role in negotiations—a crucial bargaining chip in the volatile region.

In the Arab world, soft power remains vital. More than in any other region, persuasion and education are tools of dominance. Hence the political logic of *Al-Jazeera*, and hence the huge investment of Saudi Arabia in da'wah. What Western countries accomplish via economic dominance, Saudi Arabia has accomplished through financing mosques, and Qatar has accomplished through a studied combination of media influence, economic investment, and military backing.

While the Saudi-led coalition included the shuttering of al-Jazeera as a core demand for ending the blockade, the attempt at silencing Qatar's regional da'wah seems to have only upped the ante; both Qatar and its opponents have funneled billions of dollars into PR efforts.[104] By moving the conflict into the realm of electronic da'wah, the coalition has simply played to Doha's strengths. Not only does al-Jazeera continue to spread Qatari influence throughout the region, but Doha's reputation as a feisty underdog has only been enhanced.

Endnotes

1. Sheri Berman, "Islamism, Revolution, and Civil Society," *Perspectives on Politics* 1, no. 2, June 2003, 257-272.
2. Oxford Analytica, "The Advent of Terrorism in Qatar," *Forbes*, March 25, 2005, (http://www.forbes.com/2005/03/25/cz_0325oxan_qatarattack.html).
3. Oxford Analytica, "The Advent of Terrorism in Qatar."
4. Uzi Mahnaimi, "Qatar buys off al-Qaeda attacks with oil millions," *Sunday Times* (London), May 1, 2005, http://www.timesonline.co.uk/tol/news/world/article387163.ece.
5. Uzi Mahnaimi, "Qatar buys off al-Qaeda attacks with oil millions.".
6. Uzi Mahnaimi, "Qatar buys off al-Qaeda attacks with oil millions."
7. Ben Brimelow, "Qatar wants the US military permanently in the country with a bigger air base," *Business Insider.* https://www.businessinsider.com/qatar-al-udeid-us-air-base-middle-east-permanent-2018-1
8. "Pentagon downplays plans to expand Qatar airbase," July 25, 2017, *The National.* https://www.thenational.ae/world/gcc/pentagon-downplays-plans-to-expand-qatar-airbase-1.753945

9. Elizabeth Weingarten, "Qatar: 'Worst' on Counterterrorism in the Middle East?" *The Atlantic*, November 29, 2010, http://www.theatlantic.com/international/archive/2010/11/qatar-worst-on-counterterroism-in-the-middle-east/67166/.
10. Scott Shane and Andrew W. Lehren, "Leaked Cables Offer Raw Look at U.S. Diplomacy," *New York Times*, November 28, 2010, http://www.nytimes.com/2010/11/29/world/29cables.html?_r=1.
11. Steven Emerson, Testimony before the House of Representatives Committee on Financial Services, Subcommittee on Oversight and Investigations, February 12, 2002, 8-9.
12. "Qatar Sends Billions, Hoping for an Islamic Regime in Libya," *El-Khabar* (Algeria), August 3, 2012, as translated in *Al-Monitor*, August 3, 2012, http://www.al-monitor.com/pulse/security/01/08/report-warns-about-a-serious-thr.html.
13. "Qatar deploys 1,000 ground troops to fight in Yemen," *Al Jazeera*, September 7, 2015, http://www.aljazeera.com/news/2015/09/qatar-deploys-1000-ground-troops-fight-yemen-150907043020594.html.
14. Acil Tabbara, "Qatar Emir in Gaza: Doha pushes Islamist Agenda to Detriment of Palestinian Unity," *Middle East Online*, October 23, 2012, http://www.middle-east-online.com/english/?id=55066.
15. Adam Rasgon, "Qatar coordinated payment to Hamas employees with Israel, PA," *Jerusalem Post,* July 24, 2016, http://www.jpost.com/Middle-East/Qatar-to-pay-salaries-of-Hamas-public-sector-employees-in-Gaza-462209.
16. "Inking anti-terror deal with US, Qatar vows backing for Hamas-ruled Gaza," *Times of Israel.* July 11, 2017. https://www.timesofisrael.com/inking-anti-terror-deal-with-us-qatar-vows-backing-for-hamas-ruled-gaza/
17. "After unity deal, Qatar to fund new Palestinian government HQ in Gaza," *Times of Israel,* 27 October, 2017. https://www.timesofisrael.com/after-unity-deal-qatar-to-fund-new-palestinian-govt-hq-in-gaza/.
18. Matthew Rosenberg. "Taliban Opening Qatar Office,

and Maybe Door to Talks," *New York Times*, January 3, 2012.

19. "Taliban reaffirms authority of its Qatar 'political office," *Dawn* (Karachi), January 25, 2016, http://www.dawn.com/news/1235165.
20. David Blair and Richard Spencer, "How Qatar is Funding the Rise of Islamist Extremists, "Telegraph (London), September 20, 2014, http://www.telegraph.co.uk/news/worldnews/middleeast/qatar/11110931/How-Qatar-is-funding-the-rise-of-Islamist-extremists.html.
21. "Funding al-Nusra through Ransom: Qatar and the Myth of the 'Humanitarian Principle,'" CATF Reports, December 10, 2015. http://stopterrorfinance.org/stories/510652383-funding-al-nusra-through-ransom-qatar-and-the-myth-of-humanitarian-principle.
22. David Weinberg, "Qatar is still negligent on terror finance," The Long War Journal, Aug. 19, 2015. http://mobile.businessinsider.com/qatar-is-letting-2-notorious-terror-financiers-operate-in-the-open-2015-8.
23. Blair and Spencer, op cit.
24. U.S. Department of State, Counter-Terrorism Bureau. "Country Reports on Terrorism 2014. "
25. "Funding al-Nusra through Ransom: Qatar and the Myth of the 'Humanitarian Principle.'"
26. "Funding al-Nusra through Ransom: Qatar and the Myth of the 'Humanitarian Principle.'"
27. Mariam Karouny "U.S.-led strikes pressure al Qaeda's Syria group to join with Islamic State," Reuters 26 September 2014. http://uk.reuters.com/article/uk-syria-crisis-nusra-insight-idUKKCN0HL11520140926.
28. Email from John Podesta to Hillary Clinton dated September 27, 2014, https://wikileaks.org/podesta-emails/emailid/3774.
29. "World Report 2015: Syria: Events of 2014," Human Rights Watch. https://www.hrw.org/world-report/2015/country-chapters/syria
30. David Blair and Richard Spencer, op. cit.
31. Thomas Joscelyn, "Analysis: Al Nusrah Front rebrands itself as Jabhat Fath Al Sham," The Long War

Journal, July 28, 2016. http://www.longwarjournal.org/archives/2016/07/analysis-al-nusrah-front-rebrands-itself-as-jabhat-fath-al-sham.php|.

32. Rukmini Callimachi, "Paying Ransoms, Europe Bankrolls Qaeda Terror," *New York Times,* July 29, 2014, https://www.nytimes.com/2014/07/30/world/africa/ransoming-citizens-europe-becomes-al-qaedas-patron.html; See also Ellen Knickmeyer, "Al Qaeda-Linked Groups Increasingly Funded by Ransom," *Wall Street Journal*, July 29, 2014, http://online.wsj.com/articles/ ransom-fills-terrorist-coffers-1406637010.
33. Abigail Hauslohner, "Rift Deepens Between Qatar and Its Powerful Arab Neighbors," Washington Post, March 8, 2014.
34. "Qatar-Gulf deal forces expulsion of Muslim Brotherhood leaders," *Guardian* (London), September 16, 2014, https://www.theguardian.com/world/2014/sep/16/qatar-orders-expulsion-exiled-egyptian-muslim-brotherhood-leaders.
35. "Egypt Blames Muslim Brotherhood in Qatar for Involvement in Cairo Cathedral Attack," Ahram Online, 13 December, 2016. http://www.worldaffairsjournal.org/content/egypt-blames-muslim-brotherhood-cairo-church-bombing.
36. Turkey, Iran, Qatar work on road transportation deal," *Daily Sabah,* November 9, 201.
37. "Al Jazeera blocked by Saudi Arabia, Qatar blames fake news," CNN, May 24, 2017., http://money.cnn.com/2017/05/24/media/al-jazeera-blocked-saudi-arabia-uae/index.html.
38. "Qatar denounces 'unjustified' cut of Gulf ties," *Times of Israel,* June 5, 2017, http://www.timesofisrael.com/qatar-denounces-unjustified-cut-of-gulf-ties/
39. "Qatar given 10 days to meet 13 sweeping demands by Saudi Arabia," *The Guardian,* https://www.theguardian.com/world/2017/jun/23/close-al-jazeera-saudi-arabia-issues-qatar-with-13-demands-to-end-blockade
40. "Arab states issue 13 demands to end Qatar-Gulf crisis," Al Jazeera, 12 July 2017. http://www.aljazeera.com/news/2017/06/arab-states-issue-list-demands-qatar-crisis-170623022133024.html.

41. Guido Steinberg, "Qatar and the Arab Spring: Support for Islamists and New Anti-Syrian Policy," SWP Stiftung Wissenschaft und Politik German Institute for International and Security Affairs, February 2012, 4.
42. "Qatar Sends Billions, Hoping for an Islamic Regime in Libya."
43. Terry McDermott, Josh Meyer and Patrick J. McDonnell, "The Plots and Designs of Al Qaeda's Engineer," Los Angeles Times, December 22, 2002, http://articles.latimes.com/2002/dec/22/world/fg-ksm22.
44. Brian Ross and David Scott, "Qatari Royal Family Linked to Al Qaeda," ABC News, February 7, 2003.
45. Ross and Scott, "Qatari Royal Family Linked to Al Qaeda," ABC News.
46. U.S. Department of the Treasury, "Press Release: Treasury Designates Al-Qa'ida Supporters in Qatar and Yemen," December 18, 2013, https://www.treasury.gov/press-center/press-releases/pages/jl2249.aspx.
47. Robert Mendick, "Al-Qaeda Terror Financier Worked for Qatari Government," *Telegraph* (London), October 12, 2014, http://www.telegraph.co.uk/news/11156327/Al-Qaeda-terror-financier-worked-for-Qatari-government.html.
48. David Andrew Weinberg, *Qatar and Terror Finance – Part I: Negligence* (FDD Press, December 2014), http://www.defenddemocracy.org/content/uploads/publications/Qatar_Part_I.pdf.
49. "Qatar: Wahhabi Islam and the Gulf," country-data.com, n.d., http://www.country-data.com/cgi-bin/query/r-11031.html.
50. U.S. Department of State, Bureau of Near Eastern Affairs, "Background Note: Qatar," September 22, 2010.
51. U.S. Department of State, Bureau of Democracy, Human Rights and Labor, *International Religious Freedom Report 2010* (Washington, DC: U.S. Department of State, November 17, 2010), http://www.state.gov/g/drl/rls/irf/2010/index.htm.
52. "La social-mappa del sostegno all'ISIS nel mondo arabo: più alto in Europa (ma non in Italia) che in Medio Oriente," Voices from the Blogs, November

29, 2014., https://www.voices-int.com/blog/article/2014/11/29/7609

53. "Qatar: Political Forces," *The Economist*, March 11, 2009, http://www.economist.com/node/13216406.
54. U.S. Department of State, *International Religious Freedom Report 2010.*
55. U.S. Department of State, "Background Note: Qatar."
56. U.S. Department of State, "Background Note: Qatar."
57. Azhar Unwala , "The young emir: Emir Tamim and Qatar's future," September 18, 2016. http://globalriskinsights.com/2016/09/emir-tamim-and-qatars-future.
58. "The other Wahhabi state," *The Economist,* June 2, 2016, https://www.economist.com/news/middle-east-and-africa/21699960-kinder-gentler-puritanism-some-other-wahhabi-state.
59. U.S. Department of State, "Background Note: Qatar."
60. "Qatar: Political Forces."
61. U.S. Department of State, *International Religious Freedom Report 2010*, https://www.state.gov/j/drl/rls/irf/2010/148841.htm .
62. "Qatar Court Upholds Poet Mohammed al-Ajami's Sentence," *BBC*, October 21, 2013, http://www.bbc.com/news/world-middle-east-24612650.
63. U.S. Department of the Treasury Press Center, "Remarks of Under Secretary for Terrorism and Financial Intelligence David Cohen before the Center for a New American Security on 'Confronting New Threats in Terrorist Financing'", March 4, 2014, https://www.treasury.gov/press-center/press-releases/Pages/jl2308.aspx . See also Taimur Khan, "US names two Qatari nationals as financiers of terrorism", *The National* [UAE], August 6, 2015, http://www.thenational.ae/world/americas/us-names-two-qatari-nationals-as-financiers-of-terrorism .
64. David Andrew Weinberg, "Analysis: Qatar still negligent on terror finance", *The Long War Journal,* August 19, 2015, http://www.longwarjournal.org/archives/2015/08/analysis-qatar-still-negligent-on-terror-finance.php .
65. U.S. Department of State, *International Religious*

Freedom Report 2010, https://www.state.gov/j/drl/rls/irf/2010/148841.htm ..

66. Oxford Analytica, "The Advent of Terrorism in Qatar."
67. Michael Knights and Anna Solomon-Schwartz, "The Broader Threat from Sunni Islamists in the Gulf," Washington Institute for Near East Policy *PolicyWatch* no. 883, July 25, 2004, http://www.washingtoninstitute.org/templateC05.php?CID=1761.
68. Knights and Solomon-Schwartz, "The Broader Threat from Sunni Islamists in the Gulf."
69. Barry Rubin, ed., *Guide to Islamist Movements* (London: M.E. Sharpe, 2009), 308-310.
70. Oxford Analytica, "The Advent of Terrorism in Qatar."
71. Oxford Analytica, "The Advent of Terrorism in Qatar."
72. "Qatar: Political Forces."
73. Ehud Rosen, *Mapping the Organizational Sources of the Global Delegitimization Campaign Against Israel In the UK* (Jerusalem, Israel: Jerusalem Center for Public Affairs, December 24, 2010), http://www.jcpa.org/text/Mapping_Delegitimization.pdf.
74. Tabbara, "Qatar Emir in Gaza."
75. Marc Lynch, "Muslim Brotherhood Debates," *Abu Aardvark* blog, February 28, 2007, http://abuaardvark.typepad.com/abuaardvark/2007/02/muslim_brotherh.html.
76. Reuven Paz, "Qaradhawi and the World Association of Muslim Clerics: The New Platform of the Muslim Brotherhood," *PRISM Series on Global Jihad* no. 4/2, November 2004, 1-2, http://www.e-prism.org/images/PRISM_no_4_vol_2_-_Qaradhawi.pdf.
77. Samuel Helfont, "Islam and Islamism Today: the Case of Yusuf al-Qaradawi," Foreign Policy Research Institute *E-Notes*, January 2010, http://www.fpri.org/article/2010/01/islam-and-islamism-today-the-case-of-yusuf-al-qaradawi/.
78. Samuel Helfont, "Islam and Islamism Today: the Case of Yusuf al-Qaradawi."
79. Samuel Helfont, "Islam and Islamism Today: the Case of Yusuf al-Qaradawi."
80. U.S. Department of the Treasury, "PRESS RELEASE HP-1267: Treasury designates the Union of Good,"

November 12, 2008, (http://www.treasury.gov/press-center/press-releases/Pages/hp1267.aspx).

81. Steinberg, "Qatar and the Arab Spring," 4.
82. Syria conflict: Cleric Qaradawi urges Sunnis to join rebels BBC News, 1 June 2013, (http://www.bbc.com/news/world-middle-east-22741588).
83. Nadina Shalaq, "Qatar's European Strategy," *As-Safir* (Lebanon), December 26, 2012, as translated in *Al-Monitor*, December 27, 2012, http://www.al-monitor.com/pulse/politics/2012/12/qatari-investments-in-greece-highlight-soft-power-strategy.html.
84. Harvey Morris, "Qatar's Latest Investment Stirs the French," *International Herald Tribune*, September 25, 2012, http://rendezvous.blogs.nytimes.com/2012/09/25/qatars-latest-investment-stirs-the-french/.
85. Jennifer Lambert, "Qatari Law Will Test Media Freedom," Carnegie Endowment for International Peace *Arab Reform Bulletin*, December 1, 2010, http://carnegieendowment.org/sada/?fa=42049.
86. Kristen Gillespie, "The New Face of Al Jazeera," *The Nation*, November 9, 2007.
87. Kristen Gillespie, "The New Face of Al Jazeera," *The Nation*, November 9, 2007.
88. Kristen Gillespie, "The New Face of Al Jazeera," *The Nation*, November 9, 2007; Oren Kessler, "The Two Faces of Al Jazeera," *Middle East Forum,* Winter 2012, pp. 47-56, http://www.meforum.org/3147/al-jazeera ; Sultan Sooud Al Qassemi, "Qatar's Brotherhood Ties Alienate Fellow Gulf States," *Al-Monitor,* January 23, 2013, http://www.al-monitor.com/pulse/originals/2013/01/qatar-muslim-brotherhood.html ; see also http://foreignpolicy.com/2013/07/12/al-jazeeras-awful-week/ .
89. Kristen Gillespie, "The New Face of Al Jazeera," *The Nation*, November 9, 2007; Oren Kessler, "The Two Faces of Al Jazeera; Al Qassemi, "Qatar's Brotherhood Ties Alienate Fellow Gulf States."
90. Steinberg, "Qatar and the Arab Spring."
91. Sultan Sooud Al Qassemi, "Morsi's Win Is Al Jazeera's Loss," *Al-Monitor*, July 1, 2012, http://www.al-monitor.

com/pulse/originals/2012/al-monitor/morsys-win-is-al-jazeeras-loss.html#ixzz2I3awUthS.
92. Mohammad Hisham Abeih, "Qatar on Defense over Meddling in Egypt," *As-Safir* (Lebanon), January 10, 2013, as translated in *Al-Monitor*, January 10, 2013, http://www.al-monitor.com/pulse/politics/2013/01/qatars-media-and-political-influence-over-egypt.html#ixzz2I36FW8C4.
93. U.S. Department of State, "Background Note: Qatar."
94. "Qatar: Political Forces."
95. Zvi Bar'el, "Is Al Jazeera Trying to Bring Down the Palestinian Authority?" *Ha'aretz* (Tel Aviv), February 2, 2011, http://www.haaretz.com/print-edition/features/is-al-jazeera-trying-to-bring-down-the-palestinian-authority-1.340716.
96. Gillespie, "The New Face of Al Jazeera."
97. Ayman Sharaf. "Al Jazeera staff resign after 'biased' Egypt coverage," *Gulf News*, July 8, 2013, http://gulfnews.com/news/region/egypt/al-jazeera-staff-resign-after-biased-egypt-coverage-1.1206924.
98. Al Jazeera, 12 July 2017. Op cit.
99. "Rights groups condemn demand to shut Al Jazeera," *Al Jazeera,* June 23, 2017. https://www.aljazeera.com/news/2017/06/media-watchdog-slams-demand-shut-al-jazeera-170623111049529.html
100. Bar'el, "Is Al Jazeera Trying to Bring Down the Palestinian Authority?"
101. Adel Iskandar, co-author of *Al-Jazeera: The Story Of The Network That Is Rattling Governments And Redefining Modern Journalism*, quoted in "Why Arab states want to shut down Al-Jazeera," *CBC Radio,* July 6, 2017. https://www.cbc.ca/radio/thecurrent/the-current-for-july-6-2017-1.4191665/why-arab-states-want-to-shut-down-al-jazeera-1.4191668
102. "Qatar Uses Al-Jazeera as Bargaining Chip: WikiLeaks," *The Economic Times* (India), December 6, 2010, http://economictimes.indiatimes.com/tech/internet/qatar-uses-al-jazeera-as-bargaining-chip-wikileaks/articleshow/7051690.cms
103. Hussein Ibish, "Why America Turned Off Al Jazeera," *New York Times,* February 17, 2016.

104. Hassan Hassan, "Qatar Won the Blockade," *Foreign Policy*, https://foreignpolicy.com/2018/06/04/qatar-won-the-saudi-blockade/

27 Saudi Arabia

Quick Facts

Population: 28,571,770
Area: 2,149,690 sq km
Ethnic Groups: Arab 90%, Afro-Asian 10%
Religions: Muslim (official; citizens are 85-90% Sunni and 10-15% Shia), other (includes Eastern Orthodox, Protestant, Roman Catholic, Jewish, Hindu, Buddhist, and Sikh) (2012 est.)
Government Type: Absolute Monarchy
GDP (official exchange rate): $683.8 billion (2017 est.)

Map and Quick Facts courtesy of the CIA World Factbook (Last Updated September 2018)

Introduction

Since 2015, Saudi Arabia has experienced significant changes in its domestic politics, as well as an apparent relaxation of its traditionally extreme interpretation of the Muslim faith. Following the January 2015 death of King Abdullah bin Abdulaziz Al Saud, his younger brother Salman bin Abdulaziz Al Saud ascended to the throne. Defying Saudi tradition since the 1950s, he removed his youngest (and last surviving brother) as his successor, instead naming his nephew Mohammed bin Nayef as Crown Prince of Saudi Arabia and thus his heir apparent, and his own son, Mohammed bin Salman (known as MbS) as Deputy Crown Prince. A subsequent power struggle between bin Nayef and MbS, however, led to Nayef's eventual (and apparently forced) abdication.[1] MbS, meanwhile, has attracted international attention for his apparent anti-corruption and modernization efforts. Nevertheless, doubts remain as to whether or not M.B.S. has truly renounced Saudi Arabia's long-standing practice of exporting extremist Islamist ideology in the form of Wahhabism around the world.

Islamist Activities

Islamism in Saudi Arabia is characterized by competing intellectual traditions, which—while all conservative and fundamentalist—hold significantly different, and in some ways evolving, ideas about the relationship between Islam and society.

The Rejectionists

The "rejectionists," a pietistic, lower-class Islamic intellectual movement that categorically rejects the legitimacy of the state and its institutions, opposes any role or voice for themselves in the life of the state and in the national political discourse, emerged during the 1950's and 1960's. Rejectionists believe in withdrawing from society and focusing solely on faith and ritual practice, repudiating all schools of Islamic jurisprudence (fiqh), and relying solely on the unmediated sayings of the Prophet Muhammad (hadith). They confine themselves to isolated, orthodox communities where they educate their children and pursue their distinctive lifestyle. However, they are not monolithic, and some have formed their own socio-political protest movements in spite of the trend's original doctrine.

One of these movements is the al-Jama'a al-Salafiyya al-Muhtasiba (JSM), which formed in the 1970s and was inspired by the Syrian religious scholar Nasr al-Din al-Albani.[2] In 1979, JSM, led by Juhayman al-Utaybi, orchestrated an armed takeover of the Grand Mosque in Mecca. Though the Saudis were initially reluctant to use force in one of Islam's holiest sites, they eventually raided the Mosque and ended the siege. After the Grand Mosque incident, the remaining members of JSM fled to Kuwait, Yemen, and the northern Saudi desert, returning to a state of relative isolation. However, Juhayman's ideas have continued to influence others in subsequent years. The JSM's views allegedly influenced three men who were involved in the 1995 bombing in Riyadh, as well as "senior militants" who were part of al-Qaeda's violent campaign in 2003.[3]

The Sahwa

Another intellectual tradition that developed during the 1950s and 1960s is the Sahwa ("Awakened") movement, which, unlike the rejectionists, is pragmatic, political and elitist. Sahwa clerics trace their roots back to the rise of the Muslim Brotherhood, whose members were well educated, and who established themselves in the new education and media sectors of Saudi Arabia. As a natural result of their interaction with Muslim Brotherhood members, the

Sahwa clerics' ideology became a synthesis of Salafi-Wahhabi theological teachings and the Brotherhood's political activism.[4] The spread of Sahwa teachings in Saudi universities would eventually lead to the group's political reform efforts of the 1990s. However, the Sahwa is an extremely diverse faction that includes religious scholars, scientists, doctors, and academics. Its members are commonly divided into at least two main camps: those who follow Hassan al-Banna, the founder of the Brotherhood, and those who follow his more extreme ideological successor, Sayyid Qutb. Their ability to address issues—like politics—that were traditionally outside the purview of the official Saudi religious establishment originally garnered broad public appeal.[5]

The Sahwa became widely recognized in 1990 for their virulent opposition to then-Saudi King Fahd's reliance on a non-Muslim military coalition, led by the United States, to defend the Arabian Peninsula after Saddam Hussein's Iraqi army invaded Kuwait. Prominent Sahwa clerics believed that the legitimacy of the Al Saud leadership and the official Saudi religious establishment had been permanently destroyed by this collaboration with the West.[6] Thereafter, the Sahwa called for greater Islamization of Saudi society and demanded a more prominent role in social and foreign affairs.[7]

In 1994, Salman al-Odah, Safar al-Hawali, and nearly 1,300 Sahwa affiliates were arrested for their vehement opposition to the Saudi regime.[8] To the leadership's dismay, their five years in prison only cemented the clerics' standing in the eyes of their followers and granted them even greater popular legitimacy than the official ulema. When the men were released in 1999, the Saudi government confronted them with the choice of either withdrawing from the public eye or acquiescing to the authority of the state. They chose the latter, and the Sahwa splintered as a result. Some of its members have since joined other Saudi Islamist movements, including the jihadist trend, while others abandoned Islamism entirely. For a number of years, the Sahwa took a more conciliatory tone with the Saudi Arabian regime, and rarely criticized the government.[9] But during the Arab Spring, the split amongst the Sahwa, and the challenge they present to the Saudi Arabian regime, became more apparent. In early 2011, several petitions calling for government reform were signed by leading Sahwa clerics, but none of them supported calls for the open demonstrations in Riyadh a few months later.[10]

For a few years, some Sahwa and religious scholars remained critical of the regime, but on February 4, 2014, in response to domestic condemnation of the Saudi government's support of the overthrow of Egyptian President Mohammed Morsi, the Saudi government issued a decree stating that anyone who provides support (defined loosely and in a variety of ways) to an organization categorized as extremist or defined as a terrorist group could face a prison sentence of 3 to 20 years.[11] In 2017, al-Odah was arrested and remains in Saudi custody.[12] Saudi authorities arrested al-Hawali in 2018.[13]

The jihadists

A jihadist trend exists in Saudi society, embodied by the rise of Osama bin Laden's al-Qaeda network, but it has faced considerable challenges since the ascent of the Islamic State to prominence in 2014.

From 1999 through 2001, conflicts in the Muslim world (in places such as Chechnya, Kosovo, and the Palestinian Territories) and a powerful recruiting network in Saudi Arabia enabled bin Laden to attract a wave of Saudis to al-Qaeda's training camps in Afghanistan. Al-Qaeda's operations have been well-funded by Saudi individuals and organizations. In 2004, the 9/11 Commission reported that bin Laden created an informal financial network of charities, including the Al Haramain Islamic Foundation and other non-governmental organizations, which allowed Saudi and Gulf financiers to send funds to Arabs fighting in Afghanistan and then later to al-Qaeda.[14]

In early 2002, between 300 and 1,000 Saudi al-Qaeda members returned to Saudi Arabia after the Taliban's fall compromised the network's base of operations in Afghanistan. Two independent cells subsequently formed, and the organization's operatives began preparing for operations by stockpiling weapons, renting safe houses, setting up training camps, and recruiting other "Afghan Arabs."[15] The cells consisted principally of Saudis, but maintained a small percentage of foreign nationals. The majority of al-Qaeda members were not from regions typically considered to be the most religiously conservative or impoverished rural areas. Instead, the overwhelming majority of the organization was formed by urbanites from Riyadh, most of whom shared previous combat experience in Afghanistan—first against the Soviets and later against the United States.[16]

The Saudi government's aggressive counterterrorism efforts eventually forced al-Qaeda's local branch to relocate across the border in Yemen. In January 2009, the Saudi and Yemeni branches of al-Qaeda merged to become al-Qaeda in the Arabian Peninsula (AQAP), with a number of Saudis assuming leadership positions in the new franchise.[17] AQAP grew more dangerous in its first year of operations; in August 2009, the organization nearly succeeded in assassinating then Saudi Deputy Interior Minister Prince Muhammad bin Nayef during a gathering at his home in Jeddah.[18] Then, only months later, AQAP coordinated the attempted Christmas Day bombing—carried out by a Nigerian man with explosives in his underwear—of a Northwest Airlines flight traveling from Yemen to Detroit.[19]

In 2014, after AQAP attacked a remote Saudi-Yemeni border checkpoint, the State Department determined the organization has "continued its efforts to inspire sympathizers to support, finance, or engage in conflicts outside of Saudi Arabia and encouraged individual acts of terrorism within the Kingdom."[20] Since then, the Saudi government has taken increased action to prevent Saudis from traveling abroad to support extremist groups like al-Qaeda and the Islamic State. However, after the January 2016 execution of a number of al-Qaeda suspects by the Saudi government, al-Qaeda leader Ayman al Zawahiri condemned the government and called for revenge.[21] However, in August 2018, an Associate Press investigation revealed that the Saudi-led coalition in Yemen had negotiated a series of agreements with al-Qaeda militants. These deals involved paying some al-Qaeda militants to leave cities quietly, allowing al-Qaeda militants to leave cities early with their equipment and assets, and recruiting militants to join the Saudi-led coalition itself.[22]

By his own account, Crown Prince Mohammed bin Salman (MbS) remains deeply concerned about the threat of Sunni jihadist groups to the safety of Saudi Arabia. During an April 2018 visit to the United States, MbS referred to a "triangle of evil," consisting of the Islamic Republic of Iran, the Muslim Brotherhood, and Sunni terrorist groups, including al-Qaeda and the Islamic State.[23] MbS has also claimed that Iran supports and shelters al-Qaeda operatives, including Osama bin Laden's son.[24] The relative decline of the Islamic State in 2017 and into 2018 has not assuaged Saudi concerns about the threat posed by terrorist groups.

The Shia

Another Islamic intellectual trend in Saudi Arabia is rooted in the country's Shia minority, which is primarily located in the Eastern Province, and constitutes 10-15% of the total population.[25] Having been branded as unbelievers (kuffar) since the time of Muhammad ibn Abd al-Wahhab, Saudi Shia are still severely marginalized in the modern state.[26] And while Shia Islamists have never been as organized as the Sahwa, or even the jihadists in Saudi Arabia, instances of Shia Islamist activity continue to play a significant role in Saudi society and the government's approach to dissent.

An early and frequently cited incident of Shia opposition took place in 1980, in the wake of the Islamic Revolution in Iran. Radio Tehran's Arabic channel had been broadcasting propaganda against the Saudi regime to the Shia population. The propaganda sparked a riot in Qatif, during which citizens attacked the town's central market.[27] Since that time, the Saudi government has been extremely wary of renewed violence, as well as of Iran's influence in Saudi domestic affairs.

For a brief period, the Arab Spring rekindled opposition from Saudi Arabia's Shia population. Shortly after the outbreak of protests in Tunisia in December 2011, Shia Islamists in Saudi Arabia began to organize themselves through social media tools like Facebook and Twitter, issuing petitions for political and social reforms such as the transition to a constitutional monarchy and an end to sectarian discrimination. Violent protests erupted in July 2012 in the Eastern Province—which includes not only most of the Shia population but also most of the country's oil—after security forces shot and arrested a popular Shi'ite cleric Nimr al-Nimr for instigating "sedition."[28] Shia anger continued to bubble in the weeks after Nimr's arrest, with Saudi authorities exacerbating the furor when they fatally shot two men during the demonstrations.[29] The protests in the Eastern Province escalated even further in October 2012, when tens of thousands of angry mourners carried the bodies of three young Shia men, slain by Saudi security forces, through the streets of Awwamiya while chanting "Death to al-Saud."[30]

Almost ten months after Saudi authorities arrested al-Nimr, in March 2013, he was put on trial for "sowing discord" and "undermining national unity."[31] Between the trial and the autumn of 2014, Shia protests dissipated. But on October 24, al-Nimr was sentenced to death, along with his nephew, and protests erupted again.[32] A year and four months later, on January 2, 2016, al-Nimr was executed along with 46 other people the Saudi government had labeled "terrorists." In response to the execution, protests erupted in Qatif in the Eastern Province, in Bahrain, and across the Middle East.[33] Angered by al-Nimr's death, Iranian activists attacked and set fire to the Saudi Embassy in Tehran, prompting the severance of diplomatic ties between the two countries.[34]

Saudi Arabia has often been critiqued for its poor record on human rights, particularly in the matter of executions. In response to rising sectarianism in the region and increasing tensions between Iran and Saudi Arabia, Saudi Arabia executed 158 people in 2015, up from 90 in 2014.[35] In 2016, Saudi Arabia executed at minimum 154 people, according to Amnesty International.[36] In 2017, Saudi Arabia executed at least 138 people, according to Human Rights Watch.[37] Crimes in Saudi Arabia that warrant death sentences include drug offenses, adultery, and "sorcery." Confessions to such crimes are often elicited through torture.[38] The Saudi regime has at times invoked "national security" as a catch-all defense for its execution policies.[39]

Islamism and Society

With the exception of a brief "Sahwa Insurrection" in the early 1990s, Islamist opposition or reformist movements in Saudi Arabia have failed to garner enough societal support to mount a sustained or serious challenge to the ruling House of Saud. This is largely due to the Saudi social contract, which consists of the government's use of oil wealth to provide a robust welfare state for its citizens, in return for almost complete control of all of Saudi Arabia by the ruling family.[40] Furthermore, the Saud family has always relied on proselytizing Wahhabism, a deeply radical interpretation of Islam, as part of its basis of power. MbS's determination to modernize the Saudi economy may impact this arrangement, but there were some tremors in its foundation even before the advent of the current reform effort. Since the rise of the Islamic State, there has been a renewed internal debate over the future of Wahhabism. Cole Bunzel of the Carnegie Endowment for International Peace has argued that there is a subtly emerging "correctionist" movement regarding Wahhabism within the liberal wing of the religious establishment in Saudi Arabia, and that it has been much more tolerated in society of late than in earlier years.[41] Such developments are partially due to the political leadership being preoccupied with consolidating power, but also because of the role that information technologies have played within the Kingdom.

As a social force, the Sahwa clerics rose in influence when they challenged the Islamic credentials of the ruling family and religious establishment between 1990 and 1994. Much to the Kingdom's dismay, in some cases their subsequent imprisonment only increased their status and notoriety. Increasing modernization of information technologies have changed the way that clerics have engaged with society, and expanded the cleric's influence beyond the traditional Wahhabist/Salafi international network. Between 2011 and 2014, a number of Sahwa clerics gained increasing prominence through their use of the Internet. In 2011, Forbes Middle East ranked Salman al-Odah fourth on its list of top 100 "Twitterati," who boasted more than 3.4 million Twitter followers, and by 2014 had garnered nearly 1.5 million more followers on Facebook. Today, al-Odah has 11 million followers on Twitter, and almost 7 million on Facebook.[42] Fellow Saudi clerics Muhammad al-Arife and Aidh al-Qarni have been even more successful than al-Odah on social media. Al-Arefe, who is called the "Brad Pitt" of Muslim clerics, has 16 million Twitter followers—more than the total population of the Kingdom of Jordan.[43] Likewise, al-Qarni, a social media star who is known for his self-help book, "Don't be Sad," has 14.5 million

Twitter followers.[44] After delivering a lecture in the Philippines in March 2016, al-Qarni was shot and injured in the shoulder, which only increased his notoriety.[45]

These clerics maintain tremendous influence in shaping Saudi public opinion and attitudes toward the West. On the eve of the American siege of Fallujah, twenty-six prominent clerics signed an "Open Sermon to the Militant Iraqi People" that legitimized joining the Iraqi insurgency as part of a "defense jihad" against the "aggressor" coalition.[46] Shortly thereafter, the number of Saudis who went to Iraq to fight against Western forces peaked.[47] In June 2012, a number of prominent clerics tried to organize a fundraising campaign for Syrian rebels fighting against President Bashar al-Assad's regime. However, one of the organizations facilitating the transfer of donations was the Revival of Islamic Heritage Society of Kuwait, a charity previously designated as a terrorist entity by the United States and UN for arming and financing al-Qaeda.[48] More recently, and despite the government's 2014 decree forbidding Saudis from fighting against ISIS outside of Saudi Arabia, 53 clerics and academics issued a call in the Fall of 2015 for "all those who are able, and outside of Saudi Arabia, to answer the calls of jihad" and fight against Russian forces and the Syrian government in Syria.[49]

In addition to physical and intellectual resistance, Saudi Islamists have long been implicated in terrorist financing across the globe. Since the 1970s, Saudi Arabia has spent more than 4 percent of its GDP per year on overseas aid, with "two thirds of that amount going to 'Islamic Activities'" in impoverished countries grappling with extremism, like Yemen, Sudan, Mauritania, Bosnia and Afghanistan.[50] After the events of September 11, 2001, Saudi Arabia and other Gulf countries have been repeatedly criticized for financing terrorism abroad. In 2007, then-Undersecretary of the Treasury for Terrorism and Financial Intelligence Stuart Levey said that, "If I could somehow snap my fingers and cut off funding from one country, it would be Saudi Arabia."[51] Levey's comments were a consequence of the fact that Islamic charities are commonly singled out as the primary source of illicit funds in terror financing cases. Implicating wealthy Saudis in terrorist financing cases with exact dollar amounts is extremely difficult, primarily due to the fact that Saudis prefer cash transactions and donate anonymously. Since giving charitably (zakat) is one of the five pillars of Islam, such organizations receive significant donations anonymously and from all sectors of society.

The final report of the 9/11 Commission determined that there was no evidence that the Saudi government as an institution, or the Saudi leadership as individuals, provided support to al-Qaeda, but the Commission noted that al-Qaeda raised money directly from individuals in Saudi Arabia, and through "charities with significant government sponsorship."[52] This pattern of funding allegedly stretches back for the past 30 years. In particular, the 9/11 Commission noted the "Golden Chain," a network of Saudi and other Gulf financiers used by Osama bin Laden to collect and channel funds for the anti-Soviet jihad during the 1980s in Afghanistan. The financiers used charities and other NGOs as conduits for their donations to the jihad, and this network later became influential in the establishment of al-Qaeda's base in Afghanistan in the late 1990s.[53]

In another instance of illicit financing, the Pakistani newspaper Dawn reported on a leaked 2008 cable from the U.S. Consulate in Lahore to the State Department. The cable alleged that financiers in Saudi Arabia and the UAE were sending nearly $100 million annually to Deobandi and Ahl-i-Hadith clerics in southern Punjab. In turn, those clerics were targeting families with multiple children and severe financial difficulties for recruitment, initially under the pretense of charity. Next, a Deobandi or Ahl-i-Hadith maulana would offer to educate the children in his school and "find them employment in the service of Islam." During the education phase, the clerics would indoctrinate the children and assess their inclination "to engage in violence and acceptance of jihadi culture." Parents then received cash payments of $6,500 for each son chosen for "martyrdom" operations.[54]

Throughout 2016, partially in response to legislation introduced in the U.S. Senate in 2015 as the Justice Against Sponsors of Terrorism Act (JASTA) which narrowed the scope of the doctrine of sovereign immunity to enable families of the 9/11 victims to make civil claims against a foreign state in response to an act of terrorism, Saudi Arabia aggressively pursued the issue of illicit financing. In the summer of 2016, Daniel Glaser, a former assistant secretary for terrorist financing at the U.S. Department of Treasury, testified before Congress that Saudi Arabia had emerged as a "regional leader in targeted designations."[55] Saudi Arabia's spokesperson for the Ministry of the Interior claimed that Saudi Arabia had prosecuted more than 240 suspects and froze and investigated more than 117 internal accounts.[56] These activities by the government were also in response to the growing threat of ISIL throughout the region. According to recent polling data, it is estimated that about 5% of Saudi Arabia's population—or over half a million people—support the Islamic State.[57] And in July, 2016, three suicide bombing attacks bearing the hallmarks of the Islamic State were conducted across the country; an act former CIA Director John Brennan described as "unprecedented."[58]

Islamism and the State

In 1979, the Saudi Monarchy witnessed the Grand Mosque takeover within the Kingdom's own borders, the Islamic Revolution in Iran, Shia protests in its own oil-rich Eastern Province, and the Soviet invasion of Afghanistan. Shaken by what it perceived as serious threats to its security and power, the Saudi leadership quickly took drastic measures to assert its leadership in the Islamic world and to appease rising domestic extremism. They accomplished both objectives by increasing its existing exportation of a politicized form of Wahhabism, directed as a foreign policy tool against the Soviets and competing strands of Islam alike.[59]

To bolster his legitimacy and to counter the threat of secular governance sweeping the Middle East, in the 1960s King Faysal established a policy of supporting Islamic institutions abroad. In 1962, he created the Muslim World League (MWL) to facilitate the spread of Wahhabi ideology. The Saudis also helped develop other religious organizations, including the World Assembly of Muslim Youth (WAMY), the Al Haramain Foundation, and the International Islamic Relief Organization (IIRO), among others. From 1973-2002, the Saudi government spent more than $80 billion on Islamic institutions and other activities in the non-Muslim world alone, contributing to some 1,500 mosques, 150 Islamic centers, 202

Muslim colleges, and 2,000 Islamic schools.[60]

With their unprecedented outreach campaign, the Saudis provide extremely generous support to American universities and elite institutions, which can preempt criticism from that realm.[61] However, since 9/11, Islamic institutions in the U.S. have faced increasing scrutiny. Nearly 50 organizations and institutions that have been raided, shut down, or had their assets frozen because of suspected links to terrorism. Among those institutions connected to Saudi Arabia were the Muslim World League, World Assembly of Muslim Youth, the Al Haramain Foundation, the SAAR Foundation, the International Institute of Islamic Thought, and the School of Islamic and Social Sciences.[62] There are some indications that MbS's policies may be changing the outlook of some of these groups. For example, Sheikh Mohammad al-Issa, the leader of MWL, has publicly been very supportive of MbS and his attempts at reform.[63]

After the Arab Spring

Since the outbreak of the Arab Spring in late 2010, when massive protests overthrew longtime Saudi allies in Egypt and Tunisia and heralded the rise of Islamists to power in those places, the Saudi government has worked to preempt similar demands for national reforms. As the protest movements rolled through Tunisia, Egypt, and Libya, King Abdullah rushed to avert a crisis of power by issuing subsidy packages worth an estimated $130 billion, creating a Facebook page for the population to tell him their grievances, and increasing the salaries of government workers. The king's measures included 60,000 jobs at the Ministry of the Interior, 500,000 new houses, and a minimum wage for the public sector of 3,000 Saudi Riyals ($800) per month—in contrast, the average private sector wage is only 1,000 SR per month.[64] The government also infused $10.7 billion into its development fund, which offers Saudis interest-free loans to build homes, marry, and start small businesses. An additional $4 billion was designated for the healthcare sector.[65]

To maintain order, the Saudi government also relied on help from the state's clergy, sanctioned and unsanctioned alike, who criticized activists online on Facebook and Twitter, and who issued fatwas in support of the regime. On March 6, 2011, the country's highest religious body, the Council of Senior Ulema, called on "everybody to exert every effort to increase solidarity, promote unity and warn against all causes giving rise to the opposite," and further warned Saudis about "deviant intellectual and partisan [Shia] tendencies" that could threaten Saudi stability.[66] Other clerics threatened potential protesters with violence. Saad al-Buraik, a member of the government's Counseling Program for re-educating extremists, called for "smashing the skulls of those who organize demonstrations or take part in them."[67]

The state's mix of subsidies and clerical advocacy, as well as its robust security deployments, successfully eliminated the threat of a popular uprising, but threats to the Kingdom remain. With the rise of the Islamic State, the increasing strength of Iran, the unruly nature of the Internet and online activism, and a significant power transition, Saudi Arabia continues to wrestle with how to maintain control and legitimacy in a rapidly changing geopolitical and security landscape. Unsanctioned clerics have carved out a substantial platform on social media that may prove difficult for the government to control. Because those clerics have generally played within the state's red lines, they have been largely unhindered in the messaging.[68]

Current and Future Issues

Following the death of King Abdullah on January 25, 2015, his half-brother, King Salman bin Abdulaziz, came to power and immediately began to assert his authority through various strategic policies. He released thousands of prisoners (except those deemed a threat to security), increased the salaries of public sector employees, curtailed the power of the religious police, dismissed two influential officials who had opposed Wahabi clerics, and, in a nod to ultraconservative clerics, fired the Kingdom's only female Cabinet member. He also upset the traditional succession order, forcing his brother, the Crown Prince, into retirement, and then filling the position with his nephew in 2015, and his son MbS in 2017.[69] Also in 2017, the King lifted a national ban that prevented women from driving, which came into effect in the summer of 2018.[70]

King Salman's approach to geopolitical changes has been both ideological and practical, similar to his predecessors. As King Salman has leaned more heavily on the traditional cleric establishment to maintain legitimacy, he and MbS have also moved to restructure the economy in the face of a shifting global energy landscape driven in large part by the United States' new oil independence.[71]

Increasingly concerned with the threat of Iran and its proxies in Yemen, in recent years the Saudi government has also pursued a more aggressive foreign policy defined by its call for the resignation of President Bashar al Assad of Syria, and its military efforts in Yemen beginning in 2015. Three months after coming to power, following the ouster of the Yemeni transitional government in 2015 at the hands of the Houthi rebels and backers of the former Yemeni President Ali Abdullah Saleh, King Salman initiated military strikes in coordination with nine other Middle Eastern countries.[72] Since then, despite a significant number of civilian casualties, Saudi losses, and increased tensions between Iran and Saudi Arabia, the United States supported the Kingdom in its efforts to reinstate exiled President Abdrabbuh Mansour Hadi in the ongoing conflict. Hadi is currently in Saudi Arabia. However, the relationship between Hadi and the Saudis has recently soured, as evidenced by significant restrictions on the president's movements. Saudi authorities have prevented Hadi, his sons, and his ministers from returning to southern Yemen, which is ostensibly under Hadi's control. Saudi officials indicated tensions between Hadi and the UAE led to the blockade.

In April 2016, MbS announced a long-term oil independence strategy for the country. Included among the initiatives in his "Vision 2030" was a commitment to a minor increase in the women's participation rate in the workforce—which will be raised from 22% to 30 % over 15 years. This modest proposal, according to the Economist, suggests resistance from the Wahhabi clerical establishment. For a country with a population that has been conditioned to expect oil wealth in exchange for loyalty, and a clerical establishment that is resistant to modernization, a National Transformation Program will be difficult to implement, and would rely largely on MbS to succeed.[73] However, MbS has proved his determination to do so.

MbS's first maneuver was a widespread purge, allegedly on anti-corruption grounds. Saudi police arrested over 200 people, many of them wealthy and influential, and placed them in the Ritz-Carlton Hotel in Riyadh under a kind of house arrest. Some reports suggest that the subsequent interrogations of the detainees included significant physical abuse.[74] In order to escape confinement, detainees had to pay a large sum of money and sign a non-disclosure agreement.[75] The Saudi government claimed to have regained over $100bn in this anti-corruption operation.[76] Some analysts have contended that, while MbS may have claimed anti-corruption as the motivation for this roundup, it was also intended to remove potential threats to his rule. Most prominently, the arrest of the head of the national guard, Prince Miteb bin Abdullah, left MbS in command of all three of branches of the Saudi military: the national guard, the interior ministry, and the Army.[77]

MbS attracted further international attention during his April 2018 visit to the United States. During that period, he professed reformist opinions previously unheard of among Arab leadership, including that "the Palestinians and the Israelis have the right to have their own land."[78] In that same interview with journalist Jeffrey Goldberg of *The Atlantic*, he expressed a desire to modernize Saudi Arabia's economy while preserving its culture and extreme anxiety about what he called the "triangle of evil" (Iran, the Muslim Brotherhood, and Sunni terrorist groups). However, some of his reformist zeal – at least as regards a change in Saudi Arabia's traditionally intolerant interpretation of Islam – was called into question during a particular line of questioning:

> **Goldberg**: Isn't it true, though, that after 1979, but before 1979 as well, the more conservative factions in Saudi Arabia were taking oil money and using it to export a more intolerant, extremist version of Islam, Wahhabist ideology, which could be understood as a kind of companion ideology to Muslim Brotherhood thinking?
> **MbS**: First of all, this Wahhabism—please define it for us. We're not familiar with it. We don't know about it.
> **Goldberg**: What do you mean you don't know about it?
> **MbS**: What is Wahhabism?
> **Goldberg**: You're the crown prince of Saudi Arabia. You know what Wahhabism is.

> **MbS**: No one can define this Wahhabism.
> Goldberg: It's a movement founded by Ibn abd al-Wahhab in the 1700s, very fundamentalist in nature, an austere Salafist-style interpretation—
> **MbS**: No one can define Wahhabism. There is no Wahhabism. We don't believe we have Wahhabism. We believe we have, in Saudi Arabia, Sunni and Shiite…[79]

Moving forward, the scope and authenticity of the reforms now underway in Saudi Arabia will undoubtedly become clearer, as will the commitment of the country's leadership to those goals. For the moment, observers of the changes underway within the Kingdom – including, most prominently, the U.S. government – remain cautiously optimistic about the potential moderating effect of the initiatives that have been undertaken to date by Saudi authorities under the stewardship of MbS.

Endnotes

1. Dexter Filkins,"A Saudi Prince's Quest to Remake the Middle East," *The New Yorker,* April 9, 2018, https://www.newyorker.com/magazine/2018/04/09/a-saudi-princes-quest-to-remake-the-middle-east.
2. "Saudi Arabia Backgrounder: Who Are The Islamists?" International Crisis Group, September 21, 2004, 2, http://www.pbs.org/wgbh/pages/frontline/shows/saud/themes/backgrounder.pdf.
3. Thomas Hegghammer and Stephane Lacroix, "Rejectionist Islamism in Saudi Arabia: The Story of Juhayman Al-'Utaybi Revisited," *International Journal of Middle East Studies* 39, 2007, 117, http://hegghammer.com/_files/Hegghammer-Lacroix_-_Rejectionist_Islamism_in_Saudi_Arabia.pdf.
4. Ondrej Beranek, "Divided We Survive: A Landscape of Fragmentation in Saudi Arabia," Brandeis University Crown Center for Middle East Studies *Middle East Brief* no. 28, January 2009, 3, http://www.brandeis.edu/

crown/publications/meb/MEB33.pdf .

5. Madawi al-Rasheed, *Contesting the Saudi State* (Cambridge: Cambridge University Press, 2007).
6. M. Ehsan Ahrari, "Saudi Arabia: A Simmering Cauldron of Instability?" *Brown Journal of World Affairs*, Summer/Fall 1999, 220, http://www.watsoninstitute.org/bjwa/archive/6.2/Essay/Ahrari.pdf .
7. Rachel Bronson, "Rethinking Religion: the Legacy of the U.S.-Saudi Relationship," *The Washington Quarterly*, Autumn 2005, 127, http://www.twq.com/05autumn/docs/05autumn_bronson.pdf
8. Shmuel Bachar, Shmuel Bar, Rachel Machtiger and Yair Minzili, *Establishment Ulama and Radicalism in Egypt, Saudi Arabia, and Jordan* (Washington, DC: Hudson Institute, December 2006), 18, http://www.currenttrends.org/docLib/20061226_UlamaandRadicalismfinal.pdf
9. When al-Qaeda on the Arabian Peninsula attacked three foreign housing complexes in Riyadh in May 2003, killing 34 and injuring 200, al-Odah and al-Hawali issued a statement with nearly 50 other clerics, condemning the attacks and declaring the perpetrators ignorant, misguided young men. See "Saudi bombing deaths rise," BBC (London), May 13, 2003, http://news.bbc.co.uk/2/hi/middle_east/3022473.stm; Then, in December 2004, al-Odah, Aidh al-Qarni, and 33 other sheikhs signed a statement denouncing London-based Saudi dissident Saad al-Faqih's attempts to organize demonstrations against the regime. See Toby Craig Jones, "The Clerics, the Sahwa and the Saudi State," Center for Contemporary Conflict *Strategic Insights*, March 2005, 4, http://www.nps.edu/Academics/centers/ccc/publications/OnlineJournal/2005/Mar/jonesMar05.pdf. Subsequently, in January 2005, in response to a failed attack on the Ministry of Interior in Riyadh the previous month, 41 clerics issued a statement on al-Odah's website, *Islam Today*, warning against actions and discourse targeting the Saudi regime.
10. Stephanie Lacroix, "Saudi Arabia's Muslim Brotherhood Dilemma," *The Washington Post*, March 20, 2014.
11. Lacroix, "Saudi Arabia's Muslim Brotherhood Dilem-

ma."

12. "Saudi clerics detained in apparent bid to silence dissent," Reuters, September 10, 2017, https://www.reuters.com/article/us-saudi-security-arrests/saudi-clerics-detained-in-apparent-bid-to-silence-dissent-idUSKCN1BL129.
13. "Sheikh Safar al-Hawali had been a prominent critic of American influence in Saudi Arabia," *Middle East Eye,* July 12, 2018, https://www.middleeasteye.net/news/top-islamist-cleric-detained-saudi-authorities-1156314858.
14. National Commission on Terrorist Attacks Upon the United States, "The 9/11 Commission Report," July 22, 2004
15. Thomas Hegghammer, "Islamist Violence and Regime Stability in Saudi Arabia," *International Affairs* 84, no. 4 (2008), http://hegghammer.com/_files/Hegghammer_-Islamist_violence_and_regime_stability_in_Saudi_Arabia.pdf
16. Hegghammer, "Islamist Violence and Regime Stability in Saudi Arabia," 45
17. "Al-Qaeda in the Arabian Peninsula," *Al Jazeera* (Doha), December 29, 2009, http://english.aljazeera.net/news/middleeast/2009/12/2009122935812371810.html
18. Margaret Coker, "Assassination Attempt Targets Saudi Prince," *Wall Street Journal*, August 29, 2009, http://online.wsj.com/article/SB125144774691366169.html
19. Anahad O'Connor & Eric Schmitt, "Terror Attempt Seen as Man Tries to Ignite Device on Jet," *New York Times*, December 25, 2009, http://www.nytimes.com/2009/12/26/us/26plane.html
20. U.S. State Department Bureau of Counterterrorism, Country Reports on Terrorism 2015, April 2016. The report has included similar language since the 2013 report released in April 2014.
21. "Al Qaeda Chief Tells Jihadist Fighters in Syria: Unite or Die," Reuters, May 8, 2016, http://www.reuters.com/article/us-mideast-crisis-syria-qaeda-idUSKCN0XZ0OA.
22. Maggie Michael, Trish Wilson, and Lee Keath, "AP Investigation: US allies, al-Qaida battle rebels in Ye-

men," Associated Press, August 7, 2018, https://apnews.com/f38788a561d74ca78c77cb43612d50da/Yemen:-US-allies-don%27t-defeat-al-Qaida-but-pay-it-to-go-away?utm_medium=AP&utm_campaign=SocialFlow&utm_source=Twitter.

23. Filkins,"A Saudi Prince's Quest."
24. Al-Monitor Staff, "Iran, Saudi Arabia in war of words over allegations of aiding al-Qaeda," *Al-Monitor,* March 20, 2018, https://www.al-monitor.com/pulse/originals/2018/03/iran-mbs-cbs-60-minutes-al-qaida-harboring-aid-reaction.html.
25. Graham, David. "Sheikh Nimr al Nimr and the Forgotten Shiites of Saudi Arabia," The Atlantic, January 5, 2016. https://www.theatlantic.com/international/archive/2016/01/nimr-al-nimr-saudi-arabia-shiites/422670/.
26. Ahmad Moussalli, "Wahhabism, Salafism, and Islamism: Who is the Enemy?" American University of Beirut, January 2009, 6, http://conflictsforum.org/briefings/Wahhabism-Salafism-and-Islamism.pdf
27. Rachel Bronson, *Thicker than Oil: America's Uneasy Partnership with Saudi Arabia* (New York: Oxford University Press, 2006), 147-8.
28. "Two Die During Saudi Arabia protest at Shia Cleric Arrest," BBC (London), July 9, 2012, http://www.bbc.co.uk/news/world-middle-east-18768703
29. Toby Matthiesen, "Saudi Arabia's Shiite Escalation," *Foreign Policy*, July 10, 2012, http://mideast.foreignpolicy.com/posts/2012/07/10/sable_rattling_in_the_gulf
30. For videos of the protests in Awwamiya, see http://www.youtube.com/watch?v=dPLF5fGvYNA&feature=youtu.be and http://www.youtube.com/watch?v=-JQsgTEBoH_E&feature=youtu.be
31. "Saudi Arabia: Cleric Who Backed Protests on Trial for His Life," Human Rights Watch, May 11, 2013, http://www.hrw.org/news/2013/05/10/saudi-arabia-cleric-who-backed-protests-trial-his-life .
32. Leila Fadel, "Saudi Cleric's Death Sentence Focuses Shia Anger on Ruling Family," *NPR*, October 18, 2014, http://www.npr.org/2014/10/18/357108117/saudi-cler-

ics-death-sentence-focuses-shia-anger-on-ruling-family

33. "Sheikh Nimr al-Nimr: Anger at Execution of Top Saudi Cleric," BBC, January 2, 2016, http://www.bbc.com/news/world-middle-east-35214536
34. Ben Hubbard, "Iranian Protesters Ransack Saudi Embassy After Execution of Shiite Cleric*," New York Times*, January 2, 2016, http://www.nytimes.com/2016/01/03/world/middleeast/saudi-arabia-executes-47-sheikh-nimr-shiite-cleric.html
35. Hubbard, "Iranian Protesters Ransack Saudi Embassy."
36. "China, Iran, Saudi Arabia executed most people in 2016," *Al Jazeera,* April 10, 2017, https://www.aljazeera.com/news/2017/04/death-penalty-2016-170410230144434.html.
37. "Saudi Arabia: Events of 2017," Human Rights Watch, *World Report 2018,* https://www.hrw.org/world-report/2018/country-chapters/saudi-arabia.
38. Saudi Arabia 2017/2018, Amnesty International, June 6, 2017, https://www.amnesty.org/en/countries/middle-east-and-north-africa/saudi-arabia/report-saudi-arabia/.
39. Saudi Arabia: 14 protesters facing execution after unfair trials," Amnesty International, https://www.amnesty.org/en/latest/news/2017/06/saudi-arabia-14-protesters-facing-execution-after-unfair-trials/.
40. Adel Abdel Ghafar, *A New Kingdom of Saud?* The Brookings Institute, February 14, 2018, https://www.brookings.edu/research/a-new-kingdom-of-saud/.
41. Bunzel, Cole. *The Kingdom and the Caliphate: Duel of the Islamic States, February 18, 2016.* http://carnegieendowment.org/2016/02/18/kingdom-and-caliphate-duel-of-islamic-states-pub-62810.
42. For *Forbes Middle East*'s List, see www.forbesmiddleeast.com/arabic/ اكثر-100-شخصية-عربية-حضورا-على-تويتر/; For Al-Odah's English Twitter Page, see http://twitter.com/Salman_Al_Odah ; For his Arabic page, see www.facebook.com/DrSalmanAlOadah; For his Arabic page, see www.facebook.com/SalmanAlodah
43. For al-Arefe's Twitter page, see http://twitter.com/Mo-

hamadAlarefe; For his Facebook page, see www.facebook.com/3refe

44. For al-Qarnee's Twitter page, see https://twitter.com/Dr_alqarnee; For his Facebook page, see www.facebook.com/dralqarnee?sk=wall
45. "Philippine Gunman Attacks and Injures Saudi Preacher," *Al Arabiya* (Riyadh), March 1, 2016, http://english.alarabiya.net/en/News/2016/03/01/Saudi-preacher-injured-after-gun-attack-in-Philippines.html
46. "The House of Saud: The Fatwa of the 26 Clerics: Open Sermon to the Militant Iraqi People," *PBS Frontline*, February 8, 2005, http://www.pbs.org/wgbh/pages/frontline/shows/saud/etc/fatwa.html
47. Thomas Hegghammer, "Saudis in Iraq: Patterns of Radicalization and Recruitment," *Revues.org*, June 12, 2008, http://conflits.revues.org/index10042.html
48. Jonathan Schanzer and Steven Miller, "Saudi Clerics Funnel Cash to Syrian Rebels through Terror Group," *Weekly Standard*, June 12, 2012, http://www.weeklystandard.com/blogs/saudi-clerics-funnel-cash-syrian-rebels-through-terror-group_647141.html
49. Al-Saleh, Huda, "52 Saudi clerics, scholars call to battle Russian forces in Syria," Al-Arabiya, October 5th 2015. http://english.alarabiya.net/en/News/middle-east/2015/10/05/Fifty-two-Saudi-clerics-scholars-call-for-fight-against-Russian-forces-in-Syria.html.
50. Graff, Corinne, *Poverty, Development, and Violent Extremism in Weak States*, Brookings Institution, 2010, p. 10. Accessed at: https://www.brookings.edu/wp-content/uploads/2016/06/2010_confronting_poverty.pdf
51. Brian Ross, "U.S.: Saudis Still Filling Al Qaeda's Coffers," *ABC News*, September 11,2007.
52. Christopher Blanchard and Alfred Prados, "Saudi Arabia, Terrorist Financing Issues," Congressional Research Service *Report*, December 8, 2004, http://fas.org/irp/crs/RL32499.pdf
53. Christopher Blanchard and Alfred Prados, "Saudi Arabia: Terrorist Financing Issues," Congressional Research Service *Report*, September 14, 2007, 6, http://www.fas.org/sgp/crs/terror/RL32499.pdf
54. Qurat ul ain Siddiqui, "Saudi Arabia, UAE Financing

Extremism in South Punjab," *Dawn*, May 22, 2011, http://www.dawn.com/2011/05/22/saudi-arabia-uae-financing-extremism-in-south-punjab.html

55. Kristina Wong, "Treasury Official: the Gulf states moving to cut off terrorist financing," *The Hill*, June 6th, 2016, http://thehill.com/policy/defense/282989-treasury-official-gulf-remains-important-source-of-terrorist-financing.
56. Kristina Wong, "Treasury Official."
57. "Is Saudi Arabia to Blame for the Islamic State?" BBC, December 19th, 2015. http://www.bbc.com/news/world-middle-east-35101612.
58. "Attacks in Saudi Arabia bear hallmarks of Islamic State," Reuters, July 14th, 2016. http://www.reuters.com/article/us-usa-saudi-idUSKCN0ZT2CL.
59. "Attacks in Saudi Arabia bear hallmarks of Islamic State," Reuters.
60. Alexander Alexiev, "The Wages of Extremism: Radical Islam's Threat to the West and the Muslim World," Hudson Institute, March 2011, 44, http://www.hudson.org/files/publications/AAlexievWagesofExtremism032011.pdf
61. Scott Shane, "Saudis and Extremism: 'Both the Arsonists and the Firefighters,'" *The New York Times,* August 25, 2016, https://www.nytimes.com/2016/08/26/world/middleeast/saudi-arabia-islam.html.
62. Alexiev, "The End of an Alliance," *National Review*, October 28, 2002, http://old.nationalreview.com/flashback/flashback-alexiev112602.asp.
63. David Ignatius, "Are Saudi Arabia's reforms for real? A recent visit says yes," *The Washington Post,* March 1, 2018, https://www.washingtonpost.com/opinions/global-opinions/are-saudi-arabias-reforms-for-real-a-recent-visit-says-yes/2018/03/01/a11a4ca8-1d9d-11e8-9de1-147dd2df3829_story.html?noredirect=on&utm_term=.0e07ccb361b3.
64. Steffen Hertog, "The Costs of Counter-Revolution in the GCC," *Foreign Policy*, May 31, 2011, http://mideast.foreignpolicy.com/posts/2011/05/31/the_costs_of_counter_revolution_in_the_gcc
65. Jonathan Schanzer and Steven Miller, "How Saudi

Arabia Survived – So Far," *The Journal of International Security Affairs*, May 14, 2012, http://www.defenddemocracy.org/media-hit/how-saudi-arabia-has-survivedso-far/.

66. For the full Arabic text of the fatwa, see http://www.assakina.com/fatwa/6834.html; For an English translation, see www.salafitalk.net/st/viewmessages.cfm?Forum=9&Topic=12255
67. Madawi al-Rasheed, "Preachers of Hate as Loyal Subjects," *New York Times*, March 14, 2011, http://www.nytimes.com/roomfordebate/2011/03/14/how-stable-is-saudi-arabia/preachers-of-hate-as-loyal-subjects
68. Jonathan Schanzer and Steven Miller, *Facebook Fatwa: Saudi Clerics, Wahhabi Islam, and Social Media* (Washington, DC: FDD Press, 2012) http://www.defenddemocracy.org/media-hit/fdd-releases-cutting-edge-study-of-saudi-social-media1/
69. Filkins,"A Saudi Prince's Quest."
70. Ben Hubbard, "Saudi Arabia Agrees to Let Women Drive," *The New York Times,* September 26, 2017, https://www.nytimes.com/2017/09/26/world/middleeast/saudi-arabia-women-drive.html.
71. Schanzer and Miller, *Facebook Fatwa*, 5.
72. "Saudi Arabia Launches Airstrikes in Yemen," BBC, March 26, 2016. http://www.bbc.com/news/world-us-canada-32061632
73. "Saudi Arabia's Post-Oil Future," *The Economist*, April 30, 2016, http://www.economist.com/news/middle-east-and-africa/21697673-bold-promises-bold-young-prince-they-will-be-hard-keep-saudi-arabias
74. Ben Hubbard, David D. Kirkpatrick, Kate Kelly and Mark Mazzetti, "Saudis Said to Use Coercion and Abuse to Seize Billions," *The New York Times,* March 11, 2018, https://www.nytimes.com/2018/03/11/world/middleeast/saudi-arabia-corruption-mohammed-bin-salman.html.
75. Filkins,"A Saudi Prince's Quest."
76. "Saudi Arabia claims anti-corruption purge recouped $100bn," *The Guardian,* January 30, 2018, https://www.theguardian.com/world/2018/jan/30/anti-corruption-purge-nets-more-than-100bn-saudi-arabia-claims.

77. Filkins,"A Saudi Prince's Quest."
78. Jeffrey Goldberg, "Saudi Crown Prince: Iran's Supreme Leader 'Makes Hitler Look Good,'" *The Atlantic,* April 2, 2018, https://www.theatlantic.com/international/archive/2018/04/mohammed-bin-salman-iran-israel/557036/.
79. Goldberg, "Saudi Crown Prince."

28 Tunisia

Quick Facts

Population: 11,403,800 (July 2017 est.)
Area: 163,610 sq km
Ethnic Groups:Arab 98%, European 1%, Jewish and other 1%
GDP (official exchange rate): $40.28 billion (2017 est.)

Source: CIA World FactBook (Last Updated August 2018)

Introduction

Tunisia is perhaps best-known as the site of protests that sparked the Arab Spring revolutions that swept the Middle East in 2011. The self-immolation of twenty-six-year-old fruit vendor Mohamed Bouazizi precipitated mass demonstrations in December 2010. These protests led to unprecedented social and political upheaval in Tunisia the following year. The revolution in Tunisia ended the decades-long reign of authoritarian leader Zine el-Abedine Ben Ali, thus ending the restrictive one-party structure that had been the norm since 1956. Into this newly opened field came previously suppressed opposition movements, formerly exiled politicians, and new political groups.

Following the collapse of Ben Ali's regime, Tunisia held elections to a National Constituent Assembly on October 23, 2011. Both domestic and foreign observers judged the elections to be "free and fair."[1] *The National Constituent Assembly was charged with appointing an interim government and writing Tunisia's new constitution.*[2] *In the ensuing vote, the Islamist Ennahda party won the most votes of any single party, gaining control of 90 out of the body's 217 seats.*[3] *Rather than being a strictly radical movement, Ennahda's members reflect a diversity of opinion on both religious and political issues. Furthermore, the group sought to foster cooperation among Tunisian Islamists in the post-revolutionary political environment.*[4]

Between December 2011 and January 2014, an Ennahda prime minister led the interim government in a coalition with centrist and liberal parties. The resignation of this government in January 2014 as a result of a political compromise seems to validate Ennahda's willingness to operate within established political norms. However, extremist groups have increased their activities, and a country with almost no history of political violence has had to confront Islamist-origin violent demonstrations, political assassinations, and both attempted and actual terrorism. The attack that sparked the most international attention was the assassination of 38 people in Sousse, Tunisia in June 2015. Meanwhile, non-violent Salafism has attracted many, primarily young people who are frustrated and disillusioned that the new post-revolution order has been unable to address the issues of jobs, the economy, and social justice.[5]

However, Tunisia's more dangerous role in the wider world of Islamism comes not from its domestic politics, but from its status as a major supplier of foreign fighters. The Tunisian government estimates that approximately 3,000 Tunisians have left home to fight in Syria.[6] *Independent analysts and the United Nations estimate that 6,000 – 7,000 have left Tunisia to fight in Iraq, Syria, and Libya in al-Qaeda affiliates and the Islamic State.*[7] *While exact numbers of foreign fighters are notoriously difficult to estimate, the fact remains that Tunisians make up a significant portion of the estimated 40,000 jihadi fighters that have gone to Syria and Iraq.*[8]

Islamist Activity

Ennahda

Ennahda is one of the major political parties in Tunisia today. Founded in 1981, it was originally inspired by Egypt's Muslim Brotherhood.[9] During its time in office, the government of Zine el-Abedine Ben Ali suppressed the group and exiled its leader, Rachid Ghannouchi, in 1989. After Ben Ali's ouster, Ghannouchi returned to Tunisia, and the party moved quickly to re-establish itself.

In November 1987, Zine el-Abedine Ben Ali, whom then-President Habib Bourguiba had recently appointed Prime Minister, ousted the sitting president in a bloodless palace coup. Ben Ali promised reform and democratization, and Ghannouchi, who sought to openly participate in political life, undertook to cooperate with the new President. He signed Ben Ali's "National Pact," which was essentially a social contract between the government and civil and political groups, and then sought to run a list of candidates in the 1989 legislative elections.[10] But Ben Ali soon changed course and, among other measures, prohibited any party's name to contain the words "Islam" or "Islamic" (the prohibition of religiously-identified parties remains in place today.) The MTI duly renamed itself Hizb Ennahda, the Renaissance Party. However, Ben Ali still refused to allow Ennahda to enter the elections as a recognized political party, although he did permit it to field "independent" candidates. Islamists subsequently received 15 percent of the nationwide vote (up to 30 percent in urban areas), but failed to win any seats in the legislature (by contrast, the five recognized secular opposition parties collectively received only 5 percent of the vote).[11] The unexpectedly strong performance of the Islamists within the opposition, coupled with Ennahda's increasingly strident political rhetoric, caused the regime to deny Ennahda's second request for recognition. An escalating cycle of protest and repression ensued, and Ghannouchi fled to London in 1989.[12] By 1992, virtually all of Ennahda's leadership had been imprisoned and its organizational capabilities within the country destroyed. Although it was commonly understood that Ennahda was effectively dismantled in the early 1990s, many Tunisians, including Ben Ali, believed it maintained a structure and presence in the country, albeit perhaps a "sleeping" one.[13]

Ennahda's ideology is thoroughly rooted in the ideology of its founder, Rachid Ghannouchi, who views the Koran and the Hadith as "an anchor for political thought and practice."[14] However, he appears to interpret Koranic texts in the context of Western political thinking and modern concepts of political freedoms: the dignity of human beings, human rights, and Koranic prohibitions against Muslim dictators.[15] Ghannouchi himself is a "literalist" and believes that it is the duty of Muslims to establish Islamic government where attainable; in practice, he has endorsed multi-party politics.[16] He does not advocate government by clerics, and has said that "[t]he state is not something from God but from the people... the state has to serve the benefit of the Muslims."[17] His idea of an Islamic political regime appears to be a strong presidential system with an elected president and elected parliament, and considers the parliamentary system a legitimate means of political participation.[18]

Ghannouchi's public statements since his return from exile, and those of other Ennahda figures, have been consistent with this worldview. He has said that his party will accept the outcome of fair and democratic elections, and that he himself will not run for president.[19] In a March 2, 2012 address to a civil society conference, Ghannouchi asserted that, "...We are in need of scholars and intellectuals to debate and study our issues in a climate of freedom, and accept that the legislative institution is the ultimate authority by virtue of being elected."[20] Applying his views to the prevailing political situation in Tunisia at the time, he stated,

> The fact that our revolution has succeeded in toppling a dictator, we ought to accept the principle of citizenship, and that this country does not belong to one party or another but rather to all its citizens regardless of their religion, sex, or any other consideration.[21]

However, once in power following the October 2011 elections, the Ennahda-led government (Ghannouchi himself assumed no elected or appointed position) appeared to many to be practicing the same sort of majoritarianism and attempting to control all the political levers of national power, in much the same way as the Egyptian Muslim Brotherhood would once it assumed power in Cairo the following year. At the same time, the government was seen as tolerating the disruptive and sometimes violent actions of Salafi elements while simultaneously cracking down on secular demonstrations. In a widely-cited example of this alleged, police allowed the Salafist "occupation" of Manouba University to drag on for several weeks, but quickly used force to break up peaceful anti-Ennahda demonstrations in central Tunis in April 2012.

The issue came to a head with the assassination of two leftist politicians in 2013, killings that were widely seen as the work of

Salafists emboldened by Ennahda sympathies. Popular demonstrations against the government grew. Opposition parties, which coalesced into a political umbrella called the "National Salvation Front," called for the dissolution of the National Constituent Assembly and for new elections. Also, the process of writing the country's new, post-Ben Ali constitution had proven to be both protracted and contentious, the economy was still far from robust, and the social environment was one of public frustration and pessimism. Ennahda leaders realized that some sort of national compromise was necessary, lest they go the way of the Muslim Brotherhood and President Morsi in Egypt (albeit not by the hands of the national army). Various compromises were suggested, and Ennahda offered some concessions to its political opponents. Popular demonstrations and civil disobedience waned in the Fall of 2013, and the two sides decided to negotiate a way forward. Finally, a National Dialogue led by Tunisia's labor union federation brokered a compromise in early January 2014, under which the Ennahda-led government would step down in favor of an interim, technocratic administration that would lead the country to new elections, while the Constituent Assembly (about 42% Islamist) would remain and finish the constitution.

All sides agreed to this framework, and by the end of January 2014 the new constitution was drafted and approved by the Constituent Assembly. Serious unrest was avoided, the new constitution was widely accepted, and the country appeared to be moving ahead. At the time, Ennahda appeared to indicate that it would accept the outcome of prospective power-sharing under this structure, with Ghannouchi telling a Washington, DC audience in February 2014 that:

> [T]he Tunisian experience has proven to those doubting the intentions of Islamists that Islam and democracy are compatible, and that victims of decades of repression, marginalization, and exclusion are not carrying hatred or the desire for revenge, but rather an enlightened modernist civil project as embodied in the new Tunisian constitution, which has been adopted with the widest possible consensus.[22]

However, there are indications that younger party members do not see this as a reasonable and necessary compromise, but as the secularist-compelled surrender of political Islam's "main chance" by a weak leadership.[23] Ennahda's philosophies on the relationship between religion and government, meanwhile, have continued to develop over time.

Ennahda has shown a historical unwillingness to crack down on Salafi-jihadists. This hesitance stems from Ennahda's perception that Salafi-jihadists are young and misguided, as well as from sympathy generated by Ennahda's own history of repression under Ben Ali's regime.[24] Ennahda has counseled Salafi-jihadists to follow a strategy of "bishwaya bishwaya" (slowly, slowly), worried that the aggressive tactics and rapid advance of the latter might alarm opponents. Salafi-jihadists, however, have found that argument unconvincing.[25]

At times, however, Ennahda has acted against Islamist elements. In April 2013, it declared Ansar al-Sharia, the largest Salafi group in Tunisia, a terrorist organization.[26] Since then, Ennahda has adopted a more security-oriented approach to Salafi-jihadism, entailing the forced registration of Salafis at police stations and the stationing of plain-clothes police officers in public spaces. While many members of Ennahda are uncomfortable with these measures, as well as with continuing police brutality in Tunisia,[27] the rise of Salafi-jihadism domestically and internationally has made public criticism of these policies challenging.[28] In May 2016, during its 10th party congress, 93.5 percent of Ennahda's delegates voted to separate religious and political activities into separate branches. This decision means that elected officials can no longer hold positions both in the party and in broader society, which includes mosques and Islamic organizations. Ghannouchi won reelection as party leader, and had a major hand in crafting the policy shift to split Ennahda's social and political wings apart.[29]

Other Islamist movements

While Ennahda dominates Tunisian Islamism, other Islamist groups do exist, though they tend to be small in size and loosely organized.

Salafist parties

On May 11, 2012, the Tunisian government granted a license to the Salafist Jebahat el-Islah, (JI), or "Reform Front" to operate as a party under the Political Parties Law (which requires respect for the "civil principles of the state"). It was the first Salafist group to be recognized as such.[30] During this time, Ennahda may have been more inclined to encourage pluralism in Muslim politics in order to better govern a politically diverse country.[31] JI has several leaders who were jailed during the 1980s and claims that it rejects violence, respects democracy, and does not seek to impose duct.[32] A second Salafist party, al-Rahma ("Mercy") was legalized in July 2012. Its stated goal is the establishment of sharia law. Neither al-Rahma nor JI are particularly popular.[33] JI remains unswervingly dedicated to bringing sharia law into Tunisia, but younger Salafi-jihadis tend to see the legislative route of enacting sharia as too slow and unwieldy to have much appeal.[34] Furthermore, most of JI's membership consists of older men, and the group has failed to attract younger Tunisians to its cause.[35]

El-Zeituna Party

The non-Salafist El Zeituna Party (named after the historic mosque and school in Tunis) officially announced its establishment in February 2014 and its intention to participate in the next presidential and parliamentary elections. The announcement outlined its position, which is based on the Koran and Sunnah and which "respects the legal legitimacy and the state's constitutional institutions." Its leaders are dissatisfied with the January 2014 constitution, and their goals include reform of the judicial system and establishment of an "Islamic economic system based on the just distribution of wealth."[36]

Hizb ut-Tahrir

Hizb ut-Tahrir (HuT) (in English, the Islamic Liberation Party) is another political party active in Tunisia. HuT an international movement founded in 1953 that seeks to re-establish the Islamic Caliphate. This group established a presence in Tunisia in 1973, but historically had only a few dozen members in the country.[37] It emerged publicly after the 2011 revolution and declared its goal of competing in elections and offering its "alternative constitution" to the Constituent Assembly. [38] While the group claims to renounce violence, it does not rule out rebellion and civil disobedience to establish an Islamic state. Furthermore, HuT has developed a reputation for being a pipeline for increased radicalization.[39] It advocates for the re-establishment of the Muslim Caliphate and in sharia law as the source of the constitution.[40] Its spokesman announced that HuT is preparing for an ideological and political struggle to save the nation.[41] Many Tunisians, including members of Ennahda, believe with good reason that HuT would, if it won an election, ban other parties and implement "one man, one vote, one time."[42] Its request for a license to operate as a political party was initially denied in March 2012 (as was that of the "Tunisian Sunni" party), but that decision was later and HuT became a recognized political party later in 2012.[43] The organization's cooperation with the government proved to be short-lived, however. In September 2016, the Tunisian government requested that a military court ban the group, as it has been accused repeatedly of "undermining public order" since 2012.[44] In April 2017, HuT's politburo chief Abderraouf Amri publicly stated that "Democracy no longer attracts anyone…. It is time to announce its death and work to bury it."[45] In June 2017, Tunisian judicial authorities banned HuT from party activities for one month.[46]

Islamist Militant Groups

Ansar al-Sharia Tunisiyya

Ansar al-Sharia Tunisiyya (Supporters of Islamic Law, or AST) was established in April 2011. Though there are many groups throughout the world that go by the name of Ansar al-Sharia, these organizations are not part of a united chain of command. Terrorism analyst Aaron Zelin writes: "(Ansar al-Sharia groups) are fighting in different lands using different means, but all for the same end, an approach better suited for the vagaries born of the Arab uprisings."[47] This approach allows the groups to appear to be part of a unified transnational jihadi movement, while in reality addressing the unique environment of each country.

The Tunisian group's founder, Abu Ayyad al-Tunisi, was a jihadist who had fought in Afghanistan and was subsequently arrested and deported to Tunisia as a terrorist in 2003. He was freed with many other prisoners after the revolution.[48] AST has claimed responsibility for the 2012 attack on the U.S. Embassy and the assassinations of liberal politicians Chokri Belaid and Mohamed Brahmi in February and July 2013.[49] Its most recent attack occurred in 2014, when AST militants attacked Tunisian soldiers at checkpoints near the Algerian border. 14 people were killed in that incident.[50]

AST, in general, has been less focused on violent attacks and more focused on dawa (proselytization) and community service.[51] In this manner, AST has entrenched itself and won support in a nation that feels abandoned by political elites and disappointed in the outcome of the 2011 revolution.[52] In 2013, the Ennahda-led government designated AST a terrorist organization, which limited its ability to carry out proselytization in public.[53]

In July 2014, an AST spokesman declared AST's allegiance to Islamic State emir Abu Bakr Al-Baghdadi.[54] AST has recruited heavily for ISIS in Tunisia, and encourages many young Tunisians to make the journey to Syria. Tunisians travel to Syria to wage jihad alongside a number of groups, but most commonly with ISIS.[55] ISIS also features Tunisians prominently in its own propaganda, often lauding the efforts and martyrdom of Tunisian foreign fighters.[56] However, the extent of the tactical connections between the two groups is unclear. As noted in the State Department's 2016 report on terrorist groups, AST's strength and numbers, as well as its foreign aid and financing, remain unknown.[57]

Al-Qaeda in the Islamic Maghreb

Al-Qaeda in the Islamic Maghreb (AQIM), which did not have a significant presence or recruiting base in Tunisia in the past, is now active, especially in the western part of the country. While AQIM has apparently not conducted suicide bomb-type terrorist operations in Tunisia, its "conventional" forces, armed with weapons looted from Libyan arsenals, have engaged Tunisian security forces with deadly results. In 2014, AQIM claimed responsibility for the attack on the home of the interior minister, Lotfi Ben Jeddou.[58]

AQIM has primarily regarded Tunisia as a support zone historically, and employs more defensive operations than offensive strikes.[59] Some AQIM members have defected to ISIS in recent times,[60] and the group has been weakened in recent years. In 2015, Tunisian counterterrorism operations eliminated much of the group's leadership. Furthermore, ISIS has co-opted some of AQIM's support cells along Tunisia's border with Algeria, taking supplies for themselves.[61]

The Islamic State

The Islamic State does not currently hold any territory in Tunisia, but the country still plays a vital role in the group's operations.[62] As previously discussed, a large percentage of ISIS's foreign fighters come from Tunisia; as many as 7,000 Tunisians (of a total of some 40,000 or more foreign fighters) are estimated to have gone to fight in Iraq, Syria, and Libya to date.[63] ISIS also uses the highly porous border between Tunisia and Libya, where it maintains a sizeable presence, to smuggle guns and fighters into the country.[64] In an effort to further destabilize Tunisia and its economy, ISIS fighters have attacked cities and tourists locales.[65]

ISIS has launched a number of notable attacks in Tunisia to date. In November 2014, ISIS claimed responsibility for the bombing of a presidential guard bus. The blast killed twelve presidential guards.[66] In March 2015, two ISIS-trained gunmen killed 21 tourists and one Tunisian at the Bardo National Museum in Tunis. The Islamic State also took responsibility for the 2015 Sousse shooting that killed 39 and wounded 36. In March 2016, 50 gunmen affiliated with ISIS, many of whom were part of sleeper cells coordinated attacks on "security installations and security personnel in the border town of Ben Guerdane." Security forces killed 49 of the militants, while 17 security officials and seven civilians were killed.[67] In November 2016, the Islamic State claimed the killing of a Tunisian Air Force soldier who was found dead in his home.[68] Two days after the killing, the Tunisian National Security Council announced that it had undertaken a new strategy to fight extremism and terrorism. President Beji Caid Essebsi's office said the strategy was based on "prevention, protection, judicial proceedings and retaliation." No other details about the plan have as yet been revealed.[69]

ISIS has used Libya's virtual collapse to solidify its presence in that nation. There is ample evidence that the group plans to use its base in Libya to begin to infiltrate Tunisia as well. The Ben Guerdane attack (which took place near the border with Libya) illustrates that the Islamic State is quite capable of doing so. However, ISIS's recent losses in Libya may have curtailed this interest. In December 2016, Libyan forces allied with the United Nations-backed government recaptured the coastal city Sirte from ISIS. The protracted struggle for the city took six months. Sirte was ISIS's only official holding outside of Iraq and Syria.[70]

Islamism and Society

Tunisians tend to be moderate in their views and behavior. Habib Bourguiba, the country's first president following its independence from France in the 1950s, was supported by the public and set a moderate political course. Guerrilla warfare and terrorism did not characterize the struggle, and there were no violent purges and settling of accounts among the victors of the sort that led to continued crisis and near-civil war in neighboring Algeria.

Tunisia is an unusually homogenous country for its neighborhood. Ninety-eight percent of its 11 million population is Sunni Muslim.[71] Shi'ites number perhaps in the thousands, most of them converts to the sect following the 1979 Iranian Revolution.[72] There is a small Jewish community concentrated on the island of Djerba, and there are virtually no indigenous Christians in the country. While there are differences between Arabs and Berbers, ethnicity is not a significant factor in fueling conflict. There is, however, a geographical "have/have not" gap, and the poorer southern interior has not historically been a focus of development. Most dissident movements, including Islamist forces, have originated in this region, and it was the cradle of the "Jasmine Revolution." Equitable distribution of wealth to all regions remains an important unsolved issue, especially after the revelations of corruption within the Ben Ali family, and a number of Tunisians have advocated renationalizing and relocating businesses to ensure fairness in the geographical distribution of opportunities.[73]

As previously discussed, Salafist parties such as JI and al-Rahma that focus on political action hold little appeal for Tunisians. However, Salafism as a movement and ideology still presents a certain amount of appeal. While Salafism does not necessarily manifest in terrorist acts, it is disruptive and often violent. Salafists reportedly control up to 150 mosques in the country, a development being closely watched by the Religious Affairs Ministry.[74] Some of these radical imams are calling young Tunisians to join the jihad against the Syrian regime of Bashar Assad, something of great interest to the Interior Ministry.[75] In recent years, estimates for the number of fighters who have left Tunisia to fight abroad range from 3,000 to 7,000.[76] Furthermore, nearly 700 of these fighters have since returned to Tunisia. Many of these returning fighters are sent to jail or are placed under state surveillance.[77] However, the government has never developed a clear strategy for dealing with these individuals and reintegrating them into society.[78]

Beneath the modernism and sophisticated worldview exhibited by the population as a whole, Tunisia is a traditional society that values its religion and cultural heritage. The Ben Ali regime began to recognize this and attempted to "Islamize" society and use religion to support government policies.[79] This "Official" or "Popular" Islam was designed to counter the threat of extremism and terrorism by preaching the values of moderation and tolerance and, at the same time, claiming ownership of Tunisians' Islamic identity, which had been denied by past regimes.[80] This effort was supported by many Tunisians; as an example, Radio Zeytouna, a religious station established in 2009 by the Ben Ali government as a counterweight to Islamist satellite networks, was popular with the public and had a good audience base.

Although Islamists and Ennahda failed over the years to gain the active support of the public, there is sympathy for the vision expressed by the movement—that is, political and economic reform and living by Islamic principles. Most Tunisians do not appear to consider Ghannouchi and other Islamists as saviors of society, but rather simply people who express an appealing vision.[81] Many of those who join the movement do not necessarily support the establishment of an Islamic regime.[82]

Islamism and the State

The Tunisian state was hostile to Islamism from independence in 1956 through the end of the Ben Ali regime. Habib Bourguiba, the hero of the liberation and president between 1956 and 1987, dominated the country through force of personality and an efficient political party structure organized down to the lowest grassroots. He made an early decision to devote the country's energies and limited resources to social modernization and economic growth, and not to democracy and political pluralism. Bourguiba steadily consolidated government control over political life in order to avoid the chaos and serial coups d'etat. The Tunisian people acquiesced to extensive limitations on political participation. Bourguiba's politics were strictly secular, and he insisted that the country would be also. He ignored the country's Arab/Islamic history and connected modern Tunisia directly to a pre-Islamic past—its Carthaginian heritage—while simultaneously secularizing the state and weakening traditional Islamic institutions.[83] At the same time, his regime embarked upon an economic and social development program based on a socialist model. This model failed, and the government changed course; the eventual result was impressive economic performance and very progressive social programs involving public education and literacy, economic mobility, and the position of women in society.

The process of tightening regime control accelerated after the 1987 "palace coup" by Ben Ali, who maintained that no accommodation with Islamists was possible, and who considered Islamism to be a disease against which the public must be "inoculated." The country's 2003 anti-terrorism law allowed the jailing of those threatening national security. It was used almost exclusively against Islamists, primarily Islamist-leaning young people using the Internet "illegally" (i.e., blogging or visiting jihadist websites).[84]

The pre-January 2011 state of affairs in Tunisia was one of comprehensive government domination of the public space and virtually all political activity—not just that of Islamists, but of all potential opposition groups. The state controlled mosque construction, sermon content, religious education, and appointment and remuneration of imams. While these constraints were relaxed by the Ennahda government, imams do not have carte blanche to speak freely. When several imams delivered uncensored Friday sermons attacking politicians, an official from the Ministry of Religious Affairs stated: "in the event of too many excesses, then measures will be taken. Mosques are not meant to be venues for defamation and personal attacks. An imam is not a judge, and the law is above all."[85] The post-January 2014 interim government has again, at least temporarily, limited mosque openings to prayer times only, claiming that many mosques controlled by Salafist imams were preaching jihad and takfirism (accusing another Muslim of apostasy).[86]

Although Ennahda dominated the elected Constituent Assembly and could theoretically have exerted a decisive influence over the new constitution, the Interim Government adopted the same balanced methodology used to draft the 1959 constitution. Six Constituent Assembly subcommittees focused on various parts of the constitution (e.g., the preamble and basic principles, rights and freedoms, the judiciary, legislative and executive powers, etc.). All Constituent Assembly members served in one or another of these subcommittees, in which membership was proportional to the party distribution in the Assembly. Thus, while Ennahda was well represented, it could not pack critical subcommittees with its own members. Perhaps most critically, Ennahda announced its opposition to including sharia in the constitution; the only reference to Islam repeated the 1959 Constitution's Article 1 and states: "Tunisia is a free, independent and sovereign state. Its religion is Islam, its language is Arabic, and its type of government is the Republic. This article cannot be amended."[87] As mentioned previously, Ennahda has taken further steps to separate secularism and religion in its politics, by officially splitting apart those two functions of the party. Tunisia may well continue upon a road of encouraging secular government while recognizing its population's Muslim values.

That being said, Tunisia stands at something of a crossroads. The violent Islamist tendencies in the nation have grown stronger and more prominent in recent years. The ongoing chaos and instability in neighboring Libya puts Tunisia at greater risk of attacks and increased radicalization. The government has shown a willingness to try to counteract these forces, but as Islamist forces continue to dominate the international stage, strong counterterrorism efforts will be necessary to preserve Tunisia's national identity. Though Tunisia for the moment remains the most successful example of the Arab Spring, the tenuous political gains secured there thus far threaten to be overshadowed by rising Islamic radicalism.

Endnotes

1. Issandr El Amrani and Ursula Lindsey, "Tunisia Moves to the Next Stage," Middle East Research and Information Project, November 8, 2011, http://merip.org/mero/mero110811.
2. "Tunisia's Islamist party claims election victory," *Telegraph* (London), October 25, 2011, http://www.telegraph.co.uk/news/worldnews/africaandindianocean/tunisia/8847315/Tunisias-Islamist-party-claims-election-victory.html.
3. El Amrani and Lindsey, "Tunisia Moves to the Next Stage."
4. Haim Malka and Margot Balboni, "Domestic Context: After the Revolution," Center for Strategic and International Studies, June 2016, http://foreignfighters.csis.org/tunisia/domestic-context.html.
5. Anouar Boukhars, "In the Crossfire: Islamists' travails in Tunisia," Carnegie Endowment for International Peace, January 2014, 13.
6. Haim Malka and Margot Balboni, "Tunisian Fighters: In History and Today," Center for Strategic and International Studies, June 2016, http://foreignfighters.csis.org/tunisia/tunisian-fighters-in-history.html.
7. Haim Malka and Margot Balboni, "Tunisian Fighters: In History and Today," Center for Strategic and International Studies, June 2016, http://foreignfighters.csis.org/tunisia/tunisian-fighters-in-history.html.
8. Haim Malka and Margot Balboni, "Tunisia: Radicalism Abroad and at Home," Center for Strategic and International Studies, June 2016, http://foreignfighters.csis.org/tunisia/why-tunisia.html.
9. Aiden Lewis, "Profile: Tunisia's Ennahda Party," BBC, October 25, 2011, http://www.bbc.com/news/world-africa-15442859.
10. Lewis., 101.
11. Perkins, *A History of Modern Tunisia*, 190.
12. Noyon, *Islam, Politics, and Pluralism*, 103.
13. Correspondence of previous chapter author, Larry Velte, with Tunisian academic and lawyer, September 2009.
14. Noyon, Islam, *Politics, and Pluralism*, 99.

15. Mohamed Elhachmi Hamdi, *The Politicization of Islam: A Case Study of Tunisia* (Boulder, CO: Westview Press, 1998), 107.
16. Noyon, *Islam, Politics, and Pluralism*, 101.
17. As cited in John L. Esposito and Francois Burgat, eds., *Modernizing Islam* (New Brunswick, NJ: Rutgers University Press, 2003), 78.
18. Allani, "The Islamists in Tunisia between Confrontation and Participation, 1980-2008," 266.
19. Al-Munji Al-Suaydani, "Ennahda Movement Leader Talks to Asharq Al-Awsat," *ASharq al-Awsat* (London) February 7, 2011, http://www.aawsat.com/english/news.asp?section=3&id=24070.
20. Address by Rached Ghannouchi to the Center for the Study of Islam and Democracy, Tunis, March 2, 2012.
21. Address by Ghannouchi, 2012.
22. Posted by the Center for the Study of Islam and Democracy, Washington, DC, March 18, 2014.
23. Discussion by Mokhtar Awad, Brookings Institution, Washington, DC, March 26, 2014.
24. Monica Marks, "Tunisia's Ennahda: Rethinking Islamism in the context of ISIS and the Egyptian coup," Brookings Institution Project on U.S. Relations with the Islamic World *Working Paper*, August 2015, 4, , https://www.brookings.edu/wp-content/uploads/2016/07/Tunisia_Marks-FINALE.pdf.
25. Marks, "Tunisia's Ennahda," 6.
26. Marks, "Tunisia's Ennahda," 7.
27. Marks, "Tunisia's Ennahda," 7. .
28. Marks, "Tunisia's Ennahda," 7. .
29. Sarah Souli, "What is left of Tunisia's Ennahda Party?" *Al Jazeera,* May 26, 2016, http://www.aljazeera.com/news/2016/05/left-tunisia-ennahda-party-160526101937131.html.
30. Houda Trabelsi, "Tunisia Approves First Salafist Party," Magharebia, May 17, 2012.
31. Aaron Zelin, "Who is Jabhat al-Islah?" Carnegie Endowment for International Peace, July 18, 2015. http://carnegieendowment.org/sada/?fa=48885.
32. Trabelsi, "Tunisia Approves First Salafist Party."
33. Stefano M. Torelli, Fabio Merone and Francesco Cava-

torta, "Salafism in Tunisia: Challenges and Opportunities for Democratization," *Middle East Policy* XIX, no. 4, Winter 2012.

34. Anouar Boukhars, "In the Crossfire: Islamists' Travails in Tunisia," Carnegie Endowment for International Peace *Paper*, January 27, 2014, http://carnegieendowment.org/2014/01/27/in-crossfire-islamists-travails-in-tunisia-pub-54311.
35. Aaron Zelin, "Meeting Tunisia's Ansar al-Sharia," *Foreign Policy,* March 8, 2013, http://foreignpolicy.com/2013/03/08/meeting-tunisias-ansar-al-sharia/.
36. "Tunisia: New Political Party Established" National Tunisian Television ("Alwatania"), February 15, 2014.
37. Allani, "The Islamists in Tunisia between Confrontation and Participation, 1980-2008," 258.
38. Interview by previous chapter author, Larry Veldte, with Tahrir spokesman Ridha Belhaj, Assarih (Tunis), March 11, 2011.
39. "Hizb-ut Tahrir," *The World Almanac of Islamism,* January 13, 2017, http://almanac.afpc.org/hizb-ut-tahrir.
40. "Hizb-ut Tahrir," *The World Almanac of Islamism.*
41. Belhaj interview, *Al-Jazeera* (Doha), March 10, 2011.
42. Interview with an-Nahda official Abdelfattah Moro, *Al-Jazeera* (Doha), March 10, 2011.
43. "Hizb ut-Tahrir Tunisia Spokesman: 'Our Appeal for a License has Been Accepted'," Hizb-ut Tarhri Britain, July 18, 2012, http://www.hizb.org.uk/news-watch/hizb-ut-tahrir-tunisia-spokesman-our-appeal-for-a-license-has-been-accepted.
44. "Tunisia calls for a ban on radical Islamist party," *Al Arabiya,* September 7, 2016, http://english.alarabiya.net/en/News/middle-east/2016/09/07/Tunisia-calls-for-ban-on-radical-Islamist-party-.html.
45. Agence France=Presse, "Tunisian Islamist party says time to 'bury' democracy," *Al Monitor,* April 15, 2017, http://al-monitor.com/pulse/afp/2017/04/tunisia-politics-religion.html.
46. "Tunisia radical Islamist party banned for one month," *News 24,* June 7, 2017, http://www.news24.com/Africa/News/tunisia-radical-islamist-party-banned-for-one-month-20170607.

47. Aaron Zelin, "Know Your Ansar al-Sharia," *Foreign Policy,* September 21, 2012, http://foreignpolicy.com/2012/09/21/know-your-ansar-al-sharia/.
48. Torelli, Merone and Cavatorta, "Salafism in Tunisia: Challenges and Opportunities for Democratization."
49. "Ansar al-Sharia in Tunisia (AST)," Counter Extremism Project, 2016, 13, http://www.counterextremism.com/threat/ansar-al-sharia-tunisia-ast.
50. "Ansar al-Shariah (Tunisia)" *Mapping Militant Organizations,* Stanford University, August 24, 2016, http://web.stanford.edu/group/mappingmilitants/cgi-bin/groups/view/547#note3.
51. Zelin, "Meeting Tunisia's Ansar al-Sharia."
52. Christine Petré, "Tunisian Salafism: the rise and fall of Ansar al-Sharia," *Policy Brief* No. 209, October 2015, http://fride.org/descarga/PB209_Tunisian_Salafism.pdf.
53. Petré, "Tunisian Salafism."
54. Jamel Arfaoui, "Tunisia: Ansar Al-Sharia Spokesman Backs Isis," AllAfrica, May 14, 2013, http://allafrica.com/stories/201407090299.html.
55. "AST," Counter Extremism Project, 20.
56. "AST," Counter Extremism Project, 20. .
57. "Chapter Six: Foreign Terrorist Organizations – Ansar al-Shari'a in Tunisia," in U.S. Department of State, *Country Reports on Terrorism 2016* (Washington, DC: U.S. Department of State, 2017), https://www.state.gov-/j/ct/rls/crt/2016/272238.htm.
58. Chapter Six: Foreign Terrorist Organizations – Al-Qa'ida in the Islamic Maghreb," in U.S. Department of State, *Country Reports on Terrorism 2015*, https://www.state.gov/j/ct/rls/crt/2015/257523.htm.
59. Jaclyn Stutz, "AQIM and ISIS in Tunisia: Competing Campaigns," AEI Critical Threats Project, June 28, 2016, http://www.criticalthreats.org/al-qaeda/stutz-aqim-isis-tunisia-competing-campaigns-june-28-2016.
60. Stutz, "AQIM and ISIS in Tunisia: Competing Campaigns."
61. Stutz, "AQIM and ISIS in Tunisia: Competing Campaigns."
62. Haim Malka and Margot Balboni, *Violence in Tuni-*

sia: Analyzing Terrorism and Political Violence After the Revolution, Center for Strategic and International Studies, June 2016, http://foreignfighters.csis.org/tunisia/violence-in-tunisia.html.

63. Haim Malka and Margot Balboni, "Tunisia: Radicalism Abroad and at Home," Center for Strategic and International Studies, June 2016, http://foreignfighters.csis.org/tunisia/why-tunisia.html.
64. Malka and Balboni, "Violence in Tunisia: Analyzing Terrorism and Political Violence After the Revolution," June 2016, http://foreignfighters.csis.org/tunisia/violence-in-tunisia.html.
65. Malka and Balboni, "Violence in Tunisia."
66. Malka and Balboni, "Violence in Tunisia."
67. Malka and Balboni, "Violence in Tunisia."
68. "Tunisia Takes on Extremism with New 'Terrorism' Strategy," *The New Arab,* November 8, 2016, https://www.alaraby.co.uk/english/news/2016/11/8/tunisia-takes-on-extremism-with-new-terrorism-strategy.
69. "Tunisia Takes on Extremism with New 'Terrorism' Strategy," *The New Arab*.
70. Jack Moore, "ISIS Loses Libya's Sirte, the Only City It Controlled Outside of Iraq and Syria," *Newsweek,* December 5, 2016, http://www.newsweek.com/isis-loses-libyan-city-sirte-only-city-it-controlled-outside-iraq-and-syria-528393.
71. This and other demographic statistics derived from the U.S. Central Intelligence Agency's *World Factbook,* https://www.cia.gov/library/publications/the-world-factbook/.
72. "Tunisia Islamist Trends back to the Forefront," *Al-Arabiya* (Dubai), February 1, 2011, http://www.alarabiya.net/articles/2011/01/20/134294.html.
73. Discussions by previous chapter author, Larry Velte, with civil society figures and officials in Tunis, March 10-12, 2011.
74. Michael Lukac. "Radical Islamists seize control of Tunisia mosques," *International Business Times*, November 2, 2011, http://www.ibtimes.com/radical-islamists-seize-control-tunisia-mosques-485204.
75. "Radical Mosques Call Young Tunisians to Jihad in

Syria," Agence France Presse, May 18, 2012.

76. Malka and Balboni, "Tunisia: Radicalism Abroad and at Home."
77. Sarah Souli, "Tunisia: Why foreign fighters abandon ISIL," *Al Jazeera* (Doha), March 3, 2016, http://www.aljazeera.com/news/2016/03/tunisia-foreign-fighters-abandon-isil-160301103627220.html.
78. Maghreb to tighten noose on Syria-bound jihadists," *Echourouk* (Tunis), February 9, 2014.
79. Kausch, "Tunisia: The Life of Others."
80. Correspondence of previous chapter author, Larry Velte, with Tunisian academic and lawyer, September 2009.
81. Ibid.
82. Lise Storm, "The Persistence of Authoritarianism as a source of Radicalization in North Africa," *International Affairs* 85, no. 5, September 2009, 2011.
83. Noyon, *Islam, Politics, and Pluralism*, 96.
84. Hugh Roberts, address before the Center for Strategic and International Studies, Washington, DC, March 21, 2007.
85. Quoted in *Al-Musawwar* (Cairo), March 7, 2011.
86. "The Tunisian Government is waging a campaign to restore the mosques," *Ilaf* (London) March 24, 2014, http://elaph.com/Web/News/2014/3/885206.html .
87. Duncan Picard, "The Current Status of Constitution Making in Tunisia," Carnegie Endowment for International Peace, April 19, 2012.

29 Syria

Quick Facts

Population: 18,028,549 (July 2017 est.)
Area: 199,951 sq km
Ethnic Groups: Arab 90.3%, Kurdish, Armenian, and other 9.7%
GDP (official exchange rate): $24.6 billion (2014 est.)

Source: CIA World FactBook (Last Updated June 2018)

Introduction

Islamism has featured prominently in the politics and policies of modern Syria on a number of different levels. Like other majority Sunni Muslim Arab countries governed by secular autocrats, Syria has a long tradition of Sunni Islamist opposition activity. The fact that the hereditary dictatorship of Syrian president Bashar al-Assad has long been dominated by Alawis, an Islamic offshoot sect viewed as heretical by religious Sunnis, renders it uniquely vulnerable to Islamist challenges. It has managed to survive for nearly a half-century in spite of this Achilles' heel by brutally suppressing dissent and tightly regulating Sunni religious practices.

Notwithstanding its heavy-handed treatment of Islamists at home, the Assad regime eagerly armed, financed, and sheltered foreign Islamist organizations committed to fighting its enemies abroad. These groups have had varied sectarian and ideological affiliations, ranging from the Shia Hezbollah militia in Lebanon to the Sunni Palestinian Hamas movement and al-Qaeda-aligned terrorists battling US-led coalition forces in Iraq after the fall of Saddam Hussein in 2003. By supporting these groups, the Assad regime not only advanced its regional strategic objectives, but also helped defuse Islamist militancy at home by appropriating radical causes that resonated with disaffected youth.

The eruption of a popular uprising against Assad in March 2011 and the country's subsequent collapse into civil war changed everything. Although protests were initially peaceful, multi-sectarian, and explicitly oriented around the pursuit of democratic change, the escalating violence and prolonged breakdown of law and order in many areas of the country were exploited by both indigenous and foreign Islamists, including many who had hitherto supported the regime.

Once the bane of secularists, the Syrian Muslim Brotherhood came to dominate the Western-backed Syrian National Coalition. However, more radical Islamist forces on the ground have since eclipsed its influence. Flush with financing from the Arab Gulf (in contrast to cash-starved, poorly-armed, and secular-leaning rebel forces), Salafi-jihadists close to al-Qaeda have gained dominion over key parts of northwestern Syria. Many rallied alongside Iraqi jihadists under the banner of the Islamic State, which seized control of large swathes of Iraq's Sunni heartland in 2013 and 2014. However, over the past year, military advances by the U.S.-led global coalition have helped to substantially degrade the territorial holdings and political power of the Islamic State.

Islamist Activity

More than six years of civil war in Syria have enabled an extraordinarily diverse array of Islamist actors to flourish. Broadly speaking, they can be divided into three categories: a small coterie of pro-regime Islamists, mostly Shia and non-Syrian; anti-regime Sunni political Islamists (ostensibly committed to advancing their agenda by democratic means); and Sunni Salafi-jihadists committed to either forcibly establishing an Islamic republic in Syria or using it as a stepping stone to pursue regional and international ambitions.

Pro–regime foreign Islamists

At the beginning of the uprising in March 2011, the Syrian regime retained an impressive array of foreign and domestic Islamist proxies.

In the Palestinian Territories, Syria had supported the Sunni Islamist groups Islamic Jihad and Hamas, an offshoot of the Muslim Brotherhood, for two decades. Alongside militant secular Palestinian groups, both were allowed to maintain offices and military bases inside Syria. During the Syrian occupation of Lebanon from 1976 to 2005, the Assad regime was a principal supporter and conduit to the Shiite Islamist Hezbollah movement, channeling Iranian arms and funds to the militia as it waged war against Israeli forces occupying southern Lebanon prior Israel's withdrawal in 2000, then as it waged war intermittently against Israel itself. Finally, the Syrian regime covertly supported foreign jihadists entering Iraq after the fall of Saddam Hussein's regime in 2003.[1] Many Syrian jihadists affiliated with Abu Musab al-Zarqawi's al-Qaeda in Iraq (AQI) were allowed to set up safe houses and even recruit volunteers inside Syria.[2] When the Assad regime dialed back its support for Iraqi insurgents in 2007–2008, many of these jihadis left Iraq. Hundreds were imprisoned upon their return to Syria, while some were allowed to cross into Lebanon, where they founded the group Fatah al-Islam in the Nahr al-Bared Palestinian refugee camp.[3]

When demonstrations against the Syrian regime first erupted in March 2011, most of the regime's Sunni Islamist allies remained on the sidelines.[4] Once it became clear that Assad was unable to stamp out the uprising by force, however, they abandoned the regime in droves. Hamas leaders departed their longtime home in Damascus for Doha, Qatar, in January 2012,[5] while Salafi-jihadists came out squarely in support of the uprising.

Hezbollah, on the other hand, has steadfastly stood by the Syrian regime. The movement has used its considerable political power within Lebanon's quasi-democratic system to ensure that the Lebanese Army and other state security institutions act to prevent smuggling and other pro-rebel activities in Lebanon.In 2012, Hezbollah forces began entering Syria, ostensibly to protect Shiite shrines but also to bolster pro-regime forces. In mid-2013, Hezbollah forces were instrumental in the regime's recapture of Qusayr, a predominantly Shiite Syrian town of thirty thousand, visible from the Lebanese border and essential to sealing off rebel supply routes into Lebanon.[6]

In addition to Lebanese fighters from Hezbollah, there are also Iraqi, Afghan, Pakistani, and native Syrian Shiite militias that support the regime. The most numerous and effective of these fighters beyond Hezbollah are the thousands of Iraqi Shiite militiamen.

The first major international Shia formation was the Abu al-Fadl al-Abbas Brigade, which emerged in 2012–2013.[7] Through 2013, a number of more specific formations emerged from the network of the Brigade, mostly composed of and led by Iraqi Shia. Some of these militias reflect Iranian-backed splinters from the Sadrist trend that feel let down by Iraqi cleric Muqtada al-Sadr's refusal to endorse fighting in Syria. During the same time period, older Iraqi militias such as the Badr Organization, Asa'ib Ahl al-Haq, and Kata'ib Hezbollah became involved in Syria under their own names, and new Iraqi militias in Syria like Saraya al-Khorasani, Harakat Hezbollah al-Nujaba', and Kata'ib Sayyid al-Shuhada' emerged.[8]

Following major advances by the Islamic State through northern and western Iraq in the summer of 2014, many Iraqi fighters returned to Iraq, with Hezbollah supposedly recruiting Lebanese Shiites to fill their places.[9] However, with the reversal of a number of Islamic State gains in Iraq and a relative stabilization of the situation, Iraqi fighters redeployed to Syria in considerable numbers through 2015, with a spike likely coinciding with the Russian intervention that began in October 2015.

The main units of Afghan and Pakistani Shiite fighters are Liwa Fatemiyoun and Liwa Zainabiyoun respectively. Both of these groups are affiliated with the Iranian Revolutionary Guard Corps and have mostly recruited Afghan and Pakistani Shia who are resident in Iran. The members of these groups generally lack the experience of Lebanese and Iraqi fighters and are used as frontline cannon fodder.

Among Syrian Shia, a number of formations have evolved on the basis of the idea of developing a native Syrian Muqawama Islamiya (Islamic Resistance), also known as Syrian Hezbollah. Some of these formations are directly affiliated with Hezbollah, most notably Quwat al-Ridha, which largely recruits from the Homs area; Junud al-Mahdi and the Imam al-Hujja Regiment, which recruit from the villages of Nubl and Zahara' to the north of Aleppo; and Liwa al-Imam al-Mahdi. Not all Syrian Hezbollah militias recruit only among Shia or require members to convert to Shiite Islam. For instance, some of these groups have recruited from members of the Druze population in Syria.

Anti-regime Sunni Islamists

The most prominent political Islamist group in Syria is the Syrian Muslim Brotherhood, though other groups are also active. The Syrian chapter of the Egypt-based pan-Islamic Muslim Brotherhood movement was established in 1946. Despite its status as an offshoot, the Syrian Muslim Brotherhood differs significantly from the original Muslim Brotherhood in its base of socio-economic support. Whereas the Muslim Brotherhood in Egypt traditionally drew mass support from rural areas, the Syrian Muslim Brotherhood's base lay in the Sunni urban nobility and middle class. In 1963, the secular Arab nationalist Ba'ath party seized power in Syria and began implementing land reforms and nationalizing industries, which severely threatened middle-class interests.[10] With independent political parties and media outlawed, the mosque became the one semi-protected space where dissidents could voice opposition to regime policies.[11] Assad persuaded influential Lebanese Shiite cleric Musa al-Sadr to issue a ruling certifying that Alawis are Shia Muslims and therefore eligible for the presidency.[12]

During the late 1970s, Islamist militants affiliated with the Brotherhood launched an armed insurrection against the Assad regime with the goal of replacing it with an Islamic state. Though the militants had some material support from rival Arab states, they were unable to rally support in rural areas where armed resistance was more tactically feasible. Thus, the rebellion never seriously threatened the regime. Thousands of Islamists were imprisoned, and membership in the Brotherhood was made punishable by death. When militants seized control of large parts of Hama in 1982, regime forces destroyed much of the city, killing tens of thousands.

This episode virtually eradicated the Brotherhood's influence in Syria for the following three decades. Most ranking members of the Brotherhood went into exile,[13] where they splintered into rival factions. Meanwhile, the Assad regime's soaring regional influence in the 1980s dissuaded rival governments from sponsoring armed opposition in Syria. The devastation resulting from the Brotherhood's failed insurrection made dissidents inside Syria wary of any association with Islamism in challenging the regime.

From 1996 to 2000, there was a gradual moderation of the Brotherhood's platform, rhetoric, and tactics under the leadership of Ali Sadreddine al-Bayanouni from his exile in Jordan, who was head of the Brotherhood from 1996 to 2010.[14] In 2001, the Brotherhood renounced violence. In 2004, it adopted a new political platform calling for multiparty democracy and minority rights.[15] Bayanouni also worked to improve the Brotherhood's ties with secular opposition forces. In 2005, the Brotherhood joined secular dissidents inside Syria in signing the Damascus Declaration, which was a unified statement from all Syrian opposition groups calling for a "peaceful, gradual" democratic reform process.[16]

After the Damascus Declaration initiative failed to galvanize internal opposition to the regime, the Brotherhood focused its attention on building ties with Western and Arab governments bent on bringing Assad to heel in the wake of his alleged involvement in the 2005 assassination of former Lebanese Prime Minister Rafiq Hariri.[17] In 2006, it formed an alliance with recently exiled vice-president Abdul Halim Khaddam, a Sunni ex-Ba'athist with close ties to the Saudi royal family.[18]

The outbreak of mass protests against the Syrian regime in March 2011 took the Brotherhood by surprise. As in other Middle Eastern states experiencing the so-called Arab Spring, Islamists initially played little discernable role in the unrest.[19] The Brotherhood declined to endorse the uprising for nearly two months,[20] calculating whether its interests would best be served by extracting concessions from a weakened Assad or helping achieve his overthrow. Once it became clear the regime was not going to be able to extinguish the uprising, Brotherhood leaders threw their weight fully behind the cause.

The Brotherhood's secretive and elitist structure limited how useful it could be to a popular uprising. This structure served the Brotherhood well when organizing cell-based resistance in the late 1970s and avoiding regime infiltration while in exile, but did not lend itself to mass mobilization. Furthermore, the Brotherhood's predominantly urban social base left it ill-suited to connect with a popular uprising emanating primarily from rural areas and the outskirts of major cities.

Nevertheless, the Brotherhood had an advantage over secular exile groups, due to its established organizational hierarchy, large network of members, and affiliated Brotherhood chapters around the globe, as well as burgeoning relations with Qatar and Turkey (which turned against the Assad regime several months into the uprising).[21] The Brotherhood played a prominent role in the August 2011 establishment of the Syrian National Council, which brought the exiled Syrian opposition groups under a single umbrella, and its successor organization, the Syrian National Coalition (SNC).[22]

Since then, a number of moderate Islamist currents have vied for influence with the Brotherhood within the SNC. A reformist current, which was more receptive to liberal democratic norms than the Brotherhood, included the National Action Group, an organization co-founded by Obeida Nahas, who served as political advisor to Bayanouni and was reportedly the architect behind the Brotherhood's short-lived alliance with former vice-president Khaddam. Much like members of Turkey's ruling Justice and Development Party (AKP), Nahas and his allies describe themselves as religious conservatives, not Islamists.

The Movement for Justice and Development (MJD), founded in London in 2006 in response to Bayanouni's alliance with Khaddam, actually named itself after the AKP. Its political platform calls for the Syrian constitution to declare Syria a nation of "Islamic civilization and culture," but without making sharia a principal source of legislation.[23] The Syrian National Movement (SNM), led by Emad ad-Din al-Rashid, advocates acceptance of the "Islamic reference" (al-Marja'iyya al-Islamiyya) as a source of legislation and the basis for the national identity.[24] Former SNC secretary-general Badr Jamous is affiliated with the SNM.[25]

Another current of devout (though not strictly speaking Islamist) Sunni opposition leaders is composed of ulema (traditional Sufi religious scholars) who fled Syria during the revolt, many of whom had acquired substantial followings inside Syria because Assad's regime relaxed controls over religious life in the past decade. The most notable traditionalist group is Muhammad Kurayyim Rajih's League of the Ulema of Sham (LUS), led mostly by clerics from Damascus and Homs.[26] Moaz al-Khatib of LUS, former imam of the

Umayyad Mosque in Damascus, served as the first president of the SNC. Current LUS president Sheikh Osama al-Rifai is the spiritual leader of a moderate Sufi movement called Jamaat Zayd (Zayd's Group), which the regime allowed to operate in Syria in the 1990s.[27]

In April 2014, pro-Brotherhood ulema joined together with traditionalists, reformists, and Sururis to form the Syrian Islamic Council (SIC), purporting to be an official religious authority for rebel forces. Headed by Osama al-Rifai, it is aligned with Qatar and Turkey and opposed to al-Qaeda-linked extremists.[28] Most Islamists in the SNC have avoided raising divisive social issues, such as veiling women and banning alcohol.

The perceived dominance of Islamists in the SNC alienated many secular opposition figures. Kamal Lebwany, a dissident physician released from detention in November 2011 after nearly a decade in a Syrian jail, lamented that "the Muslim Brotherhood monopolizes everything" and warned that its pretensions to democracy are "a liberal peel covering a totalitarian, nondemocratic core."[29]

Although the Brotherhood declined to establish a fighting force in Syria bearing its name, it has provided funding to a range of different militias. Its primary vehicle for providing funding was the Commission for the Protection of Civilians (CPC), established in December 2011. The Brotherhood intends less to directly control military units or promote its ideological agenda than to increase its leverage sufficiently to make gains in an internationally-brokered settlement.[30]

Although the CPC was initially the main source of external financing for the revolt, it was soon supplanted by the fundraising networks of radical Salafi preachers based in the Arab Gulf. Many of the CPC's early recipients drifted away as more sources of funding became available, most notably via the Tawhid Brigade, Ahrar al-Sham, and Suqour al-Sham.[31]

A second umbrella of Brotherhood-backed militias in and around Idlib and Hama was the Shields of the Revolution Commission, nominally loyal to the Free Syrian Army (FSA) Supreme Military Command.[32] Over the course of the war, militias affiliated with the Brotherhood have been eclipsed in strength by more radical groups. "Without a negotiated cease-fire," scholar Aron Lund wrote prophetically in mid-2013, "the real outcome of the Syrian conflict is likely to be determined on the battlefield, where the Brotherhood's failure to establish a strong presence could significantly weaken its hand."[33]

The organization that can arguably best be seen as a successor to the Shields of the Revolution Commission is Faylaq al-Sham, announced as a merger of nineteen brigades in March 2014. The group went on to become a key component of the Jaysh al-Fath (Army of Conquest) coalition set up in 2015 in Idlib province, which will be discussed further below. It also played a role in fighting in Aleppo, both against the regime and its allies as part of the reconstituted Jaysh al-Fath in 2016 and against the Islamic State in the north Aleppo countryside alongside CIA-backed FSA groups with Turkish support.

Sunni Salafi-Jihadis

The Syrian civil war has witnessed a proliferation of militant groups adhering to Salafism, an ultra-orthodox Sunni Islamist current that believes Muslims must return to the ways of al-salaf al-saleh (the righteous ancestors) from the time of the Prophet Muhammad and rid themselves of bidaa (innovations) that have taken root in the centuries since. The latter include not only such secular conventions as democracy and the nation-state, but also centuries of Islamic jurisprudence and traditions that have come to define how most Muslims practice their faith. Non-Sunni Muslims and Sufis are viewed as heretics. In sharp contrast to members of the Muslim Brotherhood and its offshoots, Salafis traditionally eschewed participation in politics, focusing instead on dawa (missionary work) to convert Muslim societies to their way of thinking.

During the late 1970s, a younger generation of Salafis in the Arab Gulf (many of them expatriates) began to reject the movement's traditional political quietism and either agitate for Islamic rule at home or fight perceived enemies of Islam abroad. Thousands went to South Asia to combat the 1979 Soviet invasion of Afghanistan. After the Soviet withdrawal and the fall of Kabul to the mujahideen, many of these so-called Arab Afghans returned home to continue fighting for their beliefs or joined Osama bin Laden's expanding al-

Qaeda network. Many Arab Afghans later went to Iraq in the wake of the 2003 US-led invasion, where they eventually coalesced into AQI, rebranded first as the Majlis Shura al-Mujahideen (Mujahideen Shura Council) in early 2006 and then the Islamic State of Iraq (ISI) in October 2006, some months after AQI leader Abu Mus'ab al-Zarqawi's death.

Today, two of the most prominent Salafi-jihadi groups are Jabhat al-Nusra and the Islamic State. In late 2011, ISI chief Abu Bakr al-Baghdadi began sending undercover operatives into Syria, many of them Syrian nationals. Those operatives released a video statement in January 2012 calling themselves Jabhat al-Nusra (The Support Front).[34] The new organization claimed responsibility for a multitude of spectacular suicide and Improvised Explosive Device (IED) bombings during the first half of 2012,.[35] Jabhat al-Nusra also displayed undeniable prowess on the battlefield, spearheading the capture of numerous regime bases and fortified installations.[36] Led by Abu Mohammad al-Golani, Jabhat al-Nusra quickly received endorsements from al-Qaeda leader Ayman al-Zawahiri[37] and other influential jihadi ideologues.[38] In sharp contrast to ISI, whose strategy during the Iraq war alienated local Sunnis, Jabhat al-Nusra developed cooperative relations with non-jihadist rebels and limited its mistreatment of civilians. When Jabhat al-Nusra was officially designated a terrorist group by the US government in December 2012, the Brotherhood and many FSA commanders publicly defended it.

In late 2012, Baghdadi became fearful that Jabhat al-Nusra was growing too independent. In April 2013, he unilaterally declared that ISI and Jabhat al-Nusra were to merge to form the Islamic State in Iraq and al-Sham (ISIS). However, Golani disputed the merger and appealed to Zawahiri to mediate, declaring a renewal of the bay'a (pledge of allegiance) to the al-Qaeda leader. When Zawahiri ruled in favor of Golani, ISIS broke away from al-Qaeda and Jabhat al-Nusra, taking most foreign fighters operating in Jabhat al-Nusra's ranks with it.

ISIS aggressively consolidated areas of northern Syria under its control, clashing frequently with other rebels, including Jabhat al-Nusra, and even executing several of their military commanders.[39]

It soon became clear that ISIS, unlike other rebel groups, was not predominately fighting to overthrow Assad—indeed, the regime's endurance had created ideal conditions for ISIS's growth. After ISIS consolidated its contiguous holdings of territory in Syria in the wake of infighting with rebels in early 2014, it went on to overrun much of northern Iraq in the spring and summer of that year. As a result, ISIS officially declared its caliphate on June 29, 2014, and changed its name to the Islamic State.[40]

In contrast to many other insurgent groups operating in Syria, the Islamic State has derived most of its income from indigenous revenue sources, not outside donations.[41] In addition to deriving revenue from taxation and confiscations, the Islamic State gained control of most of the oil-rich province of Deir az-Zor as well as other oil resources in Hasakah, Raqqa, and Homs provinces, allowing the organization to make considerable income selling off Syrian crude oil (topping up to $1.5 million a day in late 2014, going by the Abu Sayyaf records).[42] It has also allowed its oil to be resold to outside clients, including the Assad regime[43] and rebel-held areas of Syria. When ISIS took over Mosul just before the creation of the caliphate, it was reported to have looted $425 million in cash from the central bank, making it by some accounts the world's richest terrorist organization.[44] However, Islamic State finances have since been degraded by coalition airstrikes targeting "cash points" and the oil industry. Further, the Islamic State's taxation base has been reduced because local forces acting with coalition support have recaptured territory. This drop in revenue has resulted in reductions of salaries and benefits for fighters, which take up a considerable portion of Islamic State expenses.

Jabhat al-Nusra, which increasingly emphasized its al-Qaeda affiliation after Zawahiri's ruling in its favor (by doing things such as inscribing the al-Qaeda name on banners), suffered considerably as a result of the rise of the Islamic State, losing all its holdings in the east by July 2014.[45] Leaked recordings in that month suggested an impending announcement of an Islamic emirate by Jabhat al-Nusra to counter the Islamic State's project, though the emirate announcement was denied in an official Jabhat al-Nusra statement. However, the group did not collapse but rather began to show a harsher side. By November 2014, it had expelled the FSA coalition known as the Syrian Revolutionaries Front, with whom Jabhat al-Nusra had previously cooperated in expelling ISIS from Idlib.[46] In addition, Jabhat al-Nusra began setting up its own Dar al-Qada (judiciary) branches in various localities in northwest Syria and forced the Druze community of Jabal al-Summaq in northern Idlib province to renounce their faith, destroying Druze shrines in the process.[47]

In 2015, a number of Islamist, Salafi, and jihadi groups in the north came to set up the Jaysh al-Fatah coalition, primarily based in Idlib province and led by Jabhat al-Nusra and Ahrar al-Sham. Faylaq al-Sham also joined this coalition. With backing from Turkey, Qatar, and Saudi Arabia, the coalition expelled the Assad regime from Idlib city and other key towns in the province, leaving two isolated Shiite villages, Fou'a and Kafariya, under siege. The coalition failed to establish a unified governance system in the province, and Jabhat al-Nusra experienced its own internal ruptures centered around two dissident figures, Abu Mariya al-Qahtani and Saleh al-Hamawi, who were both involved in the creation of Jabhat al-Nusra but came to believe the group was not being pragmatic enough and insisted on focusing more on unification efforts.

Real unity between Jabhat al-Nusra and more mainstream factions was impeded by Jabhat al-Nusra's al-Qaeda ties. Proposals for a merger in January and February 2016 were ultimately rejected because of these connections. Around this time, Zawahiri recorded a speech entitled "Go Forth to al-Sham" (not released until May 2016) that portrayed the Syrian jihad as the best hope for establishing an Islamic government that could eventually give rise to the caliphate.[48] Unity of the mujahideen, according to Zawahiri, is paramount (an idea he had previously emphasized in a January 2014 speech on Syria in which he placed unity above temporary organizational ties).[49]

By July 2016, it had become more attractive for Jabhat al-Nusra to sever public ties with al-Qaeda, partly on account of proposed US-Russian coordination to target the group.[50] The move to break ties would put the ball in the court of the factions that objected to the al-Qaeda affiliation in discussions on mergers. In addition, Jabhat al-Nusra hoped to score a propaganda move in trying to show that Westerners objected to Islam itself, not simply to al-Qaeda links. As a result, with apparent guidance from al-Qaeda, Jabhat al-Nusra officially rebranded itself as an independent entity on July 28, 2016, changing its name to Jabhat Fatah al-Sham (Conquest of al-Sham Front).[51] The move, announced by Golani on video, was preceded several hours by an audio message from Zawahiri's deputy, Abu al-Khayr al-Masri, urging for the necessary steps to be taken to protect the Syrian jihad. The fact the message came from Jabhat al-Nusra's media wing, al-Manara al-Bayda, suggested that Masri was already in Syria, fitting in with a pattern of movement of senior al-Qaeda personnel to Syria. Some elements within Jabhat al-Nusra (for example, Abu Julaybib) rejected the rebranding out of fear of ideological dilution of the jihadist project, but they do not seem to have had the influence to divide the ranks.

"Third-way" jihadist groups

In addition to the Islamic State and Jabhat Fatah al-Sham, there have been a number of smaller jihadi factions composed partly or mainly of foreign fighters. These groups have differed in their allegiances, and most of them have merged over time with larger formations, including the Islamic State. Some groups that were more closely affiliated with al-Qaeda have merged with Jabhat Fatah al-Sham and its successor organization, Hay'at Tahrir al-Sham, or remained independent organizations. The main independent group today is the Turkestan Islamic Party (composed mostly of Uyghur refugees who have lived in Turkey).

A more mainstream current encompasses a broad array of groups funded heavily by Salafi activists in the Arab Gulf and Arab Gulf governments themselves, who see them as a means of limiting the growth potential of Jabhat Fatah al-Sham and Baghdadi's Islamic State. Most of these groups joined the Syrian Islamic Front, an umbrella coalition established in December 2012, and its successor, the Islamic Front, in November 2013. However, the Islamic Front underwent a variety of splits and mergers, with the brand currently most associated with Ahrar al-Sham and groups that have merged into it. Other Islamic Front member groups, such as affiliates of the

Aleppo-based Liwa al-Tawhid that were ideologically closer to the Muslim Brotherhood, went on to form separate coalitions like the Shami Front.

Ideologically, most of the groups that constituted the Islamic Front share much in common with hardline jihadists. They have proclaimed rejection of democracy, claimed to be fighting for an Islamic state, and refused to recognize the SNC and the opposition interim government. Unlike the transnational jihadists, however, Islamic Front groups downplayed or even denied pan-Islamic ambitions (scholar Abdul Rahman Al-Haj calls them "deferred Caliphate" jihadists[52]), avoided anti-Western demagoguery, and adopted slightly less inflammatory rhetoric concerning Syrian minorities.[53] The Islamic Front groups have had few foreign volunteers fighting in their ranks (mostly concentrated in Ahrar al-Sham), and none are known to have used suicide attacks significantly.

Most Islamic Front groups relied heavily on financing from Arab Gulf donors, most of it channeled under the guise of humanitarian aid through Kuwait, which has been the primary hub of private fundraising because of its lax regulatory environment and the political strength of Salafis.[54] The tiny, oil-rich emirate was dubbed "the Arab world's main clearinghouse" for donations to radical Islamist rebels by the *Wall Street Journal*[55] and "a virtual Western Union outlet for Syria's rebels" by the *New York Times*.[56] Due to UN sanctions and Kuwaiti regulations, these financiers' importance has been greatly diminished.

Perhaps more ambiguous in characterization is Ahrar al-Sham. Ahrar al-Sham is strongest in Idlib province and was the leading faction there alongside Jabhat Fatah al-Sham. Founded in late 2011 and led by Hassan Abboud, a former Sednaya military prison detainee, Ahrar al-Sham became a leading actor in the Syrian Islamic Front and then the Islamic Front. Though most of the first generation of the leadership was wiped out in a mysterious explosion in late 2014, the group recovered. Strongly backed by Turkey and Qatar, Ahrar al-Sham has been open to the idea of engagement on the international stage and has a foreign political relations wing dedicated to this engagement, represented foremost by Labib Nahhas (a.k.a. Abu Izz al-Deen), who was seen as embodying the more moderate wing of Ahrar al-Sham. On the other hand, remarks by Ali al-Omar, who became leader in November 2016, also situates Ahrar al-Sham within the Islamic movements that seek the revival of the caliphate. The speech framed the conflict in Syria in highly sectarian terms, stressing the need to come together to fight the "Rafidites" (a derogatory term for the Shia), and spoke highly of the Taliban in Afghanistan as a Sunni movement that could bring together Sunnis of a variety of madhahib (schools of thought).

The group maintained closer military alliances with Jabhat Fatah al-Sham than Jaysh al-Islam, but forming unified governing structures within areas taken from the regime has proven more elusive. At the local level in Idlib province, for example, Ahrar al-Sham has often acted as a local counterbalance to harsher actions by Jabhat Fatah al-Sham. The two groups also supported rival judiciary structures: while Ahrar al-Sham is linked with the Islamic Commission, Jabhat Fatah al-Sham backed the Dar al-Qada (set up in 2014 as Jabhat al-Nusra's judiciary branch). In July 2016, a number of Salafi and jihadist jurists and scholars came together to form the Assembly of al-Sham Scholars, which aimed to serve as a single, ostensibly independent judiciary body for the various factions. This development fit in with the notion of grander unification efforts among Salafi and jihadist factions—an idea that also helped give rise to the formation of Jabhat Fatah al-Sham.

However, success in the subsequent unity talks between Jabhat Fatah al-Sham and other factions, particularly Ahrar al-Sham, proved elusive. A clear reason for this failure is that Jabhat Fatah al-Sham did not appear to have fundamentally changed its conduct or ideological end goals, even though those who rejected the rebranding have feared ideological compromise of the jihadist project. This failure to change gave rise to suspicion that the rebranding was more a tactical move than a genuine break from al-Qaeda. On a key issue—namely, whether it is acceptable to coordinate operations with Turkish forces to fight the Islamic State in north Aleppo countryside—Jabhat Fatah al-Sham reiterated opposition to such action in keeping with the prior rejectionist stance of Jabhat al-Nusra, while Ahrar al-Sham's Shari'i council officially endorsed coordination. Though the endorsement does not mean everyone in Ahrar al-Sham agreed on the idea, fighters from the group participated in Turkey's Euphrates Shield operations in the north Aleppo countryside against the Islamic State, despite criticism that the Euphrates Shield drew manpower away from fronts against the regime, allowing Aleppo to fall into Assad's hands.

Jabhat Fatah al-Sham's premise for unity talks appeared to have been based on the notion that other factions should merge under its banner and lose their identities, or at least accept the group as having the main leadership role in a merger body: that is, unity should ultimately be on Jabhat Fatah al-Sham's terms. The fall of Aleppo to the regime in December 2016—a heavy blow to the wider insurgency—intensified discussions surrounding a merger between factions in the north of the country, the success or failure of which depended heavily on the roles of Ahrar al-Sham and Jabhat Fatah al-Sham. In effect, two rival unity initiatives emerged. One of these initiatives was embodied in a statement issued on December 28, 2016, by ten factions, including Faylaq al-Sham, the Shami Front, and Jaysh al-Islam's minor northern affiliates.[57] These factions have emphasized their orientation through issuing the statement in the name of the "Free Syrian Army." That is, whatever the Islamist and Salafi tendencies, the project was operating within a clear national framework.

The other unification movement represented a continuation of Jabhat Fatah al-Sham's efforts to push for unity, still clearly on its terms and with the intent of orienting the wider insurgency toward its ideological end goals. Ahrar al-Sham effectively found itself caught in the middle of these two unity initiatives. Some in Ahrar al-Sham's senior leadership are more sympathetic to the initiative led by Jabhat Fatah al-Sham, while others, in particular those associated with the group's wider political outreach efforts such as Labib Nahhas, rejected siding with Jabhat Fatah al-Sham, seeing it as an act of political suicide.[58]

Only a round of serious infighting spurred actual mergers, beginning with an attack by Jabhat Fatah al-Sham on the Mujahideen Army, a group that had received CIA support. By the end of January 2017, several groups, including the Shami Front and Jaysh al-Islam's northern affiliates, subsequently merged under Ahrar al-Sham, seeking protection from Jabhat Fatah al-Sham, while Jabhat Fatah al-Sham merged with groups that had a close working relationship with it, in addition to sympathizers in Ahrar al-Sham under Hashim al-Sheikh, to form Hay'at Tahrir al-Sham (Liberation of al-Sham Commission), led by Hashim al-Sheikh with Golani as military commander.

Despite an apparent new balance of power being struck by the mergers, Hay'at Tahrir al-Sham had seized control of important border supply routes in Idlib and had emerged the stronger actor. This reality was borne out in a subsequent round of infighting in July 2017 that saw Hay'at Tahrir al-Sham inflict some decisive defeats on Ahrar al-Sham, including forcing the latter off the key Bab al-Hawa border crossing with Turkey and expelling the group from the Idlib provincial capital.

Hay'at Tahrir al-Sham's moves against its largest rival are connected to its aim of expanding its administrative capabilities as part of a wider effort to become the face of Syria's insurgency. Hay'at Tahrir is committed to rejecting the notion of a political settlement with the regime but also trying to force the outside world to deal with it. For example, the group has taken an increasingly hardline approach towards civilian local councils operating in its areas, requiring them to become affiliated with its services administration. The group has also set up a new administration to monitor financial transfers and currency exchanges.

The long-term viability of this project is doubtful. Despite professed commitments by Hay'at Tahrir al-Sham to maintaining the independence of aid organizations and NGOs working in Idlib, these organizations and their donors will be increasingly reluctant to work in a province dominated by what is internationally considered to be an al-Qaeda front group. In turn, the growing pariah status of the province is likely to hurt Hay'at Tahrir al-Sham financially in an area lacking the lucrative resources like oil that are found in the Islamic State's remaining holdings in eastern Syria.

The formation of Hay'at Tahrir al-Sham and its growing administrative project raise issues regarding its relationship with al-Qaeda. The speed with which Hay'at Tahrir al-Sham was formed means that it is unlikely that al-Qaeda leader Ayman al-Zawahiri had a part in the creation of the merger. Since the creation of Hay'at Tahrir al-Sham, Jordanian jurist Sami al-Oraydi, who served as chief jurist for Jabhat al-Nusra and remained even after the formation of Jabhat Fatah al-Sham, has parted ways with Golani and other former comrades, accusing the successor organizations to Jabhat al-Nusra of disobeying al-Qaeda.

Further, Zawahiri has taken on a realistic view of the Syrian civil war since the insurgency's loss of Aleppo, urging the jihadists in a message released in April 2017 to pursue a strategy of guerrilla warfare rather than control of territory. Hay'at Tahrir al-Sham's policies are the opposite of this approach, indicating a clear strategic divergence between Zawahiri and the group. Only a large offensive by the regime and its allies into Idlib province, which will likely force Hay'at Tahrir al-Sham to adopt guerrilla tactics, is likely to bring about a rapprochement between Zawahiri and the group.

Ahrar al-Sham, meanwhile, has appointed a new leader (Hassan Soufan), and has vowed to continue its operations, trying to demonstrate the loyalty of its affiliates. However, it seems doubtful that the group will recover from the blows inflicted on it in July 2017.

Islamism and Society

Syria is an extraordinarily diverse country. Sunni Arabs are by far the largest ethno-sectarian group, comprising sixty-seven percent of the population. Non-Arab (predominantly Sunni) Kurds number roughly nine percent of the population. The remainder consists of non-Sunni, predominantly Arab religious minorities—Alawis comprise about twelve percent of the population; Christians of various denominations, ten percent; Druze, three percent; and various Shia denominations, around one percent.[59] Communal solidarity (*asabiya*) is very strong among all of these minorities, owing in part to centuries of oppression and discrimination at the hands of Sunni rulers.

Assad made sure that the façade of civilian government in Syria appropriately reflected Sunni demographic weight. The positions of prime minister, foreign minister, and army commander were nearly always held by Sunnis, for example, as were most parliamentary seats, judicial offices, and other high visibility posts. Many second-generation Alawi power barons later forged business partnerships with Sunnis, and some (including Bashar al-Assad) married Sunni women.[60] For most Syrians, opposition to the regime was not rooted primarily in matters of faith. The Assad regime's statist economic development and social welfare policies gave it a sufficiently strong base of rural support cutting across sectarian lines that lasted through the turn of the century.[61]

Militant Islamism certainly was not a cause of the popular uprising that erupted in 2011. There are plenty of socio-economic drivers, most notably a pronounced youth bulge. Syria's population at the time of twenty-three million was the youngest in the Middle East outside of the Palestinian Territories,[62] with fifty-three percent below the age of twenty.[63]

Bashar Assad's economic reforms solidified support for the regime among the urban elites and middle class, but at the expense of rural areas. UK-based Syrian journalist Malik al-Abdeh characterized the uprising as a "revolution of the rural Sunni working classes against the Alawi-dominated military elite and the urban bourgeoisie (both Muslim and Christian) that has profited from the Assad dictatorship."[64] It was not religion that triggered their decision to rise up to the regime after years of quiet obedience, but the "demonstration effect" of watching Egyptians, Tunisians, and Libyans overthrow their own governments.

Early in the uprising, observers sympathetic to the opposition argued that "there are few traces of radical Islamism in Syria" and that, should the Assad regime fall, "the chances of Syria turning into an Islamic state are almost nil."[65] But the secular democratic orientation of the uprising steadily eroded as the violence escalated and prospects of a peaceful solution evaporated.[66] This erosion was partly because the regime had little trouble suppressing protests in non-Sunni and mixed towns and neighborhoods, where demonstrations were never large enough to give safety in numbers. In Sunni majority areas, in contrast, demonstrations "were 20 to 30 times larger [and] organized under the semi-inviolable protection of mosques."[67] For ordinary Syrians contemplating whether to protest in the streets, ironically, it was much safer to be a Sunni than to be an Alawi.

Moreover, while it may have been the case that a majority of Christians, Druze, and Kurds—perhaps even Alawis—supported demands for political reform and human rights, they were much less willing than devout Sunnis to take great personal risks in challenging Assad. Consequently, regime repression further tilted the demographic composition of the uprising by weeding out minorities and those of little religious faith.[68] As the country rapidly slipped into full-blown civil war in early 2012 and it became a question of whether to stand up and fight the regime, the revolutionaries on the ground were almost exclusively Sunni. Sunnification was followed by Islamization as most emerging rebel groups adopted explicitly Islamic names and iconography.

Some attribute this Islamic awakening to the fact that donations from the Arab Gulf states and private Arab donors outpaced assistance from the West. According to such "resource mobilization" explanations,[69] the influx of cash from Salafi donors not only strengthened jihadist forces vis-à-vis the FSA, but also led relatively secular groups within the FSA to adopt Salafi dress and customs.[70] Many rank and file fighters of Salafi-jihadist militias are devout Sunnis with no firm extremist convictions. "Size, money and momentum are the things to look for in Syrian insurgent politics—ideology comes fourth, if even that," notes Lund.[71]

However, much as Pakistan and Afghanistan became the crucible for indoctrinating adventure-seeking youth from across the Arab world into the Salafi-jihadist path during the 1980s, Syria has perfect conditions for giving rise to a new generation of extremists. Already the effects have been felt in attacks in Europe partly caused by returning jihadists, as happened in a shooting incident at the Jewish Museum of Belgium in Brussels in May 2014, as well as the Paris attacks in November 2015. Further, the Islamic State and other jihadist groups have made a show of raising and educating children under their wings and indoctrinating them with their ideology. In addition, the large-scale Shia Islamist mobilization to aid the regime has given rise to a much more sectarian-charged atmosphere in the region than prior to 2011.

Islamism and the State

In the first three decades after the Ba'ath Party seized power in 1963, the Syrian state worked to secularize Syrian society and control Islamic religious expression, especially in the wake of the first Syrian uprising. All formal Islamic institutions were closely managed by the state,[72] while preaching outside of the mosques or outside of appointed prayer times was prohibited. There were no independent political parties, media, unions, or other associations allowed to come between citizen and state. Neutering the mosques was the final link in the chain.

Upon ascending to the presidency after his father's death in 2000, Bashar al-Assad continued efforts to promote an Islamic posture. The new president released hundreds of Islamist prisoners, lifted a longstanding ban on wearing female headscarves in Syrian schools,[73] and allowed mosques to remain open between prayer times.[74] He began favorably referencing religion in public speeches,[75] while state universities held Qur'an reading competitions.[76] The Syrian military even announced that Islamic clergy would be allowed to give lectures to military cadets for the first time in forty-three years, a decision that Defense Minister Hassan Tourkmani called a response to "the thirst for God in the barracks."[77]

Although falling well short of the kind of unfettered religious freedom that could pose direct political and security threats to the regime, state-modulated Islamization dramatically changed the public landscape of Syria, from styles of dress to architecture.[78]

Whereas the late Hafez al-Assad kept his regime's Palestinian and Lebanese Islamist clients at arms-length and never allowed them to operate unsupervised in Syria, Bashar al-Assad went much further during the Iraq war by allowing militant jihadists to preach and recruit inside Syria. The most notable was Abu Qaqaa (a.k.a. Mahmoud Qoul Aghassi), a preacher in Aleppo who was allowed to directly recruit local youth to fight in Iraq and even offer weapons training at his mosque. Some have suggested that Abu Qaqaa was, or became, a Syrian intelligence agent, as many of his recruits were tracked and arrested upon their return to Syria. His assassination in 2007 was widely seen as either payback from jihadists for betraying them or disposal by a regime that no longer needed or trusted him.[79]

During the first four months of the 2011 uprising, while thousands of pro-democracy protestors were being rounded up, the Assad regime released hundreds of Islamists from its jails, many of them Iraq war veterans who had run afoul of the authorities after returning to Syria in 2008–2009. Many of these parolees later played major roles in the rebellion. Parolees who later played roles include Zahran Aloush, the first leader of Jaysh al-Islam; Abdul Rahman Suweis of the Haqq Brigade; Hassan Aboud of Ahrar Al Sham; Ahmad Aisa Al Sheikh, commander of Suqour Al Sham; and possibly Jabhat al-Nusra commander Abu Mohammad al-Golani (whose true identity has never been confirmed).[80] Some interpreted the releases as a horribly botched effort to win the support, or at least the quiescence, of jihadists. Others believe that the releases were intended to have precisely the result they had—jumpstarting a violent Islamist insurgency that would lead the international community to think twice about aiding the Syrian opposition, while solidifying support for the regime among minorities and urban, middle-class Sunnis.

Assad had blamed foreign jihadists for the uprising from the very start, so the emergence of the Islamic State—a jihadist organization full of foreigners that makes no effort to appear civilized—was a blessing for him. There is some evidence of the regime having tried to facilitate ISIS' growth versus other rebel factions. For example, regime airstrikes against ISIS bases in some areas of Syria all but stopped when the group began targeting other insurgents in much of 2013 and early 2014.[81] However, fierce battles between the regime and ISIS in the summer of 2014 over control of oil fields, as well as the ISIS conquest of the isolated regime bases in Raqqa province and massacres of personnel in summer 2014, belied claims that ISIS was secretly in league with Assad. In addition, in 2015 the Islamic State launched a military campaign against regime positions in the Homs desert, culminating in the conquest of the ancient city of Palmyra and Qaryatayn. These towns were retaken by the regime with Russian support in the spring of 2016, though the Islamic State then recaptured Palmyra in an offensive in December 2016, while the Syrian regime and Russia were focusing heavily on Aleppo. The Syrian regime recaptured Palmyra a second time in March 2017.

Endnotes

1. Raymond Tanter and Stephen Kersting, "Syria's Role in the Iraq Insurgency," *inFOCUS Quarterly,* Spring 2009, http://www.jewishpolicycenter.org/827/syrias-role-in-the-iraq-insurgency.
2. "Treasury Designates Members of Abu Ghadiyah's Network Facilitates Flow of Terrorists, Weapons, and Money from Syria to al Qaida in Iraq," U.S. Department of the Treasury, February 28, 2008, http://www.treasury.gov/press-center/press-releases/Pages/hp845.aspx.
3. Peter Neumann, "Suspects into Collaborators," p. 19–21, *London Review of Books*, April 3, 2014, http://www.lrb.co.uk/v36/n07/peter-neumann/suspects-into-collaborators.
4. Lee Smith, "Crack-up," *Tablet,* April 28, 2011, http://www.tabletmag.com/news-and-politics/65981/crack-up/.
5. Fares Akram, "Hamas Leader Abandons Longtime Base in Damascus." *New York Times*, January 27, 2012, http://www.nytimes.com/2012/01/28/world/middleeast/khaled-meshal-the-leader-of-hamas-vacates-damascus.html?gwh=58C00E217CFD163EF15817D69C917AF0.
6. Marissa Sullivan, *Hezbollah In Syria*, Institute for the Study of War, *Middle East Security Report 19*, April 2014, http://www.understandingwar.org/sites/default/files/Hezbollah_Sullivan_FINAL.pdf.
7. Phillip Smyth, "Hizballah Cavalcade: What is the Liwa'a Abu Fadl al-Abbas (LAFA)?: Assessing Syria's Shia lInternational Brigade' Through Their Social Media Presence," Jihadology.net, May 15, 2013, http://jihadology.net/2013/05/15/hizballah-cavalcade-what-is-the-liwaa-abu-fadl-al-abbas-lafa-assessing-syrias-shia-international-brigade-through-their-social-media-presence/. See also Phillip Smyth, "Hizballah Cavalcade: From Najaf to Damascus and Onto Baghdad: Iraq's Liwa Abu Fadl al-Abbas," Jihadology.net, June 18, 2014, http://jihadology.net/2014/06/18/hizballah-cavalcade-from-najaf-to-damascus-and-onto-baghdad-iraqs-liwa-abu-fadl-al-abbas/.
8. Sullivan, "Hezbollah In Syria."

9. "Hezbollah Mobilizes to Defend Shiite Shrines in Syria," *Now Lebanon*, June 12, 2014, https://now.mmedia.me/lb/en/lebanonnews/551145-hezbollah-announces-general-mobilization-in-syria.
10. Rania Abouzeid, "Who Will the Tribes Back in Syria's Civil War?" *Time*, October 10, 2012, http://world.time.com/2012/10/10/who-will-the-tribes-back-in-syrias-civil-war/.
11. Roy Gutman and Paul Raymond, "Syria's Pro-Assad Forces Accused of Targeting Mosques in Civil War," McClatchy Newspapers, June 27, 2013, http://www.mcclatchydc.com/news/nation-world/world/article24750496.html.
12. Ari Heistein, "Iran's Support for Syria Pragmatic, not Religious (or, Who are the Alawites?)" *Informed Comment*, August 19, 2015, http://www.juancole.com/2015/08/secular-alawites-crescent.html.
13. Thomas Mayer, "The Islamic Opposition in Syria, 1961–1982," *Orient* 24, 1983; Patrick Seale and Maureen McConville, *Assad of Syria: The Struggle for the Middle East,* p. 320–338, I.B. Tauris, 1988.
14. Mohammad Saied Rassas, "Syria's Muslim Brotherhood: Past and Present," *Al-Monitor*, January 5, 2014, http://www.al-monitor.com/pulse/politics/2014/01/syria-muslim-brotherhood-past-present.html.
15. Elin Norman, "A Short Background on the Syrian Muslim Brotherhood and Its Process of Change: 1945–2012," Swedish Defense Research Agency, May 2014.
16. "Damascus Declaration in English," *SyriaComment*, November 1, 2005, http://faculty-staff.ou.edu/L/Joshua.M.Landis-1/syriablog/2005/11/damascus-declaration-in-english.htm.
17. Yvette Talhamy, "The Muslim Brotherhood Reborn: The Syrian Uprising, "*Middle East Quarterly* 19, no. 2, Spring 2012, http://www.meforum.org/3198/syria-muslim-brotherhood.
18. Ibid.
19. Nir Rosen, "Islamism and the Syrian Uprising," *Foreign Policy,* March 8, 2012, http://mideast.foreignpolicy.com/posts/2012/03/08/islamism_and_the_syrian_uprising.

20. Hassan Hassan, "In Syria, the Brotherhood's Influence Is on the Decline," *The National* (UAE), April 1, 2014, http://www.thenational.ae/thenationalconversation/comment/in-syria-the-brotherhoods-influence-is-on-the-decline.
21. Nour Malas, "Brotherhood Raises Syria Profile: Islamist Group Tries to Organize Opposition to Assad Regime, as Protests Waiver," *Wall Street Journal,* May 17, 2011, http://online.wsj.com/article/SB10001424052748703509104576327212414590134.htm; Khaled Yacoub Oweis, "Syria's Muslim Brotherhood Rise From the Ashes as Dominant Force in the Opposition," *Al Arabiya News,* May 6, 2012, http://english.alarabiya.net/articles/2012/05/06/212447.html.
22. Thomas Pierret, "Syria: Old-Timers and Newcomers," p. 76,*The Islamists are Coming: Who They Really Are*, edited by Robin Wright, United States Institute of Peace, 2012.
23. Pierret, "Syria: Old-Timers and Newcomers."
24. Pierret, "Syria: Old-Timers and Newcomers."
25. Thomas Pierret, "The Syrian Islamic Council," Carnegie Endowment for International Peace, May 13, 2014, http://carnegieendowment.org/syriaincrisis/?fa=55580.
26. Pierret, "The Syrian Islamic Council."
27. Pierret, "The Syrian Islamic Council."
28. Thomas Pierret, *The Struggle for Religious Authority in Syria*, Carnegie Endowment for International Peace, May 14, 2014, http://carnegieendowment.org/syriaincrisis/?fa=55593.
29. MacFarquhar, "Trying to Mold a Post-Assad Syria From Abroad."
30. Aron Lund, *Struggling to Adapt: The Muslim Brotherhood in a New Syria*, Carnegie Endowment for International Peace," May 7, 2013, http://carnegieendowment.org/2013/05/07/struggling-to-adapt-muslim-brotherhood-in-new-syria/g2qm?fa=searchResults&maxrow=20&tabName=pubs&qry=&fltr=&channel=&pageOn=365&reloadFlag=1.
31. Ibid.
32. Raphaël Lefèvre, "The Brotherhood Starts Anew in Syria," *Majalla*, August 19, 2013, http://www.majalla.

com/eng/2013/08/article55244734.
33. Lund, "Struggling to Adapt."
34. Bill Roggio, "Al Nusrah Front Claims Suicide Attack in Syria," *Long War Journal,* February 26, 2012, http://www.longwarjournal.org/archives/2012/02/al_nusrah_front_clai.php.
35. Most notably, the February 10 bombings in Aleppo that struck two military facilities, killing twenty-eight, and the March 17 bombings against the Air Force Intelligence headquarters and Criminal Security department in Damascus, which killed at least twenty-seven. See Bill Roggio, "Al Nusrah Front Claims Yet Another Suicide Attack in Syria," *Long War Journal*, September 2, 2016, http://www.longwarjournal.org/archives/2012/12/al_nusrah_front_clai_9.php.
36. "Syria Loses Last Idlib Army Base to Nusra Front, Other Groups," *Al Jazeera America*, September 9, 2015, http://america.aljazeera.com/articles/2015/9/9/syria-loses-last-idlib-army-base-to-nusra-other-groups.html.
37. "I appeal to every Muslim and every free, honorable one in Turkey, Iraq, Jordan, and Lebanon, to rise to help his brothers in Syria with all what he can, with his life, money, wonders, opinion, and information." As cited in Bill Roggio, "Al Baraa Ibn Malik Martyrdom Brigade forms in Syria," *Long War Journal Threat Matrix* blog, February 18, 2012, http://www.longwarjournal.org/threat-matrix/archives/2012/02/al_baraa_ibn_malik_martyrdom_b.php.
38. On March 6, 2012, prominent jihadi cleric Abu Mundhir al-Shinqiti released an online fatwa urging all capable Muslims to join the ranks of Jabhat al-Nusra. See "Fatwa by Senior Salafi-Jihadi Cleric: Muslims Are Obligated to Join the Ranks of the Syrian Jihadi Group 'Jabhat Al-Nusra'," MEMRI *Jihad and Terrorism Threat Monitor* no. 4565, March 13, 2012, http://www.memri.org/report/en/0/0/0/0/0/0/6168.htm. Other important jihadi ideologues have also given their approval, including the prominent online essayist Sheikh Abu Sa'd al-'Amil, the prominent Jordanian Salafi Sheikh Abu Muhammad al-Tahawi, and the popular Lebanese

Sheikh Abu al-Zahra' al-Zubaydi. See Aaron Y. Zelin, "Syria's New Jihadis," *Foreign Policy,* May 22, 2012, http://www.washingtoninstitute.org/policy-analysis/view/syrias-new-jihadis.

39. Other Salafi-jihadists were not immune. In May 2014, for example, ISIS militants captured and beheaded Muthana Hussein, a senior commander of Ahrar al-Sham. See "Islamist Militias Unite Under 'Code of Honor'," *The Daily Star Lebanon*, May 19, 2014, http://www.dailystar.com.lb/News/Middle-East/2014/May-19/256938-islamist-militias-unite-under-code-of-honor.ashx#ixzz35eSDD8nV.
40. Chelsea J. Carter, "Iraq Developments: ISIS Establishes 'Caliphate,' Changes Name," *CNN*, June 30, 2014, http://www.cnn.com/2014/06/29/world/meast/iraq-developments-roundup/.
41. Anne Speckhard, "ISIS's Revenues Include Sales of Oil to the al-Assad Regime," *Huffington Post*, April 28, 2016, http://www.huffingtonpost.com/anne-speckhard/isiss-revenues-include-sa_b_9789954.html.
42. Ibid.
43. Ben Hubbard, Clifford Krauss, and Eric Schmitt, "Rebels in Syria Claim Control of Resources," *New York Times*, January 28, 2014, http://www.nytimes.com/2014/01/29/world/middleeast/rebels-in-syria-claim-control-of-resources.html?_r=0.
44. Terrence McCoy, "ISIS just stole $425 million, Iraqi governor says, and became the 'world's richest terrorist group,'" *Washington Post*, June 12, 2014, http://www.washingtonpost.com/news/morning-mix/wp/2014/06/12/isis-just-stole-425-million-and-became-the-worlds-richest-terrorist-group/.
45. Daniel Cassman, "Hay'at Tahrir Al-Sham (Formerly Jabhat Al-Nusra)," Stanford University, August 14, 2017, http://web.stanford.edu/group/mappingmilitants/cgi-bin/groups/view/493.
46. Ibid.
47. "Syria Conflict: Al-Nusra Fighters Kill Druze Villagers," *BBC*, June 11, 2015, http://www.bbc.com/news/world-middle-east-33092902.
48. Thomas Joscelyn, "Ayman Al Zawahiri Discusses al

Qaeda's Goal of Building an Islamic Emirate in Syria," *Long War Journal*, May 8, 2016, http://www.longwarjournal.org/archives/2016/05/ayman-al-zawahiri-discusses-al-qaedas-goal-of-building-an-islamic-emirate-in-syria.php.

49. Ibid.
50. Lisa Barrington and Suleiman Al-Khalidi, "Syria's Nusra Front Says Ending Al Qaeda Ties; U.S. Fears for Aleppo," Reuters, July 29, 2016, http://www.reuters.com/article/us-mideast-crisis-syria-aleppo-idUSKCN108167.
51. Ibid.
52. Abdul Rahman Al-Haj, "Salafism and Salafis in Syria: From Reform to Jihad," The Afro-Middle East Centre, June 22, 2013, http://www.amec.org.za/syria/item/1229-salafism-and-salafis-in-syria-from-reform-to-jihad.html.
53. Aron Lund, *Syria's Salafi Insurgents: The Rise of the Syrian Islamic Front*, p. 22, Swedish Institute of International Affairs, January 2013, https://www.ui.se/globalassets/ui.se-eng/publications/ui-publications/syrias-salafi-insurgents-the-rise-of-the-syrian-islamic-front-min.pdf.
54. Elizabeth Dickinson, *Playing with Fire: Why Private Gulf Financing for Syria's Extremist Rebels Risks Igniting Sectarian Conflict at Home*, The Brookings Institution, December 6, 2013, https://www.brookings.edu/research/playing-with-fire-why-private-gulf-financing-for-syrias-extremist-rebels-risks-igniting-sectarian-conflict-at-home/.
55. Ellen Knickmeyer, "Kuwaiti Court Upholds Parliamentary Vote, a Setback for Muslim Brotherhood," *Wall Street Journal*, December 23, 2013, http://online.wsj.com/news/articles/SB10001424052702304244904579276383918948044.
56. Ben Hubbard, "Private Donors' Funds Add Wild Card to War in Syria," *New York Times*, November 12, 2013. http://www.nytimes.com/2013/11/13/world/middleeast/private-donors-funds-add-wild-card-to-war-in-syria.html.
57. Aymenn Jawad al-Tamimi, "Syrian Rebel Mergers: A

Harakat Nour Al-Din Al-Zinki Persepctive," *Aymenn Jawad Al-Tamimi's Blog,* January 7, 2017, http://www.aymennjawad.org/2017/01/syrian-rebel-mergers-a-harakat-nour-al-din-al.

58. Aqil Hussein, "The Syrian Revolutionary Command Council as a Replacement for the Merger Projects," *al-Modon,* December 28, 2016, http://www.almodon.com/arabworld/2016/12/28/%D9%85%D8%B4%D8%B1%D9%88%D8%B9%D8%A7-%D8%A7%D9%84%D8%A7%D9%86%D8%AF%D9%85%D8%A7%D8%AC-%D8%A8%D8%A7%D9%86%D8%AA%D8%B8%D8%A7%D8%B1-%D8%A3%D8%AD%D8%B1%D8%A7%D8%B1-%D8%A7%D9%84%D8%B4%D8%A7%D9%85

59. "Syria," , *World Factbook 2013–14,* Central Intelligence Agency, 2013, https://www.cia.gov/library/publications/the-world-factbook/geos/sy.html.

60. Eline Gordts, "Asma Assad, Wife Of Bashar Assad, Speaks Out," *Huffington Post,* February 7, 2012, http://www.huffingtonpost.com/2012/02/07/asma-assad-wife-syria_n_1260093.html.

Gregory Aftandilian, "Alawite Dilemmas in the Syrian Civil War," *Arab Weekly,* June 26, 2015, http://www.thearabweekly.com/Special-Focus/891/Alawite-dilemmas-in-the-Syrian-civil-war.

61. Raymond A. Hinnebusch, "The Islamic Movement in Syria: Sectarian Conflict and Urban Rebellion in an Authoritarian-Populist Regime," p. 150–151, in Ali E. Hillal Dessouki, ed., *Islamic Resurgence in the Arab World,* Praeger, 1982.

62. "World Directory of Minorities and Indigenous Peoples," Minority Rights Group International, October 2011, http://minorityrights.org/directory/.

63. David Kenner, "Syria Comes of Age: An Extraordinary Population Boom Fuels the Revolt Against Bashar al-Assad's Regime," *Foreign Policy,* December 8, 2011, http://foreignpolicy.com/2011/12/08/syria-comes-of-age/.

64. Malik al-Abdeh, "How I Understand the Syrian Revolution," Syria in Transition, March 1, 2012, http://syriaintransition.com/2012/03/01/how-i-understand-the-syri-

an-revolution/.

65. Hussain Abdul-Hussain, "Syria After Assad," *NOW Lebanon,* April 13, 2011, http://nowlebanon.com/NewsArchiveDetails.aspx?ID=261197.
66. This evolution can be tracked in the names of nationwide demonstrations following Friday afternoon prayers, selected each week from among slogans nominated by major activist groups in a poll on the Syrian Revolution 2011 Facebook page. Early rallies had names such as "Friday of Anger," while later on names with religious slogans began to appear, such as "If You Support God He Will Grant You Victory." Basma Atassi and Cajsa Wikstrom, "The Battle to Name Syria's Friday Protests," *Al-Jazeera,* April 14, 2012,http://www.aljazeera.com/indepth/features/2012/04/201241314026709762.html.
67. Gary Gambill, "Assad's Survival Strategy," *Foreign Policy,* April 6, 2011, http://foreignpolicy.com/2011/04/06/assads-survival-strategy-2/.
68. "While it is premature to characterize the protests as an Islamist uprising," wrote Gambill three weeks after the start of the uprising, "there is little doubt that those most eager to risk death or severe bodily harm are overwhelmingly Sunni and deeply religious." Gambill, "Assad's Survival Strategy."
69. Zach Goldberg, "Syria's Salafi Awakening: Existential Psychological Primers (Part 1/2)," *Fair Observer*, July 15, 2014, http://www.fairobserver.com/region/middle_east_north_africa/syrias-salafi-awakening-existential-psychological-primers-01474/.
70. Lund, "Syria's Salafi Insurgents: The Rise of the Syrian Islamic Front," p. 10.
71. Aron Lund, "*Islamist Groups Declare Opposition to National Coalition and US Strategy," Syria Comment, September 24, 2013, http://www.joshualandis.com/blog/major-rebel-factions-drop-exiles-go-full-islamist/*
72. Zisser, "Syria, the Ba'th Regime and the Islamic Movement," p. 45.
73. Eyal Zisser, "Syria, the Ba′th Regime and the Islamic Movement," p. 54.
74. Sami Moubayed, "The Islamic Revival in Syria," *Mid-*

east Monitor 1, no. 3, September-October 2006,http://www.nabilfayad.com/%D9%85%D9%82%D8%A7%D9%84%D8%A7%D8%AA/335-the-islamic-revival-in-syria.html.

75. For example, Assad ended a November 2005 speech at Damascus University with the popular saying "Syria is protected by God," a sentiment completely alien to decades of Ba'athist propaganda. See Bashar al-Assad, "President Bashar Al Assad's 2012 Damascus University Speech," available at Global Research, https://www.globalresearch.ca/president-bashar-al-assad-s-2012-damascus-university-speech/31250; Tabler, *In the Lion's Den*, p. 118.
76. Tabler, *In the Lion's Den,* p. 134.
77. Ibid., p. 134.
78. Lina Khatib, *Islamic Revivalism in Syria: The Rise and Fall of Ba'thist Secularism*, p. 109–142, Routledge, 2011.
79. Mohammed Habash, "Radicals are Assad's Best Friends," *The National* (UAE), January 1, 2014, http://www.thenational.ae/thenationalconversation/comment/radicals-are-assads-best-friends.
80. Phil Sands, Justin Vela, and Suha Maayeh, "Assad Regime Abetted Extremists to Subvert Peaceful Uprising, Says Former Intelligence Official," *The National* (UAE), January 21, 2014, http://www.thenational.ae/world/syria/assad-regime-set-free-extremists-from-prison-to-fire-up-trouble-during-peaceful-uprising; Raniah Salloum, "From Jail to Jihad: Former Prisoners Fight in Syrian Insurgency," *Spiegel*, October 10, 2013, http://www.spiegel.de/international/world/former-prisoners-fight-in-syrian-insurgency-a-927158.html.
81. Ben Hubbard, Clifford Krauss, and Eric Schmitt, "Rebels in Syria Claim Control of Resources," *New York Times*, January 28, 2014, http://www.nytimes.com/2014/01/29/world/middleeast/rebels-in-syria-claim-control-of-resources.html?_r=0.

30 United Arab Emirates

Quick Facts

Population: 6,072,475 (July 2017 est.)
Area: 83,600 sq km
Ethnic Groups: Emirati 11.6%, South Asian 59.4% (includes Indian 38.2%, Bangladeshi 9.5%, Pakistani 9.4%, other 2.3%), Egyptian 10.2%, Philippine 6.1%, other 12.8% (2015 est.)
Government Type: Federation of monarchies
GDP (official exchange rate): $378.7 billion (2017 est.)

Source: CIA World FactBook (Last Updated April 2018)

Introduction

In the wake of the September 11, 2001 terrorist attacks on the United States, the United Arab Emirates has been identified as significantly, if indirectly, involved in Islamic terrorism. Two of the nineteen 9/11 hijackers were residents of the UAE, while another had lived there.[1] *More than a decade-and-a-half after those attacks, much of the Arab world remains in a state of upheaval. Yet the UAE, to all appearances, remains calm. This is due in large part to the cultural setting in which the interpretation and practice of Islam have evolved in the country, as well as to the nature of its leadership since independence in 1971. The founding father of the UAE, and its president until his death in 2004, Zayid bin Sultan Al Nahyan, promoted and personified a conservative but moderate interpretation of Islam, which helped legitimize government efforts to check and contain Islamic extremism. Since 9/11, the UAE has devoted serious efforts to countering Islamic terrorism, the extreme forms of belief that promote it, and the financial support that facilitates it.*

Although concerns remain, the country's continued forceful actions to counter Islamic extremism have minimized the possibility of terrorist plots being carried out from or through the UAE, and constrained terrorist financing operations. Between December 2011 and November 2016, about 150 Islamists were arrested. They were described in government statements as belonging to an "al-Qaeda cell," and threatening militant attacks. The various charges were alleged violations of Article 180 of the UAE's penal code, which prohibits "establishing, instituting, founding, organizing, administering or joining an association or any branch thereof, with the aim of overthrowing the regime of the State."[2] *A 2014 anti-terrorism law further updated national legislation, originally formulated in 2004, allowing expanded use of the death penalty*[3] *It seems clear that the arrests and convictions stemmed more from the government's fear of the popular attraction of political Islam in the wake of the Arab Spring than from evidence of an explicit plot to overthrow the government. Since 2011, the government has energetically suppressed manifestations of dissent, criticism, and calls for political reform.*[4]

As of late 2017, the UAE clearly views the principal Islamist threats to itself as coming from Iran and its perceived proxies in the Arab world, as well as from the Muslim Brotherhood (MB) and its affiliates. It has pursued an increasingly assertive policy to counter these threats, as reflected in its leading role in concert with Saudi Arabia, Bahrain, and Egypt to effect the isolation of Qatar as well as in its Yemeni intervention.

Islamist Activity

The activity of Islamists in the UAE has historically been constrained by several factors. Islam in the UAE is generally moderate and non-political in nature, and the government closely monitors Muslim organizations, especially those with political agendas. Furthermore, the largest segment of Muslims in the country is South Asian expatriates, who have been drawn there for job opportunities and are subject to expulsion for any behavior deemed threatening to state security. Finally, astute government distribution of the country's vast hydrocarbon wealth has been effective in blunting the kind of discontent that might promote grassroots adherence to Islamism that challenges the writ of the state.

The Muslim Brotherhood

The Muslim Brotherhood (MB) has had an Emirati presence since before the UAE's independence in 1971. In the 1950s and 1960s, educated, professional MB members fleeing Gamal Abdel Nasser's repression in Egypt filled many public and private positions, especially in educational and judicial institutions, gaining significant influence in the UAE in subsequent years.[5] By the 1990s, however, whatever influence the organization exercised had largely dissipated. The Emirati government sought to curb the MB's influence in education by forcing those members employed by the Ministry of Education to renounce the Brotherhood or find employment elsewhere. In 1994, Al Islah, the UAE branch of the MB, was officially proscribed. In 2003, Mohammed bin Zayed Al Nahyan, the crown prince of Abu Dhabi, and senior MB leaders failed to strike a deal to permit the group to operate in the UAE in exchange for renouncing allegiance to its supreme guide and agreeing to halt political activities. Later the same year, UAE authorities initiated transfer of teachers associated with the MB out of the education system and, from 2006, hundreds of expatriate MB members, many in education, were deported.[6]

Subsequently, the 2008 defeat of the Brotherhood's candidates in the Kuwaiti parliamentary elections reflected a general setback for the group's attempts to gain a foothold in the Gulf, even as it continued to flounder in the UAE. An Islamist commentator lamenting negative developments for the Brotherhood observed that, in the UAE, "despite some interesting developments among the cadres and the youth of the MB, intense security obstacles prevented them from doing much by way of renewing their thought or engaging in popular actions."[7] Indeed, indications are that the UAE government views the Brotherhood as a political entity whose true aim is to establish a theocracy; thus, the organization is outlawed.[8] In the aftermath of the 2011 Arab Spring, the UAE felt very threatened by the Egyptian MB's perceived attempt to incite Islamist activity in the UAE. While Mohammed Morsi was president of Egypt (June 2012 to July 2013), relations between the two countries remained strained, on account of the Egyptian government's then-prevalent Brotherhood sympathies. As a result, the UAE gave financial aid to

President Abdel Fattah al-Sisi, after his overthrow of Morsi.[9]

In November 2014, the UAE released a list of some 83 organizations it had designated as terrorist groups. (The exact number varies slightly in various reports.) A number of allegedly MB-linked organizations were included. Among these were two U.S. groups, the Council on American-Islamic Relations (CAIR) and the Muslim American Society (MAS). The UAE, like its Gulf Arab neighbors, has been concerned that the MB is seen as a legitimate political force in the West. Their action against CAIR and MAS was meant to give support to those in the U.S. government who view negatively those groups, alleged to support the MB, and who wish to officially designate the MB as a terrorist organization. (In 2014 and again in 2015 there were unsuccessful attempts in the U.S Congress to pass legislation calling for President Obama to designate the MB as a foreign terrorist organization. Donald Trump had promised to do so during his presidential campaign).[10] After a year in office, he had failed to do so. In June 2016, the UAE Federal Supreme Court convicted a group of four Emiratis and 15 Yemenis (the numbers vary slightly in different reports) of setting up a branch of the MB in the UAE. While one report maintained that the accused intended to overthrow the government, the generally light sentences received by the accused suggest that, though the actual threat was slight, the government continues to feel the need to counter any perceived challenge from the MB.[11]

On June 5, 2017, the UAE joined Saudi Arabia, Bahrain, and Egypt in isolating Qatar by denying it land, sea, and air access to their territories. Among the reasons cited for this extreme action, Qatar's support of the MB and MB-related movements was the most salient for the UAE and Saudi Arabia. Abdullah bin Zayed, crown prince of Abu Dhabi and Saudi Crown Prince Muhammad bin Salman are the driving force behind opposition to the MB, with each viewing radicalization and extremism in the Arab world as the product of the MB and the organization's leading thinkers, like Hassan al-Banna and Sayyid Qutb.[12] Qatar maintains that MB engagement can defuse extremism, while the UAE sees the MB and other Islamists as undercutting their embrace of tolerance and modernity.[13] Qatar-UAE tensions heated up when it was revealed by

U.S. intelligence that, in May 2017, the UAE had hacked government news and social media sites in Qatar to post controversial and false quotes attributed to the emir of Qatar, Shaikh Tamim bin Hamad Al Thani.[14] At the same time, the UAE announced that a former member of the MB had confessed that the Qatari government had supported that organization's efforts to destabilize the UAE.[15] For the U.S., this contretemps has the unfortunate effect of diminishing counterterrorism cooperation in the Gulf.[16]

Al-Islah

Al-Islah, also known as the Reform and Social Guidance Association, is the largest and best-organized opposition group in the UAE. It was originally founded in 1974 as a non-governmental organization (NGO) dedicated to promoting sports and cultural activity as well as charitable work. Throughout the 1980s and 1990s, the group adopted a political reform agenda. In recent years, the government has moved to curb its influence by prohibiting al-Islah members from holding public office and other prominent positions. The government now views al-Islah as a security threat.[17] As of 2012, the organization was estimated to have as many as 20,000 UAE residents affiliated with it.[18] From December 2011 through 2012, UAE officials arrested a number of the group's members, convinced that al-Islah was actively working with the MB, especially in Egypt, to challenge the country's political system.[19] The crackdown culminated in arrests at the end of 2012 of members of an MB "spy ring" alleged to be collecting secret defense information and contemplating actions calculated to lead to regime change in the UAE. The forceful reaction of the government reflected its fear that Egypt's MB-dominated government was seeking to destabilize the Gulf monarchies by spreading its populist form of political Islam.[20]

The November 2014 list of "terrorist" organizations outlined by the UAE government, and continued arrests of suspected extremists, suggests that, well after the fall of President Morsi and the repression of the MB in Egypt, the UAE continues to perceive Al-Islah as a political threat.[21] However, the UAE appears to lack an internal consensus as to al-Islah's true identity; analysts cannot agree on whether it is a chapter of the MB, a group that embraces a similar ideology without organizational links, or is simply deeply influenced by the Brotherhood.[22] These competing views complicate governmental responses to the group. The Emirati government fears that al-Islah could become an analog to the MB in Egypt, though it is probably more accurate to characterize the organization as non-revolutionary and focused on the reform and restructuring of government. Al-Islah's base has been in Ras al-Khaimah and the other northern emirates, where resentment of the much greater wealth and opportunities in Abu Dhabi and Dubai can fuel Islamist impulses.[23]

Al-Qaeda

The terrorist attacks of September 11, 2001 highlighted links between the UAE and al-Qaeda. Two of the operatives who carried out the attacks were Emiratis, another had resided there during the planning of the attacks, and the planners had frequently transited the UAE. A further connection stems from the UAE being one of only three countries to recognize the Taliban regime in Afghanistan during its time in power (the others were Pakistan and Saudi Arabia).

Since 9/11, there have been no attacks carried out in the UAE or launched from its soil by al-Qaeda, but fairly numerous and credible threats have been reported, although not always with a high level of certainty. However, the presence of al-Qaeda operatives has been established conclusively. In November 2002, the suspected ringleader of the team that had attacked the *USS Cole* in 2000 in Aden, Yemen was captured in Dubai. The same year, credible reports claimed that a considerable number of al-Qaeda fighters captured in Afghanistan were UAE nationals, and that welfare associations in Dubai and Fujairah had been encouraging young men to join terrorist groups. These associations were also accused of sending money to radical groups in Afghanistan and South Asia. Arrests occurring in 2004 suggested that Dubai continued to be a waypoint for al-Qaeda operatives.[24] Then, in July 2005, a new group calling itself "The al-Qaeda Organization in the Emirates and Oman" issued a strong threat against rulers in the UAE, demanding that U.S. military installations in the country be dismantled immediately.[25]

In 2008, the British government issued warnings of the risk of terrorist attacks in the UAE, likely connected to threats from al-Qaeda.[26] Then, in 2009, American officials confirmed a report that

UAE authorities had broken up a major terrorist ring in Ras al-Khaimah that spring, which had been plotting to blow up targets in Dubai. In September of the same year, a Saudi tip led to interception in Dubai of explosives, which operatives of al-Qaeda in the Arabian Peninsula (AQAP) claimed to have placed on UPS and FedEx flights.[27] In 2010, there were reports that a network of "semi-legal" mosques dominated by Salafi preachers posed a jihadi threat, and there was a purported threat from al-Qaeda. The reports, though coming from backers of Shaikh Khalid bin Saqr Al Qassimi, who was contesting the succession as ruler of Ras al-Khaimah, appeared credible. These occurrences indicate that al-Qaeda still has links to the UAE. Despite some initial press speculation that members of an alleged MB spy ring arrested in December 2013 had links to al-Qaeda, no subsequent reports, official or otherwise, have given any credence to that idea.[28]

Despite these plots and threats, no terrorist group has succeeded in carrying out an operation in the UAE to date, and al-Qaeda is no exception. Some jihadi internet forum discussants have suggested that al-Qaeda's failure to strike the UAE reflects lack of popular support for the organization, owing in part to the non-militant nature of Emirati fundamentalists, which in turn constrains al-Qaeda's ability to recruit locals.[29] The government, for its part, has taken measures to counter extremism, including a public awareness campaign conducted by religious authorities about the dangers of violent extremism.[30] On December 15, 2012, in Abu Dhabi, UAE Foreign Minister Sheikh Abdullah bin Zayed Al Nahyan opened the International Center for Excellence in Countering Violent Extremism (ICECVE), also called the Hedayah (Guidance) Center. Deputy Under Secretary of State William Burns represented the U.S. at the center's launch. The center's creation was an outgrowth of the Global Counter Terrorism Forum (GCTF) created by the U.S. Department of State in September 2011, which comprises some 30 countries and seeks to help its members develop research and training in counter-terrorism. The center has, since then, promoted cooperation among members of the GCTF on issues relating to violent extremism, performed research and issued studies on the subject, and offered assistance in capacity building to counter threats. In May 2015,

Hedayah initiated implementation of a four year STRIVE Global Program funded by the EU and aimed at increasing the capacity of state and non-state actors to challenge effectively radicalization and recruitment leading to violent extremism. In December 2016, Hedayah and the United Nations Development Program (UNDP) held an international research conference in Jakarta, Indonesia to bring together researchers in the field of countering violent extremism (CVE) to share their recent research findings.[31]

The Sawab (correctness) Center, a joint UAE-U.S. initiative to combat online propaganda of extremist Islamist groups, has sponsored several social media campaigns. In the spring of 2017, it launched a campaign on its social media platforms to counteract youth recruitment by extremists.[32]

While the threats from militant Islamist groups on Emirati soil appear slight at present, the activities of AQAP in Yemen are of great concern. The UAE, in partnership with U.S. special forces, is combatting AQAP in southern Yemen through military, economic, and humanitarian support. The UAE has focused its efforts in the southern parts of Yemen, while Saudi forces have concentrated their efforts on the anti-Houthi campaign in northern Yemen. The UAE has a unique rapport with the tribes in southern Yemen, as many southern Yemenis fled the civil war in the 1960-70s and settled in the UAE. A significant number of those migrants subsequently joined the UAE's security forces.[33] Beyond these ties, the UAE perceives the Houthis to be a serious national security threat, fearing that they might provide Iran, which is currently giving the Houthi-led forces support, with a greater opportunity to destabilize the Arabian Peninsula.[34]

The UAE-U.S. partnership in combatting Islamist extremists in Yemen has been extended to Somalia, the Balkans, and Afghanistan. The UAE's military reach has been greatly expanded through the construction of bases in Africa.[35] Aspects of the UAE's vigorous initiatives against Islamist extremism in various locales are problematic for the U.S., however. For example, the UAE has embraced autocratic rulers such as General Khalifa Haftar in Libya, to whom it has given military support in contravention of a UN arms embargo.[36] Further complicating the UAE's campaign against

AQAP in Yemen is its hostility to Yemeni President Abed Rabbi Mansour Hadi, who is being prevented from leaving Saudi Arabia at the UAE's request. Hadi had pushed back against UAE efforts to establish areas of permanent influence in southern Yemen. The UAE regards his failure to cut ties with the MB in Yemen as violating the "honor pact" implicit in Yemen's agreement with the UAE and Saudi Arabia to ensure recognition of Hadi's legitimacy as president of Yemen.[37]

The Islamic State (Islamic State in Iraq and Syria, Daesh)

The UAE has also manifested its new regional assertiveness in its participation in the struggle against the Islamic State, or ISIS, now the world's leading Islamic terrorist organization. UAE participation in the anti-ISIS coalition was dramatically announced in 2014, when a female Emirati pilot flew her F-16 in the first wave of U.S.-led air attacks against ISIS targets in Syria.[38] In response, ISIS has promised action against Dubai and Abu Dhabi, and a handful of incidents have lent at least some credence to the threat. In January of 2016, the alleged leader of ISIS in the Gulf was put on trial in the UAE Federal Supreme Court, and the following month an ISIS sympathizer was detained for allegedly planning to detonate a grenade in a Dubai restaurant.[39] Also in February 2016, the same court sentenced four Emiratis to death in absentia for joining ISIS and fighting among its ranks in Syria.[40] Furthermore, there is evidence to suggest that money has been smuggled through Dubai to ISIS.[41] In coordination with the U.S., the UAE took a significant initiative in the social media front of the struggle with ISIS by establishing the Sawab Center in Abu Dhabi, designed to counter ISIS propaganda efforts online.[42] As with threats from al-Qaeda, the UAE seems reasonably protected from those of ISIS by its vigilance and its generally contented population enjoying the benefits of the country's great wealth.

However, threats do exist. In August 2017, Lebanese-Australian ISIS operatives attempted to place an explosive device on a flight from Sydney to Abu Dhabi, a plot thwarted by Lebanese police intelligence.[43]

The Taliban and Haqqani Network

Islamist activity involving South Asian residents in the UAE is significant, and reportedly has included support of terrorist groups operating in Afghanistan, Pakistan, and India. In October 2008, for example, national authorities uncovered a plot involving several individuals, including an Afghan, to provide funds to the Taliban. The U.S. government believes that the Taliban and the affiliated Haqqani Network are funded in part by donors in the UAE, drawing their support from the large Pashtun community there. The Taliban is also known to extort money from Afghan businessmen based in the UAE.[44] However, the size of both voluntary contributions and forced aid is still unknown at this time.

The Haqqani network and the Pakistani Taliban are both on the UAE's list of banned terrorist organizations, which was issued in November 2014.[45] However, there is evidence to suggest that these classifications do not seriously impede the groups' movements in the UAE. For instance, Mullah Akhtar Mohammad Mansour, the former Afghan Taliban leader who was killed in a U.S. drone strike in May 2016, frequently visited the UAE to raise funds for Taliban operations.[46] Nevertheless, these elements remain a threat to the Emirates – albeit an indirect one. In February 2017, the UAE ambassador to Afghanistan died of wounds sustained in a terrorist attack in Kandahar in January. The provincial police chief blamed the attack on the Haqqani Network.[47]

Lashkar-e-Taiba

Lashkar-e-Taiba (LeT) developed out of the Ahl-e-Hadith movement, which has roots in both the Middle East and the Indian Subcontinent.[48] The Pakistan-based Islamist LeT reportedly received large amounts of money from Gulf-based networks, including funders in the UAE.[49] There likewise appears to be a link between the UAE and the LeT's terrorist activities carried out against India; an investigation of the 2003 bombings in Mumbai revealed a Dubai connection, through which Lashkar-e-Taiba operatives in that emirate colluded with cells in India. Other urban terrorist attacks in India revealed a similar link. An important part of the equation is the set of operational ties between the Student Islamic Movement of India and militant student groups in the UAE, as well as elsewhere in the Gulf. The November 2014 list of terror organizations outlawed by the UAE included Lashkar-e-Taiba, and the UAE has worked closely with India to counter terrorist groups, notably the Indian Mujahdeen, which is closely linked with LeT. Intelligence sharing between the two countries led to the UAE turning over key operatives of the Mujahideen who had been hiding in the Emirates to India.[50] In July 2017, a suspected LeT terrorist was deported from the UAE and arrested upon his arrival in Mumbai, India.[51]

Islamism and Society

Estimates of the UAE's population vary greatly. The UN's November 2017 estimate is 9,452,850 while, for July 2017, the CIA's estimate is 6,072,475. Native Emiratis represent only 11.6% of the total population. South Asians account for 59.4%, with Indians alone accounting for 38.2 % of the country's people. Citizens are almost exclusively Muslim, and Islam is the religion of 76% of the entire population. Christians represent 9% of the population, and Hindus and Buddhists are the largest religious groups among those that comprise the balance.[52] The UAE constitution guarantees freedom of worship and declares all persons equal before the law without discrimination on the basis of religious belief. The State Department has reported that "Christian churches and Hindu and Sikh temples operated on land donated by the ruling families... Other minority religious groups conducted religious ceremonies in private homes without interference." The report added that "Within society there was tolerance for non-Muslims, including for holiday celebrations and traditions, although there was pressure discouraging conversion from Islam."[53] Sunni Emiratis adhere to the Maliki school of Islamic law, which is officially recognized in Abu Dhabi and Dubai, and the Hanbali school that predominates elsewhere (except in Fujairah, where the Shafi'i school holds sway).[54]

Attitudes toward Islamic groups in the UAE are difficult to discern since there is no significant direct popular participation on their part in government. While the constitution mandates freedom of speech, public assembly and association are still subject to government approval. Although the Emerati press is among the freest in the Arab world, it exercises self-censorship on sensitive issues, and the broadcast media are government-owned. Thus, attitudes concerning Islamic groups and their activities can be assessed mainly by inference, rather than by consideration of explicit expressions of opinion.[55]

Moreover, the identification of Islamist groups is itself somewhat problematic, because there is considerable overlap in the missions of organizations, notably in the areas of philanthropic and religious concern. Curiously, the government identifies fewer than three percent of associations in the UAE as religious.[56] Many of the groups placed under the headings "cultural," "folklore," and "human services" are to one degree or another Islamic in orientation.

The sampling of Islamic groups examined below is broadly representative of those that are active in the UAE. This stratum includes both organizations that are part of native Emirati society and those that belong to various expatriate Muslim communities. To the extent that UAE organizations are identified with the promotion of Islamic objectives, they generally reflect the conservative nature of Islam in the country. However, differences exist; organizations in Dubai tend to reflect the cosmopolitanism of that emirate, with its very large expatriate population, including more than 150,000 from Europe and the United States, while in Abu Dhabi they exhibit a generally more conservative nature in keeping with its character, and in Sharjah they reflect the ruler's commitment to upholding the strong Islamic norms of that emirate.

Emirati Islamic groups

The Mohammed bin Rashid Al Maktoum Foundation was launched in 2007 by the prime minister and ruler of Dubai, who also serves as vice president of the UAE, with a personal donation of a $10 billion endowment (one of the largest charitable donations in history). The Islamic component of the foundation's mission is not explicit, but it is nonetheless significant. A central element of the foundation is the Bayt ul-Hikma, designed to disseminate knowledge in the Arab world and named for the House of Knowledge that represented the apogee of Islamic science and learning in the Abbasid Empire of the Middle Ages.[57] In 2017, the Foundation's name was changed to Mohammad bin Rashid Al Maktoum Knowledge Foundation.[58]

In Abu Dhabi, the more modestly funded Sheikh Zayed bin

Sultan Al Nahyan Charitable and Humanitarian Foundation was established in 1992 with a $100 million endowment. Its mission is more overtly aimed at advancing Islamic goals than that of the Al Maktoum Foundation, and includes the support of mosques, educational and cultural institutions, and the financing of both Emiratis and other Muslims in performing the Hajj. In 2017, the Zayed Pilgrimage Program covered expenses for 600 UAE residents and 400 from other countries who could not afford pilgrimage costs. The foundation supports humanitarian projects, including a camp and hospital for Syrian refugees in Jordan, and assists low income Emiratis and others in building, refurbishing, and maintaining housing.[59]

The Tabah Foundation is a non-profit institution established in 2005 in Abu Dhabi that seeks to promote a more effective contemporary Islamic discourse to advance Islamic values and counter negative images of Islam. Funded by various institutions and individuals in the UAE, Tabah entered into an agreement with the Diwan (Council of State) of the crown prince of Abu Dhabi, Sheikh Mohammed bin Zayed, to develop the Zayed House for Islamic Culture, and it established a media department, comprising both a television and documentary film division.[60] In 2015, the Foundation's Tabah Futures Initiative established a partnership with Zogby Research Services to explore the attitudes of millennials in the Arab world toward religion and religious leadership. Interviews in 2017 with nearly 7,000 young Arab Muslims in 10 countries revealed distressingly, that only somewhat over 50% believed that non-Muslim citizens in a Muslim country should have equal rights with Muslims. At the same time, most young Arabs, with the exception of Omanis, identify themselves by country rather than religion.[61]

Islamic groups serving the Indian and Pakistani communities in the UAE

The very large Indian and Pakistani communities in the UAE are served by numerous organizations, each associated with varying degrees of Islamic activity. While Indians clearly constitute the largest single community in the UAE, estimates of their number vary. In 2011, there were some 60 social and voluntary organizations serving the predominantly Muslim Indian community.

By contrast, there are few Islamic organizations in the Pakistani community in the UAE. Most Pakistani organizations in the country are business or financial associations or are devoted to providing aid to earthquake and flood victims in Pakistan. However, there is an Ismaili Centre in Dubai, dedicated in 2003 by the Aga Khan, spiritual leader of the Ismaili community, whose followers in the UAE are Pakistani and Indian expatriates. The site for the center was a gift of Sheikh Mohammed bin Rashid Al Maktoum, ruler of Dubai. The Ismaili Centre, which opened in 2008, is meant to serve, in the tradition of Muslim piety, by promoting enlightenment and mutual understanding among the various elements of the Muslim world community. To that end, it carries out a program of cultural and educational activities.[62]

As the above descriptions suggest, there is little if any political aspect to the missions and activities of the Islamic organizations in the UAE, both those serving the Emirati community and those serving the large expatriate Muslim communities. None could be characterized as extreme in any sense. All would appear to fit well within the mainstream of moderate Islamic activity.

Sporadic signs of extremist activity do exist, however. In April 2010, the Federal Supreme Court sentenced five UAE nationals and an Afghan on charges of funding the Taliban, and government officials indicated that those individuals had also planned to establish an al-Qaeda network in the UAE. At the end of that year, two Pakistanis were put on trial, charged with collecting money and recruiting individuals for al-Qaeda.[63] The scope of terrorist linkage with South Asia would appear to be limited, and, as noted above, anti-terrorist cooperation between India and the UAE has been strengthened. Also, as noted earlier, the UAE has taken the fight to AQAP. While none of that organization's stated threats against the UAE has yet materialized, the possibility of a terrorist attack cannot be dismissed.

Islamism and the State

The government of the UAE funds or subsidizes the majority of Sunni mosques in the country, while about five percent are privately endowed. It employs all Sunni imams, and provides guidance to both Sunni and Shia clergy. Shia mosques are considered private, but may receive funds from the government upon request. The Shia community is largely concentrated in the emirates of Dubai and Sharjah, with the bulk of its members in the former.[64] A number of new mosques have been built, or are under construction, throughout the country. Notable among them are mosques in Fujairah and Ajman. The Shaikh Zayed Mosque of Fujairah, completed in January 2013, although located in one of the smallest and poorest of the emirates in the UAE, is the second largest in the country, accommodating 28,000 worshippers. Funded by the Zayed bin Sultan Al Nahyan Charitable and Humanitarian Foundation of Abu Dhabi at a cost of $52.1 million, it follows in the mold of its namesake, the Grand Mosque in Abu Dhabi, as an expression of local pride and the ruling family's commitment to Islam. By contrast, the much more modest mosque opened in Ajman in 2011 (designed to hold 1,500 worshippers) is being funded by a donation from Hamad Ghanem Al Shamsi, a member of a distinguished and wealthy Ajman family. In 2015 and 2016,10 new mosques, all of modest size, were built in Ajman.[65]

In December 2010, plans for four new Shia mosques were unveiled by the Khoja Shi'a Ithna-Ashari Jamaat (KSIMC) of Dubai, a private Shia religious philanthropy, with the sites for the structures provided by the government of Dubai. Typical of KSIMC activities was a 2013 seminar aimed at developing leadership skills. The members of the Shia community, through a Shia endowment fund known as the Awqaf Al Jafferiah, raised the funds to construct the mosques.[66] While there is no evidence to suggest that Shia (or Sunni) mosques have any connection with political or extremist motives, in 2012 a Khoja Shia madrasa in Dubai was closed and Shia mosque activities were restricted. The UAE government gave no explanation for these actions. These events came in the wake of numerous deportations of Shi'as from the UAE, including long-term Lebanese residents, who were forced to leave the country over fears of possible Hezbollah connections.[67]

From its birth in 1971, the UAE has been supportive of moderate, apolitical Islamic activities, while opposing those that might pose a threat to the government. Shaikh Zayed bin Sultan Al Nahyan, the father of the UAE and its president from inception until his death in 2004, embodied that philosophy both in his rule and in his personal life. He was generous in his support of religious leaders, thus arming himself and the state against attacks from secular or religious quarters. The chief threat to the UAE in the first years of its independence was secular radicalism in the region, especially as given expression by the Marxist government of the People's Democratic Republic of Yemen (PDRY), or South Yemen, and the guerrilla movements supported by the PDRY in their efforts to overthrow the government of the Sultanate of Oman, the UAE's immediate neighbor. Because of Zayed's close and positive relations with the UAE religious leadership, and the lack of extremist Islamic activity in the UAE before the events of September 11, 2001, the UAE's connections with those events was shocking and deeply embarrassing to Zayed and the UAE government.

Post-September 11th, the government reacted promptly (albeit cautiously) to the threat posed by al-Qaeda. While the generally moderate nature of Islamic belief and practice in the UAE precluded broad support for the ideology of al-Qaeda and other extremist groups, popular antipathy for some U.S. government actions in the Middle East has somewhat complicated the government's cooperation with the United States against Islamic terrorism.[68] In 2002, under Zayed's leadership, a contingent of UAE troops was deployed to Afghanistan to help in the struggle to unseat the Taliban, whose government the UAE had recognized before 9/11. Also in 2002, UAE authorities announced that they had arrested Abd al-Rahim al-Nashri, the apparent mastermind behind the October 12, 2000 attack on the *USS Cole* in Aden.[69]

In the past few years, the UAE has taken significant steps to counter Islamic terrorism, generally winning praise from the U.S. government for its efforts. While the general tendency of the UAE's rulers has been to co-opt potential troublemakers, the State Department noted that the UAE's preferred approach was to deny extremists a foothold, rather than permit their participation in the political process.[70] Abu Dhabi Crown Prince Mohammed bin Zayed also cited a threat from Islamic extremism to the country's educational system, and sought to counter this by devoting considerable resources to modernizing curricula. While, in the past, UAE funds given for house construction and humanitarian programs in Gaza may have ended up supporting activities of Hamas, including terrorism, there is evidence that the UAE's position on Hamas has dramatically shifted. The UAE was reportedly aware in advance of Israel's 2014 offensive against Gaza and urged the elimination of Hamas because of its close ties with the MB. Recent UAE support for housing in Gaza has been coordinate with the UN Relief and Works Agency (UNRWA).[71] The UAE has backed former Palestinian security chief, Mohammed Dahlan, as successor to Mahmoud Abbas as president of the Palestinian Authority, while weakening Hamas, and has reportedly committed $150 million to build a power station in Gaza.[72]

There is also concern that the UAE, while acting promptly when provided with evidence of a terrorist threat, does not have a proactive strategy for dealing with it.[73] Since 2015, however, UAE counter-terrorism measures have been robust. State Department reports have summed up UAE anti-terrorist activity by observing that "the UAE has arrested senior al-Qaeda operatives; denounced terror attacks; improved border security; instituted programs to counter violent extremism; investigated suspect financial transactions; criminalized use of the Internet by terrorist groups; and strengthened its bureaucracy and legal framework to combat terrorism."[74] In mid-2016, the UAE demonstrated its cooperation with the U.S. on this front when it accepted 15 detainees from the Guantanamo Bay prison, the largest such transfer during Barack Obama's presidency. In the UAE, the released detainees will be put in a rehabilitation program modeled after a Saudi program designed to de-radicalize the former prisoners.[75]

The UAE has exhibited considerable concern over the threat of Shia extremism, prompted largely by fears of infiltration by Iranian agents and Iran-linked sleeper cells that could sabotage critical UAE sectors, including energy and transportation. The existence of both was reportedly revealed in 2007 by a former Iranian consul in Dubai. Actions were taken in 2009, not against Iranians but against Lebanese accused of links to Hezbollah, Lebanon's powerful Iranian-supported militia. The UAE deported 44 Lebanese men, who had worked both in the public and private sectors, for sending small amounts of cash to groups affiliated with Hezbollah. The UAE Foreign Ministry said that the deportations were for violations of a type "that harms the security of the UAE." The UAE remains very concerned about a possible threat from resident Shi'as, especially those from Lebanon. This will continue to be the case as long as Hezbollah and Iran continue actively to support the Assad government in Syria, and as the Sunni-Shia divide grows more pronounced and dangerous in the Middle East.[76] It has led the UAE and Saudi Arabia to seek cooperation with Israel in opposing Iran and its support of Hezbollah and other Shia groups. The UAE has purchased considerable military equipment from Israel and agreed to establishment of an Israeli diplomatic mission in Abu Dhabi, accredited to the International Renewable Energy Agency (IRENA).[77] At the same time, the UAE has pursued better ties with Iraq and with the powerful Iraqi Shia cleric Moqtada al-Sadr, who maintains independence from Iran, in hopes of diminishing Iran's influence on Iraq's Shia community.[78]

Another area of concern is the flow of money from private donors to support extremist Sunni groups fighting in Syria, like the Islamic State of Iraq, Jabhat al-Nusra, and Ahrar al-Sham. While some of the funds are specifically targeted at assisting militias, much of the money is raised under the guise of humanitarian assistance. A Gulf-based organization, the Ummah Conference, recruits Muslim (Sunni) volunteers for Syria. Former senior military officers from the UAE head the UAE branch of the organization.[79]

The case of the Bank of Credit and Commerce International (BCCI), which was infiltrated and used for criminal money laundering and terrorist financing before its collapse in 1991, foreshadowed the complex and difficult problems that gained prominence after 9/11, when the UAE, with U.S. support and urging, tackled the problem of the financing of Islamic terrorism. Al-Qaeda was able to use a correspondent banking network to transfer funds from the Dubai Islamic bank to accounts in the United States for use by the 9/11 hijackers.[80] After 9/11, the UAE Central Bank took steps to counter money laundering. While refusing to ban the traditional hawala system of money exchange in wide use between South Asian expatriates in the UAE and their home countries, it imposed strict regulations on it.

While the UAE's efforts against money laundering and terrorist financing have been significant, cause for worry remains. Particular attention focuses on Dubai and its large Free Trade Zone, because of its potential facilitation of a variety of criminal and terrorist activities, including the use of front companies, fraud, and smuggling, as well as exploitation of the hawala and banking systems. The U.S. has closely scrutinized the operations of UAE financial institutions and, in 2012, took strong actions against two financial service companies with ties to Iran, pursuing them for alleged sanctions violations.[81] In July 2012, the UAE Central Bank issued regulations that made hawala registration mandatory with sanctions for non-compliance. Moreover, the public was cautioned about dealing with unlicensed charities.[82] In October 2014, the U.S. and the UAE established a joint financial counter-terrorism task force. In presenting the initiative, David Cohen, the U.S. Treasury Department undersecretary for terrorism and financial intelligence, stated that: "we have a very good close relationship with the Emiratis in combating terrorist financing…" [83] At the same time, concerns remain about the UAE serving as a haven for funds connected with terrorist activity. The UAE's main financial hub, Dubai, has garnered a reputation as a haven for Taliban money leaving Afghanistan.[84]

The UAE has perceived the Islamist threat in two ways—as the specifically terrorist threat of al-Qaeda and ISIS and as the broad populist threat represented by the MB and Iranian Shi'ism. Cooperation with the U.S. in combatting terrorism and drying up its sources of financing has been increasingly close and effective. There have been no reports of terrorist incidents in the UAE for the past several years. While some concerns remain, especially with respect to laundering and transfer of funds supporting terrorism, the UAE's success in countering terrorism has been impressive. The greater concern in the UAE today is with the impact of the Arab Spring and the events it set in motion. The rise to power of the MB in Egypt was alarming, especially because of the influence that the MB had exercised in the UAE in earlier years and because of the existence of an MB affiliate in the UAE, al-Islah. This accounts for the increased crackdown on dissent and the wide-ranging government identification of "terrorist" organizations, even including two U.S. NGOs. It also explains the expulsion of foreign NGOs working to help build civil society in the UAE, like the NDI and the Gallup Organization. At the same time, fear of Iranian actions and influence, given the UAE's proximity to Iran and its considerable Shia minority, has led to harsh treatment of expatriate Shi'as, especially those from Lebanon, because of possible links to Hezbollah. These perceived threats have also led to the more assertive role in the Middle East region described above, including active cooperation with the U.S. against ISIS, al-Qaeda, and the Houthi-led forces in Yemen.

The expanded, more aggressive UAE efforts to counter Islamist threats may bring enhanced risk of terrorist attacks, as ISIS, al-Qaeda, and other terrorist groups attempt to respond to the UAE's escalated attacks against them. The thwarted August 2017 "Barbie Doll" plot cited above may be an augury of things to come. Additionally, the UAE's participation in the anti-Qatar alignment, largely a reaction to Qatar's support of the MB, has split the GCC, potentially compromising in some degree the effectiveness of regional cooperation against the threats of Islamist extremists.

ENDNOTES

1. *The 9/11 Commission Report* (New York: W.W. Norton & Company, Inc., 2004), 162, 231, and 168.
2. Yara Bayoumy, "Seven alleged al Qaeda-linked plotters arrested in United Arab Emirates," Reuters, April 18, 2013, http://worldnews.nbcnews.com/2013/04/18/17806327-seven-alleged-al-qaeda-linked; Brian Murphy, "UAE sentences 69 suspects to prison in mass coup plot trial," Associated Press, July 2, 2013, http://www.foxnews.com/world/2013/07/02/united-arab-emirates-sentences-68-suspects-in-mass-trial-over-alleged-coup-plot.html; Kenneth Katzman, *The United Arab Emirates (UAE): Issues for U.S. Policy)* Washington, DC, Congressional Research Service, 2016, 5 and 6; and "UAE jails Emiratis up to 10 years

for Islamist links," November 14, 2016, https://www.yahoo.com/news/uae-jails-emiratis-10-years-islamist-links-172617458.html.

3. Courtney Freer, "The Muslim Brotherhood and the Emirates: Anatomy of a crackdown," *Middle East Eye*, December 17, 2015, http://www.middleeasteye.net/essays/muslim-brotherhood-emirates-anatomy-crack-down-1009823835.
4. Lori Plotkin Boghardt, "The Muslim Brotherhood on Trial in the UAE," Washington Institute for Near East Policy *Policywatch* no. 2064, April 12, 2013, http://www.washingtoninstitute.org/policy-analysis/view/the-muslim-brotherhood-on-trial-in-the-uae.
5. Sultan Al Qassemi, "The Brothers and the Gulf," *Foreign Policy*, December 14, 2012, http://www.tvballa.com/2012/12/.../qassemi-al-sultan-and-gulf-brothers.
6. Sultan Al Qassemi, "Qatar's Brotherhood Ties Alienate Fellow Gulf States," *Al-Monitor*, January 23, 2013, http://www.almonitor.com/pulse/originals/2013/01/qatar-muslim-brotherhood.html; Rachel Ehrenfeld, J. Millard Burr, "The Muslim Brotherhood Deception & Education," American Center for Democracy, April 18, 2013, http://acdemocracy.org/the-muslim-brotherhood-deception-education.
7. As cited in Marc Lynch, "MB in the Gulf," Abu Aardvark blog, June 10, 2008, http://abuaardvark.typepad.com/abuaardvark/2008/06/mb-in-the-gulf.html (site removed).
8. Samir Salama, "Muslim Brotherhood is Political and not Religious," *Gulf News*, September 22, 2008.
9. "The UAE and Saudi War on the Muslim Brotherhood Could Be Trouble for the U.S.," *Geopolitical Diary*, November 18, 2014, https://www.stratfor.com/geopolitical-diary/uae-and-saudi-war-muslim-brotherhood-could-be-trouble-us.
10. "The UAE and Saudi War," *Geopolitical Diary;* and Adam Taylor, "Why the UAE is calling 2 American groups terrorists," *Washington Post*, November 17, 2014; Freer, "The Muslim Brotherhood and the Emirates" and "The UAE and Saudi War;" Julian Hattem, Cruz bill would designate Muslim Brotherhood as terrorist

group," *The Hill*, November 4, 2015, http://thehill.com/policy/national-security/259099-cruz-bill-would-designate-muslim-brotherhood-as-terrorist-group; and Nahal Toosi, "Activists poke Trump to move faster on Muslim crackdown," *Politico*, January 24, 2017, http://www.politico.com/story/2017/01/trump-muslim-crackdown-234128.

11. "Verdict on 'Yemeni Muslim Brotherhood,' Group was accused of setting up a branch of the Muslim Brotherhood," Emirates 24/7 News, http://www.emirates247.com/news/emirates/verdict-on-yemeni-muslim-brotherhood-2016-06-13-1.632926.
12. David B. Roberts, "Competing Visions for the Arab Future," Policy Watch 2892, pp. 1 and 2, November 14, 2017, accessed on same date, http://info.washingtoninstitute.org/acton/ct/19961/s-047a-1711/Bet/1-0081/1-0081:/b33/ct0_0/?sid=TV2%3A7pt1Y8jYP.
13. David Ignatius, "Political Islam in the Modern World," *The Washington Post*, p. A19, July 14, 2017.
14. James M. Dorsey, "The Gulf Crisis: fake news shines spotlight on psychological warfare," p. 1, July 17, 2017, accessed on same date, https://mideastsoccer.blogspot.com/2017/07/the-gulf-crisis-fake-news-shines.html.
15. "He affirmed that Qatar's government is clearly aiding and abetting the terrorist Muslim Brotherhood," *Khaleej Times*, p.1, July 15, 2017, accessed on November 15, 2017, https:/www.khaleejtimes.com/region/qatar-crisis/qatar-plotted-to-destabilize-use-ex-muslim-brotherhood-member.
16. Maria Abi-Habib and Gordon Lubold, "Pentagon Rebukes Gulf Allies," *The Wall Street Journal*, p. A8, October 7-8, 2017.
17. Pekka Hakala, "Opposition in the United Arab Emirates," European Parliament, Directorate General for External Relations, Policy Department, November 15, 2012, http://www.europarl.europa.eu/committees/en/studiesdownload.html?...
18. Jenifer Fenton, "Al-Islah in the UAE," *Arabist*, August 4, 2012, http://www.arabist.net/blog/2012/.../4/crackdown-on-islamists-in-the-uae.html.
19. Human Rights Watch, "UAE: Crackdown on Isla-

mist Group Intensifies," July 18, 2012, http://hrw.org/news/2012/07/18/uae-crackdown-islamist; Ali Rashid al-Noaimi, "Setting the Record Straight on al-Islah in the UAE," *Middle East On*line, October 17, 2012, http://www.middle-east-online.com/english/?id=54950.

20. Al Qassemi, "The Brothers and the Gulf"; Al Noaimi, "Setting the Record Straight on al-Islah in the UAE"; Hassan Jouini, "Egypt-UAE Relations Worsen with 'Brotherhood' Arrests," *Egypt Daily News*, January 4, 2013, http://www.dailystar.com.lb/News/.../2013/Jan.../200804-egypt-uae-relations.
21. Freer, "The Muslim Brotherhood and the Emirates"; Amnesty International, "UAE: Ruthless crackdown on dissent exposes 'ugly reality' beneath facade of glitz and glamour," November 18, 2014, https://www.amnesty.org/en/latest/news/2014/11/uae-ruthless-crackdown-dissent-exposes-ugly-reality-beneath-facade-glitz-and-glamour.
22. Al Qassemi, "The Brothers and the Gulf"; Yara Bayoumy, "UAE Imprisons Islamist coup plotters," *Daily Star* (Beirut), July 3, 2013; "UAE sentences 69 suspects to prison in mass coup plot trial," Associated Press, July 2, 2013.
23. Boghardt, "The Muslim Brotherhood on Trial in the UAE."
24. Christopher M. Davidson, "Dubai and the United Arab Emirates: Security Threats," *British Journal of Middle Eastern Studies*, vol. 36, no. 3, December 2009, 444.
25. Davidson, "Dubai and the United Arab Emirates: Security Threats," 446; Reacting to the berthing of U.S. aircraft carriers in Dubai, after their planes had carried out missions to "bombard the Muslims in Iraq and Afghanistan," the organization stated that the UAE's ruling families would "endure the fist of the mujahideen in their faces" if their demand was not met.
26. Abdul Hamied Bakier, "An al-Qaeda Threat in the United Arab Emirates?" Jamestown Foundation *Terrorism Focus* 5, iss. 25, July 1, 2008, http://www.jamestown.org/single/?no_cache=1&tx_ttnews%5Btt_news%5D=5025.
27. "Terror Network Dismantled in U.A.E.," *Global Jihad*,

September 17, 2009; "AQAP Unlikely behind UPS Plane Crash - US Officials," Reuters, November 11, 2010, http://in.reuters.com/article/2010/11/11/idINIndia-52846520101111.

28. Rania El Gamal, "UAE Says it Arrested a Cell Plotting Attacks," Reuters, December 26, 2012 http://www.reuters.com/article/us-uae-saudi-plot-idUSBRE8BP08Q20121226 and "UAE arrests al-Qaeda cell 'plotters,'" *Al-Jazeera*, April 18, 2013, http://aljazeera.com/news/middleeast/2013/04/20134186290969992.html.
29. Hamied Bakier, "An al-Qaeda Threat in the United Arab Emirates?"
30. "United Arab Emirates," in U.S. Department of State, *International Religious Freedom Report 2011*, July 30, 2012, http://www.state.gov/j/drl/rls/irf/2011religiousfreedom/index.htm?dlid=192911#wrapper.
31. "First International Center for Countering Extremism Opens in Abu Dhabi," *Middle East Online*, December 15, 2012, http://www.middle-east-online.com/english/?id=56089; "Abdullah bin Zayed Opens Hedayah Centre for Countering Violent Extremism," *UAE Interact*, December 15, 2012; and "Keep Up with Hedayah," *Hedayah/LinkedIn*, nd, https://www.linkedin.com/company/hedayah.
32. "UAE Interact, "Sawab Center warns against Daesh youth recruitment," May 1, 20017, accessed on November 15, 2017,https://www.uaeinteract.com/news/default3.asp?ID=534.
33. Kyle Monsees, "The UAE's Counterinsurgency Conundrum in Southern Yemen," Arab Gulf States Institute in Washington, August 18, 2016, http://www.agsiw.org/the-uaes-counterinsurgency-conundrum-in-southern-yemen/.
34. Sigurd Neubauer, "Gulf States See Guantanamo Detainees As Policy Asset," Arab Gulf States Institute in Washington, September 9, 2016, http://agsiw.org/gulf-states-see-guantanamo-detainees-as-policy-asset.
35. "Kareem Fahim and Missy Ryan, "In the UAE, U.S. finds an ally and a headache," *The Washington Post*, p. A1, August 14, 2017.
36. Ibid.

37. Mideast wire.com, "Yemeni president joins those placed under house arrest in Saudi Arabia," p. 1, November 9, 2017, accessed on same date and translated from Arabic in *Al-Quds al-Arabi*, November 8, 2017.
38. Ian Black, "UAE's leading role against ISIS reveals its wider ambitions," *Guardian* (London), October 30, 2014, https://www.theguardian.com/world/2014/oct/30/uae-united-arab-emirates-leading-player-opposition-isis-middle-east
39. "UAE court gives four death sentence for supporting ISIS," *Al-Arabiyya* (Riyadh), February 14, 2016, http://english.alarabiya.net/en/News/middle-east/2016/02/14/UAE-Federal-Supreme-Court-sentences-defendants-for-joining-ISIS.html.
40. Ibid.
41. Paul Tilsley, "Jihadist couriers? Suspects nabbed at Johannesburg airport with $6M were ISIS-bound, say cops," *Fox News,* September 21, 2015, http://www.foxnews.com/world/2015/09/21/5-suspects-stopped-at-johannesburg-airport-with-6m-cash-headed-for-isis.html.
42. "U.S., U.A.E. launch anti-ISIS messaging center in Dubai," *CBS News,* July 8, 2015, http://www.cbsnews.com/news/us-uae-launch-anti-isis-messaging-center-dubai/.
43. Jack Moore, "Lebanon Foiled ISIS Barbie Doll Bomb Plot on Flight from Australia to Abu Dhabi," p.1, August 21, 2017, accessed on November 15, 2017.
44. "US Embassy Cables: Afghan Taliban and Haqqani Network Using United Arab Emirates as Funding Base," *Guardian* (London), December 5, 2010, http://www.guardian.co.uk/world/us-embassy-cables-documents/242756.
45. "UAE bans five Pakistan-based outfits among terror groups," *The Economic Times*, November 16, 2014, http://articles.economictimes.indiatimes.com/2014-11-16/news/56137274
46. Eltaf Najafizada, "Taliban Says Ex-Leader Often Visited United Arab Emirates, Iran," Bloomberg, May 26, 2016, http://www.bloomberg.com/news/articles/2016-05-26/taliban-says-ex-leader-often-visit-

ed-united-arab-emirates-iran.

47. The New Arab, "UAE ambassador dies of wounds from Afghanistan bombing," p.1, February 16, 2017, accessed on November 15, 2017, https://www.alaraby.co.uk/english/news/2017/2/16/uae-mbassador-dies-of-wounds-from-afghanistan-bombing..
48. Animesh Roul, "Lashkar-e-Taiba's Financial Network Targets India from the Gulf States," Jamestown Foundation *Terrorism Monitor* 7, iss. 19, July 2, 2009, https://jamestown.org/program/lashkar-e-taibas-financial-network-targets-india-from-the-gulf-states/.
49. Roul, "Lashkar-e-Taiba's Financial Network Targets India."
50. Think Chowdury, "India and the UAE: A Partnership Against Terrorism," *Swarajya*, August 25, 2015, http://swarajyamag.com/world/India-and-uae-a-partnership-against-terrorism.
51. Scroll Staff, "Suspected Lashkar-e-Taiba militant arrested from Mumbai airport," p. 1, July 17, 2017, accessed on November 15, 2017, https://scxroll.in/latest/844139/suspected-lashkar-e-taiba-militant-arrested-from-mumbai-airport.
52. CIA, *The World Factbook, United Arab Emirates,* p.3, last updated on November 6, 2017, accessed on November *16, 2017*, https://www.cia.gov/library/publications/the-world-factbook/geos/ae.html.
53. "United Arab Emirates" in United States Department of State, *2014 Report on International Religious Freedom*, October 14, 2015, http://www.refworld.org/docid/56210535a.html.
54. Malcolm C. Peck, *The United Arab Emirates: A Venture in Unity* (Boulder, CO: Westview Press, 1986), 60.
55. In the fall of 2010, through an agreement with the Crown Prince Court of Abu Dhabi, the Gallup Organization opened a new research center in Abu Dhabi to conduct inquiries into attitudes of Muslims around the world. While the initial report it issued looked broadly at the state of Muslim-West relations, the Abu Dhabi Gallup Center was set up to perform research specifically on attitudes in the UAE. Most of the UAE polling, focused on non-controversial topics like healthcare

access, although a poll on factors hindering women's entrepreneurship in the UAE and other GCC countries was conducted. However, the center was closed down in March 2012, when the UAE government ordered the closure of foreign NGOs, including the U.S.-based National Democratic Institute. Gallup reported that it "made the strategic decision to bring its efforts in Abu Dhabi back to its headquarters in Washington, DC" and that it "will continue to conduct research and publish findings about the region, and will maintain a presence in Dubai." See "Abu Dhabi and Gallup Establish New Research Center," *PRNewswire*, October 25, 2010, http://www.prnewswire.com/new-releases/abu-dhabi-and-gallup-establish-new-research-center-105668138.html and Vivian Nereim, "Gallup and think tank leave Abu Dhabi," *The National*, http://www.thenational.ae/news/uae-news/gallup-and-think-tank-leave-abu-dhabi. See also Shibley Telhami, *The World Through Arab Eyes* (New York: Basic Books, 2013), which presents some interesting results of polling done in the UAE.

56. In 1998, the country's Ministry of Labour and Social Affairs listed 103 associations with only three described as "religious." See Munira A. Fakhro, "Civil Society and Democracy in the Gulf Region," 11th Mediterranean Dialogue Seminar: Security and Development in the Gulf Region, NATO Parliamentary Assembly, Doha, Qatar, November 26-28, 2005.
57. "Mohammed bin Rashid Al Maktoum Foundation," *Revolvy*, nd (presumably 2015), https://www.revolvy.com/main/index.php?s=Mohammed%20bin%20Rashid%20Al%20Maktoum%20Foundation&item_type=topic
58. GulfNews.com, "Mohammad bin Rashid Al Maktoum Foundation renamed," p.1, February 15, 2017, accessed November 16, 2017, http://gulfnews.com/news/uae/government/mohammad-bin-rashid-al-maktoum-foundation-renamed-1.1978954.
59. WAM, "Zayed bin Sultan Al Nahyan Charitable and Humanitarian Foundation continues to assist those in need," p.2, April 16, 2017, accessed November 16, 2017, http://wam.ae/en/details/1395302608776.
60. See Tabah's newsletter, *Clarity*, its. 1, fall 2010, for a

discussion of its programs, http:/www.tabahfoundation.org/newsletter/pdfs/1/TabahNewsEn_201009.pdf.

61. Georgina Bobley, "According to a Recent Study, Young Arabs Put National Identity First: Muslim Millennial Attitudes on Religion Study," POPSUGAR Middle East Love, p. 1, May 18, 2017, accessed on November 16, 2017, https://me.popsugar.com/love/Muslim-Millennial-Attitudes-Religion-Study-43550569.
62. Aga Khan, "Speech at the Foundation Laying of the Ismaili Center in Dubai," December 13, 2003, http://www.iis.ac.uk/view_article.asp?ContentID=101003.
63. "UAE Sentences Six Convicted Taliban Agents," *World Tribune*, April 29, 2010, http://www.worldtribune/WTARC/2010/me_gulf0354_04_29.asp; "UAE Tries Two Pakistanis on Qaeda Links: Report," *Al Arabiya*, (Riyadh), December 28, 2010, http://www.alarabiya.net/articles/2010/12/28/131278.htnl.
64. "United Arab Emirates," in U.S. Department of State, *2010 Report on International Religious Freedom*, November 17, 2010, http://www.state.gov/j/drl/rls/irf/2010/148850.htm.
65. See "Large Mosque Rising in Fujairah," *Fujairah in Focus* blog, June 6, 2010, http://fujairahinfocus.blogspot.com/2010/06/large-mosque-rising-in-fujairah-uae.html; see also General Authority of Islamic Affairs & Endowments," A New Mosque for 1500 Worshippers in Ajman," March 15, 2011, hrrp://www.awqaf.gov.ae/Newsitem.aspx?Lang=EN&SectionID=16&RefID=1092; and Rezan Oueiti, "New mosques in Ajman make room for everybody," *The National*, June 16, 2016, http://thenational.ae/uae/new-mosques-in-ajman-make-room-for-everybody.
66. See KSIMC of Dubai, "Awqaf Al Jafferiah Launches Fund Raising for 4 New Mosque Projects in Dubai," December 14, 2010, http://dubaijamaat.com/latest-newsbloglayout/general-news/591-awqaf-al-jafferiah-lainches-fuind-raising-for-4-new.
67. Esperance Ghanem, "What is behind UAE deportation of Lebanese nationals?" *Al Monitor*, April 17, 2015, http://www.al-monitor.com/pulse/originals/2015/04/lebanon-nationals-deportation-uae-deci-

sion-html#ixzz40DFzmDtB; and "Over 4000 Shiites deported from UAE," *Shia World News Facebook*, February 13, 2013, https://.facebook.com/newsshia/posts/337686526342852.

68. See Malcolm C. Peck, *Historical Dictionary of the Gulf Arab States*, 2nd ed. (Lanham, MD: The Scarecrow Press, Inc. 2008), 144.
69. Sultan Al Qassemi, "The Sacrifice of Our Troops and a Need for Civil Society," *The National* (Abu Dhabi), February 28, 2010, http://www.thenational.ae/news/the-sacrifice-of-our-troops-and-a-need-for-civil-society; Mohammed Nasser, "Military Expert: Al Qaeda Present in the Gulf... but not Active," *Al-Sharq al-Awsat* (London), December 29, 2010, http://www.aawsat.com/english/news.asp?section=1&id=23598
70. "US Embassy Cables: Abu Dhabi Favours Action to Prevent a Nuclear Iran," *Guardian* (London), November 28, 2010, http://www.guardian.co.uk/world/us-embassy-cables-documents/59984.
71. "UAE, Israel have secret meeting, UAE 'offered to fund Israel's Gaza offensive,' The Peninsula, July 19, 2014, http://freedmanreport.com/?p=1651; and "600 UAE-funded housing units given to refugees in Gaza, Middle East, News, Palestine, UAE, December 7, 2015, https://www.middleeastmonitor.com/20151207-600-uae-funded-housing-units-given-to-refugees-in-gaza/.
72. James M. Dorsey, "All the UAE's men: Gulf crisis opens door to power shift in Palestine," p.1, July 9, 2017, accessed on same date, https://mideastsoccer.blogspot.com/2017/07/all-uaes-men-gulf-crisis-opens-door-to.html.
73. U.S. Embassy Abu Dhabi, "Scenesetter for Counterterrorism Coordinator."
74. Cited in Kenneth Katzman, *The United Arab Emirates (UAE): Issues for U.S. Policy*, November 28, 2016, Congressional Research Service.
75. Jess Bravin and Carole E. Lee, "U.S. Transfers 15 Guantanamo Bay Detainees," *Wall Street Journal*, August 15, 2016, http://www.wsj.com/articles/u-s-transfers-15-guantanamo-bay-detainees-1471303872.
76. Hair Nayouf, "Iran has "sleeper cells" in the Gulf:

Ex-diplomat," *Al Arabiya* News, October 30, 2007, https://english.alarabiya.net/articles/2007/10Abdul H/30/41005.html.; and Abdul Hameed Bakier, "Sleeper Cells and Shi'a Secessionists in Saudi Arabia: A Salafist Perspective," Jamestown Foundation *Terrorism Monitor* 7, iss. 18, June 25, 2009, http://www.jamestown.org/single/?no_cache=1&tx_ttnews%5Btt_news%5D=35182.; and Esperance Ghanem, op. cit. On fears of Iran and possible "fifth column" activities by UAE residents of Iranian origin, see Katzman, *The United Arab Emirates*, Congressional Research Service, June 18, 2013, p. 16.

77. James M. Dorsey, "All the UAE's men: Gulf crisis opens door to power shift in Palestine," p.2.
78. Maher Chmaytelli, "UAE pushes for better ties with cleric Sadr amid efforts to contain Iran," Reuters, pp.1-3, August 14, 2017, accessed on November 16, 2017, https://www.reuters.com/article/us-mideast-crisis-iraq-emirates.
79. Joby Warrick, "Donors boost Islamists in Syria," *The Washington Post*, September 22, 2013.
80. See Peck, *Historical Dictionary of the Gulf Arab States*, 297; Steve Barber, "The 'New Economy of Terror:' The Financing of Islamist Terrorism," *Global Security Issues* 2, iss. 1, winter 2011, 5, 9.
81. Gregor Stuart Hunter, "U.S. official to focus on illicit finance and sanctions in UAE talks," *The National* (Abu Dhabi), January 27, 2013, http://www.thenational.ae. The two financial service companies were HSBC and Standard Chartered.
82. Celina B. Realuyo, "Combating Terrorist Financing in the Gulf," The Arab Gulf States Institute in Washington, January 26, 2015.
83. Taimur Khan, "Joint US-UAE task force to choke off ISIL funding," *The National* (Abu Dhabi), October 27, 2014, http://www.thenational.ae/world/middle-east/joint-us-uae-task-force-to-choke-off-isil-funding.
84. Said Salahuddin and Erin Cunningham, "Taliban video purports to show captives' pleas to Trump," *The Washington Post*, January 11, 2017.

31 Yemen

Quick Facts

Geographical Areas of Operation: East Asia, Eurasia, Europe, Latin America, Middle East and North Africa, North America, South Asia, Sub-Saharan Africa
Strength: Estimates at year's end suggested between 12,000 and 15,000 (*These estimates only reflect membership in Syria and Iraq*)
Leadership: Abu Bakr al-Baghdadi
Religious Identification: Sunni Islam

Quick Facts courtesy of the U.S. State Department's Annual Country Reports on Terrorism, Last Updated 2016

Introduction

Yemen is a fragile Gulf state home to numerous Salafi-jihadi and Islamist groups, including al-Qaeda in the Arabian Peninsula (AQAP), a leading al-Qaeda affiliate, as well as a branch of the Islamic State terrorist group. Both al-Qaeda and the Islamic State have exploited the conditions created by Yemen's collapse into civil war. The Zaydi Shi'a Houthi movement, which has received Iranian support, is also empowered through the civil war. The Houthi movement is now a power broker in the Sana'a-based government, having seized control of state infrastructure after the collapse of the National Dialogue Conference.

Islamist extremist and separatist groups have taken advantage of Yemen's general instability to advance their political agendas and create terrorist safe-havens in the country. The Yemeni government, for its part, has coordinated closely with the United States on counterterrorism operations to target AQAP leaders, including through the use of U.S. drone strikes on Yemeni soil. An Arab military coalition intervened in Yemen in March 2015 to counter the Houthi movement and restore power to the Yemeni government. Nevertheless, AQAP, which governed certain areas for over a year, has expanded its influence, while the Islamic State now likewise has a foothold in Yemen. Both groups will continue to operate in the country as long as the civil war continues.

The economic, social and security issues that plague the Yemeni state, coupled with civil war, have paralyzed the Yemeni government. It is not able to provide effective governance and security to much of the country. The breakdown of the Yemeni state over the course of the civil war adds to historical internal challenges, including political and economic instability, declining oil reserves, severe water shortages, internally-displaced persons (IDPs), and deep-seated ethnic and religious tensions. As of April 2017, the UN had listed Yemen as having the world's largest humanitarian crisis.[1]

Islamist Activity

The land of Yemen holds religious significance in Islam. There are two hadiths (accounts of the sayings of Muhammad) directly referencing the area. The first prophesies that a Muslim army of 12,000 men will rise from Aden and Abyan in southern Yemen to give victory to Allah. The second states that two religions would not co-exist on the Arabian Peninsula, implying that Islam would overcome the other. Yemen's status in Islam has made it important to transnational Islamist groups, particularly Salafi-jihadi ones.

Yemen has served as a safe haven to opposition and terrorist groups of varying political stripes throughout its history. Prior to the unification of traditionalist North Yemen and Marxist South Yemen in 1990, the latter was used as a sanctuary for a wide array of Palestinian and terrorist organizations with the support of local authorities. Tacit support for subversive groups continued in Yemen after unification, but extremist Islamist organizations, especially those opposed to the Saudi monarchy, replaced radical Palestinian and leftist organizations.[2]

Yemen's prolonged civil conflicts, increasing sectarianism, absence of an effective central government, and continued existence of popular grievances have created the conditions for the development of homegrown Islamist militants like the Houthis, as well as a safe haven for transnational Salafi-jihadi organizations like al-Qaeda. Yemen's education system, which uses textbooks containing some degree of anti-American and anti-Israeli ideology, coupled with an unemployment rate of around 35 percent, are factors that play into the vulnerability of young men to be exploited by Islamist militant organizations.[3]

Further compounding the problem is the accessibility of weapons through Yemen's vast underground arms market; roughly three guns exist for every one person in Yemen.[4] The Yemeni political and social landscape is replete with tribal leaders and Islamist groups that have the arms and power to deny the Yemeni government a monopoly on the use of violence. Under these conditions, analysts have noted, "piracy, smuggling and violent jihad can flourish, with implications for the security of shipping routes and the transit of oil"[5] through the Red Sea to the Suez Canal.

The ouster of the country's longtime autocratic president, Ali Abdullah Saleh, and the political transition that followed his departure transformed Yemeni politics. After 33 years in power, Saleh was removed from power following widespread anti-government protests in 2011 during Yemen's version of the Arab Spring. A U.S.-backed, Gulf Cooperation Council (GCC)-brokered transition agreement led to a referendum electing former vice president Abd Rabu Mansour Hadi as Saleh's replacement. Hadi later presided over a National Dialogue Conference to lay the groundwork for a new Yemeni Constitution. The National Dialogue Conference, the forum to address longstanding grievances against the government, included a number of opposition groups and Islamist factions, including Shi'ite Houthi rebels in the north.[6]

Opposition groups decried the transition process after it did not fully shift power from the established elite. The Houthis left the negotiating table and began to militarize, advancing from their northern stronghold to Sana'a, the capital, with Saleh's support.[7] They forced the Hadi government to sign an agreement giving opposition groups, including the Southern Movement (Hirak), an umbrella group for southern opposition factions, more power in the government.[8] The Houthi coup culminated in the winter of 2015, when the Hadi government fled the country. An Arab coalition led by Saudi Arabia and including the United Arab Emirates intervened in Yemen in March 2015 in support of the Hadi government.[9] Civil war broke out between two large factions of loose, pragmatic alliances: the Houthi-Saleh faction and those opposed to it, now including the Southern Movement, the Sunni al-Islah party, local tribal militias, and al-Qaeda. The most radical actors on both sides of the civil war are actively promoting sectarianism in Yemen, where it had not been strong before.

Al-Qaeda

Al-Qaeda has a longstanding presence in Yemen. Yemenis ranked second only to the Saudis in terms of nationals serving as members of the mujahideen who fought the Soviet Union in Afghanistan in the 1980s, a war that constituted a key milestone in the consolidation of radical Islam in Yemen. Yemenis trained under al-Qaeda's high command in Afghanistan throughout the 1990s, up until the U.S. invasion of Afghanistan in 2001.[10]

From its inception until the late 1990s, al-Qaeda maintained training camps in various locations in Yemen.[11] A November 1996 autobiography of bin Laden provided to the Islamist journal *Nida'ul Islam* highlighted the terrorist chief's enduring interest in Yemen and mentioned his support for the mujahideen fighting the Communist party in South Yemen in the early 1980s and later in the early 1990s.[12] In 1997, bin Laden reportedly sent an envoy to Yemen to explore the possibility of establishing a base there in the event the Taliban expelled him from Afghanistan.[13] The al-Qaeda leader also listed Yemen as one of six countries "most in need of liberation" in 2003.[14]

In the immediate aftermath of 9/11, the Yemeni government implemented stiff counterterrorism measures and cooperated with the United States to eliminate senior al-Qaeda operative Abu Ali al-Harithi in November 2002.[15] By the end of 2003, however, Sana'a began to lag in its counterterrorism efforts, and in February 2006 twenty-three al-Qaeda terrorists, including the mastermind of the 2000 *USS Cole* bombing, escaped from a Yemeni prison.[16] An October 2009 report by the American Enterprise Institute (AEI) asserted that:

> Many Western intelligence analysts viewed elements of the Yemeni security apparatus as complicit in the prison break. The more relaxed security situation in Yemen stemmed both from complacency and the government's perceived need to reallocate security resources to address other domestic threats. Such

> circumstances made Yemen a favorable alternative location for al-Qaeda to plan, train for, and execute attacks against the regimes of Saudi Arabia and Yemen, both of which it views as hypocritical, apostate puppets of the West.[17]

In the late 2000s, Yemen was a fragile state focused on putting down the Houthi rebellion in the north. The state's distraction made the country ideal as a base of operations for al-Qaeda in the Arabian Peninsula (AQAP), which represented a merger of Yemeni and Saudi branches of al-Qaeda in January 2009. Saudi operatives had fled to Yemen after the Saudi government imposed a crackdown inside its borders following a series of terrorist attacks in the Kingdom between May 2003 and December 2004 against oil company offices, foreign targets, Saudi government offices, and security targets.[18]

Since its establishment, AQAP has been the most active of al-Qaeda's affiliates in targeting the United States. It has been implicated in a number of terrorist operations, including: a suicide bombing against a group of South Korean tourists in Hadramawt and a South Korean diplomatic convoy to Sana'a; the attempted suicide bombing targeting Saudi Deputy Interior Minister Prince Mohammed bin Nayef; and the ambush and killing of seven Yemeni security officials near the Saudi border.[19]

AQAP repeatedly attempted to attack the U.S. homeland or American interests. It claimed responsibility for the attempted Christmas Day 2009 downing of Detroit-bound Flight 253 by Nigerian extremist Umar Farouk Abdulmutallab.[20] AQAP also claimed the cargo plane bomb plot foiled in Dubai and the UK in October 2010, and asserted it was behind the September 2010 downing of a UPS flight in Dubai, although U.S. officials have found no conclusive connection between the crash and terrorism.[21] The group attempted to attack the United States again in May 2012 (an attack which was thwarted by a tip from Saudi intelligence), and was behind the threats that closed over twenty U.S. diplomatic missions across the Middle East and North Africa in August 2013.[22] Its chief bombmaker, Ibrahim al-Asiri, has trained others to share expertise with al-Qaeda groups in Syria and Somalia.[23]

AQAP is conducting an insurgency within Yemen. The group

seeks to mobilize the country's Sunnis behind it against the Yemeni state. AQAP operates within local customs and has developed local relations based on pragmatic lines of support.[24] It does not require ideological alignment to support various groups and factions. It uses asymmetrical attacks to degrade Yemeni military capabilities, as well as other forces opposed to it. The group conducts targeted assassinations against military and government leadership, as well as against intelligence officers and local powerbrokers aligned with the government. AQAP has kidnapped individuals for ransom money and could in the future use this tactic to gain political leverage over foreign powers. The kidnapping of Saudi deputy consul Abdallah al-Khalidi at his home in the south Yemeni port city of Aden in March 2012 is one such example.

The number of Yemenis claiming allegiance to AQAP is unknown. Estimates of membership have ranged from the low hundreds to a few thousand.[25] This number has increased significantly as AQAP and associated organizations active in Yemen, such as Ansar al-Sharia, have gained power and influence in southern Yemen. More recently, fighters have traveled from conflicts in Syria and Iraq to Yemen, bringing with them new skills and tactics.[26] Even before the 2011 anti-government protests swept through Yemen, AQAP had been on a path to establish links with tribes in the Marib, al-Jawf and Shabwah governorates of eastern Yemen.[27]

In the wake of the 2011 uprisings, AQAP sought to capitalize on the political transition, increasing its attacks against government targets. AQAP's insurgent arm, Ansar al-Sharia, seized key cities in the south, including the provincial capital of Abyan province, Zinjibar. Ansar al-Sharia held Zinjibar from May 2011 until the Yemeni military, aided by tribal militias known as Popular Committees, were able to overrun the al-Qaeda "emirates" in late June 2012.[28] AQAP has found a more favorable political climate in the aggrieved Sunni south, though its mass appeal remains limited in a region historically dominated by socialism. Its primary mechanism to cultivating popular support is through pragmatic relationships, where AQAP provides the local population with basic goods or services.[29]

AQAP also conducts an international outreach strategy that is much more pronounced than that of other al-Qaeda affiliates. Anwar al-Awlaki, the late American-born Muslim cleric who became a leading figure within AQAP, ran an online campaign from Yemen to recruit and aid Muslims in foreign countries to carry out attacks that led to over a dozen terrorist investigations.[30] Al-Qaeda's English-language magazine, *Inspire*, has been produced in Yemen since 2010 and provides radicalizing literature and instructions for planning and conducting terrorist attacks.[31] AQAP released a shorter "Guide to Inspire" following the June 2016 Orlando shootings and the July 2016 attack in Nice that analyzed those attacks and provided additional guidance for would-be recruits.[32] Current AQAP leaders featured in its publications include leader Qasim al Raymi, senior leader and former Guantanamo detainee Ibrahim al Qosi, senior leader Khaled Batarfi, and religious scholar Ibrahim al Banna.[33]

AQAP's strength increased significantly during Yemen's civil war.[34] It controlled al Mukalla, a major port city in southeast Yemen, from April 2015—April 2016 and also expanded its influence behind the frontlines of Yemen's war.[35] AQAP may be expanding its influence in Taiz, Yemen's third-largest city, and it continues to have sanctuary in Abyan, al Bayda, Shabwah, Ma'rib and al Jawf.[36]

A sustained UAE-led counterterrorism campaign in Yemen has attrited AQAP leadership and reclaimed territory AQAP had taken control of in 2015. The UAE military supported Yemeni forces in Aden from Fall 2015 forward to roll up the al-Qaeda and Islamic State cells in the city. The UAE has trained and equipped Yemeni security forces as part of its counterterrorism efforts. These include the Security Belt forces in Aden, Lahij, and Abyan (also known as al Hizam brigades) and the Elites in Hadramawt, al Mahrah, and Shabwah governorates.[37] U.S. and Emirati counterterrorism cooperation, along with the presence of Yemeni ground forces, has affected AQAP's operational ability[38] and removed AQAP from populated areas in Hadramawt and Shabwah. The counterterrorism operations have degraded AQAP's media capabilities as well, diminishing AQAP's output and responsiveness to current events.[39] However, the U.S.-backed Emirati counterterrorism operations have not removed AQAP's historical sanctuaries, which will leave the group permissive terrain to reconstitute should pressure against it cease. The effect of leadership attrition may not be lasting. Further, many of the conditions that enabled AQAP to spread in Yemen persist.

The Islamic State

Since its emergence as an independent entity in 2013, the Islamic State has competed globally with al-Qaeda for leadership of the Salafi-jihadi movement. Yemen is key terrain for this contest, not just because of its religious significance but also because of the presence of AQAP.[40] To this end, the late Islamic State military commander Omar al-Shishani mentioned Yemen among eight other fields of jihad in the Islamic State's celebratory June 2014 video calling for the end of borders that separate Muslims.[41]

Initial support for the Islamic State appeared in Yemen immediately after the group declared its caliphate in Iraq in June 2014. A prominent Salafi-jihadi cleric, Sheikh Ma'moun Abdulhamid Hatem, was one early supporter of the Islamic State.[42] Sheikh Hatem probably facilitated recruitment in Ibb for the Islamic State even as he remained within AQAP's network.[43] A Saudi Arabian national named Bilal al-Harbi, who was in communication with leadership in Syria by September 2014, was commissioned to gather pledges of allegiance to the Islamic State.[44] Al-Harbi is now one of the group's leaders in Yemen. Islamic State leader Abu Bakr al-Baghdadi recognized the Yemeni branch alongside four other groups in a November 2014 video.[45]

The Islamic State claimed its first attack in Yemen on March 20, 2015, simultaneously bombing two mosques in Sana'a. The attack was the deadliest terrorist incident in Yemen to-date and targeted Zaydi Shia.[46] AQAP disavowed responsibility for the attack, noting that it does not target mosques or public spaces. The Sana'a mosque bombings began a series of attacks against targets, many of them civilian, that the Islamic State labeled as being "Houthi." These attacks are part of a global strategy by the Islamic State to increase sectarianism and mobilize the Sunni behind its leadership.[47]

The group shifted its primary focus from targeting the Houthis to targeting the Arab coalition in Yemen, and thereafter the coalition-backed Yemeni military and government in October 2015. The Emiratis had led a ground offensive to reinstate the Yemeni government in Aden in July 2015 and were beginning to reestablish the internationally recognized government in the country. Islamic State militants targeted coalition and government sites in Aden on October 6, 2015.[48] The group began regular attacks in Aden through the winter and into spring 2016. It subsequently expanded attacks against the government to the southeastern port city of al Mukalla after an April 2016 Emirati-led offensive regained control of the city from AQAP.[49] The Islamic State did not conduct a mass-casualty attack in Yemen for the year after these campaigns in the south, likely due to degraded capabilities, but did engage in low-level activities. For most of 2016, the Islamic State only claimed attacks in the Hadramawt and Aden governorates, a significant decrease in activity (as well as the number of active cells) from 2015. It expanded into al Bayda governorate in central Yemen, where AQAP is also active, claiming small-scale asymmetrical attacks beginning in Fall 2016.[50] By Fall 2017, the Islamic State had established training camps in al Bayda, which the U.S. targeted with airstrikes.[51] The Islamic State regenerated an attack capability in Aden, where it conducted a mass-casualty attack in November 2017 and has continued irregular attacks.[52]

The Islamic State's expansion in Yemen has been limited because of AQAP's strong presence there and because of how the Islamic State had operated. The targeting of non-combatants, a practice generally not seen in Yemen, has helped to alienate the population. The participation in the fight in central Yemen against the Houthi movement may indicate a shift in ground operations, or may simply be because of the Islamic State's inability to generate support elsewhere. The Islamic State uses a top-down leadership approach, working with a primarily non-Yemeni leadership body. Its leaders also do not follow Yemeni tribal customs, and in fact reject them entirely. Yemeni members of the Islamic State issued a public denunciation of the Islamic State's leadership in Yemen in two letters in December 2015, rejecting the leadership but reaffirming their allegiance to Baghdadi.[53] The group's core in Yemen, however, ultimately suppressed this rebellion.

The Islamic State continues to run small cells in Aden, Yemen, and in al Bayda, in central Yemen. Broad-based support for the

Islamic State is absent. The group has been able to recruit and train cells inside of Aden that enact well-executed attacks on Yemeni security services. The Islamic State claimed a suicide vehicle-borne improvised explosive device that targeted a police force camp in Aden in November 2017, which killed at least six people, and a complex attack—suicide bombers and a small tactical team—on a Yemeni counterterrorism force headquarters building in Aden in February 2018, which killed at least fourteen people.[54] In al Bayda, Islamic State teams conduct small-arms attacks on al Houthi positions. It also had run basic military skills training camps in the area. The U.S. targeted two of these camps in October 2017, killing about 50 fighters.[55]

The Houthi Movement

Prior to the 2011 "Arab Spring" uprisings, Yemeni military and security forces were already spread thin. The Saleh regime had devoted considerable resources to suppressing a rebellion led by the Houthi family, from where the movement derives its moniker. The Houthis are Zaydi Shi'a and have a stronghold in northern Yemen. They were the most direct threat to the Yemeni state from 2004-2010. The Houthis were engaged in an on-and-off guerrilla war with the Yemeni government from 2004-2010, leading to the death and displacement of thousands. The Saleh regime accused the Houthis of receiving support from Iran and of "trying to reinstate the clerical imamate" (Shi'ite Islamic government) that ruled northern Yemen for roughly 1,000 years prior to 1962,[56] while the Houthis contend they are merely advocating "freedom of worship and social justice."[57]

Currently led by Abdul Malik al-Houthi, the younger brother of the group's late founder, Sheikh Hussein Badreddin al-Houthi, the group has accused the Yemeni government of "widespread corruption, of aligning itself too closely with the United States, of allowing too much Wahhabi (fundamentalist Sunni) influence in the country, and of economic and social neglect in predominantly Shi'ite parts of the country."[58] The Houthis couched their challenge to Saleh's rule in religious terms—Saleh is not of Hashemite descent, which made him illegitimate to rule in strict Zaydi practice—though the roots of the conflict are political.

The origins of the armed conflict trace back to 2003, when

followers of the group "Believing Youth" shouted anti-American and anti-Israeli slurs inside a Sa'ada mosque where then-president Saleh was attending service at a time when he was trying to maintain strong relations with the West.[59] The Yemeni government responded by killing Hussein al-Houthi in a firefight in September 2004. Houthi's followers took up arms for revenge. The Yemeni military's heavy hand caused collateral damage, drawing additional tribes to the side of the Houthis and mobilizing a large faction in northern Yemen.

In the years that followed, the Yemeni government and Abdul Malik al-Houthi expressed their readiness for dialogue on a number of occasions. However, several resulting ceasefire agreements proved short-lived. The Yemeni government and Houthis fought six small wars in the decade after 2004. In the fall of 2009, the conflict spilled over the Saudi border as Houthi fighters seized areas within Saudi Arabia and the Saudi military retaliated with air and ground forces to repel the Houthi incursion.[60]

Saudi Arabia has since launched an initiative to fortify its border with Yemen with motion sensors, infrared systems, and GPS trackers.[61] The initiative was launched in tandem with a March 2013 law that mandated the deportation of hundreds of thousands of illegal foreign residents.[62] The International Organization for Migration documents that almost 310,000 Yemenis returned to Yemen from Saudi Arabia between June 1, 2013 and February 28, 2014. A separate estimate found 27 percent of the deportees planned to return to Saudi Arabia when possible. Oman also perceives a security risk and is considering building a barrier along its own border with Yemen.[63]

As the conflict between the Yemeni military and the Shiite Houthis escalated, so too did accusations by the Yemeni and Saudi governments of Iranian involvement in arming the Houthis, though the evidence on this score is not conclusive. Overt, unofficial statements by Houthi officials to reporters,[64] recordings of conversations between smugglers and members of Iran's Quds Force paramilitary unit,[65] and an intercepted Iranian ship off Yemen's southern coast carrying weapons (including 10 Chinese anti-aircraft missiles) originating from Iran have been proffered as evidence of Iranian involvement.[66] Tehran has vehemently denied these accusations, and in turn condemned Saudi Arabia's involvement in the conflict. Meanwhile, Houthi rebels have accused Saudi Arabia of supporting the Yemeni government and aiding its offensives, a charge which the Saudis have denied.[67]

The Houthis were among many groups that supported the anti-Saleh protests that erupted in January 2011. As the military shifted its resources to restoring security in the capital and combating a growing threat from al-Qaeda in the south, the Houthis were emboldened to expand territorially. This led to clashes with the Sunni al-Islah party, as the two groups jockeyed for power and influence in the northern province of al-Jawf.[68] Adding to the Houthis' list of adversaries, in January 2011 the late AQAP deputy chief Saeed Ali al-Shihri declared jihad against "Iranian-backed Houthi Shiite advocates."[69] From spring 2011 through early 2013, there were reports of sectarian clashes between Houthi militants and Sunni tribes in the northern province of Sa'ada.[70] Another spike in violent activity began in October of 2013 in al-Jawf province after Houthis accused Sunni Salafis of recruiting foreign fighters.[71]

Since Saleh was ousted from power in 2011, the reconciliation process under the supervision of President Hadi granted the Houthis political recognition with 35 of 565 seats at the National Dialogue Conference.[72] The Houthis, however, rejected the outcome and continued to use military force to expand their influence throughout the process. The decision to divide Yemen into six administrative districts was inimical to Houthi interests, because the movement's stronghold would be isolated. The Houthis would also be required to compete with another powerful Zaydi family in Sanhan, Sana'a.[73]

The Houthis have had a partnership of convenience with former President Saleh and his allies since 2014 that has given them control of the capital, Sana'a, and the majority of Yemeni state infrastructure. They have sought to negotiate a political settlement to the civil war, but have repeatedly rejected the terms put forward by the international community, which favor the Yemeni government. The Houthis enjoy an out-sized level of influence over national politics compared to the small percentage of Yemenis who are actually members of the movement. They have made maximalist demands to retain this influence, including disproportional representation within the national government. Saleh and the Houthis cut a power-sharing agreement in July 2016, establishing a political council to govern the country split between Saleh's General People's Congress party and the Houthis' Ansar Allah party.[74] The al Houthi-Saleh political council announced a 42-minister "National Salvation Government" on November 28, 2016.[75]

There is increasing evidence that the Iranian regime is supporting the Houthi-Saleh faction in Yemen. The UN Yemen Panel of Experts cited Iran for violating the arms embargo on Yemen by providing the Houthis with short-range ballistic missiles.[76] The Houthis have modified these ballistic missiles and have been able to strike as far as Riyadh, Saudi Arabia.[77] Two notable ballistic missile attacks are a November 4, 2017, strike that fell just short of Riyadh's international airport and a second strike targeting the palace in Riyadh on December 19, 2017.[78] The Houthis threatened to target Abu Dhabi, UAE, with a ballistic missile on June 1, 2018.[79] In addition to the interdiction of weapons shipments transported by sea, there have been allegations that Iran is also moving weapons by land, through Oman.[80] The Houthi-Saleh forces, in turn, have used modified ballistic missiles against Saudi Arabia, a capability likely transferred from Lebanese Hezbollah, and an Iranian variant of the Chinese Silkworm missile was identified in the series of attacks against the U.S. naval presence in the Red Sea off Yemen's coast in October 2016.[81] Iran also likely provided the Houthis with sea mines found in the port of Mokha, Yemen, anti-tank missiles, and unmanned aerial vehicles (UAVs) that fly at Emirati PATRIOT systems in order to overwhelm them as part of a strategy targeting Emirati positions in Yemen.[82]

The Houthis began to meet openly with members of Iran's proxy and partner network in the region by October 2015. Houthi delegations have met with Hezbollah in Lebanon, even going so far as to take a photograph[83] with the group's leader, Hassan Nasrallah; with members of the Assad regime in Syria; and with Iranian proxy groups in Iraq like Asaib Ahl al Haq. Yemenis had been reported to have operating with Hezbollah in Syria, too, for example.[84] Additionally, Abdul Malik al-Houthi offered to send forces to support Lebanese Hezbollah in July 2017.[85]

Islamism and Society

Historically, Yemeni society has been divided along two main religious identities, the Shi'ite Zaydi sect followed in the country's north and northwest, and the Shafa'i school of Sunni Islam predominant in the south and southeast. Although no accurate and reliable statistics exist, Sunnis are generally acknowledged to represent a majority among Yemen's population of 26 million, while Zaydis claim around 35 percent of the total.[86] There is a strong Sunni Salafi trend within certain areas of Yemen. Zaydis are constituents of a Shi'a sect often described as moderate in its jurisprudence.[87]

In his studies of Islamism in Yemen, Laurent Bonnefoy of the Institut Français du Proche-Orient found that "despite episodes of violent stigmatization orchestrated by certain radical groups, the vast majority of the population is at times indirectly (and most of the time passively) involved in the convergence of the once-distinct Sunni and Zaydi religious identities."[88] He cites one such example of this as former president Saleh, who himself is of Zaydi origin but never refers to his primary identity. Bonnefoy goes on to say that: "at the grassroots level, many Sunnis do not mind praying in Zaydi mosques, and vice versa. Consequently, the religious divide only marginally structures political affiliations and adherence to specific Islamist groups."[89]

However, as anti-government protests threatened his presidency, Saleh drew on his Zaydi identity "in an attempt to rally Zaydi tribal solidarity against what he also allegedly framed as a Shafa'i-led protest movement," even going so far as to suggest that he could be the "last Zaydi president."[90] Such actions led to criticism that Saleh was "concentrating on solidifying tribal allegiances even at the cost of exacerbating sectarian divisions."[91] The increase in sectarian tensions in northern Yemen in recent years can be seen, in part, as a result of policies and governing strategies playing competing tribal and sectarian groups off of one another.

Rising sectarianism in the region against the backdrop of the wars in Syria and Iraq is also seeping into Yemen. The Islamic State has attempted to provoke sectarian furor, and Houthi and AQAP rhetoric increasingly play upon sectarian divisions. Reports from on the ground indicate that Yemenis of different sects are less likely today to practice in the same mosques.[92] For their part, both Saudi Arabia and Iran see Yemen as a space for contest, though Yemen is much more important to Saudi Arabia. Iran sees an opportunity in Yemen to expand its "Axis of Resistance" through the Houthi movement while simultaneously contesting Saudi regional hegemony. It has been able to drive Saudi responses in Yemen with minimal investment in the Houthi movement.[93]

Islamism and the State

In a March 2009 journal article for *The Middle East Review of International Affairs* (MERIA), Laurent Bonnefoy pointed to the "presence of a strong traditional 'civil society' in the form of tribal and religious groups, most of them armed or capable of opposing the state" as a source in "undermining the regime's capacity to monopolize all the levers of power and fulfilling any totalitarian dreams."[94] For years, the Saleh regime maintained such power-sharing arrangements out of self-interest (i.e., weakening its enemies, dividing political and religious groups, etc.). Such arrangements, however, have been unable to withstand a range of endogenous and exogenous shocks.

Over the past decade, divisive policies and shifting political alliances stressed an already fragile system, due in large part to the erosion of the legitimacy and power of the central government. Allegations of widespread corruption, a growing view of the government as an American and Saudi puppet by Islamist groups, and widening economic and resource inequity all contribute to the government's domestic weakness. These trends became more pronounced as the counterterrorism partnership with Washington grew. Since President Hadi's ascension to power, U.S. officials have noted "a new determination [and] a new consistency in terms of what the Yemeni government is doing on the counterterrorism front."[95]

The unification of Yemen was initially built upon a partnership between the two former ruling parties of North and South Yemen, within the framework of a power-sharing coalition. However, the Vice President of the coalition government, Ali Salim al-Baidh, who represented the south, fled to the city of Aden in 1993 and accused the government of marginalizing the south and attacking southerners. The ensuing civil war between leaders in the north and south paved the way for increased participation of Islamist groups in the government throughout the 1990s.

Sheik Abdel Majid al-Zindani was a key player during the initial infiltration of radical Islam into Yemen due to his role as a senior Islamic religious leader and prominent Islamist political figure. Zindani was a central activist in recruiting Yemeni mujahideen members for the jihad in Afghanistan, as well as being himself a combatant against the Soviets during the 1979-89 war. Upon his return to Yemen, Zindani established the al-Islah Islamic movement, which later became the major political opposition party to former President Saleh's General People's Council. The al-Islah party brought together Yemen's Salafists, Muslim Brotherhood members, and also a significant tribal faction.

After the first multiparty general elections in 1993, al-Zindani became part of the five-man presidential council, while the then-head of al-Islah, Abdallah al-Ahmar, was elected as speaker of parliament.[96] As tensions rose with the socialist leaders in the coalition, President Ali Abdullah Saleh agreed to govern with al-Islah. With the outbreak of war in May 1994 between the Saleh regime in the north and formerly Soviet-aligned separatists in the south, al-Zindani condemned the separatist movements in Yemen as a "foreign conspiracy," and stressed the need both for the unity of Yemen and for allegiance to the regime. Al-Zindani, along with the Islah party, was easily able to rally the returning veterans of the Afghan jihad behind the Saleh regime in the north as a continuation of the jihad that had been waged in Afghanistan against the Marxist regime.

After the victory of Saleh's regime over the southern separatists in July 1994, and with the reunification of north and south Yemen, Saleh rewarded the Afghan veterans for their contribution by incorporating their leaders into the government.[97] One such example of this is Tariq al-Fadli, heir of the sultan of Abyan and former Afghan mujahideen leader, who later was appointed by the president to the Majlis al-Shura, the upper house of the parliament. Veteran jihadists were thus able to strike what Bonnefoy describes as "a 'covenant of security' deal with the security services on their return home from

Afghanistan," under which they would enjoy freedom of movement within Yemen in return for a promise of good behavior inside the country's borders. During this transition, greater participation by the Muslim Brotherhood could be seen in Yemeni politics, with al-Islah members holding several important ministries, including justice, education, trade, and religious affairs.[98]

Throughout the 1990s and into the 2000s, formal and informal integration of numerous Islamist groups into the state apparatus continued. Individuals identifying with various sects of Islam gained important posts in the army and security forces. As a result, repression of Islamist groups was limited, allowing for easy access to political and tribal elites for Salafists, Sufis, Zaydi revivalists, Muslim Brothers, and some individuals sympathetic to jihadist doctrines.[99]

Al-Islah became entrenched in Yemen's political landscape and in numerous regions of the country. The party had considerable support in the former Marxist South, where a strong anti-socialist movement favored Islamist candidates and platforms over the dominant Yemeni Socialist Party and had gained influence in some areas of the north. Nationally, the Islamist party won an average of 18 percent of the vote during the 1993, 1997, and 2003 parliamentary elections. Although a lack of electoral transparency reduces the significance of these numbers, the influence of al-Islah in Yemen was very sizeable.[100]

Al-Islah gained power in the immediate post-Arab Spring reforms in Yemen. During the transition and the NDC under President Hadi, al-Islah and the Yemeni Socialist Party were the two major factions in the Joint Meeting Parties (JMP), a coalition of parties opposing Saleh's GPC. Al-Islah shared power with the former ruling GPC party and had a significant role, holding 50 seats in the NDC, negotiating and shaping the reforms that were to be instituted by the Hadi government.[101] The addition of the Houthis' party, Ansar Allah, to the NDC negotiations added to the list of Islamist groups represented in the post-Saleh government, which also included the Zaydi al Haqq party. However, it also put President Hadi at odds with many Sunni clerics, including prominent Salafi Islamist Abd al-Majid al-Zindani,[102] and some within al-Islah.[103]

There was an increase in U.S.-Yemeni counterterrorism cooperation following the ouster of Saleh, and President Hadi made statements openly supporting U.S. drone strikes against al-Qaeda.[104] The U.S. provided military assistance to Yemeni security forces in order to facilitate Yemeni ground operations against AQAP, while conducting direct action operations to eliminate imminent threats from the group.[105] The U.S. administration lauded the partnership in 2014 and described Yemen as a model for future counterterrorism alliances.[106] The model did not survive the outbreak of civil war, however. The Yemeni government now supports U.S.-backed Emirati counterterrorism operations in southern Yemen in addition to sustained U.S. direct action operations against AQAP leadership.

The outbreak of civil war has had a significant effect on Islamism in Yemen, driving Islamists to embrace more radical positions and permitting them to expand their influence. A concerning trend has been the assassinations of imams in Aden, Yemen, which has not yet been credited to a single group. Many of the imams were affiliated with al-Islah.[107] The al-Islah party has been marginalized politically[108] and many of its leading members fled the country along with some of the more moderate Salafi voices. Those remaining in Yemen are more extreme. The Houthis are empowered in northern Yemen and have expanded governance into the skeleton of the former Yemeni state through the deal with former president Saleh. They have targeted Salafis and other Islamists, placing individuals under house arrest. The more hardline faction of the Houthis is dominant, and propounds sectarian rhetoric. AQAP and other Salafi groups in Yemen also propagate sectarian messages, trying to cast the war as a religious one. Additionally, members of the Arab coalition, including Saudi Arabia and the UAE, are supporting Salafi militias in Yemen in order to counter the Houthis in the ongoing civil war.

Endnotes

1. "Yemen: We Must Act Now to Prevent a Humanitarian Catastrophe," UNOCHA, April 24, 2017, https://www.unocha.org/story/yemen-we-must-act-now-prevent-humanitarian-catastrophe.
2. Shaul Shay, *The Red Sea Terror Triangle* (R. Liberman, trans.) (New Brunswick: Transaction Publishers, 2005), 113-114.
3. Christopher Harnisch, "Denying Al-Qaeda a Safe Haven in Yemen," American Enterprise Institute Critical Threats Project, October 30, 2009, http://www.criticalthreats.org/yemen/denying-al-qaeda-safe-haven-yemen#_edn2; See also "Yemen Unemployment Rate," *Index Mundi*, n.d., http://www.indexmundi.com/yemen/unemployment_rate.html.
4. "Yemen Stems Weapons Trade," *Saba Net*, September 23, 2008, http://www.sabanews.net/en/news164686.htm; See also "Yemen Moves to Control Arms Trade," *Al-Motamar* (Sana'a), April 25, 2007, http://www.almotamar.net/en/2463.htm.
5. Ginny Hill, "Yemen: Fear of Failure," Chatham House *Briefing Paper*, November 2009, http://www.chathamhouse.org.uk/files/12576_bp1108yemen.pdf.
6. See Katherine Zimmerman, "Yemen's Pivotal Moment," American Enterprise Institute Critical Threats Project, February 12, 2014, http://www.criticalthreats.org/yemen/zimmerman-yemens-pivotal-moment-february-12-2014.
7. Alexis Knutsen, "Yemen's Counter-Terrorism Quandary," American Enterprise Institute Critical Threats Project, June 26, 2014, http://www.criticalthreats.org/yemen/knutsen-houthi-counterterrorism-quandary-june-26-2014.
8. Alexis Knutsen, "Sana'a Under Siege: Yemen's Uncertain Future," American Enterprise Institute Critical Threats Project, September 25, 2014, http://www.criticalthreats.org/yemen/knutsen-sanaa-under-siege-yemens-uncertain-future-september-25-2014.
9. See Peter Salisbury, "Yemen: Stemming the Rise of a Chaos State," Chatham House, May 25, 2016, https://www.chathamhouse.org/sites/files/chathamhouse/pub-

lications/research/2016-05-25-yemen-stemming-rise-of-chaos-state-salisbury.pdf.

10. Hill, "Yemen: Fear of Failure."
11. Lawrence E. Cline, "Yemen's Strategic Boxes," *Small Wars Journal,* January 2, 2010, http://smallwarsjournal.com/blog/journal/docs-temp/339-cline.pdf; Jonathan Schanzer, Testimony before the House of Representatives Committee on Foreign Affairs, February 3, 2010, http://www.pvtr.org/pdf/ICPVTRinNews/HouseForeignAffairsCommitteeHearing-YemenOnTheBrink-ImplicationsForU.S.Policy.pdf.
12. Bruce Lawrence, ed., *Messages to the World: The Statements of Osama bin Laden* (London: Verso, 2005), 32.
13. Jason Burke, *Al-Qaeda: The True Story of Radical Islam* (London: Penguin Books, 2004), 215.
14. Harnisch, "Denying Al-Qaeda a Safe Haven in Yemen"; See also Lawrence, *Messages to the World*, 32.
15. Gregory Johnsen, "Waning Vigilance: Al-Qaeda's Resurgence in Yemen," Washington Institute for Near East Policy *Policywatch* 1551, July 14, 2009, http://www.washingtoninstitute.org/templateC05.php?CID=3088.
16. Johnsen, "Waning Vigilance: Al-Qaeda's Resurgence in Yemen.".; See also "USS Cole Plotter Escapes Prison," CNN.com, February 5, 2006, http://www.cnn.com/2006/WORLD/meast/02/05/cole.escape/index.html; Harnisch, "Denying Al-Qaeda a Safe Haven in Yemen."
17. Harnisch, "Denying Al-Qaeda a Safe Haven in Yemen."
18. "Bombers Attempt Attack On Saudi Oil Facility," *New York Times*, February 24, 2006, http://www.nytimes.com/2006/02/24/world/africa/24iht-web.0224saudi.html; Christopher Harnisch, "Christmas Day Attack: Manifestation of AQAP Shift Targeting America," American Enterprise Institute Critical Threats Project, December 29, 2009, http://www.criticalthreats.org/yemen/christmas-day-attack-manifestation-aqap-shift-targeting-america#_ednref5; P.K. Abdul Ghafour and Essam Al-Ghalib, "Kingdom Makes Remarkable Headway in Fight Against Terror: Naif," *Arab News*, November 11, 2004, http://archive.arabnews.com/?page=1§ion=0&article=54339&d=11&m=11&y=2004.

19. Frederick Kagan and Christopher Harnisch, "Yemen: Fighting al Qaeda in a Failed State," American Enterprise Institute Critical Threats Project, January 12, 2010, http://www.criticalthreats.org/sites/default/files/pdf_upload/analysis/CTP_Yemen_Fighting_al_Qaeda_in_a_Failing_State_Jan_12_2010.pdf.
20. Kagan and Harnisch, "Yemen: Fighting al Qaeda in a Failed State."
21. "Al Qaeda Yemen Wing Claims Parcel Plot UPS Crash," Reuters, November 5, 2010, http://www.reuters.com/article/2010/11/05/us-usa-yemen-bomb-idUSTRE6A44PU20101105.
22. Katherine Zimmerman, "AQAP and the 'Parcel Plot': Assessing this Critical Threats," *AEIdeas*, November 5, 2010, https://www.aei.org/publication/aqap-and-the-parcel-plot-assessing-this-critical-threat; See also "Al Qaeda Threat to American Interests," American Enterprise Institute Critical Threats Project, August 5, 2013, http://www.criticalthreats.org/al-qaeda/zimmerman/al-qaeda-threat-to-american-interests-august-5-2013.
23. Katherine Zimmerman, Jacqulyn Meyer Kantack, and Colin Lahiff, US Counterterrorism Objectives in Somalia: Is Mission Failure Likely?" American Enterprise Institute Critical Threats Project, March 1, 2017, https://www.criticalthreats.org/analysis/us-counterterrorism-objectives-in-somalia-is-mission-failure-likely; and Ewen MacAskill, "The Saudi Chemist Sparking Fears of 'Invisible' Bombs on Transatlantic Flights," *The Guardian,* July 3, 2014, https://www.theguardian.com/world/2014/jul/03/al-qaida-bombmaker.
24. Katherine Zimmerman, "AQAP: A Resurgent Threat," Combating Terrorism Center at West Point *CTC Sentine*l, September 11, 2015, https://www.ctc.usma.edu/posts/aqap-a-resurgent-threat.
25. Yemeni Foreign Minister Abu Bakr al-Qirbi claimed in late 2008 that Yemen was playing host to more than 1,000 jihadist fighters and al-Qaeda affiliates. See Hill, "Yemen: Fear of Failure." Most Yemeni officials reported only 200-300 AQAP members as of 2010, but US estimates rose by 2015. See Ian Black, "Al-Qaida in the Arabian Peninsula: Renegades or Rising Threat?" *The*

Guardian, January 24, 2010, https://www.theguardian.com/world/2010/jan/24/al-qaida-yemen-jihad-training; and "AQAP Fast Facts," CNN, August 5, 2015, http://www.cnn.com/2015/06/16/middleeast/aqap-fast-facts/index.html.

26. Rania El Gamal, "Saudis Hardened by Wars in Syria, Iraq Join Al Qaeda in Yemen," Reuters, March 14, 2014, http://www.reuters.com/article/2014/03/14/us-yemen-security-qaeda-idUSBREA2D0XO20140314.
27. Gregory D. Johnsen, "The Expansion Strategy of Al-Qa'ida in the Arabian Peninsula," Combating Terrorism Center at West Point *CTC Sentinel* 2, iss. 9, September 2009, 8-11, http://www.ctc.usma.edu/sentinel/CTCSentinel-Vol2Iss9.pdf.
28. Jeremy Binnie, "Yemen Overruns Al-Qaeda Enclave," *Jane's Defence Weekly*, June 28, 2012; See also Katherine Zimmerman, "Al Qaeda's Gains in South Yemen," American Enterprise Institute Critical Threats Project, July 8, 2011, http://www.criticalthreats.org/yemen/al-qaedas-gains-south-yemen-july-8-2011#_edn2; Ahmed Al-Haj, "Yemen Recaptures Center of Al-Qaida-Held City," Associated Press, April 24, 2011; For a chronology of attacks by AQAP in Yemen, visit the "AQAP and Suspected AQAP Attacks in 2010, 2011 and 2012," American Enterprise Institute Critical Threats Project, n.d., http://www.criticalthreats.org/yemen/aqap-and-suspected-aqap-attacks-yemen-tracker-2010.
29. Katherine Zimmerman, "AQAP Post-Arab Spring and the Islamic State," in *How al-Qaeda Survived Drones, Uprisings, and the Islamic State*, edited by Aaron Y. Zelin, Washington Institute, June 2017, http://www.washingtoninstitute.org/policy-analysis/view/how-al-qaeda-survived-drones-uprisings-and-the-islamic-state.
30. Eric Schmitt, Mark Mazzetti, and Robert F. Worth, "American-Born Qaeda Leader Is Killed by U.S. Missile in Yemen," *New York Times*, September 30, 2011, http://www.nytimes.com/2011/10/01/world/middleeast/anwar-al-awlaki-is-killed-in-yemen.html.
31. Thomas Joscelyn, "Al Qaeda in the Arabian Peninsula Releases 12th Issue of Inspire Magazine," *Long War*

Journal, March 17, 2014, http://www.longwarjournal.org/archives/2014/03/al_qaeda_in_the_arab.php.

32. Available on www.jihadology.net.
33. Statements available through http://jihadology.net/category/al-qa%E2%80%99idah/franchises/aqap/. AQAP released Ibrahim al Banna's last statement on June 25, 2017 (http://jihadology.net/2017/06/25/new-video-message-from-al-qaidah-in-the-arabian-peninsulas-shaykh-ibrahim-al-banna-congratulations-and-a-reminder/); Ibrahim al Qosi's on November 4, 2016 (http://jihadology.net/2016/11/04/new-audio-message-from-al-qaidah-in-the-arabian-peninsulas-shaykh-ibrahim-al-qu%E1%B9%A3i-khubayb-al-sudani-fifteen-years-since-the-launch-of-the-current-crusader-campaign/); Khaled Batarfi on July 27, 2017 (http://jihadology.net/2017/07/27/new-video-message-from-al-qaidah-in-the-arabian-peninsulas-shaykh-khalid-bin-umar-bat%CC%A3arfi-abu-al-miqdad-al-kindi-we-are-at-you/); and Qasim al Raymi on May 7, 2017 (http://jihadology.net/2017/05/07/new-video-message-from-al-qaidah-in-the-arabian-peninsulas-shaykh-qasim-al-raymi-an-inspire-address-1-a-lone-mujahid-or-an-army-by-itself/).
34. See Katherine Zimmerman, "AQAP: A Resurgent Threat."
35. Katherine Zimmerman, "2016 Yemen Crisis Situation Report, May 2," American Enterprise Institute Critical Threats Project, May 2, 2016, http://www.criticalthreats.org/yemen/yemen-crisis-situation-reports-may-2-2016; See also "AQAP Expanding behind Yemen's Frontlines," American Enterprise Institute Critical Threats Project, February 17, 2016, http://www.criticalthreats.org/yemen/zimmerman-aqap-expanding-behind-yemens-frontlines-february-17-2016.
36. Maher Farrukh, "Al Qaeda's Base in Yemen," American Enterprise Institute Critical Threats Project, June 20, 2017, https://www.criticalthreats.org/analysis/al-qaedas-base-in-yemen.
37. See for example, "Map 2: South Yemen – key military, political players" in Peter Salisbury's "Yemen's Southern Powder Keg," March 2018, http://www.

chathamhouse.org/sites/default/files/publications/research/2018-03-27-yemen-southern-powder-keg-salisbury-final.pdf.

38. AQAP claimed to have conducted 40 percent fewer attacks in April 2018 than in April 2017, for example. Tweet from Elisabeth Kendall, May 3, 2018, https://twitter.com/Dr_E_Kendall/status/991996288689496064.
39. Thomas Joscelyn, "Analysis: AQAP Remains Under Pressure," The Long War Journal, May 26, 2018, https://www.longwarjournal.org/archives/2018/05/analysis-aqap-remains-under-pressure.php.
40. See Katherine Zimmerman, "Province Ties to the Islamic State Core: Islamic State in Yemen," in Katherine Bauer, ed, *Beyond Syria and Iraq: Examining Islamic State Provinces*, Washington Institute, November 2016.
41. "Islamic State Video Promotes Destruction of Iraq-Syria Border Crossing," SITE Intelligence Group, June 29, 2014, www.siteintelgroup.com.
42. Katherine Zimmerman, "Exploring ISIS in Yemen," American Enterprise Institute Critical Threats Project, July 24, 2015, http://www.criticalthreats.org/yemen/exploring-isis-yemen-zimmerman-july-24-2015, slide 5.
43. Sheikh Hatem was killed alongside AQAP militants in al Mukalla, Hadramawt, on May 11, 2015. His co-location with AQAP indicates the continued relationship.
44. United States Department of the Treasury, "Treasury Sanctions Major Islamic State of Iraq and the Levant Leaders, Financial Figures, Facilitators, and Supporters," press release, September 29, 2015, http://www.treasury.gov/press-center/press-releases/Pages/jl0188.aspx.
45. "IS Leader Abu Bakr Al-Baghdadi Rallies Fighters, Welcomes New Pledges," SITE Intelligence Group, November 13, 2014, www.siteintelgroup.com.
46. Alexis Knutsen, "ISIS in Yemen: Fueling the Sectarian Fire," American Enterprise Institute Critical Threats Project, March 20, 2015, http://www.criticalthreats.org/yemen/knutsen-isis-yemen-fueling-sectarian-fire-march-20-2015.
47. Alexis Knutsen, "Ramadan Bombings in Yemen: Part of ISIS's Global Strategy?" American Enterprise Insti-

tute Critical Threats Project, June 17, 2015, http://www.criticalthreats.org/yemen/knutsen-ramadan-bombings-part-isis-global-strategy-june-17-2015.

48. Joshua Koontz, "2015 Yemen Crisis Situation Report: October 7," American Enterprise Institute Critical Threats Project, October 7, 2015, http://www.criticalthreats.org/yemen/yemen-crisis-situation-reports-october-7-2015.
49. Jon Diamond and Katherine Zimmerman, "Challenging the Yemeni State: ISIS in Aden and al Mukalla," American Enterprise Institute Critical Threats Project, June 9, 2016, http://www.criticalthreats.org/yemen/zimmerman-diamond-challenging-yemeni-state-isis-in-aden-al-mukalla-june-9-2016.
50. Maher Farrukh and Hamsa Fayed, "Yemen Situation Report," AEI's Critical Threats Project, November 22, 2016, https://www.criticalthreats.org/briefs/yemen-situation-report/2016-yemen-crisis-situation-report-november-22.
51. Maher Farrukh, "Yemen Situation Report," Critical Threats Project at the American Enterprise Institute, October 30, 2017, https://www.criticalthreats.org/briefs/yemen-situation-report/2017-yemen-crisis-situation-report-october-30; and Maher Farrukh, Coy Ozias, and Tyler Parker, "Yemen Situation Report," Critical Threats Project at the American Enterprise Institute, August 11, 2017, https://www.criticalthreats.org/briefs/yemen-situation-report/2017-yemen-crisis-situation-report-august-11.
52. Maher Farrukh, "Yemen Situation Report," Critical Threats Project at the American Enterprise Institute, November 22, 2017, https://www.criticalthreats.org/briefs/yemen-situation-report/2017-yemen-crisis-situation-report-november-22; and Maher Farrukh and Katherine Zimmerman, "Yemen Situation Report," Critical Threats Project at the American Enterprise Institute, March 1, 2018, https://www.criticalthreats.org/briefs/yemen-situation-report/2018-yemen-crisis-situation-report-march-1.
53. See Bill Roggio and Thomas Joscelyn, "Divisions Emerge within the Islamic State's Yemen 'Prov-

ince,'" *Long War Journal*, December 23, 2015, http://www.longwarjournal.org/archives/2015/12/divisions-emerge-within-the-islamic-states-yemen-province.php.

54. Mohammed Mukhashaf, "At least six killed in Yemen suicide bombing claimed by the Islamic State," Reuters, November 14, 2017, https://www.reuters.com/article/us-yemen-security/at-least-six-killed-in-yemen-suicide-bombing-claimed-by-islamic-state-idUSKBN1DE0LP; and "At least 14 killed in attack on Yemen counter-terrorism base, Islamic State claims responsibility," ABC (Australia), February 25, 2018, http://www.abc.net.au/news/2018-02-25/14-dead-in-attack-in-yemen-islamic-state-claims-responsibility/9482912.
55. Barbara Starr and Zachary Cohen, "First US Airstrike Targeting ISIS in Yemen Kills Dozens," CNN, October 16, 2017, https://www.cnn.com/2017/10/16/politics/us-isis-training-camp-strike-yemen/index.html.
56. Hamida Ghafour, "Rebel Without A Clear Cause," *The National* (Abu Dhabi), August 21, 2009, http://www.thenational.ae/apps/pbcs.dll/article?AID=/20090822/WEEKENDER/708219838/1306; See also Christopher Harnisch, A Critical War in a Fragile Country: Yemen's Battle with the Shiite al Houthi Rebels," American Enterprise Institute Critical Threats Project, August 31, 2009, http://www.criticalthreats.org/yemen/critical-war-fragile-country-yemens-battle-shiite-al-houthi-rebels#_edn3.
57. Bonnefoy, "Varieties Of Islamism In Yemen."
58. "Yemeni Government Steps Up Assault On Shiite Rebels," *Wall Street Journal*, August 12, 2009, http://online.wsj.com/article/SB125007847389825757.html?mod=googlenews_wsj.
59. Ghafour, "Rebel Without A Clear Cause."
60. Katherine Zimmerman and Steve Gonzalez, "Tracker: Saudi Arabia's Military Operations Along Yemeni Border | Critical Threats," American Enterprise Institute Critical Threats Project, January 4, 2010, http://www.criticalthreats.org/yemen/tracker-saudi-arabia%E2%80%99s-military-operations-along-yemeni-border.

61. Glen Carey, "Saudi Arabia Barricades Its Border, U.S.-Style," *BusinessWeek*, June 27, 2013, http://www.businessweek.com/articles/2013-06-27/saudi-arabia-barricades-its-border-u-dot-s-dot-style.
62. "Saudi Arabia Deports 427,000 Foreigners in Six Months," *Gulf News*, April 27, 2014, http://gulfnews.com/news/gulf/saudi-arabia/saudi-arabia-deports-427-000-foreigners-in-six-months-1.1324727.
63. "Oman Considers Building a Fence on Borders with Yemen," *National Yemen*, June 1, 2013, http://nationalyemen.com/2013/06/01/oman-considers-building-a-fence-on-borders-with- yemen/.
64. "Houthi Official Denies Receiving Arms from Iran," *The National* (Abu Dhabi), March 16, 2012, http://www.thenational.ae/news/world/middle-east/houthi-official-denies-receiving-arms-from-iran.
65. Eric Schmitt and Robert F. Worth. "Aiding Yemen Rebels, Iran Seeks Wider Mideast Role," *New York Times*, March 15, 2012, http://www.nytimes.com/2012/03/15/world/middleeast/aiding-yemen-rebels-iran-seeks-wider-mideast-role.html.
66. "Yemen Says Intercepted Ship Carrying Weapons Was Iranian," Reuters, February 2, 2013, http://www.reuters.com/article/2013/02/02/yemen-iran-arms-idUSL5N0B22GC20130202.
67. "Yemen Says Intercepted Ship Carrying Weapons Was Iranian," Reuters; Katherine Zimmerman and Steve Gonzalez, "Tracker: Saudi Arabia's Military Operations Along Yemeni Border," American Enterprise Institute Critical Threats Project, January 4, 2010, http://www.criticalthreats.org/yemen/tracker-saudi-arabia's-military-operations-along-yemeni-border; Ariel Farrar-Wellman, "Yemen-Iran Foreign Relations," American Enterprise Institute Critical Threats Project, February 23, 2010, http://www.irantracker.org/foreign-relations/yemen-iran-foreign-relations.
68. "Islah Party, Houthi Group Sign Ceasefire Agreement in Jawf," *Yemen Post*, August 13, 2011, http://yemenpost.net/Detail123456789.aspx?ID=3&SubID=3910.
69. "Yemen al-Qaida Commander Declares War Against Shiites," Xinhua, January 29, 2011, http://news.xinhuanet.

com/english2010/world/2011-01/29/c_13711741.htm.
70. "Sectarian Violence Continues in North Yemen, 30 Killed," *Yemen Post*, February 13, 2012, http://yemen-post.net/Detail123456789.aspx?ID=3&SubID=4706; "Death Toll Rises to 20 in Sectarian Violence in Northern Yemen," Xinhua, September 23, 2012, http://news.xinhuanet.com/english/world/2012-09/23/c_131867247.htm.
71. "At Least 40 Killed in Yemen as Houthi Fighters near Capital," Reuters, March 9, 2014, http://www.reuters.com/article/2014/03/09/us-yemen-clash-idUSBREA2805920140309.
72. "Representations in the National Dialogue Conference," *Yemen Observer*, March 18 2013, http://www.yemenobserver.com/national-dialogue/227-representations-in-the-national-dialogue-conference.html.
73. Katherine Zimmerman, "A New Model for Defeating al Qaeda in Yemen," American Enterprise Institute Critical Threats Project, September 10, 2015, http://www.criticalthreats.org/yemen/zimmerman-new-model-for-defeating-al-qaeda-in-yemen-september-10-2015, 7.
74. "Signing of the National Political Agreement Between the General People's Congress and its Allies and Ansar Allah and its Allies," SABA.ye, July 28, 2016, http://www.saba.ye/ar/news434879.htm.
75. "Gulf of Aden Security Review – November 29, 2016," American Enterprise Institute Critical Threats Project, November 29, 2016, http://www.criticalthreats.org/gulf-aden-security-review/gulf-aden-security-review-november-29-2016.
76. Final Report of the UN Panel of Experts on Yemen, January 26, 2018, http://www.un.org/en/ga/search/view_doc.asp?symbol=S/2018/68.
77. Final Report of the UN Panel of Experts on Yemen, January 26, 2018,.
78. Shuaib Almosawa and Anne Barnard, "Saudis Intercept Missile Fired From Yemen That Came Close to Riyadh," New York Times, https://www.nytimes.com/2017/11/04/world/middleeast/missile-saudi-arabia-riyadh.html; and Donna Abu-Nasr and Mohammed Hatem, "Saudis Down Yemen Rebel Missile Before It

Strikes Palace," Bloomberg, December 19, 2017, https://www.bloomberg.com/news/articles/2017-12-19/missile-fired-by-yemen-rebels-downed-over-riyadh-saudi-tv-says.

79. "Gulf of Aden Security Review," American Enterprise Institute Critical Threats Project, June 4, 2018, https://www.criticalthreats.org/briefs/gulf-of-aden-security-review/gulf-of-aden-security-review-june-4-2018.
80. Yara Bayoumy and Phil Stewart, "Exclusive: Iran Steps Up Weapons Supply to Yemen's Houthis via Oman – Officials," Reuters, October 20, 2016, http://www.reuters.com/article/us-yemen-security-iran-idUSKCN12K0CX.
81. Paul Bucala, Marie Donovan, Emily Estelle, Chris Harmer, and Caitlin Shayda Pendleton, "Iranian Involvement in Missile Attacks on the USS Mason," American Enterprise Institute Critical Threats Project, October 19, 2016, http://www.criticalthreats.org/yemen/iranian-involvement-missile-attacks-uss-mason-october-19-2016.
82. Final Report of the UN Panel of Experts on Yemen, January 26, 2018, http://www.un.org/en/ga/search/view_doc.asp?symbol=S/2018/68; and "Gulf of Aden Security Review," American Enterprise Institute Critical Threats Project, March 22, 2017, https://www.criticalthreats.org/briefs/gulf-of-aden-security-review/gulf-of-aden-security-review-march-22-2017.
83. "Al Houthi Leaders Arrive in Tehran After Meeting with Hezbollah Leaders," al Masdar Online, October 5, 2015.
84. Ariel Ben Solomon, "Report: Yemen Houthis Fighting for Assad in Syria," The Jerusalem Post, May 31, 2013, http://www.jpost.com/Middle-East/Report-Yemen-Houthis-fighting-for-Assad-in-Syria-315005.
85. "Gulf of Aden Security Review," American Enterprise Institute Critical Threats Project, July 21, 2017, https://www.criticalthreats.org/briefs/gulf-of-aden-security-review/gulf-of-aden-security-review-july-21-2017.
86. "Yemen," Central Intelligence Agency *World Factbook*, April 15, 2014, https://www.cia.gov/library/publications/the-world-factbook/geos/ym.html.

87. Bernard Haykel, *Revival and Reform: The Legacy of Muhammad al-Shawkani* (Cambridge: Cambridge University Press, 2003), 151.
88. Laurent Bonnefoy, "Les identités religieuses contemporaines au Yémen: convergence, résistances et instrumentalisations," *Revue des mondes musulmans et de la Méditerranée* 121-122, April 2008, 201-15; See also Bonnefoy, "Varieties Of Islamism In Yemen."
89. Bonnefoy, "Les identités religieuses contemporaines au Yémen.
90. "Popular Protests in North Africa and the Middle East (II)."
91. "Popular Protests in North Africa and the Middle East (II)."
92. Katherine Zimmerman's conversations with NGO workers in Yemen, fall 2016.
93. Katherine Zimmerman, "Signaling Saudi Arabia: Iranian Support to Yemen's al Houthis," American Enterprise Institute Critical Threats Project, April 15, 2016, http://www.criticalthreats.org/yemen/zimmerman-signaling-saudi-arabia-iranian-support-to-yemen-al-houthis-april-15-2016.
94. Bonnefoy, "Varieties Of Islamism In Yemen."
95. John O. Brennan, interview with Margaret Warner, "U.S. Policy Toward Yemen," Council on Foreign Relations, August 8, 2012, http://www.cfr.org/united-states/us-policy-toward-yemen/p28794.
96. Bonnefoy, "Varieties Of Islamism In Yemen."
97. Peter Bergen, *Holy War Inc: Inside the Secret World of Osama Bin Laden* (London: Weidenfield & Nicolson, 2001), 190-191.
98. Bonnefoy, "Varieties Of Islamism In Yemen."
99. Bonnefoy, "Varieties Of Islamism In Yemen."
100. Jillian Schwedler, "The Yemeni Islah Party: Political Opportunities and Coalition Building in a Transitional Polity," in Quintan Wiktorowicz, ed., *Islamist Activism: A Social Movement Theory Approach* (Bloomington: Indiana University Press, 2003), 205-29; See also *Faith in Moderation: Islamist Parties in Jordan and Yemen* (Cambridge: Cambridge University Press, 2007), 280.

101. "Representations in the National Dialogue Conference."
102. Zindani remains designated by the US as a Specially Designated Global Terrorist for his role in support al Qaeda in Yemen. U.S. Department of the Treasury, "United States Designates bin Laden Loyalist," press release, February 24, 2004, https://www.treasury.gov/press-center/press-releases/Pages/js1190.aspx.
103. Ashraf Al-Muraqab, "Yemeni Clerics Disapprove of their Exclusion From the National Dialogue," *Yemen Times*, July 4, 2012, http://www.yementimes.com/en/1587/news/1092/Yemeni-clerics-disapprove-of-their-exclusion-from-the-National-Dialogue.htm; "Yemen President Offers Conditional Dialogue With Al Qaeda," Reuters, September 26, 2012, http://www.reuters.com/article/2012/09/26/yemen-qaeda-idUSL5E8KQ5LF20120926.
104. Abd Rabu Mansour Hadi, "Yemen's Transition: The Way Forward," Address at the Woodrow Wilson International Center for Scholars, Washington, DC, September 28, 2012, http://www.acus.org/event/yemens-transition-way-forward; See also Greg Miller, "In Interview, Yemeni President Acknowledges Approving U.S. Drone Strikes," *Washington Post*, September 29, 2012, http://www.washingtonpost.com/world/national-security/yemeni-president-acknowledges-approving-us-drone-strikes/2012/09/29/09bec2ae-0a56-11e2-afff-d6c7f20a83bf_story.html.
105. See Katherine Zimmerman, "Yemen Model Won't Work in Iraq, Syria," *Washington Post*, July 17, 2014, https://www.washingtonpost.com/opinions/the-yemen-model-wont-work-in-iraq-syria/2014/07/17/ba0ae414-0d18-11e4-8341-b8072b1e7348_story.html.
106. White House, Office of the Press Secretary, "Remarks by the President on the Situation in Iraq," June 19, 2014, https://www.whitehouse.gov/the-press-office/2014/06/19/remarks-president-situation-iraq.
107. Ahmed al-Haj, "Fear Grips Yemen's Aden as Deadly Attacks Target Clerics," Associated Press, April 5, 2018, https://apnews.com/cb514ded6f284e81b3776575db3ebcd2/Fear-grips-Yemen's-Aden-as-deadly-attacks-

target-clerics.

108. Hadi's vice president is now Lieutenant General Ali Mohsen al-Ahmar, a powerbroker with deep ties into Islah networks, though it is not clear whether he will act to re-empower Islah. Recent reporting indicates he has sought to recast his political affiliations away from al-Islah party.

Sub-Saharan Africa

33 Ethiopia

> **Quick Facts**
>
> Population: 105,350,020
> Area: 1,104,300 sq km
> Ethnic Groups:Oromo 34.4%, Amhara (Amara) 27%, Somali (Somalie) 6.2%, Tigray (Tigrinya) 6.1%, Sidama 4%, Gurage 2.5%, Welaita 2.3%, Hadiya 1.7%, Afar (Affar) 1.7%, Gamo 1.5%, Gedeo 1.3%, Silte 1.3%, Kefficho 1.2%, other 8.8% (2007 est.)
> GDP (official exchange rate): $79.74 billion (2017 est.)
>
> *Source: CIA World FactBook (Last Updated June 2018)*

Introduction

The U.S. Department of State has described Ethiopia as "a strategic partner in the Global War on Terrorism"[1] and welcomed "Ethiopia's dedication to maintaining security in the region."[2] The country received high-level visits from then U.S. President Barack Obama and then Secretary of State Rex Tillerson, both of whom lauded the partnership between Ethiopia and the United States in addressing governance issues, economic growth, and regional security concerns. Tillerson, speaking from the Ethiopian capital of Addis Ababa in 2018, highlighted the "many touch points where [the United States and Ethiopia] share a common interest of security, stability for the region... and opportunities for economic prosperity."[3] The encomia are more than merited, both for the Ethiopian government's actions abroad and for the challenges it faces at home, which the most recent edition of the State Department's Country Reports on Terrorism summarized as follows: "The Government of Ethiopia's 2016 counterterrorism efforts focused on fighting al-Shabaab in Somalia and pursuing potential threats in Ethiopia. Ethiopia collaborated with the United States on regional security issues and participated in capacity-building trainings."[4]

Islamist Activity

As of May 2018, Islamist threats to Ethiopia's security are primarily external and emanate from Somalia.

While a certain amount of controversy surrounds the precise details of Islamism's introduction into Ethiopia, a bridgehead seems to have been established in and around the town of Harar fairly early on in the 20th century, perhaps during the Italian occupation (1936-1942), by pilgrims returning from the hajj. Later, in the 1960s and 1970s, a number of Oromo students returning from religious studies in Saudi Arabia further propagated political Islam, not only in their native regions but also in Addis Ababa and Wollo. The May 1991 fall of the Derg dictatorship gave new impetus to these trends, as many returning Oromo exiles had been influenced by Wahhabi doctrines during their time abroad, and the new government's policies facilitated contact with coreligionists in other countries, who supported the establishment of mosques, schools, and associations.[5] Among the latter were two entities in Addis Ababa: the Ethiopian Muslim Youth Association, founded in the 1990s and linked to the Riyadh-based World Association of Muslim Youth (WAMY), and the Alawiyah School and Mission Center, owned since 1993 by the Saudi-controlled World Muslim League's International Islamic Relief Organization (IIRO).[6] IIRO has also donated food and medical relief to Ethiopia following natural disasters.[7] (In August 2006, the U.S. Treasury Department formally designated the Philippine and Indonesian branches of the IIRO for facilitating terrorism.[8])

Like their Wahhabi confrères elsewhere, Ethiopian Islamists have attacked what they regard as syncretism among other Muslims, as exemplified by certain Sufi-inspired practices like pilgrimages to various shrines and the celebration of Mawlid (the birthday of the prophet Muhammad). More recently, some zealots have pushed for a stricter observance of what they regard as compulsory practices such as the wearing of pants above the ankles and the use of face coverings by women. The tensions within the Muslim community were further aggravated when a branch of Takfir wal-Hijrah ("Excommunication and Exodus"), a radical group which originated in Egypt in the 1970s, was driven from Sudan and decamped first to Gondar and, subsequently, to a northern suburb of Addis Ababa.[9]

The group labels most fellow Muslims, including other Wahhabis, as kuffar ("non-believers"). Although it has caused less of a sensation since the 2004 death of its leader in Ethiopia, Sheikh Muhammad Amin, the group continues to exist.[10] Details of the group's activities, capabilities and resources within Ethiopia, however, remain sketchy at best, although one well-respected researcher with extensive fieldwork on the Muslim community in the country has noted that Ethiopian adherents of Takfir wal-Hijrah refuse to recognize the national constitution, pay taxes, or carry identification cards.[11]

Al-Qaeda has also been active in Ethiopia. The organization has long viewed East Africa as a priority within its overall strategy. According to the Combating Terrorism Center at West Point, the nascent al-Qaeda, then based in Sudan, sought both to establish working relations with Islamist extremists in Somalia and create training camps in ethnic Somali areas of Ethiopia in the early 1990s.[12] When Ethiopia intervened in Somalia in 2006 and again in 2014, for example, al-Qaeda renewed its interest in targeting both the Horn of Africa in general and Ethiopia in particular. However, like with Takfir wal-Hijrah (above), accurate information on al-Qaeda's organizational make-up and capabilities in Ethiopia is far from complete, at least at the open-source level. Moreover, there are indications that the foothold al-Qaeda once held in East Africa through links to al-Shabaab has eroded, particularly as the Islamic State in Iraq and Syria (ISIS) has gained ground.

Another Islamist group active in Ethiopia is the world's largest dawa (proselytizing) movement, Tablighi Jamaat. Founded in India in 1929, the group first came to Ethiopia from South Africa in the 1970s. Its activities, however, were very limited until after the fall of the Derg, the Marxist junta led by Mengistu Haile Mariam that seized control of Ethiopia after deposing the Emperor Haile Selassie in 1974 and ruled the country until its own overthrow in 1991. Little is known about the group's activities other than that its center of operations seems to be the Kolfe district of Addis Ababa, where it is especially active within the Gurage community that has migrated to the city from their mountainous homeland southwest of there.

The principal Islamist threat to Ethiopia, however, comes from neighboring Somalia. Following the January 1991 collapse of the Muhammad Siyad Barre regime, the last effective central government of Somalia, the rise of al-Itihaad al-Islamiya (AIAI, "Islamic Union") posed serious challenges to Ethiopian security—a situation that would persist throughout the 1990s. While the AIAI's primary focus was on the establishment of an Islamist state in Somalia, it also encouraged subversive activities among ethnic Somalis in the Somali region of Ethiopia and carried out a series of terrorist attacks, including the bombing of two hotels in 1996 and the attempted assassination of cabinet minister Abdul Majeed Hussein, an ethnic Somali-Ethiopian whom the AIAI accused of being a traitor. AIAI's hostility to Ethiopia arose from its toxic mix of Islamism with Somali irredentist designs on Ethiopian territory. The exasperated Ethiopian regime finally intervened in Somalia in August 1996, wiping out al-Itihaad bases in the Somali towns of Luuq and Buulo Haawa and killing hundreds of Somali extremists, as well as scores of non-Somali Islamists who had flocked to the Horn under the banner of jihad.[13]

As it turns out, the defeat was only a temporary setback for Somali Islamists, who regrouped under the banner of the Islamic Courts Union (ICU) with many of the same leaders as AIAI. One such leader was Sheikh Hassan Dahir Aweys, who had served as number two in AIAI and went on to chair the ICU's shura and later head the Eritrea-based Alliance for the Re-Liberation of Somalia (ARS), after Ethiopian forces intervened in Somalia in December 2006 in support of the country's internationally-recognized, but weak "Transitional Federal Government." The presence of Ethiopian troops in Somalia, which lasted until early 2009, occasioned an Islamist insurgency spearheaded by the radical Harakat al-Shabaab al-Mujahideen ("Movement of Warrior Youth," more commonly known as al-Shabaab), a group that was labeled a "specially designated global terrorist" by the U.S. Department of State in 2008.[14] Subsequently, in 2012, the U.S. Department of State added seven al-Shabaab leaders to its Rewards for Justice program, offering large rewards for information leading to their locations.[15] In 2014, Ethiopian forces returned to Somalia as official contributors to the African Union Mission in Somalia (AMISOM), prompting renewed calls from al-Shabaab to attack Ethiopian forces in Somalia and at home. "We defeated Ethiopia before and we know how to battle them now," al-Shabaab spokesman Ali Mohamud Rage said.[16] Mounting protests and other security concerns within Ethiopia itself may affect the country's political will to continue its participation in AMISOM. However, the withdrawal of Ethiopian and other peacekeepers, including a reduction of 1,000 troops in November 2017 from the once 22,000 strong AMISOM force,[17] could further embolden al-Shabaab activities in the Horn.[18]

Fortunately, much of the pressure from this quarter has been relieved with the military and political setbacks suffered by al-Shabaab since the terrorist organization was forced to withdraw from Mogadishu in August 2011.[19] That said, the absence of a major al-Shabaab attack in Ethiopia is not due to a lack of effort on the part of the group; in 2013, two suspected al-Shabaab operatives were killed when the bomb they were working on exploded in a home in an affluent Addis Ababa neighborhood. No one else was injured, though authorities arrested five people for their involvement and reported that al-Shabaab planned to target an upcoming football match.[20] However, the resurgence of al-Shabaab activities in Somalia, portended by the horrific October 14, 2017 truck bombings in Mogadishu that killed over 500 people, will, undoubtedly, be closely watched by authorities in Ethiopia.

While the threat from Somalia is external, it cannot be entirely separated from the internal threat to Ethiopian national security posed by dissidents who align themselves with the country's foreign enemies.

Among the latter, Eritrea falls into a category all of its own, given the bitter two-year war which the tiny state precipitated in May 1998 when it occupied a small sliver of territory that had up to then been peaceably administered by Ethiopia. While the regime of Eritrean President Isaias Afewerki is not known for its religiosity, that has not prevented it from supporting Islamist movements that serve its overall strategic objective of undermining the Ethiopian government. To this end, it has at times in the twenty-first century lent support to the Islamist insurgency in Somalia,[21] as well as to the secessionist Ogaden National Liberation Front (ONLF) in Ethiopia, which has frequently partnered with its extremist ethnic kin in Somalia.[22] A foiled March 2017 attack by a non-Islamist separatist group on the Grand Renaissance Dam, a regionally contentious project that Ethiopia deems essential to its economic future, was blamed on Eritrea (although Eritrea denies the charges).[23] In June 2017, Prime Minister Abiy Ahmed announced that his government was ready to implement a long-neglected peace deal to settle the border conflict between the two countries; Eritrea responded announcing that it would send the first delegation in years to Addis Ababa to continue negotiations.[24] While nascent, the opening could prove a boon to regional stability.

Islamism and Society

Traditionally, the dominant ethnic group in Ethiopia has been the Amhara, who, together with the Tigray, currently make up about 33 percent of the population, according to the last national census (conducted in 2007).[25] The Oromo, who live largely in the southern part of the country, constitute another 34 percent. Other important ethnic groups include the Somali (6.2 percent), Gurage (2.5 percent), Sidama (4 percent), and Welayta (2.3 percent). Religiously, more than half of the country's population is Christian, mainly adherents of the Ethiopian Orthodox Tewahedo Church, an Oriental (Monophysite) Orthodox Christian body in communion with the Armenian, Coptic, and Syrian Churches. Evangelical Christianity is the fastest growing denomination in Ethiopia, with some 14 million Protestants counted in the country's last census.[26] Another 34 percent or so is Muslim, drawn primarily from the Oromo and other southern peoples, as well as the ethnic Somali and the Afar. Given that the population of Ethiopia is estimated to number more than 100 million, the country has more Muslims than many Muslim states, including Afghanistan and Saudi Arabia.[27]

Almost all Muslims in Ethiopia are Sunni, with a plurality, if not a majority, adhering to one or another Sufi tarīqa (order). The most widely followed of these is the Qadiriyya, although the Tijaniyya, Shaziriyya, and Semaniyya orders also have significant followings. Islam is most prevalent in eastern Ethiopia, particularly in the Somali and Afar regions, as well as in many parts of the Oromo region. While institutional Islam in Ethiopia tends to be decentralized, the Ethiopian Supreme Council for Islamic Affairs, formally established (although not accorded de jure recognition) in 1976, is treated by the government as "representative of the Ethiopian Muslim community" and accorded the same courtesies as the heads of the Orthodox, Catholic, and Protestant Churches in state ceremonial matters.[28]

Overall, especially in contrast to the rough times experienced under the Derg dictatorship, the Muslim community in Ethiopia has fared better under the Ethiopian Peoples' Revolutionary Democratic Front (EPRDF) government, which lifted its predecessor's restrictions on the hajj, ban on the importation of religious literature, and obstacles to the construction of mosques and religious schools.[29] The opening "produced a new consciousness among the Muslim population, generated new religious affiliations and paved the way for Islam in Ethiopia to become more visible."[30]

By and large, Ethiopian Muslims have resisted the attempts of radical co-religionists to promote political Islam. The main reasons for this failure of Islamism to gain traction include not only the deep roots of more traditional forms of Islam, especially those represented by the Sufi orders, and the strength of social ties that cross religious boundaries, but also the fact that the extremists have failed to offer concrete solutions to many of the problems faced by ordinary Ethiopians. By contrast, the government despite its limitations, has managed to deliver impressive rates of economic growth.[31] Nonetheless, the potential does exist for religion to be exploited to mobilize greater support by various separatist or extremist movements.

Beginning in 2011, tensions escalated between some parts of the Muslim community and the Ethiopian government, with the former accusing the latter of interfering in religious matters by allegedly trying to impose the quietist al-Ahbash sect on the country's Supreme Islamic Council. Protests over more than a year drew thousands, and grievances widened to include perceived government interference in Islam and in the selection of the Supreme Islamic Council.[32] In 2015, a court convicted eighteen Muslims who had been arrested during the protests under the country's anti-terrorism law.[33] Activists and some human rights organizations suggested that the trial of these Muslim activists—in addition to other, lower-profile cases—was politicized and not held in accordance with the law.[34]

In early 2018, four major leaders of the Ethiopian Muslim Arbitration Committee were released from prison as part of a larger act of clemency for political prisoners in Ethiopia. However, turmoil after the abrupt February 15 resignation of Prime Minister Hailemariam Desalegn and a subsequent state of emergency declaration by the government precipitated confusion in Ethiopia. Almost two months later, Abiy Ahmed was sworn in on April 3 as Ethiopia's new prime minister. As both the first Oromo and first Muslim to head the government, many Ethiopians—particularly young people—have placed their hopes for political reform in Prime Minister Abiy.[35] However, inconsistent policy—particularly surrounding Ethiopia's controversial state of emergency and Anti-Terrorism Proclamation—may provide inroads to external Islamist terror organizations if progress is not forthcoming.

Islamism and the State

Following the 1974 overthrow of the Emperor Haile Selassie, the communist Derg regime of Mengistu Haile Mariam persecuted religious leaders and discouraged the practice of religion by Christians and Muslims alike. Since the defeat of the dictatorship, and the subsequent assumption of power of the current government led by the Ethiopian Peoples' Revolutionary Democratic Front (EPRDF) in 1991, the policy has shifted to one of religious tolerance, although the formation of political groups on the basis of religion is forbidden. According to the State Department's 2015 annual report on religious freedom, the Ethiopian constitution "requires the separation of state and religion, establishes freedom of religious choice and practice, prohibits religious discrimination, and stipulates the government shall not interfere in the practice of any religion."[36] Also in 2015, "some religious leaders reported interreligious tensions were at a five-year low."[37]

Despite—or perhaps because of—this lack of domestic tension, the Ethiopian government has taken a significant role in regional and international counterterrorism efforts. It served as host for the African Union's Center for Study and Research on Terrorism and in 2008 ratified the Protocol to the OAU Convention on the Prevention and Combating of Terrorism.[38] From 2006 through late 2008,

Ethiopia led the efforts in Somalia against extremists connected with the ICU, and provided "critical support" to AMISOM in its efforts against extremist groups.[39] In 2014, Ethiopia intervened again in Somalia in support of AMISOM's effort to fight al-Shabaab. The U.S. State Department has generally considered Ethiopia to be an "important regional security partner,"[40] although funds for military assistance "are explicitly limited to nonlethal assistance, training, and peacekeeping support at present."[41]

However, Ethiopia's counterterrorism efforts have drawn mixed reviews. In 2009, Ethiopia passed an anti-terrorism law designed to discourage the formation and activities of radical groups within its borders, carrying penalties ranging up to life imprisonment and even the death penalty. Expressing support for terrorism was likewise criminalized: "Whosoever writes, edits, prints, publishes, publicizes, disseminates, shows, makes to be heard any promotional statements encouraging... terrorist acts is punishable with rigorous imprisonment from 10 to 20 years."[42] The legislation, while recognized as an attempt to combat extremism, has drawn criticism from Ethiopia's international partners and from human rights organizations who claim that the law's ambiguous language, as well as its uneven implementation, is an attempt by the EPRDF to cement its power and justify oppression of opposition groups and independent media.[43]

Others have pointed to the country's recent elections as further reason for concern. In May 2010, the EPRDF and its allies won 545 out of 547 seats in the country's parliament. While the lopsided results were partially attributable to divisions within the opposition, they nonetheless raised questions among some analysts about the future of democracy in the Ethiopia.[44] In May 2015, the ruling party's victory in parliament was further cemented when the opposition did not win a single seat.[45]

As of May 2018, widespread demonstrations throughout the country's two largest regions—Amhara and Oromia—were ongoing. Protests began in late 2014 over the government's announcement of a controversial land reallocation scheme; they have continued and expanded in scope to be broadly anti-government. While primarily peaceful, some protesters have engaged in serious property damage—especially affecting foreign-owned businesses.[46] Scores were arrested, and others killed in clashes with security forces.[47] During the height of the unrest, Ethiopian authorities imposed a ten-month state of emergency from October 2016 to August 2017, which allowed expanded powers to the security services; the government has thus far blamed the unrest on "anti-peace" elements from Eritrea and Egypt.[48] While the state of emergency was lifted in mid-2017, demonstrations against the government re-started at the end of the year. The resignation of Hailemariam Desalegn in February 2018 and his subsequent replacement as prime minister by Oromo politician Abiy Ahmed are positive developments. While the declaration of a new state of emergency on February 17, 2017 was cause for concern, its repeal two four months later is promising, as was Abiy's release of political prisoners, his proposal to amend the country's restrictive anti-terrorism law, and his shake up of the security services. While there is no overt religious element to the most recent wave of demonstrations, the Ethiopian government's claims of foreign meddling bear watching.

After the fall of the communist Derg dictatorship, a constituent assembly convened by the EPRDF government adopted a constitution in 1994 that carried "a radical recognition of diversity and of a new kind of equality."[49] Each ethnic community is accorded the right and duty to manage its own affairs under the aegis of a federal government that serves as the center for state unity. While it is too early to declare the success or failure of this system of ethnic federalism, it does raise the specter of struggles for allegiance between religion and ethnicity. It also creates the distinct possibility that Islam in particular may be used by groups seeking to mobilize their ethnic kin to exercise the secession that the constitution affirms is an inherent part of the "unconditional right of self-determination" accorded to every "group of people who have or share a large measure of common culture or similar customs, mutual intelligibility of language, belief in a common or related identities, a common psychological make-up, and who inhabit an identifiable, predominantly contiguous territory."[50] Against this potential vulnerability—which external foes, both state and non-state will be eager to seize upon—the Ethiopian government will need to maintain constant vigilance, especially as the country enters a new political era and its leaders try to maintain its much-valued stability and economic growth amid rapidly changing societal expectations.

Endnotes

1. U.S. Department of State, Bureau of African Affairs, "Background Note: Ethiopia," June 2009, http://www.state.gov/outofdate/bgn/ethiopia/82233.htm.
2. U.S. Department of State, Bureau of African Affairs, "Fact Sheet: U.S. Relations with Ethiopia," June 2016, http://www.state.gov/r/pa/ei/bgn/2859.htm.
3. U.S. Department of State, Bureau of Public Affairs, "Remarks: Secretary of State Rex Tillerson and Ethiopia Foreign Minister Workneh Gebeyehu at a Joint Press Availability," March 8, 2018, https://translations.state.gov/2018/03/08/remarks-secretary-of-state-rex-tillerson-and-ethiopian-foreign-minister-workneh-gebeyehu-at-a-joint-press-availability/.
4. U.S. Department of state, Office of the Coordinator for Counterterrorism, "Country Reports: Africa," in Country Reports on Terrorism 2016, July, 2017, https://www.state.gov/documents/organization/272488.pdf.
5. See generally Haggai Erlich, Saudi Arabia and Ethiopia: Islam, Christianity, and Politics Entwined (Boulder, CO: Lynne Rienner, 2007).
6. Terje Østebø, "The Question of Becoming: Islamic Reform Movements in Contemporary Ethiopia," Journal of Religion in Africa 38, no. 4 (2008), 421.
7. David H. Shinn, "Ethiopia: Governance and Terrorism," in Robert I. Rotberg, ed., Battling Terrorism in the Horn of Africa (Cambridge, MA and Washington, DC: World Peace Foundation/Brookings Institution, 2005), 98.
8. Press Release, "Treasury Designates Director, Branches of Charity Bankrolling Al Qaeda Network," U.S. Department of the Treasury, August 2, 2006, http://www.treas.gov/press/releases/hp45.htm.
9. Timothy Carney, "The Sudan: Political Islam and Terrorism," in ibid., 122.

10. Østebø, "The Question of Becoming," 422-423.
11. See Éloi Ficquet, "The Ethiopian Muslims: Historical Processes and Ongoing Controversies," in Gérard Prunier and Éloi Ficquet, eds., Understanding Contemporary Ethiopia (London: Hurst and Company, 2015), 107.
12. Combating Terrorism Center at West Point, Al – Qa'ida's (mis)Adventures in the Horn of Africa (West Point, NY: U.S. Military Academy, Harmony Project, 2007), 38-40.
13. Medhane Tadesse, Al-Ittihad: Political Islam and Black Economy in Somalia. Religion, Money, Clan and the Struggle for Supremacy over Somalia (Addis Ababa: Meag printing enterprise, 2002), 156-168.
14. U.S. Department of State, Office of the Coordinator for Counterterrorism, "Designation of al-Shabaab as a Specially Designated Global Terrorist" (Public Notice 6137), February 26, 2008, http://www.state.gov/s/ct/rls/other/des/102448.htm.
15. U.S. Department of State, Office of the Spokesperson, "Rewards for Justice – al-Shabaab 'Leader Rewards Offers" June 7, 2012, http://www.state.gov/r/pa/prs/ps/2012/06/191914.htm.
16. "Somalia Islamists Vow to Boost Attacks as Ethiopia Joins AU Force," Ahram Online, January 25, 2014, http://english.ahram.org.eg/NewsContent/2/9/92471/World/International/Somali-Islamists-vow-to-boost-attacks-as-Ethiopia-.aspx.
17. Harun Maruf, "AMISOM Says 1,000 Troops to Leave Somalia," Voice of America, November 7, 2016, https://www.voanews.com/a/african-union-force-begins-withdrawal-from-somalia/4104674.html.
18. Colin Lahiff, "Ethiopian AMISOM Withdrawals," Critical Threats, November 4, 2016, https://www.criticalthreats.org/analysis/ethiopian-amisom-withdrawals.
19. Bronwyn Bruton and J. Peter Pham, "The Splintering of Al Shabaab," Foreign Affairs, February 2, 2012, http://www.foreignaffairs.com/articles/137068/bronwyn-bruton-and-j-peter-pham/the-splintering-of-al-shabaab.
20. Aaron Maasho, "Ethiopia Says Arrests Five Suspects in Soccer Match Bomb Plot," Reuters, Decem-

ber 19, 2013, http://www.reuters.com/article/us-ethiopia-bombers-idUSBRE9BI14F20131219.

21. J. Peter Pham, "Eritrea: Regional Spoiler Exacerbates Crisis in the Horn of Africa and Beyond," World Defense Review, October 15, 2009, http://worlddefenserеview.com/pham101509.shtml; See also Ahmed Mohamed Egal, "Eritrea's Repayment of its Fraternal Debt to the Somali People," American Chronicle, November 4, 2009, http://www.americanchronicle.com/articles/view/126773.
22. J. Peter Pham, Testimony before the U.S. House of Representatives Committee on Foreign Affairs, Subcommittee on Africa and Global Health, October 2, 2007, http://foreignaffairs.house.gov/110/pha100207.htm.
23. Conor Gaffey, "Ethiopia and Eritrea Trade Accusations Over Grand Dam 'Attack'," March 3, 2017, http://www.newsweek.com/ethiopia-dam-nile-eritrea-562895.
24. "Eritrea to Send Delegation to Ethiopia for Talks," Al Jazeera, June 20, 2018, https://www.aljazeera.com/news/2018/06/eritrea-send-delegation-ethiopia-talks-diplomat-180620064351952.html.
25. "Ethiopia," CIA World Factbook, October 21, 2016, https://www.cia.gov/library/publications/the-world-factbook/geos/et.html.
26. Emanuele Fantini, "Go Pente! The Charismatic Renewal of the Evagelical Movement in Ethiopia," in Gérard Prunier and Éloi Ficquet, eds., Understanding Contemporary Ethiopia.
27. "Ethiopia," CIA World Factbook.
28. Hussein Ahmed, "Coexistence and/or Confrontation?: Towards a Reappraisal of Christian-Muslim Encounter in Contemporary Ethiopia," Journal of Religion in Africa 36, no. 1 (2006), 11-12.
29. Hussein Ahmed, "Islam and Islamic Discourse in Ethiopia (1973-1993)," in Harold G. Marcus, ed., New Trends in Ethiopian Studies: Social Sciences (Papers of the 12th International Conference of Ethiopian Studies, vol. 1) (Lawrenceville, NJ: Red Sea Press, 1995), 775-801.
30. Østebø, "The Question of Becoming," 417.

31. See Alex de Waal, ed., Islamism and its Enemies in the Horn of Africa (Addis Ababa: Shama Books, 2004); See also World Bank, "With Continued Rapid Growth, Ethiopia is Poised to Become a Middle Income Country by 2025," November 23, 2015, http://www.worldbank.org/en/country/ethiopia/publication/ethiopia-great-run-growth-acceleration-how-to-pace-it.
32. Ficquet, "The Ethiopian Muslims," 117-18.
33. U.S. Department of State, Bureau of Democracy, Human Rights, and Labor, "Country Report: Ethiopia," in International Religious Freedom Report 2015, 2016, http://www.state.gov/j/drl/rls/irf/religiousfreedom/index.htm?year=2015&dlid=256023.
34. Morgan Winsor, "Ethiopian Muslims Accused of Terrorism, Jailed for 22 Years After Obama's Visit," International Business Times, August 4, 2015, http://www.ibtimes.com/ethiopian-muslims-accused-terrorism-jailed-22-years-after-obamas-visit-2038177.
35. "Abiy Ahmed Becomes Ethiopia's Prime Minister," BBC, April 3, 2018, http://www.bbc.com/news/world-africa-43567007.
36. U.S. Department of State, "Country Report: Ethiopia."
37. U.S. Department of State, "Country Report: Ethiopia."
38. U.S. Department of State, "Background Note: Ethiopia."
39. U.S. Department of State, "Country Reports: Africa Overview."
40. U.S. Department of State, Bureau of African Affairs, "Background Note: Ethiopia," November 5, 2010, http://www.state.gov/outofdate/bgn/ethiopia/158887.htm.
41. U.S. Department of State, "Fact Sheet: U.S. Relations with Ethiopia."
42. "Ethiopia Adopts Strict Anti-Terrorism Bill," Agence France Presse, July 7, 2009, http://www.google.com/hostednews/afp/article/ALeqM5hMqgOlskPvo1m_dSE35D1rFeICNw.
43. Leslie Lefkow, Testimony before the House of Representatives Committee on Foreign Affairs, Subcommittee on Africa and Global Health, June 17, 2010; Human Rights Watch, "Ethiopia: Terrorism Law

Decimates Media," May 3, 2013, https://www.hrw.org/news/2013/05/03/ethiopia-terrorism-law-decimates-media.

44. Barry Malone, "Ethiopia Court Rejects Final Poll Result Challenge," Reuters, July 20, 2010, http://af.reuters.com/article/topNews/idAFJOE66J0RW20100720.
45. Morgan Winsor, "Ethiopia Election 2015: Ruling Party Declares Historic 100 Percent Victory in Parliamentary Polls," International Business Times, June 23, 2015, http://www.ibtimes.com/ethiopia-elections-2015-ruling-party-declares-historic-100-percent-victory-1979220.
46. William Davison, "Dutch, Israeli Farms in Ethiopia Attacked by Protestors," Bloomberg, September 1, 2016, https://www.bloomberg.com/news/articles/2016-09-01/ethiopian-protesters-burn-dutch-owned-flower-farm-in-north.
47. "What is Behind Ethiopia's Wave of Protests?" BBC, August 22, 2016, http://www.bbc.com/news/world-africa-36940906.
48. "Ethiopia Blames Egypt and Eritrea Over Unrest," BBC, October 10, 2016, http://www.bbc.com/news/world-africa-37607751.
49. Jon Abbink, "An Historical-Anthropological Approach to Islam in Ethiopia: Issues of Identity and Politics," Journal of African Cultural Studies 11, no. 2 (1998), 121-123.
50. J. Peter Pham, "African Constitutionalism: Forging New Models for Multi-ethnic Governance and Self-Determination," in Jeremy I. Levitt, ed., Africa: Mapping New Boundaries in International Law (Oxford: Hart Publishing 2008), 188-190.

Mali

Quick Facts

Population: 17,885,245 (July 2017 est.)
Area: 1,240,192 sq km
Ethnic Groups: Bambara 34.1%, Fulani (Peul) 14.7%, Sarakole 10.8%, Senufo 10.5%, Dogon 8.9%, Malinke 8.7%, Bobo 2.9%, Songhai 1.6%, Tuareg 0.9%, other Malian 6.1%, from member of Economic Community of West African States 0.3%, other 0.4% (2012-13 est.)
GDP (official exchange rate): $15 billion (2017 est.)

Source: CIA World FactBook (Last Updated May 2018)

Introduction

Mali continues to experience significant Islamist insurgent violence as Malian and international forces struggle to adequately police a plethora of Islamist and non-Islamist armed groups active in the north of the country. The current instability can be traced back to the 2012 coup d'état and subsequent rupture between the country's north and south (though tensions between the two halves of the country existed long before the coup). In the ensuing political turmoil, Islamist groups were able to take control of the country's north, prompting an international intervention led by France in January 2013. While French forces, with the assistance of Malian and international troops, successfully regained control of the major Northern towns, large swathes of the north remain unstable and insurgent groups launch frequent attacks against Malian, French, and United Nations forces still present there, as well as against civilian targets in the south. As the Malian government struggles to implement the June 2015 peace accord, a durable peace in the country's north remains elusive and Islamist activity is likely to continue for the foreseeable future. Deadly attacks persist, including the January 2017 suicide bombing in the city of Gao that killed 47 people.[1] Furthermore, the October 2017 attack that killed four American soldiers stationed in Niger occurred near the Malian border. The attack was eventually claimed by an Islamic State affiliate group.[2] Public trust in the Malian government, meanwhile, continues to erode due to its torture and murder of civilians.[3]

Islamist Activity

Mali declared itself an independent nation in 1960. Since that time, Tuaregs (a Berber ethnic group) that live in the north have repeatedly tried to declare their independence from the Malian government. The National Movement for the Liberation of Azawad (MNLA), a Tuareg separatist group, was formed in October 2011. MNLA is a secular group, but has allied with Islamist organizations at different points in its history.

Mali's current struggles with Islamism can be traced back to the 2012 coup d'état that overthrew the country's democratically elected government. MNLA-led rebellions in the north had restarted early in 2012. Many in the military were frustrated by what they perceived as a lack of support from the government in suppressing these rebellions. The soldiers, called the Green Berets, attacked the presidential palace in Bamako and deposed President Amadou Toumani Touré.

Upon taking power, the Green Berets established the National Council for the Recovery of Democracy and the Restoration of the State (CNRDRE). The group suspended Mali's constitution and dissolved its institutions, promising to restore civilian rule.[4] Within days, the Economic Community of West African States (ECOWAS), the UN, and much of the international community had condemned the coup, and in some cases ceased operations in Mali.[5] ECOWAS suspended Mali from its membership and imposed sanctions against CNRDRE.[6]

Meanwhile, the coup caused enough chaos to benefit the MNLA's cause. On April 2, 2012, the MNLA seized several major cities in the north, including Gao, Kidal, and Timbuktu.[7] The MNLA announced a ceasefire on April 6, claiming that they had enough land to form their own state of Azawad.[8] The country was split in two, with Bamako in control in the south and the rebels holding the north.

The MNLA sought the assistance of Islamist groups in its

rebellion. These groups included AQIM, Ansar Dine, and the Movement for Unity & Jihad in West Africa (commonly referred to as MUJAO, the acronym of its French name, Mouvement pour l'unicité et le jihad en Afrique de l'Ouest). In May 2012, the MNLA and Ansar Dine agreed to merge to form an Islamist state.[9] However, the union did not last long. Within less than a week, the two groups clashed over the degree to which sharia law would be enforced. Then MUJAO similarly united with the MNLA, and similarly fell out. Thereafter, MUJAO and Ansar Dine worked together to push the MNLA out of Gao in June 2012.[10]

In early December 2012, representatives of Ansar Dine and the MNLA agreed to a ceasefire with the government.[11] However, by early January 2013, Ansar Dine suspended this arrangement, accusing the government of preparing for war.[12] The Islamists then began aggressively moving south towards Bamako. By January 10, Islamist rebels attacked and took control of Konna, a town less than 40 miles from Mopti, where the Malian army maintains a strategic base.[13]

The French government responded by announcing Operation Serval, in which the French government would support Mali in beating back Islamist forces. With French support, the Malian army regained control of Konna on January 11.[14] African troops from the Economic Community of West African States (ECOWAS) also began deployed to the country.[15] French, Malian, and ECOWAS troops quickly retook northern cities and towns in the weeks that followed. However, upon retaking Gao, the French-led forces found themselves conducting counter-insurgency measures, similar to those needed in Afghanistan and Iraq, as the Islamists mounted a counter-attack in February.[16] In August 2014, Operation Serval was replaced by Operation Barkhane. With a mandate focused more on counterterrorism, the resulting 3000-strong force is headquartered in N'Djamena, Chad, and operates across Burkina Faso, Chad, Mali, Mauritania, and Niger. Operation Barkhane was still active as of mid-2018.

The Malian government has signed a number of ceasefires with several armed Tuareg separatist groups, including the MNLA. The most recent, known as the Algiers Accord, was signed in June 2015.

Among other things, the peace deal included provisions for former separatist fighters to be integrated into the security force in the north, better representation for the north in central government institutions, and the right for the northern region to form local institutions.[17] The implementation of the peace agreement has been stalled, most notably due the ongoing insecurity in the northern regions, a product of the numerous Islamist militant groups that did not participate in the peace process. After several postponements, local elections were finally held in November 2016 amid reports of violence and at least one reported kidnapping of a candidate.[18] In August 2017, the MNLA and the Platform, a pro-government militia, agreed to a fifteen-day ceasefire and peace talks.[19] In September 2017, the two groups signed another cease-fire agreement,[20] but discord continues.

Militant Islamist groups initially did not participate in the peace process, and remain active in the north as well as, increasingly, in the south of the country. While there are a number of distinct Islamist groups, membership between them tends to be fluid. As such, multiple groups tend to credibly claim responsibility for terrorist strikes. Analysts have argued that increased counterterrorism pressure from security forces will encourage further collaboration between Mali's Islamist groups.[21]

Ansar Dine ("Defenders of the Faith")

Iyad Ag Ghaly formed Ansar Dine ("Defenders of the Faith") in 2011. Ansar Dine expanded its reach and power in northern Mali throughout 2012. In January 2013, the group was estimated to have around 1,500 fighters.[22] As previously noted, the group initially worked with the MNLA to take over the north. However, differing positions over the adoption of sharia law caused the relationship between the two to deteriorate. Ansar Dine took control of Timbuktu, Kidal, and Gao in June 2012.[23]

As Ansar Dine took control of more and more of northern Mali, the group increasingly pushed a radical interpretation of Islam on Malians. On July 10, 2012, it destroyed two tombs at Timbuktu's ancient Djingareyber mud mosque, a major tourist attraction, angering the city's residents and drawing international condemnation.[24] The Islamist group banned alcohol, smoking, Friday visits to cemeteries, and watching soccer, and required women to wear veils in public.[25] It whipped and beat those who did not adhere to its strict interpretation of sharia law.[26]

As previously discussed, Ansar Dine formed and broke a ceasefire with the Malian government in late 2012 and early 2013. As the French intervention gained momentum at the end of January 2013, there were reports that members of Ansar Dine had crossed into Darfur, Sudan through Niger and Libya.[27]

In June 2016, Ag Ghaly released his first video in almost two years, issuing new threats against the West and commending recent attacks against French forces and UN peacekeepers.[28] On October 31, 2016, Mahmoud Dicko, the president of Mali's High Islamic Council, told reporters that he has brokered a truce with Ag Ghaly.[29] However, Ansar Dine immediately denied the report, calling the claim "completely baseless."[30]

Movement for Unity and Jihad in West Africa (MUJAO)

MUJAO is a West Africa-based militant Islamist organization that is allied with Ansar Dine and has ties to AQIM.[31] The group made its first public statement on December 12, 2011. Soon after its inception, MUJAO reportedly concluded an agreement with both Ansar Dine and AQIM to pursue a common goal of spreading Islamism across the region.[32] The group appears to target West Africa more than its compatriots. The group is largely made up of black African Muslims, rather than those of Arab descent, and identifies itself as "an alliance between native Arab, Tuareg and Black African tribes and various muhajirin ("Immigrants," i.e. foreign jihadists) from North and West Africa."[33] The group appears to fund itself through kidnapping activities.[34]

Like Ansar Dine, MUJAO initially had a truce with the MNLA as they jointly fought to take control of Mali's north from Bamako.[35] But in June 2012, MUJAO and its ally Ansar Dine pushed the MNLA out of the northern Malian city of Gao.[36] While Ansar Dine appeared to have taken control of Timbuktu with AQIM, Gao was held by MUJAO.[37] In the advance to Gao, MUJAO reportedly sacked Algeria's consulate and kidnapped seven Algerian diplomats.[38] Once in control, MUJAO imposed a draconian interpretation of sharia law on Malians.[39] In August 2013, a significant faction of MUJAO merged with a militant group formerly associated with AQIM to form a new group called Al-Mourabitoun.[40]

Al-Mourabitoun ("The Sentinels")

Al-Mourabitoun was formed in August 2013 following a merger between a breakaway segment of AQIM led by Algerian commander Mokhtar Belmokhtar and a faction of MUJAO.[41] Belmokhtar's faction, known as the al-Mulathamun Battalion ("the Masked Battalion,"AMB), had previously been part of AQIM, but split into a separate organization in late 2012 after an ongoing dispute with AQIM's emir, Abdelmalek Droukdel.[42] Belmokhtar became the commander of Al-Mourabitoun, and under his command the group claimed responsibility for the January 2013 attack on the Tiguentourine gas facility near Amenas, Algeria, which resulted in the deaths of 39 civilians.

The group aims to unite Islamic movements and Muslims across Africa against secular influences, with a particular focus on attacking French interests and French allies across the region.[43] However, al-Mourabitoun's own unity has come into question. In May 2015, Al-Mourabitoun co-founder Adnan Abu Walid al Sahrawi pledged allegiance to the Islamic State and its founder Abu Bakr al Baghdadi in an audiotape that was released to the Al Akhbar new agency.[44] Several days later, however, Belmokhtar dismissed the pledge, indicating that al Sahrawi's decision had not been approved by Al-Mourabitoun's shura council, a move that seemingly indicated a split in the organization.[45] In the weeks following, local Malian media reported clashes between factions loyal to Belmokhtar and those loyal to al Sahrawi.[46] Al Sahrawi's faction continued to launch attacks in the region, including on a military outpost in Burkina Faso near the border with Mali and on a high-security prison in Niger thought to house militants from Nigeria's Boko Haram and AQIM.[47] Following the Radison Blu attack in November 2015, reports indicated that Belmokhtar reunited Al-Mourabitoun with AQIM.[48]

Al-Mourabitoun has also been involved in several high-profile attacks against foreigners in central and southern Mali, including the August 2015 attack on the Byblos Hotel in Sévaré, which killed thirteen people, five of whom where UN workers;[49] the March 2015 attack on the La Terrasse restaurant in the capital city of Bamako, which killed five,[50] and the November 2015 attack on the Radisson

Blu hotel in Bamako, in which 170 people were taken hostage and nineteen killed.[51] The group has also launched attacks outside of Mali, including collaborating on an attack on the Splendid Hotel in Ouagadougou, the capital of neighboring Burkina Faso, in January 2016 and the March 2016 attack on the Grand Bassam beach resort in Côte d'Ivoire. In January 2017, al-Mourabitoun claimed responsibility for a suicide car bombing at a military camp in Gao. The attack killed 47 people.[52]

Macina Liberation Front (FLM)

The Macina Liberation Front emerged in January 2015 and is led by Amadou Koufa, an ethnically Fulani radical Islamic preacher. In the explosion of post-coup Islamist activity in Mali, Koufa rose to prominence after he led a joint AQIM, Ansar Dine, and MUJAO offensive against the town of Konna in early January 2013, the capture of which triggered the beginning of the French intervention in the country.

Notably, the group blends an extremist Islamic ideology with a local ethnic radicalism that is a product of increased insecurity and competition between ethnic groups in central Mali.[53] The term "Macina" refers to the 19th century Fulani-led Islamic Macina Empire that stretched across central Mali, and Koufa has proven adept at capitalizing on the sense of victimization among ethnic Fulani in the central region of the country. The group is reported to target its recruiting to young Fulanis by using local radio stations to broadcast Koufa's Fulani-language sermons, which draw on a narrative of a return to a mythical time when Fulani were the masters of a prosperous Islamic faith in West Africa.[54]

Membership in the FLM is estimated to be a few hundred fighters, and the group lacks the numbers to conduct more than small-scale attacks using improvised explosive devices (IEDs).[55] The FLM does, however, often collaborate with other Islamist groups to launch high profile attacks on United Nations peacekeepers and civilian targets. The FLM claimed a role in the November 2015 attack on the Radisson Blu hotel in Bamako[56] and in the July 2016 attack on the Malian military base in Nampala area of the central Segou Region.[57] The FLM continues to recruit from within the Fulani pastoral community; local Bambara farmers support the government-supported Dozo militia. The two groups clash frequently, leading to reciprocal revenge killings.[58] The FLM also exploits the government's continual human rights abuses, such as executions and extrajudicial arrests, to curry favor with the Malian population.[59]

Al-Qaeda in the Islamic Maghreb (AQIM)

Over time, AQIM has evolved from a local terrorist group seeking to replace Algeria's government with an Islamic one to an al-Qaeda group preaching global jihad against the West. Formerly known as the Group Salafiste Pour la Predication et Combat (GSPC), AQIM has its roots in the Algerian civil war of the 1990s. In Mali, the group has taken advantage of the country's sparsely populated northern regions, where the government has a limited reach. Mali's three northern regions—Timbuktu, Gao and Kidal—contain only 10 percent of the population while accounting for two-thirds of the country's land.[60] As noted by analysts, the group has periodically turned to smuggling and criminality to raise funds, but, at its core, it has remained a highly resilient and pragmatic Islamist insurgency.[61]

GSPC/AQIM, like many Islamist terrorist groups, finances itself through crime. Prior to its merger with al-Qaeda, the group achieved international notoriety when it ransomed 15 European tourists in Algeria in early 2003.[62] It received a reported sum of 5 million Euro.[63] In May 2007, AQIM kidnapped its first foreigner since 2003. Between 2007 and 2017, there have been a number of additional, high profile kidnappings that illustrate the group's continued ability to operate in northern Mali. The kidnappings serve a dual purpose for AQIM; the activity itself drives foreign investment away from the region, while the ransom payments bring AQIM cash needed for weapons and supplies.[64] In addition to kidnapping, AQIM also engages in profitable smuggling operations in the Sahel with routes going through northern Mali.

In 2016, AQIM and its affiliates launched at least 257 attacks in West Africa.[65] This dramatic increase in attacks—nearly a 150 percent uptick from 2015—underscores the group's ability to successfully recalibrate its strategy and tactics in the face of ongoing counterterrorism efforts and competition from other Islamist groups in the region.[66] According to the Long War Journal, AQIM affiliates launched 276 attacks in West Africa in 2017.[67] This level of activity continues; in April 2018, AQIM claimed an attack that killed a United Nations peacekeeper and wounded seven French soldier, and indicated that the strike was a retaliation against French operations that had killed AQIM members.[68] At present, no credible estimates of force strength for AQIM in Mali are available. While AQIM remains loyal to Al Qaeda leader Ayman Al-Zawahiri, the group is facing increasing competition from the Islamic State (ISIS).[69]

The Islamic State

While the Islamic State has historically not demonstrated a significant interest in Mali, the group's recent losses of territory and power in Iraq and Syria suggest that this may change. In the face of setbacks on the battlefield in the Middle East, the group has broadened its territorial scope and interests, and one potential new sanctuary is the Sahel region of North Africa.[70] One attack of particular note to the United States was the October 2017 strike in Niger that killed four U.S. Special Forces soldiers, as well as four Nigierien soldiers. The attack occurred in Tongo, near Niger's border with Mali.[71] An Islamic State affiliate from northwestern Africa claimed responsibility for the attack in January 2018, according to a statement attributed to jihadi leader Adnan Abu Walid al-Sahroui.[72] While Sahraoui left al-Qaeda in 2012 and pledged allegiance to the Islamic State in 2014, the depth of the connection remains obscure. Indeed, Sahroui's announcement was issued on a website typically associated with al-Qaeda. Furthermore, the Islamic State's more official media channels did not promote the claim.[73] This discrepancy has added to confusion over how much control the Islamic State actually has over this professed affiliate.[74] Nevertheless, the potential for Mali to rise in the group's interest and strategic planning cannot be ruled out.

Islamism and Society

Mali has a significant Muslim majority, with 94.8 percent of the population adhering to the Islamic faith.[75] While the north has experienced a significant uptick in Islamist activity, it is not clear that radical ideology has actually gained a significant foothold across the country. The Islamists, their radical teachings and their imposition of justice have reportedly not been embraced by northerners, many of whom have simply fled into refugee camps in neighboring Mauritania, Burkina Faso, and Niger.[76]

Malian Islam is not typical of that found in other Islamic nations. The country's practice of the religion incorporates animist traditions from the region, including "absorbing mystical elements [and] ancestor veneration."[77] Mali's lengthy history figures prominently in the country's contemporary culture; Malians "regularly invoke Muslim rulers of various pre-colonial states and empires and past Muslim clerics, saints, and miracle-workers from the distant and more recent colonial and post-colonial past."[78] Islam and animism, in other words, have coexisted in Mali for centuries.[79]

Since Islamists took over the north, several French MPs have received reports that Qatar was financing the MNLA, Ansar Dine, and MUJAO.[80] Iran has also attempted to peddle influence in Mali.[81] Malian officials, however, have disparaged such efforts. Before his ouster, President Toure commented that: "Mali is a very old Islamic country where tolerance is part of our tradition."[82]

When Islamists were in control of the north, they sought to impose their beliefs on the region and purge Mali of religious diversity. There have been several instances of Islamist militants destroying shrines and mausoleums in the north, particularly in Timbuktu, claiming that the veneration of Sufi saints and scholars was sacrilegious. Sixteen of the mausoleums destroyed as part of this effort were listed as UNESCO World Heritage Sites.[83] The destruction of these historic shrines was recently ruled a war crime by the International Criminal Court, which sentenced one fighter involved, Ahmad al-Mahdi, to nine years in prison for his participation.[84]

While the population of the north initially welcomed the French intervention, frustrations have grown as the French and the United Nations Multidimensional Integrated Stabilization Mission in Mali (MINUSMA) peacekeepers continue to struggle to effectively provide security. There has also been discontent among northern populations regarding certain provisions of the 2015 Algiers Accord. In July of 2016, three were killed and dozens wounded when the Malian military open fired on protestors demonstrating against the nomination of former armed militants as local government authorities, as specified by Algiers Accord.[85]

Armed non-state actors remain a continual problem in Mali, and young people between the ages of 18 and 35 form the largest proportions of their ranks.[86] Almost 18 million people live in Mali, and nearly 70 percent of the population is under the age of 24.[87] A potential draw to militant groups for young people is a "governance vacuum," in which most rural communities feel ignored or abandoned by their government, while militant groups are seen as potentially providing greater protection.[88] Meanwhile, there are an estimated 140,100 Malian refugees who have been forced to flee the country, while estimates of internally displaced persons put that figure at 51,960.[89]

Islamism and the State

In keeping with the French tradition, religion in Mali "is understood as private and confessional."[90] The Malian constitution, adopted in 1992, maintains the country as a secular state. However, the 1990s saw a dramatic increase in the number of Islamic associations throughout the country, each with varying motivations and religious interpretations.[91] The government formed the High Islamic Council (Haut Conseil Islamique) in 2002.[92] While religious political parties are banned under the constitution, Mali's government supports the High Islamic Council as an "official and unique interlocutor of political authorities for all questions relative to the practice of Islam."[93]

The Bush administration began the Pan Sahel Initiative in October 2002 to train African nations in counterterrorism. [94] In June 2005, the program expanded to include more countries from the region, becoming the Trans-Saharan Counter-Terrorism Initiative (TSCTP).[95] The Initiative's Operation Flintlock provides anti-insurgency training to the armies of the seven participating states, including Mali.[96] Operation Flintlock has been reprised on several occasions, including in February 2016[97] and, most recently, in April 2018.[98]

In addition to American efforts to bolster their military capabilities, Mali and its neighbors have made efforts to coordinate their counterterrorism activities. Algeria held a conference in

March 2010 inviting leaders from Burkina Faso, Chad, Libya, Mali, Mauritania and Niger to build a joint security plan to tackle jihadists.[99] Subsequently, Algeria, Mauritania, Niger and Mali established a joint military base in Tamanrasset, southern Algeria, in April 2010.[100] Under Operation Barkhane, France has continued its counterterrorism operations and support in the region. In September 2013, in an effort to discourage the growth of radical interpretations of Islam in Mali, Malian President Ibrahim Boubacar Keita signed an agreement with the Kingdom of Morocco that would bring 500 Malian imams to Morocco for moderate religious training and make available to Malian students religious scholarships at Moroccan universities.[101] Furthermore, Mali's interim government asked the International Criminal Court (ICC) to investigate possible war crimes perpetrated by the Tuareg and Islamist rebels in the north.[102] In September 2016, the ICC convicted former fighter Ahmad al-Mahdi of war crimes.

Overall, the government response to Islamist groups has focused heavily on security solutions and building policing capacity. This has catalyzed two problems. First, heavy-handedness on the part of Malian security forces has tended to exacerbate local grievances and runs the risk of increasing support for Islamist groups. This has already happened to an extent with Mali's Fulani populations, and groups like FLM have found success recruiting among young Fulani populations disaffected after abuses by Malian security services.[103] Nevertheless, these abuses continue, including the deaths in detention of 27 men and the torture of two others in early 2018.[104]

Second, Mali's focus on security solutions has come at the expense of addressing local social and economic issues in the north of the country. Unfortunately, despite a close relationship between the Malian government and its international partners, President Keita's tenure has been hampered by allegations of corruption and nepotism.[105] Without improving trust in state institutions, service delivery mechanisms, and government accountability, it will be difficult for the government to effectively protect against the allure of Islamist groups to the young and disenchanted, and these groups will continue to capitalize on local crises and insecurity.[106]

From March 27 to April 2, 2017, Mali held a Conference of

National Understanding, as part of the requirements of the 2015 peace agreement. The conference participants recommended that the Malian government should open negotiations with jihadists, particularly Iyad Ag Ghali (a Tuareg leader associated with al-Qaeda) and Hamadou Kouffa (a Fulani leader also associated with al-Qaeda). The Malian government indicated interest in the proposal initially, but its French allies expressed a lack of enthusiasm with the idea.[107] However, some Malians remain interested in such negotiation as a possible pathway to peace, especially as military methods have failed to drive jihadists out of Mali. Furthermore, some feel that the government should accept the recommendation of the Conference as a sign of greater accountability to the Malian people.[108] Elections have been postponed repeatedly due to security concerns in years past. A new presidential election will be held on July 29, 2018. Regional elections, meanwhile, have been pushed to the end of 2018.[109] Both are likely to be affected by the current state of security in the country, and by the ongoing fight against Islamic extremism.

Endnotes

1. Angela Dewan, "Mali suicide bombing: Al Qaeda-linked group claims responsibility," CNN.com, January 19, 2017, https://www.cnn.com/2017/01/19/africa/mali-military-bombing/index.html.
2. Rukmini Callimachi, "ISIS Affiliate Claims October Attack on U.S. Troops in Niger," *The New York Times*, January 13, 2018, https://www.nytimes.com/2018/01/13/world/africa/niger-isis-green-berets-attack.html.
3. "Mali: Deaths, Torture in Army Detention," Human Rights Watch, April 9, 2018, https://www.hrw.org/news/2018/04/09/mali-deaths-torture-army-detention.
4. Adam Nossiter, "Soldiers Overthrow Mali Government in Setback for Democracy in Africa," *The New York Times*, March 22, 2012, http://www.nytimes.com/2012/03/23/world/africa/mali-coup-france-calls-for-elections.html?pagewanted=all.
5. ECOWAS, "ECOWAS Statement on the Disturbances

in Bamko, Mali," March 21, 2012, http://www.ecowas.int/publications/en/statement/mali21032012.pdf; "UN Condemns Political Instability in Mali After Armed Rebellion," UN News Centre, March 22, 2012, http://www.un.org/apps/news/story.asp?NewsID=41604&Cr=Tuareg&Cr1; Corey Flintoff, "Mali's Coup: Echoes of a Turbulent Past," *National Public Radio*, March 23, 2012, http://www.npr.org/2012/03/23/149223151/malis-coup-a-setback-for-a-young-african-democracy.

6. Emergency Mini-Summit of ECOWAS Heads of State and Government on the Situation in Mali (The Economic Community of West African States, March 29, 2012), 19, (http://www.ecowas.int/publications/en/communique_final/mini-sommet/comfinal_mali_2012.pdf.
7. Neal Conan and Ofeibea Quist-Arcton, "Turmoil in Mali Deepens After Military Coup," *National Public Radio*, April 5, 2012, http://www.npr.org/2012/04/05/150072681/a-military-coup-creates-political-crisis-in-mali.
8. "Mali Rebels Announce Ceasefire," ABC News, April 6, 2012, http://www.abc.net.au/news/2012-04-06/mali-rebels-announce-ceasefire/3936824.
9. "Mali Tuareg and Islamist Rebels Agree on Islamist State," BBC, May 27, 2012, http://www.bbc.co.uk/news/world-africa-18224004?print=true.
10. "Mali: Islamists Seize Gao from Tuareg Rebels," BBC, June 27, 2012, http://www.bbc.co.uk/news/world-africa-18610618?print=true.
11. Monica Mark, "Mali Rebel Groups Agree Ceasefire," *The Guardian* (London), December 5, 2012, http://www.guardian.co.uk/world/2012/dec/05/malian-rebel-groups-agree-ceasefire.
12. "Mali Islamist Group 'Suspends' Ceasefire," *Voice of America News*, January 4, 2013, http://www.voanews.com/content/mali-islamist-group-suspends-ceasefire/1577693.html.
13. Afua Hirsch, "French Troops Arrive in Mali to Stem Rebel Advance," *The Guardian* (London), January 11, 2013, http://www.guardian.co.uk/world/2013/jan/11/france-intervene-mali-conflict.
14. Afua Hirsch, "French Troops Arrive in Mali to Stem

Rebel Advance."

15. Christopher Isiguzo and Damilola Oyedele, "Nigeria: Air Force Sends War Planes to Mali Thursday," *ThisDay*, January 17, 2013, http://allafrica.com/stories/201301170615.html.
16. David Lewis, "In Mali Town, Counter-Insurgency Task Ties Down French," Reuters, February 14, 2013, http://www.reuters.com/article/2013/02/14/us-mali-rebels-gao-idUSBRE91D1EV20130214.
17. "Malian rivals sign peace deal," *Al Jazeera* (Doha), June 21, 2015, http://www.aljazeera.com/news/2015/06/malian-rivals-sign-peace-deal-150620173301883.html.
18. Adama Diarra and Souleymane Ag Anara, "Mali's Local Elections Marred by Boycotts, Kidnapping," Reuters, November 20, 2016, http://www.reuters.com/article/us-mali-elections-idUSKBN13F0R8?il=0.
19. Kaourou Magassa and Oliver Monnier, "Armed Groups in Mali Agree To Truce as Peace Talks Start," *Bloomberg Politics*, August 24, 2017, https://www.bloomberg.com/news/articles/2017-08-24/armed-groups-in-mali-agree-to-truce-as-peace-talks-start.
20. The Associated Press, "Rival Tuareg groups in Mali sign new ceasefire agreement," Washington's Top News, September 21, 2017, https://wtop.com/africa/2017/09/rival-tuareg-groups-in-mali-sign-new-ceasefire-agreement/.
21. Rida Lyammouri, "Attack Highlights Poor Resources of Malian Army and Underscores Collaboration between Islamist Militants," IHS Jane's Terrorism and Insurgency Monitor 16, iss. 8, September 2016.
22. "'Lion of the Desert': Ex-Partner of Germany Leads Malian Islamists," Der Speigel (Hamburg), January 13, 2013, http://www.spiegel.de/international/world/leader-of-malian-islamists-once-helped-german-government-a-878724.html.
23. "'Lion of the Desert': Ex-Partner of Germany Leads Malian Islamists," Der Speigel.
24. "Ansar Dine Destroy More Shrines in Mali," Al Jazeera (Doha), July 10, 2012, http://www.aljazeera.com/news/africa/2012/07/201271012301347496.html.
25. Michael Lambert and Jason Warner, "Who is An-

sar Dine?" CNN, August 14, 2012, http://globalpublicsquare.blogs.cnn.com/2012/08/14/who-are-ansar-dine/.

26. Adam Nossiter, "Burkina Faso Official Goes to Islamist-Held Northern Mali in Effort to Avert War," New York Times, August 7, 2012, http://www.nytimes.com/2012/08/08/world/africa/burkina-faso-official-visits-mali-in-effort-to-avert-war.html?gwh=.
27. "Chad Told France That Mali Rebels May Have Entered Sudan – Diplomat," Sudan Tribune, February 26, 2013, http://allafrica.com/stories/201302270345.html.
28. Conor Gaffey, "Who is Iyad Ag Ghaly, Mali's Veteran Jihadi?" Newsweek, June 29, 2016, http://www.newsweek.com/who-iyad-ag-ghaly-malis-veteran-jihadi-475473.
29. Idriss Fall, "Mal: Insurgent Group Accepts Ceasefire but With Conditions," Voice of America, October 31, 2016, http://www.voanews.com/a/mali-insurgent-group-ansar-dine-accepts-cease-fire/3573301.html.
30. "Mali Islamists Still Waging War, Dismiss Ceasefire Report," Voice of America, November 2, 2016, http://www.voanews.com/a/mali-dicko-ansar-dine/3576634.html.
31. Nossiter, "Burkina Faso Official Goes to Islamist-Held Northern Mali in Effort to Avert War."
32. "Some Things We May Think About MUJWA," The Moor Next Door, May 30, 2012, http://themoornextdoor.wordpress.com/2012/05/30/somethings-we-think-about-mujwa/.
33. Andrew McGregor, "Islamist Groups Mount Joint Offensive in Mali," Jamestown Foundation Militant Leadership Monitor XI, iss. 1, January 10, 2013, https://jamestown.org/wp-content/uploads/2013/01/TM_011_Issue01_01.pdf.
34. Sanders and Moseley, "A Political, Security and Humanitarian Crisis: Northern Mali."
35. "'Dozens killed' in Northern Mali Fighting," Al Jazeera (Doha), June 28, 2012, http://www.aljazeera.com/news/africa/2012/06/2012628917381524 74.html.
36. "'Dozens killed' in Northern Mali Fighting," Al Jazeera.

37. Nossiter, "Burkina Faso Official Goes to Islamist-Held Northern Mali in Effort to Avert War."
38. "Some Things We May Think About MUJWA," The Moor Next Door.
39. Serge Daniel, "North Mali Residents Ready to Resist Islamist Groups," American Free Press, August 14, 2012, http://www.google.com/hostednews/afp/article/ALeqM5jG2uPsDfGOXCBXusjGHvLzlmNvBQ?docId=CNG.5b6400c0bc73c4f95cd82e5991bf5f1a.231.
40. Bill Roggio, "Al Qaeda Group Led by Belmokhtar, MUJAO Unite to Form Al-Murabitoon," Long War Journal, August 22, 2013, http://www.longwarjournal.org/archives/2013/08/al_qaeda_groups_lead_by_belmok.php.
41. Roggio, "Al Qaeda Group Led by Belmokhtar, MUJAO Unite to Form Al-Murabitoon."
42. U.S. Department of State, Office of the Coordinator for Counterterrorism, "Country Reports on Terrorism 2013," April 2014, http://www.state.gov/documents/organization/225886.pdf.
43. Government of Australia, "Australian National Security: Al-Murabitun," November 5, 2014, https://www.nationalsecurity.gov.au/Listedterroristorganisations/Pages/Al-Murabitun.aspx.
44. Thomas Joscelyn, "Confusion Surrounds West African Jihadists' Loyalty to Islamic State," Long War Journal, May 17, 2015, http://www.longwarjournal.org/archives/2015/05/confusion-surrounds-west-african-jihadists-loyalty-to-islamic-state.php.
45. "Sahara Islamist Leader Belmokhtar Dismisses Islamic State Pledge: Report," Reuters, May 17, 2015, https://www.yahoo.com/news/sahara-islamist-leader-belmokhtar-dismisses-islamic-state-pledge-170310550.html?ref=gs.
46. Thomas Joscelyn and Caleb Weiss, "Islamic State Recognizes Oath of Allegiance from Jihadists in Mali," Long War Journal, October 31, 2016, http://www.longwarjournal.org/archives/2016/10/islamic-state-recognizes-oath-of-allegiance-from-jihadists-in-west-africa.php.
47. Conor Gaffey, "Niger Repels Attack on Prison Holding

Jihadis from Mali and Nigeria," Newsweek, October 17, 2016, http://www.newsweek.com/niger-repels-attack-prison-holding-jihadis-mali-and-nigeria-510618.

48. "Mali Extremists Join with Al-Qaeda-linked North Africa Group," Associated Press, December 4, 2015, http://www.cnsnews.com/news/article/mali-extremists-join-al-qaida-linked-north-africa-group.
49. "Mali Hotel Siege: Several Killed in Sevare, Four UN Workers Saved," BBC, August 9, 2015, http://www.bbc.com/news/world-africa-33833363.
50. "Al-Qaeda-Linked Group Claims Mali Restaurant Attack," Al Jazeera (Doha), March 9, 2015, http://www.aljazeera.com/news/2015/03/al-qaeda-linked-group-claims-mali-restaurant-attack-150309072613760.html.
51. "Two Arrested in Connection with Bamako Hotel Attack," Guardian (London), November 27, 2015, https://www.theguardian.com/world/2015/nov/27/two-arrested-in-connection-with-bamako-hotel-attack.
52. "Mali suicide bombing: Al Qaeda-linked group claims responsibility."
53. Michael Shurkin, "How to Defeat a New Boko Haram In Mali," Newsweek, September 7, 2015, http://www.newsweek.com/how-defeat-new-boko-haram-mali-369430.
54. "Mali Islamists Armed Group Push Fighting Beyond Conflict-hit North," Telegraph (London), September 23, 2015, http://www.telegraph.co.uk/news/worldnews/africaandindianocean/mali/11884570/Mali-Islamists-armed-group-push-fighting-beyond-conflict-hit-north.html; Yvan Guichaua and Dougoukolo Alpha Oumar Ba-Konaré, "Central Mali Gripped by a Dangerous Brew of Jihad, Revolt and Self-Defence," The Conversation, November 13, 2016, https://theconversation.com/central-mali-gripped-by-a-dangerous-brew-of-jihad-revolt-and-self-defence-67668.
55. Rida Lyammouri, "Attack Highlights Poor Resources of Malian Army and Underscores Collaboration between Islamist Militants," IHS Jane's Terrorism and Insurgency Monitor 16, iss. 8, September 2016.
56. "Mali: Une Seconde Revendication de L'attaque de L'hôtel Radisson," Radio France Internatio-

nale Afrique, November 23, 2015, http://www.rfi.fr/afrique/20151123-mali-revendication-attaque-hotel-radisson-front-liberation-macina-bamako?ns_campaign=reseaux_sociaux&ns_source=twitter&ns_mchannel=social&ns_linkname=editorial&aef_campaign_ref=partage_aef&aef_campaign_date=2015-11-23&dlvrit=1448817.

57. Lyammouri, "Attack Highlights Poor Resources of Malian Army and Underscores Collaboration between Islamist Militants."
58. Amanda Sperber, "What Can Save Mali?" IRIN, May 29, 2017, https://www.irinnews.org/special-report/2017/05/29/what-can-save-mali.
59. Sperber, "What Can Save Mali?"
60. William B. Farrell and Carla M. Komich, "USAID/DCHA/CMM Assessment: Northern Mali," Management Systems International, June 17, 2004.
61. J. Peter Pham, "The Dangerous 'Pragmatism' of Al-Qaeda in the Islamic Maghreb," Journal of Middle East and Africa, (2011) 2: 15-29.
62. Stephen Harmon, "From GSPC to AQIM: The Evolution of an Algerian Islamist Terrorist Group into an Al-Qa'ida Affiliate and its Implications for the Sahara-Sahel Region," Concerned African Scholars Bulletin no. 85, Spring 2010, 17, http://concernedafricascholars.org/docs/bulletin85harmon.pdf.
63. Raffi Khatchadourian, "Pursuing Terrorists in the Great Desert," The Village Voice, January 12, 2006, http://www.villagevoice.com/2006-01-17/news/pursuing-terrorists-in-the-great-desert/.
64. Michael Petrou, "Al-Qaeda in North Africa," Maclean's, May 11, 2009.
65. Caleb Weiss, "Al Qaeda linked to more than 250 West African attacks in 2016," Long War Journal, January 8, 2017, http://www.longwarjournal.org/archives/2017/01/over-250-al-qaeda-linked-attacks-in-west-africa-in-2016.php.
66. Anoar Boukhars, "How West Africa Became Fertile Ground for AQIM and ISIS," World Politics Review, November 29, 2016, http://www.worldpoliticsreview.com/articles/20556/how-west-africa-became-fertile-

ground-for-aqim-and-isis.

67. Caleb Weiss, "Al Qaeda maintains operational tempo in West Africa in 2017," Long War Journal, January 5, 2018, https://www.longwarjournal.org/archives/2018/01/al-qaeda-maintains-operational-tempo-in-west-africa-in-2017.php.
68. Associate Press, "Al-Qaida claims deadly attack on French, UN forces in Mali," The Washington Post, April 20, 2018, https://www.washingtonpost.com/world/africa/al-qaida-claims-deadly-attack-on-french-un-forces-in-mali/2018/04/20/7412b6ee-44af-11e8-b2dc-b0a403e4720a_story.html?noredirect=on&utm_term=.25d240b79d77.
69. Sergei Boeke, "Al Qaeda in the Islamic Maghreb: Terrorism, Insurgency, or Organized Crime?" Small Wars & Insurgencies 27, no. 5, 2016, 914-936, http://www.tandfonline.com/doi/full/10.1080/09592318.2016.1208280.
70. Kersten Knipp, "'Islamic State' seeks new foothold in Africa,'" Deutsch Wells, January 2, 2018, http://www.dw.com/en/islamic-state-seeks-new-foothold-in-africa/a-41977922.
71. "Islamic State affiliate claims deadly attack on U.S. troops in Niger," Reuters, January 13, 2018, https://www.reuters.com/article/us-niger-security/islamic-state-affiliate-claims-deadly-attack-on-u-s-troops-in-niger-idUSKBN1F20L3.
72. Callimachi, "ISIS Affiliate Claims October Attack on U.S. Troops in Niger."
73. Callimachi, "ISIS Affiliate Claims October Attack on U.S. Troops in Niger."
74. Callimachi, "ISIS Affiliate Claims October Attack on U.S. Troops in Niger."
75. "Mali," CIA World Factbook, January 2017, https://www.cia.gov/library/publications/the-world-factbook/geos/ml.html.
76. Kate Thomas, "In Limbo: Malian Refugees in Burkina Faso," Refugees Deeply, April 20, 2016, https://www.newsdeeply.com/refugees/community/2016/04/20/in-limbo-malian-refugees-in-burkina-faso
77. Lisa Anderson, "Democracy, Islam share a home

in Mali," Chicago Tribune, December 15, 2004, http://articles.chicagotribune.com/2004-12-15/news/0412150328_1_mali-islamic-cinq.
78. Soares, "Islam in Mali in the Neoliberal Era," 212.
79. Robert Pringle, "Democratization in Mali: Putting History To Work," United States Institute of Peace Peaceworks no. 58, October 2006, 27, http://www.usip.org/resources/democratization-mali-putting-history-work.
80. Ségolène Allemandou, "Is Qatar Fuelling the Crisis in North Mali?" France 24, January 23, 2013, http://www.france24.com/en/20130121-qatar-mali-france-ansar-dine-mnla-al-qaeda-sunni-islam-doha.
81. Willy Stern, "Moderate Islam, African-Style," Weekly Standard, August 4, 2008, http://www.weeklystandard.com/Content/Public/Articles/000/000/015/369mhred.asp.
82. Anderson, "Democracy, Islam Share a Home in Mali."
83. Joshua Hammer, "The Race to Save Mali's Priceless Artifacts," Smithsonian Magazine, January 2014, http://www.smithsonianmag.com/history/Race-Save-Mali-Artifacts-180947965/.
84. "ICC: Mali Fighter Jailed for Destroying Timbuktu Sites," Al Jazeera (Doha), September 27, 2016, http://www.aljazeera.com/news/2016/09/icc-mali-fighter-jailed-destroying-timbuktu-sites-160927093507739.html.
85. Kamissa Camara, "Violent Protests Have Erupted in Mali. Here's What is Driving Them," Washington Post, August 15, 2016, https://www.washingtonpost.com/news/monkey-cage/wp/2016/08/15/whats-the-role-for-malis-youth-after-the-2015-peace-accord-not-enough-protesters-say/?utm_term=.f9fe8717fb22.
86. Anthony Morland, "Why Some Malians Join Armed Groups," IRIN News, January 25, 2018, http://www.irinnews.org/analysis/2018/01/25/why-some-malians-join-armed-groups.
87. "Mali," CIA World Factbook, May 2018, https://www.cia.gov/library/Publications/the-world-factbook/geos/ml.html.
88. Morland, "Why Some Malians Join Armed Groups."
89. "Destabilization of Mali," Global Conflict Tracker,

May 3, 2018, https://www.cfr.org/interactives/global-conflict-tracker#!/conflict/destabilization-of-mali.
90. Soares, "Islam in Mali in the Neoliberal Era," 214.
91. Nicolas Colombant, "Mali's Muslims Steer Back to Spiritual Roots," Christian Science Monitor, February 26, 2002, http://www.csmonitor.com/2002/0226/p08s02-woaf.html.
92. Colombant, "Mali's Muslims Steer Back to Spiritual Roots."
93. Soares, "Islam in Mali in the Neoliberal Era," 215.
94. Harmon, "From GSPC to AQIM," 22.
95. Harmon, "From GSPC to AQIM," 23.
96. Harmon, "From GSPC to AQIM," 23.
97. Emanuelle Landais,"US led Flintlock counter-terrorism exercises end in Senegal, " Deutsche Welle, February 29, 2016, http://www.dw.com/en/us-led-flintlock-counter-terrorism-exercises-end-in-senegal/a-19083235.
98. U.S. Africa Command Public Affairs, "AFRICOM Announces Flintlock 2018," Press Release, march 9, 2018, http://www.africom.mil/media-room/pressrelease/30484/africom-announces-flintlock-2018.
99. "Al-Qaida Digs in to Resist Region's Armies," United Press International, July 6, 2010, http://www.upi.com/Top_News/Special/2010/07/06/Al-Qaida-digs-in-to-resist-regions-armies/UPI-14121278441085/.
100. "Brief: Saharan Countries' Cooperation Against AQIM," Stratfor, April 21, 2010, http://www.stratfor.com/node/160466/analysis/20100421_brief_saharan_countries_cooperation_against_aqim.
101. Vish Sakthivel, "Morocco's Move in Mali," Foreign Affairs, January 14, 2014, https://www.foreignaffairs.com/articles/africa/2014-01-14/moroccos-move-mali.
102. "Mali Asks International Court to Investigate Alleged War Crimes," Los Angeles Times, July 18, 2012, http://latimesblogs.latimes.com/world_now/2012/07/mali-international-court-war-crimes.html.
103. Boukhars, "How West Africa Became Fertile Ground for AQIM and ISIS."
104. "Mali" Deaths, Torture in Army Detention," Human Rights Watch, April 9, 2018, https://www.hrw.org/news/2018/04/09/mali-deaths-torture-army-detention.

105. Grégory Chauzal, "A Snapshot of Mali Three Years After the 2012 Crisis," Netherlands Institute of International Relations, June 8, 2015, https://www.clingendael.nl/publication/snapshot-mali-three-years-after-2012-crisis.
106. Anoar Boukhars, "How West Africa Became Fertile Ground for AQIM and ISIS," World Politics Review, November 29, 2016, http://www.worldpoliticsreview.com/articles/20556/how-west-africa-became-fertile-ground-for-aqim-and-isis.
107. Alex Thurston, "Speaking with Jihadists: Mali Weighs Its Options," The Global Observatory, May 25, 2017, https://theglobalobservatory.org/2017/05/jihadism-mali-al-qaeda-france-keita/.
108. Thurston, "Speaking with Jihadists."
109. "Date set for Mali presidential elections," eNCA, April 28, 2018, https://www.enca.com/africa/date-set-for-mali-presidential-elections.

35 Nigeria

Quick Facts

Population: 190,632,261
Area: 923,768 sq km
Ethnic Groups:Hausa and the Fulani 29%, Yoruba 21%, Igbo (Ibo) 18%, Ijaw 10%, Kanuri 4%, Ibibio 3.5%, Tiv 2.5%
GDP (official exchange rate): $376.3 billion (2017 est.)

Source: CIA World FactBook (Last Updated August 2018)

Introduction

Since its independence in 1960, Nigeria has been plagued by a number of organized militant groups. Among them are Niger Delta militants in southeastern Nigeria, whose grievances are based on extreme environmental degradation, as well as political and economic disenfranchisement. Additionally, there are ethnic-based militants in Nigeria's Middle Belt, where the predominantly Muslim northern region and predominantly Christian southern region meet. There are often conflicts among ethnic groups of different religions over land use. In recent years, Muslim Fulani herders have been increasingly arming themselves and killing Christian villagers in unprecedented numbers, albeit without any centralized coordination. Finally, there are Islamist militants in northern Nigeria, such as Boko Haram and also the potentially violent pro-Iranian Shi'ite Islamic Movement in Nigeria (IMN). These two groups seek to establish an Islamic state in Nigeria (for Boko Haram, a Sunni-Salafi state, and for the IMN a Khomeinist Shia state), to institutionalize Islamic law and an Islamic identity for the country, to pry Nigeria out of its alliances with Western countries, and to reorient it toward the Islamic world.

Since September 2010, Boko Haram has become the greatest threat to Nigeria's unity and has been responsible for more violence than any other militant movement in the country (although the Fulani herders may soon reach the same level of violence, if not notoriety, as Boko Haram). More than 20,000 people have been killed to date in the fighting. Millions more have been displaced, and close to 5 million need food assistance, due to Boko Haram's disruption of the local economy.[1] *Boko Haram is the most violent on the spectrum of Islamist movements in Nigeria, but it is divided internally between two factions, one of which is loyal to the Islamic State and known as the Islamic State's West Africa Province, or ISWAP. The other independent group is Jama'atu Ahlis Sunna Lidda'awati wal-Jihad (The Group for Preaching the Prophet's Teachings and Jihad, or JAS), which is loyal to Islamic State caliph Abu Bakr al-Baghdadi but is not recognized by the Islamic State as one of its affiliates. Both are referred to as "Boko Haram" by the media and government, although neither group refers to itself as such.*

Islamist Activity

In addition to ISWAP and JAS, which are northern Nigeria's most violent Salafist-jihadist groups, there are thousands of other Islamist groups in Nigeria, including millenarian mahdists, Salafists, and Shia fundamentalists. There are also many religiously moderate, albeit socially conservative, Sufi groups of the Qadiriyya and Tijaniyya orders, as well as Jama'atu Nasril Islam (JNI), a northern Nigerian Muslim umbrella organization led by the Sultan of Sokoto. In contrast to violent Islamist leaders, JNI has called on Muslims to "pray fervently for peaceful co-existence in Nigeria and for Allah to put to shame those who are bent on chaos and unrest."[2]

Nigerian universities have long been hotbeds of Islamist activity. Most leaders who are at the forefront of Islamic extremism in northern Nigeria have their roots in the universities, where they have been able to give theoretical cover to radical ideas and use academic platforms to spread their message. Two noteworthy trends in Nigeria, which are consistent with the rest of the Islamic world, are that youths are the primary demographic group susceptible to radicalization, and that men gravitate towards radicalization more than do women.

This section describes four of the most prominent Islamist groups in northern Nigeria: JAS and ISWAP (both commonly referred to as "Boko Haram" in media and government discourse); Maitatsine/

Kala Kato; Jama't Izalat al Bid'a Wa Iqamat as Sunna (Izala); and the Islamic Movement in Nigeria (IMN).

Nigerian Taliban, JAS and ISWAP (Boko Haram)

JAS and ISWAP both trace their lineage to Mohammed Yusuf, a Nigerian preacher who maintained his headquarters in northeastern Nigeria's Borno State. He primarily taught that Western education and influence were blasphemous because they contradicted the Quran, and that service in the Nigerian government was unacceptable, as Nigeria was not an Islamic State. Veteran al-Qaeda ideologue Abu Muhammed al-Maqdisi had a significant influence on Yusuf's adoption of a strain of Salafi-Jihadi ideology consistent with al-Qaeda's, although Yusuf did not explicitly cite al-Maqdisi in his sermons.[3] As Yusuf gained in popularity in the late 2000s, his teachings began to generate opposition from mainstream Salafists, who had previously mentored him; one such scholar argued that if Muslims follow Yusuf's advice, then "pagan policemen [who serve in government] will kill and injure Muslims, and when taken to hospitals pagan doctors and nurses [with Western education] will attend to them."[4]

Although Yusuf began urging his followers, who numbered in the thousands and hailed from Nigeria, Niger, Chad, and Cameroon, to prepare for conflict with the Nigerian government, he did not begin his career with a full-throated commitment to violent jihad.[5] This was different than some of Yusuf's more militant predecessors in a group then called the Nigerian Taliban, who were killed in late 2003 by the Nigerian security forces. After 9/11, they sought to engage in a jihad in Nigeria because they believed living in an un-Islamic state required immediate government overthrow.[6] They also had at least some level of communications with al-Qaeda's external operations in Pakistan.[7] Yusuf, in contrast to the Nigerian Taliban leaders, was more patient than his predecessors who were killed in 2003.

During his leadership of the organization (2003 to 2009), Yusuf's followers did not engage in coordinated violence against the state, although occasional clashes with Nigerian security forces did occur, usually because of the followers' refusal to obey local ordinances. In Yusuf's own words, he believed that sharia law "should be established in Nigeria, and if possible all over the world, but through dialogue."[8] Jihad, for Yusuf, was an option, but not as much of an obligation as it is to jihadists in groups such as al-Qaeda or Islamic State, or as it was to the Nigerian Taliban. Yusuf believed that a jihad could be delayed so long as Nigeria's Muslim rulers could still be convinced of their "infidelity" in ruling by secular laws and would be willing to change and adopt sharia laws after being convinced. However, the Nigerian rulers' continued resistance to recognizing their "infidelity" throughout the 2000s meant that jihad became an increasingly viable option for Yusuf and his followers.

Yusuf was killed along with approximately 1,000 of his followers in a four-day series of clashes with the Nigerian government in northeastern Nigeria in July 2009; Yusuf seems to have launched a jihad after he realized the current system in Nigeria was unable of changing itself to an Islamic system from within. After the clashes, Yusuf's deputy, Abubakar Shekau, and other followers announced a jihad against the Nigerian government and security forces, Christians, and moderate Muslim religious and political figures. This was the first time the group claimed a formal name: JAS. JAS's first attack took place on September 7, 2010, when approximately 50 fighters attacked Bauchi Prison and freed fellow members detained in the July 2009 clashes, making good on the organization's promise that these prisoners would not spend the holiday of Eid al-Fitr behind bars. It has since become known that Yusuf was cultivating ties to al-Qaeda in the Islamic Maghreb (AQIM) that Shekau activated immediately after he became leader. Once Yusuf died, Shekau, for example, sent high-level Boko Haram members to meet with AQIM leaders, who then offered Boko Haram financial and training support.[9] Shekau even sent a letter to thank AQIM for training and financial generosity after the Bauchi prison break.[10]

Since the Bauchi prison break, JAS has carried out more than 1,000 attacks and killed in excess of 20,000 people in an area of operations ranging from its hub of operations in northeastern Borno State to Kogi State in the geographic south of Nigeria, to Sokoto in northwestern Nigeria, to Diffa in Niger, to northern Cameroon, and to N'djamena and other villages around Lake Chad in Chad.[11] AQIM has, however, become opposed to Shekau because of his tolerance for killing Muslims or anyone who has opposed him.

At a minimum, JAS's main objectives are to: 1) remove religious authority from the Sultan of Sokoto and other traditional Muslim leaders and place religious authority in the hands of JAS's religious leaders; 2) create an Islamic state in some or all parts of Nigeria; 3) prosecute the security officers who killed Mohammed Yusuf and other Muslims; and 4) obtain amnesty for all JAS members in prison and compensation for the mosques and the homes of Muslims that have been destroyed in clashes with the government. Only the second and fourth goals have, to some extent, been achieved. Since 2014, JAS has controlled territory in parts of southern Borno State, especially around Sambisa Forest, Nigeria and as of 2017 mostly carries out sharia punishments in those areas. This is not as much territory as JAS might prefer, but may be sufficient for some of its commanders.[12] In addition, while many JAS members remain in prison, some hostage exchanges, including for 23 and 82 Chibok schoolgirls in late 2016 and early 2017, respectively, have led to the release of several key JAS members.[13]

Despite some of JAS's successes, its killings of innocent Muslims during attacks on the government and security forces—both as collateral damage and as a means to intimidate Muslims in the general population—has been one factor that has bred dissent among the movement's members. In late January 2012, a more internationally oriented faction of the group, which called itself Jama'atu Ansaril Muslimina Fi Biladis Sudan (Vanguards for the Protection of Muslims in Black Africa, or "Ansaru"), announced its formation in a video statement and in fliers distributed in Kano.[14] This occurred after Boko Haram's January 20th attacks left more than 170 civilians dead.[15] Ansaru has since been proscribed as a terrorist group by the United Kingdom for its alleged involvement in the kidnapping and killing of two British and Italian men in Sokoto State in March 2012, and for being "broadly aligned" with al-Qaeda.[16] Ansaru began raising its online media profile in November 2012, around the same time that its fighters carried out a prison break in Abuja.[17] Then, in December, Ansaru then kidnapped a Frenchman in Katsina, 30 miles from the border with Niger, and warned France that the prisoner's fate would be contingent on France rescinding the law banning the Islamic veil and ceasing its planned attack on the Islamic state in northern Mali (the Frenchman later escaped captivity).[18] In January 2013, Ansaru also kidnapped seven foreigners in Bauchi State and killed them the following month, after alleging that the UK and Nigeria were preparing to conduct a rescue attempt (one of the seven captives was British).[19] Ansaru also jointly claimed a kidnapping with the larger JAS in December 2013 of a French priest in Cameroon, who was later released for a multi-million dollar sum of money and JAS militants imprisoned in Cameroon.[20]

By 2014, however, Ansaru was virtually extinct operationally, although it continued to issue statements. Despite initially offering itself as a more "humane" alternative to JAS, three factors led to its demise: the French-led intervention in northern Mali in 2012-13, which separated Ansaru from its AQIM patrons, the arrests of key Ansaru members by Nigerian special forces, including those who received funding from AQIM, and JAS's assassinations of Ansaru commanders who defected from JAS. As the joint claim of the French priest in Cameroon suggested, Ansaru members, partly out of desperation, rejoined JAS and brought with them their kidnapping and media specialized skills, especially in the Lake Chad region. Some Ansaru members held out in Bauchi State until early 2015, when JAS leader Shekau pledged loyalty to Abu Bakr al-Baghdadi and the Islamic State. Ultimately, however, most of Ansaru appears to have been swallowed by the Islamic State in West Africa Province (ISWAP), or to have withdrawn from militancy and retreated to social media to continue propagating their beliefs.

Several months after JAS reintegrated the bulk of Ansaru into its ranks, a second major division occurred when Shekau pledged allegiance to Abu Bakr al-Baghdadi and the Islamic State.[21] In doing so, JAS officially became known as the Islamic State's West Africa Province, or ISWAP, in March 2015. Nigeria, under new president Muhammed Buhari, subsequently launched a large-scale military offensive against ISWAP, which caused the group to lose control of much of the territory in northeastern Nigeria that JAS had controlled prior to the pledge. These battlefield frustrations, as well as lingering ideological disputes between Shekau and the former Ansaru members over his tolerance for killing ordinary Muslims, ultimately led to a fracturing of ISWAP. The former Ansaru members who had rejoined JAS became recognized by the Islamic State as ISWAP in August 2016, under the leadership of Muhammed Yusuf's son, Abu Musab al-Barnawi.[22] Shekau, meanwhile, was compelled to leave ISWAP with his loyalist fighters, and subsequently announced in August 2016 that he was reverting to the name JAS.[23]

Today, both ISWAP and JAS remain active, with the former largely operating in scattered territory in the Nigerian the Lake Chad region, and the latter focused on disparate territories in Borno State. For the most part, the groups remain at odds with each other. Other factions more moderate than JAS have also reportedly offered to negotiate with the Nigerian government since 2012, but such groups have little credibility and have quickly disappeared from the scene. This is because JAS and ISWAP are behind almost all of the Islamist violence in northern Nigeria, and any truce with the factions other than JAS and ISWAP is likely to be inconsequential.[24]

Maitatsine/Kala Kato

Kala Kato, which means "mere man," in reference to the Prophet, claims to be an offshoot of the Maitatsine sect of the 1980s, which was led by the Cameroonian Mohammed Marwa. Marwa claimed to be a new Prophet of Islam and was known as the "Maitatsine," meaning "the one who damns." Even more extreme and eccentric than Boko Haram founder Mohammed Yusuf, Marwa condemned anyone who read any book other than the Quran, used watches, cars, bicycles, televisions, cigarettes or any other products that reflected Western life. An antecedent not only to Kala Kato but also to Boko Haram, Marwa and his thousands of followers clashed with Nigerian authorities in a battle in Kano in 1980 in which Marwa was killed. Subsequent battles to suppress his followers also took place in Borno State in 1982; Gongola State (present-day Gombe State) in 1984; and Bauchi State in 1985. In December 2009, Kala Kato engaged in a series of riots and clashes with the Nigerian security forces in Bauchi State, resulting in the deaths of 70 people, including soldiers, policemen, women and 15 children.[25] The cause of the clashes was Kala Kato's violation of an ordinance against preaching outdoors, which was imposed following the Boko Haram clashes of July 2009.[26] Kala Kato remains one of the most obscure Islamist groups in northern Nigeria, and its leader, Mallam Salisu, has maintained that it "has no link with the Boko Haram followers."[27] Kala Kato remains a small group of approximately 2,000 members, and likely will not have appeal to future generations of Islamists or jihadists, who are likely to see Boko Haram as a more "legitimate" group to join because of the credibility it has received from the Islamic State and its greater adherence to general Salaf-jihadi ideology. Nonetheless, Kala Kato and similar groups can be placed on a spectrum of heterodox forms of Islamic extremism that for the time being pose little threat of violence directed against the state, Muslims who disagree with them, or Christians.

Jama't Izalat al Bid'a Wa Iqamat as Sunna (Society of Eradication of Innovation and Implementation of the Sunna) (Izala)

The Izala movement in Nigeria is an anti-Sufi Salafist movement that opposes bid'a (innovation) and seeks direct interpretation of the Quran. It was established with funding from Saudi Arabia in the late 1970s, in part as an effort to quell then growing pro-Khomeinist leanings among northern Nigerian Muslims. It opposes the "Westernization" of Nigerian society, albeit while accepting modern technology and sciences and embracing women's education and financial self-sufficiency. With many institutions all over the country and influence at the local, state and even federal levels, Izala has become one of the largest Islamist societies not only in Nigeria, but also in the neighboring countries of Chad, Niger, and Cameroon. The implementation of sharia law in twelve northern states since 2000 has provided legitimacy for the Izala movement, which claims to have been the "vanguard" of the pro-sharia movement, although the inefficiencies and corruption scene in the sharia implementation since 2000 has led many Nigerian Muslims including not only those in Boko Haram to question the sincerity of Izala's sharia project altogether.[28]

Today, Izala's most important contribution to the Nigerian Islamist landscape may be simply that it is not Boko Haram and presents a credible and non-violent option for Islamists, even though in the early 2000s some Izala leaders had mentored Boko Haram leaders.[29] Nonetheless, the rising anti-Shi'a sentiment in Nigeria, coupled with broader anti-Iranian sentiment in Saudi Arabia and the Middle East, has positioned Izala also as the main anti-Shi'a group in Nigeria.[30] In this context, Izala may turn violent not so much as a facet of its Salafi-jihadism, but in an effort to clamp down on Shi'ism in Nigeria or inspire anti-Shi'a violence.

Islamic Movement in Nigeria (IMN)

The IMN is distinct from other Islamist groups in Nigeria because it is supported by the Islamic Republic of Iran, whereas most other groups (like Izala) are supported by Saudi Arabia and other wealthy Sunni Muslim sponsors. The leader of the IMN, Shaykh Ibrahim el-Zakzaky, has alleged that the IMN is only an "Islamic Movement," rather than either "Shi'a" or "fundamentalist," but the common perception of the IMN in Nigeria is that it is in fact a Shi'a movement.[31] Although the IMN's members are mostly Shi'a, the IMN resembles Izala and Boko Haram in that it believes secular authorities should not hold power and that northern Nigeria's traditional religious rulers have allowed government abuses against Muslims by supporting Christian politicians and refusing to stand up for Muslims.[32]

Throughout the 1980s and 1990s, Ibrahim el-Zakzaky and his followers petitioned for the implementation of sharia law, and sought to bring about an Islamic revolution similar to that which occurred in Iran in 1979. In the 1990s, followers associated with the IMN, who later broke away from the IMN and embraced Sunni-Salafism, carried out a series of attacks in northern Nigeria, the most gruesome of which was the 1994 beheading in Kano of Gideon Alakuka, an Igbo trader who was accused (likely falsely) of desecrating the Quran.[33] When sharia law was instituted in twelve states of northern Nigeria in 2000, el-Zakzaky believed there was an over-emphasis on corporal punishments; that the northern governors were illegitimate since they did not come to power through Islamic parties; and that the governors were dishonest people "who amputate the hands of poor people, who steal peanuts, while those who steal millions of tax-payers' money go scot-free."[34] Since 2001, the IMN has committed itself to involvement "in national or international issues that are of concern to Muslims, as well as in solidarity with oppressed sections of the Muslim Ummah such as the Palestinians and Iraqis." The movement has also voiced support for Osama bin

Laden and al-Qaeda, implying in 2001 that it would attack U.S. interests in Nigeria if the United States or Israel attacks Iran.[35] El-Zakzaky has also made frequent and well-publicized visits to Iran.[36]

After years of steady growth in followers, particularly around el-Zakzaky's base in Zaria, Kaduna State, in December 2015 the Nigerian army violently cracked down on the IMN, killing around 300 members.[37] El-Zakaky was reported to have been heavily wounded during the crackdown and taken to a military hospital in Lagos. However, rumors persist that he was killed in the incident, because in the two years that have followed he has not resurfaced, and many of his close affiliates and family members were likewise killed or missing.[38] The Nigerian government has also restricted public protests that called for more information on el-Zakzaky's whereabouts.[39] This has also led to the initiation of a #Freezakzaky campaign by his followers, and to international criticism of Nigeria for human rights abuses against the IMN.[40] The Nigerian army—possibly guided by the anti-Iran coalition of countries in the Arab World—supported the action against the IMN because el-Zakzaky had created a virtual state in Zaria, with its own police, media, and schools reminiscent of and arguably modeled after Hezbollah in Lebanon. Although unproven, there are also rumors that Saudi Arabia encouraged the elimination of el-Zakzaky in an effort to blunt Iranian influence in Nigeria.[41]

Islamism and Society

Nigeria's 170 million citizens are divided almost evenly between Muslims and Christians, with Muslims forming the majority in the northern half of the country and Christians forming the majority in its southern half. With more than 80 million Christians and a roughly equal number of Muslims, Nigeria is both the most populous Christian country in Africa, and the most populous Muslim one.[42] The Hausa and Fulani (often referred to as the "Hausa-Fulani" because of their close cultural interaction for the past several centuries) constitute the largest single Muslim ethnic group in Nigeria, and about one-fourth of its total population. The Muslim Kanuri ethnic group is most prevalent in Yobe and Borno States and is about 4% of Nigeria's population.[43] The Yorubas of southwest Nigeria are about

60% Christian and one of the three largest ethnic groups in Nigeria along with the Hausa-Fulanis and the Igbos of southeast Nigeria. At an estimated 12 million, Yoruba Muslims are second only to the Hausa-Fulanis in terms of total Muslim population in an ethnic group. There are dozens of other predominantly Muslim ethnic groups in Nigeria, including the Shuwa Arabs of Borno State, who trace their lineage to the Arab tribes who migrated into northeastern Nigeria from the Sudan centuries ago.

Almost all Muslims in Nigeria are Sunni Muslims of the Maliki school. However, about five to ten percent of Nigeria's Muslims are Shia, and they can be found throughout northern Nigeria, particularly in Kaduna State but also in large numbers in Sokoto, Kano and Yobe and in recent years also in southern Nigeria. The number of Shi'a Muslims has increased since the Iranian Revolution of 1979, which brought an Islamic government to power in Iran. Ibrahim el-Zakzaky has been the leader of the Shi'a (IMN) with the financial and ideological support of Iran. The rise of Shi'ism in Nigeria has led to a rivalry between the majority Sunni population and Shi'as, and there have been instances of Sunni mobs or Sunni leaders ordering the destruction of Shi'a mosques and attacking Shi'a communities, with the violence reaching a culmination in December 2015 with the Nigerian army's crackdown on the IMN and general approval of this action from the Nigerian Sunni community.[44] Iran's sponsorship of Shiism in Nigeria and West Africa more broadly nonetheless suggests Shiism is likely to grow in future decades.[45]

However, conflict is most frequent between Muslims and Christians as they compete for a greater share of political and economic power in Nigeria. Election season in the country tends to generate the most tension. Muslims tend to believe that, since they often claim to constitute more than 70% of Nigeria's population, the 2011 victory of the Christian presidential candidate Goodluck Jonathan over the Muslim candidate Muhammad Buhari (by 58% to 32% of the vote) was likely fraudulent. Anger over this issue contributed to an increasing sense of marginalization among Nigerian Muslims, which has since been alleviated by Muhammed Buhari's victory in the presidential elections in 2016 and Jonathan's stepping down from the position without reservation. Boko Haram has exploited this anti-democracy and anti-Christian tension by staging dozens of attacks on churches and Christians in northern Nigeria. Most recently, Muslim-Christian violence has been seen in the context of Muslim Fulani herdsmen, who are now armed with machine guns (as opposed to the sticks they traditionally carried), raiding Christian farmlands and often killing Christians they find therein. This has, in turn, led to reprisals.[46]

Over-population also contributes to religious tensions as Muslim groups from northern Nigeria migrate into Christian areas in the Middle Belt, prompting competition over land use, as well as competition between the faiths to proselytize new members. The Sultan of Sokoto, who also leads the Jama'atu Nasril Islam (JNI), has said that "The rise of secularism and the increasing activities of western evangelical organizations have made it all the more urgent that the message of Islam shall be heard loud and clear and the JNI must play a leading role in this endeavor."[47]

Islamism and the State

Although the word "secular" is not specifically used in the Nigerian Constitution, Section 101 of that document provides that, "The Government of the Federation or of a State shall not adopt any religion as State Religion." Nonetheless, in practice religion plays such a large role in the state that Nigeria is not truly secular, a status which many religious leaders and citizens acknowledge.[48]

Islam, for example, enters the governmental sphere in several ways: the country observes Islamic holidays such as Eid el-Fitr, Eid al-Adha and Milad al-Nabi; the government is involved in organizing the Hajj pilgrimage; Islamic slogans in the Arabic language are featured on the country's currency and army insignias; Islamic sermons are delivered in public places; and, most significant of all, twelve states in northern Nigeria have implemented sharia law since 2000.

This controversial implementation is inextricably linked to politics, as many northern governors seem to support sharia law less out of religious devotion than out of a desire to portray themselves as "defenders of faith" in order to gain political advantage and to mitigate their lack of support from mainstream Muslims. Through a veneer of dedication to Islam, these politicians attempt to win the support of the masses and stifle criticism or, in many cases, investigations into their corrupt behavior. Some religious scholars have argued that the traditional rulers, including the sultans and emirs, who have no formal authority but serve as political advisers and maintain influence through their social status, are really opposed to sharia law because it does not permit hereditary succession, which is the basis of their positions.[49] Izala, the IMN and Boko Haram all believe that the Sultan and other traditional rulers are apostates for accepting a version of "half-sharia" in which secular institutions like elections and democracy exist side by side with Islam.

Although Islam is not formally a state institution in Nigeria, Muslims organizations play an important role in the country. With the advent of sharia law in twelve northern states starting between 1999 and 2001,[50] these organizations have begun to challenge the secular nature of the country, although the struggle in implementing sharia has reduced the desire to completely overturn the secular system for an Islamic system, at least in the near-term future. Boko Haram, meanwhile, seeks to completely overthrow both the secular and the traditional Muslim establishment in Nigeria and create an Islamic state akin to the "caliphate" established by ISIS in Iraq and Syria. As of 2017, the group has achieved some success in controlling territory in Borno State and removing the Nigerian government's presence altogether. Although Boko Haram isn't likely to achieve this goal throughout Nigeria, Islamist groups are nonetheless gaining more and more traction in West Africa, while, in North Africa and the Arab World, pressure to adopt certain tenets of political Islam is becoming increasingly mainstream. A convergence of these forces makes it likely that the secular nature of the Nigerian state will continue to face a challenge from regional Islamist forces, which may in turn erode Nigerian Muslims' support for the secular authorities governing their country. The saving grace for Nigeria may, paradoxically, be that Boko Haram's violence has turned much of the Muslim citizenry away from jihadism so much agitation for Islamism will remain rhetoric and less violence.

Endnotes

1. Martin Cuddihy, "Major famine imminent in Nigeria as Boko Haram attacks cripple economy," *ABC News,* December 1, 2016, http://www.abc.net.au/news/2016-12-02/nigeria-major-famine-imminent-boko-haram/8085946.
2. "Ramadan: JNI Asks Muslims to Pray for Peaceful Co-Existence of Nigeria," *Sahara Reporters,* July 23, 2012, http://saharareporters.com/2012/07/23/ramadan-jni-asks-muslims-pray-peaceful-co-existence-nigeria.
3. "Ramadan: JNI Asks Muslims to Pray for Peaceful Co-Existence of Nigeria."
4. Muhammad S. Umar, "The Popular Discourses of Salafi Radicalism and Salafi Counter-radicalism in Nigeria: A Case Study of Boko Haram." *Journal of Religion in Africa* 42, no. 2, 2012 , 118-144.
5. D.N. Danjibo, "Islamic Fundamentalism and Sectarian Violence: The 'Maitatsine' and 'Boko Haram' Crises in Northern Nigeria, University of Ibadan Institute of African Studies Peace and Conflict Studies Programme, 2010.
6. Isa Umar Gusau, "Boko Haram: How it all began," *Daily Trust,* August 2, 2009, https://www.dailytrust.com.ng/sunday/index.php/35-people-in-the-news/people-in-the-news/5869-boko-haram-how-it-all-began.
7. U.S. Department of Justice, "Al Qaeda Operative Convicted Of Multiple Terrorism Offenses Targeting Americans Overseas," March 16, 2017, https://www.justice.gov/usao-edny/pr/al-qaeda-operative-convicted-multiple-terrorism-offenses-targeting-americans-overseas.
8. Emmanuel Goujon and Aminu Abubakar, "Nigeria's 'Taliban' Plot Comeback from Hide-outs," Agence France-Presse, January 11, 2006, http://mg.co.za/article/2006-01-11-nigerias-taliban-plot-comeback-from-hideouts.
9. "Letter from Abdallah Abu-al-Hamid to Abu Mus ab abd-al-Wadud," August 24, 2009, https://www.dni.gov/files/documents/ubl2017/english/Letter%20from%20Abdallah%20Abu%20Zayd%20Abd-al-Hamid%20to%20Abu%20Mus%20ab%20Abd-al-Wadud.pdf.

10. "The Initial Source of Boko Haram Funding Explained," *Medium,* (link removed) https://medium.com/@ak61/the-initial-source-of-boko-haram-funding-explained-1b142fd5a672.
11. Jacob Zenn, "Boko Haram's Dangerous Expansion into Northwest Nigeria," Combating Terrorism Center at West Point *CTC Sentinel* 5, iss. 10, October 2012, https://www.ctc.usma.edu/posts/boko-harams-dangerous-expansion-into-northwest-nigeria; "Attacks by Boko Haram continue in Niger's Diffa region, forcing more people to flee," *United Nations: Africa Renewal Online,* June 6, 2016, http://www.un.org/africarenewal/news/attacks-boko-haram-continue-niger%E2%80%99s-diffa-region-forcing-more-people-flee-%E2%80%93-un; Vincent Ehiabhi, "Boko Haram Attacks Chad, Kills 10," *Naij.com,* 2016, https://www.naij.com/384576-breaking-boko-haram-attacks-chad-for-first-time.html.
12. *North-East Nigeria: Humanitarian Situation Update,* United Nations Office for the Coordination of Humanitarian Affairs, September 2017, https://reliefweb.int/sites/reliefweb.int/files/resources/20102017_ocha_nga_ne_sitrep_no_sept_2017.pdf.
13. Seun Opejobi, "Boko Haram mocks Army, calls Buhari 'a small ant' over Shekau," *Daily Post,* September 5, 2017, http://dailypost.ng/2017/09/05/boko-haram-mocks-army-calls-buhari-small-ant-shekau/.
14. "Boko Haram: Splinter Group, Ansaru Emerges," *Vanguard*, February 1, 2012, http://www.vanguardngr.com/2012/02/boko-haram-splinter-group-ansaru-emerges/.
15. Mike Oboh, "Islamist insurgents kill over 178 in Nigeria's Kano," *Reuters*, January 22, 2012, http://www.reuters.com/article/us-nigeria-violence-idUSTRE80L0A020120122.
16. Government of Great Britain, "Proscribed terror groups or organizations," November 2012, http://webarchive.nationalarchives.gov.uk/20130128103514/http://www.homeoffice.gov.uk/publications/counter-terrorism/proscribed-terror-groups/.
17. "Declared of Jama`atu Ansaril Muslimina Fibiladis

Sudan Garki II Abuja," *YouTube*, November 30, 2012, http://www.youtube.com/watch?v=_1m5-zV3zfU.

18. Ibrahim Shuaibu, "Islamic Group Claims Responsibility for Kidnapping French Citizen," *ThisDay*, December 24, 2012.
19. "Extremist Group in Nigeria Says It Killed 7 Foreign Hostages," Associated Press, March 9, 2013, http://www.nytimes.com/2013/03/10/world/africa/extremist-group-in-nigeria-says-it-killed-7-foreign-hostages.html.
20. "Vandenbeusch Father Supporers Rally in Discretion," *RFI Africa,* December 14, 2013. http://www.rfi.fr/afrique/20131214-france-cameroun-soutiens-pere-vandenbusch-mobilisent-discretion-boko-haram.
21. Thomas Joscelyn, "Jihadists argue over leadership of Islamic State," *Long War Journal,* August 4, 2016, http://www.longwarjournal.org/archives/2016/08/jihadists-argue-over-leadership-of-islamic-states-west-africa-province.php.
22. Aaron Y. Zelin, "New audio message from Abu Bakr al-Shekau: 'Message to the World,'" *Jihadology*, August 3, 2016, http://jihadology.net/2016/08/03/new-audio-message-from-abu-bakr-al-shekau-message-to-the-world/.
23. Zelin, "New audio message from Abu Bakr al-Shekau."
24. "Statement By Boko Haram's Spokesperson Debunking Reports Of Dialogue With The Nigerian Government," Sahara Reporters, August 23, 2012.
25. Mohammed Abubakar and Ahmed A. Mohammed, "Kala-Kato crisis: How Latest Bauchi incident erupted," *The Daily Trust,* January 1, 2010, http://www.dailytrust.com.ng/weekly/index.php/report/3592-kala-kato-crisis-how-latest-bauchi-incident-erupted.
26. Aminu Abubakar, "Death toll from Nigeria clashes climbs to 70," Agence France Presse, December 30, 2009.
27. Isa Sa'isu, "Kala-Kato: Meet group with yet another perception of Islam," *Weekly Trust*, August 15, 2009.
28. "Controversies about Sharia," *Carefronting.org*, 2016, http://carefronting.org/controversies-about-sharia/.
29. Dr. Jonathan N. C. Hill, "Sufism in Northern Nigeria:

Force for Counter-Radicalization?" Strategic Studies Institute, May 17, 2010; "The Volatility of Salafi Political Theology, the War on Terror and the Genesis of Boko Haram", Diritto e Questioni Pubbliche, 15(2): 174-201.

30. "Saudi, Iran stoke Sunni-Shia tensions in Nigeria: experts"Agence France Presse, November 5, 2016, https://au.news.yahoo.com/world/a/33116829/saudi-iran-stoke-sunni-shia-tensions-in-nigeria-experts/#page1.
31. "Saudi, Iran stoke Sunni-Shia tensions in Nigeria: experts"Agence France Presse, November 5, 2016, https://au.news.yahoo.com/world/a/33116829/saudi-iran-stoke-sunni-shia-tensions-in-nigeria-experts/#page1.
32. Hill, "Sufism in Northern Nigeria: Force for Counter-Radicalization.
33. Dr. Shedrack Best, "Nigeria: The Islamist Challenge: the Nigerian 'Shiite' Movement," *Searching for Peace in Africa*, 1999.
34. Vincent Egunyanga, "El-Zakzaky Blasts Sharia Governors," *Daily Champion*, April 21, 2002.
35. Mallam Ibraheem Zakzaky, "Terrorism In The World Today, What Is Terrorism? Who Are The Terrorists?" islamicmovement.org, 2009, www.Islamicmovement.org/sheikh/terrorism2.html.
36. "Tafiyar Sheikh El-Zakzaky jamhuriyar musulunci ta Iran cikin hotuna," harkarmusulunci.org, May 30, 2009, http://www.harkarmusulunci.org/data.asp?id=101010&lang=1.
37. Ludovica Laccino, "Nigeria Zaria killings: IMN releases names of 700 missing Shias as Zakzaky returns to Abuja," *International Business Times,* January 26, 2016, http://www.ibtimes.co.uk/nigeria-zaria-killings-imn-releases-names-700-missing-shias-zakzaky-returns-abuja-1540076.
38. Garba Muhammad, "Zakzaky, wife suffer life threatening injuries – IMN," Premium Times, July 25, 2016, http://www.premiumtimesng.com/news/top-news/207519-zakzaky-wife-suffer-life-threatening-injuries-imn.html.
39. Dyepkazah Shibayan, "Zakzakys Followers teargassed in Abuja," *The Cable,* November 2, 2016, https://www.

thecable.ng/zakzakys-followers-teargassed-abuja.

40. "Nigeria: Gathering In Bauchi after a rally against 'Zaria Carnage' / Photos Part 4th," Ahlul Bayt News Agency, December 14, 2015, http://en.abna24.com/service/africa/archive/2015/12/14/724909/story.html/
41. Kit O'Connell, "Saudi Arabia Takes Proxy War With Iran To Nigeria As Shias Are Brutalized," *Mint Press News,* January 15, 2016, http://www.mintpressnews.com/saudi-arabia-takes-proxy-war-with-iran-to-nigeria-as-shias-are-brutalized/212629/.
42. Harvard Divinity School, "Islam in Nigeria," *Religious Literacy Project*, n.d., https://rlp.hds.harvard.edu/faq/islam-nigeria.
43. Matteo Figus, *A Normal Nigerian Anomaly,* Lulu Press Inc, 2017.
44. "Nigerian Shia base knocked down," *BBC*, August 1, 2007.
45. Yaroslav Trofimov, "With Iran-Backed Conversions, Shiites Gain Ground in Africa," the Wall Street Journal, May 12, 2016, https://www.wsj.com/articles/with-iran-backed-conversions-shiites-gain-ground-in-africa-1463046768.
46. Jacob Zenn, "Leadership Analysis of Boko Haram and Ansaru in Nigeria," Combating Terrorism Center at West Point, February 24, 2014, https://www.ctc.usma.edu/posts/leadership-analysis-of-boko-haram-and-ansaru-in-nigeria.
47. James Gow, Funmi Olonisakin, Ernst Dijxhoorn
48. "Nigeria is Not a Secular State," *Sun News Online*, August 25, 2011.
49. Mallam Lawan Danbazau, *Politics and Religion in Nigeria* (Kano: Tofa Commercial Press, 1991), vii.
50. Philip Ostien, Sharia Implementation in Northern Nigeria, Spectrum Books Limited, 2007, http://www.sharia-in-africa.net/pages/publications/sharia-implementation-in-northern-nigeria.php.

36 Somalia

Quick Facts

Population: 11,031,386
Area: 637,657 sq km
Ethnic Groups: Somali 85%, Bantu and other non-Somali 15% (including 30,000 Arabs)
GDP (official exchange rate): $6.522 billion (2017 est.)

Source: CIA World FactBook (Last Updated May 2018)

Introduction

The U.S. State Department's 2016 on global terrorism trends notes that, despite suffering a series of setbacks in the first half of 2015, al-Shabaab has proven resilient and "adopted increasingly aggressive tactics" aimed at both delegitimizing the Federal Government of Somalia (FGS) and weakening the resolve of the African Union Mission in Somalia (AMISOM) via an increase in attacks on AMISOM military bases in Southern Somalia, as well as attacks in neighboring AMISOM troop-contributing countries.[1] Nevertheless, the group has had to grapple with the death of several key leadership figures as a result of U.S. aerial strikes, the loss of strongholds in parts of south-central Somalia, and, in the view of U.S. authorities, increasing factionalism and defections "as the appeal of the Islamic State of Iraq and the Levant (ISIL) created divisions within al-Shabaab's core leadership."[2] ISIL itself, which retains a small foothold in Somalia, has sought to increase its presence in sub-Saharan countries such as Somalia after significant defeats in the Middle East and North Africa. Other Islamist groups, such as Hizbul Islam and the Ras Kamboni Brigades, also pose, albeit significantly lesser, threats. One reason for these groups' resilience is the weakness of Somalia's internationally-recognized FGS, whose authority is not widely accepted by Somalis. Hampering the U.S. response to this threat is not only the absence of a capable partner government in the Somali capital of Mogadishu but also Washington's failure to creatively engage effective Somali authorities, including those in the unrecognized Republic of Somaliland.[3]

Islamist Activity

Islamists active in Somalia fall roughly into one of seven principal groups:

Harakat al-Shabaab al-Mujahideen ("Movement of Warrior Youth," al-Shabaab)

Known colloquially as al-Shabaab, this movement arose out of the militant wing of the Islamic Courts Union. Following the defeat of the latter by the Ethiopian intervention in early 2007, al-Shabaab broke with other Islamists who regrouped under the sponsorship of Eritrea to form the Alliance for the Re-Liberation of Somalia (ARS) to oppose the Transitional Federal Government (TFG) then installed in Mogadishu.

Founded in large part due to the efforts of Aden Hashi Ayro, a militant who had trained with al-Qaeda in Afghanistan prior to September 11, 2001, al-Shabaab's schism with other Islamists reflects Ayro's adherence to a more radical jihadist ideology that does not countenance cooperation with the non-Muslim Eritrean regime, even against a common enemy. Although divided into several factions even before Ayro was killed by a U.S. aerial strike in May 2008, al-Shabaab was an effective fighting force overall. The senior leadership of al-Shabaab has included veteran jihadists with experience on battlefields abroad, including in Afghanistan, Bosnia, and Kashmir.[4] It managed to seize control of large sections of southern and central Somalia, including parts of Mogadishu, where it has installed a strict Islamist regime that, to the horror of many Somalis, has carried out a number of harsh punishments—among them the stoning of a 13-year-old rape victim for the crime of "adultery" in 2008.[5]

Over time, al-Shabaab's leadership split into two principal currents. The first, hard-line faction, consisting primarily of foreign or foreign-funded jihadists, follows a transnational jihadist agenda, evidenced by the attack on Kenya's Westgate Shopping Mall in 2013 and the subsequent April 2015 attack on Garissa University in Garissa, Kenya—incidents which collectively left over 200 people dead and scores injured. Ahmed Abdi Godane, also known as Mukhtar Abu Zubair, initially spearheaded this faction and proclaimed the group's formal allegiance to al-Qaeda and to Osama bin Laden's successor, Ayman al-Zawahiri, in February 2012.

The other faction, made up of clan-based militia leaders with a more "nationalist" agenda, emphasized expelling foreign forces from Somalia and focusing on local control. At the very end of 2011, the latter group declared its intention to rename itself the "Islamic Emirate of Somalia" and rejected al-Qaeda's branding and objectives, instead focusing primarily on Somalia's domestic challenges.[6]

The internal divisions within al-Shabaab helped facilitate its loss of control over Somalia. Since Kenyan and Ethiopian troops joined African Union Mission in Somalia (AMISOM) and Transitional Federal Government forces to expel Al-Shabaab from major cities beginning in late 2011, the group has surrendered its strongholds in numerous regional capitals. Defections of al-Shabaab soldiers have increased substantially. In December 2012, Godane admitted to having experienced major defeats, but pledged to continue a guerrilla war against Somali and AMISOM forces.[7]

In 2013, Godane moved against the nationalist faction of the organization, killing or forcing into hiding most of its senior leadership.[8] While Godane himself was killed by a U.S. aerial strike in September 2014, al-Shabaab continues to adhere to transnational jihadism. Under the leadership of Godane's successor, Ahmed Omar, al-Shabaab continues to focus less on holding control of territory and more on launching successful attacks both within Somalia and in neighbouring countries. These attacks include overrunning Ugandan and Kenyan-run AMISOM bases in the southern Somali towns of Janale and El Adde, attacks on hotels and FGS figures in Mogadishu, and attacks on soft targets in neighboring AMISOM troop-contributing countries, including Kenya and Djibouti.

The rise and fall of the Islamic State in the Middle East has created another challenge to the organizational unity of al-Shabaab. Several factions of the group in Puntland and Southern Somalia have pledged alliance to the Islamic State, a move that sparked a crackdown on defectors in late 2015 by al-Shabaab's senior central leadership.[9] Nevertheless, the Islamic State's media offices continue to encourage al-Shabaab-affiliated fighters in Somalia and members of the Somali diaspora abroad to support the group, and rumors continue to swirl of ongoing clashes between factions loyal to the Islamic State and those loyal to al-Qaeda.[10] After the defeat of the Islamic State in Syria and Iraq in 2017 and the collapse of its Libyan affiliate in 2016, the group has sought to expand into sub-Saharan Africa, redirecting the flow of arms and fighters to the Sahel, Maghreb, and Horn of Africa. As ISIL seeks to regroup and rebuild its networks in Somalia, the US Africa Command (AFRICOM) has received enhanced authorities to counter the group.[11] On November 3, 2017, AFRICOM conducted its first airstrikes against the Islamic State in Somalia, underscoring the potent threat this group now poses to the country.[12]

Hizbul Islam ("Islamic Party")

Led by Hassan Dahir 'Aweys, previously the military commander of Somali Muslim Brotherhood offshoot al-Itihaad al-Islamiyya (AIAI, the "Islamic Union") and subsequently the chairman of the shura of the Islamic Courts Union, Hizbul Islam is the product of a merger of several groups. Its primary difference with al-Shabaab is that Hizbul Islam does not place as much emphasis on global jihadist objectives; rather, its two principal demands are the implementation of a strict version of sharia as the law in Somalia, and withdrawal of all foreign troops from the country. Unlike the multi-clan contingency of al-Shabaab, Hizbul Islam draws its membership and support primarily from 'Aweys' Habar Gedir sub-clan.[13] By and large, Hizbul Islam has cooperated with al-Shabaab, although the two groups have come into occasional conflict over the division of spoils. Hizbul Islam lost control of the strategic town of Beledweyne to al-Shabaab in June 2010, retaining only some territory in the southern and central Somali regions of Bay and Lower Shabelle. Subsequently, during the Muslim holy month of Ramadan, the two groups cooperated on a joint offensive against TFG and AMISOM forces in Mogadishu. Reports of a merger between the two groups emerged at the end of 2010,[14] but in September 2012 a spokesperson from Hizbul Islam announced its split with Al-Shabaab, citing ideological differences and al-Shabaab's weakened position in the region.[15]

Hizbul Islam's stance with respect to the Somali government is unclear, as is the current state of the group. While 'Aweys is reported to have declared war against the regime after Sheikh Hassan Mohamud was elected president in September 2012,[16] the group's spokesman, Mohamed Moalim, was also quoted welcoming the new president and parliament as a "positive development."[17] In fact, 'Aweys came to Mogadishu in June 2013 for talks with government officials but was arrested and reportedly roughed up.[18] Since then, with 'Aweys in custody, very little has been heard from his followers.

Mu'askar Ras Kamboni ("Ras Kamboni Brigades")

Founded by Hassan Abdullah Hersi ("al-Turki"), a former military commander for the Islamic Courts, the Ras Kamboni Brigades is based in Middle and Lower Jubba Valley, where it gained control of several strategically located towns which control access to the Kenyan border, including Jilib Afmadoow, and Dhoobley. The group was aligned with Hizbul Islam until late 2009, when al-Shabaab took control of the port of Kismayo. A faction of Ras Kamboni, led by al-Turki, announced in early 2010 that it was joining forces with al-Shabaab and proclaimed its adhesion to "the international jihad of al-Qaeda."[19]

The rest of the Ras Kamboni Brigades follows Sheikh Ahmed Mohamed Islam, a.k.a. Sheikh Ahmed Madobe, who served as the former governor of Kismayo from 2006 until the fall of the Islamic Courts Union.[20] Rumored to have strong relations with the Kenyan government, the Madobe-led Ras Kamboni group played a key role in helping the AMISOM, Kenyan, and Somali government forces push al-Shabaab out of the town of Kismayo in October 2012, although some Mogadishu-based Somali government officials denied having cooperated with the "competing militants."[21] In 2013, while continuing to lead the Ras Komboni Brigades against Al-Shabaab forces in the region, Madobe was elected president of the newly established autonomous region of Jubaland.[22]

A spokesperson of the Somali government forces in Juba reported that the group subsequently allied with Ogaden National

Liberation Front (ONLF) to fight for control the port city,[23] leading to clashes with government troops in February 2013.[24] However, in August 2013, Madobe signed an Ethiopian-brokered "national reconciliation agreement" with the FGS that allowed him to remain in control of Kismayo at the head of an "interim administration" that would preside over the police forces in Jubaland, while military forces were gradually integrated into the national army.[25]

Ahlu-Sunna wal-Jama'a (roughly, "[Followers of] the Traditions and Consensus [of the Prophet Muhammad]")

The original Ahlu Sunna wal-Jama'a was an umbrella group of traditional Somali Muslims organized by General Muhammad Farah 'Aideed as a counterweight to his Wahhabi-inspired opponents in AIAI.[26] In mid-2009, the excesses of al-Shabaab led to a revival of the movement to oppose the ideology which Shabaab and other Islamist insurgents have appropriated from some of their foreign sponsors. Loosely organized into armed militias on a clan basis and with roots in the Sufi brotherhoods, Ahlu Sunna wal-Jama'a fighters in 2010 managed in a number of places to stop what had seemed to be the relentless surge of al-Shabaab forces. Trained and assisted by the defense forces of neighboring Ethiopia, which have allowed some of the movement's units the use of its territory, Ahlu Sunna wal-Jama'a emerged as a force in southern and central Somalia. However, the group's opposition to al-Shabaab should not be confused with support of the TFG. In fact, the group's formal alliance with the TFG in 2010, brought about under tremendous pressure from regional and international actors, has largely fallen apart. In any event, while Ahlu Sunna wal-Jama'a has neither the international links nor the global strategic vision of al-Shabaab, it has an Islamist agenda of its own—for example, the group has conducted operations against those who it felt were not properly observing the fast of Ramadan—that may set it at odds with the more secular elements of Somali society.[27]

The group took control of several towns and villages in Galgadud and Hiran.[28] After assisting the Somali government fight al-Shabaab for two years, in December 2012, Ahlu Sunna wal-Jama'a troops were officially integrated into Somali government forces.[29] In February 2013, the chairman of the executive committee of Ahlu Sunna wal Jama'a, Sheikh Mohamed Yusuf Hefow, passed away in a hospital in Mogadishu.[30] Since then, relations between the militia and the FGS have frayed over issues of power in Galgadud, occasioning sporadic clashes between Ahlu Sunna wal-Jama'a loyalists and Somali national government forces, notably a February 2015 clash in Guricel that left nine dead.[31]

Al-Islah al-Islamiyya ("Islamic Movement")

In 2004, the U.S. Department of State described al-Islah as an "organized Islamic group whose goal is the establishment of an Islamic state," but termed it "a generally nonviolent movement that operates primarily in Mogadishu."[32] Largely displaced during the period when the Islamic Courts Union was ascendant, al-Islah underwent something of a revival in Mogadishu with the return of Sharif Ahmed to the head of the TFG in 2009. Its chief role was the administration of schools in the capital which were supported by the group's foreign benefactors. It is not surprising, given how spectacularly state institutions have collapsed in Somalia, that "this naturally promoted fundamentalist trends (such as al-Islah) in local Islam, which had previously been largely Sufi in character, and these were encouraged by financial support from Saudi Arabia and other Middle Eastern centers."[33] Hassan Sheikh Mohamed, who was elected head of the Somali government in September 2012, has links with al-Islah.[34]

Al-Qaeda

While its earlier foray into Somalia did not prove particularly successful, al-Qaeda remains interested in Somalia both as a theater of operations and as a jumping-off point for terrorist activities in the nearby Arabian Peninsula and elsewhere in Africa.[35] An audio statement released by Osama bin Laden in 2009 in praise of the Islamist insurgency in Somalia and calling upon Muslims to support it underscored this reality.[36] More recently, Ayman al-Zawahiri, bin Laden's successor, endorsed Ahmed Omer, Godane's successor and the current leader of al-Shabaab.[37] Even analysts who previously discounted al-Qaeda's involvement in Somalia now acknowledge that, since at least early 2008, al-Qaeda advisors have played a critical role in al-Shabaab operations,[38] a fact highlighted by the

September 2009 strike inside Somalia by U.S. Special Operations Forces which killed Saleh Ali Saleh Nabhan, a Kenyan national wanted in connection with the 1998 bombings of the U.S. embassies in Dar es Salaam, Tanzania and Nairobi, Kenya. At the time of his death, Nabhan was running terrorist training camps and bringing in foreign trainers and fighters to support al-Shabaab, presumably at the behest of al-Qaeda. In February 2012, the leadership of al-Shabaab formally pledged its allegiance to al-Qaeda leader Ayman al-Zawahiri.[39] Since then, the al-Shabaab continues to receive support from al-Qaeda and carry out attacks in its name, including the 2013 assault on Kenya's Westgate Mall and a 2017 truck bombing in Mogadishu that killed over 500 Somalis.

The Islamic State (Islamic State of Iraq and the Levant, Daesh)

Although its success to date has been limited, the Islamic State has sought to re-establish itself in Somalia following major defeats in the Levant and Libya in 2017 and 2016, respectively, focusing its efforts on coopting al-Shabaab forces demoralized by their battlefield losses in recent years. In March 2016, the Islamic State claimed its first attack in Somalia, the bombing of an African Union vehicle in Mogadishu, and subsequently released a video showing what it claimed was its first Somali training camp. The group has reportedly attracted several hundred al-Shabaab defectors, as well as a number of prominent imams, especially in the northeastern part of Somalia.[40] In October 2016, a group led by Abdulqadir Mumin—a commander who broke away from al-Shabaab to declare allegiance to ISIL in 2015—captured and briefly held the port town of Qandala in northern Somalia, a major propaganda victory for the group.[41] The expanding threat of ISIL's presence in the coutnry was underscored by US airstrikes that targeted the group in Somalia for the first time in November 2017.

Islamism and Society

Traditionally, the Somali subscribe to Sunni Islam and follow the Shāfi'ī school (madhab) of jurisprudence, which, although conservative, is open to a variety of liberal views regarding practice.[42]

Up until the time of Somalia's independence in 1960, there were different movements within the Sunni Islam in Somalia. The most dominant were the Sufi brotherhoods (sing., tarīqa, pl. turuq), especially that of the Qadiriyya order (although the Ahmadiyya order, introduced into Somali lands in the 19th century, was also influential).[43] While traditional Islamic schools and scholars (ulamā) played a role as focal points for rudimentary political opposition to colonial rule in Italian Somalia, historically their role in the politics of the Somali clan structure was neither institutionalized nor particularly prominent. In part this is because sharia historically was not especially entrenched in Somalia: being largely pastoralists, the Somali relied more on customary law (xeer) than on religious prescriptions.[44] Hence, Somali Islamism is largely a post-colonial movement which became active in the late 1980s and which was strengthened by the collapse of the state in 1991 and the ensuing civil war, international intervention, external meddling, and efforts by Somalis themselves at political reconstruction. Absent this chain of events, it is doubtful that militant Islamism would be much more than a marginal force in Somali politics.

Although its adherents often appeal to the early 20th century anti-colonial fight of the "Mad Mullah" Sayyid Muhammad 'Abdille Hassan,[45] Somali Islamism is, at its origins, an import dating back at most to the 1950s. The 1953 establishment in Mogadishu of an Institute of Islamic Studies run by Egyptian scholars from Cairo's al-Azhar University introduced both Arabic language curriculum and contact with the Egyptian Muslim Brotherhood (al-Ikhwan al-Muslimoon). As is well-known, unlike the Sufis who emphasize socialization, moral education, and spiritual preparation, the Muslim Brothers stress organization, activism, and the socio-political dimension of change directed toward the creation of a modern Islamic state. After Somalia's independence in 1960, Egyptians opened secondary schools in many of the country's towns. In the 1960s and 1970s, Saudi religious and educational institutions—especially the Islamic University of Medina, the Umm al-Qura University in Mecca, and the Imam Muhammad bin Saud Islamic University in Riyadh—joined al-Azhar in offering scholarships to the graduates of these institutions. This development has parallels with the entrenchment of radical Islam in nearby Sudan via the establishment of the Sudanese Muslim Brotherhood, the precursor to the currently-ruling National Congress Party (formerly the National Islamic Front).

By the 1970s, the nascent Somali Muslim Brotherhood was so visible that the dictatorial regime of Siyad Barre took measures to suppress it, driving its adherents underground. The Somali Muslim Brothers eventually coalesced into two groups: al-Islah al-Islamiyya ("Islamic Movement") founded in Saudi Arabia in 1978, and al-Itihaad al-Islamiyya (AIAI, the "Islamic Union"), established in the early 1980s. The memberships of the two and their leadership network overlapped considerably. The differences between them were, at least initially, largely a function of the circumstances of their clandestine origins. Both sought the creation of an expansive "Islamic Republic of Greater Somalia" and eventually a political union embracing all Muslims in the Horn of Africa.[46]

The collapse in January 1991 of the Siyad Barre regime led to internecine warfare that laid waste to Somalia. AIAI was forced to withdraw after heavy fighting. This withdrawal, which coincided with the fall of the Derg in neighboring Ethiopia, allowed Somali Islamists to regroup in the Somali region of Ethiopia where there were also large numbers of refugees from Somalia proper. AIAI tried to seize control of strategic assets like seaports and crossroads. Although it temporarily held the northern port of Bosaso and the eastern ports of Marka and Kismayo, the only area where it exercised long-term control was the economically vital intersection of Luuq, in southern Somalia, near the Ethiopian border, where it imposed harsh sharia-based rule from 1991 until 1996. From its base in Luuq, the Islamists of AIAI encouraged subversive activities among ethnic Somalis of Ethiopia and carried out a series of terrorist attacks. The exasperated Ethiopian regime finally intervened in Somalia in August 1996, wiping out AIAI bases in Luuq and Buulo Haawa and killing hundreds of Somali extremists, as well as scores of non-Somalis who had flocked to the Horn of Africa under the banner of jihad. From this period emerged the cooperation between Somali Islamists and Ethiopian groups like the Ogaden National Liberation Front (ONLF), which continue to struggle against the newly established government of Ethiopia.

From its inception, the AIAI rejected the non-confessional nature of the Somali state and sought to establish an Islamic regime in the country based on a strict Wahhabi interpretation of the Muslim faith. When, in the aftermath of the collapse of the Siyad Barre dictatorship, it found the direct road to power blocked by Muhammad Farah ‘Aideed, it adopted a subtler approach based on the establishment of economic and other social programs, together with Islamic courts.[47]

Some Somalis have come to see Islam as an alternative to both the traditional clan-based identities and the emergent criminal syndicates led by so-called “warlords.” The increased influence of religion has been largely a phenomenon of small towns and urban centers, although increased adherence to its normative precepts is a wider phenomenon. Islamic religious leaders have helped organize security and other services and businessmen in particular were supportive of the establishment of sharia-based courts throughout the south, which were a precursor of the Islamic Courts Union established in Mogadishu in June 2006. The Islamists attempted to fill certain voids left by state collapse and otherwise unattended to by emergent forces like the warlords. In doing so, they also made a bid to supplant clan and other identities, offering a pan-Islamist identity in lieu of other allegiances.[48]

Given their previous experiences with Somali Islamism, especially in its AIAI incarnation, it was not surprising that, after many of the same extremists emerged in positions of authority in the Islamic Courts Union, the Ethiopians would intervene as they did in 2006 to support Somalia’s internationally-recognized but weak “Transitional Federal Government” (TFG), the fourteenth such attempt at a secular national government since 1991.[49] Unfortunately, while the intervention ended the rule of the Islamic Courts Union, it also provoked an insurgency spearheaded by the even more radical Harakat al-Shabaab al-Mujahideen (“Movement of Warrior Youth,” al-Shabaab), a group subsequently designated a “specially designated global terrorist” by the U.S. Department of State in 2008[50] and a “listed terrorist organization” by the Australian government the following year.[51] Even after Ethiopian troops withdrew in early 2009, the Shabaab-led insurgency against the TFG has continued, drawing the African Union Mission in Somalia (AMISOM) deployed to protect the transitional regime deeper into the conflict and causing them to suffer increasing casualties with terrorist attacks like the suicide bombing of September 17, 2009, which killed seventeen peacekeepers and wounded more than forty others,[52] and that of December 3, 2009, which killed three TFG ministers as well as sixteen other people attending a graduation ceremony within the small enclave of Mogadishu thought to still be controlled by the beleaguered regime.[53]

With the end of the TFG's mandate in August 2012, the Somali Federal Government was formed—depending on how one counts them, the new entity is either the fifteenth or the sixteenth interim regime since the collapse of the Siad Barre dictatorship in 1991. Hassan Sheikh Mohamud, an educator and civil society activist with ties to al-Islah as well as the earlier Union of Islamist Courts, was selected to head the new government, which was formally recognized by the United States in January 2013, the first Somali regime to be accorded that status in more than two decades. While the Federal Government of Somalia, with the help of AMISOM, has managed to roll back al-Shabaab territorial control in southern Somalia, the group continues to regularly strike SFG-affiliated targets in the capital city of Mogadishu, including an attack on the Nasa Hablod hotel in June 2016, which killed a serving government minister, among other victims.

After numerous delays due to security concerns, Somalia elected Mohamed Abdullahi Mohamed, better known as 'Farmajo,' to the presidency on February 8, 2017. Despite accusations of vote-buying and corruption in the run-up to the polls,[54] the election was marked by the peaceful transfer of power to President Mohamed, who holds dual US-Somali citizenship.[55] Despite praise by some analysts for Mohamed's previous experience in the Barre regime, the new Somali government has had difficulty in establishing legitimacy in the country and remains vulnerable to attacks by al-Shabaab.[56] On October 14, 2017, al-Shabaab was blamed for a double truck-bombing that killed an unprecedented 512 civilians, highlighting the limitations of the Somali Federal Government and its international allies in countering Islamist terror groups on its soil.

Islamism and the State

Official Somali policy toward Islamism is muddled, compromised by the complicity of the government in Islamist thought and activity. While Somali Islamism was damaged by the military defeat dealt to the Islamic Courts Union following the Ethiopian military intervention in late 2006 and early 2007, the chaos into which the Somali territories (outside Somaliland) subsequently sunk under the aegis of the TFG served to revive their standing, especially given some of the historical linkages between Islamism and pan-Somali yearning.[57] Consequently, Islamists will continue to be a competitive force among the Somalis.

In March 2009, a unity government was established between the TFG and elements of the Alliance for the Re-Liberation of Somalia (ARS). The expansion of the number of seats in the country's parliament to 550, and the election of former ICU leader Sharif Sheikh Ahmed as president, demonstrated the inclusion of a broader spectrum of Islamic ideology in government.[58] The election of Hassan Sheikh Mohamud and Mohamed Abdullahi Mohamed to the presidency of the Federal Government of Somalia in September 2012 and February 2017, respectively, has been seen as a further movement towards more moderate, albeit mildly Islamist, leadership.[59] Though Mohamud's tenure was characterized by a slow improvement in the security situation in the country, events under the Mohamed administration prove that extremist elements in Somalia continue to influence and threaten political order. This situation is exacerbated by the withdrawal of AMISOM forces (due to the respective domestic security needs of contributing countries) and a decrease in international support for their deployment in Somalia, which provide a potentially dangerous opening for the militant Islamists.

At the same time, two further topics require elucidation in the context of governmental response:

The Question of Somaliland

Although the sovereignty it reasserted has yet to be formally recognized by any other state, more than a decade and a half have passed since Somaliland (the north-western region of the former Somalia, bordering on Ethiopia and Djibouti) proclaimed the dissolution of its voluntary union with the central government. Perhaps most important, in the context of the rising tide of Islamist militancy in southern and central Somalia, is the fact that Somaliland's reliance on the older system of clan elders and the respect they command "has served as something of a mediating force in managing pragmatic interaction between custom and tradition; Islam and the secular realm of modern nationalism," leading to a unique situation where "Islam may be pre-empting and/or containing Islamism."[60] The consequence of having an organic relationship between Somali culture and tradition and Islam appears to assure a stabilizing, rather than disruptive, role for religion in society in general, and religion and politics in particular. In Somaliland, for example, the population is almost exclusively Sunni Muslim and the shahada, the Muslim profession of the oneness of God and the acceptance of Muhammad as God's final prophet, is emblazoned on the flag; yet sharia is only one of the three sources of the jurisprudence in the region's courts, alongside secular legislation and Somali traditional law. Unlike the rest of the Somali lands, the region is governed by a democratic constitution which was approved by 97 percent of the voters in a May 2001 referendum and which provides for an executive branch of government, consisting of a directly elected president and vice president and appointed ministers; a bicameral legislature consisting of an elected House of Representatives and an upper chamber of elders, the guurti; and an independent judiciary. Somaliland has held presidential elections in 2003 and 2010 and parliamentary elections in 2005, all three of which were judged "free and fair" by international observers. Initially postponed due to drought, Somaliland held its most recent presidential elections on November 13, 2017, in which the incumbent Ahmed Mohamed Mahamoud did not seek a second term. In a poll which the international community claimed "preserved the integrity of the electoral process,"[61] Mahamoud's successor in the Peace, Unity, and Development Party (KULMIYE), Muse Bihi Abdi, was elected president with 55 percent of the vote."

Not surprisingly, the relative success of Somaliland has drawn the ire of Islamists in southern and central Somalia. In 2008, on the same day that Shirwa Ahmed, a naturalized U.S. citizen from Minneapolis, Minnesota, blew himself up in an attack on the headquarters of the Puntland Intelligence Service in Bosaso, other suicide bombers from al-Shabaab hit the presidential palace, the UN Development Programme office, and the Ethiopian diplomatic mission in the Somaliland capital of Hargeisa.[62]

Since suffering defeats in south and central Somalia, al-Shabaab fighters have established footholds in Puntland, posing a major threat to the region's governing institutions and its overall stability.[63] In the past, semi-autonomous Puntland has criticized Somaliland for ignoring the threat posed by the spread of al-Shabaab militants in northern Somalia.[64] However, a number of developments—including the effective use of a small coast guard to keep Somaliland largely free of piracy, as well as the 2009 transfer of two Guantanamo Bay detainees to Hargeisa, rather than the less secure Mogadishu—indicate that Somaliland is seen as less vulnerable to militant Islam than south and central Somalia.[65] In February 2013, authorities there responded more forcefully to al-Shabaab militants by arresting approximately eighty members, including the son of a Somaliland politician.[66]

Islamism and Piracy

Although incidents of piracy have dramatically decreased since 2012, there was no evidence of anything other than opportunistic instances of cooperation between Somalia's Islamists and pirates. In early 2011, it was reported that al-Shabaab had reached a deal with one of the larger piracy syndicates for a 20 percent cut of all future ransoms from piracy and was even opening an office to specifically liaise with the pirates in the port of Xarardheere where the Islamist group would permit the hijackers to anchor seized ships while awaiting ransom payments.[67] A 2011 U.S. Congressional Research Service report cites testimony suggesting that Somali pirates were not directly allied with al-Shabaab, but did maintain many of these mutually beneficial financial arrangements.[68]

Thanks to the adoption of best practices in maritime security and increased international patrols, piracy in the Gulf of Aden has declined significantly since 2012. Moreover, al-Shabaab's loss of control of key ports including Xarardheere, Marka, Baraawe, and Kismaayo, to the Somali military and AMISOM further limit opportunities for cooperation between the Islamists and piracy networks.

ENDNOTES

1. U.S. Department of State, Office of the Coordinator for Counterterrorism, "Country Reports: Africa Overview," in *Country Reports on Terrorism 2015*, http://www.state.gov/j/ct/rls/crt/2015/257514.htm
2. "Country Reports: Africa Overview," in *Country Reports on Terrorism 2015*.
3. J. Peter Pham, "Peripheral Vision: A Model Solution for Somalia," *RUSI Journal* 154, no. 5 (October 2009), 84-90.
4. Roland Marchal, "A Tentative Assessment Of The Somali Harakat al-Shabaab," *Journal of Eastern African Studies* 3, no. 3 (2009), 389.
5. Chris McNeal, "Rape Victim, 13, Stoned To Death In Somalia," *Guardian* (London), November 2, 2008, http://www.guardian.co.uk/world/2008/nov/02/somalia-gender.
6. Brownyn Bruton and J. Peter Pham, "The Splintering of Al Shabaab," *Foreign Affairs,* February 2, 2012, http://www.foreignaffairs.com/articles/137068/bronwyn-bruton-and-j-peter-pham/the-splintering-of-al-shabaab.
7. Mojid Ahmed, "Al-Shabaab leader admits defeats," *Sabahi*, December 17, 2012, http://sabahionline.com/en_GB/articles/hoa/articles/features/2012/12/17/feature-01
8. Matt Bryden, "The Reinvention of Al-Shabaab: A Strategy of Choice or Necessity?," Center for Strategic & International Studies, February 2014, https://csis-prod.s3.amazonaws.com/s3fs-public/legacy_files/files/publication/140221_Bryden_ReinventionOfAlShabaab_Web.pdf
9. "Somalia's Al-Qaeda branch warns members against joining IS," Agence France-Presse, November 24, 2015,

https://www.yahoo.com/news/somalias-al-qaeda-branch-warns-members-against-joining-075418683.html?ref=gs

10. Stig Jarle Hansen, "Has Shabaab been weakened for good? The answer is 'yes' and 'no'," *The Conversation,* October 17, 2016, http://theconversation.com/has-shabaab-been-weakened-for-good-the-answer-is-yes-and-no-67067
11. Charlie Savage and Eric Schmitt, "Trump Eases Combat Rules in Somalia Intended to Protect Civilians," March 30, 2017, https://www.nytimes.com/2017/03/30/world/africa/trump-is-said-to-ease-combat-rules-in-somalia-designed-to-protect-civilians.html.
12. J. Peter Pham, "US Strikes on ISIS in Somalia Underscore Threat, Vulnerabilities," *New Atlanticist,* November 6, 2017, http://www.atlanticcouncil.org/blogs/new-atlanticist/us-strikes-on-isis-in-somalia-underscore-threat-vulnerabilities.
13. "Somalia: Hizbul Islam Group Withdraws Allegiance, Says 'Al Shabaab Is Weakened,'" *Garowe Online*, September 25, 2012, http://allafrica.com/stories/201209261141.html.
14. "Somali Islamists al-Shabab and Hizbul Islam 'to merge'," *BBC News,* December 10, 2010, http://www.bbc.co.uk/news/world-africa-12038556.
15. "Kenyan Amisom soldier kills six Somali civilians," *BBC News*, September 24, 2012, http://www.bbc.co.uk/news/world-africa-19698348.
16. "Somalia: Hizbul Islam Group Withdraws Allegiance, Says 'Al Shabaab Is Weakened.'"
17. "Kenyan Amisom soldier kills six Somali civilians."
18. See "Somalia and its Shabab: Are the Islamists Truly on the Ropes," *The Economist*, July 6, 2013, http://www.economist.com/news/middle-east-and-africa/21580523-new-and-much-lauded-president-finding-it-hard-bury-old-divisions-are.
19. Abdi Sheikh and Abdi Guled, "Somali Rebels Unite, Profess Loyalty To Al Qaeda," Reuters, February 1, 2010, http://www.reuters.com/article/idUSTRE6102Q720100201.
20. "The smiling warlord who Controls Ras Kamboni," *The*

Daily Nation, July 11, 2012, http://www.nation.co.ke/Features/DN2/The-smiling-warlord-who-Controls-Ras-Kamboni-/-/957860/1425264/-/12mrtirz/-/index.html

21. AbdulKadir Khalif, "Somalia in row with militias in captured town," *The Daily Nation,* October 11, 2012, http://www.nation.co.ke/News/africa/-/1066/1530598/-/14pr6i0/-/index.html.
22. "Somalia: Kismayo Residents Fear New Clan Fighting," *KeydMedia*, February 23, 2014, http://www.keydmedia.net/en/news/article/somalia_kismayo_residents_fear_new_clan_fighting/
23. AbdulKadir Khalif, "Somalia in row with militias in captured town," *The Daily Nation,* October 11, 2012, http://www.nation.co.ke/News/africa/-/1066/1530598/-/14pr6i0/-/index.html.
24. "Gulf of Aden Security Review - February 25, 2013,"American Enterprise Institute Critical Threats Project, February 25, 2013, http://www.criticalthreats.org/gulf-aden-security-review/gulf-aden-security-review-february-25-2013.
25. Andualem Sisay and Abdulkadir Khalif, "Somali Government and Jubaland Strike Peace Deal," *Africa Review*, August 29, 2013, http://www.africareview.com/News/Somali+government+and+Jubaland+strike+a+deal/-/979180/1972618/-/3a6xv7z/-/index.html.
26. Menkhaus, ""Somalia And Somaliland," 33.
27. J. Peter Pham, "Somali Instability Still Poses Threat Even After Successful Strike against Nabhan," *World Defense Review*, September 17, 2009, http://worlddefensereview.com/pham091709.shtml.
28. "Somalia's Shabaab seize third town this month after peacekeepers withdraw," Reuters Africa, October 23, 2016, http://af.reuters.com/article/topNews/idAFKCN12N0JZ .
29. "Somalia: Ahlu Sunna Wal-Jamaa Forces to Join Somali National Army," *Sabahi,* November 30, 2012, http://allafrica.com/stories/201212040647.html.
30. "Somalia: A leader of Ahlu Sunna Wal Jama'a Dies," *AllAfrica,* February 14, 2013, http://allafrica.com/stories/201302141519.html.

31. "Sufi Militias Repel Somalia Army Counterattack on Town," *Hiraan Online*, February 12, 2015, http://www.hiiraan.com/news4/2015/Feb/98127/sufi_militias_repel_somalia_army_counter_attack_on_town.aspx.
32. United States Department of State, "International Religious Freedom Report 2004," 2004, http://www.state.gov/j/drl/rls/irf/2004/35382.htm.
33. Ioan M. Lewis, *A Modern History of the Somali*, 4th rev. ed. (Oxford: James Currey, 2002), 299.
34. "Hassan Sheikh Mohamud: Somalia's new president profiled," *BBC News,* September 11, 2012, http://www.bbc.co.uk/news/world-africa-19556383.
35. Kinfe Abraham, *The Bin Laden Connection and the Terror Factor in Somalia* (Addis Ababa: Ethiopia International Institute for Peace and Development, 2006).
36. J. Peter Pham, "Bin Laden's Somali Gambit," *World Defense Review*, March 26, 2009, http://worlddefensereview.com/pham032609.shtml.
37. Thomas Joscelyn, "Shabaab's Leadership Fights Islamic State's Attempted Expansion in East Africa," *Long War Journal*, October 26, 2015, http://www.longwarjournal.org/archives/2015/10/shabaab-leadership-fights-islamic-state-expansion.php
38. Ken Menkhaus, "Somalia: What Went Wrong?" *RUSI Journal* 154, no. 4 (August 2009), 12.
39. Katherine Houreld, "Somali Militant Group al-Shabaab Formally Joins al-Qaida," Associated Press, February 9, 2012, https://www.theguardian.com/world/2012/feb/09/somali-al-shabaab-join-al-qaida.
40. Heidi Vogt, "Islamic State in Africa Tries to Lure Members from al-Shabaab," *Wall Street Journal*, October 26, 2016, http://www.wsj.com/articles/african-terror-franchise-now-has-competition-from-islamic-state-1477474200.
41. Harun Maruf, "IS Militants Seize Town in Somalia's Puntland," *Voice of America*, October 26, 2016, https://www.voanews.com/a/is-militants-seize-town-in-somalia-puntland/3566722.html.
42. Ioan M. Lewis, *Blood and Bone: The Call of Kinship in Somali Society* (Princeton, NJ: Red Sea Press, 1994),

167.
43. Ioan M. Lewis, *Saints and Somalis: Popular Islam in a Clan-Based Society* (Lawrenceville, NJ: Red Sea Press, 1998).
44. Michael van Notten and Spencer Heath MacCallum, eds., *The Law of the Somalis: A Stable Foundation for Economic Development in the Horn of Africa* (Trenton, NJ: Red Sea Press, 2006).
45. Robert L. Hess, "The 'Mad Mullah' And Northern Somalia," *Journal of African History* 5, no. 3 (1964), 415-433; see also Abdi Sheik-Abdi, *Divine Madness: Mohammed Abdulle Hassan (1856-1920)* (Atlantic Highlands, NJ: Zed, 1993).
46. Medhane Tadesse, *Al-Ittihad: Political Islam and Black Economy in Somalia. Religion, Money, Clan and the Struggle for Supremacy over Somalia* (Addis Ababa, 2002), 16-24.
47. Roland Marchal, "Islamic Political Dynamics In The Somali Civil War," in Alex de Waal, ed., *Islamism and its Enemies in the Horn of Africa* (Addis Ababa: Shama Books, 2004), 114-146.
48. Shaul Shay, *Somalia between Jihad and Restoration* (New Brunswick, NJ: Transaction Publishers, 2007), 93-127; see also Kenneth J. Menkhaus, "Somalia and Somaliland: Terrorism, Political Islam, and State Collapse," in Robert I. Rotberg, ed., *Battling Terrorism in the Horn of Africa* (Washington, DC: Brookings Institution Press, 2005), 23-47; and Jonathan Stevenson, "Risks and Opportunities in Somalia," *Survival* 49, no. 2 (Summer 2007), 5-20.
49. Ken Menkhaus, "The Crisis In Somalia: Tragedy In Five Acts," *African Affairs* 106, no. 204 (2007), 357-390
50. U.S. Department of State, Office of the Coordinator for Counterterrorism, "Designation of al-Shabaab as a Specially Designated Global Terrorist" (Public Notice 6137), February 26, 2008, http://www.state.gov/s/ct/rls/other/des/102448.htm.
51. Commonwealth of Australia, Joint Media Release of Attorney-General Robert McClelland MP and Minister for Foreign Affairs Stephen Smith MP, "Listing of Al-

Shabaab as a Terrorist Organisation," August 21, 2009, http://www.foreignminister.gov.au/releases/2009/fa-s090821.html.

52. "21 Killed In Suicide Attack On African Union Base In Somalia," CNN.com, September 18, 2009, http://edition.cnn.com/2009/WORLD/africa/09/18/somalia.suicide.attack/index.html.
53. Stephanie McCrummen, "Bombing Kills 19 In Somali Capital," *Washington Post*, December 4, 2009, A19.
54. Jeffrey Gettleman, "Fueled by Bribes, Somalia's Election Seen as Milestone of Corruption," *New York Times*, February 7, 2017, https://www.nytimes.com/2017/02/07/world/africa/somalia-election-corruption.
55. Merrit Kennedy, "In Somalia's Presidential Election, A Surprise Victor Declared," National Public Radio, February 8, 2017, https://www.npr.org/sections/thetwo-way/2017/02/08/514089778/in-somalias-historic-presidential-election-a-surprise-victor-declared
56. James Butty "New Somali Prime Minister's "Experience" Praised by Analyst," Voice of America, October 14, 2010, https://www.voanews.com/a/butty-somalia-new-pm-analysis-aligas-15october10-105009799/156109.html.
57. See J. Peter Pham, "Somalia: Insurgency and Legitimacy in the Context of State Collapse," in David Richards and Greg Mills, eds., Victory Among People: Lessons from Countering Insurgency and Stabilising Fragile States (London: RUSI, 2011), 277-294.
58. Mohammed Ibrahim, "Moderate Elected President in Somalia," New York Times, January 30, 2009, http://www.nytimes.com/2009/01/31/world/africa/31somalia.html?_r=0
59. Gabe Joselow, "Somalia Elects New President," Voice of America, September 10, 2012, http://www.voanews.com/content/somalia_parliament_votes_for_new_president/1505008.html
60. Iqbal Jhazbhay, "Islam And Stability In Somaliland And The Geo-politics Of The War on Terror," Journal of Muslim Minority Affairs 28, no. 2 (2008), 198.
61. Abdiqani Hassan, "Somaliland Picks Ruling Party's

Candidate as New President," Reuters, November 21, 2017, https://www.reuters.com/article/us-somaliland-election/somaliland-picks-ruling-partys-candidate-as-new-president-idUSKBN1DL1UH?il=0.

62. Andrew McGregor, "Somaliland Charges Al-Shabaab Extremists With Suicide Bombings," Terrorism Monitor 6, no. 23 (December 8, 2008), 7-9.
63. Yara Bayoumy, "Somalia's al Shabaab, squeezed in south, move to Puntland," Reuters, November 9, 2012, http://www.reuters.com/article/2012/11/09/somalia-puntland-shabaab-idUSL5E8M96UZ20121109.
64. Abdisamad Mooge, "Somaliland: Real terrorism threats in fictional State," Horseed Media, February 25, 2013, http://horseedmedia.net/2013/02/25/somaliland-real-terrorism-threats-in-fictional-state/.
65. J. Peter Pham, "The Somaliland Exception: Lessons on Postconflict State Building from the Part of the Former Somalia That Works," Marine Corps University Journal 3, no. 1 (2012), 27-28.
66. Mooge, "Somaliland: Real terrorism threats in fictional State."
67. Mohamed Ahmed, "Somali Rebels Agree to Ransom Deal with Pirate Leaders," Reuters, February 22, 2011, http://af.reuters.com/article/worldNews/idAFTRE71L1GO20110222.
68. Lauren Ploch et al., "Piracy off the Horn of Africa," Congressional Research Report, April 27, 2011, 16-17, http://fpc.state.gov/documents/organization/162745.pdf.

37 South Africa

Quick Facts

Population: 54,841,552
Area: 1,219,090 sq km
Ethnic Groups: Black African 80.2%, white 8.4%, colored 8.8%, Indian/Asian 2.5%
Government Type: Parliamentary republic
GDP (official exchange rate): $344.1 billion (2017 est.)

Source: CIA World FactBook (Last Updated April 2018)

Introduction

South Africa is home to approximately 1 million Muslims, constituting 1.9% of the population.[1] *The country's diverse Muslim community consists of the descendants of Malay slaves brought by the Dutch East India Company in the 17th and 18th centuries, the descendants of Indian indentured servants that arrived in the 19th and early 20th centuries, recent arrivals since the end of Apartheid, and a growing number of converts.*

Although Islamism first gained traction in the country in the 1960s, South Africa only became a haven for terrorists after the end of Apartheid. Despite their small numbers, Muslims are well represented in the leadership of the ruling African National Congress (ANC) and some have created a welcoming climate Muslim extremism. While Islamist terrorist groups rarely perceive South Africa as an enemy, they have directed violence against heterodox Muslims in the country as well as against drug dealers and businesses associated with the United States.

Islamist Activity

Islamist ideology first filtered into South Africa in the 1960s, while groups devoted to the radicalization of the country's Muslims emerged in the 1970s. Imam Abdullah Haron, president of the Muslim Judicial Council, introduced Islamist ideology to South

Africa through a newsletter called *Islamic Mirror*, which published extracts from the work of Abul A'la Maududi and Sayyid Qutb.[2] Haron also edited the *Muslim News*, a fortnightly newspaper that promoted the *Protocols of the Elders of Zion* and peddled extreme anti-Zionism.[3] In 1969, he was arrested and killed in custody for organizing the transportation of Pan-Africanist Congress (PAC) militants abroad under the guise of recruiting students for Cairo's Al-Azhar University.[4] The Muslim Youth Movement (MYM) was founded the following year, and subsequently disseminated Islamist ideology through leadership training programs that hosted foreign extremist clerics, orientation camps, study circles, and a press.[5] After the 1979 Islamic Revolution in Iran, the writings of Ali Shari'ati and the Ayatollah Khomeini were added to the MYM reading list.[6]

Qibla and People Against Gangsterism and Drugs (PAGAD)

Achmad Cassiem, a schoolteacher who had been imprisoned on Robben Island for ten years for PAC activities, founded Qibla with other PAC activists "to promote the aims and ideals of the Iranian Revolution in South Africa and in due course transform South Africa into an Islamic state."[7] Qibla members received military training in Libya and fought alongside Hezbollah in southern Lebanon.[8] It also formed the Islamic Unity Convention (IUC) in 1994, which still serves as an umbrella organization for over 250 Muslim organizations in South Africa.[9] Achmad Cassiem is leader of both Qibla and the IUC.[10] The group has boycotted government elections in South Africa "under the pretext that leaders produced by democratic means, such as elections, are illegitimate."[11] It likewise owns a radio station, Radio 786, through which it preaches and promotes its ideology.[12]

While Qibla's theocratic program attracted few adherents, its leaders were able to exploit the skyrocketing crime rates following the end of Apartheid and coopt the vigilante PAGAD, which coalesced in the Western Cape in 1995.[13] Initially, PAGAD limited its violence to attacks on gang leaders and cooperated with police.[14] However, the Qibla-controlled faction of PAGAD quickly reverted to its roots and began targeting moderate Muslims, synagogues, gay nightclubs, tourist attractions, and Western-associated restaurants.[15] Its spiritual advisor, Hafiz Abdulrazaq, was given the title emir (commander).[16] PAGAD's national coordinator, Abdus-Salaam Ebrahim, legitimized violence in his speeches. He called on Muslims to "prepare themselves with steeds of war against the enemies of Allah (SWT), the enemy of the Muslims and the oppressed people."[17]

In 1998, there were a reported 80 pipe bomb explosions in the Western Cape, with the most notorious occurring at a Planet Hollywood restaurant.[18] PAGAD was designated as a Foreign Terrorist Organization by the United States in 2001.[19] The group has not launched any violent attacks in recent years. South Africa outlawed PAGAD in 1996 and prosecuted most of its leadership in 2000, bringing the group's activities to a halt. However, as experts point out, "Since the underlying reasons for its existence were never addressed, the possible re-emergence of PAGAD or similar organizations cannot be discounted."[20]

Al-Qaeda

South Africa has provided a safe haven and financing for al-Qaeda operatives while South African jihadists have fought in Afghanistan against the Soviet Union, in Kashmir against India, as well as in Chechnya.[21] In October 1999, South African police arrested Khalfan Khamis Mohamed in Cape Town for his role in the August 1998 bombings of the U.S. embassies in Dar es Salaam and Nairobi. He had been hiding in South Africa since a few days after the embassy bombings.[22] Then, in June 2011, Fazul Abdullah Mohammad, an al-Qaeda operative and mastermind behind the 1998 U.S. Embassy bombings, was killed in Somalia. Reports indicate that he was carrying a South African passport under the name of Daniel Robinson.[23]

In January 2007, the U.S. Treasury Department designated two South African cousins, Farhad and Junaid Dockrat, as financiers of al-Qaeda.[24] In addition to acting as an al-Qaeda fundraiser, Junaid helped send South Africans to Pakistan to train with al-Qaeda, communicating via phone and email with then al-Qaeda operations chief Hamza Rabi'a.[25] In September 2009, the United States government closed its facilities across South Africa after it received credible threats against their safety.[26] The threats reportedly came from an al-Qaeda splinter group.[27] The U.S. State Department reopened its embassies and consulates a few days later.

Furthermore, evidence has come to light that demonstrates that al-Qaeda's top leadership have an interest in South Africa. In the May 2011 raid conducted by U.S. Navy Seals in Pakistan that targeted Osama bin Laden, the U.S. uncovered information regarding bin Laden's designs on South Africa. In documents retrieved during the raid, bin Laden articulated that it may be: "suitable to target Americans in South Africa, because it is located outside the Islamic Maghreb."[28]

Al -Shabaab

In 2015, documents leaked to the Al Jazeera television network revealed that the South African State Security Agency and foreign intelligence services had prevented terror attacks on South African soil between 2007 and 2010. The thwarted attacks were connected to Samantha Lewthwaite, known as the "white widow," who resided in South Africa between 2009 and 2011 on a fraudulent South African passport.[29] Lewthwaite was married to Germaine Lindsay, one of the suicide bombers responsible for the death of 26 people in the London underground in July 2005. Lewthwaite has been linked to both the al- Shabaab Westgate Mall attack in Nairobi and the attack on Garissa University in Kenya that killed 148 people.[30]

The Islamic State

In September 2015, the U.S. Embassy issued a security warning regarding a possible terrorist threat to American interests in South Africa.[31] The statement, which came as the Islamic State appealed to its followers to attack Western targets during Ramadan,[32] did not include any specifics regarding the location or timing of the attack but urged U.S. citizens to take the appropriate steps to enhance their personal security. In June 2016, the U.S. Embassy in South Africa again issued a security message to warn U.S. citizens that the U.S. government had "received information that terrorist groups are planning to carry out near-term attacks against places where U.S. citizens congregate in South Africa."[33] The British and Australian Embassies issued similar warnings the same day, encouraging their citizens to be vigilant about personal security.[34] The warnings caused a furor— the South African Department for International Relations and Cooperation (DIRCO) and the State Security Agency (SSA) feeling that the statements questioned South Africa's ability to protect foreign citizens on its soil. DIRCO questioned the credibility of the threats, raising alarm among citizens who doubted the government's capacity to advance counterterrorism efforts.[35]

In July 2016, the South African authorities arrested twin brothers Brandon-Lee and Tony-Lee Thulsie, along with two accomplices, for plotting to attack the U.S. embassy and a Jewish Building in Pretoria. South Africa's State Security Agencies had twice prevented the brothers from leaving to join the Islamic State (ISIS) in Syria. The brothers were charged with "conspiracy and incitement to commit the crime of terrorism."[36]

It is estimated that between 60 and 100 South Africans fought for ISIS and that half of them had returned by 2017.[37] South African authorities have kept details of their investigations and monitoring efforts classified. In April 2015, a 15-year old girl was removed from an aircraft leaving South Africa on suspicion that she was travelling to Turkey with the intention of joining the Islamic State.[38] There has been no documented evidence of ISIS organizing in South Africa.

Islamism and Society

The Rushdie Affair of the late 1980s/early 1990s illustrates the gains made by Islamist organizations over the past several decades. After the *Daily Mail* and Congress of South African Writers (COSAW) invited controversial author Salman Rushdie to deliver a keynote speech at a conference on censorship, the event organizers were bombarded with death threats, almost all of which were signed and included return addresses. Under Muslim pressure, the government banned the book and COSAW withdrew Rushdie's invitation.[39] The furor surrounding Rushdie has not abated over the past two decades. In 2015, three Islamists attacked South African writer Zainab Dala after she expressed admiration for Rushdie's literary style at Durban's Time of the Writer Festival. They drove her off the road, held a knife to her throat, and hit her with a brick while calling her "Rushdie's bitch."[40]

Islamists have also targeted mosques in the country that preach a tolerant form of Islam. In 2014, Taj Hargey founded Cape Town's Open Mosque, which only recognizes the Quran as authoritative, rejecting the hadith, and promotes gender equality as well as tolerance of homosexuals. In the months after its opening, Islamists firebombed the mosque three times and threatened Hargey in anonymous letters with hanging and castration.[41] The Saudi-funded[42] Muslim Judicial Council, an umbrella group with about 150 affiliated mosques, better reflects the zeitgeist of South African Muslim opinion. The organization's spokesman, Shuaib Appleby, condemned Bin Laden's killing, saying that "extrajudicial killing is totally condemned by Islam. A person must be duly tried, with a court deciding on a punishment if the person is found to be guilty. We hope that with (Bin Laden's) death, the kinds of ideas that Muslims globally were subjected to - the Islamophobia - and being associated with terrorism will cease with immediate effect."[43]

As in other countries outside the Muslim world, Islam in South Africa has been influenced by international groups and events. South Africa's position as the economic powerhouse on the continent has made it a destination for immigrants from all over Africa. Reports indicate that immigrants from Central and West Africa have "brought with them a new 'Africanised Islam' more in line with black South Africans' identities than the religion practiced by followers with closer links to Asia."[44] Islamism in South Africa appears to have been more influenced by the Iranian Revolution than by the global Salafi movement.[45] Nevertheless, South Africa's Muslims largely identify with more libertarian Sufism, which has been a long established tradition among the Islamic population in the country.[46]

A number of incidents in recent years have exposed some of the racial and ethnic cleavages in South African society. In August 2012, for example, a Muslim man was beaten to death, reportedly over the fact that he wore a beard.[47] Then, in January 2013, two Muslim students were expelled from their high school in Cape Town for refusing to remove their head coverings.[48] The South African constitution prevents schools from banning wearing certain religious garments including yamulkes and headscarves. Within weeks, however, the students were readmitted after a meeting was held between representatives from the school and education department, the parents, a local imam, and representatives from the South African Human Rights Commission.[49] Islamophobes have also vandalized mosques. In January 2017, a bloody pig's snout was found outside the historic Nurul Islam Mosque in Simon's Town.[50] Soon thereafter, blood was found smeared on the walls of a mosque in the Cape Town suburb of Kalk Bay.[51]

The legacy of Apartheid has left deep cleavages within South African society. Within the Muslim community, reports indicate that there is a growing hostility between black Muslims and other Muslims in South Africa. As Israeli scholars Reuven Paz and Moshe Terdman have noted, "[t]he grievances of Black Muslims run the gamut, from racism and exploitation to the unfair distribution of zakat (alms)."[52] The divide presents a factor that could potentially be exploited by Islamists seeking greater influence and followers.

Islamism and the State

Since the fall of Apartheid, the ANC has dominated South African politics. As many Muslims participated in the anti-Apartheid movement, they have been amply represented in government since 1994. Some of these politicians have expressed support for Islamist terrorist groups and anti-Semitism. Then-Deputy Minister of Foreign Affairs Aziz Pahad met with the chief of Hezbollah's political bureau, Mohammad Raad, in Beirut in June 2003 and characterized the group as a "legitimate liberation movement in terms of international law."[53] Then, at a January 2009 protest against Operation Cast Lead in Gaza, then-Deputy Minister of Foreign Affairs Fatima Hajaig stated that "They [ie, the Jews] in fact control [America]. No matter which government comes in to power, whether Republican or Democratic, whether Barack Obama or George Bush. The control of America, just like the control of most Western countries, is in the hands of Jewish money and if Jewish money controls their country then you cannot expect anything else."[54]

Competing with the ANC are a variety of smaller political parties representing geographic, ethnic and religious groups. Notably, some advocate the imposition of sharia law as the governing mechanism for the state. One such group is Al-Jama-ah,[55] which was created in April 2007 as a political party for South Africa's Muslim youth.[56] Ahead of the 2009 elections, Al-Jama-ah aimed its campaign at sixteen and seventeen year olds, noting that, come 2009, they would be eligible to vote. Ahead of the elections, the group posted a statement on their website calling on voters to opt for sharia law. [57] Although Al-Jama-ah did not secure any representation in either the parliamentary or the provincial elections of 2009 and 2014, they won 9 seats in the 2016 municipal elections. Controlling the balance of power in the Estcourt municipality, the party even obtained the deputy mayorship.[58]

Similar to other western states, South Africa's government does not legally recognize Muslim marriages, even those that are monogamous.[59] In 2012, the South African pension fund authority allowed a spouse a portion of their partner's pension after a Muslim divorce had been granted.[60] While the decision does not put in place any binding precedent on the South African courts, some South African Muslims "hope the case could open the way towards acknowledging the dissolution of an Islamic marriage as a divorce in terms of the Divorce Act."[61]

South Africa has porous borders and large immigrant communities that have the ability to harbor jihadists.[62] South Africa also suffers from a high crime rate.[63] This propensity towards violence, if coupled with a rise in Islamist activity, may increase the risk of Islamist-inspired attacks against targets within the country. However, the state appears to have been making efforts to reach out to the religious communities in South Africa to "manage the expression of Islam."[64] The ANC's Commission for Religious Affairs, developed in 1995,[65] meets with the President several times a year to discuss relevant issues.

In terms of counterterrorist response and readiness, however, South Africa remains lackluster. The South African government has generally hoped that its neutrality in the war on terror and a pro-Palestinian stance would spare the nation from being targeted by Islamists.[66]

Furthermore, there has long been concern that South Africa's weak intelligence services and high crime rate would render it vulnerable to large-scale terrorist attacks. In the wake of U.S. terror warnings in 2016, Minister of State Security David Mahlobo issued his own statement claiming that South Africa remains a "strong and stable democratic country and there is no immediate danger posed by the threat," further urging that there was "no need to panic."[67] The apparently contradictory messages from the South African government and international embassies do not instill confidence that the South African government is taking the threats seriously. An important first step would be the acknowledgement of potential danger from radical Islamic ideology—something currently missing from state discourse.[68]

Endnotes

1. "General Household Survey (2015)," *Statistics South Africa*. p. 28.
2. Abdulkader Tayob (1995) *Islamic Resurgence in South Africa: The Muslim Youth Movement.* Cape Town: University of Cape Town Press. p. 83.
3. Milton Shain and Margo Bastos (2012) "Muslim Antisemitism and Anti-Zionism in Postwar South Africa," in *Holocaust Denial: The Politics of Perfidy*. ed. Robert S. Wistrich. Berlin: Walter de Gruyter. p. 139.
4. Louis Brenner (1993) "Introduction: Muslim Representations of Unity and Difference in the African Discourse," in *Muslim Identity and Social Change in Sub-Saharan Africa*. ed. Louis Brenner. Bloomington: Indiana University Press. p. 4.
5. David McCormack (2010) "Africa," in *Guide to Islamist Movements: Volume 1.* ed. Barry Rubin. Armonk: M.E. Sharpe. p. 15.
6. Milton Shain (2016) "South Africa, Apartheid, and the Road to BDS," in *Anti-Judaism, Antisemitism, and the Delegitimizing Israel*. ed. Robert S. Wistrich. Lincoln: University of Nebraska Press. p. 68.
7. Anneli Botha, "PAGAD: A Case Study of Radical Islam in South Africa," Jamestown Foundation *Terrorism Monitor* 3, iss. 17, September 14, 2005, http://www.jamestown.org/single/?no_cache=1&tx_ttnews%5Btt_news%5D=561.
8. Josh Lefkowitz, "Terror's South African Front," *National Interest*. Aug. 18, 2004. http://nationalinterest.org/ar-

ticle/terrors-south-african-front-2742.

9. Lefkowitz, "Terror's South African Front."
10. Lefkowitz, "Terror's South African Front."
11. M. A. Mohamed Salih, "Islamic Political Parties in Secular South Africa," in M. A. Mohammed Salih, ed., *Interpreting Islamic Political Parties* (New York, New York: Palgrave Macmillan, 2009), 199.
12. Salih, "Islamic Political Parties in Secular South Africa."
13. McCormack, p. 18.
14. Angel Rabasa, Peter Chalk, Kim Cragin, Sara A. Daly, Heather S. Gregg, Theodore W. Karasik, Kevin A. O'Brien, and William Rosenau (2006) *Beyond al-Qaeda: Part 2, The Outer Rings of the Terrorist Universe*. Santa Monica: Rand Corporation. p. 40.
15. Beyond al-Qaeda: Part 2,p. 41.
16. Heinrich Matthée, *Muslim Identities and Political Strategies: a Case Study of Muslims in the Greater Cape Town area of South Africa, 1994-2000* (Kassel, Germany: Kassel University Press GmbH: 2008), 157.
17. Matthée, 159.
18. Goolam Vahed and Shamil Jeppie, "Muslim Communities: Muslims in Post-Apartheid South Africa," in John Daniel, Roger Southall and Jessica Lutchman, eds., *State of the Nation: South Africa 2004 – 2005* (Cape Town, South Africa: Human Sciences Research Council Press: 2005), 258.
19. Holt, "South Africa in the War on Terror."
20. Anneli Botha, "PAGAD: A Case Study of Radical Islam in South Africa," Jamestown Foundation Terrorism Monitor 3, iss. 17, September 14, 2005, http://www.jamestown.org/single/?no_cache=1&tx_ttnews%5Btt_news%5D=561.
21. *Jane's Islamic Affairs Analyst*, December 1, 2006.
22. Lynne Duke, "Ninth Suspect Charged in Embassy Bombings," *Washington Post*. 9 Oct. 1999. A02. http://www.washingtonpost.com/wp-srv/WPcap/1999-10/09/024r-100999-idx.html.
23. Peter Fabricius, "Al-Qaeda Head had SA Passport – Report," IOL News (South Africa), June 14, 2011. http://www.iol.co.za/news/africa/al-qaeda-head-had-

sa-passport-report-1.1083125#.UUnA1leE3u0.

24. U.S. Department of the Treasury, “Treasury Targets Al Qaida Facilitators in South Africa,” January 2 6, 2007, http://www.ustreas.gov/press/releases/hp230.htm.
25. “Treasury Targets Al Qaida Facilitators in South Africa,”.
26. “South Africa: Security Threat Closes U.S. Diplomatic Offices,” AllAfrica.com, September 23, 2009, http://allafrica.com/stories/200909230863.html.
27. “South Africa: Al-Qaeda Threatened U.S. Offices – Report,” AllAfrica.com, September 24, 2009, http://allafrica.com/stories/200909240664.html.
28. “SOCOM-2012-0000017-HT,” in “Letters from Abbottabad,” Translated and provided by the Combating Terrorism Center at West Point, n.d., http://www.ctc.usma.edu/posts/letters-from-abbottabad-bin-ladin-sidelined.
29. Agiza Hlongwane and Jeff Wicks, ‘White Widow’ Paid for South African Passport, *IOL Politics*, September 29, 2013.
30. Samantha Payne, “Who is White Widow Samantha Lewthwaite? Shy girl from Aylesbury who became world’s most wanted woman,” *International Business Times,* May 22, 2015, http://www.ibtimes.co.uk/who-white-widow-samantha-lewthwaite-shy-girl-aylesbury-who-became-worlds-most-wanted-woman-1502582.
31. Fred Lambert, “US Embassy in South Africa Issues Terror Attack Warning, UPI, September 9, 2015, http://www.upi.com/Top_News/World-News/2015/09/08/US-embassy-in-South-Africa-issues-terror-attack-warning/5841441748232/.
32. Reuters, May 22, 2016, Islamic State calls for attacks on west during Ramadan in audio message.
33. U.S. Embassy Pretoria, “Security Message for US Citizens: Threats to Shopping Areas and Malls,” June 4, 2016, https://za.usembassy.gov/security-message-u-s-citizens-threats-shopping-areas-malls/.
34. Adetula David, “Terrorist Attack Warnings: Here is Why South Africans Should be Worried,” *Ventures*, June 8, 2016, http://ewn.co.za/2016/06/08/Internation-

al-Relations-responds-to-criticism-on-terror-threat.
35. Chris Williams (2016) Terror threats and turmoil: a bad time for US-South Africa relations, http://theconversation.com/terror-threats-and-turmoil-a-bad-time-for-us-south-africa-relations-60804
36. Normitsu Onishi, "South Africa Charges Twins Over Plot to Attack U.S. Embassy and Join ISIS," *New York Times*, July 11, 2016, http://www.nytimes.com/2016/07/12/world/africa/south-africa-islamic-state.html?_r=0.
37. Raeesah Cassim Cachalia and Albertus Schoeman, "Violent Extremism in South Africa
Assessing the Current Threat," *Institute for Security Studies*, May 2017, https://issafrica.org/research/southern-africa-report/violent-extremism-in-south-africa-assessing-the-current-threat.
38. Ministry of State Security of South Africa, "Statement by Minister of State Security, David Mahlobo, MP, on the incident involving a South African and alleged terror links," April 6, 2015, http://www.ssa.gov.za/Portals/0/SSA%20docs/Media%20Releases/2015/Media%20Release%20Statement%20by%20Minister%20of%20State%20Security%20on%20a%20South%20African%20with%20suspected%20terro%20links%206%20April%202015.pdf.
39. Daniel Pipes (2009) *The Rushdie Affair: The Novel, the Ayatollah, and the West*. New Brunswick: Transaction Publishers. pp. 22-23.
40. Monir Hussein, "Intolerance Spreading in South Africa," *Gatestone Institute*, April 5, 2015 https://www.gatestoneinstitute.org/5495/south-africa-intolerance.
41. Gain Haynes, "Meet the British Muslim Who's Founded a Controversial Gay-Friendly Mosque," *Vice*. Jan. 15, 2015. https://www.vice.com/en_uk/article/vdpap8/open-mosque-taj-hargey-south-africa-934.
42. "Militancy Among South African Muslims," *Jane's Islamic Affairs Analyst*, October 24, 2006.
43. Deon de Lange and Michelle Pietersen, Osama's Death Exposes US Brutality," *IOL*. May 3, 2011. https://www.iol.co.za/news/world/osamas-death-exposes-us-brutality-1063414.

44. Gordon Bell, "Islam is Spreading among Black South Africans," Reuters, November 14, 2004, http://www.iol.co.za/index.php?set_id=1&click_id=139&art_id=qw1100423885802B264.
45. Michael Schmidt, "Islamic Terror is Not a Problem for SA," IOL, November 20, 2004, http://www.iol.co.za/news/politics/islamic-terror-is-not-a-problem-for-sa-227451.
46. Schmidt, "Islamic Terror is Not a Problem for SA."
47. Yusuf Abramjee, "Muslim Man Dies after Fight over Beard," News24, August 8, 2012, http://www.news24.com/SouthAfrica/News/Muslim-man-dies-after-fight-over-beard-20120808
48. "School Hijab Ban Shocks Cape Town Muslims," OnIslam, January 23, 2013, http://www.onislam.net/english/news/africa/461020-school-hijab-ban-shocks-cape-town-muslims.html.
49. "S. African School Lifts Muslim Headgear Ban," OnIslam, January 25, 2013, http://www.onislam.net/english/news/africa/461038-s-african-school-lifts-muslim-headgear-ban.html.
50. "Incidents of Islamophobia Anger S. African Muslims," *Anadolu Agency*, January 10, 2017, https://aa.com.tr/en/africa/incidents-of-islamophobia-anger-s-african-muslims/724438.
51. "'Islamophobia to Blame for Cape Town Mosque Attacks," *Al Jazeera*ˆ, January 12, 2017, https://www.aljazeera.com/news/2017/01/cape-town-mosque-attacks-islamophobia-170112105620599.html.
52. Reuven Paz and Moshe Terdman, "Islam's Inroads," *The Journal of International Security Affairs* no. 13, Fall 2007, http://www.securityaffairs.org/issues/2007/13/paz&terdman.php.
53. Lefkowitz, "Terror's South African Front."
54. Paul Trewhela, "The ANC and Anti-Semitism," *PoliticsWeb*. Jan. 28, 2009. http://www.politicsweb.co.za/news-and-analysis/the-anc-and-antisemitism.
55. "Al Jama-ah Targets Young Voters," *The Voice of the Cape* (South Africa), October 12, 2007.
56. Salih, "Islamic Political Parties in Secular South Africa," 195.

57. "Choose: The Shariah or Unruly Mix," Al-Jama-ah website, November 20, 2008, http://aljama.co.za/2008/11/choose-the-shariah-or-unruly-mix.
58. "About Al Jama-ah," Al-Jama-ah website, http://www.aljama.co.za/about-2/.
59. Megan Harrington-Johnson, "Muslim marriages and divorce." De Rebus, May 2015:40 [2015], DEREBUS 93, http://www.saflii.org/za/journals/DEREBUS/2015/93.pdf
60. "S. Africa Pensions Recognize Muslim Divorce," OnIslam, March 17, 2012, http://www.onislam.net/english/news/africa/456258-s-africa-pensions-recognize-muslim-divorce.html.
61. "S. Africa Pensions Recognize Muslim Divorce," OnIslam,
62. "S. Africa Pensions Recognize Muslim Divorce," OnIslam.
63. "South Africa ranks among the most dangerous countries in the world – and it's costing us," *BusinessTech*, September 21, 2017, https://businesstech.co.za/news/lifestyle/200044/south-africa-ranks-among-the-most-dangerous-countries-in-the-world-and-its-costing-us/.
64. Schmidt, "Islamic Terror Is Not a Problem for SA."
65. "The ANC and Religion," ANC website, n.d., http://www.anc.org.za/ancdocs/misc/anc_and_religion.html.
66. Terdman, "Factors Facilitating the Rise of Radical Islamism and Terrorism in Sub-Saharan Africa."
67. "Government on US Terror Alert: No Need to Panic," *Mail and Guardian,* June 6, 2016, http://mg.co.za/article/2016-06-06-sa-state-security-department-breaks-silence-on-us-terror-alert.
68. "Militancy Among South African Muslims."

38 Tanzania

Quick Facts

Population: 53,950,935
Area: 947,300 sq km
Ethnic Groups: Mainland - African 99% (of which 95% are Bantu consisting of more than 130 tribes), other 1% (consisting of Asian, European, and Arab); Zanzibar - Arab, African, mixed Arab and Africa
Government Type: Presidential republic
GDP (official exchange rate): $51.61 billion (2017 est.)

Source: CIA World FactBook (Last Updated April 2018)

Introduction

Tanzania's level of Islamist activity is currently low, especially as compared to its regional neighbors Egypt, Somalia, Sudan, and Kenya. However, a number of factors—among them secular nationalism, a weak parliamentary democracy, slow and uneven economic growth, and unequal opportunity—have spurred at least some Muslims in Tanzania to adhere to Islamism as an ideological alternative.[1] *The character of Tanzania's internal politics as a one-party-dominant political system and historic grievances by the Muslim Zanzibari population further strain inter-religious relations and threaten to politicize what has historically been the localized (and moderate) practice of Islam.*

Tanzania's proximity to Somalia, inside of which both al-Qaeda and ISIS are determined to vie for influence, remains a risk factor. Similarly, the presence of foreign-funded mosques and universities has only increased in recent years. Tanzanian Muslims thus experience competing forms of Islam, and more radical strains become more attractive as avenues for legitimate political expression continue to shrink.

Islamist Activity

The bombing of the U.S. embassy in Dar es Salaam in 1998, which killed eleven and injured eighty-five others, was the first indication of the existence of militant jihadi activity in Tanzania. The bombing, however, was not a plot planned inside the country, or even one organized by Tanzanian Muslims, though two Zanzibari residents were eventually implicated. Rather, the attack was planned by several Somalis, al-Qaeda operatives, and sleepers with regional links to cells in Tanzania and Kenya.[2] Although no other similarly high-profile attacks occurred for years, Tanzania is still vulnerable to radical Islamists. Since 2012, a spate of unresolved acid and explosive attacks attributed to Islamist extremists, as well as the recent discovery of suspected terror training camps inside the country, confirm these fears.[3] In 2016 and 2017, a series of violent ambushes of the Tanzanian police—not unlike some of the violent attacks on police by al-Shabaab elements in Kenya—have rattled residents but to date attribution has focused on criminal, rather than terror, groups as the perpetrators.[4]

Jihadi attacks have occurred just across Tanzania's northern border in neighboring Kenya and Uganda, and small arms and other weapons are readily available on the black market across East Africa. The Somali terror group al-Shabaab, which remains a threat to Somalia as well as the broader region, is committed to transnational expansion, including operations in, recruits from, and attacks on Tanzania. Al-Shabaab's success in Tanzania thus far has been limited.[5] Nevertheless, some weaknesses make Tanzania a relatively easy target.[6] With rudimentary border controls, a wide-open coastline and troubled neighbors, Tanzania's large coastal trade and extensive, illegal smuggling industry provide excellent logistical cover for extremists. Meanwhile, the Tanzanian police are unable, and sometimes unwilling, to provide basic public safety services, and major crimes often go unsolved; though the country's National Counterterrorism Center (NCTC) illustrates an inter-agency approach to preventing and countering violent extremists, its capacity remains limited. Corruption is a serious challenge to the effectiveness of Tanzania's security forces, notably its police force.[7] Lastly, a sense of political and economic marginalization that is especially evident among Zanzibaris has not to date led to widespread radicalization or violence, but the situation continues to evolve.

The NCTC considered the 2012 arrest of Emrah Erdogan, an al-Qaeda and al-Shabaab associate, in Dar es Salaam as confirmation that extremist organizations "have elements and plans within the country's borders."[8] A series of acid and improvised explosive device (IED) attacks targeting tourists, Christians, and moderate Muslims have occurred in both mainland Tanzania and Zanzibar since 2012, and the May 2013 bombing of St. Joseph's Roman Catholic Church in an Arusha suburb, which killed three people and wounded more than 60, further confirmed these fears.[9] While no group claimed responsibility for these attacks, some suggested that a radical Zanzibari separatist group might have, at a minimum, inspired them.[10]

At least three times between 2013 and 2016, authorities raided suspected terror training camps in Tanzania, some of which were recruiting and indoctrinating children.[11] It is unclear which group is responsible for setting them up, though authorities suggested that al-Shabaab was the prime suspect. Tanzania is not part of the African Union Mission in Somalia like its neighbors Kenya and Burundi, but it remains susceptible to the threat of Somali terror group al-Shabaab and its Kenyan affiliate al-Hijra (Erdogan, whose case is detailed above, was apprehended in part due to his links to al-Hijra members[12]). Both groups have an interest in Tanzania, evident especially in the large number of Tanzanian citizens recruited to fight for al-Shabaab in Somalia. In 2016, a cell purportedly aligned with the Islamic State (ISIS) issued a video message from a cave in Tanzania, drawing attention to a third group with its eye on Tanzania.[13] The emergence the same year of an Islamic State-affiliated group, Jahba East Africa, also bears watching, as the group claims Tanzanians among its membership. Thus far, however, Jahba East Africa is "more of an ideological threat than a physical one" and its sole attack to date was in Somalia.[14] There is little known about whether ISIS recruits in person or solely online in Tanzania, though the group's shift to inspiring and encouraging lone wolf attacks could have deadly ramifications.[15]

The potential for volatility and radicalization is higher in Zanzibar, a semi-autonomous archipelago situated off the northeastern Tanzanian coast. The islands are majority Muslim, and thus constitute a prime target for radical figures like Sheikh Ponda Issa Ponda, who has been in and out of prison for charges ranging from inciting violence to trespassing.[16] Ponda has led a smattering of Islamist organizations, including Simba wa Mungu (God's Lion) and the Council of Islamic Organizations, which in the past has forcibly taken over mosques in Dar es Salaam and violently targeted tourists.[17] He preaches jihadi Islamism and reportedly enjoys ties with al-Qaeda officials.[18]

The Zanzibari organization UAMSHO (the Association for Islamic Mobilization and Propagation, and also the Swahili word for "Awakening") first began offering public lectures on Islam in the 1990s and later expanded into the sphere of Muslim rights.[19] Its stated goals are to increase the standard of living for Muslims in Zanzibar and to ultimately achieve Zanzibari independence.[20] UAMSHO's supporters have accused the government of intervening in religious affairs in violation of Article 19 of the Constitution, and they claim that government corruption has led to the moral decline of the country. Lax enforcement of Tanzanian laws regulating dress and alcohol—especially in Zanzibar where local Muslims complain that foreign tourists flout local laws and Islamic customs—remains a grievance.[21] The government of Zanzibar, for its part, has accused the group of holding and disseminating fundamentalist views, and in 2012, Tanzanian Prime Minister Mizengo Pinda opined that UAMSHO "has of late lost direction and is propagating hatred among the people of Zanzibar."[22]

In 2012, protests following the arrest of some thirty UAMSHO members resulted in the destruction of two churches in Zanzibar; according to Zanzibari police, UAMSHO "was responsible for inciting these riots"—a charge the group denied.[23] In August 2013, the group was linked to outbreaks of violence, including acid attacks as well as religiously motivated abductions, rioting, and arson.[24] UAMSHO's popularity has reportedly risen since the formation of the 2010 government of national unity (a coalition between the ruling CCM and opposition CUF in Zanzibar), which to many Zanzibaris showed the bankrupt nature of their political system.[25] In the wake of this agreement, UAMSHO positioned itself as the only group able and willing to bring about positive change for Zanzibari Muslims. This position has only strengthened following the annulled 2015 Zanzibari elections.

The Ansar Muslim Youth Center (AMYC), based in Tanzania's Tanga region, is another group of potential importance. Thought to be led by Sheikh Salim Abdulrahim Barahiyan, the organization began as an al-Qaeda-linked group before aligning itself with al-Shabaab and al-Hijra. Its goal is to "promote moral reform through the propagation of Salafi Islam," and the group exercises considerable influence over a large network of mosques and religious schools in the country.[26] While it has been quiet in recent years, the AMYC's danger lies its network, through which it has close relations with hardline Islamic clerics, financiers, and recruiters, and has reportedly offered safe haven to jihadists passing through Tanzania.[27] Using such connections to recruit and fundraise for other radical Islamists may not be far off.

So far, however, these movements are largely ripples on the surface of theology and social life across the country. Sufi Islam and Islamic traditions remain mixed with local tribal customs, creating a formidable barrier to radical Islamists.[28] As a further preventative measure, the NCTC intends to work directly with local police to encourage respected figures in Tanzanian communities, including elders and religious authorities, to try to promote conflict resolution through dialogue rather than violence.[29] Yet it is important to note that these efforts may easily be counterbalanced by foreign influence. In recent years, expatriate Wahhabis from Saudi Arabia have been active in Muslim charitable organizations and in schools. They also finance university scholarships for Muslim Tanzanians, who often return from their studies abroad with a Wahhabist interpretation of Islam that clashes with the localized Tanzanian practice.[30] Indeed, Wahhabi-style fundamentalists have, on occasion, taken over 30 of the 487 mosques in Dar es Salaam, bombed bars, and beaten women who go out without being fully covered.[31]

Islamism and Society

Official estimates suggest that of Tanzania's population of about 54 million, about one-third are Muslim, nearly two-thirds are Christian, and a small percentage are "animist."[32] The Christian population dominates the southwest and north-central areas of the country. Many Tanzanian Muslims live along the pre-colonial and colonial trade routes. In the past, these routes were active in the transport of slaves, ivory, sisal, coffee, and tea. The Zanzibar islands, which once served as the hub of pre-colonial trade, now have a population of roughly 1.3 million, the majority of whom are Muslim.[33] In the traditional centers of Swahili culture along the coast, Muslims adhere to Sunni Islam, though a sizable minority of Tanzania's Muslims identify as Shia.[34]

Tanzania's major, simmering conflict is now the political struggle between the Tanzanian mainland and Zanzibar, which are separate former dependencies of Britain. Despite efforts to tie Zanzibar to the mainland, separatist sentiments never died in the islands.[35] Because many Zanzibaris identify culturally with their alleged Arab ancestry from across the Indian Ocean, rather than the African mainland, the potential for Zanzibari sovereignty remains a political issue linked to religious tensions and thus relevant to the question of the spread of radical Islam.

On the Zanzibar islands, Muslim religious scholars are becoming more influential in dictating social behavior, such as enforcing a dress code and attempting to shut down establishments that serve alcohol. High levels of poverty and feelings of marginalization at the hands of the mainland government on the islands continue to contribute to political discontent.[36] Zanzibar, which fared poorly from the economic liberalization of the 1990s, has fallen behind the mainland in economic growth, and its Western-focused tourist industry is small and fragile.[37] Rising crime, as well as high levels of youth unemployment (up to 85% of youth are unemployed in Zanzibar) and drug addiction (estimates suggest that some 7% of Zanzibar's population is addicted to heroin[38]) exacerbate the situation.[39] Thus its dissatisfied population is likely even more vulnerable to radicalization than are the residents of the mainland.

For nearly four decades, wealthy Gulf donors have funded Zanzibar's mosques, madrassas, health clinics, and secondary schools, as well as some scholarships to study in Sudan or Saudi Arabia.[40] Two of Zanzibar's universities are Islamic, funded by Saudi Arabians and Kuwaitis. The amount of money provided from abroad is formidable; a 2012 study estimated that Saudi Arabia spends $1 million annually on religious institutions—including schools, radio stations, and mosques—in Zanzibar.[41] As a Zanzibari parliamentarian stated, "It's very difficult for the traditional madrassas that are really in poor shape to rival the influence of those that are being funded by foreigners and Wahhabi-based institutions."[42]

Tanzania is undergoing an Islamic "revival," spawned by a set of interrelated factors.[43] First, the country's economic and political opening in the 1990s codified protections of association and assembly, leading new non-governmental organizations to flourish.[44] Second, Islamist organizations took advantage of this opening to agitate for political causes,[45] particularly those needs not being met by the state; the increasing availability of Islamic materials and media in multiple languages adds to an ability for Tanzanian Muslims to "individualize" their religion.[46] Lastly, these political realities are exacerbated by Tanzania's economic woes, as high growth rates and government services have not managed to keep up with an even higher population growth rate. This translates into a $3,300 per capita GDP, with a large percentage of the population living below the poverty line.[47]

The Islamic revival thus faces competing narratives: on one hand, Muslim traditions are threatened by a secular state as well as the "onslaught and failure" of Western values,[48] requiring a return to the "basics" to protect Islam.[49] In Zanzibar, this revival has focused primarily on munafik ("Muslims in name only") and Sufis; on the mainland, the revival targets Christians. The goal of these groups is to address what is viewed as a state failure in service provision and governance that is especially tangible among Muslim communities. At the same time, this revival clashes with the highly localized and individual practice of Islam that has flourished in Zanzibar for decades.

For the most part, a long history of cooperation in the name of nationalism has mitigated religious conflict in Tanzania. Indeed, "while there are some ethnic identities and geographic areas that coincide with a certain religious tradition, often other identities, such as class divisions or support for political parties, are cross-cutting and do not reinforce these religious divisions."[50] The legacy of the Tanganyika African National Union's (TANU) emphasis on inter-religious cooperation, has, for the most part, endured.

Yet, in the past decade, a serious political legitimacy challenge has emerged. Prior to the 2015 general elections and a scheduled constitutional referendum (which was later postponed), former President Jakaya Kikwete warned of heightened religious tensions: "the current situation, if left unchecked, could plunge our country into a major conflict between Christians and Muslims."[51] In addition to this general increase in political and sectarian tensions, which are worsened by political disagreements including the disputed Zanzibar elections, groups like al-Shabaab and ISIS have increasingly appealed to Tanzania's disaffected Muslims—many of whom are young men. In May 2016, Defense Minister Hussein Mwinyi warned about the radicalization of young Tanzanians and his concern that foreign recruits who fought for al-Shabaab or ISIS could return to Tanzania, though the government's response to date has primarily been through law enforcement.[52]

Islamism and the State

The practice of Islam in Tanzania remains highly localized, though a path remains for literal and politicized interpretations of Islam—particularly those supported by foreign Gulf state donors—to capitalize on local grievances and reinterpret them as a source of Muslim-Christian tensions. While anti-Christian sentiment thus far has not instigated a wave of Islamist radicalism throughout the rest of the population, the issue of Zanzibari sovereignty is crucial to the problem of this potentially violent reframing.

Tanganyika (the predecessor to Tanzania) came into being after achieving independence from Britain in 1962. Zanzibar achieved independence shortly thereafter, in 1963, and in the election that followed, the Zanzibar Nationalist Party (ZNP) coalition (generally representing the islands' Arab population) narrowly defeated the Afro-Shirazi Party (ASP), which represented the African "labor" class. Subsequently, an uprising of laborers and former soldiers mushroomed into the anti-Arab Zanzibari Revolution of 1964, which overthrew the ZNP government, the Sultan, the Arab elite, and the whole enterprise of constitutional monarchy.[53]

Abeid Karume, the leader of the ASP coalition, ruled by decree, warding off any challenges to the new regime. Three months later, Karume and Tanganyikan President Julius Nyerere united Zanzibar and Tanganyika into Tanzania. The rapid pace and questionable constitutionality of these origins remains a background factor to the increasing demands for full autonomy in Zanzibar, a demand which is frequently linked to the differing ethnic and religious composition of the islands' population.

During the early years of one-party socialist rule, President Nyerere insisted creating a nation without racial or religious divisions.[54] The demise of ujamaa ("community") socialism in the 1980s, as well as the rise of the multi-party system, permitted region and religion to divide the population, frustrating Nyerere's plans. Today, ethnic differences and overlapping religions have become salient rallying points in the search for the "true" identity of Zanzibar, which have faint echoes on the mainland. Across Tanzania, "people at the grassroots level advance religious identities in pursuit of their interests in regard to spiritual, material, and political interests."[55] The idea of full Zanzibari autonomy was first raised in 1994, but Chama Cha Mapinduzi (CCM), the ruling party since 1963, has constantly rejected the notion.[56]

In Tanzania, religion has taken a backseat to the unifying nationalist agenda of the CCM. In one notable exception, as a response to transferring control of the nation's education and health administration to the Catholic Church in 1992, the Council for the Propagation of the Quran (commonly known as Balukta) accused the Tanzanian government's National Muslim Organization (Bakwata) of corruption, briefly seizing its headquarters in protest. Balukta was Tanzania's first militant Islamist group, but it did not last long. President Ali Hassan Mwinyi expelled them from the Bakwata headquarters, and the group was banned in 1993.[57] Since then, most Islamists have tended to be critical of anti-government fundamentalists.

The CCM faces an ongoing challenge from the Zanzibar-based Civic United Front (CUF). A minority party whose various elements have professed their goal to be to "release Tanzanian society from the dictatorship of Christianity,"[58] the CUF's primary constituents are Zanzibaris of Arab descent. Although its supporters have clashed violently and repeatedly with the police since 1995, the CUF historically has maintained that it does not support violence as a means of gaining power, favoring instead legitimate, democratic means. Yet, it has not totally dismissed the use of violence as a means for establishing itself in Zanzibar, especially if the ongoing issues of political corruption and marginalization are not resolved.[59]

Tanzania held general elections in 2015 and, while the contest was considered well administered, the Zanzibar Electoral Commission annulled results on the island after the opposition looked poised to win (the ruling CCM won handily on the mainland). The subsequent electoral standoff resulted in heightened tensions across Zanzibar; a series of subsequent IED attacks were assumed to be politically motivated. The election annulment effectively ended Zanzibar's government of national unity and simultaneously eliminated what many felt was a last legitimate and mainstream avenue for expressing discontent.[60] There is now a chance that frustrated Zanzibaris who feel that they have been ejected from mainstream politics will seek out more radical representation.

To many, political marginalization is a reality in Tanzania. Although the Tanzanian state is officially secular and its constitution guarantees freedom of religion and prohibits religious political parties, smoldering tensions belie the effectiveness of this guarantee. Moderate groups, which offer no structural challenge to the system, are more likely to be candidates for political co-optation, while radicals are forced to work outside the system. Thus, the government risks pushing Islamists in more radical directions through sheer clumsiness: its entrenched corruption, election rigging, and alleged detentions and torture of opposition members dramatically exacerbate the perception of marginalization among moderates.

Since the end of socialist rule in the 1990s, Zanzibari Arabs have alleged that the government of Zanzibar (directed by the CCM) purposely discriminates against them, denying them access to government jobs, housing, and business licenses. Coastal Swahili and Arab populations that live on the mainland have often expressed similar concerns.[61] When the Tanzanian government signed "The Prevention of Terrorism Act" into law in December 2002 (in large part due to pressure from the United States),[62] it further aggravated this demographic and prompted waves of criticism for specifically targeting Muslims. Opponents of the law noted that it borrowed heavily from the U.S. Patriot Act, the British Prevention of Terrorism Act, and the Suppression of Terrorism Act of apartheid South Africa.[63] While some amendments were passed in 2016, "insufficient sentencing guidelines" remain.[64]

Finally, although Muslims have always held key governmental positions (and the presidency has unofficially rotated between a Christian and a Muslim), many Muslims perceive the governing elite as Christian, which contributes to the feeling of marginalization. Such frustrations with the state tend to manifest themselves in attacks upon Christians or Christian places of worship.[65] Additional dissatisfaction is aimed at the police, since in many Muslim areas, the police are often Christians that tend to disregard local customs and further alienate residents.

Tensions between Muslims and Christians, which rose parallel to an increase in political visibility and assertiveness of the Muslim community over the past decade, remained constant in 2017.[54] The potential for divisive internal politics to presage violent and dangerous radicalization remains, and it is worsened by shrinking domestic space for political opposition groups. Although there has not been a major terror attack in Tanzania in years, the overall dynamic bears watching. Al-Shabaab's continued threat to Somalia and its interest in expanding throughout the region—as well as the ideological and physical presence of ISIS and its affiliates throughout East Africa—means that Tanzania must also remain vigilant against radical external influences.

Endnotes

1. Harvey Glickman, "The Threat of Islamism in Sub-Saharan Africa: The Case of Tanzania," *E-Notes,* April 2011, https://www.fpri.org/docs/media/201104.glickman.islamismsubsaharanafrica.pdf.
2. Glickman, "The Threat of Islamism in Sub-Saharan Africa;" Andre Le Sage, "Terrorism Threats and

Vulnerabilities in Africa," in Andre Le Sage, ed., *African Counterterrorism Cooperation: Assessing Regional and Subregional Initiatives,* Washington, DC: National Defense University Press, 2007, 87.

3. "Tanzania Says 15 Are Linked to Acid Attacks," *New York Times*, September 17, 2013, https://www.nytimes.com/2013/09/18/world/africa/tanzania-says-15-are-linked-to-acid-attacks.html; Beatrice Materu, "Tanzania: Police Arrest Women, Children at 'Terrorism Training Camp,'" *The East African*, November 17, 2016, http://allafrica.com/stories/201611170829.html.
4. "Tanzania," UK Government Foreign Travel Advice, March 15, 2018, https://www.gov.uk/foreign-travel-advice/tanzania/terrorism; "Tanzania: Authorities promise retribution after latest police ambush," *Africa Times*, April 15, 2017, http://africatimes.com/2017/04/15/tanzania-authorities-promise-retribution-after-latest-police-ambush/; Asterius Banzi, "Dar on 'high alert' over terror attack claims," *The East African*, April 22, 2017, http://www.theeastafrican.co.ke/news/Dar-on-high-alert-over-terror-attack-claims/2558-3899482-10beug8/index.html.
5. "Al-Shabaab as a Transnational Security Threat," Intergovernmental Authority on Development, March 2016, https://igad.int/attachments/article/1373/1413_ISSP%20Report%20on%20Al%20Shabaab%20 2016%20FINAL3%20copy.pdf.
6. Jeffrey Haynes, "Islamic Militancy in East Africa," *Third World Quarterly* 26, no. 8 (2005), 1323; William Roseneau, "Al Qaida Recruitment Trends in Kenya and Tanzania," *Studies in Conflict and Terrorism* 28 (June 2004), 1, 4; Jodi Vittori, Kristen Bremer, and Pasquale Vittori, "Islam in Tanzania and Kenya: Ally or Threat in the War on Terror?" *Studies in Conflict and Terrorism* 32, no. 12 (2009), 1082; Bruce E. Heilman and Paul J. Kaiser, "Religion, Identity, and Politics in Tanzania," *Third World Quarterly*, August 2002, 1083; Andre Le Sage, "The Rising Terrorist Threat in Tanzania: Domestic Islamist Militancy and Regional Threats," Institute for National Strategic Studies, September 2014, http://ndupress.ndu.edu/Portals/68/Documents/

stratforum/SF-288.pdf, 6.

7. "Tanzania Corruption Report," GAN Business Anti-Corruption Portal, October 2016, http://www.business-anti-corruption.com/country-profiles/tanzania.
8. "Tanzania," in U.S. Department of State, *Country Reports on Terrorism 2012,* http://www.state.gov/documents/organization/210204.pdf, 36.
9. "Tanzania Church Blast: Saudi and UAE Suspects Freed," *BBC News*, May 14, 2013, http://www.bbc.com/news/world-africa-22522843; Le Sage, "The Rising Terrorist Threat in Tanzania," 6.
10. Mike Pflanz, Gordon Rayner, and Victoria Ward, "Zanzibar Acid Attack: Finger Pointed at Radical Islamic Group as Five Questioned Over Assault on British Teenagers," *The Telegraph*, August 9, 2013, http://www.telegraph.co.uk/news/worldnews/africaandindianocean/zanzibartanzania/10232580/Zanzibar-acid-attack-finger-pointed-at-radical-Islamic-group-as-five-questioned-over-assault-on-British-teenagers.html.
11. Beatrice Materu, "Tanzania police arrest women, children at 'terrorist training camp,'" *The East African*, November 17, 2016, http://www.theeastafrican.co.ke/news/Tanzania-police-arrest-women-and-children-for-alleged-terrorism/2558-3455612-ammrxs/index.html; Deodatus Balile, "Tanzania Dismantles Al-Shabaab Child Indoctrination Camp in Tanga Region," *Sabahi*, November 15, 2013, http://allafrica.com/stories/201311180387.html.
12. "The Future of Al-Qaeda: Results of a Foresight Project," Canadian Security Intelligence Service, May 2013, http://www.investigativeproject.org/documents/testimony/394.pdf, 66.
13. "Tanzania: Video Shows Possible New Islamic State Affiliate," *Stratfor Worldview*, May 18, 2016, https://worldview.stratfor.com/situation-report/tanzania-video-shows-possible-new-islamic-state-affiliate.
14. Jason Warner, "Sub-Saharan Africa's Three 'New' Islamic State Affiliates," *CTC Sentinel* 10, No. 1, January 2017, https://ctc.usma.edu/sub-saharan-africas-three-new-islamic-state-affiliates/.

15. "Al-Shabaab as a Transnational Security Threat," Intergovernmental Authority on Development, 21; "ISIS in Tanzanian Caves: Terror Threat Multiplication," *Intelligence Briefs*, May 18, 2016, http://intelligencebriefs.com/isis-in-tanzanian-caves-terror-threat-multiplication/. Tanzanians make up the second-largest group of foreign fighters in al-Shabaab; Kenyans are the largest.
16. Faustine Kapama, "Tanzania: DPP Directs Arrest of Sheikh Ponda for Disobeying Order," *allAfrica.com,* August 9, 2013, http://allafrica.com/stories/201308090176.html.
17. Peter Kagwanja, "Counter-terrorism in the Horn of Africa: New Security Frontiers, Old Strategies," *African Security Review* 15, no. 3 (2006), 77; Mike Pflanz, "Radical preacher wanted over Zanzibar acid attack shot in police raid, *Telegraph* (London), August 10, 2013, http://www.telegraph.co.uk/news/worldnews/africaandindianocean/zanzibartanzania/10235328/Radical-preacher-wanted-over-Zanzibar-acid-attack-shot-in-police-raid.html.
18. Simon Turner, "'These Young Men Show No Respect for Local Customs'- Globalisation and Islamic Revival in Zanzibar," *Journal of Religion in Africa* 39, no. 3 (2009), 239.
19. Thembi Mutch, "Zanzibar and the Mainland: The Shaky State of the Union," *Think Africa*, November 20, 2012, http://thinkafricapress.com/tanzania/zanzibar-tanzania-shaky-state-union-uamsho.
20. Uamsho, "About Revival," n.d., http://uamshozanzibar.wordpress.com/kuhusu-uamsho/.
21. "Uamsho Group," Terrorism Research and Analysis Consortium, https://www.trackingterrorism.org/group/uamsho-group.
22. "Tanzania: Pinda Concerned with Uamsho Group," *AllAfrica.com*, June 14, 2012, http://allafrica.com/stories/201206150142.html.
23. Fumbuka Ng'wanakilala, "Zanzibar Islamists Burn Churches, Riot – Police," *Reuters*, May 27, 2012, http://www.reuters.com/article/zanzibar-protest-idUSL5E8GR1HB20120527.

24. Nicholas Kulish, "Violent Episodes Grow in Tanzania, an African Haven," *New York Times*, June 30, 2013, http://www.nytimes.com/2013/07/01/world/africa/violent-episodes-grow-in-tanzania-an-african-haven.html?pagewanted=all&_r=1&.
25. "The Swahili Coast: Contagion of Discontent," *The Economist*, November 3, 2012, http://www.economist.com/news/middle-east-and-africa/21565641-muslim-extremism-spreads-down-east-africa%E2%80%99s-coastline-contagion-discontent?zid=304&ah=e5690753dc78ce91909083042ad12e30.
26. United Nations, "Report of the Monitoring Group on Somalia and Eritrea Pursuant to Security Council Resolution 2002 (2011)," July 13, 2012, http://www.marsecreview.com/wp-content/uploads/2012/09/UN_REPORT_2012.pdf.
27. Le Sage, "The Rising Terrorist Threat in Tanzania," 12; "The Future of Al Qaeda: Results of a Foresight Project," Canadian Security Intelligence Service, 66; United Nations, "Report of the Monitoring Group on Somalia and Eritrea Pursuant to Security Council Resolution 2060 (2012): Somalia," July 12, 2013, http://www.un.org/ga/search/view_doc.asp?symbol=S/2013/413, 15.
28. Jeffrey Haynes, "Islamic Militancy in East Africa," 1330.
29. "Tanzania," *Country Reports on Terrorism 2012,* 37.
30. Turner, "'These Young Men Show No Respect for Local Customs'- Globalisation and Islamic Revival in Zanzibar," 252-3.
31. Harvey Glickman, "The Threat of Islamism in Sub-Saharan Africa: The Case of Tanzania," Foreign Policy Research Institute, April 2011, https://www.fpri.org/docs/media/201104.glickman.islamismsubsaharanafrica.pdf.
32. "Tanzania" *CIA World Factbook.*
33. Glickman, "The Threat of Islamism in Sub-Saharan Africa;" National Bureau of Statistics – Ministry of Finance and Office of Chief Government Statistician – Ministry of State, "Basic Demographic and Socio-Economic Profile, Tanzania Zanzibar," April 2014,

http://www.tanzania.go.tz/egov_uploads/documents/TANZANIA_ZANZIBAR_SOCIO_ECONOMIC_PROFILE_sw.pdf, iii.

34. Pew Forum on Religion & Public Life, "The World's Muslims: Unity and Disunity," August 9, 2012, http://www.pewforum.org/files/2012/08/the-worlds-muslims-full-report.pdf, 30; "Tanzania," in U.S. Department of State *International Religious Freedom Report*, 2016, https://www.state.gov/j/drl/rls/irf/religiousfreedom/index.htm#wrapper.
35. Haynes, "Islamic Militancy in East Africa," 1330.
36. Glickman, "The Threat of Islamism in Sub-Saharan Africa;" Vittori et al., "Islam in Tanzania and Kenya: Ally or Threat in the War on Terror?" 1082; "Tanzania Human Development Report 2014," United Nations Development Programme, 2014, http://hdr.undp.org/sites/default/files/thdr2014-main.pdf, 10.
37. Turner, "'These Young Men Show No Respect for Local Customs'- Globalisation and Islamic Revival in Zanzibar," 259.
38. Abigail Higgins, "Fighting Heroin Addiction in Conservative Zanzibar," *Al Jazeera*, May 28, 2015, http://www.aljazeera.com/indepth/features/2015/05/fighting-heroin-addiction-conservative-zanzibar-150514102028439.html.
39. Le Sage, "The Rising Terrorist Threat in Tanzania," 8.
40. Haynes, "Islamic Militancy in East Africa," 1330; Le Sage, "The Rising Terrorist Threat in Tanzania," 81; Vittori et al., "Islam in Tanzania and Kenya: Ally or Threat in the War on Terror?" 1088. As Le Sage rightfully points out, scholars have woefully scarce data on the amount of money that has been donated from the Gulf to East Africa.
41. Katrina Manson, "Extremism on the Rise in Zanzibar," *Financial Times,* December 28, 2012, http://www.ft.com/intl/cms/s/0/c85b0054-42c0-11e2-a4e4-00144feabdc0.html#axzz2cXjw2UQ2.
42. Ibid.
43. Turner, "'These Young Men Show No Respect for Local Customs'- Globalisation and Islamic Revival in Zanzibar," 238.

44. Mohabe Nyirabu, "The Multiparty Reform Process in Tanzania: The Dominance of the Ruling Party," *African Journal of Political Science* 7, no. 2, 2002, 104.
45. Loimeier, "Perceptions of Marginalization: Muslims in Contemporary Tanzania," 143; Turner, "'These Young Men Show No Respect for Local Customs'- Globalisation and Islamic Revival in Zanzibar," 238.
46. Haynes, "Islamic Militancy in East Africa," 1331; Larson, "Introduction," 20; Heilman and Kaiser, "Religion, Identity, and Politics in Tanzania," 695.
47. 2017 measures of GDP per capita in purchasing power parity (PPP). The last available statistic for percentage of the population below the poverty line is 47% (2016). With a steady annual GDP growth rate between 6-7 percent, and as GDP per capita has increased in recent years, the number of Tanzanians living below the poverty line has decreased correspondingly, but economic poverty remains a force to be reckoned with. "Tanzania," *CIA World Factbook,* November 25, 2016, https://www.cia.gov/library/publications/the-world-factbook/geos/tz.html; "Tanzania Overview," World Bank, October 5, 2017, http://www.worldbank.org/en/country/tanzania/overview.
48. Larson, "Introduction," 24.
49. Turner, "'These Young Men Show No Respect for Local Customs'- Globalisation and Islamic Revival in Zanzibar," 240.
50. "Tanzania," *CIA World Factbook.*
51. Fambuka Ng'wanakilala, "Tanzanian President Warns of Rising Religious Tensions Before Referendum," *Reuters*, March 29, 2015, http://www.reuters.com/article/tanzania-politics-idUSL6N0WV0IM20150329.
52. At least one woman has been arrested for attempting to travel to Somalia to join al-Shabaab. Philip Muyanga, "TZ girl arrested en route to join Shabaab militants," *The Citizen*, March 31, 2016, http://www.thecitizen.co.tz/News/national/TZ-girl-arrested-en-route-to-join-Shabaab-militants-/1840392-2671154-8nmmblz/index.html. See also "Tanzania Warns of Growing Number of Terrorism Recruits," *CCTV Africa*, May 12, 2016, https://www.youtube.com/watch?v=M9t7maly0fc;

Jaston Binala, "Tanzania: Radicalism Rising in Tanzania but No Panic Yet," *The East African*, December 19, 2015, http://allafrica.com/stories/201512212852.html.

53. Greg Cameron, "Narratives of Democracy and Dominance in Zanzibar," in Kjersti Larson, ed., *Knowledge, Renewal, and Religion: Repositioning and Changing Ideological and Material Circumstances Among the Swahili on the East African Coast* (Uppsala: Nordiska Afrikainstitutet, 2009), 151.
54. Killian, "The State and Identity Politics in Zanzibar: Challenges to Democratic Consolidation in Tanzania," 115.
55. Africa Liberal Network, "Civic United Front – Tanzania," 2013, http://www.africaliberalnetwork.org/standard.aspx?i_PageID=138.
56. Killian, "The State and Identity Politics in Zanzibar: Challenges to Democratic Consolidation in Tanzania," 111.
57. Glickman, "The Threat of Islamism in Sub-Saharan Africa;" Barbara G. Brents and Deo S. Mshigeni, "Terrorism in Context: Race, Religion, Party, and Violent Conflict in Zanzibar," *The American Sociologist*, Summer 2004, 67.
58. Douglis G. Anglin, "Zanzibar: Political Impasse and Commonwealth Mediation," *Journal of Contemporary African Studies* 18, no. 1 (2000), 43-44.
59. Glickman, "The Threat of Islamism in Sub-Saharan Africa."
60. Le Sage, "The Rising Terrorist Threat in Tanzania," 8.
61. "Terrorism in Context: Race, Religion, Party, and Violent Conflict in Zanzibar," 67; Haynes, "Islamic Militancy in East Africa," 1330.
62. Glickman, "The Threat of Islamism in Sub-Saharan Africa."
63. Le Sage, "Terrorism Threats and Vulnerabilities in Africa," 87.
64. "Tanzania," in U.S. Department of State, *Country Reports on Terrorism 2016*, https://www.state.gov/j/ct/rls/crt/2016/272229.htm.
65. Glickman, "The Threat of Islamism in Sub-Saharan Africa."

Europe

40 Albania

> ### Quick Facts
>
> Population: 3,047,987 (July 2017 est.)
> Area: 28,748 sq km
> Ethnic Groups: Albanian 82.6%, Greek 0.9%, other 1% (including Vlach, Romani, Macedonian, Montenegrin, and Egyptian), unspecified 15.5% (2011 est.)
> Government Type: Parliamentary republic
> GDP (official exchange rate): $13 billion (2017 est.)
>
> *Source: CIA World FactBook (Last Updated April 2018)*

Introduction

While Albanians of all faiths have historically co-existed peacefully, the participation of Albanian fighters in ISIS—and subsequent foiled terrorist plots in Albania itself—indicate that Islamic radicalism has become an important future security challenge. The foundations for radicalism were actually laid in the early 1990s, when foreign Islamic states and organizations sought to gain influence in a country then just emerging from 45 years of Communist dictatorship. While radical Islamism has never found mass appeal, Albania has always been a place of interest for both terrorist groups and those hunting them—as was attested to as long as two decades ago by CIA operations against international terrorist cells in the country.

Islamist trends in Albania parallel similar developments in other Balkan countries. Such states share several important characteristics: a lack of employment and educational opportunities, especially for young people; indigenous Muslim populations; a transition from former autocratic socialist or communist governments; and the entrenched presence of foreign Islamist forces attempting to educate local Muslims, build mosques, provide public services, make investments, and otherwise build influence. And, as in neighboring Kosovo, the attempts of the Vatican to bolster Catholicism in Albania have angered parts of the Muslim population.

Through 2017, the number of Albanian leaving to join ISIS and the al-Nusra Front had declined significantly in response to the strategic reversals both groups have faced in the Middle East. However, as with other regional countries experiencing the same phenomenon, Albania's success in stemming the departure of foreign fighters has been offset by new problems. These include the need to deradicalize returning fighters, and to deal with terrorist plots organized from the Middle East or Western European diaspora—the most high-profile of which, so far, was a foiled plot to attack against the Israeli soccer team in a match played in Albania in November 2016.[1]

In response to the challenges posed by growing radicalism, the Obama administration during its time in office chose to create a NATO Center of Excellence in the Alliance's newest member state, to be devoted to countering radicalization. However, as of 2017, this center had not yet become fully operational, and the major elements of security cooperation against terrorism were still carried out via state engagement with the US, EU, and regional security partners.

Islamism in Albania is a particularly fascinating topic because of its historic and multi-layered nature. The still predominant Sunni branch of Islam was introduced by the Ottoman Turks, who ruled for 500 years (until 1912). Just over a decade later, the new secular Turkish Republic deported a significant number of Sufi Muslims to Albania. Following the Communist rule of Enver Hoxha, in which religion was banned, Albania returned to its Muslim, Catholic, and Orthodox faiths. But along with the Wahhabi proselytizing from Gulf states since the 1990s, Albania has recently become a place of exile for an Iranian opposition group, while the political rift between Turkish President Recep Tayyip Erdogan and U.S.-based Turkish cleric Fetullah Gülen has been felt in Albania, as in other regional states.

Islamist Activity

The population of Albania stands at 2.8 million,[2] 80 percent of whom are Muslims.[3] This cohort, in turn, is made up of three distinct groups. The Muslim Community of Albania is the major body representing the country's Sunni Muslims (and Albanian Muslims in general), and is deemed to be the most "legitimate" representative of Albanian Muslims by the state and the international community.[4] Secondly, the World Bektashi Center in Tirana officially represents the Shi'ite Bektashi Sufi order (comprising around 20 percent of Albania's Muslim population), which has a longstanding presence in the country, having been sent to Albania in the 1920s by the newly secularist Turkish Republic; this group shares some similarities with Turkey's Alevi Muslims.[5] However, the Bektashi order is considered heretical by many Muslims for its more relaxed, liberal practices and differing theology. The Bektashi are particularly despised by the third and most dangerous Islamic group present in Albania—the puritanical minority attracted to Wahhabism and other extreme forms of Islam now prevalent in the Arab world. The latter population has been involved with recruiting fighters for Middle Eastern conflicts since at least 2014.

Wahhabis comprise a minority of unknown size in Albania, as they operate largely outside of official structures. Although they continue to make determined efforts to usurp power from legitimate Islamic representatives, Wahhabis have also established parallel institutions, ranging from mosques to schools and charities. In July 2012, a Catholic charity leader voiced alarm over a perceived increase in Islamic fundamentalist attitudes among young Muslims—particularly those returning from schooling in Saudi Arabia and Turkey. This foreign training was associated with increasing fundamentalism.[6]

Recruitment for ISIS and al-Nusra in Syria's civil war, in which several hundred Albanian citizens have participated, was most notable in the capital, Tirana, and in impoverished villages in southeastern Albania, such as Leshnica, Zagoracan and Rremenj. Since 2011, some 24 young Muslims from these villages alone have disappeared into Syria, where several are presumed to have died in fighting—along with the individual responsible for their recruitment, former Leshnica imam Almir Daci.[7] When surveyed in May of 2015, 500 ethnic Albanian fighters were believed to be in Syria and Iraq, with approximately 150 of them Albanian citizens.[8] By August 2016, the number of recruits had dropped considerably, though Albanian experts viewed this decline as reflecting a relative loss of territory—and thus reduced personnel needs—on the part of the Islamic State, rather than a decline in overall radicalism in Albania itself.[9]

Indeed, as elsewhere in Europe, Albania is becoming a target for terrorist attacks. The Islamic State's territorial decline in the Middle East throughout 2016 and 2017 has increased its emphasis on creating instability in Europe. The terror group has exhorted fellow radicals to act alone toward this objective, as occurred in August 2016 when a Kosovo Albanian with a prior criminal record attacked and attempted to kidnap several people in the southern town of Vlore.[10] This episode caused significant concern among government officials, because Albania has tried in recent years to develop its coastal tourism industry, and any successful attacks would damage this much-needed source of income.

While radicalism remains low, it is significant to note that the Albanian language was one of several chosen by the Islamic State for its propaganda purposes from its earliest stages. In fact, the above-mentioned Almir Daci became a well-known propagandist for ISIS, and participated in a brigade specifically composed of Balkan recruits.[11] In Syria, the main Albanian military leader among the ranks of ISIS, the Kosovar Lavdrim Muhaxheri, became notorious after a video of him beheading a captive appeared online. Before being killed in an airstrike in 2017, Muhaxheri had remotely coordinated terrorist cells in Albania, Kosovo, and Macedonia in 2016. Police were able to prevent their plot to attack a soccer game in Albania between the Israeli and Albanian national teams in November 2016. However, the fact that an Albanian-led network from the Middle East could in fact be capable of leading such an operation came as a shock to many.[12]

Indeed, Albanians have historically taken pride in maintaining ethnic cohesion, despite being cumulatively composed of differing Christian and Muslim groups. If politically-oriented Muslim extremists (from NGO groups to actual terrorist supporters) gain influence, it could easily endanger this cooperative legacy. For the official leadership of the Muslim community, the primary challenge has been to fend off rivals both formal and informal. During the last decade and more, leadership challenges and internal conflicts within the official Albanian Islamic Community have allowed radical views to proliferate, while the official body remains occupied with its own internal problems. The Islamic Community is Albania's second-largest landowner, and some of the "scandals" surrounding the Community's leadership over the years have concerned alleged profiteering from land sales.

In recent years, this schism has divided Muslims in Albania. Rival factions arose in the Community's General Council, involving then-head mufti Selim Muca, who was in power from 2004-2014, and his opponents. On September 21, 2010, following an attempt by Muca's opponents to prosecute him for corruption, a special session of the General Council reconfirmed Muca's authority, and sacked four opponents among the Islamic leadership.[13] This decision came four years after similar infighting, which resulted in the firing of the Mufti of Shkoder, Bashkim Bajraktari. U.S. officials were concerned at the time that Shkoder's Islamic leadership was "stacked with 'extremists'" due to the local influence of an outspoken conservative NGO, the Muslim Forum of Albania (MFA), and its international links with the Muslim Brotherhood.[14]

This political jockeying has created internal frictions within Albania's Muslim community, and distracted its leadership from dealing with attempts by religious extremists to strengthen their foothold in the country. Muca, for example, was criticized for failing to stop the formation of a union of imams with reported Wahhabi leanings in Kavaja, located between Tirana and the Adriatic coast. An MFA event in Kavaja in February 2008 attracted Islamists from Kosovo, Macedonia and elsewhere.[15] A newer group, the Union of Islamic Youth, was then registered in Kavaja and was believed to be associated with Wahhabi elements (though available information about the group is sparse). Local and foreign observers agreed that the Kavaja mosque and its worshippers are increasingly wary of outsiders and seem to have more fundamentalist views.[16]

The presence of foreign-funded radical groups since the 1990s has further aggravated the internal problems of the Islamic Community. For example, following the September 11, 2001 terrorist attacks, the Bush administration asked Albania to close down charities suspected to be fronts for radical activity; one, al Haramain, was suspected of organizing the murder of a moderate Muslim Community leader, Salih Tivari, in January 2002.[17] Tivari had pledged to remove foreign Islamist elements from the country. Albanian authorities believe that local extremists trained in Islamic states actually carried out his murder.[18] In 2006, other Muslim Community leaders received death threats after an extremist group tried but failed to change one of the Community's official statutes.[19]

More recently, Albania has faced a different kind of pressure from a key regional ally: Turkey. After 2013 and a widening rift between Turkish leader Recep Tayyip Erdogan and the Pennsylvania-based cleric (and one-time Erdogan political ally) Fetullah Gülen, Ankara pressured Albania to close Gülen-affiliated schools. The request came during President Erdogan's state visit in 2015, and again after the July 2016 coup attempt against Erdogan's government in Turkey.[20] While the Albanian government refused to do so, it came under increasing pressure to tackle the alleged involvement of Gülenist 'parallel institutions' in public administration.

Turkey has alleged that Albania is serving as a stronghold for the rival movement. After the coup attempt, Turkey officially requested Albanian police "to investigate and ultimately arrest a number of individuals allegedly supporting Gülen," who media indicated "may include public figures, journalists, analysts and even high-ranking officials."[21]

A final, still-unknown commodity in Albania is the negotiated relocation of an Iranian former militant group, something that has attracted the attention of the Islamic Republic's intelligence services. Albania has a long history of doing favors for the U.S. government and, in 2013, it accepted an offer from the Obama administration to grant asylum to about 250 members of Mohajedeen-e-Khalq (MEK). This Iranian "dissident group" was formerly considered a terrorist organization, as it had targeted Americans in Iran in the 1970s, before moving into the opposition against the Islamic Republic.[22] In fact, the Albanian government has expanded this arrangement, and has taken in from 500-2,000 MEK members to date. During 2016 alone, Albania absorbed almost 2,000 MEK members as "asylum seekers" via the auspices of the UN High Commission on Refugees (UNHCR).[23]

Although this historic Marxist-Shiite group has renounced violence, it still remains a notable enemy of the Iranian state, and the latter has used proxies like Hezbollah to attack it in Iraq. While this would be more difficult for Iran to do in Albania, the presence of the MEK in the country (and the larger support given to the group by Iran's archrival, Saudi Arabia) threatens to make Albania new terrain for proxy war--although the possibility has so far received very little media coverage outside of the country. Of more immediate concern, however, "is that the MEK presence poses a risk of inflaming sectarian divides in smaller communities, a phenomenon still in its latent state among Albanian Muslims," one local expert reported in 2017.[24]

Islamism and Society

In the past decade, the number of mosques in Albania has increased rapidly, due to an ongoing process of legalizing previously non-recognized mosques. A 2009 survey stated that Albania had 568 Sunni mosques, as well as 70 Bektashi tekkes (lodges) and mausoleums.[25] By December 2015, however, officials had announced that 727 mosques existed in the country—of which at least 200 were not under the control of any official, sanctioned Muslim community organization.[26] At that time, former Muslim Community deputy director Ermir Gjinishi warned that if the clerical body did not "intervene immediately to change this situation next year, half of the mosques in Albania will pass out of its control."[27]

The following year, the country began the process of legalizing mosques that had been built since the early 1990s on state-owned land, often by shadowy foreign donors. In September 2016, it was reported that 957 structures—"most of them mosques"—were being granted property licenses by the government for the first time. Ylli Gurra, head of Tirana's Islamic Community, told media at the time that having official control of these mosques would allow the community to root out radicalism.[28] In truth, the acquisition represents a windfall for the Islamic Community (and Islamism in general), as even if many of these mosques have few attendees, their 'territorial mark' has now been cemented on the landscape, projecting a perhaps greater Islamic influence than is the case.

Albania's Muslim population accounts for 70 percent of the country's 2.8 million people. Albania also has notable Catholic (10 percent) and Orthodox Christian (20 percent) populations. The latter is located chiefly in the southern part of the country, and includes the country's Greek and Macedonian minorities. The 2009 survey reported over 1,100 Catholic and Orthodox churches in Albania.[29]

Nevertheless, secularism prevails throughout the country, especially in rapidly-modernizing Tirana, and Albanian Muslims are much less devout in their practice than are ethnic Albanians in neighboring Kosovo and Macedonia. As in these countries and throughout the wider Balkan region, however, Wahhabis have exacerbated divisions within the Muslim community since 2010, with one security official stating in June 2016 that sectarian divisions are now "at the core of the rifts between Muslim communities."[30]

While most Albanians are relatively secular-minded, an important trend for the future will be the relationship between the country's different religious groups. The government was criticized by secularists for its plan to introduce the category of religious affiliation to the 2011 national census, as doing so could exacerbate the politicking between different faiths. This has indeed occurred, with particularly religious leaders, particularly Orthodox and Evangelical ones, claiming their numbers had been underrepresented in the census. The issue became so controversial that a subsequent Council of Europe report stated that the census "cannot claim to be reliable and accurate," due to its unprofessional execution.[31]

Today, Muslims and Christian proselytizers continue to eye one another warily, and often accuse each other of inappropriate actions. In a 2012 report for the Vatican, Archbishop Angelo Massafra of the Archdiocese of Shkoder-Pult expressed concerns over rising Muslim fundamentalism in Albania, as well as the perceived involvement of countries like Saudi Arabia and Turkey. He also expressed concerns over the recent opening of a new Islamic university in Tirana.[32] (Known as Bedër University, this center opened in April 2011).[33]

It is likely that the Vatican's concern over the latter is less an expression of fear of radicalism than it is apprehensiveness over any further Islamic "re-awakening" among a relatively secular population. The Vatican has in recent years taken a proactive approach to expanding its presence in Albania, something that has involved a Papal visit of 2014 and increased involvement of (primarily Italian) Catholic schools and NGOs in Albania.[34] One key event bolstering Catholicism in Albania and beyond was the September 4, 2016 canonization of Mother Teresa; the revered ethnic Albanian nun was born in Skopje, Macedonia and had ancestry in Kosovo. Tirana's international airport is named for her, and today she is an essential part of the international Albanian brand. Anecdotal evidence suggests that this has caused an internal debate within Albanian populations of different faiths regarding Mother Teresa's rightful place in the country's national identity and history.[35]

Albania's internal struggles as a nation over religious values and broader personal and national aspirations have occasionally been heated. For example, in October 2003, the outspoken author Kastriot Myftari was arrested for "inciting religious hatred" after writing that Albanian Muslims should convert to Catholicism. (Myftari was ultimately acquitted).[36] More controversially, in November 2005, Islamists reacted sharply when then-President Alfred Moisiu, speaking before the Oxford Union in England, stated that Albanians followed a "shallow" sort of Islam, and that the country's Christian heritage has much deeper roots.[37] In response, the MFA and other Islamist groups accused Moisiu of "insulting Islam."

Inter-religious strife likewise has registered in more tangible ways. When local leaders announced that national hero Mother Teresa would be commemorated with a statue, three Muslim NGOs—the MFA, the Association of Islamic Intellectuals and the Association of Islamic Charities—condemned the initiative as a "provocation" against Islam.[38] (While the MFA was the most visible of the three, the Association of Muslim Intellectuals is older, dating from the early 1990s, paralleling the creation of other, similar Islamist intellectual organizations in Bosnia and elsewhere.[39] In 1991, it was led by the late Bashkim Gazidede, whose tacit assistance to foreign terrorist-linked entities while serving as director of Albania's national intelligence agency is discussed in detail below.)

Foreign Islamic charities still operating in the country have moved beyond the initial phase of relief and infrastructure projects, and are now becoming more involved with social issues. For example, one of Albania's intractable problems—the practice of clan vendettas in the mountainous northeast, which continues to restrict the movement and social life of entire families—has been exploited by foreign Islamists. Dedicated efforts have been made to increase Islamist teaching in these areas, which are historically associated with smuggling, paramilitary activities, and isolationism. Hundreds of students are reportedly undertaking Islamic education in rural towns like Koplik, with some going on to study in Turkey or the Middle East.[40] Taking the lead in developing programs to solve vendettas and poverty via Islamic means is the UK-registered (but globally active) charity Islamic Relief,[41] which has operated in Albania since 1991.[42]

A final aspect of note is Albania's Shiite Bektashi Dervish order, which became entrenched from the 18th century onwards, primarily in southern Albania. As a more liberal form of Islam, it in 1923 dropped Ottoman-enforced practices such as polygamy and the forced wearing of the hijab (veil) by women. Three years later, the Albanian government took in 25,000 members of the Bektashi order expelled from Turkey during Mustafa Kemal Ataturk's secularization campaign. In Albania, as elsewhere, the Bektashis are denounced by Wahhabi elements as heretical.

The Bektashi themselves do not engage in proselytizing, and are aware that they are vulnerable. However, while Iran has offered funding to help ensure their future, the Bektashi leadership claims that it has not and will not accept funds from Iran.[43] Rather, Bektashi leaders have reached out to the West to try and take on a higher profile as an example of a peaceful and tolerant movement, and the Albanian government helped to fund the establishment of the Bektashi World Centre in Tirana in November 2015. According to a U.S. State Department report on religious freedom from that year, "the Bektashi were also constructing or restoring several places of worship in Korca, Permet, Gjirokaster, and Elbasan. Property disputes with the government delayed progress."[44]

Islamism and the State

Under Ottoman rule (from the 14th to the early 20th centuries), large numbers of Albanians converted to Islam to capitalize on better opportunities for state employment and career advancement. Sunni Islam became most popular in central and northern Albania, while the Bektashi also developed a presence in the country. Under the Communist dictatorship of Enver Hoxha, however, religion was officially banned from 1967 onward, and all religious groups were persecuted by the state.

The deep history of modern Albanian engagement with Islamism is worth examining, as it is more extensive than that of any other regional state, except perhaps Bosnia, since the end of the Cold War. Thus, the most pivotal moment in the modern Albanian state's relationship with Islam came when the first post-Communist government opened its arms to outside Islamist governments and interests in the early 1990s. Then-president Sali Berisha was not himself religious, but sought out foreign investment of any kind. His election in 1992 was therefore followed by visits from Kuwaitis, who offered an "ambitious" investment plan in exchange for an opportunity to build mosques in Albania.[45] Soon after, the Islamic Development Bank (IDB) began offering substantial investment and opportunities for Albanians to learn Arabic and study in Islamic states.[46] President Berisha also made Albania the first European member of the Organization of the Islamic Conference; one momentous consequence of this decision was the "unilateral abolition" of visa requirements for citizens of Muslim countries, making Albania a desirable option for international fugitive terrorists wanting to disappear into Europe.[47] In this way, several senior al-Qaeda figures were able to establish an operational base on Albanian territory (although that specific network was dismantled in the late 1990s).[48]

By 1994, private Saudi investors in the telecom, textile, banking and transport sectors, often through the IDB, were extending multi-million-dollar lines of credit to Albania. The same year, predating similar investments by the West, the Arab-Albanian Islamic Bank was established in Tirana.[49] Osama bin Laden was reportedly the major stockholder and founder of this bank.[50] The bank built hundreds of mosques, sent Albanians to Islamic universities abroad, and paid poor Albanians on the condition that their women wear the chador (veiled outer garment).[51] Hundreds of young Albanians went to study in Islamic countries, or undertook the Hajj. In 1993 alone, more than 1,000 Albanians made the pilgrimage to Mecca.[52] Some analysts believe the true agenda of these foreign investors was to, over time, transform Albania into an Islamic state, through economic aid, proselytization, and finally the establishment of Islamic governance.[53]

Most sinister, however, was the Albanian state's relationship with the world's most dangerous Islamist terror networks. While President Berisha was not ideologically motivated, other high-level figures were in fact devoted Islamists, including the late Bashkim Gazidede, then director of the country's national intelligence agency (SHIK). By 1994, the increasing presence of foreign jihadists in Islamic charities had made Western security officials "deeply suspicious."[54] Osama bin Laden, at that time based in Sudan, visited Tirana that year, presenting himself as a wealthy Saudi businessman offering humanitarian aid.[55] However, bin Laden was actually sponsoring the charity Al Haramain, later classified as a terrorist entity by the United States government.[56]

The Albanian government likewise welcomed other dangerous charities like the Revival of Islamic Heritage Society, Muwafaq ("Blessed Relief") Foundation, the bin Laden-linked World Assembly of Muslim Youth, Taibah International and Iran's Ayatollah Khomeini Society. Another terror-linked charity, the International Islamic Relief Organization (IIRO), employed Mohammed al-Zawahiri, the younger brother of future al-Qaeda second-in-command Ayman al-Zawahiri. He had reportedly been tasked by bin Laden himself with finding legitimate cover for Egyptian Islamic Jihad members involved with assassinations or attempted assassinations of Egyptian leaders.[57] The arrival of an Egyptian foreign ministry delegation in Albania in 1995 prompted the CIA to reach out to the by-then highly-compromised SHIK. One detained Islamist became an informant, marking a temporary breakthrough on the intelligence front. The informant in turn revealed the embarrassing truth that Albania had come to be known among jihadists as a "safe hotel" where they could hide out with the tacit approval of the state.[58]

Indeed, despite the assistance provided by the SHIK on this occasion, Islamist penetration of Albanian intelligence continued, and help provided by the agency to the U.S. suffered a corresponding decline. The SHIK would only be reformed once the Berisha government was ousted; in January 1997, the collapse of an investment pyramid scheme left ordinary Albanians penniless, leading to total anarchy and the looting of state arsenals. In April 1997, the SHIK was suspended by the caretaker government. June elections saw the ascent of an Orthodox Christian prime minister, Fatos Nano, who had previously been jailed by Berisha. Ex-SHIK director and jihad sympathizer Bashkim Gazidede reportedly escaped to the Middle East, and several arrest warrants were later issued for him by the new government.

The Nano government cooled relations with the Islamic world, irritating Islamist investors when it failed to send a delegate to the 1998 OIC conference. A CIA re-training course for the SHIK, and the removal of pro-Islamist SHIK officials and Islamic Community leaders, came at a time when the result of a merger of Ayman al-Zawahiri's Egyptian Islamic Jihad and al-Qaeda was being assessed by the CIA as having produced one of the world's most dangerous terrorist entities.[59] Local experts in Albania noted that the EIJ's Tirana cell was among its most important, as it was expert in falsifying documents to facilitate the transit of suspected terrorists.[60]

In mid-1998, a renewed round of CIA-ordered SHIK kidnappings of jihadis in Tirana led to the rendition of several men to Egypt. Unfortunately, covert American involvement was leaked by "euphoric" SHIK agents, enraging the jihadist internationale.[61] A letter released by a London-based al-Qaeda newsletter on August 5, 1998 promised a violent response.[62] Just two days later, terrorists bombed the U.S. embassy in Nairobi, Kenya, killing 213 people and injuring more than 4,000. A second embassy attack, in Dar es Salaam, Tanzania, killed 11 and injured 85. These incidents revealed that ongoing counter-terrorist operations in Albania could trigger Islamist attacks globally, which put the Balkan country into the new and nebulous category of "dangerous ally." The U.S. State Department temporarily closed diplomatic facilities in Albania and Americans were warned to avoid the country altogether.

Nevertheless, Albania remained a key ally for the Clinton administration's determined efforts to arm and train Albanian separatists in the neighboring Yugoslav province of Kosovo.[63] (Ironically, at the same time, American officials were also stating openly that Albania was hosting Iranian, Chechen, Afghan, Algerian and Egyptian mujahideen who were offering their services for a Kosovo jihad.[64]) Yet U.S. support for Kosovar Muslims (and Bosnian Muslims in their own previous war against the Serbs) failed to make America beloved throughout the Muslim world. However, during the brief Kosovo refugee crisis in the spring of 1999, the U.S. government allowed massive humanitarian activity to be carried out by some of the very same foreign organizations and individuals that it had previously identified as dangerous.[65] (The connection between such charities and Albanian extremists active in the Balkans was noted over a decade later, when a radical imam was expelled from Kosovo).[66]

It was thus little surprise that adverse security conditions persisted in Albania during the following months. For example, then-Defense Secretary William Cohen had to cancel a celebratory visit to the country in mid-July 1999, as he was being targeted by remaining al-Qaeda operatives in Tirana.[67] Several months earlier, the police had detained a Saudi-trained Albanian national accused of conducting surveillance on U.S. facilities, as well as two well-armed terrorist cell members in Tirana.[68]

Soon after the September 11, 2001 terrorist attacks, U.S. government officials, speaking off the record, disclosed a connection between the al-Qaeda plotters and Albania-based Islamic terrorists.[69] In Tirana, attention turned to Yassin al-Qadi, founder and chief investor in the Muwafaq Foundation. Although he denied all charges, al-Qadi subsequently was designated a sponsor of terrorism by the U.S. Treasury Department in October 2001.[70] The multi-millionaire Saudi investor was accused of laundering $10 million for Osama bin Laden through his business interests and charities. In 2002, the Albanian government seized a 15-story business center owned by al-Qadi in Tirana and expelled his business partner, Abdul Latif Saleh; the latter had been associated with the Tirana charities created by al-Qaeda, and was accused by U.S. investigators of cooperating with al-Qaeda while in Albania.[71]

On the economic level, Albania's courtship with foreign Islamic funders continued, with the Islamic Development Bank (IDB) in October 2010 offering millions of dollars for infrastructure and other projects.[72] The announcement came only three months after then-Prime Minister Berisha hosted a high-level IDB delegation, and thanked the organization for its assistance (past and present) in development efforts in Albania.[73] In January 2012, three years after Albania had opened an embassy in the United Arab Emirates, the two countries established a Committee on Economic Co-operation. In addition to its investments in other Balkan states, the UAE in 2012 was funding the construction of the Tirana-Elbasan highway and the airport in Kukes, projects worth roughly $100 million.[74]

While Wahhabi groups remain a distinct minority, the visible presence of Albanian fighters in Syria and Iraq, and their active recruitment efforts in Albania itself, has re-oriented the government to take greater advantage of its strong relations with the U.S. and its own NATO membership. Thus, under the similarly left-leaning administrations of Barack Obama and Albanian premier Edi Rama, plans were laid for a regional center on studying the phenomenon of foreign fighters and countering violent extremism.[75]

Approved in May 2016, this new NATO Center of Excellence, once completed, will become the first of its kind in the region, and is considered a political victory as much as a security one for the Albanian government over regional rivals. However, while the Albanians are primed to take a stronger role in the region, lingering competition between Balkan states remains an impediment to greater political trust and intelligence-sharing. Thus fighting terrorism and radicalization within the country is likely to remain largely a matter of bilateral or multilateral effort, rather than a truly integrated regional one

Endnotes

1. Lizzie Dearden, "Isis attack on Israeli football team foiled by police at World Cup qualifier in Albania," *The Independent*, November 17, 2016, https://www.independent.co.uk/news/world/europe/isis-attack-israeli-israel-football-team-police-kosovo-terror-simultane-

ous-a7422696.html.
2. "Population, Total," The World Bank, 2015, http://data.worldbank.org/indicator/SP.POP.TOTL.
3. See Tracy Miller, ed., *Mapping the Global Muslim Population: A Report on the Size and Distribution of the World's Muslim Population* (Washington, DC: Pew Research Center, October 2009), http://www.pewforum.org/files/2009/10/Muslimpopulation.pdf.
4. The community's website is www.kmsh.al.
5. The official Bektashi order website can be found at www.bektashi.net.
6. "Turkey, Saudi Arabia Promoting Stricter Islam in Albania," *Catholic News Agency*, July 20, 2012, http://www.catholicnewsagency.com/news/turkey-saudi-arabia-promoting-stricter-islam-in-albania/.
7. Aleksandra Bogdani, "Albanian Villages Ponder Local Spike in ISIS Recruits," *Balkan Insight*, April 25, 2016, http://www.balkaninsight.com/en/article/albanian-villages-ponder-local-spurt-of-isis-recruits-04-22-2016.
8. Adrian Shtuni, "Ethnic Albanian Foreign Fighters in Iraq and Syria," Combating Terrorism Center at West Point, April 30, 2015, https://www.ctc.usma.edu/posts/ethnic-albanian-foreign-fighters-in-iraq-and-syria
9. Fatjona Mejdini, "Drop in ISIS Fighters Reflects 'Low Demand,'" *Balkan Insight*, August 11, 2016, http://www.balkaninsight.com/en/article/the-decline-of-albanians-fighting-with-isis-related-mostly-with-low-demand-08-11-2016.
10. Fatjona Mejdini, "Albanian Police Arrest 'Terror Attack' Suspect," *Balkan Insight*, August 16, 2016, http://www.balkaninsight.com/en/article/albania-police-charge-a-man-from-kosovo-with-terrorism-08-18-2016.
11. Joby Warrick, "In Albania, Concerns over the Islamic State's Emergence," *Washington Post*, June 11, 2016, http://www.stripes.com/news/europe/in-albania-concerns-over-the-islamic-state-s-emergence-1.414273.
12. Lizzie Dearden, "Isis attack on Israeli football team."
13. "Selim Muca Reconfirmed As Head Of Albanian Muslim Community," *Alsat Television* (Skopje), September 20, 2010.
14. "Impasse Ends After Islamic Council Votes to Dismiss

Shkodra Mufti," Wikileaks, Wikileaks Cable 06TIRANA1209. Retrieved January 2013.

15. Although it was created in the northern city of Shkodra, the MFA has long had a power base in Kavaja.
16. Vickers, "Islam In Albania."
17. U.S. Treasury Department, "Press Release JS-1703: Additional Al-Haramain Branches, Former Leader Designated By Treasury as Al Qaida Supporters," June 2, 2004, www.ustreas.gov.
18. Vickers, "Islam In Albania."
19. Karajkov, "The Young and The Old."
20. Fatjona Mejdini, "Erdogan Prods Albanian President To Fight 'Gulenists.'" Balkan Insight, December 22, 2016. http://www.balkaninsight.com/en/article/erdogan-reminds-albania-to-fight-gulenists-12-22-2016.
21. Ebi Spahiu, "Attack on Gülen Movement Increasingly a Cornerstone of Turkey's Foreign Policy in the Balkans," *Eurasia Daily Monitor*, Volume 13, Issue 141, https://jamestown.org/program/attack-on-gulen-movement-increasingly-a-cornerstone-of-turkeys-foreign-policy-in-the-balkans/
22. Chris McGreal, "Q&A: what is the MEK and why did the US call it a terrorist organisation?," *The Guardian*, September 21, 2012, https://www.theguardian.com/politics/2012/sep/21/qanda-mek-us-terrorist-organisation
23. Ebi Spahiu, "The Iranian MEK in Albania: Implications and Possible Future Sectarian Divisions," January 29, 2017, http://www.balkanalysis.com/blog/2017/01/29/the-iranian-mek-in-albania-implications-and-possible-future-sectarian-divisions/.
24. Spahiu, "The Iranian MEK in Albania."
25. Entela Resuli, "Ne Shqiperi 638 Xhami Me 1.119 Kisha (In Albania There Are 638 Mosques And 1,119 Churches)," *Tirana Observer*, December 23, 2009.
26. Fatjona Mejdini, "Uncontrolled Mosques Proliferate in Albania," Balkan Insight, December 17, 2015, http://www.balkaninsight.com/en/article/state-slams-albanian-muslim-over-uncontrolled-mosques-12-17-2015.
27. Fatjona Mejdini, "Uncontrolled Mosques Proliferate in Albania," *Balkan Insight*, December 17, 2015, http://www.balkaninsight.com/en/article/state-slams-alba-

nian-muslim-over-uncontrolled-mosques-12-17-2015.

28. Fatjona Mejdini, "Albania Starts to Legalize Unofficial Mosques," Balkan Insight, September 2, 2016, http://www.balkaninsight.com/en/article/albania-starts-the-muslim-properties-legalisation-09-01-2016.
29. Entela Resuli, "Ne Shqiperi 638 Xhami Me 1.119 Kisha (In Albania There Are 638 Mosques And 1,119 Churches)."
30. Ebi Spahiu, "Jihadist Threat Persists in Kosovo and Albania Despite Government Efforts."
31. "Third Opinion on Albania, adopted on 23 November 2011,"Council of Europe, June 4, 2012. Available here: http://www.coe.int/t/dghl/monitoring/minorities/3_fcnmdocs/PDF_3rd_OP_Albania_en.pdf
32. While the Vatican had not released the detailed report at time of writing, some comments from it were available at the Vatican Insider website: http://vaticaninsider.lastampa.it/fileadmin/user_upload/File_Versione_originale/Sintesi_2012_lingua_italiana_RAPPORTO.pdf.
33. According to the website of the university, it caters to students from 15 countries with particular focus on Albanians from home and abroad. The university has a capacity of 2000 students at present. See http://www.beder.edu.al.
34. For a detailed analysis of the role of the Catholic Church in Albania's historic development and current orientation, see Matteo Albertini and Chris Deliso, *The Vatican's Challenges in the Balkans: Bolstering the Catholic Church in 2015 and Beyond* (Balkananalysis.com, 2015), https://www.amazon.com/Vaticans-Challenges-Balkans-Bolstering-Catholic-ebook/dp/B00S30A7BQ.
35. This observation is based on numerous interviews by the author with Albanian Muslims and Catholics since 2014.
36. "Albania," in U.S. Department of State, Bureau of Democracy, Human Rights, and Labor, *International Religious Freedom Report 2004* (Washington, DC: U.S. Department of State, 2005), www.state.gov.
37. The comments that incensed Islamists were perhaps

taken out of context; the president was speaking about religious tolerance among the Albanians. Nevertheless he caused a sensation by stating "that part of the Albanians which did not convert into Islam has in its tradition not simply fifteen centuries of Christianity, but two thousand years of Christianity… The Islamism in Albania is an Islam with a European face. As a rule it is a shallow Islamism. If you dig a little in every Albanian you can discover his Christian core." The original text of the speech was published on the official website of the President of Albania, www.president.al.

38. Llazar Semini, "Mother Teresa Statue Causes Friction," Associated Press, March 20, 2006
39. Mentioned in Xavier Bougarel, "Islam And Politics In The Post-Communist Balkans," Harvard University Kokkalis Program on Southeastern and East-central Europe, January 28, 2006, 6, http://www.hks.harvard.edu/kokkalis/GSW1/GSW1/13%20Bougarel.pdf.
40. This testimony is recorded in an online summary of a recent trip to Albania by young Islamists from the Turkish IHH (Humanitarian Relief Foundation, or Insani Yardim Vakfi in Turkish), and available at the organization's website, www.ihh.org.tr. The unusually significant proselytizing efforts going on in Koplik in the 1990s were noted long ago, for example in Miranda Vickers and James Pettifer, *Albania: From Anarchy to a Balkan Identity* (New York: New York University Press, 1997), 100.
41. On its main website, www.islamic-relief.com, Islamic Relief describes itself as "an international relief and development charity which envisages a caring world where people unite to respond to the suffering of others, empowering them to fulfill their potential."
42. The charity's efforts to combat clan vendettas and develop rural places like Koplik can be seen on their website, www.islamicreliefalbania.com.
43. Vickers, "Islam In Albania."
44. Albania 2015 International Religious Freedom Report. U.S. Department of State, https://www.state.gov/documents/organization/256369.pdf
45. Miranda Vickers and James Pettifer, *Albania: from An-*

archy to a Balkan Identity, New York University Press, 1997, p 105

46. Vickers and Pettifer, *Albania: From Anarchy to a Balkan Identity*, 102-105.
47. Remzi Lani and Fabian Schmidt, "Albanian Foreign Policy Between Geography And History," *The International Spectator* XXXIII, no. 2 (April-June 1998).
48. See Christopher Deliso, *The Coming Balkan Caliphate: the Threat of Radical Islam to Europe and the West,* Praeger Security International (2007) pp. chapter 2
49. Grace Halsell, "Special Report: Albania And The Muslim World," *Washington Report on Middle East Affairs*, June 1994, http://www.washington-report.org/backissues/0694/94006020.htm.
50. J. Milton Burr and Robert O. Collins, *Alms for Jihad: Charity and Terrorism in the Islamic World* (Cambridge: Cambridge University Press, 2006), 147-149.
51. Franz Gustincich, "From Lenin To Bin Laden," *Gnosis: Online Italian Intelligence Magazine* (March 2005), www.sisde.it.
52. Damian Gjiknuri, "Albania's Counter-Terrorism Policy Options: Finding A Strategy Of Common Sense," U.S. Naval Postgraduate School Thesis, 2004, 12.
53. Damian Gjiknuri, 15.
54. Vickers and Pettifer, *Albania: From Anarchy to a Balkan Identity*, 105.
55. Chris Stephens, "Bin Laden Opens European Terror Base In Albania," *Sunday Times*, November 29, 1998.
56. United States Department of the Treasury, "Press Release JS-1703: Additional Al-Haramain Branches, Former Leader Designated By Treasury As Al Qaida Supporters," June 2, 2004, www.ustreas.gov.
57. Burr and Collins, *Alms for Jihad: Charity and Terrorism in the Islamic World*, Ibid, 146.
58. John Crewdson and Tom Huntley, "Abducted Imam Aided CIA Ally," *Chicago Tribune*, July 3, 2005.
59. Andrew Higgins and Christopher Cooper, "CIA-Backed Team Used Brutal Means To Break Up Terrorist Cell In Albania," *Wall Street Journal*, November 20, 2001.
60. Kullolli, *Proselytization in Albania by Middle Eastern*

Islamic Organizations, 58.

61. R. Jeffrey Smith, "US Probes Blasts' Possible Mideast Ties," *Washington Post*, August 12, 1998.
62. Deliso, *The Coming Balkan Caliphate*, 40.
63. Wayne Madsen, "Mercenaries In Kosovo: The U.S. Connection To The KLA," *The Progressive*, August 1999.
64. See "Kosovo Seen As New Islamic Bastion," *Jerusalem Post*, September 14, 1998, and Barry Schweid, "NATO Braces For Wider Kosovo Fight," Associated Press, June 17, 1998.
65. For example, see the following, exquisitely detailed summary of Saudi-led refugee efforts, with financial totals, activities carried out, and organizations and individuals involved. Hussein Saud Qusti, "Unsung Heroes," *Saudi Aramco World* 50, no. 4, April 1999, http://www.saudiaramcoworld.com/issue/199904/unsung.heroes.htm.
66. Kastriot Duka, an *imam* originally from Elbasan in Albania, told journalists that he had been assisted in his efforts to build mosques, teach orphans and preach in a Kosovo village during the 1999 relief efforts by a member of an Islamic charity based in Britain. See Paola Casoli, "Terror And Gratitude: Albanian *Imam*'s Kosovo Mission," www.serbianna.com, December 29, 2007. Duka, who continued to rely on funding from UK-based "charities," would be deported from Kosovo back to Albania by Kosovar authorities in March 2010 for allegedly preaching radical Islam. See Linda Karadaku, "Kosovo Deports Self-Proclaimed *Imam*, Closes Mosque," *Southeast Europe Times*, March 11, 2010, http://www.setimes.com/cocoon/setimes/xhtml/en_GB/features/setimes/features/2010/03/11/feature-03.
67. "Pentagon Chief Cancels Albania Visit Over Terror Threat," CNN, July 15, 1999.
68. The incidents were widely reported, for example see "Albanian Police Arrest More Islamists," *RFE/RL Newsline* 3, no. 33, February 17, 1999.
69. Bill Gertz, "Hijackers Connected To Albanian Terrorist Cell," *Washington Times*, September 18, 2001.
70. US Treasury Press Release, "JS-2727: Treasury Desig-

nates Bin Laden, Qadi Associate," September 19, 2005, www.ustreas.gov.

71. US Treasury Press Release, JS-2727: Treasury Designates Bin Laden, Qadi Associate" .
72. As part of this outreach, Albania—along with other IDB member states such as Pakistan, Sudan, Indonesia and Uzbekistan—is slated to receive a portion of a new $772 million tranche for development projects. See "IDB Approves $772m For New Projects," *Arab News*, October 6, 2010, http://www.gulfbase.com/site/interface/NewsArchiveDetails.aspx?n=153337.
73. See "Islamic Development Bank Expresses Interest In Albania For Increase Of Bank's Presence Through Private Sector," Balkans.com, July 6, 2010.
74. Igor Jovanovic, "United Arab Emirates To Invest in Serbian Agriculture," SETimes.com, January 19, 2013.
75. Fatjona Mejdini, "Albania to Host NATO Centre on Foreign Fighters," *Balkan Insight*, June 23, 2016, http://www.balkaninsight.com/en/article/albania-will-host-nato-center-on-foreign-terrorist-fighters-06-23-2016.

41 Denmark

Quick Facts

Population: 5,605,948 (July 2017 est.)
Area: 43,094 sq km
Ethnic Groups: Danish (includes Greenlandic (who are predominantly Inuit) and Faroese) 86.7%, Turkish 1.1%, other 12.2% (largest groups are Polish, Syrian, German, Iraqi, and Romanian)
Government Type: Parliamentary constitutional monarchy
GDP (official exchange rate): $324.1 billion (2017 est.)

Source: CIA World FactBook (Last Updated April 2018)

Introduction

In February 2015, a young man of Palestinian background attacked a public meeting about freedom of speech and subsequently a synagogue in central Copenhagen. The Islamic State claimed responsibility for the incident, which is believed to be the first Islamist attack to take place in Denmark. In recent years, the focus of Danish governments on violent Islamism has centered on the issue of foreign fighters travelling to Syria or Iraq and the potential threat they could pose when they return. According to the Danish security and intelligence service, PET, approximately 145 Danes have travelled to Syria or Iraq since 2012.[1] Due to the rollback of ISIS in Iraq and Syria, this travel pattern has stopped, and the threat of violent Islamism in Denmark has changed in nature, becoming largely one of homegrown threats and radicalization.

The history of militant Islamism in Denmark, however, dates back to the 1990s, when veterans of the Afghan jihad against the Soviet Union were granted political asylum in the country. Today, violent Islamists are few in number and vastly outnumbered by non-violent Islamist groups. Nevertheless, a majority of political parties in the Danish Parliament regard Islam and Muslims with suspicion. In October 2017, in a sign of that hostility, a majority in the Parliament expressed their support of a bill banning the burka and niqab in the public sphere.[2]

Islamist Activity:

Militant Islamism in Denmark dates back to the 1990s, when several former mujahideen from the Soviet-Afghan war (1979–89) were granted political asylum there. One of the most prominent personalities in this group was an Egyptian, Talaat Fouad Qassem, a.k.a. Abu Talal (1957–1995), who was a high-ranking member of the violent Egyptian group al-Gama'a al-Islamiyya.[3] In 1982, Abu Talal was sentenced to seven years' imprisonment in Egypt for his alleged role in the assassination of Egyptian President Anwar Sadat. He escaped during a prison transfer in 1989 and subsequently went to Afghanistan, where he joined the anti-Soviet mujahideen and fought alongside Ayman al-Zawahiri. In 1992, he migrated to Denmark, where he was granted political asylum three years later.[4]

Abu Talal was extremely well-connected to international jihadists. He had close ties to the late Egyptian cleric Omar Abdel-Rahman, the "blind sheikh" who was an unindicted co-conspirator in the 1993 bombing of the World Trade Center. Abdel-Rahman visited Denmark twice (in 1990 and 1991) ahead of that failed plot.[5] Investigations of the World Trade Center attack revealed that three other Egyptians residing in Denmark—and part of the same milieu as Abu Talal—had direct links to the perpetrators of this attack.[6] Abu Talal is believed to have been the victim of an early form of extraordinary rendition--the extrajudicial kidnapping and transfer of a person across national borders--when he was intercepted in 1995 in Croatia by U.S. intelligence agencies while on his way to Bosnia. He was sent back to Egypt, from where he subsequently disappeared. Rights watchdog Human Rights Watch believes that he was tortured and executed.[7]

Another prominent member of this first generation of jihadists was Danish-Moroccan Said Mansour. Mansour hosted Omar Abdel-Rahman during one of his visits to Denmark. An ardent supporter of the Algerian terrorist group GIA, Mansour was involved in the distribution of their newsletter, Al Ansar, and was affiliated with the notorious London-based Islamist Abu Qatada. Mansour ran a publishing house, Al Nur Islamic Information, through which he disseminated material inciting Muslims to violence. (Materials from Al Nur were subsequently found worldwide at locations related to terrorist investigations in Germany, Italy, Spain, Belgium and the United States).[8] In 2007, Mansour was convicted of "incitement to violence" and served a two-year prison term. He was released in 2009. Five years later, he was convicted for similar offences and this time stripped of his Danish citizenship.[9]

Following the 2005 London bombings, a new iteration of militant Islamism appeared in Denmark. In contrast to the first generation of this phenomenon, as embodied by Abu Talal and Mansour, this second generation was primarily homegrown in nature and often includes first-generation Danes. The first signs of Islamist terrorism in Denmark after the London bombings were homegrown plots, involving Danish citizens or residents with links to the radical activist organization Sharia4UK in London. Since 2007, however, Islamist terrorist plots have also involved "returnees" who have come back to Denmark after joining militant Islamist groups abroad or—in the aftermath of the so-called cartoon controversy—by foreigners with no prior connection to Denmark.

After the outbreak of the cartoon controversy in 2005, and in particular after the reproduction of those cartoons by several Danish newspapers in 2008, Denmark became a high-priority target of al-Qaeda as well as of like-minded groups in Europe. From 2008 through 2010, six plots targeting either the Jyllands-Posten daily newspaper or one of its cartoonists have been thwarted. The individuals behind the first two plots were Danish residents. Yet in 2009 and 2010, four plots were attempted by foreigners with no prior relation to Denmark, including one conceived by American citizen David Headley who was also involved in the 2008 terrorist attack in Mumbai, India.[10]

Although the Danish security and intelligence service has emphasized the threat of Islamist foreign fighters, the only Islamist attack perpetrated in Denmark did not in fact involve a former foreign fighter. In February 2015, a few weeks after the attack on French satirical magazine Charlie Hebdo, Danish-Palestinian Omar el-Hussein attacked a public meeting about freedom of speech and later a synagogue in central Copenhagen. Two people were killed, and several police were wounded; in those incidents. The perpetrator was subsequently killed by the police. Hussein was a petty criminal who had just been released from prison, when—apparently inspired by the Charlie Hebdo attacks—he decided to carry out violence of his own. Although there were no direct links between the two incidents, the Islamic State claimed responsibility for the events and honored Hussein by publishing a glowing obituary in their online magazine Dabiq.[11]

Since 2012, at least 145 Danish citizens and residents have joined the conflict in Syria and Iraq.[12] As ISIS has declined in those countries, travel to this region by Danish extremists has stopped. However, journalist Jakob Sheikh has collected independent data about 77 Danish citizens or residents who have traveled to Syria, with interesting results. It appears that not all of those who have traveled to this location are jihadists or Islamists. While some have joined Islamic State or the Nusra Front (now Jabhat Fatah al Sham), others have joined secular Kurdish groups or the Free Syrian Army. Irrespective of their affiliation, the vast majority of Danish foreign fighters are born and raised in Denmark. One in seven are Danish converts to Islam.[13]

These numbers confirm a general tendency. In contrast to the first and second generation of violent Islamism, milieus supportive of Islamist terrorist groups today have become more diverse. In May 2017, a seventeen-year-old Danish girl was, for instance, convicted for preparing two terrorist attacks, including an attack against a Jewish school. The girl was not, strictly speaking, part of an Islamist milieu, although she had been in contact with a returnee from Syria who had fought with both the Syrian Free Army and ISIS. While being held in custody, she wrote letters to another returnee convicted of having joined ISIS in Syria and stripped of his Danish citizenship.[14]

However, the overall number of Muslims in Denmark who actively support violent forms of Islamism is negligible. Militant Islamists are by far outnumbered by Muslims involved in non-violent Islamist groups. Among the most controversial is Hizb ut-Tahrir (HT). Hizb ut-Tahrir put down roots in Denmark in the mid-1980s, although the Danish branch of the organization was not formally established until the mid-1990s.[15] British HT members were instrumental in the establishment of the group's Danish contingent,[16] and the movement's Copenhagen leadership committee was subsequently elevated to head the group's regional affairs, as reflected in its current title, Hizb ut-Tahrir Scandinavia.[17] Although there are no reliable figures as to the actual number of HT members, the organization has an estimated 100–150 active members, but attracts around 1,000–1,200 people to its public meetings.[18]

Ideologically, HT aims to reestablish a caliphate in the Muslim world. Therefore, unlike the classical Muslim Brotherhood, the group is against the modern notion of the nation-state. HT considers democracy an un-Islamic invention and urges Danish Muslims not to engage in politics or take part in elections. The organization as a whole does not engage in violent activities, but supports "defensive jihad" in places such as Iraq, Syria, or Afghanistan. The group's public meeting in January 2011 caused considerable controversy, as it endorsed continued resistance in Afghanistan, which was interpreted by many as encouragement to kill Danish soldiers serving there.[19] Former HT spokesperson Fadi Abdullatif was convicted twice for "threats, flagrant insults and incitement to murder" against Jews, as well as against former Danish prime minister (and former NATO secretary general) Anders Fogh Rasmussen.[20] Various political parties have argued that HT should be banned, and in 2015 after the terrorist attacks in Copenhagen, the Minister of Justice, Mette Frederiksen, made yet another request to ban the group. However, the Danish attorney general has at several occasions ruled that there were no legal foundations for such a ban.[21]

Aside from HT, The Grimhøj Mosque in the city of Aarhus (Wakf) regularly attracts media attention. A majority of the men and women who travelled to Syria from the city of Aarhus apparently used to attend this mosque, which therefore has come under suspicion of being a hub of radicalization. Political initiatives to close down the mosque have hitherto been fruitless, however, because the imams have a constitutional right to free speech and therefore are deemed to have committed no infraction of the law.

Islamism and Society:

Muslim immigration to Denmark began in the 1960s and 1970s, when immigrants from Turkey, Pakistan, North Africa, and the former Yugoslavia came to Denmark to work. After the mid-1970s, a second wave of newcomers to the country was made up primarily of refugees, as well as the families of earlier immigrants who had stayed in Denmark. Conflicts and political repression in the Arab and Muslim world (including the Iran-Iraq war, as well as the civil wars in Lebanon, the former Yugoslavia, and Somalia) also prompted Muslim immigration to Denmark, as have the more recent conflicts in Afghanistan, Somalia, Iraq, and Syria.

While no official census of Muslims in Denmark exists, some preliminary data is available. As of January 2016, the proportion of Muslims in the total population was estimated to 284,000, which is 5 percent of the total population. One year before, the number was 4.7 percent, and the increase is the result of the large number of Syrian refugees who came to Denmark in 2015.[22] 70 percent of Muslims in Denmark are Danish citizens.[23] Denmark's Muslim community is ethnically very diverse. The largest group are Turks (19.9 percent), followed by Iraqis, Lebanese (Palestinians), and Syrians (9.3 percent, 8.7 percent, and 8.5 percent, respectively).[24] In 2017, the main contingents of refugees came from Syria, Morocco, Eritrea, Afghanistan, and Iran.

Since September 11, 2001, public debates on Islam and Muslims have become increasingly incendiary. The year 2001 coincided with the rise to power of a minority right wing government that—for the first time in Danish history—depended on parliamentary support from the country's anti-immigration and Islam-critical nationalist party, the Danish Peoples Party (DPP), to gain the majority. The DPP has been instrumental in articulating a "struggle of values" against Islam and Muslims, which it considers necessary in order to defend Christianity and "Danishness."[25] In public debates, politicians increasingly frame Islam and Muslims as a security threat.[26]

Yet today it is not only the far right nationalist party DPP that adopts a very critical and suspicious attitude towards Muslims, immigrants, and refugees (categories that are often conflated). Rather, a majority of the political parties in parliament do as well. A spike in the number of refugees in 2015 (primarily from Syria and Afghanistan) has prompted a public discourse that frames refugees as potential terrorists and a threat to the welfare of the Danish state, although there is no evidence available that supports this claim.[27] The discourse framing refugees as a threat culminated in January 2016 with the passage of a controversial bill allowing Danish police to seize cash and valuables from refugees to pay for expenses related to their stay in Denmark.[28]

Islamism and the State:

After the September 11 terrorist attacks and the subsequent London bombings in 2005, the Danish parliament passed two anti-terrorism acts (in 2002 and 2006, respectively).[29] The first act amended the Danish penal code by introducing a separate terrorism provision that increased the punishment for a variety of acts if carried out with the intention of "frightening a population," or destabilizing "the fundamental political, constitutional, economic or social structures of a country or an international organization."[30] The maximum sentence for committing an offense under the new terrorism provision was raised to life in prison. This anti-terrorism act also penalizes the provision of financial services to terrorist groups and gives authorities new tools to fight terrorism, including secret searches, the logging of telephone and Internet communications, easier access to computer surveillance, expanded ability to refuse or withdraw residence permits, and so forth.

Following the July 7, 2005, subway bombings in London, Danish perceptions of the threat from militant Islamism changed, and the greatest danger became seen as primarily homegrown in nature. In order to prevent the domestic processes of radicalization, a series of preventive measures was set up by the Ministry of Integration in tandem with the domestic intelligence service, PET, which established a preventive department in 2007. Over the years, this host of preventive measures has morphed into a "Danish model" that has attracted worldwide attention.[31] The Danish approach to preventing extremism and radicalization is based on extensive multi-agency collaboration between various social-service providers, the educational system, the health-care system, the police, and the intelligence and security services.[32] This approach has abandoned the idea of doing anti-radicalization—that is, changing the extremist mindset—in favor of disengagement—that is, exit-programs for persons who want to get out of extremist environments.[33]

To prevent Danish citizens and residents from going to Syria, a law was passed in 2015 that made it possible for the police to administratively confiscate passports from people who had the intention of travelling to Syria or to similar conflict areas.[34] So far, the police have confiscated only a small number of passports in this fashion, however. Additionally, a new law adopted in June 2016 criminalizes the act of entering specific areas in Syria and Iraq without a preexisting travel permit issued by the Ministry of Justice.[35]

The state does not only interfere with Islamists in security-related cases. In October 2017, a majority of the parties in the Danish parliament expressed their support for a bill banning the burqa and the niqab from the public sphere. Denmark will thus join the host of countries that recently have banned these garments.[36] Moreover, the Social Democratic Party (SDP), which is the largest party in the parliament, has recently advocated the closing down of all Muslim private schools in Denmark. The party-leader, Mette Frederiksen, argue that there are cases of headmasters and teachers promoting terrorist organizations, that the schools do not support gender equality, and that they have a hateful attitude to the Jewish minority in the country.[37]

Endnotes

1. Vurdering af terrortruslen mod Denmark [Assessment of the Terrorist Threat against Denmark], *CTA* (Center for Terror Analysis), February 7, 2017, https://www.pet.dk/Center%20for%20Terroranalyse/~/media/VTD%202017/VTD2017DKpdf.ashx.
2. Teis Jensen, "Denmark Set to Ban the Burqa Despite Fears for Religious Freedom," *Independent*, October 6, 2017, http://www.independent.co.uk/news/world/europe/denmark-ban-full-face-covering-burqa-jakob-ellemann-jensen-a7986561.html.
3. Michael Taarnby Jensen, *Jihad in Denmark: An Overview and Analysis of Jihadi Activity in Denmark 1990–2006*, p. 9, Danish Institute for International Studies,

November 2006, http://www.cie.ugent.be/documenten/jihad-dk.pdf.

4. Tribunale de Milano, "Ruling of Judge Presiding over Preliminary Investigations," p. 44, n.d., http://www.washingtonpost.com/wp-srv/world/documents/milan_warrants.pdf.
5. Taarnby, *Jihad in Denmark*, p. 17.
6. See Manni Crone and Mona Sheikh, "Muslims as Danish Security Issues," in Jørgen S. Nielsen, ed., *Islam in Denmark*, Lexington Books, 2012.
7. *Black Hole: The Fate of Islamists Rendered to Egypt*, Human Rights Watch, May 9, 2005, http://www.hrw.org/en/node/11757/section/6; Claus Blok Thomsen, "CIA's første bortførte fange kom fra Danmark" [CIA's First Abducted Catch Came from Denmark], Dagbladet Politiken, October 20, 2007, http://politiken.dk/indland/article399819.ece.
8. Søren Astrup, "Said Mansour Accepterer Dom" [Said Mansour Accepts Ruling], *Dagbladet Politiken*, April 24, 2007, http://politiken.dk/indland/art4685507/Said-Mansour-accepterer-dom; Taarnby, Jihad in Denmark, p. 22.
9. Alexander Tange, "Denmark Strips Man of Citizenship After Terrorist Conviction," *Reuters*, July 1, 2015, http://www.reuters.com/article/us-denmark-morocco-deportation-idUSKCN0PB4XI20150701.
10. "David Coleman Headley Sentenced to 35 Years in Prison for Role in India and Denmark Terror Plots," United States Department of Justice, January 24, 2013, Accessed October 20, 2017, https://www.justice.gov/opa/pr/david-coleman-headley-sentenced-35-years-prison-role-india-and-denmark-terror-plots.
11. *Dabiq*, 8, March 30, 2015, p. 5-6.
12. Vurdering af terrortruslen mod Denmark [Assessment of the Terrorist Threat Against Denmark], CTA (Center for Terror Analysis), February 7, 2017, https://www.pet.dk/Center%20for%20Terroranalyse/~/media/VTD%202017/VTD2017DKpdf.ashx.
13. Jakob Sheikh, "Syrienskrigere: danske kurdere topper listen" [Danish Foreign Fighters: A Majority with Kurdish Background], *Politiken*, September 15, 2016,

http://politiken.dk/indland/art5635830/Syrienskrigere-Danske-kurdere-topper-listen.

14. Anna Gottschalk, "Overblik: her er de nye beviser i Kundby-sagen (Overview: new evidence in the Kundby-case)," *Berlingske*, May 17, 2017, https://www.b.dk/nationalt/overblik-her-er-de-nye-beviser-i-kundby-sagen.
15. Kirstine Sinclair, "The Caliphate as Homeland: Hizb ut-Tahrir in Denmark and Britain," p. 12, doctoral dissertation, University of Southern Denmark, 2010.
16. Ed Husain, *The Islamist*, Penguin, 2007.
17. Sinclair, "The Caliphate as Homeland," p. 12.
18. Ulla Abildtrup, "Forsker: Hizb ut-Tahrir stagnerer" [Researcher: Hizb ut-Tahrir Stagnates], DR, November 16, 2010, http://www.dr.dk/Nyheder/Indland/2010/11/10/113614.htm.
19. "Hizb ut-Tahrir opfordrer til væbnet kamp" [Hizb ut-Tahrir Calls for Armed Struggle], *Information*, December 28, 2010, http://www.information.dk/telegram/254933.
20. Rigsadvokaten (The Attorney General), Supplerende redegørelse om eventuel opløsning af Hizb ut-Tahrir i henhold til Grundlovens § 78 [Supplementary Statement on the Potential Closure of Hizb ut-Tahrir in Accordance with Basic Law § 78], p. 13, 18, June 2008, http://www.rigsadvokaten.dk/default.aspx?id=58&recordid58=1190.
21. Rigsadvokaten (The Attorney General), Supplerende redegørelse om eventuel opløsning af Hizb ut-Tahrir i henhold til Grundlovens § 78, p. 43.
22. Brian Arly Jacobsen, "Hvor mange muslimer bor der i Danmark?" [How Large Is the Muslim Population in Denmark], Politiken, April 12, 2016 http://www.religion.dk/religionsanalysen/hvor-mange-indvandrer-lever-i-danmark.
23. Jacobsen, "Hvor mange muslimer bor der i Danmark?"
24. Jacobsen, "Hvor mange muslimer bor der i Danmark?"
25. Søren Krarup, Systemskiftet. I kulturkampens tegn [Systemic Shift: Characters in the Cultural Battles], Gyldendal, 2006.
26. See Crone and Sheikh, "Muslims as Danish Security

Issues."

27. Manni Crone and Maja Falkentoft, Europe's Refugee Crisis and the Threat of Terrorism: An Extraordinary Threat?, Danish Institute for International Studies, 2017, http://pure.diis.dk/ws/files/910914/Report_05_Europes_Refugee_Crisis_Web.pdf.
28. David Crouch & Patrick Kingsley, "Danish Parliament approves plan to seize assets from refugees," *The Guardian*, January 26, 2016, https://www.theguardian.com/world/2016/jan/26/danish-parliament-approves-plan-to-seize-assets-from-refugees.
29. Jørn Vestergaard, "Dansk lovgivning om bekæmpelse af terrorisme" [Danish Legislation on Terrorism], in Lars Plum and Andreas Laursen, eds., Enhver stats pligt… International strafferet og dansk ret [Duty of Every State... International Criminal Law and Danish Law], p. 391–424, DJØF Forlag, 2007.
30. Jørn Vestergaard, "Dansk lovgivning om bekæmpelse af terrorisme."
31. Bharati Naik, Atika Shubert, and Nick Thompson, "Denmark Offers Foreign Fighters Rehab Without Jail – But Will It Work?" CNN, October 28, 2014, http://edition.cnn.com/2014/10/28/world/europe/denmark-syria-deradicalization-program.
32. Ann-Sophie Hemmingsen, *The Danish Approach to Countering and Preventing Extremism and Radicalization*, p. 15, Danish Institute for International Studies, 2015.
33. Lasse Lindekilde, "Forebyggelse af radikalisering, miskendelse og muslimsk minoritetsidentitet" [Preventing Radicalization, Misrepresentation and Muslim Minority Identity], Tidsskrift for Islamforskning no. 2, 2010, http://tifoislam.dk/article/view/24593/21536.
34. Ritzau, "Overblik: Det siger loven om pas og krig" (Overview: The Law About Passports and War), *Berlingske*, February 4, 2016, http://www.b.dk/nationalt/overblik-det-siger-loven-om-pas-og-krig.
35. Ministry of Justice, "Regeringen indfører indrejseforbud i kamp mod terror" [Government Passes Law on Travelban to Fight Terrorism], September 13, 2016.
36. Teis Jensen, "Denmark Set to Ban the Burqa Despite

Fears for Religious Freedom," *Independent*, October 6, 2017, http://www.independent.co.uk/news/world/europe/denmark-ban-full-face-covering-burqa-jakob-ellemann-jensen-a7986561.html.

37. Andreas Karker Jacob Friberg, "Mette Frederiksen i brutalt opgør: Luk alle muslimske friskoler" (Mette Frederiksen in a tough confrontation: close down all Muslim private schools), *Berlingske*, August 11, 2017, https://www.b.dk/politiko/mette-frederiksen-i-brutalt-opgoer-luk-alle-muslimske-friskoler.

42 France

Quick Facts

Population: 67,106,161
Area: 643,801 sq km; 551,500 sq km (metropolitan France)
Ethnic Groups: Celtic and Latin with Teutonic, Slavic, North African, Indochinese, Basque minorities
GDP (official exchange rate): $2.575 trillion (2017 est.)

Source: CIA World FactBook (Last Updated May 2018)

Introduction

France houses a large Muslim minority, primarily of North African provenance. While many immigrants are non-observant (in line with a general French tendency toward secularism and a de-emphasis of religious affiliation), Islamist organizations actively promote a resurgence of a politicized and ideological Muslim identity. Target groups include youth, especially in the ethnic ghettos of cities where immigrant populations are concentrated. There is considerable tension within the Muslim leadership between advocates of secular French identity and proponents of the Islamist goal of a communitarian cultural separatism. In addition, the trans-Mediterranean immigration patterns and historical French colonial ties to North Africa contribute to a spillover of Islamist terrorist activity from Algeria into France. Jihadist activists with links to al-Qaeda move between Algeria and France, as well as other European countries. French Islamism, in turn, has become part of global jihadist networks.

The Islamic State, also known as ISIS, has recently become a dominant fixture in Islamist terrorist activity in the European Union, particularly France and Belgium, with its ideology often times taking root among young, isolated French or Belgian nationals with secular immigrant parents. Online networking, along with the recruitment of European nationals to train in Syria and subsequently return to the EU, has led to a surge in attacks inspired, or planned, by the Islamic State—including but not limited to the January 2015 attack on the Charlie Hebdo newspaper and a Jewish supermarket, the November 2015 Paris attack, and the July 2016 attack in Nice.

The response of the French state has evolved from earlier efforts to portray itself as the bridge between the Arab world and Europe to a more recent insistence on the value of French identity and the importance of secularism, exemplified in regulations such as the 2011 prohibition on concealing one's face in a public space. Furthermore, in contrast to the weak French response to terrorism in the 1980s, France more recently has developed an effective and robust set of counterterrorism and surveillance practices.

Islamist Activity

Union des organizations islamiques de France (UOIF)

Founded in 1983 as a small circle of foreign student activists with Islamist leanings, the Union of Islamic Organizations in France has grown into an umbrella organization claiming to represent between one to two hundred Muslim groups in France.[1] It plays a role in coordinating activities among its member associations, and is the owner of some mosques in the major cities of France. The UOIF is the French member of the London-based Federation of Islamic Organizations in Europe, active in promoting the study of Islam through its European Institute for the Human Sciences, dedicated to Islamic theology and related studies, with two campuses in France.[2] The UOIF has also established several specialized organizations, including the Young Muslims of France (JMF), the Muslim Students of France (EMF), and the French League of the Muslim Woman (LFFM).[3] These organizations contribute to the dissemination of Islamist positions and the construction of separatist communitarian identity politics. While the UOIF presents itself simply as an advocate of Muslim interests, critics point out that it engages in a "double discourse," paying lip service in public to the priority of tolerance for secular French values while at the same time promoting Islamist content (replete with intolerance, misogyny, homophobia and anti-Semitism) to its target populations.[4]

The UOIF has attained considerable public and political resonance through a disproportionate role within the French Council of the

Muslim Religion (CFCM), which was established in 2003 by then-Minister of the Interior Nicolas Sarkozy as the official representative body for Muslims in France.[5] The CFCM's responsibilities pertain to interactions between the French state and the Muslim community (e.g., the construction of mosques, oversight of halal food, provision of Muslim spiritual services in the military and in prisons, etc). In contrast to the CFCM's administrative and technical functions, the UOIF has wider cultural and political ambitions. "In France, the extremist UOIF has become the predominant organization within the government's Islamic Council where it can eclipse moderate or secular Muslim voices," experts have noted.[6] While the inclusion of the UOIF in the CFCM may have been intended as a strategy of cooptation to move the latter toward the center, it has allowed the relatively small UOIF to emerge as an influential representative of the much more diverse and generally less ideological Muslim population in France.[7]

While the UOIF's explicit goals include the religious, cultural, educational, social and humanitarian needs of the Muslim population of France, with priority given to facilitating religious practice, critics allege that it is close to the Egyptian branch of the Muslim Brotherhood and pursues a goal of communitarian separatism.[8] This agenda involves two aspects: transforming France into a safe haven for radicals engaged in militant Islamist politics in North Africa or elsewhere, especially in the Arab world, while at the same time exercising political identity pressure on the Muslims in France to conform to increasingly repressive interpretations of Islam, a sort of "reactionary and paternalist populism."[9] "The UOIF tries to rein in the Muslims of France. Some associations affiliated with the movement claim the right to say who is a good Muslim and who is, therefore, an apostate," observes Islamic studies expert Fiametta Venner. "This is all the more alarming since these people are not theologians—almost none of the directors of the UOIF pursued studies in this area—and they have a very narrow vision of Islam. They are satisfied with instrumentalizing the religion to pursue a reactionary political project of separatism."[10]

During the 2012 election campaign, Nicolas Sarkozy criticized the UOIF for ties to extremist preachers. Ahmed Jaballah, the

President of the UOIF since 2011, insisted on the apolitical character of the organization, while attributing Sarkozy's criticisms to electoral politics. In addition, he articulated a vision of a moderate Islam within the context of French secularism as an alternative to radical tendencies, implicitly carving out a space hospitable to the Muslim Brotherhood but less welcoming of Salafist positions.[11] However, the UOIF has since come under intense pressure, following its designation as a terrorist group by the United Arab Emirates in 2014. National Front politicians, specifically the party's president, Marine Le Pen, has called for the organization's dissolution.[12]

Al-Qaeda in the Islamic Maghreb (AQIM)

Al-Qaeda in the Islamic Maghreb is a terrorist group based primarily in Algeria, although it operates more widely in North Africa and has links to Europe. Over time, it has transformed from an organization committed to a local Islamist insurgency into a wider network pursuing a program of global jihad.

The precise size of AQIM's membership remains elusive. Yet even if its numbers are small, the group has acquired considerable resources thanks to profitable kidnappings and participation in drug trafficking. In 2012, General Carter Hamm, then the head of U.S. Africa Command (USAFRICOM), called AQIM "al-Qaeda's best funded, wealthiest affiliate" and ascribed to it the dominant role in the Malian insurgency.[13] The uprising began in early 2012 and involved AQIM and other Islamist groups building an alliance with Tuareg separatists. That alliance remained unstable and largely collapsed due to the participants' adherence to strict sharia.[14] Yet initially, the insurgency appeared poised to penetrate the southern part of the country and threaten the national government in Bamako. In response, French President Francois Hollande authorized a military expedition to prevent an Islamist takeover.

The French presence in Mali, a former colony, has potentially set the stage for new forms of Islamist terrorism in France itself. While France's intervention was met with considerable support from the Malian community in France, the leading French counter-terrorist judge, Marc Trévidic, expressed concern that it could contribute to the recruitment of new terrorists among Islamist sympathizers in France, especially among the young and marginalized members of immigrant communities.[15]

While AQIM is recognized a threat to Europe and the west, because of Al-Qaeda's original focus on attacking western targets an AQIM attack in Europe has not materialized. A 2013 RAND Corporation analysis of AQIM argued that the group lacked the infrastructure and willingness to launch an attack on the West while maintaining their control of the Sahel and its other North African priorities.[16] Al-Qaeda remained a strategic rival of the Islamic State, but is thought to enjoy support and loyalty of some of the same groups in sub-Saharan Africa.[17] In a 2018 audio message, the AQ leader Ayman al Zawahiri threatened to attack French interests "from Abidjan to Ouagadougu, and from the Atlas mountains to Mauritania."[18]

The Islamic State

The influence of AQIM, and other Islamist groups in France, was dwarfed by the emergence of the Islamic State. The Islamic State is a combination of Salafi jihadists and Ba'athist military and intelligence personnel who, once ousted from power in Iraq in 2003, took advantage of the civil unrest and disenfranchisement of Sunni Arabs, not only in Iraq, but also in Syria—and whose territorial control metastasized during the civil war to include nearly nine million inhabitants. That lasted only until 2016-2017, when Turkish, Iraqi and Syrian-Kurdish forces, separately, with Western support, drove ISIS fighters and officials from all of the cities it briefly held.[19]

In addition to occupying territory in Iraq and Syria, ISIS has presented a global terror threat known for inspiring attacks throughout the West, particularly in France. France has become a consistent target for ISIS-inspired attacks due to hatred and resentment towards France by Salafists caused by its colonial occupation of Algeria, its occupation in Mali, and its participation in U.S.-led coalitions intended to defeat the organization in the Middle East.[20] ISIS recruits followers through online platforms as well as through prisons and existing terror cells, and the open borders in the European Union make it easier for EU nationals to slip into Iraq or Syria for militant training. As of Fall 2017, approximately 1,700 people were estimated to have left France to join ISIS fighters in Syria and Iraq. Several hundred are thought to have been killed in battle, and several hundred more returned to France; the Foreign Minister said 500 fighters remained at the end of 2017.[21] Thereafter, the ability of those same people to return to France to recruit more followers while operating in isolated areas has led to a string of deadly ISIS-inspired attacks.[22]

The January 2015 attack on the satirical newspaper Charlie Hebdo, and the attack on a Jewish supermarket that took place in the days that followed, were carried out by three French citizens, two of whom were inspired by al-Qaeda in the Arabian Peninsula (which eventually took credit for planning the attack) and a third, Amedy Coulibaly, who was inspired by ISIS and pledged allegiance to the Islamic State.[23]

In November 2015, ISIS claimed full responsibility for the attacks on the city of Paris where eight gunmen, armed with both explosive belts as well as machine guns, killed 129 people across 6 locations throughout the city, such as the Bataclan theater and a national soccer stadium where President Francois Hollande was attending a match. The Islamic State claimed that the attacks were retaliation for French airstrikes against ISIS fighters in Syria. The attackers were a mix of French and Belgian nationals, many of whom were believed to have visited Syria, committed previous crimes, had a previous terrorism connection, and were radicalized through existing terror cells or prison encounters.[24]

ISIS inspired attacks also occurred during the summer of 2016, first with the successful attack on Bastille Day in which Mohamed Lahouaiej Bouhlel drove a 19-ton truck through a crowded street in Nice, killing 84 people. ISIS claimed Bouhlel was a "soldier of the Islamic State" and French officials believe he was radicalized through a terror cell in Nice.[25] Also in July 2016, two French nationals raided a church in Northern France and took five people hostage, eventually killing an 84-year-old priest. Both attackers pledged allegiance to ISIS, and one of the attackers was on the radar of police and intelligence agencies for over a year and tried to visit Syria at least once in 2015 before being stopped at the Turkish border.[26]

Even as ISIS waned as a military-political entity in Syria and Iraq, it continued to inspired small-scale attacks in France throughout

2017. A French soldier shot a machete-wielding man outside the Louvre in February,[27] and a police officer shot an attacker who had seized a soldier's firearm at Orly airport one month later.[28] Several other isolated assaults were committed against uniformed forces and civilians, leading to a dozen serious injuries and two deaths. Large caches of explosives and weapons were seized in Montpellier and Marseille. Though ISIS declined as a territorial power, its message has not been entirely extinguished among a subset of the French population. Counter-terrorism officials took their fight online, where radicalization had sometimes occurred, but also to prisons and social workers. Scholars of political Islam debated whether France was witnessing the radicalization of Jihad (an idea defended by Gilles Kepel) or rather, the "Jihadization" of radicalism, which was Olivier Roy's argument that Islamic terrorism was this generation's youth revolt.[29]

Islamism and Society:

Islam, barely present in France before 1945, arrived along with a wave of immigrant labor, primarily from North Africa. After Catholicism, Islam is now the most common religion in Europe. Muslims make up between five to ten percent of the total population, and Islam is the religion of two-thirds of all immigrants. Since 1872, French law has prohibited any identification of citizens by religion, even for census purposes, so precise numbers are hard to come by, but the CIA World Factbook counts 63-66 percent of the French population as Christian (overwhelmingly Catholic), 0.5-0.75 percent as Buddhist, 0.5-0.75 percent as Jewish, 23-28 percent non-affiliated, and 7-9 percent as Muslim.[30] In addition to immigration, many in France's Muslim population are indigenous citizens, having converted from another religion. The Pew Research Center, along with national polls conducted in 2010, found the number of converts at that time at between 70,000 and 110,000.[31] Of the sixteen million Muslims living in the European Union, about a third live in France, concentrated in the Ile-de-France region around Paris, in the south of France and in the country's industrial north.[32] Increased Muslim immigration and recent domestic terror attacks have taken their toll on non-Muslims' attitude towards Islam.[33] For example, an

April 2016 poll conducted by IFOP, a French polling center, found that 47 percent of French people felt that Muslims posed a threat to their national identity, up from 43 percent in 2010. The same poll also found that more than 60 percent thought Islam was both too influential and visible in France.[34]

Of the French Muslim population, about a third describes itself as "observant." An extensive secularization of the Muslim population is consistent with the decline of observant practices in other religious traditions in the country. However, there are indications that Muslim youth practice their religion at rates higher than the Catholic majority: 65% of practicing Catholics are older than 50, while 73% of practicing Muslims are younger than 54.[35] As of 2016, there were approximately 2,500 mosques in France.[36] In some instances, the construction of new mosques has led to protests, yet Muslim advocates complain that the floor space available for Muslim prayer services remains insufficient.[37]

The rise of a minority Islamism within the Muslim community can be viewed in part as a reaction against the modernization of lifestyles within immigrant communities. The mobilization of Islamist identity frequently involves younger generations rebelling against the aspirations for integration harbored by older generations of immigrants.[38] It was estimated that around one hundred Salafi prayer spaces continued to operate in 2017.[39] The number of individual Salafis in France was estimated to have tripled from 5,000 to 15,000 in the first half of the 2010s — mostly in Paris, Lyon and Marseille. "The great majority of French Salafis are quietists who condemn militant jihad," but the prayer spaces were still considered to be a sort of jihadi "airlock."[40] There were attempts to close down Salafist mosques, including some without links to violence or terrorism.[41] A French mosque in Yvelines lost its appeal to the Conseil d'Etat after it was established that it had hosted sermons of a "threatening nature" towards Christians and Jews, and which "glorified terrorism."

Islamist recruitment in France has multiple dimensions. One key venue is the mosque, although of the total number of mosques very few (approximately 120) are considered sources of potential threats.[42] In the months between December 2015 and August

2016, a total of 20 mosques were shut down by French authorities under suspicion of preaching radical Islam. In the same timeframe, France's Prime Minister, Manuel Valls, called for a temporary ban on foreign funding, the most common form of financing, for French mosques to further curb radicalization.[43] In some cases, the mosque imam provides the radical ideology, but in others jihadist recruiters may be active without the knowledge of the imam. Significant recruitment, including proselytization, likewise takes place in prisons; French prison populations are often more than 50 percent Muslim, at times reaching 80 percent in certain areas.[44] Activists reach out both to non-observant Muslim inmates, as well as to non-Muslims who are prospects for conversion. A third avenue of recruitment involves contact with French jihadis—i.e., veterans of the conflicts in Afghanistan, Bosnia, Chechnya and Iraq—who have returned to France and who may form ad hoc groups to support or carry out terrorist attacks.[45] In addition to recruitment in prison and by former jihadis, groups like ISIS target young, often disillusioned French Muslims, both men and women and often-times non-religious, through propaganda videos and social media. Recruiters target those most vulnerable and likely to be radicalized due to lack of societal integration and portray messages of strength, unity, and promise if they become ISIS fighters. Attracting younger recruits online has been incredibly successful in getting men and women to travel to Syria, causing the French government to launch an anti-ISIS communication campaign called Stop Jihadism in early 2015 to try to dissuade French youths from joining the group.[46]

The conflict between modernizing pressure and Muslim identity underlies the controversy surrounding the headscarf, or hijab. Islamist pressure to establish separatist communitarian identity focuses on symbols and practices to separate Muslims from secular French society. In 2004, facing a growing Muslim population in public schools with increasing numbers of women wearing the headscarf, the French government promulgated a law banning ostentatious religious symbols in the schools, in the spirit of laicité, [47] or France's embrace of secularism based on "freedom of conscience and freedom of worship, separation of public institutions and religious organizations, and equality before the law irrespective of their beliefs or beliefs."[48] A 2011 law banning any face covering in public places only added to the controversy around both the hijab and the burqua, and intensified the conversation around religious freedom. While the laws also pertain to Christian and Jewish symbols, the Muslim headscarf or veil has received the most public scrutiny. These controversial laws underscored the gap between French norms of secular modernity and the neo-traditionalism of Islamist behavior. A primary goal of Islamism involves the assertion of patriarchal norms and the resistance to the spread of equal rights to Muslim women.[49]

Muslim immigrant populations are frequently concentrated in the ethnic ghettos of the banlieues, the working-class suburbs surrounding French urban centers, where they remain marginalized, facing discrimination and weathering high unemployment rates. This concentration of social problems has led repeatedly to outbreaks of mass violence. In 2005, in response to the deaths of two teenagers in Clichy-sous-Bois, near Paris, local rioting erupted, spreading rapidly across the country. A state of emergency was declared, resulting in three thousand arrests. Damage to property totaled 200 million Euros.[50] Another series of riots broke out in 2009.[51] Such periodic unrest has contributed to a profound social anxiety about sécurité, a term which has implications stretching from crime-in-the-streets to terrorism. Furthermore, the banlieues serve as prime recruitment locations for groups such as ISIS, who capitalize on the lack of opportunity and upward mobility that creates discontent amongst some susceptible young Muslims. The situation has only worsened in recent times, as the communities become labeled as guilty or complacent for the recent string of terror attacks in France, creating a dangerous vacuum for radicalization.[52]

Islamism and the State

A modern liberal democracy with a tradition of secularism dating back to the eighteenth century, France is also a key ally of the United States, despite occasional foreign policy differences. French troops have played an important role in the war in Afghanistan, involvement in Libya, and the coalition to fight ISIS, even as the French state is actively engaged in resisting Islamism, both domestically and internationally.

Building on its history of colonialism, France aspired to become the European gateway to the Arab world through a systematic courting of the post-colonial regimes of North Africa. Public discourse in France, therefore, tended to be more pro-Arab than elsewhere in the West. However, the rise of an emphatically religious Islamism ran counter to French commitments to laicité, generating policy shifts under Sarkozy, an open promotion of French national identity. In October 2009, then-Minister of Immigration Eric Besson called for public debate over "the theme of what it is to be French, what are the values we share, what are the relations that make us French and of which we should be proud." He insisted on a particular valorization of Frenchness: "We must reaffirm the values of French national identity and the pride in being French."[53] This effort by the state to mobilize a focus on nationality was intended as an effort to overcome immigrant (and especially Islamist) separatism, and in the years since, this discussion has shifted increasingly toward secularism. To question the role of religion in the public sphere in France is, above all, a vehicle to inquire about the status of politicized Islam.

Yet the conflict between the republican secularism of the state and the politicization of religion inherent in Islamism continues. In 2009, a debate began over prospective legislation to ban full-length cloaks, the burqa and the niqab (the latter leaves the eyes uncovered) from public venues. Initially proposed by a Communist mayor of a town with a high Muslim population, its intention was to protect women and to defend French values of secularism. It was adopted with the support of conservative President Nicolas Sarkozy and his party, but the Socialist Party did not oppose it; current Socialist President Hollande has indicated that he does not plan to pursue a retraction of the ban, which has strong popular support.[54] Clothing bans were once again the subject of debate in 2016, when over 30 towns in coastal France imposed a ban on a full-length swimsuit, often referred to as the burkini. While the ban was overturned by some French courts, local officials as well as national figures, such as Prime Minister Valls, were vocal in their opposition to the swimsuit. In the midst of the burkini controversy, the mayor of the Riviera town at the center of the controversy told Muslim women "[i]f you don't want to live the way we do, don't come," while Prime Minster Valls referred to the swimsuit as a "symbol of the enslavement of women."[55]

French counterterrorism practices have faced criticism on civil rights and human rights grounds. The promulgation of laws criminalizing terrorist conspiracies (rather than simply terrorist attacks themselves) has elicited denunciations on the grounds that they represent an ominous expansion of state power. However, this pursuit of conspiracies has been defended as the only way to prevent catastrophic attacks, such as the successful disruption of the plans for terrorist violence at the 2014 World Cup at the Stade de France.[56] Still, Amnesty International and other watchdog groups continue to criticize France for its prosecution of conspiracy charges as a "criminal association in relation to a terrorist undertaking."[57]

With regard to any connection between terrorism and asylum seekers, it is worth noting that the countries that have been the hardest hit by terrorist attacks ranked lowest in terms of refugees accepted, including France (along with Belgium and the UK).[58] A handful of French terrorists took advantage of chaos at Europe's Southeastern border by pretending to be refugees, taking advantage of lax vetting procedures. Some had fake Syrian passports, registered as refugees in Greece, passed through Budapest on the Balkan Route. The terrorist threat came not from refugees but from thousands of native-born Muslims—roughly one-fourth of whom were converts—who traveled (or attempted to travel) to Syria or Iraq.[59] Nearly all terrorists involved in the attacks of the past two years were the products of French society, born in France or raised there from a young age.

For civil rights activists, the situation was exacerbated by 2008 legislation that authorized preventive detention in certain cases. After the completion of a sentence, an individual whom a judge deems to be dangerous may face an extended sentence for renewable periods of one year. In addition, the police were granted the authority to develop intelligence files on all individuals over the age of thirteen who are deemed to represent a threat to public order. While criticisms of this counterterrorism regime continue, France was successful in thwarting large-scale domestic attacks for several years leading up to the 2012 Toulouse shootings. Until then, there had been no return to the violence of the 1980s, when terrorists seemed able to act in France with impunity and little fear of sanction. After the Toulouse attack, it was revealed that the perpetrator, Mohammed Merah, had been under surveillance but was nonetheless able to carry out the killings, which lead to public criticism of the counterintelligence community. Marc Trévidic, the former counter-terrorism magistrate, argued that counterintelligence agencies may respond by pulling back their operations precisely in order to avoid this sort of criticism in the future: "After Merah, our policemen are afraid [...] They don't want to monitor people for a long time after they come back [from foreign travel to Islamist territories], because if they monitor someone and this guy commits a bomb attack it will be terrible a second time for [the counterintelligence agency]."[60] The alternative, an early arrest of a potential terrorist, would likely not be upheld due to a lack of sufficient evidence.

However, after it was disclosed that the extremist cell that included the Charlie Hebdo attackers had already been known to French intelligence authorities prior to their attacks, French lawmakers responded with a new law designed to intensify intelligence gathering and surveillance. In early 2015, a law was drafted to update the legislative framework to help French security services better define the purposes and types of intelligence-gathering, set up a National Commission for Control of Intelligence Techniques, and authorize new methods to collect metadata from internet providers.[61] While the law passed overwhelmingly in the National Assembly, it is particularly controversial among civil liberties groups because of its provision allowing French authorities access to "digital and mobile phone communications of anyone linked to a 'terrorist' inquiry without prior authorization from a judge." To quell the fears of vocal opponents and concerned citizens, President Hollande has pledged that the law would be reviewed by France's constitutional council to ensure its lawfulness.[62] Other elements of the counter-terrorism effort raised eyebrows amongst civil liberties lawyers. A court sentenced a French mother to two years' imprisonment for wiring money to her jihadi son in Syria. France even began target assassinations of its own jihadis nationals in Syria, sidestepping the death penalty ban and provoking no particular outcry.[63] President Macron declared an end to the State of Emergency that began in November 2015 and ended in November 2017.

In the aftermath of the 2015 terrorist attacks, France also introduced new certification procedures for preachers and closer scrutiny of mosque funding. Dozens of imams, civil servants, and teachers graduated annually from multiple anti-radicalization programs in Paris, Strasbourg, Aix-en-Provence, Lyon. In 2015, all 1,800 imams in France were assigned an obligatory educational program of 130 hours of classes over one year. The government invested another €1.5 million in sundry imam-integration projects. In the wake of the Bastille Day attack and the burkini ban controversy of 2016, former Prime Minister Hollande saw an opportunity to address the compatibility of Islam and French secularism by setting up the Foundation for Islam in France in August 2016. With the goal of improving relations between France's Muslim population and the French government, Hollande chose Jean-Pierre Chevènement to lead the foundation. In addition to the Foundation, Hollande publicly stated that France must find a way for the state to play a role in financing and building mosques and training clergy to eliminate the possibility of radicalization of imams who are trained abroad.[64] An "imam charter," meant to assist imams in combatting radicalization, was signed in March 2017.[65]

In 2017, the Foundation for Islam was given a start-up fund of €5 million to pursue "the goal of helping French Islam become autonomous, in funding and in its approach" to religion.[66] Funds could also be solicited from any Organization of Islamic Cooperation (OIC) member state to sponsor special programming — but not the CFCM's core budget itself. "France must overcome the rifts that our adversaries want to exploit," Chevènement, the foundation director, said. "The Islamic State's strategists do not hide that they want to throw our country into civil war."[67]

Chevènement added that French Imams may be "trained in those countries that fight against jihadi terrorism" so long as they fulfilled a series of specific requirements, i.e. be Francophone, obtain a diploma in legal and civic education from one of twelve French universities, and hold a degree in Islamic studies.[68] "The young people being radicalized are very removed from Islam... Only qualified theologians can help to religiously reorient them — they have become disconnected because they have broken ties to their countries of origin without having integrated in France."[69]

There has been some exchange with North African nations to assist France in anti-radicalization efforts. In May 2017, the Tunisian minister of religious affairs, Ahmed Adhoum, proposed the creation of a religious attaché to Tunisian embassies in Europe, which would allow imams and preachers to travel to European nations to combat radicalization. The French and Italian ambassadors to Tunisia expressed interest in the project.[70] Morocco offered to train fifty French imams per year at its new Mohamed VI Institute in Rabat, a religious school meant to combat radicalization, and Algeria offered to do the same at the Dar al-Imam in Algiers, or the University in Constantine.[71]

The election of a new President, Emmanuel Macron, in 2017 lent new energy to the Islam dossier. One of President Macron's future ministers wrote in 2016, "We must impose a Concordat-like set of rules so that [Islam] is totally blended into the Republic [...] French Islam means firmly accepting cutting all religious ties with foreign countries."[72] This was one of the institutional forms that the President invoked in an interview with the Journal du Dimanche when announcing that he would be revisiting the concept of the French Council for the Muslim Faith, the institution that Nicolas Sarkozy helped bring to life in 2003, based on Jean-Pierre Chevenement's own consultations with Islamic associations in the late 1990s. Among the issues still in need of resolution after thirty years of consultations: an approved place to train Islamic theologians and imams for the republic.

Endnotes

1. Fiametta Venner, OPA sur l'Islam de France: Les Ambitions de l'UOIF [OPA within French Islam: the Ambitions of the UOIF] (Paris: Calman-Lévy, 2005).
2. The website of the Institute is http://www.ieshdeparis.fr/.

3. Venner, OPA sur l'Islam de France, 133-153; Michèle Vianès, Silence, on Manipule: les Islamistes en Manoeuvre[Exploiting the Silence: Islamists in Action] (Paris: Editions Hors Commerce, 2004), 58.
4. Venner, OPA sur l'Islam de France, 158.
5. Representation in the CFCM depends on the size of mosque space controlled by an organization. See Vianès, Silence, on Manipule, 18-19.
6. Lorenzo Vidino, "The Muslim Brotherhood's Conquest of Europe," Middle East Quarterly 12, no. 1 (Winter 2005), 25-34.
7. Stéphanie Le Bars, "'Pour la Majorité des Musulmans, la Séperation du Religieux et du Politique est Acquise'" [For the Majority of Muslims, the Seperation of Religion and Politics is Artificial], Le Monde (Paris), April 4, 2011, http://www.lemonde.fr/societe/chat/2011/04/04/l-islam-est-il-soluble-dans-la-laicite_1502963_3224.html#ens_id=1460876.
8. For the objectives of the UOIF, see its official website at http://www.uoif-online.com/v3/spip.php?article20; On the radicalism of UOIF, see the interview with Fiametta Venner, "La Face Cachée de l'UOIF et des Frères Musulmans en France," [The Hidden Side of the UOIF and the Muslim Brothers in France], Le Post, March 12, 2009, http://www.lepost.fr/article/2009/12/03/1822346_la-face-cachee-de-l-uoif-et-des-freres-musulmans-en-france.html; On the influence of the Muslim Brothers, see Brigitte Maréchal, The Muslim Brothers in Europe: Roots and Discourse (Leiden: Brill, 2008).
9. Xavier Raufer, ed., Atlas de l'Islam Radical [Atlas of Radical Islam] (Paris: CNRS Editions, 2007), 13.
10. "La Face Cachée de l'UOIF et des Frères Musulmans en France."
11. "UOIF: 'Il n'y a pas de rupture avec le president de la Republique' [UOIF: 'there is no break with the president of the Republic']," Le Parisien, April 6, 2012, http://www.leparisien.fr/societe/religion-ahmed-jaballah-il-n-y-a-pas-de-rupture-avec-le-president-de-la-republique-06-04-2012-1942560.php.
12. "Islamisme : Il est urgent de dissoudre l'UOIF par-

rainée par Nicolas Sarkozy," Communiqué de Presse de Marine Le Pen, Présidente du Front National, November 18, 2014, http://www.frontnational.com/2014/11/islamisme-il-est-urgent-de-dissoudre-luoif-parrainee-par-nicolas-sarkozy/

13. David Lewis, "Al Qaeda's Richest Faction Dominant in North Mali: U.S.," Reuters, July 26, 2012, http://www.reuters.com/article/2012/07/26/us-mali-usa-africom-idUSBRE86P1IC20120726.
14. Jonathan Masters, "Al-Qaeda in the Islamic Maghreb (AQIM)", Council on Foreign Relations, n.d., http://www.cfr.org/north-africa/al-qaeda-islamic-maghreb-aqim/p12717.
15. Steven Erlanger, "French Intervention in Mali Raises Threat of Domestic Terrorism, Judge Says," New York Times, February 23, 2013 http://www.nytimes.com/2013/02/24/world/europe/french-intervention-in-mali-raises-threat-of-domestic-terrorism-judge-says.html?pagewanted=all&_r=0.
16. Christopher S. Chivvis and Andrew Liepman, "North Africa's Menace AQIM's Evolution and the U.S. Policy Response," RAND Corporation, http://www.rand.org/pubs/research_reports/RR415.html
17. Cécile De Sèze, "Daesh, Aqmi... Quelles menaces terroristes au Sahel ?" RTL, January 18, 2008, http://www.rtl.fr/actu/international/al-qaida-daesh-quelles-menaces-terroristes-au-sahel-7791887321
18. Wassim Nasr, Twitter, September 16, 2017, https://twitter.com/SimNasr/status/909138461990510592/photo/1.
19. Jessica Stern, "Why the Islamic State Hates France," PBSNewshour, November 18, 2015, http://www.pbs.org/newshour/updates/why-islamic-state-jihadis-are-enraged-by-france/.
20. Jessica Stern, "Why the Islamic State Hates France," PBSNewshour, November 18, 2015, http://www.pbs.org/newshour/updates/why-islamic-state-jihadis-are-enraged-by-france/.
21. François Grégoire, "Djihadistes français arrêtés en Syrie: la question du retour tourney au case-tête," Ouest France, January 4, 2018, https://www.ouest-france.

fr/terrorisme/djihadistes-francais-arretes-en-syrie-la-question-du-retour-tourne-au-casse-tete-5482928

22. The Soufan Group, "Foreign Fighters: An Updated Assessment of the Flow of Foreign Fighters into Syria and Iraq," December 2015, http://soufangroup.com/wp-content/uploads/2015/12/TSG_ForeignFightersUpdate3.pdf.
23. "ISIS attacks: A Timeline of Terror," CBS, n.d., http://www.cbsnews.com/pictures/isis-attacks-a-timeline-of-terror/19/.
24. Mariano Castillo, Margot Haddad, Michael Martinez and Steve Almasy, "Paris Suicide Bomber Identified; ISIS claims responsibility for 129 dead," CNN, November 16, 2015, http://www.cnn.com/2015/11/14/world/paris-attacks/.
25. Eric Kirschbaum, "Perpatrator of Nice terror attack asked for 'more weapons' before rampage, authorities say," Los Angeles Times, July 16, 2016, http://www.latimes.com/world/europe/la-fg-nice-attack-20160717-snap-story.html.
26. "France church attack: Priest killed by two 'IS militants,'" BBC, July 26, 2016, http://www.bbc.com/news/world-europe-36892785.
27. "Machete wielding 'terrorist' shot near Louvre," USA Today, February 3, 2017, https://www.usatoday.com/story/news/world/2017/02/03/soldier-louvre-paris/97436606/
28. "Orly: Un Français radicalisé tué après avoir attaqué des militaires," La Depeche, March 18, 2017, https://www.ladepeche.fr/article/2017/03/18/2538662-orly-homme-abattu-apres-avoir-derobe-arme-militaire.html
29. Adam Nossiter, "'That Ignoramus': 2 French Scholars of Radical Islam Turn Bitter Rivals," New York Times, July 12, 2016, https://www.nytimes.com/2016/07/13/world/europe/france-radical-islam.html
30. CIA World Factbook: France, https://www.cia.gov/library/publications/the-world-factbook/geos/fr.html
31. Pew Research Center's Forum on Religion & Public Life, "The Future of the Global Muslim Population Projections for 2010-2030," January 2011, 22; "France:

comment est évalué le nombre de musulmans," Le Figaro, April 5, 2011, http://www.lefigaro.fr/actualite-france/2011/04/05/01016-20110405ARTFIG00599-france-comment-est-evalue-le-nombre-de-musulmans.php.

32. "L'islam de France aujourd'hui," Contretemps, n.d., http://www.contretemps.eu/socio-flashs/islam-france-aujourdhui.
33. "Unease with Islam on the rise in France and Germany, new poll finds," France24 (April 29, 2016), http://www.france24.com/en/20160429-france-germany-unease-with-islam-rise-new-poll-finds.
34. IFOP, Regards croisés sur l'Islam en France en Allemagne, http://www.ifop.com/media/poll/3373-1-study_file.pdf
35. "Lislam, première religion en France," Le Figaro, October 24, 2012, http://www.lefigaro.fr/actualite-france/2012/10/24/01016-20121024ARTFIG00633-islam-premiere-religion-en-france.php; "En France, des jeunes de plus en plus fidèles à l'islam," Le Monde, November 4, 2012, http://www.lemonde.fr/culture/article/2012/11/01/des-jeunes-fideles-a-l-islam_1784520_3246.html.
36. Yasmeen Serhan, "France's Disappearing Mosques," The Atlantic, August 1, 2016, http://www.theatlantic.com/news/archive/2016/08/french-mosques-islam/493919/.
37. Portail Religion, http://www.portail-religion.com/islam/mosquees/mosquees-france.php.
38. Valérie Amiraux, "From Empire to Republic: the French Muslim Dilemma," in Anna Triandafyllidou, Muslims in 21st Century Europe: Structural and Cultural Perspectives (London: Routledge, 2010), 137-159.
39. Valentin Graff, "Pourquoi on ne ferme pas toutes les «mosquées salafistes" February 7, 2017 http://www.liberation.fr/france/2017/02/07/pourquoi-on-ne-ferme-pas-toutes-les-mosquees-salafistes_153886.
40. "Contre l'Islam de France," Nonfiction.fr, 30 October 2015, https://www.nonfiction.fr/article-7878-contre-l-islam-de-france.htm.
41. Vincent, Elise, "Ecquevilly, histoire d'un satanisme

français," Le Monde, 12 March 2016
42. Serhan, "France's Disappearing Mosques."
43. Amiraux, "From Empire to Republic: the French Muslim Dilemma."
44. Amiraux, "From Empire to Republic: the French Muslim Dilemma."
45. Amiraux, "From Empire to Republic: the French Muslim Dilemma."
46. Margot Haddad, French government fighting online war against jihadist youth recruiting, CNN, http://www.cnn.com/2015/02/23/europe/france-anti-jihadist-campaign/.
47. Alain Houziaux, Le Voile, que Cache-t-Il? [The Veil: What Does it Hide?] (Paris: Editions ouvrières, 2004).
48. "What is Secularism?" http://www.gouvernement.fr/qu-est-ce-que-la-laicite.
49. Vianès, Silence, on Manipule, 51-73.
50. Centre d'Analyse Stratégique, Enquêtes sur les Violences Urbaines: Comprendre les Émeutes de Novembre 2005 [Investigations into Urban Violence: Understanding the Riots of November 2005] (Paris: La Documentation Française, 2006).
51. Angelique Chrisalfis, "Three Nights of Riots in French Town After 21-Year-Old Dies in Police Custody," Guardian (London), July 10, 2009, http://www.guardian.co.uk/world/2009/jul/10/french-police-fight-rioting-youths.
52. Christina Rufini, "Les Banlieues: Searching for the seeds of terror," CBS News, January 18, 2016, http://www.cbsnews.com/news/paris-banlieues-seeds-of-terror-isis/.
53. "Besson Relance le Débat sur l'Identité Nationale" [Besson Relaunches the Debate over National Identity], Le Monde (Paris), October 25, 2009.
54. Steven Erlanger, "Has the 'Burqa Ban' Worked in France?" International Herald Tribune, September 2, 2012, http://rendezvous.blogs.nytimes.com/2012/09/02/has-the-burqa-ban-worked-in-france/.
55. Lauren Said-Moorhouse, "Burkini Ban in Nice overturned by French Court," CNN, September 2, 2016, http://www.cnn.com/2016/09/02/europe/france-burki-

ni-ban/.

56. Jeremy Shapiro and Bénédicte Suzan, "The French Experience of Counter-terrorism," Survival 45, iss. 1 (Spring 2003), 85-86.
57. See, for example, Human Rights Watch, "In the Name of Prevention: Insufficient Safeguards in National Security Removals," June 5, 2007, http://www.hrw.org/en/reports/2007/06/05/name-prevention-0; Human Rights Watch, Preempting Justice: Counterterrorism Laws and Procedures in France (New York: HRW, 2008), http://www.hrw.org/en/reports/2008/07/01/preempting-justice; "France," in Amnesty International Report 2009: State of the World's Human Rights (London: Amnesty International, 2010), http://report2009.amnesty.org/en/regions/europe-central-asia/france.
58. Belgium / France ; 10th and 17th
59. Olivier Roy, "Who are the new Jihadis?" The Guardian, April 13, 2017 https://www.theguardian.com/news/2017/apr/13/who-are-the-new-jihadis
60. Erlanger, "French Intervention in Mali Raises Threat of Domestic Terrorism, Judge Says."
61. Hugh Schofield, "Surveillance law prompts unease in France," BBC, May 4, 2015, http://www.bbc.com/news/world-europe-32497034.
62. Angelique Chrisafis, "France passes new surveillance law in wake of Charlie Hebdo attack," Guardian (London), May 5, 2015, https://www.theguardian.com/world/2015/may/05/france-passes-new-surveillance-law-in-wake-of-charlie-hebdo-attack.
63. Lhomme, Frabrice and Gérard Davet, "Qui sont les djihadistes français tués par des 'frappes ciblées?'" Le Monde, 4 January 2017; "Comment Hollande autorise 'l'exécution ciblée' de terroristes."
64. Tim Hume and Lauren Said-Moorhouse, "Hollande: Republic must create 'Islam of France' to respond to terror threat," CNN, http://www.cnn.com/2016/09/08/europe/france-hollande-islam-secularism/.
65. Une « charte de l'imam » adoptée par le Conseil français du culte musulman, March 24, 2017 http://www.lemonde.fr/religions/article/2017/03/29/une-charte-de-l-imam-adoptee-par-le-conseil-francais-

du-culte-musulman_5102903_1653130.html.

66. "Everything that is not religious for which public funding is authorized." Le 24 novembre 2015, Bernard Cazeneuve a demandé la mise en place d'une «habilitation», ou «certification» facultative des imams français par le biais du CFCM. , Zaman France, 20 March 2016.
67. Jean-Marie Guenois and Vincent Tremolet de Villers, "Jean-Pierre Chevènement, l'Islam de France," Le Figaro, 31 August 2016.
68. Jean-Marie Guenois and Vincent Tremolet de Villers, "Jean-Pierre Chevènement, l'Islam de France," Le Figaro, 31 August 2016.
69. Foundation for waqfs (Fondation des oeuvres de l'Islam de France (2005), which became the Fondation pour l'Islam de France, 2017); Jean-Marie Guenois and Vincent Tremolet de Villers, "Jean-Pierre Chevènement, l'Islam de France," Le Figaro, 31 August 2016.
70. "Le ministre des Affaires religieuses propose la creation du poste d'attaché religieux," 9 May 2017.
71. Isabelle Chenu, L'institut Mohammed VI veut former les imams d'un islam tolerant," RFI, April 19, 2017, http://www.rfi.fr/emission/20170419-maroc-institut-mohammed-vi-lutter-deviances-extremistes; http://www.aps.dz/algerie/70713-mohamed-aissa-les-imams-delegues-a-la-mosquee-de-paris-appeles-a-etre-les-ambassadeurs-de-la-paix.
72. It is the desire to Gallicanize Islam. Gérald Darmanin, "A l'islam, nous devons imposer une concorde, afin de l'assimiler totalement à la République." l'Opinion, June 6, 2016.

43 Germany

Quick Facts

Population: 80,594,017 (July 2017 est)
Area: 357,022 sq km
Ethnic Groups: German 91.5%, Turkish 2.4%, other 6.1% (made up largely of Greek, Italian, Polish, Russian, Serbo-Croatian, Spanish)
Religions: Protestant 34%, Roman Catholic 34%, Muslim 3.7%, unaffiliated or other 28.3%
Government Type: Federal Republic
GDP (official exchange rate): $3.685 trillion (2016 est)

Map and Quick Facts courtesy of the CIA World Factbook (Last Updated September 2018)

Introduction

Germany, alongside France, has the highest number of Muslim citizens in Western Europe, as well as in the member states of the European Union as a whole. It is also a hotbed of Islamist activity. Most notably, the attacks of 9/11 were organized in part in Germany by the Hamburg cell headed by Mohammed Atta.[1] *Today, Islamists from Germany, including homegrown terrorists, pose a real threat to the security of the German state.*

Islamism in Germany has deep roots, stretching back to a symbiosis between the German state and radical religious elements during the First World War. However, these connections have not always been strictly hostile. During the First World War, German diplomat Max von Oppenheim authored a guide to encourage Muslim populations to wage jihad against the entente powers, the United Kingdom, France, and Russia.[2] *These ties between Germany and Islamists endured during the Second World War, fueled by the Third Reich's close ties to the Grand Mufti of Jerusalem, Haj Amin al-Hussaini, and throughout the decades of the Cold War against the Soviet Union, before emerging to challenge the stability of the Federal Republic in the post-Cold War era. However, in more recent years, the relationship between the two has been less than friendly. Islamism and jihadism are prevalent in today's Germany, with the first significant jihadist attack in Germany taking place in*

December 2016. The Lebanese jihadi entity Hezbollah continues to maintain a strong presence in Germany, with 950 active operatives, who raise funds and recruit new members.

Islamist Activity

Both peaceful legal Islamism and violent jihadism exist in Germany today. Political Islam of the lawful variant predominates, although instances of jihadi activity have been documented as well with a serious jihadist attack with a dozen people killed in December 2016. Peaceful Islamist groups include Milli Görüs and the Gülen Movement. The Muslim Brotherhood, Salafists groups, and Iranian influencers occupy a murky middle ground on the violence spectrum. More overtly violent groups include Hezbollah, Hamas, and the Islamic State.

Milli Görüs

Milli Görüs is an Islamic political movement based on the philosophies of Necmettin Erbakan, former Turkish Prime Minister and a profoundly anti-secular and anti-Western Turkish scholar. It is popular among the Turkish Diaspora in Germany, as it is an offshoot of an originally-Turkish movement.[3] The group pegs its total European membership at 87,000, with 30,000 of them residing in Germany.[4] By its own estimate, the group maintains more than 514 mosques and cultural centers in eleven European nations. Of these, 323 are in Germany. The German iteration of Milli Görüs has stated that the group wishes to encourage a free democratic political system and help Muslims integrate into German society. However, some controversy remains. In the past, the organization has advocated anti-Semitic views through a range of media. It promotes radical television broadcasts, such as the Iranian TV series *Zehra's Blue Eyes* (which revolves around a fictional Israeli candidate for Prime Minister who kidnaps Palestinian children in order to harvest their organs for Jewish use—and glorifies suicide bombing in response).[5] It also has disseminated written anti-Semitic works, such as Turkish translations of Henry Ford's *The International Jew*.[6] Notably, the dissemination of such literature is contrary to German law, but no legal efforts to prosecute the group have taken place in that respect. At least some portion of the group also has endorsed and promoted jihadist activities abroad.[7]

In 2009, German authorities charged six Milli Görüs officials with fraud, money laundering, supporting terrorist organizations, and associating with criminals. In 2010, the charges were dropped. [8] As of 2014, The Office for the Protection of the Constitution in Hamburg, Germany, no longer views the organization as a direct threat. Manfred Murck, head of the Hamburg office, maintains that while the organization's traditions are not compatible with the fundamental principles of the German constitution, there is no evidence that the group was attempting to dismantle or damage Germany's free democratic order.[9]

However, the 2017 federal intelligence report cites Milli Görüs as having a current membership of 10,000 and is an "object of observation." The group declared its intention to pray for "the liberation of Jerusalem and from repression and occupation." Participants of two of Milli Görüs events burned Israeli flags and used anti-Semitic slogans.[10]

The Gülen Movement

The Turkish Gülen Movement has become increasingly influential in Germany. Founded by Turkish Islamist Fethullah Gülen (born 1938), it is based on the ideas of Faid Nursi (1876-1960).[11] The Gülen Movement does not publicly advocate violence, and instead espouses the gradual imposition of a sharia-based democracy.[12] The Gülen Movement runs at least 20-25 schools in Germany in all, not including some 200 groups for the coaching of pupils after school.[13] There are no official membership numbers available for the Gülen Movement, but the group is believed to be increasingly popular as a result of its educational activities.[14] According to television and media reports in June 2013, Gülen members have tried to influence and coopt democratic parties in Germany.[15]. This has clearly been the case in the city of Leipzig, where Gülen members attempted to gain a majority in the city's Social Democratic Party's youth organization, the Young Socialists (Jusos). The Gülen movement also tried to gain influence over the conservative Christian-Social Union (CSU) in Bavaria using the same method.[16]

After the attempted coup against Turkish President Recep Tayyip

Erdogan and his ruling AKP in Turkey in July 2016, however, German-Turkish alleged followers of the movement faced attacks and defamation by German-Turkish AKP supporters.[17] Germany has the biggest Turkish community outside of Turkey, with over three million Turkish people living in Germany. In August 2018, the German government cut funding to the Turkish-Islamic Union for Religious Affairs (DITIB). According to the *Deutsche Welle*, the DITIB, which is widely viewed as the long arm of Erdogan in Germany, employed imams "to spy on followers on the Gülen movement."[18]

The 2017 German intelligence report states the chief priority for Turkey's intelligence agency (MIT) is to spy on the Gülen Movement. [19] The Turkish goverment has repeatedly pressed Germany to extradite alleged Gülen supporters to Istanbul. In February, 2017, the head of MIT presented a list to the German authorities of more than a hundred alledged Gülen supporters in Germany. [20]

The Muslim Brotherhood

As of 2017, German authorities estimated that the Muslim Brotherhood (MB) has 1,040 adherents in Germany.[21] While it has no formal representation in the country, the organization is known to run Islamic centers in Nuremberg, Stuttgart, Frankfurt, Cologne, Marburg, Braunschweig, and Munich.[22]

The Brotherhood has a long history in the Federal Republic, beginning with a 1958 initiative to build a mosque in Munich—an effort which resulted in the creation of the *Islamische Gemeinschaft in Deutschland e.V.* (IGD), the "Islamic Community in Germany." Today, the IGD is headquartered in Cologne and serves as the unofficial representative of the group in national affairs. From 2002 to 2010, it was headed by Ibrahim el-Zayat; since 2010, Samir Fallah has been its head.[23] El-Zayat was general secretary of the World Assembly of Muslim Youth (WAMY), a Saudi organization active in the spread of Wahhabi ideology abroad.[24]

The IGD ostensibly tries to create a positive political climate for political Islam, and to promote a more pious way of life in Germany. However, it also collects money for Islamist causes abroad, and raised funds for Hamas during the 2009 Gaza war.[25] In 2014, the Government of the United Arab Emirates (UAE) published a list of

Islamist terrorist organizations; the only German group identified therein was the IGD.[26] The German government's intelligence report for 2017 noted that number of members—1,040—has remained the same since 2015. The federal intelligence report provides a structural chart of the Muslim Brotherhood that falls under the category of "objects of observation." [27]

Salafist elements

German authorities consider Salafism to be "the most dynamic Islamist movement," both within Germany and on a global level.[28] Salafism is a deeply conservative Islamic movement that advocates a strict return to the original practices and beliefs of the Prophet Muhammad and his first followers. Though Salafists are not necessarily violent, there has been some correlation between Salafi groups and violent jihadism.

According to the head of the Office for the Protection of the Constitution in Hamburg, Salafists are the fastest growing elements in Germany's Islamist camp.[29] This may stem from Salafists' ability to attract teenagers and young adults through music or social media events, as well as via the distribution of the Koran. Salafi groups in Germany were estimated to have increased their number of adherents from 3,800 to some 4,500 between 2011 and early 2013.[30] That growth has continued; as of 2015, some 8,350 Salafists are estimated active in Germany.[31] According to a 2017 German national intelligence report, the number of Salafists totals10,800.[32] As of July 4, 2017, some media outlets estimated the number of Salafis in the country at 10,100.[33]

This growth has brought with it an increase in militant activity. The first ever Islamist terror attack in Germany occurred in March 2011, when Kosovar Serb Arid Uka killed two U.S. soldiers at the Frankfurt International Airport.[34] Uka was discovered to have been in touch with Salafist elements via social media outlets, specifically Facebook.[35] He was convicted and sentenced to life in prison in December 2012.[36]

German authorities have begun to respond to the growing threats posed by these groups. In June 2012, the Islamist network Millatu Ibrahim was shut down by German authorities in the first action of its kind against Salafist groups.[37] In March 2013, Germany authorities proscribed the Islamist organization Dawa FFM and two other groups, Islamische Audios and An-Nussrah.[38] On April 16, 2016, two 16-year old Salafists placed a bomb at a Sikh Temple, causing an explosion that injured several people at a wedding. The best known German Salafist, a convert named Pierre Vogel, has radicalized many people.[39]

Social media and the Internet have played a crucial role in Salafist activity,[40] especially alongside activism such as the free distribution of the Koran. The "Read" Campaign, which started in 2011, was established by Cologne based Salafist Ibrahim Abou Nagie, the head of the group Die Wahre Religion (The True Religion). Its aim is to distribute over 25 million German-language copies of the Koran.[41] On May 28, 2016, the state of Hamburg was the first German state to ban the distribution, due to the organization's extremist and jihadist connections. Other German states might follow suit in the future, including in particular North Rhine-Westphalia.[42] In November 2016, Die Wahre Religion was formally proscribed by the Federal Ministry of the Interior.[43]

Iranian Influence

The influence of the Shi'a variant of Islamism propounded by the Islamic Republic of Iran can be found in Germany as well. The Islamic Center Hamburg (IZH), founded in 1962, is a pro-Iranian institution closely linked to the Islamic Republic. Its head, the Ayatollah Reza Ramezani,[44] was appointed to his post by the Iranian Foreign Ministry in April 2009.[45] The IZH, in turn, tries to spread the ideals of the Iranian Revolution via brochures, events, prayers, rallies, and other activities, and exerts an influence over a number of Islamic organizations within Germany. Furthermore, the IZH is actively involved in the following institutions:

The Council of Islamic Communities in Hamburg;
The Central Council of Muslims in Germany;
The Islamic Community of Shi'a Communities in Germany; and
The Islamic-European Union of Shi'a scholars and Theologians.[46]

In 2017, Germany's outgoing foreign minister, Sigmar Gabriel, hosted Hamidreza Torabi as part of a religious dialogue event at the ministry. Torabi heads the Islamic Academy of Germany—a part of the IZH. He is a key organizer of the annual pro-Iranian regime Al-Quds rally in Berlin that calls for the state of Israel "illegal and criminal" and features extremist anti-Western activists and Hezbollah supporters.[47]

Ever since the signing of the Joint Comprehensive Plan of Action (JCPOA) on the Iranian nuclear program in July 2015, Germany's relations with Iran have improved. Despite knowledge of ongoing Iranian attempts to buy military goods,[48] German politics now promotes a normalization of the relationship with Iran. Nonetheless, Iran has continued to seek illicit nuclear and missile technology in Germany.

According to the state of North Rhine-Westphalia, Iran made 32 attempts in 2016 to obtain proliferation technology for weapons programs of mass destruction.[49] The intelligence agency in the city-state of Hamburg stated that: "there is no evidence of a complete about-face in Iran's atomic policies" in 2016.[50] A prominent German national security reporter confirmed in October, 2016 that Iran sought technology in the federal republic to build nuclear-tipped missiles.[51] The Bavarian state intelligence agency's 2017 report stated Iran seeks to expand its weapons arsenal into a nuclear program.[52] The neighboring state of Baden-Württemberg wrote in its 2017 intelligence report: "Iran continued to undertake efforts to obtain goods and know-how to be used for the development of weapons of mass destruction and to optimize corresponding missile delivery systems."[53] The state intelligence reports contradict German chancellor Angela Merkel's belief in the efficacy of the Iran nuclear deal, formally known as the Joint Comprehensive Plan of Action.

The German government harshly criticized the Trump administration for its withdrawal from the Iran accord in May 2015. The current German foreign minister Heiko Maas reportedly sought methods to circumvent US sanctions. [54]

Many leading German politicians regularly visit Iran. Examples include Vice-Chancellor and member of the Federal Government Sigmar Gabriel, head of the Social Democratic Party, but also delegations from Saxony, Mecklenburg-West Pomerania, and Saxony-Anhalt.[55] The office of Martin Dulig, Vice-Prime Minister of Saxony, created a brochure that showed German female politicians in headscarves. The brochure prompted sharp criticism, to which officials replied that they created the brochure for a specifically Iranian audience. This defense did not hold much water, given the controversy over compulsory headscarf-wearing in Iran. [56]

Hezbollah

The Lebanese Shi'ite militia Hezbollah is also active in Germany, where it has had a presence since the 1980s.[57] Founded in 1982 after the Israeli invasion of Lebanon, Hezbollah is a Shiite militant group with deep ties to Iran.[58] The organization is both anti-Semitic and anti-Western. While it has no official representatives in Germany, the organization was estimated to have approximately 950 members and supporters as of 2017.[59] Germany's most populous state, North Rhine-Westphalia (NRW), has a variety of Hezbollah-sympathetic Islamic centers and mosques. The Imam-Mahdi Center is one high-profile example. NRW's intelligence agency wrote in its 2016 report that Hezbollah fighters have entered Germany disguised as refugees. As of 2016, there were approximately 100 Hezbollah members or supporters in NRW.[60]

Hezbollah has often acted as an Iranian proxy, and is a close ally of Syrian dictator Bashar al-Assad. Some controversy remains in the European Union over whether the group should be considered a foreign terrorist organization (FTO). For many years, Hezbollah was able to work quietly in Germany, which became its "main fund-raising center in Europe."[61] Germany has also become a source of arms for the Lebanese militia; Lebanese media outlets reported in 2012 that Hezbollah was buying weapons in Germany via Iranian-controlled companies.[62] In 2013, the European Union declared Hezbollah's military wing (though not its domestic wing) a terrorist group, a year after the organization attacked Israeli tourists in Burgas, Bulgaria.[63] The Hezbollah terrorism attack in Bulgaria resulted in the deaths of five Israelis and their Bulgarian Muslim bus driver.

While the German security forces have believed Hezbollah to be a dangerous organization for the past several years, the German government has not denounced as such and does not take action against it.[64] In 2016, both members of the Israeli Knesset and German Bundestag appealed to Thomas de Maiziére to outlaw Hezbollah's entire organization, including the domestic wing and not solely the military wing.[65] The interior minister declined.[66] The Germany left party MP Christine Buchholz has argued that both Hezbollah and Hamas represent legitimate resistance against Israel.[67] The city of Bremen's intelligence agency wrote in its 2017 report that "the Al-Mustafa-Community Center supports Hezbollah in Lebanon, especially by collection donations." [68]

Hamas

Hamas, a Palestinian militant group and political organization, has a small presence in Germany. Hamas was estimated to have 320 members in Germany as of 2016/2017.[69] In NRW, membership increased from 65 in 2015 to 75 in 2016.[70] These activists raise funds for Hamas, largely in collaboration with the Palestinian Return Center (PRC) in London.[71] While Hamas does not have any official representatives in the country, it has been known to work through like-minded organizations to raise funds and promote its political objectives there. In July 2010, for example, Germany banned the Humanitarian Relief Foundation, or IHH, due to its close ties with Hamas.[72] The IHH was noteworthy as the organization behind the controversial Gaza Flotilla of May 2010, and is accused of transmitting 6.6 million Euros from Germany to Hamas in the Gaza Strip.[73] The Palestinian Return Center (PRC), the Palestinian Community Germany (Palästinensische Gemeinschaft in Deutschland e.V.) and their allies held a conference with 3,000 participants in Berlin in April 2015.[74] After the United States government recognized Jerusalem as Israel's capital in December, 2017, thousands of German Muslims burned Israeli flags in Berlin.[75]

The Islamic State (ISIS)

The Islamic State (ISIS) is by far the most dangerous Islamist threat to Germany and Europe today. Due to its recent loss of territory and influence in Syria and Iraq, ISIS has changed its tactics, and has begun prioritizing soft targets in Europe.[76] The attacks in Paris, France in January and November 2015 as well as the 2016 bombing in Brussels, Belgium have shown the significant danger that jihadists affiliated with or inspired by ISIS pose in Europe.[77]

Germany has been a target of ISIS-related extremism. On February 26, 2016, a 16-year-old Islamist with connections to ISIS attacked a police officer in Hannover and almost killed him. She is now awaiting trial.[78] On July 18, 2016, a young ISIS follower from Afghanistan attacked five people in a local train near the Bavarian city of Würzburg, almost killing a Chinese tourist and injuring others as well.[79] Thereafter, on July 24, 2016, an ISIS-affiliated jihadist attempted to kill people at the Ansbach Open 2016 in Bavaria. Due to technical problems, his explosives detonated prematurely, killing the jihadist and injuring a dozen other people.[80] On December 19, 2016, a Tunisian jihadist affiliated with the Islamic State rammed a truck into a Berlin Christmas market, murdering 12 people and injuring over 50 people.[81]

According to the 2016 federal intelligence report, there is no firm estimate of the number of Islamic State operatives in Germany. However, the *Washington Post* reported in early 2018 that 300 Islamic State combatants returned to Germany. [82]

The head of Germany's Federal Office for the Protection of the Constitution (Bundesamt für Verfassungsschutz, or BFV), Hans-Georg Maaßen, has publicly said that Islamic terrorism is the "largest challenge" facing the federal republic.[83] In November 2016, security forces arrested a number of ISIS supporters, after several months of investigation. The supporters were accused of having recruited for ISIS in Germany, including one man and his family, who journeyed to Syria. Among the arrested is Ahmad Abdulaziz Abdullah, also known as Abu Walaa, the "preacher without face."[84] In December 2016, the worst jihadist attack in German history occurred when 23-year old Tunisian Anis Amri hijacked a truck, killed the driver and hours later he drove the truck into a Christmas market in the heart of West-Berlin at the Breitscheidplatz, killing eleven people. It turned out that the German security forces were very well informed about the criminal activities of Amri, who had been in jail in Italy for four years, and had used many identities as a "refugee" in Germany. Yet the German security forces and the police failed to prevent the massacre, despite their awareness of Amri's jihadist tendencies. After the attack on December 19, 2016, Amri went to the nearby big train station Zoologischer Garten (Zoo), was filmed by a video camera and displayed the Islamic State sign of victory, went to North-Rhine Westphalia, then via the Netherlands, Belgium and France to Italy. In the city of Sesto San Giovanni, near Milano, he was killed by police.[85]

In October 2017, Maaßen stated that over 950 jihadists had gone to Syria and Iraq to join the Islamic State. He said that, of the 950 jihadists, 20 percent were women and 5 percent were underage children. He warned: "We see the danger of children who socialized with and were indoctrinated by jihadists returning to Germany after the war zones. This could allow a new generation of jihadists to be raised here."[86] The federal intelligence agency said roughly 140 German jihadists have been killed in Syria and Iraq.[87]

The BfV is aware of the possible threat posed by the current refugee crisis in Europe, both to the EU at large and to Germany in particular.[88] However, the organization emphasizes that refugees come to Europe in search of shelter and safety, and prejudice and hatred toward them must be fought.[89] Germany's law enforcement agencies, however, remain on alert. Maaßen, has admitted that his office had in the past underestimated IS' strategy to bring jihadists to Europe and Germany.[90]

Islamism and Society

At 4.1 million, Germany's Muslim population is, alongside France's, the one of the highest in the European Union.[91] Of 4.1 million, the majority (2.56 million) is from Turkey, while roughly half a million (536,000) has roots in the former Yugoslavia. German Muslims also come from a variety of other places such as Iran, Afghanistan, Egypt, and Syria. With refugees from the Syrian crisis, Germany now houses closer to 5 million Muslims.

For decades, however, the former Federal Republic of Germany did not consider these immigrants to be true citizens, instead terming them Gastarbeiter, or guest workers. Over time, however, this fiction has become increasingly hard to sustain; Turkish workers, in particular, stayed in Germany, and their families followed them there. Racism was and remains a widespread phenomenon in Germany, due to the specific German national concept of citizenship, which until recently was defined along blood, rather than territorial, lines. Thus, being born in Germany did not necessarily mean that you were German in the popular conception. This began to change in 1999 with the passage of a new law granting the children of non-German residents citizenship by birth.[92]

Since the attacks of 9/11, and particularly over the past several years, political Islam has become a major topic of public debate in Germany. The wearing of the headscarf, honor killings, forced marriages, and support for terrorism and anti-Zionist activity are among the main topics of discussion surrounding both Islam and Islamism. Yet many newspapers, researchers, and politicians, as well as the general public at large, remain reluctant to deal with these issues.

Those political groups or parties that express their opposition to political Islam often do so out of ideological and/or racist grounds, rather than as a result of careful analysis of specific elements of political Islam. Likewise, many groups opposed to Islam are also against other foreigners (as well as those considered to be not "German" enough).

Nevertheless, a tiny but growing number of public intellectuals, scholars, activists, authors, and journalists have emerged publicly as critics of Islamism in recent years. These individuals have faced resistance on the public policy front. Some institutions, like the Berlin Center for Research on Antisemitism (ZfA),[93] have equated any meaningful criticism of Islam with anti-Semitism, often framed as Islamophobia.[94] Many journalists and mainstream scholars even compare or equate Islamist preachers of hate with pro-Western scholars, writers or activists,[95] and reject any military response to Islamism or Islamic jihad.[96] Most instead portray Islam as harmless, and look uncritically upon figures like leading Sunni Islamist Yusuf al-Qaradawi.[97]

Considerable support for Islamism and even violent jihad is visible at the grassroots level in Germany, as evidenced through sporadic rallies in German cities in support of various radical causes. Populist, racist, anti-Semitic and extremist groups such as the Pegida movement ("Patriots Against the Islamization of the Occident") or the party Alternative for Germany (AfD), are gaining massive support among the German population, with shocking electoral results. Such factions received a major showing in contests for state parliaments in Baden-Württemberg (15.1%), Berlin (14.2%), or the Eastern states of Mecklenburg-Vorpommern (20.8%) and Sachsen-Anhalt (24.3%) in 2016 alone.[98] They agitate against all Muslims and refugees and make no distinction between Islamists, Muslims, or even refugees. The relationship between German society as a whole, and Muslims, is in many ways at a historic low.

Germany has accepted over 1 million refugees since 2015, the overwhelming majority of whom come from Muslim-majority countries. Tensions arose in response to the migration of refugees and asylum seekers. In 2017, the anti-immigration, far-right party alternative for Germany entered the bundestag as the largest opposition party. Alternative for Germany secured 12.6% of the vote, nearly 6 million votes.[99] Germany's interior minister said in 2018 that migration was the "mother of all political problems."[100] His remarks came after two asylum seekers from Syria and Iraq were arrested for allegedly stabbing a man to death in the city of Chemnitz. In response, neo-Nazis and far-right protestors organized a march against migrants in the city.[101]

Islamism and the State

Some Islamist groups, such as the Muslim Brotherhood, have been present in Germany for years without engaging any real struggle for power with the government.[102] Others, however, have fared less well in Germany. Hizb ut-Tahrir, for example, was formally banned on January 10, 2003, a decision that was affirmed at the federal level in January 2006.[103] Hezbollah's dedicated television channel, al-Manar, was proscribed in hotels and coffee shops in Germany on October 29, 2008.[104] (However, private households in Germany can still watch it via Saudi and Egyptian satellites). In August 2010, the al-Quds mosque in Hamburg—a Salafi religious center known to be a significant source of Islamist indoctrination[105] —was belatedly shuttered.[106]

The German government, for its part, has also attempted to participate in—and to influence—the dialogue over Islam taking place inside the country. In 2006, it established an official "Islam

Conference," which continues to convene several times a year. At this venue, leading Muslim congregations, along with independent activists, authors, and scholars, discuss the relationship of Muslims and German society with German politicians, headed by the Federal Minister of the Interior. This approach has garnered disapproval from critics, who say that the conference itself has been co-opted by its inclusion of Islamists and suspicious groups. These include the German Islam Council (Islamrat für die Bundesrepublik Deutschland e. V., or IRD), which was excluded from the Islam Conference in 2010 due to criminal investigations against some of its members over their ties to Islamism.[107] In September 2016, the tenth anniversary of the Islam-Conference was held, but the institution remains highly controversial. "The State is not integrating Islam, but promotes Islamists," critics of the venture have opined.[108]This fragmented approach has led leading critics to contend that Germany, despite its role in international counterterrorism efforts (including Coalition operations in Afghanistan), still lacks a real anti-terror strategy.[109]

However, national security forces, with cooperation from foreign secret services, have prevented several terrorist attacks. Finally, sometimes the jihadists have simply had bad luck or have been stopped by Syrian refugees, such as in the case of an ISIS affiliated jihadist who, after a protracted chase from Saxony to Leipzig, was apprehended by authorities as a result of a tip from a Syrian refugee. Police found 1.5 kilograms of explosives in the suspect's apartment—leading to the conclusion that they had averted the worst jihadist attack in Germany's history.[110] However, the national security apparatus has had its failures. In October 2016, Syrian refugees reported a Syrian jihadists to the local police, as he was gathering heavy explosives for a suicide attack. The German police and the officials at the Leipzig jail failed to prevent the jihadist from killing himself. The German public was shocked about the failure of the German security system.[111]

The major split within Chancellor Merkel's ruling coalition centers over the question of whether Islam is integral to contemporary Germany. The German interior minister Horst Seehoffer, from Christian social union, has said "Islam does not belong to Germany." Chancellor Merkel has vehemently rejected Seehofer's positon, arguing that "these Muslims belong to Germany and in the same way their religion belongs to Germany, that is to say Islam."[112]

Endnotes

1. *The 9/11 Commission Report: Final Report of the National Commission on Terrorist Attacks Upon the United States* (New York: WW Norton & Co., 2004).
2. Wolfgang G. Schwanitz, "Germany's Middle East Policy," *Middle East Review of International Affairs*, Vol. 11, No. 3 (September 2007) http://www.rubincenter.org/meria/2007/09/4.pdf.
3. David Vielhaber, "The Milli Görüs in Germany," *Current Trends in Islamist Ideology,* Vol 13., https://www.hudson.org/content/researchattachments/attachment/1268/vielhaber.pdf.
4. Vielhaber, "The Milli Görüs in Germany."
5. "Antisemitische Hetzvideos bei der Islamischen Gemeinschaft Milli Görüs [Antisemitic hate videos of the Islamic Community Milli Görüs]," hamburg.de, July 13, 2006, http://www.hamburg.de/archiv/232516/hetz-videos-igmg-artikel.html.
6. "Antisemitische Hetzvideos bei der Islamischen."
7. ARD, "Report München," February 8, 2010, http://www.youtube.com/watch?v=-Ka6mV0-99M.
8. "Investigations into Muslim organization Milli Gorus dropped," *Deustche Welles,* September 9, 2010, http://www.dw.com/en/investigations-into-muslim-organization-milli-gorus-dropped/a-6027213.
9. Denis Fengler and Christian Unger, "Milli Görüs ab jetzt unbeobachtet," *Welt,* March 16, 2014, https://www.welt.de/print/welt_kompakt/hamburg/article126997443/Milli-Goerues-ab-jetzt-unbeobachtet.html.
10. German Federal Office for the Protection of the Constitution. Intelligence Report for 2017. Published on July 24, 2018.

https://www.verfassungsschutz.de/de/oeffentlichkeitsarbeit/publikationen/verfassungsschutzberichte/vs-bericht-2017

11. Ralph Ghadban, lecture, Aalen, Germany, May 5, 2010.
12. Ralph Ghadban, lecture, Aalen, Germany, May 5, 2010.
13. Author's correspondence with German Islamism expert Claudia Dantschke, Berlin, Germany, April 2011.
14. Claudia Dantschke, *Muslime – Ihre Einrichtungen und Vereine im Berliner Bezirk Neukölln. Überblick über die Strukturen und ihre religiösen sowie politischen Ausrichtungen. Eine Handreichung für die Jugendarbeit* [Muslims - mechanisms and associations in the Berlin district of Neukölln. Overview of the structures and their religious as well as political adjustments] (Berlin: Zentrum Demokratische Kultur, 2009), 42-44.
15. *TV Program Exakt*, June 26, 2013, http://web.archive.org/web/20140206031558/http://www.mdr.de/exakt/guelen_bewegung100.html.
16. *TV Program Exakt*.
17. "Der Kampf ist in Deutschland angekommen,“ *Stuttgarter Nachrichten*, July 20, 2016, http://www.stuttgarter-nachrichten.de/inhalt.angriffe-auf-guelen-bewegung-der-kampf-ist-in-deutschland-angekommen.1f291dbf-9e09-43e4-ab28-f135cc1af219.html; "In Deutschland häufen sich Angriffe auf Gülen-Anhänger,“ *Sueddeutsche Zeitung*, July 22, 2016, http://www.sueddeutsche.de/politik/deutschland-hetzen-drohen-denunzieren-1.3088817.
18. 18 Germany cuts funding to largest Turkish Islamic Organization. Deutsche Welle. August 30, 2018 https://www.dw.com/en/germany-cuts-funding-to-largest-turkish-islamic-organization-ditib/a-45297763?maca=en-rss-en-eu-2092-rdf
19. "German Federal Intelligence report for 2017," Verfassungsschutz, July, 24, 2018, Page 286 https://www.verfassungsschutz.de/de/oeffentlichkeitsarbeit/publikationen/verfassungsschutzberichte.
20. "German Federal Intelligence report for 2017," Verfassungsschutz, July, 24, 2018, Page 286 https://www.verfassungsschutz.de/de/oeffentlichkeitsarbeit/publikationen/verfassungsschutzberichte.
21. "German Federal Intelligence report for 2017," Verfassungsschutz, July, 24, 2018, Page 173,

https://www.verfassungsschutz.de/de/oeffentlichkeitsarbeit/publikationen/verfassungsschutzberichte

22. Federal Ministry of the Interior, *Verfassungsschutzbericht 2009 [Annual Report on the Protection of the Constitution 2015]*.
23. Federal Ministry of the Interior, *Verfassungsschutzbericht 2009*.
24. Federal Ministry of the Interior, *Verfassungsschutzbericht 2009*; For possible ties of WAMY to al-Qaeda, see "Al Qaeda linked World Assembly of Muslim Youth (WAMY) Jihad through Da'wa group working with Novib/Oxfam on Somali 'educational' initiatives," *Militant Islam Monitor*, October 16, 2006, http://www.militantislammonitor.org/article/id/2473.
25. Federal Ministry of the Interior, *Verfassungsschutzbericht 2009 [Annual Report on the Protection of the Constitution 2009]*.
26. UAE Cabinet approves list of designated terrorist organisations, groups, November 15, 2014, http://www.wam.ae/en/news/emirates-international/1395272478814.html (page removed).
27. "German Federal Intelligence report for 2017," Verfassungsschutz, July, 24, 2018, Page 210, https://www.verfassungsschutz.de/de/oeffentlichkeitsarbeit/publikationen/verfassungsschutzberichte; "Number of Salafists reaches record high," Deutsche Welle December 12, 2017, https://www.dw.com/en/number-of-salafists-in-germany-reaches-record-high/a-41733878.
28. Federal Ministry of the Interior, *Verfassungsschutzbericht 2011*, 251.
29. "Immer mehr Salafisten in Hamburg erfasst," ndr.de, August 27, 2016, https://www.ndr.de/nachrichten/hamburg/Immer-mehr-Salafisten-in-Hamburg-erfasst,salafismus154.html
30. "Immer mehr Salafisten in Hamburg erfasst," ndr.de; "Islamisten-Szene: Polizei startet Großrazzia gegen Salafisten," *Der Spiegel* (Munich), March 13, 2013, http://www.spiegel.de/politik/deutschland/islamisten-szene-polizei-startet-grossrazzia-gegen-salafisten-vereine-a-888548.html.

31. Federal Ministry of the Interior, *Verfassungsschutzbericht 2015.*
32. German Federal Intelligence report for 2017. Verfassungsschutz. Published on July, 24, 2018. Page 170. https://www.verfassungsschutz.de/de/oeffentlichkeitsarbeit/publikationen/verfassungsschutzberichte
33. http://www.faz.net/aktuell/politik/inland/bfv-warnt-vor-steigender-zahl-gewaltbereiter-salafisten-15090363.html
34. Federal Ministry of the Interior, *Verfassungsschutzbericht, 2011*, 226.
35. Federal Ministry of the Interior, *Verfassungsschutzbericht,* 255.
36. "Lebenslänglich für Frankfurter Flughafenattentäter,“ *Focus Online*, February 10, 2012, http://www.focus.de/politik/deutschland/islamistischer-anschlag-lebenslang-fuer-frankfurter-flughafenattentaeter-_aid_712754.html.
37. "Salafisten: Razzia und Vereinsverbot," n.d. http://www.bmi.bund.de/SharedDocs/Pressemitteilungen/DE/2012/06/vereinsverbot.html (page removed)
38. Reiner Burger, "Anschlag auf „Pro-NRW“-Chef verhindert [Attack on „Pro NRW“ Chief],“ *Franfurter Allemeine Zeitung*, March 13, 2013, http://www.faz.net/aktuell/politik/inland/schlag-gegen-salafisten-anschlag-auf-pro-nrw-chef-verhindert-12112847.html.
39. "Dschihad im Kinderzimmer," *Die Zeit*, June 2, 2016, http://www.zeit.de/2016/22/islamismus-salafismus-islamischer-staat-jugendliche-schutz/komplettansicht
40. "Islamismus im Internet. Propaganda – Verstöße – Gegenstrategien," December 2015, http://www.hass-im-netz.info/fileadmin/dateien/pk2015/Islamismus_im_Internet.pdf
41. "Warum Koran Verschenkaktion ‚Lies!‘ gefährlich ist," Stuttgarter Nachrichten, March 5, 2015, http://www.stuttgarter-nachrichten.de/inhalt.verfassungsschutz-warum-koran-verschenkaktion-lies-gefaehrlich-ist.69fe7409-cb59-459f-985b-c55c337a6cd3.html; "Das Missionierungsnetzwerk des Ibrahim Abou-Nagie,“ November 15, 2016, https://www.welt.de/politik/deutschland/article159513618/Das-Missionierungs-

netzwerk-des-Ibrahim-Abou-Nagie.html.

42. "Hamburg geht überfälligen Schritt: Radikale Muslime dürfen Koran nicht mehr öffentlich verteilen," *Huffington Post*, September 12, 2016, http://www.huffingtonpost.de/2016/09/12/hamburg-salafisten-lies-mich_n_11970330.html.
43. "Vereinigung 'Die wahre Religion (DWR)' alias 'Stiftung LIES' verboten und aufgelöst", https://www.bmi.bund.de/SharedDocs/Kurzmeldungen/DE/2016/11/vereinsverbot-dwr.html.
44. On the official homepage of that Islamic Center, http://izhamburg.de/index.aspx?pid=99&ArticleID=47009.
45. On the official homepage of that Islamic Center.
46. On the official homepage of that Islamic Center.
47. "German FM Hosts Iranian Official Calling for Israel's Destruction," *Jerusalem Post,* May 26, 2017, http://www.jpost.com/Diaspora/German-FM-hosts-Iranian-official-calling-for-Israels-destruction-494013.
48. Frank Jansen, "Iran will mit allen Mitteln die Atombombe," Tagesspiegel, July 4, 2016, http://www.tagesspiegel.de/politik/verfassungsschutz-iran-will-mit-allen-mitteln-die-atombombe/13829050.html.

49. Benjamin Weinthal, "Iran tried 32 times in 2016 to buy nuclear and missile technology," *The Jerusalem Post*, October 10, 2017, https://www.jpost.com/Middle-East/Iran-News/Tehran-tried-32-times-in-2016-to-buy-nuclear-and-missile-technology-507146
50. Benjamin Weinthal, "Iran still on the hunt for nuclear weapons technology across Germany," The Weekly Standard, .July, 7, 2017, https://www.weeklystandard.com/benjamin-weinthal/iran-still-on-the-hunt-for-nuclear-weapons-technology-across-germany.
51. Benjamin Weinthal, "German officials working to build nuclear armed missiles," *The Jerusalem Post* , October, 18, 2017, https://www.jpost.com/International/German-officials-Iran-working-to-build-nuclear-armed-missiles-507772?utm_source=dlvr.it&utm_medium=twitter
52. Benjamin Weinthal, "German Intel: Iran Wants to Ex-

pand Weapons into Nuclear Arsenal," *The Jerusalem Post.* July, 2, 2018, https://www.jpost.com/Middle-East/German-intel-Iran-wants-to-expand-weapons-into-nuclear-arsenal-561382.

53. Benjamin Weinthal, Intel Report: Iran Seeks Weapons of Mass Destruction Technology In Germany," *The Jerusalem Post*, June 2, 2018. https://www.jpost.com/Diaspora/Intel-report-Iran-seeks-weapons-of-mass-destruction-technology-in-Germany-558983.
54. Benjamin Weinthal, "German foreign minister in hot water over effort to bypass Iran sanctions," *The Jerusalem Post*, August, 25, 2018, https://www.jpost.com/International/German-foreign-minister-in-hot-water-over-effort-to-bypass-Iran-sanctions-565765
55. „Wirbel um Broschüre zu Iran-Reise: Auch Frauen aus Sachsen mit Kopftuch," no date available, http://www.lvz.de/Mitteldeutschland/News/Wirbel-um-Broschuere-zu-Iran-Reise-Auch-Frauen-aus-Sachsen-mit-Kopftuch
56. "Protest nach Kopftuchaffäre," June 9, 2016, http://www.bild.de/regional/dresden/kopftuch/protest-sturm-nach-kopftuch-affaere-46201142.bild.html.
57. Mark Dubowitz and Alexander Ritzmann, "Hezbollah's German Helpers," *Wall Street Journal*, April 16, 2007, http://www.defenddemocracy.org/index.php?option=com_content&task=view&id=11779494&Itemid=0.
58. Matthew Levitt, "Hezbollah," *The World Almanac of Islamism,* January 27, 2017, http://almanac.afpc.org/Hezbollah.
59. "Verfassungsschutzbericht des Landes Nordrhein-Westfalen," Ministerium des Innern des Landes Nordrhein-Westfalen, 2017, https://www.im.nrw/sites/default/files/media/document/file/vorab_vs_bericht_2017.pdf
60. Benjamin Weinthal, "Hezbollah terrorists entered Germany disguised as refugees," *The Jerusalem Post*, October, 12, 2017, https://www.jpost.com/International/Hezbollah-terrorists-entered-Germany-as-refugees-507282
61. Anti-Defamation League, "Hezbollah's International

Reach," Anti-Defamation League, December 7, 2004, http://www.adl.org/terror/hezbollah_print.asp.

62. Michal Shmulovich, "Hezbollah Drone Reportedly Manufactured on Germany," *Times of Israel*, October 17, 2012, http://www.timesofisrael.com/hezbollahs-drone-reportedly-manufactured-in-germany-and-sold-to-iran-lebanese-paper-reports/.
63. "Europäische Union setzt Hisbollah auf Terrorliste," Die Welt, July 22, 2013, https://www.welt.de/politik/ausland/article118262871/Europaeische-Union-setzt-Hisbollah-auf-Terrorliste.html.
64. http://www.tagesspiegel.de/politik/libanesische-islamisten-miliz-hisbollah-spenden-sammeln-fuer-den-terror-keinen-hats-gestoert/14555884.html.
65. Lahav Harkov, "Israeli, German Lawmakers Call to Ban Hezbollah," *Jerusalem Post,* August 7, 2017, http://www.jpost.com/Israel-News/Politics-And-Diplomacy/Israeli-German-lawmakers-call-for-Hezbollah-to-be-banned-from-Germany-501782
66. Benjamin Weinthal, "Germany to Permit Palestinian Terror Group to Run for Parliament," *Jerusalem Post,* August 31, 2017, http://www.jpost.com/Arab-Israeli-Conflict/Germany-to-permit-Palestinian-terrorist-group-to-field-Bundestag-candidates-503836
67. http://www.pnn.de/meinung/269304/
68. The Jerusalem Post. Exclusive: German Islamic center raises money for Hezbollah. June, 22, 2018. https://www.jpost.com/Diaspora/Exclusive-German-Islamic-center-raises-money-for-Hezbollah-560604
69. "Verfassungsschutzbericht des Landes Nordrhein-Westfalen," Ministerium des Innern des Landes Nordrhein-Westfalen, 2017, page 12, https://www.im.nrw/sites/default/files/media/document/file/vorab_vs_bericht_2017.pdf
70. "German Federal Intelligence report for 2017," Verfassungsschutz, July, 24, 2018, Page 173, , https://www.verfassungsschutz.de/de/oeffentlichkeitsarbeit/publikationen/verfassungsschutzberichte.
71. Federal Ministry of the Interior, *Verfassungsschutzbericht 2009 [Annual Report on the Protection of the Constitution 2009].*

72. Benjamin Weinthal, "Germany Bans IHH for Hamas Links," *Jerusalem Post*, July 12, 2010, http://www.jpost.com/SpecialSection/Article.aspx?ID=181187.
73. "Milli Görüs und die Hamas. 'Einfluss auf 60.000 Muslime' [Milli Görüs and Hamas. 'Influence on some 60.000 Muslims']," *Tageszeitung* (Berlin), July 14, 2010, http://www.taz.de/1/politik/deutschland/artikel/1/direkter-einfluss-auf-60-000-muslime/.
74. Flaggen, Leid und Heimatliebe, taz (tageszeitung), April 26, 2015, http://www.taz.de/!5010871/, Islamisten mit Nahostkarte ohne Israel, Der Tagesspiegel, April 20, 2015, http://www.tagesspiegel.de/politik/palaestinenserkonferenz-in-berlin-islamisten-mit-nahostkarte-ohne-israel/11663508.html.
75. "Anti-Semitism has no place in Germany, minister says after Israeli flags burned," Reuters, December, 10, 2017, https://www.reuters.com/article/us-usa-trump-israel-germany/anti-semitism-has-no-place-in-germany-minister-says-after-israeli-flags-burned-idUSKBN1E40ST
76. "Strategy Shift for ISIS: Inflicting Terror in Distant Lands", New York Times, November 15, 2015, http://www.nytimes.com/2015/11/15/world/europe/strategy-shift-for-isis-inflicting-terror-in-distant-lands.html.
77. Federal Ministry of the Interior, *Verfassungsschutzbericht 2015 [Annual Report on the Protection of the Constitution 2015]*.
78. 16-jährige IS-Sympathisantin angeklagt, August 29, 2016, n-tv, http://www.n-tv.de/politik/16-jaehrige-IS-Sympathisantin-angeklagt-article18519826.html.
79. Report about the Chinese victims, „Der Weg zurück ins Leben nach dem Axt-Attentat von Würzburg," November 16, 2016, http://www.augsburger-allgemeine.de/bayern/Der-Weg-zurueck-ins-Leben-nach-dem-Axt-Attentat-von-Wuerzburg-id39736352.html.
80. "12 Verletzte bei Bombenanschlag," July 25, 2016, die tageszeitung (taz), https://taz.de/Attentat-in-Ansbach/!5327637/
81. "German Federal Intelligence report for 2017," Verfassungsschutz, July, 24, 2018, Page 173,

https://www.verfassungsschutz.de/de/oeffentlichkeitsarbeit/publikationen/verfassungsschutzberichte.

82. Tim Meko, "Now that the Islamic State has fallen in Iraq and Syria, where are all its fighters going?" *The Washington Post*, February 22, 2018, https://www.washingtonpost.com/graphics/2018/world/isis-returning-fighters/?noredirect=on&utm_term=.a97f9a5146b9.
83. "Extremistische Verhaltensweisen nehmen zu," Tagesspiegel, July 4, 2017, https://www.tagesspiegel.de/politik/verfassungsschutz-bericht-extremistische-verhaltensweisen-nehmen-zu/20018900.html
84. "Anführer des IS in Deutschland offenbar gefasst", http://www.stern.de/panorama/gesellschaft/razzia--anfuehrer-des-is-in-deutschland-offenbar-gefasst-7138978.html.
85. "Flucht von Anis Amri 77 Stunden quer durch Europa," January 5, 2017, http://www.spiegel.de/politik/ausland/anis-amri-stationen-seiner-flucht-durch-europa-a-1128683.html; „Fall Anis Amri Verpasste Chancen," January 3, 2017, https://www.tagesschau.de/inland/fall-amri-verpasste-chancen-101.html.
86. "Germany says worried about new generation of Islamic State recruits," *Reuters,* October 19, 2017, https://uk.reuters.com/article/uk-germany-security/germany-says-worried-about-new-generation-of-islamic-state-recruits-idUKKBN1CO2Q6.
87. "German Federal Intelligence report for 2017," Verfassungsschutz, July, 24, 2018, Page 171, https://www.verfassungsschutz.de/de/oeffentlichkeitsarbeit/publikationen/verfassungsschutzberichte.https://www.verfassungsschutz.de/de/oeffentlichkeitsarbeit/publikationen/verfassungsschutzberichte/vs-bericht-2016
88. Statement by the German Government, May 10, 2016, http://dip21.bundestag.de/dip21/btd/18/083/1808382.pdf.
89. Statement by the German Government, May 10, 2016.
90. "Verfassungsschutz: IS falsch eingeschätzt," April 10, 2016,

http://www.tagesschau.de/inland/verfassungsschutz-is-101.html

91. Pew Research Center, *Muslim Networks and Movements in Western Europe*, September 15, 2010, http://features.pewforum.org/muslim/number-of-muslims-in-western-europe.html. France is a possible exception in this regard. However, French laws outlawing formal surveys of citizens by confession make an authoritative determination currently impossible.
92. "Staatsbürgerschaftsrecht. Reform verabschiedet [New law on citizenship passed]," *Der Spiegel* (Hamburg), May 7, 1999, http://www.spiegel.de/politik/deutschland/a-21229.html.
93. Conference of the Center for Research on Antisemitism, Technical University Berlin, Berlin, Germany, December 8, 2008, http://zfa.kgw.tu-berlin.de/feindbild_muslim_feindbild_islam.pdf.
94. The Berlin Center for Research on Antisemitism (ZfA) equated the situation of Jews in the late 19th century with the situation of Muslims today in Germany at a conference dedicated to that topic on December 8, 2008 (see footnote above). See Clemens Heni, "Antisemitism is not the same as Islamophobia," *Jerusalem Post*, December 3, 2008, http://www.jpost.com/Opinion/Op-Ed-Contributors/Article.aspx?id=122938.
95. A leading voice in equating critics of Islamism with Islamists is historian Wolfgang Benz (head of the above mentioned Berlin Center for Research on Antisemitism (ZfA) from 1990-2011). See his article "Hetzer mit Parallelen. Antisemiten des 19. Jahrhunderts und manche "Islamkritiker" des 21. Jahrhunderts arbeiten mit ähnlichen Mitteln an ihrem Feindbild. [Agitators with Parallels. Anti-Semitism in the 19th Century and some „critics of Islam" in the 21st century use similar tools in portraying their concepts of enemies]," *Süddeutsche Zeitung* (Munich), January 4, 2010, http://www.sueddeutsche.de/politik/antisemiten-und-islamfeinde-hetzer-mit-parallelen-1.59486. For more on Benz and the failure of German (and Western) academia to analyze and confront Islamism, see Clemens Heni, *Antisemitism: A Specific Phenomenon. Holocaust Trivialization*

– *Islamism – Post-colonial and Cosmopolitan anti-Zionism* (Berlin: Edition Critic 2013).

96. See the German role in the debate about Islam and the West, in David Blankenhorn et al., *The Islam/West Debate: Documents from a Global Debate on Terrorism, U.S. Policy, and the Middle East* (Lanham, MD: Rowman & Littlefield Publishers, 2005).
97. Qaradawi has been portrayed as "moderate" in the German political discourse, because he rejects suicide bombing if it is not aimed at Jews and Israel. Heni, *Antisemitism*. For an overview of German Islamic Studies after 9/11 see Clemens Heni, *Schadenfreude. Islamforschung und Antisemitismus in Deutschland nach 9/11* [Schadenfreude. Islamic Studies and antisemitism in Germany after 9/11] (published by The Berlin International Center for the Study of Antisemitism (BICSA), Berlin: Edition Critic 2011).
98. "Wo die AfD am stärksten ist – und wo am schwächsten," *Stern*, September 5, 2016, http://www.stern.de/politik/deutschland/afd-wahlerfolge--wo-die-rechtspopulisten-am-staerksten-sind---und-wo-am-schwaechsten-7043578.html; Clemens Heni, "Why Jihad and neo-Nazis embrace Brexit and "Bullshit 9.0," *Times of Israel*, June 30, 2016, http://blogs.timesofisrael.com/why-jihad-and-neo-nazis-embrace-brexit-and-bullshit-9-0/, Clemens Heni, "Germany's Hot New Party Thinks America Is 'Run by Zionists,'" *Tablet* Magazine, August 1, 2016, http://www.tabletmag.com/jewish-news-and-politics/209243/germanys-hot-new-party.
99. The New York Times. Alternative for Germany: Who are they, and what do they want?

September, 25, 2017. By Melissa Eddy.

https://www.nytimes.com/2017/09/25/world/europe/germany-election-afd.html

100. Nicole Goebel, " Migration 'mother of all political problems,' says German Interior Minister Horst Seehofer," Deutsche Welle," September, 6, 2018, https://www.dw.com/en/migration-mother-of-all-political-problems-says-german-interior-minister-horst-seehofer/a-45378092

101. Adam Pemble and Kirsten Grieshaber, "German police end march envisioned as far-right springboard," *The Washington Post,* September 1, 2018, https://www.washingtonpost.com/world/europe/far-right-to-merge-their-street-protests-in-german-city/2018/09/01/39373f0e-ade1-11e8-9a7d-cd30504ff902_story.html?utm_term=.728aaae19d34.

102. See also Ian Johnson, *A Mosque in Munich: Nazis, the CIA, and the Rise of the Muslim Brotherhood in the West* (Boston and New York: Houghton Mifflin Harcourt, 2010); see also the monograph of Stefan Meining, Eine Moschee in Deutschland. Nazis, Geheimdienste und der Aufstieg des politischen Islam im Westen, Munich: C.H. Beck 2011 [Nazis, Secret Sevices, and the rise of political Islam in the West].

103. See *Decision by German Federal Administrative Court*, January 25, 2006, http://lexetius.com/2006,604?version=drucken.

104. John Rosenthal, "Germany Does Not Ban Hezbollah TV," *Pajamas Media*, November 26, 2008, http://pajamasmedia.com/blog/germany-does-not-ban-hezbollah-tv/?singlepage=true.

105. "Salafistisches Islamseminar in der Taiba – Moschee (ehemals Al-Quds-Moschee), April 9-11,2010 [Salafist Islam seminar in Taliba mosque (former al-Quds-mosque) in Hamburg, April 9-11, 2010]," hamburg.de, April 28, 2010, http://www.hamburg.de/schlagzeilen/2231544/salafismusseminar-fhh-hamburg.html.

106. "Die 9/11-Moschee ist dicht [9/11 mosque in Hamburg has been shut down]," *Tageszeitung* (Berlin), August 9, 2010, http://www.taz.de/1/leben/alltag/artikel/1/beruehmte-moschee-ist-dicht/.

107. Statement by the Organizers of the German Islam Conference, May 15, 2010, http://www.deutsche-islam-konferenz.de/cln_117/nn_1319098/SubSites/DIK/DE/DieDIK/NeueTeilnehmer/neue-teilnehmer-node.html?__nnn=true.

108. vgl.: http://www.deutschlandfunk.de/zehn-jahre-islamkonferenz-die-bundesregierung-hofiert-die.720.de.html?dram:article_id=367026 (eingesehen: 28.09.2016)

109. Guido Steinberg, *Im Visier von al-Qaida: Deutschland braucht eine Anti-Terror-Strategie* [In the Sights of Al-Qaeda: Germany Needs an Anti-Terror Strategy] (Hamburg: edition Körber Stiftung, n.d.), http://www.koerber-stiftung.de/fileadmin/user_upload/edition/pdf/leseproben/978-3-89684-139-1_001-012_01.pdf.
110. „Syrer feiern Festnahme des Terrorverdächtigen", SpiegelOnline, October 11, 2016, http://www.spiegel.de/politik/deutschland/chemnitz-wie-syrer-bei-der-festnahme-des-terrorverdaechtigen-halfen-a-1116031.html
111. "Syrer bringt die Polizei zum festgesetzten Terrorverdächtigen", https://www.welt.de/politik/deutschland/article158660909/Syrer-bringt-die-Polizei-zum-festgesetzten-Terrorverdaechtigen.html; https://www.welt.de/politik/deutschland/article158724916/Dschaber-al-Bakr-hat-Selbstmord-begangen.html.
112. "Islam does not belong to Germany,' says country new interior minister," *The Independent,* March 16, 2018, https://www.independent.co.uk/news/world/europe/islam-germany-not-belong-muslims-interior-minister-horst-seehofer-angela-merkel-afd-a8259451.html.

44 Italy

> ## Quick Facts
>
> Population: 62,137,802 (July 2017 est.)
> Area: 301,340 sq km
> Ethnic Groups: Italian (includes small clusters of German-, French-, and Slovene-Italians in the north and Albanian-Italians and Greek-Italians in the south)
> Government Type: Parliamentary republic
> GDP (official exchange rate): $1.921 trillion (2017 est.)
>
> *Source: CIA World FactBook (Last Updated April 2018)*

Introduction

While Italy has experienced a surge in Muslim immigration over the past three years as a result of the Syrian civil war and a parallel wave of African migration, Islam in both its moderate and radical forms was already a significant presence in the country. The Union of Islamic Communities and Organizations of Italy (UCOII) has been at the forefront of the debate for the representation of the highly fragmented Italian Muslim community. With regard to jihadist activities, Italy remained primarily a logistical base until 2009, when an attempted bombing by a Libyan radical in Milan shattered popular illusions that the country was safe from extremist attacks. The event sparked significant public debate and the Italian government has begun to strengthen anti-terrorism and surveillance laws in an effort to respond more effectively to Islamism as a political and social force.

Islamist Activity

Italy's Muslim community is extremely diverse and fragmented.[1] The overwhelming majority of the country's Muslim residents are Sunni. They are predominantly first-generation immigrants, hailing from various countries. This diversity, combined with Sunni Islam's intrinsic lack of clerical hierarchy, has resulted in a low level of organization throughout the whole of the Italian Muslim community.

Consequently, the community has chronically lacked cohesive leadership. More than twenty years after the first significant wave of Muslim immigration, Italy's Muslim community has a wide variety of organizations, none of which represent more than a small fraction of the population. Relationships among these organizations are often marred by sharp disagreements and even personal rivalries, further eroding the possibility of cooperation.[2]

The one group that has repeatedly made a claim to the leadership of the country's Muslim community is the Union of the Islamic Communities and Organizations of Italy, or UCOII.[3] The union originated in the Union of Muslim Students in Italy (USMI), a small organization of Muslim students that was created in Perugia and other university cities in the early 1970s. Comprised mostly of Jordanian, Syrian, and Palestinian students, the USMI's ideology was closely related to the positions of the Muslim Brotherhood,[4] the well-known transnational Islamist movement founded in Egypt in the 1920s. By the late 1980s, when the first notable wave of North African immigrants appeared in Italy, a student organization such as the USMI could no longer satisfy the needs of the new, large Muslim population. In January 1990, representatives of USMI, six mosques from six Italian cities, and 32 individuals formed the UCOII.[5]

Since its founding, the UCOII has been active on the political scene, attempting to become the primary Muslim liaison of the Italian state. The UCOII has managed to achieve an important position within the Muslim community, thanks to the significant degree of control it exercises over Italian mosques. Its claim to control 85 percent of Italy's mosques is difficult to verify independently, but it is undeniable that the UCOII plays a predominant role in the life of Italy's practicing Muslim community and that many mosques are, to varying degrees, linked to it.[6]

While today the organization has no formal ties to the Muslim Brotherhood or any affiliated outfit in the Middle East, in many respects its worldview is still inspired by the group's ideology.[7] Like most other Brotherhood-inspired organizations throughout Europe, the UCOII aims at swaying the Muslim population of Italy to its interpretation of Islam through its far-ranging network of mosques. For many Muslim immigrants far from home, mosques provide social support and community engagement. The UCOII seeks to use its dominant position on mosques and Islamic associations[8] to spread its ideology and exercise what Italian expert on Islam Renzo Guolo defined as a "diffuse cultural hegemony" over the country's Muslim community.[9] Taking advantage of the community's considerable fragmentation, the UCOII has become the most visible, vocal, and well-run organization within Italy's Muslim community. UCOII, an active minority, has assumed control of representation of Italian Muslims, prevailing easily over an unorganized silent majority.[10]

Aside from the UCOII, other Islamist outfits operating in the country, albeit only marginally, are Hizb ut-Tahrir, the transnational pan-Islamist Sunni movement, and Tablighi Jamaat, the Islamic missionary movement that intelligence agencies worldwide suspect of having been infiltrated by radicals.[11] The Moroccan movement Justice and Charity also has a significant influence on several mosques in northern Italy.[12] Finally, at least two Shi'a organizations, Naples-based Ahl al-Bayt and its Rome-based spin-off, Imam Mahdi, attracted the attention of authorities because of their radical positions and because many of their members are Italian converts with a past association to militant right wing groups.[13] All of these groups and movements operate with various degrees of sophistication and success, competing among themselves and with non-Islamist organizations for influence in Islam in Italy.

Due to its activism and association with Italy's mosques, UCOII acts as the main representative for Italy's Muslims. However, the decentralized nature of Italy's Muslim community has led to recent rifts in representation of Islam to the Italian government. For example, in May 2016, the Italian Islamic Confederation, a Rome-based group of most Moroccan immigrants, moved forward in requesting formal recognition from the state as the main Muslim representative despite UCOIIs consistent—although unsuccessful requests. Another group, the Italian Islamic Religious Community (COREIS), based in Milan, has also made several unsuccessful requests for recognition but has also failed in both representing the Italian Muslim community as well as gaining state recognition for the religion in general.[14]

The battle that takes place for the control of Islamic places of worship and, more generally, for influence over Italian Muslims, is something that Italian authorities can only watch from afar. Authorities have recently realized this dissonance and in early 2016, Italian Interior Minister established a Council of Relations with Italian Muslims, in an advisory capacity, with the goal of helping the Muslim population integrate smoothly into Italian society. This Council is made up of Islamic religion and culture experts.[15]

As a result of the Council's work, in February 2017 community groups representing around 70 percent of Italy's Muslims signed the "National Pact for Italian Islam" with the Interior Minister. They committed to reject all forms of violence and pledged to hold Friday prayers in their mosques in Italian, or at least have them translated.[16]

With regard to jihadism, extremist networks have existed in Italy since the late 1980s, though seldom have they targeted the country. Various jihadist outfits have historically used Italy as a logistical base for acquiring false documents, obtaining weapons, and raising funds. This traditional use of Italian territory appeared to change on October 12, 2009, when Mohammad Game, a legal immigrant from Libya, detonated an explosive device hidden on his person at the gates of the Santa Barbara military base in Milan. The attack seriously injured him and lightly injured the soldier who tried to stop him.

The ensuing investigation revealed that Game had recently become radicalized. Acquaintances described how he had frequently stated that Italian troops should have left Afghanistan, framing his diatribes in increasingly religious terms. Game reportedly made similar remarks to the ambulance personnel that transported him to the hospital after the attack. Within a few days, authorities arrested two men, an Egyptian and a Libyan, who reportedly had helped Game in his plan. Forty kilograms of the same chemical substances used by Game in the attack were also retrieved from a basement to which the men had access.

Prior to October 12th, Game and his accomplices had begun to attend services at Milan's Islamic Cultural Institute (Viale Jenner mosque), a place that was at the center of terrorism investigations for almost 20 years. Yet the men did not appear to have acted under the direction of, or even in cooperation with, any established group. To the contrary, their characteristics, from their sudden radicalization to the lack of sophistication of their modus operandi, resemble that of the homegrown networks that have become common in most European countries but that had not yet then appeared in Italy.[17]

However, the growing number of immigrants and refugees arriving in Italy over the past few years has put some strain on multicultural co-existence. In general, Muslims in Italy assimilate more seamlessly then in other countries such as France, for example, which has historically lead to less radicalization and therefore less attacks. Nonetheless, with almost hundreds of thousands of migrants from predominantly Muslim countries such as Libya, and Egypt, and the expected influx of Syrian and Iraqi refugees as the EU works with Turkey to discourage arrivals into Greece, Italian citizens and politicians alike are growing concerned about the political, social, economic and security implications of the migrants. Additionally, recent attacks in France and other European countries have heightened the potential threat posed by radicalized individuals who had arrived in Italy by boat.[18]

Islamism and Society

Historically a source of immigrants to other countries, Italy only began to attract small numbers of new residents in the 1970s, with the majority coming from the Philippines and Latin America. The Muslim population consisted of diplomatic staff from Muslim countries, a few businessmen, and some students. Those numbers began to climb in the 1980s, when immigrants from North and Sub-Saharan Africa began to choose Italy as their first or final stop in their journeys to Europe.[19] Immigration has climbed since the mid-1990s, and, according to Italy's official census bureau (ISTAT), as of January 2017, there were 5,047,028 foreign citizens residing in Italy.[20] While no exact data on the number of Muslims living in Italy exists, most estimates put the number at between 1.6 and 2.6 million, corresponding to not more than 4 percent of the population.[21]

Various features characterize Italy's Muslim community, starting with its significant ethnic diversity. Morocco and Albania have historically provided the largest portion of Muslim immigrants to Italy, with 30.1 percent coming from Morocco and 16.2 percent from Albania.[22] The majority of the rest come from Bangladesh, Tunisia, Egypt, Pakistan, Senegal, Macedonia, Kosovo, Algeria, Bosnia-Herzegovina and Turkey. This ethnic diversity increased even further as a result of the 181,000 migrants who arrived in Italy by boat in 2016, with 21 percent coming from Nigeria, 12 percent from Eritrea, 7 percent from Guinea, Côte d'Ivoire, and The Gambia, 6 percent from Senegal, 5 percent from Mali and Sudan.[23]

Despite this ethnic heterogeneity, more than 95 percent of Italy's Muslims are Sunni.[24] Other distinctive characteristics of Italy's Muslim population when compared to other European Muslim communities are its higher number of non-citizens and illegal immigrants, higher percentage of males, and higher level of geographic dispersion.[25]

If there is one certainty about the future of Islam in Italy, it is that its presence will continue to grow. The influx of immigrants from North and Sub-Saharan Africa and the Middle East seems to be virtually unstoppable, given migration patterns and socio-economic conditions in the countries of departure. Italy received about 154,000 migrants in 2015, 181,000 in 2016 and is projected to receive around 125,000 refugees by the end of 2017,[26] with most coming from Africa.

Moreover, in the next few years, Italy will start to see second-generation Muslim immigrants, like most other European countries already have. Many of them will hold Italian citizenship and, furthermore, the number of Muslims carrying an Italian passport will also increase through marriages and through conversions.

It seems clear that Islam is destined to have a more visible and stable presence in the country and this is already evident in the substantial increase of Islamic cultural centers throughout Italy. According to Maria Bombardieri, the author of Mosques of Italy, Italy only has eight official mosques that are "intended as standalone structures… but there are about 800 cultural centers and musalla, which are informal prayer rooms, often housed in garages, basements, and warehouses." These cultural centers serve as proxies for mosques and provide Muslims in Italy with a place to worship as well as serve as a place to hold cultural and educational meetings.[27] In 2016, the Italian Ministry of the Interior officially identified 1,205

"Islamic structures": 4 mosques, 858 places of worship and 343 cultural associations.[28]

The UCOII's significant impact on the relationship between the Italian state and the Muslim community and the legal recognition of Islam both remain a font of political tension. Article 19 of the Italian Constitution grants all citizens the right to freely practice and proselytize for any religion (unless its rites are deemed to be against morality). All religions are free to organize themselves and, according to Article 8, their relationship with the state is regulated by law, based on agreements signed by the state with the representatives of each religious community. In order to be recognized and receive legal and financial benefits, all other religions (except Catholicism, which received these benefits by default) have to sign an agreement (known in Italian as intesa) with the government, which regulates mutual rights and obligations.

Over the last 25 years, various religious communities have done so. Islam, which is de facto the country's second largest religion, has not yet been recognized by the Italian state as a religion.[29] While the opposition of some political forces to the recognition of Islam has in some cases interfered with the process, the main reason for this seemingly paradoxical situation is to be found in the lack of a unified leadership in the Italian Muslim community. In order to sign the intesa, the Italian government needs to find a representative of the Muslim community, something the Italian Muslim community so far has been unable to produce. Intesa proposals submitted over the years by various groups that entertain cordial relationships with the Italian state have been turned down, as none of the applicants were deemed able to legitimately claim to represent the majority of Italian Muslims.[30]

Conversely, the Italian state has experienced the opposite problem with proposals of intesa submitted by the UCOII since 1990. The UCOII seems to be, prima facie, the Muslim organization with the largest following and with characteristics that make it the closest of all Italian Muslim organizations to the notion of representation that Italian authorities are looking for. Yet its intesa drafts have been turned down because authorities are skeptical of the UCOII's controversial nature and reputation (for example, the organization is often branded as anti-Semitic)[31] and also deemed the draft to be "too ambitious" in asking for state recognition of Islamic festivities, Islamic education in public schools, legal recognition of Muslim weddings celebrated as well as room for Muslims in Italian television.[32] Given these dynamics, Islam is not recognized as an official religion, a situation that creates practical difficulties and can generate the perception among many Italian Muslims that authorities discriminate against Islam.

Islamism and the State:

Even though small clusters of jihadist groups planned attacks against targets in Milan, Cremona, Bologna, Rome and other cities in the past, Italian authorities were clear in stating, as of early 2009, that the primary use of Italian soil for radical Islamists has been logistical in nature. There were no indications of networks planning attacks in Italy or from Italy against other countries. In 2009, Mohammad Game's terrorist attack in Milan changed that view. The episode came as a sort of shock to Italian authorities, who for the first time were forced to deal with a case of homegrown Islamist terrorism.

Since around 2013, authorities have seen a relative growth in homegrown networks in Italy. Growth in online activities by jihadist networks caused Italian authorities to crack down on any active members of such groups and punish them under Article 270 of the penal code, which criminalizes any facilitation of terrorist training and provides precedent for prosecuting cases where materials are exchanged online.[33]

Two notable cases of homegrown radicalization occurred in the province of Brescia, not far from Milan. The first case is that of Mohamed Jarmoune, a Moroccan-born man living in Niardo, who spent his time on the internet disseminating jihadist materials and networking with jihadist sympathizers. Italian authorities monitored Jarmoune for months and finally arrested him in March 2012, after he had narrowed in on Milan's largest synagogue as a potential target. His arrest resulted in a prison sentence of over five years, starting in May 2013, for disseminating terrorist propaganda.[34]

The other Brescia case concerns Anas El Abboubi, another active participant in jihadist networks online. Connecting with other jihadist sympathizers allowed El Abboubi to learn how to start an Italy-based extremist group, which he eventually tried to do with his blog called Sharia4Italy. El Abboubi was eventually arrested in June 2013, after Italian authorities noticed his militant online presence as well as his searches for apparent targets around the Brescia province. However, the court ruled that he had not violated Article 270 and released him.[35] A few months later, El Abboubi travelled to Syria, via Turkey, where he became a fighter of the Islamic State of Iraq and al-Sham (now the Islamic State).[36]

Unlike the majority of individuals who have been involved in radical activities in Italy before, both Jarmoune and El Abboubi grew up in Italy and were, by all standards, well integrated into Italian society. Both also ran a series of websites and Facebook pages where they shared jihadist propaganda and instructions to build explosives and use weapons. The profile of the accused and the dynamics of their networks are quintessentially homegrown, arguably signifying a shift in the jihadist threat to Italy.

Overall, today Italy has a jihadist scene that increasingly resembles that of other European countries in its homegrown characteristics but that is, for the time being, substantially smaller in size. For example, according to recent data from 2017 by the Italian Interior Ministry, 125 individuals with ties to Italy (but only a minority of them Italian citizens) have left the country to join various jihadist groups (mostly the so-called Islamic State) in Syria, Iraq and other Middle Eastern conflict zones. The number of 125 is extremely low when compared to recent estimates for other large European countries, such as France (around 1,700 foreign fighters), Germany (around 900), the UK (at least 850); and even compared to less populous countries such as Belgium (470), Austria (300) and Sweden (300).[37]

Nonetheless, various incidents that have taken place in 2016–2017 have increased the concerns of Italian counterterrorism officials because of Italian links to attacks abroad or because they indicate the growth of a homegrown scene. At least four cases are worthy of mention.[38] First, Anis Amri, the Tunisian failed asylum seeker responsible for the December 2016 Christmas market attack in Berlin, in the name of the so-called Islamic State (IS), reportedly started his radicalization process in Italian prisons. After the massacre, he returned in Italy, where he was killed in a shootout with police.

Second, Ismail Tommaso Hosni, a homeless Italian citizen born in 1996 to a Tunisian father and an Italian mother, stabbed a policeman and two soldiers with two kitchen knives after they asked to see his identity papers at Milan's central train station, on May 18, 2017. Italian authorities found that the young man was an Islamic State sympathizer and was placed under investigation for suspected terrorism. However, at this stage Italian authorities are still investigating whether a genuine terrorist motive drove Hosni.

Third, Youssef Zaghba, one of the three members of the cell that launched the London Bridge attack on June 3, 2017, was born in Morocco to an Italian mother and had dual citizenship. In March 2016, he had been stopped at Bologna airport while attempting to travel to Turkey and possibly Syria.

Lastly, Ahmed Hanachi, the Tunisian man who stabbed two women to death in Marseille on October 1, 2017, had lived in Aprilia, near Rome, for many years. His brother Anis, who had fought in Syria with IS in 2014–2016 and allegedly had indoctrinated Ahmed, was arrested in northern Italy six days later.

This evolution worries counterterrorism practitioners, who realize that in tackling the nascent homegrown threat they will not be able to extensively rely on administrative deportations, arguably one of the main legal tools used by Italian authorities in their fight against jihadism, especially since 2015.[39] But many policymakers and the public at large have, for the most part, not yet conceptualized the idea that jihadism is not just an external threat but, increasingly, an internal one.

This relative slowness in grasping the evolution of the phenomenon is not surprising. Unlike most other European countries, which, since 9/11, have engaged in a sustained debate about Islam and Islamism, Italy has followed a different trajectory. As disparate international (terrorist campaigns and conflicts in other countries) and domestic (the occasional arrest or deportation of jihadist militants) events appear on the radar, they generate a heated domestic debate that often becomes highly politicized and lacks nuance.

In response to these events, the Italian government has begun to strengthen legislation, particularly the Penal Code, in order to more effectively monitor potential militant or extremist activity. On February 18, 2015, Decree-Law No. 7 entered into effect, calling for stronger legislative and regulatory means for Italian police and armed forces to better anticipate and prevent extremist acts. This provision (subsequently converted into law, with some changes: Law No. 43 of April 17, 2015) strengthens the surveillance powers of police, and outlines new reforms for criminal punishments for those persons or groups identified as terrorists. The law also recognizes the criminality of foreign fighters, those individuals who support a terrorist organization and participate in conflicts abroad. Finally, the law gives the Ministry of the Interior the right to maintain a running list of websites and forums that may be used for recruitment for extremist activities.[40]

To be fair, Italian authorities have for the most part extensively and effectively monitored the violent aspects of Islamism in Italy since the early 1990s. Over the last 20 years, dozens of complex investigations have brought to light jihadist networks throughout the peninsula.[41] The combination of experienced security services and law enforcement agencies, proactive investigative magistrates, and adequate legal framework, such as the 2015 legislation mentioned above, have allowed Italian authorities to be among the most aggressive and successful in Europe in dismantling jihadist networks, uncovering extensive links spanning throughout Europe and the Middle East. While these successes have not always been followed by convictions and long sentences once the cases went to trial, it is fair to say that Italian authorities have been quite efficient in keeping in check violent Islamist networks.[42]

Things are quite different, however, when the focus shifts from traditional counterterrorism measures to a broader frame of analysis. While many European countries have been implementing plans to stem radicalization among their Muslim communities, Italy is severely lagging in approaching the issue. Only in the summer of 2017 did Italy's Lower House pass its first bill introducing measures for the prevention of jihadist radicalization and extremism. As of this writing, this important provision awaits final approval from the Upper House.

Moreover, the Italian debate over forms of non-violent Islamism has often shifted, with some notable exceptions, between schizophrenic overreaction, naïve whitewashing, and, most commonly, utter lack of interest. In most other Western European countries, excesses on both sides of the debate, from conflating Islamism with Islam to labeling as racist any question raised over aspects of Islamism, have slowly been replaced by more nuanced and balanced positions. Italy's public debate on the issue, on the other hand, seems still to be only occasional in nature and in many respects, less mature in its content.

Endnotes

1. See, in particular, Chantal Saint-Blancat, "Italy", in Jocelyne Cesari (ed.), *The Oxford Handbook of European Islam* (Oxford: Oxford University Press, 2014), p. 265-310.
2. Lorenzo Vidino, "Islam, Islamism, and Jihadism in Italy," *Current Trends in Islamist Ideology*, August 4th, 2008, https://www.hudson.org/research/9813-islam-islamism-and-jihadism-in-italy.
3. For a brief presentation, see Annalisa Frisina, "The Union of Islamic Communities and Organizations and Related Groups in Italy", in Frank Peter and Rafael Ortega (eds), *Islamic Movements of Europe*, London, I.B. Tauris, 2014, p. 115-118.
4. Stefano Allievi, "I musulmani in Italia: chi sono e come ci vedono [Muslims in Italy: Who They Are And How They See Us]," *Limes*, iss 3, 2004, p. 100.
5. Lorenzo Vidino, "Islam, Islamism, and Jihadism in Italy," *Current Trends in Islamist Ideology*, August 4th, 2008, https://www.hudson.org/research/9813-islam-islamism-and-jihadism-in-italy.
6. UCOII, "History of UCOII" (in Italian), http://www.ucoii.org/storia/.
7. Renzo Guolo, *Xenofobi e Xenofili: Gli Italiani e l'Is-*

lam [Xenophobes And Xenophiles: Italians and Islam], Bari: Laterza, 2003., p. 10.

8. Back in 2011, the UCOII controlled not less than 134 prayer halls in the country: Maria Bombardieri, *Moschee d'Italia. Il diritto al luogo di culto, il dibattito sociale e politico* [*Mosques of Italy: The Right to a Place of Worship, The Social and Political Debate*], Bologna: Emi, 2011, p. 29. In addition, according to its official website, today the organization gathers together 153 associations: UCOII, "History of UCOII" (in Italian), http://www.ucoii.org/storia/.
9. Renzo Guolo, *Xenofobi e Xenofili: Gli Italiani e l'Islam* [Xenophobes And Xenophiles: Italians and Islam], p. 11
10. Renzo Guolo, *Xenofobi e Xenofili: Gli Italiani e l'Islam* [Xenophobes And Xenophiles: Italians and Islam], p. 5–6.
11. 59th Report of CESIS (Executive Committee for the Intelligence and Security Services) to Parliament, January–May 2007, p. 71.
12. Lorenzo Vidino's interviews with Italian government officials and Muslim community leaders, Rome, Italy, February and July 2007.
13. "Pulsioni antimondialiste e vecchio antisemitismo [Anti-globalist Trends and Old Anti-Semitism]," SISDE GNOSIS, Iss. 4, 2005.
14. Giacomo Galeazzi and Ilario Lombardo, "Making Space for Islam in Catholic Italy," *La Stampa*, May 30, 2016, http://www.lastampa.it/2016/05/30/esteri/lastampa-in-english/making-space-for-islam-in-catholic-italy-c9wShtisWIyPP8NKbi21jN/pagina.html
15. "Italy Aims to Integrate Muslims and Shape 'Italian Islam,'" *The Local IT*, January 19, 2016, http://www.thelocal.it/20160119/italy-strives-to-integrate-muslims-and-shape-italian-islam
16. "Italian Muslims sign anti-extremism pact," *The Local IT*, February 2, 2017, https://www.thelocal.it/20170202/italian-muslims-sign-anti-extremism-pact.
17. In particular, Lorenzo Vidino, "The Evolution of Jihadism in Italy: Rise in Homegrown Radicals", CTC Sentinel, Vol. 6, Issue 11–12, 2013, p. 17-20; Lorenzo

Vidino, *Home-Grown Jihadism in Italy: Birth, Development and Radicalization Dynamics*, Foreword by Stefano Dambruoso, Milan: Italian Institute for International Political Studies (ISPI) and European Foundation for Democracy, 2014.

18. Katya Adler, "Migration Crisis: Italy Threatened by National Crisis," *BBC News*, April 19, 2016, http://www.bbc.com/news/world-europe-36080216. Cf. Lorenzo Vidino, Francesco Marone and Eva Entenmann, Fear Thy Neighbor: Radicalization and Jihadist Attacks in the West, Italian Institute for International Political Studies (ISPI) / Program on Extremism at George Washington University (PoE-GWU) / International Centre for Counter-Terrorism – The Hague (ICCT), June 2017, http://www.ispionline.it/it/file/17845/download?token=F1dOKXTC.
19. Lorenzo Vidino, "Islam, Islamism, and Jihadism in Italy," Current Trends in Islamist Ideology, August 4th, 2008, https://www.hudson.org/research/9813-islam-islamism-and-jihadism-in-italy.
20. Resident Population on 1st January, ISTAT, http://stra-dati.istat.it/?lang=en
21. "Table: Muslim Population by Country," Pew Research Center, January 27, 2011, http://www.pewforum.org/2011/01/27/table-muslim-population-by-country/; Alessio Menonna, La presenza musulmana in Italia, ISMU Foundation - Initiatives and Studies on Multiethnicity, June 2016, http://www.ismu.org/wp-content/uploads/2016/07/Menonna_Musulmani_Fact-sheet_Giugno-20161.pdf
22. "Table: Muslim Population by Country," Pew Research Center.
23. "Italy - Sea Arrivals: UNHCR Update #10," UN High Commissioner for Refugees, December 2016, https://data2.unhcr.org/en/documents/download/53633.
24. "Mapping the Global Muslim Population: A Report on the Size and Distribution of the World's Muslim Population", Pew Research Center, October 2009, http://www.pewforum.org/files/2009/10/Muslimpopulation.pdf
25. See "The Situation of Muslims in Italy," European

Muslim Union, September 2010, http://emunion.eu/emudoc/EMU%20Country%20Report%20Italy%20-%20September%202010.pdf
26. Dr. Matteo Villa, Forecast by the Italian Institute for International Political Studies (ISPI), Migration Programme, October 15, 2017.
27. Merelli, Annalisa, "There are over 1.6 million Muslims in Italy—and only eight mosques" Quartz, May 4, 2016, http://qz.com/674377/there-are-over-1-6-million-muslims-in-italy-and-only-eight-mosques/
28. Cited in Antonio Cuciniello, Luoghi di culto islamici in Italia: tipologie e dati, ISMU Foundation - Initiatives and Studies on Multiethnicity, April 2017, p. 6, http://www.ismu.org/wp-content/uploads/2017/05/Cuciniello_paper_luoghi-di-culto_aprile-2017.pdf.
29. Non-Catholic groups with an accord [with the Italian Government] include the Confederation of Methodist and Waldensian Churches, Seventh-day Adventists, Assemblies of God, Jews, Baptists, Lutherans, Mormons, Orthodox Church of the Constantinople Patriarchate, and the Apostolic Church, the Buddhist Union and Hindus, 2013, https://www.state.gov/documents/organization/222441.pdf
30. Elena Dusi, "Il fantasma della Consulta," *Limes*, Iss. 4 (2007), p.155.
31. Annalisa Frisina, "The Union of Islamic Communities and Organizations and Related Groups in Italy", p.116.
32. "The Situation of Muslims in Italy," European Muslim Union.
33. Lorenzo Vidino, *Home-Grown Jihadism in Italy.*
34. Lorenzo Vidino, *Home-Grown Jihadism in Italy.*
35. Lorenzo Vidino, *Home-Grown Jihadism in Italy.*
36. Francesco Marone, *Italy's Jihadists in the Syrian Civil War*, The International Centre for Counter-Terrorism – The Hague (ICCT), August 2016, https://icct.nl/wp-content/uploads/2016/08/ICCT-Marone-Italys-Jihadists-in-the-Syrian-Civil-War-August2016-1.pdf.
37. Lorenzo Vidino and Francesco Marone, *The Jihadist Threat in Italy: A Primer*, Analysis, Italian Institute for International Political Studies (ISPI), November 2017. See also Francesco Marone, "Ties that Bind: Dynamics

of Group Radicalisation in Italy's Jihadists Headed for Syria and Iraq", *The International Spectator*, Vol. 52, No. 3, 2017, p. 48-63.

38. Lorenzo Vidino and Francesco Marone, *The Jihadist Threat in Italy.*
39. Francesco Marone, *The Use of Deportation in Counter-Terrorism: Insights from the Italian Case*, The International Centre for Counter-Terrorism – The Hague (ICCT), Perspective, March 2017, https://icct.nl/publication/the-use-of-deportation-in-counter-terrorism-insights-from-the-italian-case/.
40. "Italy: Updated Legislation on Fight Against Terrorism," Law Library of Congress, March 24, 2016, http://www.loc.gov/law/foreign-news/article/italy-updated-legislation-on-fight-against-terrorism/
41. For an extensive analysis of jihadist networks in Italy, see Lorenzo Vidino, "Islam, Islamism and Jihadism in Italy," *Current Trends in Islamist Ideology* 7 (2008); Lorenzo Vidino, Home-Grown Jihadism in Italy.
42. See Francesco Marone, "The Italian Way of Counterterrorism: From a Consolidated Experience to an Integrated Approach", in S. N. Romaniuk et al. (eds), The Palgrave Handbook of Global Counterterrorism Policy, London: Palgrave Macmillan, 2017, p. 479-494.

45 Kosovo

Quick Facts

Population: 1,895,250 (July 2017 est.)
Area: 10,887 sq km
Ethnic Groups: Albanians 92.9%, Bosniaks 1.6%, Serbs 1.5%, Turk 1.1%, Ashkali 0.9%, Egyptian 0.7%, Gorani 0.6%, Romani 0.5%, other/unspecified 0.2%
Government Type: Parliamentary republic
GDP (official exchange rate): $6.684 billion (2017 est.)

Source: CIA World FactBook (Last Updated April 2018)

Introduction

Islam's footprint in Kosovo dates back seven centuries, to the time of the Ottoman conquest. Although much of the ethnic Albanian-majority population practices a moderate form of Islam, the slow pace of social, political and economic development since the 1999 NATO intervention has created fertile soil for Islamic radicalization. Adding to this dynamic is the fact that the post-intervention period (even after national independence in 2008) has seen amorphous and unaccountable UN and then EU missions linger on, with wide authority and influence. A smaller NATO detachment led by the United States, Kosovo Force (KFOR) also remains, though it has handed over most security duties to local government bodies. However, due to the unaccountable governance of supranational organizations, numerous Islamic states and fundamentalist-oriented charities have been allowed open access to this economically underdeveloped corner of Europe.

The result today is that, while most Kosovars are still moderate, the country has produced the highest number of foreign fighters per capita among European countries joining ISIS and al-Nusra Front, with 125 fighters for every million people.[1] *While numbers of foreign fighters have dropped sharply in the last year, due to governmental remediation efforts, the issue of countering violent extremism (CVE) and the potential for attacks from returning fighters are prominent concerns for the government and its Western backers today.*

While the Kosovar government has tended to downplay the role of Islam (and Islamic extremism) in its nation, it is taking steps to deal with security and social issues associated with radicalization, passing laws against foreign fighters and arresting scores of previous or aspiring homegrown jihadists since 2014. While there are specific connections between Kosovo and the Syrian conflict, in the long term the development of education, health and work opportunities for local youth is probably the greatest challenge Kosovo faces in countering violent extremism. At the same time, the ethnic linkages between Kosovars at home and those in Western European countries has resulted (and will result) in police actions elsewhere on the Continent involving Kosovo-related terror cells linked to ISIS. This will remain a concern going forward.

ISLAMIST ACTIVITY

Today's Islamist activity in Kosovo was, in the beginning, expedited by the 1999 NATO intervention, which replaced Serbian rule with a porous international administration that was preoccupied with matters of inter-ethnic violence, organized crime and institution-building. Relatively little attention was paid to the possibility of Islamic extremism, in part because the narrative of an ethnic nationalist liberation struggle allegedly precluded this possibility. Ultimately, though, the participation of Kosovo Muslims in modern jihad owes to the support of foreign Islamic donors, who sought to build mosques, schools and NGOs in the country following the 1999 NATO intervention. Although many of these groups have since been closed or voluntarily left, they did provide indoctrination and financial support for impoverished Kosovars at a key post-conflict time. Their influence has lingered and has created an extremist fringe that took on a leading role in the Syrian conflict.

The first foreign Islamist actors came to Kosovo in 1999 via in an assortment of Islamic charities. The most important was a Saudi government umbrella organization, the Saudi Joint Commission for the Relief of Kosovo and Chechnya (SJCRKC). It was matched by its official Kuwaiti counterpart, the Kuwaiti Joint Relief Committee (KJRC). Along with then-returning Albanian refugees, representatives of these groups (and the Islamic charities organized within them) entered Kosovo from neighboring Albania, where Albanian and U.S. authorities had been monitoring, and working to control, suspected international terrorist suspects. The Saudis initially allocated over $22.5 million for the rebuilding or new construction of mosques and schools, and also for supporting orphans in Kosovo.[2] However, Kosovo investigators of the now-closed charity found in 2016 that most of the Saudi money could not be accounted for, and that very little has ever actually been given to help orphans.[3]

Although the volume of personnel would gradually diminish over time, and in some instances disappear completely with the progressive downsizing of the UN mission, Kosovo was clearly vulnerable to foreign Islamist penetration in the early years of post-Yugoslav rule. Kosovo's internationally uncertain status also meant a no-visa policy, and with essentially open borders, Kosovo became Europe's primary "safe zone" for foreign radicals. Pressure from the EU—which Kosovo hopes to join someday—led the government to plan to impose visas on over 80 countries in 2013. But, as of August 2016, citizens from over 100 countries (including most of the Gulf states) still did not need visas to enter Kosovo.[4]

Estimates for the number of foreign fighters from Kosovo have varied widely in recent years, with the Kosovar government only admitting to the problem once it began to garner international interest in 2015. Since that time, there has been an almost complete stoppage of jihadists exiting the country.[5] Statistics in 2015 claimed some 232 Kosovo-born fighters had joined the ranks of jihadist groups, making Kosovo the highest exporter of jihadists per capita in Europe.[6] However, a U.S. Institute of Peace study from December 2016, concurring with a State Department country assessment from the summer of 2017, put the total number of foreign fighter from Kosovo at 314.[7]

Interestingly, the USIP analysis noted that "none of the five municipalities with the highest rates of foreign fighter mobilization (Hani i Elezit, Kaçanik, Mitrovice, Gjilan, and Viti) were classified as being among the municipalities with the lowest 2014 Human Development Index in Kosovo."[8] The research, which made use of official state statistics, found that "no correlation is readily observable between income and educational levels and vulnerability to mobilization."[9] While most Kosovo Muslim foreign fighters were men aged 17-30, they had relatively higher educational levels than did similar foreign fighters from Bosnia. Also, while in absolute terms urban areas (like the capital, Prishtina, and Prizren) were sources for Islamist fighters, the regular tours of Albanian extremist preachers from Macedonia created jihad pockets in tiny municipalities (Hani I Elezit, Kaçanik) that are near the border, and that turned out a disproportionate number of fighters bound for Syria and Iraq.[10]

Islamic radical activity relating to Kosovo has taken on an international profile, particularly since the Syrian war began in 2011. Yet it is not only that conflict zone that has drawn Albanians from the Balkan country to carry out jihad; in addition, the traditionally large and embedded Albanian diaspora spread throughout Western Europe is offering new potential for logistics and recruitments of terrorist bases, as has been indicated by several arrests in Italy since 2015. Most infamously, three Kosovar Albanian ISIS devotees (Fisnik Bekaj, 24, Dake Haziraj, 25, and Arian Babaj, 27) were arrested by Italian police in March 2017, after their plan to blow up Venice's historic Rialto Bridge was uncovered by Italian police.[11] According to police wiretaps, the aspiring terrorists (one of whom had returned from Syria) were inspired by the contemporaneous terrorist attack on London's Westminster Bridge.

As with other cases, all of the men were living legally in Italy—in fact, two worked as waiters in central Venice—indicating again the unique nature of Kosovo's terrorist threat.[12] Kosovo thus continues to be an exporter of instability and also faces the threat of terrorism on its own soil from returning ISIS and al-Nusra fighters. Finally, given the very high rate of economic migrants during and after the 2015 European migrant crisis, the potential for radicalization grows among both embittered forced returnees and new diaspora members attracted to radical mosques in Western Europe.

As radicalized Kosovars have forayed into the outside world, radical elements have infiltrated Kosovo's criminal network. Cooperation between ethnic Albanian drug cartels and ISIS is today a growing concern. Kosovars have historically been involved in heroin smuggling from Asia and some cocaine smuggling from South America, along with Albanians. But, as with Albania, they are most active through their extensive diaspora networks in Western Europe. After a large-scale police operation to destroy vast cannabis plantations in southern Albania, the business became fragmented, with older clans replaced by more violent adherents to radical Islam. Kosovo's most infamous ISIS member, the late Lavdrim Muhaxheri, was for several years the key link between Albanian drug operations and ISIS recruitment. This is said to mark an increasingly violent and religiously-oriented drug-smuggling outfit in the region, with ties to the Italian and other mafias.[13]

Muhaxheri (born circa 1987) had been the best-known Kosovar jihadist associated with ISIS (he previously worked for both the UN administration in Kosovo and NATO in Afghanistan before being radicalized in the small south Kosovo village of Kacanik in 2012).[14] From 2012, he became infamous worldwide—and a source of great embarrassment to state authorities—by appearing in several propaganda videos for ISIS, including one showing him beheading a captive. In an unsettling attempt to justify the crime to Kosovar nationalists, Muhaxheri claimed that he had done "the same thing" as the nationalist Kosovo Liberation Army had done against the Serbs, in 1999.[15]

In August 2014, Interpol put Muhaxheri on its wanted list. Then-U.S. Secretary of State John Kerry blacklisted the Kosovar jihadist as a threat to American national security in the Federal Register on October 2, 2014.[16] The terrorist's death was finally confirmed by family members and the Kosovo police on June 8, 2017. He had been killed by an air strike in Syria—Kosovo authorities estimated at the time that another 50 of their citizens had also been killed in fighting up to that point.[17]

Until the time of his death, Muhaxheri had led ISIS' ethnic-Albanian brigade, and headed its Albanian-language propaganda campaign. He was also the ideological protégé of the (now jailed) radical Kosovar imam Zekerija Qazimi, as was another field commander, Ridvan Haqifi.[18] In June 2017, the Kosovo authorities charged nine men (among 19 arrested the year before) for having plotted to carry out terrorist attacks in Kosovo and other regional countries; most prominent among these was a thwarted attack on an international soccer match between Israel and Albania (the match, held under heavy security, was played in a different city than originally planned). Investigators found that the arrested men had been taking their orders and funding directly from Muhaxheri in Syria, and that some had learned to make homemade explosives similar to those used in terrorist attacks in Belgium and France.[19]

An equally worrying problem for Kosovo is the prominent participation of women in the ranks of ISIS and other terrorist groups in Syria. In July 2017, it was alleged that a 23-year-old woman, Qamile Tahiri, was among the most radical of 44 known Kosovo Albanian women in Syria. She was said to be running a jihadi training camp for women in Syria and, along with another Kosovar woman, heavily engaged in recruiting newcomers to the terrorist cause from personal and internet channels. Indeed, while general media reporting of the Syrian conflict focused on the role of women as come-along "jihadi brides," examples such as Tahiri's indicate a more complex and active role for radicalized women.[20]

By May 2016, the number of Kosovars (including women and children) who had joined militant groups in Syria and Iraq had reached at least 314 persons (not counting pre-2014 fighters) according to a New York Times investigation. This report found that the development and mobilization of a Kosovar jihadist force had been accomplished by a "corps of extremist clerics and secretive associations funded by Saudi Arabia and other conservative Arab gulf states using an obscure, labyrinthine network of donations from charities, private individuals and government ministries."[21] While Kosovo's interior ministry stated in August 2016 that no new recruits were believed to have departed in the past year, some 50 Kosovars had died in battle and another 120 had returned. Over 100 of these are under investigation by Kosovar authorities.[22]

Both before and after the Syrian war, Kosovar Albanians have been involved in both terrorist cells and organized crime.[23] Despite the fact that the U.S.-led NATO intervention in 1999 liberated Kosovo from Serbia, a number of attacks and planned attacks against the U.S. military have occurred. On September 23, 2016, Kosovo citizen Ardit Ferizi was sentenced to 20 years in prison by a

U.S. district court; while based in Malaysia the year before, he had hacked into a U.S. company's database, harvesting personal data on 1,300 U.S. military and other personnel. The Kosovar admitted to having provided this data to ISIS, in the hopes of personal attacks designed to "hit them hard," an official U.S. State Department report recounted in 2017.[24] Earlier foiled attacks by Albanians against the U.S. military include the 2008 plot against Fort Dix in New Jersey,[25] and another against the U.S. Marine Corps base in Quantico, Virginia.[26] In 2012, the shadowy "Kosovo Hackers Security" group infiltrated the U.S. National Weather Service's computer networks; this was reportedly meant to be "a protest against the U.S. policies that target Muslim countries."[27]

There are also renewed fears that Western targets—and local Balkan communities— could fall victim to a new breed of Islamic terrorists inspired by ISIS. In the June 2017 issue of ISIS's magazine, *Rumiyah* (formerly known as *Dabiq*) Bosnian jihadists threatened that they would soon be bringing their war to the Balkans, targeting Christian Serbs and Croats (allegedly, in revenge for the wars of the 1990s), as well as insufficiently devout Muslims. Kosovo, Macedonia and Albania were specifically mentioned as places where terrorism would be carried out.[28] Although as of late 2017 no such attacks have occurred, police continue to make arrests.[29] Indeed, the wider threat matrix is definitely keeping regional security services busy. This will be an ongoing reality and, combined with the need to attend to migration-related issues, will have a knock-on effect, with less manpower becoming available to fight organized political violence.

Islamism and Society

The most recent estimate, from 2015, pegged Kosovo's population at almost 1.9 million.[30] Ethnic Albanians comprise 92 percent of this population, which is on average one of the youngest in any European country. However, the country's poorly-performing economy has led many Kosovars to look for options abroad, and there is a large Kosovar diaspora in Western Europe. Kosovars and Albanians sought to take advantage of the 2015 migrant crisis for economic reasons, comprising one of the largest numbers of asylum-seekers by nationality. Their asylum attempts, however, generally failed, and the individuals in question were returned to their homelands. Germany alone received 102,000 ethnic Albanian migrants in 2015.[31] Despite Kosovo's location in the Balkans, it did not receive a significant influx of migrants during the migrant crisis, because it was off the path that most migrants took to enter Europe, known as the Balkan Route. The Balkan Route runs in from Greece through the Vardar Valley corridor in central Macedonia and northwards through Serbia, reaching Hungary and Austria. Since Kosovo was not on the Balkan Route, it was never really impacted by migrant flows that passed through neighboring Macedonia and Serbia. (However, human trafficking gangs from all three countries have been active in facilitating illegal migration, according to the author's interviews with Macedonian and UN officials).

Muslims (who include small populations of Roma, Turks, Gorani and Bosniaks) in total are estimated to comprise 95 percent of Kosovo's total population.[32] Approximately three percent of Kosovo's Albanians are Catholic, though this population seems to be increasing, while various foreign Protestant denominations have tried (so far, with less success) to convert Kosovo's Muslims. The beleaguered Serbian Orthodox minority of 120,000 persons is largely concentrated in a few scattered central enclaves, and in more compact northern municipalities around the ethnically divided city of Mitrovica. However, there is also a small Serbian-speaking Slavic Muslim minority, the Gorani, who primarily inhabit the mountainous southwestern area around Dragas, nestled between Macedonia and Albania. The small Roma minority is mainly Muslim as well, but it is less active, limited by the Roma lifestyle on the margins of society.

The officially recognized Muslim organization in the country is the Islamic Community of Kosovo (in Albanian, Bashkësia Islame e Kosovës, or BIK).[33] It is intended to represent the totality of Islam in the country, though there are traditional Bektashi Sufi communities, particularly in western Kosovo, that have certain differences in doctrine and practice. Nevertheless, both the Bektashi and Hanafi Sunni Muslims generally get along and are united by a strong sense of ethnic Albanian nationalism, however, Wahhabi Muslims influenced by foreign ideologies fall outside the structure of the BIK and its control. Their numbers are notoriously difficult to calculate, as there is no strict doctrine or separate institutions governing them; they simply consider themselves "better," more committed Muslims than the rest.

Of Kosovo's approximately 800 mosques, some 240 were built following the 1999 NATO intervention—part of "a deliberate, long-term strategy by Saudi Arabia to reshape Islam in its image, not only in Kosovo but around the world."[34] This mosque-building program and other Islamic activities have been driven not only by the Saudis but by other competing actors like Turkey and Iran. Cumulatively, this rivalry between external powers has damaged social cohesion and led to increasing conservatism. A 2016 study revealed that 57% of Kosovars had greater trust in religious institutions than in state ones, while "Kosovar youth are also becoming increasingly conservative, with their main reference points for spiritual and intellectual guidance being local imams."[35]

An indication of the government's concern over religious polarization has been attested to by a new inter-faith body (led by Muslim, Orthodox and Catholic leaders) that meets regularly to discuss better cooperation and references Mother Teresa; though she was born in neighboring Macedonia, the famed nun of Calcutta is considered an ethnic Albanian national hero.[36] The Interfaith Kosovo initiative also holds annual conferences featuring high-profile international speakers, with a common aim of promoting interreligious harmony and confronting extremism; for example, its 2016 event was dedicated to the role of women in countering violent extremism.[37]

Overall, the social and political trends toward increasing Islamic conservatism in Kosovo are not surprising to anyone who has paid close attention to the country since NATO's intervention. Protecting the legacy and righteousness of that intervention has long led U.S. and NATO officials to downplay the presence of Islamism in Kosovo. Western governments in recent years tried to depict Kosovo's brand of Islam as harmless, a sort of "Islam-lite."[38] This narrative has, however, increasingly been challenged by the reality of Kosovar participation in the Syria conflict and related radicalization.

Naturally, the Kosovo government—which aspires to join the EU someday—also wishes to downplay any association with radical Islam. However, as of 2017 contemporary developments and anecdotal evidence point to a new trend toward using Islam as a way to define social identities, ideological beliefs, and cultural choices, and no longer simply as a way of making income, as had been the case with the initial Arab "investment" in Kosovo's people.[39]

Islamism and the State

The Kosovo state's disputed independent status continued in 2017 to hamper its abilities to cooperate in formal international law enforcement bodies; for example, in advance of Interpol's annual meeting in September 2017, the country's leaders had conceded that they would again have to postpone their membership bid to join the body, which was being held in "hostile" China—a country which, along with Russia, remains a strong supporter of Serbia's claim over Kosovo.[40] This effectively meant that to join the law enforcement body in 2018, Kosovo would have to lobby the Islamic country due to hold it in that year—the United Arab Emirates.[41] While it is by no means certain that Kosovo could join Interpol even in 2018, the fact that it will have to lobby one of the world's leading Islamic countries adds an interesting nuance to the state's relationship with the Muslim world in the context of fighting terrorism.

There have of course been some successes, even without formal Interpol membership, due to Kosovo's strong Western support. At the same time, these successes have also highlighted Kosovo's role as an exporter of instability, in both having sent foreign fighters to the Middle East and in exporting radicals among its diaspora in Italy, Switzerland and other countries. In August 2014, Kosovo police arrested 40 people suspected of supporting jihadists in Syria and Iraq.[42] In March 2015, the country passed a "foreign fighters" law at the U.S.'s request, as have several other Balkan countries.[43] The law penalizes the act of traveling from one's country to another to participate in a foreign conflict with punishments including prison sentences. The law is meant to be a deterrent to prevent people from going to join jihads and keep control of those who have done so and could pose a threat after returning. In May 2016, police "charged 67 people, arrested 14 imams and shut down 19 Muslim organizations for acting against the Constitution, inciting hatred and recruiting for terrorism," according to the *New York Times*.[44] One of the key radical clerics associated with ISIS, Zekerija Qazimi from Ferezaj, was found guilty of recruiting for the terror group and of inciting hatred, and was jailed for 10 years.[45] Kosovar police further targeted (in a very rare move) a Shiite organization in Kosovo run by an Iranian cleric reportedly linked to Iran's ayatollahs and accused of funding terrorism.[46]

However, the government's success in arresting returned fighters and other radicals has also created a new problem: prison radicalization. Inspections by state authorities through 2017 indicated the presence of more radical (if often, unattributed) works of theology. An RFE/RL study in 2017, quoting the country's justice minister, stated that radical Islam was drawing adherents from convicts who had been arrested for other crimes, and who had shown no previous signs of religious radicalization. To help remedy the situation, the state and prison system began a program with Kosovo's official Islamic community, to send moderate imams and religious content to the prisons.[47]

In response to this phenomenon, by 2017 a combination of governmental and NGO outreach efforts had been made in Kosovo to attempt to reintegrate foreign fighters and empower women, who in traditional Albanian society have generally been kept in a subservient position, experts say.[48] The U.S. State Department report of July 2017 noted that the country's countering violent extremism program includes "referral mechanism in the municipality of Gjilan that will bring together local officials, religious leaders, and civil society to address community concerns of radicalization to violence. Kosovo's CVE strategy includes the preparation and promotion of counter-narratives to weaken the legitimacy of violent extremist messages."[49]

Elsewhere in Europe, international cooperation with Kosovar authorities has occurred. In November 2015, Italian authorities arrested four Kosovars in the Brescia region, where they had been running an ISIS logistics network linked with Kosovo's former most-wanted jihadist, (now deceased) Lavdrim Muhaxheri.[50] At home, the Kosovar state is also seeking to counter extremism by other means. One possibility being recommended (in line with similar programs elsewhere in Europe) would offer "jihad rehabilitation" opportunities for some of the arrested men involved in the Syrian conflict.[51]

Kosovar-EU relations have been rocky in recent years, with allegations that Kosovo's top leaders profited from wartime organ trafficking and drug smuggling offset by charges of EU corruption in its own Kosovo delegation, in 2014.[52] The relationship between Kosovo's government and its Western partners has also been troubled because of internal political infighting (as when rival Kosovar parliamentarians attacked each with tear gas in 2015 and 2016).[53] The combination of internal political feuding, the unresolved international status of Kosovo and Serbia's non-recognition of the country, as well as endemic economic and social challenges all negatively affect the country's institutional capacity to deal with important but not essential challenges like Islamic extremism. However, as of late 2017, Kosovo had still avoided any sort of political transition, with former wartime allies Hashim Thaci and Ramush Haradinaj remaining key state leaders, under Western control.

Amid the turmoil, one country that also saw considerable turmoil in 2016—Turkey—has sought to increase its presence in Kosovo. Unlike Saudi Arabia and other Muslim states, Turkey has a historic and cultural legacy in Kosovo, and thus significant legitimacy there. Since 1999, it has performed considerable development work, investment and political engagement within Kisovo, with significant impact. Among other things, the Erdogan government's Justice and Development Party was the model for Kosovo's Justice Party (Partia e Drejtësisë). Although it was not significantly represented in parliament, its leader was given a cabinet minister post in the previous government. In 2010, the party attempted to pass legislation calling for an introduction of religious education and an end to the state ban on the hijab in public schools. While these attempts failed, the closeness of the vote result indicated that individual parliamentarians from a wide range of parties have sympathies with Islam on social grounds.

Kosovo's relationship with Turkey has also been complicated by the failed July 2016 military coup against President Erdogan. As elsewhere in the Balkans, in its aftermath Kosovo was asked by Ankara to close schools linked with the alleged coup mastermind, U.S.-based cleric Fethulah Gulen. The Turkish government also demanded that Kosovo punish a local journalist who had made satirical comments about the coup attempt.[54] The Kosovo government did not do either, and many in the country bristled against the perceived intrusiveness. However, the quashed coup has only increased Erdogan's popularity among average Muslims in the Balkans—and Turkey runs Kosovo's airport and electricity supply, while Turkish companies are heavily involved with its road infrastructure development. Kosovo thus faces a delicate balancing act in preserving relations with Turkey, the West and the Islamic world in the years ahead.

Indeed, in May 2017 a German parliamentarian of Turkish background upbraided her government over its perceived unwillingness to tackle Islamic extremism funded by Arab states in Kosovo, despite still keeping a German KFOR brigade there. She also noted that the Erdogan-Gulen rift has given the former "a free hand" to win support for his government among Kosovars. The German MP, Sevim Dagdalem, charged that "it is scandalous that, thanks to the presence of German troops, Saudi preachers of hate and violence have been able to, unimpeded, set up the ideological foundation" for radical Islam. [55] The hands-off attitude of Kosovo's international minders has been brought up time and time again since 1999, in the early years regarding tolerance of Albanian violence against Serbs, but since then increasingly in regards to turning a blind eye to Islamic radicalization trends.

A major issue going forward will be whether Kosovo can develop the economic and educational conditions for retaining its young and restless population. While a strong spirit of optimism characterized the country following the February 2008 unilateral declaration of independence, this spirit has long since waned as the reality of economic torpor remains. Illustrating this trend is the fact that Kosovo Albanians (along with their kin from South Serbia, Macedonia and Albania proper) comprised a significant number of asylum-seekers in Western Europe during and after the 2015 migration crisis. While many were sent home immediately, official Pew research data showed that by the beginning of 2017, some 77% of Kosovar asylum applicants in countries like Germany, Switzerland and Sweden were still awaiting a decision on their asylum applications.[56]

Kosovo's major problem, therefore, will remain creating an economically- and educationally-developed society, one in which a large young population can feel a sense of belonging and purpose. National and international authorities have identified social, economic and educational shortcomings as main drivers of radicalization here, so we can expect that counter-terrorism programs in the years ahead will continue to have this wider scope. At the same time, the proven ability of Kosovo-born radicals in Western Europe to plan and operate freely, under their own direction or from commanders in the Middle East, will pose the most significant hard security challenge to Europe and the U.S. from Kosovo-related extremists in the years ahead.

ENDNOTES

1. Joanna Paraszczuk, "Report Finds Alarming Outflow Of Kosovars To Islamic State," *Radio Free Europe/Radio Liberty*, April 15, 2015, http://www.rferl.org/content/islamic-state-kosovars-fighting-syria-iraq/26957463.html.
2. A detailed contemporaneous description of the specific Kosovar refugee relief operations undertaken by Arab groups in Albania, and their subsequent entrance from there into Kosovo, is found in Hussein Saud Qusti, "Unsung Heroes," *Saudi Aramco World*, July/August 1999. Regarding the role of U.S. and Albanian authorities targeting Islamist groups in Albania during the mid-1990s, see the *World Almanac of Islamism* chapter on Albania.
3. Carlotta Gall, "How Kosovo Was Turned Into Fertile Ground for ISIS," *New York Times*, May 21, 2016, http://www.nytimes.com/2016/05/22/world/europe/how-the-saudis-turned-kosovo-into-fertile-ground-for-

isis.html?_r=0.
4. See the official list, which is updated periodically, here: http://www.mfa-ks.net/?page=2,157.
5. "Kosovo Hails Sharp Drop in Middle Eastern Fighters," *Balkan Insight,* October 24, 2016, http://www.balkaninsight.com/en/article/kosovo-pleg-des-to-work-closer-to-islamic-comunity-to-fight-radi-calism-10-24-2016.
6. Paraszczuk, "Report Finds Alarming Outflow Of Kosovars To Islamic State."
7. Adrian Shtuni, "Dynamics of Radicalization and Violent Extremism in Kosovo," United States Institute of Peace, December 19, 2016, https://www.usip.org/publications/2016/12/dynamics-radicalization-and-vio-lent-extremism-kosovo.
8. Adrian Shtuni, "Dynamics of Radicalization and Violent Extremism in Kosovo," United States Institute of Peace, December 19, 2016, https://www.usip.org/publications/2016/12/dynamics-radicalization-and-vio-lent-extremism-kosovo
9. Adrian Shtuni, "Dynamics of Radicalization and Violent Extremism in Kosovo," United States Institute of Peace, December 19, 2016, https://www.usip.org/publications/2016/12/dynamics-radicalization-and-vio-lent-extremism-kosovo.
10. Shtuni, "Dynamics of Radicalization and Violent Extremism in Kosovo."
11. Nick Squires, "Italian police break up alleged jihadist cell that planned to attack Venice's Rialto Bridge," *The Telegraph*, March 30, 2017, http://www.telegraph.co.uk/news/2017/03/30/italian-police-break-alleged-ji-hadist-cell-planned-attack-venices.
12. Squires, "Italian police break up alleged jihadist cell that planned to attack Venice's Rialto Bridge."
13. Allan Hall and Dan Warburton, "ISIS seizes £4bn drug ring from the Mafia to fund its brutal terror campaign," *Daily Mirror* (UK), January 17, 2016, http://www.mirror.co.uk/news/uk-news/isis-seizes-4bn-drug-ring-7191800.
14. "Ekskluzive: Biografia e Lavdrim Muhaxherit" [Exclusive: Biography Lavdrim Muhaxheri]. *KosovaPress.*

com, January 28, 2014.

15. "Kosovo Albanian Who Beheaded a Man Says He Is Doing the Same Thing KLA Did," Independent.mk, August 2, 2014, http://www.independent.mk/articles/7931/Kosovo+Albanian+Who+Beheaded+a+Man+-Says+He+Is+Doing+the+Same+Thing+KLA+Did.
16. In the Matter of the Designation of Lavdrim Muhaxheri, also known as Ebu Abdullah el Albani, also known as Abu Abdullah al Kosova, also known as Abu Abdallah al-Kosovi, also known as Abu Abdallah al-Kosovo as a Specially Designated Global Terrorist Pursuant to Section 1(b) of Executive Order 13224, as Amended, FederalRegister.gov. October 2, 2014, https://www.federalregister.gov/articles/2014/10/02/2014-23534/in-the-matter-of-the-designation-of-lavdrim-muhaxheri-also-known-as-ebu-abdullah-el-albani-also.
17. Fatos Bytyci, "Kosovo Islamic State Commander Killed, Police and Family Say," *Reuters*, June 8, 2017, https://www.usnews.com/news/world/articles/2017-06-08/kosovo-islamic-state-commander-killed-police-and-family-say.
18. Labinot Leposhtica, "Kosovo Jails Hard-line Imam for 10 Years," *Balkan Insight*, May 20, 2016, http://www.balkaninsight.com/en/article/kosovo-hard-line-imam-sentenced-to-10-years-in-prison-05-20-2016.
19. Fatos Bytici, "Kosovo charges 9 men with plotting attacks at Albania-Israel World Cup match," Reuters, June 14, 2017, https://www.reuters.com/article/us-kosovo-israel-security/kosovo-charges-9-men-with-plotting-attacks-at-albania-israel-world-cup-match-idUSKBN1951PZ.
20. *Sputnik News*, "One of most radical Islamic State women comes from Kosovo," *B92*, July 17, 2017, http://www.b92.net/eng/news/world.php?yyyy=2017&mm=07&dd=17&nav_id=101825.
21. Carlotta Gall, "How Kosovo Was Turned Into Fertile Ground for ISIS," *New York Times*, May 21, 2016, http://www.nytimes.com/2016/05/22/world/europe/how-the-saudis-turned-kosovo-into-fertile-ground-for-isis.html?_r=0.
22. "Kosovo Says No New Cases Of Citizens Joining IS In

Iraq, Syria," *Radio Free Europe/Radio Liberty*, August 24, 2016, http://www.rferl.org/content/kosovo-islamic-state-iraq-syria/27943383.html.

23. The full story of this interaction is reported only partially, and in various sources. See "Kosovo Drug Baron among Terrorists," *Blic* (Belgrade), September 27, 2006. See also Genc Morina, "Radical Islam: Wahhabism a Danger to Kosovo's Independence!" *Express* (Pristina), October 15, 2006. For official reactions to the acquittal, see Nina Berglund, "Reaction Mixed to Terror Acquittal," *Aftenposten* (Oslo), June 4, 2008.
24. *Country Reports on Terrorism 2016*, U.S. Department of State, July 2017. Available at: https://www.state.gov/documents/organization/272488.pdf
25. Geoff Mulvihill, "Man pleads guilty in Fort Dix plot case," *Associated Press*, October 31, 2007.
26. See Gerry J. Gilmore, "FBI, Navy Foil Alleged Terror Plot on Quantico," American Forces Press Service, September 25, 2009. See also U.S. Department of Justice, "Kosovar National Charged with Terrorism Violations," June 17, 2010.
27. "Kosovo Group Claims Hack of US Weather Service," *Agence France-Presse*, October 19, 2012.
28. "ISIS threatens terror campaign in the Balkans," Balkan Insight, June 8, 2017,http://www.balkaninsight.com/en/article/isis-wows-to-wreak-vengeance-on-balkans-in-new-threat-06-08-2017.
29. 'Hapšenje na Kosovu: Uhapšeni Albanci pripremali TERORISTIČKE napade.' ('Arrests in Kosovo: Albanians Preparing Terrorist Attacks Arrested," Srbija Danas, May 25, 2017, https://www.srbijadanas.com/vesti/info/hapsenje-na-kosovu-uhapseni-albanci-pripremali-teroristicke-napade-2017-05-25.
30. See http://www.geoba.se/country.php?cc=XK&year=2015.
31. Sewell Chan, "How a Record Number of Migrants Made Their Way To Europe," *New York Times*, December 22, 2015, http://www.nytimes.com/2015/12/23/world/europe/migrant-crisis-europe-million.html.
32. The 2011 Kosovo census was the first internationally-recognized tally since 1981. Despite the Serb boy-

cott, the EU (which donated 6 million euros to the project) found it generally to have met quality standards. The official Kosovo government statistical office web page for the census is http://esk.rks-gov.net/rekos2011.

33. The official web site of the BIK is www.bislame.net.
34. Gall, "How Kosovo Was Turned Into Fertile Ground for ISIS," op. cit.
35. Ebi Spahiu, "Jihadist Threat Persists in Kosovo and Albania Despite Government Efforts," Jamestown Foundation *Terrorism Monitor* 14, iss. 13, June 24, 2016, http://www.jamestown.org/single/?tx_ttnews%5Btt_news%5D=45551&no_cache=1#.V77LZ6KgA3j.
36. Linda Karadaku, "Inter-faith Dialogue Expected To Advance Reconciliation," SETimes.com, August, 14, 2013.
37. The group's official website is https://www.facebook.com/Interfaith-Kosovo-403629399719855/.
38. This could be seen in media pieces printed immediately after the independence declaration, such as "Kosovo Touts 'Islam-lite,'" Associated Press, February 21, 2008.
39. Several telling examples of this trend are provided in Frud Bezhan, "A Growing Split Between Islamic, Secular Identities In Kosovo," *Radio Free Europe/ Radio Liberty*, August 7, 2016, http://www.rferl.org/content/kosovo-split-islamic-identity-secular-traditions/27906304.html.
40. Perpatim Isufi, "Kosovo Abandons Bid to Join Interpol This Year," *Balkan Insight*, September 21, 2017, https://www.balkaninsight.com/en/article/kosovo-abandons-bid-to-join-interpol-this-year-09-21-2017 .
41. Isufi, "Kosovo Abandons Bid to Join Interpol This Year."
42. Violeta Hyseni Kelmendi, "Kosovo mobilizes to fight religious radicalism and terrorism," *Osservatorio Balcani e Caucaso*, August 25, 2014, http://www.balcanicaucaso.org/eng/Areas/Kosovo/Kosovo-mobilizes-to-fight-religious-radicalism-and-terrorism-155153.
43. Una Hajdari, "Kosovo to Jail Fighters in Foreign Conflicts," *Balkan Insight*, March 13, 2015, http://www.balkaninsight.com/en/article/kosovo-law-to-punish-

fighting-in-foreign-conflicts.
44. Gall, "How Kosovo Was Turned Into Fertile Ground for ISIS," op. cit.
45. Leposhtica, "Kosovo Jails Hard-line Imam for 10 Years," op. cit.
46. Frud Bezhan, "Charges Against Cleric Put Iran's Balkan Activities Under Spotlight," *Radio Free Europe/ Radio Liberty*, August 1, 2016, http://www.rferl.org/ content/kosovo-iran-cleric-arrest/27886917.html.
47. Pete Baumgartner, "Kosovo Seeks To Root Out Radical Islam In Prison System," RFE/RL, March 7, 2017. https://www.rferl.org/a/kosovo-root-out-radical-islam-from-prisons/28356290.html.
48. Nina Teggarty, "Kosovo Looks To ISIS Wives In Order To Fight Extremism," *Huffington Post*, March 9, 2017, http://www.huffingtonpost.com/entry/kosovo-looks-to-isis-wives-in-order-to-fight-extremism_us_58c1ae33e-4b054a0ea6900dd.
49. *Country Reports on Terrorism 2016*, Ibid.
50. Matteo Albertini, "Italy and Kosovo Intensify Actions against Another ISIS-linked Group," *Balkanalysis.com*, December 6, 2015, http://www.balkanalysis.com/ kosovo/2015/12/06/italy-and-kosovo-intensify-actions-against-another-isis-linked-group/.
51. "'Offer Kosovar Fighters 'Jihadi Rehab' to Combat Extremism,'" Balkan Insight, March 24, 2016, http:// www.balkaninsight.com/en/article/offer-kosovar-fighters-jihadi-rehab-to-combat-extremism--03-23-2016.
52. Julian Borger, "EU accused over its Kosovo mission: 'Corruption has grown exponentially,'" *Guardian* (London), November 6, 2014, https://www.theguardian.com/world/2014/nov/06/eu-accused-over-kosovo-mission-failings.
53. "Opposition MPs let off tear gas in Kosovo parliament," *BBC*, February 19, 2016, http://www.bbc.com/ news/world-europe-35616745
54. Fatos Bytyci, "Turkey asks Kosovo to punish journalist over coup comments," *Reuters*, July 26, 2016, http:// www.reuters.com/article/us-kosovo-turkey-journalist-idUSKCN1061A1.
55. "Arabs are Islamizing Kosovo before KFOR's

eyes," *B92*, May 18, 2017, http://www.b92.net/eng/news/world.php?yyyy=2017&mm=05&dd=18&nav_id=101302.

56. Phillip Connor, "Still in Limbo: About a Million Asylum Seekers Await Word on Whether They Can Call Europe Home," *Pew Global*, September 20, 2017, http://www.pewglobal.org/2017/09/20/a-million-asylum-seekers-await-word-on-whether-they-can-call-europe-home.

Macedonia

Quick Facts

Population: 2,103,721 (July 2017 est.)
Area: 25,713 sq km
Ethnic Groups: Macedonian 64.2%, Albanian 25.2%, Turkish 3.9%, Romani 2.7%, Serb 1.8%, other 2.2% (2002 est.)
Government Type: Parliamentary republic
GDP (official exchange rate): $11.42 billion (2017 est.)

Source: CIA World FactBook (Last Updated April 2018)

Introduction

Ethnically- and religiously-divided Macedonia is on the front lines of the European migrant crisis, and was a major transit corridor between Greece and Serbia before that border closed in March 2016. The threat of terrorists posing as migrants has been noted by both local and international authorities. Also, over 100 ethnic Albanian Muslims have fought in jihadist groups like al-Nusra Front and ISIS in Syria and Iraq.[1] This led to the passage of a law criminalizing becoming a foreign fighter in September 2014, and increasing police activity resulting in the arrests of several alleged terrorist recruiters and fighters throughout 2017.

While only about 50 fighters from Macedonia have been killed owing to their activity as jihadists in the Middle East, some critics (such as officials in neighboring Kosovo) claim that the country's imams have been instrumental in preaching a radical agenda that has indoctrinated their own fighters.[2] This has been reflected in the arrests of several radical imams, and the admission by the country's official Islamic Community that certain mosques operate outside of its control.

Nevertheless, the West has been far less helpful in Macedonia than it has in Kosovo and Albania in donating resources or personnel toward countering violent extremism projects, instead taking a highly controversial political role in the crisis since 2015, with key security issues neglected in favor of overt political goals.

To a large extent, this Western interference has been conditioned by a desire to solve the 26-year "name issue" (Greece has vetoed Macedonian NATO and EU membership until the country changes its name). In light of the antagonism from both Greece and Albania, Turkey—always a pivotal ally of Macedonia—has taken on even greater importance. After the failed Turkish coup of July 2016, Turkish President Recep Tayyip Erdogan seems to have expanded his popularity in Macedonia, and could prove a decisive voice in national politics. The exact role Turkey will play in Macedonian politics and security remains to be seen, but it is undeniable that, in a country with over 30 percent Muslims, this appeal and power is only likely to grow.

Islamist Activity

Islamist activity in Macedonia is most widespread in areas where the Muslim population—the vast majority of whom are ethnic Albanians—is concentrated: parts of the capital, Skopje, the towns and villages between Kumanovo and Tetovo (near the border with Kosovo), and towns like Gostivar, Debar, Kicevo and Struga located along the western border with Albania. However, ethnically mixed areas exist in other regions of the country as well, such as in the central mountain massif south of Skopje. Along with some enclaves in the west of the country, a residual Turkish population dating from Ottoman times is scattered in several villages in the east, near Stip and Radovis. As is the case with neighboring Kosovo and Albania, the number of new foreign fighters originating from Macedonia has sharply declined since 2016.

The organization that officially represents Macedonia's Muslim population of approximately 675,000 is the Islamic Community of Macedonia (ICM).[3] In recent years, few altercations or inter-religious problems have occurred, though the management of the Community and its possessions remains prone to politicization among ethnic Albanian parties.

As in other regional countries, Arab-funded and -trained young radicals have challenged Macedonian authority, though this trend seems to be waning. Several violent confrontations occurred in the years following the 2001 ethnic conflict, sparked by armed extremists seeking to install their candidates in Macedonia's mosques, especially in the capital, Skopje.[4] Later, in July 2010, the ICM's leading cleric, reis-ul-ulema Sulejman Rexhepi, admitted that the ICM had lost control over several Skopje mosques, following a fight and near-riot in a mosque under Wahhabi control.[5] And in September 2010, he publicly called upon U.S. and EU representatives to help the ICM counter the growing influence of radical Islam.[6] In 2016, some of the mosques involved were targeted by police as having provided ideological indoctrination to young Muslims who would then travel to Syria to fight.[7] This police activity has gone a long way toward solving the problem, but at the same time it has been used by nationalist Albanians to stoke distrust of the predominantly Christian Macedonian majority.

While international experts have warned for years about fundamentalist threats to Macedonia's stability, until the participation of Albanians in the Syrian jihad became public in 2014, most considered Islamic infighting to be little more than internal politicking between rival ethnic Albanian parties over property proceeds and other financial interests. Nevertheless, compared to a decade ago, fundamentalist Islam (in the form of veiled women, men in traditional garb and long beards) has become increasingly visible in daily life.[8]

While there is certainly some truth to charges by skeptics that Islamism is merely "business," the participation of local fighters in Syria and Iraq has provided evidence to the contrary. In late August 2016, while announcing the arrest in Turkey of five Macedonian Albanians en route to Syria, Interior Minister Mitko Chavkov stated that at least 25 other Macedonian citizens had been killed while fighting in the Syrian civil war, and 50 were presumed to still be there.[9] In its own Country Report on Terrorism 2016, the U.S. State Department reported that Macedonia had conducted three "significant" counter-terrorism operations during that year. The most significant one, a joint operation with Kosovo and Albania, resulted in the cumulative arrests of 23 ethnic Albanians over an ISIS-led plot to attack a soccer match between Israel and Albania.[10] More recently, in the summer of 2017, ISIS announced that the Balkans would become an area of terrorist operations in future.[11]

Rather than destroying existing Islamic institutions, Wahhabi extremists have sought instead to take them over where they can. To establish control, they have historically used NGOs, charities, publishing entities, domestic and international conferences, political events, "human-rights" activities, and various demonstrations.[12] At the same time, these radicals have expedited the goals of Saudi Arabia and other Islamic states by overseeing the construction of hundreds of foreign-funded mosques.[13] The Islamist activity that led to fighters going to the Middle East was concentrated in several mosques in Skopje and Tetovo that had long been associated with radical preachers. However, in many cases, authorities have still been unable to arrest these figures because there is no solid evidence that they have done anything illegal.[14]

The complexity of Islamic affairs in Macedonia is growing, as multiple internal and external actors vie for power and influence. Aside from the ICM and their Wahhabi opponents funded by the Gulf and other Islamic states, Turkey has a deep footprint in the country, owing to five centuries of Ottoman control. With the long-simmering feud between Turkish president Recep Tayyip Erdogan and controversial cleric Fethullah Gülen finally boiling over with a failed coup against Erdogan's government in July 2016, entrenched interests in Macedonia associated with both sides came under pressure. As the enmity between the rival Turkish figures continued into 2017, Macedonia came under tremendous pressure from Ankara to close schools associated with Gulen. However, it did not do so, as this would have been politically divisive and caused problems for a wide range of people who had no involvement with either side of the conflict.

The role of Turkey is particularly important when considering that Macedonia's main ethnic Albanian party, the Democratic Union for Integration (DUI), has members privately aligned with the rival Turkish camps. Ali Ahmeti (an ethnic Albanian who led the paramilitary National Liberation Army in the 2001 civil conflict) created the DUI and has been a coalition partner in almost all Macedonian governments since 2002. Diplomatic information alleges that it was actually the DUI's Ahmeti who vetoed a governmental proposal to close Gülen entities in Macedonia.[15]

Nevertheless, Turkish foreign policy continues to take a calculated position. Minister of Foreign Affairs Ahmed Davutoglu thus praised Ahmeti as a "factor of stability" in the Balkans during a visit to Skopje on September 27, 2017, just weeks before pivotal local elections.[16] At the same time, the DUI had entered an uneasy coalition with the formerly opposition Social Democratic Alliance of Macedonia (SDSM), due to heavy U.S. pressure. This would mean mutual support for one another's local candidates—a somewhat unusual practice—because the DUI feared the growth of Besa, the new pro-Turkish party that had thrown the traditional balance of power into total disarray in the previous December's parliamentary elections, eating into the DUI's base. With Muslims in the Balkans tending to support Erdogan, and with the long-ruling DUI perceived as corrupt, Turkish influence over local Muslim populations and parties should only grow over time. The December 2016 elections (Besa's first) proved that its appeal lay with not only conservative older Muslim voters, but also with young Albanians angered by perceived corruption among the established parties.

For its part, the Turkish government and various charities have made the most of their opportunity within the country.[17] Turkey is very active through its international development agency (TIKA) and supported NGOs in reaffirming the tangible signs of its Ottoman legacy in the country.[18] The Erdogan government has long considered Macedonia a key part of its neo-Ottoman foreign policy of "strategic depth."[19] Macedonia has welcomed dozens of major Turkish investors involved in everything from construction to management of the Skopje airport. These business and political ties have strengthened the bilateral relationship tremendously; indeed, when inaugurating the third Bosporus Bridge in August 2016, President Erdogan welcomed Macedonian President Gjorge Ivanov to the ceremony—one of a very small number of leaders to receive that invitation.[20]

For his part, President Ivanov has consistently been a strong supporter of Erdogan, for example defending the latter's reaction to 2013 protests in Turkey.[21] Since Turkey is a key ally, this support has (despite Erdogan's pro-Islamist administration) actually benefited Macedonia's fight against terrorism. Indeed, Ivanov's August 25th visit to Istanbul to commemorate the bridge opening coincided with the announcement of a joint police and intelligence operation which led to the arrest of five Albanians from Macedonia in Istanbul, who had reportedly been planning to join ISIS in Syria (discussed below).

Aside from foreign relations and state-level politics, the bedrock of funding for Islamist networks was established years ago, in often opaque ways, through NGOs and other entities. The official wealth of the ICM itself, in terms of funds, real estate and other assets, is neither publicly known nor discussed. Even less well-known is the total level of funding available to radical groups and the ways in which it is transmitted.

Part of this has to do with established tradition, such as the custom of communal payments seen in the construction of village mosques; locals can simply donate anonymously, drop cash in a box, and so on. Even when police have managed to trace some funds to extremist groups abroad, authoritative figures have never been publicly disclosed. Nor do Islamists, despite their frequent calls for officials to show greater transparency, detail the provenance or amounts of their own funding.[22] As a result, investigators have had to work deductively and, to some extent, rely on anecdotal or comparative information.

In general, officials believe that Islamists in Macedonia (as elsewhere in the region) employ a creative combination of methods to move money. Police sometimes reference the use of Islamic students returning from the Gulf as cash "mules." Other financial sources include proceeds from narcotics trafficking or the sale of items ranging from plastic chairs to silver and gold. To escape the attention of authorities, Islamists sometimes eschew large bank transactions, instead breaking up payments and deposits into smaller amounts.

Finally, funds also come in through donations from ideologically sympathetic businessmen, officials and Diaspora Muslims for religious projects such as mosques, schools and publications.[23] These donations are not always a secret; indeed, the donating country or organization is often prominently displayed on the entrance of the structure in question, or in the beginning of a book.

As discussed above, Islamist activity in Macedonia over the

past 25 years has been guided largely by outside interests, such as Saudi and other Gulf state charities and proselytizers. A limited interest has also been evidenced from Pakistani and Malaysian groups.[24] Often, global Islamist NGOs registered locally or via Western Europe are used as intermediaries (with the UK serving as a major hub). However, since the 1990s, relatively fewer suspicious charities have been allowed to register in the country, in comparison to Albania, Kosovo and Bosnia, due to a measure of resistance from Macedonian security officials.[25]

Specific Islamist activity has taken different forms. One key area is the strategic construction of mosques along major highways, high ridgelines, near pre-existing churches or in close proximity to other mosques. Between 2000 and 2010, over 300 mosques were built—88 alone between Skopje and Tetovo, the main ethnic Albanian-majority city, in northwestern Macedonia.[26] The sum expended was staggering, with costs estimated at $1.5-$2.5 million per mosque. According to the same report, Saudi Arabia alone committed over $1.2 billion from 2003-2013 for building mosques, providing education, and sending local Muslims on the Hajj throughout the Balkans.[27] Later, in July 2014, the cornerstone was laid for a Saudi-style, four-minaret mega-mosque in the Skopje district of Topansko Pole. Featuring an educational center, it was expected to be the largest mosque in Macedonia and among the largest in the Balkans. As of late 2017, it remained under construction.[28]

Aside from mosque construction, Islamists in and with ties to Macedonia have been active around the world. Owing to the transnational and diaspora relations of ethnic Albanians from Macedonia, who may have kin in Kosovo, Western Europe, or elsewhere, the issue cannot be understood as simply a national one. The infamous "Fort Dix Six" plot to attack a U.S. Army base in Ft. Dix, New Jersey a decade ago involved three ethnic Albanian émigrés from Macedonia, and another from Kosovo.[29] In Switzerland, the popular 2009 referendum banning minaret construction began after an Islamist group led by another Albanian originally from Macedonia agitated in favor of such building.[30]

At the same time, even before the Syrian crisis and rise of ISIS, Muslims from Macedonia had gone to join al-Qaeda's jihad against the United States and the Coalition in Afghanistan (an estimate published in the British media in 2010 put the number at approximately 50).[31] During a joint press conference with then-Macedonian Prime Minister Nikola Gruevski in January 2010, then-Israeli Foreign Minister Avigdor Lieberman stated that radical Islam in Macedonia and the Balkans was a major concern.[32] This comment came only four months before three Muslims from Macedonia participated in the controversial "humanitarian flotilla" to break the Israeli blockade of Gaza, organized by the Turkey-based Islamic charity Humanitarian Relief Foundation (IHH).[33] The Israeli perception of an Islamic terrorism threat was evident even in the summer of 2017, when an Israeli-organized cultural event in Skopje was guarded by a Mossad contingent considered unusually large by past standards.[34]

For years, security experts have warned about rising Islamism in Macedonia—albeit without arousing much attention. In 2012, dramatic evidence attesting to these developing radical trends emerged with a series of protests. The first large-scale protest occurred in the Albanian-majority town of Struga, ostensibly in reaction to an annual carnival in the nearby Christian village of Vevchani. The carnival is traditionally light-hearted, poking fun at world leaders, social trends, and general society. However, participants at the event mocked Islam, provoking groups of angry protestors to attack churches in Albanian and Macedonian Muslim-populated villages in western Macedonia, and to even stone a group of Christians on a bus.

In a large and unprecedented protest in Struga, men waving Albanian and green Islamic flags publicly denounced Christians. Although further investigation and input from intelligence officials revealed that there was a certain amount of local politics and financial interests behind the lurid affair, the demonstration confirmed the presence of extremists and their ability to organize violently on short notice.[35] Most troubling, perhaps, was that the whole incident became a high-level security concern. Top government leaders and foreign diplomats were forced to meet extensively and reaffirm their commitment to work together and overcome ethnic and religious differences.

A second, more serious protest occurred in the capital, Skopje, on May 4, 2012, after a police press conference reported the apprehension of several Albanian "Islamic extremists." The men had been detained after a massive police operation to find the killers of a group of young Macedonian fishermen who had been murdered execution-style, along with an older man who apparently witnessed the scene. The killings sparked the biggest manhunt in Macedonian history, dubbed "Operation Monster," in which 600 police officers were deployed. At subsequent protests in Skopje (with smaller ones in Tetovo and Gostivar), several thousand ethnic Albanian youth took to the streets, waving Albanian and Saudi flags and chanting "Allahu Akbar" and "death to the Christians." Some were seen wearing provocative shirts with slogans like "Islam will dominate the world" and demanding the establishment of a Greater Albania.[36]

The protest originated at the historic Yahya Pasha Mosque, which had been under Wahhabi control for at least 10 years (and which would be targeted again in more recent raids). Since the young protesters attacked the municipal office of the local (and ethnic Albanian) mayor in the Cair neighborhood of Skopje, security experts also read this as a sign that the extremists are now beyond the control of the ethnic Albanian political mainstream.[37] There were also reports of fights on public buses between Macedonian and Albanian youth and attacks by the latter on elderly Macedonians.

The trial of the suspected gunmen was deferred twice, and witnesses and family members of those killed were only able to face the defendants in court in December 2012 and January 2013.[38] Although police did not charge him with direct involvement, longtime Islamic radical Shukri Aliu was believed to have ignited the protests by calling for an Arab Spring uprising targeting the government, and seeking the participation of imams throughout the country.[39] Aliu was extradited from Kosovo at the end of 2012 in connection with physical attacks on several imams near the village of Kondovo that took place in 2005. In December 2015, a Skopje court overruled an appeal from the five men accused of the murders, upholding life sentences for the crime. This decision sparked complaints from ethnic Albanians, but no protests on a similar level were seen. However, media alleged that the Special Prosecutor's Office (set up in September 2015 to investigate a very opaque 'government wiretapping' affair) would like to revisit the case, so there is room in the future for further ethnic and religious politicization.[40]

In fact, the specific political developments accompanying Macedonia's political crisis are bound to increase inter-ethnic and inter-religious tensions. Unfortunately, the United States has directly if discreetly furthered this process, by supporting a relatively unpopular SDSM party after 2015. The party's nominal leader (and, from June 2017, prime minister), Zoran Zaev, had run a campaign in December 2016 of trying to win ethnic Albanian votes wherever they may be found (he campaigned indeed as far as Switzerland), promising ethnic concessions which the ethnic Albanian population had not even asked for.

Zaev did not win an outright majority, and was unable to form a government in December 2016. This led ethnic Albanian party leaders to draft a platform of ethnic demands (known as the 'Tirana Platform,' as it was drafted in Albanian Prime Minister Edi Rama's office in January 2017). By appeasing ethnic Albanian demands, Zaev was able to win their political support. The demands for ethnic "rights" were seen as ultranationalist and chauvinistic not only by Macedonians, but also by the country's Turkish, Roma Serb and Vlach populations, sparking nationwide protests that lasted until a violent incident in the parliament following the illegal election of an ethnic Albanian parliamentary speaker on April 27th.[41] The West quickly rushed to recognize the new Zaev-led government, which among other concessions, offered a draft language law, expanding mandatory rights for the usage of Albanian to the large parts of the country where no Albanians live.[42]

While it appeared that U.S. policy was meant simply to create conditions for electing a government that would change Macedonia's name and thus end the 26-year "name dispute" with Greece, allowing Macedonia to finally enter NATO and the EU, one long-term side effect of further concessions to Albanian nationalist demands is inevitably going to be the expansion of Islamist goals. This, coupled with feared resettlement of international Muslim migrants into Christian-inhabited areas exclusively, animated the debate ahead of the October 2017 elections, leaving Macedonians in a state of existential doubt over the West's long-term plan for their country.

Islamism and Society

The greatest defining—and most complicating—factor relating to Islamism in Macedonia is its intimate linkage with ethnic identification and ethnic-based politics. Local attitudes toward Islamic groups, and Islam in general, are not rigidly defined and remain in a perpetual state of flux, as does the general sense of ethnic identification among different groups, Christian and Muslim alike. This unique situation arguably makes a true understanding of Islam and society more difficult in Macedonia than in any other country in Europe. The specific conflation of Albanian hardline nationalism and Muslim affiliation makes this an incredibly combustible issue, hampering law enforcement and promoting a culture in which political negotiation and a perceived need for international mediation still predominate.

Nearly 70 percent of the national population of 2 million is composed of ethnic Macedonians, a Slavic people who speak a language similar to Bulgarian and Serbian. While most are Orthodox Christian, a small number are Muslim—holdovers from Ottoman times, when those who converted enjoyed special benefits. Ethnic Albanians, who comprise 25 percent of the population, are almost entirely Muslim, predominantly from the Gheg sub-group common to northern Albania and Kosovo. Other Muslim populations include Turks (four percent of the total population), Roma (around three percent), and about 17,000 Bosniaks.[43]

However, a 2011 Pew report on global Muslim population growth trends indicates that, through 2030, Macedonia will experience a higher projected increase in number of Muslims to non-Muslims (5.4%) than any other European country. Pew expects that by 2030 some 40.3% of the total Macedonian population will be Muslim. This demographic trend will have severe political and social implications.[44] However, it should be noted that the unexpected European migration crisis of 2015 will also alter the population balance in Northern European countries, which are far more attractive targets for terrorist attacks than is Macedonia. In fact, the long-expected demographic rise of Albanians could be tempered by trends of that population's outflow (such as the large numbers of Albanian asylum-seekers during the migration crisis indicated). The fact that the vast majority of their asylum requests failed will not stop what are essentially economic migration attempts.

The chronic polarization between ethnic Macedonians and Albanians is, however, overblown and both populations have general tolerance for one another. This is where foreign (and specifically, Western) political interference has proven so negative, in deliberately politicizing and keeping alive animosities without reason. The polarization intensified during the 2001 conflict, when Kosovo-led Albanians took up arms, allegedly for more rights and civic employment opportunities, in the so-called National Liberation Army of subsequent DUI president Ali Ahmeti. Under international pressure, a peace treaty—the Ohrid Framework Agreement—was signed shortly thereafter by leaders of the four major political parties existing at that time.

The agreement stipulated a quota system for issues like public sector hiring, flag and language use, and so on. Thus followed a territorial decentralization that amounted to political horse-trading between the then-ruling coalition of the Socialist SDSM and the DUI, an ethnic Albanian party formed by the leadership of the former rebel group, the NLA. The decentralization institutionalized the ascendancy of Islam over large and territorially contiguous swathes of the population, particularly in northern and western Macedonia, where the majority of the country's Albanian Muslims live.

On a broader level, the major social issue within the Muslim community is the gap between the younger and older generations of Muslims. Young Islamists, confident in their own studies in Arab states, tend to depict older leaders of Macedonia's Islamic Community as "communists" who do not understand Islam correctly, due to their different experience growing up in the former Yugoslavia.[45] Yet the perceived discrepancy is rarely put to the test (say, through a televised theological debate). Rather, it is generally carried out through violence and intimidation. Since intimidation is often carried out subtly and occurs within tight-knit communities, it is seldom reported.[46] For the time being, therefore, the primary victims of Islamist activity in Macedonia remain the country's Muslims themselves.

Islamism and the State

In Macedonia, the state's ability to counteract extremism and engage it is conditioned by a unique factor that makes it much more complex than in other regional countries: that is, the increasing tendency of political parties from the ethnic Albanian minority to blur the boundaries between ethnic and religious identity. This tendency has been seen in social and political life, but it also has impeded the ability of Macedonian authorities to both pass counter-terrorism legislation and conduct operations. When an Albanian is arrested because of a religiously motivated crime, a backlash often arises that the individual is the victim of ethnic discrimination; and when that individual is arrested for nationalist extremism, the counter-argument is made of alleged religious bias. In this situation, police have had to tread carefully, and this more than anything else explains the relatively small number of terrorism-related arrests compared to Kosovo and Albania, where no such ethnic minority problem exists.

Because of the migrant crisis and the Syrian civil war, the Macedonian state has had to divert resources and attention away from dealing with the domestic Islamist threat. The political crisis began in early 2015, and neatly coincided with the European migration crisis, which saw some one million illegal migrants and refugees transit Macedonia from Greece en route to Western Europe. Keeping control of this flow required considerable police and military assets to be redirected to the country's southern border with Greece and its northern one with Serbia, under the law on crisis situations that was declared by President Gjorge Ivanov in August 2015 and later extended.[47]

In line with a U.S. request and legal assistance, Macedonia passed a foreign fighters law banning the participation of citizens in foreign conflicts on September 3, 2014.[48] While no one voted against it, several prominent members of the ethnic Albanian coalition partner, DUI, abstained. Similar laws have been passed in other Balkan countries since 2014. The law, which threatens any returning fighters with jail time, is meant mostly to be a deterrent to aspiring jihadis. In Macedonia, it provided a solid base for the state to begin systematically targeting known radical preachers, recruiters and returned foreign fighters from the Middle East.

The results can be seen in several related sweeps by special police, under the title Operation Kelija (Cell). In early August 2015, police targeted mosques, NGO offices and residences associated with recruiters and fighters for ISIS, in Skopje, Tetovo, Gostivar, Kumanovo and Struga.[49] Nine suspects were arrested, including Rexhep Memishi, a well-known radical imam opposed to the ICM. Another 27 suspects were at large, believed to be in the Middle East. The U.S. Embassy in Skopje praised the action as a contribution to regional and global efforts against the "evil of terrorism."[50] In March 2016, a court sentenced six of the individuals (including the self-proclaimed imam) to seven years in prison.

In July 2016, the operation continued with a further sweep and arrest of four more ISIS-related Islamists.[51] The third part was completed in August 2016, when Turkish police extradited five Macedonian Albanians suspected of having links with ISIS. They had been arrested in the Aksaray neighborhood of Istanbul while preparing to go to Syria.[52] Information from security sources indicates that this was not the first time Macedonian and Turkish police have cooperated on identifying and arresting Macedonian nationals associated with Islamist groups on Turkish soi l.

The success of these operations is ironic. While Macedonian police seem finally able to act against Islamic radicals with less danger of causing backlash from local Muslims, the fact that they have to deal with this threat at all indicates the unfortunate outcome of two decades of extremist ideology and infrastructure development in the country. The involvement of young jihadists from Macedonia and other Balkan countries in Syria since 2013 is proof of the effectiveness of the ideological, financial and logistical strategies practiced by radical supporters, years before the Syrian crisis provided a trigger for young Muslims to make the transformation from extremists to jihadists.

While Macedonia remains frozen out of the EU, owing to the unresolved disagreement with EU member Greece over the country's name (Greece has a province called Macedonia as well), it has nevertheless enjoyed robust security cooperation with neighbors Serbia, Bulgaria, and especially Turkey. Indeed, the level of security cooperation with these countries in the future will greatly influence Macedonia's ability to fight extremism at home. One of the major problems for non-EU members (like Macedonia, Serbia and Turkey) is that they are excluded from the EU's database system that has been used for cataloging asylum seekers (EURODAC). Given the vast number of migrants who have crossed through these countries in recent years, and in light of ongoing concerns that terrorists may be among them, these non-EU countries are being left to create bilateral or otherwise special methods of cooperation and intelligence-sharing. Since the mass migration phenomenon is targeting Northern Europe, not the Balkans, it would be more in the interests of the EU to cooperate with these countries than the other way around. However, for various reasons, the bloc has done an insufficient job in cooperating.[53]

In its 2017 report previously cited, the State Department notes that "Macedonia's capacity to detect and deter acts of terrorism without international support needs to be strengthened." Similarly, the report cites "uneven" implementation and a "lack of capacity" from the Macedonian side regarding development of a 2015 five-year CVE strategy.[54]

Hopefully, with the creation of a government in mid-2017 amenable to current U.S. interests, there is hope that trans-Atlantic cooperation will be more fruitful. Nevertheless, in the wake of the 2015-17 political crisis, Albanian society has become more polarized within and between ethnicities, and it is clear that Islamist factions will try to promote their own interests in the absence of national unity.

Endnotes

1. Adrian Shtumi, "Ethnic Albanian Foreign Fighters in Iraq and Syria," Combating Terrorism Center at West Point, April 30, 2015, https://www.ctc.usma.edu/posts/ethnic-albanian-foreign-fighters-in-iraq-and-syria/.
2. This consensus is based on comments for the author

made by several senior Kosovo officials since 2015.

3. The ICM's official website is www.bim.org.mk. The BIM acronym comes from the Albanian-language version of the name, Bashkesia Fetare Islame. Note that the institution is often referred to by its Macedonian name and acronym, Islamska Verska Zaednica (IVZ). International sources also refer to it as the Islamic Religious Community (IRC). All of these acronyms refer to the same official body.
4. The most infamous examples of Salafi violence date from the turbulent reign of former Skopje *mufti* Zenun Berisha, who used a sort of Islamist private guard to take over several mosques, impose preferred candidates for jobs, and generally assert his authority. Accounts of intimidation, beatings and attacks against moderates such as former *Reis* Arif Emini and former Skopje *mufti* Taxhedin Bislimi were widely reported in the local media. A comprehensive account of these events, citing some of the leaders involved, is given in Christopher Deliso, *The Coming Balkan Caliphate: the Threat of Radical Islam to Europe and the West*, p. 82-86, Praeger Security International, 2007.
5. Svetlana Jovanovska and Branko Gjorgeski, "Radical Islam In Macedonia Worries Western Observers," *WAZ/EU Observer*, July 8, 2010, https://euobserver.com/news/30446.
6. "Macedonia: Moderate Muslims Seek Help Against Sect," Associated Press, September 20, 2010, http://www.sandiegouniontribune.com/sdut-macedonia-moderate-muslims-seek-help-against-sect-2010sep20-story.html.
7. "Special forces conduct raid against IS," *The Economist Intelligence Unit*, August 12, 2015, http://country.eiu.com/article.aspx?articleid=833431267&Country=Macedonia&topic=Politics&subtopic_2.
8. See Deliso, *The Coming Balkan Caliphate: the Threat of Radical Islam to Europe and the West*.
9. "MVR so detali: makedonski drzhavjani uapseni vo turtsija planirale zaminuvane na boishtata vo sirija kako del od id," ("MOI details: Macedonian nationals arrested in Turkey planned departure battlefields in Syria as part of

ISIS,") *Kurir*, August 27, 2016, http://kurir.mk/makedonija/vesti/mvr-so-detali-makedonski-drzhavjani-uapseni-vo-turtsija-planirale-zaminuvane-na-boishtata-vo-sirija-kako-del-od-id/.

10. *Country Reports on Terrorism 2016*, United States Department of State, July 2017, https://www.state.gov/documents/organization/272488.pdf.
11. "ISIS Threatens Terror Campaign in the Balkans," *Balkan Insight*, June 8, 2017, http://www.balkaninsight.com/en/article/isis-wows-to-wreak-vengeance-on-balkans-in-new-threat-06-08-2017.
12. Islamic NGOs in Macedonia include both international franchises and local entities. Some belong to umbrella organizations, allowing them to participate in a variety of events internationally, and thereby network with likeminded ideologues from Islamic states.
13. Bojan Pancevski, "Saudis Fund Balkan Muslims Spreading Hate Of The West," *Sunday Times* (London), March 28, 2010, https://www.thetimes.co.uk/article/saudis-fund-balkan-muslims-spreading-hate-of-the-west-mdmz2lv8w0r. Further factual details are cited in "Milijarda Evra Investirani Co Radikalniot Islam (Billion-euro Investment In Radical Islam)," *Nova Makedonija*, July 6, 2010.
14. According to a senior security official, as of May 2016 some 80 such Islamists were being kept under 24-hour surveillance, as they could not be arrested, but still posed a potential threat. Author interview with Macedonian security official, May 2016.
15. Author interview with Macedonian official, August 2016.
16. "Davutoglu: Ahmeti vital for Macedonia's stability," MIA, September 27, 2017, http://www.mia.mk/en/Inside/RenderSingleNews/61/133878717#.
17. For example, in the year 2010 alone, some 80 Islamic students from Turkey were known to be studying at the *madrassa* in the eastern town of Stip—with an announced plan for increasing this number in coming years to 500, and eventually to 1,500. "Turski Studenti Go Sardisaa Stip (Turkish Students Occupy Stip)," *Dnevnik* (Skopje), December 28, 2010.

18. For one example, Turkish State Minister Faruk Celik visited Skopje in December 2010 to mark the TIKA's renovation of the magnificent 15th-century mosque of Mustafa Pasha. He also met with top leaders of the country's Islamic community. See "Turkey Says To Continue Repairing Ottoman Arts In Macedonia," *World Bulletin*, December 21, 2010, http://www.worldbulletin.net/servisler/haberYazdir/67671/haber.
19. For more on the doctrine of "strategic depth" developed by then-Turkish Foreign Minister Ahmed Davutoglu, see Ioannis N. Grigoriadis, "The Davutoglu Doctrine and Turkish Foreign Policy," Hellenic Foundation for European and Foreign Policy (ELIAMEP), April 2010, http://www.eliamep.gr/wp-content/uploads/2010/05/ΚΕΙΜΕΝΟ-ΕΡΓΑΣΙΑΣ-8_2010_IoGrigoriadis1.pdf.
20. "3rd Bosphorus bridge inaugurated," *TRT World*, August 25, 2016, http://www.trtworld.com/turkey/3rd-bosphorus-bridge-inaugurated-172455.
21. Sinisa Jakov Marucic. "Macedonians Divided Over President's Support for Erdogan," *Balkan Insight*, July 8, 2013. http://www.balkaninsight.com/en/article/macedonian-president-s-whole-hearted-support-for-endogan-divides-critics/2027/2.
22. For an example of this prevailing hostile attitude, note the comments of Islamic NGO leader Bekir Halimi to a journalist: "We are fully entitled to receive funding from both governmental and non-governmental sources from Saudi Arabia." See Pancevski, "Saudis Fund Balkan Muslims Spreading Hate Of The West," The article also notes that Halimi "refuses to name the sources of his funding."
23. Pancevski, "Saudis Fund Balkan Muslims Spreading Hate Of The West," The article also notes that Halimi "refuses to name the sources of his funding."
24. [14] Deliso, *The Coming Balkan Caliphate,* 73-78.
25. [115] For example, a former Macedonian counterintelligence chief, Zoran Mitevski, recounted that in 1996 U.S. diplomats accused him of being "undemocratic" when he blocked several terror-linked Saudi charities from registering in the country. Deliso, *The Coming Balkan Caliphate,* 81.

26. "Milijarda Evra Investirani Co Radikalniot Islam (Billion-Euro Investment In Radical Islam)."
27. "Milijarda Evra Investirani Co Radikalniot Islam (Billion-Euro Investment In Radical Islam)." These figures roughly correspond with those given in Pancevski, "Saudis Fund Balkan Muslims Spreading Hate Of The West," as well as with figures given to the author by Macedonian security officials.
28. "New Mosque Built in Topansko Pole Will Be the Biggest Mosque in Macedonia," Indepedendent.mk, July 28, 2014.
29. Three of the men involved in the plot, brothers born in the Albanian-majority town of Debar, were arrested for their role in the failed attacks on U.S. soldiers at Ft. Dix. Garentina Kraja and William J. Kole, "Brothers Behind Fort Dix Plot Were From Pro-U.S. Enclave," Associated Press, May 10, 2007, https://www.seattletimes.com/nation-world/brothers-behind-fort-dix-plot-were-from-pro-us-enclave/.
30. Devorah Lauter, "Swiss Voters OK Ban On Minarets," *Los Angeles Times*, November 30, 2009, http://articles.latimes.com/2009/nov/30/world/la-fg-swiss-minaret30-2009nov30.
31. Pancevski, "Saudis Fund Balkan Muslims Spreading Hate Of The West," *The Sunday Times (London),* March 28, 2010, https://www.thetimes.co.uk/article/saudis-fund-balkan-muslims-spreading-hate-of-the-west-mdmz2lv8w0r. See also "Vahabisti Vrvuvaat Borci Za Dzihad Vo Makedonija" ("Wahhabis Recruit Fighters For Jihad In Macedonia"), *Vecer*, March 29, 2010. These claims correspond with testimony made by different Macedonian security officials and local Muslims to the author since 2004.
32. A summary of the foreign minister's statements are available on the website of the Israeli Ministry of Foreign Affairs (www.mfa.gov.il).
33. Goce Mihajloski, "Makedonskite Humanitarsi Se Vratija Od Israel" ("Macedonian Humanitarians Returned From Israel"), *A1 Televizija* (Skopje), June 5, 2010.
34. This insight comes from the comments of a Macedo-

nian Jewish Community leader to the author, who was also present at the event and can confirm the Israeli security delegation's size.

35. See Chris Deliso, "After Macedonia's Islamic Protests, Investigators Search for Significance amidst a Confusing Array of Motives and Clues," www.balkanalysis.com, February 13, 2012, http://www.balkanalysis.com/macedonia/2012/02/13/after-macedonias-islamist-protest-investigators-search-for-significance-amidst-confusing-array-of-motives-and-clues/.
36. "Macedonia protests signal surge of radical Islam," *Euractiv*, May 14, 2012, http://www.euractiv.com/enlargement/protests-macedonia-signal-radica-news-512663.
37. Author interview with Macedonian security official, June 2012.
38. Sinisa Marusic, "Macedonia Mass Murder Trial Witnesses 'Saw Gunmen," *Balkan Insight*, January 18, 2013. http://www.balkaninsight.com/en/article/witnesses-saw-armed-men-at-skopje-s-mass-murder-site.
39. "Shukri Aliu Povikuval na Arapska Prolet vo Makedonijua," ("Shukri Aliu Called for an Arab Spring in Macedonia"), *Sitel TV*, December 6, 2012, http://www.sitel.com.mk/shukri-aliu-povikuval-na-arapska-prolet-vo-makedonija.
40. Sinisa Jakov Marusic, "Macedonia Upholds Albanians' 'Terrorist Murder' Sentences," *Balkan Insight*, December 14, 2015, http://www.balkaninsight.com/en/article/macedonia-court-confirms-terrorist-murders-sentence-12-14-2015.
41. "Macedonian Parliament's New Ethnic Albanian Speaker Enters Office," RFE/RL, May 3 , 2017, https://www.rferl.org/a/macedonia-parliament-speaker-xhaferi-enters-office/28466113.html.
42. On November 15, 2017, the Macedonian parliament began debating the draft language law, a process that was expected to be contentious and last for several months. See, "Parliament to vote on draft law on the use of languages," MIA, November 15, 2017, http://english.republika.mk/parliament-to-vote-on-draft-law-on-the-use-of-languages/.
43. These numbers derive from the 2002 national census.

The data is available in several PDF files on the official website of the State Statistical Office of Republic of Macedonia, www.stat.gov.mk.

44. *The Future of the Global Muslim Population: Projections for 2010-2030* (Pew Forum on Religion and Public Life 2011). The relevant part of the report is available online at http://www.pewforum.org/future-of-the-global-muslim-population-regional-europe.aspx.
45. "Opasnost Od Radikalizam I U Macedonikija" ("Danger From Radicalism In Macedonia Too"), *Radio Free Europe/Radio Liberty*, September 11, 2010. In the author's personal experience, the meme of "old Communists" (older, traditionalist Muslims) as being allegedly ignorant is a very pervasive one, and invoked frequently by Islamists in the country.
46. Some examples include: physical attacks against clerics deemed to be in the way of Islamists and their goals; pressure for females to wear conservative religious dress; orders for moderate Muslims not to associate with Christians; injunctions against shopkeepers against selling alcohol; perpetuation of the archaic custom of arranged marriages for teenage girls; threats against young Muslims seen to be engaging in Western "hedonism;" violence against Muslim journalists seeking to report on any such issues, and so on.
47. For a detailed account of Macedonia's security response to the migrant crisis, see Chris Deliso, "Macedonian Migration Policy and the Future of Europe," *Balkanalysis.com*, December 23, 2015, http://www.balkanalysis.com/macedonia/2015/12/23/macedonian-migration-policy-and-the-future-of-europe/.
48. See Chris Deliso, "Asymmetric Threats Challenge Macedonia before Easter and Elections," *Balkanalysis.com*, April 25, 2016, http://www.balkanalysis.com/macedonia/2016/04/25/asymmetric-threats-challenge-macedonia-before-easter-and-elections/.
49. Sinisa Jakov Marusic, "Macedonian Police Targets ISIS Suspects," *Balkan Insight*, August 6, 2015, http://www.balkaninsight.com/en/article/macedonia-launches-anti-terror-busts-08-06-2015.
50. Sinisa Jakov Marusic, "Macedonia Arrests Nine ISIS

Suspects," *Balkan Insight*, August 7, 2015, http://www.balkaninsight.com/en/article/macedonia-arrests-nine-isis-suspects-08-07-2015.

51. Maja Zuvela, "Macedonian police arrest four suspected of Islamic State links," Reuters, July 9, 2016, http://www.reuters.com/article/us-mideast-crisis-macedonia-idUSKCN0ZP0RV.
52. "Kelija 3: Five Jihadists from Macedonia, Members of ISIL, Arrested," *Vecer*, August 27, 2016, http://vecer.mk/makedonija/kjelija-3-uapseni-5-dzhihadisti-od-makedonija-chlenovi-na-isis.
53. Chris Deliso, "Mistrust and Different Priorities Vex EU-Macedonian Security Cooperation," *Balkanalysis.com*, May 27, 2016, http://www.balkanalysis.com/blog/2016/05/27/mistrust-and-different-priorities-vex-eu-macedonian-security-cooperation/.
54. *Country Reports on Terrorism 2016*, op. cit.

47 The Netherlands

Quick Facts

Population: 17,084,719 (July 2017 est.)
Area: 41,543 sq km
Ethnic Groups: Dutch 77.4%, EU 6.2%, Turkish 2.3%, Moroccan 2.3%, Indonesian 2.1%, Surinamese 2%, other 7.7% (2017 est.)
Government Type: Parliamentary constitutional monarchy
GDP (official exchange rate): $824.5 billion (2017 est.)

Source: CIA World FactBook (Last Updated April 2018)

Introduction

Historically, the Netherlands has been a country renowned for its religious tolerance. In the Golden Age of the 17th and 18th centuries, the Republic of the United Provinces served as a haven for Jews and Protestants fleeing persecution in other parts of Europe. Muslim immigrants began to join their ranks in the late 19th century. Decades later, as it sought cheap labor during the 1960s, the Dutch government actively encouraged immigration from Indonesia and Suriname, both Muslim-majority countries and former Dutch colonies. Such days, however, have long since passed; ideological conflicts abroad now serve as magnets for aspiring Dutch jihadists, while xenophobia, the refugee crisis, and the looming threat of Islamic terrorism have driven the adoption of increasingly restrictive immigration and asylum policies. Despite Dutch efforts to proactively counter radicalization and encourage integration, this social transformation has allowed Islamists to push the political envelope and expose a values gap between the Dutch majority and its immigrant Muslim population.

Islamist Activity

As in many European countries, the Netherland's current primary concern regarding Islamist activity is the foreign fighter phenomenon. Since March 2013, the Office of the Dutch National Coordinator for Counterterrorism and Security (NCTV) has tracked increasing radicalization among Dutch youth and a willingness to become "jihadi travelers:" men and women who leave the Netherlands to fight in foreign conflicts. NCTV's chief Dick Schoof has warned that, in turn, the experiences of these individuals on the battlefield is likely to make them "highly radicalized, traumatized and with a strong desire to commit violence, thus posing a significant threat to this country"[1] upon their return. Homegrown radical rhetorical movements like Behind Bars, Street Daw'ah, and Shariah4Holland have transformed into actual jihadist networks, sending core members abroad to fight, while a wider group of supporters at home supports their efforts with propaganda, hate crimes, and public demonstrations that, according to the Dutch General Intelligence and Security Service (AIVD), "encourage anti-democratic and intolerant values… creating a climate in which the use of violence becomes more acceptable."[2] These trends have prompted the NCTV to maintain an elevated "substantial" (Level 4 of 5) threat assessment since 2013.

Reports of terrorist financing activities and the dissemination of jihadist propaganda in support of al-Shabaab[3] indicates that Somalia may be a destination for some Dutch foreign fighters. However, the Middle East is the greater magnet: roughly 285 Dutch citizens are known to have joined extremist causes in Syria and Iraq. Of that number, 55 have been killed—five as suicide bombers—and roughly 50 have returned.[4] With the recapture of most ISIS-controlled territory, the AIVD expects the number of returnees to increase significantly in the coming year.[5] These battle-hardened returnees (including an increasing number of women and children)[6] may be more open to attacks either directed or inspired by ISIS, al-Qaeda, or other jihadist organizations. An online ISIS call for a terror attack on Utrecht's stadium during the 2017 European women's soccer championships confirms that the Netherlands remains on the radar of jihadist groups,[7] likely due to its involvement in the anti-ISIS coalition.[8] Moreover, throughout 2017, the NCTV warned of a higher probability of a terrorist attack after investigations discovered an increase in the number of cross-border ISIS networks along with caches of arms and ammunition.[9] The results of the Pew Research

Center's Spring 2017 Global Attitudes survey reported that 67% of Dutch citizens consider ISIS to be the top threat facing the country.[10]

Beyond the criminal foreign fighter threat, other legal Islamist organizations in the Netherlands represent causes for concern, chief among them the Dutch Salafist movement. The NCTV differentiates Salafist doctrine into three "strands:" apolitical Salafism, which encourages da'wa (proselytization) and isolation from non-Muslim society; political Salafism, which promotes engagement in society in order to advance the group's specific religious objectives; and jihadi Salafism, undoubtedly the most extreme of the three, as it glorifies violence against non-believers.[11] While the risks posed by jihadi Salafism are much greater and more immediate than those of the other two strands, the AIVD's 2017 annual report nevertheless expressed alarm with the overall movement's use of intimidation, intolerance, and deliberate polarization as well as its potential role as a recipient of unsavory foreign financing.[12] The NCTV concurred, warning that even da'wa (proselytization) undermines the democratic legal order, endorsing discrimination against outsiders and suppressing forms of dissent against the doctrine.[13]

Despite the doctrine's anti-democratic nature, liberal Dutch religious freedom laws allowed Salafism to grow largely unhindered from the mid-1980s through the early 2000s.[14] Ideological momentum appeared to slow briefly in the face of government and civilian (both Muslim and non-Muslim) opposition; after the 2004 murder of film director Theo Van Gogh, the Dutch government increased its pressure on Salafi centers that served as potential sites of radicalization, even deporting imams of the al-Fourkaan mosque whose proselytization was dangerous enough for the government to declare them personae non grata.[15] However, the movement began gaining strength again in 2014 as Dutch Salafists responded to heightened interest driven by the ongoing conflicts in the Middle East and North Africa with new recruiting tactics.[16] Savvy social media use and a new generation of traveling Salafi preachers, typically Netherlands natives who preach in Dutch, have expanded the movement's access to a greater number of potential converts. While they espouse expansion of the faith among non-practicing Muslims rather than violence and jihad,[17] the AIVD notes that even these da'wa organizations "have again hardened their tone after a period of relative moderation, becoming more anti-integration, intolerantly isolationist and hostile to any form of dissenting thought."[18]

Key Salafist institutions include the el-Tawheed mosque in Amsterdam, the al-Fourkaan mosque in Eindhoven, the as-Sunnah mosque in The Hague, and the Islamic Foundation for Education and Transmission of Knowledge (ISOOK) in Tilburg.[19] Of these, the al-Fourkaan mosque is the oldest, and the number of prominent orthodox Muslim leaders that it has produced (including Ahmad Salam, considered by many to be the most influential Salafi preacher in the Netherlands) is a sign of its influence. However, the mosque has also been linked to a number of individuals who have gone on to commit violent acts, including at least three of the 9/11 hijackers,[20] foreign fighters in Kashmir, [21] and rumored funders of al-Qaeda.[22] The AIVD remains wary of this web of al-Fourkaan associations and continues to track them in annual dossiers and reports while advising the mosque to be cautious when issuing invitations to guests. In December 2015, for example, acting on NCTV guidance, Eindhoven mayor Rob van Gijzel barred seven controversial imams from speaking at the mosque because of their past glorification of violence committed in the name of Islam.[23]

The Muslim Brotherhood is active in the Netherlands, but much less so than in other European states. In the early 2000s, the AIVD cautioned that the Brotherhood's attempted engagement with Dutch policy leaders, politicians, academics, and other public figures masked an "ultimate aim—although never stated openly—to create, then implant and expand, an ultra-Orthodox Muslim bloc inside Western Europe."[24] However, the fact that the Brotherhood has not been mentioned in any AIVD public reporting from the last decade suggests that their influence is too low to be a significant cause for concern.[25]

Other international Islamist groups may appeal to particular Muslim minority communities residing in the Netherlands because of their ties to specific ethnicities or embrace of nationalist causes. The main concern about such groups is that they threaten peaceful integration of these minorities into their host culture. A prime example is the schools and followers of Turkish scholar Fethullah

Gülen. A 2008 investigation into the movement's presence in the Netherlands found that Gülen-inspired schools promoted "anti-integrative behavior," and in response the government significantly reduced the level of funding it had previously provided to the movement.[26] Nonetheless, Gülenism continues to arouse suspicions and foster antagonism even among different elements of the Dutch Turkish community: after the failed Turkish military coup of July 2016, which Ankara alleges was masterminded by Gülen, a Turkish state news organization published a controversial list of all Gülen-affiliated organizations and individuals in the Netherlands. The Dutch government angrily denounced this foreign interference in their domestic affairs, but many concerned parents withdrew their children from the "Gülen-list" schools, resulting in a 20 percent loss to the collective student body.[27]

Similarly, the Moroccan Arrahmane mosque in Amsterdam is the headquarters of the Dutch branch of Tablighi Jama'at. Although Tablighi Jama'at is in principle an apolitical movement, the Dutch authorities have expressed concern that its ideology may further the "social isolation and radicalization" of vulnerable elements within the Moroccan immigrant community.[28] Internationally, in recent years, the movement has increasingly come to be seen as an incubator for aspiring terrorists. Many European recruits are rumored to have used Tablighi connections as a pathway into Pakistan, where they then disappeared into the jihadi training camps of the Federally Administered Tribal Areas.[29]

Finally, the radical pan-Islamist organization Hizb ut-Tahrir also maintains a small presence in the Netherlands. Although the number of its followers is believed to be in the low hundreds, the NCTV's 2016 threat assessments note increased cooperation between Hizb ut-Tahrir and various Salafist organizations, in spite of their ideological differences, driven in part by the elevated tension in the general public discourse over Islam.[30]

Islamism and Society

As of 2016 (the latest such data available), the Pew Research Center estimated that the 1.2 million Muslims in the Netherlands account for 7.1% of the total population.[31] The two largest demographics within this population are Turks (approximately 37 percent of the total Muslim population) and Moroccans (roughly 36 percent).[32] Other large Muslims communities come from Syria, Suriname, Afghanistan, Iraq, Somalia, Pakistan, and Iran.[33] Several thousand native Dutch converts and children of second-generation Muslim immigrants comprise the last piece of the multifaceted Dutch Muslim community.[34]

According to one assessment of Islam in the Netherlands, "whereas today many of the Dutch majority population support the idea of migrants adopting Dutch norms and values, the migrants themselves aspire to a combination of independent cultural development."[35] While it is certainly possible to debate the truth of this statement, there are several other important factors that create a gap between Muslim immigrant communities and the rest of Dutch society. The average age of the Muslim population is much lower than that of the country in general, at 25 years of age for Muslims and 38 for non-Muslims.[36] This age gap, taken in combination with discrepancies in levels of education achieved and language ability, poses a challenge to the seamless integration sought by the Dutch authorities, potentially even increasing the sentiments of disaffection and alienation that can lead to radicalization. The diverse nature of the Muslim community has also prevented any kind of large-scale, viable political movement from forming in support of its varied interests and concerns.[37]

At 2.4% of the country's overall population,[38] Turks make up the largest Muslim community in the Netherlands, and the infrastructure that exists to support them is quite sizable. The main Muslim organizations within the Turkish community belong to mosques under the control of the Diyanet (the Turkish religious affairs directorate in Ankara) or to the non-governmental Milli Görüs movement, which is headquartered in Cologne, Germany.[39] This directorate maintains significant power over its diaspora community in the Netherlands, including the right to appoint imams for Diyanet-controlled mosques,[40] although all imams are required by the Dutch government to take a year-long "integration course" before they are permitted to practice in the country.[41] Diyanet operates through two larger umbrella organizations: the Turkish Islamic

Cultural Foundation (TICF, founded in 1979) and the Dutch Islamic Foundation (ISN, founded 1982).[42] Diyanet mosques are heavily influenced by the course of the Turkish government; for example, Ankara's increasingly Islamist stance in recent years may be tied to the parallel increase in Salafism among the Turkish communities in the Netherlands.[43] Traditionally, the government-controlled official nature of Diyanet has kept it distinct from Milli Görüs. For decades, in fact, the Turkish government was openly hostile to the group, suspicious of the multiple Islamist parties that sprang up in its wake.

Moroccans constitute the second-largest Muslim community in the Netherlands, controlling a full 40 percent of all Dutch mosques.[44] Although the majority of Moroccan immigrants appear to have integrated well into Dutch society, the demographic is disproportionately represented in the government's threat assessments of potential jihadists. AIVD's 2014 and 2015 reports affirmed that the majority of Dutch foreign fighters in Syria are also Moroccan.[45] There has been a corresponding increase in angry public rhetoric and anti-Moroccan discrimination;[46] in one particularly high-profile example, Geert Wilders, the leader of the nationalist Partij voor de Vrijheid (Party for Freedom, or PVV), started a chant at a rally calling for "fewer Moroccans" in the country.

The Syrian conflict has catalyzed changing attitudes among many Dutch citizens as the wave of refugees seeking asylum in the EU brings the conflict closer to home. At the EU Migration Summit in 2015, the Netherlands agreed to accept over the course of two years an additional 7,000 resettled asylum seekers who had originally arrived elsewhere in Europe.[47] The Dutch government has since stated that Syrian asylum seekers represented nearly half of all the arrived refugees in the Netherlands that year (approximately 27,700 out of a total 58,880).[48] As the November 2015 attacks in Paris made clear, foreign fighters en route to Europe from Syria could easily take advantage of the chaos caused by the refugee crisis to return unnoticed.

Consequently, the famous Dutch tolerance has decreased and been replaced by rising xenophobia in the wake of the Syrian conflict and the refugee crisis. In September 2016, the Pew Research Center reported that 61 percent of Dutch citizens think that refugees will increase terrorism in the country; in the same poll, a full third of Dutch respondents said that growing diversity made the Netherlands a worse place to live.[49] As is the case across Western Europe, the presence of large Muslim communities and questions of integration have clearly provoked sentiments of unease and fear among neighbors who blame multiculturalism for increased violence and other social ills.[50] Indeed, the AIVD has noted how radical elements may attempt to exploit these sentiments:

> …the Islamists involved are indeed aware of the "favorable" polarizing effect of Islamist-inspired violent activities. Such violent activities promote the prejudices of the Dutch population about all Muslims. As a result thereof, Muslims also increasingly get the idea that they are alienated from the Dutch society and the chance that they become susceptible to radical ideas becomes bigger.[51]

The NCTV assesses that this polarized climate poses a concrete risk to Dutch society, as it may contribute to the radicalization of a lone wolf actor or small domestic cells—either from would-be jihadists or from anti-Muslim extremist groups.[52]

Islamism and the State

As attacks in Paris, Brussels, and Istanbul rocked Europe in 2014 and 2015, the Dutch government proactively took steps to lead anti-extremist efforts on the continent while simultaneously strengthening counterterrorism legislation and border security measures. The Netherlands serves as a member of the Global Coalition to Counter ISIL, conducting airstrikes on behalf of the coalition, and maintaining a liaison in U.S. Central Command. Amsterdam also recognizes the importance of travel intervention in keeping foreign fighters from leaving its territory. In 2017, the Dutch government adopted legislation that allows for harsh administrative sanctions linked to citizenship and freedom of movement, permitting: the revocation or withdrawal of a dual citizen's Dutch nationality if he or she is deemed to have joined a terrorist organization; the imposition of a travel ban on individuals whose intention in traveling poses a threat to national security (i.e., aspiring foreign fighters); and the immediate expiration of the passport for anyone who is the subject of a travel ban.[53] Notably, these penalties can be imposed even without prior criminal convictions for the individual under suspicion.

The government's second strategic goal is to isolate radicals, empower the voices of moderate Muslims, and strengthen the bonds between Muslim immigrants and the Dutch democratic political system and society.[54] The Netherlands helps lead the European Commission-sponsored Radicalisation Awareness Network and its Centre of Excellence, and it has championed EU efforts to develop protocols to counter terrorism financing. In August 2014, it began implementation of a Comprehensive Action Programme to Combat Jihadism, intended to "protect the democratic state under the rule of law, to counter and weaken the jihadist movement in the Netherlands and to eliminate the breeding ground for radicalization.[55] Among the important tactics introduced in this program are: an increase in administrative measures to block and disrupt radical imams and propagandists; the creation of support networks for those concerned or affected by the perceived radicalization of a loved one; the establishment of a center to monitor social tensions and radicalization; and the formation of an infrastructure to guide the dissemination of narratives and views that counter Islamist doctrine and promote the rule of law.

Another important tenet of the program is its emphasis on combating radicals online. By recognizing the power of social media as a recruiting and dissemination tool, the government is responding with new measures to identify and sanction online producers of propaganda, work with internet companies to proactively dismantle any sites or users violating terms of use agreements, and manage a hotline for citizens to report any online content inciting hatred or promoting violence.

The NCTV is responsible for the implementation of the Programme. The NCTV was born out of the muddled European response to the 2004 Madrid train bombings, at which point the Dutch government realized the dire need to patch the holes in its own counterterror infrastructure. In keeping with its mission "to minimize the risk of terrorist attacks in the Netherlands and to take prior measures to limit the potential impact of terrorist acts,"[56] the NCTV has since focused on the issue of counter-radicalization, launching a joint government and law enforcement operation to "disrupt" the work of the main Salafi centers in the Netherlands.[57] The Dutch counter-radicalization approach focuses both on Islamic fundamentalists and right-wing nationalists, since racially-motivated attacks against Muslims (as occurred increasingly after Van Gogh's murder in 2004) can spike hate crimes and deepen feelings of alienation and anger.[58]

This preventative outlook in the current European security environment demonstrate the Dutch government's continued adherence to its so-called "broad approach" to countering radicalization.[59] It is grounded on the idea that "no one is born a terrorist, but first goes through a short or longer process of radicalization before he or she decides to risk the life of other and his or her own for a political objective."[60] Funds allocated for this program support the goal of cooperation with Muslim communities by stimulating partnership and reducing the appeal of Islamist narratives through counter-messaging. As explicitly delineated in the Comprehensive Action Programme, law enforcement authorities are encouraged to pursue partnership with moderate mosques and imams to negate the polarization pushed by radical elements. At the same time, the government incentivizes integration by Muslim community leaders and individuals. For instance, while the government provides educational subsidies for the training of imams at Dutch universities, each participant in the program must first complete a yearlong "integration course" to familiarize themselves with local communities and customs.[61] Law enforcement officials and social workers familiar with local conditions in various towns and villages are designated as official points of contact in such approaches. Skeptics, however, have long derided the utility of the broad approach, given that it oversimplifies the motivations for at-risk individuals, may spark resentment among moderate Muslims, and has little effect on the low-profile, small study groups where such radicalization often occurs.[62] A justice ministry inspection in

2017 assessed that roughly half of all Dutch local councils (mostly in towns of 100,000 or fewer) so far have taken no action to institute programs,[63] indicating that the policy has yet to take root in small areas and will likely require greater top-down direction if it is to be effective.

At times, the narrative of the looming threat posed by potential radicals gains more ground than that of the government's constructive attempts to head it off, particularly in debates over immigration and asylum. This trend largely began at the turn of this century when the "leader of the Dutch new right" Pim Fortuyn spearheaded a campaign to restrict Dutch immigration and asylum policies.[64] Fortuyn was known not only for his aggressive stance against militant Islam, but also for a hardline belief that Dutch borders must be closed to any further Muslim immigration because Islamic values clashed irreconcilably with the permissive Dutch society.[65] After Fortuyn's murder in 2003 by a radical activist (whose motive was reportedly to stop the scapegoating of Dutch Muslims for society's problems),[66] his political mantle was quickly assumed by Geert Wilders, head of the Freedom Party (PVV). Wilders was initially able to leverage his party's crucial position in the ruling Center-right coalition to push the conversation on his priority issues and controversial proposals: stricter regulations on immigration, outlawing the burqa and the niqab, and a ban on dual nationality (which is held by an estimated 1.5 to 2 million Dutch citizens).[67] Like Fortuyn, Wilders makes no secret of his personal views of the threat that Islam poses to Dutch society and to the West, and he has faced legal action for this position. His December 2016 conviction for inciting discrimination against the Netherlands' Moroccan minority did not hurt his party's image;[68] rather, the Dutch Broadcasting Foundation reported increased support for the PVV, due in part to the fact that many Dutch citizens believed it was unfair that Wilders had been tried at all.[69]

From the low point of 2013, when the party lost 9 seats[70] in the parliamentary elections and faced significant pushback from activists opposed to the ruling coalition's restrictive immigration policy, the PVV has managed an astonishing comeback. Populist sentiments in the lead-up to the United Kingdom's 2016 Brexit vote strengthened the hand of the PVV and its ability to advance Wilders' cherished initiatives. In November 2016, for example, 132 of the 150 members of Parliament voted to outlaw wearing the niqab in schools, hospitals, government buildings, and other public places.[71] Other items on Wilders' contentious party manifesto included proposals to close all Islamic schools and mosques, ban the Koran and the wearing of headscarves, and halt all immigration from Islamic countries in pursuit of complete "de-Islamization" of the Netherlands.[72] In the 2017 parliamentary elections, this platform won the PVV twenty seats—a gain of five but still falling short of the thirty that Wilders had desired, putting it in second place in the vote count behind Prime Minister Mark Rutte's Liberal party.[73] Yet Wilders continues to play the role of spoiler. It took the Liberal Party a record 208 days to form a government[74] by patching together a coalition with three other parties whose main uniting theme was that they were "anti-Wilders."[75] This fractured leadership validates Wilders' image as the only alternative to an elite establishment willing to turn a blind eye to the existential threat to Dutch society that the PVV portrays Islam to be.[76] Under Wilders' leadership, the PVV will continue to further polarize Parliament and the public debate, spreading an ideology that undermines the government's counter-radicalization approach.

Endnotes

1. "Netherlands, Germany alarmed over Islamic extremists," Hurriyet Daily News, March 14, 2013, http://www.hurriyetdailynews.com/netherlands-germany-alarmed-over-islamist-extremists-.aspx?pageID=238&nid=42916.
2. Ministry of Interior of the Netherlands, AIVD (General Intelligence and Security Service), "Annual Report – 2012," 2012, https://www.aivd.nl/english/publications-press/@2999/annual-report-2012/.
3. AIVD, Annual Report 2012, 27.
4. National Coordinator for Security and Counterterrorism, "Terrorist Threat Assessment for the Netherlands 46 (DTN 46)," November 2017, https://english.nctv.nl/binaries/DTN46%20Summary_tcm32-294322.pdf.
5. AIVD, "Annual Report 2017," March 2018, https://

www.aivd.nl/onderwerpen/salafisme/documenten/jaarverslagen/2018/03/06/jaarverslag-aivd-2017.

6. AIVD, "The Children of ISIS," April 2017, https://english.aivd.nl/publications/publications/2017/04/26/the-children-of-isis.-the-indoctrination-of-minors-in-isis-held-territory.
7. "Dutch looking into Islamic State threat against women's soccer tournament," Reuters, July 12, 2017, https://www.reuters.com/article/us-netherlands-threat/dutch-looking-into-islamic-state-threat-against-womens-soccer-tournament-idUSKBN19X1M4?il=0
8. NCTV, "Terrorist Threat Assessment for the Netherlands 46," November 2017.
9. NCTV, "Terrorist Threat Assessment for the Netherlands 46," 5.
10. Jacob Poushter and Dorothy Manevich, "Globally, People Point to ISIS and Climate Change as Leading Security Threats," Pew Research Center, August 1, 2017.
11. AIVD and National Coordinator for Security and Counterterrorism, "Salafism in the Netherlands: Diversity and Dynamics," September 2015, 5, https://english.aivd.nl/publications/publications/2015/09/24/salafism-in-the-netherlands-diversity-and-dynamics.
12. AIVD, "Annual Report 2017," March 2018, https://www.aivd.nl/onderwerpen/salafisme/documenten/jaarverslagen/2018/03/06/jaarverslag-aivd-2017.
13. AIVD and National Coordinator for Security and Counterterrorism, "Salafism in the Netherlands: Diversity and Dynamics," September 2015, 13.
14. National Coordinator for Counterterrorism, Salafism in the Netherlands. A passing phenomenon or a persistent factor of significance? (The Hague, March 2008), 25-26.
15. NCTb, Derde Voortgangsrapportage terrorismebestrijding, December 5, 2005, 5388583/05/NCTb.
16. AIVD and National Coordinator for Security and Counterterrorism, "Salafism in the Netherlands: Diversity and dynamics," 8.
17. "Salafism in the Netherlands: Diversity and dynamics," 9.
18. AIVD, "Annual Report 2014: Not only returnees but

also 'stay-at-homes' pose a threat," May 13, 2015, 19, https://english.aivd.nl/publications/annual-report/2015/05/13/annual-report-2014-not-only-returnees-but-also-"stay-at-homes"-pose-a-threat.

19. AIVD, "Annual Report 2014: Not only returnees but also 'stay-at-homes' pose a threat."
20. Ian Johnson and Crawford, "A Saudi Group Spreads Extremism in 'Law' seminars, Taught in Dutch," Wall Street Journal, April 16, 2003.
21. AIVD, "Saudi influences in the Netherlands. Links between the Salafist mission, radicalisation processes and Islamic terrorism," 2004; Chamber of Commerce, Foundation Waqf, dossier number 41091392.
22. Chamber of Commerce, dossier number 41091392; Tareek Osama, file number 41 (Golden Chain document).
23. "Eindhoven weert zeven imams die geweld verheerlijken uit moskee [Eindhoven bans seven imams who glorify violence from mosque]," de Volkskrant, December 22, 2015, http://www.volkskrant.nl/binnenland/eindhoven-weert-zeven-imams-die-geweld-verheerlijken-uit-moskee~a4212673/.
24. Lorenzo Vidino, "Testimony - The Muslim Brotherhood in the West: Characteristics, Aims and Policy," RAND Corporation, April 2011, 7, https://www.rand.org/content/dam/rand/pubs/testimonies/2011/RAND_CT358.pdf.
25. Edwin Bakker and Roel Meijer, The Muslim Brotherhood in Europe, Oxford Scholarship Online, 2013.
26. Claire Berlinski, "Who is Fethullah Gulen?" City Journal 22, no. 4, Autumn 2012, http://www.city-journal.org/2012/22_4_fethullah-gulen.html.
27. Janene Pieters, "Dutch politicians outraged over new 'Gulen-list,'" NLTimes.nl, August 31, 2016, http://www.nltimes.nl/2016/08/31/dutch-politicians-outraged-new-gulen-list/.
28. Bakker and Meijer, The Muslim Brotherhood in Europe, 25.
29. See, for example, Omar Nasiri, Inside the Jihad: My life with Al Qaeda (Cambridge: Basic Books, 2006), 109-115.
30. NCTb, "Terrorist Threat Assessment for the Nether-

lands 42: Summary," July 2016, 5, https://english.nctv.nl/binaries/dtn42-summary_tcm32-83624.pdf.

31. Conrad Hackett, "5 Facts About the Muslim Population in Europe," Pew Research Center, November 2017, http://www.pewresearch.org/fact-tank/2017/11/29/5-facts-about-the-muslim-population-in-europe/.
32. "The Position of Muslims in the Netherlands: Facts and Figures," Institute for Multicultural Affairs (Utrecht), 2010, http://www.forum.nl/PortalsInternational/english-pdf/Muslims-in-the-Netherlands-2010.pdf.
33. "The Position of Muslims in the Netherlands: Facts and Figures," Institute for Multicultural Affairs (Utrecht).
34. "More than 850 thousand Muslims in the Netherlands."
35. Jan Willem Duyvendak, Trees Pels and Rally Rijkschroeff, "A Multicultural paradise? The cultural factor in Dutch integration policy," Paper presented at the 3rd ECPR Conference, Budapest, Hungary, September 8-10, 2005, 7.
36. "The Position of Muslims in the Netherlands: Facts and Figures."
37. Barahim and Ostawar, "The Political Participation of Dutch Muslims."
38. "Netherlands," CIA World Factbook, January 12, 2017, https://www.cia.gov/library/publications/the-world-factbook/geos/nl.html.
39. Nico Landman, Van mat tot minaret: De institutionalisering van de islam in Nederland (Amsterdam 1992), 80-82.
40. "The Netherlands," United States Department of State, 2012 Report on International Religious Freedom.
41. Freedom House, "Netherlands: Country Report," Freedom in the World 2016, n.d., https://freedomhouse.org/report/freedom-world/2016/netherlands.
42. Thijl Sunier, et al., "Diyanet: The Turkish Directorate for Religious Affairs in a Changing Environment." VU University Amsterdam, Utrecht University, January 2011, http://www.fsw.vu.nl/nl/Images/Final%20report%20Diyanet%20February%202011_tcm30-200229.pdf.
43. NCTV, "Terrorist Threat Assessment for the Netherlands 46," November 2017, 6.

44. NCTV, Salafism in the Netherlands, 25-26.
45. AIVD, "The Transformation of Jihadism in the Netherlands: Swarm Dynamics and New Strength," June 30, 2014, 26, https://www.aivd.nl/publicaties/publicaties/2014/06/30/the-transformation-of-jihadism-in-the-netherlands; AIVD, Annual Report 2015, 15.
46. "Netherlands," in United States Department of State, Country Reports on Human Rights Practices for 2015, n.d., https://www.state.gov/j/drl/rls/hrrpt/humanrightsreport/#wrapper.
47. "Dijkhoff satisfied with outcome EU migration summit," Government of the Netherlands, September 22, 2015, https://www.government.nl/topics/asylum-policy/news/2015/09/22/dijkhoff-satisfied-with-outcome-eu-migration-summit.
48. "The influx of asylum seekers is changing in terms of composition," Government of the Netherlands, March 14, 2016, https://www.government.nl/topics/asylum-policy/news/2016/03/14/the-influx-of-asylum-seekers-is-changing-in-terms-of-composition.
49. Jacob Poushter, "European Attitudes of the Refugee Crisis," Pew Research Center, September 16, 2016, http://www.pewresearch.org/fact-tank/2016/09/16/european-opinions-of-the-refugee-crisis-in-5-charts/.
50. Steven Erlanger, "Amid Rise of Multiculturalism, Dutch Confront Their Questions of Identity," New York Times, August 13, 2011, http://www.nytimes.com/2011/08/14/world/europe/14dutch.html?pagewanted=all&_r=0.
51. Erlanger, "Amid Rise of Multiculturalism, Dutch Confront Their Questions of Identity."
52. National Coordinator for Security and Counterterrorism, "Terrorist Threat Assessment for the Netherlands 46 (DTN 46)," November 2017.
53. Wendy Zeldin, "Netherlands: Three New Laws Adopted to Further Counterterrorism Efforts," Global Legal Monitor, Library of Congress, March 2017, http://www.loc.gov/law/foreign-news/article/netherlands-three-new-laws-adopted-to-further-counterterrorism-efforts/.

54. Erlanger, "Amid Rise of Multiculturalism, Dutch Confront Their Questions of Identity;" Ministry of Justice, Nota radicalisme en radicalisering, August 19, 2005; 5358374/05/AJS.
55. Zeldin, "Netherlands: Two New Sets of Administrative Sanctions Proposed to Fight Terrorism."
56. National Coordinator for Counter Terrorism of the Netherlands, "About the NCTb," n.d.,http://english.nctb.nl/organisation/about_the_NCTb/.
57. NCTb, Derde Voortgangsrapportage terrorismebestrijding, December 5, 2005, 5388583/05/NCTb; Ministry of Justice, Nota radicalisme en radicalisering, August 19, 2005; 5358374/05/AJS.
58. "Netherlands Sets Plan on Extremism," Associated Press, August 28, 2007, http://www.nytimes.com/2007/08/28/world/europe/28dutch.html?_r=0.
59. Ministry of Justice and Ministry of Interior, "Operationeel Actieplan Polarisatie en radicalisering 2007-2011," August 27, 2007, http://www.tweedekamer.nl/images/297540141bijlage01_118-182859.pdf.
60. Akerboom, "Ten Years of Dutch Counterterrorism Policy."
61. "The Netherlands," United States Department of State, 2012 Report on International Religious Freedom.
62. Ministry of Justice of The Netherlands, "Court has ruled in case of Hofstad group suspects," March 10, 2006, http://www.rechtspraak.nl/Gerechten/Rechtbanken/s-Gravenhage/Actualiteiten/Rechtbank+heeft+uit spraak+gedaan+in+zaken+verdachten+Hofstadgroep.htm; Janny Groen and Annieke Kranenberg, Strijdsters van Allah, Radicale moslima's en het Hofstadnetwerk (Amsterdam: J.M. Meulenhoff, 2006) 69-99, 127-137; Teun Van Dongen, "The Case for Tailored Interventions in the Preventative Approach: Lessons from Countering Jihadism in the Netherlands and the UK," Countering Terrorist Recruitment in the Context of Armed Counter-Terrorism Operations, S. Ekici et al. (Eds), IOS Press, 2016.
63. "Small Dutch councils not taking anti-radicalisation role seriously," DutchNews.nl, September 14, 2017, http://www.dutchnews.nl/news/archives/2017/09/

small-dutch-councils-not-taking-anti-radicalisation-role-seriously/

64. Kirsty Lang, "At home with 'Professor Pim,'" BBC, May 4, 2002, http://news.bbc.co.uk/2/hi/programmes/from_our_own_correspondent/1966979.stm.
65. Lang, "At home with 'Professor Pim.'"
66. Ambrose Evans-Pritchard and Joan Clements, "Fortuyn killed 'to protect Muslims,'" Telegraph (London), March 28, 2003, http://www.telegraph.co.uk/news/worldnews/europe/netherlands/1425944/Fortuyn-killed-to-protect-Muslims.html.
67. "Parliament to press ahead with burqa dual nationality ban laws," DutchNews.nl, May 31, 2013, http://www.dutchnews.nl/news/archives/2012/05/parliament_to_press_ahead_with.php.
68. Sheena McKenzie, "Geert Wilders guilty of 'insulting a group' after hate speech trial," CNN, December 9, 2016, http://www.cnn.com/2016/12/09/europe/geert-wilders-hate-speech-trial-verdict/.
69. "Peilingwijzer: opmars PVV zet door," Nederlandse Omroep Stichting [Dutch Broadcasting Foundation], December 21, 2016, http://nos.nl/artikel/2149429-peilingwijzer-opmars-pvv-zet-door.html.
70. "Dutch election: Pro-Europe VVD and Labour Parties win," BBC, September 13, 2012, http://www.bbc.co.uk/news/world-europe-19566165.
71. Harriet Agerholm, "Dutch government approves partial burqa ban in public places," The Independent, November 29, 2016, http://www.independent.co.uk/news/world/europe/dutch-burqa-veil-ban-holland-votes-for-partial-restrictions-some-public-places-a7445656.html.
72. Caroline Mortimer, "The Netherlands' Most Popular Party Wants To Ban All Mosques," Independent (London), August 28, 2016, http://www.independent.co.uk/news/world/europe/netherlands-pvv-leader-geert-wilders-koran-islam-mosque-ban-holland-dutch-pm-favourite-a7214356.html.
73. "Dutch election: European relief as mainstream triumphs," BBC News, March 16, 2017, http://www.bbc.com/news/world-europe-39297355.
74. "Dutch parties agree coalition government after a re-

cord 208 days," The Guardian, October 2017, https://www.theguardian.com/world/2017/oct/09/dutch-politicians-ready-form-government-election-coalition.

75. Cas Mudde, "The Dutch Election Shows How Not to Defeat Populism," New York Times, March 2017, https://www.nytimes.com/2017/03/16/opinion/geert-wilders-dutch-election-shows-how-not-to-defeat-populism.html.
76. Stefanie Marsh, "This Is Exactly What He Wants," The Atlantic, March 2017, https://www.theatlantic.com/international/archive/2017/03/geert-wilders-won-by-losing-netherlands-vote/519834/.

48 Spain

Quick Facts

Population: 48,958,159 (July 2017 est.)
Area: 505,370 sq km
Ethnic Groups: Composite of Mediterranean and Nordic types
Government Type: Parliamentary constitutional monarchy
GDP (official exchange rate): $51.61 billion (2017 est.)

Source: CIA World FactBook (Last Updated April 2018)

Introduction

The August 2017 attacks in Catalonia were the first jihadist attacks on Spanish soil since the Madrid train bombing of March 11, 2004.[1] *Prior to the Catalonian attacks, the Spanish population had a perhaps-unwarranted sense of security. In the wake of the Barcelona car attack and the Cambrils attack several days later, that sense of security has vanished.*

Spain has increased its efforts to apprehend jihadists before they strike, both domestically and abroad. Spain's location as the gateway of the Mediterranean renders it a prime destination for immigrants from North Africa and for foreign radical elements embedded among them. To many such individuals, al-Andalus—the territory of the Iberian Peninsula lost by Islam in the fifteenth century—is no longer simply an abstract cause, but rather a concrete jihadist objective.[2]

Islamist Activity

Until the late summer of 2017, Spain had not suffered a direct jihadist attack on its soil since the 3/11 train bombing in Madrid. This relative calm may have been due to the preventative efforts of Spanish law enforcement. Whatever the cause, this peaceful period ended in August 2017, when a group of jihadists attacked La Rambla in Barcelona and the village of Cambrils, causing Spain's sense of security to evaporate overnight.

The threat of radical Islamism has been present in the background of Spanish public affairs since the 2004 Madrid train bombing. Since that attack, 691 people have been arrested for crimes connected to jihadism, and over 90 percent of them have been charged with glorifying terrorism.[3] However, a wide range of Islamist activity continues to exist in Spain. It includes a broad collection of Salafist actors; elements of the Muslim Brotherhood, and extremists affiliated with both al-Qaeda and the Islamic State.

Numerous studies and investigations commissioned by city councils and the Mossos d'Esquadra (the autonomous regional civilian police of Catalonia) chronicle the advance of the Salafist movement in Spain.[4] Salafists are generally concentrated in the regions of Catalonia and Murcia and their surrounding areas. Local newspapers in these areas have reported cases of Salafi imams publicly advocating for a radical, violent ideology in their communities. In one such instance, nine men in Reus sentenced a woman accused of adultery to death by stoning. The woman managed to escape, and the men were arrested by the local Mossos d'Esquadra.[5]

Often, the most radicalized groups on Spanish soil maintain ties with different groups working in North Africa; for instance, the perpetrators of the 2004 Madrid train bombings were Salafists who received training abroad from the Moroccan Islamic Group (GICM). These connections open pathways to larger terrorist networks, including AQIM.[6] In other instances, Spain has served as an important hub for foreign Salafist organizations, including the Salafist Group for Preaching and Combat (GSPC), whose members frequently interact with the GICM as well as with radicals in Catalonia.[7]

The Muslim Brotherhood also has a significant presence in Spain. It became one of the more solidly-established Islamist organizations in the nation through its 1971 affiliation with the Spanish Muslim Association. Radical Muslim Brotherhood elements were especially active in Spain at the turn of this century; Abu Dahdah's network, an al-Qaeda hub based in Madrid, provided funding to the Brotherhood while coordinating logistics for recruits transiting Europe.[8] The Spanish Institute of Strategic Studies (IEEE) notes that the network played a significant part not only in the 9/11 attacks, but also in the attacks in Morocco in 2003 and Madrid in 2004.[9] Although their activity has faded from the media spotlight, the Brotherhood maintains a serious presence in Spain, largely in the regions of Andalusia, Valencia, and Madrid.[10]

As can be easily inferred, the level of threat against Spain has not as been low as many believed simply because no attack has occurred since 2004. In reality, the intensity and persistence of jihadist threat has been quite high. This is due to two reasons: first, the relevance within jihadist ideology of the figure of al-Andalus, a territory that encompasses the Iberian Peninsula (Spain and Portugal) and parts of Southern France. The region was under Muslim control from 711 to 1492, and is perceived as a golden moment in Muslim history. Second, and more prosaic, is the fact that Spain is the only western European nation with a land frontier with a majority-Muslim nation, thanks to the two Spanish cities of Ceuta and Melilla in Northern Africa. Consequently, Spain looms in the collective jihadi imagination.

In part due to this cultural interest, Spain faces a variety of threats affiliated with more directly violent groups, such as al-Qaeda and the Islamic State (ISIS). First, both al-Qaeda and the Islamic State have demonstrated a renewed interest in the Iberian Peninsula (known as al-Andalus when it was under Muslim governance between the early 700s and the late 1400s). In January 2017, al-Qaeda leader Ayman al-Zawahiri denounced the Spanish occupation of the North African cities of Ceuta and Melilla. He compared Ceuta and Melilla to other Muslim-majority regions under non-Muslim control, such as the Palestinian Territories (occupied by Israel), Kashmir (occupied by India), the Caucasus (occupied by Russia), and Xinjiang (occupied by China).[11] This audio recording was al-Zawahiri's first address since September 2015, and many analysts interpreted it as an attempt to challenge the Islamic State's vehement discourse.

The Islamic State has also indicated an interest in al-Andalus. In 2017, Rumiya, ISIS's magazine, highlighted the prominence of Abdallah ibn Yassin, the founder of the Almoravid dynasty that ruled the region in the late 1000s and early 1100s. The April 2017 featured The Ruling of the Belligerent Christians, which exhorted present-day Muslims to remember the errors of rule in al-Andalus that allowed Christians to conquer the region.[12] Furthermore, Amaq, ISIS's public relations arm, launched a Spanish-language channel on Telegram, as did Al Haqq, also involved in ISIS's public relations. Al Haqq likewise launched a website and a Twitter account in Spanish.

The Department of National Security warned in its 2016 report that Spain has been directly threatened by ISIS on social media, which serves a recruitment tool, and that ISIS is looking for Spanish translators to spread its propaganda among Spanish speakers. The Ministry of Interior published information on the various places throughout Spain where jihadists had been arrested between 2012 and October 2016.[13] The data set offered several interesting insights. First, out of a total of 186 people arrested, one third of the arrests happened in the autonomous region of Catalonia, and 50 of that group were arrested in Barcelona. Madrid came in second in total number of individuals arrested, at 26. The autonomous city of Ceuta had 24 arrests, Valencia had 18, and Melilla had 10. In that period, there were also 10 detainees in the autonomous Community of Andalusia and 7 in the Basque Country.[14]

Jihadi activity in Spain has varied widely. Domestically, Spain has a small population of jihadists recruiters and financiers, as well as jihadis who planned attacks on Spanish soil. On the international stage, Spain has contributed foreign fighters to the conflict in Iraq and Syria, some of whom have returned to Spain.

Recruiters work either within the Muslim community or online. In February 2016, Hamed Abderrahman Ahmed, the only Spanish national to be detained in Guantanamo, was arrested along with three of his followers. Another group took over the dismantled cell and its new participants were arrested in November 2016. One of the participants was commissioned by ISIS to recruit children as "Cubs of the Caliphate" (Ashbal al-Khilafa).[15] This was not the only recruitment effort to specifically target children. In October 2016, the Civil Guard in Ibizia arrested two Moroccan imams for radicalization and activities in support of ISIS. Their efforts targeted children at Maslid el-Fatah, a facility registered as religious center in the town of Sant Antoni de Portamany.[16] In November 2016, Moroccan Mohammed Akaarir was imprisoned for self-indoctrination for terrorist ends.[17] The National High Court's

Third Chamber for Criminal Matters sentenced him to two-and-a-half years for his support of ISIS on social media. After serving his sentence, he will also be expelled from Spain for six years.[18] In November 2016, 26-year-old Fouad Bouchihan in Roda del Ter (Barcelona) and 19-year-old Ilyass Chentouf in Madrid were sent to prison for social media activity in support of ISIS.[19]

A February 2017 CNP report describes the case of a 41-year-old Moroccan who was a veteran of jihadi wars in Chechnya and Syria, and who recruited people for Jabhat al-Nusrah and Syria. He was eventually arrested, and his last recruit joined ISIS in 2015. Furthermore, the Civil Guard arrested two Moroccans, aged 25 and 27, accused of indoctrination and enrollment via the Internet, successfully recruiting several people willing to journey to the Caliphate.[20] In April 2017, the CNP arrested a 29-year-old Spaniard in Ceuta, nicknamed. The Poison, for being a member of ISIS. His wife and three other individuals had been arrested in November 2016, all four accused of radicalizing and indoctrinating minors. At the beginning of July 2017, a 31-year-old Moroccan man was arrested by the Civil Guard in Operation Tahmil in Madrid. He was accused of propaganda work on the Internet and social media that included terrorist manuals.[21] Finally, in July 2017, the CNP arrested a Spaniard, of Palestinian descent, in Barcelona for glorifying terrorism and participating in a terrorist organization.[22]

There are jihadis who go beyond recruitment and raise money for terrorist organizations. The Civil Guard arrested two of the El Jelaly brothers on these grounds in July 2016, and a third in March 2017. The brothers had raised funds for ISIS.[23] The Civil Guard also dismantled a complex business network dedicated to jihadist financing in June 2017. Using 24 Danish shell companies with subsidiaries in Melilla, amassed nearly eight million euros in recent years. The network has sent at least ten jihadis from Spain, Denmark, and Germany to conflict areas.[24]

Some Spanish jihadists have sought to attack Spain domestically. The Civil Guard arrested two jihadis in January 2017 in connection with their possession of a submachine gun and three machetes.[25] In May 2017, a joint operation of National Police Corps (CNP) and the Moroccan intelligence service arrested three would-be jihadis. Two other men were sentenced to jail time later that month, in part due to one's intention of becoming a suicide attacker.[26] In June 2017, the CNP arrested Moroccan Rachid El Omari over his plans to organize a massacre inspired by the Manchester attacks. At the time of his arrest, he had 27 of ISIS's manuals, one of them entitled Combatant Inghimasi and Suicide Operations, which prepares jihadis for martyrdom.[27] A four-member ISIS cell was dismantled in Majorca in June 2017, as it crafted a plan to stab pedestrians in public.[28]

In August 2017, one jihadi successfully attacked La Rambla, a major street in Barcelona. Moroccan Younes Aboyaaqoub drove a van into a crowd, killing 14 and injuring 130 others. Abouyaaqoub fled the attack on foot, then killed another person as he stole the victim's car. Four days later, police killed him in Subirats, a village near Barcelona.

Spain, like many countries around the world, has had a problem with its citizens traveling to Iraq and Syria to become foreign fighters. Comparatively, Spain's problems with foreign fighters have been more limited than other European nations. The Soufan Group estimates that 204 Spaniards have left Spain and gone to Iraq or Syria.[29] In March 2015, the Spanish Criminal Code was reformed to criminalize any attempt to travel abroad for terrorist purposes, including destabilizing institutions in other countries or for training.[30] This reform gave law enforcement agencies new flexibility in handling foreign fighters.

Finally, despite the efforts of law enforcement services, some individuals do reach Iraq or Syria and then return to Spain. Given the returnees' training and combat experience, the police arrest any returning fighters immediately. In January 2017, the Civil Guard arrested a Dutch jihadist and extradited him to the Netherlands. Later that month, the CNP arrested two Moroccan returnees with the help of the Moroccan Territorial Security Directorate (DGST).[31] A number of other returnees have been arrested, as have the wives of jihadis. Assia Ahmad Mohamed, widow of ISIS jihadist Mohamed Hamduch, arrived in Spain after her arrest in Turkey as she attempted to return to Europe.

Islamism and Society

According to the Unión de Comunidades Islámicas de España (Union of Islamic Communities in Spain, or UCIDE), Spain's Muslim population as of December 2016 numbered 1.9 million.[32] Of this population, 41 percent are ethnic Spaniards, 39 percent are ethnically Moroccan, and the remainder comes from immigrant communities throughout the Middle East and Africa.[33] The largest Muslim populations reside in Andalucía in the south, Valencia in the east, Cataluña in the south, and Madrid in the center of Spain.[34] Cataluña's population is the biggest, at over 500,000. Perhaps consequently, there have been some tensions over the role of Muslim citizens in the community. A dozen Catalan towns became the first locales in Spain to ban the burqa and the niqab in municipal buildings. Lleida, a city in Western Catalonia whose population is a full 25 percent Muslim, is at the epicenter of this movement. Beyond banning the niqab, its mayor shut down the city's lone mosque because there were allegedly too many Friday worshippers. In February 2012, angry townspeople began accusing Lleida's Muslims of poisoning dogs in revenge.[35] Such regional strife has only been magnified by Catalonia's historic secessionist attitudes and Spain's recent economic woes.

Intense friction over access to mosques is not limited to Catalonia, however. Rather, it is widespread among rural Spanish communities. Between the mid-1990s and 2012, there were 60 registered disputes between Muslim communities and their Spanish neighbors over the construction of mosques.[36] Riay Tatary, president of UCIDE, has angrily protested what is perceived as a segregationist movement to "exile" mosques by relocating them to areas outside of city and residential neighborhoods.[37] The most publicized incident of this nature occurred in 2012 in Torrejon, a town of 120,000 (of which Muslims comprise nearly 10 percent). The Muslim citizens of the town purchased land to expand the city's mosque, at the time located near the town's center. However, angry protests and petitions from the rest of the town's residents, as well as a demonstration by the anti-immigration Platform for Catalonia, induced the municipal authorities to revoke the building permit and change the site to one near an industrial park outside of town.[38] In other instances, residents have strewn pig's blood and pork meat over potential mosque sites in a deliberate attempt to permanently contaminate them in the eyes of Muslims.[39] While revealing a measure of grassroots fear in some areas, these acts have the potential to alienate the moderate Spanish Muslim community, even turning some towards radicalization and retribution.

Yet simultaneously, Spanish society has shown remarkable openness to the victims of the 2015 refugee crisis, regardless of their religious affiliation. Under the EU's redistribution plan, Spain agreed to accept 15,000 resettled refugees to ease the load on Greece and Italy—a departure from the administration's original figure of just under 3,000, likely due to the pressure of Spanish grassroots organizations urged on by Prime Minister Mariano Brey's left-wing political rivals.[40] Unlike their counterparts elsewhere in Europe, Spanish groups professing a complete rejection of Islam and Muslim immigrants—including Plataforma x Catalunya, Spain 2000, and the newly arrived PEGIDA ("Patriotic Europeans Against the Islamisation of the Occident," a German movement that launched its Spanish branch in 2015)—have been unable to gain significant traction.[41]

It is vital to note that the majority of Spanish Muslims reject the use of violence and consider themselves well integrated into the broader Spanish community.[42] However, for the minority that does not share these feelings, the blend of isolation and xenophobia that they experience is dangerous. Since the Muslim community in Spain is primarily made up of immigrants, it encounters many obstacles to integration: unfamiliarity with the Spanish language, lack of documentation, an unusually high percentage of unmarried men, and frequent unemployment. All of these factors have the potential to increase frustration and estrangement, consequentially increasing the risk of radicalization.[43] As the Spanish government struggles economically, the resulting social chaos will likely cause increased perceptions of deprivation and insularism among each community—promoting more xenophobia, which will in turn promote more isolationism—which may only make the fractures between the two communities worse.

Islamism and the State

One of Spain's more unique counter-terrorism strategies has been to expel suspected jihadis from Spanish territory, even in cases when people's trials had not concluded, or when people had been acquitted of the charges against them. The Ministry of the Interior has expelled over a hundred alleged jihadis who had not been convicted of a crime since the 3/11 attacks.[44] One prominent example is Nouh Mediouni, an Algerian allegedly involved in an AQIM cell. After ten months in prison, Mediouni was released due to a lack of incriminating evidence. The Secretary of State then expelled Mediouni from Spain, citing national security concerns. Mediouni's lawyer appealed, but the Supreme Court ruled that there was sufficient evidence to ban Mediouni, if not convict criminally.[45]

Another tool in Spain's counter-terrorism efforts is the close diplomatic relationship that the nation maintains with Morocco. Morocco is undeniably a significant source of the jihadists that threaten Spain. However, Morocco has committed to working with Spain to prevent terrorist attacks and to jointly track and arrest suspected jihadists. This joint work allows Spanish authorities and Moroccan authorities to merge their capabilities and be more effective on the whole.

In spite of the effects of economic crisis, potential Catalan secession, and paralyzing political deadlock, the Spanish government under the leadership of Rajoy has nevertheless managed to pursue an effective counterterrorism strategy in terms of immigration and border control. Spain helped found the Global Counterterrorism Forum in 2011 and maintains an inter-ministerial Countering Violent Extremism (CVE) working group, described by the U.S. State Department as "tied closely to the fight against illegal immigration and the integration of existing immigrant communities."[46] Spain has also stepped up its cooperation with other Western countries through mechanisms such as the U.S. Immigrant Advisory Program and increased access to Europol information databases on terrorism and organized crime.[47]

While trying to maintain a policy of religious neutrality, the federal government has adopted an assertive stance in pursuit of jihadist cells, with varying degrees of success. In July 2015, the country's criminal code was updated to "improve its legal framework to more effectively counter the movement of foreign terrorist fighters to conflict zones, better pursue suspected terrorists without clear affiliation to a known criminal organization, and curtail terrorist preparatory activities online."[48] This legal step—which Amnesty International denounced as so vague that they would be not only ineffective but also an infringement on basic human rights[49]—was likely a response to harsh critiques over the cases described above of multiple terrorist suspects that have been released from Spanish prisons due to excessive punishment or lack of evidence.[50] An inability to convict is an unfortunate consequence of the aggressive policies of quick intervention in cases of suspected terrorism, which was a policy established in 2004 after the attacks in Madrid. In many instances, the police arrest a suspect without having the necessary evidence to guarantee a conviction.

In tandem, Spain has adopted a National Counter Radicalization Strategy, which is promulgated by the national Center for Counter-Terrorism and Organized Crime Intelligence (CITCO). This strategy recognizes that radicalization occurs at the local level and attempts to directly address the causes for grievance posed by, for example, the closure of almacabras or lack of access to mosques.[51]

Given the recent attacks in Catalonia, Spain's relative calm has been shattered. For the first time since the panic surrounding the 2004 train bombings in Madrid, the Spanish government and population are more aware of the potential threat posed by jihadist actors. Given the Iberian peninsula's significance in Islamic tradition, it is safe to assume that jihadist groups will continue to demonstrate interest in Spain in the future.

ENDNOTES

1. The author, Rafael would like to express his gratitude to the Strategic Studies Group (GEES) team working on terrorism for sharing the data from their report The Jihadi Threat Against Spain (release forthcoming).
2. In a post-9/11 broadcast, al-Qaeda leader Ayman al-Zawahiri termed the loss of Andalusia a "tragedy."

For more, see Rafael L. Bardaji and Ignacio Cosidó, "Spain: from 9/11 to 3/11 and Beyond," in Gary J. Schmitt, ed., *Safety, Liberty, and Islamist Terrorism: American and European Approaches to Domestic Counterterrorism* (Washington, DC: AEI Press, 2010).

3. Based on the annual memoir by the State Prosecutor, Justice Ministry, Madrid.
4. Ferrán Balsells, "El salafismo se hace con el control de cinco mezquitas en Tarragona [Salafism takes control of five mosques in Tarragona]," *El País* (Madrid), June 21, 2010, 31.
5. "Un 'juicio' islamista condeno a una mujer a morir por adultera en Reus [An Islamist 'trial' condemns a woman to death in Reus]," *El Periodico.com*, December 5, 2009, http://www.elperiodico.com/es/noticias/sociedad/20091205/juicio-islamista-condeno-una-mujer-morir-por-adultera-reus/print-235772.shtml.
6. See "Marruecos desarticula un grupo terrorista vinculado al 11-M [Morocco arrests terrorist cell connected with the March 11, 2004, attacks]," *La Vanguardia* (Barcelona), March 3, 2010, 17.
7. C. Echeverría Jesús, "La conexión paquistaní se consolida también en España [The Pakistani connection also solidifies in Spain]," Grupo de Estudios Estratégicos *GEES Analysis*, January 23, 2008, www.gees.org.
8. Aaron Mannes, "El Once de Marzo: A Familiar, Maddening Scene," *National Review Online*, March 12, 2004, http://www.nationalreview.com/node/209873/print.
9. Jose Maria Blanca Navarro and Oscar Perez Ventura, "Movimientos Islamistas en España [Islamist Movements in Spain]," Insituto Español de Estudios Estratégicos, January 11, 2012, http://www.ieee.es/Galerias/fichero/docs_marco/2012/DIEEEM012012_MovimientosIslamistasenEspana.docx.pdf.
10. "Movimientos Islamistas en Espana."
11. "El máximo líder de Al-Qaeda llama a reconquistar Ceuta y Melilla," *Diario de Navarra,* January 8, 2017, p. 3.
12. See Centro de Análisis y Prospectiva (CAP) de la

Guardia Civil: *Yihad: Un análisis de Rumiyah nº 9,* 2017, p. 8.

13. *Balance del terrorism en España 2016,* Cuadernos Centro Memorial de Las Víctimas del Terrorismo *2016,* pp.99-100.
14. "Un tercio de las detenciones por yihadismo desde 2012 fueron en Cataluña," ["A third of detentions for jihadism since 2012 were in Catalonia,"] *El País,* October 18, 2016, https://politica.elpais.com/politica/2016/10/18/actualidad/1476790225_493925.html.
15. Melchor Sáiz-Pardo, "La célula de Ceuta captaba niños para convertirlos en 'carne de cañón,'" [The Ceuta cell captured children to convert them to 'cannon fodder,'"] *Diario Sur,* November 10, 2016.
16. Melchor Sáiz-Pardo, "Los imanes detenidos en Ibiza radicalizaban a niños en un centro autorizado por Justicia," *Diario de Navarra,* October 26, 2016, p. 6.
17. "Detenido en Irún un camionero marroquí que residió en Barañáin," *Diario de Navarra*, December 1, 2016, p. 3.
18. BALÍN, M.: "Primer condenado en España por hacer la 'yihad mediática,'" *Diario de Navarra*, December 2, 2016, p. 5.
19. "La juez envía a prisión a los dos yihadistas detenidos el pasado sábado," *Diario de Navarra*, November 22, 2016, p. 6.
20. "Dos detenidos en Badalona por captación de yihadistas," *20 Minutos,* February 8, 2017, p. 4.
21. "Otro detenido por difundir propaganda yihadista," *Gente,* June 1 2017; Melchor Sáiz-Pardo, "Las aplicaciones para móvil del Estado Islámico llegan a España," *Diario de Navarra,* 5 de julio de 2017, p. 5.
22. "Un detenido por enaltecimiento y apoyo a yihadistas," *20 Minutos,* July 13, 2017, p. 2.
23. "El yihadista de Gerona es hermano de tres yihadistas," *Diario de Navarra,* March 16, 2017, p. 4; Melchor Sáiz-Pardo, "Un yihadista detenido en Gerona tenía tres hermanos terroristas en el Estado Islámico," *Norte de Castilla,* March 16, 2017, p. 29.
24. "Detenido en Melilla yihadista por la captación y envío de combatientes," *La Vanguardia,* June 23, 2017.

25. Melchor Sáiz-Pardo, "Los dos yihadistas arrestados en Ceuta tenían en un zulo un subfusil y tres machetes", *Diario de Navarra,* January 14, 2017, p. 5.
26. "Cárcel para los dos yihadistas," *Diario de Navarra,* May 26, 2017, p. 6;"España mantiene su nivel de alerta pese a la riada de detenciones," *Diario de Navarra,* May 24, 2017, p. 16.
27. Melchor Sáiz-Pardo, "El juez sostiene que El Omari buscaba organizar una matanza en Madrid," *Diario de Navarra,* June 24, 2017, p. 2.
28. Melchor Sáiz-Pardo, "La célula de Mallorca planeaba un apuñalamiento masivo en la plaza de Inca," *Diario de Navarra,* July 1, 2017, p. 5.
29. Richard Barrett, *Beyond the Caliphate: Foreign Fighters and the Threat of Returnees,* October 2017, http://thesoufancenter.org/wp-content/uploads/2017/10/Beyond-the-Caliphate-Foreign-Fighters-and-the-Threat-of-Returnees-TSC-Report-October-2017.pdf.
30. María Ponte, "La reforma de los delitos de terrorismo mediante la Ley Orgánica 2/2015", *Análisis GESI,* 11/2015.
31. "Detenido en San Sebastián un captador de combatientes para el ISIS," *El País,* January 16, 2017.
32. Unión de Comunidades Islámicas de España, "Estudio demográfico de la población musulmana," *Observatorio Andalusí,* December 31, 2017, http://observatorio.hispanomuslim.es/estademograf.pdf.
33. Unión de Comunidades Islámicas de España, "Estudio demográfico de la población musulmana."
34. Unión de Comunidades Islámicas de España, "Estudio demográfico de la población musulmana."
35. Such reports are still unsubstantiated. See Dale Hurd, "Under Siege? Spain resists Islamic invasion," *CBN News,* February 12, 2012, http://www.cbn.com/cbnnews/world/2012/february/under-siege-spain-resists-islamic-invasion-/.
36. Alonso, "The Spread of Radical Islam in Spain: Challenges Ahead," 480.
37. "Spanish Muslims denounce the 'exile' of their mosques," *El País* (Madrid), June 3, 2013, http://sociedad.elpais.com/sociedad/2013/06/03/

actualidad/1370260356_229615.html.
38. Guy Hedgecoe, "Local mosque row a Spanish problem," *The Irish Times*, July 10, 2012, http://www.irishtimes.com/news/local-mosque-row-a-spanish-problem-1.532693.
39. Alonso, "The Spread of Radical Islam in Spain: Challenges Ahead."
40. "Citizens Pressure the Government of Spain to Welcome in More Refugees," *The Local*, September 9, 2015, https://www.thelocal.es/20150909/citizens-pressure-spanish-government-to-act-on-refugees.
41. "Far-right extremist parties find support across Europe," Public Radio International, November 30, 2012, http://www.pri.org/stories/politics-society/far-right-extremist-parties-find-support-across-europe.html.
42. Alonso, "The Spread of Radical Islam."
43. Kern, "The Islamic Republic of Catalonia."
44. Melchor Sáiz-Pardo, "Las expulsiones sumarias, una nueva arma legal contra la yihad," *Diario de Navarra*, January 8, 2017, p. 2.
45. Sáiz-Pardo, "Las expulsiones sumarias, una nueva arma legal contra la yihad."
46. United States Department of State, *Country Reports on Terrorism 2011*.
47. Kern, "The Islamic Republic of Catalonia."; See also United States Department of State, Office of the Coordinator for Counterterrorism, *Country Reports on Terrorism 2012* (Washington, DC: U.S. Department of State, May 2013), http://www.state.gov/documents/organization/210204.pdf.
48. United States Department of State, *Country Reports on Terrorism 2015*.
49. "Spain: New Counter-Terrorism Proposals Would Infringe Basic Human Rights," *Amnesty International*, February 10, 2015, http://www.amnestyusa.org/news/news-item/spain-new-counter-terrorism-proposals-would-infringe-basic-human-rights.
50. Kern, "Islamic Supremacy Rears its Head in Spain."
51. Ministerio del Interior, "Plan Estratégico Nacional de Lucha Contra la Radicalización Violenta [National

Plan to Combat Violent Radicalization]," 7-8, 2015, http://www.interior.gob.es/documents/10180/3066463/CM_mir_PEN-LCRV.pdf/b57166c1-aaaf-4c0d-84c7-b69bda6246f5%20.

49 Contributors

ALBANIA

Christopher Deliso

Christopher Deliso is an American journalist and author concentrating on the Balkans. Over the past decade, Chris has established a dedicated presence in the Balkans, and published analytical articles on related topics in numerous relevant media outlets, such as UPI, the Economist Intelligence Unit, and Jane's Islamic Affairs Analyst and Jane's Intelligence Digest. Chris is also the founder and director of the Balkan-interest news and current affairs website, www.balkanalysis.com, and the author of The Coming Balkan Caliphate: The Threat of Radical Islam to Europe and the West (Praeger Security International, 2007).

ALGERIA

Yahia H. Zoubir

Yahia H. Zoubir is Professor of International Studies and Director of Research in Geopolitics at KEDGE Business School, France. Prior to joining KEDGE in September 2005, he taught in the United States. He has been Visiting Faculty in various universities in the China, Europe, the United States, and India, His numerous publications include books, such as North African Politics: Change and Continuity (Routledge, 2016); Global Security Watch—The Maghreb: Algeria, Libya, Morocco, and Tunisia (ABC/CLIO, 2013); North Africa: Politics, Region, and the Limits of Transformation (Routledge, 2008) and articles in scholarly journals, such as Third World Quarterly, Mediterranean Politics, International Affairs, Journal of North African Studies, Middle East Journal, Journal of Contemporary China, etc.. He has also contributed many book chapters and various entries in encyclopedias. He is currently collaborating on the Project on Rivalries in the Middle East & North Africa and another on Sahel Security and the Mediterranean.

Azerbaijan

Svante Cornell

Svante E. Cornell joined the American Foreign Policy Council as Senior Fellow for Eurasia in January 2017. He also servs as the Director of the Central Asia-Caucasus Institute & Silk Road Studies Program, and a co-founder of the Institue for Security and Development Policy, Stockholm. His main areas of expertise are security issues, state-building, and transnational crime in Southwest and Central Asia, with a specific focus on the Caucasus and Turkey. He is the Editor of the Central Asia-Caucasus Analyst, the Joint Center's bi-weekly publication, and of the Joint Center's Silk Road Papers series of occasional papers.

Cornell is the author of four books, including Small Nations and Great Powers, the first comprehensive study of the post-Soviet conflicts in the Caucasus, and Azerbaijan since Independence. Cornell is an Associate Research Professor at Johns Hopkins University's Paul H. Nitze School of Advanced International Studies. He was educated at the Middle East Technical University, received his Ph.D. in Peace and Conflict Studies from Uppsala University, and holds an honorary degree from the National Academy of Sciences of Azerbaijan. He is a member of the Swedish Royal Academy of Military Science, and a Research Associate with the W. Martens Center for European Studies in Brussels. Formerly, Cornell served as Associate Professor of Government at Uppsala University.

Bahrain

Donal Radlauer

Donal Radlauer is the foremost expert on the demographics of the victims from the phase of the Israeli-Palestinian Conflict that began in September of 2000. He is an Associate of the International Policy Institute for Counter-Terrorism (ICT) where he has published and lectured extensively on topics relating to terror finance, counter-terrorism, casualty statistics, asymmetric conflict, and radicalization via "virtual communities." Mr. Radlauer is the Lead Researcher for the ICT's "Al-Aqsa Intifada" Database Project where he developed the project's technological infrastructure and wrote the projects findings in the study "An Engineered Tragedy." Mr. Radlauer studied

History and Sociology of Science at the University of Pennsylvania. He is also a director and co-founder of the Institute for the Study of Asymmetric Conflict.

Bolivia

Joseph M. Humire

Joseph M. Humire is a global security expert, focusing on the nexus between security, defense and economic freedom. Humire's research and investigations on the crime-terror nexus, radical Islam and Iran's influence in Latin America has been sought after by various entities within the U.S. government as well as think tanks and private sector clients throughout the hemisphere. Currently the Executive Director of the Center for a Secure Free Society (SFS), Humire is developing a global network of security and defense specialists that are focused on the intersection of security, intelligence, defense and economic development. Prior to his, Humire spent seven years with the United States Marine Corps, deployed to many hot spots around the world, including Iraq and Liberia, and partook in the first multinational military exercise in Latin America—Unitas 45-04. He is also a graduate from George Mason University with a degree in Economics and Global Affairs. Humire co-edited the first English book on "Iran's strategic penetration of Latin America," scheduled to be released in the fall of 2013 by Lexington Books.

Brazil

Joseph M. Humire

Joseph M. Humire is a global security expert, focusing on the nexus between security, defense and economic freedom. Humire's research and investigations on the crime-terror nexus, radical Islam and Iran's influence in Latin America has been sought after by various entities within the U.S. government as well as think tanks and private sector clients throughout the hemisphere. Currently the Executive Director of the Center for a Secure Free Society (SFS), Humire is developing a global network of security and defense specialists that are focused on the intersection of security, intelligence, defense and economic development. Prior to his, Humire spent seven years with the United States Marine Corps, deployed to many hot spots around the world, including Iraq and Liberia, and partook in the first multinational military exercise in Latin America—Unitas 45-04. He is also a graduate from George Mason University with a degree in Economics and Global Affairs. Humire co-edited the first English book on "Iran's strategic penetration of Latin America," scheduled to be released in the fall of 2013 by Lexington Books.

CANADA

Candice Malcolm

Candice Malcolm is a best-selling author, a nationally syndicated columnist with the Toronto Sun and Postmedia papers, and an international fellow with the Centre for a Secure Free Society in Washington, D.C. She is the founder of the True North Initiative – an independent, non-profit research and educational organization in Canada that seeks to champion sound immigration and security policies for the 21st century. Candice is the author of two best-selling books, Generation Screwed and Losing True North. She is a former advisor to the Minister of Citizenship and Immigration Canada, the former director of research at Sun News Network, and the former Director of the Canadian Taxpayer's Federation in Ontario.

Born and raised in Vancouver, British Columbia, Candice is a ninth generation Canadian and loves to travel; she has visited over 80 countries. Candice has master's degrees in international relations and international law, and splits her time between Toronto and San Francisco, with her husband Kasra.

DENMARK

Manni Crone

Manni Crone is a Danish translator and holds a Ph.D. in Political Science from the Institut d'études politiques de Paris and the DEA from l'École des Hautes Études en Sciences Sociales . She has translated, among other works, Boris Vian and Francis Picabia from French to Danish together with Asger Schnack. She is an assistant professor at the Department of Political Science at the University of Copenhagen, where she conducts research in Islam, securlarism, and religious influence on policy formation.

Ethiopia

J. Peter Pham

J. Peter Pham is Vice President for Research and Regional Initiatives at the Atlantic Council as well as Director of the Council's Africa Center. From 2008 to 2017, he also served as Vice President of the Association for the Study of the Middle East and Africa (ASMEA) and was founding Editor-in-Chief of its refereed Journal of the Middle East and Africa.

France

Jonathan Laurence

Jonathan Laurence is Professor of Political Science at Boston College and Nonresident Senior Fellow in Foreign Policy studies at the Brookings Institution (Washington, DC). He is a member of the Council on Foreign Relations and an affiliate of the Center for European Studies at Harvard University, where he received his Ph.D. in 2006.

Germany

Benjamin Weinthal

Benjamin Weinthal is a research fellow at the Foundation for Defense of Democracies. A widely published journalist based in Berlin, he serves as FDD's eyes and ears in Europe. Benjamin's investigative reporting has uncovered valuable information on Iran's energy links to European firms, as well as Hamas and Hezbollah's terror-finance operations in Europe. He has also examined the growth of the Islamic State in Europe, growing anti-Semitism on the Continent, and neo-Nazism.

Benjamin's work has appeared in The Wall Street Journal Europe, Slate, The Guardian, The New Republic, The Weekly Standard, National Review Online, the Israeli dailies Haaretz and The Jerusalem Post, and broadcast outlets including the BBC and Fox News. A fluent German speaker, Benjamin has also written columns and articles in the German newspapers Frankfurter Rundschau, Berliner Morgenpost and Der Tagesspiegel.

Islamic Republic of Iran

Ilan Berman

Ilan Berman is Senior Vice President of the American Foreign Policy Council in Washington, DC. An expert on regional security in the Middle East, Central Asia, and the Russian Federation, he has consulted for both the U.S. Central Intelligence Agency and the U.S. Department of Defense, and provided assistance on foreign policy and national security issues to a range of governmental agencies and congressional offices.

Iraq

Renad Mansour

Since 2008, Renad has held research and teaching positions focusing on issues of comparative politics and international relations in the Middle East. His research at Chatham House explores the situation of Iraq in transition and the dilemmas posed by state-building.

Prior to joining Chatham House, Renad was an El-Erian fellow at the Carnegie Middle East Centre, where he examined Iraq, Iran and Kurdish affairs. Renad is also a research fellow at the Cambridge Security Initiative based at Cambridge University and from 2013, he held positions as lecturer of International Studies and supervisor at the faculty of politics, also at Cambridge University. Renad has been a senior research fellow at the Iraq Institute for Strategic Studies in Beirut since 2011 and was adviser to the Kurdistan Regional Government Civil Society Ministry between 2008 and 2010. He received his PhD from Pembroke College, Cambridge.

Israel

Micah Levinson

Micah Levinson is a Junior Fellow at the American Foreign Policy Council. Trained in government and political economy, he earned a B.A. from Harvard University and an M.A. from Washington University in St. Louis, Missouri. He also holds a certificate in counterterrorism from the Interdisciplinary Center in Herzliya, Israel. Micah's research focuses on revolutionary groups and the stability of authoritarian regimes, and he has published on these topics in Politics, Philosophy & Economics and has contributed to The Political Economy of Democracy and Tyranny, edited by Norman Schofield.

Italy

Francesco Marone

Dr. Francesco Marone is Research Fellow for the Program on Radicalization and International Terrorism at ISPI - Italian Institute for International Political Studies, in Milan, and Adjunct Lecturer in International Politics at the University of Pavia. He is also an Associate Fellow at the International Centre for Counter-Terrorism – The Hague (ICCT). He is the author of several publications in the field of security studies. In particular, his research interests focus on radicalization and terrorism.

Jordan

Ehud Rosen

Ehud Rosen is an expert on modern political Islam, focusing on the ideology and history of the Muslim Brotherhood in the Middle East and Europe. He is a senior researcher at the Jerusalem Center for Public Affairs and teaches at Bar-Ilan University. Among his relevant publications are "The Muslim Brotherhood's concept of education", Current Trends of Islamist Ideology (vol. 7, November 2008), and "Reading the runes? The United States and the Muslim Brotherhood as seen through the Wikileaks cables" (co-authored with Dr. Martyn Frampton), The Historical Journal, Cambridge (forthcoming 2013).

Kosovo

Christopher Deliso

Christopher Deliso is an American journalist and author concentrating on the Balkans. Over the past decade, Chris has established a dedicated presence in the Balkans, and published analytical articles on related topics in numerous relevant media outlets, such as UPI, the Economist Intelligence Unit, and Jane's Islamic Affairs Analyst and Jane's Intelligence Digest. Chris is also the founder and director of the Balkan-interest news and current affairs website, www.balkanalysis.com, and the author of The Coming Balkan Caliphate: The Threat of Radical Islam to Europe and the West (Praeger Security International, 2007).

Kuwait

Kristian Coates Ulrichsen

Kristian Coates Ulrichsen, Ph.D., is the Baker Institute fellow for Kuwait. Working across the disciplines of political science, international relations and international political economy, his research examines the changing position of Persian Gulf states in the global order, as well as the emergence of longer-term, non-military challenges to regional security. He is a visiting fellow at the LSE Middle East Centre and an associate fellow at Chatham House in the United Kingdom.

Coates Ulrichsen has published extensively on the Gulf. His books include Insecure Gulf: the End of Certainty and the Transition to the Post-Oil Era (Columbia University Press, 2011) and The Political Economy of Arab Gulf States (Edward Elgar Publishing, 2012). He is currently completing a book on Qatar and the Arab Spring and has been commissioned to write a textbook on the Gulf and international political economy. Coates Ulrichsen's articles have appeared several academic journals, and he consults regularly on Gulf issues for Oxford Analytica and the Norwegian Peacebuilding Resource Centre. He also authors a monthly column for Gulf Business News and Analysis.

Lebanon

Hanin Ghaddar

Hanin Ghaddar is the inaugural Friedmann Visiting Fellow at The Washington Institute's Geduld Program on Arab Politics, where she focuses on Shia politics throughout the Levant.

The longtime managing editor of Lebanon's NOW news website, Ghaddar shed light on a broad range of cutting-edge issues, from the evolution of Hezbollah inside Lebanon's fractured political system to Iran's growing influence throughout the Middle East. In addition, she has contributed to a number of U.S.-based magazines and newspapers, including the New York Times and Foreign Policy.

Prior to joining NOW in 2007, Ghaddar wrote for the Lebanese newspapers As-Safir, An-Nahar, and Al-Hayat, and also worked as a researcher for the United Nations Development Program regional office. A native of Al-Ghazieh, Lebanon, Ghaddar holds a bachelor's degree in English literature and a master's degree in Middle East studies, both from the American University of Beirut.

Macedonia

Christopher Deliso

Christopher Deliso is an American journalist and author concentrating on the Balkans. Over the past decade, Chris has established a dedicated presence in the Balkans, and published analytical articles on related topics in numerous relevant media outlets, such as UPI, the Economist Intelligence Unit, and Jane's Islamic Affairs Analyst and Jane's Intelligence Digest. Chris is also the founder and director of the Balkan-interest news and current affairs website, www.balkanalysis.com, and the author of The Coming Balkan Caliphate: The Threat of Radical Islam to Europe and the West (Praeger Security International, 2007).

Mali

Chloe Thompson

Chloe Thompson is a Research Fellow and Program Officer at the American Foreign Policy Council. She serves as the Managing Editor of the World Almanac of Islamism.

Mauritania

Martin A. Ewi

Martin A. Ewi joined the Institute for Security Studies in July 2010, as a Senior Researcher, International Crime in Africa Programme (ICAP), Pretoria Office. He previously served as a Political Affairs Officer at the headquarters of the Organisation for the Prohibition of Chemical Weapons (OPCW) based in The Hague, the Netherlands from 2005 to 2010. Before joining the OPCW, Mr Ewi was in charge of the African Union Commission's counter-terrorism programme in Addis Ababa, Ethiopia, where he was concurrently in charge of security strategic issues from 2002 to 2005.

Mr. Ewi holds a MA degree in International Peace Studies from the University of Notre Dame, at Southbend, Indiana, United States of America. He also holds a BA (with Distinction) in Peace Studies and International Politics from Juniata College in Huntingdon, Pennsylvania, United States of America. His research focus is in the area of counterterrorism and the competences of regional organisations in Africa on strategic security issues.

Morocco

J. Peter Pham

J. Peter Pham is Vice President for Research and Regional Initiatives at the Atlantic Council as well as Director of the Council's Africa Center. From 2008 to 2017, he also served as Vice President of the Association for the Study of the Middle East and Africa (ASMEA) and was founding Editor-in-Chief of its refereed Journal of the Middle East and Africa.

The Netherlands

Margot van Loon

Margot van Loon is a Junior Fellow at the American Foreign Policy Council. She conducts research, editing, and analysis in support of multiple AFPC publications. She currently serves as the Project Coordinator for AFPC's World Almanac of Islamism. A graduate of American University, her research focuses on U.S. foreign policy and public diplomacy. Her commentary has appeared in U.S. News and World Report.

Nicaragua

Rachel Echeto

Rachel is a Program Manager at the Center for a Secure and Free Society (SFS). She first joined SFS in 2014 as an undergraduate intern in the Fund for American Studies Institute on Economics and International Affairs program. As an intern, Rachel worked on translation of policy reports and op-eds on Latin American politics and the production of the 2014 book "Iran's Strategic Penetration of

Latin America."

Following her internship at SFS, Rachel worked with the US Consulate in Guadalajara, MX as an intern in the US Department of State's Virtual Student Foreign Service Program, researching economic and political data in Mexico and creating reports for the consulate. In 2015, she graduated magna cum laude from the University of Southern California with bachelor's degrees in Spanish and Linguistics, and was awarded the Senior Recognition Award for Service to the Department by the USC Department of Spanish and Portuguese. Rachel continues to work as a translator with Latin American investigative journalists and contributed to research on the 2016 special report "After Nisman: How the death of a prosecutor revealed Iran's growing influence in the Americas" by SFS Executive Director Joseph Humire.

Rachel has been certified by the Spanish government as fluent in Spanish at the B2 level, and has lived and worked in Spain and Mexico.

Nigeria

Jacob Zenn

Jacob Zenn is an analyst of African and Eurasian Affairs for The Jamestown Foundation and author of the Occasional Report entitled "Northern Nigeria's Boko Haram: The Prize in al-Qaeda's Africa Strategy," published by The Jamestown Foundation in November 2012. In 2012, he conducted field research in Nigeria, Niger, Chad and Cameroon on the socio-economic factors behind the Boko Haram insurgency. Mr. Zenn earned a J.D. from Georgetown Law, where he was a Global Law Scholar, and a graduate degree in International Affairs from the Johns Hopkins SAIS Center for Chinese-American Studies in Nanjing, China. He has spoken at international conferences on Boko Haram and is frequently interviewed and cited in international media.

The Palestinian Territories

Neri Zilber

Neri Zilber is a journalist and analyst on Middle East politics and culture and an adjunct fellow of The Washington Institute for

Near East Policy, where he was previously a visiting scholar.

He is a regular contributor to The Daily Beast, Foreign Policy, and Politico Magazine, and his work has appeared in the New York Times, Washington Post, Guardian, The Atlantic, New Republic, and Foreign Affairs, among other outlets.

He is the co-author of State with No Army, Army with No State: Evolution of the Palestinian Authority Security Forces 1994-2018, and the contributing author on Israel's social protest demonstrations for The Occupy Handbook (Little, Brown), a chronicle of the global "Occupy" movement.

In addition to reportage and analysis, Neri consults for the private sector on political and economic risk. He was previously a fellow of the Institute of Current World Affairs based in Israel, and has also worked as a researcher and analyst at the U.S. Library of Congress and the World Jewish Congress.

He is quoted regularly in the international press and has appeared on CNN, BBC, NPR, CBS, and Al Jazeera English.

Neri holds a bachelor's degree from the School of Foreign Service, Georgetown University and a master's degree from the Department of War Studies, King's College London.

Qatar

Yael Shahar

Yael Shahar is the Director for the Database Project Institute for Counter-Terrorism at the IDC Herzliya. Ms. Shahar also heads the International Institute for Counter-Terrorism's (ICT) OSINT project. She specializes in the study of technological trends as applied to terrorism and intelligence sharing. She is a dynamic speaker, and has lectured worldwide on topics related to trends in terrorism, non-conventional and techno-terrorism, threat assessment and asymmetric conflict. Ms. Shahar studied Physics and Philosophy of Science at the University of Texas and at the Hebrew University in Jerusalem. She has also served as a reservist in the IDF hostage rescue unit, and is a director and co-founder of the Institute for the Study of Asymmetric Conflict.

Saudi Arabia

Chloe Thompson

Chloe Thompson is a Research Fellow and Program Officer at the American Foreign Policy Council. She serves as the Managing Editor of the World Almanac of Islamism.

Somalia

J. Peter Pham

J. Peter Pham is Vice President for Research and Regional Initiatives at the Atlantic Council as well as Director of the Council's Africa Center. From 2008 to 2017, he also served as Vice President of the Association for the Study of the Middle East and Africa (ASMEA) and was founding Editor-in-Chief of its refereed Journal of the Middle East and Africa.

South Africa

Micah Levinson

Micah Levinson is a Junior Fellow at the American Foreign Policy Council. Trained in government and political economy, he earned a B.A. from Harvard University and an M.A. from Washington University in St. Louis, Missouri. He also holds a certificate in counterterrorism from the Interdisciplinary Center in Herzliya, Israel. Micah's research focuses on revolutionary groups and the stability of authoritarian regimes, and he has published on these topics in Politics, Philosophy & Economics and has contributed to The Political Economy of Democracy and Tyranny, edited by Norman Schofield.

Spain

Rafael L. Bardají

Rafael L. Bardají is CEO of World Wide Strategy LLC, a US based intelligence advisory firm. He was founder of the Strategic Studies Group, GEES, an independent private think tank based in Madrid; served as Senior Strategic Adviser to three different Spanish Defence Ministers and he has also been special adviser to the NATO Special Operations Command. Bardají graduated in Political Science and Sociology at the Universidad Complutense of Madrid and specialized in Strategic Issues and Military Affairs at

Oxford University, Harvard and MIT.

Tanzania

Kelsey Lilley

Kelsey Lilley is associate director of the Atlantic Council's Africa Center. Her work focuses on emerging security threats and political developments in sub-Saharan Africa, with particular interest in East Africa and the Horn.

Prior to the Atlantic Council, Kelsey worked for the Society for International Development and the Africa Center for Strategic Studies. From 2012 to 2013, she lived in Addis Ababa, Ethiopia, where she was a Princeton in Africa fellow for the International Rescue Committee.

Syria

Aymenn Jawad Al-Tamimi

Aymenn Jawad Al-Tamimi is a graduate from Brasenose College, Oxford University, and a Jihad-Intel Research Fellow at the Middle East Forum.

Follow him on Twitter at @ajaltamimi.

Tunisia

Chloe Thompson

Chloe Thompson is a Research Fellow and Program Officer at the American Foreign Policy Council. She serves as the Managing Editor of the World Almanac of Islamism.

United Arab Emirates

Malcolm Peck

Malcolm Peck has been a program officer at Meridian International Center for the past 30 years, where he helps to plan and implement professional study tours for participants in the State Department's International Visitor Leadership Program. Between 1981 and 1983, he was Arabian Peninsula analyst for the State Department's Bureau of Intelligence and Research and, from 1970 to 1981, was the director of programs at the Middle East Institute.

Earlier, he taught at the University of Tennessee, Chattanooga and was a post-doctoral fellow at the Harvard University Center for Middle Eastern Studies. Dr. Peck is a specialist on Gulf-Arabian Peninsula issues and has published three books, ten chapters, and numerous articles on the topic. He received an A.B. and A.M. from Harvard University and an M.A., M.A.L.D., and Ph.D. from the Fletcher School of Law and Diplomacy.

The United Kingdom

Tom Wilson

Tom Wilson is a Fellow at the Centre for the Response to Radicalisation and Terrorism and the Centre for the New Middle East at The Henry Jackson Society.

Tom specialises in the study of extremist groups and counter-terrorism strategy. His research has focussed on both the growth of extremism in the UK as well as terrorist organisations in the Middle East.

He regularly appears in broadcast media, including BBC, Sky and CNN, offering his analysis on the issues of extremism and terrorism, and has been published in The Wall Street Journal, the Telegraph, the Spectator, National Review, Standpoint, and other outlets.

Prior to joining The Henry Jackson Society, he worked as a Tikvah Fellow at Commentary Magazine, where he wrote about political extremism and terrorism in Europe and the Middle East.

The United States

Anonymous

AFPC thanks our anonymous authors for their generous contributions to the World Almanac of Islamism.

Venezuela

Joseph M. Humire

Joseph M. Humire is a global security expert, focusing on the nexus between security, defense and economic freedom. Humire's research and investigations on the crime-terror nexus, radical Islam and Iran's influence in Latin America has been sought after by various entities within the U.S. government as well as think tanks and private sector clients throughout the hemisphere. Currently the Executive Director of the Center for a Secure Free Society (SFS), Humire is developing a global network of security and defense specialists that are focused on the intersection of security, intelligence, defense and economic development. Prior to his, Humire spent seven years with the United States Marine Corps, deployed to many hot spots around the world, including Iraq and Liberia, and partook in the first multinational military exercise in Latin America—Unitas 45-04. He is also a graduate from George Mason University with a degree in Economics and Global Affairs. Humire co-edited the first English book on "Iran's strategic penetration of Latin America," scheduled to be released in the fall of 2013 by Lexington Books.

YEMEN

Katherine Zimmerman

Katherine Zimmerman is a research fellow at the American Enterprise Institute (AEI) and the research manager for AEI's Critical Threats Project. As the senior analyst on al Qaeda, she studies how the terrorist network operates globally. Her work is also focused on al Qaeda's affiliates in the Gulf of Aden region and in western and northern Africa. She specializes in al Qaeda in the Arabian Peninsula, the Yemen-based al Qaeda faction, and in al Shabaab, al Qaeda's affiliate in Somalia.

Ms. Zimmerman has testified before Congress about the threats to US national security interests emanating from al Qaeda and its network. She has also briefed members of Congress, their staff, and members of the defense community. Her analyses have been widely published, including in CNN.com, The Huffington Post, The Wall Street Journal, and The Washington Post.

She graduated with distinction from Yale University with a B.A. in political science and modern Middle East studies.